Marketing:
Connecting with Customers

Marketing: Connecting with Customers

Gilbert D. Harrell
Michigan State University

Gary L. Frazier
University of Southern California

Prentice Hall, Upper Saddle River, NJ 07458

Acquisitions Editor: Whitney Blake
Assistant Editor: John Larkin
Editorial Assistant: Michele Foresta
Editor-in-Chief: Natalie Anderson
Marketing Manager: Shannon Moore
Production Editor: Michelle Rich
Production Coordinator: Tara Ruggiero
Managing Editor: Dee Josephson
Manufacturing Supervisor: Arnold Vila
Manufacturing Manager: Vincent Scelta
Interior Design: Jill Yutkowitz
Design Manager: Patricia Smythe
Photo Research Supervisor: Melinda Lee Reo
Image Permission Supervisor: Kay Dellosa
Photo Researcher: Melinda Alexander
Cover Design: Jill Yutkowitz
Illustrator (Interior): ElectraGraphics, Inc.
Composition: York Graphic Services, Inc.

Acknowledgments appear on pages C1–C2.

Copyright © 1999 by Prentice-Hall Inc.
A Simon & Schuster Company
Upper Saddle River, New Jersey 07458

Library of Congress Cataloging-in-Publication Data

Harrell, Gilbert D.
   Marketing: connecting with customers / Gilbert D. Harrell, Gary L. Frazier
      p.   cm.
   Includes bibliographical references and index.
   ISBN 0-02-350251-7 (paper)
   1. Marketing—Management.   2. Consumer satisfaction.   I. Frazier,
   Gary L.   II. Title
   HF5415. 13.H356   1998
   658.8'12—dc21   98-27613
                                                      CIP

Prentice-Hall International (UK) Limited, London
Prentice-Hall of Australia Pty. Limited, Sydney
Prentice-Hall Canada, Inc., Toronto
Prentice-Hall Hispanoamericana, S.A., Mexico
Prentice-Hall of India, Private Limited, New Delhi
Prentice-Hall of Japan, Inc., Tokyo
Simon & Schuster Asia Pte. Ltd., Singapore
Editora Prentice-Hall do Brazil, Ltda., Rio de Janeiro

Printed in the United States

10 9 8 7 6 5 4 3 2 1

Contents

ABOUT THE AUTHORS   xiii

PREFACE   xv

CHAPTER 1 MARKETING: CONNECTING WITH
CUSTOMERS   2
    Objectives   3
        Connected: Surfing the Net: levi. com   4
        Career Tip: Levi Strauss Internship   4
THE CONCEPT OF MARKETING: CONNECTING WITH
CUSTOMERS   4
DEFINITION OF MARKETING   5
    The Process of Planning and Executing   5
    Product, Price, Promotion, and Place   6
    Market for Ideas, Goods, and Services   6
    Create Exchanges That Satisfy Individual and
        Organizational Objectives   8
        Connected: Surfing the Net: llbean.com   9
THE MARKETING CONCEPT: THE PURPOSE OF
MARKETING   9
    Understand the Needs and Wants of Customers   10
    Create Customer Value Through Satisfaction and
        Quality   11
    More Effectively and Efficiently Than Competitors   12
THE MARKETING STRATEGY PROCESS   12
    Situation Analysis   12
    Targeting   13
        Connected: Surfing the Net: esprit.com   13
    Positioning   13
    Marketing Mix Decisions   14
THE EVOLUTION OF MARKETING   16
    The Production Era   16
    The Sales Era   17
    The Customer Marketing Era   17
CONNECTING WITH CUSTOMERS IN THE 21ST
CENTURY   18
    Connecting Through Relationships   19
        Connected: Surfing the Net:
           americanexpress.com   20
    Connecting Through Technology   20
        Connected: Surfing the Net:
           virtualemporium.com   24
    Connecting Globally   24

Connecting with Diversity   25
Connecting Ethically   26
    Connecting with Diversity: Betty Crocker: An
        American Mosaic   27
    Connected: Surfing the Net: benjerry.com   29
Marketing: Your Involvement   29
    Connecting Through Relationships: P&G Works with
        Producers to Take the Trash out of Television   30
    Connected: Surfing the Net: Procter & Gamble   31
    Connected: Surfing the Net: General Mills   31
Chapter Summary   31
Review Your Understanding   32
Discussion of Concepts   32
Key Terms and Definitions   32
References   33
Case 1: Starbucks   34

CHAPTER 2 CUSTOMER SATISFACTION AND LOYALTY:
BUILDING VALUE WITH QUALITY   36
    Objectives   37
        Connected: Surfing the Net: mcdonalds.com   38
THE CONCEPTS OF CUSTOMER SATISFACTION, LOYALTY,
AND QUALITY   38
CUSTOMER SATISFACTION AND CUSTOMER LOYALTY   39
    Why Satisfaction and Loyalty Are Important   39
    Customer Expectations   40
    Customer Defections and Complaining Behavior   41
        Connecting Through Technology: Red Lobster Finds
        a Recipe for Customer Satisfaction with Response
        Hardware   42
    Satisfaction Ratings and Measurement   42
        Connected: Surfing the Net: jdpower.com   43
CONNECTING THROUGH RELATIONSHIPS TO BUILD
SATISFACTION AND LOYALTY   44
        Connected: Surfing the Net: saturncars.com   44
    Creating a Personal Relationship   44
        Career Tip: Hallmark   46
    Diversity and Satisfaction   47
    Global Competition and Satisfaction   47
        Connecting with Diversity: When You Care Enough
        to Send the Very Best . . . in Spanish, Hindi, or
        Chinese   48

Connected: Surfing the Net: xerox.com   48
Organizational Systems and Actions That Deliver
    Quality   49
Quality   49
    Connected: Surfing the Net: fedex.com   50
    Connected: Surfing the Net: quality.nist.gov   55
DELIVERING VALUE TO IMPROVE SATISFACTION   55
    The Value Chain   55
ETHICAL BEHAVIOR IN FULFILLING COMMITMENTS   56
    Employee and Customer Involvement   57
        Connected: Surfing the Net: Red Lobster   58
        Connected: Surfing the Net: Hallmark   58
Chapter Summary   58
Review Your Understanding   59
Discussion of Concepts   59
Key Terms and Definitions   59
References   60
Case 2: The Ritz-Carlton Hotel Company   61

CHAPTER 3 THE MARKETING ENVIRONMENT AND ITS
    GLOBAL DIMENSIONS   62
    Objectives   63
        Connected: Surfing the Net: lucasarts.com   64
THE CONCEPT OF THE MARKETING ENVIRONMENT   64
THE MICROENVIRONMENT   66
    Relationships with Stakeholders   66
        Connected: Surfing the Net: hersheys.com   66
    Industry Competition   68
        Connected: Surfing the Net: microsoft.com   69
THE GLOBAL MACROENVIRONMENT   70
    Technological Environment   70
    Economic Environment   71
        Connected: Surfing the Net: mot.com   71
        Career Tip: Recruiting   74
    Demographic Environment   74
        Connecting Through Relationships: Avon Products,
            Inc.: Around the World with 2.2 Million Avon
            Ladies   75
    Cultural Environment   77
    Connecting with Diversity: NFO Research, Inc.—First
        with a Hispanic Panel   78
    Legal/Regulatory Environment   79
        Connected: Surfing the Net: kodak.com   80
    Ethical Environment   82
        Connected: Surfing the Net: ama.org   84
    Chapter Summary   85
        Connected: Surfing the Net: avon.com   86
        Connected: Surfing the Net: amazon.com   86
    Review Your Understanding   87
    Discussion of Concepts   87
    Key Terms and Definitions   87
    References   88
    Case 3: The National Basketball Association   89

CHAPTER 4 THE STRATEGIC MARKETING PLANNING
    PROCESS: DOMESTIC AND GLOBAL   92
    Objectives   93
        Connected: Surfing the Net: disney.com   94
THE CONCEPT OF THE STRATEGIC MARKETING PLANNING
    PROCESS   94
THE ORGANIZATION VISION   95
    Core Values: The Ethical Foundation   96
        Connected: Surfing the Net: lilly.com   96
        Connected: Surfing the Net: jnj.com   97
    Business Definition (Mission)   97
        Career Tip: Lilly   98
    Strategic Direction (Intent)   98
    Strategic Infrastructure   99
        Connecting Through Technology: Kodak Adjusts Its
            Focus   104
        Connected: Surfing the Net: westinghouse.com   104
THE STRATEGIC MARKETING PLAN   106
    The Planning Team   106
    What Is Strategy?   107
    Components of the Strategic Marketing Plan   109
MARKETING MIX PLANS AND THE MARKETING CONTROL
    PROCESS   111
        Connecting with Diversity: Kraft Foods: *Su Cocina es
            Nuestra Cocina*   112
    Product Plans   114
        Connected: Surfing the Net: bandai.com;
            tigertoys.com   115
    Place Plans   115
    Promotion Plans   115
        Connected: Surfing the Net: broadway.org   115
    Pricing Plans   116
    The Marketing Control Process   116
CONNECTING GLOBALLY: ENTERING WORLD
    MARKETS   116
    Geographic Scope   117
    Strategies for Foreign Market Entry   118
        Connected: Surfing the Net: Kodak   120
        Connected: Surfing the Net: Kraft Foods   120
    Chapter Summary   121
    Review Your Understanding   122
    Discussion of Concepts   122
    Key Terms and Definitions   122
    References   123
    Case 4: Polaroid   124

CHAPTER 5 MARKETING INFORMATION AND
    RESEARCH   126
    Objectives   127
        Connected: Surfing the Net: amazon.com   128
THE CONCEPT OF MARKETING INFORMATION SYSTEMS
    AND MARKETING RESEARCH   128
MARKETING INFORMATION SYSTEMS AND DATA   129
    Turning Data into Information   130
    Information and Decision Making   132
        Connected: Surfing the Net: att.com   132
        Connected: Surfing the Net: ual.com   133

Connected: Surfing the Net:
    nielsenmedia.com   134
THE MARKETING RESEARCH PROCESS   134
  Defining the Problem   134
  Research Design   134
    Connecting Through Relationships: J.D. Power &
      Associates: A "Hate-Love" Relationship with
      Detroit   135
  Exploratory Research   135
    Connecting with Diversity: Elusive Youth:
      Researchers Find New Ways to Track Their
      Tastes   139
  Quantitative Research   140
    Connected: Surfing the Net:
      kimberly-clark.com   140
  Interpreting and Reporting Survey Findings   144
    Connected: Surfing the Net: ford.com   145
  Who Does Marketing Research?   145
    Career Tip: Market Research   146
  Technology's Effect on Marketing Research   146
  Global Marketing Research   147
  Ethics in Marketing Research and Information Use   148
    Connected: Surfing the Net:
      J.D. Power & Associates   149
    Connected: Surfing the Net:
      Bugle Boy Clothing Company   149
  Chapter Summary   150
  Review Your Understanding   150
  Discussion of Concepts   151
  Key Terms and Definitions   151
  References   151
  Case 5: Reebok   152

CHAPTER 6 MARKET SEGMENTATION, TARGETING, AND
    POSITIONING   154
  Objectives   155
THE CONCEPT OF SEGMENTATION, TARGETING, AND
    POSITIONING   156
    Connected: Surfing the Net: cocacola.com   157
MARKET SEGMENTATION   157
  Segmentation versus Mass Marketing   157
  Segmentation versus Product Differentiation   158
  Segmentation Variables   159
    Connected: Surfing the Net: future.sri.com   166
  Two Common Segmenting Methods   169
TARGET MARKETING   169
  Selecting Target Segments   170
    Connecting Through Relationships: Credit Card
      Cobranding: New Shortcut to Hitting the Target
      Market   171
    Connected: Surfing the Net:
      harley-davidson.com   172
  Finding New Markets to Target   172
  Target Marketing Strategies   172
    Career Tip: MCI   174
    Connecting Through Technology: Mining Data for
      the MicroMarket   175

Connected: Surfing the Net: bmwusa.com   176
  Ethical Dimensions of Targeting   176
  Global Targeting   176
    Connected: Surfing the Net: dominos.com   177
POSITIONING STRATEGIES   177
  The Positioning Map   177
  Positioning Business Products   177
  Steps for Positioning   179
  Bases for Positioning   179
  Repositioning   180
    Connected: Surfing the Net: Mastercard   181
    Connected: Surfing the Net: MCI   181
  Chapter Summary   182
  Review Your Understanding   182
  Discussion of Concepts   182
  Key Terms and Definitions   183
  References   183
  Case 6: Tommy Hilfiger   184

CHAPTER 7 CONNECTING WITH CUSTOMERS:
    UNDERSTANDING CONSUMER BEHAVIOR   186
  Objectives   187
    Connected: Surfing the Net: 4.nissan.co.jp   188
THE CONCEPT OF CONSUMER BEHAVIOR   188
CONSUMER INVOLVEMENT AND DECISION MAKING   188
  Consumer Involvement   188
  Consumer Decision Making   190
    Connecting Through Relationships: The Customer
      Loyalty Card Game   191
PSYCHOLOGICAL FACTORS THAT INFLUENCE CONSUMER
    DECISIONS   191
  Motivation   192
  Perception   195
  Learning   196
    Connected: Surfing the Net: conagra.com   197
  Attitudes   198
    Connected: Surfing the Net: snapple.com   198
  Information Processing   199
    Connected: Surfing the Net: nike.com   200
SOCIAL FACTORS THAT INFLUENCE CONSUMER
    DECISIONS   201
  Culture   201
  Subculture   201
    Career Tip: Ethnic Growth   202
    Connected: Surfing the Net: spiegel.com   203
  Social Class   204
  Reference Groups   205
    Connected: Surfing the Net: whymilk.com   207
  The Family   207
    Connecting with Diversity: How to Satisfy a Senior—
      Oops—I Mean a Boomer   210
USING TECHNOLOGY TO TRACK CONSUMER
    BEHAVIOR   210
    Connected: Surfing the Net: Club Med   211
    Connected: Surfing the Net: Quartermaine Coffee
      Roasters   211

THE ETHICS OF INFLUENCING CONSUMER
   BEHAVIOR   212
      Chapter Summary   212
      Review Your Understanding   212
      Discussion of Concepts   213
      Key Terms and Definitions   213
      References   214
      Case 7: The Viacom Networks   215

CHAPTER 8 BUSINESS-TO-BUSINESS MARKETING   216
   Objectives   217
      Connected: Surfing the Net: aramark.com   218
THE CONCEPT OF BUSINESS-TO-BUSINESS
   MARKETING   218
BUSINESS-TO-BUSINESS MARKETS   219
   Types of Markets   219
      Connected: Surfing the Net: envirogroup.com   221
   Business Market Segmentation   223
   Business Market Linkages: The Supply Chain   225
   Business Market Demand   226
   Globalization of Business Markets   226
      Connected: Surfing the Net: ibm.com   226
ORGANIZATIONAL BUYING   227
   Buying Decisions   227
   Steps in the Organizational Buying Process   229
   Relationships Between Buyers and Sellers   230
      Connected: Surfing the Net: kmart.com   232
      Connecting Through Relationships: Cutler-Hammer's
         Absolute Focus Proves That Less Is More   233
      Career Tip: Cutler-Hammer   234
   Functions Involved in Business Purchases   235
      Connected: Surfing the Net: ups.com   237
   Influences on Organizational Buying Behavior   238
      Connecting Through Technology: Industry.net—
         Where Business Buyers and Sellers Meet   239
      Connected: Surfing the Net: 3M.com   240
      Connected: Surfing the Net:
         Cutler-Hammer   241
      Connected: Surfing the Net: Industry.net   241
   Chapter Summary   242
   Review Your Understanding   242
   Discussion of Concepts   242
   Key Terms and Definitions   243
   References   243
   Case 8: Andersen Consulting   244

CHAPTER 9 PRODUCT DECISIONS AND STRATEGIES   246
   Objectives   247
      Connected: Surfing the Net: gm.com   248
THE CONCEPT OF PRODUCTS   248
PRODUCT DIMENSIONS   248
   Core Products   248
   Branded Products   249
   Augmented Products   249
      Connected: Surfing the Net: yamaha.com   250
PRODUCT CLASSIFICATIONS   251

Consumer Product Classification   251
      Connected: Surfing the Net: compaq.com   253
   Business Product Classification   254
PRODUCT LINE DECISIONS   255
   Product Depth and Breadth   256
   Global Products   256
      Connected: Surfing the Net: motorola.com   257
BRANDS   257
   Trademarks   258
   Trademark Piracy   259
      Connected: Surfing the Net: mtv.com   259
   Brand Strategies   260
   Brand Equity: Connecting with a Successful
      Brand   262
      Dimensions of Brand Equity   262
      Connecting Through Relationships: Starbucks
         Extends Its Brand Name Through Joint
         Ventures   263
      Connecting Through Technology: Intel Brands the
         Soul in the Machine   265
      Career Tip: Procter & Gamble   266
   Maintaining Brand Value   266
   Developing a Successful Brand Name   266
   Joint Marketing of Brands   267
   Diversity in Brand Marketing   267
PACKAGING AND LABELING   268
ETHICAL ISSUES SURROUNDING PRODUCT SAFETY AND
   LIABILITY   268
   Product Warranties   269
   Product Recalls   269
      Connected: Surfing the Web: Intel   270
      Connected: Surfing the Web: Starbucks   270
   Chapter Summary   270
   Review Your Understanding   271
   Discussion of Concepts   271
   Key Terms and Definitions   272
   References   272
   Case 9: Sara Lee   273

CHAPTER 10 PRODUCT PLANNING, DEVELOPMENT, AND
   MANAGEMENT   276
   Objectives   277
      Connected: Surfing the Net: mytwinn.com   278
THE CONCEPTS OF PRODUCT DEVELOPMENT AND
   PRODUCT MANAGEMENT   278
PRODUCT PLANNING AND TYPES OF INNOVATION   279
   Product Planning   279
      Connected: Surfing the Net: ge.com   281
   Types of Product Innovation   281
   Why Innovations Succeed   282
      Connected: Surfing the Net: ti.com   283
THE NEW PRODUCT DEVELOPMENT PROCESS   284
   New Product Strategy   284
   Idea Generation   285
      Connected: Surfing the Net: jci.com   285
      Career Tip: 3M   286
   Idea Screening   287

Business Analysis   287
Prototype Product Development   287
Market Testing   288
    Connecting Through Technology: Don't Just Look,
        Step Inside: Virtual Reality in Product Design   289
Commercialization   290
The Ethics of Product Imitation   290
Organizational Structures and Product
    Management   291
    Connected: Surfing the Net: fritolay.com   291
MANAGING PRODUCTS OVER THE LIFE CYCLE   293
Stages in the Product Life Cycle   294
    Connected: Surfing the Net: honda.com   295
Variations in Product Life Cycles   297
Extending the Product Life Cycle   298
    Connecting with Diversity: Mattel's Barbie Lures
        Girls to Computer Games   299
The Product Life Cycle in International Markets   300
CONSUMER ACCEPTANCE OF INNOVATION   301
Adoption   301
Diffusion   301
    Connected: Surfing the Net: Caterpillar   302
    Connected: Surfing the Net: Mattel   302
Chapter Summary   303
Review Your Understanding   304
Discussion of Concepts   304
Key Terms and Definitions   304
References   305
Case 10: Minnesota Mining and Manufacturing   306

CHAPTER 11 SERVICES AND NONPROFIT
    MARKETING   308
Objectives   309
    Connected: Surfing the Net: world.std   310
THE CONCEPT OF SERVICES   310
GLOBAL FORCES CREATING GROWTH IN SERVICES   312
Technology   312
Quality of Life   313
Government Deregulation of Services   313
Competition in Professional Services   314
Privatization   314
The Need for Specialization   315
    Career Tip: ARAMARK   315
Access to Knowledge   315
Growth of Franchising   315
SERVICE CHARACTERISTICS THAT AFFECT MARKETING
    STRATEGY   316
    Connected: Surfing the Net: subway.com   316
The Contrasts Between Goods and Services   316
    Connecting with Diversity: Beyond Accessiblility:
        How Hotels Win Over the Disabled Traveler   318
The Service-Goods Continuum   319
    Connected: Surfing the Net:
        barnesandnoble.com   320
Consumer Evaluation of Services   320
    Connected: Surfing the Net: carnival.com   320
Service Quality   323

    Connected: Surfing the Net: mobil.com   324
DEVELOPING THE SERVICE MIX   324
Core, Augmented, and Branded Services   324
    Connected: Surfing the Net: kinkos.com   326
Developing New Services   326
AN EXPANDED CONCEPT OF SERVICES   327
Person Marketing   328
Entertainment and Event Marketing   328
Place Marketing   330
Political Marketing   331
Cause Marketing   331
Internal Marketing   331
THE MARKETING OF NONPROFIT SERVICES   332
Types of Nonprofit Service Providers   332
The Need for Excess Revenues   332
Fund-Raising and Revenue Generation   333
    Connecting Through Relationships: The Point:
        Celebrating the Life and Culture of the South
        Bronx   334
Providing Positive Social Benefits   336
    Ethical Issues Surrounding Nonprofit
        Organizations   336
    Connected: Surfing the Net: The San Diego Zoo   337
    Connected: Surfing the Net: Hilton
        Worldwide   337
Chapter Summary   337
Review Your Understanding   338
Discussion of Concepts   338
Key Terms and Definitions   339
References   339
Case 11: Ticketmaster   340

CHAPTER 12 MARKETING CHANNELS, WHOLESALING,
    AND PHYSICAL DISTRIBUTION   342
Objectives   343
THE CONCEPT OF DISTRIBUTION CHANNELS   344
Channel Structure   344
    Connected: Surfing the Net: coach.com   345
Channel Organization and Functions   347
    Connected: Surfing the Net: airtouch.com   347
    Connected: Surfing the Net: wal-mart.com   348
    Connecting with Diversity: McDonald's®: Serving
        Diverse Communities in More Ways Than
        One   350
MANAGING DISTRIBUTION CHANNELS   351
Managing Channel Relationships: A Strategic
    Approach   351
    Connected: Surfing the Net: honeywell.com   353
Legal and Ethical Issues in Channel Management   354
WHOLESALING   355
The Importance of Wholesalers   356
    Career Tip: Arrow Electronics   356
Types of Wholesalers   357
    Connected: Surfing the Net: sysco.com   358
Wholesaling Relationships   358
    Connecting Through Relationships: W. W. Grainger's
        Alliances with Specialty Wholesalers   359

INTEGRATED LOGISTICS AND PHYSICAL
   DISTRIBUTION 359
    Physical Distribution 360
    Order Management 361
      Connected: Surfing the Net: benetton.com 363
    Global Physical Distribution 367
      Connected: Surfing the Net: McDonald's® 368
      Connected: Surfing the Net: W. W. Grainger 368
    Chapter Summary 369
    Review Your Understanding 370
    Discussion of Concepts 370
    Key Terms and Definitions 370
    References 371
    Case 12: Texas Instruments 372

CHAPTER 13 RETAILING AND DIRECT MARKETING 374
    Objectives 375
      Connected: Surfing the Net: mfa.org 376
      Career Tip 376
THE CONCEPTS OF RETAILING AND DIRECT
   MARKETING 376
RETAILING 376
      Connected: Surfing the Net: compusa.com 377
    The Importance of Retailers 377
    Retail Strategy 378
      Connected: Surfing the Net: sears.com 379
      Connected: Surfing the Net: blockbuster.com 381
      Connecting Through Technology: Peapod and
        Computer Shopping 382
    Types of Retailers 383
      Connected: Surfing the Net: staples.com 384
    Issues in Retailing 385
DIRECT MARKETING 386
    Value to Customers and Marketing 387
    Direct Marketing Databases 387
    Direct Response Media 387
      Connecting Through Relationships: The Good
        Catalog Company: Posting Great Results from
        Co-op Marketing 390
      Connected: Surfing the Net: cdnow.com 392
    The Direct Marketing Plan 392
    Ethics in Direct Marketing 394
      Connected: Surfing the Net: Peapod, Inc. 395
      Connected: Surfing the Net: Cdnow 395
    Chapter Summary 396
    Review Your Understanding 396
    Discussion of Concepts 396
    Key Terms and Definitions 397
    References 397
    Case 13: Gateway 398

**CHAPTER 14 INTEGRATED MARKETING
COMMUNICATIONS 400**
    Objectives 401
THE CONCEPT OF INTEGRATED MARKETING
   COMMUNICATIONS 402

OBJECTIVES OF INTEGRATED MARKETING
   COMMUNICATIONS 403
    Provide Information 403
      Connected: Surfing the Net: dttus.com 403
      Connecting Through Relationships: From Integrated
        Marketing Communications to "Intimate"
        Marketing Communications 404
    Create Demand for Products 404
    Communicate Value 405
    Communicate Product Uniqueness 405
    Close the Sale 405
    Build Relationships and Loyalty 406
THE COMMUNICATION PROCESS 406
    The Message Sender 406
      Connected: Surfing the Net: pepsi.com 407
    Presentation Creation: Encoding 409
    Message Characteristics 409
      Connected: Surfing the Net: rubbermaid.com 409
    Media 411
    Interpretation by Receivers: Decoding 412
    Consumer Feedback 412
THE COMMUNICATION MIX 412
    Types of Communication Activities 412
      Connected: Surfing the Net: nascarfans.com 414
    Factors Affecting the Communication Mix 414
DEVELOPING THE IMC PLAN 416
    Selecting and Understanding Target Audiences 417
      Determining Objectives and Selecting the IMC
        Mix 417
      Connecting with Diversity: Multinationals Target
        China's "Little Emperors" with Ads and
        Promotions 418
    Developing the Communication Budget 419
    Implementation 420
      Career Tip: Web search 420
    Measuring IMC Results 421
ISSUES IN COMMUNICATION 421
    Diversity 421
    Ethics 422
    Technology That Builds Relationships 422
      Connected: Surfing the Net: Snapple 423
      Connected: Surfing the Net: IBM 423
    Chapter Summary 423
    Review Your Understanding 424
    Discussion of Concepts 424
    Key Terms and Definitions 425
    References 425
    Case 14: Nike 426

**CHAPTER 15 MASS COMMUNICATIONS: ADVERTISING,
SALES PROMOTION, AND PUBLIC RELATIONS 428**
    Objectives 429
      Connected: Surfing the Net: lost-world.com 430
THE CONCEPT OF MASS COMMUNICATIONS:
ADVERTISING, SALES PROMOTION, AND PUBLIC
RELATIONS 430
MASS COMMUNICATION IN THE 21ST CENTURY 430

Technological Perspective   431
Global Mass Communications   431
  Connected: Surfing the Net: fujifilm.com   431
Ethical Issues in Advertising, Sales Promotion, and
  Public Relations   432
ADVERTISING   433
The Multiple Purposes and Roles of Advertising   433
  Connected: Surfing the Net: mercedes.com   434
Pros and Cons of Advertising   434
Categories of Advertising   435
Advertising Agencies   436
THE ADVERTISING PLAN   436
Setting Objectives   436
Developing the Advertising Budget   437
Developing the Theme and Message   437
Selecting and Scheduling Media   439
  Connecting Through Technology: Yahoo!
    Corporation: From Techie Tool to Hot New Ad
    Medium   442
  Career Tip: Tony Lee   442
  Connected: Surfing the Net: heinz.com   444
Creating the Ads   444
Assessing Advertising Effectiveness   445
  Connecting with Diversity: Breaking Taboos at
    Subaru   446
SALES PROMOTION   447
Types of Sales Promotion   447
The Success of Sales Promotion   448
Creating Customer Relationships and Loyalty Through
  Sales Promotion   449
  Connected: Surfing the Net: 7up.com   450
Business-to-Business Promotions   450
Trade Promotions   451
Retailer Promotions   452
Consumer Promotions   452
  Connected: Surfing the Net: hp.com   454
PUBLIC RELATIONS AND PUBLICITY   455
Public Relations   455
Publicity   456
  Connected: Surfing the Net: Subaru   457
  Connected: Surfing the Net: Yahoo!   457
Chapter Summary   457
Review Your Understanding   458
Discussion of Concepts   458
Key Terms and Definitions   459
References   459
Case 15: Super Bowl Advertising   461

CHAPTER 16 PERSONAL SELLING AND SALES FORCE
  MANAGEMENT   462
Objectives   463
  Connected: Surfing the Net: prenhall.com   464
THE CONCEPTS OF PERSONAL SELLING AND SALES
  MANAGEMENT   464
PERSONAL SELLING   465
Types of Sales Personnel and Selling Situations   465
  Connected: Surfing the Net: boeing.com   467

Career Tip: Hewlett-Packard   467
Relationship and Other Selling Approaches   468
  Connecting with Diversity: A Few Do's and Taboos
    for the Round-the-World Rep   469
The Responsibilities of a Salesperson   472
  Connecting Through Technology: United Parcel
    Service: Sales Reps and Laptops Create Missing
    Link   473
The Steps in Personal Selling   475
  Connected: Surfing the Net: amway.com   478
Characteristics of Strong Salespeople   480
SALES FORCE MANAGEMENT   481
Organizing the Sales Force   481
Developing the Sales Team   483
  Connected: Surfing the Net: prudential.com   484
  Connected: Surfing the Net: merck.com   485
Sales Forecasting and Budgeting   486
  Connected: Surfing the Net: whirlpool.com   486
Implementing Sales Actions   487
Overseeing Sales Force Activities   489
Sales Force Automation   491
  Connected: Surfing the Net: UPS   492
  Connected: Surfing the Net: Amway   492
Chapter Summary   492
Review Your Understanding   493
Discussion of Concepts   493
Key Terms and Definitions   494
References   495
Case 16: Duracell   496

CHAPTER 17 PRICING APPROACHES   498
Objectives   499
  Connected: Surfing the Net: nintendo.com   500
THE CONCEPT OF PRICING   500
PRICE AS PART OF THE MARKETING MIX   501
OBJECTIVES OF PRICE SETTING   501
  Connecting with Diversity: Family Bargain Uses Low
    Prices to Court the Invisible Consumer   502
Profit Objectives   503
Volume (Sales) Objectives   503
Competitive Objectives   503
Relationship (Customer) Objectives   504
MAJOR FACTORS INFLUENCING PRICE   504
Economic Factors: Demand and Supply   505
  Career Tip: Amoco   507
Legal and Ethical Influences on Pricing   509
  Connected: Surfing the Net: delta-air.com   510
  Connected: Surfing the Net: ames.com   510
Competitive Factors That Influence Pricing   513
  Connected: Surfing the Net: ticketmaster.com   514
  Connecting Through Relationships: Paying a Premium
    for Pet Care Nets Pampering, Too   516
Cost Factors That Influence Price   516
INTERNATIONAL PRICING   520
Global Market Factors   520
Global Cost Factors   521
  Connected: Surfing the Net: PetsMart   522

Connected: Surfing the Net: Amoco   522
Global Financial Factors   523
Chapter Summary   523
Review Your Understanding   524
Discussion of Concepts   524
Key Terms and Definitions   524
References   525
Case 17: Ty, Inc.   526

CHAPTER 18 PRICING STRATEGY   528
Objectives   529
Connected: Surfing the Net: pg.com   530
THE CONCEPT OF PRICE STRATEGY   530
VALUE AS THE BASIS FOR PRICING   530
Sources of Value   532
Connected: Surfing the Net: volvo.com   532
Customer Value in Pricing   532
Connected: Surfing the Net: usps.gov   533
Connected: Surfing the Net: casio.com   534
CUSTOMER, COMPETITOR, AND GLOBAL PRICING   534
Customer-Oriented Pricing   534
Connecting Through Relationships: Banks Coddle
    Some Customers and Make Others Pay Their
    Way   535

Connected: Surfing the Net: target.com   537
Competitor-Oriented Pricing   538
Connected: Surfing the Net: kelloggs.com   540
Diversity: Pricing to Attract Senior Citizens   540
Global Pricing   540
Connecting Through Technology: America Online,
    Inc.: A Tale of Two Pricing Strategies   541
IMPLEMENTING THE PRICING STRATEGY   542
Setting Prices   542
Career Tip: DuPont   544
Connected: Surfing the Net: dupont.com   544
Communicating Price   546
UNETHICAL PRICING PRACTICES   548
Connected: Surfing the Net: America Online   548
Connected: Surfing the Net: Bank of America   548
Chapter Summary   549
Review Your Understanding   549
Discussion of Concepts   549
Key Terms and Definitions   550
References   550
Case 18: Harley-Davidson   551

Photo Credits   C-1
Index   I-1

About the Authors

GILBERT D. HARRELL, Ph.D.

Gilbert D. Harrell, Ph.D., is Professor of Marketing, Eli Broad College of Business and Graduate School of Management, Michigan State University. Professor Harrell received the 1997 John D. and Dortha J. Withrow Endowed Teacher/Scholar Award, the 1996 Phi Chi Theta Professor of the Year Award, and the 1995 Gold Key National Honor Society award for teaching excellence at Michigan State University. His teaching, research, and consulting activities focus on sustainable competitive advantage, building business value, consumer satisfaction, sales management, strategic planning, and relationship marketing. Dr. Harrell's publications have appeared in the *Journal of Marketing, Journal of Long Range Planning, Journal of Marketing Research, Journal of Consumer Research, Journal of Consumer Affairs, Journal of Industrial Marketing Management, Journal of Consumer Satisfaction, Journal of Retailing, Business Topics, Journal of Logistics Information Management, Journal of Health Care Marketing, Journal of International Marketing, Journal of the Academy of Marketing Science,* and others. Dr. Harrell's doctorate degree is from Pennsylvania State University, where he was elected to the Phi Kappa Phi Honorary and the American Marketing Association Consortium. Both his Bachelor's and Master's degrees are from Michigan State University.

Dr. Harrell is founder of Harrell & Associates, Inc., a professional consulting group, which specializes in services for strategic marketing management, visioning processes, communications strategies, sales management, and executive strategy development. His firm has helped implement the strategic marketing planning systems for several Fortune 500 companies.

GARY L. FRAZIER, DBA

Gary Frazier, DBA, is the Richard and Jarda Hurd Professor of Distribution Management, School of Business Administration, University of Southern California, Los Angeles. Prior to joining USC in 1984, he was on the marketing faculty at the University of Illinois, Champaign–Urbana. Professor Frazier's research has focused on the structuring and management of channels of distribution, especially how channel relationships are coordinated to create value for the channel's customers. He has conducted research on channels of distribution in Europe and India, as well as in the United States. He heads the Program in Distribution Management at USC, supported by distributors with over $10 billion in annual sales. Gary served as chairman of the Department of Marketing at USC from 1990 to 1995. He is active in the American Marketing Association, and he has served on the editorial review board of the *Journal of Marketing* since 1984 and on the editorial review board of the *Journal of Marketing Research* since 1985. He received his MBA in 1977 and his DBA in 1979 from Indiana University, Bloomington. As a consultant, Dr. Frazier's advice has been sought by several major corporations.

Preface

Marketing is about connecting with customers. Based on the latest thinking by marketing experts and practitioners, as well as our own research, that fact will be the dominant theme in marketing in the twenty-first century. As in the past, exceptional marketing will continue to be of great benefit to customers, organizations, and society. Dramatic changes in the marketing environment are presenting immense new opportunities for organizations that really connect with customers. This book is about how companies connect with customers, particularly through relationships, through technology, with diversity, globally, and ethically.

Many fascinating stories about marketing successes and failures fill this text, but you need to know more than that to prepare for this exciting field. You need to grasp the tools, techniques, and principles of marketing, as well as how to apply them. To produce value, you have to connect with customers that you can identify and understand. Whether you are majoring in business, the sciences, the arts, or the humanities, marketing is relevant to you. Understanding marketing gives a deeper understanding of how value is formed and how you can create the greatest customer satisfaction possible in competitive environments.

CONNECTING THROUGH RELATIONSHIPS

Relationship marketing is a growing trend, and for good reason. By its very nature, a relationship requires a solid, lasting connection. Relationship marketing is introduced early in the book, emphasizing the tremendous importance of satisfied, loyal customers. Meaningful relationships with customers, happen when all employees within the organization develop the sensitivity, agility, and desire to satisfy customers' needs and wants. The ways of connecting through relationships is emphasized throughout the book.

CONNECTING THROUGH TECHNOLOGY

Technology's effect on marketing is a focus of discussion in each chapter, and it is featured seamlessly with examples of technologies that are driving progressive marketers. Internet technology is featured throughout. Chapter 1 introduces the Internet use in marketing, in such areas as scanning, communication, distribution, and research. Internet connections to more than 100 leading-edge companies are provided in opening stories and are highlighted in text examples, boxed examples, and cases.

CONNECTING WITH DIVERSITY

Diversity among organizations and customers is a source of tremendous economic strength and opportunity for marketers. An understanding of diversity is ultimately needed by all marketers, even those who do not specifically target diverse segments. Clearly, progressive companies are moving toward a better understanding of the similarities and differences among various populations. Each chapter has a diversity box, a diversity heading, or both. In addition, diversity is the subject of several chapter-opening vignettes.

CONNECTING GLOBALLY

We live in a world in which the international theme is increasingly recognized as important in all aspects of business. Marketing nearly always takes place in the international arena, so the global connection is woven into numerous principles and examples. You will find headings and references on this subject throughout. Our book is different from others because it covers this material within every chapter, rather than separately.

CONNECTING THROUGH ETHICS

Ethics are critical in all aspects of business, but particularly in marketing, because decisions in this area can affect many groups of people in very different ways. Marketers often face ethical issues. Every chapter of this book identifies ethical dilemmas marketers encounter. In each situation material is provided to help you think about the implications of marketing decisions and resolve inconsistencies. Real-life situations are discussed, and outcomes are identified.

A TOTAL TEACHING PACKAGE—IN AND OUT OF THE CLASSROOM

A successful marketing course has many challenges. Students demand a lively presentation with up-to-the-minute examples, technology provides an enormous amount of material that can be integrated into the course, and there is less time to prepare for all of it. Prentice Hall has been conducting research into the most effective ways to deliver ancillary materials for professors. Through surveys and focus groups, we have gathered a lot of information and suggestions on the most useful materials to provide to the teaching package for *Marketing: Connecting with Customers.* Your suggestions are most appreciated and will help improve these materials further.

   Note: Many of the supplements listed below are available in different formats. Print versions are available through your local PH representative along with 3.5" disk versions. You can also download many of these materials from our Web site, PHLIP. See below for a more detailed description of the Web resources which have been developed to support the marketing course.

INSTRUCTOR'S RESOURCE MANUAL

This helpful teaching resource contains chapter overviews, annotated outlines, class exercises, relevant stories and examples to help in class preparation, discussion notes for in-text company cases, and answers to end-of-chapter questions and exercises. The manual also contains a complete listing of all the ancillary teaching resources available for this course along with an overview of the PHLIP Web site.

STUDENT LEARNING GUIDE

Prepared by Gil Harrell, this study guide provides students an overview of each chapter, summarizes the major topics and concepts, and strengthens understanding through situational exercises involving cases, chapter highlights, and quizzes. A section of lecture notes reproduces the transparencies with the chapter outline for easy in-class note taking. This guide is also available as an on-line version.

CW99 AND CME

These on-line features offer study materials as well as a course manager. The Course Management edition offers the following new features: roster, gradebook, and announcements.

TEST ITEM FILE

The Test Item File, prepared by Gil Harrell, contains more than 1,400 items, including multiple choice, true-false, and essay questions. These questions are graded for difficulty and page referenced to the text. The questions are available in a Test Item File booklet and through the PH Custom Test program (in Windows and Mac versions).

POWERPOINT TRANSPARENCIES

A set of PowerPoint slides are available to adopters. The Powerpoint 4.0 files include over 175 slides and present complete lectures, transitional notes from one slide to the next, and selected key text figures (with accompanying note slides).

ACETATE/OVERHEAD TRANSPARENCIES

This first set of acetates includes hard copy of the PowerPoint slides (for those who prefer to use an overhead projector in class) along with a selection of key graphics from the text.

ADVERTISEMENT TRANSPARENCIES

A complete set of acetates of recent ads, both domestic and international, are available. Over 75 ads have been collected, together with teaching notes for each one.

ON LOCATION VIDEOS

A full video library is available to adopters. Over forty segments, focusing on major concepts in marketing, showcase a variety of companies from Nike to Starbucks. These videos are accompanied by written video cases that can be downloaded from the PHLIP Web site. A custom selection of these print video cases can also be packaged with each student copy of the text at no additional charge (custom value pack). The video segments range in length from 8 to 15 minutes and include up-to-the-minute "inside" stories of companies around the world.

PHLIP

Both professors and students can visit the best Web site for *Marketing: Connecting with Customers!* Go to www.prenhall.com/phbusiness and click on PHLIP.

ACKNOWLEDGMENTS

We would like to thank many individuals who have made important contributions to this book. Without their help it would not have been produced. Literally every aspect of the project, from planning to production, has been aided by an exceptional team of people who have dedicated their time and talent to this project.

Roger Calantone and Michael Song reviewed and contributed to the chapters involving product decisions. Richard Spreng made important contributions in the area of customer satisfaction. Robert Nason reviewed an early draft and made several suggestions that have significantly improved the final version. The following reviewers have read the entire manuscript, making detailed suggestions that have improved content, helped ensure its accuracy, and made it more interesting for the student:

David Andrus	Kansas State University
Bob Balderstone	Western Melbourne Institute of TAFE (Australia)
Richard Brand	Florida State University
William Carner	University of Texas–Austin
George Chrysschoidis	University of Wales
Howard Combs	San Jose University
John Cronin	Western Connecticut State University
Bernard Delagneau	University of Wales
Peter Doukas	Westchester Community College
Jim Dupree	Grove City College
Joyce Grahn	University of Minnesota–Duluth
Robert F. Guinner	Arizona State
Pola Gupta	University of Northern Iowa
Lynn Harris	Shippensburg University
Benoit Heilbrunn	Le Groupe ESC Lyon/Lyon Graduate School of Business (France)
Frank Krohn	Suny–Fredonia
Ken Lawrence	New Jersey Institute of Technology
Chong S. K. Lee	California State University–Hayward
Elizabeth Mariotz	Philadelphia College of Textiles and Science
Mike Mayo	Kent State University
Gary McCain	Boise State University
G. Stephen Miller	St. Louis University
Herbert Miller	University of Texas–Austin
Mark Mitchell	University of South Carolina
David Mothersbaugh	University of Alabama
Robert O'Keefe	DePaul University
Cliff Olson	Southern State College of SDA
Stan Paliwoda	University of Calgary
Eric Pratt	New Mexico State University
Mohammed Rawwas	University of Northern Iowa
David Urban	Virginia Commonwealth University
Anthony Urbaniak	Northern State University
Simon Walls	Western Washington University
Ken Williamson	James Madison University
Mark Young	Winona State University
George Zinkham	University of Houston

Elizabeth Johnston skillfully edited the entire manuscript. She made tremendous contributions by making the words come to life, by focusing material, and by sculpting the sentences to communicate what is intended. Karen Griggs, Maureen Mulvaney, Mel Hudson Nowak, Erin O'Conner, and Carrie Shimkos tirelessly and enthusiastically did library research, checked sources, found ads, and developed insightful examples. In great spirit, Cindy Seagraves and Sarah Heyer typed the manuscript, which went through many drafts. Somehow they interpreted our scratchings to produce the most professional work. Thank you all so much!

Our gratitude extends to the team at Prentice Hall. Dave Borkowski, acquisitions editor, launched the project with foresight and commitment. Whitney Blake, acquisitions editor, picked up the project midstream, and we extend our thanks for the contributions she has made. Mark Palmer, development editor, did an admirable job to ensure that all bases were covered. His experience with and sensitivity to the subject of this book were most helpful. Michelle Rich, production editor, has done a superb job in producing an attractive text. She has assembled a great team. Elaine Luthy, copy editor, did a splendid job on the final editing to make sure the entire manuscript was in alignment. Melinda Alexander, photo researcher, coordinated the photo specs, finding photographs that perfectly communicate with the points we made in the text. Monica Stipanov, permissions coordinator, obtained permissions for the ads selected for each chapter. Nancy Brandwein contributed several box examples that highlight concepts in the text. John Larkin, supplements editor, has developed the most comprehensive teaching and learning package in the industry to support this book. Steve Deitmer, director of development provided expert assistance at key times. Linda Albelli, editorial manager, provided important assistance on numerous occasions. Editorial assistants Michele Foresta, Rachel Falk, and Theresa Festa kept documents flowing smoothly among the numerous parties. Shannon Moore, marketing manager, and Brian Kibby, marketing director, have shared their insights and developed marketing and sales plans that connect with our target segments. The marketing and sales team at Prentice Hall has provided important research on the desires of faculty and students, continually emphasizing the critical nature of relationships with those parties. Sandy Steiner, President, Jim Boyd, Editorial Director, and Natalie Anderson, Editor-in-Chief, have given personal leadership to this venture. Their vision and foresight are truly appreciated.

In addition, we have had tremendous support from a broad range of business people, such as Duane Larson and Mike McGorrin at Children's World, Jerry Florence at Nissan, Rich Bell and Bob Gaylord at Cutler-Hammer, Jeanne Cole at Lucasfilms, Kenn Thieff at Flagship Group, Vinny Greco at Powerhouse Gym, and Anita Wiznuik at McDonald's® to name a few. Many of the ideas in the book have been used extensively in classes at Michigan State University and the University of Southern California, and a broad range of executive development programs. Surveys of over 2,000 students indicated that the *Connecting with Customers* theme does indeed capture their imagination. The feedback from these students and participants has been helpful, and we gratefully acknowledge their assistance.

Finally, our heartfelt thanks go to our families for their encouragement and loving support; on Gil's side, to my wife Susie and our children Rachael, Nick, and Kate; and on Gary's side, to my wife Kyoung and our daughter Jean.

Thank you all!

Marketing:
Connecting with Customers

Chapter 1

Marketing: Connecting with Customers

Objectives

1. Understand the concept of marketing, including its definition, purpose, and role in creating exchanges.

2. Learn what is involved in making marketing decisions, including examples of product, price, promotion, and place decisions to create a marketing mix.

3. Contrast the periods of marketing evolution, from the early history through the eras of production, sales, and customer marketing, leading up to today.

4. Understand the five key forces that are dramatically influencing how organizations will connect with customers in the 21st century.

5. Determine how marketing pertains to you.

It's hard to imagine that today's designer jeans originated as miners' clothes during the California gold rush, but that's exactly what happened. In 1850 Levi Strauss opened a dry goods store on San Francisco's Market Street. Among other items, he stocked blue canvas pants—the original 501 jeans—for hundreds of dusty miners. Soon these jeans were the choice of farmers, mechanics, and cowhands. Levi's now serves diverse segments that span the globe. To date, Levi's jeans has produced more value than all the gold discovered by California prospectors.

Long before the concept of marketing had evolved, Levi Strauss realized the importance of connecting with customers. He understood that innovation mattered. Therefore, he added patented nonscratch copper rivets on the pocket corners and in the crotch, promising a new pair of jeans if the rivets didn't hold. He also understood how to connect with customers using powerful imagery. In 1886 he added a patch showing two workhorses trying to rip apart a pair of jeans, depicting uncompromising quality.

Today, Levi Strauss & Co. continues to find ways to connect with a new generation of customers. It uses the power of computer technology, telecommunications, global distribution, a vast array of new marketplace options, and flexible manufacturing. It even connects with select target customers the old-fashioned way: one at a time.

Levi's isn't only after the U.S. market. Its international business has grown dramatically, contributing almost half of the company's $7.1 billion in revenues. Levi's controls more than 25 percent of the market in the United Kingdom, where consumers eagerly part with $85 for a pair of 501s. Abroad, Levi's promotes its jeans as fashion statements, which justifies their high price to consumers. It has built a major presence in such diverse areas as Europe, Russia, Japan, China, India, and South Africa.

Like most great marketers, Levi's enters a new market looking to satisfy needs and wants. If necessary, it creates a new product to connect with customers. In Brazil, the company found that women prefer a skin-tight fit, so Levi's created the Feminina jean. In Argentina, the preference for loose-fitting clothes led to the creation of the Dockers line.

Levi's also pays attention to the diversity of its home markets. A Hispanic marketing director guides Levi's into the fast-growing segment of young and brand-loyal Latinos. The company airs commercials on Spanish-language television to reach that audience. In 1992, Levi's launched its innovative "Jeans for Women" advertising campaign, using images created by women artists of women in blue jeans.

Levi Strauss might have been most proud of his company's innovative "Personal Pair Jeans" program, which connects with customers on an individual basis. Levi's recognizes that a select segment of the population seeks the ultimate in personal service. So, using a hot new marketing concept known as mass customization, *Levi's now offers made-to-order women's and men's jeans. This is how it works: Store associates enter measurements into a computer and transmit them electronically to a Levi's factory, where a pair of jeans are cut precisely to the customer's fit from a bolt of denim. The finished jeans are shipped directly to the customer. Consistent with Levi's original idea, unsatisfied customers can return their jeans for a cash refund. Levi's knows, however, that once customers have gone to the effort of providing personal data, they are likely to become loyal buyers—the connection Levi's values most. In fact, most customers are so pleased with their customized fit that they order more jeans with the same dimensions.*[1]

Levi Strauss founded a company that has become one of the world's best-known businesses. From the start, he intuitively adopted concepts that we call marketing. *Ideas like satisfying customers and personalized marketing, which seemed logical to him, have now been proven successful by scores of marketing research studies—and by billions in corporate profits.*

CONNECTED: SURFING THE NET

www.levi.com

Connect to the Levi's Web site to find out how you can be fitted for a pair of personal jeans.

CAREER TIP Most companies hope to find college graduates with experience directly related to the career they seek. Summer internships are the perfect opportunity to gain such experience. Levi Strauss & Co. offers internships that run from June through August. Most positions are in the home office in San Francisco, but some are available at other locations throughout the country. Contact Levi Strauss & Co. in March to obtain an application for a summer internship.

THE CONCEPT OF MARKETING: CONNECTING WITH CUSTOMERS

Some organizations connect with you. Nike, Coca-Cola, and McDonald's® seem to have the uncanny ability to fit into your world. They use the latest technologies to serve you; they are there when you need them—at home or abroad; they understand and accommodate diversity; and they are ethically and socially responsible. They work hard to understand what you want. They take every possible action to relate to you in order to form a lasting connection. In turn, perhaps you will connect with them. That's what they want. These organizations know you have plenty of choices, so they practice marketing at its highest level.

Ideally, organizations are created, grow, and continue to grow. In reality, some decline, and many die. For one reason or another, declining organizations fall out of favor with customers who replace them with more vibrant organizations. The common link: Winning organizations do an exceptional job of connecting with customers. They are extraordinary marketers. They understand the marketing concept, and use a full range of marketing tools and techniques. They help customers experience the tremendous satisfaction that occurs when products precisely match their needs and wants. Every time satisfaction occurs, a new connection is made or an existing connection is made stronger.

Today's business environment is global, diverse, and ethically challenging. It is based on technologies that serve customers in ways only imagined a short time ago. Therefore, marketing plays a critical role in determining where, when, and how these technological advances will be applied. Marketing is about much more than just selling a product. It is about connecting with customers in ways that are deeply rewarding for them. Marketing is also about serving the needs of society and accomplishing the goals of the organization. It includes researching potential customers' needs and wants; developing appropriate goods and services; communicating with the market; creating, selecting, and managing channels to reach customers; and pricing to deliver superior customer value. It is about satisfying customers so they will reward the business with the loyalty necessary to reach organizational objectives.

This chapter introduces marketing. As ideas are presented, chapters are referenced to provide a brief overview of the book. We begin by defining marketing and discussing its purpose. Next, we review how marketing creates and facilitates economic exchanges. Then, a section on the marketing strategy process introduces the basic elements used to build a marketing plan. This is followed by a short discussion of how marketing has evolved. We then describe how five key factors are shaping the ways in which organizations will connect with customers in the 21st century. Finally, the chapter ends with a note on the personal perspective you bring to marketing.

DEFINITION OF MARKETING

How do you view marketing? Is your impression positive or negative? Because marketing is a broad subject that can be viewed from many perspectives, it can be described in many ways. Most people have been exposed to advertising, point-of-purchase displays, and personal selling, so marketing is often seen strictly as the promotion and sale of existing products. However, marketing is much more extensive. Excellent marketing begins long before a product exists. This allows all marketing decisions—including promotion—to be made with customer needs and wants in mind. Marketing extends far beyond a purchase to ensure customer satisfaction and loyalty. You can gain a good idea about the extent of marketing by understanding each element in its definition.

The American Marketing Association (AMA), an organization of professionals interested in furthering the marketing discipline, developed the following definition. **Marketing** is the process of planning and executing the conception, pricing, promotion, and distribution of ideas, goods, and services to create exchanges that satisfy individual and organizational objectives.[2] Figure 1-1 highlights key elements of the marketing definition.

Marketing
The process of planning and executing the conception, pricing, promotion, and distribution of ideas, goods, and services to create exchanges that satisfy individual and organizational objectives.

THE PROCESS OF PLANNING AND EXECUTING

Marketing is an ongoing process. Processes are used to manage complex phenomena that undergo change. New competitors enter the market, customers change, and the economic climate shifts. What works today may be totally wrong tomorrow. Consequently, those who practice marketing must take a long view of events and see the world over time. They must not focus on a single transaction at one moment but on the enduring, systematic management of change. Marketers look for patterns, trends, and surprises that signal what is likely to

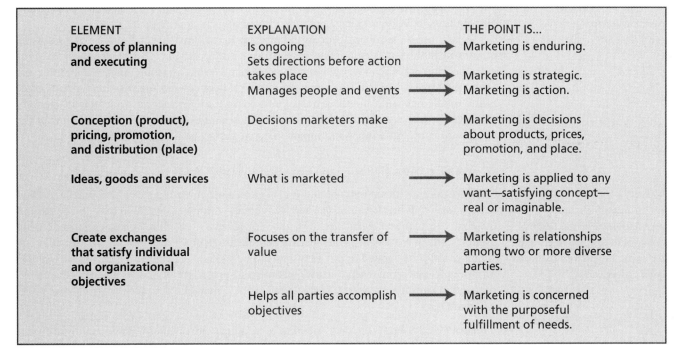

Figure 1-1 Key Elements of the Marketing Definition

happen in the future. In fact, later it will be apparent that marketing has its greatest value when it helps guide organizations in highly dynamic environments.

Consider, for example, the computer field in which the marketing plan is crucial. In 1978, the world's fastest computer processed 160 million instructions per second and cost $20 million. Twenty years later, the Sony PlayStation cost $149 and could process 500 million instructions per second.[3] There are literally thousands of similar examples in the computer, telecommunications, and other industries. In the next 20 years, speed compression and cost reduction for computing power will be even more pronounced, and the number of new products and services will be staggering. The computer industry is not alone in rapid change. No company today can enter a major market expecting that a single product and strategy will sustain it for long. Rather, it is the ability to change that separates great marketers from others.

Marketing is concerned with the process of planning, with the guidance system for companies. Planning sets direction before action takes place. It addresses what is to be accomplished and how to accomplish it. Competition forces marketing plans to be strategic, to address ways to satisfy customer needs and wants better than competitors. Later we will see that plans are created for a whole organization as well as for select products. No matter what is being planned, marketing involves a broad range of people in order for plans to be relevant. Consequently, marketing usually means working in groups rather than working alone.

Marketing is also responsible for executing or carrying out the plan. Marketing manages people and events in line with the plan, which serves as a guide. To carry out plans, marketing must acquire and develop many of the organization's human resources. Marketers are managers and doers. Marketing is action.

PRODUCT, PRICE, PROMOTION, AND PLACE

Years ago, Professor James Culliton described the business executive as a

> "decider" and "artist"—a "mixer of ingredients" who sometimes follows a recipe as he goes along, sometimes adapts a recipe to the ingredients immediately available, and sometimes experiments with or invents ingredients no one else has tried.[4]

Marketing mix
The four controllable variables—product, price, promotion, and place (distribution)—that are combined to appeal to the company's target markets.

This short passage gave Neil Borden, another noted professor, the idea that there is a list of elements the marketer mixes together. He called these elements the **marketing mix.**[5] Today, they are known as the four P's—product, price, promotion, and place. Several other elements are incorporated within this list. For example, product development, branding, packaging, and service are included in the product area. Leasing, credit terms, and price are all part of pricing. Advertising, personal selling, and sales promotion are included in promotion. Distribution, logistics, retailing, and direct marketing are part of place.

It is through the mixing process that organizations arrive at unique ways of addressing customers. In the process of mixing, marketing creativity and imagination play a key role. For example, Norcom, a school supplies company, found a market among the 40 million Americans who are left-handed. Norcom introduced a notebook with the wire binder and perforation on the right side and three holes punched on the left. Once available only in specialty stores, this creative product is selling in mass-merchandise outlets.[6] A dramatic shift in the mix produces a huge winner and minor shifts create day-to-day competition.

MARKETS FOR IDEAS, GOODS, AND SERVICES

Market
All the individuals and organizations with the desire or potential to have the desire and the ability to acquire a particular good or service.

Marketing occurs within markets and is applied to a very broad range of phenomena. A **market** consists of all the organizations and individuals with the potential to have the desire and the ability to acquire a particular idea, good, or service. Generally, we talk about marketing products, which are usually goods that are manufactured or services that are performed. Marketing can also be applied to any idea that can be used in exchange of value. These include, for example, marketing events, causes, people, and places. Ideas, goods, and services, are exchanged in consumer markets, business-to-business markets, nonprofit markets, and internal markets.

Consumer Markets Literally millions of products are marketed to many diverse consumers. Consumer marketing occurs when organizations sell to individuals or households that buy, consume, and dispose of products. Leading consumer marketers include such companies as Procter & Gamble, Johnson & Johnson, General Mills, Hewlett-Packard, and Nike.

Norcom's found a unique way to address customers with the introduction of a left-handed notebook.

You know the products of these companies very well. You have probably already purchased or used many of them and will continue to do so over the years. Because you buy, consume, and dispose of products such as these daily, you are an important part of consumer marketing. We will learn more about consumer marketing throughout this book.

Business-to-Business Markets   Business-to-business marketing occurs when a business purchases goods or services to produce other goods, to support daily operations, or to resell at a profit. Although there are many more consumers than companies, business-to-business purchases far outweigh the consumer market in dollar amount.

Organizations belong either to the public or private sector. The public sector consists of federal, state, and local government organizations. The private sector includes industrial firms, professionals, retailers, and service organizations. Utility companies, which provide water, electricity, gas, and waste disposal, fall between the public and private sectors because they are regulated by the government but may be privately owned. All these organizations rely on business-to-business marketing to purchase goods and support their operations. For example, IBM sells high-end computer solutions and services to specialized engineers and vendors.[7] Companies such as Textron Automotive purchase mostly raw materials and components. Textron buys more than $500 million per year for products from General Electric (GE) over the GE Information Services Web site.[8] In chapter 8 we will explore many of the topics and issues involved in business-to-business marketing.

Nonprofit Markets   Nonprofit marketing occurs when an organization does not try to make a profit but instead attempts to influence others to support its cause by using its service or by making a contribution. Marketing has many applications in the not-for-profit sector. Churches, museums, hospitals, universities, symphonies, and municipalities regularly create marketing plans in an effort to be more consumer oriented. The National Fish and Wildlife Foundation uses such marketing tools as fund-raisers and conferences to create partnerships with government agencies, universities, individuals, and corporations that will support its cause, which is to solve environmental problems.[9] Boston area businesses support the arts through partnerships. Recently, BayBanks sponsored the promotion of a major exhibition at the Museum of Fine Arts in Boston, and Filene's Department Stores sponsored the Boston

Ballet's *Nutcracker.* The U.S. Postal Service competes with private companies, such as Federal Express and United Parcel Service (UPS), to attract consumers, and the U.S. Army, Navy, Air Force, and Marines use their large marketing budgets for recruiting purposes.

Like businesses that seek profit, many of these organizations want to please their constituents, and they have competition. Although they may not be motivated by profit, many are interested in obtaining revenues that equal or exceed expenses. A full range of marketing decisions is often required. We will learn in chapter 11 that, in making these decisions, many not-for-profit groups seek the same quality of marketing talent as for-profit companies do.

Internal Markets   Internal marketing occurs when managers of one functional unit market their capabilities to other units within their own organization. This type of marketing addresses the needs and wants of internal customers, the employees of the firm, so these people can ultimately contribute to the external customers, who are the end users of a company's products or services. For example, Dr. Lew Dotterer, director of learning and organizational development at Sparrow Health System in Lansing, Michigan, is responsible for maintaining the knowledge and skills of employees in all units of the system. Applying marketing techniques, he first identified the key customers—doctors, nurses, administrators, and so forth. Next, he researched each group to determine its learning needs. He then created educational programs to address the learning needs of each group and promoted these programs throughout the organization. Through internal marketing, Dr. Dotterer was able to help employees better serve Sparrow's external customers (patients).

CREATE EXCHANGES THAT SATISFY INDIVIDUAL AND ORGANIZATIONAL OBJECTIVES

How an organization connects with customers has a lot to do with its value. Without customers or the ability to attract them, an organization has absolutely no value. Without customers, an organization's assets are totally wasted. Value occurs for customers and for the organization only when an exchange is created. Thus, marketing creates valuable exchanges. An **exchange** is a process in which two or more parties provide something of value to one another. At the most basic level, an exchange involves a seller who provides a product to a buyer for money or some other item. Most exchanges are much more complex than that. They involve several parties in a social system exchanging all kinds of items.[10] Marketing brings the many parties together and facilitates exchanges. This provides utility. When marketers create utility, value is created. Utility is a term economists use to describe the want-satisfying potential of a good or service. There are four fundamental types of utility—form, place, time, and ownership.

Form, Place, Time, and Ownership Utility   **Form** utility occurs when knowledge and materials are converted into finished goods and services. Marketing provides form utility when it guides decisions about what products to create and the attributes those products should possess. When McDonald's® created the Grilled Chicken Deluxe® for health-conscious consumers, the specific sandwich provided form utility. Microsoft's Windows 98™ provided form utility by combining concepts into software that possessed the attributes desired by consumers. Generally, the marketing function is responsible only for specifying what form utility the final product should possess; research and development (R&D), engineering, manufacturing, and other units are responsible for actually building it.

Place utility makes goods and services conveniently available. Fresh bananas on a remote tree are not nearly as want satisfying as those at a local supermarket, convenience store, or restaurant. They are worth many times more at those locations than where they are grown. Marketing brings products to customers for the sake of convenience. When CSX's Sea Land Service, the biggest shipping line in America, brings cargo to 75,000 cities without ports, it is providing place utility.[11] Place utility can be extremely valuable. Shopping malls provide utility by grouping stores and products together, making it convenient and sometimes fun to shop. In addition, many of these stores ship to your house, offering utility in two forms.

Time utility makes goods and services available when they are wanted. Videotapes can be watched at your convenience, which is one reason for their tremendous popularity. UPS, Federal Express, Airborne Express, and other overnight carriers offer outstanding time utility. L. L. Bean now receives an order one day and has the item at your home the next, fifteen times faster than the Sears, Roebuck & Co. mail orders that dominated the 1970s and earlier. When General Motors developed GM Access, a program that allows dealers to have a car built to customer specifications and to check inventory in minutes, it provided time utility. As a

Exchange

A process in which two or more parties provide something of value to one another.

Form utility

A want-satisfying value that is created when knowledge and materials are converted into finished goods and services.

Place utility

A want-sayisfying value that is created by making goods and services conveniently available.

Time utility

A want-satisfying value that is created when goods and services are made available when they are wanted.

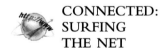

L.L. Bean provides time utility to customers with fast, efficient delivery.

result, dealers and customers can put together a car order without the time-consuming process of reading manuals and making phone calls.[12]

Ownership utility makes it possible to transfer the title of goods and services from one party to another. The most obvious way is through cash transactions, but credit card purchases and leasing are other means. Later we will learn about this function internationally. Even airplane travel is a form of ownership utility. By leasing a seat (buying a ticket), you can possess the vast resources of the air transportation system during the time required to reach nearly any destination on the planet. Marketing has progressed by finding better ways to produce increasing amounts of utility.

Ownership utility
A want-satisfying value that is created by making it possible to transfer the title of goods and services from one party to another.

Organizational Objectives All organizations have long-term objectives. Many organizations generally focus on financial measures such as profit margins and return on investment to evaluate performance. Companies must make money when they fulfill consumer needs. Profit provides the financial fuel that allows companies to innovate and grow. Nonprofit organizations, in contrast, use measures such as donation levels, membership, and services provided to evaluate performance. Although nonprofit organizations must be effective and efficient, by definition they do not seek profit as a primary goal. Still, even nonprofit organizations strive to satisfy their constituents in a cost-effective way. For example, the national organizations for Boy Scouts and Girl Scouts have rigorous financial goals. They often strive for growth in sales and in number of members as well as certain levels of customer satisfaction relative to competitors.

CONNECTED: SURFING THE NET

www.llbean.com

Visit the Catalog Quickstop and product guide on L. L. Bean's Web site and discover the advantages of time utility firsthand!

THE MARKETING CONCEPT: THE PURPOSE OF MARKETING

While the definition of marketing summarizes what marketers do, the marketing concept provides the underlying purpose. According to the **marketing concept** (philosophy), the purpose of marketing is to understand the needs and wants of customers and to create customer value through satisfaction and quality more effectively and efficiently than competitors. Applying the concept helps meet the long-term goals of the organization. The marketing concept

Marketing concept
Holds that the purpose of marketing is to identify the needs and wants of customers within markets and satisfy them in ways that ensure the long-run success of the organization.

provides the guiding reference for appropriate marketing action. In principle, it is simple; in practice, it provides the basis for an awesomely competitive system that dramatically benefits consumers. Because needs and wants are numerous, diverse, and dynamic, the concept points toward unlimited opportunities for marketing. Elements of the marketing concept are summarized in Figure 1-2.

UNDERSTAND THE NEEDS AND WANTS OF CUSTOMERS

Understanding customer needs and wants is central to the marketing concept. It is possible to implement appropriate marketing without this understanding. Marketers use a **consumer orientation**, an organizational philosophy that focuses on satisfying consumer needs and wants.

Needs and wants are not the same. **Needs** are fundamental requirements—meeting them is the ultimate goal of behavior. Of course, there are many needs, ranging from those that allow life to exist to those that produce personal enrichment. A need becomes apparent when there is a gap between a desired state and an actual state. For example, you need proper nutrition on a regular basis to have a healthy and energetic body. When nutrition drops below the desired state, your body signals the deprivation—you feel hungry. When the need is satisfied, the hunger goes away. Needs represent what people and organizations must have to survive and thrive. The degree to which needs are satisfied determines the quality of life for all people and organizations.

A **want** is the specific form of consumption desired to satisfy a need. Many different wants can fulfill a need. Each want represents an alternative way to meet goals or requirements. A want is simply one of many desires a person may have to help fulfill a need. For instance, hunger can be satisfied with a candy bar, an orange, or a chicken sandwich. Needs produce many wants. Fulfillment of a huge range of differing wants has the potential to satisfy needs.

Like people, organizations are customers with needs. All organizations have objectives that must be met. They need suppliers and employees. For-profit companies must make a sizable return on the owners' investment or they will go out of business. Nonprofit companies have other needs: The Red Cross, for example, must help increasing numbers of disaster victims if it is to meet its organizational objectives. Every organization needs customers or clients—the people they serve. There are many ways to obtain them, as well as specific types of suppliers, characteristics of employees, and profit objectives. Each way represents a potential want. Boeing addresses the need of United Airlines for aircraft by designing planes the airline will want, with attributes that satisfy United's needs. Figure 1-3 shows the relationship between needs and wants.

The marketing concept recognizes the long-run nature of successful marketing. Potential customers continuously search to satisfy wants in such a way as to produce the greatest amount of need satisfaction. Therefore, customers are dynamic. Marketing leaders facilitate

Consumer orientation
An organizational philosophy that focuses on satisfying consumer needs and wants.

Needs
Fundamental requirements the meeting of which is the ultimate goal of behavior.

Want
A specific form of consumption desired to satisfy need.

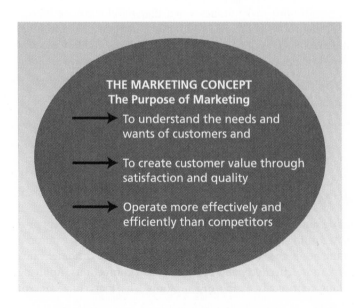

THE MARKETING CONCEPT
The Purpose of Marketing

→ To understand the needs and wants of customers and

→ To create customer value through satisfaction and quality

→ Operate more effectively and efficiently than competitors

Figure 1-2 The Marketing Concept

NEEDS Fundamental Requirements	Produce → ← Satisfy	WANTS Form of Consumption Desired to Satisfy a Need

Figure 1-3   Needs and Wants

and adjust to change rapidly by learning how to serve customers in new and creative ways. Long-term success as a marketer requires change management. The speed and effectiveness with which marketers learn how to serve customers can provide tremendous competitive advantages. Because needs and wants are numerous, diverse, and dynamic, the concept points toward unlimited opportunities for marketing.

CREATE CUSTOMER VALUE THROUGH SATISFACTION AND QUALITY

The second element of the marketing concept is to create customer value through satisfaction and quality. *Satisfaction* refers to the consumer's overall rating of his/her experience with a company and its products. *Quality* refers to the degree of excellence of a company's products or services. *Customer value* refers to what consumers perceive they gain from owning and using a product over and above the cost of acquiring it—a topic we will consider in more detail in chapter 2. In combination, satisfaction, quality, and customer value help create loyal customers. Loyal customers are a valuable asset. They provide a continuous revenue stream through repeated purchases of a product. They tell others about their satisfaction, which is one of the most effective and inexpensive forms of promotion. Pizza Hut spent $50 million in 1997 to improve the quality of its pizzas. As part of its initiative, Pizza Hut guaranteed customer satisfaction—or else the pizza was free.[13]

AT&T requires each business unit to submit reports detailing the financial effects of its efforts on customer satisfaction. The message is clear: If it doesn't contribute to satisfied customers, forget it.[14] Service Merchandise adopted a motto that proclaims its commitment to

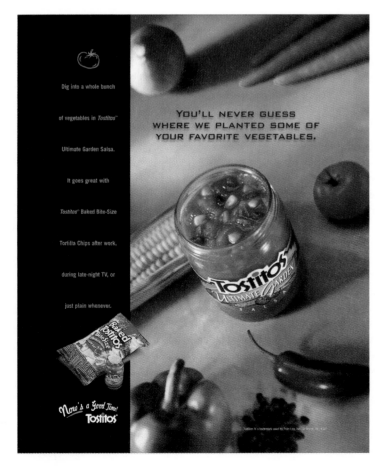

Many different wants can fulfill a need.

value: "No one offers more value at any price." Organizations that strive to implement a marketing philosophy that benefits the customer develop satisfied, loyal customers. A level of satisfaction strong enough to produce loyalty requires an organizational commitment to quality in every aspect of the business.

MORE EFFECTIVELY AND EFFICIENTLY THAN COMPETITORS

Strong marketers compete, and they measure success by the way their customers judge them, especially relative to competitors. Competition is the key to our economic system. You see aggressive global competition occurring every day: Coke versus Pepsi, McDonald's® versus Burger King, and American Airlines versus British Airways. Phil Knight, founder of Nike, has challenged its marketing team to take competition to a new level—replace Coca-Cola as the most recognized brand in the world.[15] Since Coke and Nike don't compete head to head with the same products, this competition is unique. It will be interesting to see whether Nike, Coke, or another company has the number one position in the next few years.

Don't think that only for-profit companies compete. Even nonprofit groups compete. Mail-order catalogs from the Art Institute of Chicago, the Metropolitan Museum of Art, the Smithsonian Institution, and Boston's Museum of Fine Arts all compete for your purchases. The United Way competes for your discretionary income, and political parties compete for your donations.

Effectiveness
The degree to which an organization's activities produce results that matter to consumers.

Efficiency
The degree to which activities are carried out without waste of time or money.

Marketers outperform competitors by being more effective and efficient. **Effectiveness** means that the organization's activities produce results that matter to consumers. It means doing the right things. **Efficiency** means doing these things with minimal waste of time and money. Baxter International, a hospital products company with $9 billion in annual sales, is successful on both counts. First, it recognized that customers—hospitals—were spending too much money storing and distributing supplies. Baxter developed an electronic ordering system that indicates what supplies are needed daily and where in the hospital the supplies should go. This system is effective because it meets the needs of Baxter's customers better than the competition. It is efficient because it saves both the hospitals and Baxter substantial amounts of money and time. In many cases hospitals choose Baxter as their only supplier, which leads to higher sales and profits for Baxter.

THE MARKETING STRATEGY PROCESS

The marketing concept is implemented through the marketing strategy process, the series of steps the organization takes to interface with the rest of the world. Chapter 4 defines the elements of that process in more depth. Figure 1-4 illustrates the steps of the marketing strategy process.

SITUATION ANALYSIS

Situation analysis includes all the marketing activities required to understand the global marketing environment, the customer's needs and wants, and the competition. It predicts future marketing conditions for the period covered by the strategic marketing plan. Many aspects of the global marketing environment are the same for all organizations, no matter what their line of business. Other aspects are unique to a particular industry. Both types of aspects are addressed in chapter 3.

To enhance their ability to analyze situations, organizations often build elaborate marketing intelligence systems. These capture, distill, and disseminate data to executives on an ongoing basis. Marketers also engage in marketing research, which supplies information about a particular circumstance such as planning for a new product, pricing, or the selling approach.

The situation analysis gives a good idea of the issues an organization must address. It provides the context around which plans are created, altered, and adjusted. This generally requires a thorough knowledge of consumer behavior or, in business-to-business marketing, of organizational buying behavior. Understanding consumer behavior gives marketers insight into why buyers respond to goods and services as they do. As we will see in chapter 7, consumer behavior involves not only their purchase behavior but also the ways in which consumers perceive and use information and how they arrive at feelings of satisfaction and dissatisfaction. Organizational buying behavior is more complex in terms of the functions and personnel involved in the buying decision, and marketer relationships with these buyers are

Figure 1-4   Steps in the Marketing Strategy Process

often more direct. Chapter 8 covers organizational buying in the context of business marketing.

An important function of the situation analysis is to provide the information needed to select certain customers for emphasis—targeting—which is covered next.

TARGETING

Markets usually have many types of potential customers with many different needs and wants. It is impractical to attempt to satisfy all customers. Consequently, leading marketers divide customers into groups with similar characteristics. They then select one or several unique groups to address. A **target market** is a group of potential customers with similar characteristics that the company tries to satisfy better than the competition.

The first decision that a customer-driven company makes is to choose its target markets. Fashion designer Ralph Lauren targets upscale consumers with his popular casual line. Lee, also with a line of casual clothing, targets a completely different subset of the market. Consider the different target market groups for Rolex and Swatch, Cannondale and Huffy, or Marriott and Motel 6. Esprit targets Generation Xers and teens with its line of Dr. Seuss apparel, shoes, and accessories. Because the characters from the popular Dr. Seuss children's books have a retro appeal for young people, an ideal target market exists for products with Sam-I-Am, the Grinch, and other Seuss favorites.[16] All these companies carefully cater to a specific subset of the population.

POSITIONING

One of the most useful concepts to help integrate marketing decisions is positioning. Positioning is the process of creating an image, reputation, or perception of the company or its goods and/or services in the consumer's mind. Although the idea exists in the buyer's mind, it is formed by very specific actions of the marketing organization. First, the company must identify how it wants to be positioned with a target market. Nike says "Just Do It," reinforcing the image of an aggressive, action-oriented company. It's no accident that amateur as well as professional athletes perceive Nike as producing high-quality shoes that help athletes per-

Target market
A group of potential customers with similar characteristics that a marketer tries to satisfy better than the competition.

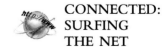

CONNECTED: SURFING THE NET

www.esprit.com

Are you a member of Esprit's target market? If so, you can explore the Esprit cyberstore where Esprit sells its Dr. Seuss apparel, shoes, and accessories on-line.

form to their maximum potential. Everything Nike does is designed to create this impression, including the use of outstanding athletes like Michael Jordan to spread their promotional message. Positioning is accomplished by creating and adjusting the product, place, promotion, and price variables so that consumers can recognize the distinctiveness of a company or its product. Potential buyers can then better determine the degree to which a product fits their desires. It is this distinctiveness that supports positioning. The next section discusses how companies use the marketing mix to create distinctive positions. Chapter 6 examines positioning strategies in more detail, including the various bases for positioning.

MARKETING MIX DECISIONS

Once the target market is selected, marketing mix decisions have to be made. How do you go about blending the elements into an appealing mix? Clearly, there needs to be a focus and a purpose. That's where the target market enters the picture. Since it is composed of similar customers, it is possible to address them with one marketing mix. Adjustments to individual customers then can be made within this framework. Figure 1-5 illustrates elements of the marketing mix and target marketing. Later we'll see that even minor inconsistencies in how marketing mix elements are blended can be disastrous. At the same time, innovation in these areas is what provides opportunities for organizations to excel.

Product Strategy Product strategy includes decisions about which products to develop, how to manage current products, and which products to phase out. It thereby determines the portfolio of goods and services the organization provides to the market. Because products go through a life cycle, product strategy decisions are ongoing. Most organizations use systematic processes to develop new products and manage products over their life cycles, including decisions regarding product attributes, warranties, package design, and customer service features.

Equally important for many companies is the establishment of brands and the creation of brand equity, the value associated with a brand. Brands send messages to consumers about the unique qualities of products. A great deal of care must be taken to establish brand names and protect their reputation. For example, in the $6 billion beverage industry, brands flourish and die quickly. Triarc recently purchased the plateaued Snapple brand from Quaker Oats with a plan to revitalize its reputation—perhaps returning it to the number three U.S. beverage.[17] Techniques for making product decisions will be discussed in both chapter 9, "Product Decisions and Strategies," and chapter 10, "Product Innovation and Management."

Place Strategy The objective of place strategy is to serve customers by providing products where and when they are needed, in the proper quantities, with the greatest appeal, and at the lowest possible cost. The first task is to determine which distribution channels to use. A distribution channel is a set of independent organizations that make a good or service avail-

*Figure 1-5 The Marketing
Mix and Target Marketing*

able for purchase by consumers or businesses. Some companies sell directly, such as your local dry cleaner, while others use longer channels with more members. For example, a company may sell to wholesalers, who sell to retailers, who sell to you. Imagine how complicated this becomes in global markets, when numerous channel members are required to move products to customers around the world. Compaq, which sells primarily through retailers, had noted that more and more people are buying direct from manufacturers. Therefore, in order to gain more direct access to customers, the company tried to acquire Gateway 2000, a major direct marketer. The *Wall Street Journal* said Compaq hoped "to better connect with buyers of its computers," with the help of Gateway's efficient distribution systems. When its acquisition plans fell through, Compaq hired 2,000 sales people to increase contact with customers. It will also push current distributors to improve services.[18]

Place decisions also involve physical distribution, which is the movement of products through the channels to consumers. To make movement efficient, companies need order entry systems, transportation, and shipping and inventory storage capacity. Sophisticated information systems are creating some extremely innovative ways of serving customers better.

Finally, companies need to manage their interface with customers. Two basic ways are retailing and direct marketing. Retailing involves selling products directly to end users, often in retail outlets such as McDonald's® or Kmart. Direct marketing uses an array of nonstore methods of connecting with customers. Marketing via telephone is one of the traditional direct marketing approaches. Today 80 percent of direct marketers use some type of "new media," such as on-line services, the World Wide Web, interactive kiosks, fax, and CD-ROM. Since customers can connect to the company so quickly through these media, direct marketers are challenged to respond more rapidly than ever before.[19] Chapter 12, "Marketing Channels, Wholesaling, and Physical Distribution," and chapter 13, "Retailing and Direct Marketing," address the place strategy.

Promotion Strategy Promotion involves communicating with customers in a variety of ways. Marketers develop integrated marketing communications by coordinating advertising, sales promotion, personal selling, and public relations to get consistent messages to all types of customers. These messages provide information necessary for the choice process. Promotion also increases demand for products, describes unique product characteristics, and helps build customer loyalty by creating expectations and reinforcing buying decisions. Heinz Ketchup recently involved kids in a promotion strategy to encourage parents' loyalty. The company sponsored a "Hey Kids, Wanna Be Famous?" contest. Ads ran in magazines nationwide, inviting kids to create a new label for its ketchup. Sixty thousand kids participated—a successful attempt to influence family buying decisions.[20]

The promotion strategy includes determining the objectives to be attained, as well as creating messages and the forms they will take. In addition, the communication mechanism or media must be selected. Will two-way communication be used, such as personal selling, the phone, or Internet or will one-way radio, television, or other media carry the message? Since many messages are carried by numerous media, these decisions can be complex and tremendously interesting. Marketers have a vast number of options when developing promotions, such as training and managing a sales force, or creating advertising. Because these mechanisms work together, coordination is vital. The promotion strategy is addressed in chapter 14, "Integrated Marketing Communications"; chapter 15, "Mass Communications: Advertising, Sales Promotions, and Public Relations"; and chapter 16, "Personal Selling and Sales Force Management."

Price Strategy Price strategy affects nearly every part of a business. The objective is to set prices to reflect the value received by customers and to achieve the volume and profit required by the organization. When prices are too high, customers are dissatisfied and refuse to buy, or switch to a competitor. When prices are too low, companies don't have money to cover costs, invest in new development, and provide a fair return to owners. So pricing strategy is extremely important.

Historically, prices were set by adding up costs and tagging on some extra for profit. That approach ignores customers and competitors, two critical elements in determining price. Pricing must focus on determining value, which is based on what customers expect and desire, what competitors charge, and the unique qualities of the products. Marketers must also determine how their prices will influence the volume sold relative to competition, and what competitors are likely to do with their prices. Consequently, we find many different pricing strategies for new and existing products and for various competitive scenarios.

Prices not only need to be set, but also must be communicated and administered. Will warranty charges be extra? What is charged for the base product or add-on? What financing is available? These questions must be answered and factored in. Pricing strategy is covered in chapter 17, "Pricing Approaches," and chapter 18, "Pricing Strategy."

THE EVOLUTION OF MARKETING

When Levi Strauss originally connected with customers, he did it personally—one-to-one. Over time his company moved to mass production and extended its reach to consumers globally. As with most organizations, the connections to customers became more complex and strained as the company expanded. Levi Strauss, much like marketing in general, has come full circle, and is again forging connections at a more personal level. Today, companies realize the importance of personal connections, and are working to establish and maintain them. In response to such challenges, marketing has developed a variety of mechanisms over the decades. A brief history will help explain how marketing has evolved in response to changing business conditions and requirements.

Marketing activities, in the broadest sense, can be traced to the trading and barter that occurred thousands of years ago. The ancient Egyptians had vending machines as early as 200 B.C.! But it wasn't until the 1500s in England and the 1600s in Germany and North America that modern marketing began. Most people lived in rural areas and produced all necessary goods themselves. Nevertheless, enterprising business people, who were actually early marketers, discovered they could make money by providing luxury items to the upper class and more practical goods to others in the population.

Although large trading companies had been around for centuries, many merchants and craftsmen built their businesses by satisfying individual customers. You often bought your shoes from a cobbler who knew the exact dimensions of your feet, your preferred shoe style, and your ability to pay. Even if the cobbler had competition, why would you go elsewhere?[21]

During the late 1700s and early 1800s, major improvements in production and transportation, along with growing urbanization, fostered the development of mass marketing. **Mass marketing** is the mass production, mass distribution, and mass promotion of a product to all buyers. A free enterprise system based on competition began to develop. Starting in the late 1800s, advertising, marketing research, improved physical distribution methods, and retailing were used to help find and develop markets for mass production. Unlike the days when the consumer came into direct contact with the producer, more goods began to be purchased through an intermediary. The producer had no contact with the end user.

During this century, the economy moved through three basic eras in terms of the focus of business: the production era, the sales era, and the customer marketing era as depicted in Figure 1-6.

THE PRODUCTION ERA

During the production era, which lasted until about 1925, companies focused on ways to make products in mass quantities. They achieved production economies that often led to lower prices. This **production orientation** emphasized new products and the efficiency of production. Businesses were primarily concerned with ways to speed physical production. Manufacturers did not address the consumer until after the goods had been made. They assumed a good product would sell itself. Salespeople were more interested in helping the manufacturer take orders than in helping the customer. Demand for these new lower-priced prod-

Mass marketing
The mass production, mass distribution, and mass promotion of a product to all buyers.

Production orientation
Historical marketing period that emphasized new products and the efficiency of production.

Figure 1-6 Eras of Marketing Since 1900

ucts was often greater than supply, which led to the growth of large manufacturing organizations.

Henry Ford's approach is a prime example of production orientation. Until Ford came along, automobiles were made one at a time in small factories. Often each car was unique; perhaps a few of each type were made. Ford standardized the design of the Model T and mass-produced it on an assembly line. This dramatically reduced costs and made cars affordable to more people. Visualizing a ready demand for this cheap form of transportation, he remarked that people "can have any color they want, as long as it's black."

THE SALES ERA

As production methods improved and more firms entered markets, competition increased. Eventually, the supply of many products outpaced demand. Since businesses had more goods than their regular customers could buy, the need for personal selling and advertising arose. The sales era focused on ways to sell more effectively. This period was marked by the Great Depression of the 1930s when spending power was drastically reduced. Consumers resisted purchasing nonessential goods and services. Sales forces and sales tactics were developed to overcome their resistance.

The **sales orientation** emphasized that consumers must be convinced to buy. Consumer tastes, preferences, and needs did not receive much consideration. Rather, companies tried to shape consumers' ideals to fit the attributes of the products offered.

After World War II, a vastly different economic environment emerged in the United States. The country was moving from the **seller's market,** where scarcity of products lets the seller control the market, to a **buyer's market,** where abundance of products lets the buyer control the market. With the emergence of the buyer's market came rewards to organizations that gave customers a prominent place in their business thinking.

THE CUSTOMER MARKETING ERA

A company with a sales philosophy focuses internally. Emphasis is placed on making the product, then on selling it. The sales force has to push existing products to the consumer through increased promotion and personal selling. In contrast, the customer marketing concept emphasizes customer satisfaction and value. After an organization determines consumer needs, it coordinates its activities so that the product will satisfy customer needs and wants.

During the past 30 years marketing has evolved into a tremendously important business function. Figure 1-7 illustrates this evolution from the viewpoint of top executives.

Before the 1960s, the prevailing economic philosophy in the United States was *caveat emptor*—"Let the buyer beware." In other words, consumers had to be cautious when purchasing a product. Once they did, they were stuck with it—and any injuries that might result. It didn't matter if the product was defective.

Sales orientation
Historical marketing period that emphasized that consumers must be convinced to buy.

Seller's market
The marketing environment in which scarcity of products lets the seller control the market.

Buyer's market
The marketing environment in which an abundance of product lets the buyer control the market.

			Connecting with customers
		Company resources	Company resources
	Competitors	Competitors	Competitors
Customers	Customers	Customers	Customers
1960s and 1970s	**1980s**	**1990s**	**2000 and beyond**

Figure 1-7 Marketing's Recent Past and Immediate Future

Led by the efforts of President John F. Kennedy, legislators began to be more responsive to consumer rights. Throughout the 1960s and 1970s, government agencies and private consumer protection groups advanced this cause. Successful companies realized they could gain a competitive edge by treating customers fairly. They also became keenly aware that a loyal repeat buyer is more profitable than a one-time buyer (which you will learn more about in chapter 2). Businesses began to realize that customer satisfaction was paramount.

In the early 1980s, executives turned their attention to competitors. For the first time in U.S. history, foreign rivals seriously threatened the dominance enjoyed for years by U.S.-based global companies. Competition, beyond mere price and promotion, was developed and refined in many ways. During the 1980s, strategic planning became widely accepted. The role of marketing was elevated from understanding consumer behavior to assessing customer expectations, learning about competitors' practices, and determining how to make the organization an industry leader in a continuously changing world.

In the early 1990s, business executives began building teams designed to focus all of the organization's resources on customer satisfaction. Achieving customer satisfaction depends on the entire organization, on how well the various parts work together. A business is like any other team; success is determined not only by individual talents but also by the ability to do well as a unit. The organization that can form fast, flexible, powerful teams is capable of competing in global markets. It is clear that an organization must be designed to maximize both the speed of its responsiveness to customers and its ability to work as a team.

Customer-driven
organization

An organization that implements the marketing concept by ensuring that all parts of the organization make the maximum contribution toward satisfying customer wants.

Customer-driven organizations implement the marketing concept by ensuring that all parts of the organization make the maximum possible contribution toward satisfying customer wants. They make sure that every part of the organization has a clear line of sight to the customer. This often involves using research tools to study customers, their satisfaction, and their loyalty to the company as well as competitors. Customer-driven organizations also make sure that all the costs they incur over the long run provide at least as much value in customer want satisfaction. For example, Microsoft is customer driven. It brings software to market that creates huge amounts of want satisfaction. Its products use the latest technology, such as the new version of Microsoft NetMeeting software. New Internet phone features enable customers to call from their Web browsers to traditional handheld telephones or other computers in Microsoft's traditional user-friendly format.[22] Microsoft willingly supports millions of users, one at a time, with customer service and 800 numbers to ensure that its products can be used as intended. Customers have rewarded Microsoft with loyalty that yields enormous profits. These, in turn, fuel additional change in Microsoft, making it one of the most competitive companies in the world. Companies like Microsoft are using their customer-driven approaches to move into the 21st century, which is described in the next section.

The last part of the 1990s finds organizations reestablishing links with customers on a massive scale. They want permanent connections so customers become assets of the organization, not just one-time buyers. How do marketers connect with huge numbers of customers? They certainly can't ask customers what they want one at a time and then provide it—that would be too expensive. So marketers must go through the steps of target marketing, positioning, and development of the marketing mix. Then they can get personal with customers in the target market. Personal attention occurs when organizations are customer driven.

CONNECTING WITH CUSTOMERS IN THE 21ST CENTURY

The future will center around better ways of connecting with customers. The single phrase—connecting with customers—captures the objective of leading-edge companies. It communicates precisely what outstanding marketers do—they connect. How marketers connect is embodied in the five supporting themes of this book, each of which will shape marketing well into the 21st century. They are

- Connecting through relationships
- Connecting through technology
- Connecting with diversity
- Connecting globally
- Connecting ethically

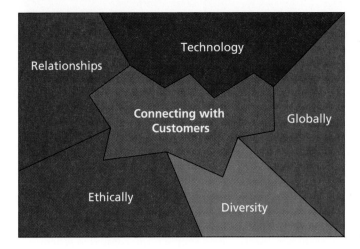

Figure 1-8   Marketing in the 21st Century

These supporting themes were carefully selected to describe how marketers build lasting connections. These five key forces, depicted in Figure 1-8, will reappear throughout the book.

CONNECTING THROUGH RELATIONSHIPS

Before the production era, marketers embraced the customer orientation. They created products, on demand, for specific customers. Relationships were built on a personal level. Consumers dealt directly with manufacturers. With mass production began the separation of manufacturers and consumers. As more levels of distribution channels were added—including retailers and wholesalers—the consumer's voice was heard less and less. In an effort to get closer—to become more connected—organizations today are enthusiastically embracing relationship marketing. Figure 1-9 describes a continuum of marketing exchanges from pure transactions to repeated transactions to relationships.[23]

A pure transaction occurs only once. When it is finished, both parties go their separate ways. Repeated transactions occur when customers have strong preferences. Many times they become loyal. But relationships create an even stronger connection. **Relationship marketing** is the development and maintenance of successful relational exchanges. It involves interactive, ongoing, two-way connections among customers, organizations, suppliers, and other parties for mutual benefit. Sony Autosound, manufacturer of car stereos, uses relationship marketing with Generation Xers. Sony spends time on the streets and in high school parking lots

Relationship marketing
The development and maintenance of successful relational exchanges through interactive, ongoing, two-way connections among customers, organizations, suppliers, and other parties for mutual benefit.

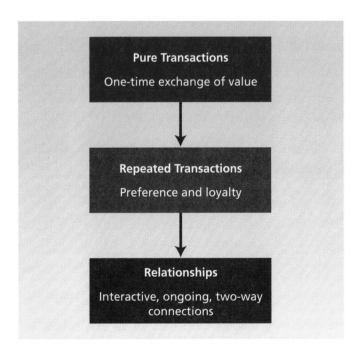

Figure 1-9   Types of Marketing Exchange

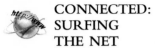
Strategic alliances

A partnership formed by two or more organizations for a new venture.

talking to young people in order to deliver unique products and maximum customer satisfaction. Building on its established reputation for quality, Sony creates relationships by addressing issues "one-on-one" with its target audience. Its Autosound Tour also gives customers personal interaction with Sony's high-quality products.[24]

Not all customers are looking for strong relationships in all exchanges. Marketers need to be sensitive to this fact. However, there is a clear trend. In recent years, marketing has evolved from transaction-based exchanges toward relationship-based exchanges. The change goes far beyond the interaction between an organization and its customers. It includes suppliers and other parties who are dependent on the customer. These relationships range from informal to contractual or even ownership. On the informal level, incentives make it difficult or inconvenient for customers to switch to a new organization. For example, Land Rover has a club for customers, with a newsletter and invitations to off-road rallies. Service managers call customers to see how their Land Rover Discovery is performing.

In business markets, suppliers develop computerized systems that are tied to a customer's manufacturing processes. If the customer selects a new supplier, the computer system will also need alterations. In some cases, these relationships are based on long-term contracts and partnerships. Prince, a manufacturer of auto components, has multiple-year contracts with Chrysler to supply specific products.[25] This arrangement gives Prince the incentive and security to commit significant investments to technology that will specifically benefit Chrysler.

In some cases, **strategic alliances** occur when a partnership is formed by two or more organizations for a new venture. For example, credit card companies often ally with airlines or automotive companies. American Express has marketed cards in partnership with ITT Sheraton, the New York Knicks basketball team, and the New York Rangers hockey team. The Rangers and Knicks cards offer discounts on games and merchandise, while the Sheraton card offers such rewards as free hotel accommodations.[26]

Some alliances may involve actual ownership arrangements. In these cases, several parties form an organization that is owned jointly. For example, Bill Gates, chairman of Microsoft, and Boeing recently invested in Teledesic Corporation's project to build a $9 billion satellite network. It will be used for high-speed mobile data and video communications of superior capability. Boeing may invest as much as $100 million in exchange for 10 percent ownership in the venture.[27] Since ownership is involved, these relationships strengthen the connections between the parent organizations.

CONNECTING THROUGH TECHNOLOGY

Peter Drucker, renowned educator and author, says that innovation and marketing are the two basic roles of every business, and all other functions (such as accounting, finance, and engineering) support these two business roles. Drucker defines innovation as rearranging the

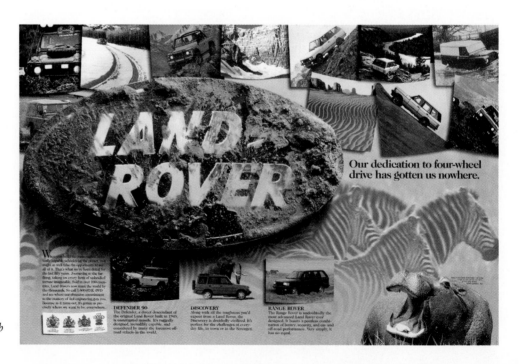

Land Rover connects through relationships with its customer club and personal service.

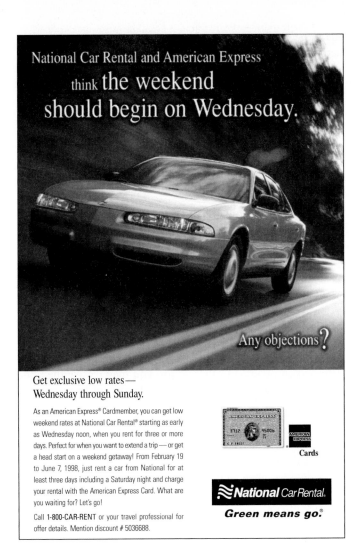
*American Express markets cards in partnership with a variety of
companies.*

old or creating the new and says that marketing is the process that delivers innovations to society. New technology is all around us, but three types are particularly noteworthy: (1) product technology that spawns new goods and services, (2) process technology that provides flexible manufacturing and distribution to adjust rapidly to customer needs, and (3) the Internet,
which facilitates two-way global connectivity with customers. Additionally, we will discuss the
concept of a marketspace that is bringing many of these technological forces into a single
focus.

Process and Product Technology   **Product technology** is technology that spawns the development of new goods and services. Product technology provides the raw material that
fuels improvements in our standard of living. Examples of innovative technology that has
produced radically new goods and services are everywhere. Farmers are beginning to use satellite technology to micromanage their crops, leading to better yields and profits.[28] Product
technology also affects sports. Speedo and Tyr, two major swimwear manufacturers, have developed new materials with nonstick resins to reduce water resistance and improve swim-
mers' times.[29] Cellular systems support telephone calls, fax, and data transmissions, as well
as global positioning from moving vehicles everywhere. Soon digital television and flat-screen
technology will support in-home theater systems superior to today's best theaters. We can
clone the "best" sheep, tomatoes, and viruses.

Process technology is technology used to make goods and services. Most typically found
in manufacturing, it is also used to enter customer orders and make sure that the appropriate products get to the right customer rapidly. Not long ago, the challenge was to forecast

Product technology
Technology that spawns the
development of new goods and
services.

Process technology
Technology used to make goods
and services.

Mass customization
The customization of a product for a specific customer by means built into a process.

the styles and quantity of goods to be produced and have them ready for customers when needed. Today, flexible manufacturing is changing all that. This type of manufacturing is often called *agile production systems*, which describes its versatility. These systems make it possible to respond to customers in a virtual environment—to build a product they request immediately.

Probably the most important marketing development due to process technology is the personalization of products. **Mass customization** occurs when customizing a product for a specific customer is built into a process. Mass customization gives companies the opportunity to produce affordable, high-quality goods and services—but with a shorter cycle time and the lower costs associated with mass production.[30] One form of mass customization occurs at the time of use. When an auto is programmed to recognize one or several drivers and automatically adjust the seat, radio, and ride, customization occurs. Today, mapping systems hooked to satellites provide customized direction finding. Voice recognition technology will soon make it possible to mass-customize a broad range of items, connecting customers with products that adjust automatically, and with direct verbal links to companies everywhere.[31]

Customization can also occur in conjunction with manufacturing. For example, Boeing uses Trilogy software to configure aircraft to a customer's specification, complete with a quoted price, in only one short sitting. This eliminates weeks of price renegotiations and saves both time and resources for both the customer and Boeing.[32]

Also impressive is the work done by direct marketer L. L. Bean. By linking a publisher's subscription list with its customer list, L. L. Bean can place ads for customers in certain magazine issues and ads for noncustomers in others. In other words, you may receive the same magazine as your next-door neighbor but with different ads targeting each of you.

The Internet Of the many technological advances that have assisted marketers in their work, perhaps the most significant to date is the Internet. It is a tremendous asset in many ways: Global, interactive, and fully integrated, it creates the opportunity to establish one-to-one relationships with customers.[33] An estimated 34.2 million people use the Internet worldwide, and the number of Web sites doubles every 50 days.[34] The Internet is home to content providers, advertisers, and you—the audience.

Internet
A global network of computers that enables the transmission of data through the use of a personal computer.

The **Internet** is a global network of computers which has been around since the 1960s, when it was first deployed by the Department of Defense as a means to send messages in case of a nuclear attack. Until the 1990s, the network was accessed primarily by researchers, who shared the capacity of supercomputers as well as electronic mail capabilities. The Web itself, with the use of hypertext, which allowed people to click on text on their screens in order to link to another computer, was introduced in the mid-1990s. The World Wide Web of today—

Zenith uses product technology to support its in-home theater systems.

Mercedes Benz "Internet cruiser" allows drivers to access computer capabilities and Internet services with their voices.

which provides graphics, sound, color, and video—is made possible by graphical browsers, such as the widely popular Netscape Communicator.[35]

Throughout this textbook you will learn many ways in which the Internet serves as a tool for marketers—including scanning, research, communication, and distribution. Figure 1-10 highlights the various uses. As a scanning tool, the Internet can be used to evaluate trends, the environment, customers, competitors, and other forces. As a research tool, the Internet can be used to conduct Web surveys, focus groups, observation, and so forth. The Internet is also a fantastic means of distributing products such as magazines, music, and video clips.

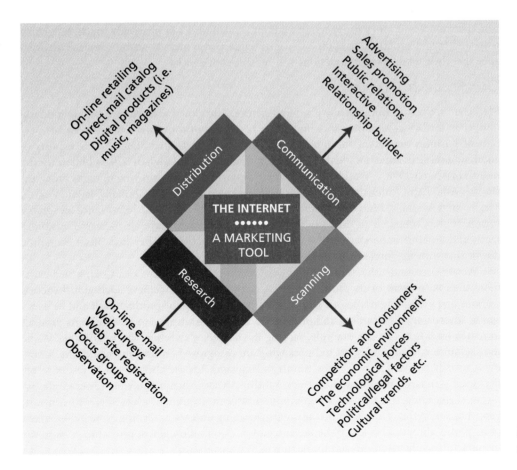

Figure 1-10   The Internet as a Marketing Tool

23

On-line retailing has become a very popular form of distribution. Marketers communicate with customers through interactive and relationship-building promotions. The Internet is a medium for advertising and public relations as well.

Marketplace and Marketspace　We tend to think of marketing as activities that occur in a physical marketplace. With the amazing new developments in technology, however, it is possible to market goods and services in **marketspace**, an electronic space where business occurs.[36]

Marketspace
An electronic space where
business occurs.

Marketspace transactions take place via the Internet, interactive television or CD-ROMs, ATM machines, on-line services, shopping channels, 800 numbers, and others. You can travel to Tower Records, Virgin, Strawberries, or any marketplace and buy music on compact discs or tapes. In contrast, you can call a music service in a marketspace—like Tower On-line—and order the same music. Some marketspaces encourage you to explore new artists and sounds.

Numerous marketspaces available on the Internet are ideal for searching for items like books and records. Browsing capabilities on Web sites are outstanding. Typing the name of a favorite artist can turn up obscure recordings not easily found in a store. You can even experience music from around the world, including Russian, Pakistani, or Chinese selections. Other Internet marketspaces provide information about nearly every other type of purchase. For instance, the Virtual Emporium brings together the best shopping sites on-line to provide more than three million products from 170 stores. Purchase decisions are simplified since the typical constraints imposed by a shopping mall—time, location, or crowds—are eliminated. Features such as the "deal monitor" and "gift picker" attempt to make shopping on-line easy and convenient. To make a purchase, shoppers fill out an on-line order form or print a fax order form. Consumers with suggestions can give the Virtual Emporium feedback as well. In addition, the Virtual Emporium promises secure on-line shopping and rigorous quality standards.

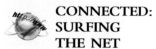

**CONNECTED:
SURFING
THE NET**

**www.virtual
emporium.com**

Here's your chance to experience a marketspace. Connect to the Virtual Emporium and browse through your choice of 170 stores and three million products.

Some predict that the growth of marketspace will eventually result in the eradication of marketplaces. By 2000, as much as 55 percent of shopping in America will be conducted in nonstore venues, such as the Internet, direct mail, catalogs, shopping channels, and many of the other marketspaces previously mentioned.[37] While this is a significant percentage, the eradication of marketplaces altogether is unlikely for several reasons. Technology does not offer the social dimension of shopping in a marketplace where consumers can interact with store personnel and other shoppers. In addition, consumers can physically touch, test, compare, and try on products. Shopping in a marketplace also gives consumers greater reassurance that their credit card transactions will remain confidential.

CONNECTING GLOBALLY

Marketers are connecting globally like never before. The global marketplace is tremendously important for U.S. companies, since more than 22 percent of consumer marketers and 44 percent of business marketers are doing business outside the United States.[38] U.S. exports of goods and services are climbing dramatically, reaching a record high of $79.41 billion for the month of March 1998.[39] Worldwide marketing opportunities are growing in many areas, including Asia, Latin America, Eastern Europe, the United Kingdom, Germany, Japan, France, Mexico, and Australia. Marketers should not ignore or lose sight of the importance of a global organization. Compared to domestic firms, global companies have an increased customer reach and a better understanding of diversity and competition. They also offset economic downturns with the implementation of appropriate strategies.[40]

We are surrounded by examples of global marketing. Consider Coca-Cola, which earns more than 80 percent of its profits abroad. Coca-Cola did not achieve such global success without first evaluating numerous global strategies, including the product itself and its packaging, advertising, distribution, and pricing. Coca-Cola's strategy is to customize its product to match local tastes by, for example, varying the degree of sweetness in the formula. While the signature curved bottle and red packaging are recognized around the world, the scripting is usually changed to reflect the country's language. Ads are also altered or reshot to reflect local standards, people, and customs. Yet the "Always" theme, showing, for example, aspiring chefs, sumo wrestlers, or a supermom, has been prominent everywhere. In contrast, Pepsi has suffered as a result of inconsistent packaging and taste, earning a mere 30 percent of its profits abroad. This led to the unveiling of a $500 million global project to revamp the manufacturing, distribution, and marketing of Pepsi overseas.[41]

Pepsi's new "Project Blue" image.

The global marketplace can be very complex. Marketers evaluate many considerations and implement well-planned strategies to ensure their success. Throughout this book, you will learn that differences need to be researched and accommodated at many levels. These include language, culture, currency, infrastructure, laws and regulations, consumer preferences, and differences in negotiating style. Marketers also need to understand the varying tastes and needs of global customers.[42]

It can be difficult to gain acceptance in new markets. Procter & Gamble found that it needed to educate Russian consumers about its products. "I was in a store in Volgograd, and people kept coming up to me asking what this or that product actually does," said Peter Smit, P&G's head of Russian operations. "You have to put yourself in the shoes of the Russian consumer. She wants to be educated."[43]

CONNECTING WITH DIVERSITY

Professor Warren Plunkett teaches what he calls "the New Golden Rule." The traditional golden rule states that you should do unto others as you would have them do unto you. But that assumes all people are the same. In an increasingly diverse society, you must be able to see others' point of view. People from different cultures or backgrounds don't necessarily have the same perceptions, needs, and wants. Plunkett's new rule is: Do unto others as they would have you do unto them. In other words, as a marketer you must remember to satisfy your customer on the basis of your customer's desires and social norms—not your own.[44]

As marketers move to a more personalized, one-to-one connection with customers, it is imperative to understand and respect diversity among customers. No two are alike. As you will learn in the consumer behavior chapter, some commonalties exist within the various subcultures and social classes. But marketers today are much more sensitive to the needs of a diverse population. It is important to understand that cultural diversity refers to far more than just ethnic groups. U.S. West Airlines, which recognizes diversity as part of its corporate culture, distinguishes among the following categories: race/color, gender, age, sexual orientation, religion, cultural heritage, veteran status, marital status, liberal/conservative, and national origin. The companies you will work for may have even more distinguishing factors. According to Marsha Farnsworth Riche, director of the U.S. Bureau of the Census, "We're all minorities now. If you count men and women as separate groups, all Americans are now members of at least one minority group."[45]

In 1997, Mattel, Inc. introduced the Becky doll, the first disabled friend of the Barbie doll. Shown here with Barbie and her African-American friend, Christie, Becky was created so that Barbie doll's world would better reflect the diversity of the real world.

Ethnic background

Subculture membership usually determined by birth and related to one or more of four elements: country of origin, native language, race, and religion.

Ethnicity

The amount of identification an individual feels with a particular ethnic group.

When marketing to ethnic groups, it is important to distinguish between ethnic background and ethnicity. A person's **ethnic background** is usually determined by birth and related to one or more of four elements: country of origin, native language, race, and religion. Hispanics are an ethnic group, but members have diverse interests and beliefs depending on country of origin, length of time in the United States, geographic placement, and other factors. **Ethnicity** refers to the amount of identification an individual feels with a particular ethnic group. According to Lafayette Jones, president and CEO of Segmented Marketing Services, Inc., marketers should "look at the market not in terms of black and white, but in terms of true ethnicity. We use terms like 'African American' because these terms really describe what we're talking about, without the social and political implications of race. . . . Every culture has its own food, music, and religious practices. They're diverse in competition, flavorings, attitudes, and expressions."[46] In the chapter on consumer behavior, we'll look more specifically at various ethnic markets. Applying what you learn can help you as a marketer cultivate and satisfy customers from varied ethnic backgrounds.

Marketers recognize that there will be tremendous diversity in markets in the 21st century. They also recognize the immense spending power of diverse groups. African Americans, Hispanic Americans, and Asian Americans spend in excess of $600 billion a year—and the amount continues to climb. Mature customers (age 50 and older) control half the U.S. buying power. Young adults spend $125 billion annually. Women make up 20 percent of the $15 billion market for golf equipment and merchandise.[47] These are just a few of the many diverse customers you will be learning about in this book.

It is both profitable and rewarding for marketers to connect and build relationships with every type of customer. By acknowledging, understanding, and accommodating the needs of diverse groups, marketers can create a loyal base of customers for future business. The diversity feature in this chapter, "Betty Crocker: An American Mosaic," highlights the efforts of General Mills to appeal to a broader spectrum of customers.

CONNECTING ETHICALLY

After emerging from the profit-oriented 1980s, marketers began to rediscover the importance of social responsibility and ethical behavior to a company's performance. In fact, ethical initiatives by businesses have more than doubled in the last five years. Responsible marketers make decisions with a clear code of ethics in mind. They must make important decisions about the standards of conduct for an organization. Approximately 60 percent of all companies and 95 percent of all Fortune 500 firms have an ethical code of conduct.[48] Ethics and

CONNECTING WITH DIVERSITY

BETTY CROCKER: AN AMERICAN MOSAIC

For 75 years, the most famous face in American grocery stores has been a paragon of white Middle America: a cheery housewife with blue eyes, creamy skin, and June Cleaver features. She has had a makeover every decade or so, but has changed little more than the style of her red-and-white wardrobe and her sensible brunette hairdo.

Now Betty Crocker is getting the wildest face-lift in the history of American marketing. It already is clear that when the new Betty emerges, her boss, General Mills, Inc., won't be serving up the same, old white bread.

To mark her 75th anniversary, General Mills will select pictures of 75 real women from across the United States, and digitally "morph" them into one new super-Betty. Since the contest is open to would-be Bettys of all races and any age from 18 to 118, the hybrid homemaker is likely to emerge with more politically correct features.

"We're hoping for ethnic diversity, which is what's happening with homemakers and society as a whole," says General Mills spokesperson Craig Shulstad. Ethnic diversity, of course, is a holy grail avidly sought by marketers everywhere in the fractious 1990s. But meshing 75 ethnically diverse women into one face is a new twist.

Russell Adams, chairperson of African-American studies at Howard University in Washington, DC, thinks General Mills' high-tech Betty will shrewdly avoid offending anybody. She will look more like the growing market of blacks and Hispanics — but not *too* ethnic, Adams says. "This will let them straddle their conservative core and their emerging market," he says.

His prediction: The neo-digital Betty will have a light tan hue, a hint of a slant to her eyes, and perhaps a bit of width in the nose. "She will be less white bread and more whole wheat."

The original Betty was born in 1921, when General Mills' precursor, the Washburn Crosby Company, decided it needed to create a spokesperson to respond to its customers' queries about baking. They came up with a fictitious character named after a popular retired director, William Crocker, and held an employee contest to choose a suitable signature for Betty, which the company uses to this day.

On Betty's 15th birthday, the company commissioned her first portrait, from prominent New York artist Neysa McMein. She did a bit of 1930s morphing, combining the features of several women in the company's Home Service Department into a "motherly image," according to a General Mills history of Betty.

Now, in this digital era, it is only natural that Betty's new look should be computer-generated, the company says. "Betty Crocker has always reflected the faces of its consumers," says Cindy Guettler, the General Mills marketing manager overseeing Betty's anniversary festivities. "We're using computer images to reflect faces from consumers across America."

Source: Reprinted from Rebecca Quick, "Betty Crocker Plans to Mix Ethnic Looks for Her New Face," *Wall Street Journal,* September 11, 1995, pp. A1, A9.

---

social responsibility go hand in hand. We will examine each of these forces more closely in the following sections.

Ethics   **Ethics** are the values or standards that govern professional conduct. **Marketing ethics** deal specifically with the application of moral standards to marketing decisions, behaviors, and institutions.[49] Nearly every area of marketing has significant ethical dimensions that raise difficult questions.[50] Throughout this book, we will evaluate many different ethical situations, including issues of fairness, equity, conflict of interest, privacy, confidentiality, product safety, and others. You will also find that every area of marketing can present an ethical dilemma, including product development, promotion, distribution, and pricing.

In order to promote ethical behavior in each area of marketing, both large and small businesses implement a code of conduct, sometimes referred to as *value statements* or *management integrity statements*. These may provide a wide range of guidelines, depending on the beliefs and values of a particular organization. For example, Johnson & Johnson established one of the first codes in 1947.[51] It embodies a commitment to ethical business practices as well as a responsibility to consumers, employees, the community, and shareholders.[52] You will learn more about Johnson & Johnson in chapter 4.

Ethics
Standards or values that govern professional conduct.

Marketing ethics
The ethics that deal specifically with how moral standards are applied to marketing decisions, behaviors, and institutions.

Aside from implementing a code of ethics, organizations try to build an ethical culture by communicating standards to employees and ensuring that ethics remain a priority. An ethical organization requires the support of top management, and many companies have training programs and seminars on ethics. Lockheed Martin, for example, utilizes ethics training for its 185,000 employees.[53] Boeing incorporates ethical standards into its company objectives through a commitment to integrity:

> Integrity, in the broadest sense, must pervade our actions in all relationships, including those with our customers, suppliers, and each other. This is a commitment to uncompromising values and conduct. It includes compliance with all laws and regulations.[54]

Because the marketing function within an organization relies heavily on interaction with customers, it is often subject to public scrutiny. This emphasizes the power of ethics as a force in making business decisions. Over the long run, it is likely that organizations with a strong ethical culture and code of conduct will be better equipped to handle ethical dilemmas.

Social Responsibility   Many people believe that a socially responsible business must satisfy the needs of customers in ways that provide profits to the owners or meet other requirements outlined by the owners. Some argue that profits represent the response of consumers to businesses that best serve their needs. As mentioned previously, social responsibility and ethics are closely related. The **societal marketing concept** seeks to balance customer satisfaction against corporate profits and the well-being of the larger society. It extends the marketing concept to include satisfying the citizen as well as the customer. Social responsibility reflects "the consequences of a person or firm's acts as they might affect the interest of others."[55]

Many companies are well known for their commitment to social causes and for acting in the best interest of the citizen as well as the consumer. Consider Ben & Jerry's, which contributes 7.5 percent of its pretax profits to charitable causes.[56] Ben & Jerry's is well known for

Societal marketing concept
The marketing concept extended to include satisfying the citizen as well as the consumer.

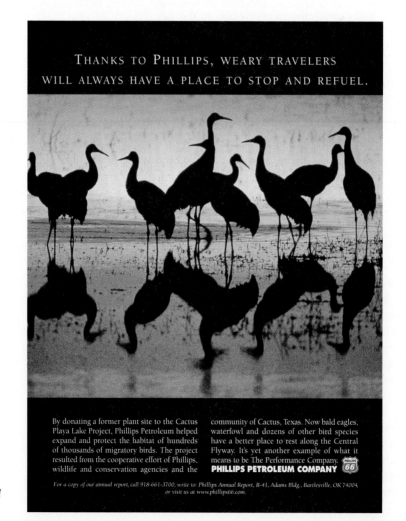

Philips Petroleum Company fulfills a social responsibility by helping reduce landfill waste and conserve natural resources.

its environmental initiatives, including innovative recycling, energy saving, and waste reduction. The company incorporated its dedication to societal marketing into this part of its mission statement:

> To operate the company in a way that actively recognizes the central role that business plays in the structure of society by initiating innovative ways to improve the quality of life of a broad community: local, national, and international.

Another example of involvement in social causes is The Body Shop, which is committed to human and civil rights, as well as protection of the environment and animals. It protests animal testing for cosmetics, campaigns for endangered species, and shows support for victims of domestic violence, among others.[57] Numerous companies express their social responsibility through donations. For example, Hewlett-Packard is recognized as a leading contributor, donating more than $72 million worldwide in 1996. Of this, $54 million went to education.[58]

Marketers have many opportunities to correct questionable behavior. Today, television shows often resort to sex, violence, and outrageousness in order to command market share. Procter & Gamble and AT&T are taking the lead in cleaning up televised trash, hoping producers will understand that positive topics are more economically viable with advertisers than salacious topics.[59] This chapter's relationships feature describes P&G's initiatives to deal with irresponsible television programming.

MARKETING: YOUR INVOLVEMENT

By now it should be clear that marketing affects you in many ways. Your exploration of marketing begins from many angles—the prospective marketer, member of a target market, customer, and citizen. Each of these roles gives you a slightly different slant, which can lead to the development of valuable marketing skills. Throughout this text we will highlight opportunities in the Career Tip feature. You'll also meet various marketers and learn from their experiences. Some, like Cynthia Palmer, who will be discussed in chapter 13, received a degree in marketing and then applied their knowledge. Others, like Vinny Greco, who will be mentioned in chapter 11, learned through experience to satisfy customers—much like Levi Strauss did 150 years ago.

One in three of you will be in a job that directly involves marketing. Your career may involve strategic marketing planning, personal selling, promotion or advertising, retailing, product development, getting products to market (distribution), or establishing pricing criteria. No matter what career you choose—working for a political campaign, a not-for-profit organization, a religious organization, or a Fortune 500 company—your job will require an understanding of marketing. Many of the ideas we will explore in this book can be applied to your personal actions.

In a sense, you are already a marketer through your everyday actions. You market yourself when you apply to schools or pursue a scholarship. You are a marketer when you seek election to an organization or attempt to influence its members. You are a marketer when you interview for an internship or job. In all likelihood, you will be applying marketing in a professional sense in the future. Since marketing is so important, this is true no matter what your college major happens to be.

You also belong to a target market, which makes you tremendously important to other marketers. You are part of a target market when political candidates on MTV ask for your votes, when the Fox network produces a television show designed to appeal to you, and when sports teams, theme parks, and movies compete for your entertainment dollars.

Marketing affects you through your role as a customer. You are a customer every time you purchase. You are a loyal customer when you have a strong preference that results in your repeated purchase of a company's good or service. You are part of a marketing relationship when a company that knows you by name wants to customize its actions to fit your desires precisely.

Finally, marketing pertains to you as a citizen. You are affected by marketing when McDonald's® selects paper over styrofoam packaging to reduce pollution. You are affected when Mothers Against Drunk Driving (MADD) reduces your chance of a serious injury from a traffic accident. You are affected when General Motors designs a Cadillac that is completely recyclable.

Marketing is a relevant, fun subject. It is filled with examples that you see every day. It touches your life directly in a million ways. We hope it connects with you—and, we hope you connect with it.

CONNECTED: SURFING THE NET

www.benjerry.com

Learn more about Ben & Jerry's efforts to fulfill the societal marketing concept by checking out its Web site. Find out about its most recent social efforts . . . . and ice cream flavors!

CONNECTING THROUGH RELATIONSHIPS

P&G WORKS WITH PRODUCERS TO TAKE THE TRASH OUT OF TELEVISION

"I'm Having Your Man's Baby," "I'm a 13-Year-Old Prostitute," and "Wild Teens." Have we piqued your interest, yet? These were sweeps episodes of the *Jerry Springer Show* and are typical fare for daytime television talk shows. Traditionally marketers like Procter & Gamble, AT&T, Burger King, and Playskool have jumped to sponsor the 20 daytime talk shows because they garner nearly half the daytime audience. Yet as these shows have become more sleazy and sensationalistic, public interest groups and industry watchdogs have begun to watch and get mad. Hence, marketers faced the ethical dilemma of either sponsoring increasingly offensive television shows or missing the opportunity to advertise to their target markets.

Finally some responsible marketers decided to put their mouth where their money is. Marketing managers at P&G, AT&T, Sears, and Kraft decided the best route to take would be to attempt to influence television content. According to R. L. Wehling, senior vice president of advertising at P&G, "If we simply throw up our hands, take away our dollars and absolve ourselves of responsibility for what these shows put on the air, then all we're doing is turning a blind eye to an increasingly serious problem. A better approach is to work constructively with producers to improve TV programming, which is what we at Procter & Gamble are doing."

When a sponsor as influential as P&G talks, producers listen. P&G developed a constructive three part approach to deal with irresponsible television programming. First, it laid the groundwork for building relationships with producers by opening communications and laying out acceptable standards. Second, it supported shows that dealt responsibly with controversial subjects. Then, it withdrew advertising on shows that did not meet its standards.

At AT&T, director of media Mike Neavill said that the company would advertise on only about eight or nine of the more than 20 daytime talk shows. He said that the long-distance powerhouse had instituted a new, stepped-up process for reviewing the content of individual episodes. "On Thursday or Friday of each week, our agency TeleVest talks to the exec producer and senior creative people of each show we're considering. By then, the shows for the upcoming week have actually been produced. We're not dealing with concepts. We're dealing with finished product, and we make our decision at that time." AT&T makes an important distinction between concepts for shows and the actual content of the finished shows. Often the topics, such as surrogate motherhood or promiscuous teens, seem safe, but when the show is actually produced they become tacky and tawdry. The move by P&G, AT&T, and others is meant to counter a strategy developed by trash television producers over the past several years: Producers would sell a couple of episodes of "clean" shows to sensitive advertisers while airing a few raunchy episodes each week to keep their ratings high.

Advertisers hope that offering a carrot rather than a stick will help turn the producers around. It appears to be working. The *Oprah Winfrey Show* began moving away from salacious topics, and other shows have adapted to what is called restrained programming. As a result of the advertisers' initiatives, "Our eyes are wide open and we constantly reevaluate what we are doing," says Burt Dubrow, vice president–programming for Multimedia Television, which distributes *Sally Jessy Raphael.*

Sources: Joe Mandese, "Talk Show Stalwart P&G Pans 'Trash,'" *Advertising Age*, November 20, 1995, pp. 1, 8; R. L. Wehling, "A Positive Impact on TV Show Content," *Advertising Age*, November 20, 1995, p. 8; "Speak up about Talk Shows," *Advertising Age*, November 27, 1996, p. 16; and William Spain, "Talk Shows Heed Loud Dissension from New Voices," *Advertising Age*, January 15, 1996, p. 28.

CONNECTED: SURFING THE NET

Procter & Gamble

www.pg.com

THIS CHAPTER'S RELATIONSHIPS FEATURE DISCUSSED THE Procter & Gamble Company's initiatives to become a socially responsible marketer. In order to extend your thinking about P&G, visit its Web site and answer the following questions.

1. Find and read P&G's history from 1945 to 1980 called "New Lands and Dynamic Growth." Relate this information to relevant periods of marketing evolution.
2. Choose a recent news release that discusses one of the five key marketing forces. Describe how this might influence or affect P&G's ability to connect with customers.
3. Locate and read P&G's pages on diversity. Why does P&G value a diverse organization? How might these values influence marketing decisions?

General Mills

www.genmills.com/index.html

THE DIVERSITY BOX, "BETTY CROCKER: AN AMERICAN MOSAIC," highlighted the efforts of General Mills, Inc., to embrace diversity. In order to extend your thinking about General Mills, visit its Web site and answer the following questions.

1. Find and read General Mills' information on its international operations. Select a strategic alliance General Mills has formed with another organization. How do you think this alliance contributes to relationship marketing?
2. Read "What's New" and select an example of General Mills using one or more elements of the marketing mix. Do you think this is an effective way to make a connection with customers? Why or why not?
3. In what types of markets does General Mills operate? Give examples.

CHAPTER SUMMARY

OBJECTIVE 1: Understand the concept of marketing, including its definition, purpose, and role in creating exchanges.

Marketing is the process of planning and executing the conception, pricing, promotion, and distribution of ideas, goods, and services to create exchanges that satisfy individual and organizational objectives. The purpose of marketing is to identify the needs and wants of customers within markets and create customer value in ways that will ensure the long-run success of the organization. Many people refer to the purpose as the marketing concept. Marketing works by creating valuable exchanges that provide utility. Utility is produced when products are created or adjusted, when goods and services are placed so consumers can discover and acquire them, when products are delivered at the right time, and when the transfer of ownership is facilitated.

OBJECTIVE 2: Learn what is involved in making marketing decisions, including examples of product, price, promotion, and place decisions to create a marketing mix.

The marketing strategy process has four steps—situation analysis, targeting, positioning, and marketing mix decisions. Situation analysis provides information about the marketing environment and specific company elements. It is based on insights gained from

the use of marketing information systems and marketing research. Targeting occurs when groups of customers with identifiable characteristics are selected for attention. Targeting helps focus resources. The best marketing strategies do an excellent job of addressing the needs and wants of customers within these targets. Positioning is used to determine what image or impression the marketer wants customers within a target segment to possess regarding the organization or its products. By blending the marketing mix—product, price, promotion, and place—marketing decisions are made to support the positioning strategy. These decisions can be blended into a vast array of combinations, each producing different results.

OBJECTIVE 3: Contrast the periods of marketing evolution, from the early history through the eras of production, sales, and customer marketing, leading up to today.

Marketing has progressed through three eras—the production era, the sales era, and the customer marketing era. As the names suggest, the production era focused on ways to efficiently mass-produce new products while the sales era focused on getting people to buy products. The customer marketing era moved management's attention toward satisfying customer needs and wants.

OBJECTIVE 4: Understand the five key forces that are dramatically influencing how organizations will connect with customers in the 21st century.

Marketing in the 21st century will be influenced by relationships, technology, ethics, diversity, and globalization. Today, more organizations are implementing the marketing concept by forging relationships with valued customers. These are creating loyalty and repeat business which help the organization to achieve its objectives. Product technology develops radically new goods and services and process technology makes it possible to be more responsive to customers by altering how marketing occurs. The Internet is a particularly noteworthy technological advance because it brings us new distribution, communication, scanning, and research capabilities. The global economy has an impact on all customers and competitors. Consequently, global factors must be considered when making marketing decisions. Ethics and social responsibility are also important forces because they help guide many marketing decisions. Ethics involve making decisions based on what is right and wrong. Social responsibility involves decisions that affect citizens as well as customers.

OBJECTIVE 5: Determine how marketing pertains to you.

You are intimately involved in marketing—as a marketer, as a member of a target market, as a customer, and as a citizen. Marketing pertains to you personally and you begin your study of the subject having already experienced many of its facets. Professionally, marketing is important no matter what major or career you choose. In a sense, you are often a marketer when you attempt to advance yourself or your views. Along with other people similar to yourself, you are part of a target market toward which certain marketers direct their attention. As a customer, you experience the actions of marketers. As a citizen, you are impacted positively and negatively by organizations whether or not you purchase their products.

REVIEW YOUR UNDERSTANDING

1. What is marketing? What are the key elements in its definition?
2. What are the four basic areas (types of markets) where marketing is typically applied?
3. What is utility? What are the four types of utility involved in marketing exchanges?
4. What is the difference between a need and a want? Give examples of each.
5. What is the marketing concept? What are its three key aspects?
6. What is a marketing strategy? Describe each of its four steps.
7. How do product, place, promotion, and price decisions form the marketing mix? Give examples of each decision.
8. What are the stages in marketing evolution. Describe each of the three marketing eras.
9. What are the five key forces shaping marketing as we enter the 21st century? Describe each.
10. How does marketing relate to you? List four ways.

DISCUSSION OF CONCEPTS

1. Describe marketing, highlighting examples from your daily life that illustrate each of its four aspects.
2. Identify one company with which you are familiar and describe four ways in which it provides utility.
3. Discuss the activities involved in implementing the marketing concept. How do they pertain to customers, competitors, and the marketing organization?
4. Describe the steps in developing a marketing strategy. Why is it important to target prior to positioning? Why is positioning important prior to marketing mix decisions?
5. Compare and contrast the various eras of marketing, assessing the role each era played in reaching the current relationship era.
6. Discuss the five forces shaping marketing by showing how they help implement the marketing concept.

KEY TERMS AND DEFINITIONS

Buyer's market: The marketing environment that exists when an abundance of product lets the buyer control the market.

Consumer orientation: An organizational philosophy that focuses on satisfying consumer needs and wants.

Customer-driven organization: An organization that implements the marketing concept by creating processes so all parts of the organization can contribute the maximum amount possible toward satisfying customer wants.

Effectiveness: The degree to which an organization's activities produce results that matter to consumers.

Efficiency: The degree to which activities are carried out without waste of time or money.

Ethics: Standards or values that govern professional conduct.

Ethnic background: Subculture membership usually determined by birth and related to one or more of four elements: country of origin, native language, race, and religion.

Ethnicity: The amount of identification an individual feels with a particular ethnic group.

Exchange: A process in which two or more parties provide something of value to one another.

Form utility: A want-satisfying value that is created when knowledge and materials are converted into finished goods and services.

Internet: A global network of computers that enables the transmission of data through the use of a personal computer.

Market: All the individuals and organizations with the desire or potential to have the desire and the ability to acquire a particular good or service.

Marketing: The process of planning and executing the conception, pricing, promotion, and distribution of ideas, goods, and services to create exchanges that satisfy individual and organizational objectives.

Marketing concept: Holds that the purpose of marketing is to identify the needs and wants of customers within markets and satisfy them in ways that ensure the long-run success of the organization.

Marketing ethics: The ethics that deal specifically with how moral standards are applied to marketing decisions, behaviors, and institutions.

Marketing mix: The four controllable variables—product, price, promotion, and place (distribution)—that are combined to appeal to the company's target markets.

Marketspace: An electronic space where business occurs.

Mass customization: The customization of a product for a specific customer by means built into a process.

Mass marketing: The mass production, mass distribution, and mass promotion of a product to all buyers.

Needs: Fundamental requirements the meeting of which is the ultimate goal of behavior.

Ownership utility: A want-satisfying value that is created by making it possible to transfer the title of goods and services from one party to another.

Place utility: A want-sayisfying value that is created by making goods and services conveniently available.

Process technology: Technology used to make goods and services.

Product technology: Technology that spawns the development of new goods and services.

Production orientation: Historical marketing period that emphasized new products and the efficiency of production.

Relationship marketing: The development and maintenance of successful relational exchanges; it involves interactive, ongoing, two-way connections among customers, organizations, suppliers, and other parties for mutual benefit.

Sales orientation: Historical marketing period that emphasized that consumers must be convinced to buy.

Seller's market: The marketing environment that exists when scarcity of products lets the seller control the market.

Societal marketing concept: The marketing concept extended to include satisfying the customer as well as the consumer.

Strategic alliances: A partnership formed by two or more organizations for a new venture.

Target market: A group of potential customers with similar characteristics that a marketer is trying to satisfy better than the competition.

Time utility: A want-satisfying value that is created when goods and services are made available when they are wanted.

Want: A specific form of consumption desired to satisfy need.

REFERENCES

1. Robert Lenzer and Stephen S. Johnson, "A Few Yards of Denim and Five Copper Rivets," *Forbes*, February 26, 1996, pp. 82–87; Michele Simpson, "Superior Jeans," *Marketing Week*, February 16, 1996, pp. 36, 38; Bruce Fox, "Levi's Personal Pair: Prognosis Positive," *Chain Store Age*, March 1996, pp. 35–36, Stratford Sherman and Jeanne C. Lee, "Levi's: As Ye Sew, So Shall Ye Reap," *Fortune*, May 12, 1997, www.fortune.com.
2. "AMA Board Approves New Marketing Definition," *Marketing News*, March 1, 1985, p. 1.
3. Don Peppers and Martha Rogers, *Enterprise One to One* (New York: Doubleday, 1997), p. 4.
4. James W. Culliton, *The Management of Marketing Costs* (Boston: Division of Research, Graduate School of Business Administration, Harvard University, 1948), cited in Neil H. Borden, "The Concept of the Marketing Mix," *Journal of Advertising Research*, June 1964, pp. 2–7.
5. Borden, ibid.
6. Ian P. Murphy, "Southpaws, Take Note," *Marketing News*, April 14, 1997, p. 2.
7. Jane Hodges, "IBM Web Test Shows Dramatic Payoff," *Advertising Age's Business Marketing*, January–February 1997, p. 1, M18.
8. Scott Woolley, "Double Click for Resin," *Forbes*, March 10, 1997, www.forbes.com.
9. "Green Model," *Forbes*, January 30, 1995, p. 26.
10. Richard P. Bagozzi, "Marketing as Exchange," *Journal of Marketing*, October 1975, pp. 32–39.
11. Anna Wilde Matthews, "One Stop Cargo Services Offer Lower Costs, Better Control," *Wall Street Journal Interactive Edition*, April 29, 1997.
12. Tom Dellecave, Jr., "Driving Sales," *Sales and Marketing Management*, January 1997, pp. 78–79.
13. "Pizza Hut to Invest $50 Million to Improve Product Quality," *Wall Street Journal Interactive Edition*, April 29, 1997.
14. Joan O. Fredericks and James M. Salter II, "Beyond Customer Satisfaction," *Management Review*, May 1995, p. 29.
15. Linda Himelstein, "The Swoosh Heard 'Round the World,' " *Business Week*, May 12, 1997, www.businessweek.com.
16. Cyndee Miller, "Seuss Characters Leap from Page into Licensing World," *Marketing News*, April 14, 1997, p. 2.
17. Christopher Caggiano, "Brand New," *Inc.*, April 1997, pp. 48–53; and Michael J. McCarthy and Richard Gibson, "Quaker to Sell Snapple for $300 Million," *Wall Street Journal Interactive Edition*, March 28, 1997.
18. Evan Ramstad, "Compaq Hires Sales Force to Compete with Direct Marketers," *Wall Street Journal Interactive Edition*, May 14, 1997.
19. Lisa Krakowka, "New Media Marketeers," *Marketing Tools*, January–February 1997, www.marketingtools.com.
20. Matt Murray, "Marketers Want Kids' Help and Their Parents' Loyalty," *Wall Street Journal Interactive Edition*, May 6, 1997.
21. Don Peppers and Martha Rogers, *The One To One Future* (New York: Doubleday, 1993), pp. 21–22.
22. "Microsoft Phone Features to Be Added to Browser," *Wall Street Journal Interactive Edition*, April 28, 1997.
23. See Frederick E. Webster, Jr., "The Changing Role of Marketing in the Corporation," *Journal of Marketing*, October 1992, pp. 1–17.
24. Shelley Reese, "The Lost Generation," *Marketing Tools*, April 1997, www.marketingtools.com.
25. Author Interview with a Prince executive, May 1997.
26. Stephen E. Frank, "Incentives, Alliances Help American Express Rebound," *Wall Street Journal Interactive Edition*, April 28, 1997.
27. Quentin Hardy, "Boeing Will Take 10% Stake in Teledesic Satellite Venture," *Wall Street Journal Interactive Edition*, April 30, 1997.
28. Barbara Carton, "Farmers Begin Harvesting Satellite Data to Boost Yields," *Wall Street Journal*, July 11, 1996, p. B4.
29. Mike Toner, "High Tech Fiters Are Faster than Skin," www.atlantagames.com/oly/news/u07cove.html on July 19, 1996.
30. Christopher Hart, "Mass Customization: Conceptual Underpinnings, Opportunities and Limits," *International Journal of Service Industry Management* 6, no. 2 (1995): 36–45.
31. Peppers and Rogers, *Enterprise One to One*, p. 2.
32. Josh McHugh, "Holy Cow, No One's Done This!" *Forbes*, June 3, 1996, www.forbes.com.
33. R. L. Wehling, "The Future of Marketing: What Every Marketer Should Know about Being On-Line," *Executive Speeches*, June–July 1996, pp. 8–12.
34. Rebecca Quick, "New Web Ads Have Become More Effective and Obnoxious," *Wall Street Journal Interactive Edition*, April 24, 1997.
35. Raymond D. Frost and Judy Strauss, *The Internet: A New Marketing Tool* (Upper Saddle River, NJ: Prentice Hall, 1997).
36. Information obtained from www.hbs.edu/smig/marketspace on July 15, 1996.
37. Budd Margolis, "Digital Commerce: The Future of Retailing," *Direct Marketing*, January 1996, pp. 41–43.

38. Rebecca Piirto Heath, "Think Globally," *Marketing Tools*, October 1996, www.marketingtools.com.
39. Robert Keatley, "U.S. Trade Deficit Widens to a Record," *Wall Street Journal*, May 21, 1998, p. A2.
40. Heath, "Think Globally."
41. Robert Frank, "Seeing Red Abroad, Pepsi Rolls Out a New Blue Can," *Wall Street Journal*, April 2, 1996, pp. B1, B6.
42. Heath, "Think Globally."
43. Celestine Bohlen, "Crash Russian Course for Procter & Gamble," *New York Times*, December 19, 1993, sec. 3, p. 5.
44. Warren Plunkett, *Instructor's Manual for Supervision*, 7th ed. (Boston: Allyn & Bacon, 1993), pp. 6–7.
45. Marcia Mogelonsky, *Everybody Eats: Supermarket Consumers in the 1990s* (Ithaca, NY: American Demographic Books, 1995), p. 185.
46. Ibid., p. 163.
47. Gerry Myers, "Mutual Respect," *American Demographics*, April 1997, www.marketingtools.com.
48. Lynette Khalfani, Dow Jones News Service, *GT Online*, September 22, 1996, www.usa.net/gtonline/archive/96-09-22/b12020.html.

49. Gene R. Laczniak and Patrick E. Murphy, *Ethical Marketing Decisions: The Higher Road* (Boston: Allyn & Bacon, 1993), p. 3.
50. See John R. Boatright, *Ethics and the Conduct of Business* (Upper Saddle River, NJ: Prentice Hall, 1997), pp. 284–315.
51. Khalfani,
52. Johnson & Johnson, New Brunswick, NJ.
53. "WorkWeek," *Wall Street Journal Interactive Edition*, April 15, 1997.
54. www.boeing.com, site visited April 23, 1997.
55. Peter D. Bennett, ed., *Dictionary of Marketing Terms* (Chicago: American Marketing Association, 1995), p. 267.
56. For an additional view regarding Ben & Jerry's, see Alex Taylor III, "Yo, Ben! Yo, Jerry! It's Just Ice Cream!" *Fortune*, April 28, 1997, www.fortune.com.
57. www.the-body-shop.com/, site visited on April 23, 1997.
58. hpcc920.external.hp.com, last updated March 6, 1997.
59. Joe Mandese, "Talk Show Stalwart P&G Cans 'Trash,'" *Advertising Age*, November 20, 1995, p. 1.

CASE 1

STARBUCKS

ODAY'S COFFEE LOVERS CAN CHOOSE an estimated 8,000 outlets that serve Starbucks, a figure up from 200 in 1989. According to the company, whose largest competitor is less than half its size, coffee is not a trend, it's a lifestyle. Starbucks has been "elevating the coffee experience" since 1971, when three men opened a gourmet coffee shop in Seattle, Washington. Many people are unaware that Starbucks has been around for so many years. In fact, it wasn't long ago that latte, cappuccino and expresso were not part of America's everyday vocabulary.

Starbuck's success can be attributed greatly to marketing efforts. In 1982, the company hired Howard Schultz as its marketer. After visiting Italy the following year, Schultz was inspired. The relationship he saw between coffee and people in Italy awakened him to the untapped markets in America. In 1987, Schultz added six Starbucks stores and planned to go national with his ideas. Was he successful? The corporation is now the leading retailer, roaster, and brand of specialty coffee, with 1,401 Starbucks stores in the United States, Canada, Japan, and Hong Kong. Starbucks supplies fine dining, food service, travel, and restaurant accounts with both coffee and equipment. Its ambitions are not small. The company plans to have 2,000 stores by 2000.

Approximately 20,000 employees, known as "partners," undergo five sessions of rigorous training. They are taught to educate customers about coffee making, to remind them to purchase new beans weekly, to explain the various blends and beverages, and most important, to serve only the highest quality drinks. Employees learn to make the drinks in an eight-hour seminar that includes lectures, demonstrations, and hands-on experience. They taste beverages that do not meet quality standards so they can be more sensitive to an unsatisfied customer.

The average customer visits Starbucks 18 times a month, and 10 percent of its clientele stop in twice a day. That's big business. A latte and scone per day adds up to $1,400 per year. Starbucks has the best success in its top markets—Seattle, Los Angeles, and Chicago—each of which has approximately 100 stores. Located mostly in urban areas and college towns, Starbucks has also ventured into alliances with other companies. It reaches an estimated 80 million travelers per year in a deal with United Airlines. The Starbucks name can be found on mobile coffee carts and in airports, bookstores, and fine restaurants. Its extended line of products includes a coffee-flavored ice cream from Dreyer's Grand, a coffee-flavored beer from Redhook Ale Brewery, and a bottled version of its Frappuccino, which was developed with PepsiCo.

Global expansion has been a large success as well. When Starbucks was introduced in Japan, as many as 200 customers lined up at a time. The company provides informational pamphlets in Japanese and posts menus in both English and Japanese. The world's fourth largest consumer of coffee, Japan is a potential $7 million market for Frappuccino alone.

Despite its rapid growth, Starbucks refuses to compromise quality. The company will not franchise, will not artificially flavor its coffee, and is very selective about business alliances. Schultz intends to maintain the Starbucks upscale image. That's why Starbucks coffee will not be sold in gas stations or convenience stores, among many other places.

From 1992 to 1996 alone, consolidated net revenues of the company grew an astounding 575 percent. How has the name become so renowned? Not only has the company put its logo out through its products, accounts, and locations, but Starbucks also has received a significant amount of positive press for community involvement, charity work, and progressive employee policies. Starbucks uses its $18.75 million in mail orders to bring its name to markets where there are no retail locations. Amazingly, traditional advertising has not played a major role in the company's success.

Starbucks seems to have found its way into coffee cups everywhere. Never tried it? Ask one of the three million people who regularly buy Starbucks coffee. They'll probably tell you what you're missing.

1. *The definition of marketing describes four types of decisions made by marketers: product, price, promotion, and place. Identify a place and promotion decision Starbucks has made.*
2. *Based on the types of retail locations selected by Starbucks, what customer characteristics form its target markets?*
3. *The marketing concept holds that the purpose of marketing is to understand the needs and wants of customers and create customer value through satisfaction and quality more*

effectively and efficiently than competitors. Given the information provided in this case, summarize how Starbucks implements the marketing concept.

4. *In 1997, Starbucks opened a new store every business day. This includes global expansion into new markets. What factors must Starbucks consider as it continues to pursue global opportunities?*

SOURCES: Ronald Henkoff and Amy R. Kover, "Growing Your Company, Five Ways to Do it Right," *Fortune,* November 25, 1996, www.fortune.com; Jennifer Reese, "Starbucks: Inside the Coffee Cult," *Fortune,* December 9, 1996, www.fortune.com; Seth Sutel, "Japan Wakes up and Smells the Latte—Starbucks Is Here," *San Diego Source,* August 2, 1996, www.sddt.com/files/librarywire/96wireheadlines/08_96/DN_08_02_fa.html; Bill McDowell, "Starbucks Is Ground Zero in Today's Coffee Culture," *Advertising Age,* December 9, 1996, www.adage.com; Kate Berry, "Starbucks Joins Fray in Miami, a Town that Knows Its Coffee," *Wall Street Journal Interactive Edition,* March 28, 1997; Starbucks History, http://occ.com/starbucks, site visited April 3, 1997; and Dow Jones Newswires, "Starbucks Corp. Jan. Same-Store Sales Rose 7%," *Wall Street Journal Interactive Edition,* January 29, 1998.

Chapter 2

Customer Satisfaction and Loyalty: Building Value with Quality

Objectives

1. Understand why customer satisfaction and loyalty are the focus of marketing in winning organizations.

2. Learn how consumer expectations influence satisfaction.

3. See why connecting with customers through relationships achieves outstanding satisfaction and loyalty.

4. Understand the ideas that help organizations market quality goods and services.

5. Define quality and describe how it is obtained.

IMAGINE THIS SCENARIO. AFTER A LONG day of work or play, a grumbling in your stomach draws your car into the nearest McDonald's®. Relishing the familiar McDonald's® atmosphere, you choose a super-sized Big Mac® value meal or another favorite. The crewmember passes you your food and change, and you find a booth to enjoy your meal. It's a typical scene that we've all been through, but now you can replay it in 109 countries around the world, and on every continent but Antarctica. The hamburger is no longer simply an American food.

McDonald's® has forged relationships with the world built upon the enduring images of Big Macs®, Ronald, and the Golden Arches®. How do you make a hamburger a global icon? McDonald's® believes that the customers' experience is critical to business success and growth. In a recent statement to shareholders, Michael R. Quinlan, Chairman and Chief Executive Officer of McDonald's admits that "by focusing on adding restaurants, we took our eye off the basics that made us famous—quality, service, cleanliness, and value." So now McDonald's® has three priorities. The first is to improve restaurant operations. The second is to re-open the value gap against competitors by offering the best prices for the total dining experience. The third is to strengthen relationships with franchisees and energize employees. These are all part of a strategy to improve customer satisfaction and enhance loyalty.

McDonald's on-line document about restaurant employee expectations starts with a telling statement: "We are a quick service restaurant business committed to 100 percent satisfaction."[1] Its focus on the customer is evident throughout the document. Specific expectations are spelled out, ranging from standards and teamwork to cleanliness and service, before a prospective employee applies. For those who reach management status in the organization, Hamburger University® provides a six-day training course in an Oak Brook, Illinois facility or in 10 other training centers worldwide.

Every day, McDonald's® employees serve more than 35 million customers around the world. Catering to the younger crowd is an important part of the McDonald's® customer strategy. From the food and fun of a Happy Meal® and Playlands® to the alliance with The Walt Disney Company, McDonald's® provides children with more than meals. "Many families visit our restaurants because of our unique ability to put smiles on their children's faces."[2] More than half of McDonald's® business is generated through people on the go. Recently chosen as the "Best Drive-Thru Service in America," McDonald's® has continued to be a leader in this area. It is matching the speedy high-quality drive-thru service with a new wheeled-logo and operational upgrades. These include such customer-sensitive modifications as face-to-face ordering windows, menus with more pictures and promotional items, and comprehensive ordering and pick-up directions.

McDonald's® is a global corporation, and almost half of its 23,000 franchises are located outside the United States. Internationally, service consistency is maintained while modifying products to meet local needs and tastes. In India, the "Maharaja Mac"® replaces the traditional Big Mac's® two all-beef patties with mutton, out of respect for the Hindu faith. Also, vegetarian items are offered, on a separate menu which is color-coded for simplicity. In Malaysia and many Middle Eastern countries, food is prepared within Muslim guidelines.

Careful food selection isn't just an international issue. In his letter to shareholders, CEO Michael Quinlan reasserted the company's dedication to food value: "We're looking at our menu to make sure it has the taste you want at a price you want to pay." A culinary staff heads up food initiatives, and recently tested items include the McDonald's® Big Extra®, or MBX®, a bigger better burger, and the McFlurry, a soft-serve ice-cream dessert mixed with cookies and candy.

One advancement with the potential to redefine McDonald's® food quality is "Made for You,"® a computerized just-in-time food preparation system. New equipment and software promise to increase food quality without decreasing service speed. The aim is to serve the customer even faster. McDonald's® expects the new system to be providing toasted buns and fresh toppings throughout the U.S. and Canada by the year 2000. McDonald's® is working with internal customers to make the transition to "Made for You"® smoother, too. By offering financing incentives, like matching the upgrade purchase costs and guaranteeing equipment buy-backs,[3] the company emphasizes partnership and long-term relationships with franchisees. It also works with suppliers to ensure "strict food-safety and quality standards"[4] by developing relationships geared toward mutual success.

Building relationships goes beyond customers and business associates. McDonald's® believes it has a role as a member of the global community. The Ronald McDonald's House Charities® supports 195 facilities in 16 countries to provide temporary housing for the families of critically ill children. The charity also supports other not-for-profit organizations, and to date it has awarded $180 million in grants to children's programs worldwide.[5] At the same time McDonald's® is very concerned about the environment. It was named the 1998 Green Lights Retail Partner of the Year for adhering to the EPA voluntary program that encourages state-of-the-art energy-efficient lighting. Through McRecycle®, McDonald's® has purchased $2 billion worth of recycled products for its U.S. restaurants since 1990, and waste reduction initiatives have kept 13.1 million pounds of waste out of landfills.

McDonald's® activities, both within their restaurants and in their communities around the world, are focused on creating customer satisfaction. The company creates a quality experience by showing respect for customers, employees, owner/operators, vendors, and the communities in which it operates. This emphasis on customer value and satisfaction has provided McDonald's® with a competitive advantage and a way to make a hamburger not just a hamburger, but an institution.

CONNECTED: SURFING THE NET

www.mcdonalds.com

Find out more about McDonald's® quality initiatives by connecting to its Web site. Take a virtual tour of its 23,000 restaurants in 109 countries around the world!

THE CONCEPTS OF CUSTOMER SATISFACTION, LOYALTY, AND QUALITY

If you want to connect with customers, you have to earn their loyalty. That means delivering goods and services worthy of their support. People have millions of choices about where to spend their money. Ultimately, the decision depends on how much value they receive for what they pay. Companies that consistently produce high value are likely to have satisfied customers who reward them with loyalty and repeat purchases.

Winning organizations go to extremes to create customer satisfaction because they know that loyalty is the single most important factor in extraordinary performance. They also know that satisfaction and loyalty are often based on the relationship they have with customers. In this chapter we will learn that satisfaction and loyalty usually go hand in hand, but not always.

Figure 2-1   Customer Satisfaction, Customer Loyalty, and Quality: Connecting Through Relationships Formed by Organizational Systems and Actions

We will also learn that leading-edge companies focus a good deal of effort on satisfaction and loyalty. How do you obtain these two goals? There is no question that they require the ability to produce quality goods and services. Without quality, it is almost impossible for goods and services to perform as expected. In order to create superior value, organizations must start with excellent products. That requires application of total quality management principles to assure that processes throughout the company support the creation and delivery of products that produce satisfaction. Figure 2-1 describes the relationships among all these factors.

What are customer satisfaction and loyalty? What are value and quality? How do relationships and technology play into these factors? As a marketer, you need a strong foundation in these concepts to be able to connect with customers. In this chapter, we'll take a look at each concept in more detail.

CUSTOMER SATISFACTION AND CUSTOMER LOYALTY

Understanding how to achieve customer satisfaction and loyalty is a focal point for scientists who study consumer behavior. A significant amount of marketing research is dedicated to measuring both aspects—but especially customer satisfaction. Satisfaction ratings are a major indicator of an organization's competitiveness. Today, every extremely successful company makes a concerted effort to satisfy customers. The race to beat competitors in customer satisfaction is a powerful business objective because satisfaction is an overall indicator of how well customers rate a company's performance. This section begins by exploring why satisfaction and loyalty are important. Next, we look at how customer expectations affect satisfaction. We then tie all of these elements together by describing precisely how connecting through relationships promotes satisfaction and loyalty. We also examine how connecting with diversity and global competition affect efforts to build satisfaction and loyalty.

WHY SATISFACTION AND LOYALTY ARE IMPORTANT

Customer satisfaction is a customer's positive, neutral, or negative feeling about the value s/he received from an organization's product in specific use situations.[6] In the past, product innovation was the major factor in gaining the competitive edge. That is no longer always true. Now, new products are copied by rivals, often within a few weeks or months, and the life span of new products is declining rapidly. Today, it is more important for organizations to conduct all aspects of their business to satisfy customers. Favorable satisfaction ratings not only boost sales but can also have a dramatic effect on company performance. One IBM location calculates that a one percentage point increase in customer satisfaction produces a $257 million gain in revenues over five years.[7]

Customer loyalty refers to how often, when selecting from a product class, a customer purchases a particular brand. Most business experts believe that customer satisfaction is a critical ingredient in building loyalty. The importance of loyalty cannot be overlooked. Fred Reichheld of Bain & Company and Earl Sasser of the Harvard Business School indicate that an increase of 5 percent in customer loyalty can double profitability. Much of this profit gain is due to the fact that roughly 70 percent of all sales come from repeat purchases of loyal customers.[8] Few firms can achieve acceptable volume or profit without a strong base of loyal buyers. These customers must be retained in the face of ever more challenging competitors. A large number of satisfied, loyal customers result in strong business performance because

Customer satisfaction
A customer's positive, neutral, or negative feeling about the value s/he received as a result of using a particular organization's offering in specific use situations.

Customer loyalty
A measure of how often, when selecting from a product class, a customer purchases a particular brand.

these customers: provide sales to increase revenues; have less concern about price; and, help reduce the organization's costs.

Sales to Increase Revenues The revenue stream from one lifetime customer can be tremendous. A loyal pizzeria patron can easily spend as much as $8,000, a Cadillac purchaser as much as $332,000, and a corporate buyer of commercial aircraft equipment literally millions of dollars.[9] If you are loyal to one coffeehouse and buy just one beverage and a breakfast muffin daily, you'll be worth more than $35,000 to the owner. When the amount a customer buys is viewed over the lifetime of a relationship, organizations understand why customer retention is so vital. In fact, many organizations develop compensation systems that tie executive and employee pay to measures of customer satisfaction and loyalty.

The importance of satisfied customers for revenue generation is magnified by their influence on other buyers. If a typical customer purchases a new car once every four years and influences one new buyer each year, the loyal, satisfied customer can be worth nearly $1 million in revenues and more than $100,000 in profit. Some companies calculate the **lifetime value of a customer,** which is the amount of profit an organization expects to obtain over the course of a customer relationship. For example, assume you are a marketing manager for a large bicycle equipment manufacturer. One of your customers, Specialized, purchases about $80,000 in equipment each month. If Specialized becomes dissatisfied and selects another supplier, how much will it cost your company? At $80,000 per month for 12 months, Specialized purchases $960,000 annually. Assuming you earn a profit of 15 percent, that equals $144,000 per year. Over two decades, your company would forfeit more than $2.8 million in pure profit and $19.2 million in revenue. If the same problem that dissatisfied Specialized results in the defection of other key customers, you face huge losses!

Less Concern About Price Customer satisfaction has become a key to making sales at appropriate prices. One study shows that U.S. firms with high customer satisfaction generally have 15 percent higher returns on investment because, for one reason, they can charge a price premium of up to 9 percent without losing customers.[10] Satisfied customers tend to be less concerned about the purchase price. In general, they are willing to pay more because they are certain they will receive valuable benefits from the product. Also, they better tolerate price increases, showing little tendency to shop around. Overall, these factors lead to higher margins and overall profits.

Reduce the Organization's Costs The percentage of loyal, satisfied customers is a very important determinant of an organization's costs and revenues. In addition to generating sales, loyal customers affect the **cost structure,** the amount of resources required to produce a specific amount of sales. The cost of acquiring a new customer is usually five to seven times more than keeping an existing one.[11] For example, about $3,000 is spent to gain a new auto customer, while keeping an existing customer often costs only a few hundred dollars. It's easy to see that you must hold on to a significant number of loyal buyers who make multiple purchases. This is why Marriott empowers desk employees to refund up to $200 for problems that may lead to a lost customer.

CUSTOMER EXPECTATIONS

Customer expectations play an important role in creating satisfaction. **Customer expectations** are consumers' beliefs about the performance of a product based on prior experience and communications. When companies fall short of those expectations, customers are dissatisfied. When companies exceed them, consumers are delighted. In both cases, customers are emotionally charged by their experience—the delighted are more likely to be loyal, and the dissatisfied are more inclined to switch.

Customer expectations are based on personal experience, observation of others, company actions, advertising, and promotion. For example, new mothers are 67 percent more likely to purchase branded products for their baby because they expect better quality from recognized brands.[12] Customers also expect companies to offer services to support their purchase decision. For example, since it is difficult for people to assess the quality of products in a catalog, companies like Williams Sonoma and Crate & Barrel make it easy for people to return products that do not meet their expectations.

Higher and more varied expectations result when competition is intense. When Lexus entered the luxury automobile segment in 1989, expectations were high because Lexus posi-

Lifetime value of a customer
The amount of profit a company expects to obtain over the course of the relationship.

Cost structure
The amount of resources required to produce a specific amount of sales.

Customer expectations
Consumers' beliefs about the performance of a product based on prior experience and communications.

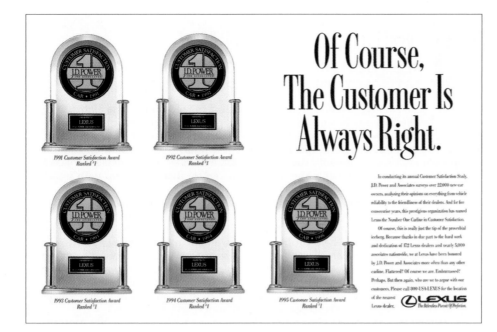

*For five years, J.D. Power and
Associates named Lexus number one
in customer satisfaction.*

tioned itself against such competitors as Mercedes-Benz, BMW, Cadillac, and Lincoln. Company executives knew the only way to succeed against the competition was to exceed expectations customers had for rival brands. The "Lexus Cares" philosophy treats customers the way they want to be treated.[13] The result has been extremely positive. In June of 1998, Lexus LS400 topped the J.D. Power & Associates Customer Satisfaction Index rating, attaining the Best Premium Luxury Car award. This is the fifth year out of the past six years that the LS400 has merited this distinction.[14]

Each time a company delights a customer, new expectations are created. Similarly, with each change in product, price, promotion, or distribution, expectations can be affected. A major challenge for companies is to create marketing strategies which give buyers high but realistic expectations. Companies must continue to do better in light of competitors' efforts and rising consumer expectations. The technology feature discusses how Red Lobster is improving customer satisfaction with better response software.

CUSTOMER DEFECTIONS AND COMPLAINING BEHAVIOR

Organizations look at **customer defections,** the percentage of customers who switch to another brand or supplier. The relationship between customer satisfaction and loyalty is complex. The two often go hand in hand. Yet, loyal customers are not always highly satisfied, and satisfied customers are not always loyal. In some cases customers continue to purchase a brand that doesn't fully meet expectations because defecting would be difficult or an alternative would be no better. In other cases satisfied customers defect because they simply want to try something new. A large number of consumers have many expectations, some of which may be met, others not. Consequently, there are degrees of satisfaction; customers may be highly or only moderately satisfied. An AT&T study indicates that 70 percent of satisfied customers still would be willing to switch to a competitor, while highly satisfied customers are much less willing to do so.[15] So, even satisfied customers may switch. The consulting firm Bain & Company found that up to 85 percent of customers who had switched were either "satisfied" or "very satisfied."[16] The point is, just focusing on satisfaction isn't enough. You must build a bond of loyalty that is based on a relationship.

Figure 2-2 illustrates that, in a study completed in Sweden, 65 percent of customers defect primarily because they are dissatisfied with the way they are treated.[17] Fifteen percent defect because they are dissatisfied with the product. The remaining defect because they prefer a different product or for other reasons unrelated to the product. This is an indicator of how extremely important it is to build relationships.

Companies committed to customer satisfaction will deal with any complaints they receive in a way that still leads to overall satisfaction. On average, nine of every 10 customer problems that are discovered and resolved immediately will result in satisfaction and loyalty. Seven of 10 customers will do repeat business with a company that makes some sort of

Customer defections
The percentage of customers who switch to another brand or supplier.

CONNECTING THROUGH TECHNOLOGY

RED LOBSTER FINDS A RECIPE FOR CUSTOMER SATISFACTION WITH RESPONSE SOFTWARE

Each morning at 8:15, John Boyd gets off the elevator on the eighth floor of the Darden Restaurants building in Orlando, Florida, and heads straight for his cubicle. Once there, Boyd, a guest relations representative for Red Lobster Restaurants, one of Darden's subsidiaries, will spend the next few hours deftly serving up comfort to people who call the restaurant's customer-feedback number. All the while, he'll click through software that documents the guest's experience, then follow up with a personalized letter and, if necessary, tuck in a gift certificate.

Red Lobster has conjured up a computer-based application that gives the $1.9 billion chain table-for-two intimacy with diners. With it, the restaurant not only tends to diners' comments but also takes swift action. That edge is crucial in the hotly competitive casual dining industry, where profit margins are napkin thin, and every customer counts. In fact, competition in the casual dining sector belies the segment's relaxed name. Red Lobster's guest relations took on new importance when the chain instituted an 800 line and began distributing customer-satisfaction surveys to diners. Callers use the telephone number pad to offer their assessment of Red Lobster's food and service on a scale of 1 to 5. Bravely, Red Lobster wanted more than just numbers.

"We wanted to know: Were the guests calm, angry, or ballistic?" says Dick Monroe, vice president of public relations. So the final survey question gives callers the option to speak with a representative and vent. Spurred by heavy promotion, 1,000 callers dialed in each week, and the guest relations department could no longer get by with its rusty DOS software. A tailored version of customer-response software was developed by Strategic Information Associates (SIA) in Northbrook, Illinois. The software empowers the staff to handle twice the number of calls.

Red Lobster, long an employer of the disabled in its restaurants, mandated that SIA make the new program mouse-free, so anyone could use it. John Boyd, for instance, operates his PC using a 5-inch wooden dowel strapped to his right hand. The software's clever mouse alternatives, which require only modest adaptation, mean full-time employment in Red Lobster's guest relations department for Boyd and 18 others whose physical disabilities prevent them from using conventional input devices. Two years ago, Boyd, 38, had never worked. Today, he adroitly handles not only data input but also the creative task of placating dissatisfied diners. His performance has been so impressive that he was promoted to lead guest representative.

In sum, Red Lobster's $80,000 software investment has paid off in enormous time savings and has provided a banquet of opportunities for its employees.

Source: Adapted from: Deborah Asbrand, "Red Lobster Finds a Recipe for Customer Satisfaction with Response Software," *Infoworld*, September 23, 1996, p. 73.

---

effort to resolve a problem. In fact, if a problem is handled satisfactorily, the average customer will tell five other people about it. A negative experience will result in nine to 20 people being told about the poor treatment or poor products and services.[18] This suggests that customers who complain and receive satisfactory attention are often more satisfied than those who don't complain at all.

It's not necessarily bad when people complain. Sometimes your most loyal customers are your biggest critics. American Demographics says that shoppers complain because they care and "because they feel connected to a particular store." According to Amanda Preus, director of research for Burke Customer Satisfaction Associates, "It seems kind of funny thinking about a complainer as someone who cares. But we've found that if you're satisfied with a store, you're more likely to complain when something goes wrong." People who take the time to let someone know about their frustration are likely to be loyal. They want the problem fixed and are willing to give the organization another chance.[19] In fact, complaining can help a relationship. J.C. Penney has found that when they patch up a disagreement, they have more customer loyalty than before.[20] Encouraging feedback and responding to complaints is one way to establish a bond of loyalty based on relationships.

SATISFACTION RATINGS AND MEASUREMENT

Satisfaction ratings

Ratings provided by testing agencies that compare purchase satisfaction with specified brands or with how well products perform.

Since satisfaction contributes so much to the success of an organization, it is no surprise that marketers are very interested in measuring satisfaction. **Satisfaction ratings** provide a way for consumers to compare brands, enable testing agencies to determine how well products

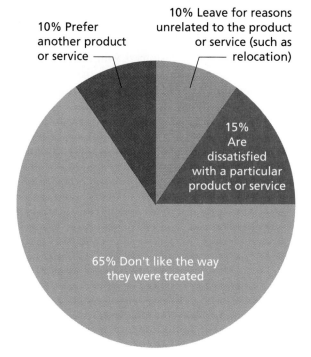

Figure 2-2 Why Customers Leave

Source: Eugene W. Anderson, Claes Fornell, and Donald R. Lehmann, "Customer Satisfaction, Market Share, and Profitability: Findings from Sweden," Journal of Marketing 58 (1994): 53.

perform, and allow companies to monitor how satisfied consumers are with their goods and services.

You may have used a rating system to help choose a stereo component, a car, or even which college to attend. Consumers have been sensitized to the importance of satisfaction by such publications as *Consumer Reports,* which routinely rates many products, and *Motor Trend,* which rates autos. Auto advertisers and others regularly incorporate satisfaction ratings into persuasive messages. The popular press runs major stories on satisfaction ratings. For example, J.D. Power & Associates produces an annual Customer Satisfaction Index for the automotive industry. It is based on evaluations by 32,000 car owners and 9,500 truck owners, and it is used to determine which vehicles best satisfy customers.[21] The American Consumer Satisfaction Index (ACSI) is a quarterly rating that measures customer satisfaction in seven sectors of the economy broken down into more than 40 industries. Even the U.S. government has entered the scene by sponsoring the Malcolm Baldrige National Quality Award, which is given to outstanding U.S. firms based largely on customer satisfaction.[22] We will discuss this award in more detail later in the chapter.

Competitive advantage comes to companies that can learn and adjust most quickly to market forces. One critical source of information is feedback from customers. It is important to know how they behave and why they feel as they do. A **customer satisfaction measurement program** is an ongoing survey of customers (and competitors' customers) for the purpose of obtaining continuous estimates of satisfaction. Simply looking at sales data can tell us whether more or fewer customers are purchasing, but it does not reveal much about underlying reasons for behavior. Consequently, in addition to sales data, companies measure such items as customer satisfaction and loyalty rates.

Marketers not only should measure their own company's performance but also should monitor that of competitors. What if your company has worked hard to improve product quality, which has been identified as critical to consumer satisfaction, yet the level of satisfaction continues to decline? It is quite possible that competitors have improved their quality much more quickly and that consumers recognize this fact.

The best consumer satisfaction program in the world is worth very little unless it feeds into the strategic and operational planning of the company. This information is then provided to all employees so that adjustments can be made to improve performance in their respective areas. Each functional area at all levels of the organization must be willing to undertake activities that lead to satisfied customers. One of the most important parts of the marketing executive's job is to get the entire organization to focus its decisions on actions that affect how much customers are satisfied. Much of a marketer's time is spent creating strategies that influence satisfaction.

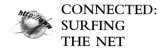 **CONNECTED: SURFING THE NET**

www.jdpower.com

Interested in information about automobiles, computers, airlines, phone services, or credit cards? Visit the J.D. Power & Associates Web site and search by industry for customer satisfaction ratings and performance reports.

Customer satisfaction measurement program
An ongoing survey of customers (and competitors' customers) for the purpose of obtaining continuous estimates of satisfaction.

CONNECTING THROUGH RELATIONSHIPS TO BUILD SATISFACTION AND LOYALTY

Just a few years ago marketers were content to sell to new customers with the goal of increasing sales faster than competitors. When one company's sales rise faster than all others, that organization's market share increases. Today, most companies realize that customer loyalty may be far more important than just market share.

The heart of the marketing concept is to address customer needs and wants. It doesn't stop there. Customer needs and wants should be addressed in a way that produces customer satisfaction and loyalty. Although not every customer seeks a relationship with every purchase, needs and wants more often are best addressed by establishing relationships.

You may try a new item for fun, but if you really like it, you will buy it again or tell others about it. The product becomes a more permanent fixture in your life and has more meaning. Without this loyalty and repeat business from customers, an organization's costs escalate, and in many cases the company fails. Very few organizations can survive on single transactions. Even companies that market products bought once in a lifetime depend on loyalty. The hospital that markets its heart surgery capabilities relies on positive word of mouth from loyal customers. Likewise, a Harley-Davidson dealer who sells a customer that one and only "dream machine" still builds the relationship after the sale. This makes it evident to other potential buyers that the Harley-Davidson organization will continue to connect with its loyal users.

Kimberly-Clark, maker of Huggies diapers, spent more than $10 million to establish a system that continually provides the name and address of more than 75 percent of expectant mothers in the United States. Information is collected from hospitals, childbirth trainers, obstetricians, and others. During pregnancy, women receive complimentary samples of baby products and parenting literature that offers tips on infant care. Even before the child is born or the first box of diapers has been purchased, Huggies has begun to develop a bond between the consumer and the brand.[23]

According to Skip Lefauvre, former CEO of Saturn Corporation, a company "must do things so astonishingly well that customers become not merely loyalists but rather outright apostles." Saturn buyers have enthusiastically embraced the company's unique customer-oriented selling philosophy. Loyalty is so great that when the company invited customers from around the country to a "Saturn Homecoming" in Spring Hill, Tennessee, more than 40,000 car owners showed up to take part in family events, plant tours, and informational meetings designed to foster trust and teamwork. According to Saturn's Corporate Communications Department, "the homecoming was just another way of building relationships and showing that we treat our customers differently from any other car company."[24]

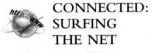

CONNECTED: SURFING THE NET

www.saturncars.com

Saturn even builds relationships with customers on the Web. If you'd like to learn more about Saturn, talk to other Saturn owners, or join its car club—connect to the Saturn Web site!

You have probably noticed that connecting through relationships creates a personal bond. That's what Saturn wants. When you buy a Saturn, your new car is cleaned and polished to perfection, and delivered to you in a special location within the dealership showroom. Your salesperson makes sure to take time, without interruptions, to discuss all of the features of your new purchase and answer any questions. And, don't be surprised to find cut flowers on the driver's seat. A personal phone call from your salesperson followed by a letter shortly thereafter provides the initial follow-through to begin furthering the relationship.

CREATING A PERSONAL RELATIONSHIP

By its very nature, a relationship is personal. It reflects the connection between two or more parties. Involvement with customers is key in relationship marketing. Chrysler is bonding with buyers at 33 jamborees nationwide, including off-roading courses in five cities and a "Camp Jeep" weekend in Colorado. "We want to win consumers' hearts, not just their pocketbooks," says Martin Levin, general manager of Chrysler's Jeep division.[25] Aside from any economic connections, relationships are socially driven as well. Empathy, trust, and commitment are important. This is true whether we are looking at consumer, business-to-business, or other markets.

Empathy Empathy is the ability to understand the perspective of another person or organization. It means putting yourself in someone else's shoes and seeing the world as that person sees it. Companies that build relationships do this in a number of ways. They use sophisticated marketing research and create a culture within the organization that is sensitive to others. But empathy works best when customers sense and know that they are under-

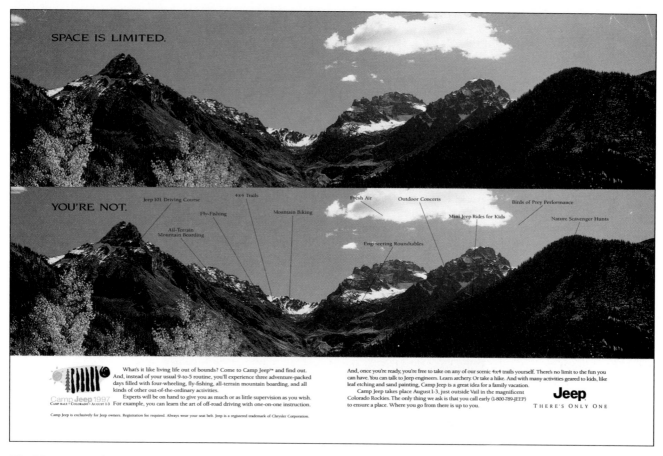

The "Camp Jeep" ads, created by Bozell Worldwide, were designed to build a relationship with the end user.

stood—that the organization has accurate knowledge of their circumstances. Marketers communicate this empathy in nearly everything they do. For example, when you call the telephone company for information and get courteous help, even if you don't spell the name correctly, the company has communicated empathy. When a company goes out of its way to make things work just for you, you experience its empathy.

Trust   Trust is being able to rely on another party to perform as promised and in the way you expect. The communications of marketers are filled with promises. For example: "Levi Strauss & Co. is committed to manufacturing products of the highest quality and ensuring the satisfaction of all our consumers. If any of our products do not meet our stringent quality standards, we want to identify the cause and take whatever corrective action is necessary."[26] Levi's backs up its promises by making it easy for you to return its products for an exchange or replacement. Companies, like people, who keep their promises earn trust. This is a tremendously important element in building lasting connections with customers.

Commitment   Companies that are committed go out of their way to serve customers. They go beyond what is promised to make sure the customer is better off because of the relationship. When things go wrong, they work hard to fix them. This is particularly critical to relationships over time. Carl Gustin, chief marketing officer at Kodak, spends 40 percent of his time traveling to visit business customers as well as channel partners and branch offices. Making an effort to stay connected with customers illustrates the company's commitment.[27]

Rewarding Loyal Customers   Relationship marketing creates connections that make it unnecessary or difficult for customers to switch to competitors. In order for relationship marketing to work, companies must understand their customers so well that competitors have little chance of offering new or unique items that would entice a trial. This means that companies must be willing to provide superior value for their best customers. Louise O'Brien and Charles Jones, vice presidents with the successful consulting firm of Bain & Company, say that if companies want to realize the benefits of loyalty they must admit that "all customers are not equal . . . a company must give its best value to its best customers. That is, customers

The Snap-On TRIBUTE CAMPAIGN which ran for three years, sought to elevate the image and trust level of professional auto technicians.

who generate superior profits for a company should enjoy the benefits of that value creation. As a result they will then become even more loyal and profitable."[28] For example, 25 percent of all households buy Diet Coke during the year. Yet, 84 percent of Diet Coke's annual sales comes from only one-third of all purchasers. Clearly, most of Diet Coke's profits come from a group of heavy users.[29] By providing lower prices for quantity purchases and coupons in packages for future purchases, the company sees to it that these loyal users benefit.

Building relationships may require specific incentives or rewards for loyal customers. MCI's Friends and Family program is a good example. It offers incentives to customers for enrolling friends and family members in the MCI long distance telephone network. All calls among the parties are discounted 20–50 percent. This encourages the introduction of MCI to new users and rewards existing and new customers for being loyal. The program was so successful in luring away AT&T customers that AT&T had to counter with its True Rewards program, which gives loyal customers free calling minutes, a 5 percent card rebate, and airline miles. Similarly, every major airline has loyalty programs that offer free upgrades into first class for the price of coach tickets and free airline tickets to domestic and international destinations. In each case the programs reward loyal customers and keep them from trying the competition.

Sometimes competitors attempt to counter loyalty programs of rivals. For example, in the summer of 1998 General Motors gave loyalty coupons worth $500 to $1000 for repurchase of a GM auto. Chrysler and Ford decided to honor these coupons for price reductions on their vehicles. At the same time, Chrysler and Ford initiated a similar loyalty program for loyal purchasers of their own cars. This neutralized the GM advantage and stimulated many GM customers to shop around.

CAREER TIP Employees at Hallmark know first hand what it means to connect with customers through relationships. Hallmark products directly promote relationships among family and friends. The employee atmosphere within Hallmark reflects this relationship philosophy. Career opportunities at Hallmark are numerous — internships, creative positions, sales, marketing, operations, corporate staff, and others. You can learn more about Hallmark career opportunities by connecting to its on-line job database at **www.occ.com/hallmark/.** Discover what positions are currently available and obtain application information for your area of interest.

DIVERSITY AND SATISFACTION

The diversity of tastes and preferences presents challenges for customer-centered marketers. Diversity helps explain why companies with the highest overall sales sometimes have lower satisfaction ratings than smaller companies. The latter can design products and services for very narrowly defined segments and can focus all their attention on those customers. These companies may have lower market share but score high satisfaction points with a few customers. As companies gain share by selling to more people, their products and services must appeal to more diversified customers with a broader range of expectations. Large companies must have the flexibility and agility to satisfy many divergent target markets while maintaining or increasing their size. Achieving satisfaction in the face of growth requires using the broadest range of marketing tools and techniques. If an organization expects impressive satisfaction scores, then it must understand all forms of diversity better than even its smallest competitors.

The success of a product or service in one market segment will not automatically transfer to consumers in another segment. The diverse nature of consumers makes universal buying preferences and behaviors very unlikely. Companies like Coca-Cola, McDonald's®, Exxon, and Levi Strauss address the individual wants and needs of people by acknowledging their unique differences. Attention to the diversity of consumers is often reflected in better market share and product sales.

Coca-Cola caters to the specific taste preferences of consumers in southern Japan by preparing a slightly sweetened version of its traditional formula. Coke found it necessary to alter the recipe so that it could better compete with Pepsi-Cola, producer of a recognized sweeter formula.[30] Companies that respect the diversity of consumers are often rewarded with strong sales and consumer loyalty.

Groups based on ethnicity have such tremendous buying power that marketers have begun to recognize the advantages of addressing each group individually. Many have even created marketing positions that focus on this. At Kraft, for example, there is a director of ethnic marketing. According to Steve Bachler, the company's direct marketing manager: "The closer you can get to the customer, the better—talk their language, represent their lifestyles, make sure the product is relevant to their lives. Targeting makes a lot of sense."[31] Today, nearly 75 percent of the nation's 50 largest firms have created diversity management positions in an effort to modify corporate culture to reflect the growth of minority segments.[32] Hallmark's efforts to reach ethnic markets is discussed in the diversity feature.

GLOBAL COMPETITION AND SATISFACTION

The success of global companies is highly dependent on customer satisfaction. Throughout the 1960s and 1970s, domestic firms dominated the U.S. market. By the early 1980s, U.S. businesses were under the false impression that success could be sustained by making only minor adjustments. This resulted in a real lack of focus on customer needs and satisfaction. Foreign companies spotted this weakness and entered U.S. markets quickly, putting customer satisfaction at the heart of everything they did. Some of the strongest U.S. companies saw their market share plummet because foreign rivals gained strong customer satisfaction ratings. These foreign competitors raised consumer expectations for quality and speed of service to new levels and often at substantially lower overall prices. Essentially, foreign competitors created new levels of customer satisfaction in the U.S. market.

No one knows this better than Xerox. In the early 1960s, Xerox introduced photocopiers to the U.S. business market. It dominated for the next 15 years with high-quality, high-priced copiers that generated satisfaction. With success, however, came a resistance to change, lack of customer focus, fewer product innovations, and unimproved quality standards. Satisfaction with Xerox declined. Japanese competitors entered the U.S. market during the mid-1970s

CONNECTING WITH DIVERSITY

WHEN YOU CARE ENOUGH TO SEND THE VERY BEST . . . IN SPANISH, HINDI, OR CHINESE

In a slow-growth business like greeting cards, ethnic marketing does more than satisfy diverse customers; it's a survival strategy. About 90 percent of greeting cards are bought by middle-aged women, and with little demographic movement in this category, there's been almost no growth in the total number of cards sold. There is opportunity, however, in the rapidly growing population of African-Americans, Latinos, and Asians, whose buying power is significant. For instance, while African Americans make up only 12 percent of the population, they purchase about 15 percent or $915 million worth of greeting cards a year.

Hallmark Card Company has created cards for African Americans since the 1960s and launched its Mahogany line in 1987. Yet, not until 1994, when the company established its Ethnic Business Center, was there a formal brand management team and marketing strategy. Hallmark now has more than 900 cards in this line. In addition, there is a line of cards called Primor for Hispanics and one called Tree of Life for Jewish customers.

How does the Kansas-based company, often seen as "white bread" and "Middle America," reach out to ethnic customers with any credibility? An inauthentic expression, a badly translated Spanish phrase, an inappropriate image—all can spell millions in lost sales. Hallmark's Ethnic Business Center calls on a stable of outside consultants and conducts extensive market research. For instance, the company has found that African Americans favor bright colors and cards that emphasize ethnic pride and social consciousness. For Hispanics, language is especially important, since word endings can be familiar or formal. Research also showed that Hispanics prefer cards without pictures of people as well as cards protected by acetate covers. For the Tree of Life line, the company sent some writers and artists to Israel to pick up cultural nuances. Cards emphasize family, religious holidays, and Jewish humor. A card for Passover features a family crowded around a table with balloons overhead, saying: "Pass the matzoh over please!" "Would you pass the salt over here?" "Hey! pass the wine over!" "Pass over the carrots." Inside the card reads: "No wonder it's called Passover. Enjoy!"

Another way Hallmark establishes credibility and attracts ethnic customers is by cross-merchandising with ethnic products. In 1996 the company slipped two free Mahogany cards into 500,000 Beautiful Beginning hair relaxer kits. At the same time, purchasers of Mahogany cards were offered $1.00 off Beautiful Beginnings if they purchased two cards in the line. The tactic was not just a hit with consumers but with retailers as well. "This cross-promotion encourages awareness and sales of two categories without expecting the retailer to be involved with any merchandising activities," says Mark Evans, marketing manager of Hallmark's Ethnic Business Center.

Hallmark's marketing possibilities are as unlimited as the growth of the ethnic population, which is expected to increase at four times the rate of the overall population. In fact, the company is currently studying the Asian market with its many subsegments, such as Asian Indian, Japanese, Korean, Cambodian, and Laotian. "We have a lot of research to do," says Evans.

Sources: Marjorie Whigham-Desir, "Boom in Black Greeting Cards," *Black Enterprise*, December 1995, pp. 104–108; Laura Liebeck, "Ethnic Selections Season Greeting Cards," *Discount Store News*, April 1, 1996, pp. 93–94; Renee Covino Rouland, "More Room for Expression," *Discount Merchandiser*, April 1996, pp. 35, 38; "Going After the Ethnic Card Market," *Discount Merchandiser*, June 1996, p. 93.

CONNECTED: SURFING THE NET

www.xerox.com

Discover how Xerox's emphasis on quality has won awards in nearly every major market where it does business. Learn more about Xerox's newest quality products and business solutions.

to take advantage of Xerox's lack of customer satisfaction. Although the Japanese first introduced low-end copiers, they slowly increased quality to challenge the high-end copiers marketed by Xerox. Satisfaction with Japanese copiers was high. By 1981, Xerox had lost 50 percent of its market share, and profits were down by $600 million, or nearly half. To combat these losses, Xerox management implemented the "Leadership Through Quality" program, which was designed to focus the entire organization on satisfying customers. An aggressive goal was set: 100 percent satisfaction across all Xerox business units by 1993. Some units had achieved this goal by 1990, and Xerox once again holds the top position in key product category of the photocopier industry. Today, many U.S. companies focus on ways to improve customer satisfaction so they can close the gap with, and in many cases surpass, foreign rivals in providing satisfaction.[33]

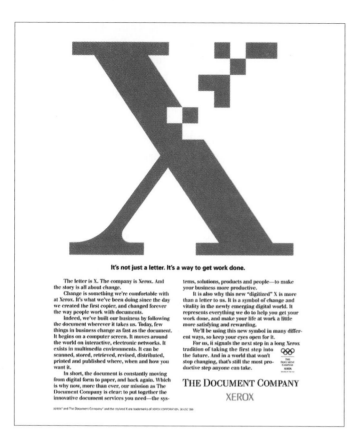

Xerox's "Leadership Through Quality" program is designed to focus the entire organization on satisfying customers.

ORGANIZATIONAL SYSTEMS AND ACTIONS THAT DELIVER QUALITY

As we discussed in chapter 1, the effects of technology are absolutely phenomenal on the creation of customer value. Overall, the functionality of products is increasing while costs are staying the same or decreasing. Today most customer oriented companies have systems and take actions that deliver quality goods and quality services to customers. And an emphasis on quality—largely made possible through technology and people—brings more satisfaction to customers. Products work as expected, last longer, and are user friendly. This section describes some of the aspects of quality that are used by leading-edge organizations to help accomplish customer satisfaction and loyalty.

QUALITY

In marketing, **quality** describes the degree of excellence of a company's goods and services. It is useful to emphasize both quality in goods as well as the special case of service quality. **Service quality** is the expected and perceived quality of all of the services an organization offers. Quality is necessary for organizations that sell physical products that are manufactured as well as organizations that only sell services. Without quality, it is nearly impossible to achieve customer satisfaction. A quality good or service performs precisely according to specifications that will satisfy customers. Consequently, quality contributes to customer satisfaction. Some companies, like Packard Electric, believe their product possesses quality to the degree that it meets or exceeds customer expectations. Elmer Reece, a former top executive at the company, introduced the "excellence concept" in a quest to deliver total quality. According to Reece, "being excellent means meeting or exceeding customer expectations in everything." Striving for excellence became a critical part of every employee's job at Packard, and Reece's philosophy turned the company into a real winner. In order to make the concept work, Reece elevated marketing from its traditional sales role to the leading force in every major decision. Reece often spoke of the problems that occurred when quality was defined from an engineering or manufacturing perspective. He said that the customer, not the company, should be the judge of quality.

Quality
The degree of excellence of a company's products or services.

Service quality
The expected and perceived quality of all of the services an organization offers.

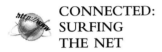

No two customers are alike. We all want quality goods and services—but we each may view quality as being slightly different. For example, if you get an urge for a Big Mac® and can even taste its flavor in your mouth, then you might define quality by consistency (which McDonald's® has perfected). But if you get an urge for a gourmet meal at a five-star restaurant, you might define quality as uniqueness and variety. Legendary restaurants such as Spago and Lutece take very different actions from McDonald's® to accomplish quality.

According to FedEx CEO Frederick W. Smith, "the quality process is the key factor that will allow FedEx to grow because our customers expect 100 percent satisfaction—not 98 or 99 percent satisfaction. And 100 percent customer satisfaction demands 100 percent employee effort to meet that goal." As defined by the customer, 100 percent customer satisfaction means 100 percent on-time delivery and 100 percent accurate information available on every shipment at every location around the world. It also means 100 percent satisfaction every time FedEx comes in contact with its customers, whether helping them locate FedEx in a foreign country or clarifying a billing problem. This is an impressive challenge, considering that FedEx moves approximately 2.5 million packages worldwide—every day![34]

In many markets, a quality product is considered the price of entry. Basically, this means that a company must offer a quality product in order to participate in a market; inferior products or services will not succeed. As more companies build quality into their products as a standard feature, it ceases to provide a differential advantage. This was not always the case, however. In the 1980s, many consumers bought Japanese cars because they were perceived to be of much higher quality than U.S. brands. Today, most experts believe that U.S. vehicles are equal in quality to Japanese cars and that U.S. manufacturers are even beginning to take the lead in new areas of quality, such as design and performance.

Quality may be evaluated in two ways, subjectively and objectively. Customers are the key to understanding the subjective analysis, while technical specifications are the focus of objective assessments.

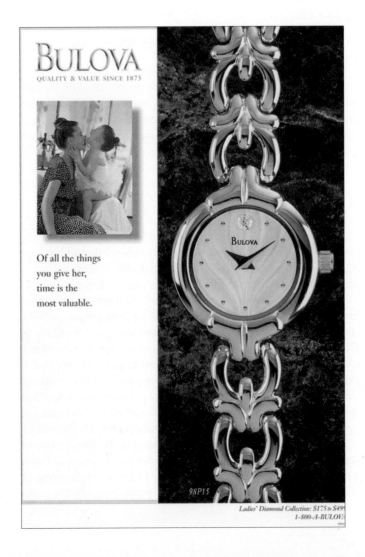

Consumers may pay more for brands they perceive have higher value.

Assessments of Quality   **Subjective assessment of quality** indicates to what degree the product does what consumers want. For example, the hamburger tastes good. In assessing quality, consumers tend to be subjective, while companies tend to be objective. After an extensive review of a number of studies, one expert defined quality as "the consumer's judgment about a product's overall excellence or superiority."[35] From this perspective, different groups may evaluate quality altogether differently. When asked, adults may say Wendy's is higher in quality than McDonald's®, while children may have the opposite response.

Subjective assessment of quality
The degree to which a product does what consumers would like it to do.

    Objective assessment of quality indicates to what degree the product does consistently what it's supposed to do. McDonald's® and Burger King make what many consider to be high-quality hamburgers because each time one is served, it consistently meets company standards. With hamburgers and other physical objects, it's possible to develop objective assessments of quality in the form of standards, such as fat and salt content or nutrition value.

Objective assessment of quality
An evaluation of the degree to which a product does what it is supposed to do.

    Even objective assessments are open to interpretation. This is particularly true globally. For example, German and Japanese products are manufactured to precise specifications and will not perform in excess of their rating. If a product is rated to lift 1,000 kg, it will do precisely that and no more. In contrast, a similar U.S. product is likely to have a safety factor of 1.5, so the product will lift 1,500 kg. The extra capacity is a sign of quality in the United States, but not in many other markets. Consequently, even measures of so-called objective quality are created in response to the subjective desires of various groups.[36]

Static and Dynamic Quality   There are at least two types of quality. **Static quality** results when an accepted practice is perfected. **Dynamic quality** results when a major change makes the existing standard obsolete. For example, Smith Corona once dominated the personal typewriter business with an extremely high-quality electric portable. All quality efforts at Smith Corona were directed at improving their typewriters. As consumers shifted to word-processors, however, Smith Corona's efforts to achieve static quality became irrelevant. A revolution had taken place as companies in the word processing business—software and hardware—created value through change, a dynamic quality shift.

Static quality
Quality that results when individuals or organizations perfect an accepted practice.

Dynamic quality
Quality that results from a change that makes an existing standard obsolete.

    Focusing activities on static quality can divert resources from new ventures, and there seems little point in perfecting technology that is about to become outmoded. At the same time, dynamic quality shifts cannot be forced; the technology needs to be perfected and the market prepared. Marketers are a company's advance scouts, signaling what is new and relevant. Marketing is also critical in defining quality from the customer's perspective. Marketers develop estimates of what attributes customers use to define quality, what minimum quality standards must be, and what various segments are willing to pay for quality.

Total Quality Management   **Total quality management (TQM)** is an organizational philosophy that helps companies produce products and services that deliver value to satisfy customers. TQM involves, first, assessing consumer needs and, second, developing products or services that meet those needs. The approach seeks continuous improvement, reduced cycle time, and analysis of process problems. It also includes quality function deployment, which attempts to ensure that customer desires are built into the final product offering.[37] When implemented correctly, TQM involves all company activities that affect customer satisfaction and ends with customer service and feedback. It deals with both deliverables (the goods and services provided) and interactions (how customers experience dealing with the provider).

Total quality management (TQM)
An organizational philosophy which helps companies produce goods and services that deliver value to satisfy customers.

Dynamic quality occurs when a major change makes the existing standard obsolete.

Continuous improvement
The enhancement process used by an organization to find the best ways of satisfying its customers.

Continuous Improvement   **Continuous improvement** occurs as the organization strives to find better ways of satisfying customers. In discussing the importance of continuous improvement, David Kearns, CEO of Xerox, has described his organization as "being in a race without a finish line."[38] FedEx uses Service Quality Indications (SQI) in its efforts to achieve continuous improvement. The index measures a number of key service factors from the customer's perspective and then weights them as to how seriously the customer will view a failure in any of those areas. Based on SQI, FedEx has set the goal of scoring better year after year. Since 1987, overall customer satisfaction at FedEx has averaged more than 95 percent and is approaching the company's goal of 100 percent.

Milliken and Company, another organization known for superior quality, pays particular attention to constant improvement. It calls its "Pursuit of Excellence" program an evolving process that continuously yields new ideas for enhancing quality, increasing customer satisfaction, and improving business performance. Through Milliken's Policy Committee and Quality Council, management creates the environment and provides the leadership necessary for quality improvement. Relying heavily on employee training and an organization structure in which employees are called associates, Milliken has instilled in every person a feeling of responsibility to find and implement quality improvement changes. Managers must respond within one day to any suggestion by an associate to enhance customer satisfaction. This form of empowerment gives each associate the opportunity to have a positive influence on quality.

Reduced cycle time
A TQM activity which helps a company move more rapidly from product inception to final delivery of the product to the marketplace.

Reduced Cycle Time   **Reduced cycle time** is a TQM activity intended to help the company move more quickly from product inception to product delivery in the marketplace. The approach pays huge dividends by reducing costs while making possible very quick shipment of products matched specifically to customer requirements. This not only allows customers more flexibility in ordering but also results in lower inventories for business customers and quicker availability of products for consumers.

Wallace Company, a Houston-based industrial distributor of pipes, valves, and fittings, has used TQM principles to achieve reduced cycle time and has seen striking results. Wallace assigns a team of outside salespeople, inside salespeople (customer service and sales representatives in the home office), and accounts receivable personnel to every customer account. This allows employees and customers to gain a great deal of familiarity with one another. Inventory turnover improved by 175 percent in five years, sales for newly introduced value-added products increased 75 percent between 1987 and 1990, and profits doubled.

Analysis of Process Problems   Analysis of process problems refers to the activities that produce the products and services. For manufactured items this includes procurement of raw materials and components that go into finished goods, the manufacture of the finished products themselves, and packaging and shipping to ensure that appropriate products get to their final destination. The International Standards Organization (ISO) has established an inclusive set of standards, called **ISO 9000**, to determine whether quality requirements are met. These standards are being introduced into laws in the European Community to ensure that firms have quality management systems in place that meet specified criteria. Individual products aren't certified. Companies must go through an arduous process to become ISO 9000 certified. Organizations such as Chrysler and Motorola require that all their suppliers be ISO 9000 certified.

ISO 9000
An inclusive set of standards established by the International Standards Organization (ISO) to ensure that quality requirements are met.

An important outcome of the analysis is to establish rigid quality control, such as the Motorola 6 Sigma standard, which sets goals so that virtually all Motorola products perform as expected. Elaborate efforts are made in product and process design to ensure that the actual manufacturing activities efficiently produce quality items. In turn, the processes are monitored to make certain that the output is produced according to specifications.

Although quality has been the focus of manufacturing for more than a decade, the same principles are now being applied to customer service. For example, at FedEx, Al White manages more than 200 employees in a state-of-the-art telecommunications center with the sole purpose of fielding customer service issues. The SQI measures at FedEx approach the mathematical rigor previously reserved only for manufacturing companies.[39]

Quality function deployment (QFD)
A process that builds customer wants and desires into the final product offering.

Quality Function Deployment   **Quality function deployment (QFD)** is used during the product or service design process to make sure that features to fulfill customer desires are built into the final offering. The three most common concerns of QFD are to make the product or service faster, better, and cheaper. Figure 2-3 shows what consumers desire in their dealings with the company and how those desires are translated into what the company delivers.

	Faster	Better	Cheaper
COMPANY DELIVERS	Availabilty Convenience	Performance Features Reliability Conformance Serviceability Aesthetics Perceived Quality	Price
CUSTOMER DESIRES	Responsiveness Access	Reliability Security Competence Credibility Empathy Communications Style	Affordability

Figure 2-3 Faster-Better-Cheaper: What the Company Delivers and What the Customer Desires

It is important to note that not all companies' TQM activities result in performance increases. According to two consulting firms, A.T. Kearney and Arthur D. Little, 80 percent of more than 100 British firms studied reported no significant effect as a result of TQM, and almost two-thirds of 500 U.S. companies had "zero competitive gains." In some cases companies focus so much attention on the TQM process that they ignore how their competitors are behaving in other areas. In other cases, so much emphasis is placed on improvements in existing products that organizations fail to innovate in all aspects of strategy.[40] Still, when customer satisfaction is increased (relative to competitors) over time, firms can expect improved profitability.

Benchmarking **Benchmarking** is the systematic evaluation of the practices of excellent organizations to learn new and better ways of serving customers. Benchmarking of **best practices**, those selected competencies for which leaders are known, has become so important that companies regularly send personnel to study and observe other organizations. Sparrow Health Systems, a leading provider in mid-Michigan, recently sent executives to Disney World to learn how to improve customer service. They also visited Saturn to obtain ideas for involving employees in the improvement process. Although Disney and Saturn are not in the same business, Sparrow was able to learn several new ways of ultimately improving health care delivery. By comparing its methods with those of known experts in other fields, Sparrow conducted benchmarking.

Benchmarking
The systematic evaluation of practices of excellent organizations to learn new and better ways to serve customers.

Best practices
The competencies of industry leaders that other organizations use as benchmarks.

Quality Awards To encourage companies to improve their quality and competitiveness, various governments have established awards. These are given to companies that demonstrate the most outstanding quality initiatives. Two very distinguished annual awards are the Deming Prize in Japan and the Malcolm Baldrige National Quality Award in the United States.

The Deming Prize Everyone has heard of quality inspectors—people who examine finished products as they roll off the assembly line and remove defective goods before they are sold to customers. In the early 1900s, most companies used inspectors as their main source of quality control. Little or no effort was devoted to correcting the manufacturing problems that caused product defects.

In the 1950s, Dr. Edward Deming took a new approach to the issue. He applied the idea of statistical quality control, a concept he learned while a statistician at AT&T's Bell Laboratories, to manufacturing. **Statistical quality control** involves using statistics to isolate and quantify production line problems that may cause defects. The idea was to improve quality in the production process so that faulty goods would not be manufactured. The Japanese openly embraced Deming's philosophy, and this is viewed by many as one of the reasons for Japan's tremendous economic success during the 1970s and 1980s. Deming's work transformed Japan from the maker of inferior products to one of the most powerful economies in the world. To honor Deming's contributions, the Japanese created the Deming Award as their highest recognition of quality.

To help business managers implement quality initiatives within their organization, Deming outlined 14 key issues, listed in Figure 2-4. Deming insisted, moreover, that top

Statistical quality control
The use of statistics to isolate and quantify production line problems that may cause product defects.

1. Create constancy of purpose toward improvement of product and service, with the aim to become competitive and stay in business, and to provide jobs.
2. Adopt this philosophy: We are in a new economic age created by Japan. Transformation of Western management style is necessary to halt the continued decline of industry.
3. Cease depending on inspection to achieve quality. Eliminate the need for inspection on a mass basis by building quality into the product in the first place.
4. End the practice of awarding business on the basis of price tag. Purchasing must be combined with design of product, manufacturing, and sales to work with the chosen suppliers; the aim is to minimize total cost, not merely initial cost.
5. Improve constantly and forever every activity in the company in order to improve quality and productivity and thus constantly decrease costs.
6. Institute training and education on the job for everyone, including management.
7. Institute supervision. The aim of supervision should be to help people and machines do a better job.
8. Drive out fear so that everyone may work effectively for the company.
9. Break down barriers between departments. People in Research, Design, Sales, and Production must work as a team to tackle usage and production problems that may be encountered with the product or service.
10. Eliminate slogans, exhortations, and targets for the work force that ask for zero defects and new levels of productivity. Such exhortations only create adversarial relationships; the bulk of the causes of low quality and low productivity belongs to the system and thus lies beyond the power of the work force.
11. Eliminate work standards that prescribe numerical quotas for the day. Substitute aids and helpful supervision.
12a. Remove the barriers that rob hourly workers of the right to pride of workmanship. The responsibility of supervisors must be changed from sheer numbers to quality.
12b. Remove the barriers that rob people in management and in engineering of their right to pride of workmanship. This means, among other things, abolition of the annual or merit rating and of management by objective.
13. Institute a vigorous program of education and retraining. New skills are required for changes in techniques, materials, and service.
14. Put everybody in the company to work in teams to accomplish the transformation.

Figure 2-4 Edward Deming's 14 Points of Quality

Source: Reprinted from The New Economics for Industry, Government, Education *by W. Edward Deming by permission of MIT and The W. Edward Deming Institute. Published by MIT, Center for Advanced Educational Services, Cambridge, MA 02139. Copyright 1993 by The W. Edward Deming Institute.*

management be involved and supportive. If quality initiatives receive only lip service, without action, they will not be successful.

The Malcolm Baldrige National Quality Award   U.S. businesses have been late to emphasize quality. During the same period that the Japanese excelled in implementing quality initiatives, U.S. firms slipped dramatically in quality. Congress finally moved to establish a quality award for American firms. It was named after the late Malcolm Baldrige, an advocate for quality and a former secretary of commerce.

While considering the passage of Malcolm Baldrige National Quality Improvement Act, the U.S. Senate Committee on Commerce, Science and Technology observed: "Strategic planning for quality improvement programs is becoming more and more essential to the well-being of our nation's companies and our ability to compete effectively in the global marketplace. Such an award would parallel the prize awarded annually in Japan."[41]

The 1987 legislation was enacted by Congress to encourage U.S. business and other organizations to practice effective quality control in the production of goods and services. At the time of passage, the Senate and House produced a declaration reiterating the need for an incentive program for U.S. businesses and affirming that these businesses had been considerably challenged by foreign competitors. Slow growth in productivity and in product and process quality had, in some industries, resulted in annual losses of as much as 20 percent of sales revenues. It was evident that U.S. businesses needed to learn more about the importance of quality.

Malcolm Baldrige National Quality Award
A program designed to raise quality awareness and practice among U.S. businesses.

The **Malcolm Baldrige National Quality Award** is widely acknowledged as having raised quality awareness and practice among U.S. companies. Some consider the Baldrige the most important catalyst for transforming American business because it promotes quality excellence, recognizes achievements by companies that effectively improve quality, and supplies a guideline that business, industry, government, and others can use to evaluate their quality improvement efforts.

The Malcolm Baldrige National Quality Award has raised quality awareness among U.S. companies.

Awards are given each year in several categories: manufacturing companies or subsidiaries, service companies or subsidiaries, and small businesses. Figure 2-5 lists companies that have received the Malcolm Baldrige Award.

In 1996, ADAC Laboratories was an award winner. The company designs, manufactures, markets, and supports consumer health care products. What makes this company a total quality winner? Among many others, customer focus is a distinguishing achievement. ADAC believes that customers come first, and its actions reflect this belief. All executives are expected to spend 25 percent of their time with customers. This means taking orders personally and inviting customers to attend weekly quality meetings. Customer satisfaction ratings at ADAC have also shown positive and improving results, including a 70–90 percent customer retention rate.[42]

DELIVERING VALUE TO IMPROVE SATISFACTION

Customer-centered marketing requires the development of unique competencies to satisfy customers within selected target market segments and to build their loyalty. Many parties are involved in contributing to the delivery of products that benefit consumers. The value chain is used to describe the chain of activities involved in bringing products to consumers. Additionally, to improve customer satisfaction and loyalty, leading-edge companies operate ethically to fulfill commitments and involve employees and customers in performance improvement efforts.

THE VALUE CHAIN

Economists use the concept of the value chain which helps marketers identify ways that the company can do a better job of satisfying the end user. The **value chain** is composed of all the activities that organizations undertake to deliver value to the customer, such as product and service development, and distribution through convenient channels. A simple value chain starts by identifying customer needs. Most people seek products that perform as desired, portray the image they want, are easy to purchase, and are priced fairly. Companies then identify the chain of events which must occur to deliver this value to customers. It is important that quality is built into each link in the chain.

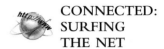

CONNECTED: SURFING THE NET

www.quality.nist.gov/

Discover what it takes to be a winner. Learn more about the Malcolm Baldrige National Quality Award and criteria by connecting to its Web site. Also, link to the home pages of several award-winning companies.

Value chain

All the activities that companies undertake to deliver more value to the ultimate consumer.

1988	Globe Metallurgical, Inc.	1992 cont.	Granite Rock Company
	Motorola, Inc.		The Ritz-Carlton Hotel Company
	Westinghouse Electric Corporation		Texas Instruments Incorporated
1989	Milliken & Company	1993	Ames Rubber Corporation
	Xerox Corporation		Eastman Chemical Company
1990	Cadillac Motor Car Company	1994	AT&T Consumer Communications Services
	Federal Express Corporation		GTE Directories Corporation
	IBM Rochester		Wainwright Industries
	Wallace Co.	1995	Armstrong World Industries Building Products Operations
1991	Marlow Industries		Corning Telecommunications Products Division
	Solectron Corporation	1996	ADAC Laboratories
	Zytec Corporation		Custom Research, Inc.
1992	AT&T Network Systems Group		Dana Commercial Credit Corporation
	AT&T Universal Card Services		Trident Precision Manufacturing

Figure 2-5   Winners of the Malcolm Baldrige Quality Award

Many activities make a major difference in the amount of customer satisfaction. These include the procurement of raw materials as well as the manufacture and delivery of products to retailers and others in the channel of distribution. Each activity has the potential to deliver added value to the customer. All functional areas—purchasing, operations, manufacturing, marketing, sales, and so on—are involved in delivering customer value. Each area must clearly understand the final consumer. And many separate organizations may be linked in the chain.

Although customers have very little knowledge of these activities, they shape the quality of goods and services as well as the price that will be charged in the marketplace. Think about Nike, whose customers want a good value at a fair price. But Nike knows that manufacturing locations make a big difference in the product cost. In the same manner, the cost of Nike's raw materials, its ability to deliver products efficiently to retail outlets, the effectiveness of its research and development, and many other activities affect the overall quality of the goods and services the company can provide to its customers. Even the quality of the ads for Nike are important, since the image of the product for users is largely shaped by the ads. Nike's competitiveness depends to a great degree on its ability, and the ability of its suppliers and distributors, to perform well on a variety of factors that influence the amount of value delivered to the marketplace. All organizations in the chain must behave with the intent of creating satisfaction for others in the chain in order that consumers can ultimately benefit to the greatest degree possible.

ETHICAL BEHAVIOR IN FULFILLING COMMITMENTS

Many organizations that promise satisfaction and quality think they should provide a remedy to customers when quality does not meet expectations. Fixing the problem is ethically correct and a good business practice. Although "satisfaction guaranteed or your money back" usually applies to such purchases as clothes or a restaurant pizza, today some colleges believe that a promise of a quality education should be backed by a guarantee as well. They are using statements about quality and satisfaction to attract students from the shrinking pool of high school graduates, which has declined from 3.2 million in 1977 to about 2.47 million today.[43]

In 1986, Henry Ford Community College in Dearborn, Michigan, became the first school to offer a guarantee for its graduates. It provides up to 16 semester hours of further training if an employer feels a graduate lacks the expected job skills. St. John Fischer College, a four-year institution in Rochester, N.Y., started featuring promotions with "The Fischer Commitment." It gives up to $5,000 in refunds to students who, after a good-faith effort, are unable to find a job within six months of graduation.

Of course, many businesses offer satisfaction guarantees. Some pay off with little hassle, like Meijer Thrifty Acres, a regional discount chain with an outstanding reputation for customer service. Others pay lip service to the offer but make it almost impossible for dissatisfied consumers to collect. Despite the satisfaction that results when a customer problem is handled well, a number of companies have tightened their rules and changed generous exchange policies. Best Buy, for example, has quit taking back goods without a sales receipt. Customers who have no receipt must pay a "restocking fee" equal to 15 percent of the purchase price of the item. Wal-Mart has changed its open-ended return policy to one with a 90-day limit.

Customers are partly responsible for these changes. Imagine people returning goods actually purchased at a garage sale or bringing back clothes worn for an entire season. Or what about customers who pull items off store shelves and bring them to the counter for a refund? Nintendo has received returned game boxes containing underwear, soap, and even a lizard. Although these are extreme examples, stores have tightened return policies to help prevent fraud. Since 10–15 percent of all retail sales are returned, the stricter policies may seem reasonable.[44] The important consideration, however, is the consumer response. If the ease of returning a defective or unwanted good is eliminated, then consumers feel negatively about the company or business. Since many aspects of satisfaction are based on how the organization and its products affect customers, it is important to make all employees aware of the importance of the customer to the overall health of the organization. That requires their involvement in knowing why products were returned and nearly every other aspect of customer evaluations.

It's pretty hard to imagine making customers satisfied without having employees who are highly involved in the process. It is also hard to imagine those same employees doing a good job with customers unless they are satisfied with their organization. Satisfied employees are much more likely to produce satisfied customers than are disgruntled employees. Thus, customer satisfaction starts with the company itself. Strong companies involve the entire organization and its customers in efforts to improve performance in ways that will promote customer satisfaction. IBM integrates customers into its improvement planning process by inviting consumers from around the world to give direct input to top-level strategic planners. Executives at Procter & Gamble take time to interview consumers at grocery stores and answer customer service calls. Hewlett-Packard recruits customers to assist in developing products that will replace current offerings. All these companies demonstrate how interaction between consumers and an organization's employees help ensure that the customer is a primary focus.[45]

The job of satisfying consumers cannot be left to the marketing or sales manager alone. According to Robert Schrandt, vice president of customer relations for Toyota Motor Sales, USA: "Achieving customer satisfaction would be impossible without a well-defined process for focusing the entire organization on the customer." As with the most important marketing functions, everyone must participate, from top management to the workers on the factory floor. In fact, most companies that are serious about improving satisfaction consider it critical to involve their top managers. They sit in on meetings about customer satisfaction and demand that everyone "walk the talk"—not just discuss issues but develop plans to address them. Compared to other organizations, managers in these companies spend more time talking with customers, and compensation structures often are based more on satisfying customers than on meeting short-term financial goals. Furthermore, all functional areas are involved, including marketing, sales, engineering, accounting, and purchasing. Other channel members, such as manufacturers' representatives, wholesalers, and distributors, often are made part of the effort. The result is a customer-centered organization working together to create satisfied purchasers.

It isn't enough to involve members of the company and its agents. Customers also must be part of the process. The biggest mistake most companies make is to assume they know what their customers want without asking them. Unfortunately, most companies that guess do so incorrectly. For a true understanding of what consumers want, a company must ask them through some sort of meaningful involvement. It is important to include not only current customers but also potential purchasers and competitors' customers. Each is likely to provide unique and enlightening information. One way to achieve involvement is through formal marketing research, such as interviews or surveys. In addition, many leading companies include customers in their planning teams.

Citizens Bank, a regional financial institution in mid-Michigan, recently developed a new strategic marketing plan in light of new and increased competition in its traditional market area. Employees from all parts of the banking organization were joined by key customers and the board of directors in a thorough and lengthy process of building new policies, services, and communication approaches. The organization went through an arduous self-assessment, and customers were part of the team in making some key decisions. The result was a plan that is very sensitive to the unique needs of the local community.

Toyota uses a well defined process for focusing its entire organization on the customer, in order to deliver value and obtain customer satisfaction.

Chapter 4 will focus on how marketing executives and managers develop strategies and plans designed to achieve customer satisfaction more effectively than competitors. Meanwhile, we will take a look at important factors in the global marketing environment that must be accounted for in the strategic planning process.

CONNECTED: SURFING THE NET

Red Lobster

www.redlobster.com

THIS CHAPTER'S TECHNOLOGY BOX DISCUSSED RED Lobster's "Recipe for Customer Satisfaction with Response Software." In order to expand your thinking about Red Lobster, visit its Web site at and answer the following questions.

1. Read the article found in "Editorials and Reviews" (www.redlobster.com/press.html) called "Quality and Service Reign As Cornerstones of Red Lobster's Continued Success." How, specifically, has Red Lobster built value with quality for its customers?
2. Learn about Red Lobster's history. Describe how building value with quality has changed and evolved over the years. How do these improvements reflect the changing needs of customers?
3. Red Lobster has hired more than 1,000 employees with disabilities at its 677 U.S. restaurants. Dick Monroe, vice president of public relations, says: "We focus on the many ways in which these employees can contribute to Red Lobster's success, rather than looking at those things they cannot do." How do you think this commitment to diversity supports or enhances the connections Red Lobster makes with customers?

Hallmark

www.hallmark.com

HALLMARK BUILDS RELATIONSHIPS WITH CUSTOMERS IN many ways, including ethnic marketing, which you learned about in this chapter's diversity box. Here is an opportunity to learn more about Hallmark. Visit its Web site and answer the following questions.

1. Read about the technology brand of Hallmark, called "Hallmark Connections." How do these unique offerings deliver value to customers?
2. What is Hallmark's reminder service, and how can it build relationships which can lead to loyalty?
3. Find the information about Hallmark's business expressions line, also referred to as "your on-line loyalty marketing resource." Read "Building Relationships" and describe why Hallmark emphasizes the importance of customer relationships.
4. Hallmark's Gold Crown Card allows customers to earn points from their purchases, which can be used toward free greeting cards or merchandise. How does this system reward customer loyalty?

CHAPTER SUMMARY

OBJECTIVE 1: Understand why customer satisfaction and loyalty are the focus of marketing in winning organizations.

Satisfied, loyal customers generate profits because they are responsible for a large percentage of sales and are less costly to develop than new customers. Loyal, satisfied customers also influence others to buy products. Similar to product innovation, customer satisfaction has become a key to competitive advantage. In addition, satisfaction ratings help consumers compare products. Finally,

loyal, satisfied customers will pay more and are less concerned about price and price increases.

OBJECTIVE 2: Learn how consumer expectations influence satisfaction.

Customers form impressions about how well companies perform in relation to expectations. If performance falls short, then customers become dissatisfied. Often they defect when they don't like the way they are treated. When customers are delighted, their expectations are likely to increase. Loyal customers are not always satisfied, and they are likely to complain. If their complaint is handled quickly, then their loyalty may be even greater.

OBJECTIVE 3: See why connecting with customers through relationships achieves outstanding satisfaction and loyalty.

The personal connection produces loyalty. Relationships are built, first, on empathy–the ability to understand another party and communicate that understanding. Second, trust is important, that is, behaving in line with promises you make and expectations you create. Third, commitment is also important. Commitment means making sure that the customer is better off because of the relationship.

OBJECTIVE 4: Understand the ideas that help organizations market quality goods and services.

Diverse customers have different expectations. Creating satisfaction requires paying close attention to various tastes and preferences. Many companies have created units to address specific groups. The variations in customer tastes and preferences are particularly challenging for large companies that want to gain high sat-

isfaction scores. They still need to address each specific segment to achieve high ratings. Satisfaction scores have historically been higher for some foreign companies in this country, reflecting their attention to quality. This has helped them gain a market foothold. Now that U.S. companies also are stressing quality and satisfaction, their scores are improving in marketing to foreign countries.

OBJECTIVE 5: Define quality and describe how it is obtained.

Quality can be assessed objectively and subjectively. Objective assessments indicate whether the product performs as designed. Subjective assessments indicate whether the product performs according to what customers want. Businesses must be careful not to focus only on static quality. The quality of change—dynamic quality— is also important. Both build value. Total quality management (TQM) is an organizational philosophy that focuses on quality. It includes several specific actions, such as continuous improvement, reduced cycle time, and analysis of process problems. Benchmarking is also important. It refers to learning from organizations considered to be among the very best and assessing how well you perform relative to them.

REVIEW YOUR UNDERSTANDING

1. What is customer satisfaction? What is loyalty? What are four reasons for an organization to stress loyalty and satisfaction? Explain each.
2. How do you calculate the lifetime value of a customer?
3. What are customer expectations? Why do customers defect? Why are complainers often your most loyal customers?
4. What are the three elements that form the personal basis of relationships? Explain each. How do companies reward loyal customers?
5. What are companies doing to address satisfaction with diversified customers?
6. Why is satisfaction important in global marketing?
7. What is customer-delivered value? Explain.
8. What is the value chain? Explain.
9. What are objective and subjective assessments of quality? Static and dynamic quality?
10. What is TQM and what are its four critical components?
11. What is benchmarking?
12. What are the Deming Prize and the Malcolm Baldrige National Quality Award?

DISCUSSION OF CONCEPTS

1. Why should companies focus on both satisfaction and loyalty? Why is satisfaction alone inadequate?
2. Imagine that you are the marketing director of a local company. How would you use the concept of customer-delivered value to improve the marketing for a product?
3. Discuss how connecting with customers through relationships relates to satisfaction and loyalty.
4. If you observed a large percentage of customer defections from a business, what might the causes be? How would you investigate?
5. Is complaining behavior good or bad? Should you encourage customers to complain?
6. What would you recommend for an organization that wishes to connect with customers through relationships?
7. What is the relationship between quality and customer value? How is quality attained?
8. Do you feel companies should allocate a great deal of effort to apply for the Malcolm Baldrige National Quality Award? Why or why not?

KEY TERMS AND DEFINITIONS

Added value: Something of value offered by a company to differentiate itself from competitors.

Benchmarking: The systematic evaluation of practices of excellent organizations to learn new and better ways to serve customers.

Best practices: The competencies of industry leaders that other organizations use as benchmarks.

Continuous improvement: The enhancement process used by an organization to find the best ways of satisfying its customers.

Cost structure: The amount of money required to produce a specific amount of sales.

Customer defections: The percentage of customers who switch to another brand or supplier.

Customer-delivered value: The perceived difference between what the customer pays and what the customer gains from a transaction.

Customer expectations: Consumers' beliefs about the performance of a product based on prior experience and communications.

Customer loyalty: A measure of how often, when selecting from a product class, a customer purchases a particular brand.

Customer satisfaction: A customer's positive, neutral, or negative feeling about the value s/he received as a result of using a particular organization's offering in specific use situations.

Customer satisfaction measurement program: An ongoing survey of customers (and competitors' customers) for the purpose of obtaining continuous estimates of satisfaction.

Customer value: The perception customers have of what they receive from owning and using a product over and above the cost of acquiring it.

Dynamic quality: Quality that results from a change that makes an existing standard obsolete.

ISO 9000: An inclusive set of standards established by the International Standards Organization (ISO) to ensure that quality requirements are met.

Lifetime value of a customer: The amount of profit a company expects to obtain over the course of the relationship.

Malcolm Baldrige National Quality Award: A program designed to raise quality awareness and practice among U.S. businesses.

Objective assessment of quality: An evaluation of the degree to which a product does what it is supposed to do.

Quality: The degree of excellence of a company's products or services.

Quality function deployment (QFD): A process that builds customer wants and desires into the final product offering.

Reduced cycle time: A TQM activity which helps a company move more rapidly from product inception to final delivery of the product to the marketplace.

Satisfaction ratings: Ratings provided by testing agencies that compare purchase satisfaction with specified brands or with how well products perform.

Service quality: The expected and perceived quality of all of the services an organization offers.

Static quality: Quality that results when individuals or organizations perfect an accepted practice.

Statistical quality control: The use of statistics to isolate and quantify production line problems that may cause product defects.

Subjective assessment of quality: The degree to which a product does what consumers would like it to do.

Total quality management (TQM): An organizational philosophy which helps companies produce goods and services that deliver value to satisfy customers.

Value: The amount of money a consumer will pay for quality in a good or service.

Value chain: All the activities that companies undertake to deliver more value to the ultimate consumer.

REFERENCES

1. www.mcdonalds.com/careers/regional/expect/expect.html, site visited May 28, 1998.
2. McDonald's Annual report, published 1998, p. 12.
3. "MCD Places Order for New Kitchen at Operator Confab," *Nation's Restaurant News*, March 30, 1998.
4. McDonald's Annual report, p. 14.
5. www.mcdonalds.com/community/rmhc/rmhc.html, site visited May 28, 1998.
6. Robert B. Woodruff and Sarah F. Gardial, *Know Your Customer* (Cambridge, MA: Blackwell Publishers, Inc., 1996), p. 20.
7. Eugene W. Anderson, Claes Fornell, and Donald R. Lehmann, "Customer Satisfaction, Market Share, and Profitability: Findings from Sweden," *Journal of Marketing*, 58 (1994):53.
8. Frederick Reichheld and Earl Sasser, Jr., "Why Satisfied Customers Defect," *Harvard Business Review*, November–December 1995, p. 88.
9. Heskett, 164.
10. Op.Cit. Anderson, et. al., p. 88.
11. Clay Carr, *Front Line Customer Service* (New York: John Wiley & Sons, 1990), p. 19.
12. Cyndee Miller, ". . . And Baby Gets Brands," *Marketing News*, March 11, 1996, p. 18.
13. Speech by Dick Chitty, "Managing Customer Loyalty," *Conference Board: Loyalty-Based Magement*, June 1, 1994.
14. www.jdpower.com/releases/80603ca2.hltm, site visited June 4, 1998.
15. Richard Whitely, "Do Selling and Quality Mix?" *Sales and Marketing Management*, October 1993, p. 70.
16. Michael W. Lowenstein, "Keep Them Coming Back," *Marketing Tools*, May 1996, www.marketingtools.com.
17. Op.Cit. Clay, p. 31.
18. Ibid, p. 19.
19. Tibbett L. Speer, "They Complain Because They Care," *American Demographics*, May 1996, www.marketingtools.com.
20. Ibid.
21. Mark Rechtin, "Once Again, Lexus Ranks No. 1 in Satisfying Buyers," *Automotive News*, July 17, 1995, p. 18.
22. Abbie Griffin, et. al., "Best Practices for Customer Satisfaction in Manufacturing Firms," *Sloan Management Review*, (Winter 1995), p. 87.
23. Jonathan R. Copulsky and Michael J. Wolf, "Relationship Marketing," *Journal of Business Strategy*, July–August 1990, pp. 16–20.
24. Andy Cohen, "It's Party Time for Saturn," *Sales and Marketing Management*, June 1994, p. 19.
25. Nichole M. Christian, "A Muddy Weekend, 52 Jeeps and Bonding with Chrysler," *Wall Street Journal Interactive Edition*, May 23, 1997.
26. www.levi.com, site visited May 13, 1997.
27. Ginger Conlon, "Getting into Focus," *Sales and Marketing Management*, January 1997, p. 43.
28. Louise O'Brien and Charles Jones, "Do Rewards Really Create Loyalty?" *Harvard Business Review*, May-June 1995, p. 76
29. Garth Hallberg, *All Consumers Are Not Created Equal* (New York: John Wiley and Sons, 1995), p. 40.
30. "Insider Trading," *Economist*, June 24, 1995, p. 10.
31. Laura Loro, "Minority Promotions Pick Up the Pace," *Advertising Age*, February 27, 1995, p. 8.
32. "A Strong Prejudice," *Economist*, June 17, 1995, p. 69.
33. Excerpted with permission from *The New Economics for Industry, Government, Education*, 2nd edition, copyright ©1994 by the Edwards Deming Institute™; and from *Out of the Crisis*, copyright ©1986, by the Edwards Deming Institute™.
34. "Interesting Facts about FedEx," wwwD.fedex.com/facts_about.html, August 20, 1996.
35. Valarie Zethaml, "Consumer Perceptions of Price, Quality and Value: A Means-End Model and Synthesis of Evidence," *Journal of Marketing*, July 1988, p. 2.
36. Michael R. Czinkote, Masaki Kotabe, and David Mercer, *Marketing Management*, (Cambridge, MA: Blackwell 1997), p. 273.
37. Arthur R. Tenner and Irving J. DeToro, *Total Quality Management* (Boston: Addison-Wesley, 1992), p. 733.
38. Meg Whittemore, "Price Achievement," *Nation's Business*, January 1990, p. 29.
39. Jack Rose, "New Quality Means Service Too," *Fortune*, April 22, 1991, pp. 99–107.

40. "The Cracks in Quality," *Economist*, April 18, 1992, pp. 67–68.
41. *Malcolm Baldrige National Quality Improvement Act of 1987*, report of the Senate Committee on Commerce, Science and Technology on HR 812 (Washington D.C., U.S. Government Printing Office, 1987).
42. www.quality.nist.gov/

43. U.S. Department of Education.
44. Louise Lee, "Sick of Scams from Shoppers, Retailers Look to Cut Returns," *Wall Street Journal Interactive Edition*, November 18, 1996 .
45. Earl Naumann, *Customer Value Toolkit* (Boise, ID: Thomson Executive Press, 1994).

CASE 2

THE RITZ-CARLTON HOTEL COMPANY

*I*MAGINE YOU'RE TRAVELING ON ONE of many overnight business trips. You like your suit pressed at 6:00 A.M. sharp, and you take your coffee black with one ice cube, among other requests. How many hotels respond to your needs with consistency and timeliness, if at all? The Ritz-Carlton does. The company uses sophisticated information technology to remember your previous requests and provide them for you again and again, in any of its hotels where you may be staying. The Ritz-Carlton prides itself on knowing and respecting your preferences, as well as providing quality and satisfaction to you on a one-to-one basis.

The Ritz-Carlton Hotel Company manages, develops, and operates luxury hotels. Based in Atlanta, Georgia, it manages 23 hotels in the United States and two in Australia. Its first resort in Asia is expected soon, and there is interest in a Cape Town location in South Africa. The Ritz-Carlton primarily targets corporate travelers and affluent vacationers. Ranked in *Forbes* as one of the top 15 U.S. city hotels and in *Fortune* as one of the top six business hotels, the Ritz-Carlton chain knows about delivering quality. In fact, the company is a winner of the Malcolm Baldrige National Quality Award, which is no small feat. It requires planning, a committed team of employees and management, and implementation of premium service.

How does the Ritz-Carlton Hotel Company accomplish all this? It starts at the top, with a team of senior executives who meet every week to review quality issues. This includes the company's products and services, customer satisfaction, growth and profits, and evaluation of the competition. In fact, Ritz executives spend 25 percent of their time working on quality-related issues. Ultimately, however, the responsibility for delivering customer value depends on 11,500 employees. In a survey, 96 percent of them noted excellence in guest services as their personal priority. Employees go through a process of orientation, on-the-job training, and certification. The Ritz-Carlton believes in rewarding employees and giving recognition for commendable work.

Being a quality leader requires a number of detailed goals and standards, all of which are integral in the performance of daily work. Extensive market research helps the company thoroughly define its objectives. In addition, customer reaction information, focus groups, and surveys provide feedback from guests. Customer needs are reflected in the "Ritz-Carlton Gold Standards," which each employee is expected not only to understand, but also to practice. Empowering employees to solve problems is another crucial element in the Ritz-Carlton's quality. They are allowed to do "whatever it takes" to make a customer happy, without first seeking management approval. No matter how large or minor the problem, all employees, regardless of job description, are expected to resolve potential conflicts and fulfill customer wishes.

Teamwork can be found at every level of the company. Each hotel has a "quality leader" who works to design and carry out quality plans. This person serves as a resource to coworkers and is an advocate for the company. Each area of the Ritz-Carlton hotel has three teams, and these are responsible for both setting and implementing quality standards in their area. Technology is also integral in achieving objectives. Production reports provide data from 720 different parts of the hotel to indicate progress or potential problems. Automated building, safety, and reservation systems as well as the history profile technology all assist in making customer value a priority.

While all Ritz-Carlton hotels work to achieve the same objectives, each can also have a unique identity. For example, the Ritz-Carlton Kapalua, Hawaii, is considered one of the finest hotels in the world. Reflecting the diverse cultural influences of its surroundings, the Kapalua offers native festivals, traditional Hawaiian music and cuisine, and hula dances. In addition, cultural classes are mandatory for all employees.

The Ritz-Carlton Hotel Company is very effective in the implementation of quality. Its 121 quality-related awards in one year alone speak for themselves. With a customer satisfaction rate of up to 97 percent, the high standards are likely to pay off in repeat business.

1. *In this chapter, requirements for creating and delivering customer value were discussed. How does the Ritz-Carlton Hotel Company meet these requirements?*
2. *Relationship marketing creates interactions with customers that make it unnecessary or even difficult for them to switch to a competitor. How has the Ritz-Carlton Hotel Company used this marketing strategy? Invent several ways the company could form one-on-one relationships with customers. How could each of these initiatives influence customer perceptions of quality?*
3. *The diversity of tastes and preferences is a challenge for customer-centered marketers. Identify several different groups (such as the elderly or handicapped) and develop initiatives the Ritz-Carlton could use to provide them with superior customer value.*

SOURCES: "Malcolm Baldrige National Quality Award 1992 Winner: The Ritz-Carlton Hotel Company," Winners Showcase, www.quality.nist.gov/, last updated May 26, 1998; Gene Sloan, "Hawaii's New Attraction: Her Rich Past," *USA Today,* March 25, 1997, web.usatoday.com/; Gene Sloan, "Asia Is Fertile Ground for Resorts," *USA Today,* March 25, 1997, www.usatoday.com/; Ed Brown, "The Best Business Hotels," *Fortune,* March 31, 1997, www.fortune.com; Don Peppers and Martha Rogers, "Welcome to the 1:1 Future," *Marketing Tools,* April-May 1994, www.marketingtools.com; Laura Bly, "A Rush to Democratic South Africa," *USA Today,* March 25, 1997, www.usatoday.com/; and William C. Flanagan, "Where Executives Love to Stay," *Forbes,* September 23, 1996, www.forbes.com.

The Marketing Environment and Its Global Dimensions

Objectives

1. Describe the marketing environment and the use of environmental scanning.

2. Understand how the roles that stakeholders play influence the accomplishment of marketing objectives. Know why marketing must address stakeholder desires when making decisions.

3. Be able to integrate an understanding of industry competition into environmental analysis.

4. Synthesize aspects of the global macroenvironment, including technological, economic, demographic, cultural, and legal/regulatory elements in order to be in step with long-term trends.

5. Recognize the importance of ethics and guides to ethical behavior.

CHANGE IS CONSTANT. SUCCESSFUL ORGANIZATIONS MUST *keep pace with changes in the environment, and leading-edge organizations often create changes that affect entire industries. Such is the story of George Lucas, who conceptualized and created digital film technology, which revolutionized the film industry and left other film organizations to wonder what he'd come up with next.*

Lucas started building the future back in the 1970s. He wanted to create a truly modern folk tale, with appropriate heroes, that would capture the imagination of children at that time. However, the traditional technology prevented George Lucas and his team at Lucasfilm from getting what was in his head onto the screen. To tell his story the way he wanted it told required a new technology. When he began his epic Star Wars *series in 1975, Lucas searched for a company that could create what he envisioned. After scanning the environment and finding a lack of technology to match his creativity, he decided to do it himself. "This was all born out of complete frustration with how the medium worked technically," says Lucas.*

To meet his creative needs, Lucas founded Industrial Light & Magic (ILM), an enterprise that would have profound effects on the entire industry and bring pleasure to millions worldwide. In 1982, ILM created the first computer-generated scene for Star Trek II: The Wrath of Khan. *Three years later came the first digital character, "stained glass man," in* Young Sherlock Holmes. *The first three-dimensional character followed in* The Abyss *(1989), created through the use of Morf, ILM's proprietary technology. Morf techniques were refined in* Terminator 2: Judgment Day *(1991). ILM developed digitally created skin for* Death Becomes Her *(1993) and "real" dinosaurs in* Jurassic Park *(1993).* Forest Gump *(1995) brought ILM its 14th Academy Award for blending historical footage with modern-day actors.* Casper *introduced the first fully digital character.*

Gordon Radley, president of Lucasfilm, observed that today Lucas is not only the owner of ILM, he is also its most demanding customer. Radley said, "He's a client of his own company. So that when he makes Star Wars, *as he does, he goes to ILM and he negotiates with his own company." This gives Lucas a very unique perspective compared to many other company heads. This orientation toward developing technology to satisfy the creative needs of clients will give ILM the leadership in the twenty-first century to continue to be the best and most preeminent in the business.*

In 1997, Star Wars Trilogy Special Edition, *was released in theaters to celebrate its 20th anniversary, demonstrating how far Lucas and digital effects have come. Lucasfilm restored the original negatives, enhanced the sound and visual, transformed backgrounds, and added a character. Harrison Ford's Hans Solo found himself in a new scene, opposite a digital Jabba the Hut. Digital technology allowed Lucas to produce the movie he had originally imagined.*

Lucas did more than change the way movies are made. With Star Wars, *he created a fantasy world, one with great marketing potential. Like Disney, Lucas told a great story, with great characters, and pushed the technological boundaries. In addition, he provided great value for consumers and a solid business enterprise. When Lucas negotiated with Twentieth Century-Fox in 1975 to make* Star Wars, *he gave up a larger salary in exchange for what the studio then regarded as worthless: ownership of merchandising, music, publishing rights—and all sequels. With that move, Lucas changed the marketing environment for movies with the concept of tie-ins.*

Since 1977, more than $3 billion in licensed Star Wars *products have been sold, including toys, books, comics, and even Franklin Mint commemoratives. Bantam Books has shipped more than 15 million copies of novels based on the movie since 1990; 16 of the 19 titles have hit the* New York Times *bestseller list. "*Star Wars *is our largest publishing franchise," says Bantam publisher Irwyn Applebaum. Bantam enriched the franchise by publishing series geared toward teens, youth, and children, each with age-appropriate language and content.*

Lucas further marketed Star Wars *and many other original titles to the computer game industry, creating the LucasArts division. It is one of the largest makers of videogames for computers, with about 10 percent of the market share. A key to success has been the application of film techniques (camera angles, lighting, editing, and so forth) to make the games look more like a movie. Constant enhancements at LucasArts keep competitors on their toes, further stimulating innovation in the entertainment industry.*

Lucas has branched into other digital arenas in movie-making by creating Skywalker Sound, the leader in this area of the industry. Because terrific effects require high-quality sound, Lucas created the THX division. It developed technology that makes viewers at home or in the theater feel as if they are in the middle of the picture. For example, in Jurassic Park, *the bushes rustle all around you, creating anticipation for another dinosaur attack.*

Forbes *estimates that Lucasfilm has annual sales of $300 million, with a pre-tax profit margin of about 40 percent and figures Wall Street would value the company at about $5 billion—and Lucas owns 100 percent of the stock!*

What's to come? Beginning in 1999, the first of three new prequels to the original Star Wars *films will open in theaters. The two additional prequels will follow in 2002 and 2005. All three movies will have a large percentage of the scenes digitally rendered. "We're going about it in a slightly more organic way," Lucas says. The estimated cost of $115 million per film is roughly half of what it would cost to do the movies using traditional methods.*

The marketing environment is composed of many forces, technology being one of the most important. It enables organizations to develop a range of products that are often only limited by one's imagination. The success of Lucasfilm shows how one organization is shaping the marketing environment by being there first. In the process Lucas and his organizations have satisfied the needs of fantasy lovers the world over.[1]

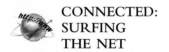

CONNECTED: SURFING THE NET

www.lucasarts.com

www.thx.com

Download demos of new games, seek technical support from "Yoda's Help Desk," and learn more about LucasArts.

THE CONCEPT OF THE MARKETING ENVIRONMENT

Change abounds. It can be your friend or enemy, depending on how it is handled. Some organizations are reactive—they do not adjust strategies until environmental changes have occurred. That can be dangerous, since it may be too late to construct a successful new strategy. Other organizations are proactive—they anticipate environmental changes and adjust ahead of time. George Lucas's ILM is the ultimate example. Proactive organizations quickly take advantage of new opportunities and minimize or eliminate damage from negative changes. Connecting with customers is best accomplished with a proactive philosophy because the forces that affect your organization are the same that affect customers. In fact, proactive companies connect best. They are in step with their customers by being in step with the marketing environment. The **marketing environment** is the sum of all factors that affect a business. Figure 3-1 depicts the marketing environment surrounding our theme: connecting with customers. First is the microenvironment, then the all-encompassing global macroenvironment. You will learn about both in the following sections.

An organization does not operate in a vacuum. Many factors can have a dramatic influence. These create opportunities, but they can also prevent the company from pursuing its desired strategy. An organization must be sensitive to its surroundings. **Environmental scanning** collects and analyzes information in order to detect any trends that may affect a company's strategy. It can be performed by the company itself, by professional or industry associations, or by one of the numerous consulting organizations that specialize in forecasting.

Kraft scans the environment constantly. If not, then it might have missed a huge opportunity in the explosive demand for fat- and cholesterol-free foods. The 1990s are notable for the immense expenditures on these healthy alternatives.[2] About 95 percent of all consumers now select at least some "light" products. But Kraft was a pioneer, and today its reduced-fat products account for about $3 billion in annual sales. A reduced-fat version of Chips Ahoy! cookies spurred 14 percent growth for that brand alone. Kraft's environmental scanning gave early warning that such foods would be important, and the company took actions that had a significant effect on the bottom line.[3]

The Internet is an extraordinary environmental scanning tool. This technology enables marketers to investigate press releases, news stories, on-line magazines, journals, newspapers, and company Web sites highlighting product offerings, as well as technical and financial data. Even company strategies can be gathered from this public information by a skilled marketing analyst.

Getting information about competitors is much faster and easier on the Internet. The U.S. Bureau of the Census Web site (www.census.gov/) provides demographic information, and such on-line magazines as *American Demographics* (www.marketingtools.com) identify cultural trends. When scanning for legal/regulatory information, marketers can check government sites for relevant material. For example, data on pending designs can be found at the U.S. Patent Office Web site (www.uspto.gov/web/patinfo).[4] The most authoritative source for economic and demographic information about foreign countries is on the CIA Web site (www.odci.gov/cia/publications/97fact).[5] The Internet also offers research, surveys, and other means for studying Web user behavior and surfing habits. All this is used extensively to collect marketing information, which we will discuss in chapter 5.

If you want help in scanning, there is plenty available. Companies that specialize in "competitive intelligence" even offer subscriptions to access data they have assembled. Subscribers

Marketing environment
The sum of all the factors that affect a business.

Environmental scanning
Collecting and analyzing information about the marketing environment in order to detect important changes or trends that can affect a company's strategy.

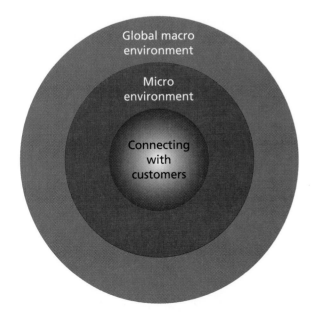

Figure 3-1   *The Marketing Environment*

give a profile of their interests (such as the automotive industry in the Midwest), and the service supplies the latest material. GE Information Services (Business Pro) and IBM (Infosage) are two leading providers of these services.[6]

THE MICROENVIRONMENT

Microenvironment

The forces close to a company that influence how it connects with customers.

The **microenvironment** is made up of the forces close to the company that influence how it connects with customers. As you'll notice in Figure 3-2, stakeholders and industry competition are part of the microenvironment. Stakeholders, as the name suggests, have a stake in an organization. Companies deal with stakeholders daily. Marketers need to understand stakeholders, recognizing that marketing decisions affect them and are affected by their influence. Marketers need to have other parties' needs in mind.

Competition is also a daily phenomenon. Competitors challenge your organization—sometimes you win, and sometimes they win. In either case, healthy competition is good because it stimulates change. Competitors, like stakeholders, must be considered in nearly every major marketing decision.

RELATIONSHIPS WITH STAKEHOLDERS

Stakeholder

A group who can influence or be influenced by the firm's actions.

Any group or individual, other than competitors, who can influence or be influenced by an organization's actions is a **stakeholder**, including customers, owners, employees, suppliers, intermediaries, action groups, and many others. In the previous chapter we stressed the importance of building relationships with customers. In this chapter we stress building relationships with other stakeholders. Marketers form interactive, ongoing, two-way connections with stakeholders. They build these lasting relationships so that stakeholders will be a positive influence on the organization. Stakeholders can help serve customer needs and wants as well as help accomplish the objectives of the organization. Consequently, marketers try to act in the best long-term interest of all the firm's stakeholders. But because stakeholders have conflicting objectives, this can be difficult. Let's examine some of these stakeholders.

Owners and Employees   Whether public or private, an organization operates for the benefit of its owners, who establish its objectives. For companies, these objectives usually stress increasing the value of the business—making substantial profit. In nonprofit organizations, the objectives usually relate to benefiting constituents. For example, the beneficiaries of Greenpeace are people concerned about the environment.

Shareholders have purchased, been given, or inherited a share of the business. Typically, owners either represent themselves or are represented by a board of directors, which is charged with the responsibility to speak for all the owners. Marketers need to understand the goals, risks, and reward levels acceptable to owners, who only invest in a company that continues to reach its objectives.[7] Hershey Foods, for example, which has one-third of the U.S. candy market, satisfied shareholders with a 40 percent increase in stock price in only one year. Hershey's made decisions that would increase the value of the company and best serve its shareholders, such as the introduction of two successful new products—Sweet Escapes and TasteTations.[8] Marketers must always take the interest of owners into consideration when making decisions.

Employees are also key stakeholders. Their livelihood depends on the company. Since every employee helps create and deliver value to the end consumer, each employee has a very

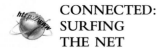

CONNECTED: SURFING THE NET

www.hersheys.com

What other decisions is Hershey making to meet the objectives of its shareholders? Connect to the Hershey Foods Corp. Web site and find out. Visit the Hershey grocery and take a trip to Chocolate Town U.S.A. while you're there.

MICROENVIRONMENT

RELATIONSHIPS WITH STAKEHOLDERS

  Owners
  Employees
  Suppliers
  Intermediaries
  Action groups
  Others

COMPETITIVE INDUSTRY

  Competitors
  Competitive groups

Figure 3-2   The Microenvironment

important influence on the organization. Companies that connect with their employees to ensure their satisfaction within the organization are often rewarded with satisfied customers. SAS, Inc., the largest privately owned software company in the United States, treats its employees as valuable stakeholders. SAS provides a state-of-the-art medical center, day care, and other facilities. In addition, each employee is guaranteed an office and is encouraged to pursue individual interests. The relationships SAS has built with employees have paid off. The company boasts a turnover rate of less than 4 percent and a 95 percent customer renewal rate. According to a SAS program manager, "What we're saying to the employee is: 'We're willing to take care of you if you're willing to take care of us.'"[9]

Contented employees are much more likely to produce contented customers. It is hard to imagine a disgruntled employee being pleasant to customers. Positive connections with customers are a result of positive connections made with employees. This is true at American Express. Marketing research director Doug Filak says the company has seen strong links between employee satisfaction and overall satisfaction.[10]

Suppliers and Intermediaries **Suppliers** are stakeholders who provide a company with necessary services, raw materials, and components. Very few organizations can exist without suppliers, who also can be a major factor in creating customer satisfaction. Ford has more than 3,000 suppliers in its automotive operations. If you like the dashboard, seats, or electronics on the new Ford Expedition, chances are a supplier worked with Ford to design it. Suppliers manufacture many of the components that go into vehicles—no matter what brand.

Companies rely on suppliers. When they have their own problems, it can mean trouble. Developing and maintaining good working relationships with suppliers can be extremely valuable. After a fire destroyed Toyota's primary supplier of valves, the company was forced to close 20 plants in Japan. Experts believed Toyota wouldn't recover for weeks, but it was running again in five days—36 suppliers cooperated to produce the valve. This closely knit family helped Toyota to make a quick recovery, which illustrates the influence suppliers can have on an organization.[11]

Since they specialize, suppliers are an excellent source of new technology and are likely to speed the introduction of the latest designs and techniques. They often provide expertise

Suppliers
An organization that provides a company with necessary services, raw materials, or components.

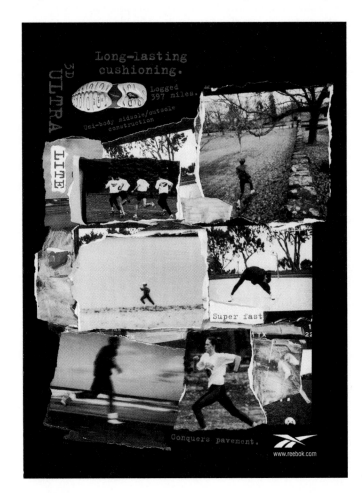

Suppliers helped Reebok develop a "bouncier" shoe.

Intermediary
A stakeholder who moves products from the manufacturer to the final user.

that helps companies compete in ways that would be impossible if they had to rely on their own resources. For example, until 1987, DuPont sold only adhesives to Reebok. Then DuPont technicians suggested that Reebok use a plastic tube technology, originally designed for the automobile industry. The tubes made Reebok shoes "bouncier" and were a hit with consumers. Chances are that Reebok never would have developed this technology on its own at the time.

Intermediaries are independently owned organizations that act as links to move products between producers and the end-user. They have an important influence on organizations because they dramatically extend the ability of marketers to reach customers at home and abroad. Book wholesalers and campus bookstores help large publishers like Prentice Hall sell textbooks to students. Beverage manufacturers such as Gatorade, Dole, and Ocean Spray use intermediaries to deliver their goods to outlets that sell them to the final consumer. Chris-Craft, 4Winns, and Sea Ray market their watercraft through dealerships.

Some intermediaries specialize in international markets, using their unique skills and capabilities to give a company global reach. An intermediary quick to establish itself in an emerging market has tremendous opportunities because it can set up channels for bringing in additional products. Companies that want to expand into untapped markets find intermediaries invaluable in delivering their product to the consumer. It is very beneficial for companies to establish solid working relationships with their intermediaries.

Action group
A number of people who support some cause in the interest of consumers or environmental safety.

Action Groups   **Action groups** are stakeholders who support some cause in the interest of consumers or environmental safety. They act as "watchdogs," making sure that companies keep the interests of people and the environment in balance with those of profit. There are hundreds of action groups. One of the most vocal and well-known consumer advocates, Ralph Nader, has fought for years to force businesses to produce safer products. The late Cesar Chavez challenged large chemical companies to protect the health of migrant workers. Many movie and television personalities lend their name and celebrity to consumer causes.

Marketers are very aware of consumer groups who frequently criticize the pursuits of business. A marketer may have to make difficult decisions when there is a conflict between the desires of action groups and other stakeholders. When Disney extended health benefits to gay couples, the Southern Baptist Convention threatened a boycott, claiming that the policy was counter to family values. Disney did not withdraw the benefits program, saying: "We question any group that demands we deprive people of health benefits."[12]

Action groups can also help marketers gain positive publicity and may help business make a greater contribution to society. Star-Kist has gained acclaim for its dolphin-safe tuna nets. Nike, in response to action groups, worked with a White House task force to sign an anti-sweatshop accord to prevent the abuse of minors in the manufacture of its apparel.[13]

INDUSTRY COMPETITION

The word *competition* brings to mind an image of two giant companies vying against each other; however, competition also involves companies of differing types and sizes. These companies, along with potential new companies, suppliers, and customers, form an industry structure that dictates the intensity of competition. Competitors may be individual companies or the industry as a whole.

An analysis of the competitive environment asks several questions. Who are the existing rivals? What new competitors may emerge? What is the relative strength of suppliers and buyers within the industry? Lastly, what substitutes are likely to appear? The answers give a complete picture of the overall nature of competition within an industry. Figure 3-3 depicts the forces that shape the competitive environment.

Existing Firms   As a marketer, you need a thorough understanding of each major competitor. This includes how each competes against your company and every other in the industry. You should examine each rival's strategy in terms of current and potential products, pricing, promotion, and distribution. You also should identify key customers and suppliers, the types of technologies used, current performance, and strengths and weaknesses. From all this information, the marketing manager attempts to determine the plans of every competitor and how every competitor will react to the marketer's actions. For example, when Holiday Inn recently renovated 1,800 facilities, a number of competitors took the same action.[14]

Potential Competitors   At any time, a company may enter an industry with similar products. In 1997, Microsoft introduced Windows CE, the software operating system for smaller computers, to compete in the market for palmtops.[15] Competitors such as U.S. Robotics, Ca-

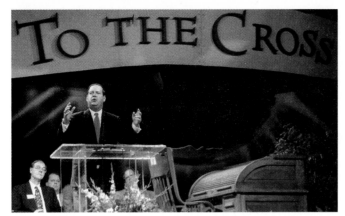

Disney faced criticism from an action group regarding its employee health coverage policy.

sio, Compaq, and NEC—who had introduced less sophisticated versions of this small PC—were clearly unhappy to see the software giant enter. An aggressive marketer like Microsoft affects the performance of these companies. One advantage is that Microsoft will draw attention to the product category so overall sales of these devices will increase. A disadvantage is that Microsoft is likely to take a large share, which will reduce the relative strength of industry rivals.

Substitutes A substitute product is any good or service that performs the same function or provides the same benefit as an existing one. For example, who competes with Federal Express for overnight delivery of letters? If you said United Parcel Service (UPS), the U.S. Postal Service, Airborne Express, or other overnight delivery companies, then you are correct, but you probably left out an important one: the fax machine.

Marketers should not limit their analysis to the same industry. Companies in other industries that make or develop substitutes may be an even greater competitive threat. For example, Merrill Lynch, a successful marketer of financial services, faces such industry rivals as Charles Schwab and Travelers Group, but it also experiences tough competition from insurance companies, banks, brokers, and others.[16] Often information about substitutes can be found on the World Wide Web.

The Bargaining Power of Buyers and Suppliers Marketers must also ask which group—buyers or suppliers—has the most power in an industry. The answer affects both company strategy and competition. Generally, buyers are the most powerful. They can be more demanding when there are several competing suppliers. For example, Wal-Mart is pow-

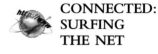

CONNECTED: SURFING THE NET

www.microsoft.com

Keep up with the latest products from the software giant, Microsoft. Visit its Web site to download free software, subscribe to newsletters, or find out how to be trained and certified on various products.

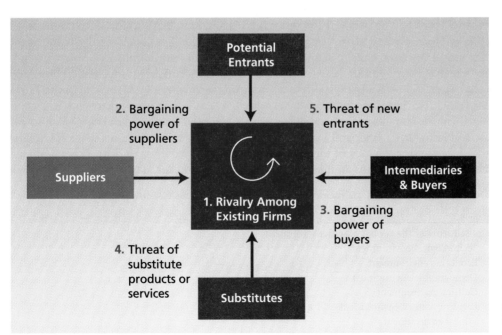

Figure 3-3 *Forces Driving Industry Competition*

Source: The Free Press, a division of Simon & Schuster, from Competitive Strategy: Techniques for Analyzing Industries and Competitors, by Michael Porter, Copyright 1980.

erful because there are fewer retailers than in the past and many, many small suppliers. Wal-Mart stores are tied electronically to more than 2,000 vendors providing goods for resale. If a vendor does not go along with policies, there are many others from which to select.[17]

When buyers are plentiful, suppliers tend to be more powerful. Since demand is great, suppliers can negotiate contracts on their terms and generally command higher prices. A supplier has most power when it offers a unique and superior product that buyers are clamoring to purchase.

THE GLOBAL MACROENVIRONMENT

Global macroenvironment
The large external influencers considered vital to long-term decisions but not directly affected by the company itself.

Like stakeholders and industry forces in the microenvironment, the global macroenvironment also influences the company, but indirectly. The **global macroenvironment** consists of large external influencers considered vital to long-term decisions but not directly affected by the company itself. It is critical for marketers to identify, anticipate, and plan for the effect of those factors. These larger forces—each of which constitutes an environment in itself—shift slowly, so they have long-term implications for the organization. Yet, they also affect day-to-day operations. Figure 3-4 lists the most important forces or environments—technological, economic, demographic, cultural, legal/regulatory, and ethical—that make up the global macroenvironment.

TECHNOLOGICAL ENVIRONMENT

Technological environment
The total body of knowledge available for development, manufacturing, and marketing of products and/or services.

As you know, technology is one of the five key elements in connecting with customers. The **technological environment** is the total body of knowledge available for use in developing, manufacturing, and marketing products. Companies spend huge sums each year to increase this body of knowledge. Merck Pharmaceutical Company, an industry leader, annually invests more than $1.5 billion (12 percent of sales) on research and development activities.[18] The government also plays a role. When President Clinton announced a war against AIDS, it included federally sponsored studies on the disease. Several pharmaceutical companies will use this basic research as the fundamental knowledge required to make patentable products. On their own, many companies would not make the very uncertain and risky investment in AIDS R&D. Basic research is expensive and so time consuming that it is often years or even decades before any revenue is received from product users.

Companies spend nearly $180 billion on R&D annually. The private sector provides about half, and the rest comes from the federal government, academic institutions, and nonprofit organizations.[19] A huge technological effect has resulted from microprocessor R&D. U.S. companies were the first to realize the importance of computers and made large investments in them. Today, the United States accounts for more than 40 percent of the world's computer investments. Americans spend approximately $850 per person on information technology—eight times the global average and more than double that of Western Europe.[20]

Investment in R&D has accelerated the rate of technological change. Products quickly become obsolete. The personal computer (PC) is an example. First introduced on a broad scale by Steve Jobs and Steve Wozniak in 1977, the PC is still evolving rapidly. Many of the first models used the same cassette technology for memory as you might use to record your favorite music. This quickly gave way to floppy disks, then hard drives, then optical disks, and compact disks. Processing capability is also growing phenomenally. At the end of the 1980s, Intel's 20 MHz chip offered state-of-the-art speed. A decade later, its popular Pentium II combined enhanced multimedia technologies with a 300 MHz Pentium Pro chip.[21] Companies are still introducing faster and faster processors. LSI's tiny microprocessors have 1.5 million transistors so thin that 300 of them placed side by side are only as thick as a strand of hair. Just one of them contains an image compressor, processor, and most circuits needed for an

---

Constituents of the Global Macroenvironment
Technological environment
Economic environment
Demographic environment
Cultural environment
Legal/regulatory environment
Ethical environment

Figure 3-4   The Global Macroenvironment

advanced digital still camera.[22] In fact, the amount of computing power a dollar can buy doubles every 18 months in direct relationship to the number of transistors on a chip.[23] Obviously, this creates quite a challenge to computer companies.

"With new processes and technologies, you want to replace [your own product] instead of letting someone else do it," says Gary Tooker, CEO of Motorola, adding that "success comes from a constant focus on renewal."[24] The rapid rate of change has important implications for businesses today. First, investment in R&D is critical to ensure you're not left behind by the competition. If a computer company cannot build a machine that processes information quickly and accommodates future additions, it will soon be as obsolete as its products. Second, companies must be creative in looking for future technologies. For example, when Microsoft held a conference for 100 top executives from 18 industries and 25 countries to discuss changing technology and implications for the future, the gathering provided a unique opportunity for Microsoft to scan the technological environment for new advances and ideas.[25]

ECONOMIC ENVIRONMENT

The **economic environment** refers to financial and natural resources that are available to consumers, businesses, and countries. An understanding of consumer economic factors like income, spending behavior, spending power, and wealth dispersion is essential in assessing opportunities that may emerge. Global marketers must also be familiar with the economic features of the world's major trading blocs.

Income and Spending Behavior   It is said that only two things are certain in life: death and taxes. **Disposable income** is the money consumers have left after paying taxes, and many marketers prefer to use this as the measure of consumer wealth. People spend some of their disposable income on necessities, such as food, clothing, and shelter; anything left over is called **discretionary income**. Consumers may choose to spend all their discretionary income or may choose to save part of it. Marketers of nonessentials, such as vacation packages, jewelry, and stereos, focus on discretionary income, because that is how much consumers have available to purchase nonessential items.

No less important than the amount of income is the willingness, or propensity, to spend. The typical middle-income American family is spending more on luxury goods. According to the U.S. Bureau of the Census, the average income of the top fifth of households rose 17 percent in the last ten years. The average family income today is more than $51,000, which is $11,000 more than in the 1960s.[26] Marketers have seized this opportunity to promote nonessential items. Patek Philippe recently sold its entire stock of $17,500 watches, using a

Economic environment
The financial and natural resources available to consumers, businesses, and countries.

Disposable income
The income consumers have left after paying taxes.

Discretionary income
The amount of money consumers have left after paying taxes and purchasing necessities.

Motorola invests heavily in R & D to keep a "constant focus on renewal."

Spending power
The ability of the population to purchase goods and services.

Gross domestic product (GDP)
The total market value of all goods and services produced by a country in a single year.

successful ad that depicted a father and child at a piano. The copy read, "Begin your own tradition," positioning the watch as a family heirloom. Hotels like ITT Sheraton have reported an increase in business at luxury resorts. Even hospitals are taking advantage of the increase in discretionary income by offering suites—for $2,000 you get a monogrammed bathrobe, wet bar, and friendly butler.[27]

Spending Power and Wealth Dispersion   Marketers must be careful not to equate a large population with a large marketing opportunity. An important consideration is **spending power,** or the ability of people to purchase goods and services. A common measure of spending power is the gross domestic product of a country. **Gross domestic product (GDP)** is the total market value of all final goods and services produced for consumption during a given period by a particular country. The U.S. GDP is approximately $7 trillion. The greatest GDP growth has occurred in the United States, at an annual rate of 2.6 percent. Europe and Japan follow, with 1.5 percent and 1.3 percent, respectively.[28]

When the GDP of every nation is added together, we have gross world product (GWP), which will be approximately $30 trillion at the turn of the century. That figure is not spread equally among countries, however. Japan accounts for 9 percent of GWP, Western Europe for about 23 percent, and the United States for around 24 percent. This figure is high, considering that the United States has only about 5 percent of the world's population. China and India, with 37 percent of the world's people, contribute merely 3.4 percent to GWP.

Many marketers do not look solely at GDP because it does not indicate how much each person in the country has to spend. For example, Mexico and Sweden have approximately the same GDP, but we know that the standard of living is lower in Mexico than in Sweden. Because the population of Mexico is large, a smaller portion of GDP can be allocated to each inhabitant. Consequently, many marketers use GDP per capita (which means "per person") to assess the standard of living. It tells how well off, on average, each citizen of a country is.

Even GDP per capita has limitations because it ignores the dispersion of wealth within a country. Often there are a few rich people and many, many poor ones. In Brazil, for example, nearly half of the wealth goes to the richest 10 percent of the population; only 2.3 percent goes to the poorest 20 percent. In the United States, 28 percent is owned by the richest 10 percent, 4.2 percent goes to the poorest 20 percent. In Japan and Poland, the dispersion of wealth is much more even.

Trading Blocs   The world's three major trading blocs—Europe, Pacific Rim, and North America—are shown in Figure 3-5. Often called the world's economic superpowers, they will compete for the mastery of international markets well into the 21st century. Combined, these three regions are responsible for about 80 percent of the world's economic activity. For example, customers in the superpower triad buy more than 85 percent of all computers and consumer electronics. The triad contains more than 600 million consumers with converging preferences. Among others, IBM, Motorola, and Gucci are found nearly everywhere in the

North America	Europe		Pacific Rim
Canada	France	Portugal	South Korea
USA	Spain	Greece	Singapore
Mexico	Germany	Ireland	Japan
	Denmark	Luxembourg	China
	Great Britain	Belgium	
	Italy	Netherlands	
	Austria	Finland	
	Sweden		
Combined GDP: 7,761,921 M	Combined GDP: 7,215,746 M		Combined GDP: 6,417,224
Combined Population: 357,256,000	Combined Population: 336,221,000		Combined Population: 1,160,044,618
NAFTA	EU		
North American Free Trade Agreement	European Union		

Figure 3-5   The Three Superpower Trading Blocs

triad. Today, each of these blocs is basically equal in terms of economic activity, but this will not be true if current trends hold. The Pacific Rim is growing the fastest, Europe next, then North America.

Despite their collective power, the triad's constituent economies are not without difficulties. Many of these countries have a mature economy, rising social welfare costs, an aging population, and escalating research and development costs.[29] Let's look at each of the trading blocs in more detail.

North America   In November 1993, when the United States, Canada, and Mexico entered into the North American Free Trade Agreement (NAFTA), they created the largest single market in the world—350 million consumers.[30] The objective of this economic alliance is to make all three nations more competitive globally by combining their strengths. The United States and Canada have capital, skills, technology, and natural resources; Mexico has low-cost labor. Proponents of NAFTA believe efficient North American companies will be able to offer lower-priced products to consumers. Overall, the open market means removal of tariffs and other trade barriers, increased investment opportunities, stronger protection of intellectual property, and more environmentally sound business practices. Recently, Central American and Caribbean nations have been pushing to join NAFTA.[31]

NAFTA is not without critics. Companies will be more mobile, and some will go where labor is cheapest. If U.S. technology does not create enough high-paying jobs at home, U.S. workers will ultimately be fighting for low-paying jobs with fewer benefits.

Pacific Rim   The Pacific Rim (PAC Rim), which comprises much of East Asia, is named for the ocean it borders. It is made up of Japan and the four "dragons"—South Korea, Singapore, Taiwan, and Hong Kong, now part of China—known for enormous manufacturing potential. Soon, depending on economic reform, Thailand, Malaysia, and Indonesia could also be included. Economic integration in the PAC Rim is based purely on market forces, not a formal agreement like NAFTA. Much of the growth in East Asia has been spurred by Japanese investors, such as Matsushita Electric, which has established 10 major operations in Southeast Asia since 1961.

East Asia has undergone explosive economic growth, although it has had a difficult economic period in the recent past. In their classic book, *Megatrends 2000*, authors Naisbitt and Aburdene call it the greatest economic expansion in world history—five times the rate of the Industrial Revolution. These economies, driven by export sales, have been growing three times faster than economies in the rest of the world, although today, with the exception of China, these economies are experiencing a recession. Yet, China is having growth as its economy benefits from deregulation, the import of new technology, and a shift from farm labor to industrial jobs.[32] China is predicted to experience nearly a 10 percent annual growth rate, making it the fastest growing area in the region.[33] Overall, experts project that by 2015, seven of the top 25 largest cities will be in Asia.

These Asian nations are feeding their home markets with the net gain in money received from other economies, which is possible when a country exports more than it imports. The domestic markets are increasing in size as companies and workers earn more money. With cash reserves of several hundred billion dollars and personal wealth, large amounts of goods can be bought from other countries. The PAC Rim Consulting Group in Hong Kong predicts that nearly 58 million Asian consumers will enter or approach middle-class status by the end of the decade, providing many additional market opportunities.[34] Although Japan has numerous cultural and regulatory barriers to foreign entry, other East Asian nations tend to be more accessible. Foreign companies can export to these countries as well as enter into partnerships or commit investments there.[35]

Europe   The European Union (EU), has occupied much of the news in Europe. Also referred to as the Maastricht Treaty and technically called the Single Market Act, it is of tremendous economic relevance there and around the world. The European Union has the goal of eliminating barriers to the flow of people, goods, services, and money within the union. The objective is to restructure Europe economically so that it can better compete against the United States, Japan, and other developed nations. The EU members are Austria, Belgium, Denmark, Finland, France, Germany, Great Britain, Greece, Italy, Ireland, Luxembourg, the Netherlands, Portugal, Spain, and Sweden. The EU unites 350 million consumers into one market with a GDP of more than $5 trillion.

The Maastricht Treaty consists of 282 directives that eliminate border controls and customs duties; strengthen external borders; establish a single European currency; coordinate defense and foreign policy; unify product standards and work conditions; protect intellectual property; and deregulate many industries, including telecommunications, airlines, banking, and insurance. This will make it much easier to move products from one region to another. Eventually, a company will be able to create a more unified marketing strategy for all of the EU, whereas its different market environments have to be addressed today.

General Agreement on Tariffs and Trade and the World Trade Organization   In 1948, the General Agreement on Tariffs and Trade (GATT) was founded under the United Nations. GATT is responsible for many of the current trade agreements among its 130 members. This organization has successfully negotiated significant reductions in trade restrictions and import duties that countries would otherwise impose in their own self-interest. GATT has been successful in reducing import duties and tariffs from more than 40 percent in 1947 to about 5 percent today. Today there are challenges in many areas of foreign trade such as foreign investment and intellectual property rights. In 1995, GATT was absorbed by the World Trade Organization (WTO), which will carry out the traditional role of GATT. The WTO deals with a broad range of issues, including pollution, tariffs, trade agreements, and trade disputes.

Natural Resources   The availability of natural sources of wealth (such as timber or oil) within a given region or nation is an important economic factor. For example, the U.S. Pacific Northwest provides a rich source of timber for the paper and construction industries. Similarly, countries in the Middle East control approximately 65 percent of the world's crude oil. In both cases, natural resources provide income to the area's inhabitants. Natural resources also include minerals, plants, wildlife, water, salt, fish, and many others. Resource availability affects a marketer's pricing strategy. If a company operates a large plant in an area where energy or raw materials are expensive, the cost of producing the product will be high, and its price must be set accordingly.

Marketers in quest of natural resources must balance these efforts against preservation of the environment. An example is the spotted owl controversy in the Pacific Northwest. Environmentalists claim that logging is destroying habitat, driving the species toward extinction. The timber industry claims that thousands of jobs and millions of dollars will be lost if its work is discontinued.

Environmental regulations also must be considered by marketers, since these may threaten current business practices or create new opportunities. For example, the Strategic Environment Initiative (SEI) recommends that the government provide tax breaks to companies using environmentally friendly technologies and levy high taxes on those using older, unsafe methods. Product and process innovations often enable companies to comply with environmental regulations. In the product area, for example, companies can retrofit antipollution devices or engineer more environmentally friendly designs.

Many marketers are developing strategies with the environment in mind. When it became known that the chlorofluorocarbons (CFCs) released from aerosol cans were thinning the ozone layer, many companies switched to pump spray bottles. Due to environmental concerns, McDonald's® discontinued its use of styrofoam sandwich containers.

CAREER TIP	Today schools are reporting a 20 percent increase in recruiter visits to campus. Top recruiters include Enterprise Rent-a-Car (5,000 projected hires); U.S. Immigration and Naturalization Service (4,000 projected hires); the Peace Corps (at least 3,500 new hires); Andersen Consulting (more than 3,300 new hires); and Boeing (more than 2,000).[36] Contact the placement office on your campus and find out which companies might be recruiting at your college.

DEMOGRAPHIC ENVIRONMENT

Demographic environment
The statistical data used to describe a population.

The **demographic environment** consists of the data that describe a population in terms of age, education, health, and so forth. Marketers examine such information to gain an understanding of current opportunities and discover trends that may indicate future opportunities. Some frequently studied demographics include population size and density, urbanization, and age structure. Avon Products, Inc., is one company that has adjusted neatly to demographic changes that nearly destroyed the company. The company had to change the way it developed relationships with customers in the United States and to expand its customer relationships around the world. See the relationships feature entitled "Avon Products, Inc.: Around the World with 2.2 Million Avon Ladies."

CONNECTING THROUGH RELATIONSHIPS

AVON PRODUCTS, INC.: AROUND THE WORLD WITH 2.2 MILLION AVON LADIES

Do the very words *Avon Lady* make you think of a neatly coifed woman calling on suburban housewives with a suitcase of lipstick samples? Think again. Avon Products, Inc., is in the vanguard when it comes to shifting with the demographic winds and changing the way it reaches and relates to customers.

Until the 1980s, "ding-dong, Avon calling," was the ad line that epitomized the company's strategy for selling cosmetics and other products door to door. The only problem was, doorbells began ringing in empty houses. American women had gone to work, in droves. Retail chains like Wal-Mart in the United States and hypermarkets in Europe were also selling similar products at discount prices. With sales plummeting, Avon had to change or die, and change it did. By 1997 the company had earnings of $2.37 per share on $4.8 billion in revenues, and its sales volume was right behind that of giants Procter & Gamble and Gillette in the consumer goods category. Under the stewardship of James Preston and a raft of top-caliber women executives, Avon accomplished a marketing makeover.

On the home front, Avon instituted the "Four Ways to be Beautiful" campaign, which gave women more choice in how and when to develop a relationship with an Avon representative. The four ways were by fax, phone, mail, or the trusty Avon Lady. An 800 number also provided a way for working women to contact a representative at a convenient time. Within a month after putting a toll-free number in print ads and catalogs in the early 1990s, consumer inquiries went from 9,000 a month to 90,000. While many women still want the attention of an Avon representative, now 50 percent of Avon's sales calls are made at the workplace.

Yet Avon still confronted a shrinking market. Its smart response has been to train sales reps globally. Of Avon's 2.2 million "ladies," the majority are in developing countries, calling on the growing number of middle-class women who can afford such luxuries as cosmetics. In the 1990s Avon entered 14 new markets, most recently South Africa and India. Combined emerging markets account for 38 percent of company sales and 49 percent of its pretax profit, and the numbers can only go up.

In each emerging global market, Avon must adopt new ways for its representatives to contact customers. In countries that lack infrastructure and retail competition, the time-honored door-to-door approach still works wonders. In China, Avon Ladies ride bicycles to key distribution points to pick up products and then pedal off to peddle their wares. In the tiny village of Registro, Brazil, Avon Lady Josina Reis Teixeira visits small wooden shacks outside São Paulo. In Russia, where people are wary of opening the door to strangers, Avon Ladies sell in parks, beauty parlors, and offices. Maria Gerasyova, a former linguist for the Red Army, now commands 15,000 Avon representatives in Moscow, St. Petersburg, and Perm. In India, Avon Ladies will also steer clear of door-to-door selling and market products to their friends, family, and office colleagues.

Avon is proving to women around the world that beauty is more than skin deep. The cosmetics company has invested $500,000 in the cause of breast cancer awareness, and its 2.2 million global reps have helped raise $25 million to combat the disease and promote other women's health issues. About $18 million of that amount came from the sale of pins, key rings, and pens emblazoned with pink ribbons, which have become the symbol for the cause. Avon does no hard-sell for its cosmetics or jewelry at events like its breast cancer summit. Still, such events and grassroots contact give the company yet another way to strengthen ties with customers around the world.

Sources: Dyan Machan, "The Makeover," *Forbes*, December 2, 1996, pp. 135–140; Rasul Bailay, "Avon Tries Twist on Sales Technique for Push into India," *Wall Street Journal*, August 2, 1996, A11; Veronica Byrd, "The Avon Lady of the Amazon," *Business Week*, October 24, 1993, pp. 93–96; Seema Nayyar, "Avon Calling, By Fax, Phone and Infomercial," *Brandweek*, February 22, 1993, pp. 22–23; and Karen Benezra, "Cause and Effects Marketing," *Brandweek*, April 22, 1996, pp. 38–40.

Population As of June 1998, there were about 5.9 billion people in the world,[37] and there are expected to be nearly 9 billion by 2020.[38] If marketing opportunities were defined solely by population size, then the prospects would be bright indeed. Other opportunity indicators must be evaluated, however, such as the income available.

Despite such huge cities as Los Angeles, Chicago, New York, and Atlanta, the United States has less than 5 percent of the world's population. China and India account for 37 percent, and they are growing at a higher rate. Population growth depends on the number of live births plus the number of immigrants entering a country. The birth rate, which is measured as the number of live births per 1,000 people, is increasing throughout the world, but, the rate of increase has begun to slow. It's estimated that about 100 million people are added to the world population each year. This translates into about 275,000 births a day. At the same time, advances in medicine and technology mean that people are healthier, and the number of deaths per 1,000 is decreasing. The longer life span, combined with births results in an even larger world population.

Movement from one country to another redistributes the world's population, and the United States is gaining considerable numbers this way.[39] Although U.S. laws have become more restrictive, immigration is still expected to contribute as much to U.S. population growth as will natural births. This will further diversify the ethnic makeup of the country. Minority groups are expected to account for about 70 percent of population growth in the United States through the end of the decade.

The U.S. population is expected to grow to 276 million in 2000 and to 372 million in 2040. Nevertheless, the average annual growth rate is expected to decrease by nearly half, from 1.1 percent in the 1990s to around .54 percent by 2045. This would be the lowest rate ever. The predicted decline is attributed to numerous factors, including the general aging of the population, increased age at first marriage, delayed childbearing, a growing proportion of childless couples, and the greater participation of women in the labor force.

Population density

The concentration of people within some unit of measure, such as per square mile or per square kilo-meter.

Density A country with a large population may seem to offer a large marketing opportunity, but it is important to know where those people live. **Population density** refers to the number of people within a standard measurement unit, such as a square mile. Canada has more than 28 million people but only 7.6 people, on average, per square mile. Yet, because many live in a few large cities, such as Quebec and Toronto, large areas of the country are quite sparsely populated. Singapore's population of three million is highly concentrated, with an average of more than 12,160 people per square mile. Where people are located within a country is also important. When they are concentrated, it's easier and more cost effective to reach them with advertising campaigns and products. When they are spread out, marketing can be difficult, time-consuming, and expensive. Consider the Pacific Rim countries, where many more people live in the coastal regions than inland. Much the same is true of Australia, with its sparsely populated Outback. Imagine the task of delivering products to consumers in these areas. Organizations are likely to focus marketing efforts on densely populated areas.

Urbanization

The shift of population from rural to urban areas.

Urbanization **Urbanization** refers to the population shift from rural areas to cities. Many countries have a high proportion of urban population. In Germany, for example, 90 percent of the population lives in urban areas; in Singapore, 100 percent. In the United States, three out of four people live in or near a city. Nearly 40 percent of the U.S. population is concentrated in the 20 largest metropolitan areas. At the top are New York City (18+ million), Los Angeles (14+ million), and Chicago (eight million). Urbanization is significant to marketers for three important reasons. First, as noted earlier, it is easier to reach a concentrated population. Second, as a group, people in cities tend to have enough income to purchase luxuries and support the arts, such as opera or theater. Third, people in urban areas tend to demand a wider variety of products than do rural inhabitants.

Metropolitan Statistical Area (MSA)

A stand-alone population center, unlinked to other cities, that has more than 50,000 people.

When the city population spills into the suburbs, neighboring cities may eventually join together. The U.S. Bureau of the Census has three terms to categorize urban concentrations. **A Metropolitan Statistical Area (MSA)** is a stand-alone population center, not linked to other cities, with more than 50,000 people. Examples are San Antonio, Texas; Montgomery, Alabama; and Spokane, Washington. A **Consolidated Metropolitan Statistical Area (CMSA)** is two or more overlapping urban communities with a combined population of at least one million. An example is the area that includes New York City, northern New Jersey, and southwestern Connecticut, with 20 million people.

Consolidated Metropolitan Statistical Area (CMSA)

Two or more overlapping urban communities with a combined population of at least one million.

Age Structure Because generations differ in their tastes, age-related marketing research has become popular. An **age cohort** is a group of people close in age who have been shaped by their generation's experience with the media, peers, events, and the larger society. Often these cohorts are divided into three groups. "Matures" were born between 1909 and 1945, "baby boomers" between 1946 and 1964, and "Generation Xers" thereafter.[40] Research reveals substantial differences among them in values, tastes, and needs.

Age cohort

A group of people close in age who have been shaped by their generation's experience with the media, peers, events, and society at large.

Globally, the average age is less than 25 years and declining. For example, because the Mexican population is growing rapidly, it is getting younger on average. In many industrial-

This ad for Sketchers was designed to appeal to the Generation X cohort.

ized nations, however, the picture is different. Children constitute a declining proportion of the German population, which is aging slowly but is older than the U.S. population. In less than 20 years, 25 percent of Japanese will be over age 65.[41] In 1994, the median age in the United States was 33.4 years; by 2030, the average age will be more than 45 years, and about 20 percent of the population will be age 65 or older.[42] This is partly due to the baby boom after World War II, which will affect U.S. demographics for many years. The U.S. age distribution varies according to race. Whereas 80 percent of Americans are Caucasian, fewer than 75 percent of Americans under age 10 are Caucasian. Among the 12 percent of all Americans who are African American, 15 percent are under age 10. Nine percent of Americans are Hispanic, and 13 percent of them are under age 10.[43] This chapter's diversity feature "NFO Research Inc.—First With a Hispanic Panel" presents a pioneering company that took an in-depth look at hispanics.

Now that U.S. baby boomers are migrating into midlife, when spending power is substantial, marketers are focusing on older consumers. Thousands of products already are being marketed to help them look and feel their best—such as Oil of Olay moisturizing cream, Ensure dietary supplement, Centrum Silver multivitamins, NordicTrack cardiovascular fitness equipment, and Weight Watcher foods. In fact, Oil of Olay based an entire promotional campaign on this concept. According to brand manager, Cindy Tripp, "before planning our last campaign, we did a lot of market research. Some people in the company thought customers still believe younger is beautiful, but we found that only 32 percent of Oil of Olay customers said they wanted to look younger; 78 percent said they wanted to look the best they could for their age. That's the direction we took with our ads."[44] In the years ahead, marketers will face the growing task of serving an aging market and addressing its unique concerns.

CULTURAL ENVIRONMENT

The **cultural environment** consists of the learned values, beliefs, language, symbols, and behaviors shared by people in a society and passed on from one generation to the next. Culture includes morals, values, customs, traditions, folkways, myths, and norms. It also includes religion, laws, economics, history, family structure, knowledge, food customs, art, music, and technology. These and other characteristics distinguish one society from another. They de-

Cultural environment
The learned values, beliefs, language, symbols, and patterns of behavior shared by people in a society and passed on from generation to generation.

CONNECTING WITH DIVERSITY

NFO RESEARCH, INC.—FIRST WITH A HISPANIC PANEL

Customer needs are constantly changing and marketers need to scan the environment to recognize and respond to trends as they occur. One trend has been a marked growth in the Hispanic population throughout the U.S. Since census data weren't even collected about Hispanics until 1970, little was known about their characteristics until the 1980s. That was when the dramatic population growth—from immigration and births—became apparent. Marketers could piece together census data and make some guesstimates, but there was a clear need for solid information.

The growing importance of Hispanics to marketers is underscored by U.S. census data. Between 1980 and 1990, the number of Hispanics rose 50 percent, to about 23 million. Between 1990 and 1995, they accounted for 30 percent of U.S. population growth. The Census Bureau predicts growth to 31 million by 2000, and to 41 million by 2010—edging out African Americans as the largest U.S. minority group.

NFO Research, Inc., a 50-year-old company, stepped up to fill the need. NFO had pioneered the use of marketing research panels—a group of prequalified people who can be called on for specific consumer information. In 1988, NFO created Nuestra Familia Opina to help marketers study Hispanic consumers. The panel consisted of about 7,500 households spread across 10 major markets—New York City, Miami, and Chicago, four Texas communities (Houston, San Antonio, El Paso, and McAllen-Brownsville), two in California (Los Angeles and San Francisco), and Albuquerque, New Mexico. This introduced the largest sample of self-identified U.S. Hispanics available for consumer research, and demographic details about each household were known. The panel was often used for targeting, and to establish meaningful demographic profiles.

The NFO panel provided specific information about a product or service, but NFO also conducts secondary research to give marketers more general data. We know that Hispanics differ from other U.S. consumers not in language but also in the way they look at life and interact with society. For example:

- Approximately half of U.S. Hispanics speak Spanish exclusively.
- Hispanics are more likely to cook from scratch and to eat dinner with all the members of their household seven nights a week.
- More than 68 percent of Hispanic teens choose their heroes from among relatives or close friends.
- Hispanics are more likely to say that all their satisfaction comes from family, that duty comes before pleasure, and that they prefer things to stay settled and stable.

NFO collects data and helps marketers interpret the findings. An analysis for a particular company shows how it can apply the information in the marketplace.

Sources: Brochure from NFO Research, Inc., August 1, 1996; Jeffrey D. Zbar, "New Research Spotlights Hispanics," *Advertising Age,* June 19, 1995, p. 12; Morton Winsberg, "Specific Hispanics," *American Demographics,* February 1994, pp. 44–53; and Marcia Mogelonsky, *Everybody Eats: Supermarket Consumers in the 1990s* (Ithaca, NY: American Demographics Books, 1995).

fine the way we think about ourselves and the world, what we want, and how we behave. Marketers must be in step with the cultural environment because it helps them to make stronger connections with diverse customers.

Most people are socialized to be part of the culture in which they grow up. The socialization process is so strong that marketers may rely unconsciously on their own values when trying to understand another culture. This is called the **self-reference criterion**. But what we do may not be acceptable elsewhere. For example, most people in the United States would not think twice about eating a candy bar as they walk down the street, but in Japan this is bad manners. In China, when people approach a bus, the first person is expected to buy tickets for the group. It is easy to embarrass yourself and others in a foreign culture unless you take the time to understand it.

Because of people's tendency to use the self-reference criterion, it's often difficult to assess opportunities in other countries. But success globally requires precisely that. McDonald's® targets the same audience around the world—young families with children—but the basic concept must be "translated" into local conditions. Beer is on the German menu. In India, where cows are considered sacred, McDonald's® markets the "Maharaja Mac,"® made of two all-mutton patties plus the usual toppings. Understanding different cultures has helped McDonald's® establish itself in the new global market.[45]

Self-reference criterion

The unconscious reliance on values gained from one's own socialization when trying to understand another culture.

In a classic article, Edward Hall notes that perceptions of time, space, things, friendships, agreements, and negotiations cause the greatest misunderstanding between people of different cultures.[46] If you do not recognize these differences and address them, then you will almost certainly fail to connect in the global marketplace.

Perceptions of Time   It's extremely important to consider a culture's perception of time, which communicates several subtle points. For example, in some cultures the most significant decisions are given the greatest amount of time. In contrast, Americans tend to operate within deadlines, and time is a scarce resource to be used efficiently. In the United States, if visitors are kept waiting, then they infer that they are unimportant. In a Latin culture, this is not the case; schedules are not rigid, and time is seen as a resource that can be used more flexibly. More recently, many Latin American countries have redefined time for business. In some cultures, a very long time may pass between customer awareness of a product and the actual purchase. Marketers need to plan a longer time frame for recapturing the investment in new product development. In cultures where decisions are made quickly, this time frame may be much shorter.

Size and Space   In the United States, size is equated with importance; the larger and taller a building, the greater the degree of status represented. The dean of a college of business is likely to be located in a spacious office on the top floor; the university president is likely to have a larger office in a taller building. In contrast, the French try to place important executives close to the scene of action, where their influence can be most strongly felt. Thus, a remote office is not equated with high status, but quite the opposite.

The distance between people during conversations also can be culturally related. In many Latin cultures, people stand close and even touch while talking. To communicate friendship, they may come to within two or three inches of one another, whereas an interpersonal space of three to five feet is considered acceptable to most people in the United States. To Latins, that great a distance could be a sign of rejection. Marketers must be sensitive to space. For example, in promotional materials, the wrong interpersonal distance among the actors or models could deliver the wrong message.

Negotiations and Agreements   Business agreements may have different meanings in various parts of the world. In highly legalistic cultures, they must be written and signed prior to acceptance. In other cultures, legal documents are viewed as inconveniences; more important is a meeting of the minds, sealed with a handshake. When people in the United States consult a lawyer, visit a doctor, or take a taxi, they assume the charge will be at the going rate. This is not the case in many cultures. For example, in the Middle East, it's best to settle the charge in advance, or the person providing the service is likely to set an arbitrary price. This can be important knowledge when developing a pricing strategy for your products. Whereas a predetermined price is expected in the United States, bartering is part of the social process elsewhere, and a preset price upsets or offends consumers.

LEGAL/REGULATORY ENVIRONMENT

The **legal/regulatory environment** is composed of international, federal, state, and local regulations and laws, the agencies that interpret and administer them, and the court system. It also includes the ethical standards and theories that guide marketing decisions. This envi-

Legal/regulatory environment
International, federal, state, and local regulations and laws, the agencies that interpret and administer them, and the court system.

McDonald's® targets families with children around the world, translating its basic concept into local conditions.

ronment reflects long-standing political and economic philosophies and varies dramatically from one country or region to another. It indicates the general outlook of government toward business practices and ethical issues as well as how cooperative it is likely to be in meeting the requests of business. It also includes the effect that legal/regulatory decisions can have on an organization, individuals, and society as a whole.

In the United States, several agencies are charged with the responsibility of regulating businesses to conform with the intentions of major laws. Among the most important are those listed in Figure 3-6. These agencies must interpret laws and develop policies and procedures to gain compliance. In some cases, the agency gives guidelines so businesses can self-regulate. Those businesses that step out of line may be taken to court by the agency. In other cases, the agency provides approval prior to marketing actions. For example, the Food and Drug Administration (FDA) must approve all drugs prior to their release in the United States.

Although the U.S. legal and regulatory sphere covers hundreds of specific practices, for our purposes these can be divided into four basic types: laws promoting competition, laws restricting big business, laws protecting consumers, and laws protecting the environment.

U.S. Laws Promoting Competition

During the 1800s and early 1900s, a few U.S. enterprises grew to the point of monopoly. Companies such as Standard Oil and Pennsylvania Railroad could exercise economic control over smaller firms, in many cases forcing them into bankruptcy by temporarily lowering prices. In 1890, due to a strong political movement led by midwestern farmers, Congress passed the Sherman Antitrust Act, which prohibits business practices designed to create monopolies or restrict trade across state lines or internationally. The Sherman Antitrust Act is extremely important because it laid the foundation for many laws that followed. The premise behind the legislation is that fair competition allows more companies to serve the market, which in turn keeps prices down and provides a greater number of choices to consumers. As you can see from Figure 3-7, many laws since 1890 are designed to ensure fair competition.

CONNECTED: SURFING THE NET

www.kodak.com

How does Kodak remain competitive? At Kodak's Web site you can read global press releases and expand your knowledge of digital photography, new products, and the company itself.

Cartel

A group of businesses or nations that work together to control the price and production of a particular product.

U.S. Laws Affecting Company Size

The U.S. approach to competition has tended to restrict company size and power. The Federal Trade Commission (FTC) has explored numerous accusations of monopolistic control. For example, it recently turned its focus on the music industry, which is dominated by six major companies that account for 80 percent of sales. Since each has retail and wholesale organizations that supply traditional stores as well, there are questions regarding possible antitrust violations and monopoly.[47]

Kodak's major competitors, Fuji and Konika, have grown largely because the U.S. government restricted Kodak's competitiveness. In June 1996, Kodak was freed from legal constraints dating back to 1921 and designed to keep it from monopolizing the U.S. photographic market. According to the Department of Justice, these constraints were necessary to allow competitors to establish a presence. Both Fuji Photo Film Company and Konica Corporation grew as a consequence. Now that these companies are strong contenders, the restrictions have been lifted to generate further competition. Fuji has invested $1 billion in facilities to manufacture its film in the United States for the first time. This will increase the speed with which U.S. orders can be filled and is part of Fuji's aggressive strategy against Kodak.[48]

Some countries promote monopoly. Many have laws that favor cartels, which are outlawed in the United States. A **cartel** is a group of businesses or nations working together to control the price and output of a particular product. The U.S. government has recognized

---

Consumer Products Safety Commission (CPSC)
Enforces regulations to protect consumers from being harmed by products.

Environmental Protection Agency (EPA)
Regulates business actions to prevent damage to the environment.

Federal Communication Commission (FCC)
Regulates communications on telephone, radio, television, and other aspects including allocations of frequencies.

Federal Trade Commission (FTC)
Enforces laws to prevent unfair or deceptive marketing practices.

Food and Drug Administration (FDA)
Enforces laws to maintain safety in food and drug products.

Figure 3-6   Federal Agencies Regulating Marketing

Sherman Antitrust Act (1890)
Outlaws monopolies and any business practice that restricts interstate or international commerce.

Federal Trade Commission Act (1914)
Declares as unlawful "unfair methods of competition in or affecting commerce, and unfair or deceptive acts or practices in or affecting commerce."

Clayton Act (1914)
Prohibits mergers and acquisitions that may "substantially lessen competition or tend to create a monopoly"; outlaws tie-in and exclusive dealing arrangements; allows violators to be held criminally liable.

Robinson-Patman Act (1936)
Developed primarily to protect small retailers. Amends the Clayton Act. Makes it illegal to sell "commodities of like grade and quality" to competing buyers at different prices if it will restrict competition. Also makes it illegal knowingly to receive an illegal price break.

Miller-Tydings Act (1937)
Protects interstate fair-trade (price fixing) agreements from antitrust prosecution.

Wheeler-Lea Act (1938)
Outlaws the pursuit of unfair or deceptive practices or actions.

Antimerger Act (1950)
Prevents corporate acquisitions or mergers that may substantially reduce competition.

Figure 3-7   U.S. Laws Promoting Competition

that laws intended to provide a fair environment for domestic competition may hamper U.S. companies competing globally. Put simply, they may be too small and lack the competitive strength to take on global rivals. In the late 1970s, the Department of Justice began to change its enforcement of traditional antitrust laws. It now permits business cooperation that would have been outlawed in the past.

U.S. Laws Protecting Consumers   Recall that the early economic philosophy in the United States was *caveat emptor*, "Let the buyer beware." Essentially, consumers were responsible for protecting themselves against the unscrupulous acts of sellers. The Pure Food and Drug Act (1906) and the Meat Inspection Act (1906) were the first attempts to protect consumers. For four decades, regulations concentrated on making the food supply safe. Laws then were extended to other products, such as automobiles and toys. Eventually, laws were passed to protect consumers from misleading advertising and deceptive labeling.

By 1960, the consumer movement was so powerful that President Kennedy issued the Consumer Bill of Rights, which guaranteed

1. *The right to choose freely* from a variety of goods and services
2. *The right to be informed* about specific products and services so that responsible purchase decisions can be made
3. *The right to be heard* when voicing their opinions about products and services offered
4. *The right to be safe* from defective or harmful products and services when used properly.

The idea was to impress upon marketers that consumers were not solely responsible for assessing the quality of a product, its safety, and the honesty of the marketer's claim.

In 1959, the FTC held a landmark conference at which consumer action groups and businesses discussed harmful practices. This activity led to the FTC assuming responsibility for enforcement of Truth in Packaging and Truth in Lending laws. The FTC tackled tobacco advertising, forcing manufacturers to include a strong warning about the dangers of cigarette smoking in ads and on packages. Shortly after, the Supreme Court ruled it illegal to create advertising gimmicks that would mislead the public or exaggerate product benefits.

Today the FTC and the Food and Drug Administration (FDA) aggressively focus on the tobacco industry. In 1997, the FTC revived an investigation of R. J. Reynolds Tobacco Company for unfair advertising with its Joe Camel campaign, allegedly aimed at minors. The campaign was part of the industry's $4.8 billion annual expenditure on ads and promotions.[49] R. J. Reynolds agreed to drop the Joe Camel cartoon figure from such items as hats, lighters, bags, and T-shirts. In addition, R. J. Reynolds will not use Joe Camel in billboard advertising or the sponsorship of entertainment events.[50] The FTC also examines the Internet for tobacco and alcohol Web sites that may violate advertising guidelines.

There are numerous consumer protection laws, and marketers need to know the ones affecting their company. Consumer safety legislation has a direct effect on important marketing decisions, such as product design, label information and design, and advertising claims. Interest in consumer safety has resulted in the development of seat belts, air bags, shatterproof windshields, antilock brakes, food labels, air quality standards, gasoline restrictions, and others. Consider the effect of air bags on marketing in the auto industry. While air bags have saved approximately 1,800 lives in the past decade, they have caused at least 60 deaths, mostly among children. As a result, Ford Motor Company was the first to introduce less forceful air bags on all 1998 models. General Motors, Chrysler, and many foreign makers are following that lead and are making marketing decisions in the interest of consumer safety.[51] Figure 3-8 lists several of the most important consumer protection laws.

U.S. Laws Protecting the Environment   By the early 1960s, it was clear that the world's natural resources were being consumed as if the supply was endless. The most basic resources—air and water—were often so polluted that they were unfit to sustain life. Although little was done internationally, the U.S. Congress enacted the National Environmental Policy Act in 1969 to direct environmental protection activities. The following year, the Environmental Protection Agency (EPA) was formed so that one agency would be responsible for enforcing all federal environmental regulation.

U.S. companies are required to make adequate disclosure of potential environmental liabilities. The EPA maintains that those responsible for environmental contamination must pay for the cleanup and subsequently protect citizens' health. The EPA's Environmental Leadership Program encourages companies to control pollution. Recent actions have focused on efforts aimed at getting companies to adopt standards to reduce 2.5 million tons of toxic air pollution, improve water quality standards in the Great Lakes, and increase by 20 percent the pace of cleanup at waste dump sites.[52]

Environmental groups such as the Audubon Society, Greenpeace, and the Sierra Club have drawn attention to numerous environmental disasters and are active participants in finding remedies and developing legislation.

ETHICAL ENVIRONMENT

Questions of ethics are not always straightforward. What is acceptable in one part of the world may not be in another. In many countries bribery is regarded as highly unethical, but in others it is considered standard business practice. There is an important difference between what

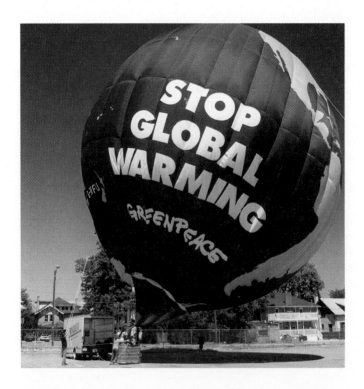

Greenpeace used this message to increase awareness of our need to protect our environment.

Pure Food and Drug Act (1906)
Regulates the manufacture and labeling of food and drugs.

Meat Inspection Act (1906)
Permits federal inspection of companies selling meat across state lines and allows for enforcement of sanitary standards.

Lanham Trademark Act (1946)
Outlaws misrepresentation of goods/services sold across state lines; forces trademarks to be distinctive.

Automobile Information Disclosure Act (1958)
Forces auto manufacturers to disclose the suggested retail price of their new cars, which keeps car dealers from inflating prices.

National Traffic and Safety Act (1958)
Provides a set of automobile and tire safety standards.

Fair Packaging and Labeling Act (1966)
Permits the FTC and FDA to create standards for packaging and labeling content.

Child Protection Act (1966)
Makes illegal the sale of dangerous toys and children's articles as well as products creating a thermal, mechanical, or electrical danger.

Federal Cigarette Labeling and Advertising Act (1967)
Requires cigarette manufacturers to label cigarettes as dangerous. Outlaws use of television media for cigarette advertisements.

Truth-in-Lending Act (1968)
Also called the Consumer Credit Protection Act. Forces lenders to disclose in writing, before the credit transaction: (1) the actual cash price, (2) the required down payment, (3) how much cash is being financed, (4) how much the loan will actually cost, (5) estimated annual interest rate, and (6) penalty for late payments or loan default.

Fair Credit Reporting Act (1970)
Allows consumers to see free of charge a copy of their credit report. Forces credit reporting agencies to remove any false information. Protects the confidentiality of the consumer.

Consumer Product Safety Act (1972)
Created the Consumer Product Safety Commission. It collects and disperses information on all consumer goods except automobiles, food, and a few others. It also has the authority to develop and enforce product standards, when deemed necessary.

Consumer Goods Pricing Act (1975)
Prevents retailers and manufacturers from entering into certain types of price maintenance agreements.

Magnuson-Moss Warranty/FTC Improvement Act (1975)
Requires the company or individual who offers a warranty to explain fully what the warranty covers and what its limitations are. This information allows consumers to file a lawsuit if the warranty is breached.

Equal Credit Opportunity Act (1975)
Forces creditors to disclose the reason for any credit denial. Credit cannot be denied on the basis of sex, marital status, race, national origin, region, age, or receipt of public assistance.

Fair Debt Collection Practice Act (1978)
Prohibits debt collectors from using harassment, abuse, or deceit when collecting a debt.

Toy Safety Act (1984)
Allows the government immediately to remove dangerous toys from the market.

Figure 3-8   Consumer Protection

is legal and what is ethical. To determine legality, you must examine the relevant law. If the meaning is unclear, then a court may have to interpret it. Without a precedent, you may have to assess whether the action would be deemed legal or illegal.

Ethical issues are not so easily defined. Is it ethical for a pharmaceutical company to charge a price for a new drug that is much higher than the cost to produce it? After all, the company has poured millions into R&D and is trying to recoup its investment. Yet the high price makes the drug unaffordable to many people who desperately need it. Is the drug company acting unethically?

The matrix in Figure 3-9 shows that marketing decisions may fall into one of four categories: legal and ethical, illegal and ethical, legal and unethical, or illegal and unethical.

	Legal	Illegal
Ethical	Market FDA-approved cold medicine	Market a safe AIDS vaccine not yet approved by the FDA
Unethical	Market a harmful drug banned by the FDA in a country with no drug review agencies	Market contraband drugs

Figure 3-9 Ethics Situations

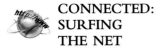

CONNECTED: SURFING THE NET

www.ama.org

Find out how you can join the American Marketing Association. Learn more about what it is, its chapters, resources, and how it can help you make connections for your career.

The appropriate behavior is easy to assess when the proposed action is clearly legal and ethical or clearly illegal and unethical. In the first case you do it, in the second you do not. However, neither legality nor ethics are always clear. What is legal and ethical may also be open to different interpretations. So marketers must be sensitive to both legal and ethical issues.

Perhaps the most difficult circumstances occur when legal and ethical standards conflict. Some people place more weight on the ethical side ("Should we do it?"), while others emphasize the legal ("Can we do it?"). Many people believe it is best to avoid altogether any actions that are either potentially illegal or unethical. Most laws that affect business are interpreted in the courts, which set precedents to be followed. Every legislative session creates new laws, which lead to new regulations, which often require new court decisions to set new precedents. So even legal and illegal may stretch along a continuum.

Many companies have developed written guidelines for employees. This helps ensure that everyone in the company is following the same set of ethical standards. The American Marketing Association also has a Code of Ethics, shown in Figure 3-10. Notice that the code goes beyond stating simply "Follow the law." It impresses upon marketers the importance of being honest and acting with integrity. It covers basic responsibilities, including a code of conduct and the importance of fairness. It describes what a customer should be able to expect from an exchange. It also describes ethical dimensions in the areas of product, promotion, place, and price—as well as in marketing research and relationships with others.

Members of the American Marketing Association (AMA) are committed to ethical professional conduct. They have joined together in subscribing to this Code of Ethics embracing the following topics:

Responsibilities of the Marketer
Marketers must accept responsibility for the consequences of their activities and make every effort to ensure that their decisions, recommendations, and actions function to identify, serve, and satisfy all relevant publics: customers, organizations, and society.
Marketers' professional conduct must be guided by:
1. The basic rule of professional ethics: not knowingly to do harm;
2. The adherence to all applicable laws and regulations;
3. The accurate representation of their education, training, and experience; and
4. The active support, practice, and promotion of this Code of Ethics.

Honesty and Fairness
Marketers shall uphold and advance the integrity, honor, and dignity of the marketing profession by:
1. Being honest in serving consumers, clients, employees, suppliers, distributors, and the public;
2. Not knowingly participating in conflict of interest without prior notice to all parties involved; and
3. Establishing equitable fee schedules, including the payment or receipt of usual, customary, and/or legal compensation for marketing exchanges.

Rights and Duties of Parties in the Marketing Exchange Process
Participants in the marketing exchange process should be able to expect that:
1. Products and services offered are safe and fit for their intended uses;
2. Communications about offered products and services are not deceptive;
3. All parties intend to discharge their obligations, financial and otherwise, in good faith; and
4. Appropriate internal methods exist for equitable adjustment and/or redress of grievances concerning purchases.

Figure 3-10 American Marketing Association Code of Ethics

Source: Courtesy of the American Marketing Association.

It is understood that the above would include, but is not limited to, the following responsibilities of the marketer.

In the Area of Product Development and Management:
- Disclosure of all substantial risks associated with product or service usage;
- Identification of any product component substitution that might materially change the product or impact on the buyer's purchase decision;
- Identification of extra-cost added features.

In the Area of Promotions:
- Avoidance of false and misleading advertising;
- Rejection of high pressure manipulations, or misleading sales tactics;
- Avoidance of sales promotions that use deception or manipulation.

In the Area of Distribution:
- Not manipulating the availability of a product for purpose of exploitation;
- Not using coercion in the marketing channel;
- Not exerting undue influence over the reseller's choice to handle a product.

In the Area of Pricing:
- Not engaging in price fixing;
- Not practicing predatory pricing;
- Disclosing the full price associated with any purchase.

In the Area of Marketing Research:
- Prohibiting selling or fund raising under the guise of conducting research;
- Maintaining research integrity by avoiding misrepresentation and omission of pertinent research data;
- Treating outside clients and suppliers fairly.

Organizational Relationships
Marketers should be aware of how their behavior may influence or impact on the behavior of others in organizational relationships. They should not demand, encourage, or apply coercion to obtain unethical behavior in their relationships with others, such as employees, suppliers, or customers.

1. Apply confidentiality and anonymity in professional relationships with regard to privileged information;
2. Meet their obligations and responsibilities in contracts and mutual agreements in a timely manner;
3. Avoid taking the work of others, in whole, or in part, and representing this work as their own or directly benefit from it without compensation or consent of the originator or owner;
4. Avoid manipulation to take advantage of situations to maximize personal welfare in a way that unfairly deprives or damages the organization of others.

Any AMA members found to be in violation of any provision of this Code of Ethics may have his or her Association membership suspended or revoked.

Source: Courtesy of the American Marketing Association.

Figure 3-10 (continued)

CHAPTER SUMMARY

OBJECTIVE 1: Describe the marketing environment and the use of environmental scanning.

The marketing environment comprises all factors that affect a business. The factors are divided into two groups—the microenvironment and the global macroenvironment. The microenvironment includes factors that marketers interact with regularly. Consequently, the microenvironment influences and is influenced by marketing. The global macroenvironment includes factors that marketers must take into account when making decisions. However, marketers seldom influence these factors. Together, the environments can facilitate or inhibit organizations from reaching their objectives. Proactive organizations anticipate changes in the marketing environment and plan accordingly. Organizations use environmental scanning in order to keep up with environmental changes. The Web is a great technological tool to help maintain currency in knowledge of the environment.

Objective 2: Understand how the roles that stakeholders play influence the accomplishment of marketing objectives. Know

why marketing must address stakeholder desires when making decisions.

Stakeholders are important parts of the microenvironment and directly participate in accomplishing the organization's goals. They include owners, employees, suppliers, intermediaries, and action groups. Stakeholders participate with the organization in order to accomplish their own goals; consequently, marketers must take their desires into consideration when making decisions. Because owners are entitled to a fair return on their investment, companies need to make a substantial profit, and nonprofit organizations must accomplish the goals their owners (sponsors) intend. Employees are also important; happy employees produce happy customers. Suppliers provide necessary services, raw materials, and components. They also provide technology in specialized areas. Suppliers have a dramatic influence on your customers. Intermediaries help move products between you and your customers. They often contact customers directly. Since they represent your organization, you must carefully interface with them. Action groups are "watch dogs" that keep the interests of the environment and people in balance with

CONNECTED: SURFING THE NET

Avon Products, Inc.

www.avon.com

THE RELATIONSHIPS BOX, "AVON PRODUCTS INC.: Around the World with 2.2 Million Avon Ladies," highlighted how Avon managed demographic changes and built better relationships with customers. In order to extend your thinking about Avon, visit its Web site and answer the following questions.

1. Locate Avon's "History." What are the company's three strategies for success? How might environmental scanning have helped Avon arrive at these strategies?
2. Avon products are available to consumers in 131 countries, and Avon is committed to further global expansion. Which markets are "Under Consideration"? List global factors that may influence Avon's final decision.
3. Imagine you are an important stakeholder in the Avon Corporation—an owner—with a significant amount of stock. Are you happy with your investment? What information did you use to reach your conclusion? How might this differ from what other stakeholders find important?
4. Avon was one of the first companies to bring women into the business world. Today, women hold 75 percent of management positions at Avon. What elements of the cultural environment do you think played a role in this decision 100 years ago?

Amazon.com

www.amazon.com

To increase your understanding of marketspaces, visit Amazon.com, a cyber bookstore, Web site and answer the following questions.

1. Upon your arrival at "Earth's Biggest Bookstore," check out the first-time visitor page. As a customer, you are a stakeholder of Amazon.com. How does Amazon.com meet objectives that are valued by most customers?
2. What environmental forces do you think have the most influence on the development and maintenance of marketspaces such as this one? Explain.
3. What do you think Amazon.com considered in order to make its site useful to consumers all over the world? How does Amazon.com handle global versus domestic orders?
4. Consumer rights are an important part of the legal/regulatory environment. How does Amazon.com protect consumers' security and privacy?

---

profit seeking. They can help marketers interface better with society. Marketers must address stakeholders' desires because stakeholders support marketers in order to attain their goals. In turn, marketers are dependent on stakeholders to accomplish the organization's objectives.

OBJECTIVE 3: Be able to integrate an understanding of industry competition into environmental analysis.

An understanding of industry competition provides an integrated picture about the major forces that determine competitive intensity. Competition involves single competitors and groups of company types that compete. We look at the rivalry among existing firms to understand one-on-one competition. Potential competitors are also viewed because firms enter and exit industries. At the same time, substitute products can play a role especially when new technologies bring new ways to perform old functions. The bargaining power of buyers and suppliers determines how a company competes. Suppliers have more power when there are few sup-

pliers and many buyers. All of these aspects of industry competition need to be understood in order to build appropriate marketing strategies.

OBJECTIVE 4: Synthesize aspects of the global macroenvironment, including technological, economic, demographic, cultural, and legal/regulatory elements in order to be in step with long-term trends.

The global macroenvironment is being influenced by many forces. The technological environment provides knowledge and tools that companies can acquire to produce better products. By phasing in new technology, progressive companies stay abreast of the best ways to create customer value. Economic factors are also important. Changes in income and spending power and other factors help determine which countries have the ability to purchase. The world has three major trading areas. The regions offer large markets, but they also compete against one another. The natural resources environment also comes into play. It provides raw materials and must be protected. Global demographics are changing. Shifts in population density and dispersion are important, as are age shifts. It is important to grasp the cultural environment and to view things from the other's perspective. The values, beliefs, and behaviors of others may differ from your own. Finally, the legal/regulatory environment is complex. Laws must be interpreted and followed. They help promote competition, influence business size, protect customers, and protect the environment.

OBJECTIVE 5: Recognize the importance of ethics and guides to ethical behavior.

Marketers often face ethical dilemmas, particularly when legal and ethical standards conflict. Many companies have developed codes of ethics for their employees to help ensure that everyone in the company is following the same standards. The American Marketing Association has a code of ethics that covers the basic responsibilities of marketers in each of the areas in which they are likely to be active. It stresses the importance of fairness and integrity.

REVIEW YOUR UNDERSTANDING

1. What is environmental scanning and what technology is being used for it today?
2. What is the microenvironment and what are its elements?
3. What is the global macroenvironment and what are its elements?
4. Who are stakeholders and why are they important? List five different types of stakeholders.
5. What are the elements of industry competition? Describe each.
6. Why is the technological environment important?
7. What are the elements of the economic environment? List three aspects that are influencing global marketing.
8. What are the three trading blocs?
9. What demographic trends are influencing marketing?
10. What is the self-reference criterion? What are some cultural differences to be aware of?
11. What are the types of laws that affect marketing?
12. What is the difference between unethical and illegal behavior?

DISCUSSION OF CONCEPTS

1. Suppose that IBM and Microsoft announced plans to merge into one company. Would U.S. laws allow this to happen? Do you think that other countries around the world would have the same reaction?
2. What is culture, and how does it affect marketing? Can you think of any products that are successful in the United States but would fail in Japan because of cultural differences?
3. In the 1980s, McDonald's® discontinued the use of styrofoam containers for its sandwiches. What other changes have occurred recently in the natural resources environment? What types of legislation do you expect in the future? How would that legislation affect marketing?
4. Do you think that General Motors should invest a significant amount of money in research and development projects? Why or why not?
5. Recently, discount stores such as Wal-Mart and Kmart have become extremely large and powerful. How does this affect industry structure and competitive intensity?
6. As the director of marketing for Dow Chemical Company, you are required to interact regularly with a number of different publics. List these publics, the concerns that each might have, and how you would address each of those concerns.
7. What effect do you expect the new European currency to have on trade among the three superblocs? Which trading relationships will be most affected? In what ways?
8. Which do you feel is more important—ethics or the law? Why?

KEY TERMS AND DEFINITIONS

Action group: A number of people who support some cause in the interest of consumers or environmental safety.

Age cohort: A group of people close in age who have been shaped by their generation's experience with the media, peers, events, and society at large.

Cartel: A group of businesses or nations that work together to control the price and production of a particular product.

Consolidated Metropolitan Statistical Area (CMSA): Two or more overlapping urban communities with a combined population of at least one million.

Cultural environment: The learned values, beliefs, language, symbols, and patterns of behavior shared by people in a society and passed on from generation to generation.

Demographic environment: The statistical data used to describe a population.

Discretionary income: The amount of money consumers have left after paying taxes and purchasing necessities.

Disposable income: The income consumers have left after paying taxes.

Economic environment: The financial and natural resources available to consumers, businesses, and countries.

Environmental scanning: Collecting and analyzing information about the marketing environment in order to detect important changes or trends that can affect a company's strategy.

Global macroenvironment: The large external influencers considered vital to long-term decisions but not directly affected by the company itself.

Gross domestic product (GDP): The total market value of all goods and services produced by a country in a single year.

Intermediary: A stakeholder who moves products from the manufacturer to the final user.

Legal/regulatory environment: International, federal, state, and local regulations and laws, the agencies that interpret and administer them, and the court system.

Marketing environment: The sum of all the factors that affect a business.

Metropolitan Statistical Area (MSA): A stand-alone population center, unlinked to other cities, that has more than 50,000 people.

Microenvironment: The forces close to a company that influence how it connects with customers.

Population density: The concentration of people within some unit of measure, such as per square mile or per square kilometer.

Self-reference criterion: The unconscious reliance on values gained from one's own socialization when trying to understand another culture.

Spending power: The ability of the population to purchase goods and services.

Stakeholder: A group who can influence or be influenced by the firm's actions.

Suppliers: An organization that provides a company with necessary services, raw materials, or components.

Technological environment: The total body of knowledge available for development, manufacturing, and marketing of products and/or services.

Urbanization: The shift of population from rural to urban areas.

REFERENCES

1. John Lippman, "News Corp.'s Profit Jumped in Period, Aided by Purchase," *Wall Street Journal Interactive Edition*, May 8, 1997; Joshua Levine, "Luke Skywalker Is Back. Let Us Pray," *Forbes*, December 30, 1996, www.forbes.com; Randall Lane, "The Magician," *Forbes*, March 11, 1996, pp. 122–128; "Starman," *Inc. Technology*, 1995, no. 2, p. 44; Joseph Garber, "Virtual Superstar," *Forbes*, March 13, 1995, p. 152; Jeff Jensen, "'Star Wars' Empire Shows New Strength," *Advertising Age*, December 5, 1994, p. 33; Thomas Jaffe, ed., "Telephone Assault," *Forbes*, December 5, 1994, p. 20; and A.D., "LucasArts Entertainment," *Fortune*, July 11, 1994, pp. 129–130; Interview with Jeanne Cole, Lucasfilms, May, 1998; and, Dan Fost, *Marin Independent Journal*, December 29, 1977, p. D5.
2. "Lots of Low-Fat Intros," *Marketing News*, March 25, 1996, p.1.
3. Cindee Miller, "Food Producers Appeal to Fat-Free Crowd," *Marketing News*, August 14, 1996, p. 3.
4. Raymond D. Frost and Judy Strauss, *The Internet: A New Marketing Tool* (Upper Saddle River, NJ: Prentice Hall, 1997), p. 41.
5. Ibid, p. 91.
6. Tom Dellecave, Jr., "Gaining a Net Advantage," *Sales and Marketing Management*, October 1996, pp. 104, 106.
7. Gene R. Laczniak and Patrick E. Murphy, *Ethical Marketing Decisions: The Higher Road* (Boston: Allyn & Bacon, 1993), pp. 14–15.
8. William Heuslein, "Timid No More," *Forbes*, January 13, 1997, www.forbes.com.
9. Randall Lane, "Pampering the Customers, Pampering the Employees," *Forbes*, www.forbes.com.
10. Ian P. Murphy, "Amex Looks Beyond Satisfaction, Sees Growth," *Marketing News*, May 12, 1997, p. 6.
11. Valerie Reitman, "Toyota Motor Shows its Mettle after Fire Destroys Parts Plant," *Wall Street Journal Interactive Edition*, May 8, 1997.
12. Mary Foster, "Baptists Warn of Disney Boycott," *Boston Globe*, June 13, 1996, p. 3.
13. Greg Rushford, "Nike's Enemies: The Usual Suspects," *Wall Street Journal Interactive Edition*, May 7, 1997.
14. Rebecca Piirto Heath, "The Competitive Edge," *Marketing Tools*, September 1996, www.marketingtools.com.
15. Walter S. Mossberg, "Windows CE Tries to Beat Laptops with Hand-Held PCs," *Wall Street Journal Interactive Edition*, May 1, 1997.
16. Matthew Schifrin, "Merrillizing the World," *Forbes*, February 10, 1997, www.forbes.com.
17. Hiawatha Bray, "That Wal-Mart Feeling," *Boston Globe*, February 8, 1996, p. 60.
18. Erick Schonfeld, "Merck vs. the Biotech Industry: Which One Is More Potent?" *Fortune*, March 31, 1997, www.fortune.com.
19. Thomas Karier, "The R&D Gap," *Challenge*, July-August 1995, p. 60.
20. Kim Clark, "These Are the Good Old Days," *Fortune*, June 9, 1997, pp. 74–86.
21. Christopher Grimes, "Intel's 300 Megahertz Pentium II Prices at $1,981," *Wall Street Journal Interactive Edition*, May 7, 1997.
22. Andrew Pollack, "More Complex Superchips Put Premium on Designs," *New York Times*, May 26, 1997, p. C1.
23. John Verity, "Deconstructing the Computer Industry," *Business Week*, November 23, 1992, p. 90.
24. Terrence E. Deal and Allan A. Kennedy, *Corporate Cultures: The Ethics and Rituals of Corporate Life*, Reading, MA: Addison-Wesley Publishing (1982), p. 8.
25. David Bank, "Gates Invites CEOs to Hear about Future of Technology," *Wall Steet Journal Interactive Ediiton*, May 7, 1997.
26. Clark, "These Are the Good Old Days."
27. Cyndee Miller, "Baubles Are Back," *Marketing News*, April 14, 1997, pp. 1, 10.
28. U.S. Bureau of the Census; and Rik Kirkland, "America in the World: Still on Top, with No Challenger," *Fortune*, June 9, 1997, pp. 86–87.
29. Kenicki Ohmae, "Becoming a Triad Power: The New Global Corporation," *International Marketing Review*, Autumn 1986, p. 7.
30. *Business America*, October 19, 1992, p. 2.
31. AP–Dow Jones News Service, "El Salvador Pres to Visit Mexico in Hopes of Joining NAFTA," *Wall Street Journal Interactive Edition*, May 21, 1997.
32. Andrew Tanzer, "Stepping Stones to a New China?" *Forbes*, January 27, 1997, www.forbes.com.
33. AP–Dow Jones News Service, "PECC: Asia-Pacific Growth at 'High, Sustainable Plateau,'" *Wall Street Journal Interactive Edition*, June 3, 1997.
34. Bill Saporito, "Where the Global Action Is," *Fortune*, Autumn-Winter 1993, p. 62.
35. Karl Schoenberger, "Has Japan Changed?" *Fortune*, August 19, 1996, pp. 72–82.
36. Carl Quintanilla, "For '97 Grads, Spring Brings a Flood of New Job Offers," *Wall Street Journal Interactive Edition*, May 16, 1997.
37. www.census.gov/cgi-bin/ipc/popclock visited on June 1, 1998.
38. Otto Johnson, ed., *Information Please: 1996 Almanac* (Boston: Houghton Mifflin, 1996).
39. Claudette Bennett, *Current Population Reports* (Washington, DC: Bureau of the Census, U.S. Department of Commerce, January 1995), p. 2.
40. S.W. Smith and A. Clurman, "Generational Marketing," *Inc.*, April 1997, www.inc.com.
41. Kirkland, "America in the World."
42. Bennett, *Current Population Reports*, Jan 1995, p. 30.
43. Marcia Mogelonsky, *Everybody Eats* (Ithaca, NY: American Demographics Books, 1995), p. 154.
44. "The New Idea of Beauty: It's Bigger, Broader . . . and More Inclusive," *Glamour*, May 1996, pp. 220–225.
45. Cyndee Miller, "Chasing Global Dream," *Marketing News*, December 2, 1996, p. 1.
46. Edward T. Hall, "The Silent Language in Overseas Business," *Harvard Business Review*, May-June 1960, p. 87.
47. John R. Wilke and Patrick M. Reilly, "Music Firms Face Problems in U.S. Over Prices of CDs," *Wall Street Journal Interactive Edition*, May 7, 1997.
48. Emily Nelson, "Fuji in Challenge to Kodak, Plans to Make Film in the U.S.," *Wall Street Journal Interactive Edition*, May 8, 1997.
49. Bruce Ingersoll, "FTC and FDA Team Up Against Tobacco," *Wall Street Journal Interactive Edition*, May 1, 1997.
50. Chicago-Reuters, "Children Smoking Linked to Promotional Items," Infoseek News Channel, www.infoseek.com, December 15, 1997.
51. Associated Press, "Ford Plans for All 1998 Models to Have Less Forceful Air Bags," *Wall Street Journal Interactive Edition*, April 24, 1997.
52. "Recent Accomplishments of the U.S. EPA," U.S. Environmental Protection Agency home page, www.epa.gov/.

THE NATIONAL BASKETBALL ASSOCIATION

*P*ICTURE AN NBA TEAM, SUCH as the Chicago Bulls, playing for a half-empty arena. Or imagine the league's premier event—the championship games—being shown on tape delay against *The Tonight Show* due to a lack of interest from fans. Seem impossible? Amazingly, the NBA has not always been the worldwide phenomenon we know today. According to *Sales and Marketing Management,* just 12 years ago the NBA "was a product about as appealing as a week-old banana." How did it become an overnight international success? Many attribute the transformation to the marketing savvy of Commissioner David Stern. Since he took over, the league has expanded from 24 to 29 teams, gross revenues have risen from $181.8 million to $1.1 billion, and average attendance per game has grown from 11,141 in 1985 to more than 17,000. According to Pat Williams, senior executive vice president of the NBA's Orlando Magic, "David Stern has a tremendous marketing mind, and he is one of the great sports stories of the twentieth century."

During the 1970s and 1980s, marketing efforts by most NBA teams were minimal. Today, kids are wearing Chicago Bulls T-shirts in Casablanca, Phoenix Suns caps in Punta del Este, and Los Angeles Lakers jackets in London. NBA stars such as Michael Jordan, Shaquille O'Neal, and Dennis Rodman are recognized around the globe. And worldwide sales of NBA merchandise amount to more than $3 billion a year. David Stern has spent the last decade creating a global brand, and he has succeeded. The NBA of the 1990s has emerged as the first truly global sports league. Today, says Stern, "we're okay in Melbourne, Tokyo, and Hong Kong, but we've got to beef up our operations in Singapore, Jakarta, and Kuala Lumpur." This was a league that ranked third in fan popularity only 12 years ago.

When Stern became commissioner in 1984, he immediately saw the NBA's global potential. In addition to worldwide requests for more games to telecast, Stern noted a number of environmental changes: the collapse of communism and the growth of market economies, the globalization of American consumer products, and a worldwide television revolution that created new cable and satellite channels. A more recent development is the growth of the global Internet, where the NBA has an official Web site. It offers programming in Spanish, French, and Italian and draws 35 percent of its traffic from outside the United States.

How has this vast international opportunity been exploited? Television is the number one tool. In addition to the traditional game broadcasts, a variety of programs are produced by the NBA. For example, kids and teens are targeted with two weekly programs, *NBA Action* and *NBA Jams.* The NBA also sells television rights to local broadcasters, even in countries where it does no other business. In such countries as Spain, France, Mexico, and Japan, the NBA collects more than $1 million in rights fees. Given the intensity of media competition, these numbers are expected to grow. In 1970 the NBA sold cable rights for $400,000. Today, it commands an astounding $90 million.

Based on the exposure made possible by television, the NBA has moved into a number of live events, attractions, and grassroots activities. The latter are part of the NBA's effort to reach a broad demographic scope of fans and to allow them to connect with the brand. Among these activities is "2Ball," a program that teaches basic basketball skills to children, in which more than 100,000 kids in 31 states have participated. In 1996, the NBA tested "2Ball" in 500 schools in the United Kingdom where 25 percent of the participants touched a basketball for the first time. The next year, 2,400 schools in Germany, France, and the United Kingdom signed up. Since only 2 percent of fans have the opportunity to attend pro games each year, there is a need to reach consumers in alternate and meaningful ways. Other attractions include events such as the McDonald's® championship, which is telecast worldwide. In the October 1997 McDonald's® championship, the Bulls played teams from Spain, Greece, Argentina, Italy, and France.

A number of factors have facilitated the worldwide growth of the NBA, including electronic media, sports marketing, and foreign-born players. David Stern wants the NBA to be a part of pop culture in "every global medium that matters." He believes "the real-time delivery of data and statistics about the NBA on a global basis via the Web is about as exciting as it gets." Stern himself has participated in on-line chat sessions. In addition to the popularity of interactive media, sports marketers such as Nike have complemented the NBA's global presence. According to Stern, "they have an enormous marketing, distribution, and manufacturing capability that we borrow. And to the extent that that's associated with their brand, it makes our brand stronger. We're sort of borrowing each other's equity." Cultural diversity in the league has also facilitated the NBA's global growth. For example, while the Bulls are visibly led by Michael Jordan and Scottie Pippen, they heavily rely on Toni Kukoc from Croatia and Luc Longley from Australia. These players attract intensive media coverage at home, as do players Georghe Muresan in Romania, Arvydas Sabonis in Lithuania, and Detlef Shrempf in Germany.

Managing the NBA is a dynamic role. It requires interfacing with apparel companies, licensees, U.S. and global media companies, and corporate giants such as McDonald's®, Coca-Cola, Nike, and Disney. The NBA is not just a provider of sports programming; it is also in the sporting goods, sponsorship, consumer products, and trading card businesses, among others. With these relationships comes the need to defend property rights, and the NBA has been the most active league in that regard. This includes even digital rights. Stern says: "I just want to be standing with this big bundle of carefully protected rights. . . . I had owners in 1979 that didn't want me to get involved with cable, but if you can be part of the growth pattern, you will always do better."

Growth often brings difficult management decisions. Stern tries to incorporate ethical choices into the league's expansion. "You must be on the ground in every continent exploiting your brand with sensitivity towards local issues. But there's nothing easy about that," he says. "We want to play into the existing infrastructure, not supplant it. We do not wish to injure or disrupt the Italian League, Spanish League, or any other league."

Stern predicts that one-third of the NBA's revenues could come from abroad within the next ten years. Today's staff of 105 is double the number that ran the league in the 1980s. International sales of NBA licensed merchandise alone rose 22 percent in 1996. The NBA is known as a selling sport. The game is played nearly everywhere, and it is easily understood. The phenomenal popularity and worldwide presence of the NBA is all about marketing. As the league continues to grow, fans will continue to cheer for the *mate* in Latin America, the *trofsla* in Iceland, and the *smash* in France. And the Chinese will continue to root for the Bulls, better known as the "Red Oxen."

1. *The global macroenvironment consists of large external influencers vital to long-term decisions but not directly affected by the company itself. Identify these influencers and note several ways each has affected or may affect the NBA's global expansion.*
2. *What considerations does the NBA need to address before entering a particular country or region? Suggest several adjustments that may be required to serve customers successfully in those markets.*

3. *Stakeholders include groups such as owners, employees, suppliers, intermediaries, and action groups. Identify the groups with a stake in the NBA, making assumptions when necessary. How may each of these influence marketing decisions?*

SOURCES: Marc Gunther, "They All Want to Be Like Mike," *Fortune,* July 21, 1997, www.fortune.com; Jeff Jensen, "Experiential Branding Makes It to the Big Leagues," *Advertising Age,* April 14, 1997, pp. 20, 24; Terry Lefton, "At Age 50, Stern Looks Ahead," *Brandweek,* October 28, 1996, pp. 34–38; Bob Ryan, "Hoop Dreams," *Sales and Marketing Management,* December 1996, pp. 48–53; Michael Schrage, "David Stern," *Adweek,* May 26, 1997, pp. 24–26; and the NBA Web site, www.nba.com, visited October 29, 1997.

The Strategic Marketing Planning Process: Domestic and Global

Objectives

1. Understand how the strategic marketing planning hierarchy fits together to provide a complete planning system.

2. Describe the four elements of an organization's vision that provide guidance for all actions.

3. Integrate components of the strategic marketing plan with the vision.

4. Understand why elements of the marketing mix must be integrated and outline the steps of the marketing control process.

5. Identify the four major ways that organizations enter and cultivate global markets.

ALMOST 60 YEARS AGO, WALT DISNEY founded his company based on three precepts: Tell a great story, tell it with great characters, and push the technological bounds. His characters formed the basis of the movies, cartoons, theme parks, and merchandise that would propel Disney into the forefront of entertainment. His creative vision was easily summed up: Demand the impossible! And his marketing vision for the Disneyland theme park, opened in 1955, was far ahead of its time: Exceed guests' expectations.

On the one hand, Walt's visionary zeal created a number of businesses—movies, cartoons, television shows, theme parks, and merchandise—held together by the Disney brand. On the other hand, the company lacked any real marketing strategy. Walt's autocratic leadership and unchallenged control in every detail of the operation simply didn't focus on the long term. When Walt Disney died in 1966, the company floundered. As one senior employee put it, "Everyone looked to the past, asking, 'What would Walt have done?' No one looked to the future and asked the visionary question, 'What if . . . ?'"

It wasn't until the mid-1980s that a new team of executives, led by CEO Michael Eisner, began strategic and marketing planning for The Walt Disney Company. Eisner separated the organization into strategic business units (theme parks and resorts, filmed entertainment, and consumer products) so that it could focus on what it did best. Instead of short-term planning, long-range plans became the norm. It's not unusual for a Disney division to have 5-, 10-, and 15-year plans to help it stay focused. While the business press was writing off Euro Disney (now called Disney Paris) when it first opened, Disney officials could see that they were actually ahead of their 30-year plan!

One of Disney's strategies is partnering with major marketers. In 1996 Disney inked a 10-year mega-deal with McDonald's® for joint marketing of Disney movies with Happy Meals.® Disney also negotiated with George Lucas to win the rights to co-market a new series of Star Wars movies scheduled to begin appearing in 1999. That's in addition to many licensing agreements, including those with Mattel and Hallmark for toys and cards using Disney characters.

Disney's global strategy continues to expand as well. The Disney Channel is now available in Taiwan, Great Britain, and Germany, and more countries will be added to the list in the near future. The Disney Store has more than 450 retail outlets in 10 countries. Disney's publishing operations include more than 180 magazines in 28 languages in 32 countries. With theme parks in Tokyo and France, Disney continues to search for further expansion possibilities.

And Disney continues to recognize diversity. The Disney Store recruiting brochure maintains that it is "committed to supporting cultural diversity in the workplace because . . . 'It's a Small World After All.'" Even the animated films of the 1990s have moved from the exclusively white characters: Aladdin *focuses on Arabs,* Pocahontas *celebrates Native Americans,* The Lion King *relates to the African experience, and* The Hunchback of Notre Dame *empathizes with the disabled.*

The "Magic Kingdom" didn't get that way through magic. Rather, Disney developed a strategic marketing plan aimed at exceeding customer expectations. Along the way, it developed short-term tactics to keep the plan in focus.[1]

CONNECTED: SURFING THE NET

www.disney.com

Check out the many features of the Disney Web site. You'll find links to the Disney Store, Walt Disney World, the Disney Channel, Walt Disney Pictures, Disney Publishing, and much more.

THE CONCEPT OF THE STRATEGIC MARKETING PLANNING PROCESS

Connecting with customers requires a sustained, concerted effort by organizations over the long term and the short term. Long-run plans concentrate on developing the resources an organization needs to win. Short-run plans describe how these resources will be deployed. An effective planning system addresses both the development and use of resources. The five forces that determine how well organizations connect with customers can be effective only with careful planning. The strategic marketing plan provides the guidance necessary to build relationships, develop and use technology, court diversity, and ensure ethical behavior in domestic as well as global markets.

Marketing can be described as philosophy, as strategy, and as tactics. Leading-edge businesses like Children's World, Disney, Eli Lilly, and Johnson & Johnson develop marketing plans that address each of these aspects to help them connect with customers. Figure 4-1 outlines the type of planning that corresponds with each aspect of marketing, including the people who usually implement each.

Marketing as philosophy can be viewed as the organization's marketing concept. It is embodied within the organization's vision statement, which articulates what customer value will be delivered, the codes of conduct guiding organizational behavior, and the resources that will be developed and deployed to build value. The vision describes the fundamental contributions the business intends to make to society, its position relative to competitors, and the attributes that make the organization unique from others. The vision is usually developed by top executives. In many organizations, this often includes the board of directors. Input from all organization levels may be sought as well.

Strategic marketing plan

The document describing the company's objectives and how to achieve them in light of competitive activities.

Marketing as strategy is formalized in the **strategic marketing plan**, a document describing the company's objectives and how to achieve them in light of competitive activities. Essentially, this plan outlines the decisions executives have made about how the vision will be accomplished. The strategic marketing plan generally requires input and guidelines from marketing executives and a planning team of top- and middle-level personnel.

Marketing as tactics refers to precisely how each part of the marketing mix (product, price, promotion, place, and customer service) will be managed to meet requirements of the strategic marketing plan. Marketing mix plans are developed by specialists in each component, such as product managers, advertising executives, and sales personnel.

The owner may perform all these planning roles in a small company while several hundred people may be involved in companies like Johnson & Johnson or General Electric, two global giants known for exceptional marketing planning. You will find that companies tend

Marketing Aspect	Type of Planning	Responsibility
Marketing as philosophy	Vision	Top executive and top management team
Marketing as strategy	Strategic marketing plan	Marketing executive and other members of the strategic marketing team
Marketing as tactics	Marketing mix plans	Managers responsible for product, price, promotion, and place programs

Figure 4-1 Types of Marketing Planning

to blend philosophy, strategy, and tactics into a range of planning appropriate for the organization. Still, all three aspects are found within leading organizations.

The hierarchy shown in Figure 4-2 describes what takes place as companies develop plans to address the three aspects of marketing: philosophy, strategy, and tactics. Each of the major components of the vision, strategic marketing plan, and marketing mix plans depicted here is examined in detail in the following sections. The final section of the chapter focuses on the strategies companies use to enter and build strength in foreign markets.

THE ORGANIZATION VISION

Outstanding performers have a vision that focuses marketing efforts purposefully. The **vision** helps everyone maintain consistent direction despite volatile market environments. When President John F. Kennedy said "We will put a man on the moon," he created an effective vision. He provided a picture that inspired the U.S. space program, largely because the vision was simple, clear, and easy to remember. If Kennedy had described the enormity of the challenge in detail (how many people were needed, what talents they must possess, what type of equipment would be required), it's doubtful the venture would have succeeded. Instead, Kennedy's vision was fulfilled in 1969, when Neil Armstrong took "one small step for man, one giant leap for mankind," and walked on the moon.

Take a few minutes to visualize your life now and in five years, 15 years, and beyond. You are forming a personal vision. To make that vision a reality, what values will guide your behaviors? What will you contribute to people around you? What is your idea of excellence? What skills and attributes do you possess or will you develop? These same questions must be answered by organizations. This is the visioning process. Discovering the vision is critical for companies (or people) who wish to deliver superior value.

The corporate vision provides a common understanding of what the organization is trying to accomplish in the broadest sense. Duane Larson, president of Children's World Learning Centers, a division of ARAMARK Corporation, says of his company's vision about providing child care:

> Just as the rudder determines the direction a boat will take, our Vision determines what direction our organization will take. Without it there is effort but no progress. At Children's World, it includes our Core Values, which are the things we hold sacred, like our concern for the safety of the children in our care. It also includes our mission, that which we are trying to accomplish. It sounds easy to delineate; it isn't.

Vision

The desired image of the company in the minds of employees.

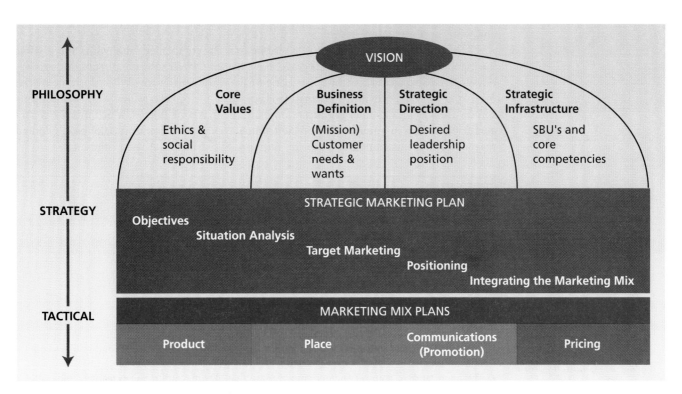

Figure 4-2   Marketing Planning Hierarchy

Core values

A set of statements describing
the type of behavior expected of
the company and its employees.

CONNECTED:
SURFING
THE NET

www.lilly.com

Eli Lilly invites you to learn
more about its global
research-based
pharmaceutical corporation.
Visit Eli Lilly's Web site and
find out more about its
company philosophy,
corporate citizenship, and
treatment of employees.

Most company visions are composed of four parts: a set of core values, a business definition, the strategic direction of the company, and the strategic infrastructure.

CORE VALUES: THE ETHICAL FOUNDATION

Core values describe the type of behavior expected from a company's employees. Core values are the articulation of ethics and social responsibility, which were discussed in chapter 1. Everyone must live them every day. L. L. Bean's values are to "sell good merchandise at a reasonable price and treat customers like friends." Employees believe that if they do this, business will take care of itself. Core values often express the company's philosophy about societal well-being, good corporate citizenship, and treatment of employees.

"Values are the way a company does things," says Randall Tobias, CEO of Eli Lilly, adding that in order for them to work, "values must be both defined and lived."[2] Eli Lilly executives have clearly articulated the organization's core values.

Eli Lilly Core Values

Long established core values guide us in all that we do as we implement our strategies and pursue our mission

- Respect for the people that includes our concern for the interests of all the people worldwide who touch—or are touched by—our company: customers, employees, shareholders, partners, and communities.
- Integrity that embraces the very highest standards of honesty, ethical behavior, and exemplary moral character.
- Excellence that is reflected in our continuous search for new ways to improve the performance of our business in order to become the best at what we deliver.

Recently, as the first step in their strategic planning process, a team of top executives and managers from Children's World gathered to undertake the difficult task of developing their core values. The result is shown in Figure 4-3. Notice that each of the many stakeholders of the organization is explicitly addressed.

Core values provide an ethical guide that may be particularly useful in a crisis. It is possible Johnson & Johnson would not be around today if it had not adhered to its core values when Tylenol capsules laced with cyanide were linked to several deaths. The company's values are described in a credo, developed in the early 1940s, which reads in part: "We believe our first responsibility is to the doctors, nurses, and patients, to mothers and all others who use our products and services. In meeting their needs, everything we do must be of high quality." That credo represents the organization's main purpose, to produce products responsibly and with consumer safety in mind.

The tragic Tylenol situation in 1982 is one that few companies could withstand. By following the guidelines set forth in its credo, however, Johnson & Johnson did not just survive, but emerged stronger. This ethics issue, one of the most heavily covered of this type by the *Wall Street Journal*, provides a fascinating classic example of core values.[3] Johnson & Johnson owns McNeil Consumer Products Company, the maker of Tylenol, which in 1982 generated $500 million in annual sales and contributed 8 percent of Johnson & Johnson's annual revenues. It was outselling Bayer aspirin, Bufferin, Excedrin, and Anacin combined.

*Figure 4-3 Children's World
Learning Centers, Inc.
Corporate Vision*

CORE VALUES
We hold sacred . . .
- Our paramount and uncompromising concern for the safety, health, and emotional and educational well-being of our customers and employees.
- Our dedication to making a positive difference in children's lives.
- Our responsibility to operate with honesty and integrity with all publics:
  —Parents   —Employers
  —Children   —Suppliers
  —Communities   —Management
  —Employees   —Government
- Our respect for the uniqueness of the individual.
- Our commitment to excellence in the delivery of our service to our customers and results to our shareholders.
- The importance of empowering our employees so that they may utilize their creativity and initiative to deliver on the company's commitment to excellence.

Tylenol's comeback can be attributed to Johnson & Johnson's early decision to stand by its credo.

On September 30, 1982, when Extra-Strength Tylenol capsules laced with cyanide were reported as linked with five deaths and one serious illness, McNeil immediately and voluntarily withdrew from the market the lot of 93,000 units from which the two bottles came. That same day, 500 sales agents were sent to remove the product from store shelves. By midafternoon, the company had sent half a million messages to physicians, hospitals, and distributors notifying them of the deaths and indicating the lot number.

Tougher times were ahead. Another death occurred in April that was linked to poisonous Tylenol. The company removed from the market all 22 million bottles of Tylenol capsules, valued at $79 million. To offset the loss in consumer goodwill, the marketing focus shifted to selling Tylenol tablets and voluntarily exchanging these for bottles of capsules. Nevertheless, by October 25, 1982, sales of *all* Tylenol products had slipped more than 25 percent. A letter was sent to approximately 61,000 doctors nationwide in which McNeil's Dr. Thomas N. Gates outlined the steps taken in response to the product tampering. In addition, two million pieces of literature were sent to doctors, dentists, nurses, and pharmacists emphasizing that the company was not the source of the poison. A special promotion offered coupons for Tylenol, and customers who had thrown away their bottles following the scare could have them replaced for free by calling an 800 number. Investor confidence improved and Johnson & Johnson stock, which had fallen 17 percent immediately after the first deaths were reported, bounced back on the New York Stock Exchange. Johnson & Johnson had all stores restocked with tamper-proof capsules by January 1, 1983.

Tylenol's comeback can best be attributed to Johnson & Johnson's early management decision to both stand by its credo and not let the brand die. The credo concludes: "We are responsible to the communities in which we live and work and to the world community as well. . . . We must experiment with new ideas. Research must be carried on, innovative programs developed, and mistakes paid for."

CONNECTED: SURFING THE NET

www.jnj.com

Johnson & Johnson is well known for its adherence to core values set forth by the company. Learn more about Johnson & Johnson and read its credo in its entirety on the company's Web site.

BUSINESS DEFINITION (MISSION)

The **business definition**, also referred to as the company mission, describes the fundamental contributions the organization provides to customers. Merck Pharmaceuticals says: "We are in the business of preserving and improving human life. All our actions must be measured by our success in achieving this." Children's World says: "Our mission is to enrich the quality of family life by providing peace of mind to parents and by enhancing the life experiences of the children in our care."

Noted scholar Ted Levitt has had a tremendous influence on how companies develop their business definition. In a classic *Harvard Business Review* article, "Marketing Myopia," he explains why a customer orientation is absolutely critical to a company's business definition. **Marketing myopia** occurs when executives focus on their company's current products and services rather than on benefits to consumers. Levitt uses U.S. railroads as an example. They didn't stop growing because the need for passenger and freight transportation declined; in fact it grew. They got into trouble because they saw themselves in the railroad business rather

Business definition
Describes the contributions the business makes to customers and society; also called the company mission.

Marketing myopia
A focus on company products rather than on how these benefit consumers.

than the transportation business. They were product oriented, not customer oriented. Trucking and airline companies took customers away from railroads because they better met their needs. In addition, the railroads' failure to focus on customer needs created a situation whereby they also failed at making railroads themselves as competitive as could be. If the railroads had defined their business as transportation, then maybe Penn Central or some other company would have invented the truck or the airplane or served customers' transportation needs in other innovative ways with the railroads themselves. Levitt adds that "the entire corporation must be viewed as a customer-creating and customer-satisfying organization. Management must think of itself not as producing products but as providing customer-creating value satisfactions."

The organization's business definition should be stated in basic, benefit-rich terms and should focus on consumer benefits, not product features. It should always answer this question: "What business are we really in?" For example, is a cereal company in the "food" business (product focused) or the "nutrition" business (focused on consumer needs)? Benefits are based on what customers receive, not on the work companies do. Microsoft has grown dramatically and received substantial profit because of the benefits its software provides. Customers don't care how much raw material Microsoft uses or what it costs to produce the software. Michael Jordan, Shaquille O'Neal, and Juwaan Howard make hundreds of millions of dollars because of the entertainment they provide, not just the points they score. Figure 4-4 contrasts myopic business definitions with customer-centered business definitions.

> **CAREER TIP** The Eli Lilly corporate mission states that "the company's objective is to attract and retain outstanding people at all levels and in all parts of the organization."[4] As a part of this effort, Eli Lilly offers a summer internship program which has grown and become more diverse each year. Interns are challenged to become actively involved in order to develop individual talents, leadership, and communication skills. Internships are offered in marketing and many other career areas. For further information, you can contact: Summer Intern Coordinator, Eli Lilly & Company, Lilly Corporate Center, Indianapolis, IN 46285.

STRATEGIC DIRECTION (INTENT)

Strategic direction
The desired leadership position of an organization as well as the measures used to chart progress toward reaching that position.

Strategic direction is the desired leadership position of an organization and the measures used to chart progress toward reaching this position. Strategic intent is another term for strategic direction: "Strategic intent captures the essence of winning."[5] Strategic direction addresses the competitiveness of the organization and often sets specific growth, profit, share, or scope goals relative to the competition and market opportunities. Eli Lilly's strategic direction is to become the global leader in providing "optimal clinical and economic outcomes" to con-

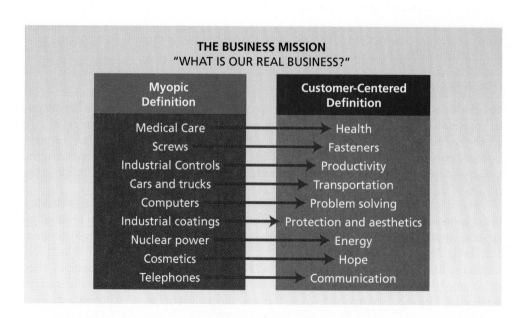

Figure 4-4   The Business Definition

THE BUSINESS MISSION
"WHAT IS OUR REAL BUSINESS?"

Myopic Definition	Customer-Centered Definition
Medical Care	Health
Screws	Fasteners
Industrial Controls	Productivity
Cars and trucks	Transportation
Computers	Problem solving
Industrial coatings	Protection and aesthetics
Nuclear power	Energy
Cosmetics	Hope
Telephones	Communication

sumers. It plans to focus primarily on three strategic dimensions: achieving a global presence, using its critical capabilities, and concentrating its resources on the five disease categories in which the company believes it can have the greatest effect.[6]

Strategic direction may identify competitors by name or by type. Fuji's strategic direction is aimed at overtaking Kodak, and Toyota is intent on surpassing General Motors. Or strategic direction may guide organizations toward becoming one of the largest in an industry. General Electric wants to be either a leader or close follower in each venture it pursues. Netscape and Microsoft's strategic direction involves a battle for dominance of the Web. Both companies have recently introduced new versions of their Internet software, intensifying the competition to be the largest in the industry.[7]

STRATEGIC INFRASTRUCTURE

Executives must develop and organize the company's **strategic infrastructure**, the corporate configuration that produces the company's distinctive or core competencies and provides the resources necessary to satisfy customer wants. This often means dividing the business into functional units and determining which core competencies to develop. The idea is to provide the products, services, and talents necessary to satisfy customer needs and create customer value.

Strategic Business Units (SBUs) Most medium-sized and large companies have several strategic departments or units. A **strategic business unit (SBU)** is a part of the firm that can be managed separately for marketing purposes; it may be a division within the company, a separate product or product line, a distinct group of customers, or a unique technology. Johnson & Johnson has three SBUs: consumer, pharmaceutical, and professional products. The consumer SBU concentrates its efforts on marketing consumer products such as Band-Aids, No More Tears shampoo, and Tylenol. The pharmaceutical SBU mainly markets prescription drugs to the health care industry. The professional SBU produces sutures, surgical equipment, and medical supplies for physicians, dentists, and others. The Walt Disney Company also has three SBUs: theme parks and resorts, filmed entertainment, and consumer products.

Consider the corporation illustrated in Figure 4-5. It has two divisions: ground transportation and air transportation. The ground transportation division can be divided into SBUs according to products (motorcycles, trucks, and cars), types of markets (business, consumer, and military), and technology (electric and gas). The air transportation division can be divided similarly (products are passenger planes, fighter planes, and training planes; markets are military, airlines, and consumers; and technologies are conventional and stealth). The

Strategic infrastructure
The corporate configuration that produces the company's distinctive or core competencies and provides the resources necessary to satisfy customer wants.

Strategic business unit (SBU)
A part of the firm that can be managed separately for marketing purposes; it may be a division, a product or product line, a distinct group of customers, or a unique technology.

Figure 4-5 Strategic Business Units

total SBUs possible for this company is 36, but not all combinations would make sense (such as an SBU that produces stealth passenger planes for consumers).

There are several ways to structure the SBUs in this company. Grouped by technology, there would be four (electric, gas, conventional, and stealth); based on products there would be six (motorcycles, trucks, cars, passenger planes, fighter planes, and training planes); according to type of market, there would be four (airlines, other businesses, consumers, and the military). Many companies, lacking a customer focus, form SBUs by product line. In market-oriented companies, SBUs often address specific segments. That's why UPS World Wide Logistics is organized by the industries it serves: automotive, pharmaceuticals, computer, and so forth.

Typically, an SBU is managed by a team from several different functional areas, such as marketing, accounting, and manufacturing. The corporate executives are responsible for managing the collection of SBUs—often called a portfolio— that make up the organization. The general health of the company depends on how well the SBU portfolio matches the needs of the market.

Portfolio planning tools

Tools that measure the contribution each SBU makes to the overall performance of the company.

Portfolio planning tools measure the contribution each SBU makes to the overall performance of the company. We will discuss two that are widely used: the growth-share matrix developed by the Boston Consulting Group (BCG) and the attractiveness-strength matrix developed by General Electric.

Assessing SBUs: The Growth-Share Matrix   Marketers need to understand market opportunities and the strength of their organization's resources relative to competitors. The growth-share matrix, shown in Figure 4-6, uses market growth as a measure of opportunity and the company's market share as the measure of resource strength. SBUs are placed in a matrix according to their scores on these two dimensions. Different actions are recommended, depending on the category into which the SBU falls.

In the low-share/high-growth category are SBUs termed question marks. Although they are in a market that is growing fast, most have not yet achieved competitive advantage or begun generating substantial revenues. Iomega's Zip drive falls in this category. The revolutionary new product is a substitute for a computer's internal hard drive. It stores data like a disk but has enormous capacity. Despite relatively low sales at this point, investors are paying high prices for stock in the company because of its huge potential. Since question marks are very risky, marketers may choose to (1) invest a little in the SBU and hope for the best; (2) spend time, energy, and patience on developing the SBU; (3) invest everything and keep their fingers crossed; or (4) get more information before doing anything.

Stars (high-share/high-growth SBUs) are a lot like movie personalities—give them lots of attention and expect a lot of success. Because they're growing, stars require a high investment, but it can result in a high return. Products like Sony's PlayStation and Windows 98 are examples.

Cash cows (high-share/low-growth SBUs) require a relatively small investment but should yield fairly substantial returns. Although the market is growing at a very low rate, the SBU has enough share to generate substantial cash flow. Companies want at least one product in this category and often have more, since revenues from these products can support the de-

Figure 4-6 Boston Consulting Group Growth-Share Matrix

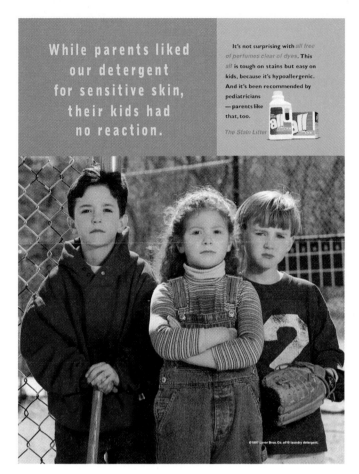

While parents liked our detergent for sensitive skin, their kids had no reaction.

It's not surprising with *all free of perfumes clear of dyes.* This *all* is tough on stains but easy on kids, because it's hypoallergenic. And it's been recommended by pediatricians —parents like that, too.

The Stain Lifter

Lever Brothers' laundry detergent All is an example of a cash cow.

velopment of others. Two huge cash cows are the DOS operating system for Microsoft and Ivory soap for Procter & Gamble.

Dogs (low-share/low-growth SBUs) typically provide less than desirable returns. They're often considered competitively disadvantaged and unlikely to generate profits. They may actually consume resources, becoming cash drains that create negative value for the company. An example is *Playboy* magazine. It loses lots of money, so why keep it? Because it's the cornerstone of the profitable activities of Playboy Enterprises. The astoundingly profitable playmate videos (an SBU star) and other Playboy businesses are possible only because of the magazine.

Assessing SBUs: The Attractiveness-Strength Matrix   The growth-share matrix says nothing about competitive behavior or market characteristics, and for this reason most marketing strategists use the attractiveness-strength matrix. As illustrated in Figure 4-7, the marketer first examines such factors as market size, market growth, competitive pressure, price levels, and government regulation to develop a composite industry attractiveness score. Next, the business strengths of each SBU are assessed based on estimates of the company's market share, customer and market knowledge, customer satisfaction with the company, cost efficiency, level of technology, product quality, and financial strength. Each SBU is then graphed in the matrix based on these several measures.

The attractiveness-strength matrix uses colors to signal whether executives should stop (red), be cautious (yellow), or go ahead (green) with the SBU. Unfortunately, during the 1960s and 1970s, "red" SBUs were sometimes categorically denied the resources required to compete, dooming them to failure. At the same time, "green" SBUs were allowed to charge ahead, irrespective of the vision of the company. All that was important was the amount of investment required and the SBU's potential return.

Today, portfolio planning tools are considered useful indicators, not predictors. Even SBUs that fall in the same category may need vastly different strategies. Portfolio techniques are helpful in identifying the current business situation, but they are inappropriate for making

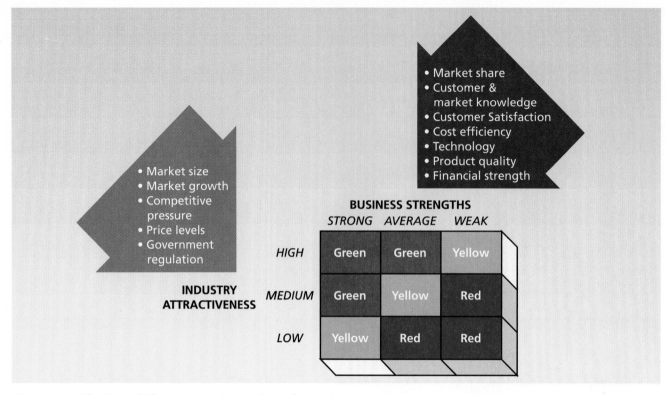

Figure 4-7   The General Electric Attractiveness-Strength Matrix

Companies such as GE assess its SBUs based on estimates of market share, customer and market knowledge, customer satisfaction, cost efficiency, level of technology, product growth, and financial strength.

resource allocations. These, as we shall see later, should be made only after the strategic marketing plan has been developed. Because portfolio techniques say little about strategy, they should be used only as a first step in strategic marketing.

Core Competencies   As was shown in Figure 4-2, core competencies are the other important aspect of strategic infrastructures. **Core competencies** are the unique resources a company develops and employs to create superior customer value. They are the fundamental building blocks of competitive advantage. As Duane Larson of Children's World explains:

> In developing a strategic marketing plan for Children's World, it was important that we had a clear idea of what we did well, and how those competencies fit with our overall strategic direction. This process was valuable because more than telling you what you did well, it highlighted the holes we had that needed to be filled in order to deliver on our plan.

Children's World identified several core competencies that are kept confidential as part of their strategy. McDonald's® core competencies in food distribution and preparation give it the ability to reproduce precisely the same taste, texture, and service millions of times a day, anywhere in the world. FedEx has developed a core competency in computerized information and tracking system technology so it can determine the location of any package worldwide within seconds.

Core competencies underlie the success of any one SBU and also span several SBUs or corporate divisions. Core competencies allow new products to grow. Marketing's role is to interpret market forces so that the proper core competencies can be developed to provide maximum benefit to consumers in the marketplace. When this role is performed well, companies are rewarded with the profit necessary to support continued improvement and growth. Kodak's ability to thrive through the consolidation of corporatewide technology is discussed in the technology feature.

An understanding of core competencies is necessary to comprehend how technology is shaping marketing practices. Through the rapid growth of technologies, companies build the millions of products and services that produce superior customer value. The many types of core competencies can be grouped into five categories: (1) base technologies, (2) process technologies, (3) product technologies, (4) people systems, and (5) information systems.

Base Technologies   The research and development skills of companies can be applied to an endless array of product areas. For example, one of Canon's core competencies, vision optics, can be used to deliver outstanding cameras, copiers, and numerous inventive products. DuPont, known for basic chemistry, has developed multitudes of industrial and consumer products. Westinghouse is skilled in the wave technology necessary for radar and other types of vision systems. General Electric has spent billions of dollars developing its extensive

Core competencies
The unique resources a company develops and employs to create superior customer value; the fundamental building blocks of competitive advantage.

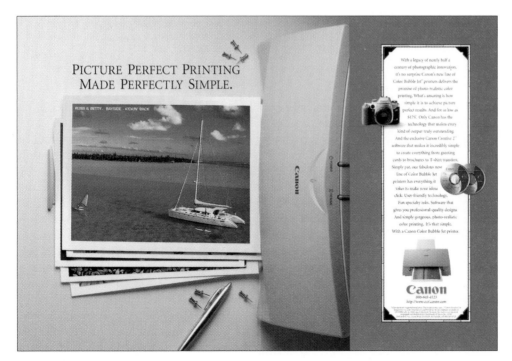

One of Cannon's core competencies is vision optics.

CONNECTING THROUGH TECHNOLOGY
KODAK ADJUSTS ITS FOCUS

More than a century ago, "You push the button, we do the rest," was the slogan—and vision—that introduced photographic technology to the public and pushed Eastman Kodak to one of the top brands in the United States. By the mid-1990s, however, Kodak had strayed dangerously from its core competency: photo imaging. It had ventured into a host of unrelated businesses, such as household products, clinical diagnostics, and pharmaceuticals, and it posted a $1.5 million loss in 1993. Enter CEO George Fisher, former top gun at Motorola. Charged with reinventing the company, Fisher decided not only to refocus on what made Kodak great in the first place—imaging—but also to push the limits of digital imaging technology to give customers greater value. With respectable earnings of $1.3 billion on $15 billion sales in 1995, it looks like Fisher's strategy is paying off.

The first thing Fisher did was to sell off Kodak's unrelated businesses. Next, he made Kodak's leadership in developing digital imaging a priority. Kodak joined forces with competitors Nikon, Minolta, Canon, and Fuji to develop Advanced Photo Systems (APS), hailed as one of the best products of 1996 by *Business Week*. This new digital imaging system gives customers easy drop-in film loading, improved print quality, three print formats, and the ability to have certain data recorded digitally on the film. Although the five-company consortium developed APS together, Kodak owns approximately 60 percent of the patents and has contributed the most marketing muscle—a splashy television and print campaign for its own Advantix brand.

Each and every Kodak ad now features the line "Take Pictures Further," and the vision has been as crucial to Kodak's strategic reinvention as was "You push the button" at its founding. The slogan expresses Kodak's broader mission to increase the number of photos customers take—whether through digital or traditional technology—and to get customers to use their pictures by enlarging them, putting them on T-shirts, in newsletters, on computer screens—you name it. More than 60 billion pictures are taken each year, but only 2 percent are enlarged, used commercially, or displayed. Part of the APS appeal is the ability to order prints from a contact sheet so that only the pictures you want to use get printed.

Kodak's mission, however, is not confined to its digital imaging strategic business unit. Fisher centralized marketing for all nine of the company's SBUs; all report to a chief marketing officer, and each is charged with delivering value to its customers, as opposed to delivering technology. "We have a number of technologies, but we have to be technologically transparent," says Bill Gray, manager of corporate branding. "What we deliver is pictures. And how we will get growth and how we will serve people is to explain to them how they can, in our words, 'take pictures further.'" To back up this unified marketing strategy, Kodak is using an ad campaign that spotlights every one of its SBUs—a first for the company. The ad features vignettes of the many ways people and companies get value with imaging, whether they're capturing memories or improving business communications.

Sources: Linda Grant, "The Bears Back Off Kodak," *Fortune*, June 24, 1996, pp. 24–25; Ginger Conlon, "Getting into Focus," *Sales and Marketing Management*, January 1997, pp. 40–45; and Steve Gelsi, "Imaging Is Everything," *Brandweek*, February 26, 1996, pp. 22–23.

CONNECTED: SURFING THE NET

www.westinghouse.com

Learn more about base technologies by visiting Westinghouse's Web site. Discover how the company has applied its research and development skills to develop innovative products.

knowledge of physics. Base technologies can be applied simultaneously to a number of diverse industries and product areas.

Process Technologies   Process technologies allow the firm to produce quality products in the most effective and flexible manner possible. Marketing's job is to make sure that the development of processes is consistent with market trends and is in the customer's best interest. McDonald's® has nearly perfected the process of quickly delivering quality food to consumers, but the company does not consider current standards fast enough. It is now shooting for order fulfillment within 90 seconds and a customer wait of no more than 3.5 minutes, including the drive-thru.[8] This improvement requires extensive changes in employee training, as well as the technologies used to process food. ARAMARK set a world record of its own when it used its superior process technologies to serve more than five million meals to athletes from 198 countries at the Centennial Olympic Games in Atlanta in 1996. WearGuard designs thousands of new products each year for the custom clothing market. An order for a shirt with a company logo or Little League team name can be received over the phone and shipped within 24 hours. Its production is tied so closely to the customer order process that no time is spent without contributing value to the customer.

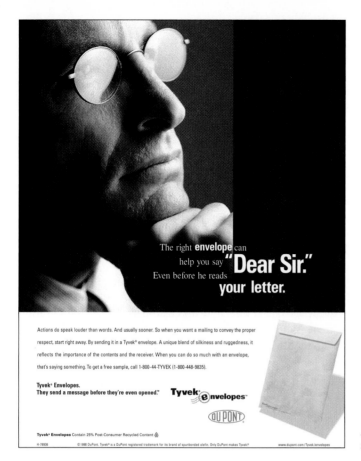

DuPont's core competencies in chemistry have enabled it to develop a number of industrial and consumer products.

Product Technologies   The company's ability to create new goods and services is supported by product technologies. Many organizations have worked hard to develop competency in moving quickly from the idea stage through a series of well-defined steps to commercialization. Others follow the leader, copying competitors' products, possibly improving upon them slightly. Followers benefit from the innovation of leaders without having to invest substantially in developing their own product technology.

Nokia, second to Motorola in the fierce and fast-growing mobile phone industry, spends less than half the amount of its rivals on research and development. It acquires and copies product technologies developed by others. According to Merrill Lynch analyst Neal Barton, "Motorola and Ericsson are pioneers in technology. Nokia is much closer to customers. It doesn't pioneer technology; it just gives customers what they want." This includes special products, such as phone accessories and unique products for special market segments. Like many companies, Nokia is faced with the challenge of constantly providing better features at increasingly lower prices. It does this by carefully crafting its marketing to meet local tastes and appeal to consumer segments, leaving the responsibility of large-scale innovation to its competitors.[9] Eli Lilly, on the other hand, invests heavily in research and development to be a leader in product technology. Currently the leader in protein therapeutic products, Eli Lilly has a five-year plan to spend $70 million to create new medicines from proteins.[10]

People Systems   The procedures that provide the human connection between companies and consumers are called people systems. Jan Carlzon from Scandinavian Airlines said the "moment of truth" occurs each time an employee has contact with a customer. He meant that encounter results in either a good or bad impression being formed. Therefore, Carlzon invested in employee training to ensure that the moment of truth resulted in a positive experience for customers. He pulled his company into a leadership position by using people systems that provide outstanding customer service.

The Walt Disney Company has always placed high value on its team of employees. Walt once said: "The whole thing here is the organization. Whatever we accomplish belongs to our entire group, a tribute to our combined effort. I feel that there is no door with which the kind of talent we have cannot be opened." His successor, Michael Eisner, updated those sentiments: "The Disney name—and the image it conveys—is one of our greatest assets, second only to the people who have contributed their talents and dreams toward the achievement of the goals we have set for ourselves."[11]

The importance of Disney's employees is reflected in the organization's retail operation. To foster a spirit of teamwork, employees are called *cast members*. On the retail floor, they are *on stage*; in the storeroom they are *backstage*. Customers are *guests*. Such role-playing helps employees keep the desired goal in mind: Exceed guests' expectations.[12]

Two companies often cited for excellent people systems are ARAMARK, with 140,000 employees, and UPS, with nearly 300,000 employees, both of whom have extensive contact with customers and their customers' customers. Andersen Consulting, a company that provides computer information systems for a broad range of clients, also has developed a core competency in people systems. After an elaborate centralized recruiting process, every Andersen employee who may potentially have contact with clients receives training aimed at minimizing any personality conflict. Personnel policies, operating procedures, and consulting approaches are designed in such a way that a large number of consultants can be mobilized rapidly, around the world, to work inside client organizations. This provides both efficiency and speed of operations.

Information Systems An exceptional information system can be a core competency. Historically, companies were located close to their customers, so information about them was easy to obtain firsthand. Even executives talked directly with customers. Today, the situation is vastly different because of the increasing diversity of products, customers, and competitors. Especially important in global marketing, information processing technologies put vast amounts of data at our fingertips rapidly. Companies that don't possess this core competency will be at a dramatic competitive disadvantage.

FedEx has satellite technology that enables it to track packages instantaneously. Route drivers equipped with scanning devices provide information on exactly when a package is picked up or delivered. If you want to know where your package is, simply get on the Web and go to the FedEx home page. This information benefits not only the customer but also FedEx. Management teams determine what types of services are used most often, which destinations are most common, where more drivers may be needed, and so forth.

Basing the marketing strategy on core competency gives companies the longer-term flexibility required for sustained leadership. Technological advances can be shared throughout the company. SBUs should be treated as relatively temporary reservoirs of competencies that may be phased in, phased out, or adjusted radically in accord with strategic marketing conditions. According to Prahalad and Hamel, noted educators, "The real sources of advantage are to be found in management's ability to consolidate corporate-wide technologies and production skills into competencies that empower the individual business to adapt quickly to changing opportunities."[13]

THE STRATEGIC MARKETING PLAN

As we have mentioned, implementing the marketing concept is the responsibility of everyone in the organization. Consequently, many people are involved in developing and executing strategic marketing plans. Marketing isn't conducted only within a marketing department. As noted scholar and business consultant Frederick Webster, Jr., says: "Everyone in the firm must be charged with responsibility for understanding customers and contributing to developing and delivering value to them."[14] Marketing is so pervasive in customer-focused, competitively driven companies that it's often carried out in cooperation with marketers by teams from diverse areas of the firm, such as accounting, finance, engineering, and manufacturing.

THE PLANNING TEAM

Cross-functional planning team
Employees from several areas responsible for developing the company's strategic marketing plan.

There cannot be a strategic marketing plan unless someone produces it. In the past, the planning process included only marketing personnel. Today, strong marketers generally assemble a **cross-functional planning team.** This team works together with a total understanding of the market and the organization's capabilities. Just as relationships with stakeholders outside the company are important, so are internal relationships. Since each member of the planning team brings a unique perspective, these people must bring all parts of the picture together. Figure 4-8 gives each person's functional area and a short description of his or her main responsibility.

TITLE		RESPONSIBILITY
Marketing	→	Development of strategic plan and team leader
Engineering	→	Technological product development
Manufacturing	→	Efficient manufacturing
Finance	→	Financial modeling of strategies
Marketing Intelligence	→	Estimate competitor strengths, vulnerabilities
Marketing Research	→	Customer and consumer requirements
Sales	→	Potential sales strategies
Promotion & Advertising	→	Support program development
Procurement	→	Available supply partners and costs
Human Resources	→	Union and employee relations
Logistics	→	Distribution systems approaches
Accounting	→	Analysis of cost data

Figure 4-8 A Cross-Functional Strategic Planning Team

WHAT IS STRATEGY?

Before we talk about strategic marketing plans, we need to discuss one of the most overused and misused terms in business. The military defines *strategy* as "the art of meeting the enemy in battle under advantageous conditions." Although there are several "correct" definitions of strategy, we will use the following: A **strategy** is the development and/or deployment of resources with the intent of accomplishing goals and objectives in competitive arenas. Because companies have limited resources, executives must determine how best to use them to accomplish organizational goals. Note that "competitive arena" implies the presence of competitors. They are striving to achieve their own goals, perhaps the same ones set by your company. Certainly, their actions affect your ability to achieve your goals. Japanese companies tend to be acutely aware of competitors. Consider Honda's public statement, "*Yamaha No Tsubusu*"—"We will crush, squash, and slaughter Yamaha." But beating competitors with the intent of hurting them is not really what strategy is all about. The idea is to win out by serving customers better—by connecting better—through relationships and technology, with attention to diversity, globally and ethically.

Strategy is not just about meeting competitors fact to face. It's also about seizing the moment to create change in a timely manner. Hang around any group of planners and you're sure to hear someone refer to the strategic window. Derek Abell, noted business strategist, coined the term **strategic window** to describe the moment when requirements of the market and competencies of the firm fit together to create a significant opportunity.[15] Now, more than ever, the strategic window is important. Products and technologies are changing so rapidly that organizations late to introduce advances are likely to spend millions in product development only to see it go down the drain. Competitors who get there first will obtain the sales, while the late product sits on the shelf.

For example, in 1996, the U.S. Federal Communications Commission (FCC) took actions that allow television broadcasters to transmit programs using digital signals, a new technology that provides a sharper image. Both it and the existing analog technology are permitted for 15 years, at which point analog transmissions will be stopped.[16] Manufacturers know that consumers will have to purchase television sets that can handle the digital signals. Current sets won't work 15 years from now. This began a scramble among manufacturers to be among the first to market the digital sets. Savvy marketers know that the strategic window will be open for a relatively short period as consumers begin to replace their televisions.

Strategy
The development and/or deployment of resources with the intent of accomplishing goals and objectives in a competitive arena.

Strategic window
The time during which market needs and the competencies of the firm fit together to create a significant opportunity.

Low-cost strategy
Strategy whose objective is to be the low-cost leader, thereby allowing the company to have higher margins than competitors and pass some savings on to customers through lower prices. Works through efficiency.

Differentiation strategy
Strategy based on delivering customer value in a way that clearly distinguishes the product from competitors. Works through effectiveness.

Sustainable competitive advantage
The cost position or superior value in a product that competitors cannot easily duplicate or surpass.

Even though strategic windows are open only for a short time, the objective is to create a sustainable strategy. Two generic approaches are a low-cost strategy and a differentiation strategy. **Low-cost strategy** focuses on winning through efficiency. The objective is to be the cost leader, which allows the company to have higher margins than competitors and to pass some savings on to customers through lower prices. There are many ways to gain a favorable cost position:

- *Process technology.* Invent a low-cost way to create and deliver a product.
- *Product design.* Create a product that provides the same level of functionality with lower cost, often through new materials or miniaturization.
- *Consolidation of the value chain.* Combine several steps in the value chain into one.
- *Low-cost suppliers.* Lower costs by purchasing materials and other inputs more cheaply.
- *Location.* Put facilities in low-wage areas or nearer markets to lower distribution costs.
- *Economies of scale and scope.* Produce more and market in a larger area so costs are spread over more units and customers.[17]

A **differentiation strategy** involves delivering customer value in a way that clearly distinguishes the product from its competitors. Differentiation works through effectiveness. It is usually achieved by giving superior benefits or reducing customer cost rather than price. There are several ways to achieve differentiation.

- *New functional capabilities.* Create products that do new things.
- *Improved performance.* Make products that work better, have less maintenance, or are cheaper to operate.
- *Product tailoring.* Make products that more closely suit the needs of select groups.
- *Mass customization.* Use a process that creates products precisely to the specifications of individual customers.

These various strategies are meant to create sustainable competitive advantages for the company. **Sustainable competitive advantage** is the cost position or superior value in a product that competitors cannot easily duplicate or surpass. Once it is attained, competitors gen-

Bailey, Banks, and Biddle uses a low-cost strategy for its Swiss Army brand watches.

erally try to copy it or develop their own advantages. Organizations that create sustainable advantages have less volatility and better long-run performance.

COMPONENTS OF THE STRATEGIC MARKETING PLAN

Guided by the corporate vision, the strategic marketing plan essentially describes how to accomplish that vision. Keep in mind that many organizations are complex and may have many strategic marketing plans. Similar planning steps are used for the entire company or for an SBU within a company. Delphi, a General Motors division that designs auto components, has one strategic marketing plan for the division and additional ones for each SBU: engine systems, exteriors, interiors, and chassis. Each plan has a similar structure.

The planning team has to address several areas: objectives, situation analysis, target markets, positioning, and integration of the marketing mix. The first step is to state the objectives the business will pursue and the specific goals it expects to obtain. The second step usually is a situation analysis, which describes the current business environment and how well the company will be able to compete in it. The third step is to determine target markets, or which customers the organization plans to serve. The fourth step is to decide positioning relative to competitors, that is, the image the organization wants customers to have about it and its products. The fifth step is to develop plans for each aspect of the marketing mix and integrate these into the overall strategic plan. We will discuss each step in detail following this logical order, but as actual plans are developed, the various steps usually interact with one another. For example, objectives are stated first but may later be changed to reflect information uncovered during the situation analysis. Finally, like a baseball pitch, a good strategic marketing plan needs follow-through, or control measures that provide feedback on how well the plan is working.

Objectives   The strategic marketing plan must support the business definition laid out in the organization's vision. For example, Delphi defines its business as personal transportation. One of its SBUs supplies steering mechanisms for vehicles. Today that SBU manufactures mechanical and hydraulic systems, but because it is moving toward electronic and computerized systems, it is in the business of directional control. Another SBU is in the vision business— headlamps—but is researching other technologies, such as radar, infrared, and satellite positioning. Although each SBU has a separate strategic marketing plan, all contribute to Delphi's business definition of personal transportation.

Since the objectives are an outgrowth of the vision, they tend to be stated up front. But remember, they must take into account all of the remaining parts of the plan as well. Companies usually set objectives in terms of desired profit, market share, or total sales. Profit is the most common choice and may be stated in various ways, such as return on investment, cash flow (amount of cash returned to the business), or profit margins. Market share refers to a proportion relative to competitors that the company captures: the percentage of customers within a given market, the percentage of dollars spent on similar products, or the percentage of all similar product units that are sold (unit sales). Finally, businesses determine a total sales objective, defined as either a dollar amount or a product quantity sold. Most organizations state objectives in one of these ways, but they may add others: number of loyal customers, customer retention rates, and customer satisfaction scores.

A company's market share, profit, and sales objectives are important because managers from various functional areas (such as production and distribution) often base their activities on them. Falling far short of objectives can spell disaster. The objectives stated up front usually are reviewed when the entire plan is completed and adjustments may be made. This makes sense, since implementing a realistic plan is important.

Often, it's appropriate to state very specific objectives, such as "44 percent market share by 2000." Certain ARAMARK divisions intend to increase sales by 10 percent annually for the next five years, called the 10-5 objective. In other cases, objectives may reflect customer satisfaction goals such as "99 percent satisfaction rating by 1999" or "90 percent customer retention through the next four years."

Notice that objectives always provide a time frame and must be verifiable. Verifiable means that it will be possible to determine precisely whether the objective has been met or not. You will see why this is important when we talk later about the marketing control process.

Situation Analysis   All marketing activities required to understand the marketing environment, customer needs and wants, and the competition are examined in the situation analysis. This analysis predicts market conditions for the period that the strategic marketing plan is in effect. If the plan extends through 2005, for example, then predictions should be made up to that time. Developing possible scenarios generally requires bringing together data and expertise from different parts of the company to provide an accurate picture.

The analysis can be very elaborate or fairly simple, depending on the circumstances. At a minimum, it should give the planning team a general idea about the future, including potential size of the market, types of customers, competitors, technology, channels of distribution, economic conditions, governmental regulations, and the resources the company will have at its disposal, both globally and in individual countries. Mike McGorrin, vice president of marketing at Children's World, describes the major forces that affect his organization.

> Children's World Learning Centers' performance is influenced by demographic trends (e.g., birth rate, number of dual income families, number of single-parent families, delayed child-bearing resulting in more disposable income), economic variables (e.g., new job creation and unemployment), parents' expectations/attitudinal factors (e.g., families' preferences for "socialization" and "academic readiness" for their children), competitive activity (e.g., pricing, advertising, promotion and new center development strategies), the public sector (e.g., public elementary school programs, public grants criteria, etc.), the development of new technology (e.g., availability of new computer hardware and software applications which improve our ability to communicate within our organization, etc.).

In order to develop a competitive marketing plan that will succeed, Children's World personnel examine each of these factors and determine their potential influence on the organization. In fact, McGorrin adds, "effective business strategies are rooted in a 'market-driven' mindset. Our new services, pricing, promotions, creative and targeting strategies have all been highly influenced by the marketplace." In other words, Children's World builds effective strategies because it keeps in mind the market forces at work.

As a final step in the situation analysis, the planning team must determine how well the company's skills and resources match the predicted market opportunities. This is typically called a **SWOT analysis,** which is military jargon for Strengths, Weaknesses, Opportunities, *and* Threats. An example is shown in Figure 4-9. Strengths and weaknesses are defined by such measures as market share, number of loyal customers, level of customer satisfaction, and rate of product introduction success. Strengths describe the unique resources or circumstances that can be used to take advantage of opportunities. Weaknesses suggest aspects of the organization or product that need improvement or, if that is not possible, ways to minimize any negative effects. The opportunities portion proposes advances that can be made in new or existing markets and identifies areas in which competitive advantages can be gained. The threats section describes how the competition, new technology, the business environment, or government possibly may impede the company's development.

Companies are constrained by their weaknesses. For example, Westinghouse has been hampered in building its defense business because it lacks the capital to fund product development. Companies are also vulnerable to threats. When the government eliminated the use of certain environmentally hazardous resins in the manufacture of recreational boats, irate customers complained that colors faded in the sun. Many stopped purchasing designer-style boats for that reason. White didn't fade, but the lack of color reduced much of the excitement

SWOT analysis

An analysis of strengths, weaknesses, opportunities, and threats to determine how well the company's skills and resources match the predicted market opportunities.

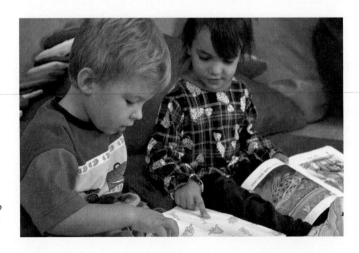

Children's World Learning Center's vision is "translated" into outstanding learning environments for children.

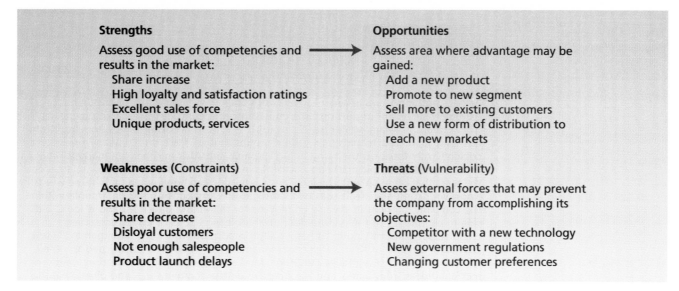

Strengths	Opportunities
Assess good use of competencies and results in the market:	Assess area where advantage may be gained:
Share increase	Add a new product
High loyalty and satisfaction ratings	Promote to new segment
Excellent sales force	Sell more to existing customers
Unique products, services	Use a new form of distribution to reach new markets
Weaknesses (Constraints)	**Threats** (Vulnerability)
Assess poor use of competencies and results in the market:	Assess external forces that may prevent the company from accomplishing its objectives:
Share decrease	Competitor with a new technology
Disloyal customers	New government regulations
Not enough salespeople	Changing customer preferences
Product launch delays	

Figure 4-9 An Example of SWOT Analysis

of new models and designs. Today, technological breakthroughs in environmentally friendly but stable colors have eliminated this threat.

Target Marketing   Once the situation analysis is complete, the planning team determines the characteristics of customer groups on whom to focus attention. Businesses cannot be "all things to all people"; given their competencies, they must choose which segments have the greatest potential. **Target marketing** is the process of selecting which market segments the firm will emphasize in attempts to satisfy customers better than its competitors. In August 1996, Ford released its first full-size sport utility vehicle, the Expedition. Ford specifically aimed at winning customers from GM's client base. Until that time, GM owned this market with its Tahoe, Suburban, and Blazer lines. Vice president of Ford Truck, Jim Englehart, says: "The Ford Expedition boasts a roomier interior, better fuel economy, wider back doors, and an optional third-row seat not available in the Tahoe." With these options, Ford is attempting to satisfy the customer better than its rival.[18] Another example is Kraft, which actively targets ethnic communities, as discussed in the diversity feature.

> **Target marketing**
> The process of selecting which market segments the organization will emphasize in attempts to satisfy customers better than its competitors.

Positioning   Planning teams often decide to pursue different positioning strategies with different target market segments. **Positioning**, as you recall, refers to creating a perception in the minds of consumers about the company and/or its products relative to competitors. A common word for positioning is image, often evoked by the brand name. For example, the Ralph Lauren Company wants to convey an image of high quality and status. If consumers see the company that way, then the marketing team has been successful in its positioning efforts.

> **Positioning**
> Creating an image or perception in the minds of consumers about the organization or its products relative to the competition.

In today's competitive business world, positioning is extremely important. "Everyone is after everyone's business. The mind of your customer or prospect is the battleground and that's where you win or lose," says Jack Trout, author of numerous marketing books and president of Trout & Partners, Ltd. According to him, "just as each product needs to be positioned in the mind [of consumers] against competitors, so does a company need to be positioned. Customers want to know where you're going. So do your employees."

MARKETING MIX PLANS AND THE MARKETING CONTROL PROCESS

Once the desired positioning is established, the marketing mix—product, place, promotion, and price—must be integrated to make the strategy happen. Taken alone, each mix element does not represent a strategy. A strategy combines all the mix elements to create a unified effect on customers in the market.

There are numerous excellent examples of companies that have integrated all elements of the marketing mix into an effective strategy. Disney offers multiple products—amusement parks, MGM Studios, Epcot Center, Blizzard Beach, Discovery Island, and others. Each pro-

CONNECTING WITH DIVERSITY

KRAFT FOODS: *SU COCINA ES NUESTRA COCINA*

Perhaps nothing seems as American as Kraft's Cheez Whiz, yet Kraft Foods USA has been extremely successful in putting its products into the pantries of Hispanic Americans—from Cubans in Miami to Puerto Ricans in New York to Mexicans in Los Angeles. Kraft has long marketed to different ethnic groups, but in 1992 the company realized it couldn't truly focus on the burgeoning Hispanic and African-American markets unless it centralized all ethnic marketing activities in one department. Luis Nieto, Jr., headed the team that came up with the idea, and his mission can be summed up in three words: Know your consumer. Kraft uses two strategies to carry out this mission: It looks within the company, tapping its diverse employees for marketing direction, and it looks outside to capture up-to-the-minute data on the buying habits of ethnic consumers.

"Diverse cultural input is especially important for food companies," says C. L. Reid, director of Kraft's Diversity Management. "Food is so closely tied to ethnicity and culture . . . Essentially, our Ethnic Marketing people solicit advertising and promotional ideas from blacks and Hispanics inside the company . . . and direct them to the brand groups, who implement them with the sales force, who in turn execute them in specific markets." One example is the company's annual presence at Calle Ocho in Miami's "Little Havana," billed as the biggest block party in the world. With the theme of *Su Cocina es Nuestra Cocina* ("Your Kitchen is Our Kitchen"), Kraft sponsors on-site food preparation by one of Miami's premier Latino chefs, who cooks up savory items using Kraft ingredients.

Of the $15 million Kraft has invested in targeting the Hispanic market, most money goes to ongoing marketing programs. Some capitalize on what the company already knows about the Hispanic consumer. For instance, with data from Strategy Research Corporation, Kraft learned that Hispanics consume twice as many gelatin products as caucasians and African Americans, so it markets Jell-O aggressively through television ads and samples at events. Other programs seek to introduce Hispanics to Kraft products not traditional in their culture, such as macaroni and cheese. Yet others introduce new products developed specifically for Hispanics, such as mango-flavored Tang.

With so much invested in these targeted marketing programs, it's crucial that the company be able to track the results. Until recently, there was a serious lack of data on Hispanic buying habits, but Kraft's Nieto came up with a remedy. The company pioneered with market researcher A. C. Nielsen to create a store scanner system. "What the Nielsen data does," says Nieto, "is give us essentially the same kind of information we have for the general market." For six key Hispanic markets, based on the Nielsen sample, "we're able to read store volume and share results for all our key categories in what we describe as a sample of key stores." The scanner system promises to push Kraft's ethnic marketing into what Nieto calls "the results-driven phase," yet he isn't content to stop there. The next step will be to gather information on the missing piece of the puzzle: individual Hispanic households.

Sources: "Opening Doors to Ethnic Category Management," *Progressive Grocer*, May 1996, pp. 124–125; Becky Ebenkamp and Gerry Khermouch, "Why Major Marketers are Latin Lovers," *Brandweek*, August 5, 1996, pp. 20–24; and C. L. Reid, "The Advantages of Taking a Proactive Approach to Diversity," *Executive Speeches*, October-November 1994, pp. 26–28.

vides a high-quality experience, whether for vacations, weddings, or business meetings. And new products are constantly added, closely related to current consumer lifestyles. Disney carefully chooses theme park locations (place) that are easily accessible to consumers. It also makes information about its products readily available through Web sites and thousands of travel agents around the world. The variety of pricing options—deluxe, moderate, or economy—makes it easy for customers from all walks of life to purchase. And Disney takes care to promote its products to a variety of customers. Some are aimed directly at children, others at young singles, yet others at married couples whose children have left home. This communicates to consumers that Disney parks are for everyone. Clearly, the integrated strategy is paying off: Disney's earnings in 1997 increased by 6 percent to reach $22.5 billion.[19]

A plan is needed for each part of the company's marketing mix: product, place, promotion and price. The plan for each element often is developed within specific functional areas of marketing, such as the pricing department. In some cases, all these plans are combined into one. Each marketing mix element will be covered in depth in future chapters, but a brief discussion of the issues is provided here. Figure 4-10 illustrates some of the questions marketers face when developing plans for each aspect of the marketing mix. There are many, many more, some of which will be covered in later chapters.

Disney's team of employees are "cast members" while customers are "guests."

Each plan for an element of the marketing mix deals with both strategies and tactics. For example, the decision to enter a new product area or distribution channel is strategic. Changes to an existing product or the addition of a new retailer in distribution are tactical. Tactics are used to achieve strategies. Strategies are long term and broad in scope; **tactics** are short-term,

Tactics
Short-term actions and reactions to specific market conditions through which companies pursue their strategy.

Marketing Mix Element	Types of Decisions
Product/Service	What new products/services should we introduce?
	Which ones should we drop?
	What are our objectives with each product or service?
	Are any new technologies available to improve our product/service?
	What type of service do our customers expect or desire?
	What policies should we implement in terms of product returns, spare parts, or repairs?
Place	Where do our customers shop? Should our product/service be available at all these places or just a few?
	Should we sell directly to our customers or through middlemen, such as retailers, wholesalers, or dealers?
	How should we ship the product—by rail, truck, air, ship, or others?
	How should we handle customer complaints?
Promotion	What are our promotion objectives? Are we trying to create awareness, encourage purchases, or others?
	What medium should we use: television or radio advertising, coupons, free trials, personal selling, public relations campaign, or a combination of these?
Price	What type of message do we want to send out? What is our overall pricing philosophy? Do we want to exceed, meet or under price our competitors?
	Is our price consistent with the amount of value we deliver to our customers?
	Should we change our prices? How will this affect demand for our product or service?
	Do our prices allow the organization to make a profit and invest in improved performance?

Figure 4-10 **Examples of Marketing Mix Decisions**

well-defined actions suited to specific market conditions. Strategies describe how we will compete to serve customers, while tactics describe who will do what and when. Duane Larson, president of Children's World Learning Centers, says: "Selling a product or service today is like a war, even in the child care arena. Those armies with the best tactical plan will win more frequently than those without one. Lose enough battles and you won't have to wait for your competitors to put you out of business because the buying public will have already done that."[20]

Companies usually employ several tactics to accomplish a given strategy. McDonald's® strategy is to provide high-quality, moderately priced food and friendly, fast service to families. One tactic is to have a miniplayground at some of its restaurants. Another is colorful packaging of children's meals and personal appearances by the popular Ronald McDonald clown. Subway, which targets a more adult audience, pursues a strategy of preparing customized sandwiches quickly. Their assembly-line tactic allows patrons to build their own. Another tactic is to preassemble the meat element of the sandwich, leaving only the toppings to be added, which speeds the process but maintains patron selection. It would be tactically inconsistent for McDonald's® to add gourmet items to its menu or for Subway to offer complicated meals.

PRODUCT PLANS

A company may sell physical goods (such as automobiles or textbooks) or intangible services (a college education, legal counsel, or health care). Many companies sell both. In the business world, the word *product* has come to mean services as well as physical goods, and when marketers refer to product decisions, they are also referring to services. Unless specified otherwise, we shall use *product* to mean either goods or services. A **product** is any physical object, service, idea, person, event, place or organization offered to satisfy consumers' needs and wants.

Product decisions are critical for most companies and they are among the most difficult to make. Marketers must help determine which products or product lines to develop and which ones to drop. A **product line** consists of several closely related products marketed by an organization. For example, Nabisco offers many different types of snack foods, including Oreos, Fig Newtons, Chips Ahoy!, and Ritz crackers; each of these is a separate product line. Items are constantly being added, such as Nabisco's Ritz Bitz crackers, a product designed to fulfill customer demand for a smaller snack.

Marketers must take consumers into account when making product decisions. Ford did an extremely good job of accommodating consumer requests in 1996 when it redesigned the Taurus and its sister car, the Mercury Sable. The company had been flooded with customer complaints about the legibility, size, and accessibility of instrument panel controls. Ford employed a team of stylists, ergonomists, and engineers to create a driver-friendly dashboard that would be easier to see and to reach as well as aesthetically pleasing. According to Ford, the redesigned instrument panel has been so well received by car buyers that it is being considered for other models. David Hoffmeister, Ford ergonomist, thinks consumer input is very

Product

Any physical object, service, idea, person, event, place, or organization offered to satisfy consumer needs and wants.

Product line

Closely related products marketed by the organization.

More than four million virtual pets have sold in Japan. Marketers hope for the same success in the United States.

important. He notes that conventional wisdom holds that larger knobs or buttons placed close to the driver are superior to buttons farther away and smaller. "But if we followed all of our own rules all the time, we'd probably have a very ugly car and we wouldn't sell a single one, so we're always compromising."[21]

Technological product plans challenge marketers to continuously monitor, assess, and make decisions based on the ever-changing technological environment (and other factors). Technological products are developed, introduced, and dropped rapidly. This requires marketers to make frequent, and sometimes difficult, product decisions. Bandai Ltd. and Tiger Electronics have recently introduced a new product—the virtual pet. The "pets," attached to key chains, range from cats and dogs to chimps and dinosaurs. A menu allows the owner to feed, nurture, and even put the pet to bed at night. Pets that are fed too much and exercised too little will turn fat and lazy, while pets that are ignored may die. In Japan, more than four million have sold. Product plans and decisions will play an important role for marketers who are hoping for the same success in the United States.[22]

PLACE PLANS

Physical distribution is the movement of finished products through channels of distribution to customers. It involves getting the right product, in the right condition, to the right customer, at the right time, for the minimum cost. This is one of the fastest growing and most important areas of marketing. U.S. companies spend more than $700 billion annually on logistics, and that amount is expected to grow.[23] The tremendous growth in this industry can be attributed to the rapid increase of new technologies, such as the Internet. The Internet offers several advantages over older technologies. These include speed, accuracy, and the ability of suppliers and distributors to share information.[24]

Physical distribution decisions can greatly affect the profitability of the company. For example, excess inventory in the channel increases storage costs. It is marketing's job to help ensure that an optimal amount of inventory moves through the channel. Of course, some companies are more successful at this than others. Procter & Gamble does an excellent job of inventory control through the Internet. For example, it uses the Internet to track how many Pampers Wal-Mart sells daily. When an outlet's stock gets low, more diapers are shipped from the factory. This system helps Procter & Gamble maintain optimum inventory with minimum inventory levels in the channel.[25]

Distribution channels are the set of independent organizations involved in making the product available for purchase. A channel describes the route a product follows as it moves from manufacturer to consumers. First, marketers must determine where target customers shop: malls, shopping centers, downtown areas, discount outlets, drive-thrus, or at home via mail or telephone. People also shop in many different types of stores: supermarkets, merchandise marts, hyperstores, specialty shops, and outdoor markets. In each area of the world, consumer shopping patterns are unique. Parisians buy bread baked daily at small shops located throughout the city. The Japanese prefer to purchase fresh fish, caught within hours of eating, from small neighborhood retailers. Suburban Americans usually shop once a week and freeze many items for use days or even weeks later. They like one-stop supermarkets and are willing to drive to them. Obviously, it's important for marketers to know where consumers prefer to shop for the types of products or services that their company makes.

PROMOTION PLANS

The third element of the marketing mix, promotion, provides information about a company's product or service in an effort to encourage purchase. Media advertising, direct mail, coupons and samples, personal selling, or public relations may be used. Many companies employ several forms simultaneously. Broadway shows, once only promoted in theater directories, use several forms of promotion today. Marketing a Broadway show has taken on a new importance. Today ads appear on water towers and subways, while many consumers are reached by direct mail. Jeffrey Seller, a producer of the Broadway show *Rent*, says "You have to get the word into the consciousness of many different people and that involves many different outlets, like magazines, radio, outdoor, print, publicity." *Rent* used a unique promotional strategy. A major subway advertising campaign was designed to reach teenagers and consumers in their 20s. This market was considered the "non-Broadway-going public." Print ads explained the show's story line and how to purchase tickets. Radio spots were also used on the integrated marketing mix plan to reach consumers.[26]

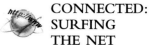

CONNECTED: SURFING THE NET

Bandai's Tamagotchi: www.bandai.com

Tiger Electronics: www.tigertoys.com

Here's your chance to find out what owning a virtual pet is all about. Keep up with the product plans of Bandai and Tiger Electronics by visiting their Web sites.

Physical distribution
The movement of finished products through channels of distribution to customers.

Distribution channel
A set of independent organizations involved in making the product available for purchase.

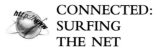

CONNECTED: SURFING THE NET

www.broadway.org

Marketing Broadway has taken on a new importance as plays and musicals gain new audiences. Learn more by visiting The League of American Theaters and Producer's Web site.

PRICING PLANS

When Reebok aerobic shoes were first introduced into the women's market segment, demand was disappointing. The product was priced incorrectly, in this case too low. When prices were raised, demand increased. Prices send strong signals to buyers. Consumers equate low price with poor quality, while higher prices signal unique and positive characteristics as well as higher quality. Raising price to increase demand is not unusual. Porsche did it in the United States. Ralph Lauren found it worked with men's and women's clothing. The perfume industry has used this technique since its inception.

In other cases, price increases can be devastating to sales volume. Think about the airline industry, with many different providers offering service between the same cities. What do you think would happen to ticket sales at United Airlines if it raised its prices above those of Delta or Northwest? Demand would probably start dropping. That's why a price shift in one airline triggers shifts in most others.

THE MARKETING CONTROL PROCESS

Control process
Procedures designed to provide feedback on how well the marketing strategy is working.

Control review meeting
Meeting of members of the planning team to see whether objectives are being met.

Once a strategic marketing plan is implemented, results seldom occur precisely as expected. The **control process** provides feedback on how well the strategy is working. In a typical **control review meeting**, members of the planning team assemble to see whether objectives are being met. As described in Figure 4-11, the team reviews the original objectives, including sales volume projections, order quantities, customer loyalty rates, customer satisfaction rates, and market share projections. These numbers for each target market segment and in total are compared to actual results. This procedure is often called *metrics,* which connotes metering what actually happened. This process gives a picture of what has occurred.

By comparing actual results to the stated objectives, the team can assess the organization's performance. During these reviews, trends can be spotted. For example, sales and market share may be higher than expected because competitors were late in launching a new product, or sales may be low because the company's price was too high in relation to competitors. If it's not apparent what caused the results, additional marketing research may be needed.

Next, the team may decide to adjust objectives or plans. If results are strong, then objectives may be elevated. If not, objectives can be lowered, but the team usually resists this step because it can be viewed as a sign of weakness.[27] Adjustments to the plans usually are tactical rather than strategical, done through changes in the marketing mix elements. If a change in overall strategy is required, then a more involved and lengthy process starts. Sometimes, teams go back to ground zero and start fresh. In either case, time is critical. One executive says that adjusting plans and taking action can be "like changing a flat tire on a moving automobile." It happens rapidly in companies that are flexible, efficient, and competitive.

CONNECTING GLOBALLY: ENTERING WORLD MARKETS

Today, you find that global activities are incorporated into planning, just like market segments or products, although sometimes they may be documented separately.

Figure 4-11   The Marketing Control Process: Assessing the Strategic Marketing Plan

Once the domain of a few corporate giants, global marketing is fast becoming a requirement for most companies. Why? First, world markets offer tremendous opportunities. Many foreign market segments are larger and growing more rapidly than segments in the United States. Second, like it or not, U.S. business is no longer safe from global competitors. In comparison with other countries, the United States has few restrictions on foreign entry. Most U.S. companies must deal with some form of global competition, even within local markets. Third, a company intent on becoming an industry leader must operate globally or be placed at a severe competitive disadvantage.

GEOGRAPHIC SCOPE

World trade has skyrocketed in recent years. U.S. exports exceeded $786 billion in 1995,[28] and the U.S. Department of Commerce hopes that figure will surpass $1.2 trillion by 2000.[29] The United States also imports a large amount of foreign goods and services—nearly $892 billion worth.[30] From a planning standpoint, marketers must identify the **geographic scope** of the strategy, which is the extent of a company's international activities. Generally, geographic scope is divided into four categories, as outlined in Figure 4-12.

Geographic scope
The extent of a company's international activities.

International Scope   When a company conducts business in one or a very few foreign countries it has an international scope. Generally, international companies treat foreign business as a supplement to their domestic operations, rather than as a strategic necessity. Yet expansion in even one country can provide useful experience for further global activity at a later date. For example, Forestry Systems, Inc., of Greensboro, North Carolina, began international operations by selling its timber products in Canada and Mexico and is now considering additional markets in South America.[31]

Regional Scope   Operations in several adjacent countries give a company regional scope. In essence, regional companies are competing within one large market that crosses national borders, and generally only in one area of the world. Regional operations tend to be efficient because the markets are close together. The benefits of large market size can be combined with localized production and distribution to provide a viable strategy. This is the approach of Starbucks Corporation, the specialty coffee chain, as it expands outside the United States. The company has opened its first Pacific Rim outlet in Tokyo and from there, hopes to expand into other parts of the Asian-Pacific region, including Singapore, Hong Kong, Taiwan, and Indonesia. According to Kathie Lindemann, director of international operations for Starbucks, "Asia . . . is full of emerging markets; consumers' disposable income is increasing as their countries' economies grow. Most of all, people are open to Western lifestyles."[32]

Multinational Scope   When companies operate in several countries around the world, their scope is multinational. The markets are not concentrated in one region. For example, Westinghouse sells satellite telephones to Mexico and Australia; nuclear power plants to the Czech Republic, Spain, and Taiwan; and defense-related equipment within North America. It markets many other products to many other countries as well. Multinational companies carefully pick their target areas and choose not to enter many countries. They tend to operate differently within each area of the world.

Global Scope   Operations in nearly all countries around the world constitute a global scope. Kenichi Ohmae, global consultant for McKinsey & Company, describes global scope with the mental image of hovering like a satellite over the earth.[33] Global businesses develop totally integrated strategies that maximize competitiveness worldwide over the long term. The Quaker

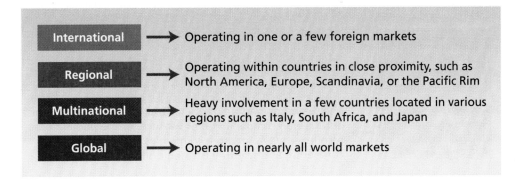

Figure 4-12   Geographic Scope

Oats Company has committed to this type of integrated global strategy. Its Quaker International Branding Program is designed to ensure that the Quaker name means "healthy," no matter where you live. The company has a basic advertising, packaging, and promotion plan that is tailored to meet local conditions. This helps keep the Quaker image consistent around the globe. The approach seems to be working, as Quaker's international business has surpassed $6 billion.[34]

A global market reaches nearly all countries. Differences among market areas are recognized, but so are similarities, so that similar segments of buyers within the various regions can be targeted. This helps marketers achieve vast economies of scale, especially in advertising, packaging, and distribution. Consider Gillette, which has "won the loyalty of 700 million shavers in the world." About 70 percent of Gillette's sales and profits come from a global market in 200 countries. The company identified similar segments of buyers and successfully markets its razors to these clusters.[35]

Global marketing is based on the notion that consumers around the world are growing more alike and that modern technology has created a degree of commonality. Travel and communication have exposed more and more people to the same types of goods and services. Global companies appreciate the differences in consumer preferences, shopping behavior, cultural institutions, and promotional media, but they believe that these preferences and practices can and will become more similar.[36]

STRATEGIES FOR FOREIGN MARKET ENTRY

There are several different approaches for entering and developing markets. Small companies may use only one or two methods, while larger companies may use several simultaneously. Figure 4-13 outlines the most important approaches.

Exporting and Importing   Exporting and importing are the least risky and most common forms of international marketing. **Exporting** sends domestically manufactured products into foreign countries for resale. **Importing** brings products from foreign countries for resale within the home market, usually as part of another product. Exporting and importing are relatively easy ways to enter foreign trade because the investment is lower than for most other methods. In addition, most governments offer support and expertise to help domestic companies with these activities.

Because foreign trade can involve many complicated details, most firms use **export and import intermediaries**, which are firms with expertise in this area. There are two types. **Indirect export intermediaries** are located in the domestic market and help send products abroad. They specialize in knowledge about foreign customs, regulations affecting businesses and products, laws, and market conditions. **Direct export intermediaries** are located in the foreign market. Since they are very familiar with the local business environment, they can help clients in special ways, such as unique government contacts. Intermediaries can be very

Exporting
Sending products to a foreign country for sale.

Importing
Receiving products from a foreign country.

Export intermediary
Domestic or foreign firm that assists with exporting activity.

Import intermediary
Firm set up to help guide importing actions.

Figure 4-13   Approaches for Entering and Building Foreign Markets

beneficial because they assume many of the risks involved with distribution. At the same time, the exporting company must give up a significant amount of control over how its product is distributed.

Trading companies are large intermediaries that facilitate the movement of goods in and out of countries. Hall and Hall Global Trading, located in Colorado Springs, facilitates the sale of a variety of goods to more than 45 countries around the world ranging from chicken to Egypt, sugar to Russia, and blue jeans to just about anywhere.[37]

Foreign Licensing and Franchising   **Foreign licensing** assigns the rights to a patent, trademark, or manufacturing process to a foreign company for a fee, often called a royalty. Licensing allows companies to gain entry into a foreign market at almost no cost or risk, but control of the marketing strategy is turned over to the licensee. **Franchising** is a special type of licensing arrangement whereby the marketer provides not only the product, technology, process, and/or trademark but also most of the marketing program. In nearly any major city around the world, you are likely to find McDonald's®, Burger King, and Kentucky Fried Chicken, or Holiday Inn, Hilton, and Marriott. They are there because local entrepreneurs have bought the franchise. Franchising allows companies to maintain marketing control while passing along many of the costs, risks, and responsibilities to the foreign licensees. These often function quite autonomously from the parent company but benefit from being part of a large corporation.

Overseas Marketing and Production   Also called subsidiaries, overseas marketing and production operations are owned by a parent company in foreign countries, whether a small sales office or something more elaborate. A subsidiary operation may simply assemble finished goods or may function as an independent business, responsible for product development, manufacturing, marketing, and so on. For example, General Motors operates assembly plants for automotive components in Mexico, while its German and British subsidiaries produce entire automobiles. Subsidiaries can be very costly to establish and very risky to operate, since the owner is liable for any mishaps. Foreign operations also are subject to a host of

Trading companies
Large intermediaries that facilitate the movement of goods in and out of countries.

Foreign licensing
Assigning the rights to a patent, trademark, or manufacturing process to a foreign company for a fee, often called a royalty.

Franchising
A special type of licensing arrangement whereby the marketer provides not only the product, technology, process, and/or trademark, but also the entire marketing program.

Star Alliance is a network of United Airlines, Air Canada, Lufthansa, SAS, and THAI.

Joint venture

An alliance of two companies who combine resources to provide products and services more cometitively than either could do independently.

circumstances beyond the company's control. For example, several oil companies lost billions of dollars when their Iranian subsidiaries were closed after invasion of Kuwait. The major advantage of a subsidiary is that the parent company retains control and can carry out its own strategy.

Foreign Strategic Alliances   Strategic alliances involve partnering. A **joint venture** occurs when two companies combine resources for a new venture. They are formed to provide products and services more competitively than a single organization could do independently. Typically, a foreign joint venture has one company in each of two countries, but more partners or countries are possible. National laws often require any business to have a certain percentage of domestic ownership. Sony develops many of its innovative computer and communications products through strategic alliances and ventures with companies in the United States.[38] When the Soviet bloc dissolved, joint ventures were formed rapidly as foreign firms attempted to gain access to these markets. Often, the first strategy was to buy ownership, which Volkswagen did in the Czech Republic, for example. The Germans beat out other contenders, like Renault of France, and acquired 31 percent of the Czech auto leader Skoda. Together, Volkswagen and Skoda planned to produce nearly 400,000 autos in 1997.[39]

Global strategic alliances are joint ventures that involve actions taken internationally by two or more companies contributing an agreed amount of resources. The arrangement often resembles a well-funded start-up operation. This approach may be preferred when competition is tough or technology and capital requirements are relatively large for one partner. General Motors has global alliances with Suzuki, Isuzu, and Toyota. Ford has allied with Nissan and Mazda, Chrysler with Mitsubishi and Honda.[40] General Mills created an alliance with

---

 CONNECTED: SURFING THE NET

Kodak

www.kodak.com

THIS CHAPTER'S TECHNOLOGY FEATURE DISCUSSED KODAK'S strategic reinvention. Here is an opportunity for you to learn more about Kodak. Visit its Web site and answer the following questions.

1. In Kodak's annual report you will find the company vision, mission, and values. List them. Discuss several ways Kodak has fulfilled its vision, mission, and values using the Web site as your resource.
2. List Kodak's strategic business units. How are its business units structured? Explain.
3. After exploring Kodak's Web site, products, and services, determine what you think its core competencies are. Explain your choices.
4. Under the "History of Kodak" menu, select and read "Kodak . . . The Company." Which strategy did Kodak use at the firm's beginning, low cost or differentiation? Does it use this same strategy now? Explain.

Kraft Foods

www.kraftfoods.com

KRAFT FOODS HAS BEEN VERY SUCCESSFUL at knowing its customers and developing products to meet the needs of various target markets. In order to expand your thinking about Kraft Foods, visit its Web site and answer the following questions.

1. What market does Kraft appear to be targeting with its Web site? What features does the site offer that may be of particular interest to this segment? How might these features help Kraft build relationships with customers?
2. The Kraft strategy is to provide "good food for busy lives." What are some of the tactics Kraft has implemented recently to accomplish this strategy?
3. Peek inside Kraft's virtual refrigerator and pantry, which you'll find loaded with products. Using the Boston Consulting Group growth-share matrix, select a product that is appropriate for each of the four categories—star, question mark, cash cow, and dog.

Nestlé in Europe, called Cereal Partners Worldwide (CPW), to compete against Kellogg's growing global share. General Mills and Nestlé agreed to pool part of their product lines and distribution system.

A global strategic alliance may be formed between or among companies that compete in some regions of the world but decide to cooperate in others. Toshiba, for example, is allied with a number of U.S. firms in the United States (United Technologies, Apple Computer, Sun Microsystems, Motorola, and National Semiconductor) and European firms in Europe (Olivetti, Seimens, Rhore-Poulenc Ericcson, and SGS-Thomson).[41] Notice that many of these are rivals in various markets, but each works with Toshiba.

Whether its scope of operations is global or local, the company needs in-depth knowledge of its targeted markets in order to shape the strategic plan and meet its goals. In the next chapter we will look at the important role of marketing research in providing needed information for strategic planning and other marketing decisions.

CHAPTER SUMMARY

OBJECTIVE 1: Understand how the strategic marketing planning hierarchy fits together to provide a complete planning system.

Strategic marketing proceeds from a company's vision, to the strategic marketing plan, to the marketing mix plans. The vision describes what the organization is trying to accomplish in the broadest sense. It includes the organization's marketing philosophy. The strategic marketing plan is developed in line with the vision by a cross-functional team representing several business areas, such as manufacturing, accounting, finance, and engineering. The plan describes the company's goals and states how the company will achieve them. Specialists in each component of the marketing mix prepare a plan for that area.

OBJECTIVE 2: Describe the four elements of an organization's vision that provide guidance for all actions.

The vision statement expresses the company's core values, business definition, strategic direction, and strategic infrastructure. Core values reflect the company's beliefs about the types of behavior acceptable from employees and the company as a whole as well as its relationship to employees, customers, and society in general. A business definition describes the contributions a company seeks to make to customers and society. It is important to avoid marketing myopia when developing a mission statement. Marketing myopia occurs when executives focus on the company's products and services rather than on the benefits these provide to consumers. Strategic direction is the desired leadership position of an organization as well as the measures used to chart progress toward reaching that goal. It captures the "essence of winning" and addresses the competitiveness of the organization. A company's strategic infrastructure consists of both strategic business units and core competencies. SBUs can be managed using portfolio planning tools, such as the growth-share matrix or the attractiveness-strength matrix. Core competencies are the unique resources a company develops and employs to create superior customer value. They are the fundamental building blocks of competitive advantage and can be developed in one or more of the following areas: base technologies, process technologies, product technologies, people systems, or information systems.

OBJECTIVE 3: Integrate components of the strategic marketing plan with the vision.

The strategic marketing plan describes how to accomplish the vision for a particular part of the business. It has five components: objectives, situation analysis, target marketing, positioning, and integration of the marketing mix. Objectives are developed in line with the vision and the situation analysis. They state aims regarding profit, market share, and total sales as well as customer satisfaction and loyalty. The situation analysis describes the marketing environment for the period that the plan is in effect. It gives all the information required to estimate possible business scenarios, including market size, customer characteristics, competitors, and technology. A key part of the situation analysis is to examine strengths, weaknesses, opportunities, and threats (SWOT). The target marketing phase of strategic marketing planning focuses the organization on select groups of customers. In the positioning phase, the image of the organization relative to the competition is developed. The final step is to integrate the marketing mix plans to accomplish the overall strategy. It is important to look at the total effect of the marketing mix, rather than a single element, on the market.

OBJECTIVE 4: Understand why elements of the marketing mix must be integrated and outline the steps of the marketing control process.

Plans for each part of the marketing mix are usually developed by specialists in the respective areas. Often a separate plan is created for product, place, promotion, and price, but sometimes these plans are combined. Plans for any of these elements are both strategic and tactical. Strategies are long term and broad in scope, while tactics are short-term actions suited to specific market conditions. Several tactics may be used to carry out a single strategy.

To determine whether the strategic marketing plan is accomplishing the intended objectives, a marketing control process is needed. It has five steps. First, the original performance objectives are reviewed. Second, measures indicate what performance has occurred. Third, performance is evaluated by interpreting the results obtained and looking for any trends. Fourth, it is decided whether actions or objectives should be altered. Fifth, the strategy proceeds as planned or another course is developed and implemented.

OBJECTIVE 5: Identify the four major ways that organizations enter and cultivate global markets.

Organizations enter and cultivate global markets through exporting and importing, foreign licensing and franchising, overseas marketing and manufacturing, and joint ventures and strategic alliances. Exporting involves sending domestically manufactured products into foreign markets. It is usually the low-risk and low-cost way to enter markets. There are many forms of help for companies just getting started in exporting or importing. Foreign licensing and franchising simply assign the rights to a patent, trademark, or process to a foreign company. Overseas marketing and production involves setting up operations in a foreign country. This requires the commitment of direct investment in a foreign country. Strategic alliances and joint ventures involve sharing resources with a partner to enter markets. Often the partner has strong contacts in the country or region where the venture takes place. Joint ventures can simply involve contracts between companies or shared ownership of new organizations. In some cases these can involve huge investments and substantial risks.

REVIEW YOUR UNDERSTANDING

1. What are the elements of the marketing planning hierarchy?
2. What are the components of a vision?
3. What is marketing myopia? How is the company's mission related to myopia?
4. In what ways can strategic business units be structured?
5. What are portfolio planning tools and how are they used?
6. What are core competencies? Give examples of five types.
7. Which people in an organization create the strategic marketing plan?
8. What is the difference between a strategy and a tactic? How do they work together?
9. What are the components of the strategic marketing plan? Describe each.
10. What are the elements of a SWOT analysis?
11. How are mix plans strategic and tactical?
12. What is the marketing control process, and what are its steps?
13. In what four ways can foreign markets be entered? Describe each.

DISCUSSION OF CONCEPTS

1. Define strategy. Define tactics. How is strategy related to tactics? What strategy do you think Coca-Cola is following? What tactics is it using to support this strategy?
2. How are a company's core values, business definition, strategic infrastructure, and strategic direction interrelated? Do you think it is important for a company to develop an explicit statement about each of these?
3. Imagine that the following companies describe their business as shown: (a) Black & Decker: drills and sanders; (b) Sherwin-Williams: paint; (c) Schwinn: bicycles; (d) U.S. Post Office: mail delivery. Do you think these companies are suffering from marketing myopia? How may they better define their business?
4. Why is it important for a company to have a well-defined strategic direction? In your opinion, what may happen to a company that lacks strategic direction?
5. How would you assess the contribution made by each strategic business unit? Do you think it is important for technology to be shared among SBUs? Why or why not?
6. Who should be involved in the development of a strategic marketing plan? Why?
7. What is the purpose of a situation analysis? What type of information should be included?
8. Why do most companies engage in some type of target marketing? Who do you think Nintendo is targeting with its Game Boy product line?

KEY TERMS AND DEFINITIONS

Business definition: Describes the contributions the business makes to customers and society; also called the company mission.

Control process: Procedures designed to provide feedback on how well the marketing strategy is working.

Control review meeting: Meeting of members of the planning team to see whether objectives are being met.

Core competencies: The unique resources a company develops and employs to create superior customer value; the fundamental building blocks of competitive advantage.

Core values: A set of statements describing the type of behavior expected of the company and its employees.

Cross-functional planning team: Employees from several areas responsible for developing the company's strategic marketing plan.

Differentiation strategy: Strategy based on delivering customer value in a way that clearly distinguishes the product from competitors. Works through effectiveness.

Distribution channel: A set of independent organizations involved in making the product available for purchase.

Exporting: Sending products to a foreign country for sale.

Export intermediary: Domestic or foreign firm that assists with exporting activity.

Foreign licensing: Assigning the rights to a patent, trademark, or manufacturing process to a foreign company for a fee, often called a royalty.

Franchising: A special type of licensing arrangement whereby the marketer provides not only the product, technology, process, and/or trademark, but also the entire marketing program.

Geographic scope: The extent of a company's international activities.

Importing: Receiving products from a foreign country.

Import intermediary: Firm set up to help guide importing actions.

Joint venture: An alliance of two companies who combine resources to provide products and services more cometitively than either could do independently.

Low-cost strategy: Strategy whose objective is to be the low-cost leader, thereby allowing the company to have higher margins than competitors and pass some savings on to customers through lower prices. Works through efficiency.

Marketing myopia: A focus on company products rather than on how these benefit consumers.

Physical distribution: The movement of finished products through channels of distribution to customers.

Portfolio planning tools: Tools that measure the contribution each SBU makes to the overall performance of the company.

Positioning: Creating an image or perception in the minds of consumers about the organization or its products relative to the competition.

Product: Any physical object, service, idea, person, event, place, or organization offered to satisfy consumer needs and wants.

Product line: Closely related products marketed by the organization.

Strategic business unit (SBU): A part of the firm that can be managed separately for marketing purposes; it may be a division, a product or product line, a distinct group of customers, or a unique technology.

Strategic direction: The desired leadership position of an organization as well as the measures used to chart progress toward reaching that position.

Strategic infrastructure: The corporate configuration that produces the company's distinctive or core competencies and provides the resources necessary to satisfy customer wants.

Strategic marketing plan: The document describing the company's objectives and how to achieve them in light of competitive activities.

Strategic window: The time during which market needs and the competencies of the firm fit together to create a significant opportunity.

Strategy: The development and/or deployment of resources with the intent of accomplishing goals and objectives in a competitive arena.

Sustainable competitive advantage: The cost position or superior value in a product that competitors cannot easily duplicate or surpass.

SWOT analysis: An analysis of strengths, weaknesses, opportunities, and threats to determine how well the company's skills and resources match the predicted market opportunities.

Tactics: Short-term actions and reactions to specific market conditions through which companies pursue their strategy.

Target marketing: The process of selecting which market segments the organization will emphasize in attempts to satisfy customers better than its competitors.

Trading companies: Large intermediaries that facilitate the movement of goods in and out of countries.

Vision: The desired image of the company in the minds of employees.

REFERENCES

1. The Disney Store recruiting brochure, 1996; Kate Fitzgerald, "License to Sell," *Advertising Age*, February 12, 1996, pp. S1, S40; Matthew S. Scott, "Wonderful World At Disney," *Black Enterprise*, December 1995, pp. 58–64; Rachel Parker, "Disney Finds Upgraded Database System More Agreeable," *Infoworld*, November 13, 1995, p. 94; Patricia A. Scussel, "Disney Tunes Up Catalog Unit," *Catalog Age*, October 1995, p. 6; Wendy Marx, "The Co-Marketing Revolution," *Industry Week*, October 2, 1995, pp. 77–81; George Pitcher, "Disney's Road to Damascus," *Marketing Week*, August 11, 1995, p. 25; Meg Carter, "Disney Shows Its Networking Skills," *Marketing Week*, August 11, 1995, pp. 16–17; and Bill Kelley, "Destination Disney," *Sales and Marketing Management*, July 1995, p. 40.

2. Randall L. Tobias, "Communicating Core Values," *Public Relations Strategist*, Spring 1996, p. 19.

3. Michael Waldholz and Dennis Kneale, "Tylenol's Maker Tries to Regain Good Image in Wake of Tragedy," *Wall Street Journal*, October 8, 1982; "Johnson & Johnson to Scrap all Capsules in its Effort to Save the Brand Name," *Wall Street Journal*, October 8, 1982; "It Could Have Been Anyone," *Wall Street Journal*, October 8, 1982; Michael Waldholz, "Johnson & Johnson Officials Take Steps to End More Killings *Linked* to Tylenol," *Wall Street Journal*, October 4, 1982, p. 16; "Johnson & Johnson Pulls Tylenol Lot from Market in Wake of Five Cyanide Deaths," *Wall Street Journal*, October 1, 1982; "Authorities Say Cyanide-Laced Tylenol Likely Was Planted at Individual Stores," *Wall Street Journal*, October 4, 1982, p. 3; Michael Waldholz, "Johnson & Johnson Can Weather Tylenol Storm—If It Hurries," *Wall Street Journal*, October 5, 1982, p. 22; "Tylenol Containing Strychnine is Found In California as Consumer Fears Mount," *Wall Street Journal*, October 6, 1982, p. 2; "J&J Tries Ads to Revive Sales of Tylenol," *Wall Street Journal*, October 25, 1982, p. 20; Michael Waldholz, "Drop in Johnson & Johnson Shares is Linked to Belief that Fears Over Tylenol Will Linger," *Wall Street Journal*, October 29, 1982; Michael Waldholz, "Tylenol Maker Mounting Campaign to Restore Trust of Doctors, Buyers," *Wall Street Journal*, November 12, 1982, p. 33; Michael Waldholz, "Johnson & Johnson Plans to Reintroduce Tylenol Capsules in More Secure Package," *Wall Street Journal*, November 12, 1982, p. 4; and Michael Waldholz, "Tylenol Regains Most of No. 1 Market Share, Amazing Doomsayers," *Wall Street Journal*, December 24, 1982, p. 1.

4. www.lilly.com, site visited on June 6, 1997.

5. Gary Hamel and C. K. Prahalad, "Strategic Intent," *Harvard Business Review*, May-June 1989, p. 64.

6. "Eli Lilly and Strategic Focus," May 23, 1996, http://www.lilly.com/strategic.html.

7. Don Clark, "Microsoft, Netscape Get Ready to Launch New Browser Battle," *Wall Street Journal Interactive Edition*, June 4, 1997.

8. Richard Gibson, "McDonald's Approaches '96 with Goal of Making Its U.S. Service 'Hassle Free,'" *Wall Street Journal*, December 1995, p. A1.

9. Rahul Jacob, "Nokia Fumbles, But Don't Count It Out," *Fortune*, February 19, 1996, p. 86.

10. William M. Bulkeley, "Eli Lilly Plans to Invest in Unit of Millennium Pharmaceuticals," *Wall Street Journal Interactive Edition*, May 29, 1997.

11. Recruiting brochure for The Disney Store.

12. Ibid.

13. C.K. Prahalad, and Gary Hamel, "The Core Competence of the Corporation," *Harvard Business Review,* May/June 1990, p. 81.

14. Frederick E. Webster, Jr., "The Changing Role of Marketing in the Corporation," *Journal of Marketing*, October 1992, p. 14.

15. Derek F. Abell, "Strategic Windows," *Journal of Marketing*, July 1978, p. 21.

16. Albert R. Karr, "FCC's Digital Plan May Be U.S. Bonanza," *Wall Street Journal*, July 26, 1996, p. 2.

17. Based on Michael Porter, *Competitive Advantage: Creating and Sustaining Superior Performance* (New York: The Free Press, 1985).

18. James R. Healey, "Ford Expedition to Land at Dealers in August," *USA Today*, May 9, 1996.

19. www.disney.com/investors/index.html, site visited on May 29, 1998.

20. Personal interview with Duane Larson, 1995.

21. John Pierson, "Ford Labors over Tiny Buttons and Dials in Quest for a Driver-Friendly Dashboard," *Wall Street Journal*, May 20, 1996.

22. Joseph Pereira, "Retailers Bet Virtual Pets Will Be Next Toy Craze," *Wall Street Journal Interactive Edition*, May 2, 1997.

23. Ibid., p. 58.

24. Scott Woolley, "Replacing Inventory with Information," *Forbes*, March 24, 1997, pp. 54–57.

25. Ibid.

26. Pamela Ellis-Simmons, "Broadway Means Business," Special Advertising Section, *Fortune*, June 9, 1997, pp. 49–56.

27. Jeff Schmitt, Ph.D. dissertation, Michigan State University, 1996.

28. FT900 (95) (CB-96-98), Bureau of the Census, Foreign Trade Division, Final 1995.

29. USDOC, International Trade Administration, "Implementation of the National Export Strategy," IT TPCC Part 3, October 19, 1995.

30. FT900 (95) (CB-96-98), Bureau of the Census, Foreign Trade Division, Final 1995.

31. Karl Kunkel, "Go Global, Young Man," *Triad Business News*, May 17, 1996.

32. "Starbucks Considers Expanding Its Chain in Asian-Pacific Area," *Wall Street Journal*, August 29, 1996.
33. Kinichi Ohmae, *The Borderless World* (New York: Harper Business, 1990), pp. 17–31.
34. Betsy Spethmann, "Brand Builders," *Brandweek*, December 4, 1995, pp. 17–18.
35. Linda Grant, "Gilette Knows Shaving—And How to Turn Out," *Fortune*, October 14, 1996, www.fortune.com.
36. David A. Erickson, "Standardized Approach Works Well in Establishing Global Presence," *Marketing News*, October 7, 1996, p. 9.

37. Roberta Maynard, "Hot Markets Overseas," *Nation's Business*, June 1995, p. 219.
38. "Sony Electronics Inc.: Leading the World to 'What's Next' in Technology," Special Advertising Section, *Fortune*, June 9, 1997, p. 176.
39. "Costs Dispute with Prague Sours SKODA Deal," *Financial Times*, September 9, 1993, p. 4.
40. "Japan Braces Itself for the US Roadshow," *Financial Times*, August 19, 1993, p. 17.
41. "How Toshiba Makes Alliances Work," *Fortune*, October 4, 1993, p. 116.

CASE 4

POLAROID

REVITALIZING A BUSINESS IS NO small challenge. Polaroid's traditional product line of instant cameras was losing popularity, but the company has recently found rejuvenation by focusing more attention on existing and new markets. In 1995, Polaroid instant film sales in the United States fell 22 percent, while global sales slipped 3 percent. Often referred to as a tired product, Polaroid's instant camera and film needed to be revived. A four-part strategy was created to restore the company to recognized world leadership in instant imaging. Early indications are that the new strategy is working. Polaroid had earnings of more than $202 million in 1996, nearly double the 1995 level.

Historically, Polaroid has created innovations with consumer benefits in mind. Founders Edwin Land and George Wheelwright introduced one-step black-and-white photography in 1947. In 1952 they introduced full color and stereographic movies complete with 3-D glasses. By 1963 the company had the first instant color film, followed by sonar autofocus technology in 1978. Four years later came the first video printer, which could display diagnostic images useful in industrial and medical markets.

Over the years, Polaroid has found its greatest success in instant imaging, which is how it defines its business today. Piggybacking on a history of innovation, Polaroid has tremendous core competencies that are at the heart of its rejuvenation strategy.

Chairman and CEO Gary T. DiCamillo has made a point of listening to Polaroid users, dealers, retailers, employees, investors, suppliers, and even competitors on four continents in order to design the best revitalization strategy. Striving for a competitive plan that would be more responsive, DiCamillo identified opportunities in core consumer markets, selected global commercial markets, developing country markets, and new imaging businesses that required new products. Since all these initiatives were consistent with Polaroid's mission of instant imaging, they worked well together; success in one area helped support strategies in other areas.

Efforts to revive sales among traditional consumers, especially in North America, Japan, and Western Europe, built on the desire for a product that records an important moment but also enhances the moment itself by involving people in the imaging experience. Through ads that reinforce this positioning of instant photography, Polaroid has generated both positive consumer awareness and a strong increase in camera sales. "See what develops" is a creative tagline that describes the technology of instant film and suggests the benefits of integrating instant photography with life experiences. In one ad, a dog uses a Polaroid photo to prove to its owners that it was the cat who got into the trash. Today, the average Polaroid customer is approximately 53 years old and has had experience with the product over the years. The new campaign is designed to create awareness among younger consumers as well as a fresh interest in mature markets and around the world. The expenditure of approximately $40 million on advertising seems to be paying off in the United States, Western Europe, and Japan. In 1996 Japan was a tremendous success story, with Polaroid camera sales up nearly 50 percent, mostly among younger consumers.

Among businesses with a clear need for instant photography, careful attention was paid to selecting market segments that could benefit dramatically from the Polaroid technology. The demand for instant film is exploding in such commercial markets as real estate, insurance, advertising, mail order, automotive design, and aircraft maintenance. These businesses often want an instant record without the time, cost, and inconvenience of developing film. Polaroid focused on large-scale identification systems and business imaging in technical markets. Examples are driver's license bureaus in the United States and auto registration programs in several Chinese provinces. By carefully tackling the 11 countries that contain over half the world's population Polaroid preempted other competitors from gaining a solid foothold. Strong sales in these markets are expected for years to come.

Piggybacking on success in these commercial markets, Polaroid is expanding into consumer markets in the same 11 countries. There is high demand for some of Polaroid's additional products, such as XOOR polarized sunglasses, as well as instant cameras and film.

To develop new imaging businesses, Polaroid sought out strategic alliances, licensing agreements, and joint marketing arrangements that allow it to strengthen and profit from its brand name as well as extend its technical expertise to new applications. For example, Polaroid has a joint venture with Immunomatrix, a privately held biotechnology company, to develop and manufacture instant diagnostic tests for use in doctor's offices or clinical laboratories. Polaroid technology will help physicians obtain accurate results within a matter of minutes rather than hours or days. Polaroid also is partnering with Roboticvision Systems Inc., a world leader in machine vision, to produce products that can be used in the manufacture of a variety of industrial and consumer goods.

Polaroid's revitalization plans have committed the entire organization to a market focus. All product innovations start with market dynamics in mind. Polaroid is leveraging its technology in instant imaging to produce a range of new product applications in such areas as instant image cameras and films, digital imaging (hardware and software), medical diagnostics, graphics, polarizing, and holographics.

Polaroid has done an excellent job of applying its core competency in each of these arenas. DiCamillo is quick to point out the extensive use made of new product development teams, which bring together key players from marketing, sales, research, engineering, and manufacturing. The teams are required to listen to customers in order to provide them with imaging solutions that meet specific needs. The team approach speeds the product development process, enabling Polaroid to introduce 40 to 50 new products or line extensions annually. These new products are expected to provide up to 25 percent of Polaroid's sales by the end of 1998.

Where is Polaroid headed? By focusing on new growing markets and by reinvigorating promotion and product development, Polaroid is trying to stay ahead of competitors such as Fuji, who have benefitted from expirations of Polaroid patents. The plan is to stick with the company's core competency in instant photography and to maintain about 90 percent of sales and profits in this solid business. Polaroid expects to grow not only in developing markets but also in North America, Western Europe, and Japan. With the introduction of new products and others on the drawing board, Polaroid intends to be a permanent innovative presence in all the markets.

1. *The corporate vision provides a common understanding of what the organization is trying to accomplish in the broadest sense. Using what you've learned from this case, describe the current Polaroid vision.*
2. *There are several ways to structure SBUs. How does Polaroid structure its business units? How could portfolio planning tools be used to assess the effectiveness of the company's business units?*
3. *Core competencies are critical aspects of strategic infrastructure. Identify Polaroid's core competencies. Into which categories can they be grouped?*

SOURCES: Polaroid Web site, www.polaroid.com, visited October 28, 1997; Shelly Reese, *Marketing Tools,* June 1996, www.marketing-tools.com; Mark Maremont, "Polaroid: Ready for a Reshoot," *Business Week,* April 1, 1996, p. 6; Joan Voight, "Polaroid Yuks up with $40M Push," *Brandweek,* February 26, 1996, p. 6; Michael Wilke, "Polaroid Pins Its Revival to Brand, Product Lineup," *Advertising Age,* December 2, 1996, p. 20; and Otis Port, "Digital Finds Its Photo Op," *Business Week,* April 15, 1996, p. 71.

Marketing Information and Research

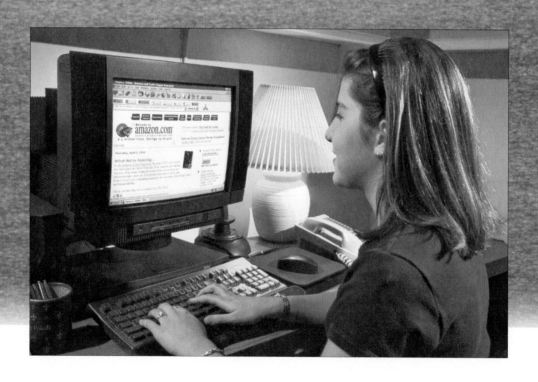

Objectives

1. Understand the roles that marketing information systems (MIS) and research play in marketing decision making.

2. Recognize how data are transformed into information to be used in a variety of marketing decisions.

3. Understand the types of research and the steps of a typical marketing research process.

4. Describe widely used marketing research techniques.

5. Explore how marketing information is being influenced by technology and is obtained globally.

6. Understand that ethical issues surround the use and dissemination of research.

WHEN YOU ENTER THE BOOKSTORE, YOU'RE *met with a familiar greeting: "Welcome back, friend, these are your recommendations." The bookseller suggests several titles that may interest you and points you in the right direction. You quickly find information about the books, author and publisher notes, price information, and even reviews by other customers. You choose two titles, quickly pay with a credit card, and leave the store. The strange thing is you never left home.*

Welcome to Amazon.com, the hottest on-line business to hit the World Wide Web. Started in 1995 by Jeffery Bezos, Amazon.com has grown at incredible rates. During the first quarter of 1998, it reported revenues of $87.4 million, an increase of 32 percent over fourth quarter 1997, and up 446 percent over the previous year. Investors have also rewarded the firm. The stock price has risen more than 450 percent since it was first offered at $18 per share.[1]

While a great deal of Amazon.com's success can be attributed to overwhelming growth in the Internet, its use of marketing information systems provides a strong competitive advantage. The ability to record and remember customer preferences allows it to offer specialized services that elude other retailers. Amazon gets to know its customers like few other businesses can.

The Amazon.com marketing information system is a two-way street. While Amazon gathers information about users, users are also given plenty of information about the bookseller and even about other customers' tastes and preferences. When customers enter the Web site they are recognized from their original registration (a simple process that asks for name, e-mail address, and a password), and their buying history is accessed. Next, based on that history and the buying behavior of other Amazon.com customers, a list suggests books that are likely to interest the customer.

Users who have never purchased books at Amazon.com are led to six other ways to discover great reads. The most interactive is the BookMatcher system. The simple five-minute process collects information on your reading habits and opinions by asking you to rate genres and specific titles. Once you enter this information, you can rate any book that's recommended or that you find while searching. The data are cross-referenced with the ratings of others to provide an increasingly solid reader profile of you.

Amazon.com delivers information to users even when they are not visiting the site. The service allows readers to choose among more than 40 categories that may interest them. It automatically sends them e-mail with new information about those categories, including recommendations, reviews, author notes, interviews, chapter samples, and best-seller lists.

Another suggestion device is MoodMatcher, which uses an index of themes like "Fantastic Voyages" and "It Was a Dark and Stormy Night" to guide readers to authors and titles. Customer Buzz lists books by genre that have been heavily reviewed by Web site visitors and separates the list into two categories: "Divided Over" and "Raving About." There also is an option that provides searchers with a way to link well-liked authors to similar writers they may not know about. Yet another section provides title synopses and critical thinking questions that can be used as a framework for group discussion.

The Amazon system also allows users to search for specific titles. The On-line catalog contains 2.5 million books and is searchable by author, title, subject, publisher, publication date, and ISBN. After you type in the information required, the search engine supplies the three most likely matches, plus any additional items that you may have intended. Each listed title is a link further information including price, and commentary from other reviewers, positive and negative. One customer even commented, "you do a wonderful job. Recently, I didn't purchase a book I'd been planning to order from Amazon because rather than hyping it, you provided balanced assessments about its strengths and weaknesses. My experience has been that you are a company customers can trust."[2] By posting public reviews, Amazon is able to get feedback on the books it carries, and makes that information available to customers.

The use of technology to gather information extends beyond the borders of Amazon.com through third-party associates. For example, a Web site specializing in gardening can create a link that takes Amazon.com users directly into a page displaying the latest titles on flowers, lawn care, and botany. The program is growing fast, due in large part to the commissions associates receive for each book purchased in this way. Currently over 35,000 affiliate sites are earning commissions of up to 15 percent.

Jeff Bezos admits, "We're never going to have sofas; we're never going to have latte."[3] Although Amazon.com can't provide the atmosphere of a local bookstore, what it does have can be even more powerful. The information interface allows it to gather customer-specific information and provide users with a more complete service. In a technological age, Amazon.com proves that marketers can understand customers through the Web and perhaps serve them even better than if they were face-to-face.

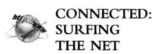

CONNECTED: SURFING THE NET

www.amazon.com

Amazon.com is an extraordinary company that has been on-line since 1995. This leading online book retailer offers over 2.5 million titles and provides book reviews, gift suggestions, and more. Get connected to Amazon.com and learn more about their services.

Marketing information system (MIS)

A computerized system used to collect and analyze marketing data.

THE CONCEPT OF MARKETING INFORMATION SYSTEMS AND MARKETING RESEARCH

Connecting with customers requires vast amounts of information. You can't connect if you can't locate, understand, and respond to customers. That's where marketing information systems and marketing research enter the picture. Technology has changed the way the business world views marketing information. Data gathering and dissemination occur at the speed of light. Information is at the fingertips of anyone with a personal computer and a modem; access is as easy as dialing the telephone. The director of strategic planning at a large midwestern hospital commented recently: "We have access to more information than we can possibly use. The trick is to determine which information will be useful to us in making decisions that positively affect our future."[4] In fact, a major problem for executives today is data overload—access to so much that their minds simply can't process all of it. To help decision makers, most companies carefully structure the way data are collected, stored, and made available through marketing information systems and marketing research.

Marketing information systems (MIS) are computerized systems that collect and organize marketing data on a timely basis to provide information for decision making. For example, executives at Pizza Hut use MIS to constantly monitor customer satisfaction. The restaurant chain distributes more than 2.5 million customer surveys annually, or about 50,000 per week. Pizza Hut also asks some customers to call an interactive 800 number that appears at the bottom of a dining receipt. The call line focuses on issues that unit managers can control, such as service, food, and overall dining experience.[5] The results become part of the MIS so that executives have constant feedback.

Companies capture data for MIS to provide information for decision making.

Note that the abbreviation MIS can be confusing because many organizations have a **management information system,** also called an MIS. Many times the marketing information system is considered part of that larger system. Management information systems usually contain additional data, such as employee records and various internal documents.

Marketing research is the formal assembly and analysis of data about specific issues surrounding a marketing strategy. It is called for when managers face a complex marketing situation for which little or no information is available. All the data gathered focus on the problem at hand. For example, to open an upscale dating service, Andrea McGinty wanted the names of a select group of singles in the Chicago area. She hired R. R. Donnelley & Sons, a marketing research group, to gather information about the dating public. She needed to know names, addresses, and telephone numbers of singles between the age of 25 and 50 who earned at least $50,000 annually and either owned their own residence or paid more than $975 in rent per month. McGinty obtained a list of more than 165,000 singles clustered in 10 zip codes in Chicago's downtown and Lincoln Park neighborhoods. This information was used to launch her business, It's Just Lunch, a unique service that arranges prescreened luncheon dates for busy professionals.[6]

The type of research described above addresses a specific issue with a clearly identified objective regarding marketing strategy. Once the research is completed, it's typically saved as part of the MIS. Figure 5-1 depicts the relationships of MIS and marketing research to marketing decision making. This chapter starts with an examination of marketing information systems and their role in marketing decisions. This is followed by a discussion of the marketing research process, which is also a key in decision making. The chapter concludes with sections on the all-important technological, global, and ethical dimensions of information generation and usage.

MARKETING INFORMATION SYSTEMS AND DATA

Marketing information systems often include a **marketing decision support system (MDSS),** which allows decision makers to access raw data from the MIS and manipulate it into a useful form. A typical MDSS consists of a computer database, data retrieval and modeling soft-

Management information system (MIS)
A computerized system used to collect and analyze the data needed for management decision making. The marketing information system is often considered a part of this system.

Marketing research
The formal assembly and analysis of information about specific issues surrounding the marketing of goods and services.

Marketing decision support system (MDSS)
A two-way communication bridge between the people who collect and analyze information and the executives who use it.

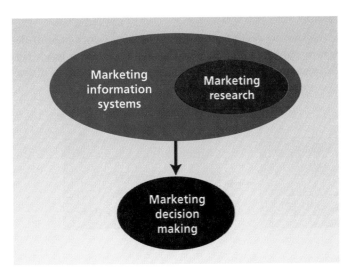

Figure 5-1 **Marketing Information and Decision Making**

1. What types of decisions do you make regularly?
2. What types of information do you need in order to make those decisions?
3. What types of useful information do you get regularly?
4. What types of information would you like to have that you are not getting now?
5. What types of information do you get now that you don't really need?
6. What information do you want daily? weekly? monthly? yearly?
7. What topics would you like to be kept informed about?
8. What databases would be useful to you?
9. What types of information analysis programs would you like to have?
10. What are the four most helpful improvements that could be made in the present information system?

Figure 5-2 How to Determine Marketing Information Needs

Source: Philip Kotler and Gary Armstrong, Principles of Marketing, 7th ed. © 1994. Adapted by permission of Prentice Hall, Inc., Upper Saddle River, NJ.

ware, and a user-friendly graphical interface. Let's say that a marketing manager wants to know how the price of the company's downhill skis compares to that of a competitor. The information is probably in the MIS on a store-by-store basis. It would be difficult for her to wade through all the raw data and draw any conclusions. Instead the manager sits down at a computer and accesses the company's MDSS. A user-friendly display appears and, through interactive directions, helps the user determine how to manipulate the raw data. The marketing manager may want to compare average prices across the entire country or for one region or state. Once that is decided, the MDSS software retrieves and models the relevant data. Now the manager is able to interpret the data and make an informed decision.

A specialized type of MIS is a **transaction-based information system (TBIS),** which is a computerized link between a firm and its customers and/or distributors and suppliers. Originally designed for ordering, billing, shipping, and inventory control, these systems are now designed to provide data on customer preferences, loyalty, sales trends, and an array of marketing issues.

Transaction-based information system (TBIS)

A computerized link between a firm and its customers and/or distributors and suppliers.

To develop an excellent MIS and design a useful MDSS, the organization needs to assess its marketing information needs. This assessment begins by identifying the types of executive decisions, what information will help make them, and the best formats and time tables for presenting it. Figure 5-2 describes the types of questions used to assess marketing information needs.

TURNING DATA INTO INFORMATION

In order to comprehend marketing information systems and marketing research, you must understand the nature of data and how they become information useful for decision making. Keep in mind that data and information are not the same. Data are simply facts. Information is data that have been analyzed and put in useful form, as depicted in Figure 5-3. "Data served up in tabular form, which is the way business was being done not so many years ago, will no longer suffice," says Gerald Kanovsky, president of Career Consulting Group, Inc. "Today's executives need information they can act on."[7] In other words, market analysts and researchers need to interpret data—turn it into information—to assist upper-level managers and executives in making quick, informed decisions.

Types of Data   Data provide the starting point from which marketing information is derived. **Data** can be any set of facts or statistics obtained from outside (external) or inside (internal) the company. Usually the data are stored in a **database,** which is a collection of material that can be retrieved by a computer.

Data

Facts or statistics obtained from outside or inside the company.

Database

A collection of data that can be retrieved by a computer.

Types of Data	Data Analysis	Information and Decision Making
External and internal Primary and secondary	Data sorting Statistics Models	Marketing planning Marketing mix decisions Performance monitoring

Figure 5-3 How Data Become Information

External data come from outside the company. Popular external databases include CompuServe, LEXIS®-NEXIS®, Dow Jones News/Retrieval Service, and Dialog. They provide raw data as well as articles, newsletters, breaking news stories, financial reports on companies, and nearly any other type imaginable. For specific needs, you can use sources like *Neighborhood Report CompuServe*, which provides summaries of demographics for any zip code in the United States: population, race, age, occupation, and housing patterns. You can also use one of the many on-line services to discuss a variety of subjects with knowledgeable people. Forums such as newsgroups and Web-based message boards allow people to tap into expertise around the globe on any issue—from scientific discoveries to new business ventures.

To track competitors, one approach is the source in the NEXIS® service, which analyzes specific industries and companies. If you're interested in business customers, Dow Jones News/Retrieval Service can provide Dun & Bradstreet information on 8.7 million U.S. businesses and professionals. It can give in-depth financial and operational reports on most of the companies. The databases generally have a cost. Companies charge either for time on-line or for each piece of data, such as a name or news release.

Internal data are found within a company. Sales data, accounting records, and sales force call reports are examples. Internal data are likely to reside in several different departments. For example, the accounting department has detailed records of sales costs and how much cash is generated by each product. In some cases these figures are available for each market segment. The manufacturing and shipping departments track production schedules, amount of capacity utilized, shipping dates, and inventory levels. In many companies the supply chain management department provides detailed records of the flow of goods into the company and out to each customer, including the frequency of orders, stock levels, and purchase rates. The marketing department will usually have such data as type and frequency of sales calls, orders received from each location, and advertising schedules.

Primary data are those gathered for the first time for a particular issue being addressed. As a result, they tend to be slower and expensive to collect. **Secondary data** are those that already have been collected. Nearly all marketing information falls into this category. For example, the National Trade Data Bank, with data from numerous government agencies, is a wonderful resource for international research.

External data
Data obtained outside the company.

Internal data
Data obtained within the company.

Primary data
Information collected for the first time.

Secondary data
Information that already has been collected.

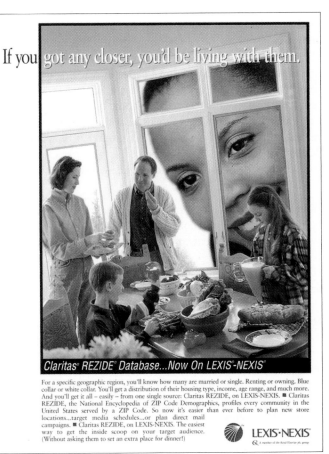

LEXIS®-NEXIS® provides external data such as articles, newsletters, breaking news stories, and more.

Data Analysis Data analysis transforms material into a usable form, so insights can be developed. It usually involves data sorting, statistics, and/or models. Data sorting uses several tools for grouping data. For example, Burger King may want to know sales by time of day to determine whether certain items are more popular at certain times.

Statistics help describe data in more detail or tell us how representative certain occurrences are relative to overall patterns. Most information systems have readily available statistical packages that can easily be applied to the data. In some cases they simply count frequencies of occurrence or describe the averages. For example, although Folger's coffee is purchased by 38 percent of all households over the course of a year, 70 percent of its total volume is accounted for by only 15 percent of all households.[8]

Models are miniature representations of marketing phenomena. They simplify complex situations by presenting key facts and ignoring unnecessary details. Marketers need models for the same reasons that architects need blueprints. With a blueprint, the architect can visualize various parts of the building without actually being there. Marketing models describe which variables are important for specific marketing situations. For example, Children's World evaluates consumer satisfaction in order to predict loyalty. Its model indicates that satisfaction leads to customer loyalty. The important thing is that the data analysis should be insightful, so it will lead to innovative marketing decisions, and easy to use, so executives will be more inclined to incorporate it into their decision making.

INFORMATION AND DECISION MAKING

Using information is not easy; however, it's absolutely critical to have good information if you expect to connect with customers. Marketers have historically relied on their own intuition. While experience is still important, the world is more complex today. So experience must be supplemented with marketing information. Good information helps executives make key marketing decisions. As was illustrated in Figure 5-3, marketing information is generally used in three key areas: marketing planning, marketing mix decisions, and performance monitoring. Let's take a look at each of these in more detail.

Marketing Planning Marketing planning requires information at nearly every stage of the process. The situation analysis needs input about customers, competitors, market trends, technology, channels of distribution, and economic conditions. Marketing information also helps marketers make better decisions about which segments to target and how to position the organization. Often, marketing information affects the competitive thrust of the company. For example, research at AT&T indicates that customers want help managing their increasingly busy lives. This includes understanding new technology, convenience in reaching others, and easy access to information and entertainment services. To address these wants, AT&T is working to supply such services as electronic bill payment using the home television screen; automatic redialing on calls that receive a busy signal or no answer; and a message recording system for the home workplace that stores faxes or data on the computer if lines are occupied by personal voice calls. Through marketing information, AT&T is able to better understand consumers in order to build customer relationships and provide consumers with valuable products.[9]

Marketing Mix Decisions Marketing mix decisions are another area in which marketing information is required. In fact, it is so critical to decisions about product, place, promotion, and price that expertise has evolved in each area. For example, Booz, Allen & Hamilton, a large consulting firm, has a department that focuses primarily on product research. The University of Tennessee funds the Center for Logistics Research, which concentrates on distribution channels. The way marketing information aids each of the marketing mix decisions is discussed below.

Product Decisions Marketing information on new products is essential. Frito-Lay tests some of its new products with at least 100,000 consumers before releasing them. Drawing annually from more than 250 community groups (such as churches, scouts, and soccer clubs), researchers assemble about 100 testers every weekday evening. They analyze the feedback overnight and relay the information to more than 70 Ph.D.'s and a 200-person marketing support group. The test results help refine new products or alter existing brands.[10] One outcome was the Frito-Lay decision to spend $225 million to make low-fat foods an integral part of its business. It hopes these new health alternatives will eventually account for one-third of its $6 billion salty snack food line.[11]

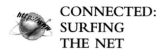

CONNECTED: SURFING THE NET

www.att.com

AT&T's research has led to the development of many products we use every day. Visit the AT&T Web site to look inside the AT&T labs, where you can participate in demonstrations and experiments.

Marketing information also helps identify opportunities for new products. Kodak Gold was created to supplement the company's line of color film. Of professional quality, it can be reproduced and enlarged without the graininess or distortion of commercial color film.[12] In another case, Annette Zientek created Christine Columbus, a mail-order catalog that offers specialty items for women travelers, such as compact curling irons and makeup mirrors. Before leaving on a vacation in Europe, she spent nearly six weeks trying to find the travel accessories she needed. Wondering whether all women had the same difficulty, Zientek set out to collect marketing information. She found that women make up nearly half of all travelers and that the growth rate of their market share is expected to outpace that of men over the next five years.[13]

Place Decisions Marketing information helps with place decisions such as determining the appropriate distribution channel, either directly to consumers or through intermediaries, such as wholesalers and retailers. In can be used to identify specific distributors or the inventory requirements for selected channels. One form of marketing information tracks every item sold in every store. "It captures the entire retail marketing area," says Donald Stuart, partner at Cannondale Associates. "Manufacturers are able to identify the stores that are most important to their category, least important to their category, or that hold the best opportunities for brand or category development." Marketers can identify similar consumer clusters in individual stores and determine which products do better in which stores. Information such as this "gives manufacturers a definitive read on their business in any account," says Joe Battoe, president of sales and retail services at IRI Research.[14] Once executives gain a good understanding of market phenomena, they are able to make quality decisions regarding the distribution of their products and services.

Promotion Decisions Vast amounts of information are necessary in the area of promotions. For example, executives must determine the budget required to accomplish desired objectives. They have to decide the proper combination of advertising, personal selling, or other promotion approaches. For advertising, they need to determine the most effective amounts of print, television, and/or radio ads to reach targeted consumers.

Marketing information also provides valuable feedback. "Without indicators like increased sales or market share gain, we really have no way of knowing how effective our plan for a brand really is," says Dana Anderson, media buyer for United Airlines at Leo Burnett Company, Inc., a major advertising agency. "Marketing information also tells us how well an advertising plan meets specific marketing objectives, like an increase in company or product awareness or an improved image of a brand. . . . We also evaluate the effects of our promotional campaign on competitors."[15]

Pricing Decisions Because prices send strong signals to the market about the value of a product, information on pricing is critical for almost every marketing decision. In many cases, pricing is specific to a region. Wal-Mart and Toys "Я" Us advertise that they will meet or beat competitors' prices. They monitor these locally, feeding the information into a centralized MIS. They also collect ads that consumers bring in. Automobile companies look not only at the prices of major competitors but also at finance and leasing terms. Information is collected about the effectiveness of cash discounts and rebates as well as the likelihood of buyers switching from one brand to another at various price points. The airline industry, whose profits are highly sensitive to volume, continually monitors how price affects demand in local, national, and international markets.

Monitoring Performance The third area supported by marketing information is performance monitoring. This helps managers make sure that plans and programs are moving ahead on target. Information is required to track progress, identify unsuspected obstacles, and make corrections to accomplish objectives. After Frito-Lay launches a product, 10,000 employees make 400,000 calls weekly in the United States. Using scanner data, the company also tracks sales almost instantly, correlating the data by market segment. Frito-Lay can immediately judge the effectiveness of its advertising, packaging, and pricing decisions and make adjustments as needed.

Today, nearly every organization monitors customer service levels. Marketing information provides data on customer expectations and how well the company meets them. American Express Financial Advisors, Inc., uses client satisfaction surveys to gauge their quality of service. Client names are selected at random, and telephone interviews identify any areas needing improvement. Information such as this helps marketers track the effects of customer service on sales and satisfaction.[16] To determine optimum service positioning, Hilton conducted

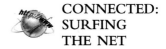

CONNECTED: SURFING THE NET

www.ual.com

What are the Friendly Sky's latest promotional decisions? Visit the United Airlines Web site and find out. You'll also have an opportunity to obtain flight information, make reservations, and much more.

customer and employee surveys to identify market needs and expectations. This led to Hilton's unique service clusters, which are classified by the purpose of the visit and the origin of the guest. Hilton International strives to provide a variety of services to customers from 130 nationalities at 150 locations around the world. For example, it caters to Japanese guests by giving them "comfort and service, the Japanese way."[17] Hilton captures this by providing "Wa No Kutsurogi" brand name service which includes a Japanese-speaking staff, oriental food selections and the availability of Japanese newspapers.[18]

Outside rating services can provide unbiased information on how consumers evaluate performance. You're probably familiar with the Nielsen ratings, which usually appear weekly in publications such as *USA Today*. Nielsen Media Research, the leading international television information services company, monitors approximately 5000 homes. A "Nielsen People Meter" is installed on each television to record tuning records for every channel: the time of day, duration of tuning, and which household members are watching. The company retrieves the information through the phone lines. The result is television show rankings, weekly ratings, and season to date rankings.[19]

Just think of the usefulness of the Nielsen service to marketers. A company can decide to advertise during programs and time slots when they can be certain targeted consumers are watching. It is important for such services to keep an arm's-length relationship with the companies they rate. To see how J. D. Power & Associates accomplishes this for the automotive industry, check out the relationships feature, "J. D. Power & Associates: A 'Hate-Love' Relationship with Detroit."

THE MARKETING RESEARCH PROCESS

Marketing research is a key aspect of the organization's ability to make good marketing decisions. It starts with a clear understanding of the problem to be addressed and ends with an interpretation of findings that will aid in decision making. Each step is shown in Figure 5-4.

DEFINING THE PROBLEM

When asked what he recommended for ensuring high-quality marketing research, an experienced executive at Upjohn Corporation answered: "Never begin a research process with a search for market information. Always start by understanding the decisions to be made and the managerial circumstances surrounding those decisions." This isn't as easy as it sounds, but it's a critical step in the research process. As Albert Einstein said, "the formulation of a problem is often more essential than its solution."[20]

The marketing researcher and key decision makers should work together to specify the problem. The researcher usually must ask probing questions to identify objectives. What is the environment of the problem? When must it be solved? What resources will be committed to the final course of action? It does no good to recommend a remedy clearly beyond the capacity of the company.

Care must be taken to isolate the symptoms from the actual problem. Imagine that Pepsi sales decline rapidly. This sounds like a problem, but it's only a symptom. The real problem may be a new promotional campaign by Coca-Cola that Pepsi has failed to address. Or perhaps many Pepsi customers are switching to bottled water. Just as a fever is a sign of the flu, declining sales usually indicates a deeper problem. Once it is isolated, the variables or factors causing it can be identified. This helps define the problem before any marketing research begins.

RESEARCH DESIGN

A **research design** is an outline of what data will be gathered, which sources will be used, and how the data will be collected and analyzed. The research design is, in effect, a master plan for the research project as shown in Figure 5-4.

Most designs call for two types of research: exploratory and quantitative. **Exploratory research** clarifies the problem and searches for ways to address it. **Quantitative research** provides the information needed to select the best course of action and forecast the probable results. Research generally starts with an exploratory study, may include a pilot phase, and ends with quantitative research. A **pilot study** is a small-scale project that allows the researcher to refine and test the approaches that ultimately will be used.

Research design
An outline of what data will be gathered, what scores will be used, and how the data will be collected and analyzed.

Exploratory research
Research designed to clarify the problem and suggest ways to address it.

Quantitative research
Research designed to provide the information needed to select the best course of action and estimate the probable results.

Pilot study
A small-scale project that allows the researcher to refine and test the approaches that eventually will be used.

CONNECTING THROUGH RELATIONSHIPS

J. D. POWER & ASSOCIATES: A "HATE-LOVE" RELATIONSHIP WITH DETROIT

A common blind spot of marketers is to look for research that confirms what they think, not research that points up what they don't know. This was certainly the case when independent researcher John David Power presented his data to the automotive industry 25 years ago. Power approached the nation's automakers with extensive independent surveys on customer satisfaction. Instead of embracing Power and his work with open arms, the Big Three gave him the cold shoulder. The surveys highlighted America's dissatisfaction with U.S.-made cars, and Detroit didn't want to hear about it. Ironically, it was Power's insistence on maintaining an arm's-length relationship with the auto industry that finally brought Detroit around. Today, the J. D. Power & Associates Customer Satisfaction rating is the most coveted, and credible, seal of approval in the business.

A former financial analyst at Ford Motor Company, Power struck out on his own in 1968. His idea was to pay for his own customer surveys of the automotive industry and later sell the results. Says J. Ferron, a former Power executive and now partner-in-charge of Coopers & Lybrand's auto practice, "Dave's genius was not to depend on companies to finance proprietary studies, but to do independent studies and publish the results." Detroit turned a blind eye, but the Japanese were only too happy to see what the surveys had to say about their competitors. Power's data were a crucial step in their campaign to break into the U.S. auto market, which they did.

By the mid-1980s, Japanese cars were overtaking U.S. models in sales, and the Big Three were forced to listen to Power. "Our goal has always been to improve the quality of cars," says Power. "People like Ralph Nader [the consumer activist] wanted to protect consumers, too, but I always thought he was anti-Detroit. We wanted to work with Detroit." Today, automakers whose cars receive a top rating are happy to fork over the $250,000 licensing fee that Power requires when they advertise his results. It's actually a small price to pay, since a J. D. Power & Associates number one rating has been known to double sales of a particular model.

Drawing on the success of his car ratings, Power is taking his $42 million company in some exciting new directions. He is extending his arm's-length handshake to the nation's 21,000 new car dealerships, giving them the chance to compete for their own J. D. Power awards. The Power Information Network (PIN) is a computerized program that collects details of every transaction made by participating dealers. PIN gives carmakers and dealers an accurate picture of what cars are selling where and at what price. It's a far cry from tabulating survey results at the kitchen table, which is what Power and his wife did when he first started out.

J. D. Power is also hoping to sell his surveys in Europe and become a brand name there. If his initial reception is any clue, it looks like he'll be a success. At a presentation to the top brass of Italy's auto industry, Power briefed them on how his consumer surveys could help them learn more about their customers and sell more cars. Flashback to Detroit 25 years ago: "During the question and answer period, they blatantly told me I didn't understand their market," says Power. If history repeats itself, in a few years the Europeans will be forking over big eurodollars to brandish the J. D. Power rating in their own ads.

Sources: Larry Armstrong, "Rating J. D. Power's Grand Plan," *Business Week*, September 2, 1996, pp. 75–76; and David Carnoy et al., "Know Your Customer," *Success*, February 1997, pp. 36–38.

EXPLORATORY RESEARCH

Exploratory research enables investigators to obtain a better understanding of the issues. Specifically, it helps

determine the exact nature of the problem or opportunity,

search for causes or explanations for the problem,

define the magnitude of the problem,

create hypotheses about underlying causes,

describe why or how the causes may affect the situation,

understand competitors' actions and reactions to company strategies, and

estimate how courses of action may affect the market.

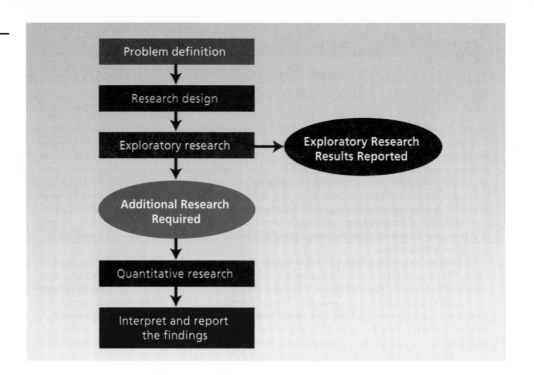

*Figure 5-4   The Marketing
Research Process*

Exploratory research seeks information that will enlighten marketers in the decision-making process. For example, sports marketing is an increasingly visible and rapidly growing business. Sports event spending was about $3.5 billion in 1996, up 17 percent from 1995, and media spending by advertisers was another $3.5 billion. To better understand consumers, exploratory research segmented the seemingly homogeneous sports enthusiast market. It revealed that people who actually participate in sports tend to be receptive to advertising, and aggressive, emotional messages are the most appropriate. In contrast, those who only watch sports seem to be less interested in what advertising has to offer.[21]

Exploratory research generally begins by finding and reviewing secondary data. This information already has been collected, so it's usually the quickest and most cost-effective way to get started. Sometimes the entire research question can be answered with secondary data, but the collection of primary data usually is required.

Although exploratory research seldom quantifies the best solution, it clearly defines the problem and suggests options. With that information, the executive may be able to choose a course of action, and many projects end at this stage.

Exploratory research is conducted with focus groups, interviews, projective techniques, observation, and case analysis. Each is discussed below.

Focus group

A group, usually composed of eight to 12 people, whose opinions are elicited by an interviewer to provide exploratory insights into a problem.

Focus Groups   A **focus group** usually involves eight to 12 people whose opinions provide qualitative insights into a problem. This approach is particularly useful in clarifying problems with a company's products, services, advertising, distribution channels, and the like. It's possible to gather a wide range of information about customers' feelings on these subjects and discover the reasons for their attitudes or purchase behaviors. Techniques are used that probe into thoughts and feelings. Researchers ask questions and encourage participants to interact with one another to uncover unexpected attitudes, behaviors, and ideas that may suggest innovative marketing strategies. In a sense, the group interviews itself. The social interaction often yields insights that could not be obtained through one-on-one interviews.

Focus groups have been used for a variety of purposes. After the 1992 riots in Los Angeles, the L.A. Vons supermarket chain took the lead in opening stores in the central city, an area it traditionally had ignored. Vons conducted extensive focus group research on nearly every aspect of its business—including product mix, security, and hiring policy—in order to develop ideas for matching outlets with the needs of the local community.[22] *Buzzworm*, an environmental magazine, uses focus groups to determine what current subscribers like and dislike about the publication.[23] Rodale Press, Inc., gathers information from focus groups on customer preferences, to brainstorm new book titles, and to generate precisely targeted prod-

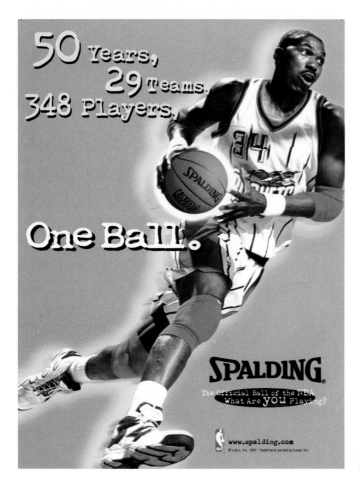

Sports marketing is an increasingly visible and rapidly growing business.

ucts through direct mail and state-of-the-art testing. The diversity feature focuses on ways to handle focus groups with young people.

While most focus groups are conducted in person with a facilitator, other formats can be used, such as video conferencing through television monitors, remote control cameras, and digital transmission. Approximately 100,000 video-conferenced focus groups are conducted annually, and the number is expected to double by 2000.[24] The Internet is another popular format. For example, consumers can click on 3-D images on their PCs to evaluate and give feedback on new toothpaste package designs. A number of companies today use interactive focus groups as a part of their product development process.[25] You'll learn more about this unique format in the technology section.

When selecting participants for a focus group, it's generally best to choose those with similar demographics, since common experiences provide the basis for more in-depth discussion. Most exploratory research calls for more than one focus group. In fact, a single session is likely to produce erroneous information. The researcher should use several groups to ensure that the findings are somewhat representative. Even though many individuals may be involved, the unit of analysis is the group and not the individual. Six groups with eight people each, in effect, yields six interviews, not 48.

Depth Interviews **Depth interviews** are relatively unstructured conversations that allow researchers to probe into a consumer's thought processes. Often they are used to investigate the mechanisms of purchase decisions. Although the discussion may appear casual to the participant, the skilled researcher exerts a great deal of control. Often the interview is designed to cover all aspects of the participant's attitudes, opinions, or motivations. The marketer uses these results both as individual case studies and as comparative data to examine commonalities among respondents.

Projective Techniques **Projective techniques** enable respondents to project their thoughts onto a third party, or through some type of contrived situation. This is often done using word associations, sentence completion, and role-playing. Because projective approaches do not re-

Depth interview
A relatively unstructured conversation that allows the researcher to probe deeply into a consumer's thoughts.

Projective technique
A technique that enables respondents to project their thoughts onto a third party or object or through some type of contrived situation.

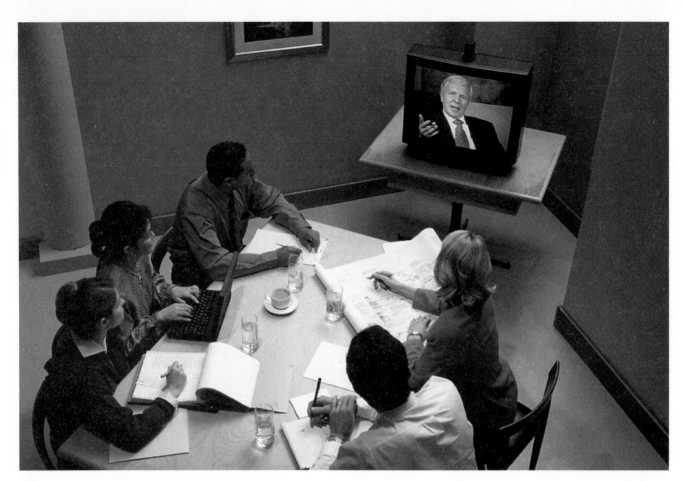

Focus groups provide qualitative insights.

quire respondents to provide answers in a structured format, people are more likely to interpret the situation creatively and in the context of their own experiences and emotions. When asked directly why they purchase a particular item, they may describe a far more rational process than the one that actually occurs. For example, if a recent college graduate is asked why she purchased a Chrysler LeBaron convertible, she may cite performance, gas mileage, and overall value of the product. But if asked to project the feelings of a person who purchases this kind of automobile, she may focus on status, self-esteem, and the need to be noticed.

Observation

A research technique whereby researchers simply watch the participants they are studying.

Observation   **Observation** is a technique whereby the participants are simply watched. In one classic study, researchers stationed themselves in both crowded and uncrowded supermarkets to discover whether buying behavior differed. In uncrowded stores shoppers tended to use the information on labels and shelves, whereas in crowded conditions they tended to make decisions more hastily. This exploratory observation was followed by a more formal survey that enabled conclusions to be drawn about buyer behavior in crowded situations.[26]

Structured observation is made through mechanical means. Galvanometers record electrical resistance in the skin, associated with sweating and other responses. Tachistoscopes measure visual stimuli. Special cameras often are used to study eye movement as a subject reads advertising copy. By observing pupil dilation and blinking responses, it is possible to judge what receives attention in ads or on packaging.[27]

Case analysis

The in-depth study of a few examples.

Case Analysis   **Case analysis** is the in-depth study of a few examples. This technique is particularly appropriate for complex buying and competitive situations. For example, how industrial companies make decisions for particular components or capital goods is often studied this way. A single researcher may spend several days interviewing a firm's employees who purchase and use the product in question. In addition, buying policies, documents, and actual purchase history are investigated. When a few (perhaps 10) companies are examined in this way, researchers obtain a more complete understanding of why and how certain suppli-

CONNECTING WITH DIVERSITY

ELUSIVE YOUTH: RESEARCHERS FIND NEW WAYS TO TRACK THEIR TASTES

To get a bead on the buying habits of teens and 20-somethings, or to catch the next trend wave before it rolls into the stores, market researchers are now talking to kids in clubs, pizzerias, concert ticket lines, and, of course, the mall.

"We tried focus groups in a traditional conference-room setting," says Mitchell Fox, publisher of the hip New York magazine *Details*. "They understood we were there for something. Teens and youth in their 20s are a tough nut for market researchers to crack. More than previous generations, they are aware of themselves as targets for marketing and advertising. This makes them very knowledgeable and outspoken about what they like and don't like—the perfect focus group subjects—but also very wary of being sold to, conned, or labeled." According to Liz DiPilli, a market researcher who conducts roving focus groups, "Young people want to get their opinions out. They feel that the media perception of them as being these slackers . . . sitting around watching *The Real World* and eating nachos all day is not really them." But who are they, what do they want, and how do you find out without ticking them off?

Companies like Evian and Comedy Central are paying DiPilli a $4,900 fee to take part in "Project X" and get the answers to these questions. In her tour of five American cities, DiPilli ditches the traditional sites and holds partylike gatherings in trendy hotel suites. She also chats up kids on the street, at roller blade rental stands, or at volleyball games. "This way you're dealing with them on their terms," says DiPilli. "There's no client looking at them through a two-way mirror or people taking notes." *Details* publisher Fox holds focus groups in people's living rooms.

Bugle Boy Clothing Company goes a step farther and turns young subjects into researchers of their own life. Working with Chilton Research, Bugle Boy plucked four young men out of obscurity, handed each of them an 8 mm video camera, and told them to do a documentary on themselves. The young filmmakers were given only broad categories to work with such as school, home, and shopping. The videos were then used to spur discussions of product and lifestyle issues in free-form focus groups held at unconventional venues, such as restaurants. "I think it really allowed us to get a handle on what these kids do," said Bugle Boy's ad manager, Sue Scheimann. "It lets us see what their lives are all about, their awareness of the Bugle Boy brand, and how they perceive the brand."

Researchers are using unorthodox methods not only to track the tastes of "every kid" but also to spot trends months in advance. Fads and fashions used to be dictated by designers, but now trends are just as likely to pop up from the street, particularly among urban kids. More and more market research firms are getting assignments to seek out today's coolest youngsters. For instance, Cheskin + Masten/ImageNet gave three of its researchers cameras and sent them off to a rock concert in San Francisco's Golden Gate Park. There they checked out offbeat clothing colors, tattoos, and body piercing patterns. One trend they spotted was service-station attendant uniforms or "mechanicwear."

This type of research can pay off big. Burlington Industries learned from the New York–based market research firm Sputnik, Inc., that cool urban kids were wearing stiff, unwashed jeans because they liked the darker color. Burlington soon began producing denim in deeper hues. Now the color is showing up where all the teen trends eventually are played out—the suburban mall.

Sources: Cyndee Miller, "Sometimes a Researcher Has No Choice but to Hang Out in a Bar," *Marketing News*, January 3, 1994, pp. 16–17; Roger Ricklefs, "Marketers Seek Out Today's Coolest Kids to Plug into Tomorrow's Mall Trends," *Wall Street Journal*, July 11, 1996, pp. B1–2; and Cyndee Miller, "Researcher Reaches Xers with Her Focus Groups on the Road," *Marketing News*, January 2, 1996, p. 10.

---

ers are selected. The information can help suppliers determine the appropriateness of various marketing approaches.

Case analysis can also be used to study the competition. Researchers may select two or three activities of key competitors and examine them in depth. By knowing all aspects of the strategies used to introduce a couple of products, researchers can assess competitors' strengths and weaknesses and also predict how they might behave in the future with other products. Benchmarking is also a form of case analysis. For example, the Big Three automakers benchmark such competitors as Nissan, Honda, and Toyota because these companies are substantially more efficient. In fact, one report estimated that if the Big Three could match Nissan's efficiency, Ford could save $1.7 billion; Chrysler, $1.45 billion; and GM, $5 billion annually.[28]

QUANTITATIVE RESEARCH

Quantitative research provides information that helps decision makers select the best course of action and estimate the probable results. As the name suggests, numbers are involved. Rigorous statistical procedures allow researchers to estimate how confident they can be about their conclusions. Since quantitative research uses widely accepted methods, duplicating the study should arrive at approximately the same results. Certain techniques also indicate how closely the findings represent the views or attitudes of the whole population at large, not just the sample studied.

Quantitative research played an enormous role in the successful positioning and launch of Kimberly-Clark's Expressions facial tissue line. In the face of increasing competition from products, the company began looking for an innovative way to increase market share for its Kleenex brand. Nearly 37 percent of buyers said they disliked the look of tissue boxes and often hid them in closets or bathrooms, where they wouldn't clash with household decor. The Expressions line introduced packaging with about 50 different motifs that range from Native American animal drawings to Amish quilts to an impressionistic Manhattan skyline. Product testing in eight U.S. cities revealed consumer preferences for six styles: traditional, country, southwestern, contemporary, Asian, and Victorian. Expressions was ultimately a great success, partly because marketers took the time to learn the opinions of consumers.[29]

Quantitative research usually follows the scientific method to ensure that faulty conclusions are not drawn. The **scientific method** is a systematic way to gather, analyze, and interpret data in order to confirm or disconfirm a prior conception. Essentially, it is a two-step procedure. First, researchers develop a hypothesis about an issue based on a limited amount of information. A **hypothesis** is a tentative assumption about a particular event or issue. Second, rigorous tests are conducted to determine whether the hypothesis is supported by the information.

Let us say we have an idea that more men and women shop in malls on the weekend because they're not working, so we hypothesize that greater sales volumes will be obtained on Saturday and Sunday than on weekdays. We then gather information to test the hypothesis. The key is for researchers to state beforehand what they believe the results may be and why. This enables appropriate data to be gathered and analyzed to assess whether the hypothesis is true.

Data Collection Methods Two of the most common methods for collecting quantitative data are experiments and surveys. **Experiments** usually take place either where the marketing problem occurs or in a laboratory setting that is contrived to match research needs. To test new packaging for a pain reliever, for example, the manufacturer may invite consumers to "shop" in a simulated supermarket. In that way shopping patterns can be observed to see whether the packaging is eye catching. Experiments are often used for causal research. **Causal research** attempts to find a cause-and-effect relationship between two events. One of the most

Kimberly Clark used product testing to reveal consumer preferences for its Expressions line.

INSTRUCTIONS: Please put an X in the space that indicates how strongly you agree or disagree with the following statements about MTV.

	Strongly Disagree	Disagree	Neither Agree Nor Disagree	Agree	Strongly Agree
MTV is fun to watch	_____	_____	_____	_____	_____
MTV is less educational than most evening programming	_____	_____	_____	_____	_____
MTV appeals more to those with higher income	_____	_____	_____	_____	_____
Jenny McCarthy is a real plus for MTV	_____	_____	_____	_____	_____

Figure 5-5   A Typical Likert Scale

important forms of causal research is test marketing. A test market provides a limited trial of a product strategy under realistic conditions.

Surveys are the most popular way to collect data. When researchers want to ensure that each subject is asked for the same information, they prepare a written survey questionnaire. It is a measurement device, much like a thermometer or a ruler. Two common units of measure for questionnaire items are the points along Likert scales and bipolar adjective scales

Likert scales are simple to develop and easy to interpret. **Likert scales** allow the intensity of feelings to be expressed and tend to provide information about a person's attitude toward something. Subjects are asked to indicate the extent to which they agree or disagree with each statement in the survey. The Likert scale shown in Figure 5-5 has five points (units of measure). A seven-point scale often is used, adding "somewhat disagree" and "somewhat agree" on either side of the middle point.

Bipolar adjective scales allow respondents to choose along a range between two extremes. Figure 5-6 shows a typical bipolar adjective scale. In general, there are three, five, or seven points in the scale. Many dimensions can be measured in a relatively short questionnaire. Perhaps that is why this scale is so frequently used in marketing research.

The wording of an item can make quite a difference. A classic example occurred in the 1980s during the battles between Burger King and McDonald's®. Burger King asked respondents: "Do you prefer your hamburgers flame-broiled or fried?" The three-to-one preference for flame-broiled was touted extensively by Burger King in an ad campaign. The results were completely different when McDonald's® researchers asked: "Do you prefer a hamburger that is grilled on a hot stainless-steel grill or cooked by passing the warmed meat through an open-gas flame?" McDonald's® frying method received a clear majority. When the question was modified to include the fact that the gas-flame burgers were warmed in a microwave oven prior to serving, McDonald's® won seven to one.[30]

Likert scale
A scale that measures the respondent's intensity of agreement with a particular statement.

INSTRUCTIONS: Please put an X in the space that most appropriately indicates your feelings about shopping at the GAP.

	Very	Moderately	Slightly	Neither One Nor the Other	Slightly	Moderately	Very	
Inexpensive	—	—	—	—	—	—	—	Expensive
Helpful Salespeople	—	—	—	—	—	—	—	Unhelpful Salespeople
High-Quality Products	—	—	—	—	—	—	—	Low-Quality Products

Figure 5-6   A Typical Bipolar Adjective Scale

Figure 5-7 Comparative
Advantages of Interviews,
Mall Intercepts, Telephone
Surveys, and Mail
Questionnaires

	Personal Interviews	Mall Intercepts	Telephone	Mail
Speed of Completion	Slowest	Fast	Fastest	Moderate
Response Rate	High	Moderate	Moderate	Low
Quality of Response	Excellent	Good	Good	Limited
Interviewer Bias	High	Moderate	Moderate	Low
Geographic Reach	Limited	Limited	Excellent	Excellent
Cost	Very expensive	Moderate	Moderate	Very inexpensive

Administering Surveys A survey can be administered through personal interviews, mall intercepts, telephone, or mail. Each technique has benefits and disadvantages, as shown in Figure 5-7. The researcher needs to select the method most appropriate for the current project.

Personal Interviews Personal interviews require face-to-face two-way communication between the interviewer and the respondent. This method is particularly useful in probing complex answers or observing the respondent's behavior. The setting usually is comfortable, and the respondent is given undivided attention. Sputnik, Inc., is a New York market research firm that specializes in projecting trends among teenagers. It conducts personal interviews with hip teens, often in underground dance clubs or other trendy venues. Participants may be paid up to several hundred dollars for videotaped interviews. Questions are asked about clothing preferences, fingernail polish colors, body piercing, and other issues.[31] Marketers believe that the opinions of this group can be used to predict future fashions among mainstream teens.

One benefit of personal interviews is the high participation rate. It's unlikely that any questions will go unanswered, and props or visual aids can be used. But there are several disadvantages. Subjects may be influenced by the interviewer, and they give up anonymity when meeting face to face, so they may withhold information or answer in unnatural ways. Interviewing is expensive, since professionals must be trained and then sent to the various locations. The cost can range from $25 per average consumer to thousands of dollars per top executive, surgeon, legislator, or others.

Mall Intercepts Mall intercepts, as the name implies, occur at a shopping mall, and the interviewer chooses respondents on some objective basis, such as every fifth person encountered. Mall intercepts are simple to conduct, and data can be collected quickly and cost effectively. Questions can be asked about actual purchases during some specified period. This helps the researcher determine actual behaviors as well as opinions and attitudes. One variation of this method is a shopping basket study, or simply looking at what a consumer purchases during a particular trip to the store. Grocery stores often want this kind of informa-

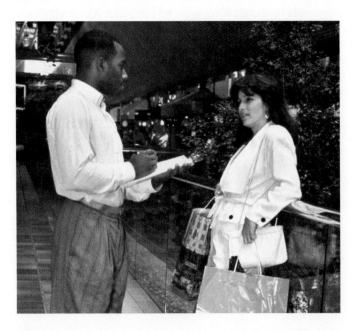

Sputnik, Inc. specializes in projecting trends, often through personal interviews in trendy venues.

tion in order to identify which products are purchased together, the total amount of spending, and the shopping patterns of individuals while in the store.

Telephone Surveys Telephone surveys offer speed and relatively low cost. Using banks of telephones, marketers can contact a large number of people at approximately the same time. This method is particularly effective with professionals, who tend to be articulate and willing to discuss things over the telephone. By prearranging the call, it's possible to gain considerable cooperation from respondents. Now that fax machines and the Internet are so prevalent, a common procedure is to call ahead, fax the information or ask respondents to get it from a Web site, and obtain reactions over the telephone. This enables interviewers not only to probe for thoughts and ideas but also to elicit responses to printed materials. Another advantage of the telephone is that a second call can be arranged easily if the individual cannot respond at that moment. Today, computer-assisted technology allows respondents to register their answers using the touch-tone pad, which works particularly well with a large panel of subjects. Also, computerized systems that are voice activated save on telephone charges and make on-line data analysis possible.

The major drawback of telephone interviews is the increase in unlisted numbers, which makes it very difficult to obtain a valid sample. In some cities more than half the population has an unlisted number. One way to overcome this is through *random digit dialing* by a computer although many consumers are adding Caller ID service to screen out unwanted surveys. In addition, phone surveys have an obvious limitation if respondents are required to see something, as in evaluating ads or product renderings.

Mail Surveys In mail surveys, a questionnaire is sent directly to the respondent's home or place of business. An advantage is that people can answer at their own pace and at a convenient time. Mailed questionnaires can be extremely useful for surveying professionals, who have a high response rate and tend to give thoughtful answers. Publishers regularly survey professors by mail concerning textbooks they have adopted, teaching methods, and their ideas about innovative materials that can be created. Associations often obtain good response quality and return rates from membership surveys by mail.

Many techniques are used to encourage people to answer mail questionnaires. Often a cover letter explains the purpose of the study and why it will be beneficial to them. A little gift or a small amount of money can improve return rates. A study sampling owners of small construction subcontracting companies revealed that one dollar significantly increased the response rate; as the monetary incentive increased, so did the rate.[32] Research also reveals that the rate can be boosted considerably by multiple prior notification, while sending only one has no influence. Mailing a second survey has a significant effect on response rates as well.

It helps to have the surveys sponsored by a legitimate organization, such as a professional association. A study reported in *Industrial Marketing Manager* examined this effect. The mean response rates for the questionnaires from a university and an honor society sponsor were significantly higher than for those sponsored by a marketing research firm and an unidentified source.[33]

Despite every effort to improve the percentage of responses, many people refuse to answer mail questionnaires. This is a serious problem, since those who do respond may differ from the rest of the population. For example, they may be motivated to answer because they intensely like or dislike a product.

Sampling Surveys are conducted to draw insights about the people being studied. The **population (universe)** is comprised of all the individuals or organizations relevant to the marketing research project. For example, if the Bureau of the Census wants to know the average number of jobs a U.S. resident holds during the first 10 years out of high school, the relevant population is all U.S. residents age 28 or older. There are millions in this age group. The bureau could attempt to interview all of them, but that would be impractical if not impossible and far too costly. Researchers have developed methods for surveying a subset of people from whom they draw inferences about the larger population.

The first step is to obtain a **sampling frame,** which is a list of people in the universe who potentially could be contacted. From this, researchers select the sample. A **sample** is the group of people who are asked to participate in the research. Since focus groups usually are very small, it is difficult to determine whether the opinions expressed truly represent those of the larger population.

There are two categories of samples: probability and nonprobability. In a **probability sample,** the chance of selecting a given individual can be calculated. One popular method is

Population (universe)
All the individuals or organizations relevant to the marketing research project.

Sampling frame
A list of people in the universe who potentially could be contacted.

Sample
The group participating in a research project that represents the entire population of potential respondents.

Probability sample
A sample in which the chance of selecting a given individual from the sampling frame or population can be calculated.

Simple random sampling
A sampling technique in which each member of the study population has an equal and known chance of being chosen.

Stratified random sampling
A sampling technique in which each member of a selected subgroup of the population has an equal chance of selection.

Nonprobability sample
A sample in which the likelihood of selecting a particular respondent from the sampling frame cannot be calculated.

Judgment sample
A sample selected by the researchers or interviewers based on their belief that those chosen represent a majority of the study population.

Convenience sample
A sample composed of people who happen to come along, such as shoppers in a store at a given time, whoever answers the doorbell, or travelers passing through an airport.

simple random sampling, whereby each individual has an equal chance of being chosen (say, every third name is selected). Another is **stratified random sampling,** whereby each individual within a selected subgroup of the sample has an equal chance of selection (say, every third household with income of $50,000+). This method is often used in marketing since much research focuses on market segments. If some form of random sampling is adopted, then statistics can be used to determine the likelihood that responses from the sample will be similar to the responses of the larger population.

When using **nonprobability samples,** the researcher does not know the likelihood of selecting a particular respondent. The two most common types are judgment and convenience samples. **Judgment samples** are chosen by the researcher based on the belief that these people represent a majority of the study population.

Convenience samples are people who happen to come along, such as shoppers in a given store at a certain time or travelers passing through an airport. Convenience samples are relatively inexpensive, and the selection can be purposely unrepresentative, such as interviewing only females. In general, this method does not provide data reliable enough for quantitative research. Even probability samples can become like convenience samples if care is not taken regarding the smallest details, such as when interviews are conducted. Tom Brokaw remarked during the 1992 elections that polls could not be taken on Friday night. It seems the results would be skewed because so many Republicans go out that evening.

INTERPRETING AND REPORTING SURVEY FINDINGS

Once the research is completed, the results must be reported to the appropriate decision makers. No matter how sophisticated or reliable, marketing research is of little use unless it can be easily understood by the people who act upon it. Most managers and executives have little experience with research techniques and little interest in learning about them. Thus, presentation of understandable research results is an important skill for marketers. Good research moves from data to information to insight. Unfortunately, to demonstrate the hard work that has gone into a project, many researchers give too much extraneous information. A report that describes each table in detail instead of using the information to reach conclusions is not likely to meet the needs of executives.

Experience pays off in interpreting research. When the Museum of Fine Arts in Boston held focus groups on an upcoming exhibition of Winslow Homer, the researchers found that the public did not know about the artist and would not attend. A museum executive used her experience, including the MFA shop's sales records of items linked to Homer, to demonstrate that the public may not know his name but does know his pictures and would turn out for the show. Because the museum relied on the executive's experience, not the focus groups, it was prepared for the 1996 blockbuster. Yet, sometimes research is right when the experts are wrong. Ford didn't listen to marketing research in the mid-1950s. The Edsel was built with features that consumers said they wanted, but the car itself did poorly in several rounds of consumer testing. Ford went ahead anyway, believing it could push the car with a strong sales force. The mistake cost about $350 million (in 1950s dollars)!

There is some debate about whether marketing researchers should recommend action. Whether marketing researchers make recommendations must depend on the total data available, the inclinations of the researcher, and the desires of decision makers. In keeping with the team spirit, most executives would like knowledgeable people to provide as many insights

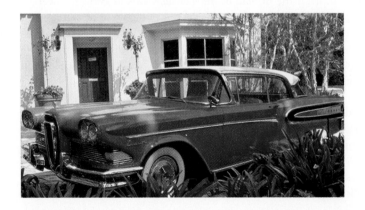

The Edsel: A marketing mistake.

as possible. If recommendations are made, then all the underlying assumptions should be clearly stated.

WHO DOES MARKETING RESEARCH?

The first commercial research department was founded in 1911, at the *Saturday Evening Post*, when Charles C. Parlin completed his now famous study of Campbell's soup users. He undertook the research because Campbell's executives refused to purchase advertising in the *Post*, believing that its working-class readership did not represent a significant market for the company. The soup sold at 10 cents a can, a cost they believed only wealthy consumers could afford. By counting cans in the garbage from different neighborhoods, Parlin proved they were wrong. He showed that canned soup was bought mainly by the time-constrained working class, whereas the wealthy enjoyed homemade soup prepared by servants. Campbell's became a big advertiser in the magazine and one of the top brand names in the United States.

In-Company Research   An AMA survey indicates that three out of four large companies have a formal in-company marketing research department. In fact, nearly all consumer products manufacturers, retailers, wholesalers, advertising agencies, and publishers have such a department. Most were created within the last decade. According to the AMA, the average marketing research budget is about $2 million per firm.[34]

Most in-company marketing research departments are headed by experienced personnel who report to top executives. The research staff usually includes project directors, analysts, and specialists. The project director is responsible for designing projects, which may be conducted within the department or by outside agencies. The position of analyst is an entry-level job with the function of interpreting specific types of data for select decisions. Analysts usually are part of a marketing team from several units or divisions, although they report directly to the head of their department. Marketing research specialists have expertise in one aspect of a project, such as survey design, data collection, statistics, modeling, and/or marketing science.

Marketing research has become so sophisticated that few organizations are willing to rely entirely on their internal capabilities. Consequently, research is conducted by both in-house personnel and outside agencies, who may or may not work together. Often it's not cost effective for companies to hire employees with all the different skills required to conduct a broad range of research. This is especially true regarding data collection. Numerous companies offer field services in that area. Even if external agencies are used, however, most companies still need internal staff to help identify the research problem and interface with the outside agency.

External Research   Companies often hire out marketing research. As you can see from Figure 5-8, conducting research can be a very lucrative business.

Outside agencies include consulting companies, full-service research firms, specialty research firms, and syndicated data companies. Such consulting companies as Deloitte & Touche, Andersen Consulting, and Electronic Data Systems (EDS) often conduct all phases of marketing research but only for clients with whom they have an ongoing relationship. Full-service firms focus on all aspects of data collection and analysis, and their personnel can handle the entire project. Specialty research firms concentrate on certain aspects of a project.

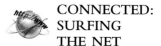

CONNECTED: SURFING THE NET

www.ford.com

Ford has come a long way since the Edsel. Find out what cars it creates for consumers today by visiting "Showroom Boulevard" at the Ford Web site.

Rank	Organization	Headquarters	Total Research Revenues (millions)
1	A. C. Nielsen Corp.	Stamford, CT	$1,358.6
2	Cognizant Corp.	Westport, CT	$1,223.8
3	Information Resources, Inc.	Chicago, IL	$405.6
4	The Arbitron Co.	New York, NY	$153.1
5	PMSI/Source Informaties	Phoenix, AZ	$152.2
6	Westat Inc.	Rockville, MD	$146.5
7	Maritz Marketing Research	St. Louis, MO	$133.6
8	NFO Research, Inc.	Greenwich, CT	$109.2
9	The Kantas Group	London, UK	$99.6
10	Market Facts, Inc.	Arlington Heights, IL	$83.8

Source: "The Top 50 U.S. Marketing/Ad/Opinion Research Firms Profiled," Marketing News, June 9, 1997, p. H3.

Figure 5-8 Top 10 Marketing Research Organizations

Some only conduct surveys, relying on others to supply questionnaires and yet others to perform data analysis. Certain specialty research firms help marketers better understand diversity or particular segments. For example, Hispanic Marketing Communication Research studies consumer satisfaction in Spanish-speaking markets in the United States and Latin America; SIS International Research provides field coverage in more than 100 countries; and Impact Media does door-to-door sampling of specific demographic groups.[35] Syndicated data companies research one type of information or a single industry. For example, the Bureau of the Census and the Bureau of Labor Statistics are experts on census data and use it to model various scenarios for clients. Neurocommunication Research Laboratory specializes in customized information about how broadcast and print advertisements trigger the maximum responses in viewers.

Because marketing research is critical for good decision making but expensive to conduct, most companies build a long-term association with one or more outside sources. This enables the agency to become familiar with the typical problems faced by the organization and to establish a good working relationship with in-company marketing research staff.

> **CAREER TIP** Bob Walker, of the market research firm Surveys and Forecasts, says: "Researchers need to be able to synthesize information from a variety of sources and tell a cohesive story." Marketing research is a challenging and exciting field. Businesses today are not only spending more in this area but also are adding staff researchers and paying higher salaries.[36] The increased demand is providing numerous career opportunities. If you think you might be interested in marketing research, then investigate one of the top ten organizations listed in Figure 5-8.

TECHNOLOGY'S EFFECT ON MARKETING RESEARCH

Technology has brought many changes to marketing research. Today's marketers can acquire and analyze more information faster than ever before. Technology also has made it easier for them to connect with an increasing number of customers and information sources. In the past, marketing research was a relatively static process in the face of constantly changing markets. Now marketers can know in real time what is happening in the marketplace. Data are quickly converted to information that can be used in a specific decision.[37]

Technology has not merely speeded up the research process. Advances in computerized 3-D modeling make it easy to simulate retail stores on computer screens. Virtual shopping is inexpensive to create when compared to the cost of setting up an actual store. Consumers can make product selections as they scroll through the computer image. You can change brand assortment or features in minutes. The virtual store gives marketers a no-risk way to exercise their imagination early in the product development process.[38] Technology helps reduce the cost as well as the risk of marketing innovations.

The Internet's World Wide Web can be an excellent source of marketing data. In fact, it is sometimes referred to as the world's largest resource library. It contains information on literally millions of topics and is updated daily. The trick is to sift through all of it to find what you need.

Marketers do this through the use of a search engine such as Yahoo!, America Online, WebCrawler, and Netscape Navigator Net Search. You type a keyword into the search engine, and it scans all the Web sites to which it's linked, providing you with a list of available information matching the keyword. For example, the keyword *distribution* is likely to produce thousands of sources ranging from companies that provide distribution services to consultants in the distribution industry. You can scan through the sources and generally find the information you need. All marketers should learn how to surf using keyword searches. Still, marketers need to know the limitation of search engines. A single search engine is likely to find only a third or less of the available information on a topic. Multiengine search devices like Metacrawler (www.metacrawler.com) and Savvy Search (guaraldi.cs.colostate.edu:2000) give results from several search engines.[39]

The Internet is an amazing research tool. It has two major advantages over traditional methods—speed and cost effectiveness.[40] According to a survey by LEXIS®-NEXIS®, 81 percent of marketing researchers use on-line services.[41] There is information on nearly every industry, from agriculture to zoology. In addition, quantitative and exploratory research can be conducted through e-mail surveys, on-line focus groups, Web site registration, and observation of discussions among Net users. Marketers often research on-line to divide Internet users into meaningful segments.

The advantages of Internet research are quickly apparent. For example, WP-Studio, an on-line entertainment company, took to the Net when traditional focus group work seemed unsuccessful. The results were amazing. Janice Gjertsen, director of marketing, found the on-line sessions were cheaper, more accurate, and fast. She believes that anonymity allows on-line participants to be honest. Furthermore, special software allowed her to send the moderator messages without the participants knowing. The on-line sessions cost one-third the price of a traditional session, and Gjertsen received a full report in one day as opposed to four weeks.[42] The cost is reduced because participants can dial in from nearly any global location, eliminating the costs of travel, accommodations, and facility rental.

E-mail surveys are another popular method. Such companies as Decisive Technology Corporation offer software that allows e-mail surveys to be conducted with speed and ease.[43] Telephone and mail surveys can cost more than $100,000, but e-mail does away with labor, telephone, postage, and printing costs.[44] Marketers also observe discussions among Net users to gather information about current and prospective customers. Many companies encourage customers to fill out a Web site registration form. The participant is usually asked to volunteer some personal information in exchange for a free gift, coupon, or some other incentive. The information helps the marketer to understand Internet behavior and habits. Banyan Systems, for example, has a Web site registration form that profiles customer interests. Not only can the information be used for research, but also relevant e-mail can be automatically forwarded to those who want it.[45]

GLOBAL MARKETING RESEARCH

Global marketing research involves the same process as any other kind—from research design to the interpretation and presentation of results. And usually the same techniques are employed—interviews, focus groups, and surveys. The big difference is that global marketing research is very difficult.

It is not easy to locate secondary data in foreign countries. Sometimes, it simply isn't collected in a country. For example, Ethiopia and Chad don't gather population statistics.[46] Many developing countries lack mechanisms for collecting data about retail and wholesale activities. And even if secondary data are available, they may be incomplete or their accuracy questionable. The data may be manipulated by the government for political reasons: Russia reported inflation at 2 percent when the International Labor Organization found it was actually more than 10 percent.[47] Industrialized nations usually have sophisticated collection procedures, at least for basic statistics on population and economic activity. In developing countries, data are likely to be based on estimates or outdated processes.[48]

Because secondary data are difficult to find, global research most often requires the collection of primary data. This, too, presents many challenges. One of the most obvious is that of language. It's very hard to ensure an exact translation, especially when slang is used. Many researchers use a technique called *back translation*: The research question is translated into the foreign language by one person, and then it is put back in the original language by a second person. This helps catch any errors. It certainly helped an Australian soft drink company hoping to market its product in Hong Kong. Its slogan, "Baby, it's cold in here," translated

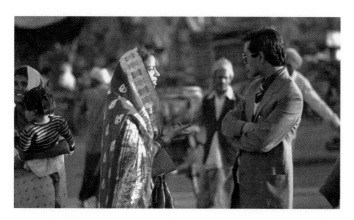

Global marketing research can present numerous challenges.

into Chinese as: "Small mosquito, on the inside it is very cold."[49] Needless to say, that would have been an embarrassing marketing blunder!

Once the survey instrument is translated, participants must be found. Again, this isn't easy. In Mexico, there are only eight phones per 100 citizens, compared to 50 per 100 in the United States. And the phone service in Mexico is extremely unreliable. In Brazil, nearly 30 percent of all mail is never delivered. Postal service is equally poor in other developing countries. Even if the mail gets through, literacy can be another barrier. Sometimes, even individual interviews present challenges. In many cultures, it's considered embarrassing to discuss personal hygiene, such as which shampoo or soap you use. The Germans tend to avoid conversations about personal finances and the Dutch would rather talk about sex than money.[50]

Nevertheless, companies that avoid global marketing research find themselves in trouble. Consider the U.S. baby care company advertising its bath soap in Hungary. The ad, which showed a mother holding her baby, caused an uproar. Why? Because the mother had a wedding band on her left hand, and Hungarian women wear wedding bands on their right hand. The ad was interpreted as an unwed mother holding her baby, and women refused to buy the product.[51] Marketing research probably would have caught the mistake.

Global marketing research is becoming more and more prevalent as companies expand their scope of operations. The time it takes to conduct worldwide research has been reduced by computer-based interviews via the Internet, the spread of telephones and fax machines, and express delivery services. For example, one software company conducted a worldwide survey of more than 80 clients in only three weeks. This amazing feat involved modeling tasks, computer programming, list development, respondent recruiting, diskette distribution, and data retrieval, analysis, and reporting. As a result of the research, the company was able to improve its pricing strategy.[52]

ETHICS IN MARKETING RESEARCH AND INFORMATION USE

J. D. Power is paid by automakers to provide research on customer satisfaction. This information is then used in publications to promote autos. Some magazine editors receive "consulting fees" from auto companies and write reviews of car performance. These are certainly legal practices, but are they ethical?

With the information explosion comes an increasing amount of potentially deceptive research that can be used to alter consumers' opinions. Historically, studies were sponsored by scientists, the federal government, and academic institutions. Today, with government and universities on tight budgets, private companies fill the void with so-called objective research for hire. Corporations, litigants, political candidates, trade associations, lobbyists, and special interest groups can buy research to use as they like.[53]

A study by the Boston Center for Strategy Research reveals that some marketing managers believe market research is likely to reflect biases rather than present objective information. They also believe much of it is conducted to confirm a preconceived conclusion or validate a client's position. In other words, it arrives at the desired answer, no matter what the facts may indicate. Research of this nature is confirmation, not exploratory.[54] The scientific method is supposed to prevent this type of bias, because anyone duplicating a study or experiment should come up with the same results.

More and more of the information available to consumers is created to sell a product or advance a cause. Buying and selling information to advance a private agenda demonstrates how the modern sense of truth may be warped.[55] Privately sponsored research tends to emphasize positive results and downplay negative ones. Companies obviously want their products to look good.[56] If study results contradict the sponsor's agenda, then they may be suppressed. Yet, if the information indicates potential harm to consumers, then ethical and possibly legal issues arise.

Although consumers are increasingly suspicious about "facts," they often have little basis for questioning them. The average consumer does not have enough personal knowledge to dispute the research that almost daily shapes our beliefs about social, political, economic, and environmental issues. That is why many groups exist to assist and protect consumers. Interested in truth, objectivity, and accuracy, these groups consist of representatives from industry, individual companies, academia, and the government. They have taken action to regulate the content of information and to defend the average consumer from distorted messages. Some industries have collectively formulated policies in order to reduce litigation, prevent mandatory regulation, and increase consumer trust. Still, questionable information finds its way to consumers.

Consider a 1990 study sponsored by Procter & Gamble, the leading maker of disposable diapers. For several years, the company had been fighting a public relations battle against environmentalists and the cloth diaper industry. Between 1988 and 1990, sales of cloth diapers skyrocketed, and more than a dozen state legislatures were considering various regulations for disposable diapers. Under pressure, Procter & Gamble decided to finance a public policy study.

The researchers found that disposable and cloth diapers were environmentally equivalent, when factors such as energy and water use were taken into account. The media disseminated the results and the sale of disposables improved. In 1992, Gerber Products, the largest supplier of cloth diapers, closed three plants and laid off 900 workers. Gerber's CEO said: "There was a dramatic change in the cloth diaper market caused by reduced environmental concern about disposable diapers."[57] Procter & Gamble won back lost market share and gained, at least temporarily, acceptance of disposables.

Although a marketer may occasionally benefit from biased information, those who connect ethically are more likely to create a profitable long-term relationship based on trust and

---

CONNECTED: SURFING THE NET

J. D. Power & Associates
www.jdpower.com

THIS CHAPTER'S CONNECTING THROUGH RELATIONSHIPS feature discusses J. D. Power & Associates, the international marketing information firm. Learn more about the company by visiting its Web site and answering the following questions.

1. Read "About J. D. Power & Associates." In what two areas has the company been recognized for its marketing information and consulting? What other marketing information services does the company offer? How do these services benefit its customers?
2. A number of industries are served by J. D. Power & Associates. Read "Friends of J. D. Power & Associates." List three of the companies—each from a different industry. What kind of marketing information might each company you've listed be interested in obtaining?
3. Since J. D. Power & Associates is an international firm, what difficulties may it encounter when collecting information? In what ways can technology facilitate the company's marketing research efforts?

Bugle Boy Clothing Company
www.bugleboy.com

THE DIVERSITY FEATURE IN THIS chapter discusses the Bugle Boy Clothing Company's unique method of conducting research. To expand your thinking about Bugle Boy, visit its Web site and answer the following questions.

1. Bugle Boy is one of the largest privately held apparel companies in the United States. Read its history. To what does the company attribute its success? What role do you think marketing information and research have played in this success?
2. Read about the evaluation of products at Bugle Boy. How have its products changed through the years? How might exploratory research have contributed to Bugle Boy's product decisions? List ways the company may have collected this research.
3. Play Bugle Boy's on-line game. How does the company use this game as a means of collecting marketing information? Would you say that this is an effective method? Why or why not?
4. In order to connect with customers, Bugle Boy must understand and accommodate diverse needs. Choose and discuss a press release that shows Bugle Boy connecting with diversity. How does marketing research strengthen this connection?

loyalty. Often, as companies seek to build such relationships, the first question they must answer is: What customers are we trying to reach and how do we go about it? In the next chapter we will discover ways in which marketing information supports the selection and targeting of desirable market segments.

CHAPTER SUMMARY

OBJECTIVE 1: Understand the roles that marketing information systems (MIS) and research play in marketing decision making.

You can't connect with customers if you can't locate, understand, and respond to them. MIS are critical in making informed decisions about nearly every aspect of marketing. They are used to systematically collect and analyze data to support decision making. An MIS often includes a marketing decision support system (MDSS), which puts information in convenient form for executives to use. MIS are ongoing and encompass all information. Marketing research is conducted to address a particular opportunity, problem, or issue. Marketing information is used in planning, marketing mix decisions, and performance monitoring.

OBJECTIVE 2: Recognize how data are transformed into information to be used in a variety of marketing decisions.

Data and information are not the same. Data must be translated into information before they are useful for decision making. External data come from outside the firm, and internal data originate inside the firm. Both types are stored in databases so they can be retrieved through a computer. Primary data are collected for the first time to address a specific issue. Secondary data already exist and can be accessed immediately by a broad range of users. Once data are assembled, they must be analyzed through data sorting, the use of statistics, and models. All of this is done with particular issues and decision areas in mind.

OBJECTIVE 3: Understand the types of research and the steps of a typical marketing research process.

The marketing research process starts with the problem definition, which focuses on the needs of decision makers to ensure that the research will be useful. The research design is then based on what decisions need what information, what data and data sources will provide that information, and how the data will be collected and analyzed. Next, exploratory research helps investigators better understand issues by defining problems, searching for possible explanations, and creating hypotheses. Quantitative research yields information to help decision makers select the best course of action. Because it is quantitative, estimates usually can be made of the likely results of actions. This requires appropriate measurement and sampling. The last steps are to interpret and report findings. Experience and insight are useful at this stage because the same information can be interpreted in various ways.

OBJECTIVE 4: Describe widely used marketing research techniques.

Exploratory research techniques include focus groups, depth interviews, projective techniques, observation, and case analysis. A focus group usually has eight to 12 people. Several sessions must be used since the group, not individuals, provide the data. Depth interviews are one-on-one conversations. Researchers spend a lot of time probing a few respondents about their opinions and actions. With projective techniques, subjects are asked to analyze contrived situations or to give opinions about how they believe others may respond. Observation provides insights by watching consumers in a range of situations. Finally, case analysis is the study of a few situations in depth. It is particularly useful for benchmarking. Quantitative research often involves using the scientific method. Surveys and test markets are common in this type of research. Survey data are usually collected from a sample of the population. Questionnaire design is important. Likert scales or bipolar adjective scales frequently are used in questionnaires.

OBJECTIVE 5: Explore how marketing information is being influenced by technology and is obtained globally.

Both internal and external marketing research are being dramatically influenced by technology. It facilitates the faster collection and analysis of greater quantities of information than was possible in the past. The Internet is a revolutionary way of interacting with customers. Research in global markets is complicated because secondary data may be scarce. Surveys must be carefully translated, and data collection is often difficult. Still, global research is becoming more and more important.

OBJECTIVE 6: Understand that ethical issues surround the use and dissemination of research.

There are many ethical issues surrounding marketing research. One problem is that it sometimes can reflect the biases of marketers. When research is conducted to confirm a preconceived conclusion or validate a position, the results are not likely to be objective. The scientific method can eliminate this type of bias. A number of groups exist to prevent the manipulation of marketing research. They are interested in accuracy and want to protect consumers.

REVIEW YOUR UNDERSTANDING

1. What is a marketing information system (MIS)? What is a marketing decision support system (MDSS)? What is a transaction-based information system (TBIS)?
2. What is marketing research? How is it different from an MIS?
3. How are data transformed into information? What are the three steps?
4. What are the differences between primary and secondary data? Give examples.
5. What are the three major uses of marketing information? Explain.
6. What are the steps in a typical marketing research project?
7. What is exploratory research? What are five exploratory research methods?
8. What is quantitative research? What are two quantitative methods?
9. Give two challenges associated with global marketing research.
10. What are the pros and cons of each type of survey data collection?

1. How is a MIS used? What are the two components of a typical MIS? Describe them.
2. What is the difference between data and information? Why is it important for marketers to provide executives with information rather than data?
3. Explain the objective of the marketing decision support system.
4. List and describe the four types of information MIS provides. What is the importance of each type for decision making?
5. Describe each step of the marketing research process. Why is it so important to lay out each step in detail prior to beginning any research project?
6. Select a marketing problem and design a marketing research approach suitable to address it.
7. After completing an exploratory research study, how would you decide whether quantitative research is in order?
8. What would be the major considerations in developing a marketing research capability for a small company?
9. Under what circumstances would you consider it to be ethical to withhold marketing research from interested consumers? When would it be unethical?

KEY TERMS AND DEFINITIONS

Case analysis: The in-depth study of a few examples.

Causal research: Research that attempts to prove a cause-and-effect relationship between two phenomena.

Convenience sample: A sample composed of people who happen to come along, such as shoppers in a store at a given time, whoever answers the doorbell, or travelers passing through an airport.

Data: Facts or statistics obtained from outside or inside the company.

Database: A collection of data that can be retrieved by a computer.

Depth interview: A relatively unstructured conversation that allows the researcher to probe deeply into a consumer's thoughts.

Experiment: A test conducted under controlled conditions in order to prove or disprove a marketing hypothesis.

Exploratory research: Research designed to clarify the problem and suggest ways to address it.

External data: Data obtained outside the company.

Focus group: A group, usually composed of eight to 12 people, whose opinions are elicited by an interviewer to provide exploratory insights into a problem.

Hypothesis: A tentative assumption about a particular event or issue.

Internal data: Data obtained within the company.

Judgment sample: A sample selected by the researchers or interviewers based on their belief that those chosen represent a majority of the study population.

Likert scale: A scale that measures the respondent's intensity of agreement with a particular statement.

Management information system (MIS): A computerized system used to collect and analyze the data needed for management decision making. The marketing information system is often considered a part of this system.

Marketing decision support system (MDSS): A two-way communication bridge between the people who collect and analyze information and the executives who use it.

Marketing information system (MIS): A computerized system used to collect and analyze marketing data.

Marketing research: The formal assembly and analysis of information about specific issues surrounding the marketing of goods and services.

Nonprobability sample: A sample in which the likelihood of selecting a particular respondent from the sampling frame cannot be calculated.

Observation: A research technique whereby researchers simply watch the participants they are studying.

Pilot study: A small-scale project that allows the researcher to refine and test the approaches that eventually will be used.

Population (universe): All the individuals or organizations relevant to the marketing research project.

Primary data: Information collected for the first time.

Probability sample: A sample in which the chance of selecting a given individual from the sampling frame or population can be calculated.

Projective technique: A technique that enables respondents to project their thoughts onto a third party or object or through some type of contrived situation.

Quantitative research: Research designed to provide the information needed to select the best course of action and estimate the probable results.

Research design: An outline of what data will be gathered, what scores will be used, and how the data will be collected and analyzed.

Sample: The group participating in a research project that represents the entire population of potential respondents.

Sampling frame: A list of people in the universe who potentially could be contacted.

Scientific method: A systematic way to gather, analyze, and interpret data in order to confirm or disconfirm a prior conception.

Secondary data: Information that already has been collected.

Simple random sampling: A sampling technique in which each member of the study population has an equal and known chance of being chosen.

Stratified random sampling: A sampling technique in which each member of a selected subgroup of the population has an equal chance of selection.

Transaction-based information system (TBIS): A computerized link between a firm and its customers and/or distributors and suppliers.

REFERENCES

1. Sources: Virginia I Postrel, "The Big Uneasy," *Forbes ASAP*, August 26, 1996, p. 32, Kathy Rebello, "A Literary Hangout—Without the Latte," *Business Week*, September 23, 1996, (from on-line BW) p. TK; Michael H. Martin,

"The Next Big Thing: A Bookstore?," *Fortune*, December 9, 1996, pp. 168–170.

2. www.amazon.com/exec/obidos/subst/misc/comments.html/May, 1998.

3. Kathy Rebello, "A Literary Hangout—Without the Latte," *Business Week,* September 23, 1996.
4. Personal interview with Olga Dazzo, Sparrow Health System, Lansing, MI.
5. Chad Rubel, "Pizza Hut Explores Customer Satisfaction," *Marketing News,* March 25, 1996, p. 15.
6. Suzanne Oliver, "Yuppie Yenta," *Forbes*, March 25, 1996, p. 102.
7. Cyndee Miller, "Research Spending Up, Staffs Down," *Marketing News,* January 29, 1996, p. 8.
8. Garth Hallberg, *All Consumers Are Not Created Equal* (New York: John Wiley & Sons, 1995), p. 40.
9. Internet: Webmaster@ATT.com, June 27, 1996.
10. Gary Jacobson, "How Frito-Lay Stays in the Chips," *Management Review,* December 1989, p. 11.
11. Cyndee Miller, "Food Producers Appeal to Fat-Free Crowd," *Marketing News,* August 14, 1995, p. 3.
12. Nancy K. Austin, "Getting the Picture," *Incentive,* April 1995, p. 44.
13. Michelle Ortiz Ray, "Catalog Focuses on Women Travelers," *Marketing News,* February 26, 1996, p. 12.
14. Leah Haran, "Grocery Category Management Made Better by Census Data," *Advertising Age,* May 6, 1996, p. 16.
15. Personal interview with Dana Anderson, Leo Burnett Company, Inc., Chicago, IL, July 3, 1996.
16. Rubel, "Pizza Hut Explores Customer Satisfaction."
17. "Hilton's Home Away from Home," *Library Management* 15, no. 5 (1994): 16.
18. Richard Feare, "Promoting Service Excellence Through Service Branding," *International Journal of Contemporary Hospitality Management,* 1992, p. III–VII.
19. "Nielsen Media Research Interactive Services" http://www.nielsenmedia. com.
20. A. Einstein and L. Infeld, *The Evolution of Physics* (New York: Simon & Schuster, 1942), p. 95.
21. Melanie Wells and Dottie Enricho, "Marketers Tie Brand Names to Major Events," *USA Today,* December 8, 1995, p. B1.
22. Bradley Johnson, "Supermarkets Move Back to Inner Cities," *Advertising Age,* January 25, 1993, p. 41.
23. Joseph E. Daniel, "Becoming One with Your Readers," *Folio,* August 15, 1993, p. 90.
24. Rebecca Piirto Heath, "Future Focus Groups," *American Demographics,* January 1994, p. 6.
25. Charlie Hamlin, "Market Research and the Wired Consumer," *Marketing News,* June 9, 1997, p. 6.
26. Gilbert D. Harrell, Michael D. Hutt, and James C. Anderson, "Path Analysis of Buyer Behavior under Conditions of Crowding," *Journal of Marketing Research,* February 1980, p. 47.
27. For a discussion of human mechanical observation techniques see Gilbert A. Churchill, Jr., *Marketing Research,* 5th ed. (Chicago: Dryden Press, 1991), p. 349.
28. Valerie Reitman, "Big Three Auto Makers Shrink Productivity Gap With Rivals," *Wall Street Journal Interactive Edition,* June 12, 1997.
29. Raju Narisetti, "Plotting to Get Tissues into Living Rooms," *Wall Street Journal,* May 3, 1996, p. B1.
30. Christy Marshall, "Have It Your Way with Research," *Advertising Age,* April 4, 1983, p. 16.
31. Roger Ricklefs, "Marketers Seek Out Today's Coolest Kids to Plug into Tomorrow's Mall Trends," *Wall Street Journal,* July 11, 1996, pp. B1–2.
32. Jeannine M. James and Richard Bolstein, "Large Monetary Incentives and Their Effect on Mail Survey Response Rates," *Public Opinion Quarterly,* 1992, pp. 442–452.
33. Sudhir K. Chawla, P.V. (Sundar) Blakrishnan and Mary F. Smith, "Mail Response Rates From Distributors," *Industrial Marketing Management,* Nov. 1992, p. 307–310.
34. Thomas C. Kinnear, ed., *1994 Survey of Marketing Research* (Chicago: American Marketing Association 1995), p. 30.
35. "Services Index to the 1995 Marketing News Directory of Customer Satisfaction Measurement Firms," *Marketing News,* October 23, 1995, p. 10.
36. Cyndee Miller, "Study: Firms Adding Researchers but Continue to Outsource," *Marketing News,* June 9, 1997, pp. 1, 7.
37. Chad Rubel, "Technology Forces Changes in Marketing Research," *Marketing News,* October 23, 1995, p. 38.
38. Raymond R. Burke, "Virtual Shopping: Breakthrough in Marketing Research," *Harvard Business Review,* March-April 1996, p. 120.
39. Gina Kolata, "It's Confirmed: Web's Size Bogs Down Searches," *New York Times* (Circuits section), April 9, 1998, p. G3.
40. Ian P. Murphy, "Interactive Research," *Marketing News,* January 20, 1997, pp. 1, 17.
41. "Researching Researchers," *American Demographics,* September 1996, p. 34–36.
42. Sarah Schafer, "Getting a Line on Customers," *Inc.* (Technology Supplement), Nov. 19, 1996, p. 102.
43. Jerry Rosa, "Decisive Technology: Surveys over the Internet, Intranet," *Computer Reseller News,* October 7, 1996, p. 146.
44. Peter Krasilovsky, "Surveys in Cyberspace," *American Demographics,* November-December 1996, pp. 18–22.
45. "Snaring Customers on the Web," *Sales and Marketing Technology* (A Sales and Marketing Management Supplement), June 1996, p. 11.
46. Jeannet Henessey, *Global Marketing Strategies*, 3rd ed. (Boston: Houghton Mifflin, 1995), p. 202.
47. "Politics and Current Affairs," *Economist,* February 5, 1994, p. 4.
48. "The *Good* Statistics Guide," *Economist,* September 11, 1993, p. 65.
49. Sak Onkvisit and John J. Shaw, *International Marketing,* 2nd ed. (Upper Saddle River, NJ: Prentice Hall, 1993), p. 398.
50. Robin Cobb, "Marketing Shares," *Marketing,* February 22, 1990, p. 44.
51. Tara Parker-Pope, "Ad Agencies Are Stumbling in East Europe," *Wall Street Journal,* May 10, 1996, p. 82.
52. John B. Elmer, "Travel the High-Speed Road to Global Market Research," *Marketing News,* June 9, 1997, p. H11.
53. Cynthia Crossens, *Tainted Truth: The Manipulation of Fact in America* (New York: Simon & Schuster, 1994), p 19.
54. "Repondents Assail Quality of Research," *Marketing News,* May 8, 1995, p. 14.
55. Crossens, *Tainted Truth,* p 14.
56. Ibid., p. 19.
57. Jeffery Kluger, "Poll Vaulting," *Discover,* May 1995, p. 46.

CASE 5

REEBOK

*I*MAGINE HOW REEBOK MARKETING EXECUTIVES felt when they discovered they had shipped 53,000 pairs of shoes bearing a name that means "an evil spirit that makes sexual advances to women while they are sleeping." The company annually picks about 1,500 new names for products, and "Incubus" was selected after a legal search found that it wasn't trademarked. Unfortunately, no one had taken the obvious first step of looking it up in the dictionary. This is unusual for Reebok, which knows the importance of marketing research and uses it in some very creative ways.

The "Incubus" blooper, however, is minor compared to the many challenges Reebok has faced. In 1995, Paul Fireman, CEO of Reebok International Ltd., told an angry group of shareholders he would resign if he failed to turn the company around within two years. At that time, profits were declining, and sales were relatively flat. In the 1980s Reebok sold about one-third of the sports

footwear in the lucrative U.S. market. By the mid-1990s, it commanded a mere 20 percent, while rival Nike had increased by 6 percentage points. Roger Best, senior vice president and general manager of Reebok, says the brand had lost definition. "We've been a little too much like vanilla ice cream, which is a nicer sounding term than mud." This allowed competitors to gain share, largely at Reebok's expense.

Part of the company's problems stem from its success in the mid-1980s as a fitness-based brand. By the 1990s it needed to become a more broadly based sports brand. As a part of this effort, Reebok decided to target young, physically active men and women and trend-setting teens. In order to accomplish its objectives, Reebok relied strongly on marketing research and information gathering. Fireman believed that one of the first questions to answer was whether Reebok is a sports/performance brand or a fitness/fashion brand. Based on research, he opted for sports/performance. Reebok needed a leadership product to take on Nike's Air system. The result was the DMX Series 2000, a running shoe that some believe contains breakthrough technology.

How did Reebok use research to design a leadership product? In the 1980s, the company discovered a neglected market niche by studying how women used their leisure time. The results revealed that aerobic exercise was one of the hottest markets for women, so Reebok developed the first women's aerobic shoe. Its success made the company an industry contender and proved the value of understanding time-use in identifying needs and creating products. Today, Reebok does a lot of time-use marketing research. Sue Prakken, senior marketing research manager at Reebok, says: "We track what people are doing with their leisure time very carefully, particularly with regard to exercise." Prakken manages an extensive program of telephone interviews, mall-intercept surveys, and in-depth interviews at consumers' homes in order to understand precisely how people use their time.

Reebok's time-use research has paid off. In 1991, the company followed the off-season activity of basketball players and found that they played on asphalt rather than indoor hardwood courts. This led to the creation of Reebok's successful blacktop basketball shoes. Research also revealed that adults were spending less time in exercise clubs and more time working out at home. So, Reebok marketed a "home step" product and exercise video. When it learned more people were walking for exercise, it responded with a line of walking shoes.

Marketing research is critical in the highly competitive $6.8 billion U.S. shoe market. Nike and Reebok sneakers used to come out yearly, but now there are new styles every season and for almost every sport. On average, Nike issues more than one new shoe style every single day. To keep up with the fierce competition, Reebok often uses the names of athletes with broad market potential. For example, the company will offer the first signature footwear with female endorsers, including basketball players Rebecca Lobo and Saudia Roundtree. Reebok also plans to introduce high-end cleats tied to its top female soccer endorsers, Julie Foudy and Michelle Akers. But these moves don't ensure success. Fila and Adidas are also looking for athletic footwear signature superstars, and Nike is probably among the most aggressive in this area, featuring such WNBA players as Lisa Lesley. Nike projects that its women's sports business will make up 40 percent of its total within five years and is a tough, tough competitor.

Perhaps Reebok's most interesting research technique today is the Cool Hunt. Who decides what's cool? At Reebok, the answer is certain kids in certain places, and Baysie Wightman, general merchandise manager, knows where to find them. Places like Stratton, Vermont, and California's Summit County are on her list. Cool hunting is not about a clearly defined statement but a collection of observations and predictions. A *New Yorker* reporter recently went on a Cool Hunt with Baysie, who took along a canvas bag with 24 different shoes Reebok planned to bring out. At Dr. J's, the cool place to buy sneakers in the Bronx, Baysie solicited opinions from consumers who gathered around. She asked one question after another as she displayed each pair of shoes. Reebok's new DMX RXT, a low-cut walking and running shoe in white and blue, with mesh and a translucent ice sole, was well received by the men. Interestingly, the DMX RXT was a women's shoe that had not done well, so their interest was particularly useful.

On the surface, it appears that Baysie's research is unscientific. Certainly, it's hard to know whether this method really provides useful marketing data. Is it appropriate for a company that wants to position itself technologically for the serious athlete? E. Scott Morris, senior designer for Reebok, believes it's important for an organization to stay in touch. "The kid in the store would say, 'I'd like this shoe if your logo wasn't on it.' That's kind of a punch in the mouth. But we have all seen it. You go into a shoe store, the kid picks up the shoe and says, 'Ah, man, this is nice.' Eventually he says, 'Ah, this is Reebok,' and 'I ain't buying this,' puts the shoe down, and walks out." Somewhere along the way, Reebok lost its cool and must rebuild its image.

Reebok's cool hunting takes various forms. For example, a recent Emmett Smith shoe, designed for football players, had a piece of molded rubber on the end of the tongue as a design element. When Reebok gave the shoes to the Boston College football team for wear testing, it got them back with the rubber tongue piece cut out. It wasn't cool, and on the final version of the shoe it was eliminated. The cool hunters at Reebok have a rule of thumb: If kids in Chicago, New York, and Detroit like a shoe, it's a guaranteed hit. When Baysie returns from a Cool Hunt, she sits down with marketing experts, sales people, and designers to reconnect them to the street. She tries to make sure they have the right shoes at the right price. But Baysie isn't alone. Her friend Didi Gordon, who works for Lambiss, an advertising agency in Delmar, California, is also a cool hunter. Didi says to be a good cool hunter you must somehow just know. She said she once tried to hire someone as a cool hunter who was not cool. It was a disaster. He just didn't have the instinct, the sense that told him what was cool.

Marketing research at Reebok is continually evolving. In the past two years, the company has made investments in produce research and development centers at both corporate headquarters and in Korea. In addition to Reebok's time-use research and other creative methods, the centers will help Reebok return to cutting-edge thinking and true product innovation. According to Bob Meers, president and CEO of the Reebok division, the company is developing "a continuous stream of evolving product based on well researched technological and design platforms, opening up a host of possibilities for the Reebok brand." With this focus, perhaps Reebok can regain its cool.

1. *How do the research approaches and methods described in the case support or not support the positioning being sought by Reebok? Explain.*
2. *Identify the components of a marketing information system you believe are necessary for Reebok to remain competitive.*
3. *What type of research method is a Cool Hunt? What additional steps are required to provide reliable data for making key product development and merchandising decisions within Reebok?*

SOURCES: http://www.reebok.com, visited October 30, 1997; Malcolm Gladwell, "The Coolhunt," *New Yorker*, March 17, 1997, pp. 78–88; Joe Schwartz, "How Reebok Fits Shoes," *American Demographics*, March 1993, http://www.marketingtools.com; "What You Didn't Learn in Marketing 101," *Sales and Marketing Management*, April 1997, p. 14; Silvia Sansoni and Lori Bongiorno, "Reebok Is Tripping Over Its Own Laces," *Business Week*, February 26, 1996, pp. 62–66; Patricia Sellers, "Reebok Gets a Lift," *Fortune*, August 18, 1997, http:fortune.com; Terry Lefton, "Nike Uber Alles," *Brandweek*, December 9, 1996, pp. 25–36; Jeff Jensen, "Reebok Readies Women's Signature Shoes," *Advertising Age*, April 7, 1997, pp. 3, 53; Randall Laqne, "You Are What You Wear," *Forbes*, October 14, 1996, pp. 42–46; and Steve Gelsi, "Everyone's Still Shooting at the Swoosh," *Brandweek*, February 5, 1996, p. 30.

Market Segmentation, Targeting, and Positioning

Objectives

1. Understand the advantages of target marketing and how it differs from mass marketing and product differentiation.

2. Describe how to do market segmentation and select target markets.

3. Explore three basic target marketing strategies: undifferentiated, differentiated, and concentrated marketing.

4. Know how to do positioning and describe several approaches marketers use to create valuable, lasting images of their products.

"AS AMERICAN AS APPLE PIE" IS a cliché in need of an image makeover. America is no longer just pie. It is also burritos, wontons, fritters, and papadums. And it is no longer just apples. Try mangoes, star fruit, lingonberries, or lichees. The tastes of ethnic and racial minorities, and the way they influence all things related to food, is creating great changes in the supermarket—in product mix, displays, and even the products themselves.

Food manufacturers and grocers are paying much more attention to minorities than ever before. In fact, Americans are paying more attention to one another. Multiculturalism starts early—in day care centers, on television, in kids' coloring books, and in videos. All around the world, children are the heralds of the diversity connection. They are encouraged to learn about their similarities and differences through games, books, toys, and even food.

In the United States, immigrants are usually young, and minorities tend to have large families. Therefore, the younger population is likely to be more ethnically diverse than the population in general. According to the 1990 census, 80 percent of all Americans are nonminorities, but less than 75 percent of the population under age 10 are nonminorities. Although 12 percent of all Americans are African American, the figure is 15 percent for those under age 10. And Hispanics account for 9 percent of the general population but almost 13 percent of those under age 10.

Food is one of the most obvious characteristics of a culture. It is also one that spreads the fastest. Today, all sorts of ethnic foods find their way into the shopping carts of all sorts of Americans. This was not always the case. During the 1950s, adventurous cooks might try a few classic French dishes. Other "exotic" fare in home kitchens was Italian and Chinese—in the form of canned pastas and chop suey. Only the most daring prepared such radical recipes as Polynesian pork or Spanish paella.

Now salsa is as common as ketchup; pizza and spaghetti are so mainstream that they're old hat. Kosher-certified labels appear on everything from colas to hot dogs. Just about every self-respecting fast-food place offers a range of multicultural dishes from tacos to bagels to croissants.

Two topics interest marketers when looking at ethnic foods. First, there is the issue of marketing to minority groups themselves. African Americans, Hispanics, Asians, and others have their own distinct food cultures, tastes, and traditions. They also have distinct economic and social parameters that set them apart when it comes to eating, cooking, and shopping. Second, minorities are not the only ones interested in regional and ethnic cuisine. People of all backgrounds are crossing boundaries to try the latest foods.

Some manufacturers are adapting ethnic recipes to suit nonethnic tastes, while others are pushing cross-ethnic hybrids like Mexican pizza and Chinese pasta. Some products originally aimed at specific minorities have been "discovered" by shoppers looking for something different. Gerber found that its line of "Tropical"—juices, fruits, cereals, and desserts in such flavors as passion fruit, mango, and papaya—sold well not only to Hispanics, for whom the product was designed, but also to other parents.

Ethnic marketing has taken on new dimensions as different groups move from urban ethnic enclaves to more mixed suburbs and rural areas. Marketers are encountering a broader variety of shoppers with different needs. Reaching these consumers requires a crash course in diversity. The results can be well worth the effort—as everyone, not just the minority shopper, begins to experiment with new products, tastes, and cooking ideas.[1]

THE CONCEPT OF SEGMENTATION, TARGETING, AND POSITIONING

In the early days, General Motors' philosophy was "a different auto for every need." At that time, each GM division focused its creative energies and economic might on satisfying loyal customers in separate market segments. They connected with customers by targeting clearly defined groups of buyers. Today, GM's 10 lines of cars and trucks (Chevrolet, Chevy Trucks, Geo, Pontiac, Oldsmobile, Buick, Cadillac, GMC, Saturn, and EV_1) have several models each. In fact, GM markets 82 different names of cars and trucks.[2] When GM was founded, the American social class system had a good deal of upward mobility and GM had a brand targeted at each class. Typically, a young family might buy a Chevy, followed by a Pontiac. Years later, a Buick or Oldsmobile would be purchased. Finally, as a mark of economic accomplishment came the ultimate in status and prestige—a Cadillac. America is no longer defined largely by social class, so while the relative costs of GM models still reflect, to some degree, the pricing hierarchy of previous years, their target markets are vastly different.

Among other products, Procter & Gamble markets 10 different laundry detergents, seven brands of hand soaps, six shampoos, four types of dishwashing soaps, four toothpastes, and three toilet tissues. How many of these can you name? See the footnote for answers.*

Why would strong companies like General Motors and Procter & Gamble develop so many brands? Do these compete with one another or primarily take on rival brands? The answer is that each brand is designed for a different market segment. A **market segment** is a homogeneous group of customers with similar needs, wants, values, and buying behavior. Each segment is an arena for competition. Both GM and P&G have a tradition of building marketing strategies around strong brands that match the uniqueness of diverse segments. And you can bet there's some competition among the organization's own products, but that's minor in comparison to other brands. The approach has worked well—GM is the largest auto company on the planet and P&G dwarfs its competitors.

Through **segmentation,** the market can be divided into several groups of people with similar characteristics. Each segment will vary in size and opportunity. Since it may be difficult to appeal successfully to each segment, companies select certain ones for emphasis and will try to satisfy them more than competitors, which is called target marketing. For example, the nation's first health and fitness mall opened recently in Norcross, Georgia. It is targeting health-conscious consumers with similar needs, wants, values, and buying behaviors. **Positioning** means creating an image, reputation, or perception in the minds of consumers about the organization or its products relative to the competition. The company appeals to customers in the target segments by adjusting products, prices, promotional campaigns, service, and distribution channels in a way consistent with its positioning strategy. The Norcross

Market segment
A homogeneous group with similar needs, wants, values, and buying behavior.

Segmentation
Division of a market into homogeneous groups with similar needs, wants, values, and buying behavior.

Positioning
Creating an image or perception in the minds of consumers about the organization or its products relative to the competition.

*Bold, Cheer, Dash, Dreft, Era, Gain, Ivory Snow, Oxydol, Tide, and Solo; Camay, Coast, Ivory, Kirk's, Lava, Safeguard, and Zest; Head & Shoulders, Ivory, Pantene, Pert, Prell, and Vidal Sassoon; Dawn, Ivory, Joy, and Liquid Cascade; Complete, Crest, Denquil, and Gleem; Banner, Charmin, and White Cloud.

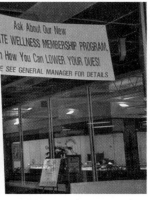

Norcross fitness mall targets health and fitness minded consumers.

fitness mall identified a segment of health and athletic consumers and positioned itself by constructing a 160,000-square-foot, two-story complex featuring health food, sporting goods, sports medicine, and a gymnasium.[3]

Segmentation, targeting, and positioning give organizations the means to connect with customers by identifying and understanding their characteristics, by focusing resources to meet their needs and wants, and by establishing how customers will view the organization. Let us say a company simply compiles data on consumers, averages it, and tries to develop one brand that appeals to the average consumer. In the U.S. marketplace alone, there are approximately 280 million people. You can find the average for certain of their characteristics—age, gender, income, location, and so forth—but what about ethnic origin, home life, and taste in music, clothing, and food? The "average" American represents few, if any, real people. Efforts to connect with this mythical average consumer probably wouldn't have appeal for any customer. Thus, marketers generally cannot use averages. Instead, they use segmentation, targeting, and positioning to define unique consumer groups, select those they wish to serve, and then integrate the marketing mix to establish a unified image of the product relative to the competition.

To be a leader in the 21st century, companies know that they must connect with customers by identifying, selecting, and relating to them in highly innovative ways. That's why segmentation, targeting, and positioning—three sequential stages summarized in Figure 6-1—are critical. You simply can't be a leading-edge marketer without these steps. The activities required to accomplish each stage are described in the sections that follow. Under market segmentation, we include descriptions of mass marketing and product differentiation as general marketing approaches that are contrasted with the more preferred segmentation methods. We also introduce several ways to identify diverse market segments. The section on target marketing describes how to select targets and focus resources where they will accomplish the most. The last section looks at positioning. It also describes how to reposition when things change.

MARKET SEGMENTATION

In the 21st century, most leading-edge companies will take great care to focus on specific market segments. That hasn't always been the case. Historically, there has been a movement from mass marketing, to product differentiation, to market segmentation, targeting, and positioning. In the following sections you'll explore how these approaches differ.

SEGMENTATION VERSUS MASS MARKETING

We know from chapter 1 that many companies once pursued **mass marketing,** which is the mass distribution and mass promotion of the mass product to all potential customers. Coke, introduced in 1886, pioneered this strategy, and was successful in reaching most consumers with the same product formula, price, promotion, and distribution strategy. Today, however, Coke's success depends on recognizing the tremendous diversity of the market. During the 1996 Olympic Games, Coke aired more than 100 different television commercials targeting different market segments. One day of broadcasting was designated "One World Day" by Coke, and the advertisements depicted people from many countries drinking Coke in their home environments.[4] The hallmark "Always Coca-Cola" melody was changed to incorporate the

CONNECTED: SURFING THE NET

www.cocacola.com/home.htm

Coca-Cola recognizes the tremendous diversity of its global market. Its Web site reads: "A Coke is a Coke no matter where on the planet you drink it. But a Coke light can be a diet Coke and a Mello Yello can be a Lychee Mello. Fanta is a dozen different things—peach in Botswana, passion fruit in France, and flower-flavored in Japan. Other countries have their own flavors—only Italy can pour a Beverly (and some travelers who've tried it are just fine with that)." Visit the Coca-Cola Web site to learn more.

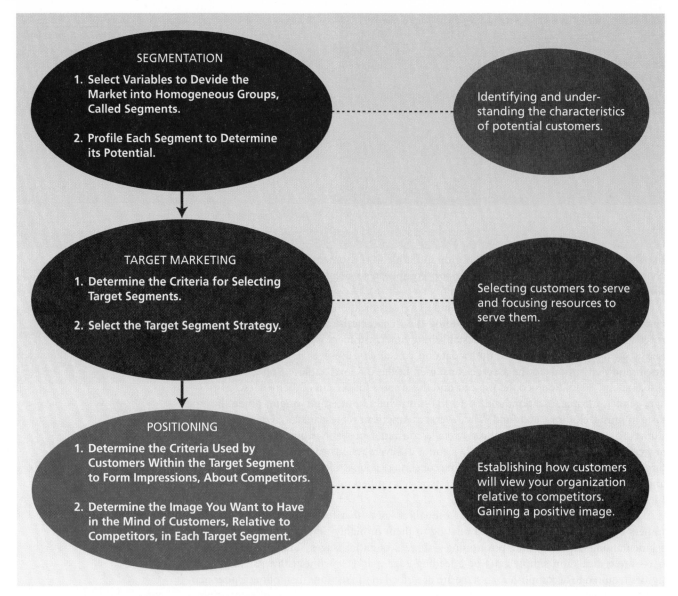

Figure 6-1   Connecting with Customers by Identifying, Selecting, and Relating to Them

musical styles of many countries. Although mass marketing was useful decades ago, competition that appeals to consumer diversity prevents this from being a viable strategy today.

Be sure not to confuse mass customization, discussed in chapter 1, with mass marketing. They have nothing in common, except the word "mass." Later in this chapter we will see that mass customization is a form of target marketing that takes advantage of many technologies to uniquely serve customers.

SEGMENTATION VERSUS PRODUCT DIFFERENTIATION

Product differentiation

A marketing strategy with which companies attempt to make their products appear unique relative to the competition.

Eventually, companies realized that mass marketing didn't provide enough variety and they began to follow a product differentiation strategy. **Product differentiation** makes a product appear unique relative to others, whether produced by the same company or the competition. This uniqueness is then used as a major factor in appealing to customers. The belief is that by offering choices, the company will attract more of the mass market. Notice that product differentiation implies a recognition that consumers may seek variety. But unlike market segmentation, the leading dynamic is a difference in the product, not in buyer characteristics. The pain reliever market is dominated by product differentiation. Aspirin comes in plain formula or with caffeine, buffered or not, with and without sleep aids, with or without a cold remedy, and in standard or extra strength. You can also find it in caplet, liquid, tablet, chewing gum, or capsule form, coated or noncoated, flavored or not. The objective is to offer an aspirin for every preference imaginable. And hundreds of millions of dollars are spent each year by companies like Bayer to promote its different product configurations.

It is important to keep the distinction between product differences and market segments in mind. Market segments should not be defined by product names or characteristics. Markets are made up of people and organizations. Consequently, market segments are described according to their characteristics, not according to the products they buy. Misunderstanding this distinction is a common and often deadly flaw for the marketing strategist. For example, a marketing consultant once asked the chief engineer of an air conditioning manufacturer to describe the company's target segments. The engineer responded with product categories: heavy, medium, and light-duty units. When asked questions about the characteristics of current and potential buyers, the engineer had little knowledge. The consultant knew immediately that this client did not fully understand market segmentation, a key reason customers were buying fewer of the engineer's new product introductions. When executives equate product categories with market segments, they tend to a focus attention on what they want to make, which may not meet customer requirements. The result is often products that please the people who make them but disappoint customers.

SEGMENTATION VARIABLES

The total market is **heterogeneous,** meaning it has many types of buyers. Market segmentation divides the total market into **homogeneous** subgroups, or clusters with similar characteristics. We then can inspect each subgroup in greater detail. Without a well-focused picture of the market, it's virtually impossible to create a powerful marketing strategy. Essentially, segmentation allows marketers to focus on relevant aspects of potential buyers. It's a critical step in connecting with customers.

Heterogeneous group
Buyers with diverse characteristics.

How is segmentation done? First, the marketer must select a way to categorize potential customers into subgroups. A **segmentation variable** is any descriptive characteristic that helps separate all potential purchasers into groups. Examples include gender, age, and income. Variables are then subdivided into categories. For example, within the gender variable, the two categories are male and female. Categories may be very broadly or very narrowly defined. Income can be classified generally as low, moderate, and high, or more specifically as, for example, up to $5,000, $5,001 to $20,000, $20,001 to $40,000, $40,001 to $60,000, and above $60,000.

Homogeneous group
Buyers with similar characteristics.

Segmentation variable
Any distinguishing market factor that can vary, such as gender, age, or income.

Think about how colleges segment students for recruiting and admissions. Like companies, they do this to gain a better understanding of potential customers. At the most basic level, the segmentation variables are grade point average in high school, SAT or ACT scores, and high school class rank. These variables can be subdivided into categories, as shown in Figure 6-2. The categories then can be grouped together in various ways to form several market segments, which often are named descriptively. For example, the market segment in the third categories column of Figure 6-2 might be called the "cream of the crop." Or students with above average SAT/ACT scores but in the bottom of their class and with a low GPA might be the "underachiever" market segment.

Most colleges add other variables, and these can dramatically change the segmentation structure. For example, what seems to be a fairly uniform market turns out to be a lot of segments. From our example in Figure 6-2, 27 market segments emerge (3 GPA categories × 3 SAT/ACT categories × 3 class rank categories = 27 segments). Adding just two residence categories (in and out of state) would produce 54 segments.

Variables need to be chosen with care, because each segment must meet certain criteria in order to be useful to a marketer.

- Members should have similar needs, wants, and preferences, because these are what marketers want to understand and influence.

Variable	Categories		
High School GPA	Below 2.0	2.0–3.5	3.6–4.0
SAT/ACT Score	Below average	Average	Above average
High School Class Rank	Lowest 25%	Middle 50%	Top 25%

Figure 6-2
Segmenting the College Market

- Members should have similar information-gathering and media usage patterns, because this allows marketers to communicate with the segment.
- Members should have similar shopping and buying patterns, because marketers then can find efficient places to sell and service their products.
- The number of members should be large, because marketers need to generate a profit.
- Data about the segments should be available, because marketers need to know about customers in order to build marketing strategies.

Segmentation typically is based on geographic, demographic, diversity, psychographic, and behavioristic factors and/or benefits-sought. Figure 6-3 lists the variables and categories commonly used to segment. All of these apply to consumer markets. Additional variables and categories that are primarily useful to segment business markets are provided in chapter 8 on business-to-business marketing.

Geographic Segmentation One of the most common ways to analyze a market is by geography. It can reveal some interesting facts. For example, consider this odd statistic about the difference in the size of men's suits. In New York the most typical size is 42 regular; in Paris, 40 regular; in San Francisco, 38 regular; and in Chicago, a strapping 44 long.[5]

Segmentation by city is often used by global companies. Coke knows that soft drink consumption relates to population size. With the exception of New York City and Los Angeles, all metropolitan areas of more than ten million are located outside the United States. So it's no mystery why Coke markets globally. A city's population size alone doesn't always provide enough segmentation information, so marketers think about other factors. Some metropolitan areas are known for their industry expertise: In Hollywood it's movies; in Silicon Valley, computer software; and in Philadelphia, pharmaceuticals. Auto components suppliers, like Bosch and Eaton Corporation, know that virtually all major buying decisions are made in fewer than 20 cities located in a handful of countries. A presence in Stuttgart, Detroit, Los Angeles, Wiesbaden, Paris, Osaka, and Seoul gives the supplier substantial global coverage.

Geodemography

Combining geographic information with demographics to identify segments with common consumption patterns.

Geodemography combines geographic information with data on consumer expenditures and demographics to identify segments with common consumption patterns. A geographic information system (GIS) employs computer mapping to identify targets. It uses data from the Bureau of the Census, which provides computerized street maps that contain economic and population data per city block. For $12,700 you can buy maps and data covering the entire United States. For considerably less, you can buy information for a smaller region of the country. Arby's uses GIS data to select restaurant locations, and the former Chemical Bank used it to target neighborhoods. According to Michael Marvin, an executive at MapInfo Corporation, with this technology, "Quaker Oats found that 80 percent of their ethnic customers lived in 18 of their 55 sales territories."[6] The information allows Quaker to develop highly targeted segment strategies.

Zip code segmentation

Division of a market into specific geographic locations based on the demographic makeup of the zip code area.

Zip code segmentation divides the market according to the demographic makeup of the zip code area. One marketing firm grouped all U.S. zip codes into one of 40 clusters based on family size, income, age, age of the home, type of housing, and so forth. Each cluster is described by the typical consumption practices of its residents. For example, in zip code 48236 (Grosse Pointe, Michigan), the cluster type is "Young Influentials":

> Up and coming young professionals living in townhouses and apartments. Residents like to sail, ski, and play tennis. Lots of joggers and airline travelers. A good place to sell yogurt and mutual funds but not wall paneling, motorcycles, or guns and ammunition. Residents buy 3.8 times the average number of Rolls-Royces.[7]

If you need to get even more specific, similar methods can be used to identify customers by city block based on street addresses. The LEXIS®-NEXIS® electronic information database now provides a service called REZIDE, which segments customers by any variable the user requests (zip code, area code, city, and so forth), and supplies the information electronically.

Demographic segmentation

Division of the market according to such characteristics as gender, family life cycle, household type, and income.

Demographic Segmentation Characteristics like gender, family life cycle, household type, and income are used in **demographic segmentation.** This type of information is readily available. Demographics are very useful in categorizing different tastes and preferences. An added benefit is that it's relatively easy to project the composition and size of demographic segments for the next five, 10, or even 15 years. Consequently, this kind of segmentation is an excellent tool for long-range strategic planning as well as short-term marketing.

Variable	Examples of Categories
Geographic	
World region	Pacific Rim, Europe, North America
Economic stage	Advanced, developing, subsistence
Nation	U.S., England, Japan, Mexico
City	Tokyo, Paris, Mexico City
City size & density	Large and dense, small and spread out, suburban, rural
Region	New England, Mid-Atlantic, South Atlantic, East South Central, Midwest, Mountain Pacific
Climate	Northern Equator, Southern Equator
Zip Code	10001, 10002, etc.
Demographic	
Gender	Female, male
Age	1–5, 6–11, 12–19, 20–34, 35–49, 50–64, 65–72, 72+
Income	Poverty, up to $15,000, up to $20,000, up to $30,000, up to $50,000, up to $100,000, $100,000+
Family size	1, 2, 3, 4, 5, 6
Family life cycle	Young single, young married no children, young married with children (under 6), young married with children (over 6), older married full nest, older married empty nest, retired, middle-aged, single, divorced, sole survivor
Occupation	Unemployed, homemaker, student, retired, clerical, blue collar, white collar, professional, proprietor
Education	Grade school (or less), some high school, high school graduate, some college, college graduate, postgraduate degree
Diversity	
Religion	Protestant, Catholic, Jewish, Muslim
Race	Anglo, African, Asian, Hispanic, Native American
Social class	Lower-lower, upper-lower, lower-middle (working class), middle, upper-middle, lower-upper, upper-upper
Psychographic	
Lifestyle	Actualizer, fulfilled, achiever, experiencer, believer, striver, maker, struggler
Personality	Compliant, aggressive, detached, sensory, intuitive, thinking, feeling
Behavioristic	
Readiness	Unaware, aware, interested, knowledgeable, desirous, intend to buy, trial
Ability and experience	None, novice, expert, professional, nonuser, first-time user, regular user, former user
Loyalty	Switcher, moderate, high
Media and shopping habits	Magazine subscriber, cable user, mall, convenience stores
Usage	Daily, weekly, monthly
Rates	Heavy, medium, light
Benefits Sought	
Delivery	Convenience, speed, flexibility
Service	No questions asked returns
Price	Low, medium, high

Source: Philip Kotler, Marketing Management: Analysis, Planning, Implementation, and Control, *9th ed. © 1997. Adapted by permission of Prentice Hall, Inc., Upper Saddle River, NJ.*

Figure 6-3 Ways to Segment Consumer Markets

Segmentation by Gender The buying behavior of men and women is unique. Some of this uniqueness can be attributed to the roles each performs. As these roles shift, marketers adjust. That's why Procter & Gamble markets diapers to dads today, but wouldn't even think of it a decade ago. Women are, in many ways, a prime segment for thousands of products. Judann Pollak has traced the "fitful pursuit of American women" by auto companies.[8] She begins with a 1907 ad for a Franklin showing women in long skirts behind the wheel and the caption "Notice how much room there is to get in or out of the driver's side." In 1930 Chrysler research found women to be a "potent factor" in 75 percent of new car purchases, and themes focusing on them were credited with raising company sales by 33 percent. By 1948, all major automakers were advertising in *Women's Home Companion,* the number one magazine targeted at women. Robert Austin, director of marketing communications for Volvo Cars of North America, says the industry has come a long way from the "Hi, sweetie, here is a pink car mentality." Today, women are the principal drivers of 26 percent of light trucks, including sport-utility models. According to Sean Fitzpatrick, vice chairman of McCann-Erickson Worldwide advertising agency, the popularity of these vehicles with women is largely due to "straight-shooting" advertising directed at them.[9]

The issue has never been whether to segment by gender—only how to address women. Chrysler formed a Women's Advisory Committee composed of 30 women from disciplines such as finance, manufacturing, and marketing. The company pioneered driver's side sliding doors and integrative child seats on the 1996 minivan. Sometimes women are targeted by accident. Dianne Romanelli, advertising coordinator at Saturn, says the company didn't start out targeting women: "The strategy was to show people how the Saturn shopping experience is different . . . (i.e., no-hassle, no-haggle policy). It just so happens that women really respond to that."

Even the NFL and NHL plan to test market feminine versions of team-logo apparel in order to capitalize on the growing number of female fans. A recent study indicated that the NBA's popularity increased 70 percent among adult women between 1989 and 1993, and the NFL posted a 45 percent increase. The hockey and football leagues decided to maintain the nongender-specific look of apparel but to produce it in sizes, fabrics, and colors appealing to women.[10]

Men are also a unique segment. Traditional products include sports tickets, hunting and fishing equipment, and auto supplies. Sometimes men buy products traditionally sold to women. Cosmetic companies are gaining ground with male skin care products. In the United States, men have been afraid to buy these for fear of being labeled vain. But careful segmentation has resulted in significant increases in business.[11] Sales of men's hair dye have quadrupled since 1986, to about $80 million.[12]

Segmentation by Family Life Cycle Families pass through stages, from young single adults, to marriage, to childbearing, to later life. The next chapter describes the specific categories in depth. For now, it is important to note that these family stages are excellent segmentation categories. America Online (AOL) differentiated itself as a service provider by putting to rest the growing parental fear about inappropriate material for young children on the Internet. AOL developed a filter application that allows parents to monitor and block the display of material. They also can screen e-mail sent to their children and monitor their children's visits and interactions in cyberspace. The filter can detect improper language and react by instantly logging off.[13] The system has helped AOL appeal to many parents, and other services have followed suit. By directing attention specifically to families, AOL has gained leadership in this important segment.

Using the family life cycle as a guide, marketers are beginning to promote adult products to young groups. For example, Mylanta addresses mothers with a children's formula in bubble gum and fruit-flavored chewable and liquid forms.[14] Other adult brands for young people include Benadryl, Sudafed, and Motrin.[15] Kleenex and Dial for Kids are just the tip of the iceberg for children's products.

Segmentation by Age As mentioned in chapter 3, age cohorts are people of similar age and life experience. Heroes, music, and even economic times are somewhat unique for each generation. Tastes, preferences, and product choices reflect those differences. Other generational similarities include physical capacity and earning power. You've probably heard of baby boomers, baby boomlets, and baby busters. Figure 6-4 describes various age cohorts frequently discussed today.

The baby boomers are a huge market segment in the United States. By 2010, more than 26.5 percent of the population will be older than 55, an increase of nearly 25 million people

Cohort	Born	Proportion of Population	Comments
GI generation	Before 1930	14%	Came of age during the Depression; many fought in WWII; frugal and patriotic.
Depression generation	1930–1939	8%	Moved from hard economic conditions as children to prosperous postwar years in adulthood.
War babies	1940–1945	6%	The worst-defined generation, it is usually described in terms of those that followed or preceded.
Baby boomers	1946–1964	30%	Largest U.S. generation; also known as the Vietnam, Woodstock, or Sixties generation.
Baby busters	1965–1976	17%	Often described as cynical about their future; also known as Generation X or Gen X.
Baby boomlet	1977–1995	25%	Primarily children of baby boomers: called boomlet because births began to rise in the late 1970s and are gradually decreasing.
Echo bust	Born after 1996	Not available	Children of the post–baby boomers, echoing the bust of 1965–1976, births will decline as baby boomers leave their childbearing years. The drop could be significant if, on the average, parents of this generation have fewer than two children.

Source: Adapted from Diane Crispell, "Where Generations Divide—A Guide," American Demographics, May 1993, pp. 9–10. Reprinted with permission. © 1993 American Demographics, Ithaca, NY.

Figure 6-4   Age Cohorts

in that category compared to today. Cadillac has its eye on baby boomers with its new entry-level luxury car, the Catera. It was developed specifically to fulfill their wants: sporty, safe, luxurious, and long-lasting vehicles. Cadillac realizes the importance of this market since two-thirds of all vehicle sales will soon be to people over age 45.[16]

People with higher spending power, born before World War II, are called *WOOFS* (*Well Off Older Folks*). This age cohort is often the target of major marketers. J. C. Penney has a clothing line called Easy Dressing, which uses velcro fasteners instead of buttons and zippers. Barnes & Noble carries large-print paperbacks, and travel agencies market special trips for the elderly. McDonald's® introduced the Arch Deluxe® to this segment.

As for Gen X, the baby busters, their purchasing power will peak about the time the boomers retire. Many busters are finding it difficult to establish independence and may rely on parents for some support.[17] Marketers need to realize that incomes have not increased rapidly for this generation. As a relatively small group it may have trouble paying for the government-sponsored health and retirement benefits that will be due to the large cohort of baby boomers when they reach eligible age. Social security payments made over the years by baby boomers were not invested for them. These payments were used to pay benefits to current

Cadillac targets baby boomers with its entry level luxury car.

social security recipients, so little will remain when they retire. That issue is spurring efforts to change the social security system in the United States.

The baby boomlet is a growing segment in the work force, adding spending power to the economy. The number of teenagers will grow at twice the rate of the rest of the population during the next 10 years. This $100 billion annual market is very attractive.[18] Much of the teenager's average weekly income of $60 is spent on "feel good" products—cosmetics, entertainment, and fast food.[19] And the under-17 age group does like to shop, spending an average of $25 per outing. About 55 percent of the trips are during the weekend, and this concentrated shopping provides a good targeting opportunity. The right price is the top concern of teens, followed by quality, style, and variety. Teenagers represent 59 percent of sneaker sales, 58 percent of compact disk players, and 53 percent of video games; they also account for more than 25 percent of toys/games, sports equipment, jeans, toothpaste, and shampoo. The snack industry certainly knows this market. Oreo snack packs, Mini Chips Ahoy, Ritz Bits, Ritz Ark Animals, Dizzy Grizzlies, Teddy Grahams, and Nutter Butter Bites all have attributes kids want—great taste, portability, value, and fun.[20]

Age is a useful segmentation variable for high-technology services. As you would expect, most Internet users have high levels of income and education. You also might think that no one over age 30 goes on-line. "Not so" says Thomas Miller, vice president of the Emerging Technologies Group, at Find/SVP.[21] A whopping 53 percent are in their 30s and 40s. Another 31 percent are age 18 to 29 and only 3 percent are older than 50. According to Miller, younger and older users focus on communicating via the Net, while the middle group is seeking information. Younger users are nearly three times as likely to publish their own Web sites, and they spend 36 percent of their time socializing in chat rooms and through e-mail. They also are more interested in Web music and entertainment, downloading photos, video clips, and music clips. Miller predicts that as they mature, they will grow to value information as the baby boomers do today. Like most of us, their needs will change with age.

Segmentation Based on Diversity[22]

Some people hesitate to segment markets based on ethnic heritage, race, or religious factors. Yet a wonderful fact of life is the world's tremendous diversity. Marketers know that the character of many markets is dramatically influenced by these factors.

It's important to remember that ethnic segments are not homogeneous. There are demographic differences within ethnic groups. For many people of color, race has nothing to do with their buying behavior. Consequently, other forms of segmentation may work much better.

African Americans, Hispanics, and Asian Americans account for much of the current population growth in the United States. Within 25 years, each is estimated to be approximately the same size—about 42 million people. Compared to the general population, African Americans will grow at about twice the overall rate, Hispanics at 4.5 times the rate, and Asians at more than 8 times the rate. Whites will increase at about 60 percent the rate of other groups.[23] Many people will maintain their high ethnicity by living among and associating within these groups. High ethnicity results in attractive market segments.

In 1994, minorities represented nearly 25 percent of the U.S. population, and the Bureau of the Census estimates that figure will rise to nearly 64 percent by 2020.[24] Minorities are now a majority in one of every six U.S. cities. Most immigrants settle in urban areas along with people from their home country. This produces concentrations of new ethnic populations, as the examples in Figure 6-5 show.[25]

According to Market Segment Research of Coral Gables, Florida, ethnic buying power totals nearly $600 billion. Moreover, this money is often spent in distinctive ways. Studies show that African Americans, Asian Americans, and Hispanics typically spend more on groceries than the average family. Hispanics and Asians tend to purchase more expensive, branded products rather than discounted items.[26]

De-ethnicization

The result of targeting a product heavily associated with one ethnic group to other segments.

De-ethnicization occurs when a product heavily associated with one ethnic group is targeted at other segments. Products like bagels, salsa, and egg rolls have become favorites of many people other than Jews, Mexicans, or Chinese. Kikkoman soy sauce was originally marketed to Chinese groceries and restaurants. Now that ethnic foods have become more mainstream, Kikkoman products are sold in grocery chains to consumers from many different backgrounds.

Services also can be de-ethnicized. Many artists, for example, begin by performing for their own ethnic group and then broaden their appeal. Gregory Hines, an African-American

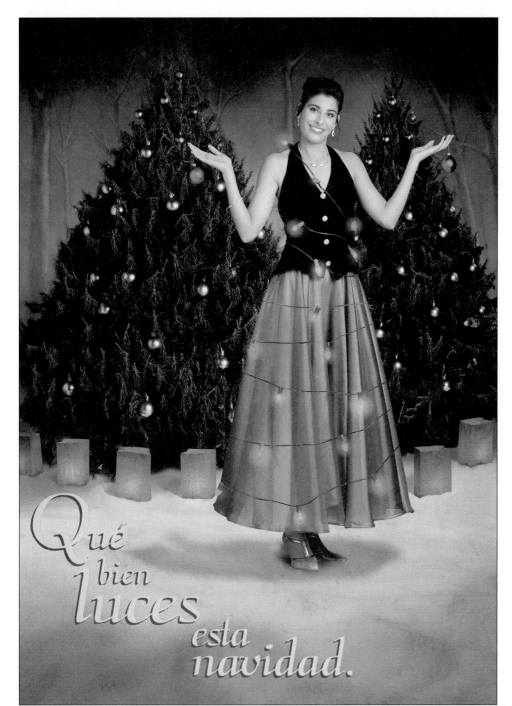

Qué bien luces esta navidad.

Many companies hire specialists to help target various ethnic groups.

tap dancer, started out in traditionally black venues and eventually became well known to most of the general public.

Psychographic and Lifestyle Segmentation Psychographic and lifestyle segmentation links geographic and demographic descriptors with a consumer's behavioral and psychological decisions. Psychographic variables used alone are often not very useful to marketers; however, they can be quite powerful when joined with demographic, geographic, and other data. *Lifestyle* is a person's distinctive mode of living. It describes how time and money are spent and what aspects of life are important. The choice of products, patterns of usage, and the amount of enjoyment a person gains from being a consumer are all part of lifestyle. Consider the difference between people who are physically fit from exercise and proper nutrition and those who are out of shape from high-fat diets, smoking, and sedentary living. Messages like "Just Do It!" or "No pain, no gain" are received very differently by these two groups. Of course, since there are so many lifestyles, the trick is to identify them in the context of your company's marketing strategy.

City	Origin
Atlanta	Vietnam, South Korea
Baltimore	South Korea
Chicago	Mexico, Philippines, South Korea
Denver	Mexico, Vietnam
Dallas	Mexico, Vietnam, India
Jersey City	Cuba
Los Angeles	Mexico
Miami	Cuba
Minneapolis/St. Paul	Laotians
New York City	all immigrants
Seattle	Philippines, Vietnam, South Korea

*Figure 6-5   New Ethnic
Populations in Selected Cities*

Psychographics
Marketing approaches and tools
used to identify lifestyles based
on measures of consumers'
values, activities, interests,
opinions, demographics, and
other factors.

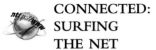

**CONNECTED:
SURFING
THE NET**

www.future.sri.com

Here's a fun way to learn
about psychographic
segmentation. Learn which
VALS™ 2 segment you fit by
completing an on-line
questionnaire. You will
answer 35 general attitude
statements, 10 Internet-
specific statements, and six
demographic questions. In
only seconds, you will see a
description of your VALS™
type. You'll also be presented
with options for exploring
the kinds of media, products,
and services your segment
prefers.

Psychographics are marketing approaches and tools used to identify lifestyles based on measures of consumer values, activities, interests, opinions, demographics, and other factors. Figure 6-6 shows one scheme for identifying types of lifestyle, including examples of what people in each category seek, and ways to reach them.

Another way of classifying lifestyles emerged from a Roper/Starch Worldwide survey of about 2,000 Americans for insights into views about money. Seven distinct profiles were discerned: hunter, gatherer, protector, splurger, striver, nester, and idealist. The hunter takes risks to get ahead and equates money with happiness. The gatherer is better safe than sorry, a conservative investor. The protector puts others first and uses money to protect loved ones. The splurger is self-indulgent. The striver believes that money makes the world go around and equates it with power. The nester isn't very interested in money except to take care of immediate need. The idealist believes there is more to life than money; material things aren't all that important.[27]

There are many ways to define lifestyles using psychographics, so marketers must use a combination of research and creativity to develop useful segments.

The best psychographic segmentation approaches are based on accepted consumer psychology and sound research methods. One of the most popular systems is SRI Consulting's VALS™, which stands for *Values And Lifestyles*. This second version of earlier research segments consumers into groups that think and act differently. VALS research found three major categories of consumers, each with a different self-orientation.[28] *Principle*-oriented consumers' follow their own beliefs; *status*-oriented consumers are influenced by others, and *action* oriented consumer's seek variety, action, and risk taking. In addition, VALS considers a consumers' resources, which are education, age, income, energy, self-confidence, eagerness to buy, and health.[29] Figure 6-7 illustrates the VALS™ 2 segmentation system and Figure 6-8 provides summary descriptions of the segments. The VALS battery of attitude items is used in survey research to discover the product choices, media preferences, and leisure activities of each of the VALS consumer groups. Marketers, advertisers, media planners, and new product designers use VALS to discover who is naturally attracted to their product or service and then to design communication strategies, advertising, and distribution plans that will be attractive to their particular consumer target. VALS refreshes its product, media database twice a year.

Typology	What They Seek	Possible Spokesperson	Source of Advertisement
Intellectual	Superpremium unique products	Luciano Pavarotti	*Wall Street Journal*
Conformist	Products with large market share	Mickey Mouse	*Sports Illustrated*
Popularity Seeker	Trendy products	Bart Simpson	MTV
Active Lifestyle	Good service Healthy body	Barbara Walters	*Travel & Leisure*
Relief Seeker	Fantasy escape	Madonna	HBO
Sentimentalist	Old fashioned products	Bob Hope	*Family Circle*
Pragmatist	Functional products	Merle Haggard	*Prevention*

*Figure 6-6   Psychographic
Segmentation*

Source: John Mortan, "Brand Quality Segments: Potent Way to Predict Preference," Marketing News, September 14, 1992, IR-8.

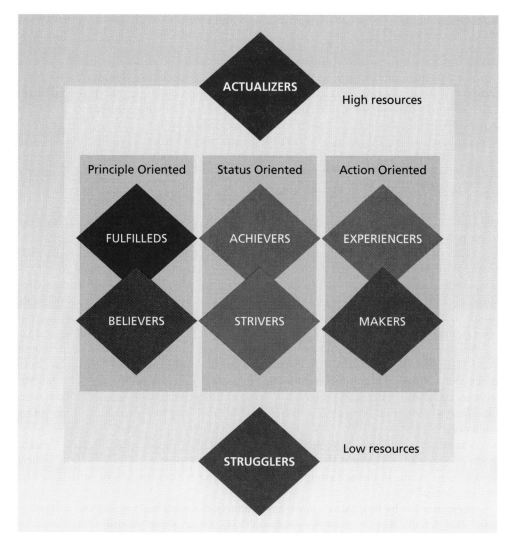

Figure 6-7 The VALS™ 2 Segmentation System
Source: Printed with permission from SRI Consulting, Menlo Park, CA.

The connected: surfing the net box describes how you can obtain your profile. If you answer the questions on the VALS™ 2 questionnaire, you can find out whether you are an Actualizer, Fulfilled, Believer, Achiever, Striver, Experiencer, or Struggler. Additionally, you can explore the types of media, products, and services your profile prefers. This is just an example of how psychographic segmentation helps companies connect with customers.

Using sophisticated computer technology, GeoVALS™ allows marketers to profile a city, metropolitan area, and/or zip code.[30] It has been adjusted for use in other countries. The

Segment	Orientation	Description	Median Age	Portion of U.S. Population
Actualizer	All	Successful, sophisticated	43	8%
Fulfilled	Principle	Satisfied, comfortable, abundant resources	48	11%
Believer	Principle	Focus on family, religion, and social group	58	16%
Achiever	Status	Committed to jobs, family, in control, abundant resources	26 26	12%
Striver	Status	Unsure of self, needs approval of others, low resources	34	13%
Experiencer	Action	Fashion conscious socializers	30	13%
Maker	Action	Practical, traditional, family oriented		
Struggler	No particular	Older, uneducated, concerned, low resources	61	14%

Source: Printed with permission from SRI Consulting, Menlo Park, CA.

Figure 6-8 The VALS™ 2 Approach to Segmentation

Japanese version shows categories of buyers according to product adoption as well as the VALS™ 2 categories.[31]

Behavioristic Segmentation

Behavioristic segmentation categorizes consumers based on people's awareness, product and media uses, and actions. Past behavior is one of the best predictors of future behavior, so these variables require an understanding of what consumers have previously done. The variables include purchase volume, purchase readiness, ability and experience, loyalty, media habits, and shopping behaviors.

Segmentation by Usage Rates   You have probably heard about the "80-20" rule: 20 percent of buyers purchase 80 percent of the volume of any product. It is amazing how true this is for many products. Heavy users can be extremely important to companies. Consequently, most marketers divide the market into heavy, moderate, and light users, and then they look for characteristics that may explain why some people consume vastly greater amounts. It usually costs no more to reach heavy users than light users. Therefore, the marketing costs are lower per unit of sales.

Still, marketing strategists need to realize that competition for heavy users can be extreme. If medium or light users are being ignored, they may provide a marketing opportunity. For example, giants like Coke and Pepsi are always targeting the college crowd. They spend big bucks to be represented on campus in order to capture students. Royal Crown Cola avoids this segment altogether because of the stiff competition. Instead, it concentrates on older adults, who tend to be lighter users of cola.

Broadway is now targeting a younger market in order to expand business. According to Dave Mulryan, a New York advertising executive involved with the effort: "They don't have much choice. If you look at the average person going to plays, it's a 70-year-old suburban woman, and Broadway is asking itself where its new audience is coming from."[32] Productions like *Bring in 'Da Noise Bring in 'Da Funk* and *The Lion King* are intended to reach young audiences.

Sometimes marketers mistakenly assume that certain segments are light users. A recent study of Generation X surprised some financial advisors. Often regarded as passive, cynical complainers, people in this age group have been investing at rates equal to or surpassing that of their elders.[33]

Segmentation by Readiness   For many products, potential users go through a series of stages that describe their readiness to purchase. These stretch all the way from being unaware of a product, through trial, leading up to loyalty. Readiness is a useful segmentation variable particularly for newer products. This scheme is often used in adjusting the communications mix. Chapter 14 addresses this issue in depth, so it is only mentioned here.

Segmentation by Ability and Experience   The performance of products is determined by the ability and experience of its user. Consequently, ability is an excellent segmentation variable for almost any skill based product. For example, the marketing of skis, tennis racquets, golf clubs, and most other sports equipment is targeted to ability segments. This is due in large part to the performance requirements of these products. As performance requirements increase, new technologies produce products with higher performance capabilities but generally require more skill. There are 1,709 United States Golf Association approved balls, yet nearly 75 percent of those playing in the 1997 U.S. Open selected Titleist. With amateur players spending more time at the range, these types of higher-priced balls are increasing favorites. Wilson and Spalding are taking advantage of the reputation of titanium drivers with the introduction of balls made with titanium.[34]

Segmentation by Loyalty   As we have discussed, a key goal of firms is to create brand loyalty. Some consumers are naturally loyal to particular product categories. There are many ways to look at loyalty, but the most popular seems to be the most straightforward. It looks at switchers, moderately loyal, and highly loyal categories. Switchers may select a separate brand with nearly every purchase. They may actually seek variety or they simply don't care which brand they buy. Moderately loyal customers have a preference for a brand but will switch if it is convenient to do so. Loyal buyers have strong preferences. Not all buyers are loyal to a single brand within a product class. Some people have two or three that are equally acceptable. This type of segmentation may include more than the three categories described.

Segmentation by Media and Shopping Habits   A broad range of media and shopping habits can be used to categorize shoppers. For example, some people subscribe to cable, others don't; some prefer shopping in malls, others at department stores; and so forth. These variables focus on accessibility of target customers. Those who shop only in mall settings are accessed differently from those who prefer catalog shopping at home.

Segmentation by Benefit Benefit segmentation divides the market into homogeneous groups based on the attributes consumers seek from a particular product class. Russell Haley popularized this method in the 1960s by dividing the toothpaste market into segments based on whether the consumer wanted flavor, brightness of teeth, dental health, or low price. A benefit segmentation of auto buyers might group them according to the importance they place on economy, performance, styling, or reliability. When a lot is known about the attitudes and perceptions of buyers, it is possible to develop a benefit profile, or what product attributes are considered most important. This can be a useful first step in segmentation because customers in a benefit segment are likely to have other identifiable characteristics. For example, people who desire convenience are likely to be members of a dual career family or single parent household.

When only benefits are addressed, this technique is not always consistent with good segmentation procedures. Because the benefits are often described according to product characteristics, we learn very little about the buyers themselves. For example, you could say that Apple addressed the user-friendly computer benefit segment. Then again, you could say that Apple products are user-friendly. A good rule of thumb is that segments should not be defined solely by product characteristics. In fact, when benefit segmentation is based on product attributes, it may be confused with product positioning, which will be discussed later in this chapter.

Nevertheless, benefit segmentation can be useful when it leads to descriptions of the *consumers* who prefer each benefit. In order to create these descriptions, researchers generally start with benefit segments and then use the other segmentation schemes to define each group. In this way, the focus is ultimately on buyers, not products.

TWO COMMON SEGMENTING METHODS

Segmentation can be quite complicated because most markets are complex. There are many different types of customers, and, as we have seen, literally thousands of variables can be used to segment them. Marketers typically use one of two approaches in selecting variables and grouping customers.

The **take-down segmentation method** starts with all consumers and seeks meaningful variables for subdividing the entire market. For example, a cosmetic company may segment by gender. It may choose to target women, believing they have a significantly greater buying potential than men. It then may further segment women by age, type of user, or skin shade. In the early 1990s, cosmetic manufacturer Covergirl recognized the vast potential of marketing to nonwhite women. Until then, it had almost completely ignored the special needs of dark-skinned women. Had it not broken down the market and looked specifically for smaller niches with unmet needs, it might have continued to overlook this huge segment. Today, Covergirl offers more than 72 shades designed specifically for nonwhites, and it leads the ethnic market with over 29 percent of total sales.[35]

Take-down segmentation method
Method that starts with a set of variables and assigns all consumers to one of them.

The **build-up segmentation method** starts with a single potential customer and adds others with similar characteristics. Anyone without those characteristics is placed in a new segment, and the process continues. In other words, rather than the whole market, the focus is on one segment at a time. Brian Maxwell, the developer of Powerbar, had high-performance athletes in mind when he first created the nutrient-rich, low-fat food. He wanted a healthy alternative to fat-laden breakfast and candy bars that would supply reserve energy during competition. The Powerbar quickly gained popularity as a nutritious snack or quick meal for health-conscious consumers. Flavors have been added to appeal to new segments, and distribution has expanded to hundreds of retail outlets.[36] The build-up segmentation method has helped Powerbar become a success.

Build-up segmentation method
Method that starts with a single potential customer's characteristics and adds a segment for each new characteristic found in other customers.

TARGET MARKETING

While segmentation is an analytical process, target marketing is a decision-making process. The company must choose the segment(s) on which it will focus its energy. At one extreme, all segments may be selected; at the other, only one. Clearly, most companies would like everyone to buy their product. But even giants like Coca-Cola and Pepsi must battle for customers, and each devotes different effort to specific market segments. Pepsi has a long history of concentrating on youth—"Generation Next." It has spent billions trying to woo the young and nearly young, implying that Coca-Cola is for the older generation. Similarly, The Limited focuses on young, trendy women; Gerber on infants and young toddlers; McDonald's® on fam-

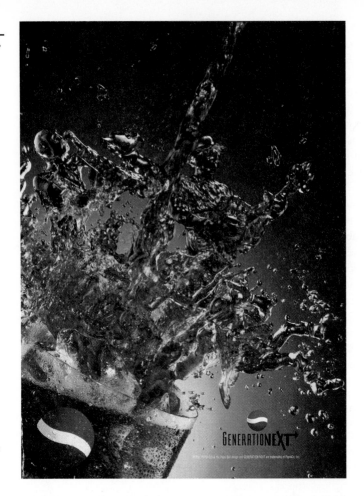

*Pepsi has a long history of
concentrating on youth, referred to
by the company as "Generation
Next."*

ilies; and Lexus on quality-conscious, high-income adults. The relationships feature, "Credit Card Co-Branding: New Shortcut to Hitting the Target Market," discusses a new spin on target marketing.

SELECTING TARGET SEGMENTS

Market segment profile
Information about a market
segment and the amount of
opportunity it represents.

How do companies decide which market segments to target? Once the segmentation scheme is developed, you need to describe, or profile, each group in more detail. The **market segment profile** compiles information about a market segment and the amount of opportunity it represents. The profile may include: (1) the number of current and potential buyers; (2) the potential number of products these buyers may purchase; (3) the amount of revenue the segment may provide; and (4) the expected growth rate. In addition to size and growth, other criteria used to select targets include competitive factors, cost and efficiency factors, the segment's leadership qualities, and the segment's compatibility with the company's vision, objectives, and resources.

Size and Growth Market segments vary considerably by size and growth rate. Although a segment must be large enough to generate revenues and profits, the biggest is not always the most attractive. Competition may be very tough there. A slightly smaller segment may have enough revenue to ensure a satisfactory profit. In the 1980s, Japanese companies gained strong footholds in many countries (including the United States) by targeting smaller segments that were being ignored. These were large enough to support sustained marketing efforts and included people whose spending power would increase over time.

Competitive Factors In general, the less competition within a segment, the better. Marketers must be aware not only of who is currently serving the segment but also of who is likely to do so in the future. A company may decide not to serve a particular segment in order to avoid competitors known for their aggressiveness and strength. In other cases, a company may choose to challenge rivals. Church & Dwight decided to take on Procter & Gamble and Colgate-Palmolive by introducing its Arm & Hammer baking soda toothpaste. It felt the product was just different enough to be successful with certain segments.

CONNECTING THROUGH RELATIONSHIPS

CREDIT CARD COBRANDING: NEW SHORTCUT TO HITTING THE TARGET MARKET

Credit card issuers are finding it a lot easier to target someone else's loyal customers than to inspire loyalty in their own. After all, with the flood of cut-rate cards filling mailboxes and the ease of transferring balances, consumers have little incentive to stick with a particular one. But what if a card gives something back? That's the principle behind credit card cobranding, a marketing strategy that's taken the business world by storm since it appeared in 1990.

Co-branding works like this: An issuer such as MasterCard or Visa teams up with a partner. It can be a retailer, a mail-order company, an airline, a university, or a nonprofit group. In a typical cobranding program, the issuer develops a marketing campaign that targets the partner's customers. The issuer also contributes about 1 percent of its sales to the partner's reward program, which may be merchandise discounts, cash rebates, gift certificates, or donations to a particular cause. Even manufacturers have caught the fever: General Motors has sold 600,000 cars with award points generated from its GM credit card.

Cobranding flourishes because it's a win-win-win situation. The card issuer can easily target and reach a new base of customers and net a steady stream of revenue from transaction fees. The partner gains increased customer loyalty, higher average orders, and more frequent purchases. And the consumer gets free toys, air miles, or a host of other perks for using the cobranded card. One couple charges thousands of dollars of private-school tuition and is able to book the family on a yearly Caribbean vacation using frequent flier miles from UAL's Mileage Plus Visa card.

Of course, perks only draw customers if the brand appeals to them in the first place. The cobranding relationship taps into consumer loyalty or emotional ties to a cobrand sponsor, says Leslie Dukker Dory, senior vice president and director of marketing for Sun Trust BankCard of Orlando, Florida. "A well-established, well-identified, easily reached target," if provided the right perks, says Dory, "will gravitate to a card."

Sun Trust's own specialty is cobranding cards that target leisure-activity niches. Two of the cards it issues are the Cool Country Visa, aimed at fans of 11 major country music artists, and the Daytona USA MasterCard, aimed at motor sports enthusiasts. Sun Trust reaches these people through direct mail as well as promotions, special event tie-ins, album inserts, and take-one dispensers.

Although country music fans and motorcycle mavens represent rather narrow niches, they can be very profitable. Cobranded cards that target populations likely to carry balances can pull in substantial revenues even among a small customer base.

The new Wal-Mart Visa card issued by Chase Manhattan Bank is expected to become one of cobranding's biggest success stories. "Wal-Mart has a large group of intensely loyal customers who will line up to get a cobranded bank card carrying the Wal-Mart name," says Robert McKinley, an industry analyst. And with point-of-purchase promos at more than 2,000 Wal-Mart stores nationwide, it will be pretty hard for Chase Manhattan not to hit the bull's-eye of this target market.

Sources: Kelly Shermach, "Cobranded Credit Cards Inspire Consumer Loyalty," *Marketing News,* September 9, 1996, p. 12; Kate Fitzgerald and Mark Gleason, "Wal-Mart Leaps into Credit Cards," *Advertising Age,* September 30, 1996, pp. 1, 62; Kathleen Kiley, "Branded!" *Catalog Age,* June 1996, pp. 77–80; and Renee Covino Rouland, "Toys 'R' Free," *Discount Merchandiser,* October 1995, p. 70.

Cost and Efficiency Factors It is more efficient to target some segments than others. When Citibank set its sights on chief financial officers of several worldwide corporations, costs ran into the millions for research, product development, and personal selling. This sounds expensive, but it was a very efficient use of funds. This extremely compact segment consists of a few known and very influential people, so all the marketing dollars could be aimed directly at the targets. If the message reaches all sorts of consumers, then the result is higher cost and/or reduced efficiency. For example, alcohol abuse prevention advertisements are seen by responsible drinkers and teetotalers, not just the target audience.

Segment Leadership Qualities Some segments set the trend for adopting new ideas and products. Professional sports teams influence the dress and equipment of college athletes, who, in turn, influence high school teams. Marketers often choose a target segment with leadership qualities, hoping that other segments will follow suit.

Compatibility Factors Companies often select segments they believe are particularly compatible with the company's vision, objectives, and resources. Thus, to a significant degree, target segments reflect the qualities and character of the company. In the early 1980s, Honda recognized that Harley-Davidson was attracting customers who didn't appeal to much of the general population. Honda took advantage of this by targeting younger, well-educated buyers with the theme: "You meet the nicest people on a Honda." This segment was consistent with Honda's image. Other Japanese motorcycle companies, such as Yamaha and Kawasaki, did the same and captured a large number of U.S. customers. Today, Harley-Davidson is trying to erase its Hell's Angels image, says a spokesperson for the Milwaukee-based company. The old image of tough bikers is definitely a fading emphasis.[37]

FINDING NEW MARKETS TO TARGET

A major innovation occurs when companies discover new market segments. You can probably think of many examples. A recent headline in the *Wall Street Journal* read: "Big Beer Makers Go After the Sober Set." Nonalcoholic beer (near beer) has been available for a long time. Heileman Brewing Company has sold Kingsbury for nearly three decades, but only when Anheuser-Busch and Miller Brewing introduced O'Douls and Sharp's, respectively, did sales take off. Why were they successful when Heileman was not? Both Miller and Anheuser-Busch segmented the market, chose target segments, and designed strategies to appeal directly to their targets. Miller selected the bar market, while Anheuser-Busch chose those purchasing in supermarkets. Both used sizable marketing budgets. Each company targeted people who enjoy the lifestyles associated with beer drinking—evening entertainment and socializing—but who want to avoid the adverse effects of alcohol. When Coors saw its archrivals' sales climbing, eroding the sales of regular beer, it decided to enter the fray with Cutters. Thus, a new segment had been discovered.[38]

TARGET MARKETING STRATEGIES

A targeting strategy defines the number of markets and the relative amount of resources allocated to each. Strategies usually fall within one of the three categories shown in Figure 6-9: undifferentiated marketing, differentiated marketing, and concentrated marketing. Two others are used less frequently: niche marketing and micromarketing. Mass customization

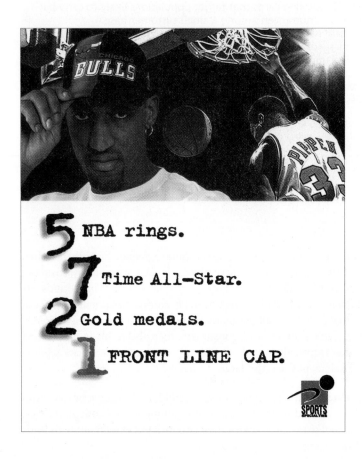

Professional sports teams often influence the dress of college and high school teams.

Undifferentiated   Differentiated   Concentrated

| Single mass market | Several well-defined markets | Single well-defined market |
| One approach for all | Different approach for each | One approach for the particular market |

Figure 6-9   Target Market Strategies

may be the wave of the future. Figure 6-10 illustrates the way the marketing mix is targeted in each of the three most common strategies.

Undifferentiated Marketing   Similar to mass marketing, **undifferentiated marketing** treats all customers the same. Companies look for desires that are common to most potential customers and then try to design products that appeal to everyone. By focusing internally on a single or a few products, companies can streamline manufacturing, distribution, and even promotion in order to improve quality and gain cost efficiencies. But the standardized product may fail to meet individual customer needs. For years United Parcel Service (UPS) used this strategy. Users benefited from the cost-effective operations but were upset by the company's inability to fulfill unique customer requirements.

As long as companies keep the price relatively low and competitive alternatives are unavailable, an undifferentiated marketing strategy can be successful. Today, however, competition is tough. Companies that once thrived are being threatened by rivals who use more targeted approaches, such as differentiated or concentrated marketing.

Differentiated Marketing   **Differentiated marketing** serves each segment with marketing mix elements matched specifically to its desires and expectations. When Federal Express

Undifferentiated marketing
A strategy that views all potential customers as though they were the same.

Differentiated marketing
Marketing to each of several segments with a marketing mix strategy matched specifically to its desires and expectations.

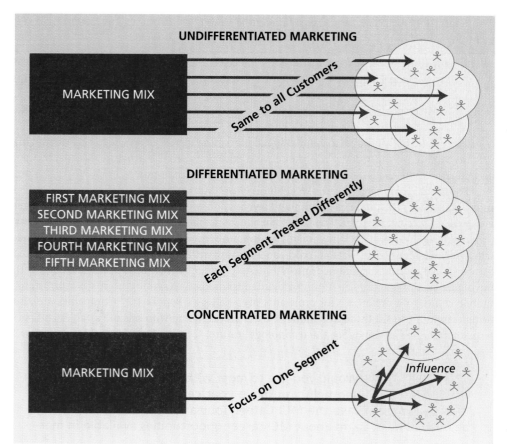

Figure 6-10   How the Marketing Mix is Used in Common Targeting Strategies

and others entered the market with differentiated strategies, UPS executives had to make a choice. Should the company settle for slowly eroding sales, or should it choose the risk, hard work, and uncertainty of a new course? UPS decided on a differentiated marketing strategy. It carefully selected targets and designed services to meet their different needs. Some of its operations are applicable to all segments, such as its computerized tracking system and extensive aircraft fleet. Other elements differ, such as product mix, personal selling, and pricing. This approach allows UPS to serve all its customers better.

The advantage of differentiated marketing is that needs and wants are better satisfied for each targeted segment. The disadvantage is that it may also be higher cost, because several marketing mix strategies are typically required. Differentiated marketing requires decentralized decision making. **Centralized decision making** involves a small group of executives who make all the major decisions for the whole company. **Decentralized decision making** permits numerous groups, each dedicated to a specific segment, to make the decisions for their particular segment. This gives marketers a lead role in the company, as they need to ensure that customers' needs and wants are considered in every decision. When UPS decided to engage in differentiated marketing, the first step was to create a much stronger role for marketing. This meant educating large numbers of executives about the latest marketing techniques.

Concentrated Marketing Focusing the organization's marketing mix on one or two of the many possible segments is called **concentrated marketing.** Companies must make sure they have a great deal of knowledge about their core market segment, as this major target is called. While most of the marketing is aimed at the core, substantial revenues and profits may be gained from other segments. This is because segments with leadership qualities are often selected for concentrated marketing in hope they will influence the behavior of others. Ralph Lauren has used concentrated marketing successfully to target high-income, well-educated professionals and their families. Wanting to emulate them, consumers in the noncore segment are drawn to Lauren products as well.

Concentrated marketing has worked extremely well for new companies or companies entering new areas of the world. By gaining a foothold in a core market, a company can build the financial strength, experience, and credibility needed for expansion. When Tower Records opened its first music store in Thailand, it concentrated on young people. "They made it a real hip thing to buy a record," says Kamol Su KosolClapp, chief of Bakery Music Company, a popular Thai label.[39] Success in this segment is leading to further expansion in Thailand, including a host of additional outlets catering to listeners of all types.

Niche Marketing and Micromarketing Niche marketing and micromarketing are two other strategies worth mentioning. A **niche** is a very small market that most companies ignore because they do not perceive adequate opportunity. For example, Mazda decided to serve a niche market with its Miata sports model, although it sold fewer than 40,000 annually. Suzuki, with its Samurai model, and Subaru, with its SVX and other models, used the same approach. General Motors discontinued niche marketing of the Fiero, which sold at roughly half the volume of most other GM models. Because of their cost structure, Mazda, Suzuki, and Subaru could make money at low volume, while GM could not.

The smallest possible niche is the individual. Marketing to one customer is called **micromarketing.** Advances in technology have made it possible to adjust marketing strategies to meet individual needs. "Tell me someone's zip code, and I can predict what they eat, drink, drive—even think," claims Jonathon Robbin. He is creator of the PRIZM cluster system, which matches census data and consumer surveys with the 36,000 zip codes in the United States. Consumers are partitioned into 40 lifestyle groups, which in turn are matched with buying behaviors. The information can be used to predict everything from a person's automobile choice to a preference for croissants over Kellogg's Pop-Tarts.[40] Companies are also using computers to sift through billions of bytes and come up with sets of variables and patterns that boggle the mind. See the technology feature, "Mining Data for the Micromarket."

Centralized decision making
Management process in which a small group of executives make all the major decisions for the whole company.

Decentralized decision making
Management process in which numerous groups, each dedicated to a specific segment, make decisions about their segment.

Concentrated marketing
Focusing the organization's marketing mix strategy on one or only a few of many possible segments.

Niche
A very small market segment that most companies ignore because they fail to see any opportunity.

Micromarketing
Marketing to an individual customer.

| CAREER TIP | Would you like to meet with MCI "fast-trackers" who can help you move your career ahead? On the MCI Web site you can take the MCI Career Tour and find out where it will be headed next. Learn about MCI career opportunities available in mar- |

keting, computers, networking, sales, engineering, legal, finance, accounting, and human resources. You can even apply on line. Visit the MCI Web site at **www.mci.com.**

Imagine the possibilities of micromarketing. Printing technology is so flexible that neighbors can receive the same magazine with different pages targeted to their own consuming patterns. For example, if the people next door shop at discount stores and you do not, then they may receive a copy with ads featuring price promotions, while your copy features upscale items with no mention of price. Even more impressive is the work done to pinpoint loyal customers. By linking a publisher's subscription list with a company's customer list, marketers can substitute special ads for loyal customers in place of the general ad being carried in the magazine.

Mass Customization Probably the most important technological development for marketing is the personalization of mass merchandise. As you learned in chapter 1, mass customization serves one or several markets while efficiently responding to the needs and de-

CONNECTING THROUGH TECHNOLOGY

MINING DATA FOR THE MICROMARKET

Like most phone companies battling for market share, MCI is determined to keep its best customers from defecting to rivals. If it could identify them before they jump, and offer them special rates and discounts, then MCI would have a formidable edge over the competition. Well, that micromarketing edge has become a reality for MCI through data mining and data warehouse technology.

Using data mining software, MCI can comb marketing information on 140 million households, each evaluated on as many as 10,000 attributes, such as income, lifestyle, and past calling habits. Then, to see which attributes may signal defection, whether it's an increase in calls to customer service or a steadily declining bill, the company can boot up its IBM SP/2 supercomputer. This data warehouse identifies the most important variables to look at, and so far it has come up with 22 detailed and top-secret statistical profiles.

This kind of technology fulfills a dream marketers have had since the 1960s. With these client/server systems, immense volumes of information can be collected in one database. Cross-indexing that data in any combination can be done within tens of minutes—not days or weeks—to get almost any view you can imagine. For instance, Bank of America's data warehouse has 800 billion characters of data, culled by separate computers that handle daily checking, savings, and other transactions. Now, whenever a phone rep fields a customer call—and the company receives about 100,000 calls a day—the rep can reach into the data warehouse and pull up information on that customer's banking patterns. Let's say you call just to check your balance, but the rep notices that you repeatedly bounce checks. You are likely to get a sales pitch on overdraft protection.

The biggest market for these $100,000+ systems (still cheaper than a mainframe, mind you), is retailer powerhouses like Sears, Wal-Mart, and Burlington Coat Factory. "The retail industry is very very competitive," says David Skeels, Computer Science Corporation's retail consultant. "The selling space per person is at an all-time high and consumers are getting smarter—they are highly value driven and not especially loyal."

With its new data mining capabilities Wal-Mart, the country's largest retailer, is getting smarter, too. The company has just begun recording every sale for every one of its 2,268 stores in a data warehouse. The corporation uses the data to fashion targeted marketing strategies and to distribute products to the stores where the most people are likely to buy them.

Every time you make a transaction in a store or over the phone, by snail mail or e-mail, chances are that you're feeding some company's massive data warehouse. In turn, the data will be used to send you targeted promotions or telephone pitches for products you're likely to buy. These trillion-byte marketing weapons yield so much insight into customer behavior that Bank of America's vice chairman Luke S. Helms says "It's like you're cheating."

Sources: John W. Verity, "A Trillion-Byte Weapon," *Business Week,* July 31, 1995, BW Online; Rosemary Cafasso, "Sears Roebuck and Co.," *Computerworld Client/Server Journal,* special issue, August 1996, pp. 12–13; Laurence Zuckerman, "Do Computers Lift Productivity? It's Unclear, But Business Is Sold," *New York Times,* January 2, 1997, p. C15; and John W. Verity, "Coaxing Meaning Out of Raw Data," *Business Week,* February 3, 1997, pp. 134–138.

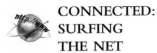

CONNECTED: SURFING THE NET

www.bmwusa.com

Customize a BMW to *your* specifications on the Internet. You will have an opportunity to select the colors and features you desire in a car. Shortly after you submit your options, you will be presented with the suggested retail price and have an opportunity to order a brochure. Visit the BMW Web site to check it out.

sires of individual consumers. By creating a process that can respond to uniquely defined needs of targeted consumers, mass customization gives customers tremendous individualized attention. Companies can make affordable, high-quality products tailored to a customers needs—but with the short cycle time and low costs associated with mass production.[41]

Andersen Corporation, for example, offers millions of possible combinations for windows. In reality, the number of unique configurations shipped has risen from about 10,000 to more than 160,000. Andersen's multimedia system, called Windows of Knowledge, has an icon menu with more than 50,000 features. Distributors work with customers to design windows, and the multimedia component shows exactly how they will look. The computer then generates error-free quotations and manufacturing specifications, which are electronically transmitted to the factory.[42]

BMW uses mass customization as well. The company believes customer needs are neglected when salespeople are under pressure to sell vehicles off a lot. At some of its dealerships BMW has implemented a new approach that emphasizes selling customized vehicles. By using a single "customer counselor" to deal directly with the client, BMW wants to accomplish "bonding in such a personal way that customers will want to come only to that franchise." The company uses a multimedia computer system to place, track, and display orders for the customized vehicles. If all BMW dealers choose to adopt the new retailing plan, then the company may increase its market share an estimated 1.5 percent by 2000.[43]

ETHICAL DIMENSIONS OF TARGETING

It makes sense that manufacturers should want to target ethnic segments, but this creates trouble for some companies. They are coming under fire for campaigns aimed at specific groups. The alcoholic beverage industry frequently is criticized in this regard. For example, in the early 1990s, G. Heileman breweries began distributing a new malt liquor, Power-Master, in minority neighborhoods.[44] Twenty-one consumer and health groups tried to call a halt. The beer contained 5.9 percent alcohol, compared to no more than 5.4 percent for other malt liquors. Critics denounced the positioning of the beer toward minorities, especially given its alcoholic strength. "The ethics of targeting a single demographic group with a brand is a much stronger issue than even five years ago," says Rob Klugman, vice president of brand marketing at Coors Brewing Company. "The response to PowerMaster should have surprised no one."[45] Shortly after, the product was discontinued.

Similarly, the tobacco industry has come under intense fire due to targeting. With more than 400 cigarette brands and/or styles available in the United States, many of the products could not survive without appeal to very specific consumer groups. Lorillard, Inc., aims Newport Stripes specifically at women. Cartier Vendome is promoted by Philip Morris as a cigarette for the wealthy or aspiring rich. These brands effectively target subsets of the larger population. When R. J. Reynolds introduced a menthol cigarette for African Americans called Uptown, the result was public scrutiny and condemnation by the U.S. secretary of health and human services and numerous African-American and community groups. There were demands that the government bar tobacco companies from designing and promoting cigarettes targeted at this market segment. The fight stopped short of litigation when Reynolds agreed to cancel the brand at an estimated cost of $5 to $7 million. Not all business people believe this should have happened. Caroline Jones, president of her own advertising agency in New York, a company owned predominantly by blacks, said that it is insulting to ignore the African American community and *not* target it. "Marketers could and should advertise products to blacks, and that includes cigarettes and alcohol as well as bread and candy."[46]

Are there differences between products such as Uptown cigarettes and Kmart's line of private label health and beauty care items aimed specifically at African Americans? There are varying opinions among consumer groups and industry manufacturers. One thing is certain. Tobacco and alcohol companies find it increasingly difficult to introduce, position, and market their products to ethnic consumers.

GLOBAL TARGETING

Major U.S. companies have expanded efforts to reach carefully targeted foreign market segments. Vast amounts are being spent to create a presence in areas where middle-class consumers are growing by leaps and bounds.[47] Frito-Lay is changing the snack food business in Thailand by marketing its traditional potato-based products. It also is changing agriculture: Potatoes weren't traditional food in Thailand, so it is teaching farmers to grow special seeds and educating them on all aspects of potato culture.[48] Anticipating a growth in the Russian middle class, Pepsi is trying to dominate the market for soft drinks. It plans to invest $550 million in building new plants and a new distribution system. There may even be a deal in the works to create a "space billboard" on the orbiting *Mir*.[49]

Domino's Pizza focuses on various global segments by tailoring its service to different cultural needs. Consider that in Iceland most households are without a telephone, the British consider it rude for a delivery person to knock on the door, and Japanese homes are not numbered sequentially. These cultural differences require Domino's to adjust its strategies. To find addresses in Japan, wall maps up to three times the size of those used in the United States were developed. In Iceland, Domino's paired up with drive-in movie theaters: Employees bring cellular phones to cars with a flashing turn signal, and customers then order pizzas for delivery right to their vehicle.

PepsiCo has been testing the Chinese market, which finds the cheese flavor undesirable, with such Cheeto flavors as Peking duck, fried egg, and dog. Procter & Gamble provides Japanese mothers with thin diapers, since they change their babies twice as often as Americans do. Green Giant advertisements picture corn falling off the cob into salad and pasta in France but being sprinkled over ice cream in Korea.[50]

POSITIONING STRATEGIES

Once the segmentation process gives a clear picture of the market and the target marketing strategy is selected, the positioning approach can be developed. Positioning is the process of creating in the mind of consumers an image, reputation, or perception of the company and/or its products relative to competitors. Positioning aligns a marketing strategy with the way the marketer wants buyers in a given target market to perceive the value they will receive from the company's products.

Positioning helps potential customers understand what is unique about the company and its products relative to competitors. Most important, it helps buyers connect mentally with the brand by understanding the brand. **Product position** refers to the characteristic that consumers associate with a brand. For example, Snickers is positioned as the snack to give energy, while Three Musketeers can be shared with a friend. BMW is positioned on prestige performance, while Mercedes projects prestige luxury.

THE POSITIONING MAP

A **positioning map** is a diagram of how consumers in a segment perceive specific brand elements they find important. This gives marketers a picture of how their products are viewed. Essentially, the idea is to graph where each brand falls regarding important attributes relative to other brands. To understand this, follow the process used to complete a perceptual map of television talk shows (the product) based on input from executives attending a seminar at Syracuse University.[51] They were asked to give their perceptions of talk shows. The anchors for the graph were social value and intellect. The combined results are shown in Figure 6-11. You can probably think of other talk shows. How do you perceive them relative to the ones listed in the figure?

Once the perceptions are plotted, most marketers want to know the consumer's ideal position. The ideal position is the one most preferred by each consumer. In one example, the star near Larry King marks the positioning many executives preferred. Oprah Winfrey faced a dilemma when she realized that her own show had migrated toward the lower left quadrant, which she felt was out of alignment with her own values. Shows like *Ricki Lake* have a sensationalism that appeals to many viewers, but many believe their value to society is questionable. Oprah decided to move her show back to its original position in the upper right quadrant. Rosie O'Donnell has been credited with single-handedly saving daytime TV from itself by taking the trash out of talk shows. Her program, which is designed to offer intelligence and social value, has won not only great reviews, but also huge ratings.[52] Yet Jerry Springer has recently picked up in the ratings. Where would you put that show?

POSITIONING BUSINESS PRODUCTS

In addition to the same positioning dimensions used by consumers, business customers look at three other product classifications: commodity, differentiated, and specialty. Commodity products have no uniqueness. These classifications are shown in Figure 6-12. Buyers make

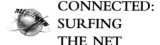
Product position

The characteristics consumers associate with a brand based on important attributes.

Positioning map

A diagram of how consumers in a segment perceive brands based on specific elements they consider important.

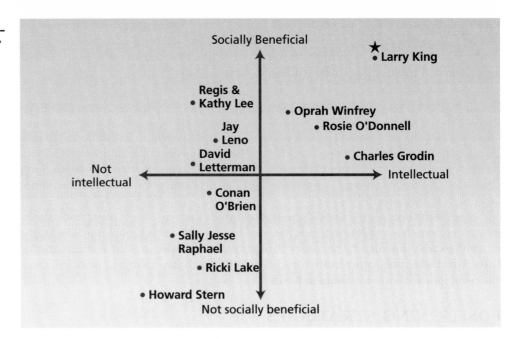

*Figure 6-11 Examples of a
Positioning Map: TV Talk
Shows*

selections according to the lowest price and reliable delivery. The differentiated position requires buyers to evaluate, compare, and contrast the products from various suppliers. The specialty position is for a unique product that can be customized to user needs.

The Delphi division of GM markets auto components to various GM groups such as Oldsmobile, Cadillac, and Opel, as well as to manufacturers around the world. BMW, Renault, and Ford buy components from Delphi. Depending on the product line and target segment, Delphi uses all three positioning strategies. In some cases it positions products as commodities, such as simple wire harnesses that connect parts of the electrical system. For these commodities Delphi tries to keep costs low by using standard technologies. Delphi also markets seating systems that are differentiated from those of competitors and require state-of-the-art technology. Delphi's specialty products are unique. By working closely with the de-

*Television talk shows are
positioned by selecting guests and
content that appeal to particular
target markets.*

Category	Commodity	Differentiated	Specialty
Product Characteristics	No hidden qualities, similar to other suppliers	Comparisons with other suppliers show advantages	Unique
Technology	Standard	State-of-the-art	Customized

Figure 6-12 Positioning of Business Products

signers of drive trains (engines and transmissions) in their customers' companies, Delphi produces engine fuel systems tailored to specifications. These products ensure compliance with EPA standards while producing the performance demanded by consumers.

STEPS FOR POSITIONING

Consumers' perceptions are influenced by the categories people use to sort through the massive amounts of product information. Music, for example, is categorized as rock, country-western, jazz, classical, and so forth, while other dimensions help differentiate one artist or group from another. Consumers also evaluate a brand relative to others based on their impression of whether it is more or less similar. Finally, they look at a brand according to their preferences—or how close it comes to their ideal position. The following steps can be used to position a brand.

1. Identify the attributes or characteristics used by buyers in a segment to understand brands.
2. Diagram the most important dimensions on a grid (map).
3. Locate the brand relative to others based on how it is perceived by buyers.
4. Identify the ideal position for buyers in the segment.
5. Determine the fundamental way to position the product.
6. Develop the marketing mix that supports the positioning strategy selected.

BASES FOR POSITIONING

Two noted marketing scholars have identified the following seven fundamental bases that can be used to position products.[53] Each basis is described in more detail below.

	EXAMPLE OF USE	
Positioning Basis	Characteristic	Brand/Product
Benefit (Attribute)	Safety	Volvo
Price/Quality	Value	Wal-Mart
Time of Use	After a workout	Gatorade
Product User	Mature	McDonald's® Arch Deluxe®
Direct Comparison		MCI vs. AT&T
Product Class	Thirst quencher	Orange juice
Country of Origin	Jamaica	Jamaican rum

Positioning by Benefit   Benefits (attributes) can be used to describe the appeal of a product. For example, Procter & Gamble uses medical testimony to position Crest as a cavity-fighting toothpaste. SmithKline Beecham positions Aqua Fresh as a cavity fighter and a breath freshener. Glad trash bags are positioned to be more durable than the competition. Fisher-Price toys are positioned as safe and educational. Energizer batteries are positioned to keep going and going.

You must carefully select the benefits to associate with your product. Describing benefits that satisfy wants tends to work better than merely describing product attributes, because consumers can relate the benefits to themselves.

Positioning by Price or Quality   Sam Walton made $25 billion by identifying underserved geographical market segments and then positioning Wal-Mart as consistently lower priced than competitors. Other retailers, such as Neiman Marcus, position themselves as high priced to signal higher quality.

Positioning by price is common in the pharmaceutical industry. Typically, branded drugs (usually marketed by firms that first develop them) are priced much higher than generics (usually marketed by companies that copy drugs when the patent expires). The product is basically the same. The generics are positioned on price, while the branded products are positioned on quality.

Positioning by Time of Use or Application   Marketers frequently position products on the basis of how they are used or applied. Gatorade, Powerade, and All-Sport are positioned for drinking while exercising. Wrigley's positions its gum for use by smokers when smoking is not permitted—on airplanes, in car pools, or in nonsmoking workplaces.

Often, sales can be increased by positioning a product for more than one use or application. For example, McDonald's® discovered a huge opportunity when breakfast service was added. Arm & Hammer expanded baking soda sales by positioning the product as an odor fighter in the refrigerator, auto, or cupboard, in addition to its uses in toothpaste, laundry detergent, and baking. V-8 juice, originally consumed at breakfast, is now the "Wow, I could have had a V-8!" anytime beverage.

Positioning by Product User or Spokesperson   In the mind of some people, products take on meanings associated strongly with the spokesperson. For example, Nike used Michael Jordan, an extraordinary athlete, to position Nike as extraordinary. Andre Agassi and John McEnroe, both considered tennis rebels, were used to help position Nike athletic shoes as an alternative to the conservative models sold by competitors.

Sometimes spokespersons are not even real, such as Betty Crocker and Mr. Goodwrench. At other times, the person's area of expertise may be more significant than the unknown individual. Cat or dog breeders are shown in ads for pet food. The Club, a device to prevent auto theft, was introduced in a national ad campaign by actual police officers.

Positioning by Direct Comparison   Nearly all customers create impressions about a brand by comparing it to another. Marketers need to determine how they want their brand to be evaluated relative to the competition. In a few cases, competitors are named, although many believe they should not be given "free" publicity. More often, the comparison is general—one brand is stronger, brighter, and so forth, than "the others." Pontiac brags of "European" styling, inviting comparison with BMW. The "Avis tries harder" positioning strategy moved the company to number two in the car rental industry.

Positioning by Product Class or Category   Cereals can be categorized as natural or sweetened. Consumers are likely to position the natural cereals, such as All-Bran or granola, relative to one another. They tend not to consider sweetened cereals, such as Froot Loops or Frosted Flakes, at the same time. When determining a positioning strategy, it is important to understand how consumers categorize products.

Positioning by Country of Origin   A company's image can be affected by the mental association people make with its country of origin. We think of German precision engineering, Japanese cost and quality, Italian fashion, French taste, and U.S. technology. Certain countries are associated with certain products: the United States with movies, Germany with automobiles, Japan with electronics, the Netherlands and Belgium with beer, France with perfume and wine, and Italy with shoes.

Companies may create a subsidiary in a nation associated with a product, or they may use a brand name that sounds like it's from that country. For example, Little Caesar's is a U.S. pizza company with an Italian-sounding name.

REPOSITIONING

For nearly 40 years, Procter & Gamble's Crest toothpaste has dominated. However, by mid-1997 its share had fallen nearly 2 percent each year for five years, and was down to 26 percent. Crest was facing a positioning problem. Some marketing experts contend that in toothpaste, P&G has lost its edge. One reason is that Crest was positioned on the attributes gum care and tartar control while rivals stressed brightening power attributes. Expect to see new Crest formulas as we enter the 21st century. But there is speculation whether Crest will maintain its health-oriented positioning or move closer to the brightness positioning of rivals.[54]

Repositioning may become necessary over time as competitive forces, customer tastes and preferences, and the marketing environment change. Repositioning can be difficult and very expensive because it's hard to alter old impressions and create new ones. Thom McAn, a shoe manufacturer, underwent the difficult process of repositioning. According to Nick Cohen, creative director for McAn's ad agency, "Getting people to believe you've changed is no easy task, especially if your worthy reputation is covered in as much dust as Thom McAn's. In partnership with our client, we decided the best way to convince people that Thom McAn really had fundamentally improved was to cheekily admit the charges."[55] McAn ran two ads with that theme. One headline read "Please excuse some of our shoe styles in the past. Through a fluke computer error, the office supply store sent us the wrong desk calendars and we still thought it was 1976." The other began with the same sentence and continued: "For years, our new and updated shoes were re-routed by a disgruntled postal worker and abandoned under a bridge near Chicago."[56] Whether the company is positioning a new product or repositioning an old one, the ultimate goal of its decision making is to persuade the targeted consumer to make a decision as well — the decision to purchase the product. The complex psychological and social factors that influence consumer decision making and buying behavior will be examined in the next chapter.

 ## CONNECTED: SURFING THE NET

Mastercard

www.mastercard.com

THE RELATIONSHIP FEATURE IN THIS CHAPTER discusses credit card cobranding, a popular marketing strategy for developing customer loyalty. One of the many companies teaming up with partners is MasterCard. Visit its Web site and answer the following questions.

1. How many markets does MasterCard target? What specific offerings does the company provide to reach them?
2. In this chapter you learned the variables and categories commonly used to segment consumer markets. Which one(s) does MasterCard use? Select a market the company does not currently target. Does it meet the segmentation criteria listed in the chapter? Do you think this would be a successful market? Explain.
3. Read "New Ways to Pay." How has MasterCard led the way in this area, and how has connecting through technology facilitated its advances?
4. MasterCard is accepted in more locations around the world than any other card. List some of its global initiatives. Link to the Web site of MasterCard Australia. How does this site differ in the way it connects with customers?

MCI

www.mci.com

IN THIS CHAPTER YOU LEARNED ABOUT MCI's use of data mining and data warehouse technology to identify and target potential customers. Visit the MCI Web site and answer the following questions.

1. Seven fundamental ways to position products were described in this chapter. Read the overview of MCI products and services and select three listed. Identify how each is positioned. Explain.
2. MCI's "Connections" allows Net users to interact on-line. What features does MCI offer to encourage customer involvement with the Web site? How, specifically, do these features help MCI build relationships with customers?
3. In what four areas does MCI invite you to explore your interests? Is the company successful in targeting the unique interests of consumers in this part of the Web site? List other ways MCI could reach diverse consumers through the Internet.

OBJECTIVE 1: Understand the advantages of target marketing and how it differs from mass marketing and product differentiation.

Mass marketing treats all customers as though they have the same needs and wants. A single marketing strategy is designed to appeal to all potential customers. This strategy does not generally work well because customers with differing characteristics have different needs and wants. Product differentiation is a strategy that alters products to stress their uniqueness relative to competitors. It recognizes that customers have differing needs and wants, but it doesn't start with an understanding of them. Target marketing focuses on select groups of customers so marketers can more clearly understand their specific needs and wants and adjust accordingly.

OBJECTIVE 2: Describe how to do market segmentation and select target markets.

Market segmentation separates potential customers into several groups or segments with distinctive characteristics. Customers within a segment should have similar needs, wants, and preferences; they should have similar media habits and shopping and buying patterns; the group should be large enough to justify attention; and data about individuals in each segment should be available.

Typical segmentation variables are geographic and demographic factors, ethnic and other diversity-related factors, psychographic and behavioristic factors, and benefits desired. Two common segmenting methods are the take-down method and the build-up method. The take-down method begins by selecting segmentation variables and assigning customers to the category they fit. The build-up method starts with the unique characteristics of one potential customer. Each time someone with unique characteristics is discovered, a new segment is added.

Segments are selected as target markets based on such factors as their size and growth potential, competition, cost and efficiency, leadership qualities, and compatibility with the organization.

OBJECTIVE 3: Explore three basic target marketing strategies: undifferentiated, differentiated, and concentrated marketing.

Undifferentiated marketing treats all customers alike and is similar to mass marketing. In order for this strategy to work, companies generally must have significant cost advantages. Differentiated marketing involves serving several segments but adjusting the marketing mix for each. It usually requires decentralized decision making. Concentrated marketing focuses on one segment or only a few. Companies can use all their resources to gain advantage within that group. Because differentiated and concentrated strategies consider customer needs and wants, they are far superior to an undifferentiated strategy.

OBJECTIVE 4: Know how to do positioning and describe several approaches marketers use to create valuable, lasting images of their products.

Positioning creates in the mind of consumers an image, reputation, or perception of the company and/or its products relative to competitors. It helps customers understand what is unique about a company and its products. Marketers can use a positioning map to depict how customers perceive products according to certain characteristics. For business products, a commodity, differentiated, or specialty positioning strategy can be used. Products are often positioned by benefit, by price and quality, by the time of use or application, by user or spokesperson, by direct comparison with a competitor, by product class, or by country of origin.

1. Define mass marketing, segmentation, and targeting. How are they different?
2. What are the steps in segmentation, targeting, and positioning?
3. What variables are used to segment markets? Give examples of each.
4. What are the three basic marketing strategies associated with segmentation?
5. What is VALS™ 2? What major categories of consumers does it profile?
6. What is the difference between the take-down and the build-up segmentation methods?
7. What characteristics are used to select target markets?
8. What is micromarketing and how does it differ from mass customization?
9. What are positioning strategies? List three used in business markets.
10. What is a positioning map and how do organizations use it to position products?

1. Why do marketers use market segmentation to summarize information about large numbers of consumers? Why not just use averages?
2. Are segmentation techniques used by companies who follow a mass marketing strategy? A product differentiation strategy?
3. Imagine that you are the marketing manager for a company that wants to produce a new line of men's and women's dress shirts. Which segmentation variables would be relevant for this market? What categories would you use? Describe five or six market segments that may emerge.
4. What is a segment profile? Develop one for each market segment you listed in question 3.
5. Which segments in question 3 would you select as target markets?
6. Once target markets are chosen, what different strategies are available? Which would work best for your target markets?
7. Why is positioning important? What are some of the different ways to position dress shirts in your target markets?
8. Positioning is typically done relative to the competition. If you have no important competitors, then how can the concept still be useful?

Build-up segmentation method: Method that starts with a single potential customer's characteristics and adds a segment for each new characteristic found in other customers.

Centralized decision making: Management process in which a small group of executives make all the major decisions for the whole company.

Concentrated marketing: Focusing the organization's marketing mix strategy on one or only a few of many possible segments.

Decentralized decision making: Management process in which numerous groups, each dedicated to a specific segment, make decisions about their segment.

De-ethnicization: The result of targeting a product heavily associated with one ethnic group to other segments.

Demographic segmentation: Division of the market according to such characteristics as gender, family life cycle, household type, and income.

Differentiated marketing: Marketing to each of several segments with a marketing mix strategy matched specifically to its desires and expectations.

Geodemography: Combining geographic information with demographics to identify segments with common consumption patterns.

Heterogeneous group: Buyers with diverse characteristics.

Homogeneous group: Buyers with similar characteristics.

Market segment: A homogeneous group with similar needs, wants, values, and buying behavior.

Market segment profile: Information about a market segment and the amount of opportunity it represents.

Micromarketing: Marketing to an individual customer.

Niche: A very small market segment that most companies ignore because they fail to see any opportunity.

Positioning: Creating an image or perception in the minds of consumers about the organization or its products relative to the competition.

Positioning map: A diagram of how consumers in a segment perceive brands based on specific elements they consider important.

Product differentiation: A marketing strategy with which companies attempt to make their products appear unique relative to the competition.

Product position: The characteristics consumers associate with a brand based on important attributes.

Psychographics: Marketing approaches and tools used to identify lifestyles based on measures of consumers' values, activities, interests, opinions, demographics, and other factors.

Segmentation: Division of a market into homogeneous groups with similar needs, wants, values, and buying behavior.

Segmentation variable: Any distinguishing market factor that can vary, such as gender, age, or income.

Take-down segmentation method: Method that starts with a set of variables and assigns all consumers to one of them.

Undifferentiated marketing: A strategy that views all potential customers as though they were the same.

Zip code segmentation: Division of a market into specific geographic locations based on the demographic makeup of the zip code area.

REFERENCES

1. Adapted from Marcia Mogelonsky, *Everybody Eats: Supermarket Consumers in the 1990s* (Ithaca, NY: American Demographics Books, 1995), pp. 153–155. Reprinted with permission. ©1995 American Demographics, Ithaca, NY.
2. Rebecca Blumenstein and Gabriella Stern, "GM Decides to Reposition Its Brands Rather Than Eliminate Most Models," *Wall Street Journal,* August 30, 1996, A3, A4.
3. News Digest, "Mall Targets Health-Conscious," *Marketing News,* August 14, 1995, p. A1.
4. Associated Press, "Coke Plans 100 Different Commercials during Olympics Broadcast," 1996. Retrieved from URL www.nando.net/newsroom/ap/oth/1996/oth/oly/feat/archive/071596/oly12977 on August 29, 1996.
5. *Chicago,* March 1996, p. 22.
6. David Churbuck, "Geographics," *Forbes,* January 6, 1992.
7. Bob Minzesheimer, "You Are What Your Zip Is," *Michigan: The Magazine of the Detroit News,* May 15, 1983, pp. 22–26.
8. Judann Pollack, "In Fitful Pursuit of American Women," *Advertising Age,* January 8, 1996, p. 54.
9. Ibid.
10. Sandy Shore, "NHL, NFL Design Products for Women Fans," *Marketing News,* August 26, 1996, p. 8.
11. Mary Tannen, "Fears of Buying," *New York Times,* September 24, 1995.
12. Andrew Wallenstein, "Boomers Put New Life in Hair Dye for Men," *Advertising Age,* September 25, 1995, p. 1.
13. Joshue Quittner, "How Parents Can Filter Out the Naughty Bits," *Time,* July 3, 1995, p. 45
14. Michael Wilke, "Mylanta Targets Children," *Advertising Age,* May 27, 1996.
15. Pam Weiss, "Eau de Toilette for the 12-and-Under Set," *Brandweek,* February 13, 1995, p. 30.
16. Ian P. Murphy, " 'Downscale' Luxury Cars Drive to the Heart of Baby Boomers," *Marketing News,* October 7, 1996, pp. 1, 19.
17. Michael R. Solomon, *Consumer Behavior* (Upper Saddle River, NJ: Prentice Hall, 1996), p. 503.
18. Laura Zinn, "Teens, Here Comes the Biggest Wave Yet," *Business Week,* April 11, 1994, p. 76.
19. Solomon, *Consumer Behavior,* p. 510.
20. "Biscuit Vision," published by Nabisco, Inc., Summer 1995, as told by Rachel Mantle, summer intern at Nabisco.
21. Thomas E. Miller, "Segmenting the Internet," *American Demographics,* July 1996, pp. 48–52.
22. For a review, see Solomon, *Consumer Behavior,* pp. 463–493.
23. Robert Pear, "A New Look at the U.S. in 2050: Bigger, Older, and Less White," *New York Times,* December 4, 1992, p. A1.
24. Leah Rickard and Jeanne Whalen, "Retail Trails Ethnic Changes," *Advertising Age,* May 1, 1995, p. 1.
25. Michael J. McDermott, "Marketers Pay Attention! Ethnics Comprise 25% of the U.S.," *Brandweek,* July 18, 1994, p. 26.
26. Leah Rickard, "Minorities Show Brand Loyalty," *Advertising Age,* May 9, 1994, p. 29.
27. Robert Sullivan, "Americans and Their Money," *Worth,* June 1994, p. 60.
28. Joel R. Evans and Barry Berman, *Marketing,* 7th ed. (Upper Saddle River, NJ: Prentice Hall, 1997), pp. 270–271.
29. Michael Gates, "VALS Changes with the Times," *Incentive,* June 1989, p. 27.
30. "The Best 100 Sources for Marketing Information," *American Demographics,* January 1995, p. 29.
31. Lewis C. Winters, "International Psychographics," *Marketing Research,* September 1992, pp. 48–49.
32. Cyndee Miller, "Broadway Increases Marketing to Reach Younger Theater Crowd," *Marketing News,* September 9, 1996, pp. 1–2.
33. Vivian Marino, "Young Adults are Targets of Financial Advisors," *Marketing News,* September 9, 1996, p. 1.
34. Seth Schiesel, "Teeing Up New Technology," *New York Times,* June 21, 1997, pp. 23–25.

35. Leon E. Wynter, "Business and Race," *Wall Street Journal,* July 3, 1996.
36. Jeff Reiter, "New Powerbar Flavors Can Mean Big Profit for Health Food Retailers," *Food Service Product News,* August 1995, p. 18.
37. Associated Press, "Biker Sues Harley-Davidson for Trying to Yank Business," *State News,* Michigan State University's Independent Voice, April 10, 1996, p. 6.
38. Marj Charlier, "Big Bear Makers Go After the Sober Set with Assortment of Nonalcoholic Brews," *Wall Street Journal,* March 30, 1992. p. B1.
39. G. Pascal Zachary, "Major U.S. Companies Expand Efforts to Sell to Consumers Abroad," *Wall Street Journal,* June 13, 1996.
40. Michael J. Weiss, *The Clustering of America* (New York: Harper & Row), p. 1.
41. Christopher Hart, "Mass Customization: Conceptual Underpinnings, Opportunities and Limits," *International Journal of Service Industry Management* 6, no. 2 (1995): 36–45.
42. B. Joseph Pine II, "Serve Each Customer Efficiently and Uniquely," *Network Transformation,* January 1996, pp. 2–5.
43. Nichole M. Christian, "BMW Aims to Double U.S. Sales by Overhauling Dealer Network," *Wall Street Journal Interactive Edition,* June 12, 1997.
44. "Distilling Truth about Alcohol Ads," *Business & Society Review,* Fall 1992, pp. 12–17.
45. Rinler Buck, "PowerMaster Trips ANA's Dewitt Helm," *Adweek's Marketing Week,* July 8, 1991, p. 12.
46. Judann Dagnoli, "RJR's Uptown Targets Blacks," *Advertising Age,* December 18, 1989, p. 4.
47. G. Zachary, "Strategic Shift," *Wall Street Journal.*
48. Ibid.
49. "Pepsi Aims for the Stars," *Marketing News,* June 3, 1996, p. 1.
50. Tara Parker-Pope, "Custom Made: The Most Successful Companies Have to Realize a Simple Truth: All Customers Aren't Alike," *Wall Street Journal,* September 26, 1996, pp. R22–23.
51. Graduate School of Sales Management and Marketing, sponsored by Syracuse University and Sales and Marketing Executives International, June 9–20, 1997. The exercise was done for the purpose of creating an example and does not necessarily reflect how executives perceive these shows.
52. Rick Martin, "Coming Up Roses," *Newsweek,* July 15, 1996, pp. 45–48.
53. David A. Aaker and J. Gary Shansby, "Positioning Your Product, " *Business Horizons,* May-June 1982, p. 56.
54. Dana Canedy, "P&G Seeks to Stem Loss of Smile Share," *New York Times,* June 20, 1997, p. C1.
55. *Communications Arts,* March-April 1995, p. 53
56. Ibid.

CASE 6

TOMMY HILFIGER

*I*N 1984, TOMMY HILFIGER LAUNCHED his line of menswear with an ad campaign that communicated his vision. It proclaimed: "The 4 Great American Designers for Men are: Ralph Lauren, Perry Ellis, Calvin Klein, Tommy Hilfiger." It was a big joke with the New York designer crowd but Hilfiger is now one of fashion's hottest designers. With 1997 sales of almost $500 million, he has found tremendous success with his original target—young professional men. Recently, he entered new market segments—hip-hop teens, women, and children.

In the early years, companies like Calvin Klein, Ralph Lauren, and Bill Blass targeted higher-income professionals, so Hilfiger went after younger professionals of more modest means. He positioned his clothing as classic casual wear, with just enough new style to make it modern, at an affordable price. This meant building in the quality young professionals desired and adding a slight twist to differentiate his product line. The "twist" might be striped fabric lining the inside of polo shirt collars or colored fabric on a traditional oxford shirt. Thanks to the integration of design and manufacturing, Hilfiger could cash in on the Lauren trend with similar quality, but for a more price-sensitive market.

The Tommy Hilfiger Corporation was formed in 1989 in partnership with Silas Chou, a member of one of Hong Kong's oldest textile and apparel families. The Chou family had built a fortune on private label contracting but was beginning to lose business to lower-wage countries like India, China, and Vietnam. Teaming with former Ralph Lauren executives Lawrence Stroll and Joel Horowitz, Chou and Hilfiger integrated design, manufacturing, and marketing. By 1995 the Hilfiger vision was realized; the Council of Fashion Designers of America voted Tommy Hilfiger the menswear designer of the year. In 1997, company sales exceeded $660 million, up 38 percent in a single year.

POSITIONING

In the 1980s, the Hilfiger image was ingeniously associated with such great menswear designers as Ralph Lauren, thereby reaping benefits it had taken those designers years to achieve. Hilfiger has now gained legitimization in his own right, and the Tommy Hilfiger name stands on its own, its positioning based on design themes and association with people who wear the clothes.

Hilfiger often uses a red, white, and blue theme and visualizes his clothes as "celebrating the individuality and creativity that defines America." He puts a spin on the classics. Hilfiger positions his designs as an extension of himself. "I want people to feel comfortable yet unique. It's new-age funk combined with traditional style that give my clothing an edge. This enhances people's individuality and enables them to stand out." He notes that "preppy kids started wearing classics in a different way, very oversized. City kids took it another level by going giant sized." So Hilfiger created another size category, giant, which is considerably larger than XXL. In keeping with the theme, Hilfiger made his logos bigger and extremely graphic.

Hilfiger is worn by a diverse range of public figures. For example, President Bill Clinton, Michael Jackson, Harry Connick, Jr., and Mick Jagger sport his logo. Hilfiger brings together a crossover market of young professionals, preppies, and the urban hip-hop crowd. The prep-urban style runs through many of his lines. Hilfiger says: "I think it's very cool that I can walk down Fifth Avenue and see a messenger wearing my rugby shirt five sizes too big, and then go to Wall Street and see an investment banker wearing my pinstripes." Hilfiger's street popularity was boosted in March 1994, when Snoop Doggy Dogg wore a red, white, and blue rugby shirt on *Saturday Night Live.* Hilfiger has even been labeled "hip-hop's favorite haberdasher."

In advertising, Tommy always wants his models to seem spirited and fun. Referencing to a typical Hilfiger ad, *Adweek* wrote: "Notice the group of wet and wild funsters just up from a dunk in their local stone quarry, their big ol' WASP prepster style Tommy underwear soaked to the eh—groin. There must be something about the large white teeth gleaming in the mouths of all of these nice, clean, young, 'ammuricans' that makes the otherwise revealing image seem *spirited,* as if people pose for their dentist in their underwear."

TARGETING A NEW SEGMENT

Russell Simmons, the founder of Def Jam Records, says that "Tommy's clothing represents the American dream to black kids. They're not interested in buying holey jeans; they want high-quality merchandise." While Hilfiger has been successful in a variety of markets, of particular interest to many is his success among urban youth. Hilfiger focuses on true "hip-hoppers," a group that may seem too small and too poor to target. But millions of suburban kids follow inner city trends—ranging from music to clothing. Hilfiger has used gangsta' rap to tap into the inner-city market. In exchange for free wardrobes to rap artists, Hilfiger's name is mentioned in the lyrics of various songs, and The Fugees prominently displayed his logo in the September 1996 issue of *Rolling Stone.* Hilfiger also has used rap stars as runway models. According to Yankelovich African-American monitor, there are six segments of black consumers based on income and attitudes. The "hip-hopper" segment accounts for 27 percent of U.S. blacks, and they are twice as likely as others to keep up with new styles. Hilfiger is said to have taught marketers that "bragging rights in the 'hood are worth far more than the dollars generated there."

TOMMY TARGETS WOMEN

Hilfiger has expanded into the professional women's market with a positioning strategy very similar to that used for men. This could be a very smart move given the strong trend among women toward casual dress. The brand, which features larger than life logos and varsity styling, is outselling more sophisticated sportswear offerings. Michael Toth, president and creative director of Toth Design and Advertising, which has been Hilfiger's agency for

five years, says "Tommy is a lifestyle brand that transcends the genders." The ads use cheerful, fresh-faced young models against the red, white, and blue background. This defines Tommy as being American, youthful, honest, charming, and mischievous, according to Toth. Positioning around the fun theme has done well in the women's market. Hilfiger also has launched the Tommy Girl fragrance, and a line of infant clothing is due out soon. If he follows the pattern of Calvin Klein and Donna Karan, children's clothing, home furnishings, cosmetics, and even candles may follow. Using a $25 million ad budget, Hilfiger's jeans and sports wear for women are expected to exceed $100 million in sales in the first year.

1. *Identify the core target markets of Tommy Hilfiger, historically and today. What subsegments are targeted within each core target?*
2. *Develop an overall segmentation scheme, using variables and categories that describe the Tommy Hilfiger market. How do the Hilfiger target market segments differ from those of Calvin Klein?*
3. *Describe the traditional positioning strategy Hilfiger used for the professional men segment. Use a positioning map to represent it. Why did you select each of the axes? How is Tommy Hilfiger differentiated from Calvin Klein and Bill Blass?*
4. *How is Tommy positioned in the women's target market segment? What are the similarities and differences with Tommy Hilfiger's positioning with men?*
5. *How has Hilfiger's positioning with the urban market influenced other aspects of the positioning strategy?*

SOURCES: Justin Doebele, "A Brand Is Born," *Forbes,* February 26, 1996, pp. 65–66; Elaine Underwood, "Tommy Hilfiger on Brand Hilfiger," *Brandweek,* February 5, 1996, pp. 23–27; Joshua Levine, "Badass Sells," *Forbes,* April 21, 1997, http://www.forbes.com; Shelley Reese, "The Quality of Cool," *Marketing Tools,* July 1997, http://www.marketingtools.com; Marc Spiegler, "Marketing Street Culture: Bringing Hip-Hop Style to the Mainstream," *American Demographics,* http://www.marketingtools.com; Woody Hockswender, "Prep-Urban," *Esquire,* March 1996, pp. 131–132; Martha Duffy, "H Stands for Hilfiger: The Former Mens Wear Laughing Stock Expands into the Women's Market," *Time,* September 16, 1996, p. 66; and Barbara Lippert, "Beyond Critical," *Adweek,* March 18, 1996.

Chapter 7

Connecting with Customers: Understanding Consumer Behavior

Objectives

1. Appreciate the importance of involvement in the decisions consumers make.

2. Evaluate the effect on consumer behavior of such psychological factors as motivation, perception, learning, attitudes, and information processing.

3. Explain how such social factors as culture, subculture, social class, reference groups, and family help explain consumer behavior.

FEW PURCHASES IN LIFE ARE AS EXCITING—or as hard to make— as buying a car. You are thrilled by the thought but dread haggling with a stereotypical car salesperson. You look at several models and find one that seems made just for you—the right style, features, and price. Was that luck? Or did marketers at the auto company understand consumer behavior so well that the car was created "for you"?

Think about that for a moment. In 1996, around 9 million cars were bought in the United States. Consumers chose from 406 car and truck models, spending an average of about $20,000 per purchase. For an ordinary household, that's 63 percent of annual income! Yet the overwhelming majority are not just satisfied with their purchase but proud of it. How do marketers satisfy so many consumers?

Although Nissan claims to make cars "for the human race," it doesn't try to satisfy all 6 billion people on the planet. Instead, like other auto manufacturers, it is an expert at understanding very narrow target markets. Nissan's Maxima, Altima, Sentra, Pathfinder, 240SX, and others made for the U.S. consumer are created to satisfy those markets. Packages and options are based on buying behavior. Well-researched showroom design encourages the right person to make the right purchase. Specific types of vehicles with specific packages are displayed.

Nissan understands the importance of targeting women, who purchase 50 percent of all cars and influence up to 80 percent of all vehicle purchases. In fall 1995, the company launched a direct marketing program to make buying a car easier and less stressful for women. Called Altima:Extra, it attempts to address focus-group complaints about lack of information on the buying process and the treatment women sometimes receive at dealerships. The Altima:Extra shopping kit includes a video, a card entitling the bearer to perks and services at participating dealers, coupons for discounts on parts, and "owner reassurance plans." Nissan is pleased with the response.

Nissan also differentiates its markets in other countries. Due to regional variations in regulations and preferences, it has research and development centers in the United States and Europe. The Primera, with more conservative packaging and responsive performance, was developed for the European market. In the United States, where softer suspensions and advanced styling sell, the J30 model is popular. But the J30 doesn't do well in Japan, where its size is considered too small for the price.[1]

What makes you choose a particular model or style of automobile? According to some sources, emotion is the main reason for up to 85 percent of us. Good marketers understand that many things influence emotions: social upbringing, jobs, family and friends, and culture. In this chapter, we'll explore the numerous factors that affect consumer buying decisions.

THE CONCEPT OF CONSUMER BEHAVIOR

In the 21st century there will be vastly greater diversity among a growing number of consumers in expanding global markets. The challenge leading-edge organizations face is to enhance the life experiences of consumers with products that live up to their expectations. Every action must contribute in some way toward consumer well-being. This doesn't happen with wishful thinking or intuition. It requires a thorough knowledge of consumer decision making and the forces that influence it. To connect with customers, we must understand the societal and psychological factors that determine their decisions. And as we approach the next millennium, leading-edge organizations are bundling their knowledge of all these factors into systematic ways of influencing customer satisfaction, loyalty, and relationships.

Connecting with customers requires a thorough understanding of consumer behavior. **Consumer behavior** involves the actions and decision processes of individuals and households in discovering, evaluating, acquiring, consuming, and disposing of products. Consider the key parts of that definition. First, it looks at both actions—what people do—and decision processes—how they think and feel. For example, only 28 percent of consumers rent one video at a time; 47 percent rent two, and 24 percent rent three or more.[2] Marketers want to know how often this occurs and for what reasons. Second, the definition refers to individuals and households. Usually an individual makes the purchase, but those decisions are often related to household considerations. When a mother shops she may buy Pepsi for one person, Coke for another, bottled water for a third, and so forth. Third, evaluating, acquiring, and consuming products are important parts of the process, but we need to remember that consumer behavior starts with discovery and proceeds through disposal.

Figure 7-1 provides an overview of the main topics covered in this chapter. We begin with the relationship between consumer involvement and decision making. Since involvement can be low or high, decision making can be relatively passive or very active. Next we deal with five psychological factors that influence consumer behavior: motivation, perception, learning, attitudes, and information processing. The third major section, on social influences, describes how culture, subculture, social class, reference groups, and family members affect the decisions of individual consumers. In the last sections, we look at ways in which technology is used to track consumer behavior, as well as ethical issues related to attempts to persuade consumers.

CONSUMER INVOLVEMENT AND DECISION MAKING

Decision making and involvement are closely related processes. Knowledge about them provides insight into how and why consumers behave as they do. Involvement is a function of how important, complex, and/or time-consuming a purchase may be. As we will see, decision making varies with the degree of involvement. For high-involvement purchases, the consumer is likely to devote time and attention to each of five steps in the decision process.

CONSUMER INVOLVEMENT

Think about the difference between buying a box of breakfast cereal and a new home. Which purchase would you spend more time researching and generally care more about? Not all purchases have the same importance; some mean more to us than others. **Low-involvement pur-**

Consumer behavior
The actions and decision processes of individuals and households in discovering, evaluating, acquiring, consuming, and disposing of products.

CONNECTED: SURFING THE NET

www4.nissan.co.jp

Take the Nissan global cybercruise. Link to Nissan North America, Asia, Europe, or Japan and then take a plant tour. Read about Nissan milestones, vehicle design, manufacturing, marketing, and much more.

Low-involvement purchase
A routine buying decision.

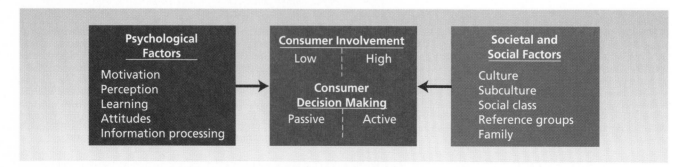

Figure 7-1   Connecting with Customers: Understanding Consumer Behavior

Nickelodean stores, a new extension from the Viacom Flagship store, feature branded merchandise that reflects the network's humor and irreverence.

chases require only routine decision making. Cereal, soap, soft drinks, and similar items don't require much thought. Many people purchase the same brand every time they shop, which underscores the importance of brand awareness. **High-involvement purchases** demand extensive and complex decision making. Buying a car, a computer, or even a television set requires a good deal of thought. The product is expensive, and you probably will have to live with it for a long time. Nontraditional products often fall in this category. Viacom's flagship entertainment store in Chicago sells such "showstoppers" as a $10,000 Star Trek ship model, a $2,800 Nickelodeon bed, and a costume worn by Lucille Ball. The store offers "hooks to draw consumers in and let them experience and connect with the brands directly."[3] Through these connections, Viacom helps make the products meaningful to customers despite the complexity of the purchase decision.

Figure 7-2 shows how involvement influences decision making. The level of involvement with any product depends on its perceived importance to the consumer's self-image. High-involvement products tend to be tied to self-image, whereas low-involvement products are not. A middle-aged consumer who feels (and wants to look) youthful may invest a great deal of time in her decision to buy a sport-utility vehicle instead of a station wagon. When purchasing an ordinary light bulb, however, she buys almost without thinking, because the purchase has nothing to do with self-image. The more visible, risky, or costly the product, the higher the level of involvement.

Involvement also influences the relationship between product evaluation and purchasing behaviors. With low-involvement products, consumers generally will try them first and then form an evaluation. With high-involvement products, they first form an evaluation (expectation), then purchase. One reason for this behavior is that consumers do not actively search for information about low-involvement products. Instead, they acquire it while engaged in some other activity, such as watching television or chatting with a friend. This is called **passive learning,** which characterizes the passive decision making process. Only when they try the product, do they learn more about it. In contrast, high-involvement products are investigated through **active learning**—part of an active decision making process—in order to form an opinion about which product to purchase.

Figure 7-3 shows that products fall on a continuum between low and high involvement. Moving toward the high end, decisions are made about more expensive, permanent, and com-

High-involvement purchase
A complex buying decision made after extensive thought.

Passive learning
Learning in which little energy is devoted to thinking about or elaborating on information.

Active learning
Learning in which substantial energy is devoted to thinking about and elaborating on information.

Figure 7-2   Low/High Involvement and Passive/Active Decision Making

Figure 7-3   *Examples of Products on an Involvement Continuum*

plex products that also are more related to self-concept. Consumers give these purchases more thought.

CONSUMER DECISION MAKING

For a better understanding of consumer buying behavior, marketers have broken the decision process into the five steps described below. These are shown in Figure 7-4, along with a description of how one consumer, Erin, made a high-involvement purchase. For low-involvement purchases, the first three steps may be skipped. As involvement increases, each step takes on greater importance, and more active learning occurs.

Problem recognition
Becoming aware of an unfulfilled need or desire.

Information search
Thinking through a situation by recalling information from stored memory or obtaining it from external sources.

Alternatives evaluation
Use of decision rules that attempt to determine which product would be most likely to satisfy goals.

Problem recognition occurs when a consumer becomes aware of an unfulfilled desire. In a low-involvement situation, such as the purchase of a compact disk, you might immediately go to a place like Tower Records and casually select recordings by two or three of your favorite artists. Or, if you're thirsty, you may simply run out and buy a soft drink. In a high-involvement purchase the recognition of a need may arise long before it is acted upon. In the case of a house, the cost may prevent you from acting on your need for several years.

The **information search** consists of thinking through the situation, calling up experiences stored in memory (internal search), and probably seeking information from friends, salespeople, advertisements, on-line services, and other sources (external search). Each source has its benefits and drawbacks. Experience is a good teacher, but you may not have enough information in memory. External search is beneficial, but friends may have preferences different from yours, salespeople may push the product that earns them the highest commission, and ads are often incomplete.

Alternatives evaluation is based on decision rules about which product or service is most likely to satisfy goals. These rules are personal; that is, they vary according to what the indi-

Figure 7-4   *The Consumer Decision-Making Process*

CONNECTING THROUGH RELATIONSHIPS

THE CUSTOMER LOYALTY CARD GAME

More and more people are discovering that there *is* a free lunch—or coffee, haircut, video, or even lube job—if you patronize certain shops and get your frequent-customer card punched. More than three in ten adults take advantage of business freebies, and 56 percent of past or current users say the cards influence their buying decisions, according to a survey by Market Facts of Arlington Heights, Illinois.

Customer loyalty is in the cards. Retailers are finally realizing that building relationships with customers they already have is more profitable than luring first-timers with splashy ad campaigns or costly discounts. "Repeat business is like compounding interest," says S. Todd Burns, owner of Time-It Lube in Shreveport, Louisiana. Because his business is based on repeat customers and new business from word-of-mouth referrals, Burns doesn't have to spend much money on advertising. Instead, he relies on incentives like a frequent-user card, good for $3.00 off the $24.95 service price on your third visit, $5.00 off on your fourth. Burns estimates that 90 percent of his customers return.

At Quartermaine Coffee Roasters in Rockville, Maryland, owner Roger Scheumann surveyed customers to see if they wanted rewards. Armed with that information, Quartermaine started two programs in 1994, one for people who buy bags to brew at home, and another for those who get their coffee to go. Since then, Quartermaine has redeemed tens of thousands of frequent-customer cards. That's a lot of free coffee. Yet, companies in the customer loyalty business consider freebies an investment in an extremely valuable asset—a customer database. Each time someone fills out a card, the name, address, and vital stats are punched into a computer. Mailings to advertise specials and new products go to the people most likely to buy: true-blue customers.

Of course, for a program to work, businesses must give customers a reason—like superior service—to be loyal in the first place. And the card game isn't for every business. Only those with enough volume are likely to make incentives pay off. But customer loyalty is still the name of the game. Foot Traffic, a chain based in Kansas City, Missouri, relies almost entirely on impulse purchases, since its stores are located in tourist-center malls. Even so, owner Charles Barnard makes sure all customers are treated as if they will return. Salespeople and managers are armed with knowledge about sock fabrics and trends. So many customers began telephoning orders that Foot Traffic started a small mail-order business. "Satisfied customers find a way to get back to you," says Barnard.

Sources: Jennifer Fulkerson, "It's in the Customer Cards," *American Demographics*, July 1996, pp. 44–47; and Michael Barrier, "Building Your Customer Portfolio," *Nation's Business*, December 1996, pp. 45–46.

---

vidual consumer considers important. At this point, complex thinking is likely to occur. Using the results of the information search, the consumer weighs the pros and cons of each choice.

The **purchase decision** emerges from the evaluation of alternatives. The consumer may decide not to buy and save the money or spend it on a different item altogether. Or s/he may want to play it safe by deciding to purchase a small amount for trial purposes, or by leasing rather than buying. The decision to buy often occurs some time before the actual purchase. The **purchase** is a financial commitment to make the acquisition. It may take time to secure a mortgage or car loan, or the dealer may be temporarily out of stock.

The **purchase evaluation** stage results in satisfaction or dissatisfaction. Buyers often seek assurance from others that their choice was correct. Positive assurance reinforces the consumer's decision, making it more likely that such a purchase will be made again. Positive feedback confirms the buyer's expectations.

PSYCHOLOGICAL FACTORS THAT INFLUENCE CONSUMER DECISIONS

Although the decision making process appears straightforward, it is influenced by many psychological factors. We will look at the most important ones: (1) motivation, (2) perception, (3) learning, (4) attitudes, and (5) information processing.

Purchase decision
The decision whether or not to buy, and which competing product to buy that is arrived at after carefully weighing the alternatives.

Purchase
A financial commitment to acquire a product.

Purchase evaluation
The process of determining satisfaction or dissatisfaction with a buying choice.

MOTIVATION

Marketers first conducted "motivation research" during the 1950s and early 1960s in an attempt to identify buyers' subconscious reasons for purchasing various products. This work has since been discredited because it was based on a very limited theory and poor research techniques. Early motivation researchers depended on the ideas of Sigmund Freud. This pioneering psychoanalyst suggested that most human behavior is determined not by conscious thought but by unconscious urges, passions, repressed feelings, and underlying desires. Based on these beliefs, motivation researchers declared that men purchase a convertible as a substitute for a mistress, and women make cakes as a symbol of giving birth. About the best that can be said for this early work is that it inspired marketers to develop new concepts of motivation. Today, motivation theories are much sounder, and they provide several basic insights for marketers.

Motivation
An internal force that directs behavior toward the fulfillment of needs.

Motivation is an internal force that directs behavior toward the fulfillment of needs. It involves the needs (or goals) a person has and the energy that is triggered to drive the person to action. The needs that underlie motivation can be classified as either biological or psychological. *Biological needs* have been called primary or innate needs because they seem to exist in all people, regardless of environment. Needs in this category include food, water, shelter, fresh air, and at least some degree of comfort. Products like Evian spring water, Kellogg's Special K, and various brands of bedding were developed in direct response to this type of need. **Psychological needs** are often called secondary or learned needs because they result from socialization. Needs in this category include friendship, a sense of self-worth, and achievement or self-fulfillment. The U.S. Army slogan "Be all that you can be" appeals directly to psychological needs.

Psychological needs
A need that arises in the socialization process.

Maslow's Hierarchy of Needs   Abraham Maslow's famous classification is often used by marketers to help categorize consumer desires. According to Maslow, five basic needs underlie most human goals. He ranked them in a hierarchy, to indicate that higher-level needs tend to emerge only after lower-level needs are satisfied. Figure 7-5 illustrates Maslow's hierarchy in the form of a pyramid.

At the base of the pyramid are physiological needs essential to survival such as food, clean air and water, warmth, and sleep. Evian produces bottled spring water to fulfill the need for clean, unadulterated water.

On the next level is the need for safety, which includes basic security and freedom from physical abuse. These needs are both biological and psychological. Insurance companies appeal to them with such slogans as "You're in good hands with Allstate" and "Get a piece of the rock" (Prudential).

The third level of the pyramid is the need for love and belonging. Humans seek out companionship to fulfill this psychological need. Family and friends are extremely instrumental in satisfying it. Advertisements for Hallmark cards and FTD florists play on our need for human interaction, love, and belonging.

The fourth level is the need for esteem, which comes from prestige, status, and self-respect. Many consumers maintain and exhibit their social status through high-visibility products. Designer labels or symbols on clothing and recognizable automobile designs are two ways marketers have attempted to fulfill this need.

Figure 7-5   Maslow's Hierarchy of Needs
Source: Adapted from Abraham H. Maslow, Motivation and Personality, 2nd ed. Copyright 1970 by Abraham H. Maslow. Reprinted by permission of Harper & Row Publishers, Inc.

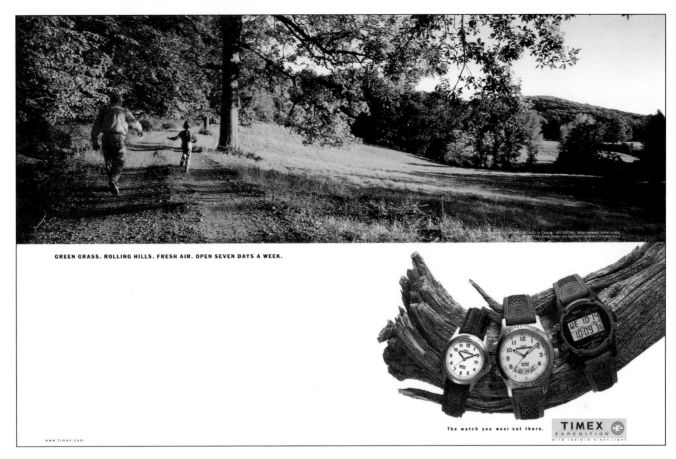

This Timex ad appeals to the need for self-actualization.

The final level of Maslow's hierarchy is the need for self-actualization. As people begin to feel physically satisfied, safe and secure, accepted, and esteemed by others, they may need a higher level of personal satisfaction. They are motivated by a desire to develop themselves and use their abilities. Education is directed toward this need by helping people attain knowledge and experiences that improve self-worth, sharpen talents, and promote personal growth. Self-actualization also may come from coaching youth soccer or playing in a basketball league. Backpacking, writing, skiing, painting, and composing are other examples. The Nike ad campaign, "I Can . . . ," is aimed at consumers who are motivated by self-actualization. The Peace Corps offers a challenge as well as a reward: "The toughest job you'll ever love."

Motivational Conflict   People are motivated to attain some ends and avoid others. In marketing terms, consumers approach activities that help them attain desired outcomes but avoid activities that have negative consequences. Yet, because human needs and wants are so varied, consumers may be faced with outcomes that combine both desirable and undesirable features. Three types of such motivational conflict have been identified: approach-approach, avoidance-avoidance, and approach-avoidance. These are summarized in Figure 7-6.

Approach-approach conflict occurs when a consumer desires two objectives but cannot have both. Suppose George wants sports-car styling but family comfort in a new car. Unless he can afford to buy a Viper and a Caravan, he will have to resolve this conflict by choosing one or the other. Chrysler promotes its Town & Country as having "leather in places luxury cars don't even have places."[4] This type of promotion is aimed at consumers who want luxury features in a practical family car.

Avoidance-avoidance conflict results when a choice must be made between two undesirable alternatives. Elaine's car has a bad muffler. The noise draws disapproving looks from strangers, and her friends are starting to make jokes about it. But the repair will deplete Elaine's savings account. She will have to resolve this conflict by selecting the least adverse choice. Midas muffler says, "America's favorite mufflers are Midas® Mufflers. Period. And quality is one reason." The appeal is to consumers who don't want engine problems yet also don't want to spend extra money on maintenance.

Approach-approach conflict
Motivational conflict that occurs when a consumer desires two objectives but cannot have both.

Avoidance-avoidance conflict
Motivational conflict that occurs when consumers must choose between two undesirable alternatives.

Type	Description	Sample Situation	Possible Marketing Response
Approach-Approach	Two objectives are desired, but the consumer cannot have both	Toothpaste Health with fluoride Sex appeal with breath freshener	*Provide both benefits:* Toothpaste with fluoride and a breath freshener.
Avoidance-Avoidance	The consumer must choose between two undesirable alternatives	Muffler repair Depleted savings Bothersome exhaust noise	*Stress unpleasantness of one alternative to get desired action:* Muffler ads that emphasize how embarrassing a defective muffler can be or that offer financing or delayed payments.
Approach-Avoidance	The consumer's goal has both positive and negative aspects	College education Hard work and expense Greater earnings opportunities	*Emphasize positive benefits of desired action:* A college ad campaign that illustrates how long-term earnings compare for a college graduate and a nongraduate.

Figure 7-6   Types of Motivational Conflict

Approach-avoidance conflict
Motivational conflict that occurs when a consumer desires an alternative that has certain negative qualities.

Approach-avoidance conflict occurs when a consumer desires an alternative that has positive and negative qualities. If Jim works out on his NordicTrack, then his body will be stronger, but at the cost of time-consuming strenuous exercise. Many types of purchases cause approach-avoidance conflict because they have drawbacks, side effects, or other undesirable features. In a way, all purchases can be considered a mixed blessing, since the buyer must forfeit some money sooner or later. Consider the National Guard, which may offer tuition assistance and enlistment bonuses but requires training obligations and a period of service.[5] The approach-avoidance conflict for people who join up involves positive rewards in exchange for hard work and sacrificed time.

By understanding motivational conflicts, marketers can respond with new products as well as advertising, pricing, and distribution plans that help minimize these buyer conflicts.

The Navy offers positive rewards in exchange for hard work and time— an approach-avoidance conflict.

Human beings use their sensory organs to see, hear, smell, taste, and touch an almost infinite variety of sensations. The sensations are caused by stimuli—the sound of a jackhammer, the fragrance of a flower, the texture of material, and so on. **Perception** is the process of recognizing, selecting, organizing, and interpreting these stimuli in order to make sense of the world around us.

We constantly receive so many stimuli that only a limited number can be processed. Therefore, consumers must select—either consciously or subconsciously—the stimuli on which to focus. Typically, this selection occurs in four stages: selective exposure, selective attention, selective comprehension, and selective retention. At each stage, a product or message may be screened out, disregarded, misinterpreted, or forgotten by the consumer. Figure 7-7 illustrates the perception process.

Selective Exposure   U.S. companies spend more than a billion dollars every day in the hope of communicating messages to consumers. However, a large portion of these messages are screened out in the first stage, when consumers choose whether to ignore or receive the message. How often do you reach for the remote and channel surf whenever an ad appears on television? Marketers call the consumer's ability to seek out or avoid information **selective exposure.** For example, Soloflex advertises extensively on television, but you can choose to watch, tune out mentally, or change the channel. You decide whether to be exposed to Soloflex information. This happens to you hundreds of times a day with other media—billboards, radio, newspapers, and so on.

Selective Attention   Consumers do not pay attention to very many messages. Noticing every one of them would lead to mental exhaustion from information overload. So consumers are extremely skilled at screening out irrelevant messages.

Through **selective attention,** people have a strong tendency to heed information that supports their current views. Democrats listen more often to Democratic than Republican politicians, and vice versa. Similarly, consumers attend to advertising for products they have already purchased or intend to purchase. They screen out much of the information that conflicts with their experience or goals because it is irrelevant and distracting. One of the most important challenges faced by any marketer is gaining the consumer's attention. Without it, no matter how well crafted, the message will have no effect on the intended target.

A good example is the ineffectiveness of smoking prevention campaigns. One-fourth of Americans smoke, despite millions of dollars spent trying to dissuade them, including warnings from the U.S. surgeon general and proof that smoking increases the risk of heart disease, cancer, and other health problems.[6] Each year, smoking causes 400,000 deaths and the loss of 5 million years of potential life.[7] Yet, consumers continue to buy cigarettes. Smokers may tune into advertisements about their brand but ignore prevention ads. This selective attention reinforces the likelihood that they will continue to smoke, since the negative messages about health implications do not get through.

Perception
The process of recognizing, selecting, organizing, and interpreting stimuli in order to make sense of the world around us.

Selective exposure
The tendency to seek out or avoid information sources.

Selective attention
The tendency to heed information that supports current views and behaviors.

Figure 7-7   Process of Perception

To help gain attention, a marketer should initiate the message in a way relevant to the consumer—by using a known sports figure, a common activity, an attractive person, or humor. Then the brand name can be related to that attention-getter. Next, it is important to maintain attention by keeping the ad meaningful or interesting to the consumer. Shimano does an excellent job of attracting attention with its mountain bike ads. The logo is eye-catching and the simple, direct ads have unusual visuals.

Selective Comprehension   Marketers must take care to ensure that their products and messages are understood by consumers in the way intended. **Selective comprehension** refers to consumers' tendency to interpret messages based on their biases. If a message runs counter to a consumer's strong beliefs, then it is perceived as being farther from the buyer's point of view than is really the case. Consumers are likely to reject any information that contradicts their current beliefs or past behaviors. That is why many ads keep it simple and avoid controversial images. A notable exception is political ads, since selective comprehension can work in the marketer's favor.

Selective Retention   **Selective retention** means that consumers remember some messages and forget others. The way information is understood determines how well it is remembered. People tend to recall what agrees with their own beliefs, desires, or behaviors.

Once information is retained, it is held until replaced or altered. Old information may be forgotten when new, conflicting messages are received, or it may be reshaped if the new information is more consistent with the person's beliefs or goals. Joan wants a Macintosh laptop computer but has heard it will be very expensive. She reads an ad comparing the cost of laptops and sees that Macintosh is not the highest. As a result, she discards the idea that Macintosh laptops are expensive and retains the information that other brands cost more. The "Nobody Beats Midas—Nobody" advertisement was designed by the muffler giant to achieve such an effect.

Subliminal Perception   Since our conscious perceptions selectively and routinely filter messages, is it possible to bypass that level and market to the consumer's subconscious? The belief in subliminal persuasion began in 1957, in a New Jersey movie theater. Market researcher Jim Vicary claimed to flash messages such as "Drink Coca-Cola" and "Eat Popcorn" on the screen too fast to be recognized by the naked eye. According to him, the messages still registered in the brain, resulting in sales increases of 18 percent for Coke and almost 60 percent for popcorn. Vicary then coined the term *subliminal advertising*. Researchers were never able to replicate his study, and there is no evidence to support his claim.[8]

We do have evidence that subliminal messages do not work. A 1991 psychology study set out to determine whether self-improvement tapes really help people lose weight, improve memory, raise self-esteem, or quit smoking. Researcher Anthony Greenwald found that roughly half the people who listened to the audio tapes claimed improvement in the area specified on the label. But the labels had been deliberately switched, so any effect has to be attributed to the power of suggestion, not the tapes themselves.[9] It is still debated whether subliminal messages are effective in changing the minds of consumers.

Learning

Consumers learn how to acquire and use products. The process starts at an early age and continues throughout life. It is through learning that consumers select the patterns of behavior that determine when, where, and how they purchase, consume, and discard goods. **Learning** is any change in consumers' behavioral tendencies caused by experience. There are two basic types of learning: cognitive and behavioral. Cognitive learning emphasizes perception, reason, and problem solving. It focuses on knowledge, insights, ideas, opinions, and goals. High-involvement and challenging purchases incorporate active learning that focuses attention on problem-solving behavior. The five decision steps outlined in Figure 7-4 dealt with this type of learning. Behavioral learning occurs through either classical or operant (sometimes called instrumental) conditioning when consumers react to external events. Behavioral learning primarily concerns what consumers do, not what they are thinking.

Classical Conditioning   Classical conditioning gets its name from an early (and therefore classical) experiment by the Russian physiologist Ivan Pavlov in the 1920s. He presented meat paste to a dog, and the dog salivated. He then presented the paste while ringing a tuning fork.

Selective comprehension
The tendency to interpret products and messages according to current beliefs.

Selective retention
The tendency to remember some and forget other information.

Learning
Any change in consumer behavior caused by experience.

Again, the dog salivated. Pavlov repeated this several times. Eventually, when the tuning fork was rung without the meat paste, the dog still salivated.[10] The basic idea behind **classical conditioning** is that people can learn to respond to one stimulus in the same way they respond to another if the two stimuli are presented together.

Classical conditioning is used extensively in marketing.[11] Think for a minute about the ad that featured young people on a hot day drinking Mountain Dew and jumping off a steep cliff into a river. Marketers were trying to get consumers to associate the soft drink with excitement and refreshment in summer weather, in much the same way that Pavlov's dogs associated the tuning fork with meat paste. Then, when a hot day comes along (stimulus), you will want to drink Mountain Dew.

Consumer preferences are often influenced by advertising features (stimuli) rather than the product itself. Marketers say that music often helps define the emotional appeal of a certain brand. Classical music is often used to convey comfort, luxury, and distinctive taste.[12] Chevrolet developed an advertising campaign for trucks around Bob Seger's "Like a Rock," which now is identified with the reliability and strength of Chevy trucks.

Marketers need to understand that consumers may generalize stimuli or discriminate among them. **Generalization** occurs when people make the same response to different stimuli. **Discrimination** occurs when consumers make different responses to different stimuli. For instance, when oat bran cereals were first found to reduce cholesterol levels, the oat bran image was generalized to other oat cereals, like Cheerios, and to other bran cereals, like Raisin Bran. With experience, however, consumers began to discriminate, aided by advertisers. Health Valley says its Oat Brand O's® cereal has "More Healthy Benefits: fat-free; cholesterol free; good source of fiber; low sodium; good source of six B-vitamins; and, made with organic oat bran and oats."[13]

To take advantage of a strong brand name, marketers establish visual consistency across categories. The various products in ConAgra's Healthy Choice™ line, including pasta sauces, cereals, breakfast bars, frozen dinners, and ice cream, are branded under the distinctive green Healthy Choice™ label. Consumers can readily identify the brand and are able to generalize the health benefits of Healthy Choice™ products even across product categories.

Marketers also try to take advantage of a buyer's ability to discriminate among brands. For example, Burger King and McDonald's® each spend millions to help consumers distinguish between their products. When a survey revealed that 72 percent thought McDonald's® had the best burger for kids but only 18 percent considered it the best burger for adults, the company went after the adult segment with the Arch Deluxe®.[14]

Operant Conditioning   Even before Pavlov gained fame, the noted psychologist, Thorndike published work showing how rewards encourage certain responses and punishment discourages others. Behavior that is intermittently rewarded (positive or negative reinforcement) will be repeated in the expectation of eliciting the reward. Behavior that is punished will be avoided and thus will diminish in frequency. Psychologist B. F. Skinner later termed this type of conditioning "operant" because the learning occurs as the subject responds to or "operates on" the environment. Thus, **operant conditioning** is the use of reinforcement or punishment to shape behavior. Today, marketers know that consumers associate positive and/or negative consequences with the items they consume.

There are several ways positive reinforcement can occur. The first is through a product satisfying a need or want. If you drink Lipton's iced tea and your thirst disappears, then that behavior is reinforced. The next time you are thirsty, you are likely to reach for Lipton's. The second reinforcer is information or knowledge. Many organizations publish magazines to support their business: Northwest Airlines has *The World Traveler*, Ticketmaster issues *Live! Entertainment Magazine*,[15] and ESPN publishes *Total Sports*.[16] These offer information that will reinforce purchases and stimulate new interests while maintaining brand loyalty. A third way consumer behavior can be reinforced is by seeing results. For example, the LifeCycle computerized bike is promoted as burning 750 calories per hour of exercise.[17] The 20-minute daily workout required to see results actually becomes a reinforcer because consumers know they are making progress toward getting in shape. Yet another way companies reward purchasers and encourage repeat purchases is the frequent-customer card promotion. This is discussed in the relationships feature, "The Customer Loyalty Card Game."

Punishment may result from such things as a product that fails to perform as advertised; a service agent who acts in a curt, unfriendly manner; or even news stories that cast the corporation in a bad light and undermine the consumer's pride in owning its products.

Classical conditioning
After two stimuli are presented together repeatedly, people learn to respond to one in the same way as the other.

Generalization
Making the same response to different stimuli.

Discrimination
Making different responses to different stimuli.

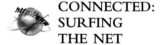

CONNECTED: SURFING THE NET

www.conagra.com

Visit the Web site of ConAgra, the largest independent food company in the United States. ConAgra produces such brands as Healthy Choice™, Hunt's, Van Camp's, Orville Redenbacher's, and many more. Read company information and news or link to the Healthy Choice™ or Butterball Web sites.

Operant conditioning
The use of reinforcement or punishment to shape behavior.

Attitude

A state of readiness, with cognitive, emotional, and behavioral components, that reflects the beliefs of the consumer with regard to messages, brands, products, product characteristics, and so forth.

Belief

A conviction that something is true, or that descriptive statements are factual.

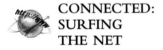

CONNECTED: SURFING THE NET

www.snapple.com

Make the "liquid connection" and visit the Snapple Web site. Create your own Web page, obtain Snapple information, and take an opportunity to play games and win prizes.

ATTITUDES

An **attitude** is a state of readiness with cognitive, emotional, and behavioral components, that reflects the beliefs of the consumer with regard to messages, brands, products, product characteristics, or other aspects of life. Attitudes are often described as consumer preferences—a like or dislike for products or their characteristics. Marketers usually think of attitudes as having three dimensions: cognitive, affective, and behavioral. The cognitive aspect refers to knowledge about product attributes that is not influenced by emotion. The affective component relates to the emotional feelings of like or dislike. The behavioral element reflects the tendency to act positively or negatively. In other words, attitudes toward purchasing a product are a composite of what consumers know about its attributes; whether they like or dislike them; and how positively or negatively they feel about the purchase.

Figure 7-8 shows how attitude can affect the purchase of a mountain bike. Attitudes are important because they help us understand why a particular action is taken. And notice that attitudes are not the same as beliefs. A **belief** is a descriptive thought or conviction that expresses an opinion about the characteristics of something. For example, a consumer may believe that rapid-fire shifters are a feature of a Specialized brand bicycle. Beliefs may help shape attitudes but don't necessarily imply like or dislike. Attitudes also influence beliefs: If rapid-fire shifters increase the price, then a consumer who dislikes high cost may believe they are not a very useful feature.

Consumers frequently form attitudes to help evaluate whether products and brands fit into their lifestyle. These attitudes are drawn from a broad range of ideas, not just the characteristics of a product.

Generally, marketers use their knowledge of consumer attitudes to make sure that strategies are consistent with consumer tastes and preferences. From time to time, marketers attempt to change consumer attitudes, usually by influencing one of the three components. A common approach is to use promotion to influence the cognitive component. During the early 1980s, Ford experienced record losses mainly because competitors' products were seen as being of better quality. Consumers thought (cognitive) that if they purchased a Ford, they would not be getting the quality they deserved, which led to negative overall attitudes toward Ford. A companywide strategy was developed to combat the problem. Ford made design and manufacturing changes, enlisted the cooperation of key parts suppliers, and established employee work programs to improve quality. Information about these improvements was communicated to consumers through an advertising theme: "At Ford, Quality is Job One!" Today, Ford is the second largest car and truck producer in the world and ranks second on the Fortune 500 list of largest industrial corporations, based on sales.[18] Ford has recently jettisoned its 17-year-old "quality is job one," for a new tagline "Better ideas. Driven by You." Ford believes this new tagline will be consistent with messages about the importance Ford places on the environment, safety, and personal security.[19]

Marketers also try to influence the affective component of consumer attitudes. For example, as the health and fitness craze swept the United States, many people developed a dislike for beef, believing it to be high in fat and cholesterol. The industry launched a campaign showing that beef is nutritional and easy to prepare, hoping to make consumers feel good about eating it. "Beef. It's what's for dinner" was a recognizable slogan for 70 percent of Americans less than four years later. The demand for beef has increased ever since the commercials began running.[20]

| Product Attribute | ATTITUDE COMPONENT | | |
	Cognitive (Does the bike have this attribute?)	Affective (Do I like this attribute?)	Behavioral (Am I likely to buy this bike?)
Rapid-fire shifters	Yes	Like very much	Very positive
Light weight	Yes	Like very much	Very positive
Rigid frame	Yes	Neither like nor dislike	Neutral
Durability	No	Like somewhat	Somewhat negative
Vibration absorption	Yes	Like somewhat	Somewhat positive
High cost	Yes	Dislike somewhat	Somewhat negative

Figure 7-8 Attitudes About a Mountain Bike Purchase

To change the behavioral aspect of consumer attitudes, often a coupon or free sample is offered. Research indicates that once a product is purchased or used—even if only a free sample—the likelihood of future purchase is greater. When Quaker Oats owned Snapple, it spent $40 million on a three-month program that sent a "squad of Snapple samplers" to parks, offices, and Little League games. The plan was to give away 10 million bottles in hope that once consumers tried the drink, they would be more likely to purchase it.[21]

INFORMATION PROCESSING

Information processing refers to ways in which consumers acquire, store, and evaluate the data they use to make decisions. The human mind has a remarkable ability to process (understand and apply) the information it takes in. Perception, motivation, behavioral learning, and attitudes are integrated into the human thought system, which acquires, stores, and analyzes data to arrive at goal-directed behaviors. Key to information processing is the encoding of information and its use in memory.

Encoding **Encoding** is the process of converting information to knowledge. The brain is sometimes described as having two relatively distinct ways of encoding information.[22] These enable it to handle pictorial, geometric, and nonverbal information as well as verbal, symbolic, and analytical thinking. The mind combines all this information and produces integrated perceptions.

The mental images encoded are thoughts held in "picture" form, called episodes. Episodes are not like pictures taken with a camera, and they can be felt and known without words. Aesthetics, tastes, and symbolic meaning are represented this way. Ads and other phenomena are also likely to be retained as episodes.[23] Nike traditionally uses a highly visual format for its advertisements. These images capitalize on consumer emotions and attempt to link personal value to the wide array of Nike products. Advertising is never just about Nike, the brand. It is carefully constructed to draw in consumers. According to a recent survey by Teenage Research Unlimited (TRU) of Northbrook, Illinois, 42 percent of respondents age 12 to 19 chose Nike as the top brand. "Nike's equity transcends its status as a product marketer," says Peter Zollo, TRU president. "No other brand from any category comes close to benefiting from such

Information processing
The process whereby consumers acquire, store, and evaluate the data they use in making decisions.

Encoding
The process of converting information to knowledge.

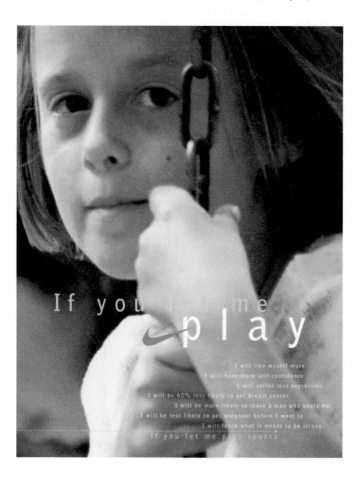

Nike usually uses a high visual format for its advertisements.

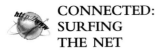

CONNECTED: SURFING THE NET

www.nike.com

Check out the ever-changing Nike Web site and discover what's new. Visit the locker room and have a look at Nike products, or take the Nike trivia challenge.

Memory
The brain function that stores and recalls encoded information; includes sensory, short-term, and long-term capacities.

top-of-mind positive imagery."[24] The Nike swoosh symbol is a highly recognized trademark that may elicit desired effects because of an episode encoded earlier in the consumer's brain.

Verbal encoding occurs when words or symbols are stored in what is called semantic memory. General knowledge, facts, and principles gleaned from experience are held there. Many believe that such information as package size, the meaning of brand names, prices, and so forth, are stored this way. For example, advertisements for Johnson & Johnson's ultrasensitive products use facts and statistics to appeal to concerned mothers. One ad states: "Three leading pediatric dermatologists helped develop it. 200 babies with dry, easily irritated skin clinically tested it. Today, nearly 2 million babies can benefit from it."[25] Many mothers may form an impression in their semantic memory based on this information and call upon it later to make a purchase decision.

Marketers must remember that consumers encode both verbal and pictorial information about the world.[26] In the early stage of information processing, the pictorial tends to dominate. In later stages, verification and more analytical thoughts dominate. Therefore, visual, musical, creative, and pictorial elements of ads catch the consumer's attention. Then, facts, reasoning, and details of product messages are likely to be picked up.

Memory   **Memory** is the brain function that stores and recalls encoded information (knowledge). There are three types of memory: sensory, short-term, and long-term. Each operates differently and can be considered a separate step in the process of memory formation.

The first and most basic stage is *sensory memory,* which takes in an almost unlimited amount of encoded information. These sensory impressions decay (are forgotten) within a fraction of a second. But when attention is focused on a few stimuli, sensory information about them is transferred to short-term memory, where it can be coded and interpreted.

Short-term memory interprets what is sent from sensory memory. It usually can hold information for only a short time, and its capacity is much smaller than that of sensory memory—about four to seven chunks of information at once.[27] A chunk is a unit of organized information that can be recalled to solve specific problems of short duration. A chunk may vary greatly among persons focusing on the same object. A first-time buyer of a used car is likely to have a more difficult time than a person who has purchased several. For example, the experienced buyer probably will ask for past service receipts to learn about repair history, whereas the novice may not think of it.

In *long-term memory,* a vast amount of information may be held for years or even indefinitely. It remains there until replaced by contradictory information through a process called interference. For example, you go to your favorite restaurant and receive a poor meal or poor service. This interferes with your positive memory of the place, and you then reclassify it to a lower status. Once a brand is stored in long-term memory, consumers can add relevant information to help with future choices. Makers of Chapstick often associate their product with the elements (sun, wind, dryness). That way, when outdoor enthusiasts need lip protection from the elements, they often think of Chapstick.

Consumers are bombarded with promotional messages. Marketers hope that the more often their brand name is seen, the more likely consumers will be to process information about it. In Colorado Springs, school children get unusual exposure to advertising. Marketers are allowed access to schools in exchange for supplemental funds that will help pay for everything from basic equipment to extracurricular activities. Mountain Dew and Marriott Food

Some children receive exposure to advertising at school.

Services have each hung banners in the hallways, while Frito-Lay has built an "Enter the Crunch Zone!" display.[28] It is hoped that the constant presence of the brand name will reinforce memory and stimulate future purchases.

SOCIAL FACTORS THAT INFLUENCE CONSUMER DECISIONS

Social factors have a great influence on how individual consumers and households behave. Consider something as simple as a pair of earrings. In some societies, children's ears are pierced at birth; other societies frown on ear piercing altogether. Some social groups regard earrings as a symbol of wealth and refinement; others consider them showy and in poor taste. Some people wear them to indicate membership in a group, others to enhance status, yet others to make a fashion statement. Some people have many sets and change earrings almost daily; others wear the same pair forever. Many different social influences affect our purchase decisions, but for marketers the most notable ones are culture, subculture, social class, reference groups, and the family.

CULTURE

Perhaps the most pervasive influence on human beings is culture. **Culture** is the learned values, beliefs, language, symbols, and patterns of behavior shared by people in a society and passed on from generation to generation. It produces manners and actions that are often taken for granted as the "appropriate" way.

> **Culture**
> The learned values, beliefs, language, symbols, and patterns of behavior shared by people in a society and passed on from generation to generation.

Culture changes very slowly unless outside forces intervene. Historically, such forces have included political and religious wars and natural disasters. Today, global economics and technology are having an enormous effect. They have made the world much smaller and culture more uniform. In an ingenious experiment that demonstrated the growing similarity of cultures, the New York advertising agency BSB Worldwide took pictures of the bedrooms of teenagers from 25 different countries. These revealed that posters, clothing, sports gear, and music tastes were much the same. Executives at the agency had a hard time differentiating one room from another, and most could not tell whether the pictures came from Los Angeles, Tokyo, or Rome.[29] In fact, young people all over the world have many of the same concerns, interests, and activities. Of children surveyed in the United States, Germany, the United Kingdom, Japan, China, and France—55 percent responded that "being with friends" was their favorite activity. And, 90 percent of those surveyed said they watch television at least three days a week.[30] Global companies like PepsiCo, Reebok International, MTV, and many others are taking advantage of this emergent world culture.

By taking cultural values into account, companies adjust to the particular customs of people in different societies. **Values** are the shared norms about what is right to think and do. They reflect what society considers to be worthy and desirable. Marketers need to understand values so their actions are not counter to what consumers in a given market consider acceptable. Ford must be conscious of the values of Asian consumers in marketing the Taurus. "We know in Singapore that styling is going to be important, and in Hong Kong, it's safety," says John Fitzpatrick, director of sales and marketing for the Pacific Rim. The automaker must make consumers believe that it is sensitive to their values. "The problem with Ford is that it has come to Asia believing that consumers know the brand," says Peter Boardman, a senior industry analyst in Tokyo. "But customers don't know what kind of company it is or what products Ford sells." The plan is to localize in each country, since consumers have different demographic characteristics and buying behaviors. Ford has already started running commercials in South Korea that focus on safety features and environmental policies, two issues important to consumers there.[31]

> **Values**
> The shared norms about what is right to think and do; what culture considers to be worthy and desirable.

SUBCULTURE

Understanding a culture provides marketers with an overall picture, but they also need more specific information. A **subculture** is a group of people with shared values within a culture. In the United States, these groups may be defined by ethnicity, age, religion, geographic location, and national origin. In this section we will focus on ethnicity and look at three groups: Hispanic, Asian, and African-American consumers.

> **Subculture**
> A subset of people with shared values within a culture.

It should be noted that an ethnic subculture can be a very broad category. For example, the U.S. Hispanic community includes Cubans, Puerto Ricans, Mexican Americans, Tejanos, and Chicanos, among others. Within such groups are further distinctions—low or high ethnicity, length of time in the United States, immigrant or native-born, and place of residence, to name a few. A marketer may want to target Cubans with high ethnicity living in New York City—as Miller beer does.

Marketers know that ethnic subgroups are much more likely to buy branded products and spend more for what they perceive as quality. Immigrants are often perplexed by the wide variety of choices, so they tend to stick with the major brands they knew at home. Gary Berman, president of Miami-based Market Segment Research, says that "these groups define nationally advertised brands as being quality products and are more likely to select quality over price."[32]

Groups with strong ethnicity form some of the most important subcultures. As we learned in chapter 6, marketers are interested in identifying segments of the population with common needs, wants, and buying behaviors. Marketing strategies can then be developed to appeal directly to these segments. Therefore, it's critical for marketers to identify people of high ethnicity—who identify strongly with their ethnic subculture—rather than simply those with a certain skin color or national origin. A thorough understanding of ethnic backgrounds can lead to the formation of homogeneous segments. Figure 7-9 illustrates the spending power, income, and population percentages of several ethnic groups in the United States.

> **CAREER TIP** With the increase in ethnic populations, companies that produce, sell, and market ethnic products may see a considerable growth. Use your knowledge of diversity to your advantage in interviews and by writing targeted cover letters. Remember that companies in growth areas may offer you better opportunities for advancement.

Hispanic Consumers Hispanics are a booming subculture. Their number is growing rapidly due to births and immigration. The U.S. Bureau of the Census predicts the figure of 23 million in 1990 will reach 31 million by 2000 and 41 million by 2010—edging out African Americans as the largest U.S. minority group.

Although Hispanics come from many countries, they share certain norms. Socialization is high. They frequent parks as social centers, not just as places to take the kids. This means that parks are a good venue for promoting products and connecting with customers through sponsoring a community event. Food marketers can gain market share among Hispanics by acknowledging festivals and traditions as well as by carrying foods specific to that subculture. Because Hispanics share a common language, Spanish (except for Brazilians, who speak Portuguese), radio or television stations that program in Spanish are obvious media choices for promotional messages. Hispanics exhibit exceptional brand loyalty: nearly three-quarters prefer products made by well-established companies, and 71 percent are reluctant to switch once they find a brand they like.[33]

Many Hispanics view shopping as a social event. It's a way of keeping in touch with news about the community and the "old country." It's not unusual for suburban Hispanics to drive to shopping areas closely associated with their own heritage. Only 4 percent like to shop in small grocery stores. Most prefer full-sized supermarket chains or warehouse-style stores, where the large packages and low prices are draws.[34]

A study by the National Hispanic Corporate Council revealed that among the top 1,000 U.S. companies surveyed, only 36 percent target the $300 billion Hispanic market—but that

Figure 7-9 Subculture Spending Power in the United States

	All Groups	White	African American	Hispanic	Asian
Percentage of U.S. Population	100%	83.2%	12.4%	9.7%	3%
Average Household Income	$30,786	$32,368	$18,660	$22,848	$42,240
Annual Spending Power	$1.7 trillion	$1.33–1.38 trillion	$220–270 billion	$300 billion	$100 billion

is changing.[35] Nissan aimed a national campaign at these consumers on Univision Network, with spots featuring celebrities from television and the movies. AT&T has sponsored a documentary during Hispanic Heritage Month, and McDonald's® used Spanish-language ads in promoting its Arch Deluxe®.[36] Although many Hispanics are fluent in English, most marketers believe that it is better to sell in Spanish. Research shows that most bilingual Hispanics prefer it.[37]

Asian-American Consumers Imagine a market segment that's highly educated, affluent, and geographically concentrated. That describes Asian Americans, whose number has doubled in the past 20 years. A growth rate of 4 percent annually is expected through 2050. They are the best-educated U.S. subculture: 39 percent of those over age 25 have completed four years of college, compared with 22 percent of whites. They also earn the most: Their median family income is $42,240, compared with $36,910 for whites. And two-thirds live in just five states: California, New York, Hawaii, Texas, and Illinois.

Like other ethnic groups, Asians can be differentiated by country of origin, length of time in the United States, and other factors.[38] They also have common norms, such as looking to key opinion leaders in their community for decision making. Most Asians are brand-conscious, and high-income groups associate brands with social status.[39] They also search for businesses that want to get involved in their community.

The Bank of America has been very successful in this market. Asians are impressed that the organization was founded long ago by an immigrant who achieved the American dream. "Many Asian people admire that," says Bill Imada, president of the Los Angeles ad agency Imada Wong Communications Group. "They like to know everything there is to know about a company's history, is it successful, is it stable, is it likely to be around for awhile."[40] According to Eleanor Chang, vice president for Asian markets at Bank of America, one cultural norm is that you don't spend what you haven't got. Thus, a promotion featuring special financing may not have the same appeal for Asians as for other subcultures.[41]

Information from other people is important to Asians in making purchase decisions. Bill Imada estimates that "90% of nonacculturated Asian communities get a majority of their information from a relative, a friend, a business associate, or their church or temple." Television and newspapers are the next main source of information, followed by a growing interest in radio.[42]

Like Hispanics, Asians should not be considered homogeneous. Chinese, Koreans, Vietnamese, Filipinos, Indians, Japanese, and Polynesians all have different backgrounds. They also feel differently about acculturation into U.S. society. Many Japanese who come to work in the United States consider themselves transients. Since they plan to return to Japan, they resist changing their culture or learning the language. Marketing to such a clientele in a personalized manner can reap great rewards.

African-American Consumers African Americans represent about 12 percent of the U.S. population and have an annual buying power of perhaps $270 billion. In 1996, national advertisers spent more than $865 million on advertising to African-American consumers.[43]

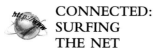

**CONNECTED:
SURFING
THE NET**

www.spiegel.com

Spiegel on-line allows you to shop at the "speed of life." Discover what Spiegel has to offer for work, play, and home. Or link to other Spiegel sites and learn what's new.

Bank of America has successfully personalized branches in Asian communities to better serve local needs.

Until the 1990s, it was believed that minority groups did not respond to direct mail. But when Spiegel teamed up with *Ebony* magazine to target African Americans with a new catalog, *E-Style,* it met with great success. Spiegel research had revealed that African Americans felt no catalog on the market was aimed specifically at their needs. In addition to speaking with 800 customers and conducting nine focus groups, researchers also measured how clothing fit on more than 1,300 volunteers to determine any differences from the general population.[44]

Marketers also connect with African Americans through products designed for Kwanzaa, the annual holiday that combines American customs with African traditions. About 15 million people celebrate it, and the market has grown from $100 million to $500 million in just a few years. It is said to be the "fastest growing holiday in America." Hallmark includes Kwanzaa cards in its line for African Americans, called Mahogany.[45]

Other large companies are paying attention to this segment. Microsoft, for example, teamed up with Black Entertainment Television to deliver interactive information and entertainment for African Americans, including CD-ROM titles and on-line services. Nissan also is targeting this market with a multimillion-dollar radio, newspaper, and magazine campaign.[46]

SOCIAL CLASS

Social class
A relatively stable division of society based on education, income, and occupation.

The third major social influence on consumer behavior is social class. A **social class** is a relatively homogeneous grouping of people based on similarities in income and occupation. Members tend to share values, interests, and behaviors. How would you rank the following occupations by status: salesperson, high school teacher, and accountant? What about a physician, a professor, or a lawyer? Your views agree with research findings if, in both groups, you

Social Class	Percentage of U.S. Population	Description	Examples of Purchases
Upper Upper	Less than 1%	Often called the "old rich," upper-upper class families have been wealthy for generations and are born into wealth. People in this group do not have to work for a living.	Jewelry, fine wine, luxury cruises, yachts
Lower Upper	About 2%	Often called the "new rich" because their fortunes are not inherited, these self-made millionaires tend to be executives, athletes, consultants, movie stars, and high-technology entrepreneurs.	Highly visible products such as cars
Upper Middle	12%	Comprised of doctors, professors, lawyers, veterinarians, state politicians, and business executives, this class is upwardly mobile and success oriented.	Condominiums, skiing, travel, home computers, outdoor furniture, camcorders, cellular phones
Middle	32%	In addition to white- and blue-collar workers, the middle class includes such professions as clerk, bank teller, public school teacher, and nearly all nonmanagerial office positions and other such occupations.	Brand-name clothing, family vacations
Working Class	38%	Largely blue collar, the working class has jobs that can be defined as fairly routine and not requiring advanced education. Many in this class are union members.	Used trucks & motorcycles
Upper Lower	9%	Living standards are just above poverty. Work is predominantly unskilled and low wage. The members of this class are often poorly educated.	Fundamental necessities: food, rental housing, medical care
Lower Lower	7%	At the bottom of the social class system are the visibly poor, many of whom are third-generation welfare recipients. Typically underemployed or unemployed, they rely on public aid or charity to survive.	Food, used clothing, minimum necessities

Source: Based on Richard P. Coleman, "The Continuing Significance of Social Class to Marketing," Journal of Consumer Research, December 1983, pp. 265–280, © Journal of Consumer Research, Inc., 1983.

Figure 7-10   A Breakdown of Social Classes

ranked them from highest to lowest in the order presented. Feelings about the relative prestige of these occupations reflect the tendency in most cultures to make social class distinctions. Figure 7-10 describes various social classes and gives examples of purchases for each.

Global Social Class Dimensions   Marketers increasingly look at social class from a global perspective. In some societies—such as India, South Africa, and Brazil—class distinctions are clear, and status differences are great. In others—such as Australia, Denmark, and Canada—differences are less extreme. In countries with strong class differences, where people live, the cars they drive, the restaurants they frequent, the sports in which they participate, the types of clothing they wear, how much they travel, and where (or whether) they go to college is largely determined by social class.

Commercial activity, particularly interpersonal relations, also can be greatly influenced by class associations. For example, the president of a French company expects to deal only with the top executives of another firm. More than once, U.S. companies have failed at marketing in France because they did not know or ignored this. In some cases, the French were offended when the Americans sent lower-level managers to important meetings. In other cases, the Americans lost status when high-ranking executives communicated with middle-level French managers. In a country with a more homogeneous class structure, such as Sweden or Denmark, it is not uncommon for executives from all levels to work as a team, so Americans of various rank are accepted as well.

Marketers study global social class dimensions in order to understand consumer profiles, habits, interests, and purchasing behavior. In 1997–1998, three national surveys costing more than $30 million were mailed to more than 24 million British homes by ICD Marketing Services. The research was designed to give insight into consumer preferences for cars, finance, travel, and other purchases.[47]

REFERENCE GROUPS

Another major influence on consumer behavior is reference groups. We all live with, depend on, and are nurtured by other people. We influence and are influenced by those with whom we have frequent contact—friends, coworkers, and family members. We also are influenced

The "milk mustache" ads use a diverse collection of celebrities to bring success to the campaign.

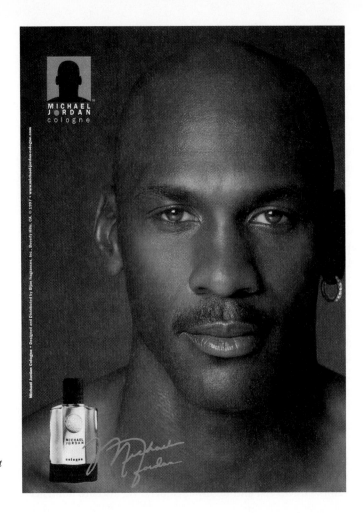

Michael Jordan is one of the most highly recognized and influential athletes for product endorsement.

by people we know only indirectly, through the mass media. Research shows that groups have an immense effect on the purchasing behavior of their members, including their search for and use of information, their response to advertisements, and their brand choices.[48]

Reference groups are people whose norms and values influence a consumer's behavior. Consumers depend on them for product information, purchase comparisons, and rules about correct or incorrect buying behavior. College fraternities and sororities are examples of reference groups. Although each member is unique, each adheres to certain group norms and standards.

Marketers distinguish between two types of reference groups. **Associative reference groups** are those to which people *want* to belong, although they may be prevented by income, occupation, or education. In contrast, **disassociative reference groups** are those to which people do *not* want to belong. The same reference group can be associative to some people and disassociative to others. For example, a widely publicized concern about the world of some rock 'n' roll artists is the use of heroin. There is a possibility that teens who are drawn to some rock artists may become more accepting of heroin despite the obvious hazards. Keyboardist Jonathon Melvoin of Smashing Pumpkins died of an overdose, and many other musicians and groups are known to be current or past users, including The Red Hot Chili Peppers, Steven Tyler of Aerosmith, and the late Kurt Cobain.[49] Teens may choose these bands as associative or disassociative reference groups.

Advertisers capitalize on the human tendency to rely on groups. In one form or another, groups are a part of almost all mass media advertisements and are used in many personal selling presentations. The "milk mustache" ads by the dairy industry have used a diverse collection of celebrities for a successful campaign. Featuring athletes such as Steve Young and Gabriela Sabatini as well as television celebrities such as *Friends* stars Lisa Kudrow and Jennifer Aniston, the campaign targets a number of different reference groups.[50]

Promotions that appeal to associative tendencies command a good deal of attention. Ads in youth-oriented magazines often depict people who belong to admired groups. Because consumers are full of hopes and dreams for the future, the use of associative reference groups is

Reference groups
A set of people whose norms and values influence a consumer's behavior.

Associative reference groups
A group with which people want to identify.

Disassociative reference groups
A group with which people do not want to identify.

206

very effective. Consider the number of advertisers that use famous spokespersons to tout their messages about products. Professional athletes are often seen as being members of associative reference groups. A recent survey, conducted by American Sports Data, ranked Michael Jordan and Tiger Woods as the most highly recognized and influential athletes for product endorsement. Consumers rated Tanya Harding the lowest, preceded by O. J. Simpson; others ranking below average were Dennis Rodman, Mike Tyson, and Pete Rose.[51]

THE FAMILY

How much has your family influenced the way you behave, speak, or dress? Often the family in which you grow up—known as your *family of orientation*—teaches you certain purchase habits that continue throughout your life. Many consumers buy the same brand of soap, toothpaste, mayonnaise, laundry detergent, or gasoline that their mother or father did. Later, people start their own family, called the *family of procreation,* and it also influences purchase habits.

The family is especially important to marketers because it forms a **household,** which is the standard purchase and consumption unit. If you do not already have a household, chances are great that someday you will purchase or rent a home, buy appliances and durable goods, and require banking and insurance services. In other words, your household will be a consumption unit.

Not all households consist of a mother, a father, and children. Many have only one person, or several nonrelatives, or a single parent with children. This section, however, focuses on the traditional nuclear family. Marketers generally look at three important aspects:

- How do families make decisions as a group?
- What roles can various members play in a purchase decision?
- How does family purchase behavior change over time?

Family Decision Making Family decision making is "one of the most underresearched and difficult areas to study within all of consumer behavior."[52] How does your family make buying decisions? Most purchases are probably conceived and carried out by one member with little influence from the others. These are called *autonomous* decisions. In other cases, several family members may be involved. These are called *joint* decisions.

Marketers must remember that gender roles affect how family decisions are made. Decisions are termed *syncratic* when both spouses are jointly and equally involved; *autonomous* when either one of them makes the decision independently; and *husband-* or *wife-dominant* depending on which one has the influence. Research has found that gender especially affects financial decisions and that men and women approach finances differently. In general, men perceive themselves as advisors, active in business and in influencing their friends' financial decisions. Men are more likely to take independent financial risks, and they often place value on ego-gratifying opportunities. Women are more likely to discuss finances with friends and others before making a decision. They are less likely to take risks and are more open to advice. Directing marketing activities to the wrong person in the household could be as wasteful as directing them to the wrong market segment.[53] For this reason, it's important for marketers to understand the decision-making roles within a family.

Family Purchasing Roles When children ask a parent to buy a certain type of cereal, they are influencing the purchase, but the parent still makes the final decision. In contrast, when teenagers go to the mall to buy clothing, while they certainly may be influenced by their parents, they usually make the final decision. Family members play certain roles in certain purchases and play different roles for different products. There are five key roles:

- *Initiator.* First suggests that a particular product be purchased.
- *Influencer.* Provides valuable input to the decision-making process.
- *Decision maker.* Makes the final buying decision.
- *Purchaser.* Physically goes out and makes the purchase.
- *User.* Uses the product.

The role a consumer plays is not always obvious. While men have been the traditional focus of Black & Decker marketing efforts, research shows that women are a large secondary market. They buy tools not only for gifts but also for their own use.

Household
Family members (and occasionally others) who share the same housing unit; for marketers, the standard purchase and consumption unit.

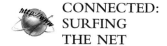

CONNECTED: SURFING THE NET

www.whymilk.com

Want to know how "got milk" got started? Read the story behind the award-winning ads. You also can watch a 30-second ad, courtesy of the American Dairy Association.

Children have a significant effect on family decisions. In fact, for certain products, the marketer may decide to focus on them rather than parents. Reebok is among the many companies that have formed a club targeting kids. Club Reebok offers a spectrum of sports-related activities, and Shaquille O'Neal is a prominent member. Kids identify with "their" brand, and the next time a parent purchases shoes for them, Reebok can be assured it has developed a young influencer in the purchasing decision.[54] Cereal manufacturers also recognize the important role young children play. Eye-catching boxes and cartoon characters are designed to appeal directly to children. The influence of children continues as they grow, but usually for a different set of products—clothes, video or computer games, and such services as family vacations or video rentals.

Family Life Cycle   As families age, they progress through a series of predictable stages, called the family life cycle. At each point, unique problems and life situations must be addressed. An understanding of each stage gives marketers powerful insight into the needs and expectations of families.

Only a few decades ago, everyone was expected to move in orderly progression from youth, to marriage, to childrearing, to retirement. Today, the picture is more complex because of widespread divorce and single parenting, as shown in Figure 7-11. As you can imagine, a family's needs and purchase decisions vary at each stage. Let's look at these in more detail.

Young Singles   Young singles are in the process of setting up their first household. Items they buy tend to be easily transportable from one location to another as living arrangements change or they find a new job. During this stage, courtship activities make social events, recreation, and entertainment important. Advanced education and training also may be purchased to further a career. This market category, when combined with middle-aged singles and sole survivors, has shown high growth from 18 percent of all households in 1970 to 25 percent in 1990. The U.S. Bureau of the Census predicts the figure will be 27 percent by 2010.

New Couples   Young married people without children generally try to build an economic foundation for later responsibilities. By combining resources, a new couple may have enough discretionary income to enjoy recreational activities while still saving for the future. This group spends more than other households on furnishings, new cars and trucks, and alcohol.

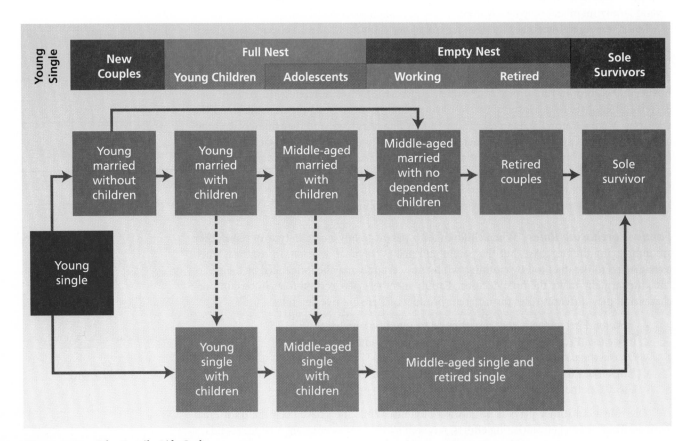

Figure 7-11   The Family Life Cycle

Full-Nesters   Whether you are single, divorced, or married, a great deal changes once children enter the picture. They are expensive and consume great amounts of time. Household budgets for full nesters increase for nearly every category of purchase, and new expenses emerge—diapers, day care, toys, piano lessons, and so forth. As children reach adolescence, their sports activities may cost from several hundred to several thousand dollars per year. Many families prepare for the cost of college, which can consume 30–40 percent of annual household income for each child.

Of course, purchase behavior will differ according to family structure—traditional family, divorced or widowed parent, or single parent. The latter group often has very limited spending power. A divorced or widowed parent may have some child support or death benefits to ease the burden a little, but often s/he must work long hours to make ends meet and has very little free time. In traditional families, both parents usually work to provide for their children. Their earnings tend to increase over time as they become well established in a career.

Working Empty Nesters   This category consists of three types of consumers: middle-aged singles, married couples with no children, and married couples with grown children who have left home. These households are in their prime wage-earning years. Once overlooked, this market accounts for half of U.S. buying power and controls three-quarters of the nation's assets. The group has discretionary income of $150 billion annually.[55] Without children around, empty nesters are free to travel, pursue hobbies, and explore new lifestyle options. As baby boomers turn 50, this market will grow even more. For details on how to capture it—whether empty or full nesters—see the diversity feature, "How to Satisfy a Senior—Oops— I Mean a Boomer."

Retired Empty Nesters   Consumers at this stage of the family life cycle are economically and socially diverse. The bottom 20 percent live at or near the poverty level, while the top 20 percent have an average net worth nearly 90 times higher. In fact, 70-year-olds today are consuming nearly one-fifth more than 30-year-olds.[56] This wealthier group has changed the image of the retired couple over the last decade. Retirees are now viewed as financial investors willing to assume some risk, mobile and daring, physically active and health conscious, and willing to pamper themselves. It was once thought that advertising dollars were wasted on this segment but no longer; it's a powerful niche that is targeted in television programming and advertising campaigns. The wealthy elderly are the focus of luxury cruise lines, automobile manufacturers, and land developers.

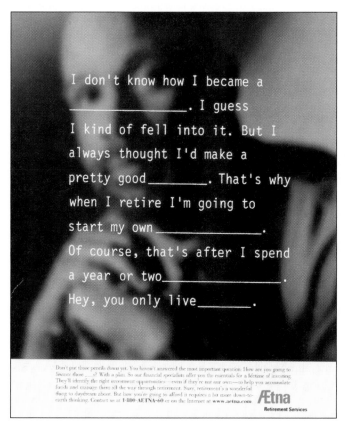

Retired empty nesters are now viewed as financial investors, physically active, health conscious, and willing to pamper themselves.

CONNECTING WITH DIVERSITY
HOW TO SATISFY A SENIOR—OOPS—I MEAN A BOOMER

Call them young at heart, in their prime, or maybe even mature. Just don't call them seniors. Marketers who treat the aging baby boomers like previous generations of seniors are in for a shock. Boomers are reinventing senior citizenship in their own young image, and their numbers are too great to be ignored. In the next 25 years, the segment of Americans over age 50 will increase by 47.2 million, to a total of 115.4 million.

The marketing community needs to be reminded that there's gold in those golden years. Mention the 50+ age group and "most marketers see some doddering 90-year-old," says Candace Corlett, president of the special markets division at Research 100, in Princeton, New Jersey. The stereotype of a penny-pinching senior on a fixed income isn't true of many people. Spending power is progressively more concentrated among those age 50 and older—household income averages $59,600 for the age group 45–54. Furthermore, baby boomers are more active and fit than their parents were at the same age. Market researchers are finding that life stage is a better definition. For example, a man over 50 may be divorced and suddenly alone, or starting a second family, or remarrying into a new family, or a full nester with responsibilities for young children and aging parents, to name a few possibilities.

But boomers do seem to have one common denominator: denial of aging. Corlett says: "They think they can defy age if they just exercise or eat healthier." Older people used to perceive themselves as 10 years younger than their actual age, but that gap is widening as boomers lop off a good 20 years. Successful marketing must take this gap between self-perception and reality into account. For instance, a Tylenol commercial depicting a 40-something man jogging after knee surgery appeals to boomers, who feel the aches and pains of age but won't let that slow them down. Nike spots show older runners talking about being "wrinkled but not old." Keds has a "forever young" campaign, and the same name is used for a Club Med program targeted at boomers. After a failed attempt to push vacations to seniors through the American Association of Retired Persons, Club Med refashioned its Forever Young packages to appeal to the more active 50+ set.

But the future for boomers won't be all fun in the sun. Research commissioned by Sun City retirement communities, located in five states in the South and West, found that two-thirds of the oldest baby boomers would like employment after they retire, three-quarters of them in a part-time capacity. Sun City has noticed this trend already and is offering more homes with a guest cottage—not so the grandkids can visit, but for a home office. The company also plans to prewire new homes for stereo systems since boomers will bring along a cherished passion of their youth—rock music by singers like Mick Jagger, who also belong to the 50+ cohort.

Sources: Cyndee Miller, "Boomers Come of Old Age," *Marketing News*, January 15, 1996, pp. 1, 6; Paula Mergenhagen, "Sun City Gets Boomerized," *American Demographics*, August 1996, pp. 16–20; Lisa Krakowka, "Modern Maturity," *American Demographics* (Marketing Tools Supplement), May 1996, pp. 31–33; Terry Lefton, "Empty Nests, Full Pockets," *Brandweek*, September 23, 1996, pp. 36–40; Gary Kass, "Call Me Mature," *American Demographics*, November 1996, p. 22; and Richard A. Lee, "The Youth Bias in Advertising," *American Demographics*, January 1997, pp.47–50.

Sole Survivors   Sole survivors are men and women whose spouse has died as well as older single people who never married. Their net worth and buying power have increased over the past decade due to the stock market boom of the mid-1980s and mid-1990s and the rise in home values. A number of sole survivors are senior citizens, who today are targeted heavily by marketers. The growing number of products designed to appeal to seniors include home health care, which is growing at a rate of 20 percent per year.[57] Television fitness programs are also targeted to the elderly, as well as a variety of diet supplements.

USING TECHNOLOGY TO TRACK CONSUMER BEHAVIOR

Technology not only helps marketers better understand consumers but also is having a direct influence on how companies build relationships. More than 7 million young people in North America use the Internet, and the number who go on-line internationally doubles every six months. Dubbed the Net Generation, they are primarily children of the baby boomers. About 90 percent of this group in the United States has access to the Internet through home, school, or library computers. The proportion is expected to reach 100 percent by 1998.[58]

CONNECTED: SURFING THE NET
Club Med
www.clubmed.com

THIS CHAPTER'S DIVERSITY FEATURE DISCUSSED BABY boomers, a segment marketers are defining by life stage rather than age. Visit the Web site of Club Med, one of the many organizations targeting this group, and answer the following questions.

1. Which three stages of the family life cycle does Club Med present as options for a customized tour of the Web site? How does this feature enable the company to make a stronger connection with customers?
2. Visit the "All You Need to Know" page to learn what Club Med offers. Using Maslow's hierarchy as a guide, explain how the company appeals to each need.
3. What is a Club Med village like? How do these villages differ to meet the diverse needs of customers? How does the Web site help customers select a village that matches their preferences?
4. Imagine you are taking a Club Med vacation. Is this a low- or high-involvement purchase? Explain. Describe the steps you would go through in deciding whether to take the trip. Give examples.

Quartermaine Coffee Roasters
www.quartermaine.com

THIS CHAPTER'S RELATIONSHIPS FEATURE, "THE CUSTOMER Loyalty Card Game," discussed how frequent-customer cards help build loyalty. Quartermaine Coffee Roasters is one of many companies that considers freebies a valuable investment. Learn more about the company by visiting its Web site, then answer the following questions.

1. The use of associative reference groups is a very effective way to reach consumers. What groups or spokespersons would be good choices for Quartermaine? Explain.
2. How might global customers differ in their taste and preferences for coffee? How do Quartermaine's coffee varieties accommodate these differences?
3. Marketers develop strategies that form relationships through customer satisfaction. Explain the stages a customer might go through in establishing a relationship with Quartermaine. What actions could the company take to ensure the customer is satisfied?

What implications does this have for marketing? NPD Group has developed PC Meter Service, which records such information as software programs, on-line services, Web usage, and the age and gender of users. This meter service allows marketers to track consumer behavior. For instance, Web surfers visited an average of 22 different sites in January 1996, typically looking at about 3.7 pages per site. Marketers are spending up to $100,000 to use the service to target consumers on the Web.[59] Knowledge Discovery and Net Angels are introducing similar technologies to study the interests of Internet users. This information not only will assist marketers in identifying consumer behavior but also will improve search results for frequent users.[60] Names, addresses, and other data requested when a Web site is accessed become a reservoir of information about consumers.

Marketers also offer software that can take a consumer straight to a company's home page on the Web. Soon these customized Web browsers will be everywhere—sent through the mail, tucked in the glove compartment of new vehicles, included in the product carton, and so on. This technology allows marketers to connect with their customers through quick and easy access to company information.[61]

Ultimately, the growing use of new technologies will provide marketers with greater insight into consumer behavior. Categorizing user behavior as well as providing consumers with easy Web access enables marketers to reach many of their targeted audiences. This will benefit both consumers seeking information and the companies supplying it.

THE ETHICS OF INFLUENCING CONSUMER BEHAVIOR

For a long time, marketers have used sexual themes to heighten brand awareness and influence consumers. Today, ethical questions are being raised about some of these promotions, which many people find offensive. A notable example was a Calvin Klein campaign using ads with heavy sexual undertones and partial nudity. Despite the bans by television networks, magazines, and retailers, sales of CK products neared $1 billion in 1995.[62] Klein's shock tactics got the attention of most consumers, whether they were disgusted or intrigued. Among 120 advertising agency employees polled in one survey, 63 claimed that the CK jeans campaign was "tacky," "went too far," "was in poor taste," or was "offensive."[63]

Controversial promotion risks losing consumers in the selective comprehension phase of perception. Some people screen out ads altogether that conflict with their values. At the same time, controversy generates free publicity, perhaps worth millions of dollars in the case of Calvin Klein.[64] Klein was quoted as saying "jeans are about sex," and added that he planned to continue to market his products accordingly.[65]

Although consumers are free to seek out or avoid information, people often feel that children should not be exposed to objectionable images. When these are plastered on billboards or the side of a bus, it is hard to avoid them. Marketers face a challenge when deciding whether to promote a product with a sexual theme or shock tactics. They must weigh the risk of losing customers and crossing ethical boundaries against the advantages of gaining attention and strongly influencing purchase behavior.

Many of the factors that influence consumer decision making also play a role in the buying decisions of businesses, because businesspeople are, after all, individuals with psychological motivations, perceptions, and attitudes. Overall, however, the buying behavior of businesses is quite different from consumer buying behavior. As we will see in chapter 8, it often follows formalized procedures, involves many persons and functions, and requires more personalized communication with the selling firm.

CHAPTER SUMMARY

OBJECTIVE 1: Appreciate the importance of involvement in the decisions consumers make.

Marketers know that an understanding of consumer behavior lies at the heart of nearly every successful strategy for connecting with customers. Consumer behavior is the actions and decision processes of individuals and organizations in discovering, evaluating, acquiring, consuming, and disposing of products. Consumers behave differently in low- and high-involvement purchasing situations. When involvement is high, they use an elaborate five-step decision process, and their attitudes are learned actively. When involvement is low, they make choices without much effort, and learning is passive.

OBJECTIVE 2: Evaluate the effect on consumer behavior of such psychological factors as motivation, perception, learning, attitudes, and information processing.

The five important psychological factors influencing consumer behavior are motivation, perception, learning, attitudes, and information processing. Motivation is an internal force that directs behavior toward the fulfillment of needs. Marketers often use Maslow's hierarchy to categorize needs. Consumers may experience one of three forms of motivational conflict: approach-approach, avoidance-avoidance, or approach-avoidance. Perception is the process of recognizing, selecting, organizing, and interpreting stimuli in order to make sense of the world around us. It occurs in four stages: selective exposure, selective attention, selective comprehension, and selective retention. Learning is any change in behavioral tendencies due to previous experience. The two basic types of learning are cognitive learning and behavioral learning. Behaviors can be learned (conditioned) by classical conditioning and operant conditioning. Attitudes have cognitive, affective, and behavioral components. Information processing involves encoding and memory processes. The human brain encodes information differently depending on the type of data. It processes nonverbal, emotional, and visual concepts in one way, while it handles general knowledge, facts, and justifications in another. Memory consists of sensory, short-term, and long-term memory.

OBJECTIVE 3: Explain how such social factors as culture, subculture, social class, reference groups, and family help explain consumer behavior.

Subcultures are groups that display homogeneous values and behaviors that diverge from the surrounding culture. Social class is a relatively stable division into groups based on such factors as education, income, and occupation. Reference groups provide norms and values which become the perspectives that influence a consumer's behavior. Associative groups are ones with which people want to be associated, while disassociative groups are ones with which people do not want to identify. Families have a profound influence on consumer behavior.

REVIEW YOUR UNDERSTANDING

1. What is involvement? How does it influence passive and active learning?

2. Describe the five steps in decision making.

3. What is motivation? Describe Maslow's hierarchy of needs.

4. Describe the four elements of the perception process.
5. What is learning? Describe cognitive learning and two types of behavioral learning.
6. What are attitudes? What are their three components? How does knowledge of the components help in creating attitude change strategies?
7. What is information processing and how does it work?
8. What social influences are most important to marketers? List and define each.
9. How is social class measured?

DISCUSSION OF CONCEPTS

1. Name several subcultures in the United States. Which companies have target-marketed to them?
2. Why must marketers distinguish between a person's ethnic background and ethnicity?
3. How does social class affect consumer behavior? Which social classes exist in the United States? The values and beliefs that must be addressed to market a products to each.
4. What are the different ways families make purchase decisions? How do these affect marketing?
5. Imagine that you are the marketing manager for the Pontiac Firebird sports car. What product features would you include to meet each of the five types of needs described by Maslow's hierarchy. (For example, air bags might fulfill the safety need.)
6. What types of motivational conflict might be associated with the purchase of this Pontiac Firebird? How would you try to resolve the conflict?
7. You are in charge of marketing for a Major League baseball team. How might you apply the principles of cognitive learning to your job? Could you also apply the principles of classical conditioning or reinforcement learning? How?

KEY TERMS AND DEFINITIONS

Active learning: Learning in which substantial energy is devoted to thinking about and elaborating on information.

Alternatives evaluation: Use of decision rules that attempt to determine which product would be most likely to satisfy goals.

Approach-approach conflict: Motivational conflict that occurs when a consumer desires two objectives but cannot have both.

Approach-avoidance conflict: Motivational conflict that occurs when a consumer desires an alternative that has certain negative qualities.

Associative reference groups: A group with which people want to identify.

Attitude: A state of readiness, with cognitive, emotional, and behavioral components, that reflects the beliefs of the consumer with regard to messages, brands, products, product characteristics, and so forth.

Avoidance-avoidance conflict: Motivational conflict that occurs when consumers must choose between two undesirable alternatives.

Belief: A conviction that something is true, or that descriptive statements are factual.

Classical conditioning: After two stimuli are presented together repeatedly, people learn to respond to one in the same way as the other.

Consumer behavior: The actions and decision processes of individuals and households in discovering, evaluating, acquiring, consuming, and disposing of products.

Culture: The learned values, beliefs, language, symbols, and patterns of behavior shared by people in a society and passed on from generation to generation.

Disassociative reference groups: A group with which people do not want to identify.

Discrimination: Making different responses to different stimuli.

Encoding: The process of converting information to knowledge.

Generalization: Making the same response to different stimuli.

High-involvement purchase: A complex buying decision made after extensive thought.

Household: Family members (and occasionally others) who share the same housing unit; for marketers, the standard purchase and consumption unit.

Information processing: The process whereby consumers acquire, store, and evaluate the data they use in making decisions.

Information search: Thinking through a situation by recalling information from stored memory or obtaining it from external sources.

Learning: Any change in consumer behavior caused by experience.

Low-involvement purchase: A routine buying decision.

Memory: The brain function that stores and recalls encoded information; includes sensory, short-term, and long-term capacities.

Motivation: An internal force that directs behavior toward the fulfillment of needs.

Operant conditioning: The use of reinforcement or punishment to shape behavior.

Passive learning: Learning in which little energy is devoted to thinking about or elaborating on information.

Perception: The process of recognizing, selecting, organizing, and interpreting stimuli in order to make sense of the world.

Problem recognition: Becoming aware of an unfulfilled need or desire.

Psychological needs: A need that arises in the socialization process.

Purchase: A financial commitment to acquire a product.

Purchase decision: The decision whether or not to buy, and which competing product to buy that is arrived at after carefully weighing the alternatives.

Purchase evaluation: The process of determining satisfaction or dissatisfaction with a buying choice.

Reference groups: A set of people whose norms and values influence a consumer's behavior.

Selective attention: The tendency to heed information that supports current views and behaviors.

Selective comprehension: The tendency to interpret products and messages according to current beliefs.

Selective exposure: The tendency to seek out or avoid information sources.

Selective retention: The tendency to remember some and forget other information.

Social class: A relatively stable division of society based on education, income, and occupation.

Subculture: A subset of people with shared values within a culture.

Values: The shared norms about what is right to think and do; what a culture considers to be worthy and desirable.

REFERENCES

1. Consumer Union of U.S., Inc., on-line car-buying quiz, downloaded from AOL, May 7, 1996; Susan B. Garland, "The NAACP Bets on a New Breadwinner," *Business Week*, January 8, 1996; "1995 Echo Awards: The Front-runners," *Direct Marketing*, November 1995, p. 19; Colleen Cooper, "Nissan Targets the Female Car Buyer," *Incentive*, October 1995, p. 14; Jo-Anne Walker, "Nissan's Direct Route," *Marketing Week*, March 10, 1995, pp. 28–30; Tom O'Sullivan, "Wheel Meet Again," *Marketing Week Customer Loyalty*, November 18, 1994, pp. 29–30; and Larry Armstrong, "New From Nissan: Reverse Sticker Shock," *Business Week*, May 23, 1994, p. 27.

2. Ian P. Murphy, "The Average Consumer," *Marketing News*, April 14, 1997, p. 2.

3. Cyndee Miller, "Surreal but So Real: Viacom Is Latest to Make Retailing Entertaining," *Marketing News*, June 23, 1997, pp. 1, 20.

4. Chrysler Town & Country advertisement, *Fortune*, May 27, 1996, pp. 54–55.

5. Louisiana Army National Guard Recruiting Home Page, home.gnofn.org/"/ang/, site visited on January 23, 1997.

6. Kai Maristed, "Nicotine, An Autobiography," *American Scholar*, Summer 1996, p. 389.

7. David Satcher and Michael Eriksen, "The Paradox of Tobacco Control," *Journal of the American Medical Association*, February 23, 1994, p. 627.

8. John Vivian, *The Media of Mass Communication* (Boston: Allyn & Bacon, 1993), p. 296.

9. A.G. Greenwald et al., "Double-Blind Tests of Subliminal Self-Help Audiotapes," *Psychological Science* 2 (1991): 119.

10. Ivan Pavlov, *Conditioned Reflexes: An Investigation of the Physiological Activity of the Cerebral Cortex*, trans. G. V. Anrep (London: Oxford University Press, 1927).

11. For further discussions, see Walter R. Nord and J. Paul Peter, "A Behavior Modification Perspective on Marketing," *Journal of Marketing* 44 (1980): 36–47; and J. Paul Peter and Walter R. Nord, "A Clarification and Extension of Operant Conditioning Principles in Marketing," *Journal of Marketing* 46 (1982): 102.

12. "Stand by Your Fans," *Advertising Age*, April 29, 1996, p. M1.

13. Package by Health Valley Foods, Inc., Irvindale, California, 1997.

14. Richard Gibson, "McDonald's Plays Catch-Up with BLT Burger," *Wall Street Journal*, May 2, 1996, p. B1.

15. Deirdre Carmody, "Ticketmaster is Trying Publishing with Live!" *New York Times*, January 22, 1996, p. C7.

16. Mark Adams, "The Sporting News," *Mediaweek*, January 1, 1996, p. 9.

17. LifeStyle 5500 advertisement, *Parenting*, December-January 1997, p. 96.

18. www.ford.com/archive/FordHistory.html, site visited on January 21, 1997.

19. Robyn Meredith, "Advertising—Ford is Jettisoning its 17-year-old 'Quality is Job One' Tagline for 'Better Ideas. Driven by you'," *The New York Times*, May 4, 1998, p. C10.

20. "Checkoff-Funded Beef Promotion Covers the Bases," http://www.ncanet.org/press_releases/nr_beefpro_bic.html, site visited January 30, 1996

21. Judann Pollack, "New Marketing Spin: The PR 'Experience'," www.adage.com, site visited January 21, 1997.

22. Flemming Hansen, "Hemispherical Lateralization: Implications for Understanding Consumer Behavior," *Journal of Consumer Research* 8 (June 1981): 23–36; and Sidney Weinstein, "A Review of Brain Hemisphere Research," *Journal of Advertising Research* 22 (1982): 59

23. Morris B. Holbrash and William L. Moore, "Feature Interactions in Consumer Judgments of Verbal versus Pictorial Presentations," *Journal of Consumer Research* 8 (1981): 103.

24. "The Coolest Brands," *Marketing News*, July 1, 1996, p. 58.

25. Advertisement in *Parenting*, December-January 1997, p. 60.

26. Allan Piave, "A Dual Coding Approach to Perception and Cognition," in Herbert L. Pich, Jr., and Elliot Saltzma, *Modes of Perceiving and Processing Information* (Hillsdale, NJ: Laurence Frilliaum, 1978), p. 16.

27. Herbert A. Simon, "How Big is a Chunk?" *Science*, February 8, 1974, p. 183.

28. Melanie Wells, "Ad Pitches Target Teen Consumers," *USA Today*, May 9, 1996, p. A1.

29. Shawn Tully, "Teens, the Most Global Market of All," *Fortune*, May 16, 1994, p. 90.

30. Nancy Ten Kate, "Are All Children the Same?" *American Demographics*, June 1997, www.marketingtools.com.

31. Fera Warner, "Ford Promotes Taurus Model in Asia Markets," *Wall Street Journal*, July 22, 1996, p. A76.

32. Leah Richard, "Minorities Show Brand Loyalty," *Advertising Age*, May 9, 1994, p. 29.

33. The Market Development/Yankelovich Hispanic MONITOR 1992, quoted in Marcia Mogelonsky, *Everybody Eats* (Ithaca, NY: American Demographics Books, 1995), p. 177.

34. Ian P. Murphy, "Mom & Pop Grocery Stores," *Marketing News*, March 3, 1997, p. 2.

35. "Hispanic Study," November 1, 1996, www.adage.com

36. "Nissan Targets Hispanics," October 17, 1996; "AT&T Backs Hispanic Special," April 23, 1996; and "Hispanic Arch Deluxe," May 23, 1996, http://www.adage.com.

37. Ted J. Rakshs, "The Ethnic Boom: Marketing to the Target," *Kiwanis*, February 1994, pp. 32–34.

38. John Steere, "How Asian-Americans Make Purchase Decisions," *Marketing News*, March 13, 1995, p. 9.

39. Bill Britt, "Asian Consumers Display Collective Behavior," June 11, 1996, www.adage.com.

40. Penny Lunt, "What Asians Like and Dislike about Banks," *ABA Banking Journal*, July 1994, pp. 62–65.

41. Ibid.

42. Ibid.

43. Valerie Lynn Gray, "Going After Our Dollars," *Black Enterprises*, July 1997, p. 68–78.

44. Diane Cyr, "Cutting across Ethnic Lines," *Catalog Age*, July 1994, pp. 155–162.

45. www.hallmark.com, site visited on January 21, 1997.

46. "BET, Microsoft Tell Plans," February 2, 1996; "Nissan Hires Black Agency," *Advertising Age*, June 26, 1996, www.adage.com.

47. "Giant Lifestyle Survey to Hit U.K.," December 4, 1996, www.adage.com.

48. J. Paul Peter and Jerry C. Olson, *Consumer Behavior and Marketing Strategy*, 2nd ed. (Burr Ridge, IL: Richard D. Irwin, 1990), p. 370.

49. Karen Schoemer, "Rockers, Models, and the New Allure of Heroin," *Newsweek*, August 26, 1996, pp. 50–54.

50. Chad Rubel, "Mustache Ads Change Attitude Toward Milk," *Marketing News*, August 26, 1996, p. 10.

51. Ian P. Murphy, "It Must Be the Shoes," *Marketing News*, March 17, 1997, p. 2.

52. William L. Wilkie, Elizabeth S. Moore-Shay, and Amardeep Assar, *Family Decision Making for Household Durable Goods* (Cambridge, MA: Marketing Science Institute, 1992), p. 1.

53. Richard E. Plank, Robert C. Greene, Jr., and Joel M. Greene, "Understanding Which Spouse Makes Financial Decisions," *Journal of Retail Banking*, Spring 1994, p. 21.

54. Stephan A. Butscher, "Welcome to the Club: Building Customer Loyalty," *Marketing News*, September 9, 1996, p. 9.

55. U.S. Bureau of the Census.

56. Howard Gleckman, "Spending in the Golden Years," *Business Week*, July 22, 1996, pp. 43–44.

57. Peter Weaver, "Opportunity Knocks as America Ages," *Nation's Business*, August 1996, pp. 80–83.

58. Dan Tapscott, "Opinion: The Rise of the Net-Generation," www.adage.com, site visited on January 23, 1997.

59. Kim Cleland, "NPD's PC Meter Tracks Individual Web Site Visits," www.adage.com, site visited on January 23, 1997.

60. Kim Cleland, "Search Tools Get Personal," www.adage.com, site visited on January 23, 1997.

61. Wendy Marx, "Marketer's Home Page Advantage", www.adage.com, site visited on January 23, 1997.

62. Joshua Levine, "Let Linda Do It," *Forbes*, September 11, 1995, p. 254–256.

63. Robert Gustafson, Johan Yssel, and Lea Witta, "Ad Agency Employees Give Views on Calvin Klein, Benetton Ads," *Marketing News*, September 23, 1996, p. 16.

64. Ibid.

65. Ibid.

THE VIACOM NETWORKS

THE MTV NETWORKS—MTV, NICKELODEON, and VH1—produce huge profits for Viacom by catering to moody teenagers, fickle kids, and music-loving baby boomers. With nearly $625 million in earnings, Viacom has become part of the entertainment lifestyles of three consumer generations. The key is connectivity with the mindset of each core market segment. Profit margins, which are growing at 25 percent annually, have been the envy of other broadcast networks and Hollywood studios.

Nearly 3 million households around the world tune into MTV, whose corporate philosophy is "Think Globally but Act Locally." The network stays in tune with a staff of young executives, whose success depends on pleasing young viewers much like themselves. In MTV's free flowing corporate culture, ideas count more than tradition, and even interns get heard. Tom Freston, CEO of MTV Networks, is confident about the organization's continued growth, as long as it retains the loyalty of kids, teens, and 20-something's—TV's most faddish viewers. This means staying fresh and being open to change. The average employee is age 28, and the corporate climate is more like a college dorm—or romper room, in the case of Nickelodeon. If you walk the halls, you'll see backpacks, not briefcases, and more nose rings than neckties.

To stay current, MTV uses the usual ratings, polls, focus groups, and on-line chats, but it also sends researchers into the field to dig through dorm rooms, closets, and CD collections of 18- to 24-year-olds. This consumer group is a target because younger teenagers aspire to be like them, as do people in their late 20s and 30s who want to stay hip. These researchers spotted trouble with fading hits like *Beavis and Butt-head*, *The Real World*, and *Singled Out*. MTV eliminated several shows and ushered in new ones, such as the animated *Daria* about a sarcastic 16-year-old.

Even poorer shows did five times better than the video hours, but viewers still complained that it was hard to find music on MTV. The problem with music videos is that viewers surf them so rapidly that the ratings don't pick them up, while the shows are recorded by the ratings. So the network ratings can be hurt dramatically with music videos. The answer was more music, shown live from studios and hosted by new VJ's. These music content shows reduce channel surfing.

Despite lower ratings, ad rates have grown by 10 percent, but sponsors are willing to pay a premium to connect with hard-to-reach consumers age 12–34. Judy McGrath, MTV's president, says that "advertisers want to be on there [MTV] for association, not absolute numbers or eyeballs."

"We're not really in show business," Freston says, "we're in the networking business. All these networks are marketing machines." You can expect up to six more networks similar to MTV, each featuring its own musical genre, such as country and oldies.

McGrath knows she needs to please the young, so she hires 60 interns a year, age 18 to 22, to create a laboratory of youthful tastes and styles. McGrath says that "one year they look like hippies. The next year they're wearing black, the next nobody has any hair, the next you can't tell the genders apart." Her job is not to judge, but "make an environment where the interns feel welcome." Based on their input, *The Real World* and *Road Rules* are being restyled to show kids as more respectful of their parents and dressed in a more civilized manner. *Real World* cast members are now filmed working at day care centers or volunteering.

Nickelodeon is in the enviable position of being able to extend its brand name to everything from kids' toys to macaroni and cheese. Ad spots sell out almost two seasons ahead. Despite a lot of new competition, Nickelodeon has been cable's top-rated network since 1995. It has several new ventures, such as *The Good Burger,* a movie backed by Burger King, which will promote the film in its outlets. Nickelodeon's assets have made it a clear cable star: intimate knowledge of kids, promotion clout, and inventive playfulness.

VH1 is geared to MTV graduates, the baby boomers who want a channel that plays their music—not just the oldies but contemporary artists like Jewel and the Wallflowers. VH1 president John Sykes says that "music is in our culture. Music is our social conscience. That's why you see our music selling every product on television today." VH1 tends to have chronically low ratings due to channel surfing but collects a steady stream of fees from cable operators, who pay up to 10 cents a month for each of the 60 million subscribers. Revenues from fees and advertising have more than doubled in three years, to $150 million, and earnings have quadrupled to $40 million.

In developing VH1, Sykes wanted "a focused adult music channel with a singular vision . . . music first. Music drives everything we do. Number one, I saw that the MTV generation had grown up, and had no where else to turn for music on cable TV. Number two, I saw that the baby boomers got older and were driving consumption and making decisions about cable TV. So I saw a huge opportunity to reach young, active, affluent adults with music." Sykes adds: "We're the generation that grew up with Woodstock, with Vietnam, and with a lot of tension. The music of those times really stuck to us. It wasn't just pop fodder, it was woven into our culture, and as a result we stay with that music. It's part of our existence." He believes these adults are looking for entertainment with context, such as information about songs. Approximately $50 million will be spent on original program production in 1998. Aimed at the inquisitive, sophisticated, adult viewers who watch NBC's *Dateline* or ABC's *20/20,* shows like *Behind the Music* or *Hard Rock Live* will be key elements in the programming.

1. *How are the stages of the family life cycle used by each of the MTV networks in order to reach viewers successfully?*
2. *List three possible viewer reference groups for each MTV network. How do the networks use reference groups to influence consumer behavior?*
3. *Discuss why advertisers would select each of the MTV networks and how attitudes, learning, and perception about the sponsor's brand might be influenced by the network.*

SOURCES: Marc Gunther, "This Gang Controls Your Kids' Brains," *Fortune,* October 27, 1997, pp. 172–182; Dyan Mchan, "A More Tolerant Generation," *Forbes,* September 8, 1997, pp. 46, 47; and Donna Petrozzello, "VH1: and the Brand Plays On; Channel Has Remade itself to Put Music First for Adults," *Broadcasting and Cable,* September 1, 1997, p. 43.

Chapter 8

Business-to-Business Marketing

" ANYONE WOULD HAVE SEEN
A PARKING LOT. FORTUNATELY, ARAMARK SAW
AN OLYMPIC DINING HALL. "

John Scanlan from ARAMARK: "Remember, this is Atlanta 1996. The Centennial Games. This has to be great. We have no intention of duplicating what we did in Barcelona four years ago. Or Mexico City in '68. Or any of the Games in between. We're here to help 15,000 athletes and coaches from 197 different cultures. Athletes who have prepared for a lifetime to be better than they've ever been in that lifetime. We know that takes more than just a standard issue menu. Or a standard issue effort, for that matter. This is the Olympic Games. You're either prepared to be great. Or you haven't." We don't just rely on a book for all the answers at ARAMARK. We have no magic "Olympic Games Menu" to dust off every four years. In Atlanta, we'll customize a menu for every single athlete if that's what it takes. We'll even put a world-class kitchen and dining hall on a parking lot. It's a mind-set that makes it possible for John to add, "In just over four weeks, we'll prepare over one million meals designed for peak athletic performance. Quite possibly a world record." **ARAMARK**

OF COURSE THERE'S MORE TO TELL ABOUT THE WAY WE WORK. PLEASE CALL 1-800-ARAMARK.

Managed Services. Managed Better.

Objectives

1. Describe the types of organizations and products involved in business-to-business marketing and understand the importance of this market.

2. Understand the link between consumer demand and business-to-business marketing.

3. Describe the organizational buying process.

4. Know how buyer-seller relationships work, including informal and contractual partnerships.

5. Learn what functions and roles within organizations influence the purchase of a broad range of products.

WITHOUT EVER KNOWING IT, MOST OF *you have been served by ARAMARK. The company sells to thousands of colleges, schools, hospitals, and sports arenas. It provided food service for the 1996 Olympic Games in Atlanta, and it even serves people in prisons! Every day, it connects with more than 15 million people through its more than 5,000 worldwide locations.*

You may not have heard of the name, however, because ARAMARK partners with a business to provide expertise on-site. You may be eating at Boston University Food Services, but ARAMARK is behind the scenes, providing the management, employees, menus, nutritional guidance, cost analysis, inventory management, and food safety procedures—everything needed to deliver the service.

ARAMARK's biggest and best-known partnership is with the Olympic Games. In summer of 1996, for the 10th time, the company partnered with an Olympic Committee to provide all food services for athletes and visitors. It actually turned down the Moscow Olympics, since the Russians could not provide the quality hardware required to produce safe, quality food.

To serve the 1996 athletes, ARAMARK built the world's largest temporary food facility on a parking lot at Georgia Tech. The 150,000-square-foot operation served 3,500 athletes per hour and was open 24 hours a day. The logistics of constructing and staffing such a place is mind-boggling: For the Olympic Village alone, resumés and applications totaled 500 pounds of paper!

The "world menu" that ARAMARK created for the Atlanta Games took more than 100,000 hours of planning. The result was 550 recipes rotated every five days—a staggering 110 dishes to prepare. Foods needed to suit the nutritional requirements of athletes, as well as make the diverse group feel "at home." Overall planning took three years. Starting with Atlanta's unique needs, the company worked to achieve its corporate goals: Exceed customer expectations, and create enduring relationships.

Such lofty goals are also a means to an end: Olympic press coverage garnered ARAMARK free publicity worth about $5 million. Don't forget: The reporters were fed as well, and the positive impression the company made was mentioned nightly in the news. The Olympic effort also helped win business for other ARAMARK business units. The Health Support Services division (HSS) landed an $11 million partnership with a network of health care facilities in St. Louis. HSS director of business resources Ed Kelly said: "They wanted to know that they were making the right decision in selecting ARAMARK. Our Olympic Games record, great food, and reputation reinforced to them that they were."

Serving the community is part of any great business. In Atlanta, ARAMARK formed partnerships with more than 60 nonprofit groups, who staffed concession stands with volunteers and in exchange received a percentage of sales. Under the leadership of general manager Mark Pevan, one-quarter of the 2,400 members of the company's team at Olympic Stadium events consisted of volunteers, whose work earned funds for local church groups.

You have probably heard of service guarantees, but ARAMARK goes a step farther than most: guaranteed results, including guaranteed savings. After deciding how it can best service a customer, the company quantifies its suggestions. A baseline is created, and the savings are shown. In some markets the savings are shared, underscoring the importance between results and partnership.

ARAMARK makes its people responsible to their customers. Many managers share in company ownership. In the Uniform Services division, route drivers are empowered to take full accountability for customer relationships. If there is a problem with the bill or delivery, the route driver fixes it on the spot. Customers like the approach, and the drivers see themselves as account managers rather than as simply delivery personnel.

ARAMARK is an excellent example of an organization dedicated to helping its customers excel in their own businesses. Although the company seldom sells directly to consumers, its own consumers do. Like many business marketers, the company forms lasting relationships with its clients and plays a major role in how well they compete. This chapter describes the challenges of business-to-business marketing and shows its importance to the world economy.[1]

THE CONCEPT OF BUSINESS-TO-BUSINESS MARKETING

Business-to-business marketing Marketing goods and services to other producers of goods and services.

In the 21st century there will be spectacular growth in business-to-business marketing. DuPont, General Electric, Sun Microsystems, and Westinghouse, like thousands of other companies, are connecting with customers through selling to other businesses. And they will market even more in this arena in the next millennium. The marketing of goods and services to other businesses, governments, and institutions is known as **business-to-business marketing.** It includes everything but direct sales to consumers. Globally, it's the largest market by far. In the United States, more than 13 million business organizations spend trillions of dollars on goods and services each year—a whopping 70 percent of total sales volume.[2] That means the business market is about four times larger than the consumer market.[3]

Most consumer goods are made from a variety of components and processes. The products are marketed from one organization to another, until the one at the end of the chain sells to the final consumer. Let's follow the production of an automobile. It begins with a steel manufacturer marketing its product to a company that makes rivets and other metal fasteners, which are sold to a company that makes radiators. That business then markets its products to an automobile manufacturer. In the factory, the radiators are combined with other components that have much the same history, and the finished car is shipped to a dealership, where the final customer buys it. At each step, money, time, and effort are spent on marketing, and value is created.

In other cases of business-to-business marketing, a finished product is simply sold and resold down the line until it reaches the end consumer. For example, a deck of playing cards is purchased by a wholesaler, who resells it to a retailer like Kmart, who then sells it to the final consumer. Again, time, money, and effort are expended at each step. In still other cases, one company sells products directly to another for its own internal use—whether copy machines, laptop computers, or toilet tissue.

Consumers may never take physical ownership of the item at all, but they benefit just the same. A telephone call is one example. Consumers can place a call to and from nearly anywhere in the world, yet they own only their telephone, and sometimes not even that. The switching network, satellite communications equipment, and cable that process the call belong to a company such as AT&T or MCI. With the exception of the consumer's monthly service fee and telephone, the other items are part of business-to-business marketing.

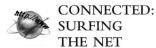

CONNECTED: SURFING THE NET

www.aramark.com

Visit the Web site of ARAMARK, the world's largest managed services company. Learn more about its people, services, and partnerships. And for fun, you can play ball against "Fenway's Green Monster."

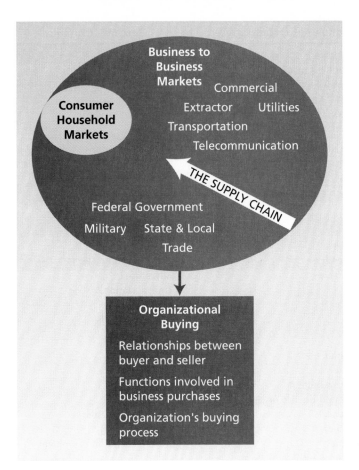

Figure 8-1 Connecting with Customers through Business-to-Business Marketing

Many types of organizations buy business products. For example, General Motors alone purchases nearly $200 million worth each day from its own divisions and outside companies. Other for-profit and nonprofit organizations—from the Fortune 500 to small private firms—do the same and add to this total volume. Finally, the government market makes purchases nearly as large as all private organizations combined, ranging from country road repairs to army boots to toothbrushes. The business market offers tremendous opportunities.

The key elements of the business-to-business market are depicted in Figure 8-1. In the early sections of the chapter we will look at the various industries that comprise the overall market and at possible approaches to segmenting this market. We will see how supply linkages between companies create a supply chain reaching all the way from raw materials extractors to neighborhood retailers; how consumers ultimately determine business market demand; and how the globalization of business markets creates new requirements as well as new opportunities.

We then turn our attention to organizational buying, beginning with an examination of the decisions to be made, and the steps in the buying process. Good buyer-seller relationships are key in business-to-business markets; we will see how these relationships develop in phases and may involve interaction with many functions and personnel in the buying organization. This part concludes with a look at several important factors—including interpersonal conflict—that often influence organizational buying behavior.

BUSINESS-TO-BUSINESS MARKETS

TYPES OF MARKETS

The business market is divided into the seven categories shown in Figure 8-2: commercial market, extract industries, trade industries, institutions, utilities, transportation and telecommunications, and government. Each category is comprised of organizations with similar business circumstances and general purchasing requirements.

Commercial Market The **commercial market** category consists of organizations that acquire goods and services that are then used to produce other goods and services. Many of these products are used in finished products purchased by consumers. For example, Ford has

Commercial market
Organizations and individuals that acquire goods and services to produce other goods and services sold to an end consumer for profit.

Category	Examples of Organizations	Purchase Examples
Commercial	Fabricators	Raw materials
	Component manufacturers	Component parts
	Processors	Processing equipment
	Original equipment manufacturers	Transportation
	Designers	Consulting services
Extractor	Agriculture	Fertilizer and pesticides, seeds
	Forestry	Heavy- and light-duty equipment
	Mining	Pipe
	Drilling	Aircraft and transportation
	Water	Real estate, mining rights
		Products for resale
		Loading equipment
Trade	Retailers	Computer systems
	Wholesalers	Buildings/real estate
	Dealerships	Advertising
		Transportation
		Warehousing
		Pharmaceuticals
		Equipment
Institutions	Hospitals	Food
	Schools	Consulting
	Day care centers	Health care
	Banks and finance organizations	Suppliers
	Insurance	Computer systems
	Churches	Nuclear fuel
	Charities	Power generation equipment
Utilities	Electric utilities	Electric components
	Gas utilities	Motors
	Water and waste disposal plants	Computers
		Chemicals
		Testing equipment
		Fuel
		Equipment
Transportation and Telecommunications	Airlines	Computers
	Trucking	Real estate
	Rail companies	
	Telephones	
	Cellular	
Government		
Federal	Senate and House	Consulting
	Judicial	Offices
	Agencies	Forms
	Military	Computers
		Energy
		Aircraft
		Radar communications
		Health care items
		Food
		Logistics
State and Local	Highway commissions	Equipment
	Health and social services	Energy
	Schools and universities	Books
	Prisons	Sports equipment
	Police	Restoration
	Libraries	
	Park and recreation	
	Museums	

*Figure 8-2 Types of
Business-to-Business Markets*

more than 3,000 suppliers of products used to build automobiles. These, in turn, have other suppliers. All the marketing activities leading up to and including the sale of goods and services to Ford are part of the commercial market.

Extractor Industries   The **extractor industries** category includes organizations that obtain and process raw materials, as in forestry or mining. Extractor companies are separated from the commercial segment because they acquire much of their supply from the earth. They require expensive equipment such as drilling rigs, and instrumentation. These industries are huge consumers of nearly every product imaginable. Many of the companies in this category have global operations, such as Mobil Oil and Exxon.

There are often unique demands on extractor organizations to be environmentally sensitive. Petroleum Development Corporation (PDC) of West Virginia drills for natural gas and markets it to local power companies, who in turn sell it for residential use. To obtain funds for drilling wells, PDC creates general partnerships with qualified clients. The company won first place in the reclamation award given by the Environmental Protection Agency of West Virginia for 1992–1995.[4] There are numerous opportunities in this category for marketing ecological products. EnviroGroup is a firm that provides both consulting and testing services. Soilsorb, an environmental risk assessment tool used by EnviroGroup, measures contaminants in soils over time. With its expertise and advanced equipment, EnviroGroup manages environmental issues for clients worldwide.[5]

Trade Industries   The **trade industries** category is made up of organizations that acquire or distribute finished products to businesses or to consumers. It includes retailers, wholesalers, and other intermediaries. These companies play an important role in the "place" component of the marketing mix. The importance of **resellers**, companies that purchase a product and sell it in the same form for profit, has been gaining more and more recognition recently. The computer industry, for example, is now emphasizing the role of resellers in distribution and increasingly relies on them to install and service products. Apple developed a marketing campaign called the Premium Service Reseller Program, and IBM also is moving

Extractor industries
Industries that obtain and process raw materials.

CONNECTED: SURFING THE NET

www.envirogroup.com

Learn more about EnviroGroup, the environmental solutions company. Discover how it manages ecological issues for clients worldwide.

Trade industries
Industries comprised of organizations that acquire finished products and distribute them to others.

Reseller
A company that purchases a product and sells it in the same form for profit.

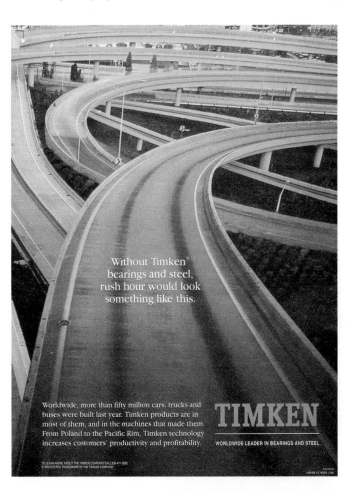

Without Timken® bearings and steel, rush hour would look something like this.

Worldwide, more than fifty million cars, trucks and buses were built last year. Timken products are in most of them, and in the machines that made them. From Poland to the Pacific Rim, Timken technology increases customers' productivity and profitability.

TIMKEN
WORLDWIDE LEADER IN BEARINGS AND STEEL

Timken, a worldwide leader in bearings and steel, is part of the commercial market.

toward providing resellers with more information and support. For both companies, this form of marketing is expected to drive an increase in sales through the resellers.[6]

In many cases, resellers repackage products to suit the needs of particular market segments. For example, Kroger buys meat in bulk and cuts it into sizes and forms for household use. The Cappuccino Cafe buys coffee in 100-pound units and sells it by the pound or freshly brewed.

Institutions
Public and private organizations that provide services to consumers.

Institutions   The **institutions** category covers public and private organizations that provide health, education, and welfare services to consumers. It includes universities, hospitals, churches, nursing homes, and museums. Institutional buyers purchase a broad range of products with funds of their own or from third parties, such as donors, insurance companies, and government grants.

Because of third-party funding, institutions may have unique purchasing requirements. Consequently, companies often establish very specific strategies for marketing to these organizations. For example, most pharmaceutical firms have separate units that market to hospitals. ARAMARK has a separate food service division that markets specifically to universities. Its expertise in nutrition, understanding of the college-age population, and knowledge of how universities make decisions combine to create unique, highly targeted marketing programs.

Utilities
Companies that distribute gas, electricity, or water.

Utilities   The **utilities** category is comprised of companies that distribute gas, electricity, and water. Once highly regulated by government, utilities are being given the opportunity to operate more like private organizations. Public service commissions continue to provide oversight, however, because even private utilities are considered to be part of the public sector to some degree. Consolidated Edison and Florida Power & Light are huge buyers of business products. Westinghouse sells billions of dollars in nuclear fuel, power generation equipment, and design services to both public and privately owned utilities.

Transportation and Telecommunications   Transportation and telecommunications make up another business market category. The transportation portion is comprised of companies that provide passenger and freight service such as Union Pacific Railroad and United Airlines. Telecommunications companies supply local and long-distance telephone service as well as cable and broadcasting. CBS, Time-Warner, Northwest Airlines, AT&T, and Ameritech are

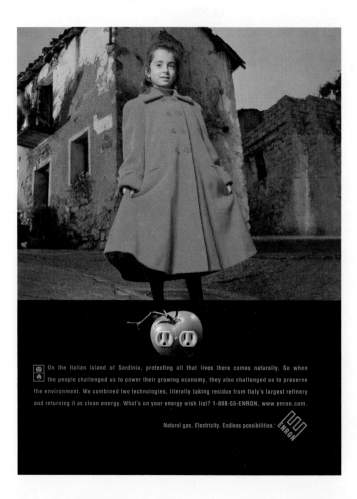

Enron sells natural gas and electricity in the utilities category of business-to-business markets.

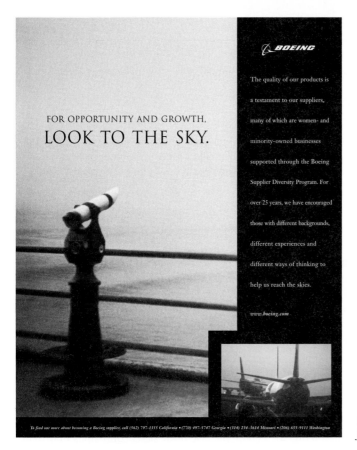

Boeing purchases billions in parts, equipment, and services each year from other businesses.

somewhat like utilities. This category was once subject to extensive government regulation that has been relaxed in recent years.

Although there are relatively few companies in this category, their purchases are huge. In 1996, Boeing alone purchased more than $20 billion worth of parts, equipment, and services from approximately 50,000 U.S. companies located in all 50 states.[7] The cable and broadcast companies purchase satellite capacity, equipment, and a huge range of services necessary to develop state-of-the-art telecasting.

Government Markets In the United States, the subdivisions in the **government market** category are (1) the federal government, (2) the 50 state governments, and (3) 8,700 local units. Together, they make more purchases than any other group in the United States. In 1997, the U.S. government spent more than $1.3 trillion. The national military is by far the largest purchaser of goods and services, accounting for 40 percent of U.S. spending.[8] For many corporations, the federal government is an essential customer. Defense companies like Lockheed Martin Astronautics are dependent on government contracts. In December 1996, the U.S. Air Force Space and Missile Systems Center awarded the Lockheed Martin Corporation contracts totaling $120 million to produce designs for the new Evolved Expendable Launch Vehicle (EELV) rockets. Boeing also receives large government contracts, many of them through NASA for components of the International Space Station.[9]

Government markets
The federal, state, and local governments in their role as purchasers of goods and services.

BUSINESS MARKET SEGMENTATION

Business markets differ from consumer markets in several important ways: number of buyers, size of purchase, supplier relationships, geographic concentration, purchasing approaches, and buying influences. Figure 8-3 shows the characteristics of each. Although the business market is segmented using procedures much like those used to segment the consumer market (discussed in chapter 6), its distinctive characteristics are used to categorize business consumers along different dimensions—by company demographics, geographic scope, buying approach, and product/technology—as outlined in Figure 8-4.

Segmentation by Company Demographics In describing a company, we usually think first about its demographics: industry, size, financial stability, place in the distribution channel, and ownership. Industry is defined by the company's products. Ford, GM, and Honda

Characteristic	Business Market	Consumer Market
Number of buyers	Few	Often millions
Supplier relationship	Long-term contracts and supplier involvement	Many single purchases
Size of purchase	Often extremely large	Usually small
Geographic concentration	Usually near population centers	Widely dispersed
Purchasing approach	Technically trained buying agents follow policies and constraints. Tend to buy directly from manufacturer	Nontechnical purchasing to satisfy personal preferences
Buying influences	Committees, technical experts, and management are all involved in decision making	The individual, household members, or friends and relatives

Figure 8-3 How Business and Consumer Markets Differ

are in the automotive industry, while Mack and International are in the heavy truck industry. Large companies may have strategic business units (SBUs) in different industries. Johnson & Johnson, for example, makes consumer health care products as well as medical supplies for professionals. The federal government's Standard Industry Classification (SIC) codes can help identify a company's industrial category. Industry classification reveals a great deal about an organization—the types of problems it is likely to face, the kinds of products it purchases, its economic cycles and regulatory environment, and the types of competitive practices it is likely to encounter.

Company size is based on dollar amount or volume of sales, number of employees, or units produced. Size affects purchase procedures and requirements such as delivery schedules and inventory capacity. Large firms often do much of their own engineering, and their purchasing department uses formal buying arrangements. Medium-sized companies may be interested in value-added services a seller can provide. Small firms often use less formal procedures and may want the seller's help with tracking and restocking inventory.

Another demographic characteristic is financial stability and profitability. Marketing to a company in difficulty may not be worth the effort and risk. If sales volumes are substantial, delays in payments can cause the seller financial hardship. The profitability of a company is often used as an indication of its ability to pay as well as other characteristics.

Channel membership refers to whether the organization is a distributor, original equipment manufacturer (OEM), or one of the tier suppliers. Each type has significantly different needs. Distributors acquire to resell, OEMs want to develop a final product, and tiers typically have unique needs as well.

Ownership influences how organizations buy. Since private companies can set policies as they see fit, we find many purchasing strategies. In the public sector, governmental units and utilities must follow very strict guidelines.

Basis	Example
Company Demographics	
Industry	food, mining, automotive, computer
Company size	large, medium, small
Financial stability and profitability	strong, medium, weak
Channel	distributor, OEM, first tier, second tier
Ownership	private, public
Industry leadership	leader, close follower, laggard
Geographic Scope	local, regional, national, international, global
Buying Approach	
Centralization	centralized, decentralized
Functional involvement	finance, marketing, manufacturing
Partnering approach	bid, relationship oriented, contracts
Product/Technology	
Level of technology	high, medium, low
Configuration purchased	components, modules, subsystem
Design source	internal, external

Figure 8-4 Segmenting the Business Market

Segmentation by Geographic Scope When we discussed geographic segmentation in chapter 6, it was in terms of locating clusters of targeted consumers. In the case of businesses, however, we are concerned with the geographic scope of the customer's business, whether local, regional, national, international, or global. The range of operations clearly affects how an organization buys. General Motors has a global scope, so sellers must be able to think in terms of manufacturing plants around the world—and of reaching buyers who may come from various cultures. Saab, which manufactures only in Sweden, has a much more localized set of needs.

Segmentation by Buying Approach Organizations also can be differentiated according to their buying approach. This takes into account their degree of centralization, what functional areas are involved, and what kind of partnering arrangements they have. A centralized organization generally has one purchasing unit with very set policies, whereas a decentralized organization is likely to allow local buying decisions using various procedures and policies. Functional involvement refers to a company's orientation—manufacturing firms use one set of criteria, while a financial institution or a consulting firm may use others. Partnering can range from simple bid purchases to a long- or short-term contract that may or may not contain detailed specifications and other requirements, such as an exclusivity clause.

Segmentation by Product/Technology Product/technology can affect purchasing in numerous ways, but three of the more important are level of technology, configuration purchased, and design orientation. First, firms vary dramatically in technological capability. This is primarily due to their hiring, training, retention, and technical practices. A high-tech firm has very different expectations from a low-tech firm. Consequently, marketing to each group is different. Second, buying configurations differ. Some companies want to purchase only components, and base their decisions on price and delivery specifications. Others buy modules that already combine many components and make it easier to add the supplier's product at the time of manufacturing. Yet others prefer to purchase a system that enhances the functionality of their products, as when Chrysler buys traction control products from Tevis. This variable is related in some ways to design. Some organizations want to do their own, some want suppliers to do it, and some work closely with suppliers to develop a design. A company such as Delphi Automotive Systems has extensive design capabilities but sometimes relies on suppliers for the design of certain components, modules, and systems.

BUSINESS MARKET LINKAGES: THE SUPPLY CHAIN

The **supply chain** links organizations involved in the creation and delivery of a product. Figure 8-5 is a simplified diagram of the supply chain for automobiles. The original equipment manufacturer, such as GM or Ford, is in the middle of the chain. There are supply activities both upstream and downstream. In business-to-business marketing, the word **tier** refers to the degree of contact between suppliers and the OEM. In the automotive industry, there are third-tier suppliers (extractors who process steel from ore), second-tier suppliers (manufacturers of components such as fasteners), and first-tier suppliers (makers of radiators). The last is a direct supplier to the OEM. Other examples of direct or first-tier suppliers in this in-

Supply chain
The linkage of organizations involved in the creation and delivery of a product.

Tier
The degree of contact between the supplier and the OEM.

Figure 8-5 An Example of the Supply Chain in Automotives

dustry are the makers of leather seats, radios, and carpeting, each of whom deals with its own group of suppliers.

Supply chain management involves establishing or improving linkages to maximize efficiency and effectiveness. Marketers view the supply chain in terms of activities that need to be coordinated to provide the greatest value to the consumer, who is at the end of the chain. UPS World Wide Logistics, for example, works with many companies to improve supply chain management. Its experts help clients with systems design, transportation, information systems, and other services.

BUSINESS MARKET DEMAND

The demand for products in the business market is not based solely on what happens in the business sector. As you will see, demand is based largely on what happens to consumers.

Derived demand

A demand, like the demand for business-to-business products, which depends ultimately on the demand of end consumers.

Derived Demand Business marketers must rely on derived demand to create opportunities for their products. **Derived demand** means that the amount of sales for business-to-business products ultimately depends on (is derived from) the demand for products by consumers. For example, when automobile sales increase, so does the need for materials, components, and subassemblies. The first (original) demand occurs among consumers and is reflected in the business-to-business market. This ripple effect is felt all along the supply chain, and it drives economic growth.

Inelastic demand

Demand that is little influenced by price changes.

Inelastic Demand Certain products are so essential that they are less responsive than others to changes in the economy. **Inelastic demand** refers to products so necessary that a change in price has relatively little effect on the quantity demanded. If the price of sugar or another cola ingredient rises, it's doubtful that Coke or Pepsi will use less of it in making their product. The cost has little to do with their decision about what to buy, although it may affect the price charged to consumers.

Fluctuating Demand: The Accelerator Principle Some business products are highly sensitive to changes in consumer demand. We see the accelerator principle operating when a small fluctuation (increase or decrease) in consumer demand has a larger effect on business demand. Suppose that the economy is sluggish. In an effort to save money, consumers are closely watching their energy consumption—turning off lights when not in use, running the air conditioner as little as possible, and so forth. Obviously, this will affect the revenues of local power plants. A few dollars saved by each customer quickly mount when multiplied by thousands of people in the utility's service area. Even a small drop in consumer demand may be enough to force the plant to postpone the purchase of multimillion dollar equipment. Of course, if consumer demand exceeds expectations by only a little, the result may be brownouts, power outages, or the need to buy energy from outside the system.

GLOBALIZATION OF BUSINESS MARKETS

The growth of international business has provided companies with a number of business-to-business marketing opportunities overseas. The United Kingdom and the Netherlands, among the first to deregulate their telecommunications industry, are potential markets that AT&T is said to be eyeing. Despite recent economic problems in the Pacific Rim, South Korea is the sixth largest market for U.S. exports, and the United States is the major importer of products from South Korea. Indonesia, Malaysia, and Thailand have also provided markets for U.S. goods. Business products being successfully exported from the United States currently include computer hardware and software, aircraft, electronics, medical equipment, oil and gas field machinery and equipment, and analytical instruments.[10]

Strong business marketers must be able to support their customers' business efforts globally. One major media company is used by IBM solely to execute global campaigns. Companies such as International Data Group (IDG), a computer publisher, are becoming more capable of providing global coverage. IDG currently has 225 publications in 75 countries, which makes it possible for advertisers to connect with customers around the world.[11] Caterpillar, manufacturer of earth movers and other heavy equipment, also launched an international campaign to send consistent messages throughout Europe. Stressing reliability, with a "you can count on us" tagline, Caterpillar is targeting the United Kingdom, France, Italy, Spain, and Scandinavia in an effort to win sales.[12]

Strong global connections with customers require marketers to establish brand identity. This is as just as important in business-to-business markets as consumer markets. New tech-

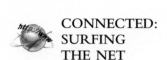

CONNECTED: SURFING THE NET

www.ibm.com

For more information about IBM's worldwide activities, visit its Web site and select from more than 50 countries. Also discover how IBM is making it safe to shop on the Web.

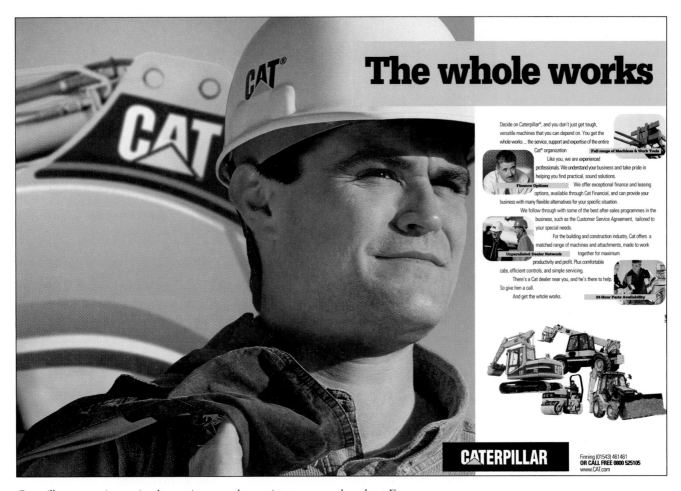

Caterpillar uses an international campaign to send a consistent message throughout Europe.

nologies have created numerous worldwide business opportunities, from supplying satellites to building computer chip factories. Business-to-business marketers must develop and position their brands to differentiate themselves from competitors. Allianz, a highly recognized insurance company in Germany, was challenged to publicize its brand name when it expanded into global markets. Dana Corporation, a supplier of automotive components, learned the importance of brand identity when it began to lose business to global competitors. Since Dana sold components, not systems, it developed a strategy to strengthen its brand image. Today its diamond logo symbolizes the value of its brand.[13]

ORGANIZATIONAL BUYING

BUYING DECISIONS

Business-to-business marketing is strongly influenced by two organizational considerations. First, a company must decide whether it is better to seek outside suppliers, or to make the product(s) in-house. Second, if suppliers are used, then different types of situations require varying involvement by people within the buying organization. Furthermore, the type of situation also may be a factor in whether competitive bidding is used.

The Make or Buy Decision   **Make or buy decisions** occur when companies must decide whether to supply products or services in-house or to buy them from other businesses. **Outsourcing** is the purchase of products from other companies. Many organizations choose this route so they can focus on their core business. A number of factors influence the make or buy decision. A company must evaluate its need for direct control over production or quality, and it must examine the costs associated with supplying internally versus externally. There are also issues of supplier reliability, design secrecy, and workforce stability. For example, General Motors buys 70 percent of its parts from Delphi Automotive Systems, which it owns.[14] Outsourcing could cost thousands of jobs at Delphi. Workforce considerations are very important if a strong union is involved.

Make or buy decision
The decision whether to supply products in-house or to purchase them from other businesses.

Outsourcing
Purchasing products and services from other companies.

227

Approximately 86 percent of major corporations use outsourcing so they can focus on their core business.

Outsourcing has become widely popular—86 percent of major corporations used it to some extent in 1996, up from 58 percent in 1992. ARAMARK has been a leading provider of external services to cafeterias in companies, colleges, and hospitals, since the 1960s. TeleTech handles customer service calls for companies such as AT&T, and Automatic Data Processing supplies payroll functions for a large list of clients.[15] Outsourcing can cut costs and allow more attention to be directed toward primary business activities. In order to sustain a competitive advantage, more and more businesses are turning to this option.

The Outsourcing Decision   Outsourcing may involve the purchase of a product on a routine basis, changes in suppliers, or purchase of a product for the first time. This involves the three kinds of situations—straight rebuy, modified rebuy, and new task situations—summarized in Figure 8-6. A **straight rebuy** is a routine purchase with which the organization has had a great deal of experience. For example, an exclusive furniture manufacturer may purchase leather for its sofas from only one supplier, who has a reputation for the highest quality. The two organizations have done business for years, and the manufacturer has made hundreds of purchases. In this case, a buying decision may take less than a week and involve only one or two people from each organization. In fact, it's normal for a purchasing agent to handle the entire transaction.

Suppose that the furniture manufacturer is dissatisfied with the leather supplier or doesn't want to depend on only one. A **modified rebuy** situation involves purchasing a familiar product from an unfamiliar supplier or a new or different product from a familiar sup-

Straight rebuy

A routine purchase with which the organization has considerable experience.

Modified rebuy

Purchase of a familiar product from an unfamiliar supplier or a new or different product from a familiar supplier.

Type	Description	People Involved
Straight rebuy	Reorder from current supplier	One purchasing agent
Modified rebuy	Evaluate alternative suppliers of a product purchased before or a new or different product from a current supplier	Puchasing agent plus one or a few others
New task	First-time purchase of a product	Many people from several areas of the organization

Figure 8-6 Organizational Buying Situations

plier. Usually more people will be involved in a modified rebuy decision, and more time and energy will be expended.

Finally, let us say the furniture manufacturer decides to add a line of fabric sofas. This **new task situation** involves purchasing an unfamiliar product from an unfamiliar supplier. Since there is a great deal at risk, many people will likely provide input to the decision process, which may take several weeks, months, or even years.

Competitive Bidding Some organizations use competitive bidding, especially for purchases over a certain amount. They want to obtain the lowest price rather than establish long-term relationships with suppliers. Most government purchases must be made this way by law. Many companies, such as General Motors, have purchasing rules that require a minimum number of bids—usually three—for certain types of purchases. Often exceptions can be made so long as the rationale for noncompliance with the bidding policy is documented.

In straight rebuy situations in the private sector, competitive bids are seldom required. They are likely in modified rebuys that involve the evaluation of alternative suppliers and are common in new task situations. In any of these cases, if the amount is very large, then the bidding procedure will probably be used.

Competitive bids may be sealed or negotiated. For the sealed bids, each seller is given a request for quotation (RFQ), which describes all the product and purchase specifications. The responses are due on a given date, when envelopes are opened, and the lowest bidder is awarded the order. Negotiated bids differ in that suppliers may be invited to comment on the specifications, modifications are possible, and the two or three most appropriate bids are then negotiated to determine the best choice—not necessarily the lowest bidder.

STEPS IN THE ORGANIZATIONAL BUYING PROCESS

An organization may go through eight different stages when making a buying decision, but every purchase does not require all of them. New task situations may involve all eight, modified rebuys fewer, and straight rebuys the fewest. The eight possible steps in the organizational buying process are shown in Figure 8-7: problem recognition, general need description, product specifications, supplier search, proposal solicitation, order routine specifications, purchase and use of product, and performance review and feedback.

Problem recognition occurs when the buying organization realizes that a situation can be improved by acquiring a good or service. Potential problems include unsatisfactory materials, machine failure, or development of a new product that requires new equipment. A gen-

New task situation
Purchase of an unfamiliar product from an unfamiliar supplier.

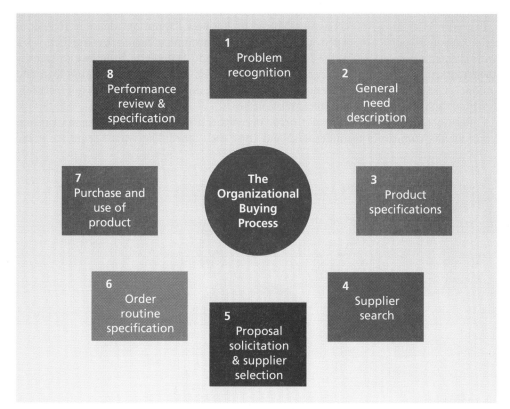

Figure 8-7 Steps in the Buying Process

eral need description is developed that identifies the basic characteristics of what is wanted, such as reliability, price, range, and durability. Next, the organization prepares product specifications, which usually are technical and/or very detailed: precise dimensions, tolerances, quantity, or the objectives of a consultant's study are examples.

Unless it has been decided to make the product in-house, the search for suppliers now begins. Some may have been involved in the previous stages, but the organization usually looks for more to be certain no options are missed and to encourage price competition. New products may require a lengthy search, and straight rebuys may involve a very limited one. During the proposal solicitation and supplier selection stage, the buying organization invites bids and assesses these according to the criteria set forth in the specifications. The lowest price usually wins, especially in the government sector, but such considerations as a reputation for quality and/or reliability may enter as well.

When a supplier has been selected, the buying organization negotiates the final terms of the agreement, called order routine specifications. Some fine-tuning may occur, now that a particular supplier has been chosen. During the purchase and use of product stage, the buyer signs the contract, takes the delivery, and begins to evaluate whether the product does the job as anticipated. At this point, follow-through by the seller is critical to resolve any problems that may arise. The final step is performance review and feedback. After making a formal analysis, the buyer lets the supplier know how well the product meets the needs of the organization.

As the buying organization moves through this process repeatedly, creeping commitment may occur. If there is consistent satisfaction with a seller's products, the two parties may begin to build a lasting relationship. In that case, the buying process becomes simpler for both organizations, as modified or straight rebuys are more likely.

RELATIONSHIPS BETWEEN BUYERS AND SELLERS

As in the case of consumers, business marketing relies on connecting through customer relationships. These relationships are built up in phases as the buying and selling organizations learn to work together. A seller who understands the buyer's strategies, problems, and opportunities can help the company be more competitive in its own markets. Authors Don Peppers and Martha Rogers describe a business that treats and interacts with customers individually as a one-to-one enterprise. They say building this type of relationship takes time and effort. Repeated interactions with buyers provide a company with feedback that enables it, over time, to learn how to meet customer preferences even better.[16]

Many business marketers focus on building relationships. Hallmark, known for its excellence in relationship marketing, introduced its Business Expressions division in 1992 to help companies connect more personally with business customers. Hallmark researchers work with clients as large as NASA, the New York Yankees, and State Farm Insurance to identify their marketing goals and then design customized cards with the organization's logo and unique characteristics. These can then be used to mark different events, show appreciation, or simply enhance a growing business relationship.[17]

Relationships in business do not occur overnight. It may take weeks, months, or even years for the companies to understand and trust each other. The typical sequence is the

Hallmark's business expressions division helps companies connect more personally with business customers.

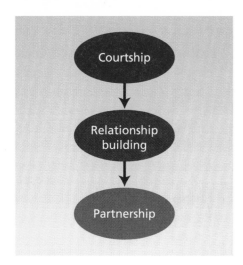

*Figure 8-8 Building Business-to-Business
Partnerships*

courtship phase, the relationship building phase, and the partnership phase. Figure 8-8 illustrates these steps. For example, the UPS World Wide Logistics (WWL) group supplies warehousing and shipping services. Usually, a customer begins by purchasing only a few services. As the business comes to realize that WWL services can help satisfy its customers in many ways, more are purchased. Over time it is not unusual for WWL to supply all of a customer's warehousing and transportation needs. WWL's high-technology information systems are not the only reason; WWL works to understand each customer's business thoroughly. This means that strategies and plans must be shared freely, and the client must trust WWL to keep them confidential. In many cases, WWL even helps customers develop the strategies and plans.

The Courtship Phase During courtship, purchasers express their desires to sellers, who develop proposals designed to satisfy the buyers' needs. This phase often begins when a company is placed on the buyer's approved supplier list, which means it meets at least minimum standards The criteria usually include financial health, size, licensing qualification, and delivery capabilities.

Because quality has become so important, suppliers are often required to demonstrate quality control methods and records as a prerequisite to being approved. Each of the Big Three automakers used to have its own set of standards, but these have been replaced with QS-9000, which specifies requirements to prevent product defects. Uniform criteria for the auto industry simplify compliance for suppliers yet assure quality components.[18]

Unlike many people, businesses tend to look before they leap. Often courtship takes a good deal of time. Each company is trying to understand the other's requirements, so there are many discussions about product specifications, product design, and order routines. Eventually, the social distance begins to narrow. Often the buyer will grant the supplier a small order to test the waters, including the response to any problems that occur.

The Relationship-Building Phase The buyers and sellers work together for the first time in the relationship-building phase, which strengthens the bond between them. Unlike consumer marketing, business-to-business marketing tends to involve customizing the product, its delivery, and its terms and conditions to each individual buyer. Buyers often grow to rely on suppliers for additional expertise, especially regarding new technologies. That is why trust, loyalty, and compromise become so important in organizational buying activities.

Due to the complexity and technical nature of most organizational purchasing, buyers and sellers must learn to work together. Each party may even adjust its internal practices to better satisfy the other's needs. Understanding the customer—and its customers—is critical. The Kaleidoscope Media Group of San Rafael, California, is a business that facilitates business-to-business marketing. The firm helped *California Lawyer* magazine attract Xerox as an advertiser by discovering that (1) lawyers produce the most photocopies of any professionals, (2) there are more lawyers in California than any other state, and (3) the number of lawyers representing corporations is especially high in California.[19]

During the relationship-building phase, the purchasing organization does not always have the upper hand. In fact, the relationship is sometimes said to be symmetrical—that is, the

He deletes a comma as *S*he adds a caption as

*S*he changes a word as *H*e makes the photo bigger.

REAL-TIME DOCUMENT CONFERENCING

Businesspeople everywhere can now work together like never before. With networkMCI Document Conferencing,* you can simultaneously create, discuss and edit documents and PC files on your computer, with people all over the world. Without having to exchange overnight deliveries, faxes or e-mails. You don't even have to be an MCI long distance customer to use it. It's amazing what people can do when they put their heads together.
  For more information, visit www.mci.com. To learn about our special offers, call 1-800-475-3555.

Is this a great time, or what? :-)

MCI

MCI expanded its business efforts to provide a number of additional services, such as real-time document conferencing.

buyer and the seller may have equal power.[20] Both frequently feel a very strong need to interact in order to explore all options before signing a contract. This is particularly the case if a formal partnership is being considered. Sellers generally offer information to help buyers formulate ideas about the purchase decision. Buyers provide information that helps the sellers do a better job of matching products to needs.

Many suppliers expand their business efforts to build stronger relationships. MCI once offered only telecommunications services but now provides marketing and merchandising expertise, billing, and customer service operations. MCI wins business customers by asking them what they want and then adjusting its basic services to meet those wants. This ability to customize plays an important role for MCI in building and strengthening business relationships.[21]

In many cases, computerized order entry systems are developed to link the buyer with the seller's manufacturing facilities. Nearly all Kmart suppliers have such a link. Quick's Candy, a specialty lollipop manufacturer, monitors twelve Kmart distribution centers. When inventory is low in one of these centers, Quick's can replenish the stock without prior approval from Kmart. Through close relationships with its suppliers, Kmart can keep costs down and speed product distribution to avoid lost sales.[22]

The Partnership Phase After numerous purchases have been completed satisfactorily and long-term agreements are reached, the partnership phase begins. Because the buyer and seller have extensive experience with each other, they spend less time on the relationship itself and more time on ways to improve the productive aspects of the exchange. The buying process becomes routine. The seller may become an exclusive supplier or blanket orders may guarantee that the buyer will purchase a certain amount within a certain period.

The seller can commit resources to the buyer because the business relationship will continue. Chrysler's partnerships with its suppliers have resulted in product development costs equal to 2.7 percent of revenues—half that of the competition. Chrysler suppliers work with platform teams in the early stage of product development to minimize or eliminate problems later on.[23] Another terrific example of connecting with customers can be seen in the relationship feature, "Cutler-Hammer's Absolute Focus Proves Less Is More."

CONNECTED: SURFING THE NET

www.kmart.com

Learn more about Kmart's relationships with its suppliers by exploring its Web site. Read the latest headlines, find out more about Kmart celebrities, or window shop in a virtual Kmart.

CONNECTING THROUGH RELATIONSHIPS

CUTLER-HAMMER'S ABSOLUTE FOCUS PROVES THAT LESS IS MORE

Building relationships between buyers and sellers is critical in business-to-business marketing. One savvy company found that some relationships are more profitable than others, to the tune of a whopping 100 percent increase in sales. Pittsburgh-based Cutler-Hammer, a manufacturer of electrical distribution and industrial control equipment, used to have 40 sales and service reps calling on several thousand potential customers. Although sales were a respectable $90 million, marketing vice president Rich Bell was convinced that fewer but more concentrated relationships with the most attractive customers would pay off—in sales and customer satisfaction.

Bell's brainstorm was a strategy called "absolute focus." Cutler-Hammer segmented the market and identified 256 clients who could benefit dramatically from superior customer service. They buy Cutler-Hammer components and use them to manufacture products. The idea was for salespeople and engineers to show them how best to use the components to craft top-quality equipment.

Bell says that building value for these customers "requires knowing all about the customer's business, the challenges it faces and the customers it serves. It means not just being a supplier but becoming a partner with them in their business." The first step Cutler-Hammer took was to choose 25 sales and service reps for these accounts. These highly knowledgeable reps and engineers work out of the company's new OEM Response Center. With a centralized database of customer information at their disposal, they serve as the link between the outside sales force and the OEM customers.

Perhaps a better name for their workplace would be the OEM "anticipation" center. Thanks to cutting-edge marketing technology, you won't hear a phone ringing at the response center. When a call comes in, an interactive phone system puts the customer's data on the computer screen of a preassigned service area. Before the customer can voice a concern, the service team has a record of previous transactions.

Next, an "expert system"—a computerized bank of questions and answers—is on-line to help isolate any detail the customer may want to discuss. Martine Rawlings, a recent college graduate, works at the center. Her responsibilities include daily communication with several key customers and the salespeople who service those accounts. To learn every facet of her customers' business, she even visits their offices. Her next move up the Cutler-Hammer career ladder will be to outside salesperson and then to an upper management position.

"Our goal," states the OEM Response Center literature, "is to create a competitive advantage for you and for Cutler-Hammer by consistently overwhelming every customer with caring." Although this goal seems rather warm and fuzzy for a relationship between large manufacturers, it is the attention of people like Martine that has sent sales soaring. Two years after Cutler-Hammer began its absolute focus, sales were up 94 percent to $175 million and customer satisfaction was at an all-time high. And company profits are higher because of more highly focused marketing with fewer people.

Source: Interview with Rich Bell and Bob Gaylord of Cutler-Hammer; and OEM Response Center literature.

Cutler-Hammer has many electrical products used by industrial and construction businesses.

CAREER TIP Rich Bell, vice president of marketing at Cutler-Hammer, says the company hires "friendly people, who have the capacity to overwhelm the customer with caring." He defines caring as "understanding whatever customers perceive as their problems, identifying them immediately and making sure customers know that those problems become 'my' problem too. It means having the competency within the Cutler-Hammer organization to make sure we help customers achieve their goals." Bell says you should let recruiters know you realize the importance of caring about customers. Furthermore, let them know it goes beyond courtesy to true partnering with the customer.

Partnerships can be informal or contractual. Informally, each party may work without any guarantee of long-term business. Usually, the benefits are such that the relationship is likely to last. A good example is an advertising agency and its client. Both invest a lot of time and energy, and share important information, so it's costly for either party to end the relationship.

A contractual partnership is formed when the buyer signs an agreement with a supplier for a specified period, usually three to five years. The trend in purchasing today is toward fewer suppliers, the use of programs that certify the qualifications of suppliers and long-term contracts. Close relationships with suppliers help ensure quality. Many buying organizations find that contractual partnerships have considerable advantages. The long-term relationship with suppliers allows the buying organization to concentrate energy on its customers. The buyer and supplier work as a team, each contributing its own expertise, to provide products that better meet consumer needs. The longer the relationship, the better are the results in terms of cooperation, efficiency, quality control, and profits. Contractual partnerships were a major part of Ford's campaign to improve quality and enhance its competitive position in global automobile markets.

Many suppliers also find contractual partnerships advantageous, but there are risks. The organizations often share highly secret market and technological information as well as sensitive strategic marketing plans. Contracts safeguard a supplier against an unethical buyer who might reveal those secrets to the supplier's competitors in an attempt to receive price reductions. When this occurs, most strong suppliers will refuse to market their newest technology to unethical buyers or in some cases refuse to sell to them altogether. Partnerships can have other hazards. Strong relationships mean greater dependence. If one partner experiences downsizing, strikes, or financial failure, then the other party feels the consequences.

Sometimes the partnership phase results in strategic alliances, including joint R&D, licensing agreements, joint ventures, and others. Consider the 1996 deal termed a "historical global marketing alliance" between Disney and McDonald's®. For ten years, McDonald's® will have exclusive rights in the fast-food industry to promote Disney products. The partnership will likely yield large profits to both corporations.[24]

Typically, alliances are formed because each company can offer something of value to the other. Suppose a Frito-Lay supplier has an idea for making chips stay fresh longer but lacks the money to conduct the necessary research. A joint R&D project might benefit both orga-

For the next ten years, McDonald's® has the exclusive rights in the fast food industry to promote Disney products.

nizations. Four Baby Bells (Ameritech, BellSouth, U.S. West, and Pacific Bell) have formed an alliance on the Internet by developing a "shared" Yellow Pages and information service. The companies hope this will protect their on-line businesses from the onslaught of Internet start-ups. Each company will benefit from the strong brand name of its partners. In addition, they can provide customers with a richer source of information.[25]

Ethics and Business Relationships Unethical decisions can have a destructive effect on business relationships. Purchasing agents are often very familiar with the trade secrets, production plans, and technologies of an organization. Misuse of this information has both ethical and legal implications. Consider the legal battle between General Motors and Volkswagen which began when GM's purchasing chief of North American Operations, José Ignacio López, suddenly moved to Europe's biggest automaker in 1993. López was accused of stealing thousands of pages of documents and computer diskettes from GM. The dispute was resolved when VW agreed to pay GM a $100 million settlement and to purchase $1 billion in parts over seven years.[26]

Turning over trade secrets to a competitor is a serious breech of ethics with numerous repercussions. For example, many industry experts did not expect GM's lawsuit to go to trial because negative publicity was likely to damage the two companies.[27] The image of both the company and its individual executives may be tarnished. Legal disputes consume large amounts of money as well as management's time and energy. A long-running dispute also can hinder normal business practices and competitive relationships between the companies involved. An individual who steals and betrays company information may face serious criminal charges. While López was not charged in GM's civil suit, VW agreed not to use his services until 2000. By which time, it is speculated he will either be exonerated or found guilty.[28]

FUNCTIONS INVOLVED IN BUSINESS PURCHASES

Many employees are important to the purchasing process. Because of their different functions, they do not have the same motives for purchasing and do not use the same criteria. This section highlights those who are most often involved in organizational buying: purchasing agents, functional managers, and the buying center.

Laterally, people at about the same level of management, but from different functional areas (such as purchasing, engineering, production, sales, and marketing) may take part in a purchasing decision. Although their status is roughly similar, their influence on a particular purchase can vary considerably. Imagine that several vice presidents meet to select a strategic marketing consultant. Comments by the vice presidents of manufacturing and purchasing are certainly valuable, but the vice president of marketing probably will have the most influence on the final decision.

Vertically, people at different management levels within one functional area may participate in a buying decision. For example, the need for a new piece of equipment may be pointed out by a production floor worker to the foreman, who relays this to the production manager. S/he seeks approval from the plant manager. If the purchase is costly, then the vice president of manufacturing or even the company president might be involved. If not, then the production engineer may have authority to approve the purchase.

Purchasing Agents Purchasing agents are hired to help the organization buy a broad range of products most effectively. They establish and enforce policies and procedures that help maintain consistent purchase arrangements with all suppliers. Often they make the initial contact with sellers. They interact with many suppliers and gain a good deal of experience in negotiations. Through training programs, purchasing agents can learn how to obtain the best delivery schedules, prices, and financing, while still meeting product specifications.

Purchasing agents are extremely important executives in some major corporations. In others, they simply process procurement requests. This function has received more attention in recent years, partly because of restricted supply in some industries and a greater general recognition of the cost savings from effective purchasing. College programs emphasizing the buying function have been developed, and graduates with this specialized education are finding increasing opportunities in global purchasing.

Most of us don't think of educational institutions as big spenders, but in 1996 alone, Georgetown University processed 43,500 purchase orders and bought $53 million in goods and services. Faculty and staff convey their needs through requisitions, or purchase orders, which are then processed by buyers. At Michigan State University, the purchasing department maintains a list of 20,000 suppliers who send representatives to consult with the university's purchasing agents.[29]

Functional Managers   Functional managers have a position in a specific operational area of the buying organization. At one time or another in their career, most will be involved in negotiations to buy equipment or supplies. Typically, they come from the following areas:

- *Administration (including accounting and finance).* Help evaluate the cost effectiveness of projects.
- *Design engineering.* Buy equipment and material for products the company is marketing.
- *Research and development.* Look at basic materials and supplies rather than specific applications.
- *Manufacturing.* Often responsible for production equipment and processing approaches.
- *Technical specialists.* Advise others regarding the best brands and suppliers for a particular product type.

The Buying Center   A group of people in the organization who make a purchase decision are said to form the **buying center**. These people may play one of six important roles: gatekeeper, information seeker, advocate, linking pin, decision maker, or user. It's important to note that buying center membership changes, depending on the type of purchase being considered. Often the selling organization that wins the order is the one that has made contact with each of the buying influencers. Figure 8-9 depicts the buying center roles.

Gatekeepers   A **gatekeeper** controls the flow of commercial (outside) information into the buying organization. Purchasing agents have been referred to as gatekeepers because they are often the first people that sales representatives contact. They are responsible for screening all potential sellers and allowing only the most qualified to gain access to key decision makers. When the purchasing department is very small, and unusual or complicated products are being purchased (such as high-tech parts), the gatekeeper may be a specialist outside the purchasing area. For example, the head of engineering may recommend that only suppliers with whom the company has a working relationship should be contacted for engineering consulting services. General Motors uses this approach to control purchases of computer hardware. Because of GM's size, hundreds of selling organizations attempt to market mini- and

Buying center
The group of people from the buying organization who make a purchase decision.

Gatekeeper
A person within the buying center who controls the flow of commercial (outside) information into the buying organization by screening all potential sellers and allowing only the most qualified to have access to decision makers.

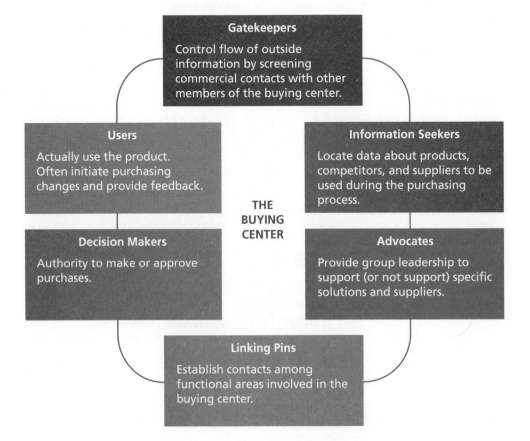

Figure 8-9   The Buying Center Roles

personal computers to the company. To assure the compatibility of the internal communications system and to obtain the best pricing and delivery terms, GM has its computer experts screen out unwanted vendors. When a department plans to buy computer hardware, it usually calls the gatekeeper to ask which suppliers to contact.

Clearly, a skilled salesperson is one who succeeds in working around and through the gatekeeper. Generally, gatekeepers understand the roles played by various people in the organization. When they are cooperative, they can direct salespeople to the appropriate decision maker.

Information Seekers   A great deal of information about products, competitors, and suppliers is required for major purchases. **Information seekers** locate data that they or others can use during the purchasing process. Often the purchasing department is responsible for obtaining lists of firms or alternative types of products, but this task can also be performed by others. Think about the fundamental changes technology has brought to business-to-business marketing. Both FedEx and UPS, for instance, use the World Wide Web to provide information about their companies, as do General Electric, Hewlett-Packard, and AT&T. The Web can satisfy some of an information seeker's needs in only seconds.[30]

The role of information seeking differs from that of gatekeeper. The former looks for sources of information, while the latter tends to reject sources of information and limits the number of people and companies allowed access to the buying firm. Naturally, marketers can make the job of the information seeker easier by clearly presenting relevant product data in an accessible way.

Advocates   The **advocate** exercises a powerful influence over buying center decisions. Advocates participate the most in group discussions, have high status, and play a leadership role. They often obtain their power from the amount of interaction they have with outside organizations and from their expertise on particular topics. Advocates sometimes use their position to inhibit the communications (or recommendations) of less powerful people in the organization. Thus, they may support one seller's offering while restricting the influence of competitors' presentations. Consequently, sellers often seek high-status, knowledgeable, and articulate people within the buying organization to help promote their products. If salespeople are to succeed, then one or more advocates must take their side during purchase deliberations.

Linking Pins   Contact among the functional areas involved in a buying center is provided by **linking pins**. They are particularly important to marketers of products that affect several parts of the buying company, such as electronic data-processing and telecommunications equipment. Linking pins communicate with one another both formally and informally. In many cases, information from the seller to one linking pin is then spread throughout the buying organization. A cooperative linking pin makes the seller's job easier.

Users   **Users** are those within the buying center who actually will use the product being purchased. In manufacturing firms, for example, they are the employees who operate or service production equipment. When components are purchased, the users assemble the parts. In hospitals and other health care facilities, users may be nurses, physicians, or the technicians who operate medical equipment. In other professional organizations, they may be programmers or technical support staff who interface with computers. There are almost as many types of users as there are job descriptions, and their influence on the purchasing process varies.

Users with a high degree of expertise may help develop product specifications. They are especially important in the last phase of the buying process, follow-through. They can provide valuable feedback to sales representatives about how well the product performs. The sophisticated salesperson seeks out such feedback, in turn providing users with information to make the product function as smoothly as possible.

Decision Makers   Sometimes it is difficult for the seller to identify **decision makers**, the persons with authority to make or at least approve the purchase decision. It is also hard to determine when the decision is actually made. Often the selling organization solidifies its relationship with the buying center over time, which is called creeping commitment. The seller gradually wins enough support to obtain the order. In competitive bidding situations, the decision to purchase occurs when the envelopes are opened. In these cases, however, much depends on how the specifications are drawn up in the first place. Some salespeople work closely with the buying organization at that stage to tilt the specs and ultimate decision in their favor. Sellers also spend large amounts of money for promotional items, often unrelated to the product being sold. Companies invest about $6 billion in such business-to-business promo-

Information seeker
A person within the buying center who locates data that can be used during the purchasing process.

Advocate
A person within the buying center who exercises a powerful influence over group decisions.

Linking pin
A person within the buying center who establishes contact among functional areas formed within the buying organization.

User
A person within the buying center who actually uses the product.

Decision maker
A person within the buying center who has the authority to make or approve a purchase decision.

tional giveaways as hats, key chains, coffee cups, and posters—to keep their name in front of decision makers.[31]

In many cases the salesperson can identify exactly who will make the buying decision. In some organizations the decision maker is the purchasing agent. In most cases, however, the choice is made by a buying center or by someone who has budgetary authority and long-term experience with the product. Retail organizations often use a buying committee. Salespeople are invited to make a presentation or to supply information so that a committee member can decide.

INFLUENCES ON ORGANIZATIONAL BUYING BEHAVIOR

The buying process is seldom the same from one firm to the next, or even from one purchase to the next within a given firm. In each case, the decision making process of the buying organization is affected by a number of factors.[32]

Background of Buying Center Members The background of the buying center members affects the buying process. Purchasing agents, engineers, users, and others in the organization have expectations that are formed largely by their experiences. These expectations, in turn, influence the criteria used for decision making. Specialization has a great deal to do with the way people look at problems. Engineers see things differently from financial professionals. Engineers are highly trained in technical areas and are likely to judge a product accordingly. Financial managers are inclined to evaluate products on the basis of profitability.

Role orientation, which refers to the way people see themselves, is also a factor. For example, a member of the buying committee and a minor influencer in the purchase process have a different degree of involvement in the decision. Furthermore, position or rank within the organization obviously can have an effect—one vice president among several lower-level managers has a stronger say in buying center decisions.

Finally, personal characteristics play a role. The lifestyles interests, activities, and general opinions of buying center members affect the buying process.

Information Sources Organizational buying is influenced by the sources of information—salespeople, exhibitions and trade shows, direct mail, press releases, journal advertising, pro-

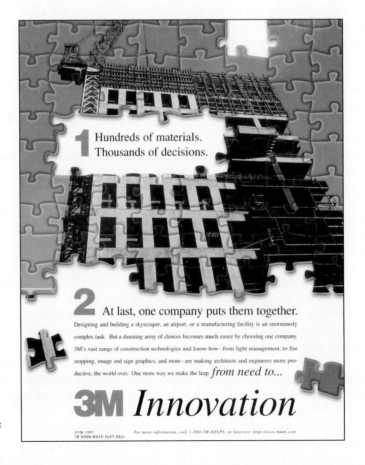

To reduce perceived risk, 3M creates products that meet business needs.

CONNECTING THROUGH TECHNOLOGY

INDUSTRY.NET—WHERE BUSINESS BUYERS AND SELLERS MEET

It's a gold rush on the World Wide Web, and the businesses most likely to get the gold are marketing their wares to other businesses. In fact, business-to-business marketers are leading the way in using new media technologies, particularly Web sites, to promote brand values, reduce paper and printing costs, attract and qualify prospects and leads, and foster customer loyalty. On the purchasing end, Web sites allow corporate buyers to advertise their needs and get the most competitive bids from suppliers. For instance, General Electric estimates that its Web Based Trading Process Network will account for about $1 billion in purchases during only the first 12 months of operation.

The most adventurous prospectors in this new terrain are larger cybermarts, such as Industry.net. Offering a kind of on-line matchmaking service for business buyers and sellers, Industry.net boasts more than 180,000 registrants at more than 36,000 company locations. It also promotes up-to-date product information from more than 250,000 U.S. suppliers.

The concept, spearheaded by the former CEO of Lotus Development, Jim Manzi, is deemed no less revolutionary than Lotus spreadsheets were in the early 1980s. Steve Johnson of Andersen Consulting says that systems like Industry.net "give the ability to invert the traditional purchasing process. Companies can post their supply requirements at a Web site where anyone can bid on them. 'Here's what I need. Hit me!' That could have a huge impact." Already Industry.net is drawing in 3 million "hits" a month.

Strategic alliances and partnerships, spurred by the Web's extraordinary networking capabilities, are making Industry.net even more valuable. It recently forged an alliance with Thompson Publishing, a trade heavyweight that offers on-line catalogs and information on more than 150,000 companies under 52,000 product headings. By joining forces with Thompson and other trade publishers, Industry.net can provide editorial content to help boost its electronic commerce.

The Industry.net system is taking business-to-business marketing leaps and bounds ahead. Typically, most companies have only used Web sites to provide the kind of corporate information traditionally available in print. In contrast, supersites like Industry.net offer a one-stop shopping environment—an on-line industrial cybermall—where you can get comprehensive information on whatever part you want and order it then and there. Transactions are executed at electronic speed, not at the snail's pace and expense of paper. And, this cybermall is global: Buyers and sellers from around the world can meet and trade without the need for expensive brokers or air travel.

Of course, the mother lode belongs to the software makers who facilitate the development and operation of electronic buying and selling. Companies like Netscape Communications, TradeWave, TSI International, and OpenMarket are chasing a market that should hit $750 million in 1999.

Sources: John W. Verity, "Invoice? What's an Invoice?" *Business Week Online*, June 10, 1996; B. G. Yovovich, "Online Alliances Sell Their Wares," *Advertising Age's Business Marketing*, April 1996, pp. 1, 4; and David Stipp, "The Birth of Digital Commerce," *Fortune*, December 9, 1996, pp. 159–164.

fessional and technical conferences, trade news, word-of-mouth, and others. Like direct selling, exhibitions provide one-on-one contact with a company's target audience.[33] While sales calls reach four to five potential customers per day, exhibitions can reach that many per hour. Direct marketing is also useful. Of the total spending in this category, 60 percent is used for direct mail, and 20 percent is for database marketing.[34]

The Internet is playing an increasing role in business-to-business marketing. Web sites enable organizations to promote brand values, reduce printing costs, attract and qualify prospects and leads, and foster customer loyalty. Sites also can expand the customer database, provide customer service, and showcase and sell products.

The interactive age is providing businesses with the potential to strengthen relationship marketing and generate new customers. The media services available today can be the key to staying ahead and maximizing profits. The reach provided by the Internet is tremendous. Learn more about it in this chapter's technology feature, "Industry.net—Where Buyers and Sellers Meet."

Product Factors: Time and Risk

Product and company factors tend to influence the organizational buying process. **Product factors** include time pressure and perceived risk. Time pressure relates to the speed with which a purchase must be made. When more members of

Product factor

A factor such as time or perceived risk that influences the organizational buying process.

the buying organization are involved in the decision, more time is required to make it. Perceived risk refers to what can be lost rather than gained when making the purchase. To reduce perceived risk, 3M invents products that will meet business needs. It builds customer relationships through teams with representatives from all functions, including R&D and sales, who consult with buying organizations about desired products. In response to requests from doctors for a fabric that would block fluids yet allow water vapor to pass through, 3M came up with gowns that protect them from patients' blood but let perspiration escape.[35]

Five types of uncertainty or risk aversion have been identified among buying organizations:

1. *Acceptance uncertainty.* Buyers are not sure of their need for a product.
2. *Need uncertainty.* The buying organization has not yet established product specifications.
3. *Technical uncertainty.* Buyers are unsure about the performance of a product in their own particular environment.
4. *Market uncertainty.* Buyers are unsure of the possible offerings from which they can select.
5. *Transaction uncertainty.* Buyers are unsure about the terms of the sale and product delivery.

When uncertainty is high, buyers strive to reduce perceived risk by either purchasing less or learning more. Decreasing the amount at stake means smaller orders or a reluctance to pay top prices. When much is at stake, others in the organization may be included in the purchase decision, thus spreading the personal risk.

Company Factors Three company factors have particular influence on the purchasing process: the organization's orientation, its size, and its degree of centralization. An organization's orientation, or dominating function, is very important. Some companies are production oriented, while others are marketing oriented. In still others, finance or accounting control the decisions. When marketing dominates, sales factors tend to be very important in making purchase decisions. In production-oriented organizations, production factors are most important. In finance-oriented organizations, decisions are likely to be made on the basis of cost and other financial concerns. The seller must understand the organization's orientation in order to determine the basis for purchasing decisions and which members of the buying center are most influential.

The size of the organization is also likely to influence the number of people involved in purchasing. In very small companies, the purchasing process tends to be informal. Decisions are often made by a key executive at the top. Very large organizations use a formal purchasing process, and decisions often are made by members lower in the managerial structure.

Finally, highly decentralized organizations are likely to give various departments or divisions the autonomy to make their own purchases. Nevertheless owing to the need for accountability, even these companies have formal buying procedures that can involve red tape.

Joint Decisions and Conflict Resolution Whenever several people are involved in decision making, there is a potential for conflict. Purchase decisions are no exception and can be affected by how conflict is handled. When it occurs, members of the buying organization negotiate with one another to arrive at a solution. These negotiations can be shaped by task or nontask motives. Task motivation refers to solving the organization's problem, while nontask motivation refers to the personal needs of the buying group members. Organizations usually attempt to resolve conflicts through problem solving and persuasion. The objective of this task-oriented and constructive approach is to make the best decision for the company. Non-task-oriented approaches to conflict involve bargaining and politicking. Each party is attempting to "get its own way" without considering the organization's goals or engaging in open communication. Sellers who are sensitive to the prevailing negotiating mode can plan their approach accordingly.

Problem solving in the buying context occurs when all decision makers agree on the goals of the particular purchase. Sellers address those goals and show how their product can help meet them. This is very straightforward.

Persuasion occurs when buying center members do not agree on purchase goals, and each tries to convince the others that his or her own goals should take precedence. In the case of buying a computer, for example, the purchasing agent may consider cost most important,

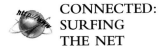

CONNECTED: SURFING THE NET

www.3M.com

Check out 3M's worldwide operations in any industry when you visit the company Web site. Surf its image graphics or obtain information on hundreds of products.

Problem solving

A task-oriented method of conflict resolution whereby all parties agree to put the organization's goals first.

Persuasion

A task-oriented mode of handling conflicts in which persons with different goals attempt to convince the others that their goals should take precedence.

while a user may put software compatibility first. When the two discuss the merits of the various tradeoffs, they are engaging in persuasion. The seller needs to understand both parties and address both sets of goals.

Bargaining occurs when people in the buying center cannot arrive at a solution. Through dialogue, one person may try to obtain his or her preferred product by agreeing that someone else can choose the supplier for a different product. The supplier needs to make sure to address all individuals who might ultimately be in a good bargaining position.

Politicking occurs when buying center members of the organization have strong ego needs. In their search for power or self-esteem, they place their own goals before those of the organization as a whole. Such people are looking for support rather than the most functional purchase choice. What usually results is a "pecking order" within the buying firm, in which an employee's influence on the purchase is proportional to his or her status in the company. The seller's claims about product superiority will go unnoticed because personalities are more important. The seller must be very sensitive to personalities if they wish to conduct business under this circumstance.

In this chapter we have focused on *how* buying takes place in business markets. In chapter 9, we will look more closely at *what* businesses buy, in a section devoted to the three categories of business products: capital products, production products, and operations products.

Bargaining
A nontask-oriented mode of handling conflict in which one person obtains his or her goal by agreeing to allow the other's goal to prevail at another time.

Politicking
A nontask-oriented mode of handling conflict in which personal ego needs take precedence over problem solving.

CONNECTED: SURFING THE NET

Cutler-Hammer

www.cutlerhammer.com

THIS CHAPTER'S RELATIONSHIPS FEATURE INTRODUCED YOU to Cutler-Hammer, a manufacturer of electrical distribution and industrial control equipment. To expand your understanding, visit its Web site and answer the following questions.

1. What business-to-business markets interest Cutler-Hammer? List the products the company sells. Give examples of likely prospects for Cutler-Hammer.
2. Read "What's New." How does E-Bill enable Cutler-Hammer to connect with its customers?
3. Visit the advanced products support center. How does Cutler-Hammer's communications system help it build relationships with buyers?

Industry.net

www.industry.net

THIS CHAPTER'S TECHNOLOGY FEATURE, "INDUSTRY.NET—Where Business Buyers and Sellers Meet," discusses one of the largest on-line business marts. In order to learn more about it, visit its Web site and answer the following questions.

1. What tools/resources does Industry.net offer? How can these assist a company in the organizational buying process?
2. Recall the five types of purchase uncertainty or risk that buying organizations may experience. How does Industry.net help reduce them?
3. Would Industry.net be most useful in a straight rebuy, modified rebuy, or new task situation? Could it be useful in all three? Explain.
4. After exploring the Industry.net web site, do you think businesses can effectively connect with one another in this format? What are the advantages and disadvantages of an on-line business relationship?

OBJECTIVE 1:   Describe the types of organizations and products involved in business-to-business marketing, and understand the importance of this market.

A large number of companies sell most of their products to other companies, which is known as business-to-business marketing. In total volume, business-to-business marketing is much larger than consumer marketing. Types of business markets include the commercial market, extractor industries, trade industries, institutions, utilities, transportation and telecommunications, and government markets. These markets can be segmented according to company demographics, geographic scope, buying approach, and product/technology. Multiple steps bring the final product to consumers as businesses sell materials and processes to each other along the supply chain.

OBJECTIVE 2:   Understand the link between consumer demand and business-to-business marketing.

Business markets rely on derived demand to create opportunities for their products. When consumers purchase more, businesses buy more in order to produce more. The demand for business goods and services tends to be inelastic, which means that a price change does not greatly affect the types of products purchased. The accelerator principle recognizes that some business goods and services are highly sensitive to changes in consumer demand.

OBJECTIVE 3:   Describe the organizational buying process.

Organizations make purchases to support their production requirements and business needs. Buying decisions often start with the make or buy decision. Decisional situations in outsourcing include straight rebuy, modified rebuy, and new task situations. The buying process can involve as many as eight steps: problem recognition, need description, product specification, supplier search, proposal solicitation and supplier selection, order routine specification, purchase and use, and performance review and feedback. Good buyer-seller relationships are key to facilitating the process.

OBJECTIVE 4:   Know how buyer-seller relationships work, including informal and contractual partnerships.

The buyer-seller relationship between businesses develops over time, usually in three sequential phases: courtship, relationship building, and partnership. During courtship, buyers express their desires to sellers, who propose products to satisfy the purchaser's needs. In relationship building, the two parties work together for the first time, customizing the product, its delivery, and conditions. In the partnership phase, long-term agreements are reached either informally or contractually, and closer cooperation develops lasting relationships.

OBJECTIVE 5:   Learn what functions and roles within organizations influence the purchase of a broad range of products.

Different functional areas may be involved in business purchases, ranging from operational units to a purchasing department. The group of people who make a purchase decision form the buying center. Having different backgrounds and functions in the company, they have different buying motives and use different criteria in evaluating products. Purchase decisions may be made laterally, through the interaction of people from different functional areas, or vertically, at one or more level in the corporate hierarchy. Various buying center members play different roles: gatekeeper, information seeker, advocate, linking pin, decision maker, and user. It is important that the salesperson identify exactly who will make the purchase decision, whether the purchasing agent, a buying committee, or someone with budgetary authority.

REVIEW YOUR UNDERSTANDING

1. What is business-to-business marketing? How does it differ from consumer marketing?
2. List the types of business-to-business markets.
3. What is the supply chain? Give an example.
4. What is derived demand? Inelastic demand? How do they apply to business markets?
5. What are two ways that globalization affects business marketing?
6. What is a make or buy decision?
7. What are three types of decisional situations in outsourcing?
8. What are the steps in the organizational buying process?
9. List the phases in buyer-seller relationships.
10. List six functions performed in the buying center.
11. What are purchasing agents? Functional managers?
12. List and explain five types of purchase uncertainty.

DISCUSSION OF CONCEPTS

1. Why is business-to-business marketing larger than consumer marketing? Explain the process of business-to-business marketing.
2. The private sector is composed of several classes of organizations. List examples of these classes, along with companies in each, and explain their importance within business-to-business marketing.
3. Explain the accelerator principle and how it relates to business-to-business marketing. Give an example.
4. When making a purchase, an organization generally goes through a number of steps. Describe these and explain why some purchases require more than others.
5. Describe an informal partnership and a contractual partnership. What are the advantages and disadvantages to both buyer

and seller of each type? How does price-only purchasing come into play?

6. Why are many employees within a buying organization essential to the purchasing process? Explain the different levels of involvement in business purchases. What roles do purchasing agents and functional managers play?

7. Several roles that people play within the buying center are essential to the purchasing process. Define these and explain why they are necessary. Is one more important than the other? Which has the most influence on the purchase decision?

8. Numerous factors influence the buying process. Explain the relevance of each in purchase decisions.

KEY TERMS AND DEFINITIONS

Advocate: A person within the buying center who exercises a powerful influence over group decisions.

Bargaining: A nontask-oriented mode of handling conflict in which one person obtains his or her goal by agreeing to allow the other's goal to prevail at another time.

Business-to-business marketing: Marketing goods and services to other producers of goods and services.

Buying center: The group of people from the buying organization who make a purchase decision.

Commercial market: Organizations and individuals that acquire goods and services to produce other goods and services sold to an end consumer for profit.

Decision maker: A person within the buying center who has the authority to make or approve a purchase decision.

Derived demand: A demand, like the demand for business-to-business products, which depends ultimately on the demand of end consumers.

Extractor industries: Industries that obtain and process raw materials.

Gatekeeper: A person within the buying center who controls the flow of commercial (outside) information into the buying organization by screening all potential sellers and allowing only the most qualified to have access to decision makers.

Government markets: The federal, state, and local governments in their role as purchasers of goods and services.

Inelastic demand: Demand that is little influenced by price changes.

Information seeker: A person within the buying center who locates data that can be used during the purchasing process.

Institutions: Public and private organizations that provide services to consumers.

Linking pin: A person within the buying center who establishes contact among functional areas formed within the buying organization.

Make or buy decision: The decision whether to supply products in-house or to purchase them from other businesses.

Modified rebuy: Purchase of a familiar product from an unfamiliar supplier or a new or different product from a familiar supplier.

New task situation: Purchase of an unfamiliar product from an unfamiliar supplier.

Outsourcing: Purchasing products and services from other companies.

Persuasion: A task-oriented mode of handling conflicts in which persons with different goals attempt to convince the others that their goals should take precedence.

Politicking: A nontask-oriented mode of handling conflict in which personal ego needs take precedence over problem solving.

Problem solving: A task-oriented method of conflict resolution whereby all parties agree to put the organization's goals first.

Product factor: A factor such as time or perceived risk that influences the organizational buying process.

Reseller: A company that purchases a product and sells it in the same form for profit.

Straight rebuy: A routine purchase with which the organization has considerable experience.

Supply chain: The linkage of organizations involved in the creation and delivery of a product.

Tier: The degree of contact between the supplier and the OEM.

Trade industries: Industries comprised of organizations that acquire finished products and distribute them to others.

User: A person within the buying center who actually uses the product.

Utilities: Companies that distribute gas, electricity, or water.

REFERENCES

1. "The ARAMARK Unlimited Partnership: The Centennial Olympic Games," video, Summer 1996; ARAMARK Web site, www.aramark.com; and Phyllis Bermand with Joe Gorham, "Sweaty Equity," *Forbes*, December 10, 1997, www.forbes.com.

2. Bob Donath, "Where Business-to-Business Leads the Way," *Marketing News*, June 23, 1997, p. 12.

3. Philip Kotler, *Marketing Management* (Upper Saddle River, NJ: Prentice Hall, 1997), p. 204; and Michael R. Solomon and Elnora W. Stuart, *Marketing* (Upper Saddle River, NJ: Prentice Hall, 1997), p. 226.

4. PDC investment literature.

5. www.envirogroup.com/about.html, site visited on January 6, 1997.

6. Charles Waltner, "Computer Makers Shift Strategy: Growth of Networks Heightens Reseller Role," *Business Marketing*, June 1996, pp. 1, 16.

7. "Boeing Spent $20 Billion with U.S. Companies in 1996," September 8, 1996, www.boeing.com/news-releases-1997_news_release_9709086.html.

8. Soloman and Stuart, *Marketing*, p. 239.

9. "Air Force Selects Lockheed Martin to Design New Launch Vehicle Family," December 20, 1996, www.mmc.com/Astro/press/1996/9647.html, and www.boeing.com/dsg.station.html.

10. Laura Mazur, "Hot Prospects: Top 9 Countries and What They Need the Most," *Business Marketing*, May 1996, pp. 1, 5.

11. Bradley Johnson, "Global Mindset Expands," *Business Marketing*, February 1996, pp. 1, 4.

12. Char Kosek, "Caterpillar European Campaign Puts the Emphasis on Reliability," *Business Marketing*, March 1996, p. 2.

13. Peter Hirsch, "Global Industries Must Foster Brand Identity," *Marketing News*, June 23, 1997, p. 6.

14. "Has Outsourcing Gone Too Far?" *Business Week*, April 1, 1996, pp. 26–28.

15. Ibid.

16. Don Peppers and Martha Rogers, "The $15,000 Rug," *Marketing Tools*, May 1997, www.marketingtools.com.
17. Mark Ingebretsen, "Brand Strength Lures Corporations," *Business Marketing*, October 1996, p. 13.
18. Jayanta Bandyopadhyay, "Quality System Requirements QS9000, The New Automotive Industry Standards," *Production and Inventory Management Journal*, Fourth Quarter, 1996, pp. 26–31.
19. Kelly Shermach, "Practice Makes Perfect and Dilbert Makes for Bonding," *Marketing News*, November 6, 1996, p. 6.
20. Hakan Hakanson and Bjorn Wootz, "A Framework of Industrial Buying and Selling," *International Marketing Management* 8 (1979):39–49.
21. Kim Cleland, "MCI Keeps an Open Line to Customer Base," *Business Marketing*, June 1996, pp. 5–14.
22. Zachary Schiller and Wendy Zellner, "Clout! More and More, Retail Giants Rule the Marketplace," *Business Week*, December 21, 1992, pp. 66–72; and Wendy Zellner and Marti Benedetti, "The Meek Who Make Good with the Might," *Business Week*, December 21, 1992, p. 73.
23. Jerry Flint, "Company of the Year," *Forbes*, www.forbes.com, site visited on June 26, 1997.
24. Stuart Elliott, "Disney and McDonald's as Double Feature," *New York Times*, May 24, 1996, pp. D1, D6.
25. Leslie Cauley and Jared Sandberg, "Bells Hope Fingers Will Walk to Their On-Line Yellow Pages," *Wall Street Journal Interactive Edition*, June 25, 1997.
26. Dow Jones News Services, "GM Confirms It Has Settled Dispute with Volkswagen," *Wall Street Journal Interactive Edition*, January 9, 1997; and Gabriella Stern, "Volkswagen to Pay GM $100M in Lopez Settlement," *Wall Street Journal Interactive Edition*, January 9, 1997.
27. Michelle Maynard, "Suprise End to Feud over Trade Secrets," *USA Today*, January 10, 1997, p. B1.
28. Ibid.
29. http://adminweb.georgetown.edu/facility/#purchasing, site visited on January 6, 1997; and http://usdinfo.msu.edu/pur/aboutpur.htp, site visited on January 6, 1997.
30. "Direct Marketing Aids Business-to-Business Web Sites," *Business Marketing*, July/August 1996, p. A7.
31. CNN Headline News, December 2, 1996, 3:45 P.M. (EDT) business report.
32. Jagdish N. Sheth, "A Model of Industrial Buyer Behavior," *Journal of Marketing* 37 (October 1973): 50–58.
33. Liona Kinzing, "Creating a Beautiful Harmony," *Business Marketing*, April 1996, p. B6.
34. Laura Loro, "Mail Favorite Tool in Direct Marketing Circles," *Business Marketing*, June 1996, pp. 5–16.
35. Thomas A. Stewart and Melanie Warner, "3M Fights Back," *Fortune*, February 5, 1996, http://pathfinder.com/@@8jzhQAQAUzkBe/fortune/magazine/1996/960205/3mfignt.html.

CASE 8

ANDERSEN CONSULTING

GEORGE SHAHEEN, CEO OF ANDERSEN CONSULTING, believes that knowledge or intellectual capital will be the business currency of the 21st century. The company is positioning itself to be the leading organization in this area. Andersen differentiates itself from other consulting firms with a service model known as *business integration*. It looks at the client as a total enterprise and attempts to align the client's technology, people, and processes with an overall business strategy. Andersen works not just with top management but with nearly all the functions within an organization.

Management consulting is a $20 billion industry that has grown by more than 10 percent annually for almost a decade. Andersen Consulting has been growing at an annual rate of approximately 22 percent. It employs more than 45,000 people globally, 55 percent of them in the Americas, 35 percent in Europe, and 10 percent in Asia. With more than 12,000 partners and managers located in 47 countries, Andersen has revenues of nearly $6 billion, making it larger than many of its major clients and one of the largest business-to-business professional organizations in the world.

The "Andersen Way" is to educate and train people to work in teams using very unified approaches. As consultants move from client to client, they execute projects from the same fundamental knowledge platform. This requires spending approximately 6.5 percent of the company's annual revenue on employee education and development. In addition, nearly $50 million a year is spent on R&D to develop knowledge capital.

Knowledge also is developed by learning what works in the field and applying it to new challenges as they come along. Andersen's information system collects in one centralized location nearly all the project descriptions and reports produced for clients. In this way, teams can tap into what has been done before they work on new projects. Information is applied from client to client, industry to industry, and globally. This is believed to be one of the keys to Andersen's strength. According to Shaheen,

"We've never been more effective in the marketplace. I've got to believe it's a function of how much easier it is to communicate with each other and the information we have at our disposal, to target customers, prepare proposals, and consummate deals." Andersen's information technology plays a major role in addressing customer needs and solving a broad range of customer problems.

Shaheen started at Arthur Andersen in the mid-1960s. The client list was highly focused on Fortune 500 corporations, whose global operations and complex technologies required expert advice on state-of-the-art computer systems. Today, states *Fortune* magazine, "the company will be re-tooling management systems, reorganizing business processes, restructuring work forces, and leveraging knowledge capital in ways that transform entire industries."

Consulting can be so specialized, however, that even a complex organization like Andersen must form joint ventures with others, in some cases competitors, to satisfy a large client's needs. One alliance was put together by a major customer, J. P. Morgan and Company. Andersen Consulting is responsible for applications development, AT&T Solutions covers network management, and Bell Atlantic Network Integration is responsible for desktop computing. Called the Pinnacle Alliance, it is an example of a new trend in team outsourcing by many corporations. In another case, DuPont formed an information technology partnership with Andersen and Computer Sciences Corporation (CSC). The DuPont contract with Andersen to handle all its data processing is worth $4 billion.

One product Andersen has developed is the "virtual corporation," a group of hypothetical companies brought together to pursue a specific business opportunity. The computer simulation model, named DaVinci, is located at Andersen Consulting Center for Strategic Technology in Palo Alto, California, where it is being demonstrated to about 2,000 business customers. It is designed to help executives think though complex business issues in a simulated environment. Much as simulations are used to train pilots, Andersen hopes that DaVinci will help the business customers tie technology and strategy together to create insightful ways of looking at the world.

Business simulations have been around for decades and have provided organizations with a very useful means of understanding business dynamics. The approach is not new, but Andersen is doing it on a scale of unusual proportions. DaVinci shows how technology can be used to expand the relationship between customers and suppliers in the consumer market. It demonstrates how database software, multimedia, and customer service kiosks can be used in product development and many other applications. Andersen Consulting expects that early adopters of the technology will be in the retailing, finance, and transportation sectors.

1. *What types of business markets does Andersen serve? How is its business integration approach used to serve these markets?*

2. *Once Andersen Consulting has identified a potential client, how do you think the organization goes about developing relationships with key buying influences within the organization?*

3. *How is outsourcing changing/influencing business-to-business marketing? Discuss the advantages and disadvantages, using the Pinnacle Alliance as an example.*

4. *What types of issues could be addressed using Andersen's DaVinci virtual reality simulation?*

SOURCES: J. P. Donlon, "Shaheen's Advice Machine," *Chief Executive*, May 1997, pp. 52–56; David Whitford, "Arthur, Arthur . . . ," *Fortune*, November 10, 1997, fortune.com; Esther Shein, "Outsourcing, Team Style," *PC Week*, November 3, 1997, pp. 84–85; Ann Marsh, "Business Services, and Supplies," *Forbes*, January 13, 1997, http:www.forbes.com; and Jane Bird, "Simulating, Simulating," *Management Today*, January 1996, pp. 62–64, 74.

Product Decisions and Strategies

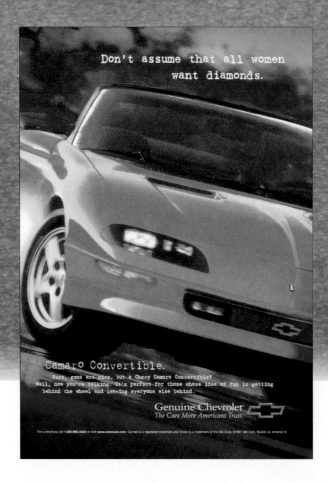

Objectives

1. Describe the major dimensions used by marketers to differentiate their products from competitors. Understand bundling and unbundling.

2. Understand consumer and business product classifications based on how and why products are purchased and consumed.

3. Know how organizations make product line decisions that determine what will be sold, including the degree of standardization chosen for global markets.

4. Recognize that branding and brand strategies are important aspects of building and maintaining a brand name.

5. Know how to create brand equity—the value associated with a product's name.

6. Discuss the many legal and ethical issues surrounding brand and packaging decisions.

A NEWSWEEK SURVEY ONCE ASKED WHICH *invention of the past 100 years you couldn't live without. The answer by far was cars and trucks—which scored even higher than the lightbulb! And while about 70 percent of people chose vehicles, fewer than 10 percent picked personal computers.*

In the automotive industry, a basic car or truck is a core product. Among all the companies making hundreds—if not thousands—of models, General Motors is the world's largest. It offers 82 brands in the United States and scores more for the global market.

Not long ago GM sold its interest in Hughes, the aerospace giant, and in Electronic Data Systems Corp. (EDS), the information systems company. This allowed GM to focus primarily on its core product. The company's extensive line of autos is produced by six marketing divisions, each with its own dealership system: Chevrolet, Pontiac, Oldsmobile, Cadillac, Buick, and Saturn. Each of these varies in depth, that is, in the number of brands. The Buick line offers only four: Century, Park Avenue, Regal, and Riviera. Chevrolet has at least 15, including the Cavalier, Lumina, Tahoe, Suburban, Monte Carlo, Corvette, and Camaro.

Keeping track of all the differences among these varied products is tough for consumers. So GM has worked for several years to restructure its North American vehicle unit. It will try to define more sharply the differences between a Pontiac and a Chevrolet or a Buick and an Oldsmobile, using a brand management strategy. According to G. Richard Wagoner, an executive vice president who has led the restructuring, "Over the past 10 to 12 years, we haven't gotten full value out of [the brands] because we have tended to blur products. The game plan now is to recognize that the brands are of great value."

Wagoner believes that GM's ability to target more products at more narrowly defined market segments than its competitors will be a marketing advantage. GM plans to redesign many of its midsized models. Both the products themselves and the images used to market them will be more sharply differentiated. For example, Pontiac introduced in 1996 a completely redesigned Grand Prix sedan, whose sporty look is a departure from its staid predecessor.

GM has a greater number of products than competitors and is reluctant to cut back. The company believes each model has a potential customer base and doesn't want to abandon those customers. Keith Dennis, a Pontiac dealer in Columbus, Ohio, says that GM's product depth is "a two-edged sword." Although dealers want lots of different products to appeal to a variety of customers, there is a flip side: "If you have a product that doesn't appeal to the intended segment, it becomes an albatross."

GM has dropped a few models. In late 1996, the Chevrolet Caprice, Buick Roadmaster, and Cadillac Fleetwood were eliminated. But the extra manufacturing capacity will be used to make more light trucks and minivans. Environmental scanning has shown the company that light trucks will soon represent half the U.S. light-vehicle market. Since GM has 55 percent of its product line in cars, it wants to bring its portfolio more in tune with the market.

GM has found some unexpected benefits from its global efforts. In 1993, the company's U.S. and European engineers and designers were brought together to create a minivan that would sell well in the United States and also capture a share of the emerging European market. Europeans want a minivan suitable for their narrow roads and small garages. And since they pay a lot for fuel, the vehicle has to be light. GM used lightweight metals and made the seats out of magnesium. To its delight, the company discovered that the easy-to-lift seats appealed to U.S. customers as well.[1]

CONNECTED: SURFING THE NET

www.gm.com

At the GM Web site you can select a car, locate a dealer, choose a finance plan, meet the family, discover new terrain, and invest in the company—all in one place! Get connected to learn more.

Product

Any physical object, service, idea, person, event, place, or organization offered to satisfy consumers' needs and wants.

THE CONCEPT OF PRODUCTS

Product decisions and strategies are challenging and exciting. They affect nearly every aspect of the business and are major factors in connecting with customers. This chapter defines products and how they are managed from a marketer's perspective. The next chapter addresses new product development, and chapter 11 focuses on services, which is a special case. A **product** is any physical object, service, idea, person, event, place, or organization that can be offered to satisfy consumers' needs and wants. Products can be aggregated into packages that perform important functions for individuals, families, or organizations. In the broadest sense, anything that is purchased or sold can be considered a product. Corn, corn flakes, and Kellogg's Corn Flakes are all products. A silicon chip, a transistor, and a computer are all products. A movie, a baseball game, and airplane travel are also products. For many people, the term *product* refers to a tangible item, but are actually services, a special category of products. Today, services represent more than 70 percent of U.S. GDP, and nearly 75 percent of the U.S. workforce is employed in service industries, such as restaurants, lodging, health care, and law.[2]

Figure 9-1 presents the topics covered in this chapter. First we explore the three dimensions of a product. Then we turn our attention to product classifications and global product line decisions. We will then take a look at branding, packaging, and labeling. The chapter concludes with a discussion of ethical issues surrounding product safety and liability.

PRODUCT DIMENSIONS

Most marketing experts describe products in terms of three dimensions: core, branded, and augmented.

CORE PRODUCTS

Core product

The essential physical item or intangible service that the customer receives.

A **core product** is the physical item or intangible service that the customer receives. It refers to functions and benefits at the most basic level. A core product can be a tennis racket, a subcompact automobile, a bowling center, a life insurance policy, or a physical examination. The core product is the essential item or service purchased and does not include the brand name, styling features, packaging, or any other descriptive aspects.

A core product is often called the *generic product,* which means it conforms to the basic description that specifies the function it performs. A bicycle has two wheels and can function as a mode of transportation. Although mountain bikes have specifications different from touring bikes and racing bikes, all of them perform the generic function of transportation. One of the most common examples is generic pharmaceuticals, which are drugs sold without reference to a particular manufacturer. Usually the company that discovers or invents a drug will patent and then brand it. Once the patent expires, other companies can simply copy the pharmacological formula and sell it as a generic drug. It usually costs much less than the branded drug since its price doesn't have to reflect the research or advertising costs associated with developing and introducing new drugs.

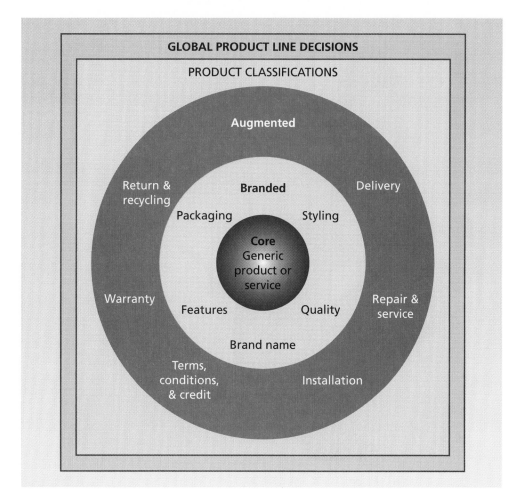

Figure 9-1 Concept of a Product

BRANDED PRODUCTS

A **branded product** is the core product plus the characteristics that allow the consumer to differentiate it from similar products. Most important is the brand name, although styling, quality, features, and packaging are additional ways to distinguish brands. The branded product also can be called the *identified product,* for branding confers an identity on products just as a rancher's brand identifies his herd. Most branded products not only carry the value of the core product but also have a distinctiveness that allows consumers to recognize them and recall their experiences with them. Nearly every teenager recognizes the name Nike. In a 1996 national survey of teenagers, Nike was ranked the "coolest" product brand. Since the teenage market spends more than $65 billion a year, marketers seek to establish a "hip" image for their products.[3] Today, brands such as Girbaud, Levi Strauss, Guess, and CK are recognized widely by consumers buying a pair of jeans.

Some branded products are identified purely by the need for the function they perform, such as Morton's salt. Others may be identified through styling. For example, most of us easily recognize the distinctive lines of a Porsche or a Corvette. When Volkswagen dropped the popular Beetle model and used new styling, the result was confusion in the marketplace. Quality and reliability also tend to be associated with brands. For many decades, Maytag has promoted its product reliability by depicting the lonely repairman who never gets to visit a customer. Finally, packaging may differentiate one product from another. We all recognize immediately the distinctive script lettering of Coke.

AUGMENTED PRODUCTS

An **augmented product** has characteristics that enhance value beyond that of the core and branded product. Delivery methods, warranty terms and conditions, and credit terms are ways to augment a product. A dishwasher from Sears can be delivered, installed, covered by a lim-

Branded product
The core product plus the characteristics that allow the consumer to differentiate it from similar products.

Augmented product
Product with characteristics that enhance its value beyond that of the core and branded product.

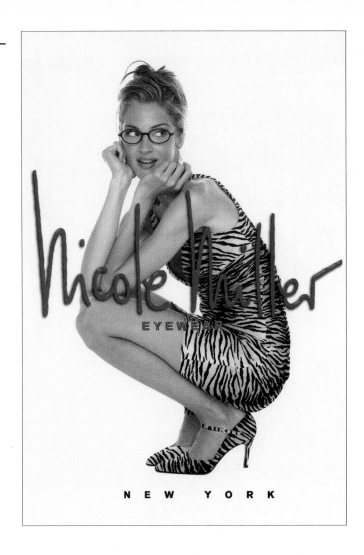

Nicole Miller Eyewear is an example of a branded product.

Bundling strategy

A strategy in which several products are combined into a single offering.

ited warranty, and paid off on credit. Many products also require extensive installation, such as an in-ground swimming pool. Once a product has been purchased, installed, and used, it may require service or repair. That's why warranty conditions and the availability of service are significant in augmenting products. Eastman Kodak guarantees that any photos taken with its film and printed on its paper will be reprinted at no charge if they are damaged in any way. Advertisements show them being destroyed by a dog or churning around in a washing machine.[4]

Another aspect of augmentation is product bundling. A **bundling strategy** combines many products into a single offering. GM's A. C. Rochester Division sells engine management systems to automotive manufacturers. Although these systems are made up of several components (products), they are sold as one unit. The functionality of all the products is improved by combining them, and the sale is larger than if they were sold separately. More important, product bundling enables manufacturers to add value.

Consumer marketers also decide whether to bundle. Stereo equipment, for example, can be sold as a system or as individual components. Maybe in the purchasing process you find that Harman/Kardon speakers sound better, but you prefer the Pioneer receiver and a Sony CD player. In this case, you want to buy an unbundled product. Yamaha's strategy is to market a whole stereo system, with components specifically designed to work together for maximum sound quality.

For environmentally conscious consumers, an increasing appeal is augmentation through recycling. Product disposal is becoming a more important issue. Many consumers want a product that can be returned for recycling at the end of its usefulness. A common example of recycling is automobiles that flow to the used car market and eventually into reclamation centers, where usable parts are extracted and such raw materials as metal and rubber are recycled. In response to consumers' environmental concerns, nine European car manufacturers (including BMW, Mercedes, Ford/Jaguar, Rover, and Volvo) cooperate with dismantlers to reduce automotive waste, generate demand for materials currently being sent to landfills, and eliminate pollution risks from the disposal process. Through the program, carmakers and dismantlers are finding new ways to design and recycle vehicles to minimize waste, producing both economic and environmental advantages.[5]

251
Product Classifications

PRODUCT CLASSIFICATIONS

Products are classified according to how they are purchased and used. These classifications usually require a certain type of marketing strategy. We'll start with consumer products and then move on to business products.

CONSUMER PRODUCT CLASSIFICATION

Marketers need to understand the different types of products that consumers buy. One useful scheme divides products into the five categories listed in Figure 9-2.

Unsought Products **Unsought products** are items not thought about frequently and not perceived as very necessary. The need is usually felt just before purchase and only briefly. These goods may be novelties, such as T-shirts or "over the hill" gag gifts. They also may be things buyers don't like to think about, such as cemetery plots. In any case, consumers don't seek information on their own, so personal selling and prominent promotions are very important. Heavy sales effort may be required to persuade potential buyers to consider the item.

A special category of unsought products is impulse items. As the name suggests, these purchases are made on a whim, with very little thought. In most cases impulse items are relatively inexpensive and have little to do with need fulfillment, other than the buyer's immediate enjoyment at the time of purchase. How many times have you been grocery shopping and tossed into your cart a box of Chips Ahoy! or Twinkies? You're not alone! One study estimates that more than half of all supermarket purchases are unplanned and can be considered impulse items.[6]

Emergency Products **Emergency products** are purchased when an unexpected event takes place and the consumer has an urgent need for a product. When an ambulance or tow truck is needed, the buyer is unlikely to compare prices and probably has little choice about the supplier. From the marketer's standpoint, it's crucial to have telephone numbers and other means of access available to buyers when an emergency occurs. A good example is the 911 service that local police, fire, and ambulance agencies promote. American Express provides consumers with phone numbers that allow lost traveler's checks to be replaced immediately. Many automobile companies now provide toll-free numbers for emergency roadside service.

Convenience Products **Convenience products** are relatively inexpensive items that consumers purchase frequently and with minimum effort. Often, they are referred to as *staples*

Unsought product
An item that consumers don't think about frequently and for which they don't perceive much need.

Emergency products
A product purchased due to an unexpected event and for which the consumer has an urgent need.

Convenience products
A relatively inexpensive item that consumers purchase frequently and with minimum effort.

Classification	Repurchase Planning	Number of Comparisons Made	Frequency of Purchase	Location of Purchase	Examples
Unsought	None	Few or none	Seldom	At buyer's home or at store checkout	Cemetery plots Pet rock
Emergency	Unexpected need	None	Very rarely or once	Closest to emergency	Ambulance Towing service
Convenience	Little	Several (but over many purchases)	Often and regularly	Close to home, travel, work	Soft drinks Chewing gum Fast food
Shopping	Moderate	Many	Infrequent	In areas with many similar products	Automobiles Televisions Appliances Furniture Clothing
Specialty	Extensive	Few	Infrequent	Buyer travels to merchant's location	Fine watches Gourmet restaurants

Figure 9-2   A Product Classification Based on Consumer Purchase Behavior

because people always need them—milk, toilet paper, gum, soft drinks, and so on. Convenience items are usually bought close to home, or work, or travel routes. Typically they are purchased only when the consumer's supply is low. For example, when your tube of toothpaste is almost gone, you'll probably buy another. Most of you won't have an inventory of three or four tubes on hand.

Brand name is very important for convenience products because buyers don't spend much time selecting their purchase. They tend to be brand loyal but will choose a substitute if their favorite is unavailable. Consider the national drugstore chain CVS. Since drugstore supplies are items that buyers want to purchase with minimum effort, CVS provides one-stop shopping for a multitude of pharmaceutical and beauty needs. CVS also offers its own brand, which reduces purchase decision time as well as cost. Marketers must ensure that convenience items are widely distributed and prominently displayed so they are noticed and easily purchased. Eye-catching packaging also can be important.

Shopping product
A purchase generally made only after the consumer has compared several alternatives.

Shopping Products   **Shopping products** are generally purchased only after the consumer has compared several alternatives. Comparisons are made on such elements as style, quality, features, and packaging. Buyers compare prices to select the product providing the best value. Most shopping products are purchased less frequently and cost more than convenience items. Automobiles, televisions, appliances, furniture, and clothing are all considered shopping goods. Although people may do some prepurchase planning at home, they are likely to visit

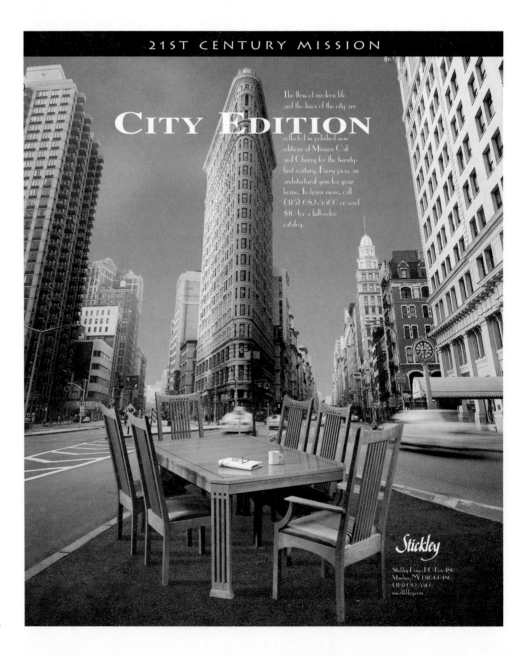

Furniture, like most shopping products, is purchased less frequently and is more expensive.

stores to examine shopping goods. That's why stores offering similar types of shopping goods tend to be located near one another. There may be several shoe stores in the same wing of a shopping mall, or several automobile dealerships not far apart on the same street. This makes it easier for consumers to make comparisons and increases the chance that one of the outlets will make the sale.

Because shopping goods tend to be relatively durable, consumers don't want them to clash with what they already own. Selecting just the right piece of furniture to complement a room or finding an item of clothing that coordinates with one's wardrobe can require extensive shopping. Many people take along friends or family to help with the decision, and there tends to be interaction with salespeople. Most of us wouldn't purchase a car or a business suit without first consulting a salesperson. Many retailers and manufacturers recognize this and train their salespeople to identify buyers' needs and help them find exactly the right item.

Because comparisons are made among shopping goods, many manufacturers market several similar products at different price points. Compaq Computer Corporation has three lines—economy price, middle range, and top end. Compaq structures its offerings to be in tune with the marketplace and to be suitable for various consumer incomes.[7]

Specialty Products   **Specialty items** have unique characteristics that provide unusual value to the purchaser. Most carry meanings that buyers associate with their self-image. Consequently, customers are brand loyal and often refuse to accept substitutes. They are willing to travel long distances and pay high prices to obtain particular products. Some examples are Movado watches, Gucci purses, Godiva chocolates, Louis Vuitton luggage, and Armani suits. A lobster and filet mignon dinner, a dress from Saks Fifth Avenue, a stay at the Plaza Hotel, or a luxury cruise also can be considered specialty items.

Most consumers spend a considerable amount of time on prepurchase planning for specialty items. They must acquire the necessary funds and select a particular style or model of the brand. Marketing a specialty product requires heavy involvement of the retailer to ensure the right fit between the individual model and the customer's needs. To justify the expense of this service, marketers work hard to create customer loyalty. Repeat purchases generate enough profit over time to offset the cost of the first sale.

CONNECTED: SURFING THE NET

www.compaq.com

Visit the Compaq showroom and discover what specifically tailored products and solutions the company has to offer. Learn about both business and home computing or "go inside" Compaq for corporate information, news, and publications.

Specialty item
A product with unique characteristics that provides unusual value to the purchaser.

for store locations or more information call 1-800-388-6785

Gucci purses are considered a specialty item.

Service professionals often try to achieve the status of a specialty provider. There are physicians who practice only internal medicine, oncology, or cosmetic surgery. The specialty classification signifies a great deal more value to most customers and in turn commands a much higher price. Certain types of lawyers, architects, consultants, and accountants usually charge more than their nonspecialized counterparts. Buyers often seek these suppliers not only for their status but also because of the unique qualities of the product or service they provide.

BUSINESS PRODUCT CLASSIFICATION

Business products are purchased by an organization for its own use. The seven types listed in Figure 9-3 are grouped into three categories according to function. These are the products needed to start a company and keep it running for a long time.

Capital product

A costly item that lasts a long time but does not become part of any finished product.

Capital Products **Capital products** are costly items that last a long time but are not part of any finished product. They usually are built or used to manufacture, distribute, or support the development of products. For accounting purposes, these items are depreciated over several years. Capital products are subdivided into installations and equipment.

Installations house operations; examples include office buildings, factories, and distribution centers. Since they cost a lot and are intended to last for a considerable time, they are carefully selected by top management. Salespeople for these products use technical expertise to communicate with buyers. Marketing generally requires a team approach, an understanding of the prospective client's business, and customization of the product to meet the unique requirements of each customer. Providers range from a small construction firm that may put up an office for a local dentist to companies like Bechtel, a huge multinational. It has offices in most world regions and relies on marketing skills to find opportunities and win business globally.

Equipment is movable capital goods used to manufacture or maintain other products. Drills, computers, fork lifts and die presses fit this category. ABB and AO Smith sell robotics designed for specific tasks to many types of manufacturers. GM, Ford, and Chrysler have purchased thousands of robots for welding alone; other functions include sorting, lifting, and inspecting. Of course, products that bring information to businesses represent a huge equipment marketing opportunity. Companies like Sun Microsystems sell computerized workstations for professional and clerical workers. These products are connected through elaborate networks that allow personnel around the globe to tie into the company system. Airline reservations in Japan, France, the United States, and the Czech Republic are likely to be made this way. It is not unusual for these equipment systems to cost hundreds of millions of dollars.

Category & Type	Description	Examples
Capital Products		
Installations	Facilities that contain operations	Office buildings, factories, stores, distribution centers
Equipment	Items used to manufacture products and support the business	Drills, computers, desks, robots, lifts, trucks, airplanes
Production Products		
Raw materials	Substances in natural state	Crude oil, sand, gas, water
Processed materials	Basic substances used to manufacture products	Refined oil, steel, plastic, aluminum
Component Parts and Subassemblies		
Operations Products	Products that are elements of other products	Brakes, transmissions, computer chips, switches, lights, cords
Operating services	Activities purchased to help run the business	Consulting, accounting, waste removal, employee food service
Operating supplies	Consumable items used by the business	Paper, pens, file folders, cleaning products

Figure 9-3 A Classification of Business Products

Production Products Production products—raw materials, processed materials, component parts, and subassemblies—become part of other goods. Few manufacturers extract the raw materials they need or make all the components for a finished product. Instead, they rely on outside suppliers. Raw materials are basic substances used in the manufacture of products, such as ore or grain to produce steel or flour, or cotton and wool for textiles, or soybeans for food products. Companies like Archer-Daniels-Midland (ADM) claim that they "feed the world" because their agricultural products go into so many food items. Processed materials undergo an intermediate treatment—such as refining, chemical combination, purification, crushing, or milling—before reaching the manufacturer.

Component parts and subassemblies are manufactured goods that are elements of other products. Brake linings are components of antilock brake systems. Since these have several components and are part of still another product—vehicles—they are called subassemblies. Companies like Eaton and North American Rockwell make components and subassemblies. Although each part is relatively inexpensive, manufacturing companies are likely to purchase large quantities at one time, numbering thousands or even millions of units.

Quality control and delivery of component parts can be very complicated, so successful companies must perform these operations at a high level of precision. Marketers stress this aspect of their product when selling to businesses, which usually is done by highly trained sales representatives. As noted in chapter 8, suppliers frequently form close ties with manufacturers and produce components or subassemblies tailored to their needs.

Operations Products Operations products are purchased to help run the business and are not included in finished products. These range from very inexpensive items, such as paper clips, to an expensive product like nuclear waste removal from power plants. Operations products are subdivided into supplies and services. **Supplies** are consumable items and may seem relatively unimportant, but in total they can involve large sums. In banks, printed business forms alone often cost several hundred thousand dollars a year. Items such as pens, folders, and cleaning products can contribute significantly to company costs. Every year, American offices use enough paper to build a wall 12 feet high stretching from Los Angeles to New York.[8]

Operations services are activities purchased to help run the business. Examples are legal, accounting, advertising, and billing services. Some companies now outsource their entire logistics operations. Andersen Consulting, EDS, and McKinsey & Company all compete for lucrative contracts involving R&D, tactical and strategic plans, and design of information systems. Companies such as ARAMARK and Marriott supply food service and other products. Many companies have outsiders handle customer service; for some of its clients, UPS World Wide Logistics repairs computers returned to the manufacturer. IBM is a world leader in operational services. One of its ads shows an executive asking: "Will a 14-year-old sociopath bring my company to its knees?" It goes on to describe the dangers of "Information Superhighwaymen," who can destroy a company's information and computer network, embezzle funds, and otherwise wreak havoc. It then offers a brochure about IBM's Secure Way™ family of products and services that can eliminate the risk.[9]

PRODUCT LINE DECISIONS

Product lines must be configured for domestic and global markets. Decisions about how many lines to carry, how many products in each line, and the degree of standardization across markets shape the overall offering of an organization. A **product line** consists of the closely related products marketed by an organization. A company may have one line or several, but a single line usually focuses on the same type of benefit, such as hair care. An **item** is a specific version of a product within a product line. Each item, in turn, consists of several units. A unit refers to the specific product amount, container size or type, and formula. Retailers call these stockkeeping units (SKUs) to identify the variations they regularly have on the shelves.

Consider a line of products in the hair care category made by Procter & Gamble, Pantene, which includes several items—mousse, styling gel, hair spray, and shampoo. Pantene's shampoo product line consists of formulas for regular hair, permed or color-treated hair, and dry or damaged hair; moisturizing shampoo; highlight-enhancing shampoo; and shampoo for frequently washed hair. Procter & Gamble carefully manages the entire line and recently experienced record sales for its hair care products. For the fiscal year ending in June 1996, Pantene's market share increased by 20 percent over the previous period.[10]

Supplies
Consumable items used for business operations.

Product line
Closely related products marketed by the organization.

Item
A specific version of a product within a product line.

Depth
The number of items in a product line.

Breadth
The number of different lines a company markets.

PRODUCT DEPTH AND BREADTH

Most companies need to consider how broad and deep their product lines should be, as described in Figure 9-4. The **depth** of a product line refers to the number of items. Since the Pantene shampoo product line consists of many items, it is said to be deep. A product line with only a few items is called shallow. **Breadth** of product lines refers to the number of different lines a company markets. Since Procter & Gamble markets many, ranging from laundry detergent to toothpaste to a variety of foods, it is considered to have a broad number of product lines. General Electric has an even broader set of product lines, marketing household products to consumers, nuclear power plants to foreign governments, and hundreds of other product lines as well.

Hershey's candies can be considered a narrow and shallow product line. The products fall in a single product category, candy, and there are a fairly limited number of items—chocolate bars, Kisses, and hard candy, all with a few types each. Organizations such as Kodak compete with narrow but deep product lines. Nearly all of Kodak's products relate to one category: imagery. It manufactures and sells nearly every kind of film imaginable. In addition, Kodak makes products and processing equipment for film development, such as paper and chemicals. Kodak lost money when it attempted to broaden into pharmaceuticals, copiers, and chemicals, lines in which it does not dominate.[11] Sales appeared sluggish in 1996 due to declining use of film by its traditional customer base.[12] But Kodak is taking its strength in a narrow but deep product line to developing markets. Based on the 28 percent increase in the number of Russian families owning a camera, around 700 Kodak express laboratories have been established to cover the Russian Federation.[13]

Most companies with a broad product line are large, although there are exceptions. Small organizations usually lack the resources for competing across diverse product categories. Brunswick is a large company that uses a broad and deep product line strategy. One of its lines, recreational boats, is marketed under the brand name Sea Ray. Sea Ray produces several different types of boats, ranging from 12 feet to more than 50 feet. It also owns Brunswick Bowling & Billiards, which markets a line of products ranging from alleys with automatic pinsetters to bowling balls and other equipment. Another Brunswick product line is fishing equipment, marketed under the Zebco brand name, with several types of rods, reels, and related items. Brunswick also markets a number of other product lines with several items each.

Now think about Kmart. It carries a broad product line, but the variety of items within each is limited. In other words, Kmart carries a broad and shallow product line. In some instances, product lines may be too deep or too broad. Procter & Gamble reduced its consumer lines after deciding it offered too many different items. Its product roster is one-third smaller than in 1990, which probably explains its increased market share over the last five years.[14]

GLOBAL PRODUCTS

The globalization of business creates several product-related dilemmas. Among the most critical is determining the optimal amount of standardization for individual products and lines across market regions. Different areas of the world vary greatly in terms of consumer and business purchasing approaches, media exposure, and tastes and preferences. In addition, product standards and regulations, measurements and calibration systems, and economic factors vary immensely. Despite these differences, however, many firms like to standardize products to achieve economics of scale in R&D, production, and marketing.

| | | PRODUCT LINE BREADTH | |
		Narrow	**Broad**
PRODUCT LINE DEPTH	**Shallow**	Few product lines with a few items in each	Many different product lines with a few items in each
	Deep	Few product lines with a number of items in each	Many different product lines with a number of items in each

Figure 9-4 Product Line Depth and Breadth

Standardization plays a major role in global company strategy. Pizza Hut refuses to alter its spice and dough formulations despite pleas from its Japanese joint venture partner, Asahi Breweries. It also refuses to alter its line by adding hamburgers, chowder, or chips. In contrast, Kentucky Fried Chicken found success in Japan by adjusting its product line to include smoked chicken and fish.[15] Curiously, both companies are owned by the same parent organization, PepsiCo.

While the advantages of modifying products usually center around meeting customers needs and conforming to local standards, the costs can be very high. In the electronics area, Europe and the United States are different. Consequently, products made for one market simply will not work in the other. R&D costs to conform to standards run into the hundreds of millions for companies like Seimens in Germany and General Electric. In an effort to avoid the problem, Ford has developed what it calls the world car, Taurus, which it sells in most major markets. Although there are still minor differences between the European and U.S. versions, Ford believes its costs are reduced enough to pass savings on to consumers, increase market share, and meet profit goals.

The depth and breadth of the product line has a lot to do with successful global competition. The marketing battles between Coke and Pepsi involve two different strategies. Coke appears to be winning out, at least for the time being. *Fortune* says "Coke is kicking Pepsi's Can."[16] Pepsi has three product lines: snack foods (Frito-Lay), restaurants (Pizza Hut, Taco Bell, and Kentucky Fried Chicken), and beverages. Coke concentrates on beverages and obtains 71 percent of its revenues internationally. Pepsi obtains the same percentage domestically.

Some believe Coke's global strategy—a narrow line with geographic variations—is one reason for its success. Pepsi, in contrast, has standardized its beverage line globally. Clearly, product line breadth doesn't determine why one company outsells another, but the issue is important in developing global strategy. And some believe that eventually Pepsi's broader line will translate into global growth as the mass markets in Europe, Asia, and Latin America choose local varieties of Cheetos, Doritos, Fritos, Ruffles, and Sunchips.[17] Whether they wash them down with Coke or Pepsi remains to be seen.

IBM also has a global product strategy. It adds products designed to span geographic regions. It introduced the widely popular Lotus Notes for the IBM global network to coincide with the 1996 Olympics. This software gives companies the ability to share information and collaborate on projects from locations around the world.[18]

Even some companies with deep domestic product lines find additions are in order when going international. Rubbermaid, known for its large number of products, wants to increase its global participation from 18 percent in 1996 to 30 percent by 2000 through aggressive marketing in Europe, Asia, and Latin America.[19] Experience with a deep and broad product line in the consumer, industrial, and health care fields will be important as companies seek to connect with the needs and tastes of consumers in these diverse regions.

Emerging economies like China present their own problems from a product standpoint, because large and risky investments in design and manufacturing are often necessary. Motorola finished work on a $560 million semiconductor component plant in Tianjin, China, in 1998. Since it is estimated that China will become the world's largest consumer market for new personal computers, television sets, microwaves, and telephones sometime in the 21st century, Motorola believes the plant will position it well to support a broad range of technologically sophisticated products there.[20]

BRANDS

A **brand** is a distinguishing name and/or symbol intended to identify and differentiate products from those offered by competitors.[21] Philip Morris purchased Kraft in 1988, the same year Nestlé bought the British company Rowntree. What was unusual about these takeovers was the tremendous premium paid for the brand name. Philip Morris paid four times more than the tangible assets of Kraft, and Nestlé paid more than five times the assets of Rowntree.[22] More recently, Procter & Gamble purchased the Eagle brand name and trademark from Anheuser-Busch for an estimated $10 to $20 million.[23] Why did these companies pay so much? They wanted the long-term cash generation potential of these names. Many brands are now recognized globally, producing dramatic returns around the world.

Can you name the top ten brands in the world? Does your list match Figure 9-5? No matter what criteria are used in creating such a list, the same brands tend to emerge as leaders.[24]

CONNECTED: SURFING THE NET

www.motorola.com

Learn about "what you never thought possible" by visiting the Motorola Web site. Take a look at the company's product portfolio and business units, or explore its global community.

Brand

A distinguishing name and/or symbol to identify and differentiate products from those of competitors.

1990	1996
1. Coca-Cola	McDonald's®
2. Kellogg's	Coca-Cola
3. McDonald's®	Disney
4. Kodak	Kodak
5. Marlboro	Sony
6. IBM	Gillette
7. American Express	Mercedes-Benz
8. Sony	Levi's
9. Mercedes-Benz	Microsoft
10. Nescafé	Marlboro

Figure 9-5   The World's Top Ten Brands

Source: Interbrand.

Brands are very powerful concepts in business. They send strong signals about what the product represents. A brand image can make or break a company's reputation. To a consumer, a trusted brand promises high quality, but a "tainted" reputation means poor quality or bad service. Since customers spend an average of only four seconds examining a shelf in a grocery store, brands play a crucial role.[25] According to James Lenehan, worldwide chairman of Johnson & Johnson's consumer pharmaceuticals and professional group: "If you have a brand that you know and trust, it helps you make choices faster, more easily. Can you imagine going shopping without them?"[26]

Historically, brands were used to identify a product's manufacturer. They also protected both the customer and the producer by ensuring that the products met certain quality standards and came from a reputable source. Companies with early success in building brands include P&G, IBM, Anheuser-Busch, Sony, American Express, Volkswagen, American Airlines, Pepsi, and Kodak. Such companies created a brand perceived by consumers as having more intrinsic value.

In the 1960s, the strategy was simple: The greater the perceived value, the greater the sales. This strategy is still used today, but companies must work hard to ensure that the products themselves provide the added value communicated by the name. Brand strategies help businesses such as Coca-Cola, Disney, Gillette, and Hewlett-Packard develop credibility with customers. The role of brands grew in importance in the 1990s. Advertisers spent $174.1 billion in 1996 to promote brands, an increase of 7.8 percent over 1995.[27]

Today, brands do far more than identify the manufacturer. They have become "personalities" with a character much greater than the products they represent. An early example of successful branding is Ivory soap, introduced in 1879 by Harvey Procter. With its claim of "99.44% pure," it has long been the leader. Estimates are that the Ivory brand has brought more than $3 billion in profit to Procter & Gamble over the years. In some cases the brand name becomes the product itself to many people: Xerox, Kleenex, and Rollerblade are synonymous with their functions. And such brands as Nabisco, Kellogg, Kodak, Gillette, Campbell's, and Goodyear have all outlived the specific items they represented when introduced. While the products themselves may have altered due to changing technology, customer preferences, and modernization, the brand name has stayed the same.

TRADEMARKS

Trademark (brand mark)
A distinctive form or figure that identifies the brand.

People tend to use the words *brand* and *trademark* interchangeably, but there are some notable differences. The brand name is the wording attached to the product. Coke, Pepsi, and Chiquita are brand names. The **trademark** (brand mark) is a distinctive form or figure that identifies the brand. A picture is called a trademark symbol; distinctively shaped letters are called a logo: IBM, HBO, GE. Coca-Cola uses white script on a red background. Burger King uses a crown, and McDonald's® uses golden arches. Other examples are NBC's peacock, Fila's blue-and-red letter *F*, Chrysler's five-pointed star, and Nike's swoosh symbol. Intel has found that, in the quickly changing world of technology, the "Intel Inside" symbol has endeared it to customers. It reassures them about a purchase that is often filled with confusion and anxiety.[28]

A trademark or logo can provide immediate recognition and credibility even when it is applied to products owned by other companies. The American Cancer Society is selling its red dagger logo for approximately $4 million to endorse NicoDerm antismoking products

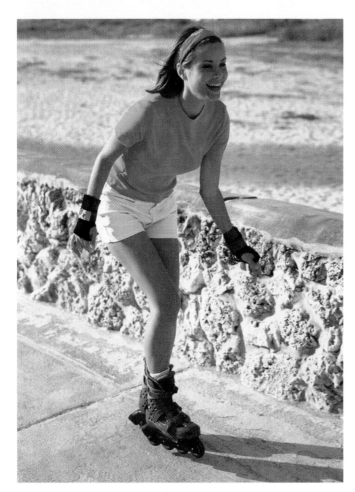

Many brands today seek association with an active lifestyle—certainly not a Couch Potato.

and Florida Orange Juice. Groups such as the American Dental Association and the American Heart Association have done the same. These endorsements, however, raise an ethical issue. Should nationally respected health groups use their logo to give products instant credibility?[29]

Trademark Piracy

The brand name and the trademark symbol or logo are protected by law if they are registered. That gives the owner sole right to use them any way s/he chooses. Just as most people want to protect their reputation, companies are careful to protect a brand. It is property they own and competitors may not use or imitate it. For example, a federal court in Milwaukee ruled that the Hog Farm, a motorcycle parts and repair shop, had to change its name. It infringed on the rights of Harley-Davidson, whose motorcycles are widely known as "hogs."

Recently there was a dispute over the Original American Couch Potato, a pillow with the slogan "This Spud's for You." Anheuser-Busch considered this an infringement on its trademark slogan, "This Bud's for You," which took many years and millions of dollars to build. To avoid confusion over the true manufacturer of the product, the pillow's creator agreed to change the slogan.[30]

In the entertainment industry, property rights and reputation are no less important. The wording "Steven Speilberg presents" is used to brand the famous director's cartoon shows, *Tiny Toons* and *Animaniacs*. Networks also brand products. MTV came out with the movies *Joe's Apartment* and *Beavis and Butthead Do America* as well as books, T-shirts, and CDs with the MTV trademark.

Securing trademarks globally can be very tricky. People throughout the world recognize Mickey Mouse and Donald Duck as Disney characters, but a court in Indonesia ruled that the duck's picture could be used by a local company. This situation occurs frequently, particularly in developing countries where more pressing problems command government attention. In advanced economies, trademark protection is considered essential for sound competitive industrial policy. Elsewhere trademarks may be viewed as merely a tool to stimulate

CONNECTED: SURFING THE NET

www.mtv.com

Connect to MTV on-line. Stay on top of the music world by checking out the latest headlines, news releases, weekly features, and more. You can also "feed MTV news" and surf through your favorite shows.

commerce. No single world policy has yet been developed that takes into account the perspective of all nations.

The International Trade Commission reports that intellectual thievery costs U.S. business huge amounts annually in lost exports, domestic sales, and royalties.[31] Pirated products range from computer software and designer goods to soaps and candies. Packaging closely resembles that of the American-made counterpart, and often logo designs are stolen and used. Individual firms may or may not choose to file an international suit against offenders.

Much of the trouble occurs in Asia. It is estimated that as many as 200 million illegal compact disks are sold each year, with almost 60 percent coming from China. Machines used to copy movies, music, and computer disks flood into China illegally, mostly from Europe.[32] Kmart Corporation wrestled for ten years in court before settling against a store owner in Singapore who had been using its name, logo, and "The Savings Place" tagline since the 1970s. The company decided not to seek damages, estimated at more than $2 million, but the store owner had to remove all disputed references within seven days, rename his business, and refrain from any future copyright infringements.[33]

Counterfeiting has become so widespread that *Fortune* has coined the term *brandnapping* for copying products and affixing illegal labels. An estimated 5 percent of all products sold worldwide fit this category, totaling about $200 billion annually. This represents huge losses to legitimate owners of the brands.

Unfortunately, some fakes can have very serious consequences. For example, the Federal Aviation Administration has found quantities of substandard counterfeit airline parts in commercial planes. Since the U.S. government has been relatively ineffective in preventing this type of problem, companies have turned to private agencies to help stem the flood of knock-offs from high-tech bandits in countries like South Korea, Vietnam, and Russia.[34] U.S. trade negotiations have lessened the occurrence of infringements, but developing countries have little incentive to enforce laws. Efforts continue through such organizations as GATT and the United Nations to develop international norms.

BRAND STRATEGIES

There are a number of brand strategies, as shown in Figure 9-6. In addition to a generic or nonbranded approach, the most common types are individual, family, manufacturer (national), private, and hybrid.

Generic brand strategy
Strategy in which no brand name is used.

Generic Strategy A **generic brand strategy** uses no brand name whatsoever. Firms generally select this approach when they want to gain a low-cost commodity market position. As mentioned before, pharmaceutical companies often adopt this strategy. Some grocery stores devote entire aisles exclusively to generic products, packaged in plain black and white. Many consumers prefer generics because they cost so much less than name brands.

Individual brand strategy
Strategy in which there is a unique name for each major product or product line.

Individual Brand Strategy An **individual brand strategy** assigns a unique brand name to each major product or product line. There are three situations in which this approach is likely to be used. First, companies may have different product lines that compete against one another. For example, General Motors builds total market share with several individual brands: Chevrolet, Cadillac, Pontiac, Buick, and Oldsmobile. Second, products within one line may be matched with unique market segment needs. For example, Procter & Gamble's nine laundry detergents appeal to different segments. Third, a company may make highly dissimilar products. For example, Kellogg markets breakfast cereals under its name, toaster pastries under the Pop-Tarts brand, and pies under the Mrs. Smith's label.

Family brand strategy
Strategy in which a single brand name covers the entire group of products in the company's line(s).

Family Brand Strategy A **family brand strategy** uses a single brand name for the entire group of products in the company's line(s). This can be very cost effective because advertising, promotion, and distribution resources can be focused to create a single image in the marketplace. The result is increased consumer awareness of the company and its products, such as Black & Decker tools.

The family brand strategy is used when products are similar. Dole markets more than 20 mainstream fruits and vegetables as well as numerous exotic fruits under one name. The Sony name covers hundreds of products, from high-priced stereos to inexpensive alarm-clock radios. The family brand approach has allowed Sony to introduce and eliminate products fairly rapidly while almost guaranteeing that its new products will at least be tried. Both Dole and Sony have sought to make their name synonymous with quality, regardless of the specific product.

Type	Description	Reasons for Use	Examples
Generic	No brand name is used.	Lower cost. Commodity position.	Pharmaceuticals Vegetables
Individual	Unique brand name for each major product or line.	Company has dissimilar products. Each product is matched to a segment. Products compete against one another.	Procter & Gamble's Tide, Bold, Cheer, Dreft, Era, Gain, Ivory, Oxydol, and Solo laundry detergents.
Family	Umbrella name covers all products in the line.	Economical way to create one brand identity for all existing and new products. Increase awareness and market presence by using one image for all.	Dole Sony Campbell's Sara Lee Black & Decker
Manufacturer (National)	Brand name synonymous with the owner.	Ties R&D, manufacturing, and company reputation to the product.	McDonald's® Kodak Fisher-Price Johnson & Johnson General Motors General Electric
Private (labels)	Brand name applied to supplier's product by wholesaler or retailer.	Lower cost. Builds on and enhances reputation of firm. Enhances firm's buying power.	Meijer A&P: Aunt Jane Wal-Mart: Sam's American Choice ACE Hardware IGA Stores Spartain Stores Sears: Kenmore
Hybrid	Two or more approaches are used.	Merger and acquisition. Gain benefits of all approaches.	Kraft

Figure 9-6 *Types of Brand Strategies*

Manufacturer's Brand Strategy **Manufacturer's brands,** as the term implies, are named after the maker. Sometimes they are called national brands, since the products often are found throughout the country. We've already mentioned a few in this chapter, such as Kodak and General Electric, but manufacturer's brands also can be local, such as Hanover pretzels. The company's reputation is closely tied to the product. Benetton, McDonald's®, and Johnson & Johnson use public relations, advertising, and other means to ensure that the public connects their products with the policies of the firm. Usually this means creating a singular image for the company and the products it makes. Kodak's brand name revolves around imaging; Fisher-Price is known for products that relate to child development and safety; and Gerber is famous for baby food.

Manufacturer's brand (national brand)
Brand named after the manufacturer.

Private Brand Strategy When wholesalers or retailers place their own name on a product it's called a **private brand** (or private label). Since these are promoted locally rather than nationally, they can be sold at a lower price than manufacturer's brands. Private labels allow the reseller to build and enhance its own reputation. By carefully selecting suppliers and developing quality control mechanisms, Wal-Mart can promote Sam's American Choice products as being high quality at a low price. This strategy increases Wal-Mart's buying power, since the company can shop among competing suppliers for the best price and pass on some of the savings to consumers. In addition, private brands enable retailers and wholesalers to differentiate themselves from competitors.

Private brand (private label)
The name wholesalers or retailers attach to products they resell for numerous suppliers.

Companies that use private labels believe they understand consumers better than national marketers in several key respects, especially in their knowledge of local or regional consumer needs and shopping habits. Yet they do not have the resources to innovate far beyond current brands.[35] Their goal is to increase in-store brand sales. For their national brand competitors, the challenge is to persuade consumers not to be drawn by the low prices.[36]

The rivalry between in-store and national products has come to be know as the "battle of the brands." Many manufacturers fear being undercut by private labels, although branded goods do more for retailers because they help a store become more profitable. Coca-Cola explained to retailers across the country that brand shoppers spend three to four times more on groceries

Hybrid brand strategy
A combination of two or more brand strategies.

than do private label shoppers.[37] The "battle" started when large manufacturers gained power by selling products through a broad range of distribution channels, and their size allowed them to place many demands on retailers. Large retailers retaliated by creating private labels.

Hybrid Brand Strategy Many firms employ a **hybrid brand strategy,** which is a combination of two or more approaches. Often this happens when mergers and acquisitions join organizations using different strategies. In these cases, executives must decide whether to blend the acquired brands into the company's portfolio or let them maintain their identity.

General Motors uses a strategy mix. The individual brand approach generally applies for Chevrolet, Pontiac, Buick, Oldsmobile, and Cadillac, although the Geo individual brand was introduced within the Chevrolet family brand. Saturn cars were introduced as a family brand with loose ties to GM. The company also promotes the manufacturer brand—General Motors automobiles. At the same time, many GM products, such as spark plugs, are sold under the Delco name or to resellers for private branding.

BRAND EQUITY: CONNECTING WITH A SUCCESSFUL BRAND

Brand equity
The assets linked with the brand name and symbol that add value to the product.

Brand equity refers to the assets linked with the brand name and symbol that add value to the product or service.[38] It indicates how valuable the brand is to the parent company. Be aware that a brand carries denotative and connotative meanings. It denotes (identifies) what the brand is, such as Head & Shoulders or Selsun Blue shampoo. It also connotes (produces an image of) the brand's relationship to the consumer's lifestyle. Connotative meanings grow over time and become tremendously valuable. Ideally, brands will achieve enough connotative meaning to endure forever if they are supported properly. Names like Gillette, Morton's salt, and Betty Crocker predate your grandparents.

DIMENSIONS OF BRAND EQUITY

When people gradually purchase their home from the mortgage company, we say that they are earning or gaining equity. The homeowner is investing in the property. In a similar fashion, companies must invest in developing brands. Through sustained communication of the brand's connotative qualities, value is increased. Brand equity is an intangible asset with five dimensions, as shown in Figure 9-7. Let's look at each dimension in more detail.

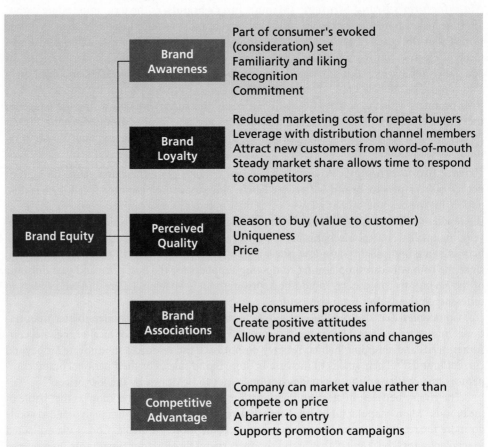

Figure 9-7 The Five Dimensions of Brand Equity

Source: Adapted from David A. Aaker, Managing Brand Equity *(New York: The Free Press, 1991), inside cover.*

Brand Awareness   Brand awareness is the extent to which consumers recognize the name and are likely to include it among the set of brands they consider. High awareness means a greater probability of purchase. If consumers are familiar with a brand and like it, they will have positive attitudes about the product(s) with that name. Consider the warmth and no-fail reliability of the Betty Crocker mother figure or Pillsbury's Poppin' Fresh baker. Because strong brands are often global, they may be recognized around the world and provide traveling consumers with ready access to a familiar item. High brand awareness also represents the commitment of the company to maintaining long-term standards of excellence for the consumer.

Even established companies work to sustain broad awareness. Kraft is doing this through a food-related Web site called "Interactive Kitchen," which will provide recipes, news, and information. The company is hoping for 5 million Web site visits from consumers every year. On-line customers who choose to add their address to a marketing list will receive product information, promotions, and coupons through the mail.[39] This increased accessibility to Kraft's brand name is intended to heighten brand awareness.

Newer companies or brands always have to create awareness. Since a surprising percentage of software users don't know the Microsoft name, the company has been trying to change

Brand awareness
The extent to which consumers recognize the brand and are likely to include it among the set of brands they consider.

 # CONNECTING THROUGH RELATIONSHIPS

STARBUCKS EXTENDS ITS BRAND NAME THROUGH JOINT VENTURES

As the stellar Seattle coffee company seeks to extend its brand name, Starbucks is showing up in ice cream, cold drinks, and on the trays of United Airlines' food service.

With 100 stores across the United States and 20 times as many planned for the new millennium, Starbucks coffee seems to be everywhere. Yet the company figures that perhaps only 1–2 percent of Americans have even tried its product. Spearheaded by the senior vice president of marketing, Scott Bedbury, the strategy is to push the Starbucks name onto grocery shelves through a series of carefully planned joint ventures.

Rather than spend money and energy developing new products, Starbucks is forming relationships with key organizations in the product categories or venues it wants to enter. The company's most ambitious joint venture is its 50–50 partnership with PepsiCo. It started in 1994 and hopes to cash in on the Starbucks reputation for specialty coffee and Pepsi's bottling and distribution muscle. Their first product, a carbonated coffee drink called Mazagran, was a flop. "Weird," "nasty," and "strange" were some of the unpromising comments when it was test-marketed. Now the companies are banking on their newest ready-to-drink coffee, a bottled version of Frappucino. This frothy blend of ice, milk, and coffee sent summer sales through the roof at Starbucks stores when it was introduced in 1996. With the formula nailed down, Starbucks is counting on Pepsi's command of prime shelf space in the soft drink and iced tea aisles.

After making the leap from hot coffee to bottled drink, Starbucks figured a cold coffee dessert was a natural next step. It teamed up with Breyer's Grand Ice Cream, Inc., in another 50-50 deal. Espresso Swirl, Javachip, and three others flavored with Starbucks coffee hit grocery store freezers in summer 1996. Within eight months, the brand became the nation's top-selling coffee ice cream.

Starbucks is also trying to package the atmosphere of its coffee bars. The company has collaborated with Capitol Records, Inc., on two jazz CDs played and sold in Starbucks stores.

There is a risk that Starbucks may extend its name too far and dilute its brand identity. Bedbury admits that this is his biggest worry. Some Starbucks-struck stock analysts are a tad nervous about the deal with United Airlines. The company that has made its name marketing, preparing, and serving coffee will now entrust the job to United flight attendants. Allan Hickock, managing director of Piper Jaffrey in Minneapolis, cautions: "Leaving your concept in the hands of people who don't share your culture is a big risk." Starbucks views the deal differently; they see the chance to reach about 80 million travelers a year in an environment in which coffee traditionally has been crummy. Even Hickock thinks that if any company can pull it off, Starbucks can. "They pay a lot of attention to detail," he says, "and everything the consumer touches drips with quality."

Sources: Kelly Shermach, "Coffee Drinking Rebounds; Specialty Blends Lead Way," *Marketing News,* September 12, 1994, p. 2; "Starbucks Has Breyer's Over for Dessert," *Los Angeles Times,* November 1, 1995, p. D2; Ian James, "One Part Coffee, One Part Soda, Mix in Some Marketing Muscle," *Los Angeles Times,* September 20, 1995, p. D4; Seanna Browder, "Starbucks Does Not Live by Coffee Alone," *Business Week Online,* August 5, 1996; and Jennifer Reese, "Starbucks: Inside the Coffee Cult," *Fortune,* December 9, 1996, pp. 190–200.

Brand loyalty
A dimension of brand equity that causes consumers to choose one brand over others available.

that with MTV-like advertising. Microsoft has spent more than $200 million on this endeavor.[40] The relationships feature shows how "Starbucks Extends Its Brand Name through Joint Ventures."

Brand Loyalty **Brand loyalty** occurs when consumers select a particular brand over others on a regular basis. In effect, the firm's customers are an asset. Brand loyalty leads to lower overall marketing costs because it's much less expensive to persuade repeat buyers than create new ones. Distribution channel members are more likely to provide a good location within their outlet for the sale of an item with high brand loyalty. Furthermore, companies with faithful customers tend to be less susceptible to economic downturns or new competitors. Loyal buyers are not immediately inclined to look at other options, staying with the product even in times of economic hardship.

According to one poll, 74 percent of consumers "find a brand they like, then resist efforts to change."[41] Loyalty produces sales that enhance the earning power of the company. Cheerwine is a nonalcoholic carbonated drink produced by Carolina Beverage Corporation and sold in 11 southern states. While Cheerwine does not even register in national market share polls, where Coca-Cola (41 percent share) and Pepsi (32.8 percent share) dominate, it can claim up to 15 percent of sales on some weekends in its hometown. How is this possible? Carolinians are so loyal to the drink that those who relocate often write the company asking where Cheerwine can be bought. Loyalists tell others about their favorite brand, which has such a following that 9.4 billion gallons have been sold.[42]

Even Mother Nature's own fruits have been branded—bananas by Chiquita and oranges by Sunkist. Why buy these rather than just any banana or orange? Why are names like Kodak and Coca-Cola so well received in every part of the globe? Customers don't merely know them but prefer them. For a brand to be valuable to a company, a significant number of customers must prefer it over competitive brands.

Brand insistence
A dimension of brand equity that makes consumers unwilling to accept substitutes for the brand.

The best kind of loyalty for a company is when consumers insist on its brand. **Brand insistence** means that buyers are not willing to accept substitutes. This degree of loyalty is more likely for specialty items, such as Polo shirts or branded pharmaceuticals. Brand insistence is an enviable position and gives the company a valuable asset that will produce significant future cash flows. In recent years, some unlikely products have gained brand insistence status. It used to be that technology products, such as electrical components, did not have much brand awareness to say nothing of brand loyalty. Intel Corporation, the pioneering semiconductor company, gave technology branding a boost. Through an innovative marketing campaign, it has persuaded consumers to insist upon Intel microprocessors in their PCs. See the technology feature, "Intel Brands the Soul in the Machine."

Perceived quality
The degree to which a brand consistently produces satisfaction by meeting customer expectations.

Perceived Quality The third dimension of brand equity is **perceived quality,** the degree to which brands consistently produce satisfaction by meeting customer expectations. This is one of the most important reasons consumers buy a product. The high or unique quality of a brand is directly related to what consumers are willing to pay and to whether the firm can charge a premium. A New Zealand study indicates that having and using a major accounting firm is associated with premium audit fees. In effect, names such as Arthur Andersen or Price Waterhouse serve as a brand name. Companies are willing to pay higher fees for the perceived higher quality of a Big Eight audit, even when the identical service could be carried out by another firm.[43]

Cheerwine has such a following of loyal customers that 9.4 billion gallons have been sold!

CONNECTING THROUGH TECHNOLOGY

INTEL BRANDS THE SOUL IN THE MACHINE

Before 1992—when it wasn't cool to be a cybergeek—not many computer users knew or cared about the microprocessor powering their PC. Then Intel Corporation gave them a reason to care. The $20 billion company, which now owns a 90 percent share of the microprocessor market, revolutionized corporate branding with its "Intel Inside" marketing campaign. Never before had an electrical component company tried to create brand identity with the end user.

The motto of the company owner is "only the paranoid survive," and Intel's success rests on its obsession with making its own products obsolete. The goal is to come out with a new, more powerful microprocessor every eighteen months. By 1992, however, Intel needed to convince consumers who had the old 286 chip that a 386 is better—and, looking ahead, that the next generation will be better yet, and the next. So Intel decided to educate buyers with a two-tiered marketing campaign, one aimed at computer manufacturers and the other at end users. For corporate purchasers and PC experts, Intel inserted "technology briefing" pamphlets in PC magazines, featuring a new topic every six to eight weeks. For consumers, Intel television and print ads showed dramatic swooping views of a computer powered by an Intel microprocessor. The goal: Take away the fear and make Intel's technology accessible or, better yet, indispensable.

But the biggest branding brainstorm was Intel's offer of co-op advertising money for every PC maker who put the "Intel Inside" sticker on its products or in its ads. Intel pays up to 5 percent of the ad costs, and now the logos are almost as common as floppies. The move shook up the whole industry. "The microprocessor has become a consumer product," said Intel's hard-driving CEO Andy Grove, adding that "its role in contemporary society is not a passing phenomenon." Five years after the campaign began, Intel still uses advertising to connect with consumers and educate them about new products. During Super Bowl XXXI in 1997, viewers were treated to a funky spot advertising quite a different type of chip—the MMX Pentium.

To be sure, there were skeptics when Intel first tried to make consumers care about technology. One analyst asked: "If you buy a BMW, who cares about the spark plugs?" Ironically—and to the distress of PC makers—the consumer now often cares more about the "spark plugs" than the name on the disk drive. Intel has beefed up its brand identity even more by designing and building entire motherboards, the circuitry at the heart of PCs. Dozens of computer companies, including IBM, Digital, Compaq, and Hewlett-Packard, are selling machines with Pentium chips. They were forced to march to Intel's beat since they couldn't produce their own motherboard designs as quickly. And that beat is picking up tempo. According to David House, a senior vice president at the chip-making giant: "Twice a second somebody buys an Intel-based computer."

Sources: Robert D. Hof, "The Education of Andrew Grove," *Business Week Online*, January 16, 1995; Lawrence M. Fisher, "Intel Doubled Its Earnings in 4th Quarter," *New York Times*, January 15, 1997, p. D1; Tim Clark, "Inside Intel's Marketing Machine," *Business Marketing*, October 1993, pp. 14–19; Robert D. Hof, "Intel Unbound," *Business Week Online*, October 9, 1995; and Michael Treacy and Fred Wiersema, *The Discipline of Market Leaders* (Reading, MA: Addison-Wesley, 1995), pp. 103–121.

Brand Associations   Brand equity also involves establishing **brand associations** that evoke positive attitudes and feelings in consumers' minds. This enables firms to create messages that gain consumers' attention more easily. It also allows the brand equity to be extended to additional products. Procter & Gamble marketed only 13 advertised brands in 1950. By 1991, there were more than 100, not counting minor variants of major brands.[44] In a hard-hitting campaign against Yamaha motorcycles, Honda used brand associations with its automobiles. It quickly produced a great number of motorcycles of every type in an effort to crowd Yamaha out of the market. This was a feasible strategy because consumers already had a positive feeling about the Honda brand name.

Brand associations also can facilitate product changes. For example, Tide gradually altered its detergent from a bulky powder to concentrated powder and liquid forms. Positive brand associations help consumers make the transition. Buyers are more willing to try these products and accept them with different features or in new forms.

Competitive Advantage   Finally, brand equity can lead to **competitive advantage,** since a company can sell value rather than compete on the basis of price alone. The firm can charge a premium for many of the intangible dimensions associated with the brand. Brand equity also creates competitive advantages by serving as a barrier to entry. In other words, it may be

Brand associations
The positive attitudes and feelings a brand evokes in consumers' minds.

Competitive advantage
A dimension of brand equity that permits the product to be sold on a value basis rather than a price basis, and may serve as a barrier to entrance against competitive products.

too risky or expensive for another company or brand to compete in the same market. In the 1980s, a battle of the brands among beer companies created an environment in which only the strong survived. Within only 10 years, hundreds of small and local breweries were put out of business by such companies as Anheuser-Busch, Strohs, Miller, and Coors. Nearly every beer company that relied on product processing and procedures rather than building brand equity fell out of contention.

> **CAREER TIP** At Procter & Gamble, "a job is not just a job, it's a career. That's why we recruit the very best people from around the world—and work closely with them to help find their place in the company." P&G is a leading-edge company in developing brand equity. At P&G, careers in brand management allow you to contribute to the growth of the business and the growth of people. Brand managers work with product development, marketing research, sales, finance, and other functions. Check out the career center at the P&G Web site to learn more. **www.pg.com**.

MAINTAINING BRAND VALUE

How many times have you requested a Coke in a restaurant and been asked whether a Pepsi would be okay? Coca-Cola has gone to great lengths to make sure that the Coke brand name does not become a generic name. This is always a danger. Believe it or not, the following used to be brand names: aspirin, escalator, kerosene, nylon, and zipper. To prevent brand names from becoming available for general use, a company must continuously inform the public about its exclusive ownership. Consequently, Coca-Cola waged court battles against retailers who substituted Pepsi when Coke was ordered. Without such efforts, Coke could have lost its trademark exclusivity. Similarly, General Foods, owner of the Jell-O brand, tries to keep the name proprietary.

Often, the first manufacturer of a new technology or product becomes synonymous with the entire product class. How many times has a friend invited you to go Rollerblading, when in fact you would be in-line skating? Did you grow up believing that Kleenex was another name for facial tissue? Do you ask for a Band-Aid when you want an adhesive bandage? Many people say they are going to Xerox something, but they may be using a Canon or some other brand of copier. To avoid the loss of its exclusivity, Xerox runs advertisements explaining that "Xerox" is its registered trademark and should be used only when referring to the company and its products as opposed to a general process.

DEVELOPING A SUCCESSFUL BRAND NAME

Choosing a brand name may not be easy. In 1997, more than 65,000 new names were added to the 775,000 existing trademarks registered in the United States—that's 250 new names for every day of the week! This poses a challenge to companies that want a memorable and meaningful brand name.[45] Name Lab, Inc., a specialist in this area, identified Geo as a globally ori-

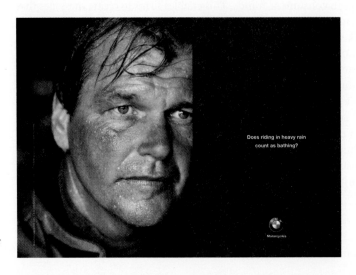

BMW has tried to develop a global brand promotion on a single name known around the world.

Product/Service	Brand Name
Exercise equipment	Soloflex
Vegetables	Green Giant
Batteries	Eveready
Fabric softener	Stay Fresh
Refrigeration trucks	Thermo King
Sweetener	NutraSweet
Oil change service	Jiffy Lube
Reclining chair	La-Z-Boy
Mufflers	Midas

Figure 9-8   Brand Names That Communicate Benefits

ented name for GM's Chevrolet Division to use. It also developed Acura for Honda.[46] In both cases the names are easy to remember, distinctive, positive, and can be used around the world. Because every language has a *k, o,* and short *a* sound, names like Acura, Geo, Coca-Cola, Compaq, and Kodak fit well on the international scene.

Some firms have chosen brand names that communicate product attributes or benefits. For example, Wheaties describes the ingredients of the cereal. When "Breakfast of Champions" is added, we get an image of wholesomeness or goodness. The name Weight Watchers communicates a direct consumer behavior, and it carries strong associations with weight control and health. Recognizing the company's value, Heinz purchased it in 1978 and built it into a major product line by the 1990s.[47] Figure 9-8 identifies several products whose brand name is related to a particular benefit.

Brand names must represent quality and commitment. That's why extensive research is usually conducted to identify whether the name is appropriate and can be used internationally. Standard Oil tested Exxon in 54 languages and more than 150 foreign markets before making a final decision. Marketers must be acutely aware that not all brand names carry the same meaning when translated. For example, the new General Mills cereal, Fringos, designed to be eaten with your fingers, translates into a less than appetizing word for Hungarians. Also consider Chevy Nova, which in Spanish-speaking countries meant "no va" or "no go."

Some brand names are successful because of what they say about the user. Many convey a personality trait that makes the connection directly. Magazines like *Playboy, Cosmopolitan,* and *Glamour* represent attributes readers consider desirable.

JOINT MARKETING OF BRANDS

Joint marketing is cooperation between two companies to sell their brands. A common form of partnership occurs between two goods manufacturers. Since coupons and short-term promotions (such as refund certificates) often cause disloyalty and confusion among customers, replacing those tactics with joint marketing can build business for the cooperating companies. Kraft and Kodak, for example, teamed up in a "Holiday Homecoming" promotion. The partnership hoped to accomplish increased supermarket sales for Kodak products as well as 25 Kraft food items. This type of cooperation is expected to become more frequent.

Some partnerships are established between manufacturers and retailers, such as the team promotion of Tide laundry detergent and the Target brand name. Rubbermaid is another company that has collaborated with large retailers, such as Wal-Mart, Home Depot, and Venture Stores. Kraft Foods, among others, intends to follow suit.[48]

DIVERSITY IN BRAND MARKETING

As U.S. society becomes more diverse, companies are turning their attention to increasing brand equity by meeting the needs of various cultures, nationalities, and age groups.

Marketers are spending increasing amounts of money to promote their brands to ethnic markets. Kraft set aside $24 million for that purpose in 1996. The spending went hand in hand with the development of a new ethnic marketing division within the company.[49] By expanding its menu, Weight Watchers wants to extend its brand name to reach a number of cultural markets new to the company. Its International Selections line offers Italian, Mexican, and Chinese recipes, among others.[50]

Even the Yellow Pages brand recognizes ethnicity. Both AT&T and BellAtlantic have published and distributed telephone directories in foreign languages, such as Russian, Hebrew,

Joint marketing
Cooperation between two companies to sell their products, which tend to be complementary.

Spanish, Portuguese, Chinese, and Malay.[51] This improves service to customers who frequently place international calls.

Generation Xers also are being targeted to increase brand equity. Intel, the world's biggest computer chip maker, has formed a partnership with MTV to target the 18–25 age group. Intel is piggybacking on brand awareness of the widely popular MTV name. In one of its MTV spots, featuring an alternative rock band, a musician can be seen backstage opening e-mail from fans on his laptop.[52] Intel hopes to reach a number of potential customers. Kodak also has a new campaign to bring a high-tech and "cool" appeal to its brand for Generation Xers. The plan is to lure younger buyers, who often have mixed brand loyalties.[53]

PACKAGING AND LABELING

"People don't buy spray paint, they buy spray paint cans." That statement was made in a marketing research report for a major manufacturer in the industry to dramatize the importance of packaging. The research found that most buying decisions were made at the point of purchase. By looking at the color and design of the cans and by reading labels, consumers quickly determined which spray paint would best suit their needs.

Packaging and labeling once served simply to protect and identify the product inside. Now their role has been expanded to seven functions:

- Contain and protect items
- Communicate messages to customers
- Make the product more convenient to use
- Facilitate product storage
- Be environmentally friendly
- Contain product codes
- Protect against misuse

Labels

Information printed on a product's package to inform consumers and help promote the product.

The **labels** on a package inform consumers and help promote the product. The Fair Packaging and Labeling Act of 1966 requires that consumer products carry clear and easily understood labels. They should contain the brand name and symbol, the manufacturer's name and address, the product content and amount, and recommended uses. The law also requires adequate information when value comparisons are made among competitive products.

In 1990 Congress passed the Nutritional Labeling and Education Act, which applies to food.[54] Excluded are meat, poultry, and eggs (covered by U.S. Department of Agriculture regulations) as well as restaurants, delicatessens, and infant formulas. Additional legislation that year required the FDA to develop standard definitions of terms commonly found on products, such as "reduced calories," "high fiber," and "low fat."[55] These laws affect about 15,000 U.S. food packagers as well as many importers. Food labels must say how much fat and saturated fat, cholesterol, carbohydrate, and protein the product contains. They also must specify vitamin content and the percentage of the daily recommended allowances a serving represents. European standards on "diet" claims are even more strict than in the United States. Research shows that the people most likely to read food labels are women who have more education, live with others, are more knowledgeable about nutrition, are concerned about the quality of food they purchase, and believe that current dietary recommendations are important to their health. Less likely readers are men who have less education, live alone, are less concerned about food quality, are less knowledgeable about nutrition, and believe that the current dietary recommendations are unimportant.[56]

The Labeling of Hazardous Art Materials Act (LHAMA) of 1990, addresses another product category. The U.S. Public Interest Research Group (PIRG) lobbied for this legislation because it believed that a wide variety of suppliers inadequately warned consumers of chronic and long-term health risks related to certain chemicals used in their products.[57]

Marketers must take care to ensure that packages are properly labeled.[58] Both consumers and marketers benefit, particularly when health and safety issues are involved.

ETHICAL ISSUES SURROUNDING PRODUCT SAFETY AND LIABILITY

The Consumer Product Safety Act of 1972 created the Consumer Product Safety Commission (CPSC) to police consumer goods. It has broad authority over the end-product, can require recalls and redesigns, and even inspects production facilities. For example, on September 5, 1992, the CPSC recalled 3.5 million smoke detectors because of a possible defect.[59] Of significance is its ability to bring criminal charges against companies and individuals who develop unsafe products.

Product liability refers to the fact that marketers and manufacturers are held responsible for injuries and damages caused by a faulty product. In one case the CPSC found that more than 7,000 people were being injured monthly on three-wheel all-terrain vehicles (ATVs), most of them made by Honda and Kawasaki. Although the number of accidents was well known to dealers and distributors, only when the CPSC applied pressure did the makers agree to stop marketing the product in the United States. Many people believe consumers had the right to know about the ATV injuries. Clearly, wider publicity about the hazards would have meant lost sales.

The liability issue involves the right to safety and the manufacturer's responsibility for designing safe products and for informing the public about any dangers. Most companies fulfill this obligation through the product warranty and, in extreme cases, product recalls.

Product liability
The responsibility of marketers and manufacturers for injuries and damages caused by a faulty product.

PRODUCT WARRANTIES

Warranties are written or implied expectations about product performance under use conditions. An *express warranty* is a written statement about the content or quality of a product and the manufacturer's responsibility to repair or replace it if it fails to perform. For example, an express warranty may indicate that an item is handcrafted in the United States, or may use such general terms as "unconditionally guaranteed" or "fully guaranteed," or may be a technical description of the goods. In the past, when consumers made claims under a warranty, some unethical manufacturers made it very difficult for them to receive satisfaction. General warranty statements came to lack meaning in many cases.

To combat this problem, Congress passed the Magnuson-Moss Warranty–Federal Trade Commission Improvement Act in 1975. Essentially, the law requires that express warranties be written in clear language and indicate which parts or components are covered and which are not. If repair is included in the express warranty, it must occur within a reasonable time, free of charge. A full warranty states that either the merchandise will be repaired or the purchase price refunded if the product does not work after repair.

Many retailers pressure their suppliers to take back any product a customer returns for any reason. Companies like Wal-Mart have a very liberal return policy. This provides feedback on product performance and builds good customer relations, which in turn helps gain market share.

An *implied warranty* is an unwritten guarantee that the product or service will do the job it is intended to do. All products, even if not accompanied by a written statement, have an implied warranty based on the Uniform Commercial Code (UCC). Adopted in 1952, the UCC is a federal statute affecting the sale of goods and giving consumers the right to reject a product if it does not meet their needs. Many states also have laws protecting consumers.

Warranty
Implied or written expectations about product performance under use conditions.

PRODUCT RECALLS

A **product recall** is the withdrawal of a potentially harmful product from the market, by either a manufacturer or the federal government, for its repair, replacement, or discontinuation. The Consumer Product Safety Commission (CPSC) is the federal agency responsible for protecting consumers from product-related injuries. It establishes standards for product design and instructions. It also requires manufacturers to meet safety standards through product testing. Manufacturers and retailers are required by law to notify the CPSC if they find a defective product that may result in injury.

When a manufacturer realizes a product is defective, its response can inspire consumer confidence and actually *promote* sales. In chapter 4 we described the actions of Johnson & Johnson during the Tylenol scare in 1982.[60] The unprecedented recall brought tremendous positive publicity to the company. When Tylenol went back on the shelves, consumers made it the top-selling pain reliever.

Consumers do not always respond to product recalls. For instance, Chrysler recalled 4.5 million minivans with defective tailgate latches in March 1995. After 12 months, only 28 percent of affected customers had responded. A recall of defective seat belts by 11 automakers, which involved 8.8 million vehicles, received an even weaker response—only 5.7 percent among Nissan owners.[61] Much disinterest may be due to a notice that doesn't convey a sense

Product recall
The withdrawal from the market, by either a manufacturer or the federal government, and repair, replacement, or discontinuation of a potentially harmful product.

of urgency. In its recall letter, Chrysler did not mention a "defective" part or that passengers had fallen out the back of the vans in accidents, as was shown on news broadcasts.[62]

In contrast, Sears realized in May 1996 that dishwashers manufactured for it by Whirlpool had a defective wiring harness that could cause a fire. The Sears recall proclaimed in large red letters: "Important Safety Notice. Dishwasher Rework—Potential Fire Hazard. Please Give This Your Immediate Attention." Within three days the response rate was 20 percent.[63] Even when a company meets its legal obligations, the ethics of the situation may require more.

Throughout this chapter we have explored a wide range of strategies—from bundling products into special value units to assuring product safety—that marketers employ to build strong brand equity and give appeal to existing products. In chapter 10 we will look at the special challenges involved in introducing new products and managing products appropriately throughout their life cycle.

 CONNECTED: SURFING THE NET

Intel

www.intel.com

INTEL, THE TOPIC OF THIS CHAPTER'S technology feature, was the first electronic component company to create a brand identity with end users. To learn more about Intel, visit its Web site and answer the following questions.

1. Examine Intel's home page. Without exploring the site farther, what features can you identify that may help the company connect with diversity? Now, try the features. How do they appeal to diverse consumers? Explain.
2. How do the owners' club and Intel forums help the company build customer relationships? Are there any other features on the site that facilitate this connection?
3. Check out "Connected PC." Use a product line depth and breadth matrix (introduced in Figure 9-4) and position Intel in the appropriate box. Explain your choice.
4. Which type of brand strategy does Intel use? Also note its branding approach and the possible reasons for this particular choice.

Starbucks

occ.com/starbucks/index.html

THIS CHAPTER'S RELATIONSHIPS FEATURE is "STARBUCKS Extends Brand Name through Joint Ventures." Learn more about Starbucks at its jobline site and answer the following questions.

1. Check out the various departments in the "Home Office." How does it describe Starbucks' marketing department? Relate it to what you have learned about branding in this chapter.
2. Read about the history of Starbucks, where you will also learn about locations, accounts, business ventures, product line, and so forth. One useful marketing scheme to help develop effective strategies is consumer product classifications. How can Starbucks' products be classified? Explain.
3. How do you think the company's community involvement supports connections with customers?
4. What are other Starbucks business ventures, not mentioned in this chapter's relationships feature? How can they help build business for the company?

CHAPTER SUMMARY

OBJECTIVE 1: Describe the major dimensions used by marketers to differentiate their products from competitors. Understand bundling and unbundling.

Products can be core, branded, and augmented. The core prod-

uct represents the most basic functions and benefits. Some call this the generic product. The branded product adds characteristics that help consumers differentiate it from others. The augmented product includes such features as delivery, warranty, and customer service. A bundling strategy combines several products into one offering sold together. When products are bundled, they provide more value to the buyer than if each were sold separately.

OBJECTIVE 2: Understand consumer and business product classifications based on how and why products are purchased and consumed.

Five categories are used to classify consumer products. Unsought products are bought on the spur of the moment. They include novelty, impulse, and low-involvement items. Emergency products are bought because of unexpected events, such as an accident or theft. Convenience products are inexpensive and are usually purchased near home. Brand name and wide distribution are very important for these items. Shopping items are selected after comparisons are made. They tend to be carefully chosen and are kept for a long time. Specialty products have unique characteristics and value. They are often high-involvement purchases.

Business products are divided into capital, production, and operations products, depending on their primary use. Capital products include installations such as offices and factories, and equipment such as delivery vans and computers. These products last for a long time. Production products become part of other products. This category includes raw and processed materials, components, and subassemblies. Operations products help run the business. These include services such as accounting and waste removal, and office supplies like business forms and cleaning products.

OBJECTIVE 3: Know how organizations make product line decisions that determine what will be sold, including the degree of standardization chosen for global markets.

A product line may comprise one item or a number of related products. Companies may have one or more product lines, each with many or few items. The term *depth* refers to the number of items in a product line; the term *breadth* refers to the number of lines the company offers. Most companies with broad lines are relatively larger; those with narrow lines may be large or small. The degree to which products should be standardized is a major consideration for global firms. Some organizations pursue standardization to benefit from the resulting scale economies while others use a local strategy to respond to local needs.

OBJECTIVE 4: Recognize that branding and brand strategies are important aspects of building and maintaining a brand name.

A brand is distinguished from the product in general or other brands. Brands signify the "personality" of a product. The brand name and trademark can provide immediate recognition and credibility. Consequently, companies must register and protect trademarks. This is particularly challenging in global markets because stolen brand names and counterfeit products are so prevalent. There are several brand strategies. The generic approach involves no brand name. The individual strategy uses a unique name for each product line. The family brand is one name that covers all products in the line. Manufacturer brands are synonymous with the company that owns them. Private label brands are names used by wholesalers or retailers for products supplied to them. Combining two or more of these strategies is called a hybrid approach.

OBJECTIVE 5: Know how to create brand equity—the value associated with a product's name.

A strong brand name is extremely valuable, but developing that name is not simple. First, the name must be selected with care. It should be acceptable globally, represent quality and commitment, and be protected legally. A good brand can easily be extended to additional products as they are developed. Second, brand equity must be created by devoting company resources to each of its five dimensions: brand awareness, brand loyalty, perceived quality, brand associations, and competitive advantage. Third, care must be taken to protect the brand so it does not become a generic name for the product.

OBJECTIVE 6: Discuss the many legal and ethical issues surrounding brand and packaging decisions.

Federal laws and codes require that labels clearly identify the brand and manufacturer and warn consumers of safety hazards associated with use. Product liability holds marketers responsible for injuries and damages caused by a faulty product. Warranties refer to how products perform when used. In many cases, manufacturers are legally obligated to replace or repair faulty products. Express warranties are in writing. An implied warranty is unwritten. Essentially, a product should perform as it was designed. A product recall is instituted by the government or manufacturer to withdraw or modify a product. This occurs when a product is defective, especially if the potential for injury exists.

REVIEW YOUR UNDERSTANDING

1. What is a product? Give several examples.
2. What are core, branded, and augmented products?
3. What is bundling and unbundling?
4. What are five categories of consumer products? What are three categories of business products? Give examples.
5. What is a product line? Unit? SKU?
6. What is a broad and deep product line? What is a narrow and shallow product line? Give examples.
7. What are global products and brands?
8. What is joint marketing of products? Give an example.
9. What is brand equity? How is it developed?
10. Why is it important to secure trademarks?
11. Name and describe five brand categories.
12. What are the functions of packaging?
13. What is product liability?

DISCUSSION OF CONCEPTS

1. Imagine that you are a marketing manager at IBM responsible for the sale of personal computers to individual consumers. How would you describe your product in terms of core, branded, and augmented characteristics? Which of these do you feel is most important?
2. What are some advantages of a bundling strategy over an unbundling strategy? Disadvantages?
3. Name the five categories of products based on consumer buying behavior. Why is it so important for marketers to understand the category of their product?
4. Discuss the differences between product line breadth and depth. What are some advantages and disadvantages of each combination of breadth and depth?
5. Classify each of the following companies in terms of product

line breadth and depth and explain your reasoning: Sears, 7-Eleven, Hallmark Cards, Wal-Mart, Kmart, Victoria's Secret.

6. If you were the marketing manager at a company with a broad product line, which of the six brand strategies would you likely select? What factors would affect your decision? What if the product line were narrow?

7. What are the most important activities involved in developing a successful brand name? Once the name is developed, how is brand equity formed?

8. Name the key functions of packaging. Which do you feel is most important? Does this vary by product?

9. The Consumer Product Safety Commission is a government entity with the power to bring criminal charges against companies and individuals who develop and market unsafe products. Is it fair to consider marketers criminals if consumers are injured by their company's products? Why or why not?

KEY TERMS AND DEFINITIONS

Augmented product: Product with characteristics that enhance its value beyond that of the core and branded product.

Brand: A distinguishing name and/or symbol to identify and differentiate products from those of competitors.

Brand associations: The positive attitudes and feelings a brand evokes in consumers' minds.

Brand awareness: The extent to which consumers recognize the brand and are likely to include it among the set of brands they consider.

Brand equity: The assets linked with the brand name and symbol that add value to the product.

Brand insistence: A dimension of brand equity that makes consumers unwilling to accept substitutes for the brand.

Brand loyalty: A dimension of brand equity that causes consumers to choose one brand over others available.

Branded product: The core product plus the characteristics that allow the consumer to differentiate it from similar products.

Breadth: The number of different lines a company markets.

Bundling strategy: A strategy in which several products are combined into a single offering.

Capital product: A costly item that lasts a long time but does not become part of any finished product.

Competitive advantage: A dimension of brand equity that permits the product to be sold on a value basis rather than a price basis, and may serve as an entry barrier to competitive products.

Convenience product: A relatively inexpensive item that consumers purchase frequently and with minimum effort.

Core product: The essential physical item or intangible service that the customer receives.

Depth: The number of items in a product line.

Emergency product: A product purchased due to an unexpected event and for which the consumer has an urgent need.

Family brand strategy: Strategy in which a single brand name covers the entire group of products in the company's line(s).

Generic brand strategy: Strategy in which no brand name is used.

Hybrid brand strategy: A combination of two or more brand strategies.

Individual brand strategy: Strategy in which there is a unique name for each major product or product line.

Item: A specific version of a product within a product line.

Joint marketing: Cooperation between two companies to sell their products, which tend to be complementary.

Labels: Information printed on a product's package to inform consumers and help promote the product.

Manufacturer's brand (national brand): Brand named after the manufacturer.

Perceived brand quality: The degree to which a brand consistently produces satisfaction by meeting customer expectations.

Private brand (private label): The name wholesalers or retailers attach to products they resell for numerous suppliers.

Product: Any physical object, service, idea, person, event, place, or organization offered to satisfy consumers' needs and wants.

Product liability: The responsibility of marketers and manufacturers for injuries and damages caused by a faulty product.

Product line: Closely related products marketed by the organization.

Product recall: The withdrawal from the market, by either a manufacturer or the federal government, and the repair, replacement, or discontinuation of a potentially harmful product.

Shopping product: A purchase generally made only after the consumer has compared several alternatives.

Specialty item: A product with unique characteristics that provides unusual value to the purchaser.

Supplies: Consumable items used for business operations.

Trademark (brand mark): A distinctive form or figure that identifies the brand.

Unsought product: An item that consumers don't think about frequently and for which they don't perceive much need.

Warranty: Implied or written expectations about product performance under use conditions.

REFERENCES

1. S.L. Mintz, "What's Good for General Motors . . . ," *CFO*, August 1996, pp. 20–24; Rebecca Blumenstein, "While Going Global, GM Slips at Home," *Wall Street Journal*, January 8, 1996, pp. B1, B4; and Rebecca Blumenstein and Gabriella Stern, "GM Decides to Reposition Its Brands Rather than Eliminate Most Models," *Wall Street Journal*, August 30, 1996, pp. A3, A4.

2. U.S. Department of Commerce, Bureau of the Census, *Statistical Abstract of the United States* (Washington DC: Government Printing Office, 1989), p. 423.

3. "The Quest for Cool," *USA Today*, September 4, 1996, p. B1

4. "Promoting a Sure Thing: Guarantees Multiply," *USA Today*, August 13, 1996, p. B1.

5. "Car Manufacturers Announce the CARE Initiative," www.tecWeb.com/wlibrary/care.htm. Site visited August 10, 1997.

6. Lori Petersen, "Study Confirms Impulse Buying on Rise," *Promote*, October 12, 1987, p.6.

7. Karen Blumenthal, "Compaq to Unveil Three New Lines at Lower Prices for Business Market," *Wall Street Journal Interactive Edition*, July 22, 1996.

8. http://nw.opp.psu.edu/oper/asrv/rcyc/rcycgd3.htm, site visited January 8, 1997.
9. Advertisement, *Fortune*, May 27, 1996, pp. 60–61.
10. "P&G Sees Record on Shampoo Sales," *Nation*, June 28, 1996, p. B3.
11. Riccardo A. Davis, "Kodak Rethinks Strategy: Marketer Will Focus on Core Photo Brands, New Products," *Advertising Age*, May 10, 1993, p. 48.
12. "Kodak Zooms in on Younger Customers," *Wall Street Journal*, April 12, 1996, p. B5.
13. "Kodak Competes with Fuji on the Russian Market of Films for Cameras," *Izvestiia*, May 21, 1996, p. F2.
14. "Make it Simple," *Business Week*, September 9, 1996, p. 96.
15. Susan P. Douglas and C. Samuel Craig, *Global Marketing Strategy* (New York, NY: McGraw-Hill, 1995), p. 214.
16. Patricia Sellers and Patty De Llosa, "How Coke is Kicking Pepsi's Can," *Fortune*, October 28, 1996, p. 70–84.
17. Glen Collins and Stephanie Stram, "Can Pepsi Become the Coke of Snacks?" *New York Times*, November 3, 1996, p. 5.
18. "IBM Unveils Global Lotus Notes," *Computer Reseller News*, June 17, 1996, p. 71.
19. "Rubbermaid Inc. Reorganizes its Global Marketing Efforts," *Cleveland Plain Dealer*, June 28, 1996, p. 2.
20. Karl Schoenberger, "Motorola Bets Big on China," *Fortune*, May 27, 1996, pp. 116–124.
21. David A. Aaker, *Managing Brand Equity*, (New York: The Free Press, 1991), p. 7.
22. David Arnold, *The Handbook of Brand Management*, (Reading, MA: Addison-Wesley, 1992) pp. xvii.
23. "Can P&G Make Eagle Fly in Snack Market?" *Chicago Tribune* (National Edition), May 8, 1996, p. B3.
24. "Broad, Deep, Long, and Heavy," *Economist*, November 16, 1996, p. 72.
25. Diane Crispell and Kathleen Brandenburg, "What's in a Brand?" *American Demographics*, 1993, pp. 26–29, 31–32.
26. Betsy Morris, "The Brand's the Thing," *Fortune*, March 4, 1996, p. 72.
27. Ibid.
28. Ibid.
29. "Cancer Society's Deal to Sell Its Name Sparks Protests," *Marketing News*, September 23, 1996, p. 5.
30. Stacy Kravetz, "Spoofing Ads is Risky for Entrepreneurs," *Wall Street Journal*, December 12, 1996, p. B1.
31. "Whose Idea is It Anyway," *Economist*, November 12, 1988, p. 73.
32. Robert S. Greenberger and Craig S. Smith, "Illegal Disk Piracy Thrives Despite Efforts by Chinese," *Wall Street Journal Interactive Edition*, April 24, 1997.
33. Mark K. Magner, "Kmart Wins Trademark Feud in Singapore," *Journal of Commerce* (November, 1991): p. A1.
34. David Stipp, "Farewell my Logo," *Fortune*, May 27, 1996, pp. 128–140.
35. Gerry Meyers, "Another View on Private Labels: They're Not Going to Fade Away," *Advertising Age*, April 25, 1994, p. 26.
36. Jonathon Berry, "Attack of the Fighting Brands," *Business Week*, May 2, 1995, p. 125.
37. Morris, "The Brand's the Thing," p. 84.
38. Adapted from Aacker, *Managing Brand Equity*, p. 4.
39. "Make Room in the Kitchen for yet Another Appliance," *New York Times*, September 16, 1996, p. C6.
40. Morris, "The Brand's the Thing," p. 82.
41. Crispell and Brandenburg, "What's in a Brand?"
42. Hannah Miller, "Soft Drink Has No Wine, but Plenty of Cheer," *Advertising Age*, June 1, 1992, p. 3, 4.
43. Michael Firth, "Price Setting and the Value of a Strong Brand Name," *International Journal of Research in Marketing*, December 1993, pp. 381–386.
44. William M. Weilbacher, *Brand Marketing* (Lincolnwood, IL: NTC Business Books, 1993), p. 51.
45. Gene Koprowski, "The Name Game," *Marketing Tools*, September 1996, http://www.marketingtools.com.
46. Susan Moffat, "Foreign Car Sales Go Vroom in Japan," *Fortune*, April 9, 1990, p. 10.
47. Warren Burger, "The Big Freeze at Heinz," *Ad Week's Marketing Week*, August 21, 1989, pp. 20–25.
48. Raju Narisetti, "Joint Marketing with Retailers Spreads," *Wall Street Journal Interactive Edition*, October 24, 1996.
49. "Kraft Hopes Hispanic Market Says Cheese," *Wall Street Journal*, December 13, 1995, p. B5.
50. "Weight Watchers Goes Decidedly Gourmet in Appeal to Boomers' Changing Palate," *Quick Frozen Foods International*, April 1996, p.104.
51. "Diversity Pays Off in a Babel of Yellow Pages," *New York Times*, December 3, 1995, p. A1.
52. Sally Goll Beatty, "Advertising: Intel Targets Ad Campaign at Savvy MTV Viewers," *Wall Street Journal Interactive Edition*, October 28, 1996.
53. "Kodak Zooms in on Younger Customers," *Wall Street Journal*, April 12, 1996, p. B5.
54. Chris Baum, "NLEA Compels Food Packagers to Redesign," *Packaging*, May 1994, p. 21.
55. Andrea Dorfman, "Less Bologna on the Shelves," *Time*, November 5, 1990, p. 79.
56. Pam Demetrakakes, "Packaging Field Gears up for New Labeling Rules," *Packaging*, January 1993, p. 3.
57. Mark Hartley, "For the Sake of Invisible Ink," *Occupational Health & Safety*, December 1993, p. 4.
58. Frances J. Cronin, Cheryl Achterberg, and Laura S. Sims, "Translating Nutrition Facts into Action: Helping Consumers Use the New Food Label," *Nutrition Today*, September-October 1993, p. 30.
59. "3.5 Million Smoke Detectors Recalled," *New York Times*, September 6, 1992, p. 48.
60. "Tylenol Containing Strychnine Is Found in California as Consumer Fears Mount," *Wall Street Journal*, October 6, 1982, p. 2.
61. Oscar Suris and Nichole M. Christian, "Will Consumers Respond to Ford's Recall Notice?" *Wall Street Journal*, May 8, 1996, p. B1.
62. Ibid.
63. Recall letter from Sears, on file with authors.

CASE 9

SARA LEE

WHAT DO THE FOLLOWING BRANDS have in common? Ball Park, Hilshire Farms, Jimmy Dean, Douwe Egberts, Hanes, Leggs, Playtex, Champion, Coach, and Kiwi? They are all part of the $20 billion Sara Lee Corporation, which has leading positions in packaged meats, frozen baked goods, shoe care, coffee, hosiery, and underwear. An interesting question is how all these Sara Lee brands have become household words around the globe. Sara Lee now has operations in more than 40 countries employing more than 141,000 people, and markets branded products in more than 140 nations. The company attributes much of its success to its ability to build and maintain leadership positions through innovation and responsiveness. Consider the tremendous amount of product development that goes into maintaining each one of these product lines. The four major lines of business at Sara Lee are shown below. Each is organized as a discreet profit center, as are some of the products within those lines, and each is led by operating executives with a high degree of authority and accountability for performance. Those who succeed at Sara Lee are measured by how well they perform.

Sara Lee's product depth and breadth are key parts of its overall strategy. Through both acquisition and product development, it has supported a full-line strategy. Product lines do not stand on their own. Their growth strategies are designed to meet or exceed product goals by the following means:

- Build brands and new channels in new ways.
- Achieve and maintain low-cost production worldwide.
- Concentrate development and marketing efforts behind high-margin, value-added products.
- Increase business internationally, focusing on growth in strongly developing economies.

Essentially the Sara Lee focus is on value-added product development, brand-building advertising programs, and strategic acquisitions. Over the years it has enjoyed outstanding success.

The Sara Lee Corporation has had 20 years in a row of record sales and profits.

Recently, the company announced a major restructuring program to focus more resources on key branded leadership positions. Essentially, capital demands on the company will be reduced through less vertical integration within operations. In other words, Sara Lee will divest assets to reduce its manufacturing functions while providing more resources for marketing of leading brands. Resources will be moved away from fixed costs and put into brand building. Management also is considering the divestiture of several businesses with products that have not been able to establish a prominent position in the market.

Sara Lee's Four Major Lines of Business

PACKAGED MEATS AND BAKERY
Packaged Meats:

Aoste	Hillshire Farm	Nobre
Argal	Hygrade	Rudy's Farm
Ball Park	Imperial	Sara Lee
Best's Kosher	Jimmy Dean	Seitz
Bill Mar	Justin Bridou	Sinai 48
Bryan	Kahn's	State Fair
Comby	King Cotton	Stegeman
Dacor	Kir	
Galileo	Marcassou	
Gallo Salame	Mr. Turkey	

Bakery:
Sara Lee
Wolferman's

Food Service:
Monarch

HOUSEHOLD AND BODY CARE

Shoe Care:

Bama	Meltonian
Eri	Tana
Golden Rooster	Tuxan
Kiwi	

Body Care:

Aqua Velva	Radox
Badedas	Sanex
Body Mist	Satina
Brylcreem	Savane
Delial	She
Duschdas	Williams
Quenty	

Baby Care:

Femar	Sanex
Fissan	Zwitsal
Petit Cheri	

Insecticides:

Bloom	Ridsect
Catch	Vapona

PERSONAL PRODUCTS
Intimates and Accessories:

Bali	Lovables
Coach	Playtex
Daisyfresh	Polo/Ralph Lauren
Dim	Rien
Hanes Her Way	Rosy
Just My Size	Wonderbra

COFFEE AND GROCERY
Coffee and Coffee Systems:

Bravo	Maison du Café
Chat Noir	Marcilla
Douwe Egberts	Merrild
Friele	Mocoona
Harris	Piazza d'Dro
Jacqmotte	Soley
Kanis & Gunnink	Superior
	Van Nelle

Tea:
Harris
Pickwick

Grocery:

Bénénuts	Natreen
Borrelnootjes	Natrena
Duyvis	Tijgermootjes
Felix	
Lassie	

Air Fresheners:
Ambi-Pur
Parry's
Tolett

Direct Selling:

Avroy Shlain	Nutri-Metics
House of Fuller	Nuvo Cosmetics
House of Sara Lee	Swissgarde
Hom Care	

Oral Care:
Prodent
Yijianxi
Zendium

Specialty Products:

Abel Auto	Kitten	Valma
Behold	Kiwi/Peli	White King
Biotex	Neutral	
Bloo	Nuclear	
Closan	Tolett	
Endust	Ty-D-Bol	

Knit Products:

Abanderado	Dim	Princesa
Beefy-T	Hanes Her Way	Rinbros
Carter's	HanesWear	ShowToons
Champion	Just My Size	Spalding
Champion Jogbra	Liabel	

Hosiery:

Bellinda	L'eggs	Sheer Comfort
Bonds	Little L'eggs	Sheer Energy
Cameo	Nur Die	Silk Reflections
Diam's	Philippe Matgnon	Smooth Illusions
Dim	Pretty Polly	Smooth Silhouettes
DKNY Coverings	Razzamatazz	Spaniel
Donna Karan	Reliance	
Elbeo	Resilence	
Filodoro		
Hanes		
Hanes Her Way		
Just My Size		
Legacy		

Source: www.saralee.com/corporate/brands/content.htm.

After downsizing, Sara Lee will outsource many of its products and concentrate on building each product line through its distribution, advertising, and selling skills. *Forbes* points out that an earlier experiment with this strategy did not work very well for the company. In 1993, in an attempt to double sales and profits within five years, it closed Aris-Isotoner's highly productive glove factory in the Philippines and purchased products from suppliers in other parts of the world. They proved to be more expensive, however, and difficulties with manufacturing, distribution, and marketing coordination further decreased profits.

One reason for Sara Lee's greater emphasis on marketing is the changing nature of shoppers and new channel options that require greater attention and flexibility. For example, the L'eggs brand already participates in two Internet shopping ventures and has a Web site stocked with health, political, family, career, and other news of interest to women. A spokesperson for Sara Lee says: "Pantyhose is a pretty boring subject unless you work for the company [so] they wanted to build brand recognition with users in general by providing useful, entertaining information." Another channel option is being pursued by Hillshire Farms through a "country smokehouse" located at 200 new Phillips 66 gas stations. In yet another case, Ball Park brands are being developed for vending machines. Sara Lee wants to free up resources to concentrate on these and other ways to market its brands.

1. *In looking at the Sara Lee brands, would you categorize the organization relative to its competitors as having a broader or narrower line, a deeper or shallower line? Why?*

2. *What are the issues Sara Lee has faced historically in developing successful brands? What issues will it face in maintaining brand value and in reaching its objectives?*

3. *How does Sara Lee use the concept of core products, branded products, and augmented products as elements in its marketing strategy?*

4. *Do you believe Sara Lee's strategy of moving resources away from manufacturing and into marketing will enhance its competitiveness and provide better opportunities to build brand equity? In your analysis, assess the role of manufacturing in supporting strong brands in the marketplace. What steps should Sara Lee take to ensure that the problems with Aris-Isotoner are not repeated?*

SOURCES: Sara Lee Web site, http://www.saralee.com; Gretchen Lorgenson, "Been There, Tried That," *Forbes*, October 20, 1997, www.forbes.com; Jerry Khermouch, "Jordan Goes On-line for Gatorade: Leggs Site Expansion Is Lifestyle," *Brandweek*, February 19, 1996, p. 14; and Stephanie Thompson, "Hillshire Grows Line with TenderSmoked," *Brandweek*, October 28, 1996, p. 5.

Sara Lee Contribution to Revenues by Line of Business

Sales: $19.7 Billion 1997 Worldwide Sales	Profit: $1.9 Billion 1997 Worldwide Income
Packaged Meats and Bakery: 39%	Packaged Meats and Bakery: 23%
Coffee and Grocery: 14%	Coffee and Grocery: 23%
Household and Body Care: 9%	Household and Body Care: 12%
Personal Products: 38%	Personal Products: 40%

Source: www.saralee.com, site visited January 9, 1998.

Product Planning, Development, and Management

Objectives

1. Provide a framework to evaluate the extent to which existing or new products are marketed to existing or new market segments.

2. Understand how the characteristics of innovation influence the speed with which they are accepted.

3. Know the steps used to develop new products from the initial idea through commercialization.

4. Show how the product life cycle concept can be used to build and adjust marketing strategies over time.

5. Recognize how innovations are adopted by consumers by being spread from group to group.

HAVE YOU EVER HAD AN IDEA for a great product? If you're like most people, you have. Then, months or years later when you see it on store shelves, you want to kick yourself for not pursuing it. Well, the partners of The Flagship Group in Englewood, Colorado have lots of great new product ideas. And The Flagship Group makes sure their ideas become reality before anyone else thinks of them. This is the story about how Flagship found a terrific idea and brought it to market.

In 1987, The Flagship Group was organized to develop new products. According to them, new products don't just happen. They are developed through clear research efforts. Successful new products can be created if you know the process and are aware of the traditional kinds of potholes along the road to success.

The Flagship Group established a relationship with a corporation to explore for, identify, and develop new product ideas. Through the development phase, Flagship essentially acted as a general partner. Flagship designed the consumer research, identified core competencies of the corporation, contributed expertise and experience, and developed marketing strategies, the product, promotion programs, and target marketing. The corporation functioned as a limited partner and put up the money to explore and develop the new opportunities. When the product was ready to launch, the corporation took over using its existing distribution channels and marketing infrastructure, and Flagship received royalties.

Around the same time, in Southern California, an emergency-room doctor noticed that children coming to the hospital were often clutching a doll. To take their mind off their injury or illness, the doctor would often talk to the children about why that doll was their favorite. Frequently the children would say that the doll looked like her or had hair like hers. The doctor's fiancée, a birthday-party consultant, also noticed that lonelier children used dolls as their alter ego and as a self-esteem builder. From these simple observations came the pioneering idea of custom-made, personalized dolls made to look like that particular child.

The couple put together their ideas in an inexpensive brochure, bought a small local mailing list, sent out the brochures, and went on a five-day vacation. They returned to find their mailbox crammed with orders. Now they had to turn their idea into reality. Then went to doll shows to learn how to make dolls: molds, wigs, clothes, and the like. While they continued to operate with some success over the next 22 months, they were very undercapitalized.

To create a doll that looks just like a child, My Twinn asks for a photo and a "Personal Profile" (the order form). This includes face shape; skin tone; color of eyes, lashes, and brows; eyebrow thickness and shape; hair color, length, and style; and birthmarks, moles, and freckles. An artist uses the information to create the individual doll. As you can see from the picture, My Twinn does extraordinary work.

Meanwhile, one of the Flagship partners received a mailing from My Twinn. He liked the idea and ordered a doll for his child. A year later, two Flagship partners were passing through the town in which the doll was made, and, on a whim, stopped by to meet the owners. The founders had great vision, but clearly realized their resources limited that vision. As they were driving away, the partners looked at each other with a "Are you thinking what I'm thinking?" look, then went back and started the dialogue about buying the company. Flagship bought My Twinn and moved it to Littleton, Colorado.

Flagship jumped right into the doll business, learning it from A to Z. They accessed many face shape resources, including doctors, dentists, photographers, anatomists, sculptors, ophthalmologists, and artists. They found a company that makes eyes for people that lost eyes and spent weeks studying eyes. They found the best hair they could, of high quality vinyl. They hired local artisans to create the high-quality, custom look.[1]

Like Flagship, most organizations must come up with new products. When a business ceases to innovate it is usually only a matter of time before decay sets in. Therefore, most companies have systematic ways of ensuring that new products enter the stream of business activities. This chapter describes how companies remain vital by constant focus on developing and managing new products.

THE CONCEPTS OF PRODUCT DEVELOPMENT AND PRODUCT MANAGEMENT

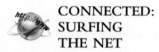
Product mix

All the product lines and products a company offers.

A winning company doesn't rest—it innovates. New products invigorate organizations. They create enthusiasm among employees even before they excite the market. They are absolutely essential to competitive advantage. Companies that fail to innovate usually fail, period. Even those that are slower than competitors will find their customer connections strained or broken as leading-edge organizations step in and step ahead. At the same time, winning companies don't prematurely abandon their existing products. They nurture and support them like old friends. Organizations make direct connections with customers through products. Without these, no relationship can exist. Products form the fundamental substance of all business exchanges. Whether these connections remain solid depends largely on the ability of marketers to introduce and manage products. In fact, 81 percent of chief executives say innovation is the key to growth in their organization.[2] This chapter explores how long-term, tight connections are made through technological innovations and product management that fulfill market potential.

Speed and responsiveness make sheer company size a major force shaping the marketplace today. The ability to develop products quickly is extremely important in gaining a competitive advantage.[3] Companies are compressing the amount of time required to turn an idea into a marketable product. This is multiplying the number of products offered as well as shortening the life of products in the market. Because of these trends, executives are emphasizing the firm's **product mix.** They also are adjusting the depth and breadth of product lines in response to rapidly changing market forces. Excellent product management is considered essential for creating superior customer value.

Organizations must continue to manage existing products, and they must have the ability to identify, find, or create new ones. In a classic study, the consulting firm of Booz, Allen & Hamilton found that 28 percent of company growth comes from products introduced in the past five years.[4] Yet, new product development is risky and expensive. About 56 percent of introductions fail within five years, and about 45 percent of new product development resources are spent on failures. In fact, companies usually have to come up with 13 new product ideas before they hit on one that works.[5] Research shows that a common reason innovations fail is the lack of strategic direction.[6] With the right strategy products can provide sufficient profits necessary to reach the organization's objectives and cover the costs of developing and growing new products.

The main objective of product management is to ensure a steady flow of products that support the company's mission. New technologies that were once restricted to a few giant corporations are now accessible to numerous small and midsized firms. In addition, markets are expanding both domestically and internationally through global networks of communication, distribution, and business relationships. All these factors allow both large and small organizations to introduce products very rapidly. Companies entering the 21st century will be making even more new and innovative product introductions.

There are many important elements to consider in product development and management as shown in Figure 10-1. This chapter begins with a look at how the product mix affects growth. Organizations sometimes grow by focusing on existing products and segments, but much more growth comes from innovation in products and markets. Next we explore types of innovations and factors that affect how rapidly they are accepted by potential customers. Once a company decides the role of new products for accomplishing objectives, it employs a new product development process. We explore a successful process—from formulation of new product strategy to product launch. This is followed by a section on product management approaches, particularly the policies and organizational structures that foster innovation. Finally, we examine how the product life cycle and the diffusion process relate to decisions ranging from introduction to discontinuation.

PRODUCT PLANNING AND TYPES OF INNOVATION

PRODUCT PLANNING

Every business needs to develop a product plan consistent with its overall marketing strategy. **Product planning** outlines the focus given to core businesses (current products in current segments); market development (new segments for current products); product development (new products for current segments); or diversification (products totally new to the company for new segments).

Product planning
The focus given to core businesses, market development, product development and diversification.

Product planning decisions are influenced by market segment strategies. Marketers must decide how much emphasis to place on the existing product lines and segments and how much on developing new products and markets. Figure 10-2 depicts these fundamental choices.

Core Business Focus   A core business focus emphasizes the marketing of existing products to existing market segments. Even this requires careful decisions about whether to maintain, expand, or eliminate current products, depending on market conditions, the age of the product, and competitive factors. Firms that do not make these adjustments usually must retreat.[7] This may become evident in plant consolidations, fewer and fewer products, divestment of lines of business, and/or withdrawal from certain markets.

Many strong companies achieve success by focusing on their core products and market segments. This doesn't mean that all avenues for expansion are closed off. The core business

Figure 10-1   The Concepts of Product Planning, Development and Management

	Existing Products	New Products
Existing Market Segments	**Core Product Focus** Maintain, expand, or harvest current products	**Product Development** Improve products Add to product line
New Market Segments	**Market Development** Add new market segment(s)	**Diversification** Add new product lines Expand into unrelated businesses

Figure 10-2   Product Planning Options

can provide earnings to support other options, such as Coke's aggressive global strategy. Rather than rely on its U.S. operations, Coke moved into new markets to become one of the best-known companies in the world. Sometimes companies move away from their core business and then return to their traditional focus. In the mid-1990s, Eastman Kodak sold three major business units it had acquired or recently developed, accounting for more than 23 percent of its sales and $3.7 billion in annual revenues. The Sterling Winthrop drug unit, L&F Products, and clinical diagnostics division were peddled in an effort to refocus on Kodak's imaging operations. This action reversed nearly a decade of diversification and showed the company's determination to regain prominence in its core business.[8]

Market development

Offering existing products to new market segments.

Market Development   **Market development** occurs when existing products are offered to new segments. Firms may sell directly to these or use new channels of distribution. They also may expand from local markets to regional, national, international, or global markets. Nike is targeting a new segment: Brazilian soccer players and fans. It has closed a $200 million sponsorship deal with the Brazilian team, one of the best in the world. Nike replaces the current sponsor, Umbro, a prominent marketer of soccer equipment, as Brazil's sponsor in the category. Nike is using its ties with the team to forge a cultural connection with Hispanics and soccer fans in the United States. The company targets this new segment with its existing apparel line, simultaneously reaching both national and international markets. In the last two years Nike has signed sponsorships with soccer organizations in the Netherlands, Italy, Russia, South Korea, and Nigeria as well.[9] Studies have shown that successful market development need not involve the same products as long as there is a fit between brand concept and the extension products.[10] For example, Nike could decide to produce badminton and volleyball equipment and easily connect its reputation for footwear with sports that require fast footwork.

Product development

Offering new products to existing market segments.

Line extension

A new product closely related to others in the line.

Product Development   **Product development** occurs when companies make new products for existing market segments. This may take the form of simple improvements to older products or extensions of the product line. A **line extension** is an innovation closely related to other products in the line. Most software companies are continuously introducing improved versions. For example, Microsoft has upgraded its popular Word software several times. Examples of extensions are also numerous. Consider Intel's MMX multimedia chip, which improves PC graphics, video, and audio performance. Intel saw it as an addition to a product already in the marketplace. Unlike the Pentium chip, the MMX was not "the next generation," so incorporation was expected to occur rapidly.[11]

Whether in the consumer or business market, product lines are continuously expanding. Minnesota Mining and Manufacturing recently added fly-fishing rods to its leisure products. These were available by the time trout season opened and were a huge success against competitors' offerings.[12] Even pizza has product line extensions. Domino's experiments with different sauces, doughs, and exotic toppings to create such new varieties as Garlic Crunch.[13] In the business arena, General Electric has added computer networking and other technology services for its government and commercial customers. Because these services require extensive personal attention to the unique needs of large customers, they are being provided through

GE's new Capital Information Technology Solutions company. GE is thus expanding its product line to benefit a market segment with which it has strong relationships.[14]

Diversification Diversification occurs when new products are introduced into new market segments. Sometimes this is done with extensions of the current business, and sometimes it occurs with totally new ventures. Liz Claiborne, Inc., traditionally a designer of upscale merchandise, is diversifying with the Emma James budget label for department stores. Claiborne also will introduce a new women's wear collection exclusively for Sears and a low-priced line of women's casual knitwear for Wal-Mart. These new segments are expected to generate an additional $200 million in sales within two years.[15]

Often companies diversify by expanding into totally new business product areas. The multibillion-dollar conglomerate Philip Morris has acquired several food companies in order to diversify from its leading brand, Marlboro cigarettes. Given the potential legal liability faced by the tobacco industry, the company may be making wise investments in Miller beer, Post cereals, Maxwell House, General Foods International Coffees, Kraft, and Jell-O. Consistent with the old adage about not putting all of the eggs in one basket, diversification spreads the risk associated with one industry. DuPont Co., historically a slow moving chemical company, is turning to diversification on the theory that diversification breeds growth and stability. DuPont has expanded into biotech agriculture and pharmaceuticals. This adds to the life sciences part of its business. To pay for new acquisitions in this area DuPont sold 20 percent of its wholly owned subsidiary Conoco, Inc. This makes DuPont far more recession-resistant than other companies.[16]

TYPES OF PRODUCT INNOVATION

Marketers classify innovations according to the effect they are likely to have on consumers. **Continuous innovation** is a minor change in an existing product, such as a new style or model, that can be easily adopted without significant alterations in consumer behavior. The product usually is familiar. Kraft Foods is reinventing frozen pizza with DiGiorno, which uses new technology that allows the crust to bake rather than be reheated when prepared at home. Since the pizza tastes more like takeout, the ad theme is "It's not delivery, it's DiGiorno."[17] The product is new, but it requires little or no consumer behavior change.

Red Devil—"the first hand tool that didn't forget the hand"— also used continuous innovation. The company worked with Deskey Associates to ergonomically redesign its entire product line, beginning with wood scrapers and drywall tools. Deskey's executive vice president said the new design adhered to the foremost principle of product development: "Touch the consumer in the most direct way; the more physical the connection, the better."[18]

A **dynamically continuous innovation** endows a familiar product with additional features and benefits that require or permit consumers to alter some aspect of their behavior. When auto companies introduced the antilock braking system (ABS), consumers needed to adjust driving habits. Rather than pump the brakes in an emergency, they had to learn that ABS works best when the brakes are totally compressed. Manufacturers were careful to educate drivers about the benefits and requirements of ABS so that reaction to the new system would be positive. Another example is plain paper fax machines. Users no longer had to stock special heat-sensitive paper. Regular paper would do, which made it easier to write on and photocopy a fax.

A **discontinuous innovation** is an entirely new product with new functions. Sometimes called "new to the world," these products require behavioral changes by users. The high degree of novelty makes consumers think about the product's benefits and costs prior to adoption. Examples include cellular telephones, satellite-transmitted maps for autos, and heart pumps. When automobile airbags were introduced, buyers had to evaluate the benefits carefully before committing the additional funds for the optional purchase. Eventually airbags became standard equipment and were included in the vehicle price.

The Internet is a discontinuous innovation that has affected nearly every aspect of life, including entertainment, education, and business. It has led to the development of other entirely new products, such as Internet kiosks, sometimes called Internet cyberbooths. Atcom/Info developed this equivalent of a pay phone, now installed in 167 locations across the country. The kiosks enable the two-thirds of business travelers who do not carry laptops to check the stock market or e-mail the office between flights for only 33 cents a minute.[19]

Dictation software is another example. The technology known as general-purpose continuous-speech recognition enables users to speak into a microphone at a normal pace

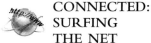

CONNECTED: SURFING THE NET

www.ge.com

Visit the Web site of the company that "brings good things to life." You'll find answers to questions about General Electric products for the home, business and industry services, and company information. Also be sure to explore GE in Germany—now on-line!

Continuous innovation
A minor alteration in an existing product, such as a new style or model, that can be easily adopted without significant changes in consumer behavior.

Dynamically continuous innovation
A familiar product with additional features and benefits that require or permit consumers to alter some aspect of their behavior.

Discontinuous innovation
An entirely new product with new functions.

and read the words on a screen as they are said. If the computer makes an error, it can be corrected with spoken commands.[20] This revolutionary program is not widely available yet, but once its benefits become apparent to consumers, it may be as commonplace as the Internet.

WHY INNOVATIONS SUCCEED

Research reveals novelty alone does not ensure new product success. What matters most is how well innovation meets customer needs.[21] Several specific factors influence consumer acceptance of new products: relative advantage, compatibility, complexity, trialability, and observability.

Relative Advantage Relative advantage is the amount of perceived superiority of the new product in comparison to existing ones. Marketers must make it easy for consumers to recognize the benefits of switching from the old product. Often this entails a trade-off. A new word-processing program may be easier to use but requires additional training. Consumers need to be persuaded that the training investment will yield benefits, like time savings and ease of use. Otherwise, they probably won't purchase the new program.

To increase the perceived superiority of its upgraded software versions, Microsoft offers counseling sessions that explain the benefits and how the upgrade will meet user needs.[22] It's especially important for computer software to have a relative advantage, considering the overwhelming number of offerings. Microsoft's Office 97 was designed to be more "Web Savvy" and includes tools to import Web site graphics. Considering the Web's popularity and usefulness, consumers easily saw the advantages of this updated version.[23] In 1998, the U.S. Department of Justice filed suit against Microsoft, claiming essentially that it uses Windows to dominate other markets—for example, to gain a choke hold on the Internet. According to the Department of Justice, by combining a Web browser with the Windows operating system, Windows 98 would have an unfair advantage over companies like Netscape which only has a browser. According to this claim, ultimately the consumer could suffer because of less competition in the market.[24] Microsoft counters that it is doing what the consumer wants which will help increase its market share.

Compatibility Compatible products fit easily into the consumer's current thinking or system. To succeed, a new product should be consistent with the values and beliefs of target consumers. Furthermore, if additional products are required to make a product usable, they should be included in the package. Consumers who have to seek out these additions or who find installation difficult are likely to reject the product. This is one reason many organizations now have 800 numbers to answer questions.

"Cyberbooths" are popular among business travelers who do not carry laptops.

When deciding to purchase an automobile, most people consider safety important. Understanding that this is a value, companies are working on high-tech ways to make driving safer. For example, GM's Delco division has created a blind-spot radar to warn drivers when it's unsafe to change lanes. Texas Instruments has developed a thermal-image camera that eliminates glare from oncoming headlights. These innovations are consistent with a strong consumer value. Since the products are included in the vehicle purchase, the issues of installation and additional purchase are avoided.

Product Complexity Complexity is the degree to which a new product is easy to understand and use. User-friendly items have a great advantage over products with many parts and difficult instructions. It's important for designers to keep the user in mind, a major factor in the success of Macintosh computers. Many people have sat down at a Macintosh, followed the simple instructions, and quickly learned to use elaborate programs. It wasn't until Microsoft developed its Windows interface that the DOS platform provided similar ease of use.

For complex products, understandable owner's manuals and directions are essential. The streamlined layout of switches, buttons, and knobs is also important. A major innovation in cameras was the automation of complicated focusing and lighting mechanisms. By designing a product that matches the photographic needs of most people, companies substantially reduced the complexity and promoted huge growth in 35 mm equipment and films.

Web TV is a new company that hopes to bring the World Wide Web and e-mail into millions of living rooms via the television. Sony and Philips will deliver the hardware, which consists of a set-top box and remote control. Technological challenges still exist, such as significant resolution to read Web pages easily. Once these are overcome, adoption of Web TV is expected to occur rapidly.[25]

Trialability Trialability refers to the ease with which potential users can test a new product at little or no expense. New product acceptance can be speeded up through free samples, low-cost trials, interactive showroom techniques, or loaners. Computer retailers usually place equipment on display so consumers can interact with it. Nearly every car buyer test drives an automobile before purchasing it.

Trialability is critical for software vendors, because only through use can potential buyers understand the features they would gain. Several software programs can be downloaded for free from the Web, used a few times or in a limited way, and then purchased. In the magazine world, free trial issues are common. Food companies often provide free samples in supermarkets. When Kentucky Fried Chicken launched its $150 million campaign for Colonel's Rotisserie Gold, it wanted to make the product a cornerstone of its new nonfried menu, which caters to health-minded consumers. KFC ran coupons for free samples in magazines such as *People, Ladies' Home Journal, Newsweek, Good Housekeeping, Better Homes & Gardens,* and *Readers' Digest.*[26]

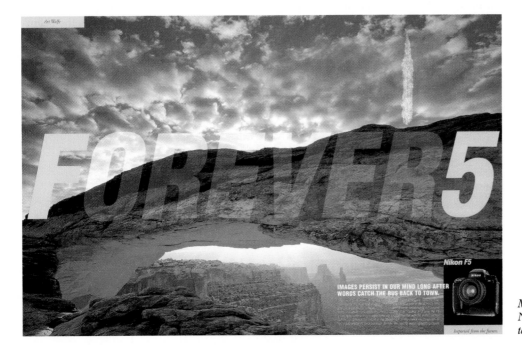

Many camera companies, like Nikon, reduce product complexity to match the needs of consumers.

Observability Observability means that the product's benefits can be easily seen by potential buyers. It is particularly useful to be able to see others using the product. New products with obvious advantages are adopted rapidly. When benefits are more subtle, it's more difficult to gain acceptance. Weight-loss plans that show quick results are popular because users can see the results and acquaintances are likely to make positive comments. In comparison, the effects of fitness training may not become apparent for some time, so it's more difficult to gain consumer acceptance.

Another product with high observability is the BMW 5-Series, a winner of the 1996 Edison Best New Products award. The new model is larger on the outside, roomier on the inside, and features extensive innovations in "virtually every area of the vehicle." [27] Friends, family, and other passengers can quickly observe its obvious benefits.

THE NEW PRODUCT DEVELOPMENT PROCESS

Success with new products depends on translating the organization's core competencies into goods or services that provide superior value to the customer.[28] The competitiveness of most markets requires a stream of new products, processes, and ventures. It's difficult to pinpoint exactly why some organizations are more innovative than others. Nevertheless, researchers have suggested the following will improve the chances of bringing innovations to market successfully:[29]

- A champion who believes in the new idea and will keep pushing no matter what the roadblocks
- A sponsor high enough in the organization to provide access to major resources: people, money, and time
- A mix of bright, creative minds (to generate ideas) and experienced operators (to keep things practical)
- A process that moves ideas through the system quickly so that they get top-level endorsement, resources, and attention early in the game
- A focus on customers at every step
- A team orientation

Figure 10-3 describes the elements in the new product development process beginning with the new product strategy and going through commercialization.

New Product Strategy

Leading-edge companies have a strategy for new product development. In forming that strategy, top executives must answer a number of questions: Will the organization be a market leader, close follower, or also-ran? Will it have broad or deep product lines? How rapidly must the product stream flow, given competitive conditions and market expectations? How much will be invested in R&D over time? The business vision discussed in chapter 4 is the beginning point, since most company missions require that new technologies and innovative processes be used to create superior customer value.

AT&T's business vision of "anywhere, anytime communications" clearly implies that new products must be developed. Fulfilling that vision requires increasingly smaller, more pow-

Figure 10-3   The New Product Development Process

erful devices for access to data, audio, and visual communications globally. Telephone wire lines are being replaced with fiber-optic cable, which is being replaced by wireless radio frequencies, which are being replaced by satellite beams. And plans are already under way by companies like Motorola to replace high-earth-orbit satellites with more energy-efficient medium-earth-orbit technology and very elaborate lower-earth-orbit systems.

Fulfilling the company mission requires that marketers have the courage to bring out newer and more advanced technologies. The value statements of many corporations recognize the social responsibility of providing more functional, cost-effective, environmentally sound, and safe products. How do those goals become a reality?

IDEA GENERATION

Organizations will not find an adequate number of significant new product ideas without an appropriate system. **Idea generation** is the use of a range of formal and informal methods to stimulate concepts from a number of sources. Among the many possible sources are employees, customers, technology analysis, distributors and suppliers, competitors, R&D, environmental trend analysis, and outside consultants. Marketers must ensure that ideas flow continuously from these groups. Often a reward is provided to individuals who make significant contributions.

A system based on four general principles seems to work quite well.[30]

- Systematically seek and ask for new product ideas.
- Make sure that all ideas, no matter how trivial or elaborate, reach the individual or group responsible for collecting them.
- Provide timely feedback to all people contributing ideas.
- Build rewards and recognition into the organization scaled according to the number and quality of ideas.

Employees, who work with products every day, are likely to identify many minor improvements that can result in cost savings, better quality, and higher sales. They should constantly be encouraged to submit ideas. At a Johnson Controls plant in Kentucky, every employee submitted at least one idea in 1996.[31] The Kinko's incentive is a Disney vacation for the employee with the best suggestion of the year, while the CEO or a vice president fills in at the store.[32] Company salespeople are in the field where they can learn about new trends or ideas that may lead to the development of a new product.

Customers are a logical source of new product ideas. This is particularly true in business-to-business marketing, since customers rely on suppliers to improve their own products and processes. By training salespeople to explore customer problems, and creating a system for feedback, companies are likely to discover numerous new concepts. Surveys, focus groups, and other marketing research techniques can be used. Parker Hannifin advertises its business as "working in partnership with our customers" in order to solve problems and add more value to the company's wide variety of products.[33]

A technology analysis forecasts the speed of advances as well as possible areas of application. The result can be novel products to improve the standard of living. Any number of products have changed the way people live, from indoor plumbing and telephones to four-wheel-drive automobiles, and personal CD players. True innovations like the Internet are rare, but in the consumer and services sector they tend to be in areas where the bulk of exploration is focused, such as electronics or pharmaceuticals.[34]

Distributors and suppliers have a personal interest in the number of products a company makes. They often are asked to serve on the council that many organizations establish to generate new product concepts. At semiannual meetings, ideas are exchanged, and concrete lists of innovations and new approaches are developed. Sun Microsystems has a program that involves suppliers at the idea stage and allows them to qualify as providers of the new product. Suppliers also have helped Sun introduce new technology into its own workstations and microprocessing servers.[35]

Competitors can be a major source of ideas. It's not enough for marketers simply to compare products and prices. They need to anticipate rivals' innovations by systematically monitoring and projecting the approach the competition is likely to take. For example, by recognizing progressive changes in miniaturization, Allen-Bradley Corporation has been able to surpass competitors and develop new robotics that leapfrog entire generations. Japanese firms often imitate and improve on the products of U.S. companies rather than develop their own.

Idea generation
The gathering of suggestions for new products from a number of sources using a range of formal and informal methods.

 CONNECTED: SURFING THE NET

www.jci.com

Explore the Web site of Johnson Controls, Inc., the global market leader in automotive systems and building controls. Learn how its "70,000 employees at more than 500 locations around the world are dedicated to exceeding customer expectations."

R&D personnel–scientists, engineers, designers, and others–have a clear interest in new product development, since that's a large part of their job. Companies that encourage innovation make sure they provide ample opportunity for scientists to explore on their own. When a percentage of their time is free from routine tasks, R&D staff often identify major breakthroughs. One company famous for this is 3M. It allows employees to spend 15 percent of their week on whatever projects they choose. Management also urges them to seek new product ideas from everywhere, even failed experiments. The very successful Post-it notes were invented this way. Scientists were trying to invent a strong adhesive but kept failing. Rather than scrap the research, a way was found to use the less sticky glue.[36]

> **CAREER TIP** 3M says: "We foster an individual, entrepreneurial spirit that leads to the development of innovative processes and products. We encourage the exchange of ideas, teamwork across different functions, and empowerment of our employees with the freedom to take risks." 3M is famous for its product development and innovations. You can get a detailed look at the company's employment opportunities on-line. The company's Web site will fill you in on the varied career opportunities and corresponding job requirements. You can also obtain an application on-line, or send an e-mail directly from the site for further inquiries. Check it out at **www.3m.com**.

An environmental trend analysis estimates how major social forces may affect an industry. The organization then can project ways in which it can provide timely products. One example is to identify pollutants in a current product, find substitute ingredients and components, and develop a new version that will appeal to "green" consumers. Seventh Generation is a company that sells bathroom tissue made from 100 percent recycled paper rather than trees.[37] As of 1996, at least two dozen types of tree-free paper were available for printing, copying, and writing.[38]

Outside consultants specializing in new product development obviously focus much of their work on idea generation. They use a broad range of techniques to help companies de-

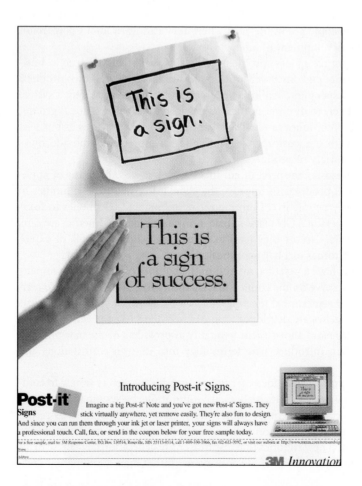

3M recently introduced Post-it signs, an addition to its list of innovations.

velop concepts: surveys, brainstorming, focus groups, and others. Each method provides a structured way of discovering innovative products. The consulting firm Booz, Allen & Hamilton has gained a global reputation for its ability to identify commercially viable solutions to customer problems.

IDEA SCREENING

A good system will provide hundreds of new product ideas each year. The **idea screening** process identifies those with the strongest potential for success. Companies usually apply certain criteria to judge each concept. The criteria generally fall into several categories: the market, competition, required resources, technology, the environment, legal and liability issues, and financial factors. Multiple scales measure how well a product performs on each dimension.

Usually, a cross-functional team examines the limited information about the idea, using both experience and subjective judgment. The team may weight certain factors more than others, and a summary total is provided with qualitative comments to support the evaluation. Once this is completed, the team looks at the scores for all new products under consideration. As a rule, those with higher scores are chosen for further development. The team then provides feedback to everyone who contributed an idea, including an explanation of why it was accepted or rejected. The various team members take different responsibilities over the course of a new product project. Involving several functions at the idea stage greatly increases the likelihood of picking the best ideas and developing a great product. Each member of the team has specific skills (engineering, marketing, manufacturing) that contribute to product success.[39]

BUSINESS ANALYSIS

A **business analysis** assesses the attractiveness of a product from a sales, cost, profit, and cash-flow standpoint. Business analysis starts with the **product concept,** which refines the idea into written descriptions, pictures, and specifications. Marketing and R&D work diligently to define the benefits, form, features, and functions the product will have. The product concept is then presented to consumers, distributors, and retailers, who provide input regarding the product's potential as well as its description and visual representations. In the process, the description is likely to undergo changes. **Concept testing** helps identify the facilitators and inhibitors to a product's success. While testing concepts to sell its new cake batters, Duncan Hines stumbled upon the theme of moistness. After hundreds of hours of concept testing, one homemaker said the cake was so moist, it stuck to the fork. From this, a successful campaign emerged.

Once the concept has been fully defined, an initial marketing strategy is developed. Success depends not only on the product but also on the strategy for marketing it. This includes examining the opportunities for segmentation, product positioning, and other aspects of the marketing mix. It's also important to look at production and materials acquisition needs as well as the time required before launch. A key feature of strategy development is to project long-term profitability under different scenarios. At this point, the likelihood of success or failure becomes more apparent. Doubtful products must be weeded out at this point, because the next stages can be very expensive.

PROTOTYPE PRODUCT DEVELOPMENT

A prototype is a working model of the product, usually created by a team of marketing, manufacturing, engineering, and R&D personnel. Prototypes can be extremely expensive because handwork rather than automation is used. They may cost 10 or even 100 times more than a product made on the production line. Although costly, these models are necessary for the all-important next step, market testing. Openness among team members and a clear sense of direction, led by a product champion, greatly increase the chances for prototype success regardless of the competitive situation.[40]

Prototype development has been influenced greatly by technology, which has made the design and building process faster and less expensive. Three-dimensional (3-D) digitizers that translate physical models into a computer enable cross-functional teams to thoroughly understand and adjust the design. Augmented reality systems are emerging that will allow diagrams or textual information to be superimposed on a prototype as if it were painted there.

Idea screening

Identifying the new product ideas that have the most potential to succeed.

Business analysis

Assessment of the attractiveness of the product from a sales, cost, profit, and cash-flow standpoint.

Product concept

A product idea that has been refined into written descriptions, pictures, and specifications.

Concept testing

Testing the new product concept to evaluate the likelihood of its success.

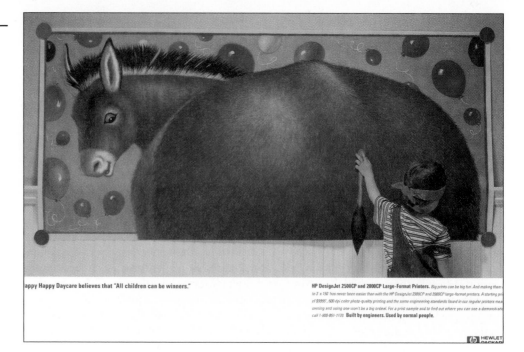

*Hewlett-Packard has used the
venture team approach to
develop printers.*

These systems are the joint project of Boeing Computer Services, Honeywell, Virtual Vision, and Carnegie-Mellon University.[41] The technology feature, "Don't Just Look, Step Inside: Virtual Reality in Product Design," discusses this fascinating area.

MARKET TESTING

Test marketing is a limited trial of the strategy for the product under real or simulated conditions. Up to this point, champions may be able to push a weak product through the system. Now reality sets in. A **test market** is a small geographical area, with characteristics similar to the total market, where the product is introduced with a complete marketing program. Test marketing allows companies to implement the product strategy on a limited basis under real conditions. In fact, a test may involve trying two or more marketing strategies in separate areas to identify which works best.

Test market

A small geographic area, with characteristics similar to the total market, in which a product is introduced with a complete marketing program.

In carefully designed test marketing, consumers are unaware that they are part of an experiment. Retailing, distribution, and promotion activities are similar to what would occur at the national or international level. When the results are in, marketers can forecast how long it will take for the product to be adopted in the general market. That kind of feedback was obtained when Motorola used test marketing for its AirWeb Wireless Software, which allows a Netscape Navigator browser to operate over wireless data networks.[42]

Test market sites are selected very carefully to represent the segments that eventually will be targeted. For example, manufacturers testing toys would avoid Sarasota, Florida, which has a large elderly population. Snowshoes are more likely to be tested in Wyoming than in Georgia. A popular site is Boise, Idaho, where there may be up to 15 test products on the shelves at once. Pillsbury tried its All Ready pie crust there. The idea of selling kitchen towels and oven mitts in supermarkets was tested in Boise. Audit services in more than 125 cities throughout the United States monitor test market results. Figure 10-4 lists the top 20 test markets with a population of 50,000 or more.

By the time an organization enters a test market, substantial funds have been spent on the new venture. There is a very strong probability of committing to a full-scale product launch—unless the test is a total failure. The results mainly help predict adoption rates among consumers and channel members. McDonald's® is test-marketing an idea aimed at the "computer literate and on-the-go eater"—a combination gas station/fast-food store. At the gas pump, a computer screen asks whether customers would like to "McOrder" something. The test will give McDonald's® an indication of whether consumers will like the concept.[43] Such experiments also help identify factors that facilitate or hinder product adoption and may yield surprises about who the users will be.

CONNECTING THROUGH TECHNOLOGY

DON'T JUST LOOK, STEP INSIDE: VIRTUAL REALITY IN PRODUCT DESIGN

Sometimes a product designer has to go into a cave before the "Eureka!" light goes on. We're not talking about homes for bats, but a Cave Automatic Virtual Environment (CAVE). At Caterpillar, product design teams are moving beyond computer-animated models and physical prototypes to full immersion in virtual reality (VR). With CAVE, they can get into a virtual traction cab and test-drive new designs safely and quickly. CAVE is a projection-based VR system that surrounds the viewer with screens arranged in a cube. Images, with correct perspective and stereo projections, are displayed on the front and side screens and on the floor. The images change in response to the operator's head motion and use of controls, creating a truly interactive environment.

In the old days Caterpillar had to build physical prototypes. With the VR system, it not only saves time and money but also frees up designers to try more innovative ideas. The company's new Model 914G wheel loader, developed using CAVE technology, features 57 percent more glass in the cab to improve visibility. While only a few pioneering and capital-rich companies can afford to use VR technology, it is generally considered the wave of the product development future. Estimates are that the VR market will grow from $249 million in 1994 to more than $1 billion by 1997. Organizations forging ahead with the technology range from Boeing and McDonnell Douglas to Honeywell and NASA.

Virtual reality not only spurs innovation but also complements the trend toward concurrent engineering: using multidisciplinary teams to design products. For many team members, especially those without an engineering background, visualizing designs in 3-D can be difficult. Helping them "see" the product early in the development cycle means that changes can be made faster and at less cost. When a marketer looks at the chassis of a virtual car and asks how it would look if the hood were sleeker, the designers don't stomp back to the drawing board to prepare a sketch by next week. According to Joshua Larson-Mogal, manager of the Enabling Technology Group of Silicon Graphic's Advanced Systems division: "Before, to design the interior of a car, you had maybe three or four revisions you could do with the mock-ups before you had to commit to something. With VR you could do 20, maybe 30 or more." It also is easy to incorporate feedback from potential customers about product design long before anything is built. After customers "try out" a VR prototype, designers can make revisions and ask those same customers to reevaluate the update within a matter of hours. The certain result, says Larson-Mogal, will be "products that are better accepted by the market."

Sources: Barbara M. Schmitz, "Great Expectations: The Future of Virtual Design," *Computer-Aided Engineering*, October 1995, pp. 68–74; Barbara M. Schmitz, "VR Accelerates Caterpillar's Design Testing," *Computer-Aided Engineering*, June 1995, p. 8; and Joshua Larson-Mogal, "VR at Work Today," *Computer-Aided Engineering*, October 1994, pp. 64–68, 70.

There are several drawbacks to using test markets. First, it takes time, and product development costs rise with every delay in full-scale launch. Second, competitors become aware of the new product, and the element of surprise is lost. Sometimes a rival will jump in with a similar product or use tactics that spoil the results. For example, when a competitor test-marketed a new item, Vicks pulled all its similar products off the shelves, leaving no basis for judging whether the test was successful. Other tactics are flooding the market with unusual promotions, point-of-purchase displays, and price cuts. Third, it's impractical to use test marketing for many products because prototypes are too costly. Automobiles are an example. Fourth, it is extremely expensive to make the trial products, stock stores, train salespeople, run ads, and so forth.

A **simulated product test** is an experiment in artificial conditions. This may be done before or instead of a full test. At Interplay Productions, video games are sometimes tried out by a limited number of players before being shipped to retailers. This simulated product testing helps identify flaws and provides feedback.[44] The food industry often sets up a replica of a supermarket, asks consumers to shop as if they were in a natural environment, and interviews them afterward. Although simulations are not as effective as a test market, they do provide useful information at dramatically reduced costs. Furthermore, competitors are less likely to find out about a company's plans prior to product launch.

Simulated product test
Experimentation with the marketing strategy in artificial conditions.

Rank	Place	1990 Population
1.	Tulsa, OK	367,000
2.	Charleston, WV	57,000
3.	Midland, TX	89,000
4.	Springfield, IL	105,000
5.	Lexington-Fayette, KY	225,000
6.	Wichita, KS	304,000
7.	Bloomington, IL	52,000
8.	Oklahoma City, OK	445,000
9.	Indianapolis, IN	731,000
10.	Rockford, IL	139,000
11.	Longview, TX	70,000
12.	Lafayette, LA	94,000
13.	Omaha, NE	336,000
14.	Phoenix, AZ	983,000
15.	Gastonia, NC	55,000
16.	Dallas, TX	1,007,000
17.	Jacksonville, FL	635,000
18.	Edmond, OK	52,000
19.	High Point, NC	69,000
20.	Salt Lake City, UT	160,000

Figure 10-4   Top 20 Test Markets with at Least 50,000 Residents

Source: First Data Solutions, Naperville, IL, based on 1990 census.

COMMERCIALIZATION

Commercialization

Final stage in the new product development process, when the product is introduced into the market.

During the final stage of the process, **commercialization** introduces the product to the market. Launching consumer products requires heavy company support, such as advertising, sales promotions, and often free samples and price promotions. Consider the $30 million commercialization of Frito-Lay's Sunchips brand, which included television spots and the company's largest ever direct mail sampling program to more than six million households. After a decade of development, Sunchips breezed through test marketing in six months, indicating to Frito-Lay executives that this multigrain snack had the potential for overnight success. In this industry new products rarely achieve even $40 million in sales, but Sunchips topped $100 million in the first year and continues to bring in huge profits.[45]

THE ETHICS OF PRODUCT IMITATION

Some argue that since companies make substantial investments in new products, they should be the only ones allowed to market them. Recognizing this, intellectual property laws and patent laws afford some protection. Others argue that imitation results in healthy competition. It forces market leaders to keep up with technology, contend with lower-priced substitutes, and respond to smaller and faster challengers. Organizations that want to remain competitive need to keep a keen eye on competitors' new products. Many times it helps to emulate their products, a totally ethical approach under many circumstances.

Protecting a firm's products from imitation is increasingly difficult. This tactic has become a recognized part of business strategy across the globe. Software development giant and market leader Microsoft is said to have greatly benefited from the inventions of others.[46] Its Windows 95 operating system, which has become the standard program that runs nearly all personal computer operations, is considered very similar in user friendliness and visual format to Apple's Macintosh system.

Not all imitations are created equal. Some are illegal duplicates of popular products, and some are truly innovative products merely inspired by a pioneering brand.[47] The makers of knockoffs or clones often copy original designs but may leave off important attributes. In the computer industry, reproductions of IBM PCs carry their own brand names. The clones are often the same basic product, but they retail at lower price and without the prestigious IBM label. Clones are legal because protective patents, copyrights, and trademarks are absent or have expired.

Some copies play on the style, design, or fashion of a popular product. This type of imitation is common in the automobile industry. In the 1980s several Japanese automakers in-

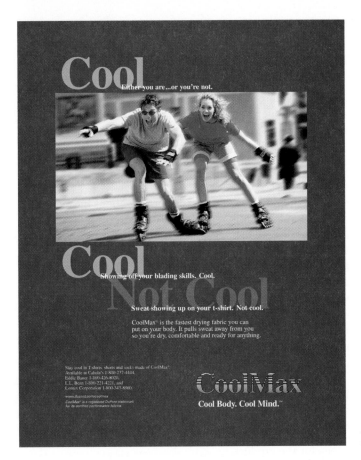

DuPont used a creative adoption to develop CoolMax—a fast drying fabric.

troduced lines to challenge Mercedes-Benz and BMW. Toyota's Lexus, Nissan's Infiniti, and Honda's Acura closely mirror the design and features of the German luxury cars. When technical products are copied, reverse engineering is often used to learn how the original was designed or made.

Creative adoptions innovate beyond an existing product. These may occur as a technological development or as an adaptation to another industry. Initially, DuPont developed Teflon for the nose-cones of spacecraft but soon extended its uses to coatings for consumer products. W. L. Gore, who was researching Teflon uses, left DuPont in 1958 and eventually developed Gore-Tex fabric. It is used in clothing that keeps rain out but "breathes" to let body moisture escape.[48]

ORGANIZATIONAL STRUCTURES AND PRODUCT MANAGEMENT

Simultaneous new product development occurs when people from a number of functional areas work together. Marketing coordinates the team, which usually represents R&D, engineering, production, procurement, legal and human resources, financing, and so on. This approach has many advantages over the old technique of **sequential new product development,** which passes responsibility from one functional area to the next. Companies can produce better products at lower cost and gain returns more quickly. Consequently, the marketing function should attempt to ensure teamwork across all major departments of the business.

Recent Organizational Trends   There are many ways to manage existing and new products. Today, companies make creative use of computer and communications technologies to support a flexible organizational structure. This enables them to respond quickly to buyer demands. It also provides access to global technologies and the ability to adapt to competitive forces. There are three notable organizational trends.

1. *Downsizing.* Several product lines are brought under a single management team, and/or product offerings are reduced to those that generate strong and increasing revenues.
2. *Delayering.* The number of personnel/positions between top executives and those who manage market activities is reduced.

CONNECTED: SURFING THE NET

www.fritolay.com

Check out the Frito-Lay Web site for recipes, "fun stuff," products, company information, and a peek at the dream site where Madame Nozitall tells your fortune! You'll also have an opportunity to learn more about the PepsiCo family.

Simultaneous new product development
People from all functional areas work together to develop products.

Sequential new product development
People from various functional areas work on different stages of product development.

3. *Fewer functional silos.* When one function works in isolation of others it is called a functional silo. Organizations are stressing cross-functional synergy and personnel with experience in multiple areas. Marketers no longer work only with other marketers, or accountants only with other accountants.

Fundamental Structures There are many acceptable organizational structures. Today, most companies prefer a structure that supports strategy changes. As strategies alter to meet new challenges, organizational structures need to change with them. The most fundamental structures for new product development are the product or market manager, the new product department, the new product committee, and the venture team. Companies may combine elements of several of these, and may use consulting organizations as well.

Product or Market Managers Some of the most successful organizations have used the product manager or market manager structure. **Market managers** are responsible for one or several similar product lines targeted at defined market areas. **Product managers** oversee one or several products targeted at all market segments. In either case the structure is similar. The manager works closely with individuals from a range of functions to build integrated strategies. The system was pioneered by Procter & Gamble, which developed teams of experts loosely tied but headed by a very strong manager. Each team was responsible for building the equity of a given brand. Product managers compete almost as strongly with other teams in the organization as they do with competitors on the outside. For example, the Crest product manager is in competition with the Gleem product manager, and the Tide product manager is in competition with all product managers for the other detergents made by Procter & Gamble. However, since each product is positioned to address a particular benefit—Crest for tooth decay prevention and Gleem for brightness—competition may not be direct.

Product managers or market managers have the following specific responsibilities:

- Achieve the sales, profit, market share, and cash flow objectives for the product line.
- Develop the market strategy for the product.
- Prepare a written marketing plan, develop forecasts, and maintain timely updates of progress.
- Integrate all functions necessary to implement a synergistic marketing strategy.

One difficulty with this system is that the manager has responsibilities beyond the traditional lines of authority. Figure 10-5 illustrates why this occurs. The product manager can be described as the hub of a wheel. Notice that the spokes are all the functional areas that help make a good marketing strategy work. Product managers have no formal authority over these people, who report directly to managers in their own functional area.

What makes the system work? First, the product or market manager must have the necessary interpersonal and business skills to gain the team's respect. In fact, the lack of direct authority is what makes this system effective. Through team play and networking, strong product or market managers can tap into very specialized talents from a range of people. Second, the manager must report to someone high enough in the organization to obtain the status required. While unable to govern the activities of team members, product and marketing managers can make their presence felt through communication with top executives and across functional areas of the company.

The system's strength is also its weakness. Product managers must rely on functional managers from various areas of the organization to help them build a strong team. New product prospects may receive low priority from managers in the spokes. Their reward structures may inhibit working on innovations. Experience has shown that without proper attention by top management, the product or marketing manager may be relegated to relatively mundane tasks. When there is appropriate executive leadership, the system can be a flexible way to address numerous market situations.

New Product Department The **new product department** is responsible for identifying ideas, developing products, and preparing them for commercialization. The members generally report directly to top executives and include individuals with experience in many aspects of the business. This structure separates the responsibility of new product development from the rest of the organization. It helps eliminate redundancies that occur when the same ideas are developed in different product areas. These personnel have a firm grasp of the methods and risks involved in developing new products. In reality, these departments are often formed with great expectations but some quickly become a functional silo neglected by top

---

Market manager

A manager responsible for one or several similar product lines targeted at specific market segments.

Product manager

A manager who oversees one or several products targeted at all market segments.

New product department

The organizational unit responsible for identifying product ideas and preparing them for commercialization.

management. This is particularly the case when top management is preoccupied with current products or when the new product department does not set aggressive goals regarding commercializable products. Such a department usually operates best when it has strong executive involvement and concentrates its efforts on finding strategies to make product ideas commercial successes.

New Product Committee   The **new product committee** consists of key functional personnel who are brought together from time to time to develop new products. Because this activity is often not considered a strong factor in building a career, participants may give it less attention than required. Further, the committee often lacks the authority to make things happen. However, ideas and expertise can be contributed by many different key people, and committee members can be brought into a project as needed.

Venture Team   A **venture team** is a group formed for a set period to accomplish a set objective. A venture team is headed by a manager who reports very high in the organization. The manager selects team members from various areas of the company, and each is given release time for the assignment. Because the venture team has very specific objectives and a limited time frame, it tends to focus on getting the job done. Strong leadership and decision-making power allows the team to commit resources in a timely fashion. And the release time enables members to devote attention to the project. Unfortunately, in many organizations managers are unwilling to permit their best people to participate. In addition, the team is dissolved once a given task is completed. The new venture team must start over without the benefit of experience. Hewlett-Packard used this approach to develop the first low cost laser printer.

Consulting Organizations   Full service or specialty consulting firms can be hired to set up new product development systems, facilitate the process, or conduct all or part of the development task. In many cases, consulting groups have outstanding talent with experience in the area of new products. Because of that experience, companies can save vast amounts of time and money in the innovation process. Unfortunately, employees sometimes resist implementing consulting firm recommendations because they were not involved in the decision-making process. Consulting organizations like Booze, Allen and Hamilton, and McKinsey and Company often make strong efforts to involve their clients in all phases of their new product consulting.

MANAGING PRODUCTS OVER THE LIFE CYCLE

One of the oldest and most useful concepts for marketers is the product life cycle, depicted in Figure 10-5. Like living organisms, products move from birth to infancy, adolescence, maturity, old age, and death. The **product life cycle** consists of four stages: introduction, growth, maturity, and decline. It's important to recognize that this is only a conceptual tool, and not all products move through a complete life cycle. Some marketers question the usefulness of the idea, but it remains one of the most common notions in marketing strategy. It has been applied to generic products, suppliers, industries, and individual brands.

New product committee
A group of key functional personnel who are brought together periodically to develop new products.

Venture team
Personnel from various areas of the company who are given release time to work on a specific assignment.

Product life cycle
The four stages a product goes through: introduction, growth, maturity, and decline.

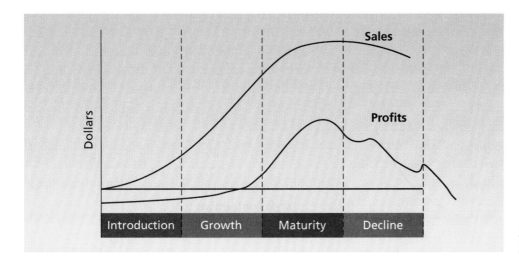

Figure 10-5   The Product or Market Manager's Team

Recall from our definition of marketing that firms seek to satisfy customers more profitably than competitors in order to increase the value of the business. Figure 10-6 illustrates the sales and profits for a typical product as it moves through its life cycle. Before introduction, large sums are likely to be expended on development. In the pharmaceutical industry, it may take 15 years or more for R&D, testing, and FDA approval. Biotech R&D in this area is running $5 billion annually.[49]

An executive at NovAtel Carcom estimates that it costs a vertically integrated company about $40 million in base technology and $5 million per product to develop new cellular phones. In other words, five new products cost $65 million.[50] In other industries the development process may be less costly, but every product begins its life by taking cash from some other part of the business.

STAGES IN THE PRODUCT LIFE CYCLE

Each of the four stages in the product life cycle is associated with its own opportunities, costs, and marketing strategies. In this section we examine each stage in more detail.

Stage 1: Introduction During the introductory phase of the product life cycle, sales slowly take off and grow. Shipments from the factory may be high, and channels of distribution are filled as wholesalers and retailers stock the item. Since the product is new, marketers scramble to create consumer awareness and encourage trial. This often involves heavy advertising campaigns, samples, and educational sales techniques. During this critical period, marketers attempt to build share quickly to gain first-mover advantages. As numerous studies have shown, whoever introduces a product is likely to become the future industry leader in that area. Chrysler introduced minivans and now controls more than half the market. Yet, Chrysler as a whole accounts for only 10 percent of the car market. The first products on the market often are so dominant that they become generic names: Kleenex, Jell-O, Xerox, Formica, and Gore-Tex.[51]

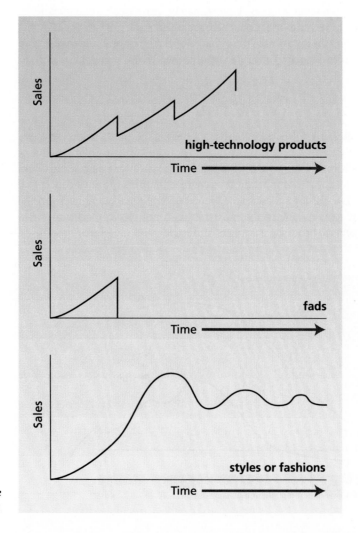

Figure 10-6   Traditional Life Cycle Curve

*Chrysler controls more than half
the market with its minivans.*

Typically, there are few competitors during introduction, so marketers concentrate on achieving customer acceptance of the entire product class. Less emphasis is placed on gaining competitive advantage through differentiation. When car phones were introduced, most advertising focused on selling the idea. Later advertising attempted to distinguish the various products from one another. Most organizations introduce only one or two items in a new product line so they can gain experience and monitor progress. Furthermore, global markets offer such vast opportunities for new products that some rivals may elect to avoid confrontations by selecting an untapped area.

As a rule, introductions represent advances in technology, manufacturing, and service. Product design also tends to be very innovative. Firms should make sure, however, that the design is easy to try and to use. It's also important to have flexible manufacturing that can match production to highly uncertain demand. Distributors don't want to be left with unsold units. But if demand is not met, buyers may lose interest, or competitors may enter the market. Finally, customer service efforts must seek out and correct problems.

Profits may be negative during all or most of the introductory phase. Sales usually grow slowly, and consumers need to be made aware of the product's existence, which requires relatively costly promotion. It can also be very expensive to develop distribution channels and to educate people about the product's use.

Stage 2: Growth During the growth stage, the pace of consumer acceptance and sales quickens. This is an especially critical time because rivals, noticing the increase in sales will develop competitive products and aggressively pursue distribution channels. Consumers begin to make comparisons among the various products, so companies attempt to gain preferred status and brand loyalty. Strong companies like Microsoft and Dell Computers seek dominance during this period. Many organizations believe that if they don't emerge from the growth stage as number one or two, then they should abandon that line of business. Competition is extremely aggressive. Honda's Cub motorcycle, introduced in 1958, is still experiencing growth, especially in Pacific Rim countries. The company has gained preferred status and brand loyalty among consumers and continues to seek dominance among new users and market areas.[52]

Product technology often enters its second generation during the growth stage. The first-generation technology applied to the original products is improved as companies gain experience. Usually, second-generation technology produces greater customer satisfaction through both cost savings and enhanced functionality. The first car phones had to be mounted permanently, and an antenna was attached to the outside. The next generation included bag phones that could be transferred from vehicle to vehicle. Now, hand-held phones that fit in your pocket can be purchased.

With growth come product designs that differ substantially from one manufacturer to the next. Also, product lines begin to deepen as models and styles are developed to satisfy

**CONNECTED:
SURFING
THE NET**

www.honda.com

Get to know Honda by visiting its Web site. You'll be able to see the model lineup, "drive one home," learn about Honda's owners, and much more. Or search the site for what interests you.

tastes and applications in target segments. For example, when a successful upgrade of Microsoft's Windows NT was launched in September 1996, industry experts anticipated it would continue to grow at a 44 percent annual rate through 2000. Second-generation technology enabled Microsoft to provide greater customer satisfaction through the enhanced functionality of Windows NT.[53]

Manufacturing processes undergo change during the growth phase. The flexibility of the previous stage gives way to assembly lines and more automation. Higher sales volumes mean that standardized production can be used to achieve economies of scale and cost savings. Since forecasting is more accurate, just-in-time delivery and advanced quality control systems are possible. Motorola strives for six sigma quality rates, which equates to 3.4 defects per one million products. Of course, it's important that firms have the manufacturing capacity to meet increasing demand. Otherwise, competitors may step in.

Promotion and sales take on a whole new dimension during growth. Aggressive head-to-head competition forces organizations to show their uniqueness, and the augmented product becomes extremely important. Financing, installation, and training in product use are critical promotion activities. Advertising shifts to substantive messages that describe the benefits, functions, and features of the product relative to competitors' offerings.

The companies that emerge as leaders tend to provide uncompromising customer service. They build trust in the distribution channel and with end users. Sometimes repeat purchases are based more on service satisfaction than on product performance and styling. Most consumers expect problems with any product. How they are handled makes the difference. If service is performed correctly the first time, then consumers are likely to feel an affinity toward the supplier. In fact, as discussed in chapter 2, loyalty may be strengthened when problems occur and are handled well.

Stage 3: Maturity As products mature, sales level off and may remain flat for long periods. Overall market growth is relatively small, so a sales increase for one company usually comes at the expense of another. That's why firms with loyal buyers tend to have the greatest longevity. Yet, loyalty also indicates that consumer interest in the product is subsiding, which makes it very difficult and costly to build market share. Most firms are happy if they simply hold their own in this phase. Weaker competitors are likely to lower prices, while stronger rivals may sacrifice market share to maintain a satisfactory profit level. Strong rivals also engage in dramatic cost containment to preserve profits. Often this results in a standardized product design with less costly components and more efficient manufacturing.

At maturity, weaker rivals may drop out and use resources on more promising products. Even strong companies may exit if profit margins suffer too much, as GE did with its consumer line of light bulbs. The maturity phase may last several months, years, or even decades, and a low-cost position is critical for long-term success. This is particularly true if low-cost foreign competitors enter the business.

Product line size becomes especially important during the mature phase. Companies need to drop products with low-volume sales, high production costs, or little competitive viability. But many buyers want to deal with a supplier who offers a full product line. This leads many organizations to employ outsourcing; that is, they purchase certain items from other companies and affix their own label. In this way they continue to mass-produce the lower-cost standardized items while depending on smaller firms to make the rest. Competitors may even buy from one another during the mature stage in order to gain an overall cost advantage, often called co-opetition. For example, some replacement parts for Chrysler cars may be produced by GM and vice versa. Co-opetition combines rivalry and cooperation to create a maximum business benefit.[54] Honda and Rover also use this approach. Rover competes with Honda's newly introduced sport-utility vehicles, but the two companies supply each other with engines and components.[55]

The technology used for mature products tends to be older. Many firms have invested so heavily in the past technology that they resist committing more resources to an aging product. The primary focus is on improving the manufacturing process. For example, some organizations move from assembly line and batch-oriented production to a continuous-flow system. This integrates people, paperwork, computerization, and manufacturing into a seamless operation that maintains production at the greatest level of efficiency.

Promotional campaigns focus more on reminder advertising than on new themes, since most buyers are now loyal to a particular brand or company. Sometimes, companies resurrect messages that were used to build the brand's name. By adding a novel twist, the firm can keep its product in the forefront. For example, Wheaties, the traditional "Breakfast of Champions," regularly updates its package to show the latest sports superstars. The objective is to create a link to younger consumers while maintaining its strong brand identity.

Service usually is standardized for mature products. In many cases, new service firms are formed to specialize in a particular product area. Even though Otis or Westinghouse installs most of the elevators we use, it is private service companies that keep them in tip-top condition. Many organizations elect to hire local service firms to perform repairs. The marketing of replacement parts may become extremely profitable at this stage. During economic recessions, customers often prefer to fix an existing product rather than buy a new one. In the United States, movable furniture systems from such companies as Steelcase, Herman Miller, and Hayworth have entered the maturity phase. Local firms are now purchasing and refurbishing the units for resale.

The rapid sales increase in the growth stage peaks during early maturity. Profits are likely to decline because of price competition, both domestically and internationally. This is particularly true in industries with high exit barriers. That means it costs companies a lot of money to leave the line of business because of their high fixed investment. Since it is costly to stop making the product, prices often are lowered to maintain demand. Furthermore, such trade promotions as point-of-purchase sales and discounting may be used. By the end of the maturity phase, a product may be losing money or have a very thin profit margin because of low demand.

Stage 4: Decline   In the decline stage of the product life cycle, sales of new units diminish. For some products, such as earlier models of computers, the decrease may be very rapid. For others, it may be slow and steady, as with black-and-white television sets. Or it may be slow and then rapid, which was the case with vinyl records. Their sales dropped gradually and then plummeted as more and more titles became available on CDs. The speed of decline is related to the types and value of substitute products.

Most companies with a declining product want to maintain the lucrative replacement market but are willing to give up market share in exchange for earnings. Fierce price wars are likely to result in losses for all competitors. Low-cost producers that minimize new activities are in a much better position than high-cost competitors. Product design is nearly always standardized. Changes are intended to reduce the cost of components, which helps the company maintain earnings.

Companies are likely to return to a much shallower product line at this stage, focusing on the products that generate adequate cash flow. Old technology is kept in place, and manufacturing runs are limited, which frees up production capacity for more profitable items. To keep costs down, very little promotional activity occurs, so buyers may have to seek out the product themselves. Service is likely to be handled by independent companies. Because replacement parts still generate a profit, the firm is likely to maintain a supply that affords some level of earnings.

The "profit life cycle" implies that companies should have products in all stages at all times. Firms with only mature and declining products can expect dwindling profitability. Yet product development and the introductory stage are likely to absorb much of the profit generated from growing and mature products. Strong companies plan ahead and add products at various stages in the life cycle to ensure a viable business. This is particularly important for companies whose products are patented. In 1993, Upjohn faced such a challenge. The patents on four drugs that made up 32 percent of its 1992 sales were due to expire in mid-1994, opening the door for generics. Analysts speculated that the company didn't have any new drugs in the works to offset the sales decline that was sure to occur. Upjohn then purchased the rights to market several new ibuprofen products that had been developed but never sold. The market for these general pain relievers was growing, and this move gave Upjohn products in the introductory and growth stages.[56]

VARIATIONS IN PRODUCT LIFE CYCLES

By looking at extinct products, we know that several kinds of life cycle are possible. By understanding the different types, marketers can make general predictions about the challenges they face. Several types are illustrated in Figure 10-6. The first curve is typical of high-tech products, such as computer software. Just when sales achieve a healthy pace, another generation hits the market. General acceptance of the product grows with each wave, however, which explains the successively higher peaks. Each generation usually lowers the cost to consumers.

The second curve illustrates the life cycle of a fad. Sales rise sharply in the introductory and growth phases, then quickly fall. Marketers of such products are careful not to base the longevity of their company on one or two items. They realize the fad is likely to be a passing windfall. For example, Sears stocked its stores with conservative levels of World Cup Soccer merchandise and monitored inventory levels carefully before ordering more. Once the World Cup was over, consumers would probably lose interest.[57]

Clothing fashions follow yet another kind of curve. When a style is first introduced it is likely to experience relatively fast growth and then tail off, only to be resurrected a few years later. The width of neckties has gone from narrow, to medium, to wide, and back to narrow. Skirt lengths rise and fall. Marketers of these products must be aware of constantly changing consumer preferences and build strategies accordingly.

Although the product life cycle gives marketers a rule of thumb, it is not an exact science. To obtain more precise forecasts, researchers have developed mathematical and statistical models that examine market size, the number of initial buyers, and the time between first and repeat purchase. These can be very useful, particularly for products that behave similarly to those modeled.

EXTENDING THE PRODUCT LIFE CYCLE

Firms that resist change sometimes keep products going far beyond their usefulness. But there are times when it's good business to extend the product life cycle. The four most common ways to do this are to sell to new market segments, to stimulate more frequent use, to encourage more use per occasion, and to promote more varied use.

Selling to New Segments One way to give a product a new lease on life is to find new buyers. For example, in-line skates were originally used primarily by males to simulate ice hockey, but now they have been adopted widely by females. The truck market has undergone a similar change. Realizing the popularity of smaller pickups with women, Ford acknowledges the importance of "female friendly" vehicles and promotes the F-150 models to this segment.[58] The diversity feature centers on how Mattel entered the market segment of CD-ROM games for girls.

Stimulating More Frequent Use After a decade of declining sales nationwide, the milk industry needed a marketing campaign to stimulate use. From this the well-known "Got Milk?" campaign was born. Research indicated that the product played only a peripheral role in people's lives. The only time they gave it a second thought was when they didn't have any. The campaign theme chosen was "milk deprivation"—a man agonizing over a milkless bowl of cereal, deciding whether to rob his baby's bottle or his cat's dish. Or Santa entering a home, eating a brownie, finding no milk, and taking the Christmas presents away. These award-winners not only heightened awareness by 91 percent but also increased the frequency of use.[59]

The makers of cellular phones encourage more frequent use by marketing the importance of owning several instruments. Telephone communication once was limited to the home, office, or a pay phone. Now people can have constant access. One Web site for Motorola's cloning capabilities suggests: "A cell phone in each car and a smaller cell phone so you can carry it with you—A cell phone for your spouse for emergencies—A cell phone for your kids when they are away from home."[60] Marketers want to convince consumers to purchase several phones for the sake of both convenience and safety.

Encouraging More Use per Occasion Have you ever purchased a Snickers bar offering 20 percent more candy for free? That is one way to encourage more use per occasion. Many companies promote on this basis. McDonald's® offers a "Super Sized®" meal, with a larger order of french fries and a larger beverage. Coca-Cola encourages greater consumption with 20-ounce sizes in vending machines. Claussen, a division of Campbell's, recently introduced a giant crinkle-cut pickle slice to "blanket" hamburgers. The 69 percent of Americans who enjoy pickle on their burgers will now have a bigger option.[61]

Promoting More Varied Use Arm & Hammer dramatically extended the life cycle of baking soda by using it as an ingredient in toothpaste, laundry products, room fresheners, and deodorant. Furthermore, ads recommend it for absorbing odors in refrigerators and closets.

CONNECTING WITH DIVERSITY

MATTEL'S BARBIE LURES GIRLS
TO COMPUTER GAMES

Developing a successful new product is hard enough, but what about creating one for a market that doesn't exist? This was the challenge faced by Mattel, Inc., when it came up with its new Barbie Fashion Designer CD-ROM. Males account for more than 80 percent of the CD-ROM game market, and no company had yet successfully marketed one of these products to girls. But had they stayed away because there were no appealing products or because they simply weren't interested in computers?

The spectacular success of the Barbie CD-ROM proves that appeal was the problem. With retail sales of 200,000 units in November 1996, Barbie Fashion Designer sold more in its first month than any other educational CD-ROM and is shaking up an industry dominated by products for boys.

One of the keys to Mattel's success was paying attention to girls' computer use and play patterns. Until age six, they use computers as much as boys and even develop superior concentration and skills. Around age seven, when gender differences begin to emerge, girls drop out of the market. They become more interested in socializing, story-telling, and particularly emulating heroines they read about and see on screen. In sharp contrast, games on the market—like Doom, Duke Nukem, or Quake—feature kick-boxers, guns, and buckets of blood to capitalize on boys' interest in competitive, spatial games.

The Barbie Fashion Designer CD-ROM, developed by Mattel in conjunction with Hollywood special effects company Digital Domain, is one of the few titles that addresses girls' desire to use the computer for creative expression. Now girls age five and older can design Barbie clothes on the computer and print them out on a light fabric with any computer printer. Another CD-ROM, the Barbie Storymaker, uses a number of favorite Barbie haunts to let girls create hundreds of different stories around Barbie and her friends.

Developing a unique product was only half the battle. Mattel and other makers of new CD-ROMs for girls have had the added challenge of reaching this huge untapped market. Girls don't hang out at Egghead Software Co. They don't cruise the CD-ROM aisle of Toys "R" Us or read techie magazines. One tactic is to leverage the power of an established brand, as Mattel has done by basing its product on the popular fashion doll. Using its considerable clout, Mattel persuaded retailers to place the product in both the toy and computer departments.

Her Interactive was not so fortunate when it launched its McKenzie & Co. CD-ROM a full year before Barbie's debut. Designed for the 10–15 age group, it features a group of girls dating, shopping, and applying makeup. McKenzie & Co. couldn't find shelf space. Retailers didn't know where to place it. Now, Her Interactive is happily riding on Barbie's coattails. Marketers at Simon & Schuster Interactive have adopted a grassroots approach, using nontraditional sites to attract preteens and teenagers. Their interactive girls' handbook *Let's Talk About Me* is available in Contempo Casual and Wet Seal clothing stores and is sold right next to clothes and makeup.

It's clear that Barbie's success will spark a host of other companies to develop CD-ROMS for girls, a market with $42 million in disposable income. And girls who want to have fun on the computer couldn't be happier. "The great thing about these products is, they put the girl in control," said Barbie media marketing vice president Pam Kelly. "She's making the decisions, and she can use the products to interact with friends, which is how girls like to play."

Sources: Lisa Bannon, "Barbie, Dressed to Kill, Beats CD-ROM Rivals," *Wall Street Journal*, December 18, 1996, B1:3; Lisa Bannon, "Mattel Bets Barbie Can Sell Girls on Computer Games," *Wall Street Journal*, February 9, 1996, B1:3; Maria Matzer and Bernhard Warner, "Newmedia: Where the Girls Are," *Brandweek*, October 14, 1996, pp. 18–24; Cyndee Miller, "Guys on Game for Girls Don't Do Karate Kicks," *Marketing News*, December 4, 1995, p. 2; and "Girls Just Want to Have Fun—New Software Gives It to Them," *Discount Store News*, January 1, 1996, p. 43.

Once used only for cooking, today baking soda has far more applications. Even when it is being disposed, it helps sanitize the drain. Another example is the "I could have had a V-8" campaign, which popularized the traditional breakfast drink as a refreshment for any time of day. And Yellowstone Park, traditionally viewed as a summer attraction, now advertises snowmobile trips in the winter.

THE PRODUCT LIFE CYCLE IN INTERNATIONAL MARKETS

A product's stage in the life cycle has important implications for international trade, not only in terms of marketing, but also in terms of design and manufacture.

New products tend to be designed, manufactured, and sold first in advanced economies, where there is sufficient wealth to underwrite development costs, and where markets accept innovation more readily. For example, personal computers were developed largely in the United States and sold primarily in the more upscale U.S. and Western European markets. As sales grew, however, Pacific Rim manufacturers developed clones, produced them with lower-cost labor, and became important competitors in Western markets. The lower prices that resulted in turn opened up new international markets in less-advanced economies like Russia and Eastern Europe.

A product at the peak of its popularity, with many brands competing for market share, may be manufactured far from its primary market if it can gain a competitive advantage through lower manufacturing costs. Athletic shoes, for example, were pioneered in the United States—which remains their largest single market. But as product sales burgeoned and new competitors entered the market, both Nike and Reebok moved their production to low-wage countries to reduce costs.

Maturing products tend to be exported to less-advanced economies looking for lower-priced goods. As these markets grow, companies are likely to establish production facilities there, using their already standardized processes. We see this in Mexico, where both Nissan and Volkswagen have assembly plants that produce for the local market—and export to the United States as well. As manufacturing skills and processes are absorbed locally, local companies may set up their own plants and begin producing for the home market, thereby increasing competition.

Products that have reached the end of their life cycle in one economy may still be needed in another. Few U.S. households still do their laundry with washboards and tubs, but in poorer parts of the world, particularly in rural areas that have no access to electricity, such products remain useful and desirable.

Some countries are more suitable markets early in a product's life and others are more suitable later. Where products are made and marketed depends on their stage in the life cycle and on the economic characteristics of the location.[62]

Arm and Hammer products make brighter, fresher environments.

CONSUMER ACCEPTANCE OF INNOVATION

ADOPTION

The **adoption process** comprises the five steps that consumers go through in making a product choice: knowledge, persuasion, decision, implementation, and confirmation. First, the consumer becomes aware of the product and learns about it. Second, the person forms a favorable or unfavorable attitude toward the product. Third, the product is chosen or rejected. Fourth, the consumer tries the product. Fifth, experience confirms or disconfirms the wisdom of the choice and whether the item will be purchased again.[63]

The major point is that product adoption takes time. The speed of adoption depends on buyer characteristics, and other factors. Because people are different, it is possible to categorize them according to how long it will take them to adopt an idea. We know, moreover, that product acceptance is passed from one group of consumers to the next. To explain this process, marketers have developed a concept similar to the product life cycle except that it focuses on consumers: the diffusion process.

Adoption process
The steps an individual consumer goes through in making a product choice.

DIFFUSION

The **diffusion process** describes the spread of innovations from one individual or group to another over time. Marketers are keenly aware of how diffusion affects the introduction and long-term adoption of products. We know that sales are influenced dramatically by the interaction of buyers, through word of mouth, as well as by promotions and messages from marketers. Often managers focus only on organizing the firm to develop new and/or improved products. Yet they must also pay attention to understanding how consumers evaluate innovations. Otherwise even very beneficial products may not be diffused throughout the market.[64]

Figure 10-7 illustrates the five groups of consumers who can be expected to purchase a product over time. The approximate distribution is 2.5 percent innovators, 13 percent early adopters, 34 percent early majority buyers, 34 percent late majority buyers, and 16 percent laggards. The illustration is based on standard deviations, but the proportions may differ with various products.

Diffusion process
The spread of innovations from one group of consumers to another over time.

Innovators The first consumers to purchase a new product are **innovators**. As you can guess, they are more adventurous than most of the population. They have higher incomes and thus can afford to try relatively expensive introductions. They are technically competent and in some cases are almost obsessed with the details of new products. At the same time, many innovators are rather eccentric. This small group has only minor influence over others, but it provides proof that the product functions properly. Marketers can point to that experience in attempting to educate other buyers. The marketer of a new computerized vision system for detecting manufacturing flaws first installed the system at a small innovative firm that makes electronic parts. The company later cited successful use there in selling the product to a leader in the industry.

Innovators
The first group of consumers to purchase a new product.

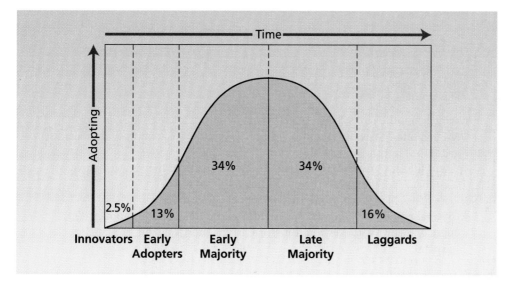

Figure 10-7 Life Cycles for Various Types of Products

Early adopters

The second group of consumers to purchase new products.

Early majority

The third group of adopters, who are more risk averse in purchase decisions than innovators and early adopters.

Late majority

The more skeptical consumers who purchase products after the early majority.

Early Adopters **Early adopters** are the second group to purchase new products and are critical to marketers. They are the key to good word-of-mouth publicity and wider acceptance. They are well respected in their community, so other categories of buyers are likely to emulate them. Consider the video-conferencing products that were launched in 1996 by a number of companies, such as Intel, Microsoft, Apple, and C-Phone. The goal was to jump-start visual communications on PCs and follow through with a wide range of new items.[65] Early adopters help determine the success and adoption rate of such offerings.

Early Majority Buyers **Early majority** consumers tend to be more risk averse than innovators and early adopters. They wait to see how something new works for others before purchasing it themselves. They also tend to read extensively about various products and compare different brands before reaching a decision. For the most part, these consumers are followers rather than leaders. Think about the recent development of the Advanced Configuration and Power Interface (ACPI), which will bring more flexibility to PC use. The ACPI permits instant access as well as automated functions after the computer is turned off.[66] Early majority consumers are likely to wait until a technology such as the ACPI is in widespread use before making the purchase, despite the extensive benefits it offers.

Late Majority and Laggards The more skeptical consumers tend to fall into the **late majority** group. They have little faith in new products, so they wait until half the population has purchased it before they do. However, even more resistant to new products is the last group

---

CONNECTED: SURFING THE NET

Caterpillar

www.caterpillar.com

IN THIS CHAPTER'S TECHNOLOGY FEATURE, "Don't Just Look, Step Inside: Virtual Reality in Product Design," you learned how Caterpillar uses this technique. To learn more about the company, visit its Web site and answer the following questions.

1. Without exploring the site farther, what does Caterpillar's product line include? What markets does it serve?
2. Now, read about the company's products. Caterpillar says it is "entering the 21st century with the most extensive machine lineup ever." Which product line growth option(s) does the company use for its equipment? Explain.
3. Read "Caterpillar Around the World" and explore some of its global markets. Pick two and explain how they may differ.

Mattel

www.hotwheels.com

THIS CHAPTER'S DIVERSITY FEATURE, "MATTEL'S BARBIE Lures Girls to Computer Games," discusses the uphill battle the company faced in developing a new product for a new market. Visit Mattel's Hot Wheels Web site and answer the following questions.

1. Check out the Hot Wheels '98 lineup. How many different lines of cars does Mattel offer? Why do you think it needs to continuously improve or make additions to product lines?
2. Read the Hot Wheels history. Give several examples of how Mattel managed products over the life cycle. Try to give an example for each phase.
3. How does Mattel use its Web site to connect with collectors?
4. Several groups are influential in the idea-generation stage of product development. Which do you think may be the most valuable to Mattel? Explain.

of consumers to purchase, the **laggard:** little, if anything, can be done to convince laggards to purchase a new product.

U.S. farmers can be viewed using the diffusion cycle. Innovators and early adopters stay current on all developments in agriculture. They go to trade shows and read everything they can get their hands on. These consumers are the first to buy a new piece of equipment or pesticide. On the other extreme lie the laggards. They feel "if it ain't broke, don't fix it" and tend to stay brand oriented. They influence little or none of the market. Marketers have used different strategies to reach each group. The innovators and early adopters prefer advertising with a lot of good information or copy. Laggards, on the other hand, need attention grabbing ads and coupons as an incentive to purchase new products.[67] Since laggards are often low income and a relatively small group many marketers simply avoid marketing to this group altogether. The fact that they have low education and low income often makes them bad credit risks as well.

Laggards
Consumers who resist new products the longest.

The diffusion cycle can also be applied to the pharmaceutical industry. When a pharmaceutical firm introduced a new pain reliever, salespeople were asked to identify physicians who fit the early adopter profile: younger, heavy prescribers, on hospital boards, with modern offices and equipment. Special attention was given to these physicians through direct mail, sampling, and sales calls. Because early adopters are more cosmopolitan than average, they are more inclined to accept information and interact with innovative firms. They agreed to test and evaluate the new product, quickly gave it their support, and set in motion rapid diffusion throughout the medical community.

When we think of product innovation and new product introductions, our tendency is to think in terms of manufactured goods. But services, too, are products—as you are aware from the marketing definition in chapter 1 and the many examples of services encountered thus far. The next chapter is devoted to exploring the distinctive features of service products, including the functional and interactive features that marketers need to consider when developing new services.

CHAPTER SUMMARY

OBJECTIVE 1: Provide a framework to evaluate the extent to which existing or new products are marketed to existing or new market segments.

Every organization needs to develop a product mix consistent with its overall strategy. It must match current and new products with current and new segments. This produces four basic options for marketing mix management. A core business focus maintains, expands, or harvests current products in current markets. Market development seeks new market segments for existing products. Product development improves or adds new products for sale to current segments. Diversification introduces new products into new market segments. Organizations can use this framework to help allocate resources to obtain the best overall performance.

OBJECTIVE 2: Understand how the characteristics of innovation influence the speed with which they are accepted.

Product innovations are of three types. Continuous innovations are minor changes in existing products that require no alterations in how consumers use them. Dynamically continuous innovations have added features and benefits that require minor changes in behavior. Discontinuous innovations are new to the world and may require major changes.

How rapidly a product is accepted depends on several factors. If its relative advantage over other products is high, then faster acceptance can be expected. If the product is compatible with current thinking, then quick adoption is likely. Also, less complex products and those that can be easily tried are more readily accepted. Finally, if the product can be observed in use by others, then it is more likely to be adopted rapidly.

OBJECTIVE 3: Know the steps used to develop new products from the initial idea through commercialization.

The new product development process has seven steps. First, a strategy is outlined by top management. This indicates the importance of new products to the organization. Second, idea generation provides a list of possibilities. These can come from numerous sources, especially if they are actively sought. Third, idea screening narrows the list to those most compatible with the organization's need. Several criteria are used in screening. Fourth, business analysis develops a product concept and performs a financial analysis to assess feasibility and estimate profitability under numerous assumptions. Fifth, prototype product development involves all the steps leading up to and including the creation of a working model. Sixth, test marketing provides a limited trial of the marketing strategy under real or simulated conditions. The objective is to see whether the strategy will work or needs to be refined before full-scale launch. Seventh, commercialization occurs when the product is formally introduced into the market.

OBJECTIVE 4: Show how the product life cycle concept can be used to build and adjust marketing strategies over time.

Products can be viewed as moving over a life cycle with several stages. In the introduction phase, sales usually take off slowly despite heavy promotion. Marketers concentrate on getting consumers to be aware of and accept the product class. During the growth stage sales increase, and product technology often enters its second generation. Manufacturing and promotion are adjusted. Leading producers focus on customer service. At maturity, sales begin to slow and level off. Gains in market share for one company come at the expense of another. A few companies exit at this point. Low cost really counts now in manufacturing and marketing. The decline stage is marked by a downward sales trend. While a good replacement parts market may exist for some products, many companies choose to exit or harvest.

OBJECTIVE 5: Recognize how innovations are adopted by consumers by being spread from group to group.

People go through a series of steps in adopting a new product. The speed depends on personal characteristics. Individuals can be grouped into five categories that comprise the diffusion process. Innovators are the first to adopt. They are usually a small group and tend to be eccentric. Early adopters, a larger group, are next. They have high income, and education levels, and others respect them. This group is key to the success of new products. The third category is early majority buyers, a larger segment that generally follows the leadership of the early adopters. The last two categories, late majority buyers and laggards, are the last to adopt. The late majority group is numerous, so it is important.

REVIEW YOUR UNDERSTANDING

1. What are the four product mix options? Describe each.
2. What are the three product innovation categories? What are the characteristics of each?
3. What product characteristics speed the adoption of an innovation?
4. What are the new product development steps? Describe each.
5. What are test markets?
6. List five organizational structures for new product development.
7. What are the differences between simultaneous and sequential methods of new product development?
8. What is the difference between a product manager and a market manager?
9. What are the stages in the product life cycle? Describe them.

DISCUSSION OF CONCEPTS

1. What is the difference between continuous innovation, dynamically continuous innovation, and discontinuous innovation? What are the main activities for marketers when introducing each type?
2. Assume you are senior vice president of marketing for General Electric. What four product mix management options might you consider? Give specific examples of each.
3. Describe the typical profit scenario as a product moves through its life cycle. Do you think it's important for companies to have products in all stages? Why or why not?
4. What are some problems with using the product life cycle concept to make marketing decisions? Why do you think so many companies use the concept?
5. What are some ways to extend the product life cycle? Can you think of any companies that have used these techniques?
6. Many marketers use the diffusion cycle concept and the product life cycle concept. How are they different?
7. When introducing a new product, how may a marketer facilitate consumer acceptance?
8. Describe each organizational structure for new product development. What factors would influence your decision to select one structure over another?

KEY TERMS AND DEFINITIONS

Adoption process: The steps an individual consumer goes through in making a product choice.

Business analysis: Assessment of the attractiveness of the product from a sales, cost, profit, and cash-flow standpoint.

Commercialization: Final stage in the new product development process, when the product is introduced into the market.

Concept testing: Testing the new product concept to evaluate the likelihood of its success.

Continuous innovation: A minor alteration in an existing product, such as a new style or model, that can be easily adopted without significant changes in consumer behavior.

Diffusion process: The spread of innovations from one group of consumers to another over time.

Discontinuous innovation: An entirely new product with new functions.

Dynamically continuous innovation: A familiar product with additional features and benefits that require or permit consumers to alter some aspect of their behavior.

Early adopters: The second group of consumers to purchase new products.

Early majority: The third group of adopters, who are more risk averse in purchase decisions than innovators and early adopters.

Idea generation: The gathering of suggestions for new products from a number of sources using a range of formal and informal methods.

Idea screening: Identifying the new product ideas that have the most potential to succeed.

Innovators: The first group of consumers to purchase a new product.

Laggards: Consumers who resist new products the longest.

Late majority: The more skeptical consumers who purchase products after the early majority.

Line extension: A new product closely related to others in the line.

Market development: Offering existing products to new market segments.

Market manager: A manager responsible for one or several similar product lines targeted at specific market segments.

New product committee: A group of key functional personnel who are brought together periodically to develop new products.

New product department: The organizational unit responsible for identifying product ideas and preparing them for commercialization.

Product concept: A product idea that has been refined into written descriptions, pictures, and specifications.

Product development: Offering new products to existing market segments.

Product life cycle: The four stages a product goes through: introduction, growth, maturity, and decline.

Product manager: A manager who oversees one or several products targeted at all market segments.

Product mix: All the product lines and products a company offers.

Product planning: The focus given to core businesses, market development, product development and diversification.

Sequential new product development: People from various functional areas work on different stages of product development.

Simulated product test: Experimentation with the marketing strategy in artificial conditions.

Smultaneous new product development: People from all functional areas work together to develop products.

Test market: A small geographic area, with characteristics similar to the total market, in which a product is introduced with a complete marketing program.

Venture team: Personnel from various areas of the company who are given release time to work on a specific assignment.

REFERENCES

1. Material given by permission of the Flagship Group, February 1998.
2. Russell Kern, "Nurturing Creativity for Powerful Marketing," *Marketing News,* March 31, 1997, p. 18.
3. George Stalk, Jr., and Thomas N. Hout, *Competing Against Time* (New York: The Free Press, 1990), p. 253.
4. Booz, Allen & Hamilton, *New Product Management for the Eighties* (New York: Booz, Allen & Hamilton, 1982).
5. Christopher Power, "Flops—Too Many New Products Fail. Here Is Why—And How to Do Better," *Business Week,* August 16, 1993, pp. 76–82.
6. Edwin E. Bobrow, "Innovation Is a Strategic Move," *Marketing News,* March 17, 1997, p. 13.
7. Stalk and Hout, *Competing Against Time,* p. 253.
8. Wendy Bounds and Stephen D. Moore, "Kodak to Sell Sterling Winthrop Drug and Two Other Units to Focus on Film," *Wall Street Journal,* May 4, 1994, p. A3.
9. Jeff Jensen, "Deals in U.S., Abroad Aid Nike's Apparel Business," *Advertising Age Interactive Edition* (Features), November 8, 1996, www.adage.com; and Brian Trusdell, "U.S. Soccer Signs Nike Deal," *Associated Press,* www.athens-newspapers.com/1997/102397/1023.s4soccer.html; site visited June 10, 1998.
10. N. Dawar and P. Anderson, "Order and Direction of Brand Extension," *Journal of Business Research* 30 (1994): pp. 119–129.
11. Carmen Fleetwood, "Intel Sends Much Anticipated MMX Chip Into Market," *Wall Street Journal Interactive Edition,* January 8, 1997.
12. Thomas A. Stewart and Melanie Warner, "3M Fights Back," *Fortune,* February 5, 1996, http://pathfinder.com/@@8jzhQAQAUZkBe*e3/fortune/magazine/1996/960205/3mfight.html, site visited January 7,1997.
13. Daniel McGinn, "Here's to Pie in the Sky," *Newsweek,* January 13, 1997, p. 54.
14. "GE Forms Company to Offer Networking, Tech Services," *Wall Street Journal Interactive Edition,* November 8, 1996.
15. Teri Agins and Wendy Bounds, "A Flashier Liz Claiborne Fashions a Turnaround," *Wall Street Journal Interactive Edition,* November 11, 1996.
16. Amy Barrett, "The Corporation's Strategies—It Expands into New Field While Bolstering Its Old Reliables," *Business Week,* September 29, 1997, p. 107; and Joseph Chang, "DuPont Begins To Sell Conoco In Effort to Focus on Biotech," *Chemical Marketing Reporter,* May 18, 1998, pp. 1–22.
17. Judann Pollack, "Kraft's DiGiorno Aiming for Takeout Pizza Dollars," *Advertising Age* (Interactive Edition), November 1996.
18. "Red Devil, Deskey Roll Out Ergonomic Hand Tools," *Marketing News,* March 17, 1997, p. 14.
19. "Cool Companies: 25 Outfits to Watch," *Fortune* (Interactive Edition), July 2, 1997.
20. Walter S. Mossberg, "Dragon Systems Bridges Gap In Speech Recognition Software," *Wall Street Journal Interactive Edition,* June 12, 1997.
21. R.J. Calantone, C.A. diBenedetto, and S. Bhoovaroghaven, "Examining the Relationship between Degree of Innovation and New Product Success," *Journal of Business Research* 30 (1994): pp. 143–148.
22. Stephanie Losee, "Burned by Technology," *Fortune,* September 9, 1996, pp. 105–112.
23. Chris Jones, "Excel, Power Point to Pack Interactive Tools," *Infoworld,* September 23, 1996, p. 29.
24. Michael Krantz, "The Main Event," *Time,* June 1, 1998, pp. 32–37.
25. Janice Maloney, "Married . . . with Internet?" *Fortune,* September 30, 1996, pp. 218–220.
26. Matthew Grimm and Mary Huhn, "KFC Backs New Chicken with $55M in Marketing, Including Magazine Buys," *Media Week,* July 19, 1993, p. 3; and Rona Gindin, "Year of the Roaster," *Restaurant Business,* April 10, 1993, p. 139.
27. Supplement to the March 17, 1997, issue of *Marketing News,* p. E4.
28. George Stalk, Philip Evans, and Lawrence E. Shulman, "Competing on Capabilities: The New Rules of Corporate Strategy," *Harvard Business Review,* March-April 1992, pp. 57–69.
29. Power, "Flops"; and Howard Schlossberg, "Fear of Failure Stifles Product Development," *Marketing News,* May 14, 1990, pp. 1, 16.
30. Michael J. McCarthy, "U.S. Companies Shop Abroad for Product Ideas," *Wall Street Journal,* March 14, 1990, pp. B1, B4; Jack Wagner, "New Products Are Not the Only Way to Grow," *Marketing News,* May 14, 1990, p. 17; and Power, "Flops."
31. "Kentucky Plant Workers Are Cranking Out Good Ideas," *Wall Street Journal,* August 13, 1996, p. B1.
32. Michael H. Martin, "Hip, Hot, 'N' Happening," *Fortune,* July 8, 1996, p. 102.
33. *Wall Street Journal,* August 15, 1996, p. B2.
34. William M. Weilbacher, *Brand Marketing* (Lincolnwood, IL: NTC Business Books), p. 22.
35. James Carbone, "Sun Shines by Taking Out Time," *Purchasing,* September 19, 1996, pp. 34–35.
36. Power, "Flops."
37. "Seventh Generation, Inc.," *Marketing News,* April 25, 1994, p. E8.
38. Jack Weiss, "It Isn't Easy Being Green," *Communications Arts,* September-October 1996, p. 123.
39. R. Calantone, S. Vikery, and C. Droge, "Business Performance and New Product Development Activities: An Empirical Investigation," *Journal of Product Innovation Management* 12 (June 1995): pp. 214–223.
40. T. Haggblom, R. Calantone, and C.A. DiBenedetto, "Do New Product Managers in Large or Hi-Market Share Firms Perceive Marketing R&D Interface Principles Differently?" *Journal of Product Innovation Management* 12 (September 1995): pp. 323–333.
41. "Wearable Computer Systems with Head-Mounted Displays for Manufacturing, Maintenance, and Training Applications," http://eto.sysplan.com/ETO/TIA/Factsheets/BoeingTRP.html, November1996.
42. Ken Yamada, "New Motorola Unit Test Markets Wireless Stations," *Computer Reseller News,* June 17, 1996, p. 63.
43. John F. Yarbrough, "Fill 'er up," *Sales and Marketing Management,* September 1996, p. 126.

44. Damon Darlin, "Wanted: Opinionated Pains in the Butt," *Forbes*, September 23, 1996, pp. 102–104.

45. Jennifer Lawrence, "The Sunchip Also Rises," *Advertising Age*, April 27, 1992, p. S2; and Jennifer Lawrence, "Big Push for Sunchips," *Advertising Age*, February 24, 1992, p. 2.

46. Bob Trott and Ed Scannell, "Courtroom Showdown: Antitrust Action Already Affecting Microsoft Rivals," *InfoWorld*, May 25, 1998, pp. 1–7.

47. Steven P. Schnaars, *Managing Imitation Strategies* (New York: The Free Press, 1994), p. 5.

48. Frank Shipper and Charles C. Manz, "WL Gore and Associates, Inc.," 1992, in Henry Mintzberg, James Brian Quinn, and John Voyer, *The Strategy Process* (Upper Saddle River, NJ: Prentice Hall, 1995), pp. 488–498.

49. Lawrence A. Armour, "Finding New Life In Health Stocks," *Fortune*, September 29, 1997, p. 292.

50. Jennifer Glasse, "Balancing Act: Keeping Size and Cost Down Has Cellular Manufacturers Walking a Fine Line," *Dealerscope*, January 1993, pp. 58–62.

51. Al Ries and Jack Trout, *The 22 Immutable Laws of Marketing* (New York: Harper Collins, 1993), pp. 6–7.

52. Valerie Reitman and Reginald Chua, "Honda's Cub Reigns as King of the Road," *Wall Street Journal*, July 26, 1996 p. B1, B13.

53. Dean Takahashi, "PC Makers See Holiday as Corporate Demand Surges," *Wall Street Journal Interactive Edition*, November 8, 1996.

54. Adam M. Brandenburger and Barry J. Nalebuff, *Co-opetition* (New York: Doubleday, 1996).

55. AP–Dow Jones News Service, "Honda to Stop Selling Sport-Utility Vehicle," *Wall Street Journal Interactive Edition*, November 8, 1996.

56. Ron Stodghill II, "At Upjohn, a Grim Changing of the Guard," *Business Week*, May 3, 1993, p. 36; and Patricia Winters, "Upjohn Buys McNeil's R&D and Runs," *Advertising Age*, January 25, 1993, p. 4.

57. Tim Triplett, "World Cup Winners: Marketers Could Score with Audience of Billions," *Marketing News*, June 20, 1994, pp. 1, 9.

58. Paul Lienert, "Car Talk," *Detroit News*, August 23, 1995, http://detnews.com/AUTOS/0823/talk.htm.

59. Paula Mergenhagen, "How 'Got Milk' Got Sales," *American Demographics*, September 1996, www.marketingpower.com/publications/MT/96_MT/9609_MT/9609MD02.HTM.

60. www.Webprofit.com/common_html/index.htm, site visited on January 9, 1997.

61. Ian P. Murphy, "Super-size It Was the Answer," *Marketing News*, June 9, 1997, p. 2.

62. Raymond Vernon, "International Investment and International Trade in the Product Life Cycle," *Quarterly Journal of Economics* (May 1986) p. 199.

63. Evertt M. Rogers, *Diffusion of Innovations*, 3rd ed. (New York: The Free Press, 1982), pp.164–175.

64. R. Olshavsky and R. Spreng, "An Exploratory Study of the Innovation Evaluation Process," *Journal of Product Innovation Management* 13 (November 1996): 512–529.

65. Dow Jones News Service, "Apple and C-Phone Roll Out Video-Conferencing Products," *Wall Street Journal Interactive Edition*, January 8, 1996.

66. "Intel, Microsoft and Toshiba Publish Specification for Easy, Flexible Power Management on Desktops, Laptops and Servers," January 6, 1997, www.microsoft.com/corpinfo/press/1997/Jan97/acpipr.htm.

67. Brian F. Blake, "They May be Innovative, But They're Not The Same," *Marketing News*, April 15, 1991, p. 12.

CASE 10

MINNESOTA MINING AND MANUFACTURING

*I*NNOVATION IS REQUIRED AT 3M, where 30 percent of annual sales must come from products less than four years old. New products are a critical part of 3M, but the company also believes in forming innovative relationships with suppliers and customers. 3M has made the top 10 list in *Fortune*'s "Most Admired Corporations" for 10 of the last 12 years. Much of its success can be attributed to aggressive new product development. 3M introduces more than 500 new products each year.

According to Dave Beal, a business reporter in Minneapolis–St. Paul, where 3M is headquartered, the company is "stepping up its effort to leverage its technology, in a sweeping drive to boost its sales." Essentially, the strategy is to get to market first with one-of-a-kind products that can be premium-priced to increase the company's profit margins. To help accomplish this, 3M restructured the organization. Many traditional products that faced price competition were put into a separate company, Emation, while less price-sensitive products remained with the parent. In this way, 3M executives can focus attention on higher value-added, unique products.

With a new worldwide technology and product development process, "Pacing Plus," 3M is trying to enhance its competitiveness by bringing successful products to market more rapidly. The program is designed to bring ideas to successful commercialization in half the time. This means products with significant functionality for customers and value that can generate high profits for the corporation. Pacing Plus cuts through the red tape and focuses on products with a high probability of success. 3M has approximately 50 major initiatives in the works and just two of them are expected to bring in more than $400 million in new sales by 2000. Ron Mitsch, 3M's vice chairman, believes that new products will soon increase the company's annual growth rate to more than 10 percent. With at least $1 billion a year invested in R&D,

these new products must be successful in the global marketplace. If 1997 is any indication, the approach is on target. U.S. sales rose approximately 9 percent, and sales abroad increased more than 12 percent.

3M certainly has the talent to make things happen. Its 6,500 R&D personnel have backgrounds in chemistry, electronics, biochemistry, microbiology, genetics, pharmacology, and material sciences. They are scattered among 71 R&D laboratories around the world, the largest of which houses approximately 4,000 at 3M's Maple Wood campus in Austin, Texas. Many new product ideas emerge from scientists working closely with customers who have specific needs. To help focus R&D talent efforts, 3M groups technologies into 37 "platforms." Some are large, such as the adhesive platform, which includes the sticky substance on Post-it notes and thousands of other 3M products. The micro-replication platform focuses on new technologies that provide opportunities to reinvent many existing 3M products through enhanced benefits.

3M R&D chief, William Coil says that "one of our goals is to increase our speed to market. But, we're not trying to increase our speed before we decide to take something to market, because that could have a real negative implication for innovation." 3M spends a good deal of time making sure that market conditions can support a new product. The risks are gigantic, given the large number of people and huge budgets involved, but 3M personnel are taught to understand and assume risk. In one training session, students are given real money and asked to wager it. In one scenario, a small amount of cash is placed at the end of a long plank laid on the floor, and an employee is given the opportunity to walk along the plank to get the loot. Then the students are asked if a huge amount of money were at stake, would they walk the same plank if it were stretched between two seven-story buildings. "The downside risk . . . ," someone might begin; but the leader responds, "What risk? You've already proven it's very easy to do it."

By creating a safe environment for risk-taking entrepreneurship, 3M has been able to accomplish 30 percent of sales from very young products. Still, it is interested in raising the bar, and Pacing Plus is one way to do this. It requires coordination throughout the organization. According to Marc Adam, head of marketing, "there's progressively more in common between R&D and marketing." 3M's major customer teams include representatives from R&D all the way through sales. This helps the company understand even unarticulated customer needs, so it can create products to meet them.

1. *Imagine you are in charge of product development at 3M. Explain why innovation is a critical part of your company's strategy.*

2. *How is Pacing Plus expected to improve 3M's product development process?*

3. *How does 3M manage risk? Suggest additional ways the company can promote risk-taking entrepreneurship.*

4. *How might 3M use the product life cycle concept to build and adjust its marketing strategies over time?*

SOURCES: Dave Beal, "To Boost Sales, 3M Steps up Effort to Capitalize on Its Technology Edge," *St. Paul Pioneer Press–Knight-Ridder/Tribune Business News,* March 31, 1997, p. 331; Thomas A. Stewart, "3M Fights Back," *Fortune,* February 5, 1996, www.fortune.com; and the 3M Web site, www.mmm.com, visited on June 10, 1998.

Chapter 11

Services and Nonprofit Marketing

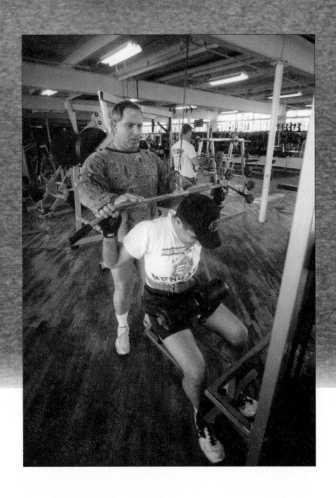

Objectives

1. Identify the forces that have produced and will continue to create tremendous growth in the service economy.

2. Understand which characteristics of services must be adjusted for successful marketing.

3. Know how to develop the service mix.

4. Explore the expanded concept of services.

5. Appreciate the importance of nonprofit marketing and the uniqueness of this important marketing arena.

WITH SEVERAL HUNDRED GYMS SERVING ABOUT *two million people in the greater Boston area, you have to be doing something right to attract clients and win awards. Vinny Greco's Powerhouse Gym, in the small suburb of Watertown, Massachusetts, understands that emphasizing service is the key to success. The Powerhouse brand name may draw people in, but it's the individual facility that keeps them coming back. "You have to love what you do," says Greco, who created the mix of services, enthusiasm, level of comfort, and atmospherics for his clientele. A real people person, he enjoys helping clients meet their personal health and fitness goals. Not only that—he's proud of his business and has fun, too. "I'm the curator of an adult playground," says Vinny, "so I've gotta have fun!"*

Serving customers on a personalized basis has resulted in higher-than-average retention rates and numerous awards for Greco's gym. Located in a town with a dozen competitors, Vinny won four newspaper awards in 1997 (based on voting by readers). The awards were for best gym, best coach (Vinny Greco), best trainer (Vinny Greco), and best bartender (part-time staffer John Sementelli, a marketing major at Bentley College). No wonder the gym is in the top 10 in the greater Boston area.

Vinny's love for gyms began more than 20 years ago. At age 24 and almost 260 pounds, Greco realized he had to do something. He joined a local gym and taught himself about proper nutrition and training programs. Armed with his knowledge—and the experience of shedding many pounds—he became one of the first personal trainers in Massachusetts. His approach to personalizing the workout experience made him popular with clients.

But Vinny had set an even higher goal: own his own gym. He saw the need for a facility that targeted the local community—a diverse array of blue-collar workers, immigrants, professionals, and students living just 10 minutes away from Boston. From his personal training and work at another gym, he saved $25,000 in eight years. Still short of the money needed, Vinny wrote a business plan and approached family members about a loan, offering 10 percent annual interest in addition to repaying the principal. With the necessary capital in hand, he called some of the major franchises.

Vinny talked directly with owners of Powerhouse Gyms International, Inc., and felt an immediate rapport. He shared similar goals with the organization: providing a high-quality, personalized service. As a licensee, Vinny paid a set amount up front plus a yearly fee. In return, he received help from the experts at Powerhouse in setting up the gym, marketing, and *merchandising—not to mention a 10 percent discount on all gym equipment. For Vinny, that made a big difference when he bought $75,000 in equipment to get started. In addition, Powerhouse franchisees offer support and advice to one another.*

Of course, Powerhouse is a large organization, with more than 320 global locations. The name is an asset in recruiting clients. The company promotes its national image through sponsoring major fitness and bodybuilding events. On a regional level, Greco underwrites an annual bodybuilding competition each fall. In late 1996, Powerhouse also launched a nationally distributed magazine, Balance.

Vinny runs his service as four separate business units: memberships, clothing, tanning, and the juice/protein bar. As he puts it: "Four ways to make money." The membership fees are clearly the bread and butter. A small part of the gym is set aside to sell branded Powerhouse clothing (muscle shirts, sweatshirts, T-shirts, pants, and lifting gloves). There are some tanning beds for use on a fee basis. And the 29-foot juice/protein bar includes dietary supplements like protein shakes and MetRx bars.

Over the years, Greco's gym has seen its share of famous people. Former members include Danny Woods (from New Kids on the Block), Major League baseball player Ellis Burkes, and Ted Arcidi—the first person to bench press 700 pounds. Olympic athletes and professional bodybuilders have stopped by on occasion. And writer Chris Radant immortalized Vinny's gym in a chapter of her best-selling book, Home for the Holidays.[1]

Greco's gym is successful because Vinny understands the key ways to market a service. He understands the personal nature of a service and how to offer value by addressing the unique requirements of his customers. In this chapter we will explore how the marketing of services differs from the marketing of goods. We will identify many types of services and learn about how consumers evaluate services.

THE CONCEPT OF SERVICES

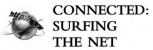

CONNECTED: SURFING THE NET

www.world.std/ ~jyocum/vinny.html

Locate Vinny Greco's Powerhouse Gym on the Internet or use a search engine to visit the Web site of a Powerhouse Gym near you.

Products can be either goods or services. Goods are physical objects. **Services** are intangible ideas, tasks, experiences, performances, or activities that one party can offer another. A major difference between a service and a good is that services generally involve suppliers connecting directly with consumers for performance of the service. Your barber, your doctor, and your professor all require your involvement in order to perform their service. They connect with you personally. When you think about it, even goods are more valuable when accompanied by excellent service. Consequently, goods and services often go hand in hand.

To serve means to benefit a receiving party through personal acts. The marketing of services, by its very nature, concerns the development of beneficial relationships. Interpersonal skills are critical, because for a service to be performed well, these skills must help support the customer relationship. And the marketers of services are likely to fail if they do not embody all the principles of good marketing in their activities.

For more than a quarter century, the dollar volume of services in the U.S. economy has grown at nearly 4 percent annually, approximately double the growth rate for products. This torrid pace is expected to continue well into the 21st century. Services are responsible for 74 percent of GDP and 79 percent of all jobs.[2] More than 10 million U.S. workers are employed in the travel and hospitality industries alone.

Countries such as the United States, Japan, and Germany rely upon the production, sale, and consumption of services for domestic growth.[3] Since services account for $600 billion in international trade, the global market also is very important.[4] The United States has emerged as a world leader in services. Foreign countries pay approximately $70 billion more for U.S. services than Americans pay them for theirs. That trade surplus is five times greater than it was in 1986, and some analysts expect it to be even greater by 2000.[5] Global marketing, therefore, is particularly important for many U.S. service providers. The Carlson Co. is a good example of how U.S. service companies have gone international. Carlson owns T.G.I. Friday's, a popular "all-American" restaurant chain with a casual format that has done well at home and abroad, including the Far East. Sales volume in Seoul, Korea, for example, is double that

TGI Friday's is an international service provider that has done especially well in the Far East.

of the chain's average U.S. restaurant. The atmosphere is the same, the walls are decorated with remnants of American culture, and the staff is just as lively as in the States.[6]

Figure 11-1 provides an overview of this chapter. We begin by looking at forces that have created and will continue to produce explosive growth for services. This is followed by a section that explores service characteristics in depth. It will show how services are differentiated, their relationships to goods, the attributes consumers use to judge them, and what quality service is. Next, we will describe the aspects marketers consider when developing the service mix. You will extend what you learned in chapters 9 and 10 to services by looking at core, augmented, and branded services and the development of new offerings. Keep in mind that services are as important in business-to-business marketing as they are in consumer marketing. Such traditional services as health care, insurance, energy, telecommunications, garbage and snow removal, accounting and tax preparation, auto service, and restaurants have been the backbone of the service economy for a long time. The first part of the chapter provides an understanding of how these kinds of services are marketed. The next sections discuss the

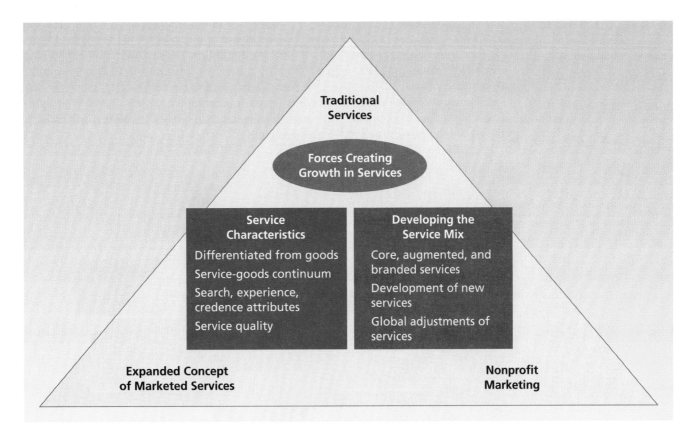

Figure 11-1   The Concept of Services

expanded concept of services, which includes person, entertainment, event, place, political, cause, and internal marketing. We conclude by looking at the important area of nonprofit marketing.

GLOBAL FORCES CREATING GROWTH IN SERVICES

The service economy is not unique to the United States. In developed countries around the globe, more and more of total economic well-being is based on services. As nations become more sophisticated, the demand for services grows. The Industrial Revolution brought about productivity gains through the substitution of machines for human and animal labor. The technology revolution that followed went far beyond the mere substitution of labor. It resulted in the creation of products that exceeded human and animal capabilities. A century ago, who would have imagined that millions of business travelers would routinely fly six miles above the earth and use plastic cards to charge phone calls while in flight? Air transportation and telecommunications are examples of services that have brought us closer to the reality of a global community. Figure 11-2 depicts the global forces that are influencing growth in services.

TECHNOLOGY

On the eve of the 21st century, technology is producing more sophisticated services more rapidly. Until recently, more advanced nations were still dedicated to the production of goods. Today, many of the goods that are produced support services for thousands, and even millions of consumers. The technologies of today can't be used by consumers without the services of highly trained professionals. For example, jet aircraft produced in the '60s, still carry millions of passengers annually, while planes being produced today are likely to still be flying half way through the 21st century. Smaller percentages of the population are now able to produce greater quantities of more valuable goods thereby shifting the emphasis to value-added services. Some of these services include entertainment, travel, health, and education in the consumer sector and consulting and environmental controls in the business-to-business sector.

The technological revolution is making an information revolution possible, which now facilitates nearly every human endeavor. Soon, transmitters in today's microprocessors will be replaced by transmitters that operate 10 million times faster. This could alter the commercial landscape to a point nearly unrecognizable by many of us.[7] Today one of the largest service industries is computer software, and this sector will almost certainly expand exponentially in future decades. Consider the new service on the Internet which allows you to download a single song from a CD for about $1.00. By 2002 this type of cyber tunes business is expected to reach $1.6 billion. And secure links will provide instantaneous funds transfer. A two-hour computer card can be filled with single songs from your favorite artists.[8] Amazingly, the service industry already dominates spending for on-line computer services, totaling $520 million and topping 25 industries.[9] The information and technological revolution will assist in the creation of services presently unimaginable.

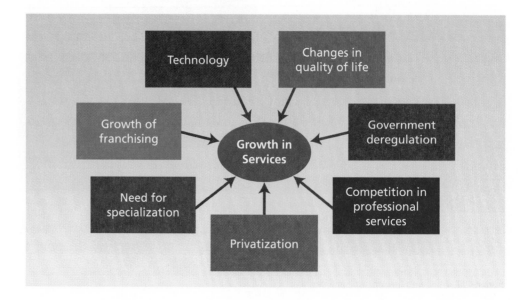

*Figure 11-2   Global Forces
Creating Growth in Services*

In many cases, technology eliminates the need for personal interaction between a buyer and seller. For example, according to the Federal Deposit Insurance Corporation, the number of commercial banks has declined from 14,200 in 1986 to 9,500 today. This can be attributed in part to automated teller machines, computer banking, and other services. Despite the decline, consumers still prefer to do business face-to-face. A recent study by KPMG Peat Marwick indicated that 73 percent of consumers prefer to bank in a staffed branch. Another 64 percent said they would rather not use technology for certain transactions.[10]

QUALITY OF LIFE

Quality of life is not defined by how much is consumed but by how people feel and experience life. For example, our thinking about basic services such as health, education, and mobility has expanded dramatically. Health once meant the absence of sickness but today's perception of health has expanded to include fitness, increased physical performance, and enhanced mental well-being. Education, once the domain of the elite few, has become accessible to a significant percentage of the population. Many people find expenditures at bookstores as valuable as the purchase of a microwave oven was in the 1970s. Mobility, expressed in the 1950s by a high-performance car, now includes psychological mobility provided by movies, cellular phones, and the Internet. Internet cafes illustrate yet another change in the quality of life, providing customers with two popular services in one—specialty coffees and the world wide computer network.

The fast pace of family life has placed a tremendous premium on services of all types. As more women move into the work force, there is less time available for traditional responsibilities such as child care and cooking. Nearly all the women who entered the workplace in the last two decades have joined the service sector, which has increased the demand for services. Most people would prefer to use their leisure time for activities other than shopping and cooking. Today, American's eating patterns are changing from three square meals a day to five smaller meals. An increasing percentage of these meals are consumed in the car. This has resulted in an increase in the availability of convenient food options for on-the-go consumers, such as fast food restaurants.[11] Because of time constraints, sales in traditional supermarkets are declining dramatically, while companies like Peapod Delivery Systems, which delivers full grocery baskets to people's homes, are growing. Others, such as Waiter on Wheels, Room Service Deliveries, Takeout Taxi, and Door 2 Door work with restaurants to deliver meals. Many families enjoy the convenience of a home service for grooming their pet. Cindy Sommerville brings her pet grooming service to the customer's home for $40–$55, depending on the type of pet.[12] Today, 42 percent of pre-school age children are in day care facilities, allowing both parents to work. As a result of the increase in dual-career families, the need for quality day-care services has grown dramatically and services to support the family in leisure time have also become more valuable.

GOVERNMENT DEREGULATION OF SERVICES

Another factor profoundly influencing growth in services is industry deregulation that has occurred over the past 15 years. This trend, started in the United States, has now spread throughout Europe. Understanding that competition provides vast opportunities for economic growth, legislators have deregulated many services that were traditionally controlled by government agencies. As expected, numerous private companies have stepped in to seize

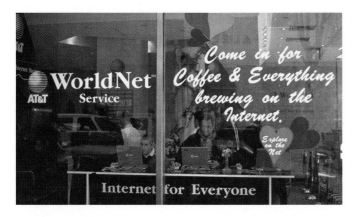

"Cybercafes" are an example of a change in the quality of life, offering customers specialty coffees and the opportunity to connect to the Internet.

and create opportunities. For example, the spectacular growth in cellular phones was stimulated by deregulation of the telephone industry. In fact, the deregulation of the telephone industry has led to competitive phone wars. SNET (Southern New England Telephone Company) of Connecticut estimates the average family will soon spend $200 a month on communications and entertainment. SNET, which once served 98 percent of all the homes and businesses in Connecticut, now faces serious competition from companies like AT&T. Other companies have formed alliances in order to provide bundled services, such as the alliance formed by Sprint, TCI, Cox Communications, TCG, and Comcast. These bundled services can include local, long distance, cellular, and cable among other services. In the future it is expected that the more services a consumer buys in a bundled package, the cheaper each becomes.[13] Consumers should emerge as winners in the midst of increasing competition due to improved services and lower prices. Major deregulation also has occurred in:

- Transportation—air freight, airlines, trucking, and shipping
- Finance—banking, securities, and insurance
- Telecommunications—radio, television, and telephones
- Energy—electricity and gas

Competition stimulated by deregulation results in a better selection at a better price, which improves demand and creates jobs. For example, when the government deregulated the airline industry, companies expanded the number, location, and pricing approaches of flights, among other changes. The result has been better prices, better schedules, and overall improved service levels for consumers. Increased competition has made it necessary for companies to deliver greater value to consumers, which in turn has stimulated demand for these services. For example the telecommunications industry has become one of the three fastest growing industries in the United States. Spending on communications alone is expected to reach $353 billion by the year 2000.[14] Overall, consumers and businesses both win.

COMPETITION IN PROFESSIONAL SERVICES

Not long ago, doctors, lawyers, and other professionals were prohibited from marketing their services in the media. Only subtle means were allowed, such as sports team sponsorships or word-of-mouth. All this changed in 1974, when the Supreme Court ruled that a ban on lawyer marketing was unconstitutional.[15] Today, nearly every profession engages in some form of marketing. Health care is a good case in point.

Hospitals, preferred provider organizations, and health maintenance organizations compete vigorously for patients, and there are elaborate educational campaigns designed to teach doctors how to market services. The availability of information via technology has enhanced marketers' opportunities to promote health care services. Users will be able to access medical specialists and information as well as interact with visuals and audio. Touchscreens will walk the patient to the health care provider electronically.[16] Marketers must exercise care in the promotion of health goods and services. Since the health care industry is complex and often confusing, consumers usually know very little about products and services offered. Without this knowledge and expertise about the industry, consumers must rely, to some degree, on marketers to inform them. This places great emphasis on the importance of truthful and reliable information. The use of puffery to increase market share or profits could have serious ethical implications.[17]

The legal profession also promotes itself. The largest section in most urban Yellow Pages is attorneys. Although prestigious law firms still tend to use community activities as their main source of promotion, many attorneys use all forms of promotion, pricing, and distribution approaches. In some areas, lawyers distribute their services through 900-number phone lines, which consumers call for advice at $3.00 per minute. In Canada, some law firms engage in advertising through direct mail, billboards, and magazines.[18]

PRIVATIZATION

Privatization occurs when government services are contracted to private organizations for them to manage. The concept originated in the United Kingdom as an effort to revitalize the economy by shifting many bureaucratic services to aggressive private firms. The British railroad, telecommunications, and transportation industries were privatized, among others. Privatization also occurred in East Germany when the Berlin Wall came down and in Russia when the Soviet Union was dissolved. Both countries immediately began to transfer ownership of huge, government-controlled service institutions to private companies. Consulting organizations from the United States, Europe, and Japan have been working diligently to help these private companies succeed. In Kuwait, members of the parliament have been lobbying for privatization in the mobil telephone market. Kuwait Mobile Telephones recently signed a contract with Motorola which more than doubles Kuwait's subscribers in a market it currently monopolizes.[19] Lobbyists want private organizations to manage the mobile telephone market to allow competition to occur.

In the United States there is a definite trend toward privatization of local, state, and federal government services. Many hospitals and jails, once owned and maintained by cities and counties, are now operated by private companies. Likewise, prisons are often run more economically by private firms than by the government. In Baltimore, Maryland, eight public schools were contracted out to a private organization, Education Alternatives, to operate for profit. They, in turn, subcontracted cleaning and maintenance to Johnson Controls and accounting to KPMG Peat Marwick.[20] Minnesota-Based Educational Alternatives, Inc. (MEAI) also competes for business from communities willing to transfer public school management to private hands.[21]

THE NEED FOR SPECIALIZATION

Specialization occurs when an organization chooses to focus its resources on core business activities. In order to utilize resources and build strength in their core business, many organizations rely on service providers for basic support of their business. Personnel agencies hire and assess employees, accounting firms do the books, systems consultants set up the computers, and so forth. Most companies find it economical to farm out some of the services they previously performed themselves. ARAMARK, featured in chapter 8, is one of the world's largest service companies. It has chosen the strategy of marketing services that are not core to their clients' business. For example, ARAMARK offers security, cleaning, grounds maintenance, catering, and snow removal services. For large stadiums and amusement parks, it handles everything from parking lots to food, maintenance, and cleaning. The firm even supplies hospitals with physicians for emergency rooms, a particularly difficult area of hiring and management for hospitals. Companies realize that just as they specialize in a certain aspect of business, there are service providers who do the same.

| CAREER TIP | ARAMARK is the world's leading managed services provider with a portfolio of career opportunities in nearly every service area. Since ARAMARK has units in thousands of locations, it can offer companywide, nationwide, and worldwide opportunities. Check out current employment listings and submit your qualifications on-line at **www.aramark.com/employment/home.htm**. Or, send your resume to Dept. GRWBAR291, ARAMARK Corporation, P.O. Box 41796, Philadelphia, Pennsylvania, 19101. |

ACCESS TO KNOWLEDGE

Today, fundamental competencies required to run many service businesses are accessible to individuals or small groups of experts. At one time, these competencies were only available to large corporations. Through computerized subscription services on the Internet, experts everywhere have access to vast quantities of information. At one time, General Motors (GM) provided its own internal information service, but as it grew more complex, GM acquired EDS, a service group, to help develop and maintain its information system. By providing expertise in mainframe computers and centralized control, EDS brought many unique skills that GM required to manage its vast information needs. Today, much of that same type of information is available to anyone with a good PC. Although GM recently sold EDS, it now helps GM connect a vast array of PCs in a "distributed information system." The system allows thousands of GM employees access to company information. This increased accessibility to the system gives employees all the information that is needed to do their jobs right at their fingertips.

GROWTH OF FRANCHISING

A **franchise** is a contractual agreement in which an entrepreneur pays a fee and agrees to meet operating requirements in exchange for the franchise of name and marketing plan.

Franchise
A contractual agreement whereby an entrepreneur pays a fee for the franchise name and agrees to meet operating requirements and use the organization's marketing plan.

CONNECTED: SURFING THE NET

www.subway.com

Learn about Subway franchise opportunities by visiting its Web site. Browse the electronic library, read about international Subway franchises, or request a brochure. And, for fun, play the amazing virtual Subway game.

Franchising is another major trend influencing the service industry. National and international franchisers have developed aggressive growth strategies, particularly in the sectors of fast food and cleaning. Franchising allows companies like McDonald's®, Subway, Service Master, and Jiffy Lube to increase quickly the number of locations where customers can purchase their services. Food service chains were expected to see a growth between 5–6 percent in 1996, which would contribute to the $900 billion food industry.[22] Of course, this also means that more and more employees are required to deliver the service.

Another area of franchise growth will be seen in the distribution channels for car sales. Since customers value pressure-free shopping when purchasing an automobile, third parties, superstores, and on-line buying have provided alternatives.[23] These alternatives have taken a fixed price approach without aggressive sales tactics. The increase in the use of these franchises may result in a decline of traditional dealerships and a change in the way today's dealers serve customers.

SERVICE CHARACTERISTICS THAT AFFECT MARKETING STRATEGY

Several aspects of services should be considered when marketing strategies are developed. First, services can be clearly contrasted from goods in several ways. Second, services should be looked at from the perspective of a service-goods continuum, not simply as services. Some products are all service, others are half of each, and still others are pure goods. Third, consumers use several strategies to evaluate a service. They look at its attributes to find clues about its expected performance. Fourth, service quality plays a key role in success.

THE CONTRASTS BETWEEN GOODS AND SERVICES

Most of our discussion in this book has referred to products, meaning both goods and services. This is because the marketing of both is very similar. What works for one generally works for the other. In addition, as we will see later, an organization's product mix usually has products with characteristics of both goods and services. Even so, there are six sharp distinctions between the two. The uniqueness of services lies in their intangibility, the relationship with the consumer, the importance of the service encounter, their aspect of simultaneous production and consumption, their perishability, and the type of quality controls they entail.

Marketing Intangibles Physical goods have form and mass; they can be seen and touched. Prior to sale, services exist primarily as an offer or promise of some experience that will occur in the future. They only become "real" when performed. Insurance is a good example of an intangible product. The paper on which the policy is printed describes the promise the company makes to the person paying the premiums. Only when the consumer suffers a loss is the product delivered—in the form of money or a replacement for an insured item.

Many services take shape in unexpected ways over time. Think about a computerized dating service. The purchaser may have high expectations, but it may be weeks, months, or even years before the potential benefit is realized. This intangibility makes it difficult to assess the value of services or compare alternatives prior to purchase. And after the service is performed, it is too late to change the decision. Consider bungee cord jumping. Until you step onto the platform, have the cord attached, and jump, you cannot experience the sensation. Once you leave the platform, it is too late to reject the service.

Relationship of Provider to Customer Services are performed on or with customers personally or on what is theirs—children (day care, youth sports camps), animals (vets, stables, feedlots), things (lawn care, car wash, auto repair), and so forth. Whereas most goods are manufactured at a plant far from customers, most services are created in their presence or with their personal knowledge of how they were performed. Consequently, there is an inseparable relationship between the provider and the user. In some cases this interaction may be very personal, such as the relationship between parents and the provider of their child's care. Consumers may develop a strong preference about who performs the service. Most of us have a favorite barber or hair stylist and dread trying someone new. In fact, we may be willing to pay extra to have our usual stylist cut our hair. Much the same holds true for the family dentist, lawyer, and doctor.

The Service Encounter Connection   One of the most important aspects of service marketing is the **service encounter**, the contact between the consumer and the seller. Jan Carlzon, former president of Scandinavian Airline Systems (SAS), speaks of service encounters as "moments of truth." Carlzon led SAS toward a strong customer focus, pointing out that the airline came face to face with consumers 65,000 times each day. He estimated that each passenger had contact with five SAS employees over the course of a year. Although the typical service encounter lasted only about 15 seconds, the outcome of each one ultimately translated into success or failure for the company. His fervent conviction has made SAS one of the most customer-oriented carriers in the industry.

The service encounter concept reinforces the importance of customer relationships in marketing a service. Employees not only must have the interpersonal skills to treat consumers well but also must be oriented toward solving the customer's problem. At the most elementary level, salespeople need to be cordial and gracious. At a more fundamental level, they have to be helpful in discovering and meeting service needs during the encounter. Each moment contributes to the customer's experience with the service. If these moments are positive, then satisfaction with purchase and service delivery is likely to be positive as well.

At SAS, Carlzon realized that in order to satisfy a customer in 15 seconds, employees had to have the tools and the authority necessary to make certain decisions. He rearranged the organization so that front-line personnel could quickly serve any customer. Managers, who typically hold power and responsibility, became supporters for those employees. Similarly, Wal-Mart managers support employees in efforts to maintain exceptional service encounters. At Wal-Mart, the company receives letters daily from customers pleased with their service encounter, which may include an associate who remembers their name or carries out a purchase for them. Some customers write letters in appreciation of a simple smile. Sam Walton, the company founder, insisted that associates practice "aggressive hospitality" in order to offer better service. Wal-Mart believes even brief service encounters can make enough difference to keep the customer coming back.[24] The diversity feature, "Beyond Accessibility: How Hotels Win Over the Disabled Traveler," shows how crucial the service encounter can be.

Simultaneous Production and Consumption   The fact that many services are made and used at the same moment creates interesting situations. First, the buyer and seller have to cooperate. In some cases this involves power dynamics. When you tell your stylist how you want your hair cut, you accomplish a managerial act. Second, since buyers vary and services depend on the recipient, the same service may be dramatically different from one situation to the next. A provider may operate one way with one consumer and then adjust the service considerably to meet the needs of another. Consider the role of a personal fitness trainer. Since people have different goals and varying personal needs, a trainer must adjust a fitness program to suit each individual. Finally, since the buyer must be present in order for at least part of the service to be performed, consumers invest time. This places a premium on the speed of delivery and the importance of correct performance the first time. For example, satisfaction with automobile repair services depends largely on whether the car is ready when promised. Or think about how annoying it is to wait in a physician's crowded office when you have other things to do.

No Storage and Inventory   Although goods can be stored until needed, services cannot. Services are extremely **perishable**—their value exists for a short time. When an airplane takes off with several empty seats, those fares can never be recovered. Therefore, accurate forecasting and the need to match supply with demand are important. When the demand for a service is stable, there is little difficulty in meeting supply requirements, but most services have erratic demand. For example, on very hot days almost all consumers turn on their air conditioner, creating a surge in energy demand. Should the utility company build enough capacity to supply its peak load or its average load? In the first case, there will be many periods when resources are unused; in the latter case, blackouts can result. When you telephone on Mother's Day or Thanksgiving, it may be difficult to get through right away because of an unusually high demand for connections. At peak hours of Internet demand, the speed at which you can access information decreases significantly. Similarly, cellular phone users often have problems during rush hour, when everyone tied up in traffic decides to make calls. If the service provider cannot meet the peak load, then customers are likely to go elsewhere.

Service encounter
The interaction between the consumer and the seller.

Perishable
The temporal nature of services, whose value exists for only a short time.

CONNECTING WITH DIVERSITY

BEYOND ACCESSIBILITY: HOW HOTELS WIN OVER THE DISABLED TRAVELER

To prepare for the 1996 Little People of America Conference, the Adams Mark Hotel in Indianapolis spent thousands of dollars to make check-in desks, elevator buttons, urinals, and other fixtures accessible to people as short as three feet. It also coached employees in being sensitive to dwarves, who often face rejection and ridicule. The Adams Mark is one of a number of hotels taking a proactive approach to the Americans with Disabilities Act (ADA) passed in 1990. With no federal enforcement—but the threat of a lawsuit if a hotel is found not to be accessible—some facilities have only grudgingly complied. Others, like the Adams Mark, are finding there is good reason not just to meet but to exceed the expectations of disabled customers.

The almost 50 million Americans with disabilities comprise a virtually untapped and ignored market. Furthermore, about 77 million baby boomers are approaching the age at which chronic illness sets in. As the disabled organize for social, legal, and educational purposes, they are holding more and larger conventions, and these tend to last longer than a week. While staying at a hotel, the disabled make more use of dining and bar facilities than other guests do. As Oral Miller, executive director of the American Council of the Blind, points out: "Because 98 percent of our members are blind or visually impaired, we're not as likely to go out and hit the town." After hosting the sixth annual meeting of the Society for Disability Studies, the Embassy Suites hotel near Seattle had the most profitable week of the year in its restaurants.

This doesn't mean that hotels can treat the disabled as a captive market. Like any guests, the disabled complain if they're unhappy, but their complaints can escalate into ADA-related lawsuits. Hotels that court these travelers consult with several disabled groups before they make structural changes, train employees, or host conventions. The Chicago Hilton & Towers talked with several before it undertook a $1.5 million full-scale ADA renovation. Lighthouse, an organization that works with the visually impaired, had very practical suggestions, such as Braille and enlarged-letter information sheets at the front desk. The hotel has since won kudos from *Access to Travel* magazine for successfully hosting a convention of more than 3,000 blind people.

Carol Duke, creator of Opening Doors, a training program for hotel employees, emphasizes that the hospitality industry must go beyond structural issues, like making a toilet seat low enough or doors wider "You can have the Taj Mahal of accessibility and a manager who can recite every nuance of the law," she says, "but if your employees are uncomfortable around persons with disabilities, it doesn't matter." Duke's program is based on what she calls the "forgotten section" of the ADA, requiring businesses to modify behavior, practices, and policies to overcome fear and ignorance of the disabled.

Accessible and sensitive, hotels are rewarded with a loyalty surpassing that of most guests. Disabled people tend both to return to trusted hotels and to spread the word fast among other groups. The Little People's convention at the Adams Mark ended with hugs between happy attendees and staff and an assurance that the 900-plus group would return and recommend the hotel to others. Beyond these tangible rewards, however, is the simple pleasure service employees feel when they give someone a week of feeling "normal," surrounded by their peers in an hospitable atmosphere.

Sources: Grace Wagner, "Taking a Lead on ADA," *Lodging Hospitality,* October 1993, pp. 47–48; Kevin Helliker, "Catering to the Disabled at Convention Time Is a Lucrative Niche,"*Wall Street Journal,* September 19, 1996, A1; and Grace Wagner, "Hilton's Leading Role," *Lodging Hospitality,* April 1994, pp. 55–56.

Service Quality Control The quality of goods is usually monitored by human inspectors or the electronic eye of machinery. That close monitoring is virtually impossible in the case of services. Unique quality control techniques, which are discussed in detail later in the chapter, are necessary for services. For now, it is important to remember that many services cannot be performed again if a mistake is made. An 18-year-old who emerges from high school poorly educated is unlikely to start all over again. In addition, because services are so people-intensive, quality can depend directly on those who supply them. For example, companies like National Seminar Group, Skill Path, Inc., and Career Trak provide educational services nationally, and much of the quality relies on the competence of individual instructors. In some service companies, people at one level of the organization train others, who train others, and so on. But despite all efforts to ensure good training, it may not be possible to standardize a service and ensure quality every time. If one employee at a dry cleaning shop ruins your suit or dress, then you probably will go elsewhere the next time.

Globally, training methods often need to be adjusted to ensure quality service. For example, sales reps in China often sell products solely on price, fail to ask consumers business-related questions, and demonstrate little product knowledge. They also have little training or marketing support. In the United States, sales reps are trained to understand customers needs and emphasize product benefits, have extensive product knowledge, and help the customer understand the value of the potential purchase. The Chinese and American training methods produce two distinct types of service. Differences in culture also play an important role in consumer perceptions of quality service.[25]

Service quality control is monitored by trained observers during and after service delivery. Chances are that you have phoned a company and heard a recording saying the call may be monitored to be sure you receive appropriate service. This type of feedback lets the organization know whether service is being performed consistently and as it was intended. When there are difficulties, most customer-oriented service providers give employees additional training, supervision, and help.

THE SERVICE-GOODS CONTINUUM

While there are differences in marketing goods and services, there are also many similarities. In fact, few organizations market only one or the other. Most purchases fall somewhere along the continuum between almost pure goods and almost pure services, as illustrated in Figure 11-3.

Notice the word *almost* at each end of the continuum. Even in their purest form, goods and services still contain some aspect of the other. Almost pure goods are physical products that can be described by their form, mass, and function. There are thousands of types, ranging from computer chips to ocean liners. A gym supplies several different products that can be considered almost pure goods, such as clothes, equipment, and health food.

Next along the continuum are goods with services. These are physical products accompanied by the supportive services required to make them work. For example, automobiles play a major role in our economy not only because of their sales revenues but also because of the services they require. Chrysler's success has been due in part to its warranty strategy. Nintendo succeeded where Atari failed because of its return policy and 800 numbers. In Boulder, Colorado, Robb's Music offers free delivery and assembly of electronic keyboards and pianos.[26]

Half goods and half services are products that require both elements equally to succeed. Restaurants provide a certain level of service, which includes the atmosphere, and goods such as food and beverages. Key topics at a National Restaurant show emphasized just that. Customers want to anticipate as well as enjoy their dining experiences, which means it is impor-

Almost Pure Goods	Goods with Services	Half Goods, Half Services	Services with Goods	Almost Pure Services
Physical products that are purchased and consumed with little or no service	Products supported with repair, maintainance, add-ons, and advice	Products that consist of both goods and services	Intellectual property or equipment to make goods work	Experiences that are consumed during delivery
Groceries Gasoline (self-serve) Steel	Autos Auto repair Video games	Restaurants Bookstores Movie theaters Prepared food delivery	Rental movies Training books Software Electronic mail Fax service	Health clubs Medical care Consulting Legal services Day care

Figure 11-3 Continuum of Goods and Services

Source: Adapted from Valarie A. Zeithaml, "How Consumer Evaluation Processes Differ Between Goods and Services," in Marketing of Services, *ed. James H. Donnelly and William R. George. Reprinted with permission of the American Marketing Association, 1981.*

tant for marketers to appeal to customer expectations about entertainment, a unique atmosphere, or interactive opportunities. Since people "eat with their eyes, ears, and other senses" before the meal, food and service quality are equally important.[27] Bookstores provide not only products (books) but also guidance in searching out unique topics. In addition, their spatial arrangement, background music, and atmosphere all contribute to the "feelings" that sell. Coffee and beverage shops have been added to many bookstores to encourage customers to spend hours on a self-actualizing experience.

Services with goods are usually intellectual properties or equipment required to make goods work. Examples include rental movies, training books, and software. They are significant not so much because of their physical aspects but because of the messages they contain. Electronic mail or Internet services such as Netscape can be included in this category. In 1995 the consumer market for on-line services was very attractive, but the original Microsoft Network failed due to a lack of Web content. Microsoft has since reintroduced its network to include communications, technical information, references, and other services lacking in the previous version.[28] Another example of services with goods is importing and exporting companies. Export services are the fastest growing sector of global businesses for both industrialized and less advanced economies. Countries such as the United States, Japan, and Germany rely on these services to maintain and expand economic growth.[29]

Almost pure services provide consumers with experiences that are consumed during the delivery process. Among the many items in this category are health clubs, legal services, and education. Although a haircut is considered the classic example of a pure service, even that ordinarily takes place in an establishment selling styling and beautification products. Services such as air and train travel involve such goods as meals and soft drinks as well as tickets that can be exchanged. Even though Southwest Airlines does not offer meals or assigned seats, consumers still have a very high perception of quality and service value. How can this be? When asked, customers usually cite the great service, such as frequent departures, on-time arrival, friendly employees, and low fares. Southwest has achieved the highest level of on-time arrivals and the fewest complaints of any airline.[30] This is an almost pure service that passengers value highly, which contributes to customer loyalty at Southwest.

CONSUMER EVALUATION OF SERVICES

Product Qualities Affecting Consumer Evaluation   Products can be viewed as having three types of qualities—search, experience, and credence—that affect consumer evaluation. Search attributes can be evaluated prior to purchase. Experience qualities can be assessed only during or after consumption. Credence qualities are almost impossible to evaluate even after purchase and consumption. As Figure 11-4 illustrates, most goods are high in search and experience qualities, while most services are high in experience and credence qualities.[31]

Search Qualities   Search qualities are found mostly in goods. They make it easy for consumers to judge one product relative to another. People can use their sense of smell, hearing, sight, touch, and taste to note differences in attribute quality. Many products are compared and studied in detail before a selection is made. For example, if you are shopping for new stereo speakers, you can listen to different models at the retail store to decide which pair sounds best. Similarly, you can test-drive different cars or try out a pair of in-line skates in the store parking lot. Even after purchase, items high in search qualities allow the consumer to assess their value. Best Buy, the nation's leading volume specialty retailer, devotes up to 58,000 square feet in its stores to allow for hands-on displays.[32] These are meant to increase the customer's knowledge of product features. Since Best Buy offers a number of items high in search qualities, its format enables consumers to compare and contrast products easily.

Experience Qualities   In the combined categories (goods with services, half goods and half services, and services with goods), products are high in experience qualities. Consumers cannot assess the amount of pleasure or satisfaction derived from them until they have used them. Then they can decide whether the product met or exceeded their expectations and can describe desired improvements or changes. As the name suggests, products high in experience qualities involve the customer, and promotional efforts usually create an image of people taking part in the experience. Cruises are a good example. Advertising campaigns for Carnival Cruise Lines often display consumers participating in a wide variety of activities. Carnival attracts more clients than any other line—more than a million per year from all over the world. These consumers can assess their experience only after the cruise has ended, but more than 98 percent of Carnival customers say they were well satisfied.[33]

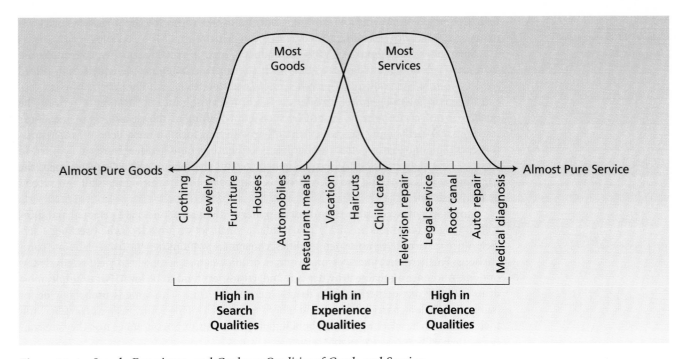

Figure 11-4   Search, Experience, and Credence Qualities of Goods and Services

Source: Valarie A. Zeithaml, "How Consumer Evaluation Processes Differ between Goods and Services," in Marketing of Services, ed. James H. Donnelly and William R. George. Reprinted with permission of the American Marketing Association.

Credence Qualities   Credence qualities are found only in services and cannot be evaluated before, during, or after consumption. A medical diagnosis, for example, is almost impossible for consumers to assess, since most people have little or no knowledge of pathology and must trust in the ability of others. The outcomes of credence qualities are largely unobservable to the customer until indirect benefits emerge, such as higher sales as the consequence of hiring a consultant. Of course, there can be negative effects from the service, such as an IRS audit because of an accountant's error. The more intangible the result, the higher the credence qualities involved. In other words, customers must have a high degree of faith that the exchange has been worthwhile.

Consumer Evaluation and Buying Behavior   Because services are high in credence qualities, consumer buying behavior tends to be different for services than for goods. Specific differences, described below, range from the more personal nature of the information sources relied upon to the fact that the customer is often a competitor of the service provider.

The Personal Factor   In selecting services, buyers rely more on information from personal sources. Because services tend to be personal, this is not surprising. Suppose you are going to court in an important lawsuit. Would you select your lawyer from an ad on television or a recommendation from your best friend? Consumers not only relate better to personal information sources but also give them more credence.

Postpurchase Evaluation   Because services are not easily evaluated before purchase, most assessments are made during or after the fact. Lawn care companies are careful not only

Credence qualities
Product qualities that buyers find almost impossible to evaluate even after purchase and consumption.

Best Buy's format enables customers to compare and contrast items which are high in search qualities.

to do a good job of mowing and trimming but also to clean away the clippings, leaving a well-manicured look with very little the consumer can criticize.

Surrogates for Judgment   When a product is high in credence quality, consumers use surrogate cues to make judgments. One such cue is price. Many people equate high-priced services with greater value, low-priced services with less value. Another cue is physical features, such as how the service provider dresses or the appearance or location of offices. The quality of car service may be judged by such a small thing as the cleanliness of the shop's restroom. An inefficiently run physician's office with new furniture may send off more positive cues than one that is better run but has poor lighting, outdated furniture, and clutter. In this case, the cues are used to make judgments about the quality of medical treatment the consumer will receive, and the office decor is a surrogate for measuring the skill and success of the physician.

Small Sets of Acceptable Brands or Suppliers   Because services are personal and difficult to judge, consumers are likely to consider a small set of providers when seeking a service. Since services have no search qualities, consumers will not benefit from elaborate comparisons. Furthermore, their personal sources of information are likely to yield relatively few options. And once a reliable provider is found, customers tend to be loyal. For example, most of us use only one or perhaps two dry cleaners all the time. The same is probably true for hair stylists, tailors, party planners, and other types of providers. Some business travelers limit their choice when selecting a hotel, booking only Marriott or Sheraton because they are confident they will receive acceptable service.

Slow Adoption   Because prepurchase evaluation is almost impossible, the risk of buying a service is greater than for goods. Therefore, many new services are adopted very slowly by consumers. People want to wait and see how the new service performs. Many consumers were initially reluctant to use the automatic teller machines (ATMs). They anticipated problems like lost deposits or theft and preferred contact with a human being. Over time these fears diminished, and many consumers now do all their banking through ATMs.

The situation is the same when the service is not an innovation but simply new to the consumer. Someone who has never had a facial or a body massage may be reluctant to try it. To overcome this reluctance, gyms may offer a free month of membership to encourage customers to join. Hair stylists often give discounts to first-time clients, and financial planners frequently offer free consultations before charging for their services.

Strong Brand Loyalty   As noted above, the personal nature of services includes a built-in loyalty factor. People are more loyal to other people than to things. They also tend to stick with what they know. In addition, because consumers participate in the service, they may attribute any problems that occur to their own behavior, relieving the provider of some responsibility. For example, if your hairdresser cuts your bangs too short, you may partially blame yourself for not being explicit about what you wanted. Furthermore, the high degree of credence qualities in services makes it difficult to know whether the provider has done a poor job unless something goes wrong, such as your car failing to start the day after it was fixed. Without a negative signal, consumers are likely to assume that the provider did at least a good job. In general, there is less complaining behavior from consumers about services as opposed to goods. We know from earlier chapters, however, that it is very important to seek out and respond to consumer complaints about any type of product.[34]

The Customer as Competitor   Services usually involve activities that consumers can do for themselves. Parents may elect to stay home with their young children or have relatives take care of them, in which case, they are "competing" with day care centers. People can mow their own lawns, clean their own cars or homes, prepare their own tax returns, or prepare food for their own parties. Or they may select a service provider to do it for them. In many instances the trade-off is between time and money. This is why so many providers stress the amount of time their services will save consumers. For example, Video Express of Birmingham, Michigan, not only rents video tapes but also offers delivery and pickup service for an additional $3.99.[35]

Providers also may emphasize the improvements possible through an outside service compared to what consumers can do for themselves. Such claims may be based on larger and more sophisticated equipment or safety, as in tree removal. Especially in business-to-business marketing of services, cost savings may be cited. For example, companies too small to have a personnel department may hire a resume bank, such as SkillSearch, which provides a larger pool of potential candidates than they would be able to obtain on their own.[36]

Since service quality plays a significant part in the purchase decision for most consumers, it is crucial for marketing success. One study shows that service is "irrelevant" to customer perception of quality in only 15 percent of markets.[37] The Marketing Science Institute, through international conferences and research with major corporations, has identified how consumers assess overall service quality. The results, outlined in Figure 11-5, indicate that assessments have three aspects: dimensions of service quality, consumer factors, and quality perception. Dimensions of service quality are elements that consumers are most likely to perceive when making judgments, such as reliability and responsiveness. Consumer factors refer to customer needs and information acquisition. Quality perception depends on how closely the buyer's expectations are matched (or exceeded) by the service actually delivered, a concept very similar to customer satisfaction. Each of these is discussed below.

Dimensions of Service Quality   The dimensions of service quality fall into five categories: tangibles, reliability, responsiveness, assurance, and empathy. It's important for marketers to consider each of these as they evaluate the quality of the services they provide to consumers.

Tangibles   It has been noted already that services are intangible but often are associated with physical facilities, equipment, personnel, and promotional materials. These tangibles have a very significant effect on customers. Organizations that provide tangibles of high quality communicate an impression of their nontangible offerings as well. For example, the way an office is designed and equipped, its cleanliness, and the personal appearance of employees all play a major role in conveying quality.

Reliability   The ability to perform the promised service dependably and accurately is critical to service quality. Reliability involves, for example, returning calls and meeting deadlines. It also means performing activities precisely as outlined, such as sticking to the script in training programs, producing credit card statements free of errors, and doing a task correctly the first time. Research has shown that completing all car repairs when promised is more important than the quality of the work itself.

Responsiveness   The willingness of providers to be helpful and give prompt service is very important to buyers. Waiting time is critical to buyer satisfaction and evaluation of service quality. What managers view as a short wait may seem long to customers.[38] It is important to respond in a timely manner to customer requests and needs. If the customer finds an error on a financial statement, is it resolved quickly and with an adequate explanation? Are salespeople willing to answer questions about what to expect from a service? Do they help resolve difficulties if they arise?

Assurance   The knowledge and courtesy of employees and their ability to convey trust and competence are essential for services which have high credence qualities. A very important factor is whether customers are treated with dignity and respect. Another is credibility— whether the provider conveys sufficient knowledge, experience, and trustworthiness to perform the service. Finally, assurance is related to security, the belief that the services will be

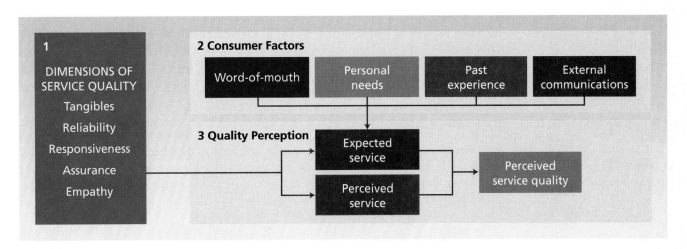

Figure 11-5   The Customer's View of Service Quality

Adapted from Valarie A. Zeithaml, A. Parasuraman, and Leonard L. Berry, Delivering Quality Service, Balancing Customer Perceptions and Expectations, (New York: The Free Press, 1990), p. 26.

performed safely and confidentially and that a free exchange of ideas between the provider and the consumer is possible. Relationship marketing has become an integral part of services during the last several years. By focusing on the needs of customers, well-developed and long-term relationships can be established.[39] Providing assurance is a major component in a company's ability to build and maintain these relationships.

Empathy The caring, individualized attention that a firm provides its customers encompasses a number of dimensions. It is particularly important for service providers to convey that they understand the customer. It is through their ability to listen, communicate clearly, and relate well to the client that they transmit empathy.

Consumer Factors Factors that influence the consumer's view of service quality include word of mouth, personal needs, past experience, and external communication. Word of mouth is particularly important because services are not readily observable and must be described verbally. Because they lack search qualities, they are likely to be discussed with friends when consumers are seeking a provider. These discussions tend to carry considerable credibility. Personal needs are also important. These deal with the motives that determine the nature and strength of what a consumer wants from a service. Past experience refers to what consumers have learned through personal interaction with a service provider. This is particularly important in shaping expectations, a topic covered below. The final element is external communication, that is, such marketer-dominated sources as personal selling and advertising. How a service is positioned and what is communicated through paid messages can influence consumer perceptions.

Quality Perception Because perceptions of service quality depend on the service meeting or exceeding customer expectations, service providers must take care in shaping those expectations. Because the product is intangible and people cannot readily observe for themselves what to expect, the messages and examples from service providers contribute much to developing expectations. It is critical that the provider describe outcomes as clearly and accurately as possible before purchase. Organizations that create unrealistic expectations in an effort to sell a service are likely to find that customer satisfaction is low. Those unhappy consumers will tell others, and the credibility of the business will be hurt.

To ensure high perceived quality and a loyal customer base, providers need to be accurate and reasonable about what they lead customers to expect. They also need to do a good job in the areas of tangibles, reliability, responsiveness, assurance, and empathy. Because the personal nature of services makes them very difficult for competitors to emulate, those companies that invest resources and energy in building strong service quality are most likely to be winners. Mobil, recognizing consumer interest in quality service, has hired "Friendly Serve" attendants at its gas stations to clean windows, give directions, and direct drivers to open pumps at no extra charge. The campaign is intended to add a personal touch, so that a pleasant experience will bring customers back. Mobil hopes that its investment in these attendants will help its stations outperform the competition with exceptional service.[40]

DEVELOPING THE SERVICE MIX

Services, like goods, usually occur as a mix. They often rely on branding to communicate uniqueness. At the same time, several qualities must be considered when developing a new service. These include the service itself, the brand, and factors that enhance the fundamental service. This section explores these dimensions more extensively.

Core, Augmented, and Branded Services

Recall from chapter 9 that products have core, augmented, and branded dimensions. Let's relate these concepts to services. We can use the example of birthing in a hospital, as depicted in Figure 11-6. The **core service** is the basic benefit, in this case delivery of a healthy baby and safety for the mother. That is the main objective of the service. But, in today's competitive health care arena, the augmented and branded product also plays a key role. The augmented service is the package of bundled goods and services that differentiate one provider from another. It has a great deal to do with how well service providers connect with customers. Since the core service is the same for all providers, the augmented features are critical.

In chapter 9 we discussed the importance of brand equity for goods. It is equally if not more important to build brand equity for a service. Because a service is intangible, a customer

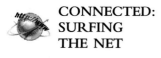

CONNECTED:
SURFING
THE NET

www.mobil.com

Find out about Mobil's consumer and business services by connecting to its Web site. And, discover Mobil worldwide—the company does business in more than 125 countries on six continents.

Core service
The basic benefit delivered.

Figure 11-6 *Example of a Core, Augmented, and Branded Service*

comes to know its value through the symbols and cues around it. McDonald's® has achieved name recognition not only because of the reliability of its products but also because of its customer service, personnel management, cleanliness, child-oriented image, and so forth. Its brand equity reflects the interactive service element as well as the functional dimensions of the physical goods sold. Consider the growing brand equity of Kinko's, which now has more than 850 locations in the United States, Canada, Japan, Australia, United Kingdom, Korea,

It would take us all day to list all of our services.
(Fortunately, we're open 24 hours.)

Presentation Materials. Training Manuals. Oversize Color. They're just a few of the ways Kinko's has become the most complete business service center around. Your Kinko's Corporate Account Manager is ready to analyze the ways in which you produce and use documents, and offer solutions that streamline your workflow and reduce costs. In addition, our dedicated staff has the resources to help you get your work done efficiently and effectively. And of course, Kinko's is open 24 hours so you can count on us all the time, every time. Find out why every day, more than 200,000 businesses use Kinko's.

The new way to office.

Open 24 hours, 7 days a week.   Visit Kinko's web site at http://www.kinkos.com
More than 850 locations worldwide. For the location nearest you call 1-800-2-KINKOS.

Kinko's provides a range of services to more than 700 copy centers in the United States, Canada, Japan, and the Netherlands.

Functional element

What a service is supposed to
accomplish.

Interactive element

The personal behaviors and
atmosphere of the service
environment.

Service complexity

The number and intricacy of
steps involved in producing a
service.

Divergence

The degree to which a service
involves customization beyond
routine or standardized
procedures.

and the Netherlands. Others provide copy services, but Kinko's has become synonymous with a customer-oriented philosophy. It has expanded services to include desktop publishing, computer rental with high speed ISDN Internet access and Worldwide network video-conferencing, among others. Customers rely on the Kinko's name for value and service.[41]

Marriott extended its branded line by developing three chains with lower complexity than the original service. Courtyard has become an identifiable service mark associated with high-quality motel accommodations and limited services. Fairfield Inns are positioned as the least complex, no-frills part of the chain. Residence Inns cater to an extended stay of five days or more; 80 percent of their guests are business travelers. With these three brand names, the company has developed services consistent with the target markets for which each is intended.[42]

The U.S. Postal Service provides a core service of mail delivery. It leverages a certain amount of brand equity and maintains high quality by being dependable. It augments its services through 50 nationwide business centers. These are designed to help small and medium-sized companies improve the efficiency of their mailings as well as learn new techniques, such as how direct mail can benefit them.

DEVELOPING NEW SERVICES

Just as with goods, new services need to be developed. Certain functional and interactive elements have to be considered. The **functional element** of a service relates to whether it accomplishes what it is intended to do. (Does the orthodontist straighten a patient's teeth? Does a shoe get repaired?) The **interactive element** involves the personal behaviors and physical atmosphere of the service environment. Each element is discussed below.

Functional Elements in Service Development   The functional element in service product development is influenced by the complexity and divergence of the service. **Service complexity** refers to the number and intricacy of steps involved in producing a service. For example, a muffler shop that adds brake lining and transmission repair to its services is increasing complexity. The service a defense lawyer provides a murder suspect is much more complex than a house cleaner's activities. **Divergence** relates to the amount of routine procedure involved in providing a service. A very customized service has high divergence, such as a consultant who tailors staff development advice to each person in a company. A standardized service has low divergence. For example, Fred Pryor Seminars, Inc., gives a set presentation on various topics to groups representing many organizations.[43]

Figure 11-7 illustrates complexity and divergence for four services. Since most local barber shops do approximately the same thing, and cutting hair is not highly complicated, divergence and complexity are very low. Dentistry has low divergence due to standardized procedures, but it tends to be high in complexity. House cleaning is highly customized (divergent) but low in complexity, whereas litigation tends to be high in both divergence and complexity.

Interactive Elements in Service Development   The interactive element is often more important than the functional aspect in creating service excellence. Walt Disney Enterprises has attempted to produce a strong interactive service by using a stage (the environment) with actors (Disney employees) to involve the audience (consumers). Through extensive role playing, the Disney people have learned to connect in a way that produces strong customer satisfaction. One part of this interaction is simply the desire to help customers have fun.

Many companies use atmospherics, the environment in which the service is performed, to enhance the interactive element.[44] Originally applied to retail stores, atmospherics has

	Complexity (Degree of Intricacy)	
	Low	High
Low	Local barber	Dentistry
High	House cleaning	Litigation

DIVERGENCE (Degree of Standardization)

Figure 11-7 Complexity and Divergence in Services

important implications for all types of services outside the consumer's home. Such features as color, music, and layout are all part of the atmosphere. It not only influences the selection of a service provider but also, and more important, determines whether service outcomes are satisfying.

The physical components of atmosphere have an emotional dimension. The mood created greatly influences whether consumers want to enter and explore the environment, communicate with personnel, and gain satisfaction from the service encounter.[45] Retail stores such as Banana Republic, Bath & Body Works, and Eddie Bauer emphasize music as a way to increase sales. AEI Music Network, Inc., a service provider to many retailers, researches the demographics and psychographics of a store's customers and then creates suitable sound. The music is designed to encourage customers to shop longer and also creates an atmosphere for each retailer.[46] The next time you visit a Nine West, Coach, or Victoria's Secret outlet, note the music program created especially to appeal to you.

Structuring New Services The functional and interactive aspects of services affect how organizations structure new offerings. Marketers determine where each new service attribute fits on the continuum from low complexity/divergence to high complexity/divergence. Figure 11-8 shows an example of structural alternatives in the restaurant business. The standard restaurant can be viewed as falling in the middle. The restaurant's marketing manager can choose to move in one of two directions for each area shown: more upscale (higher complexity/divergence) or more downscale (lower complexity/divergence). By conducting this type of analysis, the organization can make clear choices in developing new services.

AN EXPANDED CONCEPT OF SERVICES

Services of all types are marketed to you daily. In addition to the traditional offerings, service marketing is used to promote people, entertainment and events, places, political candidates and ideas, and different causes. It can even be used within an organization, through internal

Lower Complexity/Divergence	Current Process	Higher Complexity/Divergence
No reservation	← Take reservation →	Specific table selection
Self-seating; menu on blackboard	← Seat guest, give menu →	Recite menu; describe entrees and specials
Eliminate	← Serve water and bread →	Assortment of hot breads and hors d'oeuvres
Customer fills out form	← Take orders; prepare orders →	Taken personally by maitre d' at table
Prepared; no choice	← Salad (4 choices) →	Individually prepared at table
Limited to 4 choices	← Entree (15 choices) →	Expand to 20 choices; add flaming dishes; bone fish at table; prepare sauces at table
Sundae bar; self-service	← Dessert (6 choices) →	Expand to 12 choices
Coffee, tea, milk, and sodas	← Beverage served (6 choices) →	Add exotic coffees; wine list; liqueurs
Serve salad and entree together; bill and beverage together	← Serve orders →	Separate course service; sherbet between courses; hand-grind pepper
Cash only; pay when leaving	← Collect payment at table →	Choice of payment, including house accounts; serve mints

Figure 11-8 Structural Alternatives in the Restaurant Business
Source: Adapted with permission from G. Lynn Shostack, "Service Positioning through Structural Change," Journal of Marketing 51 (January 1987): 34–43.

Person marketing
Promoting an individual's
personality, character, and
appeal, which in turn may assist
in the promotion of a product.

marketing, to promote one group's capabilities to another. The following sections describe these additional types of service in more detail.

PERSON MARKETING

Person marketing involves promoting an individual's character, personality, and appeal, which in turn may be used to promote a service or product. Michael Jordan, whose endorsements may have a lifetime value of more than a billion dollars, is probably the most notable sports figure to date. Even the Internet makes use of his appeal. Jordan recently signed a 10-year contract to create and manage his own official Web site for SportsLine USA, a news and information service. SportsLine hopes that Jordan, among other big name athletes, will attract advertisers and boost the number of paying subscribers.[47]

The multiethnic appeal and charisma of Tiger Woods has struck a chord with diverse customers across the globe, creating opportunities for companies to market Tiger's image to promote golf-related products. This includes Nike, which pays him $8 million a year in endorsements. According to Phil Knight, Nike CEO: "Today's world is a lot more wired. There are so many ways for [Tiger] to touch people . . . that he could easily be as widely known around the world as any athlete today—and in a fraction of the time." Nike has been overwhelmed with unsolicited product orders from Africa, Japan, and Europe for its golf apparel.[48] The entire golf industry is making connections with customers, hoping to sell more rounds of golf, apparel, and equipment than ever before.

Michael Jordan and Tiger Woods both have agents who help market their exceptional appeal to various companies and to consumers. For them and other Olympic or professional athletes, much of their attraction is due to their skills and character. In addition, however, service providers who market sports personalities contribute a great deal. Person marketing is often a two-way process in which promotion of the individual increases his or her value as a product endorser. Public exposure that enhances reputation leads to more lucrative endorsements, contracts, and vice versa.

ENTERTAINMENT AND EVENT MARKETING

During the 1996 Thanksgiving weekend, *101 Dalmatians,* Disney's remake of its 1961 animation, opened at theaters. It immediately brought in $50 million, giving Disney the biggest single weekend revenues on record. Nothing was left to chance. Nearly every aspect of the

*A number of companies, including
Nike, market Tiger Woods' image
to promote golf related products.*

movie was the result of careful planning, from promotion to the precise timing of its intro-duction. Glenn Close, a huge draw in her own right, was selected for the lead and was fea-tured prominently in every advertisement. The target audience could relate well to the unique quality her character represented.

Television and radio also thrive on sophisticated marketing. The popular television show *Seinfeld* was successful because it provided comic relief. Jerry Seinfeld wrote much of the show, being careful not to let intellectual material interfere with the light humor enjoyed by so many loyal viewers. At the other end of the spectrum is *ER,* whose appeal is serious drama. Both shows are designed with target audiences in mind. Careful monitoring makes sure that from week to week a show reaches the audiences advertisers desire.

Event marketing is the promotion of an event in order to generate revenues and enhance the reputation of an organization. It has become a huge factor in the entertainment world, with sporting events at the forefront. Ohio State University characterizes its athletic depart-ment as being in the entertainment business.[49] As at many universities, sports at Ohio State are big business. They generate the revenues that support student athletes and contribute pos-itively or negatively to the university's reputation. College athletics are a multibillion-dollar industry, with revenues from stadium attendance, television and radio, concessions, ap-parel, and signage at stadiums. The University of Michigan earns several million in royalties from its logo alone.

One of the most successful event marketers is the National Basketball Association, which in 1985, had earnings of $181 million from tickets, television contracts, and sponsors. By 1995 that figure was $1.1 billion, and NBA-licensed products (mostly apparel) had gone from $200 million to more than $3 billion.[50] While most NBA games are played in the United States, the 1996 NBA All-Star game was televised in 170 countries in 39 languages. With an average attendance of 17,000, arenas are filled at 90 percent capacity, and more than half a billion households in 180 countries watched the games on television during the 1996–1997 season. Given these numbers, Shaquille O'Neal gets the equivalent of about 20 cents per household with his $100+ million salary from the Los Angeles Lakers. The NBA has assisted in basketball theme movies as well: *Forget Paris* starring Billy Crystal, *Celtic Pride* star-ring Whoopi Goldberg, *Space Jam* starring Michael Jordan, and *Kazzam* starring Shaquille O'Neal.

Sponsorships allow companies to link their name with the outstanding experience peo-ple associate with the event. Coke, Pepsi, and General Motors are likely to be seen support-ing college athletics. A great example was Coca-Cola's sponsorship of the 1996 Summer Olympic Torch relay. Aside from seeing the torch, few spectators could forget the sponsor. Coca-Cola lined the streets with posters announcing when the relay would arrive, while ad-vance trucks sold bottles of Coke. The company also gave out posters and stickers to kids and handled press coverage.

Event marketing
Promoting an event in order to generate revenues and enhance the reputation of an organization.

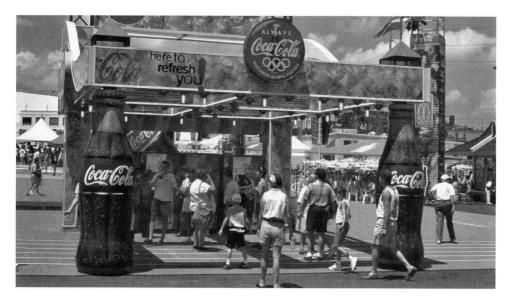

Sponsorships enable companies to associate their name with outstanding events, such as the Olympics.

Place marketing
Promoting a geographical
location in order to appeal to
businesses, investors, and/or
tourists.

PLACE MARKETING

Place marketing enhances a location in order to appeal to businesses, investors, and tourists. Check out "The Smart State For Business," at http://smart.state.ia.us and you'll learn about Iowa's cutting-edge business environment, such as technology centers at the University of Iowa, Iowa State University, and the University of Northern Iowa. With the theme "Pride and Prosperity," Iowa is marketed as "the smart state for business." Partners in the endeavor are Pella Windows and Doors, Maytag, Winnebago, the Principal Financial Group, MidAmerica Energy, Monsanto, IPSCO, John Deere, Rockwell, Vermeer, Sheaffer, Postitech, APAC, Quantum Chemical, Amana, and RUAN Transportation Management Systems. Iowa is also trying to persuade other businesses, cities, and counties to join in.[51]

Maybe you want to find an area for financial investment, locating a company, or tourism. Panama, like many countries, is marketing itself to appeal to all those interested. It points to its location as a global hub for international shipping, and to its valuable real estate, government privatization policies, and free trade zone. It also targets consumers and travel agencies by catering to people who want cruises and ecotourism destinations of natural landscapes, rain forests, and undeveloped beauty. Panama has a unique marketing challenge as a result of the recent withdrawal of the United States from the canal. Autoridad de la Region Interoceanica (ARI), has the task of marketing many properties formerly associated with the United States. It is also marketing a strategic vision.[52]

Vacation places receive tremendous marketing attention. Countries, states, cities, and resorts all participate. Few put it all together as well as Disney does. "It's a small world after all" in any one of several unique resort hotels at Walt Disney World near Orlando, Florida. You can walk from country to country experiencing, for example, a British pub or German restaurant. The Theme Parks and Resorts division of Disney had revenues of nearly $4 billion in recent years. This includes Disneyland near Paris and Tokyo, two newer developments.

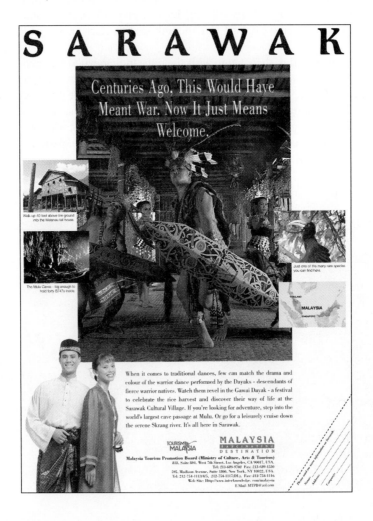

*Malaysia uses place marketing to
draw tourists to Sarawak.*

Political marketing involves the promotion of an individual or idea with the aim of influencing public policy and voters. Politicians use political marketing in order to present themselves and their ideas in the best possible way. The 1996 presidential campaign brought two political unknowns into the race for the nation's highest office. Following the same approach of Ross Perot in 1992, Steve Forbes and Morry Taylor used their personal fortunes to fund their quest. And they did what most businesses do for products—they developed carefully planned marketing strategies. Both candidates used a full array of marketing tools to communicate their ideas.[53]

Of course, elections are not always won or lost based on the character of candidates or their ideas. In 1996, total spending on campaigns for the U.S. Congress was nearly $1 billion. The political arena is a highly competitive environment, and both positive and negative advertising is accepted. Few companies would ever bad-mouth competitors' products so aggressively. At least one political commentary indicated that Steve Forbes forgot a basic lesson: Consumers are unlikely to support marketers "whose sales pitch relies on trashing the competition."[54]

The marketing talent a candidate can attract may have a lot to do with the number of votes s/he is likely to receive. For example, less than a month before the election, trailing in the polls, Bob Dole found it difficult to hire a top-quality marketing firm. Phil Dusenberry, who headed Ronald Reagan's team, and Tom Messener, who worked with George Bush, rejected Dole because they said they were busy with consumer products campaigns.[55]

Just how commercial is the political process? Political marketing involves the same steps we find in other areas. The objectives should be clearly stated in terms of influencing issues and/or getting elected. Just as mass marketing of products seldom works, mass marketing of issues or candidates will likely fail. The first step is to identify the various target segments, called *constituencies* in political terms. Then it is important to pinpoint the salient issues for each constituency and understand their thoughts and feelings. This usually involves considerable marketing research, including surveys (political polls) and focus groups. Of course, the campaign itself usually requires advertising and direct marketing, with an army of volunteers making calls in person or by telephone to targeted voters.

Political marketing
Promoting an individual or idea motivated by the desire to influence public policy and/or voters.

CAUSE MARKETING

Cause marketing involves gaining public support and financing for a cause in order to bring about a change or a remedy. You are familiar with many of the marketing campaigns to combat AIDS, drunk driving, drugs, domestic violence, and smoking among teens; to promote the use of seat belts; and to prevent cruelty to animals, to name a few. Cause marketing is used for blood drives, Community Chest drives, and charities that feed and clothe the homeless or combat various diseases. The overall objective is to remedy a situation by gaining public support for change.

Cause marketing is challenging because it usually confronts two very difficult tasks: raising money and changing harmful behavior. For example, AIDS activists have been somewhat successful in educating people about the disease to help reduce its spread. Personalities like Earvin "Magic" Johnson have heightened awareness. Efforts by the gay, lesbian, and heterosexual community have pressured the government into allocating more money to HIV and AIDS research.

Cause marketing
Gaining public support and financing in order to change or remedy a situation.

INTERNAL MARKETING

Internal marketing occurs when one part of an organization markets its capabilities to others within the same firm. For example, imagine that you are a human resources manager. Your job, among other responsibilities, is to provide training and career development for employees in all the company's different divisions and departments. An effective approach is to use marketing concepts. The only difference is that you are aiming your efforts at internal customers—the employees of the firm—rather than end users of the company's products. This is not the same as internal communications, which are also important; all the marketing tools and techniques tend to be used, even marketing plans.

For example, Dr. Lew Dotterer at Sparrow Health System in Lansing, Michigan, was responsible for developing learning programs for the organization. He employed marketing

Internal marketing
The marketing of a business unit's capabilities to others within the same firm.

concepts to make this happen. First, he identified the key customers—doctors, nurses, administrators, and so forth. Next, he spoke with each group to determine its learning needs. He then created training programs that addressed those needs and promoted them throughout the system. Through internal marketing, Dr. Dotterer helped his internal customers better serve their external customers.

THE MARKETING OF NONPROFIT SERVICES

Marketing of nonprofit services is a huge area. Today, the more than one million nonprofit organizations in the United States generate $1.1 trillion in revenue each year. About $130 billion is contributed by private donors. Americans allocate almost 3 percent of their income to charitable giving, and nearly everyone gives something. About 96 percent of middle-income households ($60,000–$75,000) give an average $1,600 per year.[56] Nonprofit services account for more than 7 percent of all economic activity in the United States. As you can see from Figure 11-9, the United States has the highest percentage of nonprofit workers to total employment and to total service employment in the world. The U.S. nonprofit sector employs seven million people, compared to 1.4 million in Japan and about one million in France.

Nonprofit marketing

The activities performed by an organization not motivated by profit in order to influence consumers to support it with a contribution.

Nonprofit marketing is performed by an organization that is not motivated by profit and is exempt from paying taxes on any excess revenues over costs. Marketing has many applications in the nonprofit sector. Churches, museums, foundations, hospitals, universities, symphonies, and municipalities regularly create marketing plans in an effort to gain funds and public support. Nonprofit organizations often use person marketing, entertainment and event marketing, and place marketing. Nearly all political and cause marketing, as well as marketing of the arts, fits the nonprofit description. For example, the National Fish and Wildlife Foundation uses a full range of marketing tools to create partnerships with government agencies, universities, individuals, and corporations to help solve specific environmental problems.[57]

TYPES OF NONPROFIT SERVICE PROVIDERS

Figure 11-10 shows several categories of nonprofit service providers and gives examples of each. As you can see, marketing skills are required by a very broad range of nonprofit organizations. For example, your university probably has a fairly elaborate marketing plan, and chances are that many of the administrators have attended American Marketing Association seminars on how to promote higher education. At a recent seminar in Nashville, Tennessee, participants covered subjects ranging from marketing research techniques to using the university as a brand name.[58]

THE NEED FOR EXCESS REVENUES

Nonprofit service organizations are usually tax exempt and may appear to be less concerned about pricing and cost structures. Yet they need to generate revenues in excess of costs for several reasons. First, their revenues (money for services and from contributions) tend to fluctuate from year to year. For example, the Museum of Fine Arts in Boston, discussed in more detail in chapter 14, relies on blockbuster shows every few years to boost revenues. Likewise, the Leona King Gallery in Scottsdale, Arizona, put together a silent auction in conjunction with Super Bowl XXX. By planning ahead, the gallery had time to commission local artists to paint Native American scenes on footballs, which were later purchased by donors. Some

	Percentage of Total Employment	Percentage of Service Employment
United States	6.8	15.4
France	4.2	10.0
United Kingdom	4.0	9.4
Germany	3.7	10.4
Average	*3.4*	*8.9*
Japan	2.5	8.6
Italy	1.8	5.5
Hungary	0.8	3.0

Figure 11-9   Nonprofit Jobs as a Percentage of Total and Service Employment

Source: Stephen Greene, "Nonprofits Group Expanding World," *Chronicle of Philanthropy,* June 28, 1994, pp. 1, 28–29. Reprinted with permission of *The Chronicle of Philanthropy.*

Category	Example	Product
Arts/Culture/Humanities	Metropolitan Museum of Art, New York Chicago Symphony	Exhibits Musical programs
Education/Instruction	Michigan State University Executive Education University of Southern California Undergraduate Program	Executive programs Classes, degrees
Environmental Quality/ Protection/Beautification	Smokey the Bear (U.S. Forest Service) Greenpeace	Fire safety Saving the environment
Animal-Related	San Diego Zoo People for the Ethical Treatment of Animals (PETA)	Species preservation Animal rights
Health	Listening Ear Alcoholics Anonymous (AA)	Cure for AIDS Stop alcoholism
Consumer Protection	Consumer Hotline	Legal aid
Crime Prevention	Neighborhood Watch Crime Tip Hotline	Discourage criminals Catch criminals
Employment/Jobs	U.S. Army	Volunteer recruitment
Public Safety	State of Michigan State of Florida	Drive safely Wear seat belts
Recreation/Sports	Silverdome American Youth Soccer Organization	Football Youth sports programs
Youth Development	Boy Scouts of America Big Sister/Big Brother programs	Scouting jamborees Companionship and role models
Community/Civic	Bring Your Company to . . . Kiwanis Club	Community enhancement Economic development
Grant Agencies	Rockefeller Foundation Robert Wood Johnson Foundation	Arts development Medical research
Religious Organizations	Catholic Church Evangelists	Membership Spirituality
Other Cause-Based Groups	National Organization of Women (NOW) American Civil Liberties Union (ACLU)	Women's rights Individual rights

Figure 11-10   Types of Nonprofit Service Providers

of the money covered costs incurred earlier, but $2,375 went to the arts program of the local Hopi Indian High School.[59]

Second, you can't raise money if you aren't solvent. The United Way wants the organizations it supports to have at least a three-month safety net. That means a full quarter's expenses have to be earned and set aside—no small task for most organizations! Fund-raising operations must be run in a financially sound manner in order to gain support from large donors. That means efficiency and documentation identifying the costs of items as well as the revenues received.

Third, nonprofits hire professionals to help the organization grow. Similar to any business, growth generally requires capital and the ability to access funds from financial institutions. Lenders look at nonprofits much the same way they look at any other organization. Underwriters Laboratory, a well-known nonprofit company, made $17.1 million from revenues of $281 million in 1994.[60] This type of financial performance not only attracts managerial talent but also affords the company access to all the services required by a for-profit company.

FUND-RAISING AND REVENUE GENERATION

Nonprofit organizations may raise revenues in two ways. First, they acquire funding from third parties, such as governments, private and public agencies, and individual contributors. Second, they may expand into a number of business operations.

A considerable amount of funding comes from donations by individuals, families, or businesses. Microsoft CEO Bill Gates is recognized for making contributions to nonprofits. He recently formed his own nonprofit, the Gates Library Foundation, which contributed $200 million to public libraries in low-income communities for computer hardware and software to access the Internet. Microsoft Corporation pledged to match the donation.[61]

CONNECTING THROUGH RELATIONSHIPS

THE POINT: CELEBRATING THE LIFE AND CULTURE OF THE SOUTH BRONX

"We're the hottest, most interesting nonprofit in the country," says Paul Lipson. That's how The Point's cofounder likes to describe this emergent community development corporation in the Hunt's Point section of New York's South Bronx. And his description is not just the boasting of a proud father. In the three years since its inception, The Point has garnered almost $400,000 from a wide array of donors and captured the attention of ABC's *Nightline*. More important, it has harnessed the talents of the community it serves—from the young people who participate in and stage its hugely popular hip-hop performances to the budding entrepreneurs who use street-corner smarts to sell their wares in the Point's Marketplace.

According to Paul Quintero, chairman of the board, The Point has succeeded by turning the standard nonprofit model on its head. In the past, most social agencies used a "What's wrong with this picture?" approach to the South Bronx. They saw the neighborhood only in terms of its crime, poverty, poor schools, and substandard housing. They tried to put a Band-Aid on problems or fill in gaps. In contrast, the Point's four cofounders asked: "What are the assets—the raw assets of the community?" The answer was simple: a wealth of abandoned buildings and the passion and talents of at-risk youth.

With seed money from The Kaplan Foundation, The Point's first project was to turn an abandoned old mint, the former American Banknote Company, into their headquarters. Now a stylishly renovated building, it has a 220-seat theater for its "Live from the Edge" performance series and a 4,000-square-foot arts and business incubator. For the renovation and for every program housed within it, The Point has drawn on the assets of the neighborhood and its residents. Where someone else might see a boiler room, the Point's young aspiring hip-hop and rap artists see a future recording studio. Where someone else might see an abandoned lot full of wood and debris, the Point sees a business enterprise. At the Hunt's Point Farm, local youths use a machine to chop up wood, which they sell for use in fireplaces at restaurants in the metropolitan area.

Developing proposals for concrete projects like these is a big factor in The Point's success in obtaining funds. "We're building incrementally, project by project, in a very tangible way," says Quintero. "People can relate to that, and that has been a very key piece of our marketing approach. We're not saying 'buy our vision.' The vision is nice, but people can't relate to it." For instance, rather than say "We want to develop arts and enterprise in the community," they go to a donor with a specific proposal and say "We want to have a cross-cultural theater exchange with a group in Poland" (now a reality), or "We want to start an Internet center."

The Point is also able to attract donors because of its joint ventures with more established nonprofit partners. Working with the renowned International Center for Photography, The Point will soon have a darkroom, photo studio, monthly exhibitions in the atrium, and a budding photography business. Kids who never held a camera will be selling their photos in calendars, date books, and postcards. This ability to help turn interest into skills and then into enterprise is what is most exciting to Quintero. "There's new life, new activity, and new hope. That's the bottom line. For so many people, there is hope now where there wasn't any before."

Sources: Patrick Queen, "Paul Quintero: Making a Difference at the Point," *Columbia* Winter 1997, pp. 38–39; and interview with Paul Quintero, the Point's chairman of the board.

Understanding donor profiles helps nonprofit groups target fund-raising efforts. Figure 11-11 lists six categories of donors, the types of charities they most often support, and why they give. The largest group, communitarians, believe in supporting their community. As government has decreased its support of social services and the arts, nonprofits in these areas must compete against one another for private dollars. Just as new ventures need a well-honed marketing strategy and innovative approach to entice venture capitalists, new nonprofits need to do the same to capture the attention of donors besieged by requests. The Point Community Development Corporation, in the Hunt's Point section of New York's South Bronx, is only three years old but has rustled up a significant amount of funding. It uses "out of the box" thinking and cultivates relationships within both the neighborhood and the nonprofit community. See the relationships feature, "The Point: Celebrating the Life and Culture of the South Bronx."

In addition to fund-raising, many organizations develop business ventures that provide substantial revenues. These are often unrelated to the basic nature of the core activity. Your

Category	Percentage of All Major Donors	Who They Are and What They Support	Why They Give
Communitarians	26%	*91% male* Local charities, cultural, religious, and educational concerns	To improve the community Good for business relationships
Devout	21%	*80% male & business owners* Religious organizations	Moral obligation
Investors	15%	*87% male, 75% business owners* Wide variety	Rather support them than the government No moral obligation
Socialites	11%	*62% female* Arts, education, and religious projects	Believe that giving is part of personality and provides entry into a desirable social circle
Repayers	10%	*65% male* Educational institutions & medical facilities	Loyalty or obligation due to an event that happened later in life
Dynasts	8%	*50% male, 50% female* Many have inherited wealth and give to wide range of groups	Believe everyone should support nonprofits Family traditionally supports nonprofits

Source: Adapted from "One Study's Analysis of 7 Types of Wealthy Donors," *Chronicle of Philanthropy*, March 8, 1994, p. 14. Reprinted with permission of *The Chronicle of Philanthropy*.

Figure 11-11 Categories of Donors to Nonprofit Groups

high school band, drama club, or sports team probably has used some type of retail operation at one time or another—a car wash, a food stand at the local fair, or a candy sale—to raise money for uniforms or a special trip. We all are familiar with Girl Scout cookie sales. In fact, these activities often compete with the for-profit sector. Because the service labor is donated, the price charged by the nonprofit group can be substantially lower than the normal retail price. In some cases, for-profit businesses simply cannot compete while the fund-raiser is going on. At the same time, nonprofits are good customers for many for-profit businesses.

Sometimes the revenue-generating venture fits nicely with the core activity of the nonprofit. For example, private schools and universities have bookstores and other merchandising operations. Museums and musical organizations (symphonies, opera companies) may have shops and mail-order catalogs. Some groups license their name or logo for a fee. Zoos, museums, sports teams, and others often charge admission.

Finally, membership fees represent a large source of revenue. Most associations are formed for the benefit of members, whether individuals or organizations. For example, a member of the American Marketing Association pays $130 annually to the AMA in addition to chapter dues. Students are given a special rate. This entitles the member to obtain AMA publications and attend conferences at substantially reduced rates. The AMA is the world's largest professional society of marketers, with more than 45,000 members in 92 countries; there are 500 chapters in North America. The association works to promote education and assist in career development among marketing professionals.[62]

Most professions have a similar organization, and in many cases companies can be members. For example, firms interested in service quality are likely to join the First Interstate Center for Services Marketing at Arizona State University. It is North America's leading university-based program for the study of services marketing and management. The center conducts research, offers specialized education and training, and works to provide firms with applicable principles, concepts, and tools.[63]

PROVIDING POSITIVE SOCIAL BENEFITS

Another challenge for nonprofits is to provide maximum positive social benefits to their constituency. This can be difficult because constituents may have differing objectives and needs. For example, the San Diego Zoo must balance the public's desire to see certain animals with the interests of environmentalists in species preservation. Expenses to house, care for, and in some cases help rare animals reproduce can be very high. Zoo personnel traveled to China to find a suitable mate for Shi Shi, their rare panda.[64] Likewise, groups concerned with spouse or child abuse must allocate funds to serving families as well as to promoting their cause.

Having a good understanding of constituent needs is not always easy. The Internet is a particularly useful marketing tool for nonprofit groups. Many use it as a virtual community to communicate, share information, educate, collaborate, and interact. It is an excellent format for publishing, sharing perspectives on issues, assisting in community development, and increasing participation.[65]

A good example of the importance of serving constituency needs can be found in the arts. These include a long list of services—museums, theaters, opera, symphonies, dance companies, exhibitions, public radio and television, and others. A major indicator of the quality of life in many communities is the availability of the arts. Numerous cities have a symphony orchestra, which can be an important factor in attracting businesses and people to the area.

Customers for the arts are called *patrons*. Attracting them is a critical aspect of marketing the arts, but that is only part of the challenge. Equally important is finding sponsors of all types, since revenues from ticket sales seldom generate enough money. Yet patrons may have many choices about which arts events to attend, and sponsors may have a broad range of requests for donations. Ultimately, successful organizations are those that can show the benefits they bring to their constituents.

ETHICAL ISSUES SURROUNDING NONPROFIT ORGANIZATIONS

Today, many types of organizations claim nonprofit status, which entitles them to tax exemption. While a majority of these benefit society, a growing number have little or no resemblance to traditional charities. In fact, of the 45,000 new organizations that apply for tax-exempt status each year, many make a considerable profit. This raises the question of whether it is ethical for money-making nonprofits to pay no taxes. Consider professional golfing's PGA Tour, which grosses $180 million a year. It could afford to pay its commissioner $4.2 million over the last two years, partly at the expense of the American taxpayer. The PGA Tour, Inc., is a nonprofit organization and is not required to pay federal tax on tour operations. Some nonprofits are very rich, indeed. The J. Paul Getty Trust in Los Angeles has $5.7 billion in assets.

Although nonprofits are taxed on income from businesses unrelated to their function, fewer than 5 percent report such income. The revenue for most nonprofits comes from investments and business operations. Nonprofit executives say they have shifted toward profit-making schemes in order to survive. Many others feel that there are too many nonprofits taking advantage of tax-exempt status, but efforts to change the law have failed repeatedly in Congress.

You may be familiar with many nonprofit organizations, such as National Geographic, the Academy of Motion Picture Arts and Sciences (which presents the Oscars), and the Humane Society. Nonprofits are not limited to charity, however. Many are found in retail, restaurant, hotel, insurance, and even laundry services. Most nonprofits do not pay taxes on investment income as well. Competitors of these organizations find the tax exemptions unfair and unethical. Nonprofits in competition with normal for-profit companies have a clear financial advantage. Consider the difference between a nonprofit hotel operated by George Washington University and other tax-paying hotels in the area. In fact, Washington, DC, houses 1,800 nonprofits. If they were to pay taxes on the land and buildings they use for operations, then approximately $94 million a year would flow to the city. Critics point out that they use city services just as other organizations do.

The nation's nonprofit sector generates an amazing $1.1 trillion every year, and controls $1.475 trillion in assets. While many of these organizations directly benefit Americans, for others the tax-free status remains an ethical issue.[66]

This chapter dealt with services and nonprofit organizations. The next chapter explores how products and services are made available to customers by looking at marketing channels, wholesaling, and physical distribution.

CONNECTED: SURFING THE NET

The San Diego Zoo

www.sandiegozoo.org

IN THIS CHAPTER YOU LEARNED THAT marketing has many applications in the nonprofit sector. In order to expand your thinking about nonprofit organizations, visit the Web site of the San Diego Zoo and answer the following questions.

1. What three parts make up the Zoological Society of San Diego, and what service is it dedicated to fulfilling?
2. There are several categories of nonprofit service providers. In which one(s) does the San Diego Zoo belong? Using information from the Web site, list several benefits the zoo provides to society.
3. An important challenge faced by nonprofit organizations is fund-raising and revenue generation. List specific ways the San Diego Zoo accomplishes this. How do you think understanding donor profiles might help fund-raising efforts? Explain.
4. Read "Society Sponsorship," found in the membership information. How does the San Diego Zoo connect through relationships, and what are the advantages of these connections?

Hilton Worldwide

www.hilton.com

THIS CHAPTER'S DIVERSITY FEATURE, "BEYOND ACCESSIBILITY: How Hotels Win over the Disabled Traveler," discussed a proactive approach to the Americans with Disabilities Act. In order to learn more about one of these hotels, visit the Hilton Web site and answer the following questions.

1. Upon your arrival at the Web site, note the variety of offerings. Next, place as many of these as you can on a service-goods continuum. Explain your choices.
2. Read about Hilton's guest reward program. How does it help the company connect through relationships? In what specific ways does Hilton build relationships with customers?
3. Select a press release or news article that relates to Hilton's service quality. Explain how the company might meet or exceed customer expectations in this regard.
4. Find the Hilton background and read about the company's milestones. How do you think the forces creating growth in services have contributed to its success and accomplishments?

CHAPTER SUMMARY

OBJECTIVE 1: Identify the forces that have produced and will continue to create tremendous growth in the service economy.

The service economy is growing at about twice the rate of the sale of goods. First, technological advances and the accompanying information revolution are creating vast opportunities in the service sector. Technology often can only be used with the help of service specialists who have the necessary knowledge and skills. Second, the quality of life is being measured by how people feel and experience life. Third, governments around the world have deregulated services. Fourth, professional service providers such as lawyers are turning to marketing as a way to conduct their business operations. Fifth, privatization of government functions is opening up service opportunities. Sixth, there is a need for outside specialists by companies that want to concentrate resources on their core business. Finally, there is a strong growth in franchising, which tends to focus on service-based products.

OBJECTIVE 2: Understand which characteristics of services must be adjusted for successful marketing.

Services are differentiated from goods on five key dimensions that must be considered in successful marketing. First, services are intangible, so evidence of benefits may occur long after purchase and may be difficult to assess. Second, there is a unique relationship between the service provider and customers, who are either present when the service is performed or have knowledge of how it was performed. Third, the service encounter is a crucial point of connection between provider and consumer, in which each moment must contribute to meeting customer needs. Fourth, since production and consumption often occur simultaneously, the same service may be different each time it is performed and may be adjusted to the unique circumstances of each consumer. Fifth, because there is no storage or inventory with a service, demand forecasting is important so that service providers are ready when needed. Finally, service quality control is extremely important but it is complicated. It requires thorough training of personnel and careful monitoring.

Most products contain elements of both goods and services and can be placed on a service-goods continuum. Consumers tend to evaluate services differently from goods. Generally, services are high in credence qualities, which means it is difficult to evaluate them even after they have been consumed. Therefore, consumers tend to rely on personal references for information, engage in post purchase evaluation, develop surrogates for judging quality, select providers from a small set of choices, and actually serve as a competitor to the service provider. They are slow to adopt new services but eventually develop strong brand loyalty.

Judgments of service quality usually have three aspects: the dimensions of service quality, consumer factors, and quality perceptions. The dimensions of service quality include tangibles, reliability, responsiveness, assurance, and empathy. Customer factors—word of mouth, personal needs, past experience, and external communication—help form customer expectations. Quality perception is based on the difference between what is expected and what is received.

OBJECTIVE 3:   Know how to develop the service mix.

Service mix development requires understanding in two areas. First, services have core, augmented, and branded dimensions similar to goods. Brand equity is equally if not more important for services than for goods. Second, when developing new services, marketers must give careful consideration to both functional and interactive elements. The functional element is influenced by the complexity and divergence of a service, which must provide benefits that match customer needs and wants. The interactive element involves such concerns as the consumer's personal behaviors and the atmosphere in which the service will be performed.

OBJECTIVE 4:   Explore the expanded concept of services.

There are many types of service marketing including person marketing, entertainment and event marketing, place marketing, political marketing, cause marketing, and internal marketing. Person marketing promotes an individual, often a sports figure or movie personality, who in turn generally helps market another product. Entertainment marketing promotes movies, television programming, and the like. Event marketing, like that for sporting events and concerts, is a major category. Through sponsorships of events, companies also market other products. Place marketing promotes a geographic location, such as a city, state, or country. It is often connected to investment or travel products. Political marketing promotes politicians or political ideas and policy issues. Cause marketing attempts to gain support for a cause, such as research on HIV and AIDS. Internal marketing occurs when one business unit markets its capabilities to others within the same firm.

OBJECTIVE 5:   Appreciate the importance of nonprofit marketing and the uniqueness of this important marketing arena.

Nonprofit marketing accounts for more than 7 percent of economic activity in the United States and is growing. It is performed by organizations that are tax exempt, such as churches, museums, foundations, hospitals, universities, and orchestras. Even nonprofits need revenues in excess of their costs. These revenues provide service continuity from year to year and allow nonprofits to access the talent and funding required to serve their constituents. Consequently, fund-raising and revenue generation from donors, patrons, and members is often a focal point. At the same time, nonprofits must provide benefits to all constituents, which can be difficult because different parties have varying expectations and needs. Ethically, there is a question about tax-exempt status for at least some nonprofits, especially when they compete against for-profit organizations.

REVIEW YOUR UNDERSTANDING

1. List the seven forces that are producing explosive growth in services. Very briefly describe each.
2. What are the differences between goods and services?
3. What is the services-goods continuum? What are the categories of the continuum?
4. What are search, experience, and credence attributes of services? List a product example in each attribute category.
5. What are the five dimensions of service quality, the four consumer factors, and the three elements of quality perception that shape the customer's view of service quality?
6. What are the functional and interactive elements of services?
7. List three examples of person marketing.
8. What are entertainment and event marketing?
9. Give an example of cause marketing.
10. What is internal marketing?
11. What differentiates nonprofit services?
12. Why do nonprofit organizations need excess revenues over costs?

DISCUSSION OF CONCEPTS

1. List three of the seven forces driving the explosive growth of the service economy. How will each force influence the nature of college education?
2. Select two differences between services and goods and detail how each affects marketing strategy development.
3. Do you think it is possible for a product to be either a pure good or a pure service? Why or why not?
4. What are the differences between search, experience, and credence qualities of products? How does each affect marketing strategy development?

5. Name a service high in credence quality. What type of buyer behavior would you expect to encounter?
6. Imagine that you are the marketing manager for a major hotel chain. What steps would you recommend to help ensure success in each of the five dimensions of service quality?
7. Select a target market and design the core, augmented, and branded aspects of a restaurant.
8. Do you consider it appropriate for politicians to develop sophisticated marketing campaigns in order to be elected to office?

KEY TERMS AND DEFINITIONS

Cause marketing: Gaining public support and financing in order to change or remedy a situation.

Core service: The basic benefit delivered.

Credence qualities: Product qualities that buyers find almost impossible to evaluate even after purchase and consumption.

Divergence: The degree to which a service involves customization beyond routine or standardized procedures.

Event marketing: Promoting an event in order to generate revenues and enhance the reputation of an organization.

Franchise: A contractual agreement whereby an entrepreneur pays a fee for the franchise name and agrees to meet operating requirements and use the organization's marketing plan.

Functional element: What a service is supposed to accomplish.

Interactive element: The personal behaviors and atmosphere of the service environment.

Internal marketing: The marketing of a business unit's capabilities to others within the same firm.

Nonprofit marketing: The activities performed by an organization not motivated by profit to influence consumers to support it with a contribution.

Perishable: The temporal nature of services, whose value exists for only a short time.

Person marketing: Promoting an individual's personality, character, and appeal, which in turn may assist in the promotion of a product.

Place marketing: Promoting a geographical location in order to appeal to businesses, investors, and/or tourists.

Political marketing: Promoting an individual or idea motivated by the desire to influence public policy and/or voters.

Service: An idea, task, experience, or activity that can be exchanged for value to satisfy the needs and wants of consumers and businesses.

Service complexity: The number and intricacy of steps involved in producing a service.

Service encounter: The interaction between the consumer and the seller.

REFERENCES

1. Interview with Vinny Greco, August 27, 1997.
2. U.S. Bureau of Labor Statistics.
3. Douglas L. Fugate and Alan Zimmerman, "International Services Marketing: A Review of Structural Barriers, Regulatory Limitations, and Marketing Responses," *Journal of Services Marketing* 13, 2 (1996): 33–58.
4. Eileen Bridges, Renee A. Florsheim, and Claudette John, "A Cross Cultural Response to Service Promotion," *Service Industries Journal*, July 1996, pp. 265–286.
5. Ronald Henkoff, "Finding, Keeping and Training the Best Service Workers," *Fortune*, October 3, 1994, pp. 110–122.
6. Howard Banks, "Surprises in Foreign Sales of U.S. Services," *Forbes*, March 28, 1994, p. 41; Ralph T. King, Jr., "U.S. Exports Are Growing Rapidly But Almost Unnoticed," *Wall Street Journal*, April 21, 1993, pp. A1, A6; and James E. Ellis, "Why Overseas? 'Cause That's Where Sales Are," *Business Week*, January 10, 1994, p. 62.
7. Bill Gates, *The Road Ahead*, (New York: Viking), 1995, p. 33.
8. Richard Turner, "Selling a Little Net Music," *Newsweek*, July 14, 1997, pp. 54–55.
9. Char Kosek, "On-line Spending in Expansion Mode," *Business Marketing*, June 1996, p. S5.
10. Eleena De Lisser, "Tellers vs. ATMs: People Prefer Doing business Face to Face," *Wall Street Journal Interactive Edition*, May 16, 1997.
11. Robert Posten, "Consumers Will be Picky About Packaged Goods," *Marketing News*, December 2, 1996, p. 7.
12. Julie Candler, "It Pays to Delivery," *Nation's Business*, December 1992, pp. 46–50.
13. Brian O'Reilly, "First Blood in the Telecom Wars," *Fortune*, March 4, 1996, p. 124.
14. Ian Murphy, "Yearly 7% Growth Seen for Communications Spending," *Marketing News*, October 7, 1996, pp. 8, 11.
15. Adam Shell, "7 Years after Landmark Ruling, Professional Firms Look to Marketing," *Public Relations Journal*, February 1992, p. 10.
16. John F. O'Malley, "Telecommunications and Health Care Marketing," *Marketing News*, December 2, 1996, p. 8.
17. Kirk Davidson, "Health Care Industries Pose Ethical Problems," *Marketing News*, December 2, 1996, p. 5.
18. Shell, op. cit., p. 10. Crawford, Michael, "The Law and the Jungle," *Canadian Business*, February 1992, pp. 42–47.
19. AP-Dow Jones News Service, "Kuwait Mobile Telephone Signs Contract with Motorola," *Wall Street Journal-Interactive Edition*, December 5, 1996.
20. Joan C. Szabo, "New Approaches to Education Reform," *Nation's Business*, March 1994, pp. 30–32.
21. Connie Leslie with Debora Rosenberg, "Taking Public Schools Private," *Newsweek*, June 20, 1994, p. 77.
22. Greg Burns, "All Together Now: 'Make That To-Go'," *Business Week*, January 8, 1996, p. 105.
23. Alex Taylor III, "How to Buy a Car on the Internet . . . and Other New Ways to Make the Second Biggest Purchase of Your Life," *Fortune*, March 4, 1996, pp. 165–168.
24. www.wal-mart.com/, site visited on January 14, 1997.
25. Chip E. Miller, "U.S. Techniques Not Best for Chinese Sales Reps," *Marketing News*, November 4, 1996, p. 5.
26. Julie Candler, "It Pays to Deliver," *Nation's Business*, December 1992, pp. 46–50.
27. Mitch Schechter, "Making the Most of Merchandising, Promotions, and Special Events," *Food Management*, September 1996, pp. 52–66.
28. Peter Burrows, "David vs. Goliath on the Infobahn," *Business Week*, December 5, 1994, p. 94E.
29. Fugate and Zimmerman, "International Services Marketing,"; and Rex Baldazo, "The New MSN Goes Web-Wild," October 17, 1996, www.cnet.com/Content/Reviews/Hands/101496/msn.html.
30. James L. Heskett, et al., "Putting the Service-Profit Chain to Work," *Harvard Business Review*, March-April 1994, pp.164–174.
31. Valarie A. Zeithaml, "How Consumer Evaluation Processes Differ between Goods and Services," in *Marketing of Services*, ed. James H. Donnelly and William F. George (Chicago, IL: American Marketing Association, 1981).
32. www.bestbuy.com, site visited on January 17, 1997.

33. "What to Expect on Carnival Cruises," www.bvt-usa.com/cruises/c-expect.html, site visited on January 13, 1997.

34. Valerie Zeithaml, "How Consumers Evaluation Processes Differ."

35. Candler, "It Pays to Deliver."

36. Janine S. Pouliot, "A Computerized Hiring Search," *Nation's Business*, February 1994, p. 32.

37. Sundar G. Bharadwaj and Anil Menon, "Determining Success in Service Industries," *Journal of Services Marketing*, 7, no. 4 (1993): pp. 19–40.

38. Julie Baker and Michaelle Baker, "The Effects of the Service Environment on Affect and Consumer Perception of Waiting Time," *Journal of the Academy of Marketing Science*, Fall 1996, pp. 338–349.

39. Maria Holmlund and Soren Kock, "Relationship Marketing: The Importance of Customer Perceived Service Quality in Retail Banking," *Service Industries Journal*, July 1996, pp. 287–304.

40. Chad Rubel, "Quality Makes a Comeback," *Marketing News*, September 23, 1996, p. 10.

41. www.halcyon.com/dbonner/kinkos/welcome.html, site visited on December 19, 1996.

42. Louise I. Driben, "The Service Edge," *Sales and Marketing Management*, June 1993, pp. 80–84; Russell Shaw, "Courtyard Rethinking F & B," *Hotel & Motel Management*, September 7, 1992, pp. 1, 34; Russell Shaw, "Marriott to Merge Courtyard With Fairfield Inns," *Hotel & Motel Management*, January 13, 1992, pp. 1, 56; and Jenny Campbell, "Marriott Making Mark in Philadelphia," *Hotel & Motel Management*, January 11, 1993, pp. 4, 10.

43. G. Lynn Shostack, "Service Positioning through Structural Change," *Journal of Marketing* 51 (January 1987): 34–43.

44. Philip Kotler, "Atmospherics as a Marketing Tool," *Journal of Marketing* 40 (Winter 1973–1974): 50.

45. M. Mehrabian and J. A. Russel, *An Approach to Environmental Psychology* (Cambridge, MA: MIT Press, 1974).

46. Chad Rubel, "Marketing wtih Music," *Marketing News*, August 12, 1996, pp. 1, 21.

47. Stefan Fatsis, "Can NBA Star Michael Jordan Score on the World Wide Web?" *Wall Street Journal Interactive Edition*, June 24, 1997.

48. Roy S. Johnson, "Tiger!" *Fortune* (Interactive Edition), May 12, 1997.

49. Mission statement of Ohio State University Athletic Department.

50. Bob Ryan, "Hoop Dreams," *Sales and Marketing Management* (December 1996), pp. 48–51; and Craig Copetas, *Wall Street Journal*, November 29, 1996, p. B5.

51. "Iowa," *Fortune*, March 4, 1996, special edition section.

52. "Panama: Putting a Global Hub to Work," *Fortune*, March 18, 1996, special advertising section following p. 102. For further information, ARI invites you to contact the Marketing and Promotion Department, ARI, P.O. Box 2097 Balboa, Ancón, Panama, R.P. or e-mail: ari@ns.sinfo.net.

53. Judy Keen, "Two Unknowns Sink a Fortune into Recognition," *USA Today*, October 15, 1996, p. A2.

54. Steven W. Colford, "Forbes' Faux-pas," *American Advertising*, Spring 1996, pp. A2, 23.

55. Martha T. Moore, "Dole Campaign Looking for Messenger for Its Message," *USA Today*, October 15, 1996.

56. Joel R. Evans and Barry Berman, *Marketing*, 7th ed. (Upper Saddle River, NJ: Prentice Hall, 1997), p. 346.

57. "Green Model," *Forbes*, January 30, 1995, p. 26.

58. American Marketing Association, "Seventh Symposium for the Marketing of Higher Education," Chicago, IL.

59. David Ressner, "Painted Pigskins Pay Off," *Decor*, August 1996, pp. 79–82.

60. Edward T. Pound, Gary Cohen, and Penny Loeb, "Tax Exempt," *U.S. News and World Report*, October 2, 1995, p. 36.

61. "Gates to Give $200 Million for Library Computers," *Wall Street Journal Interactive Edition*, June 24, 1997.

62. www.ama.org/index.html, site visited on January 16, 1997.

63. www.asu.edu/aad/catalogs/graduate/research-centers.html, site visited on January 16, 1997.

64. www.sandiegozoo.org/zoo/panda_research.html, site visited on January 17, 1997.

65. "Establishing a Presence: Local Nonprofits Online," www.uwm.edu/People/mbarndt/npdev.htm, site visited on December 19, 1996.

66. Pound, Cohen, and Loeb, "Tax Exempt," *U.S. News and World Report*, pp. 36–51.

CASE 11

TICKETMASTER

TICKETMASTER KNOWS WHAT IT MEANS to serve customers through the development of beneficial relationships. It is the world's leading computerized ticketing service, with more than 3,500 clients—including 77 pro sports franchises—in the United States, Canada, Mexico, Europe, and Australia. The corporation sells nearly 60 million tickets annually through more than 2,500 retail outlets, 16 nationwide call centers, licensees, client box offices, and its Web site. Its customers fill hundreds of leading arenas, stadiums, performing arts venues, and theaters.

Not long ago, buying tickets for a major event was often associated with a long drive, standing in an endless line, and sometimes even camping out overnight. In 1985, *Time* magazine wrote a story about computerized ticketing, which was quickly becoming the industry standard: "Queuing for hours in the sub-freezing cold to buy a pair of hard-to-get tickets may have once been a mark of theater-going dedication, but increasingly, it is a mere sign that you are behind the times." Ticketmaster, formed in 1978 by two Arizona State University students, had a competitive drive to be at the forefront of improvements in its industry. Arenas often had poor inventory control, and concert organizers could not accurately predict demand for shows. Ticketmaster helped change all this and became the industry benchmark. President and CEO, Fredric D. Rosen, saw to the introduction of advanced technology, service, and innovations that have pushed the company's annual sales from $1 million in 1982 to more than $1.6 billion today.

Ticketmaster's computerized operating system is upgraded approximately five times a year. Buyers can order by phone, through ticket centers, from box offices, or via the Internet. Ticketmaster Online enables customers to check event schedules and seating charts, chat with celebrities, shop for tour merchandise, or check on breaking tour information. The site receives an amazing 650,000 visits a day. Through the Ticketmaster system, customers can obtain the best available tickets, no matter where they live. The company typically receives more than a million calls in the first hour after a major rock tour goes on sale. To meet such demand, the more than 4,000 employees regularly receive computer training.

Ticketmaster has expanded from its core ticketing business into related entertainment and marketing opportunities through the creation of sponsorship and promotional programs. The company publishes *Live!*, a monthly event guide, and merchandises through Entertainment to Go. It continually looks for new markets and new ways to serve customers with a wider variety of events. Recently, Rosen has promoted the idea of turning Ticketmaster into a home shopping channel for retail goods as well as tickets. The company announced plans in November 1997 to issue a credit card in conjunction with MasterCard, asking for partnership proposals from more than 15 banks.

Scheduled for launch is a companion to Ticketmaster Online, developed jointly with Intel to deliver "rich, interactive content to live event fans on their desktops, using Intel-based computing and 'push' technology." The system features customized event listings, virtually reality, and panoramic seating charts that allow fans to "see" the view from any vantage point or "tour" their favorite facilities. Subscribers will be able to access information on more than 30,000 Ticketmaster events at a speed far surpassing the Internet. Personalization technology will enable users to select precisely which type of news they want, whether about Broadway, sports, museums, or rock and roll. According to Rosen, "This is a tremendous breakthrough in the delivery of live-event information, tickets, and merchandise. The success of Ticketmaster Online, which now sells over $3 million worth of tickets per month, inspired the creation of the new service, which will help us meet the growing demand of computer-based ticketing. And with this new technology, learning about live entertainment will also become a form of entertainment in itself." Ron Whittier, Intel's senior vice president and general manager, content group, says that such technology enables retailers to "deliver visually rich product information to consumers in a responsive and individually customized fashion, and, what's more, they can make the sale."

Ticketmaster introduced its Mobile Ticket Van, donated by General Motors, at Lollapalooza in August 1997. This specially equipped vehicle gives the company yet another way to reach consumers who may not live near a Ticketmaster outlet. Executive vice president Claire L. Rothman believes "there is an unlimited number of promotional tie-ins we could initiate. I think we'll find so many uses for this that one won't be nearly enough to cover L.A., and I wouldn't be surprised if we roll them out in major cities throughout the country." To promote ticket sales, the van will likely appear at tourist attractions, festivals, or sporting events.

Ticketmaster's partnerships are numerous. In addition to the ventures with Intel and MasterCard, the company has paired up with Samsung Electronics America, Calvin Klein, R. J. Reynolds, Microsoft, Pepsi, Ford, Apple Computer, and others. The aggressive pursuit of marketing opportunities has sometimes been perceived as monopolistic, especially since Ticketmaster has acquired at least 12 of its closest competitors in the past decade and controls approximately two-thirds of major stadiums, arenas, and amphitheaters in urban centers. It has grown 20 percent annually for the past five years and is often the only operation large enough to land major contracts. According to Richard Schrader, a former New York commissioner of consumer affairs, "If you've got exclusive access to two-thirds of the available seats in venues nationally, you're able to exert incredible market pressure in the industry." That pressure is apparent in ticket surcharges, which have outpaced ticket prices in the last five years.

Rosen says, "There's nothing wrong with being competitive—fighting for what you believe in." For competitors, their only change may be technological innovation, but Ticketmaster remains ahead of the pack with its ability to mail up to 100,000 tickets an hour and an unparalleled distribution network, just to name a few. Ticketmaster will continue to pursue new ways to build relationships with customers and to provide service that is second to none in the industry.

1. *Discuss how the forces creating growth in services may have affected Ticketmaster's business over time. Which has probably been the most significant influence?*
2. *How does Ticketmaster address each of the five dimensions of service quality? Make assumptions when necessary.*
3. *The interactive element is often more important than the functional aspect in creating service excellence. How does Ticketmaster achieve a strong interactive connection with customers?*

SOURCES: Doug Reece, "Ticketmaster Offers Sales on Wheels," *Billboard,* August 30, 1997, p. 74; "Ticketmaster and Intel Jointly Developing Advanced Online Ticketing Service," September 30, 1997, http://mktnews.nasdaq.com; United Press International, "Ticketmaster to Issue Credit Card," *USA Today,* November 3, 1997, www.usatoday.com; Ticketmaster Web site, www.ticketmaster.com; and Linda Himelstein and Ronald Grover, "Will Ticketmaster Get Scalped?" *Business Week,* June 26, 1995, pp. 64–68.

Chapter 12

Marketing Channels, Wholesaling, and Physical Distribution

Objectives

1. Learn why companies frequently use intermediaries to reach targeted customers.

2. Attain insight into how channel relationships should be managed over time.

3. Appreciate the economic importance of wholesalers.

4. Know the different types of wholesalers and the distinct roles they play.

5. Understand what physical distribution entails and why it is critical for any business organization.

6. Learn the steps in the order management process.

WHEN MILES CHAN FOUNDED COACH IN 1962, he needed a way to get his leather goods to consumers. He knew his choice of distribution channel would influence where and when the new products were sold. His line of designer handbags was unique, and he believed the best outlet would be department stores. Because his company was new, Chan decided on personal selling as the best way to persuade buyers for the stores to give his products a chance. So he hired Dick Rose as his lone salesperson, and they put together what was probably the first "designer" collection of handbags under the Bonnie Cashin label. She was a top sportswear designer of that era, and she created for Chan a highly innovative line of soft, squishy leathers.

Rose fondly recalls his start. "I had been selling encyclopedias door to door and didn't know a thing about merchandising or retailing. But I was young and brash and bold and newly married—so very desperate for a real job. So I sold myself. I think Miles saw a freshness in me." Rose quickly confronted his first major obstacle: Handbag buyers had no interest because they were unfamiliar with a designer from the sportswear area. He then changed his strategy.

My first call was to Norman Wexler at Saks Fifth Avenue because I knew Bonnie [Cashin] had a shop there on the third floor. He returned my phone call with the comment, "I didn't know Bonnie Cashin was making handbags," to which I responded, "Yes sir, she is, and I'm just trying to figure out whether you'd prefer to house them on the third floor with the sportswear or in the main floor handbag department." My first order from Saks was for $900 and with that ammunition, I called up the handbag buyer at Neiman Marcus and told her that Saks was featuring the bags in both the sportswear and handbag departments. Before I knew it, I was up in Stanley Marcus's office. I laid the bags down, he sat there studying them and scratching his beard and finally said, "You know, this is something very different: I want to feature it in the windows on Main Street; can I get an exclusive in Dallas and Houston?" Could he get an exclusive? — we had no other customers! So that was the beginning. From there, I got on planes to every department store in the country, dropping names like crazy. We put the collection in maybe a couple of dozen department stores and it died in all of them. The country wasn't ready for it yet.

Times changed, and so did the Coach strategy. Rose did all he could to see that the stores stayed with it, and eventually the products began selling. The leather bags were repositioned as "not for every women but only for those who truly love the smell and feel of genuine leather. It was a whole new concept." And it worked. But with continued growth, Coach needed more than one salesperson to get its product out. Then it added its own chain of outlets across the country. After its acquisition by Sara

Lee in 1984, Coach began to reach customers through a mail-order catalog. Ads featuring the bags and an 800 number underscored the direct marketing approach. Eventually, Coach factory outlet stores were created to handle the product returns from department stores. As the need arose, Coach altered its distribution channel strategy, always in the interest of finding the best way to reach the customer. The multiple or "hybrid" channel approach has proven successful for Coach. By 1995, sales reached $500 million, with a goal of a billion by 2000.[1]

This example illustrates the importance of distribution channels to all manufacturers and service providers. Most customers must have access to goods before they can be observed, evaluated, and purchased. New companies face a major challenge in getting their goods distributed. Once established, distribution channels must be adapted over time to parallel changes in customer needs and competition. Frequently, more than one channel is needed to make a product available to targeted customers.

THE CONCEPT OF DISTRIBUTION CHANNELS

A **distribution channel** is a set of interdependent organizations that make a product or service available for purchase by consumers or businesses. The distribution channel serves to connect a manufacturer, such as Coach, or a service provider, like AT&T, with consumers or users. In simple terms, a distribution channel is a pipeline or pathway to the market.

Distribution channels are needed because producers are separated from prospective customers. An example is Mattel's star product, Barbie, which is targeted to girls age 4 through 10 and, of course, their parents. Barbie is made available to consumers in 140 countries through a host of different retail establishments, such as Wal-Mart, Toys "R" Us, Kay-Bees, and neighborhood toy stores. These retailers are both members of the distribution channel and customers of Mattel.

A distribution channel that enables a company to deal efficiently and effectively with separations in time, place, form, and possession will be successful. To accomplish that end, the channel must be organized and managed properly. Physical distribution activities, such as inventory management and product delivery, are essential for connecting with customers.

A distribution channel consists of at least a producer and a customer. Most channels, however, use one or more intermediaries to help move products to the customer. **Intermediaries** are independently owned organizations that act as links to move products between producers and the end-user. The primary categories are brokers, wholesalers-distributors, and retailers. **Brokers** do not purchase the goods they handle but instead actively negotiate their sale for the client. A familiar example is real estate brokers, who negotiate the sale of property for their customers. Companies have more control over the activities of brokers, including the final price to the customer, because brokers do not own the goods they sell. **Wholesalers** (also referred to as distributors) take title to products and resell them to retail, industrial, commercial, institutional, professional, or agricultural firms, as well as to other wholesalers. A good example is Ingram Micro, Inc., a large wholesaler of computer hardware and software based in Santa Anna, California. Its salespeople contact a variety of companies to sell and distribute such products as IBM personal computers, Hayes modems, and Microsoft's Windows 98. **Retailers** take title to products for resale to the ultimate consumer. These range from discounters like Wal-Mart and large department stores to specialty chains such as The Limited and local boutiques.

CHANNEL STRUCTURE

Direct and Indirect Channels Distribution channels are of two fundamental types. In **direct channels** (also called integrated channels), companies use their own employees (e.g., salespeople) and physical assets (e.g., warehouses, delivery vehicles) to serve the market. For example, IBM's sales force sells computer systems and software directly to large companies like Bank of America. Sherwin-Williams owns and operates a majority of the outlets where its paint is sold. In **indirect channels** (also called nonintegrated channels), companies make use of independent agents to serve markets. General Motors sells aftermarket components through a variety of channels such as independent parts distributors, autobody repair shops, and independently owned dealerships.

Distribution channel
A set of interdependent organizations involved in making a product available for purchase.

Intermediary
Independently owned organization that acts as a link to move products between the producer and the end user.

Brokers
A firm that does not take title to the goods it handles but actively negotiates the sale of goods for its clients.

Wholesaler
A firm that takes title to products for resale to businesses, consumers, or other wholesalers or distributors.

Retailer
A firm that takes title to products for resale to ultimate consumers.

Direct channel
A distribution channel in which the producer uses its own employees and physical assets to distribute the product directly to the end-user.

Indirect channel
A distribution channel in which the producer makes use of independent organizations to distribute the product to end users.

Distribution channels can be described by the number of **channel levels,** or the number of distinct units (producers, intermediaries, and customers) in a distribution channel. By definition, a direct channel has two levels: the producer and its targeted customers. Indirect channels are longer with at least three levels. Figure 12-1 illustrates common channel arrangements for consumer goods, business-to-business goods, and services.

Companies must decide whether to use direct channels or intermediaries. Direct channels are most attractive when the following conditions obtain:

- Customers and/or orders are large, especially if concentrated in a few geographical areas.
- Resource constraints are not severe.
- Environmental uncertainty is low to moderate.
- Investments in direct distribution will produce a high return.
- Significant value-added is required in the channel, including specialized investments.
- Customers prefer or demand to deal directly with manufacturers, Wal-Mart being a prime example.

Many markets are simply too small to make it economically feasible for companies to establish a direct channel. Consider independently owned convenience stores, whose average order from a company like Procter & Gamble or Gillette would be tiny relative to supermarket or discount chains. The manufacturer's costs of selling, processing orders, and delivering products to mom-and-pop stores would be larger than the revenues generated. The problem is intensified because convenience stores are so geographically dispersed.

Intermediaries assemble merchandise from a variety of manufacturers and sell in smaller lots at a regional or local level. Therefore, an order from a small convenience store represents a relatively larger sale to a wholesaler than to an individual manufacturer. Moreover, wholesalers often have greater cost efficiencies than manufacturers due to their smaller size (lower overhead) or proximity to customers (lower selling and logistics costs.) The result is that wholesalers can make money serving smaller customers whereas manufacturers cannot. The same rationale applies to retailers. Figure 12-2 shows that four manufacturers selling directly to 10 retailers would need to make 40 contacts to conduct business. Each one consumes resources. That compares to four contacts if they do business with one wholesaler, who in turn makes 10 contacts with the retailers for a total of 14.

Intermediaries tend to require less of the company's resources. Intermediaries make investments in inventory, offer credit to customers, and manage accounts receivable. They also pay for sales personnel and other employees, allowing the producer to avoid these costs. More and more companies are relying on the use of intermediaries. Honeywell, Intel, and Texas Instruments are among those who have recently increased the use of intermediaries as opposed to company-owned or direct channels.[2]

Channel levels
The number of distinct units (producers, intermediaries, and customers) in a distribution channel.

CONNECTED: SURFING THE NET

www.coach.com

Learn more about Coach's history, craftsmanship, and distribution by connecting to its Web site. Locate a Coach store near you, request a catalog, or visit the questions and comments page.

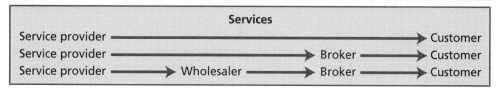

Figure 12-1 Common Channel Configurations

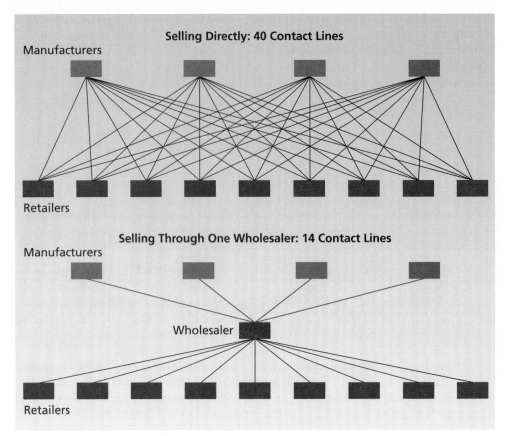

*Figure 12-2   Contractual
Efficiency*

Source: *Louis Stern, Adel El-Ansary, and
Anne Coughlan,* Marketing Channels,
*5th ed. © 1996. Adapted by permission
of Prentice Hall, Inc., Upper Saddle
River, NJ.*

The use of intermediaries is attractive to companies when it is difficult to make accurate predictions about the future. This lowers the risk level for the company because the intermediary is sharing the investment burden. Adapting to change is also easier, since companies have less fixed investment and, therefore, more financial flexibility. Warehouse facilities are an obvious example. If owned by the company, then the building, equipment, and personnel are a significant drain on resources when the economy takes a downturn.

Many customers prefer to deal with intermediaries, to save money and time. For example, Price Club prefers to buy computer products and software from wholesalers like Ingram-Micro, Tech Data, and Merisel rather than deal directly with manufacturers. This avoids the expense of hiring professional buyers knowledgeable about features and comparative value. Price Club notifies wholesalers about the quality, quantity, and price it needs, and the intermediaries locate the best deal. Manufacturers like IBM, Compaq, and Hayes have little choice but to use these wholesalers if they want to do business with Price Club.[3]

Multiple channel systems

The use of more than one channel to access markets for the same product.

Multiple Channel Systems   Many manufacturers want to connect with customers in as many ways as possible. **Multiple channel systems** are the use of more than one channel to access markets for the same product. For example, Ben & Jerry's distributes its premium ice cream through company-owned stores, wholesalers that resell to supermarkets and convenience stores, and franchised outlets. It even sells by mail, packing the order in dry ice.[4]

A leading manufacturer of personal computers, Compaq uses direct channels to reach large companies like Goodyear or large government agencies that want to deal directly with producers. It also uses wholesalers like Ingram-Micro and Intelligent Electronics to reach companies that prefer one-stop shopping for all their computer and software needs. Compaq deals with "value-added distributors," who assemble customized hardware and software packages, to reach specialized markets (such as dentists). Through retailers like Best Buy, CompUSA, and Computer City, it reaches small to medium-sized businesses as well as consumers. In addition, Compaq sends mail-order catalogs out to certain customer groups.[5]

Reverse channel

A distribution channel that flows from the end user to the wholesaler and/or producer.

Reverse Channels   Most distribution channels flow from the manufacturer to the end user, but goods sometimes move in the opposite direction. A **reverse channel** flows from the end user to the wholesaler and/or the manufacturer. An example is recycling of bottles and cans.

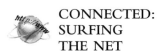

Compaq offers value added service by dealing with distributors who assemble customized hardware and software packages.

A company called Advanced Recovery takes computers apart and sells the semiconductor chips to parts wholesalers and maintenance shops.[6]

Channel Dynamics and Technology   Companies must continually evaluate whether their channels need adjustment to deal with changing conditions. If this is ignored, then the whole foundation of the company can be weakened. Alterations are required as products progress thorough the life cycle. For example, Intel introduces new microprocessors about every two years. In the introductory phase, only a direct channel is used. The supply of new chips is limited until production is slowly scaled up. Large computer manufacturers get them first, as a reward for being very important customers. In the growth and maturity phases, both direct and indirect channels are used; wholesalers sell to smaller manufacturers and the replacement market. Finally, Intel relies primarily on indirect channels in the decline stage. Then the next generation of microprocessors is launched and the cycle repeats.[7]

Companies also need to alter their channels as the industry evolves. AirTouch Communications began offering cellular service in the Los Angeles market in 1984. Its channel mix at the time consisted of four salespeople who focused on *Fortune* 100 accounts, wholesalers who bought airtime and resold it under their own name, and a group of independent agents. Since the small to medium-size business segment was not being covered very well by existing channels, AirTouch also established direct sales offices in several communities in the late 1980s.

Technology is also having a tremendous influence on channel operations. Many companies now send orders electronically rather than have salespeople submit handwritten sheets. Caller-identification systems give inside salespeople updated information on customers when they phone in orders. Hand-held computers let sales reps take inventory on retail shelves and submit orders to manufacturers via satellite. For $3,000 or less, a company can print its own bar-code labels for incoming goods and use scanners to find and retrieve them.[8] Automated conveyor systems and robots have brought enormous efficiencies to many companies. Fax machines, toll-free numbers, e-mail, and the Internet have made it much easier and more efficient for all companies to reach customers all over the world. For example, Sharper Finish, Inc., a $3 million manufacturer of commercial laundry equipment, can stay in ready contact with about 300 foreign wholesalers in 30 countries.[9] Technology that improves sales and distribution capability is helping to level the playing field for smaller competitors.

CHANNEL ORGANIZATION AND FUNCTIONS

In a **conventional channel system,** efforts to coordinate actions are seen as unimportant by channel members. Loosely aligned and relatively autonomous manufacturers, wholesalers, and retailers bargain aggressively with one another over each transaction.[10] Once a deal is

CONNECTED: SURFING THE NET

www.airtouch.com

Around the world, demand for wireless communications is on the rise as more people everywhere discover the benefits of wireless services for business and personal uses. AirTouch Communications, Inc., has emerged as a global leader in this dynamic, fast-growing industry, and at the end of second quarter 1997 reached over a million customers worldwide. Visit the company's Web site and learn more about how it manages its diverse mix of channels.

Conventional channel system
A channel system in which efforts to coordinate the actions of channel members are seen as unimportant.

reached, there is not much concern about what others in the channel are doing. Most giftware, furniture, and motion pictures move through conventional channels, where channel members tend to follow traditions.

In contrast, **vertical marketing systems (VMS)** are networks that emphasize channel coordination. VMS have grown in importance over the past two decades. More and more companies realize that customer satisfaction is impossible without efficient and effective distribution. There are three types of VMS: administered, contractual, and corporate.

Administered Channel Systems   Members of an **administered channel system** coordinate with others in the channel and facilitate activities. Marketing programs, such as cooperative advertising and sales training, are developed and offered to channel members.[11] Black & Decker, General Electric, and Sealy (the mattress company) are among the manufacturers known for their administered channel systems. Wal-Mart has invested heavily in coordinating relationships with its suppliers. When channel members have roles that are rather complex and challenging, greater coordination is needed.

Contractual Channel Systems   In a **contractual channel system,** relationships are formalized, often with a written contract. Retail cooperatives, wholesaler-sponsored voluntary chains, and franchises are three common forms.

Retail Cooperatives   A **retail cooperative** unites a group of small retailers into a wholesaling operation to increase buying power. Compare a hardware retailer who buys 20 Black & Decker power drills a year to 100 stores that buy 2,000. Obviously, the group will have more clout in bargaining on price. Ace Hardware and SERVISTAR are examples. Retail cooperatives also are common in the grocery industry, such as Associated Grocers and Topco Associates.

Wholesaler-Sponsored Voluntary Chains   In a **wholesaler-sponsored voluntary chain,** a wholesaler takes the initiative to unite a group of retailers. Typically, the wholesaler remains under private rather than cooperative ownership.[12] Again, enhanced buying power is the main objective. Such channels are prominent in the automotive accessory market (Western Auto), the grocery trade (Independent Grocers Alliance, Red and White, and Super Value), and the hardware arena (Pro, Sentry). More than 3,000 independent drugstores are aligned with McKesson Drug Co., a wholesaler of pharmaceuticals and health care products, under the Valu-Rite name.[13]

Franchise Systems   In a **franchise system,** a formal contract ties the franchiser to franchisees. The franchiser holds the product trademark and licenses it to franchisees. They pay royalty fees and promise to conform to standards and guidelines laid out in the contractual agreement. This usually covers such issues as the fees required, rights and responsibilities of both parties, transfer of the franchise, and grounds for termination.

There are two types of franchise systems. In product and trade-name franchising, the franchisee acquires some of the identity of the franchiser. Vinny Greco's Powerhouse Gym, discussed in chapter 11, is an example. Others are automobile dealerships, gasoline stations, motorcycle dealerships, and soft-drink bottlers. Business format franchising involves not only the product and trademark but also the entire business concept—marketing, strategy, training, merchandising, and operating procedures.[14] This is especially prevalent in the service arena: fast-food restaurants (McDonald's® and Burger King), hotels and motels (Holiday Inn), diet programs (Nutri-Systems), real estate (Century 21), travel services (Uniglobe), and vehicle rental (Hertz).

The roughly 2,500 franchisers and more than 540,000 outlets in the United States account for more than $750 billion in annual sales.[15] About 40 percent of all U.S. retail sales flow through a franchise system. Business format franchising is growing at a phenomenal rate. U.S. franchisers have been particularly successful in establishing indirect channels in global markets. For example, Coca-Cola gets 80 percent of its beverage profits from overseas, where it commands a three-to-one market share lead over Pepsi. The main reason is its long relationships with independent franchised bottlers in each market, who buy the syrup concentrate and then carbonate, package, and sell the product to retailers. Coke's new breed of regional intermediaries, called *anchor bottlers,* have deep local ties, huge capital budgets, and finely tuned distribution systems.[16] On a broader scale, McDonald's® has developed an excellent program for recruiting and developing a diverse mix of franchisees. See the diversity feature, "McDonald's®: Serving Diverse Communities in More Ways Than One."

Vertical marketing system (VMS)
A system in which channel members emphasize coordination of behaviors and programs.

Administered channel system
A vertical marketing system in which channel members devote effort to coordinating their relationships.

Contractual channel system
A vertical marketing system in which relationships among channel members are formalized in some fashion, often with a written contract.

Retail cooperative
An alliance of small retailers for wholesaling purposes.

Wholesaler-sponsored voluntary chain
A group of retailers that have been united by a wholesaler.

Franchise system
A type of distribution channel in which the franchiser holds the product trademark and licenses it to franchisees who contract to meet certain obligations.

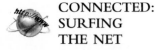 **CONNECTED: SURFING THE NET**

www.wal-mart.com

Learn more about Wal-Mart's relationships with suppliers by visiting the company's Web site. And stop by its virtual store, where you'll find everything from music to automotive, lawn and garden, jewelry, and pet products.

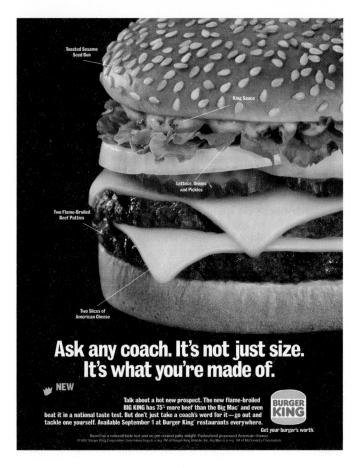

Business format franchising is prevalent in fast food restaurants such as Burger King.

Corporate Channel System   In a **corporate channel system,** the corporation runs and operates organizations at other levels in the channel. It is very similar to a direct channel, and great emphasis is placed on coordinating activities. Examples are Goodyear, Hart, Shaffner & Marx, Sherwin-Williams, and Tandy, which operate such systems in whole or in part.[17]

Corporate channel system
A vertical marketing system in which a company owns and operates organizations at other levels in the channel.

Channel Functions   Channel functions are the tasks that must be performed within a distribution system to facilitate sales with ultimate customers. Common channel functions are illustrated in Figure 12-3, broken down into four categories: selling, financing, order management, and postsales service.

Based on the nature of the target market and products, the company must determine the functions to be performed in the channel. For example, Timex does not have to worry much about the product repair function, since its watches are priced so low that customers merely discard them once they stop working. Rolex, in contrast, must ensure that customers have access to reliable repair services.

Distribution Intensity   **Distribution intensity** refers to the number of locations through which a company sells its products in a given market area.[18] There are three strategic options. **Intensive distribution** uses many outlets in each geographical area. **Selective distribution** uses several outlets per area. **Exclusive distribution** uses only one outlet in each trading area.

The choice is driven to some extent by the nature of the product. Many consumer and business-to-business products are relatively low price and are purchased frequently, requiring little value-added in the channel. Commonly referred to as *convenience goods,* they require intensive distribution.[19] Numerous sales outlets per trade area will minimize travel time and acquisition costs for customers. Examples are coffee, detergent, chewing gum, motor oil, soft drinks, and toilet tissue. Other products, referred to as *shopping goods,* require some search on the part of the customer. Different brands are compared on price, quality, and other features at the time of purchase. Selective distribution is appropriate for these goods, which include bicycles, cameras, and motorcycles. Finally, *specialty goods* have unique qualities that induce high customer loyalty. Since people are willing to exert considerable effort to seek out and purchase them, exclusive distribution can be used. Luxury items and top-of-the-line cosmetics are examples.

Distribution intensity
The number of locations through which a company sells its product in a given market area.

Intensive distribution
Making the product available through every possible sales outlet in a trade area.

Selective distribution
The use of a limited number of sales outlets per trade area.

Exclusive distribution
Distributing a product through only one sales outlet in each trading area.

CONNECTING WITH DIVERSITY

MCDONALD'S®: SERVING DIVERSE COMMUNITIES IN MORE WAYS THAN ONE

During the Los Angeles riots in spring 1992, one company remained untouched. Of the 30 McDonald's® restaurants located in the inner city, not one was torched. "We were spared—if we can use that term—because of our involvement in the community," said Leighton Hull, owner-operator of two McDonald's® in the Lynwood section of Los Angeles. "The folks know we're involved in the community. To them, we aren't the guys who just take the money and leave."

Founder Ray Kroc said that owner-operators should reflect the diversity of the communities in which they do business; he even insisted that all restaurants and company officials participate in community affairs. Since that time, McDonald's® has gained kudos for effectively bringing in minorities and women at all levels. Those two groups account for 25 percent of franchisees. McDonald's® also has a program that encourages select managers to buy franchises for less than one-third of the usual start-up cost of around $610,000. Many in the program are minorities. In fact, McDonald's® has the best record in the fast-food industry for helping African Americans advance. In many black neighborhoods, overwhelmed by crime and poverty, fast-food restaurants have emerged as one of the more stable institutions, offering jobs and role models.

A case in point is Phil Hagans, who started by flipping burgers at a Houston McDonald's® and eventually realized his goal of owning a franchise—now two—in his old neighborhood. When he was promoted to manager, Hagans spurred sales in ways a white manager in the same neighborhood might never have done. He doubled sales by hiring a gospel group to serenade black churchgoers while eating Egg McMuffins® on Sunday morning. The gospel breakfast became so popular that local ministers complained their parishioners were showing up late for church. To avoid upsetting these powerful community leaders, Hagans moved the gospel sessions to Sunday afternoon. In 1992 he bought his first franchise and he's planning a third. The days of buying furniture one piece at a time are over—Hagans now pulls in six figures.

Hagans and other successful inner-city franchisees are determined to give back to the community whose patronage has helped drive their success. In Houston, Hagans is a one-man social service agency, giving financial planning classes for workers, offering advice to employees battling alcoholism, and conducting a kind of boot camp for job seekers at the local high school. In Los Angeles, Leighton Hull assists community-based organizations as well as local service organizations by providing scholarship donations, food, and other incentives. It's easy to see why McDonald's® was serving coffee and Egg McMuffins® the day after the riots. Clearly, businesses can thrive in the inner city when they capitalize on the strengths of community members and give neighborhood youth role models with whom they can identify.

Sources: Charlene Marmer Solomon, "McDonald's® Links Franchisees to the Community," *Personnel Journal,* March 1993, pp. 61–64; Jonathan Kaufman, "A McDonald's® Owner Becomes a Role Model for Black Teenagers," *Wall Street Journal,* August 23, 1995, pp. A1, A6; Barbara Robie, "The Women Behind McDonald's®," *New York Times,* March 27, 1994, p. F23; and careers page on McDonald's® Web site, www.mcdonalds.com, November 16, 1996.

The brand strategy of the company also will influence the decision. As Figure 12-4 indicates, different brands of the same product can have widely different distribution patterns. Brands positioned for high quality and price, and requiring significant value-added in the channel, require more selective distribution to protect them against rampant price competition.[20] Generally, the more prestigious the brand, the fewer the number of outlets used by the manufacturer.

When a company uses independent wholesalers and retailers in its channel system, selective and, especially, exclusive distribution breeds considerable loyalty. For example, Caterpillar uses only 65 dealers in North America and 183 worldwide. Some dealers have two or three entire states as their exclusive domain. They are like extensions of Caterpillar, willing to support the company in any way they can.

Companies that use independent intermediaries must be careful in moving from a selective to a more intensive strategy. The loyalty of traditional channel members can quickly vanish. For example, Vidal Sassoon hair care products used to be distributed only in beauty salons. When the company decided to distribute through major supermarket and drugstores, the salons dropped the line in a flash.[21] Similarly, when Gitano Group made its jeans and

Selling

Advertising
Generating leads
Qualifying leads
Personal selling (face-to-face)
Personal selling (over the phone)
Customer education

Financing

Offering credit
Collecting accounts receivable

Order Management

Holding inventory
Transmitting and entering orders
Screening and prioritizing orders
Filling orders
Invoicing
Loading
Delivering

Post Sales Service

Training in product use
Installing
Assisting with applications
Handling product returns
Repairing product

Figure 12-3   Common Channel Functions

sportswear available to discount stores like Wal-Mart and Kmart, full-priced retailers no longer wanted to carry the line for fear of hurting their store image.[22] Also, wider distribution is likely to increase price competition and thus reduce profit margins of current channel members.

MANAGING DISTRIBUTION CHANNELS

MANAGING CHANNEL RELATIONSHIPS: A STRATEGIC APPROACH

Companies must think strategically about relationships with intermediaries. Guidelines for channel management are outlined in Figure 12-5. Interdependence, trust, and support are prerequisites.

Interdependence   Each channel member depends to some degree on other channel members to achieve desired goals.[23] This need is high when a large amount of a channel member's sales and profits can be attributed to the arrangement.[24] High interdependence means that each has the potential to influence the decisions of another.[25] Gaining attention and support is easier in that case, because each party has a vested interest in continuing the relationship. Procter & Gamble and Wal-Mart have a highly dependent relationship, and both commit considerable effort and resources to ensuring that it works smoothly.[26]

When a channel relationship is unbalanced, the firm that is less dependent has a power advantage. If the producer has the advantage, then the intermediary is likely to be very receptive to its salespeople and their plans. In the semiconductor industry, Intel has that kind of power over wholesalers like Arrow Electronics and Hamilton-Hallmark. Sometimes the intermediary is in the driver's seat. Royal Appliance, a small manufacturer, has 27 percent of its sales in Wal-Mart stores and 16 percent in Kmart stores.[27] No doubt, Royal is very concerned about satisfying the desires of Wal-Mart and Kmart management.

When dependence is low for all parties, each lacks power in the channel relationship. All are unconcerned about the others and offer little or no support. Therefore, producers need to establish channel systems in which the dependence of associated firms is reasonably high.

Trust   Another important factor in channel relationships is trust, or confidence in the reliability and integrity of channel members.[28] High trust is the belief that words and promises

Product Category	Exclusive-Selective Distribution	Intensive Distribution
Bicycles	Cannondale	Huffy
	Kestral	Murray
	Klein	Ross
Cameras	Hasselblad	Minolta
	Leica	Pentrax
	Rolleiflex	Polaroid
Golf equipment	Callaway	Dunlop
	Power Bilt	Spalding
	Taylor Made	Wilson
Hair care products	Joico	Clairol
	Matrix	Helene Curtis
	Paul Mitchell	Vidal Sasson
Stereo speakers	Audiophile	Advent
	N.E.A.R.	Bose
	Thiel	KLH
Pet food	IAMS	Alpo
	Nutro	Friskies
	Science Diet	Purina
Ski equipment	Lacroix	K2
	OTA	Rossignol
	Wolf	Solomon
Watches	Ebel	Bulova
	Rolex	Citizen
	Toumeau	Timex

Figure 12-4   Variation in Distribution Intensity Across Brands

Source: Gary Frazier, consulting project in conjunction with Economic Analysis Corporation, Century City, California, conducted in 1995.

can be relied upon. It makes the coordination of channel relationships much easier. The credibility of information exchanged need not be questioned. For example, Wal-Mart agreed to share point-of-sale information with VF Corporation, a leading manufacturer of jeans, because it trusted the company.[29]

Lack of trust creates serious problems. Intentions and basic honesty are likely to be questioned. Recently, Anthony Conza, a cofounder of Astor Restaurant Group, discovered he was

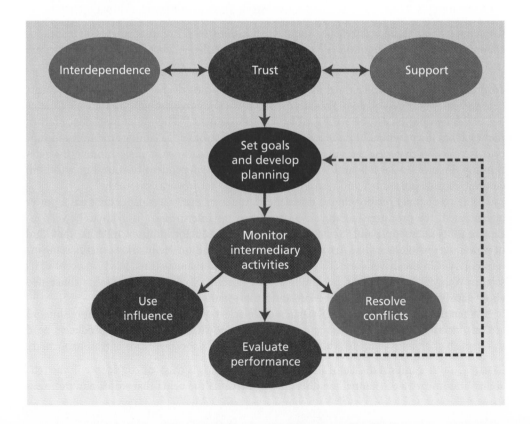

Figure 12-5   A Process for Managing Channel Relationships

losing the trust of many of his 600 Blimpie franchisees. He responded by improving communications. He established a franchisee advisory council, a newsletter called *No Baloney News,* and a toll-free hotline for franchisees. These changes increased trust—as well as sales growth and franchisee satisfaction.[30]

Support   A company may lack power with an intermediary because of low dependence, but it can grab attention with the right kind of support. Cooperative advertising is a common means. The producer reimburses intermediaries for expenses when they submit proof of the ad along with media invoices. Usually, certain standards must be met. For example, motorcycle manufacturers do not reimburse dealers if ads mention more than one brand.[31] For eligible ads, half the expense is normally reimbursed, although limits are set on the amount per year, ordinarily based on the intermediary's percentage of annual sales for a product. Many manufacturers supply prepared advertising material to ensure quality.

Market development funds may be provided to intermediaries for general promotion purposes, such as brochures, mailings, and training related to a product. Even laptop computers for salespeople may qualify.[32] Again, the amount made available is usually based on the percentage of company sales the intermediary contributes.

Incentive programs offer special rewards for extraordinary commitment and effort in selling the company's products. These are often referred to as *spiffs.* For example, NEC of Wood Dale, Illinois, ran a 1996 spiff program for its MultiSynch XV17 computer monitor by offering wholesaler salespeople $25 for every unit sold and covering the freight charges.[33] Kodak wins exclusive arrangements with certain retailers, such as Eckerd Corporation and Price/Costco, Inc., through up-front cash payments and rebates.[34] Frito-Lay takes a similar approach.[35]

Another form of support is to invite intermediaries to sales conferences to mingle and attend sessions devoted to new products or marketing techniques. Although some business is conducted at these events, the main purpose is to socialize and build personal relationships. As another way to foster goodwill, many companies help fund sales conferences sponsored by intermediaries. Support also may be offered through inventory management and sales training programs, hotlines, and toll-free numbers.

Goal Setting and Planning   Channel management is facilitated when members meet formally to set joint goals and develop plans for the coming year. This works best when interdependence and trust are high. During these sessions, intermediaries make a commitment to a set of goals, often including accounts and products that will get special emphasis. Specific business plans are developed regarding the activities and investments intermediaries will make to help achieve the goals. At the same time, the producer agrees to assist intermediaries through support programs and marketing efforts.

A number of companies use this approach. Honeywell's Home and Business Control division has a group of loyal wholesalers, many of whom are former Honeywell employees. The planning sessions are truly "joint," with confidential information on new products and company strategy shared with the wholesalers. As a result, they are truly committed to the goals and business plans developed during such meetings.[36] Procter & Gamble has more than 100 sales teams that work with major wholesale and retail accounts. A key part of their mission is to reach agreement on goals and plans with these intermediaries.[37] The division of Texas Instruments that sells laptop computers and printers takes special steps. At the beginning of each year, sales personnel meet at headquarters with top management of intermediaries to set goals and develop plans. Then, other sales personnel visit individual branch managers to communicate the goals and plans and discuss how they might be fine-tuned.[38]

Monitoring Intermediary Activities   Once the business plan is in place, company sales personnel must keep abreast of the marketing and selling efforts of each intermediary. Deviations from the plan must be noted. How well the intermediary is doing in reaching the goals established must be constantly evaluated.

For example, McDonald's® has company personnel visit franchisee locations and order food as a regular customer. They rate the facility on a variety of dimensions, including friendliness of the staff, quality of the food, and cleanliness. Similarly, Holiday Inn evaluators stay overnight and rate performance. Monitoring such as this gives a company leverage in channel relationships.

Conflict Resolution   Channel conflict occurs when members disagree about the course of their relationship. It often arises due to business pressures, policy changes, and the use of co-

CONNECTED: SURFING THE NET

www.honeywell.com

Honeywell is the global leader in control technology. Learn more about its residential and commercial divisions by visiting its Web site. You'll also have an opportunity to explore its global connections.

ercion. For example, Motorola suffered a drop in market share in cellular phones in 1996 due to intense competition from European competitors, such as Finland's Nokia and Sweden's LM Ericsson. It insisted that wholesalers carry its full line before being allowed to sell StarTac, its hot new miniature. This caused a minirebellion among some intermediaries.[39]

Unilever Group's Elizabeth Arden division planned a September 1995 launch of Elizabeth Taylor's Black Pearls fragrance. In late summer, it began an elaborate $12 million ad campaign, featuring a blitz of 42 million scent strips and black-and-white print ads with Ms. Taylor immersed in what the company called a Tahitian lagoon. Suddenly the launch was canceled because such major department stores as Dillard's, Federated, and May refused to carry the perfume. They were retaliating for a decision by Arden's president a month earlier to cut the amount contributed to sales force salaries in cosmetic departments from 5 to 3 percent of retail sales.[40]

Some conflict is inevitable. Channel members recognize that some policies will not be changed, as in the case of Motorola, and get on with their business. Sometimes company sales personnel can help by explaining policies to intermediaries. In other cases, companies recognize they made a mistake and try to correct it. Arden's president left soon after the failed launch, the company restored the 5 percent, and Black Pearls was introduced in 1996 with some success.

LEGAL AND ETHICAL ISSUES IN CHANNEL MANAGEMENT

United States antitrust laws and other regulations designed to promote competition and consumer welfare affect distribution practices. Legislation in other countries varies widely.

Resale Price Maintenance Resale price maintenance is an attempt by companies to compel channel members to charge certain prices. The practice is illegal when title to the product changes hands. Since wholesalers and retailers normally purchase the products they sell, they can charge any price they choose. If manufacturers cross the line between persuasion and coercion, then legal problems can arise. For example, a manufacturer should never threaten to take a product line away if prices are not raised.

Collusion among channel members to pressure a wholesaler or retailer to charge higher prices is against the law. Therefore, company personnel should never consult with channel members to find out whether any are discounting prices. They also should not solicit the support of intermediaries in persuading another channel member to maintain a certain price level.

Differential Pricing and Support Programs A company must give prices and support programs on "proportionally equal terms" to competing channel members unless two conditions are met. First, a price differential is justified if it costs less to serve one channel member versus another. Costs are usually lower in dealing with large distributors and retailers due to economies of scale. Therefore, quantity discounts are justified. Second, variations are legal if they are required to meet a competitive offer.

Companies can provide differential pricing and support programs to intermediaries who are not in competition. For example, a computer manufacturer can charge one price to a local wholesaler in San Diego and another to a local wholesaler in Seattle. Whether this makes good business sense is another matter.

Territorial and Customer Constraints A *territorial constraint* exists when a company assigns an intermediary a specific geographic area in which to sell its products. That is, it can sell there but nowhere else. Such constraints are legal, as they are seen as protecting the investment of all neighboring intermediaries who sell the company's products.

A *class-of-customer constraint* is a company limit on the customer groups to which an intermediary can sell its product. For example, a manufacturer of medical equipment may direct a wholesaler to sell to physicians and nursing homes in New York City but not to hospitals. This constraint is illegal, as the courts have found that it limits competition and harms consumer welfare. A company is allowed to suggest that an intermediary focus on certain targets: "We are looking for you to cover primarily these customer groups."

Exclusive dealing

Restricting intermediaries from carrying competitive lines.

Exclusive Dealing Exclusive dealing occurs when a company restricts intermediaries from carrying competitive lines. Such constraints are legal, unless they are proved to be a substantial limit on competition in the marketplace. Furthermore, terminating intermediaries for failure to perform can be difficult if exclusive dealing is a requirement. The intermediary may have passed up opportunities to add other lines and may be very dependent on the channel relationship as a result.

Tying Arrangements and Full-Line Forcing   A **tying arrangement** exists when a company conditions the purchase of a superior product on the purchase of a second and less desirable product. For example, a copier company may refuse to sell a high-quality machine unless the customer buys a service agreement. Such arrangements are illegal.

Full-line forcing occurs when a company requires intermediaries to carry and sell its complete line. This practice has been generally upheld in the courts, especially when it is common within an industry. It may be challenged, however, if it entails quantities to be purchased and inventory levels to be maintained. It also may be challenged as an illegal tying arrangement if it involves unrelated product lines.

Intermediary Termination   In many channel systems, agreements commonly allow either party to terminate the relationship with 30 days' notice. In franchise systems, contracts are more complex. Whatever the case, companies need to document the reasons for termination. Usually, the intermediary fails to meet standards or is a poor credit risk. The termination may be challenged if based on intermediary noncompliance with illegal restraints on trade.

Ease of termination varies considerably by state. Wisconsin has a very strict law. If a company's product comprises 12 percent or more of an intermediary's sales volume, then the company cannot terminate it. This has led many manufacturers to establish direct channels in Wisconsin, though they generally use indirect channels elsewhere.[41]

Ethics   It is illegal for companies to impose certain constraints on channel members. Other practices may not be against the law but are ethically questionable. For example, franchisers often confront the issue of how close to place outlets. Market coverage improves with a greater number, but existing franchisees may be hurt. They have committed time and money to building their business, and they do not want to be crowded out by competition from their own company.[42]

Another ethical issue arises when companies set territorial constraints and then choose to ignore them. They lack the courage to confront large intermediaries for selling outside their assigned territory. Such intermediaries often claim they will drop the product line and switch to competitors if they cannot broaden their market area.

Certain intermediaries abuse the use of market development funds. Industry analysts believe that some commonly charge about 10 to 15 percent above actual cost. Intelligent Electronics, a distributor of computer products in Pennsylvania, created a controversy by billing manufacturers far more than its marketing expenses on advertising, brochures, and mailings.[43]

Every company must take a deep look at itself. Competitive pressures aside, what is good ethical business practice and what is not must be carefully spelled out to all employees. Companies must recognize that short-term sales increases makes no sense if they weaken existing channel members. And policies must be enforced. To maintain the integrity of the entire channel system, violators must be terminated.

WHOLESALING

Wholesaling affects our lives every day, but we rarely notice. We may buy aspirin at Good Neighbor retail pharmacies, not knowing it was purchased from Bergen Brunswig Corporation, a large pharmaceutical wholesaler. We order a pepperoni pizza at a small neighborhood restaurant, not knowing most of the ingredients were acquired from SYSCO, a large wholesaler of food products.[44] Parents in Europe shop in retail stores for Incredible Hulk and X-men action figures by Toy Biz, a U.S. company with a licensing agreement from Marvel Comics, not knowing the retailers acquired them through European toy wholesalers.[45] Most of us never see these intermediaries, but they are very important to us.

Many wholesalers are relatively small, filling a certain niche. Others are multibillion dollar companies serving global markets. Wholesalers help thousands of companies connect with millions of customers. Whatever their size or scope, they all face competition. Their ability to make decisions about target markets, service level, pricing, business locations, merchandise assortment, credit management, use of technology, and image will influence their survival.

Wholesaling is selling goods for resale or use by retailers and other businesses. Producers have a number of options in making sales to retailers and other businesses, includ-

Tying arrangement
The purchase of a superior product is conditioned on the purchase of a second product of lower quality.

Full-line forcing
Requiring intermediaries to carry and sell the company's complete line.

Wholesaling
Selling goods for resale or business use to other businesses.

ing company-owned sales branches, brokers, and wholesalers. The focus of this chapter is on the latter.

As mentioned earlier in the chapter, a wholesaler is an intermediary that takes title to the products it carries and makes a majority of sales to retailers or other businesses. Many wholesalers make no sales directly to consumers. For others, these sales may be a significant part of revenue. For example, Smart and Final, Inc., sells food products and related merchandise to small businesses and consumers. Since more than half of its sales come from small businesses, it is classified as a wholesaler. A pure wholesaler organization does not manufacture any goods.

THE IMPORTANCE OF WHOLESALERS

Wholesalers play an important role in the economy. The roughly 280,000 such organizations in the United States employ approximately 5.8 million people. Annual sales approach $2 trillion.[46] Wholesalers are prominent in a wide variety of product categories, including beverages, climate control equipment, computer hardware and software, electrical products, electronic components, fabrics, flowers and florist supplies, food, giftware, medical supplies, movies, pharmaceuticals, telecommunications, tools, and toys. They provide value to customers and suppliers, as depicted in Figure 12-6. We will also see that they provide value for one another.

For wholesalers of consumer goods, the primary customers are retailers and service businesses, such as restaurants, hospitals, and nursing homes. In business-to-business markets, the primary customers are manufacturing organizations and service firms, such as accountants or contractors.

Assortment

A wholesaler function that entails selling a range of merchandise from a variety of sources.

Allocation

A wholesaler function that entails purchasing products in large quantities and reselling them in smaller quantities.

Wholesalers are important for product assortment and allocation. They fulfill their **assortment** function by purchasing merchandise from a variety of suppliers for resale. This makes available in one place a range of products so customers do not have to shop at many locations. They fulfill their **allocation** function by purchasing large quantities to resell in smaller amounts. This means savings for customers in both purchase price and storage costs. In essence, wholesalers make a wide variety of goods available in amounts that can be afforded and handled effectively.

Wholesalers also perform other functions, depending on customer needs. They may provide credit, education on product benefits, training in product use, and technical assistance. Hamilton-Hallmark recently opened a Technical Support Center near Phoenix staffed by electrical engineers. Customers call an 800 number if they have questions about specific applications for semiconductors.[47]

Wholesalers are needed because small or medium-sized companies in many industries cannot buy directly from manufacturers. Either direct channels are unavailable or minimum orders are too large. For example, approximately 100,000 original equipment manufacturers (OEMs) in the United States purchase semiconductors to incorporate into products such as automobiles, computers, televisions, and video cassette recorders. Roughly 96,000 of these buy from wholesalers like Arrow Electronics, Hamilton-Hallmark, and Wyle Laboratories because manufacturers cannot afford to serve them directly.[48]

> **CAREER TIP** Arrow Electronics says: "As our company continues to grow, we encourage qualified applicants to explore the opportunities, training programs, and career rewards available within the Arrow family." Various kinds of positions are available in five North American operating groups. For example, at Gates/Arrow Distributing, asset managers play an important role in processing daily buys, managing stock, maintaining proper inventory levels, and acting as a front-line contact for the sales department. To learn more, visit Arrow's career page at **www.arrow.com/careernf.htm.**

Some believe that wholesalers only add to the price of goods. Actually, their price is lower than what individual manufacturers would have to charge on most orders if they were made directly. Wholesalers get a discount for buying in quantity, and part of that is passed on to consumers. Furthermore, overhead is normally lower for wholesalers than for manufacturers. Therefore, wholesalers can serve small or medium-sized companies and still make a profit, whereas most manufacturers cannot.

Figure 12-6   Wholesalers Add Value for Suppliers and Customers by Performing Important Channel Functions
Source: *Adapted from Bert Rosenbloom,* Marketing Functions and the Wholesaler-Distributor, (*Washington, DC: Distribution Research and Education Foundation, 1987*): p. 26.

Wholesalers often do business with one another. Sometimes this is just a matter of courtesy. A wholesaler may need a Black & Decker power drill for an important customer and can get it most quickly by calling a nearby wholesaler. In other cases, the transactions are systematic. Small wholesalers may find it easier to do business with large wholesalers than with manufacturers. As a result, in a number of industries other wholesalers are a primary target market. For example, Tech Data, a multibillion-dollar computer hardware and software wholesaler headquartered in Clearwater, Florida, targets smaller intermediaries that assemble specialized systems for various market niches (such as dentists, hospitals, and hotels). Tech Data also sells to retailers and other businesses.[49]

Master distributors are wholesaling companies given the right by manufacturers to develop certain geographical areas and recruit other distributors. These, in turn, are called *subdistributors.* All sales to subdistributors go through the master distributor. The system is often used by manufacturers entering a global market, especially if they lack the resources to serve it directly. Joico, Inc., a Los Angeles–based manufacturer of high-quality hair products, uses independently owned Joico-Canada, located in Vancouver, British Columbia, as its master distributor.[50]

TYPES OF WHOLESALERS

Full-service wholesalers perform a wide range of tasks for their customers. **Limited-service wholesalers** provide only some of the traditional channel functions, either eliminating others entirely or passing them to someone else to perform. Within each category, several types of wholesalers can be identified. Figure 12-7 summarizes the functions performed by different types of wholesalers.

Full-Service Wholesalers   **General line wholesalers**   General line wholesalers carry a wide variety of products and provide a full range of services. Bosler Supply of Chicago and W. W. Grainger are good examples. They stock thousands of different industrial products, provide technical advice on product applications, and expedite shipments when necessary. Another example is SYSCO, which sells a broad array of frozen, dry, and refrigerated products to the food industry. It can provide special packaging and delivery schedules. Its cruise ship customers, for example, can receive plastic-wrapped pallets of food at any time of day or night.

Full-service wholesaler
An intermediary who performs a wide range of functions or tasks for its customers.

Limited-service wholesaler
An intermediary who performs only some of the traditional channel functions, either eliminating others or passing them on to someone else.

Type of Wholesaler	Personal Selling	Carry Inventory	Product Delivery	Offer Credit	Specialized Services
Full Service					
General line	yes	yes	yes	yes	yes
Specialty	yes	yes	yes	yes	yes
Rack jobbers	yes	yes	yes	yes	yes
Limited Service					
Cash and carry	yes	yes	no	no	no
Drop shippers	yes	no	no	yes	no
Truck jobbers	yes	yes	yes	no	no
Mail-order	no	yes	no	sometimes	no

Figure 12-7   Functions Performed by Different Wholesalers

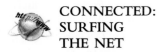

Specialty Wholesalers   Specialty wholesalers focus on a narrow range of products, carry them in great depth, and provide extensive services. Ryerson is the largest metals wholesaler in the world, with 50 distribution centers across the United States. It performs a variety of specialized services for customers, such as cutting metals to specification.[51] Ingram-Micro and Tech Data focus on computer hardware and software products, while providing many customer services.

Rack Jobbers   Rack jobbers, who sell single product lines to retail stores on consignment, set up product displays and keep them stocked with goods. Retailers pay for the goods only after they are sold to consumers. L'eggs pantyhose are distributed this way. Rack jobbers are common in the music industry and part of their role is to listen to new albums for offensive language. That is how Wal-Mart learned of a Sheryl Crow lyric suggesting that it sold guns to children and pulled the album from the shelves.[52]

Limited-Service Wholesalers   **Cash-and-Carry Wholesalers**   Cash-and-carry wholesalers are located near customers. They do not extend credit and do not use an outside sales force. Customers perform certain functions for themselves, such as bagging their own goods and delivery. Costs are tightly controlled in order to offer excellent prices.

Drop Shippers   Drop shippers arrange for shipments directly from the manufacturer to the customer. They do not physically handle the goods but take title to them, assuming all associated risks (such as damage and theft) while in transit. They do offer credit terms. Drop shippers are prominent in the lumber, chemicals, and petroleum industries, where goods are bulky and sold in large quantity.

Truck Jobbers   Truck jobbers specialize in the speedy delivery of perishables or semi-perishables, such as candy, bakery goods, fresh fruits, potato chips, and tobacco products. They use their own vehicles and offer virtually all services except credit. They focus on smaller customers that full-service wholesalers tend to ignore.

Mail-Order Wholesalers   Mail-order wholesalers sell through catalogs distributed to retailers and other businesses. They are most popular among small businesses in outlying areas, who are not regularly contacted by salespeople. These wholesalers are prominent in the clothing, cosmetics, hardware, office supply, jewelry, sporting goods, and specialty food industries.

WHOLESALING RELATIONSHIPS

Wholesalers are successful to the extent they develop strong customer loyalty. Sometimes, relationships with other wholesalers are used to serve their customers. For example, W. W. Grainger has developed alliances with a number of specialty wholesalers. The relationships feature explains Grainger's program and the special efforts of its internal sourcing group to satisfy customer needs.

Rack jobbers set up product displays for L'eggs pantyhose and keep them stocked with goods.

CONNECTING THROUGH RELATIONSHIPS

W. W. GRAINGER'S ALLIANCES WITH SPECIALTY WHOLESALERS

Grainger Integrated Supply Operations (GISO) is a division of W. W. Grainger, a large industrial wholesaler. GISO's goal is to handle the acquisition, materials management, and warehouse activities for major customers through a broad range of maintenance, repair, supply, and operating services. The diverse products it provides customers include forklifts, plastic tubing, oil and grease, electric drills, road salt, and toilet tissue. It takes special requests as well. GISO's primary customers are original equipment manufacturers, such as Caterpillar and General Motors. Whenever possible, GISO fulfills customer orders from its own distribution centers, but it has relationships with a network of independent specialty wholesalers. These focus on a narrow line of products, such as janitorial supplies or electrical products.

When GISO receives an order, it immediately checks the central computer to see whether the items are available from one of its distribution centers. If not, then GISO turns to an associated wholesaler, depending on the product and the geographical location of the customer.

Written contracts with each wholesaler specify the products it will supply. GISO pays the wholesaler immediately upon delivery and then collects from the customers. Strong relationships have developed between GISO and its network members.

When GISO gets an order that cannot be filled by its distribution centers or aligned wholesalers, it turns to its internal sourcing group. The group routinely scours the world to satisfy requests for unusual products and services. For example, in summer 1995, ARCO Alaska requested bear repellent for pipeline workers. GISO's sourcing group found a small manufacturer in a remote part of Alaska. They then determined whether spray or steam applicators would be most useful and what size containers would be most economical. Once these decisions were made, GISO figured out how to get the repellent from the manufacturer to the workers as quickly as possible. Talk about going the extra mile!

Sources: James Morgan, "Is This the Age of the Super Distributor?" *Modern Distribution Management,* April 10, 1994, pp. 5–7; James Narus and James Anderson, "Rethinking Distribution," *Harvard Business Review* (July-August 1996): 116; and Grainger's Web site, www.grainger.com, August 15, 1996.

Developing strong connections with suppliers is also important to more effective and efficient business operations. Southwestern Supply, an industrial products wholesaler in Las Vegas, and Milwaukee Electric Tool, a manufacturer of portable power tools, have developed an outstanding working relationship. Southwestern relies on Milwaukee to develop annual business plans, identify potential customers, develop new marketing strategies, and train its sales force. In exchange, Southwestern employees promote Milwaukee over other brands carried by the company.[53]

The decision to add new suppliers can sometimes alienate current partners. For example, in summer 1996, Bell Industries signed an agreement to sell semiconductors from Samsung, a Korean company. National Semiconductor, a U.S. manufacturer, immediately terminated its relationship with Bell. National's stated policy is not to distribute through wholesalers carrying foreign products. Bell presumably knew about the policy and preferred a relationship with Samsung.[54] In such a situation, the wholesaler must weigh the pros and cons to determine which supplier is a better match for the future.

INTEGRATED LOGISTICS AND PHYSICAL DISTRIBUTION

Physical distribution involves only finished products, whereas logistics is a broader concept. **Logistics** is the movement of raw materials, components, and/or finished products within and between companies. **Integrated logistics management** is the coordination of such activities in a company. It is very important because each part of the process is highly interrelated with others. If the movement of goods needed as inputs is not properly managed, then physical distribution of output to customers will be impeded. Coordination is equally important when goods move between plants, distribution centers, warehouses, wholesalers, and retailers.

Logistics
The movement of raw materials, components, and/or finished products within and between companies.

Integrated logistics management
The coordination of all logistical activities in a company.

The challenge of integration is to establish effective communications among companies, departments, and people whose decisions affect logistics. Even within the company, there can be problems. Salespeople may be so worried about late deliveries that they pad their forecasts. Concerned about costs, purchasing, and production, departments are conservative in their projections. In many companies, the people deepest in the organization and farthest from the customer, production planners, develop the final estimates used to hire workers and build inventory.[55]

Integrated logistics management is only as strong as a company's understanding of its customers and the ability of its people to work together. Cross-functional teams in purchasing, production-warehousing, marketing, and sales often produce excellent results. By sharing information on purchasing, production schedules, marketing and sales plans, customer service standards, and customer preferences, the team can make logistical decisions that are truly integrated and beneficial to the company. Even without teams, integration can occur if communication from and about customers flows throughout the company in the form of market research reports, sales activity, forecasts, and orders. This information can be refined into specific purchasing and manufacturing plans.[56]

PHYSICAL DISTRIBUTION

Physical distribution

The movement of finished products through channels of distribution to customers.

Physical distribution is the movement of finished products to customers. Although the concept is simple, accomplishing this task effectively and efficiently is often complex. For example, Mattel must process and ship orders for Barbie from its four Asian factories to distribution centers, wholesalers, and retailers in 140 countries around the world.[57]

Although physical distribution obviously plays a dominant role in the operations of any wholesaling organization, it is very important to any company involved in making or selling goods. In fact, when performed well, it can provide a competitive edge.[58] For example, Domino's Pizza, with 1,160 stores in 46 countries, has achieved a leadership position in the pizza industry based on its home delivery capabilities, even while others like Pizza Hut try to emulate it.[59] Based on its strong dealer and physical distribution network, Caterpillar gets repair parts to customers the same day or the next, while it takes competitors like Samsung several days or more.

The primary objective of physical distribution is to get the right products to the right locations at the right times at the lowest total cost. An effective distribution system can contribute to customer satisfaction and, in turn, increased sales revenues. A poor performance will alienate customers, who will switch allegiance to competitors.[60]

Compaq Computer estimates it may have lost up to $1 billion in sales in the early 1990s because its laptops and desktops were not available when and where customers were ready to buy them. The company put renewed emphasis on managing its physical distribution operations with a $100 million reengineering effort. In its 350,000-square-foot Houston distribution center, sophisticated software matches customer orders to inventory on hand. Radio signals tell drivers of Aisle Rangers, the 30-foot-high trucks that run on tracks between shelves in the warehouse, which items to pick up in filling customer orders. As a result, the company's performance in making products available through around 31,000 wholesalers and retailers worldwide has significantly improved.[61]

While revenue generation is important, no less significant is careful control of the costs of processing orders, maintaining warehouses, carrying and handling inventory, and shipping products. Physical distribution can account for up to 40 percent of total cost and more than 25 percent of each sales dollar.[62] Achieving high customer service levels at the expense of company profitability makes no sense. Therefore, physical distribution management involves a delicate balance between effective customer service and efficient operations.

Toyota's Lexus division is an excellent example of striking the right balance. The typical car dealer has more than $200,000 in parts inventory, a heavy financial burden. At the same time, stock-outs frequently occur. Understanding this, Lexus designed a system that better serves the company, its dealers, and its customers. Lexus requires dealers to have AS400 computers and satellite dishes that connect them to company headquarters in Torrance, California. Specialized inventory control software helps dealers have the right parts on hand. If an item is unavailable in inventory, then it can be ordered electronically one day and received by air freight the next. Although Lexus dealers have only $100,000 tied up in parts inventory, there are few stock-outs, and customer satisfaction levels are higher.[63] The systemwide costs of computers, satellite dishes, software, and air freight are more than offset by lower inventory costs and increased sales through better customer service.

ORDER MANAGEMENT

Order management refers to how the company receives, fills, and delivers orders to customers. The design of the physical distribution system—including order processing, warehousing, materials handling, inventory control, and transportation functions—determines how well the company manages orders, as outlined in Figure 12-8. New technologies, such as electronic data interchange and bar coding, have had a remarkable effect on system design, which in turn has improved the effectiveness and efficiency of order management. **Electronic data interchange (EDI)** is an intercompany computer-to-computer exchange of orders and other business documents in standard formats.

Customer service standards will have a major bearing on the design of the physical distribution system. Companies that want high marks on order fill rate, order cycle time, delivery reliability, and invoice accuracy must be prepared to invest heavily in network design. Often, managers find they must lower desired standards somewhat because the costs of achieving an ideal level are prohibitive. One approach is to recognize that all customers are not equal. As a general rule, a small percentage of a company's customers, often 20 percent or less, provide over 80 percent of its revenues.[64] Customer service standards can be set higher for the firm's most important customers. Scarce resources can be saved by lowering customer service standards, at least to some extent, with less important customers.

Order Processing   The distribution of products cannot begin until the company receives an order. Order processing includes all the activities and paperwork involved in transmitting and entering, screening and prioritizing, and invoicing orders.

Orders received from customers, channel members, or company personnel are entered into the company's recordkeeping system. Traditionally, salespeople wrote the orders by hand and delivered them to the office in person or by mail, phone, or fax. New technologies have dramatically changed all that. EDI connects many companies directly with customers, who key in the order and submit it electronically. Order cycle time is significantly reduced. Furthermore, since no one has to reenter the information, errors are minimized, and invoice accuracy is improved. Labor and material cost for printing, mailing, and handling paper-based transactions are lower. An EDI system helped Texas Instruments reduce order cycle time by 57 percent, resource requirements by 70 percent, and shipping errors by 95 percent.[65] Companies like Marshall Industries and Motorola supply their outside salespeople with laptop computers. They can access price information instantly rather than check price lists or call the office. They can enter an order, plug into phone lines, and transmit it electronically. Inside salespeople input telephone orders directly into the system. Order cycle time, invoice errors, and order processing costs are all reduced.

Order management
The means by which a company receives, fills, and delivers orders to customers.

Electronic data interchange (EDI)
Intercompany computer-to-computer exchange of orders and other business documents in standard formats.

Physical Distribution Functions	Steps in the Order Management Process
Order processing	Transmitting orders Entering orders Screening orders Prioritizing orders Invoicing orders
Warehousing	Filling orders
Materials handling	Filling orders
Inventory control	Filling orders
Transportation	Shipping orders

Figure 12-8   Order Management

EDI systems help connect companies directly with customers.

Orders must be screened in terms of the customer's ability to pay. Traditionally, this was done after order entry, but EDI now allows companies to screen orders immediately. For example, Vanstar's system is connected to the banks and flooring companies of its customers. (Flooring companies such as ITT grant credit lines to businesses.) If they place an order that exceeds their bank account or credit line, the order is automatically put on hold. The computer then rechecks the account or credit line twice that day to determine whether sufficient funds have been added. If so, the order is processed. If not, the order remains in limbo.[66]

The telephone-computer technology known as caller ID enables an inside salesperson to know who is calling before picking up the phone.[67] A variety of information about the caller appears on a computer screen, including payment history and credit information. If a problem is apparent, then the salesperson can notify the customer before entering the order. This avoids a good deal of wasted time on everyone's part. After screening, many companies prioritize orders based on the importance of the customer or the order cycle time requested. For example, Vanstar customers can request same-day delivery on orders, at a premium price. The computer system transmits these orders to distribution ahead of next-day orders.[68]

Bills are prepared once it is known how much of the order can be filled from available inventory. Today, advanced computer systems keep track of inventory and the latest prices continuously. Invoices are automatically printed out. Order cycle time is reduced, while invoice accuracy is dramatically improved. And interestingly, invoices are becoming a hot promotion tool. They have a 100 percent readership rate, and companies are including special information and offers on them.[69]

Warehousing

The storage of inventory in the physical distribution system.

Distribution centers

A location where inventory is maintained before being routed to individual sales outlets, or customers.

Private warehouses

A storage facility owned and operated by the company.

Public warehouses

A storage facility owned and operated by businesses that rent space.

Cross-docking

Sorting and loading an incoming shipment from a supplier for delivery to customers without its being stored in any warehouse.

Warehousing **Warehousing** is the storage of inventory in the physical distribution system. Many companies perform this function with a mix of distribution centers and warehouses. **Distribution centers** are where the bulk of a company's finished-goods inventory is maintained before being routed to individual sales outlets or customers. These are of two types: **Private warehouses** are owned and operated by the company, and **public warehouses** rent space to store products. Preferences for fixed versus variable costs help determine a company's mix of private and public warehousing.

With technology, many companies can provide better customer service with fewer warehouses. National Semiconductor recently closed six distribution centers around the globe and is air-freighting its microchips to customers from a new, 125,000-square-foot center in Singapore. This has cut standard delivery time 47 percent, reduced distribution costs 2.5 percent, and increased sales by 34 percent.[70] Benetton Group, Italy's integrated fashion manufacturer and retailer, ships 80 million items each year directly to 7,000 stores in 100 countries with an order cycle time of as little as seven days. Most items are sent from a single automated distribution center.[71]

Cross-docking involves sorting and reloading an incoming shipment from a supplier for delivery to customers without its being stored in any warehouse. The method is used most frequently in truck transport. EDI and specialized information systems allow for the close coordination that makes cross-docking efficient. This practice is on the increase because it reduces inventory carrying costs and order cycle time. Furthermore, the fewer times the product is handled, the lower the potential for damage. Compaq, for example, increasingly relies on cross-docking at its Houston distribution center.[72] The technique affects warehousing design: Larger parking lots are needed for transferring products from truck to truck, and buildings are smaller.

Materials Handling   **Materials handling** is the moving of products in a warehouse in the process of filling orders. Traditionally, the facility manager would receive the paperwork and assign it to a worker. With a handcart or motorized forklift, the worker would go through the warehouse, picking up products and checking them off on the order forms. If some were unavailable, that would be noted on the form, and a *back order* would be generated. These were filled and shipped when a new supply arrived.

Bar codes, radio frequency technology, and hand-held scanning devices are having a remarkable effect on materials handling. Bar-code labels for identification purposes can be placed on everything from cardboard boxes to plywood sheets. Hand-held scanners with display panels receive orders directly from the mainframe computer through radio waves and guide workers to the appropriate locations. Workers then scan in the bar codes to make sure the right product and quantity are selected. If not, the scanner will beep. Errors and order cycle time are reduced. Back orders are processed much more quickly. This system is a must for any company interested in boosting quality control and customer satisfaction.[73]

Inventory Control   **Inventory control** is the management of stock levels. For each product, company management must decide how much inventory will be carried in each distribution center and warehouse. Carrying too little inventory leads to poor order fill rates, too many back orders, and poor customer service. Carrying too much leads to higher than necessary costs. Many companies fail because they have too much capital tied up in inventory; this reduces cash flow, which means that bills cannot be paid.[74]

Inventory levels are often determined with the help of the *ABC classification* approach. Stockkeeping units (SKUs) are divided into three categories based on their sales volume and/or profitability. Inventory levels are kept relatively high for the A category, moderate for B, and relatively low for C. The trap to avoid is a large inventory of less profitable SKUs purchased by fringe or noncore customers.

Part of inventory control is to determine reorder points and order quantities. A *reorder point* is the inventory level at which a replenishment order is generated. The standard formula is

Reorder point = Demand or usage rate × Order cycle time + Safety stock

In other words, there should be enough inventory to supply customers during the time required to get more stock, plus a margin of safety. More formally, safety stock is the inventory kept on hand in case of forecasting error or delayed delivery of replenishment stock. For example, if the average daily demand rate is 50 units, order cycle time is 4 days, and safety stock is 20 units, then the reorder point is $(50 \times 4) + 20 = 220$ units. Whenever inventory drops to that level, a replenishment order should be made.

The **economic order quantity (EOQ) model** is a method for determining how much product to order each time. It compares ordering costs to inventory carrying costs, with the objective of minimizing total costs. The standard formula is:

$$EOQ = \frac{2 \times CO \times D}{CI \times U}$$

where CO = Cost per order
   D = Annual sales volume in units
   CI = Annual inventory carrying cost
   U = Unit cost

Materials handling
The moving of products in and around a warehouse in the process of filling orders.

Inventory control
Management of stock levels.

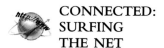

CONNECTED: SURFING THE NET

www.benetton.com

Explore the Benetton Web site, where you can learn the details of its distribution network as well as the role of information systems in its business practices. You can also check out the company's fan and hate mail, send a postcard, read about its corporate background, and much more.

Economic order quantity (EOQ) model
A method of determining the amount of product to be ordered each time.

Automated distribution centers reduce errors in filling orders and order cycle times.

The cost per order is calculated by determining purchasing costs, computer costs, and accounts payable costs associated with placing individual orders. Annual inventory carrying costs are calculated by summing expenses associated with warehouse space, insurance, taxes on inventory, obsolescence and shrinkage, materials handling (including wages and equipment), and costs of money invested. The lower the cost per order relative to inventory carrying costs, the lower the order quantity.

The EOQ method should be used only as a guideline. It works particularly well for products with consistent demand patterns throughout the year. For seasonal items or for products on which suppliers give discounts at certain order quantities, EOQ estimates need some adjustment. A just-in-time (JIT) system also skews the EOQ method. In a JIT system the necessary unit is delivered in the necessary quantity at the necessary time. The fundamental objective is to eliminate waste of all sorts, especially excess inventory. Products are delivered in just enough quantity to cover demand for a short period. Shipments are made frequently and are scheduled precisely; 100 percent delivery reliability is sought because little safety stock is carried. Total cost of ownership is stressed. Per-unit price is less important than the costs associated with extra handling, warehousing, and inventorying. JIT requires companies to meet specific deadlines, supply exact quantities, and adjust deliveries and quantities to meet changing needs, all with a minimum of paperwork. Strong relationships between the companies, including high trust, are critical to the success of such systems.

The Japanese popularized JIT delivery for materials and parts used in manufacturing, but it is now used for a variety of consumer and business-to-business products. If done well JIT can reduce inventory carrying costs by well over half.[75] The increase in transportation costs is offset by inventory reductions. Compaq, Saturn, and Wal-Mart are among the companies that rely on JIT today.

Transportation   In a physical distribution system, transportation is the movement of goods to channel members and customer locations. That is the largest distribution expense for many manufacturers, especially if heavy, bulky products are involved, since transportation fees are charged by the pound. The cost of transporting weight training equipment and exercise bicycles, for example, is often more than that of the equipment itself.[76] Deregulation of the transportation industry increased competition among carriers, which has led to greater efficiency and real cost savings for U.S. manufacturers, wholesalers, retailers, and consumers.

The methods for moving products are motor vehicles, railroads, airlines, water carriers, and pipelines. Figure 12-9 depicts the share of U.S. freight traffic and shipping revenues by each mode. While railroads have the highest share of traffic, trucks dominate in share of total shipping revenues in the U.S. market.

Figure 12-10 contrasts the advantages and disadvantages of the various modes. Managers choose among them based on customer service versus cost trade-offs. Different modes can be used to serve different clients. For example, orders to core customers may be go via fast, reliable air service, while orders to noncore customers may be delivered by less expensive ground transportation.

Trucks   The major advantages of trucks are door-to-door service and speed. Trucks also are dependable and widely available, making frequent shipments possible. Their major disadvantage is cost. Given these characteristics, trucks are ideally suited for high-value manufactured products. Companies can purchase and operate their own fleet of trucks or use the services of independent companies. The trade-offs have to do with level of control and fixed versus variable costs. When uncertainty is high, the use of independents is preferable. In Brazil, for example, Coca-Cola's bottler piggybacks its products on beer trucks; the Pepsi bottler owned 700 trucks until it declared insolvency in 1996.[77]

Transportation Mode	Share of Freight Traffic (billions of ton miles)	Share of Shipping Revenues
Trucks	28%	80.2%
Railroads	38%	8.0%
Air	less than .5%	4.0%
Water carriers	15%	5.4%
Pipelines	18%	2.3%

Figure 12-9   Transportation Modes: Share of U.S. Freight Traffic and Revenues

Source: *Statistical Abstract of the United States* (Washington, DC: U.S. Department of Commerce, 1995), pp. 625, 626.

	Trucks	Railroads	Air	Water Carriers	Pipeline
Transportation Cost	high	average	very high	very low	low
Door-to-door service	high	average	average	low	high
Speed of service	high	average	very high	very low	low
Dependability in meeting schedules	high	average	very high	average	high
Availability in different locations	very high	high	average	low	very low
Frequency of shipments	very high	low	average	very low	high
Need for intermodal transfer for door-to-door service	no	often	almost always	often	often
Primary advantage	door-to-door service and speed	low cost for long hauls of bulk commodities	fastest and highest quality	low cost for long hauls of bulk commodities	low cost and dependability

Figure 12-10   Comparison of Different Modes of Transportation

Railroads   Railroads represent the most efficient mode of land transportation for bulky commodities, such as chemicals, coal, grain, iron ore, lumber, sand, and steel. Major U.S. railroads haul more than 250,000 carloads of goods in an average week, with coal accounting for about 40 percent of the total.[78] The major disadvantages of railroads are transit time and lack of door-to-door service, although rail spurs can be built to some customer locations. *Unit trains* run back and forth between a single loading point, such as a coal mine, and a single destination, such as a power plant, to deliver one commodity. Leading U.S. companies providing rail transportation include Burlington Northern, CSX, and Union Pacific.

Air Transport   Air transport is offered by the airlines and cargo service companies. Speed and dependability in meeting schedules are very high relative to the other modes. Air is the most costly, however. Fashion merchandise, fragile and highly perishable items, emergency shipments, and expensive industrial goods account for the majority of products shipped air freight.

Water Carriers   Water carriers include transoceanic ships as well as barges used on inland waterways. Their transportation cost is the lowest among the various options, often the only way to ship large volumes must balance speed versus balance. Furthermore, only channel members and customers in port cities can be reached directly. Water carriers are used for bulky commodities, like cement and petroleum. Ore barges, for example, are a common sight on the Great Lakes. The mode also is used to carry mass-produced products, like automobiles and toys, overseas.

Pipelines   Pipelines transport natural gas and petroleum by land from production fields to refineries. Up to 40 different grades of product can be shipped through the same pipeline simultaneously and separated at destination points. Pipelines are very dependable and offer door-to-door service. They are the least labor intensive of any mode, and maintenance expenses are low. They can be used only for a narrow range of products, however, and delivery speed—less than 5 miles per hour—is slow.

Intermodal Methods   Intermodal transportation, the combination of two or more modes in moving freight, is gaining popularity. The objective is to exploit the major advantages of each. Piggybacking truck trailers on rail cars, for example, joins the benefits of long-haul rail movement with the door-to-door service of trucks. Express delivery often uses trucks and air to rush shipments from source to destination. Federal Express, the pioneer in overnight delivery, has developed a thriving business running transportation services for such clients as National Semiconductor, Laura Ashley, and Vanstar. Other companies offer a variety of intermodal options. For example, CNF Transportation, headquartered in Palo Alto, California, owns and operates Conway Transportation Services, which focuses on trucking services, and Emery Worldwide, which offers global air freight, ocean transport, and air charter.

Intermodal transportation
The combination of two or more modes in moving freight.

The transportation modes used by companies is sometimes influenced by laws and government pressure. Coca-Cola uses three-wheeled motorbikes for deliveries in Shanghai, China, because truck use is restricted during daylight hours.[79] The Japanese government is campaigning against frequent truck deliveries because of extreme traffic congestion in major cities.[80]

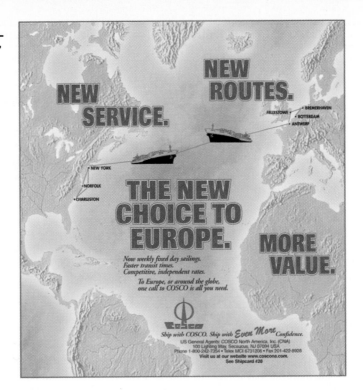

COSCO ships cargo around the globe.

New technologies are influencing how the transportation function is being performed. Progressive trucking companies install on-board computers in vehicles. Ryder System, which provides transportation services to such companies as Saturn, gives its drivers plastic keys loaded with electronic data. When these are plugged into the on-board computer, a screen informs the driver exactly where to go, which route to take, and how much time to spend getting there.[81]

Satellite communication systems are also having an important effect, providing a fast and high-volume channel for information movement around the globe. Schneider National, a U.S. trucking company, uses communication dishes on the top of its trucks to link drivers and dispatchers.[82] The real-time interaction provides up-to-date information to customers regarding location and delivery time. Furthermore, dispatchers can redirect trucks in response to need or traffic congestion. Federal Express, Roadway, and United Parcel Service are among the many companies that track shipments electronically to ensure that all customers remain fully informed about deliveries.

Efficient consumer response (ECR) programs

Programs to improve the efficiency of replenishing, delivering, and stocking inventory in the distribution channel, while promoting customer value.

Efficient Customer Response **Efficient consumer response (ECR) programs** are designed to improve the efficiency of replenishing, delivering, and stocking inventory while promoting customer value.[83] Enhanced cooperation among channel members in order to eliminate activities that do not add value is a primary goal. A 1994 study found that ECR could yield as much as $24 billion in operating cost reductions and $6 billion in financial savings. Potential savings ranged from about 3 percent for manufacturers to 12 percent for retailers.[84]

Traditionally, retailers and wholesalers have used professional buyers to decide what and when to order from suppliers. To curry favor, suppliers frequently offered buyers price deals. *Forward buying* became commonplace: a large order for a product at a special price per carton and then a long delay until the next order. This led to a wide variation in order patterns for manufacturers and great uncertainty. Because of inefficiencies, stock-outs occurred much too frequently, even though inventory levels for many products were high throughout the channel.

ECR requires a change in the roles played by channel members. Wholesalers and retailers give up some of their buying authority. On a daily basis, they send information on stock levels and warehouse shipments to their suppliers over EDI networks. Personnel in the supplier organizations use this information to decide what and when to ship. Order quantities are determined with the objectives of providing sufficient safety stock, minimizing total logistics costs, and eliminating excess inventory in the channel. Before shipments go out, wholesalers and retailers can review and edit orders if they desire, via EDI. Fewer special prices are offered by suppliers to reduce the incentive for forward buying, which is disruptive to ECR. Instead, everyday low pricing may be used.

If done effectively, ECR can reduce inventory costs and stock-outs in the channel. Furthermore, wholesalers and retailers can reduce the number of professional buyers they employ, since suppliers assume more ordering responsibilities.

Procter & Gamble has been a leader in developing and implementing ECR programs with supermarket customers. In the five-year period from 1992 to 1996, it more than doubled inventory turnover for such products as Crest, Pampers, Tide, and Prell, and order fill rates rose from 90 to 99 percent. By 1996 P&G's overall sales were up 33 percent, with more than 40 percent of orders shipped automatically based on withdrawals from customer warehouses. Such moves helped the company cut its annual production and distribution costs by $1.6 billion, or about 8 percent since 1992.[85]

GLOBAL PHYSICAL DISTRIBUTION

It is difficult enough to distribute products in one's own country. When doing business abroad, the challenge is multiplied. Uncertainty increases because of greater transport distances, longer lead times, and complex customs requirements and trade restrictions. The most important factor from a physical distribution perspective, however, is a country's infrastructure, which influences how products are stored and transported.

China is the world's third largest economy, after the United States and Japan. Nearly 50 million Chinese have an annual income above $18,000 (adjusted for purchasing power). Unfortunately, China's infrastructure has not kept up with the growth in consumer demand. The state, usually at the provincial level, controls more than 90 percent of warehousing capacity. The majority of buildings, designed in the 1950s, are single-story and poorly lit. They are subject to flooding, have no temperature control, minimal or no fire protection, and poor pest control. Goods are typically floor-stacked, which leads to damaged cartons and inefficient use of space. Manual loading and unloading of trucks is the rule, without even forklifts.[86]

The Chinese road system covers more than 600,000 miles, but only 3,600 miles are modern paved highway. Typical freight haulage is in tarpaulin-covered trucks. A team of two drivers, working a 16-hour day, can cover only about 300 miles, averaging under 20 miles per

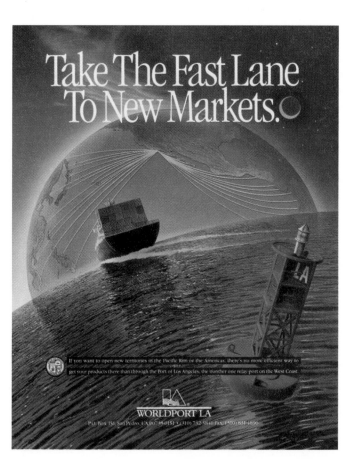

The Port of Los Angeles advertises efficiency in moving products globally, especially the Pacific Rim.

hour.[87] China's railways cover more than 33,000 miles and are tremendously overburdened. It takes about 17 days to go by train from Shanghai to Guangzhou (1,125 miles). The State Planning Commission controls rail scheduling and gives priority to basic commodities. At certain times of the year, such as after major harvests, commercial capacity is simply unavailable. The number of airports is insufficient. Air freight and express services are mainly provided by passenger aircraft. Domestic telecommunications are of uneven quality. Integrated information technology does not exist.

Because of this infrastructure, companies find it very difficult to get their products quickly, safely, and reliably to customers in China. Customer service standards must be set with reality in mind. Proper packaging is extremely important to protect goods. Relationships must be developed with government officials to persuade them to devote resources to the infrastructure. More than $230 billion in infrastructure investment is needed to sustain continued economic growth through the next five years.[88] Similar problems are found in Africa, Asia, Eastern Europe, and elsewhere.[89] For example, there are 14,172 kilometers of road per million people in the United States. In Latin America, the figure is 670 kilometers; in East Asia, 231 kilometers.[90]

CONNECTED: SURFING THE NET

McDonald's®

www.mcdonalds.com

THIS CHAPTER'S DIVERSITY FEATURE, "MCDONALD'S®: SERVING Diverse Communities in More Ways Than One," discussed how the franchise thrives in inner city locations. To expand your thinking about marketing channels and franchising, visit McDonald's® Web site and answer the following questions.

1. How might McDonald's® use physical distribution to bridge the separation between manufacturers and prospective customers?
2. Check out "McWorld®." What does it offer? How does it make a personal connection with customers?
3. How may channel length differ in McDonald's® global markets? List several of the company's highly successful global markets.
4. As you learned in this chapter's diversity feature, McDonald's® has been successful in developing a diverse mix of franchises. Read the company's franchise information. What percentage of McDonald's® restaurant businesses is owned and operated by franchisees? On what premise is the corporation's franchising system based?

W. W. Grainger

www.wwgrainger.com

THIS CHAPTER'S RELATIONSHIPS FEATURE, "ALLIANCES WITH SPECIALTY WHOLESALERS," W. W. Grainger's discussed the company's partnerships with a number of large specialty wholesalers. To learn more about Grainger's alliances and supply operations, visit its Web site and answer the following questions.

1. W. W. Grainger's on-line catalog provides access to more than 189,000 items for more than one million customers around the world. What other services does Grainger offer? How do you think these have helped the company become a leading business-to-business distributor in the United States?
2. Read the company overview. How does Grainger meet the primary objective of physical distribution? How can an effective system impact the company? An ineffective system?
3. How does Grainger go "Beyond the Basics" to establish lasting connections with its customers?
4. Read the company's "'no excuses' guarantee." Which companies have awarded Grainger for its excellence? What customer service standards does Grainger use?

Of course, a major challenge for many companies is moving products into other countries. **Freight forwarders** are cargo specialists, and their services are often used. Domestically, they pick up partial shipments at the customer location, consolidate all these into truckload or carload size, and arrange for delivery at destination points. Their gross margin is the difference between the rates they charge customers and what they pay carriers. Many exporters rely on freight forwarders to handle the documentation, insurance, and other aspects of delivery abroad. For example, they ensure that letters of credit are issued at the buyer's bank and properly transferred into the sellers account. Leading global freight forwarders include Nippon Express and Kintetsu World Express (Japan), Danzas AG and Kuhne and Nagel (Switzerland), Schenker (Germany), Lep International and MSAS (United Kingdom), and Burlington Air Express and Air Express International (United States).[91]

Freight forwarders
Service companies specializing in the movement of cargo from one point to another, often country to country.

Regardless of geographic location, the ultimate goal of distribution is to make the product readily available to the consumer or end user. For the majority of consumer products, this has traditionally meant delivering goods to the retail outlets where consumers shop. Today, however, direct marketing—including sales via the Internet—is a growing force in consumer as well as business-to-business sales. In chapter 13 we will focus on retailing and direct marketing, including the distinctive strategies used by marketers in these fields.

CHAPTER SUMMARY

OBJECTIVE 1: Learn why companies frequently use intermediaries to reach targeted customers.

Indirect channels involving independent intermediaries are frequently used, especially when the targeted market is small and geographically dispersed, companies face severe resource constraints, environmental uncertainty is high, the anticipated return from investments in direct channels is low, the level of value-added activities is low, and customers prefer dealing with intermediaries. Deciding whether to use direct or indirect channels in foreign markets is especially challenging, but culture, market structure, entrenched channels, and legal regulations have a significant effect on the choice.

OBJECTIVE 2: Attain insight into how channel relationships should be managed over time.

Coordinating relationships within the distribution channel is a challenge. The company must think strategically and develop a management plan. Interdependence, trust, and support will influence the success of coordination. Joint goal-setting and planning, monitoring, the use of influence, conflict resolution, and performance appraisals are steps that need to be taken.

OBJECTIVE 3: Appreciate the economic importance of wholesalers.

Wholesalers are intermediaries who take title to the products they carry and make the majority of their sales to businesses. Wholesalers purchase large amounts of merchandise from a variety of suppliers and offer it for resale in smaller quantities. They often provide credit, extensive information on product benefits, training on product use, and technical assistance. They are needed because small to medium-sized companies in many industries do not buy in sufficient quantity to deal directly with manufacturers. Many large companies also buy from wholesalers because of convenience, lower personnel costs, and better customer service.

OBJECTIVE 4: Know the different types of wholesalers and the distinct roles they play.

A wide range of functions is performed for customers by full-service wholesalers, a category that includes general line wholesalers, specialty wholesalers, and rack jobbers. In contrast, limited-service wholesalers perform only some of the traditional channel functions. In this category are cash-and-carry wholesalers, drop shippers, truck jobbers, and mail-order wholesalers.

OBJECTIVE 5: Understand what physical distribution entails and why it is critical for any business organization.

Physical distribution, the movement of finished products through channels of distribution to end customers, entails order processing, warehousing, materials handling, and transportation. The primary objective is to get the right product to the right customer location at the right time at the lowest total cost. Physical distribution management involves a delicate balance between effective customer service and efficient operations. Order fill rate, order cycle time, delivery reliability, and invoice accuracy are four commonly used measures of customer service proficiency.

OBJECTIVE 6: Learn the steps in the order management process.

Order management is concerned with how the company receives, fills, and delivers orders to customers. New technologies have dramatically changed the way orders are transmitted, entered, screened, prioritized, invoiced, and filled. Many orders are now sent electronically. Hand-held scanners with display panels often are used by warehouse workers in filling orders. There are automated distribution centers with mechanized picking equipment controlled by computers in conjunction with conveyor systems. Inventory control is essential to assure maximum fill rates at minimum cost. In transporting orders to customers, the major advantage of trucks and airplanes is speed, but they are relatively costly. Railroads and water carriers are the most efficient modes for the movement of bulky commodities. Gaining in popularity is intermodal transportation, the combination of two or more modes in moving freight.

Efficient consumer response programs attempt to eliminate activities that do not add value in distribution channels. Wholesalers and retailers give up some of their buying authority. They send daily information via EDI to their suppliers on stock levels and warehouse shipments. Personnel in the supplier organization then decide what and when to ship.

1. What are intermediaries? List three primary categories of intermediaries.
2. What is a reverse channel? Give an example.
3. What is a conventional channel system? Give an example.
4. What do members of an administered channel system do?
5. List three common forms of contractual channel systems. Briefly describe each.
6. What are the guidelines for managing channel relationships?
7. What is a wholesaler? Briefly explain why wholesalers are important.
8. What is a full-service wholesaler? A limited-service wholesaler? List three types for each.
9. What is integrated logistics? What is physical distribution? Name the primary objective of physical distribution.
10. What is order management? Name a technological advance that has improved its effectiveness and efficiency.
11. What is warehousing? Name two types of distribution centers.
12. What is economic order quantity? What is its formula?
13. List five modes of transportation used in a physical distribution system.
14. What is efficient consumer response?
15. Name an important factor in global physical distribution.

1. What is a distribution channel? Why are distribution channels so important to companies and consumers?
2. How do direct channels differ from indirect channels? Under what conditions are indirect channels preferred to direct channels?
3. Why do channels vary in length or number of levels? What are multiple channels? Why are they being relied on by more and more companies today?
4. What are vertical marketing systems? Discuss the three types of VMS.
5. Describe the three distribution intensity options available to companies and give examples of each.
6. What is interdependence? Why is it such an important concept in managing channel relationships? What role do support programs play in the distribution channel?
7. Explain how conflicts can be resolved in channel relationships.
8. Compare the businesses of limited-service and full-service wholesalers. Can limited-service wholesalers be just as successful financially as full-service wholesalers?
9. What is EDI? How is it influencing the effectiveness and efficiency of order processing?
10. Explain how bar codes, radio frequency technology, and scanning devices are improving the effectiveness and efficiency of the materials handling function.
11. How are efficient consumer response programs changing the way business is conducted between manufacturers and retailers?
12. What is the major challenge to integrated logistics management? How can companies overcome this challenge?

Administered channel system: A vertical marketing system in which channel members devote effort to coordinating their relationships.

Allocation: A wholesaler function that entails purchasing products in large quantities and reselling them in smaller quantities.

Assortment: A wholesaler function that entails selling a range of merchandise from a variety of sources.

Broker: A firm that does not take title to the goods it handles but actively negotiates the sale of goods for its clients.

Channel levels: The number of distinct units (producers, intermediaries, and customers) in a distribution channel.

Contractual channel system: A vertical marketing system in which relationships among channel members are formalized in some fashion, often with a written contract.

Conventional channel system: A channel system in which efforts to coordinate the actions of channel members are seen as unimportant.

Corporate channel system: A vertical marketing system in which a company owns and operates organizations at other levels in the channel.

Cross-docking: Sorting and loading an incoming shipment from a supplier for delivery to customers without its being stored in any warehouse.

Direct channel: A distribution channel in which the producer uses its own employees and physical assets to distribute the product directly to the end user.

Distribution center: A location where inventory is maintained before being routed to individual sales outlets or customers.

Distribution channel: A set of interdependent organizations involved in making a product available for purchase.

Distribution intensity: The number of locations through which a company sells its product in a given market area.

Economic order quantity (EOQ) model: A method of determining the amount of product to be ordered each time.

Efficient consumer response (ECR) programs: Programs to improve the efficiency of replenishing, delivering, and stocking inventory in the distribution channel, while promoting customer value.

Electronic data interchange (EDI): Intercompany computer-to-computer exchange of orders and other business documents in standard formats.

Exclusive dealing: Restricting intermediaries from carrying competitive lines.

Exclusive distribution: Distributing a product through only one sales outlet in each trading area.

Franchise system: A type of distribution channel in which the franchiser holds the product trademark and licenses it to franchisees who contract to meet certain obligations.

Freight forwarders: Service companies specializing in the movement of cargo from one point to another, often country to country.

Full-line forcing: Requiring intermediaries to carry and sell the company's complete line.

Full-service wholesaler: An intermediary who performs a wide range of functions or tasks for its customers.

Indirect channel: A distribution channel in which the producer makes use of independent organizations to distribute the product to end users.

Integrated logistics management: The coordination of all logistical activities in a company.

Intensive distribution: Making the product available through every possible sales outlet in a trade area.

Intermediary: Independently owned organization that acts as a link to move products between the producer and the end user.

Intermodal transportation: The combination of two or more modes in moving freight.

Inventory control: Management of stock levels.

Limited-service wholesaler: An intermediary who performs only some of the traditional channel functions, either eliminating others or passing them on to someone else.

Logistics: The movement of raw materials, components, and/or finished products within and between companies.

Materials handling: The moving of products in and around a warehouse in the process of filling orders.

Multiple channel systems: The use of more than one channel to access markets for the same product.

Order management: The means by which a company receives, fills, and delivers orders to customers.

Physical distribution: The movement of finished products through channels of distribution to customers.

Private warehouse: A storage facility owned and operated by the company.

Public warehouse: A storage facility owned and operated by businesses that rent space.

Retailer: A firm that takes title to products for resale to ultimate consumers.

Retail cooperative: An alliance of small retailers for wholesaling purposes.

Reverse channel: A distribution channel that flows from the end user to the wholesaler and/or producer.

Selective distribution: The use of a limited number of sales outlets per trade area.

Tying arrangement: The purchase of a superior product is conditioned on the purchase of a second product of lower quality.

Vertical marketing system (VMS): A system in which channel members emphasize coordination of behaviors and programs.

Warehousing: The storage of inventory in the physical distribution system.

Wholesaling: Selling goods for resale or business use to other businesses.

Wholesaler: A firm that takes title to products for resale to businesses, or other wholesalers or distributors, and sometimes consumers.

Wholesaler-sponsored voluntary chain: A group of retailers that have been united by a wholesaler.

REFERENCES

1. Adapted from Karen Alberg Grossman, "The Ultimate Coach . . . ," *Accessories,* November 1995, pp. 10–16.
2. Based on consulting experiences with each company.
3. Discussion with John Thompson, Merisel vice president, January 1995.
4. "Ben and Jerry's Homemade, Inc.," case in Bert Rosenbloom, *Marketing Channels,* 6th ed. (Fort Worth: Dryden Press, 1995), pp. 665–670.
5. Based on consulting experience.
6. Steve Lohr, "Computers Greening with the Times," *Chicago Tribune,* April 18, 1993, p. 3.
7. Personal conversations with Dennis Reker, head of distribution at Intel, in 1993.
8. Merrifield Consulting Group, "Infotech Applications for Distribution Channels," www.merrifield.com, August 26, 1996.
9. William Holstein and Kevin Kelly, "Little Companies, Big Exports," *Business Week,* April 13, 1992, p. 71.
10. William Davidson, "Changes in Distribution Institutions," *Journal of Marketing* (January 1970): 7.
11. Rosenbloom, *Marketing Channels,* 6th ed. (Fort Worth: Dryden Press, 1995), pp. 486–487.
12. Ibid.
13. Barnaby Feder, "McKesson: No. 1 but a Doze on Wall Street," *New York Times,* March 17, 1991, p. 10.
14. Louis Stern, Adel El-Ansary, and Anne Coughlan, *Marketing Channels,* 5th ed. (Upper Saddle River, NJ: Prentice Hall, 1996), p. 373.
15. U.S. Department of Commerce, *Statistical Abstract of the United States,* 113th ed. (Washington, DC: U.S. Government Printing Office, 1993), p. 780.
16. Robert Frank and Jonathan Friedland, "How Pepsi's Charge into Brazil Fell Short of Its Ambitious Goals," *Wall Street Journal,* August 30, 1996, pp. A1, A6.
17. Rosenbloom, *Marketing Channels.*
18. Gary Frazier and Walfried Lassar, "Determinants of Distribution Intensity," *Journal of Marketing* 60 (October 1996): 39–51.
19. Stern, El-Ansary, and Coughlan, *Marketing Channels.*
20. Frazier and Lassar, "Determinants of Distribution Intensity."
21. Discussions with top management in Joico, Inc., a manufacturer of hair care products, in October 1994.
22. Gretchen Morgenson, "Greener Pastures," *Forbes,* July 6, 1992, p. 48.
23. Gary Frazier and Raymond Rody, "The Use of Influence Strategies in Interfirm Relationships in Industrial Product Channels," *Journal of Marketing* 55 (January 1991): 52–69.
24. Gregory Gundlach and Ernest Cadotte, "Exchange Interdependence and Interfirm Interaction: Research in a Simulated Channel Setting," *Journal of Marketing Research* 31 (November 1994): 516–532.
25. Frazier and Rody, "Use of Influence Strategies."
26. "Wal-Mart Typifies Cooperation between Supplier, Retailer," *Commercial Appeal,* July 14, 1991, p. C1.
27. Zachary Schiller and Wendy Zellner, "Clout! More and More Retail Giants Rule the Marketplace," *Business Week,* December 21, 1992, pp. 66–73.
28. Robert Morgan and Shelby Hunt, "The Commitment-Trust Theory of Relationship Marketing," *Journal of Marketing* 58 (July 1994): 20–38.
29. Liz Seymour, "Custom Tailored for Service: VF Corporation," *Hemispheres,* March 1996, pp. 25, 26, 28.
30. Laurel Touby, "Blimpie Is Trying to Be a Hero to Franchisees Again," *Business Week,* March 22, 1993, p. 70.
31. Based on a consulting project for Santa Monica Honda-Kawasaki in 1996.
32. Based on a consulting project for Hewlett-Packard in 1996.
33. William Terdoslavich, "Monitors: The Squeeze Is On," *Computer Reseller News,* January 1, 1996, pp. 55, 56.
34. Wendy Bounds, "Film Exposures," *Wall Street Journal,* July 31, 1995, pp. A1, A5; and Emily Nelson, "Kodak Signs Pact with Price/Costco, Dealing Fuji Blow," *Wall Street Journal,* December 5, 1996, p. A5.
35. Robert Frank, "PepsiCo Unit Says It Is Part of U.S. Probe," *Wall Street Journal,* September 6, 1996, p. B2.
36. Based on discussions with Steve Arnholdt, general manager of the Perfect Climate division of Honeywell, throughout 1995 and 1996.
37. "Wal-Mart Typifies Cooperation."
38. Based on a consulting assignment for Texas Instruments in 1996.
39. Leslie Helm, "Motorola Again Predicts Lower Results," *Los Angeles Times,* September 12, 1996, pp. D1, D3.
40. Teri Agins, "Arden Cancels Fall Launch of Liz Taylor's Fragrance," *Wall Street Journal,* August 30, 1995, p. B1.
41. Based on discussions with Susanne Haas, a corporate lawyer at Honeywell, in 1994.

42. Frederick Reichheld, *The Loyalty Effect* (Boston: Harvard Business School Press, 1996).

43. Raju Narisetti, "Intelligent Electronics Made Much of Its Profit at Suppliers' Expense," *Wall Street Journal*, December 6, 1994, pp. A1, A5

44. David Fondiller, "The Pizza Connection," *Forbes*, October 21, 1996, p. 202.

45. Suzanne Oliver, "A Marvelous Annuity," *Forbes*, November 4, 1996, pp. 178–180.

46. U.S. Department of Commerce, *1992 Census of Wholesale Trade, Geographic Area Series* (Washington, DC: U.S. Government Printing Office, 1995), p. US-2.

47. Based on consulting experience in the computer industry.

48. Ibid.

49. Based on discussion with Ed Raymund, founder and chairman emeritus of Tech Data, August 1996.

50. Based on a consulting assignment with Joico, Inc., 1995.

51. Discussion with Terrence Mulholand, vice president of western region at Ryerson, August 1996.

52. James Bates and Chuck Philips, "Wal-Mart Bans Album over Gun Sale Lyrics," *Los Angeles Times,* September 10, 1996, pp. A1, A15.

53. "Quality . . . A Critical Part of a Successful Distributor Partnership," *Today's Distributor,* June 1995, pp. 4–5.

54. "Bell Industries Responds to Supplier Termination," *Modern Distribution Management,* August 25, 1996, p. 4.

55. Benson Shapiro, V. Kasturi Rangan, and John Sviokla, "Staple Yourself to an Order," *Harvard Business Review,* July-August 1992, pp. 113–122.

56. Donald Bowersox and David Closs, *Logistical Management* (New York: McGraw-Hill, 1996), p. 33.

57. Ron Tempest, "Barbie and the World Economy," *Wall Street Journal*, September 22, 1996, pp. A1, A20.

58. Ronald Henkoff, "Delivering the Goods," *Business Week,* November 28, 1994, pp. 64–78.

59. John Cortez, "The New Direction for Domino's," *Advertising Age,* January 4, 1993, pp. 3–5; and Jeanne Whalen, "Domino's Turnaround Master Exits,"*Advertising Age,* January 24, 1994, p. 4.

60. Bowersox and Closs, *Logistical Management.*

61. Henkoff, "Delivering the Goods."

62. Stern, El-Ansary, and Coughlan, *Marketing Channels,* p. 119.

63. Reichheld, *Loyalty Effect,* p. 263.

64. Zachary Schiller, "Make It Simple," *Business Week,* September 9, 1996, pp. 96–104.

65. Clay Youngblood, "EDI Trial and Error," *Transportation and Distribution* 4 (1993): 46.

66. Based on consulting experience with Vanstar in 1996.

67. Gordon Graham, *Distributor Survival in the 21st Century* (Richardson, TX: Inventory Management Press, 1992), pp. 5–12.

68. Based on consulting experience with Vanstar in 1996.

69. Beth Wade, "That's No Invoice; That's a Marketing Tool," *Marketing News,* September 9, 1996, pp. 10, 11.

70. Henkoff, "Delivering the Goods."

71. Thomas Foster, "Global Logistics Benetton Style," *Distribution* 92 (October 1993): 62–66.

72. Henkoff, "Delivering the Goods."

73. Merrifield Consulting Group, "Infotech Applications for Distribution Channels."

74. Graham, *Distributor Survival*; and Reichheld, *Loyalty Effect*, p. 25B.

75. Rosenbloom, *Marketing Channels.*

76. Interview with Vinny Greco, owner of Vinny's Powerhouse Gym, 1996, Watertown, MA.

77. Frank and Friedland, "How Pepsi's Charge into Brazil Fell Short."

78. "Weekly Loadings of American Railroads," *Commerical Appeal,* January 11, 1993, p. B5.

79. Joseph Kahn, "The Pioneers," *Wall Street Journal,* September 26, 1996, p. R12.

80. "Lean and Its Limits," *Economist,* September 14, 1996, p. 65.

81. Henkoff, "Delivering the Goods."

82. Bowersox and Closs, *Logistical Management,* p. 77.

83. Kurt Salmon Associates, *Efficient Consumer Response: Enhancing Consumer Value in the Grocery Industry* (Washington, DC: Food Marketing Institute, 1993), p. 2.

84. Stern, El-Ansary, and Coughlan, *Marketing Channels,* p. 119.

85. Schiller, "Make It Simple."

86. Lawrence Alberts and Hugh Randall, "China Logistics: Creating Competitive Advantage," *Logistics,* Spring 1996, p. 4.

87. Ibid., p. 5.

88. Ibid., p. 8.

89. Cyndee Miller, "Chasing Global Dream," *Marketing News,* December 2, 1996, pp. 1, 2

90. "Infrastructure in Latin America: Privacy Please," *Economist,* July 27, 1996, pp. 54, 55.

91. David Bovet and Roland Henneberger, "Going Global? International Freight Forwarders Can Help," *Logistics,* Spring 1996, pp. 21–25.

CASE 12

TEXAS INSTRUMENTS

TEXAS INSTRUMENTS, INC. (TI), WITH HEADQUARTERS in Dallas and operations in more than 30 countries, markets semiconductors, defense electronics, software, computers and peripheral products, custom engineering, electrical controls, and consumer electronics products. Recently, TI has consolidated several businesses to free up resources for the lucrative semiconductor business. In that arena, the company has transformed itself from a maker of commodity memory chips to a producer of more specialized chips that are higher in value added. For example, TI's newest chipset technology will speed up Net access and enable equipment vendors to develop their own asymmetrical digital subscriber line (ADSL) products. While it appears that the chip industry is slowing, TI has predicted sales growth of 10 percent in 1998, double its 5 percent growth the year before. In order to reach its goal, TI must take into account dramatic shifts in distribution in the semiconductor industry.

In the United States, most major distributors have historically carried either U.S. or Asian semiconductor products. Few distributors have carried both. The five leading U.S. chip manufacturers sold approximately 83 percent of the nearly $4 billion worth of chips sold in the United States. The five top Asian manufacturers reported selling approximately 17 percent. In some cases, U.S. manufacturers have allowed their distributors to share shelf space with Asian manufacturers, particularly to fill out a complete line. For example, TI has been willing to share shelf space with Asian manufacturers for years. In October 1997, Motorola relaxed a decade-long prohibition against sharing space with Asian manufacturers. Thus, after decades in which OEMs had to source domestic and Asian semiconductors from two or more distributors, it is now possible to source products from both areas with a single distributor.

The ability of Japanese organizations to use distributors of U.S. products within the United States has global repercussions as well. There are obvious advantages to the Japanese chip manufacturers who have had difficulty selling to several large global OEMs with major operations in the United States. They have been inhibited because multinational customers often want a single point of contact worldwide. Now those manufacturers are able to use a single large distributor with a global presence. Dick Skipworth, managing director at Memec International Components group, Essen, Germany, a large European and PAC Rim distributor, believes that distributors everywhere now may face the problem of creating differentiation. "There is going to be an increased need for specialization as blindcards [product lines] begin to look more and more alike. I think there is going to be more specialization on the sales and marketing side of any semiconductor manufacturer that relies on distributors to actively sell their product."

The changes in distribution policies have occurred largely because of changes in OEM inventory strategies. OEMs have reduced inventories from a 10-week supply 10 years ago to a 2.2-week supply today; the brunt of the inventory reductions took place in 1996–1997 and the trend is continuing. Companies like Dell, which build products to order, are demanding virtually no inventory. Consequently, there is a need for distributors that can supply customers' immediate needs while finding new ways to differentiate themselves. Arrow, for example, a large national distributor, has recently realigned itself into seven customer-driven units. Each unit is designed to provide specialized services for a unique market segment. Marshall, another large distributor, will continue to differentiate itself through technology, support, and service. Rob Rodin, chief executive of Marshall, indicates, "We are trying as always to be the low cost producer. On the delivery front, we are trying to bring the most unique and reliable delivery systems to the marketplace, including value-added programs, programming services, JIT inventory management, 24-hour-a-day service coverage, Internet, intranets, extranets, and delivery." Arrow and Marshall both carry TI plus other major semiconductor manufacturers' products.

TI has targeted its memory chips and complex digital signal processors, high-value-added chip-based products at OEMs that incorporate semiconductors into everything from VCRs, personal computers, and toys, to navigational systems in automobiles and boats. TI sells semiconductors through two channels—direct to OEMs and indirectly to OEMs through a network of electronics distributors including Arrow and Marshall Industries. Approximately 30 percent of TI's semiconductor sales in the United States are through the distributor channel and this percentage is growing rapidly. Since distributors sell a mix of competitive products including Advanced Micro Devices, Intel, Motorola, and National Semiconductors, TI must fight to get its share. Marshall Industries, for example, emphasizes TI and Toshiba semiconductors. TI has approximately 300 field personnel that focus both on OEMs and distributors. Since the top 100 OEMs in North America use approximately 50 percent of all semiconductors, they are covered directly by TI personnel as major accounts. The next 4,000 OEMs, which use 44 percent of all semiconductors, are covered by distributors who play a vital role for TI. The remaining 6 percent in sales are made up of approximately 100,000 small OEMs, which are targeted by TI with several distributors.

Over the past several years, semiconductor manufacturers have asked distributors to develop better technical expertise, and the response has been to hire more field application engineers. Since they must deal with an array of different products from a number of manufacturers, their depth of knowledge is limited. This is even more true for ordinary sales reps, who lack the background necessary to understand the technical nuances of the complex products they are selling. Typically, distributors have about 10 sales reps for every one field application engineer, so TI devotes significant resources to helping distributor personnel when technical and sales questions arise.

Distributor personnel can contact the TI sales rep assigned to their account or geographic area, and s/he either answers the question or gets the information from others in the organization. Many distributors also inform customers about the Product Information Center at TI, accessible through an 800 number, where the staff is supposed to provide an answer within 24 hours. Marketing and product managers at TI spend considerable time on technical questions that arise in the field. Another concern is to get distributors to specify TI. An area where distributors tend to perform poorly is getting the TI product specified during the OEM's design phase. If this does not occur, TI might not become the preferred supplier.

John Szczsponik, TI's director of North American distribution for semiconductors, has been discussing the industry changes and the specification issue with a number of people throughout the organization. Four possible options have been identified.

Option 1: Put additional pressure on distributors to enhance their technical capability. Each should hire more field application engineers and train them more effectively. TI would contribute by providing the necessary training. TI also could take the responsibility of generating sales leads for distributors through ads and bingo cards.

Option 2: Lower expectations of what distributors can accomplish. Their role should be redefined as primarily fulfilling demand. TI should be responsible for creating demand and winning designs. TI should hire at least 30 more technical and field reps and assign them accounts that appear to have greatest potential.

Option 3: Change TI's policy about sharing competitive information. Give distributor salespeople more information about product applications and hold workshops for their customers; pay distributor salespeople a bounty of $50 for every customer they can motivate to attend. Competitors like Analog Devices are making great use of tactics such as this.

Option 4: Include distributors in the design phase. They should send out direct mail to their customers not only to raise awareness of TI but also to identify application needs. With their detailed knowledge of customers, distributors can help TI focus resources on products and markets with greatest potential.

Szczsponik sees some merit in each of the options and also is trying to identify others not yet considered.

1. *Explain the basic problem(s) TI faces in its distribution channel.*
2. *How should TI address the movement toward distributors that carry both U.S. and foreign competitors' products?*
3. *Would you choose one of the four options, combine some of them, or develop a new approach? Support your recommendation.*

SOURCES: Discussions with Greg Delagi, Pat Moran, Briant Regan, and John Szczsponik of Texas Instruments in 1996 and 1997; Ismini Scouras, "Chain Reaction—Model Prompts OEMs to Keep Inventories Low," *Electronic Buyer News,* December 15, 1997, p. 1; Allen Myerson, "Company Reports: Chip Maker's Operating Net Is Up Sharply," *New York Times,* January 22, 1998, p. D4; Barbara Jorgensen, "New Rules Put OEMs a Step Closer to One-Stop Shopping—Industry Ponders Future as Shelf-Sharing Restrictions Ease," *Electronic Buyer News,* December 15, 1997, p. 41; and "Texas Instruments Speeds Up Net Access with New ADSL Chips," *Newsbytes News Network,* www.newsbytes.com, January 27, 1998.

Retailing and Direct Marketing

Objectives

1. Appreciate the important role retailers play in our economy and society.

2. Understand strategy issues confronted by retailers when making marketing decisions.

3. Recognize the diverse array of retailers that compete with one another.

4. Learn what direct marketing entails, its value, and how it differs from mass communication.

5. Be familiar with the different types of direct response media.

6. Understand the marketing decisions made by direct marketing companies.

WE ALL DREAM ABOUT A JOB that bridges the gap between our personal interests and our desire to live well. Take Cynthia Palmer, assistant general manager of retail operations at the Museum of Fine Arts (MFA), in Boston. Her creative side loved the arts, but her practical nature led her to major in marketing. When the MFA's posting for a marketing assistant appeared at Boston University's career center, Cynthia jumped at the chance. That was back in 1983, when the MFA had a fledgling retail operation—one store and a small catalog—bringing in about $4 million. Realizing the growth potential for the market, Cynthia stayed on, steadily moving upward. And, she has been a major factor in a business that now brings in $37 million a year and is one of the top museum retail operations in the world.

How can a museum succeed in the competitive world of retail? According to Palmer, "the homogenization of the market has created a demand for unique product." The MFA features some of the world's greatest French Impressionist paintings, Egyptian artifacts, and Asian treasures. Says Cynthia: "The museum's mission is to market quality products that relate to the collection, possess intrinsic beauty, educate the customer, and bring optimum revenue to the museum." MFA Enterprises consists of retailing, direct mail, and a site on the Internet. Through various activities, it reaches more than 7.5 million people a year—about 2.5 percent of the U.S. population!

The MFA's retail stores have visitors estimated at more than a million annually. The flagship shop, a 5,7000-square-foot store in the museum, serves 250,000 customers a year. A smaller shop, devoted to major exhibitions, serves another 80,000 patrons a year. The MFA also has five satellites in major malls around Boston and plans to expand. In keeping with the modern retail environment, the MFA has an additional outlet near its warehouse.

The major thrust of business comes through the direct-mail catalog. The MFA sends out four editions per year, for a total of 12.5 million copies. These help them reach the bulk of their customers in New York and California. The target market is women (85 percent), highly educated (many have graduate degrees), in their mid-30s, married, with children—people who appreciate the uniqueness of the products only a museum can offer. Catalog fulfillment is done from a 100,000-square-foot warehouse. That's also the number of mail orders the MFA receives, plus 275,000 phone orders. More than 435,000 packages are shipped each year.

The MFA began selling on the Internet in 1996. Although sales are currently small, it is important to be available in multiple marketplaces. Palmer is negotiating with major on-line services to join an electronic mall.

A major part of Cynthia's work involves creating strong ties with suppliers. She travels to Japan and Italy to meet with long-term suppliers. Since the MFA's products are unique, and many require expert craftsmanship, "it's crucial to have good supplier relations. Good business is built upon good relationships," says Palmer. "You have to understand the capabilities and the drive behind the person on the other side of the table. Understanding what motivates them will make them excel to a greater level than they would with an ordinary customer."[1]

Like MFA Enterprises, modern retail organizations strive to understand and meet the needs of targeted customers. Often this requires establishing multiple channels, including direct marketing and Internet sites. Competition is too intense for retailers to ignore any viable way to connect with and serve customers.

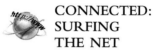

CONNECTED: SURFING THE NET

www.mfa.org

Check out how MFA sells on the Internet by visiting its Web site. You'll also find information on its collections, exhibitions, school, and more.

CAREER TIP Working in a museum has advantages. You can work in a field that may be of great interest to you. There is the satisfaction of bringing money to an institution devoted to making art more accessible to everyone. And from a career standpoint, non-profits allow you to get involved with a broader spectrum of activities than is typical in for-profit organizations.

THE CONCEPTS OF RETAILING AND DIRECT MARKETING

Retailing and direct marketing touch our lives almost daily. Retailing is involved whenever you purchase a burger at McDonald's®, rent a movie at Blockbuster, or buy a pair of jeans at The Gap. Direct marketing is involved whenever you receive a catalog from Dell Computer, watch QVC, or place an Internet order with CDnow for R.E.M.'s latest release. Retailers and direct marketers provide us with the goods we need to survive and prosper.

Operating a retailing organization in today's fast-paced world is challenging. Competition is intense, with different types of retailers going after many of the same customers. Retailers must make decisions about target markets, service levels, pricing, merchandise assortment, store locations, image, and the use of direct marketing, among others. They must stay abreast of new technologies that affect the efficiency and effectiveness of store operations. They must decide whether to follow increasing numbers of retailers into global markets.

More and more companies such as IBM or Wal-Mart, are using direct marketing to connect with customers. And, companies that specialize in this area are on the rise. Customers like the convenience, and technologies like the Internet are opening new avenues. Direct marketing plays an important role in selling to consumers as well as in the business-to-business market. This vibrant and exciting field has a bright future.

RETAILING

Retailing
The activities involved in selling products and services directly to end users for personal or household use.

Retailing refers to selling products directly to consumers for personal or household use. It does not include the sale of products to other resellers or businesses, which is the domain of wholesaling. A retailer is a firm that makes the majority of its sales to consumers. Many discounters and warehouse clubs sell to small businesses as well, such as restaurants and small independent stores, but if more than half their sales are made to consumers, they are classified as retailers. CompUSA, Home Depot, Staples, and Price Club are examples of retailers that have a significant amount of sales to business customers.

As the MFA example illustrates, many retailers use direct mail and catalogs to supplement their store sales. Texas-based Neiman Marcus sends out a Christmas Book every October to its credit card customers. Over the years it has included such exotic products as camels, his-and-her airplanes, mummy cases, windmills, and submarines. In 1996, custom 1997 Jaguar XK8 convertibles at $74,975 were featured; all 50 of the cars sold within eight days.[2] CompUSA and Wal-Mart are among the retailers that have recently established Web sites on the Internet to sell select groups of products.[3]

The Home Depot is a popular retailer of household products.

THE IMPORTANCE OF RETAILERS

Retailers are vital to our economy. Sales in the United States through retail stores were well over $2.6 trillion in 1997.[4] Throughout the world, retail sales exceed several trillion per year. Retailing also is one of the largest U.S. industries in terms of employment. According to the Bureau of Labor Statistics, about 20 million people work in retailing—approximately one out of every seven full-time workers.

Retailing is the final stage in the distribution channel for the majority of products sold to consumers, everything from chewing gum to insurance to automobiles. As retailing practices develop and become more refined, better products are provided to consumers at better prices. Retailers perform a variety of functions that increase the value of products to consumers. Similar to wholesalers, they play two critical roles in the mix of goods. They perform an allocation function by purchasing products in large quantities from suppliers (manufacturers, wholesalers, or brokers) for resale to consumers in smaller quantities. They perform an assortment function by purchasing merchandise from a variety of suppliers and offering it for sale in one location. Therefore, retailers make a broad variety of goods available to consumers in amounts they can afford and effectively handle.

Although packaged goods such as cereal, detergent, milk, and toothpaste are purchased off the shelf by consumers, retailers still provide information about such products through advertising, displays, and unit prices posted on the shelves. Other consumer products, especially durable goods and services like insurance, require that retailers use salespeople to provide information and answer questions about product benefits.

Well-located stores increase the convenience of shopping for customers. Furthermore, many retailers facilitate transactions by investing in scanner technology and offering credit. They also may customize products, as do clothing retailers who alter suits or insurance agents who develop specialized packages. Repair services are provided by retailers like Sears, Circuit City, or Radio Shack.

Time, place, possession, and form utilities are provided to consumers by various retailers. They help make our life more manageable and pleasurable. Without them, acquiring the basic necessities would be difficult in terms of both time and money.

Some manufacturers, such as Sherwin-Williams in the paint industry and Liz Claiborne in the apparel industry, own their outlets, at least in part. Others, like Dell Computer, sell directly to consumers, bypassing retailers. For a majority of consumer good manufacturers, however, retailers are essential for product distribution. Most producers cannot afford to access consumer markets themselves. Their capital is tied up in operations, and it makes no sense for even large manufacturers like Procter & Gamble to open up outlets. Retailers do this for them, investing in land, buildings, fixtures, and personnel. Furthermore, retailers typically take title to the goods they resell, incurring the inventory carrying costs and sales risks otherwise held by the manufacturer. Retailers often sell goods to consumers on credit, assuming the risks associated with accounts receivable and bad debts. Retailers also promote the products they carry. In other words, retailers make it economically feasible for manufacturers of consumer goods to operate.

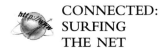

CONNECTED: SURFING THE NET

www.compusa.com

Check out "The Virtual Computer Superstore" by visiting CompUSA on-line. You'll have access to information about the latest computer technology, as well as facts about the company and its 130 stores across the country.

RETAIL STRATEGY

The **wheel of retailing** is one way to describe how retailers emerge, evolve, and sometimes fade away. According to the theory, new retailers locate their no-frills stores in low-rent areas to keep costs down. Those that succeed start to change. They add more services, move to more expensive real estate, upgrade facilities, and raise prices. This makes them vulnerable to new low-price entrants and the wheel goes round and round. The wheel can be broken if retailers carefully develop a strategy. They must choose a target market and create a marketing mix that satisfies it. Upgrading services, locations, and prices can be defended only if that is what the target market demands. The steps in formulating a retail strategy are shown in Figure 13-1.[5] Invariably, successful retailers have a sound retail strategy.

Target Markets and Positioning   Like any business, retailers must understand their customers to be truly successful. As a first step, they must carefully analyze the general market and decide the segment or segments on which to focus. For example, Autozone, based in Memphis, is an auto parts retailer that targets low-income consumers who repair their own cars.[6] Nordstrom's, headquartered in Seattle, is a department store chain that targets middle- to high-income households desiring superior service. Wet Seal, Inc., based in Irvine, California, operates several hundred apparel stores throughout the country and targets young women ages 13 through 18.[7]

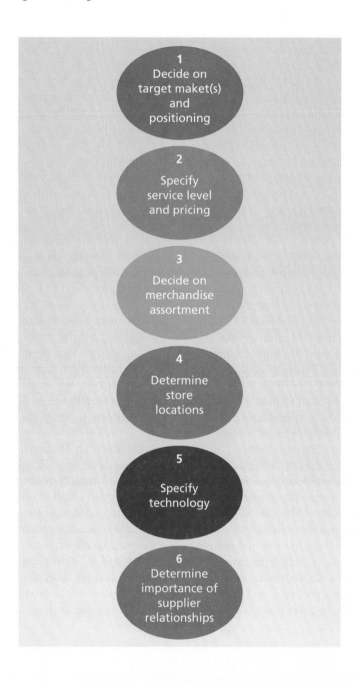

Figure 13-1   Developing a Retail Strategy

Todo para tu estilo único

Blusa marca Mirrors,
tallas S-M-L, $24.
Falda marca Star City,
tallas 3-13, $26.
Precios pueden variar en Puerto Rico.

SEARS *Todo para ti*

Sears is at the forefront in connecting with diverse segments of customers.

Whatever the overall targeting strategy, individual outlets may face different mixes of customers. The primary trade area is the geographic territory in which the majority of a store's customers reside. The trade area can vary in circumference from less than one mile for a convenience store to 20 miles for a specialist such as Toys "R" Us.[8] Each store manager must understand primary trade areas and react accordingly. For example, Target has a sophisticated computer system that tracks customer buying habits and tailors merchandise in each primary trade area of its 714 stores.[9] Sears sends out direct mailings in Spanish for stores whose trade area has a high proportion of Hispanics.[10]

Retailer positioning is the mental picture consumers have of the retailer and the shopping experiences it provides. Retailers must decide what image they want with customers — high prestige, superior service, friendly atmosphere, low prices, or whatever. Then they must determine how to get this image established in the minds of their customers. Decisions on service level and pricing, merchandise assortment, and store location will influence the retailer's image.

Service Level and Pricing The target market and positioning will influence decisions on service level and pricing. Many retailers follow a discount-oriented strategy, offering products and service of acceptable quality at low prices. The objective is to keep service costs and overhead down in order to make prices competitive. Lucky Stores is a supermarket chain in southern California that offers low prices and few amenities. Wal-Mart and Kmart have a discount-oriented strategy. Crown Books offers discounts up to 40 percent. Competitors such as Barnes & Noble and Borders may provide coffee shops or sell compact disks as well—and discount no more than 30 percent.[11]

A service-oriented strategy emphasizes quality products and value-added functions, with prices to match. It is successful to the extent that this is what the target market wants. In the jewelry business, Cartier offers unique jewelry, and its well-trained sales force caters to the specific needs of each customer. Nordstrom's is well known in the Northwest for its quality of service, such as ironing shirts for customers immediately after purchase. Many retailers

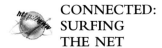

CONNECTED: SURFING THE NET

www.sears.com

Find out more about how Sears connects with diversity by checking out its Web site. While you're there, "explore the many sides of Sears." See what's new in products and services, and learn more about the company.

such as Mr. Hesel's Toy Shop in Concord, Massachusetts, and Miller's Toys in Mamaroneck, New York, are doing very well against giants like Toys "Я" Us and Wal-Mart by offering unique products and high levels of service. Certain toys sell better when demonstrated in the cozy confines of a neighborhood store by owners who know the product thoroughly—or who may be willing to help with assembly![12]

Yet other retailers follow a hybrid strategy, combining quality products, value-added services, and low pricing in some manner. Autonation, Carchoice, and Carmax (a division of Circuit City) offer huge inventories of used cars marked with low, no-haggle prices. Their stores have such amenities as child care centers, coffee bars, and touch-screen computers. Home Depot offers competitive prices and knowledgeable salespeople who can give sound advice on home improvement projects.[13] With this knowledge, they can help customers select materials and tools and then give advice on how to use this information for home repair.[14]

Merchandise Assortment   Retailers must take great care in deciding what merchandise to offer. Those with the right assortment have greater sales revenues and customer satisfaction. Merchandise breadth, the variety of product lines offered, and merchandise depth, the number of products available within each line, must be determined. Department stores have considerable breadth but only moderate depth. Retailers like Circuit City and CompUSA have limited breadth but great depth.

A **scrambled merchandising** strategy means that the product lines carried seem to be unrelated. The goal is to facilitate one-stop shopping for customers and achieve competitive advantage. For example, in the new "Super Kmart" stores, traditional goods are combined with a well-stocked supermarket of food products. Meijer, a chain in the Midwest, has used this strategy since its inception.

Part of the assortment of many retailers is private label merchandise. J. C. Penney's St. John's Bay jeans and Sears, Roebuck & Company's Canyon River Blues jeans are two examples. Sales of private label products exceeded $37 billion in the United States in 1995 and are growing at about 5 percent a year.[15] Private labels are especially common in the apparel, food, home appliance, and drug industries. In apparel, private labels serve to build the image of the retailer rather than the manufacturer. Ann Taylor and The Gap have taken this a step farther, to vertical retailing. These companies design, manufacture, and market their own products in their own stores.

Store Location   The location decision is very important for any retailer. Among other things, it affects how convenient shopping will be for customers. The target market dictates the choice to some degree. Autozone, for example, places its stores directly in low-income neighborhoods.[16] In contrast, specialty toy stores and clothing boutiques locate in well-to-do suburbs.[17] And, the location decision can be a source of competitive advantage if it preempts competitors from moving to an area with high sales and profit potential. Wal-Mart's strategy was to establish stores in small towns that could not support more than one large discount operation. It froze out competition while building a strong sales base.[18] It then spread to larger cities in the early 1990s. Dillard Department Stores concentrates primarily in secondary markets, where competition is not so fierce.[19]

Some retailers use a destination location strategy; that is, stores are put in low-rent areas off highways and some distance from other retailers.[20] Because the store is off the beaten path, consumers make it their destination when they want to shop there. In contrast, a competitor location strategy puts stores near those of major competitors. The rationale is that even more consumers will be drawn to the area. For example, Borders is likely to place its superstores as close as possible to a Barnes & Nobles outlet. They often compete for the same retail site.[21] Diamond merchants cluster along 47th Street in New York City, antique stores line the Place du Grand Sablon in Brussels, and a Planet Hollywood usually can be found near a Hard Rock Cafe.[22] In general, retailers with large stores, a large amount of merchandise, and attractive pricing can use a destination location strategy effectively. Retailers selling goods that consumers want to compare on quality and price are usually wise to locate close to competitors.

Of course, many retailers choose a local or regional shopping mall rather than a freestanding location. A **shopping mall or center** is a group of retail stores in one place marketed as a unit to shoppers in a trade area. Shopping malls, especially regional ones, have immense pulling power. The diverse mix of stores offers a wide array of merchandise. Merchants can pool resources to provide entertainment, such as pianists or clowns or even a supervised

Scrambled merchandising
A retail strategy that entails carrying an array of product lines that seem to be unrelated.

Shopping mall (shopping center)
A group of retail stores in one location and marketed as a unit to shoppers in a trade area.

Some retailers use a competitor location strategy, putting their stores near those of major competitors.

indoor playground, as at the huge Mall of America in Minneapolis. This supermall has 2.5 million square feet of retail space, equivalent to four regional shopping malls, and chartered flights bring consumers from all over the world.[23] The West Edmonton Mall in Alberta, Canada, is another example of a supermall.

Technology   Retailers must keep abreast of new technologies and adopt those that promote customer satisfaction at a reasonable cost. Custom Foot, with three shoe stores in the Westport, Connecticut, area, sells custom-made Italian shoes. Each store carries 150 style samples, but no inventory. A computer is used to measure each foot in 14 different ways—both feet are not the same on most people. Sizes range from women's 4AAAA to men's 16EEEEE. Customers choose style, color, grade of leather, and sole. All the information is transmitted electronically to one of a dozen factories in Italy. Shoes are shipped directly to customers within two weeks.[24]

As noted earlier, Target's sophisticated computer system tracks customer buying habits and preferences for its 714 outlets. It has become a master of micromarketing, a consumer-driven approach that tailors merchandise in individual stores to the preferences of patrons. The Target in affluent Scottsdale, Arizona, sells child-toting bicycle trailers but no portable heaters. In Mesa, twenty minutes away, the portable heaters are a big seller, and bicycle trailers are nowhere to be seen. Successful micromarketing has helped Target grow more rapidly than its competitors.[25]

Database marketing is the process of building, maintaining, and using computerized information to contact customers in a personalized fashion.[26] Advances in technology have enabled more and more retailers to take advantage of database marketing. A custom profile is kept on each person, which can include demographics (age, income) and past purchases as well as psychographics (activities, interests, opinions). Customized product offerings then can be developed with individualized messages and incentives. For example, Blockbuster Video requires customers to use "personal identification cards" when renting movies. These offer the company some protection from theft, but their more important function is to provide database information. Blockbuster keeps track of the types of movies customers rent and sends personalized promotions based on their tastes. Staples follows a similar approach in serving its customers.[27]

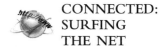

CONNECTED: SURFING THE NET

www.blockbuster.com

"Technology is a tool, or an enabler for people to enjoy the content that constitutes entertainment or other engaging experiences. Blockbuster is committed to participating in developing, testing, and retailing new technologies that improve entertainment experiences for our members." Find out more about how the company connects through technology by visiting its Web site.

Shopping malls have immense pulling power, especially when they are as large as the Mall of America in Minneapolis.

CONNECTING THROUGH TECHNOLOGY
PEAPOD AND COMPUTER SHOPPING

Beth Mansfield of Libertyville, Illinois, owns a sports-equipment franchise and works 60-hour weeks. She also has two young daughters. Because of her hectic schedule, she used to shop at the local supermarket in the late evenings. Then a company named Peapod made her life a little easier. Beth now shops for and orders groceries from her home computer.

Peapod, Inc., headquartered in Evanston, Illinois, is a five-year-old retail company providing a computer shopping and delivery service to customers in the Chicago and San Francisco metropolitan areas. It hopes to add Boston very soon. Peapod enables its roughly 10,000 customers to shop their local Safeway or Jewel Osco from a personal computer. For this they pay a $29.95 startup fee, $4.95 per month, and $6.95 plus 5 percent of their total order each time. Peapod's 450 employees are mostly shoppers and drivers who fill the orders and make deliveries. Almost 75 percent of the customers are women in households with high income, but little time. The company has retained over 80 percent of the people who try the service.

Peapod's supermarket partners electronically zap it daily price updates on 25,000 grocery and drugstore items, from laundry detergent to aspirin. Customers can shop at any hour, sorting through the items by product category or attributes, such as cost per ounce, fat content, calories, nutritional content, and sugar. Comparison shopping is easy. Customers inform Peapod whether substitutes are acceptable if preferred items are out of stock. They also select one of six time slots for next-day delivery. Peapod forwards the order to the nearest participating store.

A new interactive marketing division of Peapod enables sponsors such as Kraft Foods, Bristol-Meyers Squibb, and Ore-Ida Foods to offer coupons. These appear on the screen when customers select certain items or are about to choose. Sponsors also can send product samples along with the order through the home delivery service. According to Tim Dorgan, who heads the interactive division: "We can drop a sample to your home because we know you eat chocolate-chip cookies. Then, when you go on-line, that cookie will be on the shelf."

In June 1995, Microsoft CEO Bill Gates startled a group of top food retailers by predicting that one-third of food sales will be handled electronically by 2005. Peapod hopes he is right. Now, less than 1 percent of groceries are bought from home and mostly by phone rather than computer.

Sources: "Delivery System," *Brandweek,* August 15, 1995, pp. 22, 26; Susan Chandler, "The Grocery Cart in Your PC," *Business Week,* September 11, 1995, pp. 63, 64; W. Frank Dell, "Home Delivery Gets a Reality Check," *Grocery Marketing,* February 1996, pp. 36, 37; and Peapod's Web site, www.peapod.com, June 6, 1996.

The technology feature describes Peapod's PC-based grocery shopping service. Several supermarket chains see it as a viable alternative channel to serve certain customers. Some experts believe that by 2005, nearly 30 percent of consumers will be purchasing more than $47 billion in groceries from their home via computer.[28]

Supplier Relationships Developing strong relationships with suppliers is a strategic imperative for many retailers. Partners go out of their way to serve one another. Supplier loyalty pays off when the retailer gets the goods it needs in a quick and efficient manner. Wal-Mart has long been known as a retailer that values close partnerships with its major suppliers.[29] Whatever the strength of a relationship, however, tough bargaining issues are likely to arise between suppliers and retailers.

Cost and pricing issues are the most common areas of friction. Retailers have a targeted **markup,** the difference between merchandise cost and the retail price. For example, if Wet Seal buys blouses from California Concepts, a manufacturer in Gardena, at $12 each and prices them in stores at $20 each, the markup is $8, or 40 percent of the selling price ($8 ÷ $20 = .40). The formula is:

Markup
The amount added to the cost of acquiring a product that determines its retail selling price.

$$\text{Markup Percentage} = \frac{\text{Amount added to cost (markup)}}{\text{Selling price}}$$

Markdown
A reduction from the original retail selling price of a product.

Goods that do not sell as expected require a **markdown,** a reduction in the original retail price. Wet Seal may sell some of the blouses at $20 but then lower the price to $15 in order to sell the rest. The markdown in this case is $5, and the markdown percentage is 25 percent ($5 ÷ $20). That is the discount amount typically advertised for a sale item, and it is computed as follows:

$$\text{Markdown Percentage} = \frac{\text{Amount of markdown}}{\text{Previous selling price}}$$

The retailer typically goes back to the supplier and asks for markdown money, a credit to the retailer's account to adjust for the unanticipated price reduction.

TYPES OF RETAILERS

There are several ways in which to classify retailers. Form of ownership distinguishes between small independents (often called mom-and-pop stores) and **chain stores,** which are a group of centrally owned and managed retail outlets that handle the same product lines. Level of service can be used, whether full, limited, or self. Price level can be used as well. However, the most informative classification is based on the merchandise assortment, whether retailers sell a limited line or general merchandise. Within each category, different types of retailers exist based on their service level and pricing strategy, as outlined in Figure 13-2. A number of successful companies have stores of more than one type, such as Dayton Hudson, Kmart, and Wal-Mart.

Limited-Line Retailers   Limited-line retailers focus on one product category. The four types are specialty stores, franchises, superstores, and automated vending retailers.

Specialty Stores   **Specialty stores** offer merchandise in one primary product category in considerable depth. Examples are Wet Seal and The Limited, Florsheim and Women's Foot Locker, and Champ's Sports and Roller Skates of America. Since their strategy generally is service oriented, payroll expenses may approximate 35 percent of sales.[30] Goods are of moderate to high quality. Prices tend to be high and comparable to department stores.

Many specialty stores are franchisees, who sign a contractual agreement with a franchiser organization to represent and sell its products in particular retail locations. Examples include Blockbuster Video stores, the vast majority of fast-food restaurants (some outlets are company-owned), and automobile dealerships.

Superstores   Sometimes called category killers, **superstores** focus on a single product category but offer a huge selection and low prices. They tend to range in size from 50,000 to 75,000 square feet. Service levels are normally low to moderate. Examples include Barnes & Nobles, CompUSA, Home Depot, IKEA, Staples, and Sportsmart. Superstores have been particularly successful in taking business away from traditional discount stores as well as wholesalers.[31] Customers like the wide selection of brands which makes price and feature comparisons easy.[32]

Automated Vending Operators   **Automated vending** retailers use machinery operated by coin or credit card to dispense goods. The placement of machines is critical, and airports, hospitals, schools, and office buildings are among the most popular locations. Traditionally, vending has focused on beverages, candy, cigarettes, and food, but the industry is expanding into new areas, such as life insurance policies in airports, movie rentals in supermarkets, and lottery tickets. ARAMARK and Canteen Corporation are two leading automatic vending retailers.

In Japan, vending machines are more important in retail trade. Homes and apartments are small, with little storage space, and consumers often travel on foot or by mass transit. The

Chain store
One of a group of centrally owned and managed retail stores that handle the same product lines.

Specialty store
A retailer offering merchandise in one primary product category in considerable depth.

Superstore
A retailer that focuses on a single product category but offers a huge selection and low prices; also called a *category killer.*

Automated vending
The use of machinery operated by coins or credit cards to dispense goods.

Limited Line	General Merchandise
Specialty stores	Department stores
Franchises	Convenience stores
Category killers or superstores	Supermarkets
Automatic vending operators	Warehouse clubs
	Discount stores
	Variety stores
	Hypermarkets

Figure 13-2   Classification of Retailers

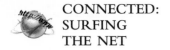
Department store

A retailer with merchandise of broad variety and moderate depth and with a relatively high level of customer service.

Convenience store

A small retailer with moderately low breadth and depth of merchandise.

Supermarket

A large, departmentalized, food-oriented retail establishment that sells beverages, canned goods, dairy products, frozen foods, meat, produce, and such nonfood items as health and beauty aids, kitchen utensils, magazines, pharmaceuticals, and toys.

Warehouse club

A large, no-frills store that carries a revolving array of merchandise at low prices.

Discount store

A retailer offering a broad variety of merchandise, limited service, and low prices.

Off-price retailer

A seller of brand-name clothing at low prices.

Catalog showroom

A discount retailer whose customers shop from catalogs and can view floor samples of items held in stock.

convenience of location and small quantities is appealing, and a wider variety of products can be bought. Octopus dumplings, pizza, beer, and yogurt drinks are among the most popular food and beverage items. The machines often play a tune or talk to buyers while dispensing products.[33]

General Merchandise Retailers   General merchandise retailers carry a number of different product categories. There are seven types: department stores, convenience stores, supermarkets, warehouse clubs, discount stores, variety stores, and hypermarkets.

Department Stores   **Department stores** carry a broad array and moderate depth of merchandise, and the level of customer service is relatively high. Merchandise is grouped into well-defined departments. Both soft goods, such as apparel and linens, and hard goods, such as appliances and sporting goods are normally sold. The intention is to provide one-stop shopping for most personal and household items. While often situated in downtown areas at a stand-alone location, department stores also are prevalent in shopping malls, where they are considered anchor tenants who draw customers.

Target markets and pricing strategies vary considerably among department stores. Some seek the upscale customer such as Bloomingdale's, Neiman Marcus, and Saks Fifth Avenue. Their decor is plush, with an ambiance and prices to match. Others such as Dillard's and May Company, appeal to a somewhat broader middle-income clientele and focus on mainstream tastes.[34] Yet others, like J. C. Penney and Sears, seek an even broader array of customers. Finally, department stores like Mervyn's, Upton, and Byron's focus primarily on low-income households, featuring low prices and frequent promotions.[35] Specialty stores provide the most competition to upscale department stores, while at the lower end there is intense rivalry from discounters.

Convenience Stores   **Convenience stores** are small and have moderately low breadth and depth of merchandise. Sandwiches, soft-drinks, snack foods, newspapers and magazines, milk, and beer and wine are among the most popular products carried. They are open long hours, prices are high, and their location is their primary advantage. Some are part of large corporate chains, including 7-Eleven, Circle K, and Dairy Mart. Some large oil companies have established their own operations, such as Arco's AM/PM stores and Texaco's Food Mart. Many convenience stores are mom-and-pop businesses, family owned and operated.[36]

Supermarkets   **Supermarkets** are large, departmentalized, food-oriented retail establishments that sell beverages, canned goods, dairy products, frozen foods, meat, produce, and such nonfood items as health and beauty aids, kitchen utensils, magazines, pharmaceuticals, and toys. Many have in-store bakeries and delicatessens. Merchandise breadth and depth are moderately high. Since gross margins are generally low, supermarkets attempt to maximize sales volume. Typical after-tax profit is about 1.5 percent of sales.[37] In the United States, regional chains dominate, such as Hughes, Kroger, Safeway, and Winn-Dixie.

Warehouse Clubs   **Warehouse clubs** are large, no-frills stores that carry a revolving array of merchandise at low prices. They are typically 60,000 square feet or more. Consumers must become members before shopping in the clubs. Brands carried vary by day and week, depending on the deals arranged with suppliers so product selection is somewhat limited. By carrying only the most popular items in a merchandise category, clubs strive for high asset turnover (net sales divided by total assets) with gross margins as low as 8 percent. Products are often sold in bulk. Price Club/Costco and Sam's Club (part of Wal-Mart) now control 90 percent of the warehouse club industry.[38] These retailers give supermarkets stiff competition.

Discount Stores   **Discount stores** offer a broad variety of merchandise, limited service, and low prices. Merchandise depth is low to moderate. Service levels are minimal. Operating costs, including payroll, are normally 20 percent or less of total sales.[39] Discounters concentrate on low- to middle-income consumers. The goal is asset turnover and sales volume per store. Wal-Mart, Kmart, and Target (a division of Dayton Hudson) are the major U.S. discount stores.

There are two specialized types of discounters. **Off-price retailers** sell name-brand clothing at low prices. Their inventory frequently changes as they take advantage of special deals from manufacturers selling excess merchandise. Examples are Loehmann's, Marshall's, Men's Warehouse, and T. J. Maxx. **Catalog showrooms** have only samples on display, and customers shop from catalogs. They often write up their own order and present it to clerks. The merchandise is then brought from the storage area. Best Products Company and Service Merchandise are examples.

Variety Stores   Variety stores offer an array of low-priced merchandise of low to moderate quality. There is not much depth. These retailers are not as numerous as they used to be because of intense competition, mainly from larger discounters. Examples of variety stores are Everything's A Dollar and Pic'N'Save.

Hypermarkets   Hypermarkets are giant shopping facilities offering a wide selection of food and general merchandise at low prices. They have at least 100,000 square feet of space, some of them three times that. The concept was developed by a French company, Carrefour, which is very successful throughout Europe and Latin America. Hypermarkets have not thrived in the United States, partly because there is so much competition. Furthermore, consumers often complain about too much walking and limited brand selections. The costs of operating the giant facilities are high.[40] Nevertheless, hypermarkets are likely to become more popular in the United States because they offer one-stop shopping. Existing hypermarket operations include Super Kmart Centers and Hypermarket USA.

Variety store
A retailer offering a variety of low-priced merchandise of low to moderate quality.

Hypermarket
A giant shopping facility with a wide selection of food and general merchandise at low prices.

Issues in Retailing

Retailing changes constantly and rapidly. It is important for retailers not to lose sight of such important factors as diversity, legal and ethical issues, and global retailing.

Diversity and Retailing   Because retailers deal directly with consumers, most of them realize that staffing and marketing programs must reflect the nature of the population they serve. Recognizing diversity and its implications for business practice is a must for top-performing retailers. Sears is at the forefront in connecting with diverse markets. Its stores in California serve a significant number of Hispanics, and Sears has bilingual salespeople and signage. It also advertises in Spanish in local newspapers. The effort is paying off: Sales gains in its California stores with a large Latino customer base have been twice those at its other stores. Sears also is stocking smaller dress sizes in stores that serve a large Asian population.[41]

In another approach to diversity, Marriott International, Inc., has a program in the inner cities called Pathways to Independence. It recruits, screens, and trains welfare recipients. To qualify, applicants must have a sixth-grade reading ability, pass a drug test, and demonstrate a desire to work. Nearly 600 people entered the program the past several years and assumed responsible positions in the hotel chain. They have a lower turnover rate than the average Marriott worker. The company believes the program more than pays for itself and has significant social benefits.[42] Opryland Hotel and J. C. Penney are developing similar programs.[43]

Legal and Ethical Issues in Retailing   Retailers face a range of legal and ethical issues. It is important that they understand and comply with the laws applicable to them. For example, title companies perform a variety of services in consumer real estate transactions. Recently, some California title companies were found guilty of giving kickbacks, such as cash payments, computers, and free printing of sales literature, to real estate brokers in exchange for recommending them to customers. Under federal law, no one may receive or charge any fee, kickback, or thing of value for referring business in mortgage transactions.[44]

Ethical dilemmas often arise over the goods sold by retailers. Consumer action groups often lobby them to stop carrying certain products. In an unprecedented move, Target eliminated all cigarette sales in its 714 stores in September 1996. The decision was influenced by the growing stigma attached to smoking and mounting pressure to comply with laws barring the sale of tobacco to minors.[45] From the start, Blockbuster Video has refused to rent or sell pornographic films. Depending on community standards, many stores do not carry certain magazines, or keep them under the counter, away from children. Wal-Mart stopped carrying guns in its 2,265 stores in 1994. It still sells them through catalogs, which offends many consumer advocates. The company banned Grammy winner Sheryl Crow's album in 1996 because of a lyric suggesting it sells guns to children. Record industry executives estimated this move would cost Crow a staggering 400,000 album sales.[46]

Employee relations are another area in which ethical questions arise, such as steps taken to prevent unionization or reduce employee theft. Whatever the issue, if employees are not treated with fairness and respect, then major problems can result. The National Labor Relations Board recently found that Dayton Hudson Corporation of Minneapolis used unfair labor practices during a campaign to defeat unionization in its Michigan stores. Management used surveillance, threats of job loss, and coercive interrogations. As a result of the

*A number of U.S. companies are
putting up multiplexes in Japanese
suburbs.*

NLRB judgment, Dayton Hudson is refocusing efforts on developing better employee relationships.[47]

Global Retailers   A number of U.S. retailers, such as McDonald's® and KFC, have had successful operations in global markets for many years. Others, such as The Gap and Toys "R" Us, have only recently ventured overseas. Similar to doing business at home, the global retailer must focus on targeted customers in each market. In many cases, consumer tastes vary considerably across countries for the same product or service. McDonald's® found that it had to add beer to the beverage menu in Germany and Cadbury chocolate sticks to its ice-cream cones in England.[48]

Gaining a foothold in foreign markets can be quite a challenge. It requires a strong and properly implemented retail strategy. A number of U.S. companies have recently opened movie theaters in Japan, among them AMC Entertainment, Time Warner, Inc., and UCI (a joint venture between Paramount and Universal Studios). They have met staunch resistance from movie giants Toho and Shochiku Company, which own or control the vast majority of outlets. One of the major problems for the newcomers is obtaining a steady supply of first-rate films from Japanese film distributors. But the U.S.-owned theaters are doing well because of what they offer for the price. They are putting up multiplexes in Japan and are locating many theaters in the suburbs. They offer advanced sound and cinematic technology, and they are open later in the evenings. Their concession stands are modern. All this is available at ticket prices as low as $10, compared to the average of $18 in theaters operated by Toho and Shochiku. Previously, movie attendance was declining in Japan due to high prices, aging theaters in downtown neighborhoods dominated by adult entertainment and bars, and competition from television and VCRs.[49]

DIRECT MARKETING

Direct marketing

The use of various
communication media to
interact directly with customers
and generally calling for them to
make a direct response.

Direct marketing uses various methods to communicate with consumers, generally calling for a direct response on their part. Direct marketing is both a form of communication and a channel of distribution. Direct mail and catalogs have been used for many years. Telemarketing is another prominent method. Advertisements in print media or on television and radio that include toll-free numbers for placing orders have become very popular. The field is being revolutionized by technology—fax machines, e-mail and voice mail, electronic catalogs on diskettes and compact disks, infomercials, home television shopping channels, and the Internet.

Many organizations can benefit from direct marketing. A growing number of companies, called direct marketers, conduct business primarily or solely in this way. Excellent examples are CDnow on the Internet and Dell Computer. This kind of direct marketing is most powerful when it communicates product and pricing information, along with guidance for placing orders. The sale is completed by delivery of products via computer (such as software) or through services like Airborne Express, DHL, and Federal Express.

Direct marketing sales to consumers and in business-to-business markets are expected to exceed $1.6 billion by the year 2000.[50] Sales growth in this field has been outpacing U.S. retail sales growth by about two to one. Today, for every $15 in sales in the U.S. economy, roughly one dollar is generated by direct marketing techniques, and that figure is expected to grow dramatically in the next century. Some industries are more affected than others. For example, in 1996, personal computer sales rose by 50 percent in mail-order channels but less than 10 percent in traditional retail outlets.[51]

VALUE TO CUSTOMERS AND MARKETING

Direct marketing offers consumers a convenient way to shop from the comfort of their home or office. The fast-paced lifestyle of many people leaves little time or energy for shopping trips. Driving costs keep increasing. Traffic congestion and parking are problems. Checkout lines are growing as many retailers reduce staff to cut costs. All these factors have increased the importance of convenience. The widespread availability of credit cards, toll-free numbers, and overnight delivery service has made direct marketing to consumers even more viable. Convenience is also important in business-to-business markets. Direct marketing allows business customers to gain information on products and place orders efficiently. It requires much less time than meeting with a variety of salespeople.

Direct marketing also can improve the quality of products offered to customers. For example, Calyx & Corolla is a mail-order florist. Its flowers are generally fresher than those offered by retail outlets because its network of growers and Federal Express can get orders to customers quickly.[52] Another advantage of direct marketing is competitive prices. A company can operate out of an unadorned warehouse in an inexpensive location, keeping overhead low. Many Japanese consumers save money by ordering from U.S. catalog companies like L. L. Bean.[53]

Direct marketing is of increasing value to many entrepreneurs as retailers cut back on inventory. For example, there are currently about 2,000 CD-ROM titles for children, yet major outlets have room for no more than 250 titles.[54] Wholesalers are overloaded as well. Even if they agree to add a product, there is no guarantee the product will get much support from salespeople.

Direct marketing allows small businesses to access markets without the assistance of retailers, wholesalers, or a company sales force. Consequently, the investment required for product launch is relatively low. For example, Ziff-Davis Publishing in New York City, puts out a large monthly catalog, *Computer Shopper,* in which companies can advertise. A full-page ad can cost as little as $13,000 to reach well over one million consumers. *Computer Shopper* has enabled several small companies to start and successfully maintain their business.[55]

Large organizations also benefit from direct marketing. Some use it as their primary means of doing business. Others use it in combination with other channels. Victoria's Secret, a division of The Limited, Inc., has retail stores in major shopping malls throughout the country and also mails out several catalogs per year.

DIRECT MARKETING DATABASES

All direct marketing companies maintain a database with customer name, address, and purchase history. These are often supplemented with lists purchased from market research companies like Zeller's and Dun's. Some direct marketers have taken the art of database management to a new level. Firefly Network, Inc., headquartered in Boston, sells compact disks on-line and builds vivid profiles of the people who use its Web site (www.firefly.com). Visitors assign themselves an alias and begin to register their likes and dislikes in movies and music. Software programs known as "intelligent agents" take over, sifting through lists logged in by other visitors with similar interests, and using that information to recommend films and music to each individual on a personalized basis. Firefly had an estimated 300,000 users in its first 10 months.[56]

DIRECT RESPONSE MEDIA

Several media are used in direct marketing. Figure 13-3 provides estimates of 1995 sales through various direct response media. Direct mail, including catalogs, generated the highest revenues in consumer markets, while telemarketing was the leader in business-to-business markets. The "other" category in Figure 13-3 includes electronic commerce over the Internet, which will grow in prominence very quickly. By 1997, direct marketers were already indicating that 40 percent of their budget would be allocated to the Internet.[57]

Medium	Consumer Markets	Business-to-Business Markets
Direct mail and catalogs	$225.7	$130.4
Telemarketing	159.3	226.3
Newspapers	84.9	52.2
Magazines	30.9	29.9
Television	43.8	28.9
Radio	14.4	11.1
Other	35.6	19.4
Total	$594.4	$498.1

Source: *Economic Impact: U.S. Direct Marketing Today* (New York: Direct Marketing Association, 1997), p. 43.

Figure 13-3 U.S. Direct Marketing Sales by Medium and Market (in billions of dollars)

Direct Mail   Each year, billions of paper-based pieces are sent to prospective customers through the U.S. Postal Service. Usually, a cover letter and brochure are included but audio tapes, videotapes, and computer disks may be used. America Online mails out diskettes so consumers can try the service. Orders can be placed by calling a toll-free number, filling out and mailing back an order form, or faxing the order form.

Mail contact is popular because it hits a select market at a reasonably low cost. Selective mailing lists can be developed or purchased. Direct mail also can be personalized, is flexible, and allows early testing and response measurement. But 58 percent of those surveyed in a recent *Direct* magazine poll said they do not even look at their direct mail before throwing it away.[58] An order-response rate of 2 percent is generally considered good, though the standard varies by product category and the skills of the direct marketing firm.

Three forms of mechanized mail are becoming popular with marketers. Fax mail is sent from one fax machine to another. Fax numbers are published in directories that can be purchased from market research companies. This method has the advantage of speed, as do the two others. E-mail is sent from one computer to another. Messages arrive almost instantly and are stored until individuals access the files. Voice mail is a verbal message sent via telephone and stored until it is retrieved. The public is less enthusiastic than direct marketers about these techniques. Many people resent paper being used to print unsolicited messages, or the time wasted reading, listening to, and deleting messages. These forms of direct mail are best used to communicate with regular customers or people who express an interest in a product. For example, it is appropriate to send customized e-mail to people who regularly access a company's Web site, or request to be included on e-mail messages.

Mail-order catalog

A collection of product and price information that is published in paper form.

Catalogs   **Mail-order catalogs** publish product and price information, in paper form. Annually, more than 12 billion copies of more than 8,000 different paper-based catalogs are sent through the U.S. Postal Service. Some feature general merchandise, such as those by J. C. Penney. Others focus on a narrow range of products. Omaha Steaks sells beef, seafood, pork, lamb, chicken, pastas, and desserts in its catalog.[59] Eddie Bauer catalogs include men and women's apparel, luggage, footwear, and accessories.

Some companies, like airlines and hotels, assemble products from various sources and hire third parties to publish paper-based catalogs. United Airlines provides *High Street Emporium* to passengers. It is a collection of upscale, unique merchandise from a number of catalogs, including Brookstone, Disney, Healthrider, Hammacher Schlemmer, and Sharper Image. Customers call an 800 number to order.

A major disadvantage of catalog marketing is the expense. Paper and postage prices are so high that many entrepreneurs find it impossible to issue their own, and it's very hard to get products included in brand-name catalogs. The Good Catalog Company has filled a need by partnering with producers who can't afford to publish and distribute on their own. See the relationships feature: "The Good Catalog Company: Posting Great Results from Co-op Marketing."

Electronic catalogs store product information on computer diskette or compact disk. They are becoming popular, especially in business-to-business markets. W. W. Grainger's 1996 paper-based catalog of 3,500 pages was mailed to more than two million businesses. The company also mails a CD format to more than 52,000 customers.[60] These provide tremendous convenience for fast-paced businesses who can search electronically for the precise items they want. Businesses are likely to put several catalogs on their system for maximum speed of access.

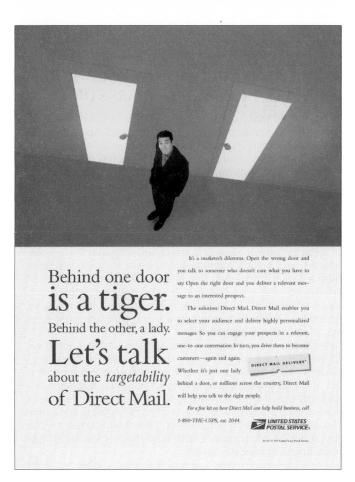

The United States Postal Service advertises the targetability and individualized benefits of direct mail.

Mail order catalogs are a popular way of communicating product and price information to consumers.

CONNECTING THROUGH RELATIONSHIPS

THE GOOD CATALOG COMPANY: POSTING GREAT RESULTS FROM CO-OP MARKETING

In 1991 Barbara Todd sold her successful mail-order catalog business, Orchids Only! She was swamped with calls from would-be entrepreneurs asking her to keep it alive. But with rising postage and paper costs, the business was tougher to enter than when Todd started out in the 1980s. Realizing this harsh reality, Todd came up with a marketing brainstorm. Why not create a catalog in which anyone—from garage inventors to Fortune 500 companies—could pay to advertise? The Good Catalog Company was born in 1992, and since that time it has posted not just good but great results.

In 1995, bucking bad times for the direct marketing industry, The Good Catalog Co. increased its sales by 92 percent and increased its profits by 345 percent. In 1996 *Chain Store Age* called it the fastest-growing private retailer in the country. By allowing wholesalers, distributors, manufacturers, and private individuals to purchase space, the catalog provides many companies access to this marketing channel while sharing the financial risk with other advertisers. It's a win-win situation: Todd's company supplements its sales with a steady stream of ad revenue, and advertisers get an inexpensive way to test the waters with their products. "It's really as good as a focus group because people are actually buying," says Todd. "It's not hypothetical."

The Good Catalog's 63 employees are really more like business partners for their clients. At rates of about $3,000 for one-sixth of a page and a 20 percent sales commission, the company takes a set amount of merchandise on consignment and then handles everything from product photography and copywriting to shipping, customer service, and even business consulting. For example, advertiser Mary Zellem, whose Executive Accents company crafts animal-shaped pillows, asked the staff to help gauge consumer sensitivity when she wanted to raise the price of her product. Zellem had turned to The Good after being rejected by about 70 other houses, and now she has leveraged her exposure there to get into two brand-name catalogs.

While the Good Catalog is open to anyone who can pay the price, it does not pool a hodgepodge of merchandise. It actually publishes nine "books" under names like Westbury Collection, Somerset Collection, Good Kids, and Good Finds. Since each is directed at separate market segments, advertisers can target certain groups of consumers. Another tactic is to contact these buyers again and again, mailing a title every other week or so in which about 40 percent of the merchandise offered is new. "We observed that the industry as a whole was mailing less so we mailed more," says Todd. "When other catalogs zig we zag." And with its unconventional approach, the Good Catalog Co. seems likely to continue its zigzag to the top.

Sources: "Good Catalog Co. Achieves 'Unreasonable' Goals," *Chain Store Age,* June 1996, p. 36; "Good Catalog Company: A Cataloger with a Unique Niche," *Direct Marketing,* September 1996, pp. 16–23; and Cyndee Miller, "Co-op Catalog Marketing as Good as a Paid Ad," *Marketing News,* September 23, 1996, p. 2.

Telemarketing

Using the telephone to contact leads (potential customers) from a list.

Telemarketing **Telemarketing** occurs when salespeople make telephone calls to leads provided by marketing services or from others lists. The timing of calls is very important. Late morning and early afternoon are normally the best times for reaching businesses, while evenings between 7:00 and 9:00 are best for contacting households—from the marketer's standpoint. You probably have had more than a few interruptions at that time from telemarketers. When people are out, messages are often left on voice mail.

Telemarketing has a higher cost per contact than direct mail or catalogs. Furthermore, many consumers view unsolicited telephone calls as an annoyance and resent unwanted clutter on voice mail. Salespeople often are poorly trained and cannot answer questions. In fact, they may be instructed not to deviate from prearranged script regardless of what they are asked.

Automated telemarketing uses machines to dial numbers, play recorded messages, and take orders either via answering machines or by forwarding calls to live operators. Outbound automated calls meet with strong resistance, and the system is better used for incoming calls—that is, consumers are reached by other means and then place orders through the automated systems.

Precise list selection and development are critical for telemarketing. The sales message must be simple and strong. Salespeople must receive at least some training on how to make calls and handle customer concerns. Person-to-person telemarketing is best used in the consumer market with current customers who prefer this mode of communication. In business-to-business markets, especially when targeted at employees outside the purchasing area, telemarketing is not very successful. But some professional buyers prefer it to face-to-face dealings because less time is involved. In the business setting, it is especially important that telemarketers be carefully selected, well trained, and adequately compensated.

Advertisements in Print and Broadcast Media

Print ads in magazines and newspapers are used a great deal in direct marketing. Along with information on products and prices, toll free numbers are given. For example, Horizon Instruments of Fullerton, California, sells digital engine tachometers and other instrumentation to owners of private planes through ads in leading aviation magazines.

Direct marketers also rely on television and radio spots, usually ranging from 10 to 60 seconds. Exercise equipment from NordicTrack and Soloflex, publications such as *Sporting News* and *Sports Illustrated*, and music CDs are among the products frequently advertised on television. Oreck Corporation of New Orleans, uses radio ads to sell vacuum cleaners.

Infomercials are long advertisements that resemble documentaries. They range from 15 to 60 minutes and often include celebrity endorsers and testimonials from satisfied customers. Such products as smoking cessation, weight-control programs, cosmetics, and exercise equipment are promoted this way. Established companies like Chrysler and Mattel are beginning to use the technique to communicate in depth about product benefits. Some direct marketers use it to obtain distribution in retail stores. For example, Peter Bieler's infomercials on the Thighmaster Exerciser featuring Suzanne Somers generated national publicity—including a mention in David Letterman monologues and George Bush speeches. Bieler then gained distribution through Kmart, Wal-Mart, and other big chains, selling six million units in less than two years.[61]

Infomercial
A programmatic advertisement of considerable length that resembles a documentary.

Televised Home Shopping

In the past several years, home shopping via cable television has come into prominence. The two largest marketers are Quality Value Channel (QVC) and the Home Shopping Network (HSN), with others including the Home Shopping Mall, Teleshop, and Value Club of America. Themed programs are telecast 24 hours a day, seven days a week, to more than 54 million households in the United States. Program hosts, including such celebrities as Julia Child and Hugh Downs, offer products ranging from books to computers, jewelry to lamps, clothing to power tools. Customers send orders over toll-free lines, enabling companies to adjust inventory minute by minute, not just season by season. Orders are usually shipped within 48 hours. Annual sales through this medium are about $3 billion. QVC alone receives more than 70 million phone calls each year and ships 46 million packages, resulting in sales of $1.6 billion.[62]

Videotext links a consumer's television with a seller's computerized catalog of products by cable or telephone lines. Consumers can place orders through special keyboard devices. The use of videotext in direct marketing has not yet been successful, partly because the systems are costly to install and are available in only a few markets.

The Internet

Most companies are still using their Web site only to communicate information,[63] but the Internet is gaining ground as a medium for electronic commerce. Consumers are already comfortable with other types of direct response media, which helps make them receptive to the Net. Security is an issue, however. Many people are reluctant to provide credit card numbers on-line. In addition, massive amounts of data are clogging the Internet. Some predict gridlock, which would hardly make electronic commerce convenient.[64]

Furthermore, the consumer cybermarket is still fairly limited because not every household has a personal computer. And beyond our borders, the Web's heavy U.S. accent grates on many cultures. As the Web becomes more global, however, this problem also provides an opportunity for enterprising marketers who can operate across boundaries in many languages.

Despite drawbacks, electronic commerce is expected to thrive in the 21st century. Already, many companies are creating and maintaining storefronts on the net. A 1996 survey of 1,100 Web-based businesses by ActivMedia, a market research company, found that 31 percent claimed to be profitable, and 28 percent more said they would be in the next 12 to 24 months.[65]

Companies must decide whether to set up their own Web operation or turn to a provider. The trade-off is between greater control and no fees to outside Internet resellers, on one hand, and expertise and an existing subscriber base on the other. An annual fee plus some percentage of the company's on-line sales, typically 2 percent, is paid to the on-line service.

Arrangements vary. J. C. Penney has relationships with CompuServe to sell certain products on-line, while Wal-Mart has its own operation. Microsoft allows Cybersource to sell some of its most popular titles. This enhances market coverage without a large fixed investment in time and personnel to process thousands of small orders.[66]

In the consumer market, CDnow, Inc. of Fort Washington, Pennsylvania, is an Internet reseller with more than 300,000 compact disk and cassette titles, T-shirts, videos, and laser disks for sale through its site on the World Wide Web. Shoppers make purchases by credit card through a secure encryption system. CDnow owns no inventory; instead it relies on a network of wholesalers to ship orders, normally within 24 hours.[67]

The Internet is a great interactive medium. In the 21st century, electronic commerce will have its greatest effect. Less than 1 percent of all travel is currently booked on-line, but demand is growing. American, Northwest, and USAir began selling tickets through the Net in 1996 to unload some of the thousands of seats that go unsold daily. The cyberfares are as much as 70 percent below those available through travel agents or the usual airline reservation system.[68] TravelBids is an on-line system that allows travelers to save money by bidding their travel to many travel agents at one time. Travelers make a reservation directly with any airline or resort, and don't pay or provide a credit card. They then put the information with TravelBids and the winning (low priced) agent will take over your reservation.[69] Microsoft recently teamed with American Express to launch a service that allows clients to book travel and do expense reporting on a laptop.[70]

THE DIRECT MARKETING PLAN

Direct marketers make several decisions when developing a marketing strategy. The most important relate to target markets, database management, merchandise assortment, pricing, choice of media and other channels, message design, and payment methods and delivery. The steps are depicted in Figure 13-4.

Target Markets   Every excellent marketing strategy begins with an understanding of the intended audience, whether baseball hobbyists, newlyweds, cooking buffs, or outdoor enthusiasts. Therefore, the first decision is which customers to target.[71] Many direct marketers are small companies content to serve a narrow group of customers in their home territory. Others expand nationally or globally once a strong business foundation is established. Dell Computer Corporation began in 1983 by serving small and medium-sized businesses in Austin, Texas, who needed upgrades on IBM-compatible computers. Dell branched out to serve large businesses and government agencies throughout the United States in the mid-1980s. Today, Dell is doing business in all major international markets and is especially successful in Western Europe.[72]

Database Management   Maintaining a strong customer database is essential. Addresses and preferences must be current. Duplicate names must be removed. Those with poor credit

*Dell began its company serving a
small target market, later branching out
to serve all major international
markets.*

Target markets
Database management
Merchandise assortment
Pricing
Choice of media and other channels
Message design
Payment methods and delivery

393

Direct Marketing

Figure 13-4   Direct Marketing Decisions

histories must be flagged, and inactive customers must be noted. A record must be kept of those who do not want to be contacted.

Another critical function of a database is tracking. For example, Austad's, a North Dakota direct marketer of golf equipment, started analyzing its overseas sales. Japan surfaced as a major market, and Austad's began to increase its presence, initially with catalogs in English and later in Japanese. Today, Japan is an even larger market for Austad's.[73]

Merchandise Assortment   The choice of target markets goes hand in hand with decisions on merchandise assortment. Baseball enthusiasts will be attracted to fantasy baseball camps and memorabilia. Cooking buffs are interested in exotic ingredients and hard-to-get equipment. Companies need to review and adjust the assortment in light of economic trends, competition, and changes in preferences of the target market. Omaha Steaks initially sold beef but responded to the trend toward lower fat foods by offering seafood, lamb, and chicken.[74] Dell Computer, which focused on desktop computers for years, had to add laptops and local area network (LAN) servers in the mid-1990s when it expanded to many user segments.[75]

Pricing   Direct marketing companies often follow a low-price strategy, facilitated by their low overhead. Gateway, Inc., headquartered in Sioux City, South Dakota, is the nation's seventh largest maker of personal computers. Customers are attracted by low prices and the convenience of ordering. Facility and labor costs are relatively inexpensive in Sioux City. Furthermore, Gateway is a pure assembler of components. It has a narrow product line and spends little money on R&D, which keeps costs and prices down.[76]

In contrast, some companies emphasize merchandise quality and follow a premium price strategy. Brigandi Coin Company in New York City has a strong direct marketing business in baseball cards, team-signed baseballs, and autographs. It has developed a reputation for selling only the finest quality, authentic memorabilia. This is important, since fraud is a major problem in the industry. Many collectors will pay Brigandi's high prices because of their confidence in the company.

Media and Channels   Direct marketing companies normally start with one promotion medium. QVC started with a home television shopping channel. Over time, many branch out to multiple media. Lands' End now uses the Internet as well, and QVC not only has an online service through the Microsoft Network but also sends out catalogs.

Some direct marketers use traditional channels. Gateway recently decided to offer its new 31-inch monitor through retailers like CompUSA.[77] Omaha Steaks has established 28 company-owned retail stores in eight midwestern states.[78]

Message Design   Whatever medium is used, message design and presentation is most important. For paper-based mail, attention must be paid to the envelope, the cover letter, and the product brochure. Envelopes of standard size and appearance are often discarded unopened, especially when mailing labels are used. An illustration or an important reason for opening the envelope often helps. The cover letter should be short and clear, using bold type to identify key product or service benefits. Brochures must be of high quality in appearance and content.[79]

Catalogs vary in quality of production depending on the company, its merchandise, and its targeted customers. For example, Victoria's Secret sells high-quality lingerie and women's apparel, targeted to an upscale market. Paper, design, and photographs are of high quality. Hello Direct sells telephone productivity tools, such as cordless headsets and speakerphones, to businesses. It emphasizes low prices, and its catalog is produced at low cost.

On the Web, the home page must be eye-catching and provide different categories of information the user can access. Sites must be easy to navigate. One rule of thumb is that content should never be more than three clicks away. Getting back to the home page must be simple. One guideline in creating content is to think of how the best salesperson would sell the company and its products. The site must provide a clear overview of the company and why its products are a good buy. Testimonials from satisfied customers is a good idea. Finally, sites must be updated regularly so that users will keep coming back to see what's new.[80]

Finally, the diversity of a company's customers must be considered when designing direct marketing messages. For example, in 1996 Montgomery Ward & Company sent 70,000 mailers in Spanish to Hispanic households in Los Angeles. Recipients were encouraged to call a toll-free number to place orders, and bilingual support staff took the calls. Sears also has directed a variety of direct marketing activities to reach Hispanics.[81]

Payment Methods and Delivery Direct marketing companies serving the consumer market often offer several different payment methods—check, money order, or credit card. Installments also may be possible, especially when the product is relatively expensive, although the final cost to the consumer is greater under that option. Oreck Corporation allows a free trial period of two weeks for its vacuum cleaners.

In business-to-business markets, customers often have an account with the direct marketer, and a monthly bill is sent. Typically, if the invoice is paid within ten days, a 2 percent credit will be applied to the next bill. Payment is normally due within 30 days.

Customers usually have several delivery options. The standard mode at Sharper Image is Federal Express second-day air; the delivery charge is based on the dollar value of the order. For an extra fee, they can select next-day air or Saturday delivery. Eddie Bauer offers standard delivery (3 to 5 days), express (3 days), or express plus (2 days) at progressively higher charges. Free delivery is declining as the service providers increase their fees, although some catalog companies calculate an average and quote prices as inclusive of delivery.[82]

ETHICS IN DIRECT MARKETING

A number of ethical problems confront the direct marketing industry, such as the right to privacy and the confidentiality of personal information. When you order products by mail, enter a sweepstakes, apply for a credit card, or buy a magazine subscription, chances are the information is entered into a huge database that can be accessed by many companies. In September 1996, thousands of callers jammed the phone lines at the Ohio headquarters of LEXIS®-NEXIS®, demanding to be removed from P-Trak, a personal database offered commercially by the firm. It is targeted to law enforcement officials and lawyers trying to track down witnesses, but it can be bought by anyone willing to pay a search fee.[83] You and virtually every American adult are in P-Trak which has current and former addresses, birth dates, and maiden names, among other information.

Another ethical issue is misrepresentation. Contests and sweepstakes are sometimes worded to make people believe they have won a prize. Only after making expensive 900-number calls do consumers discover that they have won little or nothing.

Some direct marketers bombard consumers with unwanted messages. People subscribing to one of the commercial on-line services often find loads of junk e-mail waiting for them, a practice called *spamming* in the industry.[84] In response to complaints, America Online denied access in 1996 to the biggest junk e-mailers. They filed a lawsuit, and a federal court ordered AOL to lift the blockade pending the suit's resolution.[85] A higher court finally ruled AOL had the right to protect subscribers.

In some countries, direct marketing has a very poor reputation because of past abuses. For example, many Japanese consumers view direct marketers as fly-by-night operators that cannot be trusted.[86] The industry must police itself if it is to thrive. With this in mind, the Direct Marketing Association (DMA) in Washington, D.C., has established ethical guidelines, which are summarized in Figure 13-5. Companies must sign the code and agree to uphold it before becoming members of the association. The DMA has an executive committee that reviews direct marketing materials. If any are found to be misleading, then the company is asked to change the message. The DMA also provides a service to help consumers block unwanted mail and catalogs.

You may notice that the basic principles underlying the DMA guidelines—such as honesty, clarity, fairness, and accuracy—are relevant not only to direct marketing but to marketing communications in general. In chapter 14 we will take an in-depth look at this broad and important topic. In addition to presenting an integrated conceptual framework for marketing communications, we will examine the communications process itself and the ways in which the communications mix can be orchestrated to send a powerful, unified message to the target audience.

HONESTY: All offers should be clear, honest, and complete so that the consumer may know the exact nature of what is being offered.

CLARITY: Simple and consistent statements of all the essential points of the offer should be clearly displayed in the promotional material. When an offer illustrates goods that are not included or that cost extra, these facts should be made clear.

PRINT SIZE: Print which by its small size, placement, or other visual characteristics is likely to substantially affect the legibility or clarity of the offer or exceptions to it should not be used.

PHOTOGRAPHS AND ARTWORK: Photographs, illustrations, artwork, and the situations they represent should be accurate portrayals and current reproductions of the products, services, or other subjects in all particulars.

SPECIAL OFFERS

When the term "free" or other similar representations are made (for example, 2-for-1, half-price. 1-cent offers), the product or service required to be purchased should not have been increased in price or decreased in quantity or quality.

PRIZES

No award should be held forth directly or by implication as having substantial monetary value if it is of nominal worth. The value of a prize given should be stated at regular retail value.

PREMIUMS

A premium, gift, or item should not be called or held out to be a "prize" if it is offered to every recipient of or participant in a promotion.

PRICE COMPARISONS

Price comparisons such as those between one's price and a former, future, or suggested price, or between one's price and the price of a competitor's comparable product should be made fairly and accurately.

Figure 13-5 A Summary of Direct Marketing Association Guidelines for Ethical Conduct
Source: A handout from the Direct Marketing Association, October 1996.

 ## CONNECTED: SURFING THE NET

Peapod, Inc.

www.peapod.com

THIS CHAPTER'S TECHNOLOGY FEATURE DISCUSSES PEAPOD, Inc., an on-line shopping and delivery service. To learn more about this type of retailing, visit Peapod's Web site and answer the following questions.

1. Peapod is the number one on-line grocery shopping and delivery service. In order to achieve that success, the company must provide value for consumers. How does it accomplish this? Give examples.
2. List several companies that have partnered with Peapod. How do you think these alliances help the company bring better service to its customers?
3. Successful retailers like Peapod must have an effective plan. Imagine you are responsible for developing Peapod's retail strategy. What steps would you take? Give examples.
4. What are some pros and cons of electronic commerce? How does Peapod create appeal for the advantages of on-line shopping?

CDnow

www.cdnow.com

IN THE DIRECT MARKETING SECTION OF this chapter, you learned about CDnow, an Internet reseller with more than 112,000 CD and cassette titles. To expand your thinking about direct marketing, visit CDnow's Web site and answer the following questions.

1. How does CDnow use its site to call for a direct response from the consumer?
2. In what ways is the CDnow site both a communication device and a channel of distribution?
3. How does direct marketing provide value to consumers? What, specifically, does the CDnow site offer to deliver value?
4. What ethical issues might CDnow face in direct marketing?

OBJECTIVE 1: Appreciate the important role retailers play in our economy and society.

Retailing is the final stage in the distribution channel for a majority of products sold to consumers. Time, place, possession, and form utilities are provided to consumers by retailers. In addition, retailers may promote the general welfare of society through efforts to recruit a diverse workforce. A number of U.S. retailers have been very successful in global markets by understanding important variations in consumer tastes across cultures.

OBJECTIVE 2: Understand strategy issues confronted by retailers when making marketing decisions.

Retailing strategy must cover a variety of issues. Each retailer must decide on the target market(s) and positioning, then adopt a distinct service level and pricing approach and decide what type of merchandise assortment it will offer. The geographical location of stores is a very important decision. Some retailers locate stores in low-rent areas off highways and at a distance from other retailers, while others place stores close to competitors. Well-run shopping centers have immense pulling power and are good locations for many retailers. New technologies, such as sophisticated computer systems that allow merchandise to be tailored in individual stores, help improve retailer performance. Furthermore, effectively managing relationships with suppliers—whether manufacturers, wholesalers, or agents—is critical.

OBJECTIVE 3: Recognize the diverse array of retailers that compete with one another.

Limited-line retailers include specialty stores, superstores, and automated vending operations. General merchandise retailers include department stores, convenience stores, supermarkets, warehouse clubs, discount stores, variety stores, and hypermarkets. An understanding of each type is useful in tracking and predicting competitive trends. A number of successful retailers have stores of different types.

OBJECTIVE 4: Learn what direct marketing entails, its value, and how it differs from mass communication.

Direct marketing is a powerful selling approach, especially when media are used to communicate information on products and prices, and how to place orders. Growth in sales through direct marketing channels is outpacing growth in U.S. retail sales by about two to one. Direct marketing offers consumers and businesses a convenient way to shop. It enables many small companies to access markets they could not reach through traditional retail and wholesale organizations. It is popular in many parts of the world. In fact, the largest direct marketing companies are foreign-based. International direct marketers must adjust their strategies to the unique characteristics of each country they serve.

OBJECTIVE 5: Be familiar with the different types of direct response media.

A large number of direct response media are available. Paper-based mail, fax mail, e-mail, and voice mail are options. Mail-order catalogs are used by many companies, and electronic versions are gaining in popularity. Telemarketing is a major force, especially in business-to-business markets. Advertisements in print and broadcast media are important in direct marketing activities. Infomercials can be used effectively to sell products and gain distribution through retailers. Television shopping channels have done well. The Internet is an intriguing medium still in its infancy. Each medium has its strengths and weaknesses that must be considered by companies choosing which one or which mix to use.

OBJECTIVE 6: Understand the marketing decisions made by direct marketing companies.

Direct marketers make a number of decisions when developing a marketing strategy. They must carefully select the target market(s). Strong customer databases must be developed and maintained. In particular, direct marketers can put database marketing to great use. Decisions on target markets go hand in hand with merchandise assortment and pricing. Multiple direct response media should be used, with great attention paid to the content of messages in each medium. Each medium has unique challenges with regard to message content. Finally, payment methods and delivery options must be decided upon.

REVIEW YOUR UNDERSTANDING

1. What is retailing? What is a retailer? List two reasons retailers are important.
2. What are the steps in developing a retail strategy?
3. What is a markup? Markdown?
4. What are the four types of limited-line retailers? What are the seven types of general merchandise retailers?
5. List three ethical issues in retailing.
6. What is direct marketing?
7. List several ways direct marketing provides value to customers.
8. List several media used in direct marketing.
9. List the seven decisions direct marketers make when developing a marketing strategy.
10. What are two ethical problems in the direct marketing industry? Briefly explain each.

DISCUSSION OF CONCEPTS

1. Explain the Pathways to Independence program of Marriott International, Inc. What are its main benefits?
2. Is following a hybrid strategy on service and price more difficult for a retailer than either a discount-oriented or service-oriented strategy? Explain.
3. What are the pros and cons of following a destination loca-

tion strategy? Under what conditions would locating stores close to the competition be preferable?

4. Among the various types of limited-line and general merchandise retailers, which have the strongest competitive position. Why?

5. Some experts view electronic shopping over the Internet as a major threat to retailers. Do you agree or disagree?

6. What are the major reasons for the growing importance of direct marketing in the United States?

7. What are the pros and cons of using fax mail, e-mail, and voice mail? Would you recommend their use to a direct marketing company? Why or why not?

8. What are infomercials? Can they be misused? How?

9. Explain how effective database management can improve the performance of a direct marketing company.

10. Are the efforts of the Direct Marketing Association to promote ethics among its members worthwhile? What else can be done to encourage ethical behavior in the industry?

KEY TERMS AND DEFINITIONS

Automated vending: The use of machinery operated by coins or credit cards to dispense goods.

Catalog showroom: A discount retailer whose customers shop from catalogs and can view floor samples of items held in stock.

Chain store: One of a group of centrally owned and managed retail stores that handle the same product lines.

Convenience store: A small retailer with moderately low breadth and depth of merchandise.

Department store: A retailer with merchandise of broad variety and moderate depth and with a relatively high level of customer service.

Direct marketing: The use of various communication media to interact directly with customers and generally calling for them to make a direct response.

Discount store: A retailer offering a broad variety of merchandise, limited service, and low prices.

Hypermarket: A giant shopping facility with a wide selection of food and general merchandise at low prices.

Infomercial: A programmatic advertisement of considerable length that resembles a documentary.

Mail-order catalog: A collection of product and price information that is published in paper form.

Markdown: A reduction from the original retail selling price of a product.

Markup: The amount added to the cost of acquiring a product that determines its retail selling price.

Off-price retailer: A seller of brand-name clothing at low prices.

Retailing: The activities involved in selling products and services directly to end users for personal or household use.

Scrambled merchandising: A retail strategy that entails carrying an array of product lines that seem to be unrelated.

Shopping mall (shopping center): A group of retail stores in one location and marketed as a unit to shoppers in a trade area.

Specialty store: A retailer offering merchandise in one primary product category in considerable depth.

Supermarket: A large, departmentalized, food-oriented retail establishment that sells beverages, canned goods, dairy products, frozen foods, meat, produce, and such nonfood items as health and beauty aids, kitchen utensils, magazines, pharmaceuticals, and toys.

Superstore: A retailer that focuses on a single product category but offers a huge selection and low prices; also called a *category killer*.

Telemarketing: Using the telephone to contact leads (potential customers) from a list.

Variety store: A retailer offering a variety of low-priced merchandise of low to moderate quality.

Warehouse club: A large, no-frills store that carries a revolving array of merchandise at low prices.

Wheel of retailing: A descriptive theory about how retailers emerge, evolve, and sometimes fade away.

REFERENCES

1. Interview with Cynthia Palmer, August 12, 1997.
2. Laura Bird, "Forget Ties; Catalogs Now Sell Mansions," *Wall Street Journal,* November 7, 1996, pp. B1, B4.
3. "Virtual Wal-Mart," *USA Today,* July 30, 1996, p. B1.
4. "Estimated Total Annual Retail Sales," Washington, DC: Bureau of the Census, www.census.gov/svsd/retlann/view/artssal.txt, site visited June 10, 1998.
5. Michael Levy and Barton Weitz, *Retailing Management* (Chicago: Richard D. Irwin), 1995, p. 129.
6. David Bolotsky and Matthew Fassler, *Exploring the Future of Hard Goods Specialty Retailing* (New York: Goldman, Sachs & Company, 1993), pp. 2–4.
7. Conversation with Ed Thomas, president of Wet Seal, November 26, 1996.
8. Levy and Weitz, *Retailing Management,* p. 129.
9. Gregory Patterson, "Target Micromarketing Its Way to Success: No Two Stores are Alike," *Wall Street Journal,* May 31, 1995, pp. A1, A8.
10. George White, "The Ethnic Side of Sears," *Los Angeles Times,* January 29, 1996, pp. D1, D4.
11. Zina Moukheiber, "The Price Is Right," *Forbes,* December 16, 1996, pp. 52, 53.
12. Joseph Pereira, "Toys 'R' Them: Mom and Pop Stores Put Playthings Like
Thomas on Fast Track," *Wall Street Journal,* January 14, 1993, pp. B1, B7.
13. Michael McCarthy, "Home Depot's Do-It-Yourself Powerhouse," *Wall Street Journal,* July 17, 1990, p. B1.
14. Levy and Weitz, *Retailing Management,* p. 619.
15. Bruce Horovitz, "Value-Minded Consumers Call the Shots," *USA Today,* September 10, 1996, pp. B1, B2.
16. Bolotsky and Fassler, *Hard Goods Specialty Retailing,* pp. 2–4.
17. Pereira, "Toys 'R' Them."
18. Levy and Weitz, *Retailing Management,* p. 258.
19. Louis Stern, Adel El-Ansary, and Anne Coughlan, *Marketing Channels,* 5th ed. (Upper Saddle River, NJ: Prentice Hall, 1996), p. 62.
20. Adam M. Brandenburger and Barry J. Nalebuff, *Co-opetition* (New York: Doubleday, 1996), p. 34.
21. Patrick Reilly, "Where Borders Group and Barnes & Noble Compete, It's a War," *Wall Street Journal,* September 3, 1996, pp. A1, A6.
22. Consulting assignment for Planet Hollywood during 1995; and Brandenburger and Nalebuff, *Co-opetition,* p. 33.
23. Paul Doocey, "Mall of America Fallout," *Stores,* May 1993, pp. 44–47.
24. "Restructuring Is Out, Replaced by Growth," *Wall Street Journal,* December 9, 1996, p. A1; and business report on CNN Headline News, August 14, 1996.

25. Patterson, "Target Micromarketing."

26. Don Peppers and Martha Rogers, *The One to One Future* (New York: Doubleday, 1996).

27. Frederick Reichheld, *The Loyalty Effect,* (Boston: Harvard Business School Press, 1996), pp. 82–83.

28. Tim Triplett, "Smart Store Challenges Executives to Change," *Marketing News,* July 4, 1994, p. 6.

29. "Wal-Mart Typifies Cooperation between Supplier, Retailer," *The Commercial Appeal* (Memphis), July 14, 1991, p. C1.

30. Stern, El-Ansary, and Coughlan, *Marketing Channels,* p. 44.

31. John Cortez, "Kmart Unleashes Its Category Killer Chains," *Advertising Age,* February 1, 1993, pp. S4, S5.

32. Cyndee Miller, "Retailers Do What They Must to Ring Up Sales," *Marketing News,* May 22, 1995, pp. 1, 10, 11.

33. Andrew Tanzer, "War of the Sales Robots," *Forbes,* January 7, 1991, pp. 294–296.

34. Francine Schwadel, "As Retailing's Chic and Indebted Stumble, Bland May Co. Thrives," *Wall Street Journal,* January 19, 1990, p. A1.

35. Levy and Weitz, *Retailing Management,* p. 40.

36. See, for example, Marcia Mogelonsky, "Asian-Indian Americans," *American Demographics,* August 1996, pp. 32–39.

37. William Schoell and Joseph Guiltinan, *Marketing* (Upper Saddle River, NJ: Prentice Hall, 1995), p. 408.

38. Stern, El-Ansary, and Coughlan, *Marketing Channels,* p. 43.

39. Ibid., p. 44.

40. Walter Levy, "Are Department Stores Doomed," *Direct Marketing,* May 1991, pp. 56–60.

41. White, "Ethnic Side of Sears."

42. Dana Milbank, "Hiring Welfare People, Hotel Chain Finds, Is Tough but Rewarding," *Wall Street Journal,* October 31, 1996, pp. A1, A6.

43. Catherine Yang, "Low-Wage Lessons," *Business Week,* November 11, 1996, pp. 109–111, 114, 116.

44. Debora Vrana, "State Investigating Title Company Kickbacks," *Los Angeles Times,* September 11, 1996, pp. D1, D11.

45. George White and Myron Levin, "Target Stores to Stop Selling Cigarettes," *Los Angeles Times,* August 29, 1996, pp. A1, A28.

46. James Bates and Chuck Philips, "Wal-Mart Bans Album over Gun Sale Lyrics," *Los Angeles Times,* September 10, 1996, pp. A1, A15.

47. Marjorie Kelly, "Dayton Hudson Corp. Is Caught Doing Good—and Not So Good," *Star Tribune* (Minneapolis), September 2, 1996, p. D3.

48. Tara Parker-Pope, "Custom Made," *Wall Street Journal,* September 26, 1996, pp. R22, R23.

49. Evelyn Iritani, "A Reel Challenge: U.S. Firms Make Big Push into Japan Theater Market," *Los Angeles Times,* July 28, 1996, pp. D1, D4.

50. Data reported in *Economic Impact: U.S. Direct Marketing Today* (New York: Direct Marketing Association, 1996).

51. Alice Cuneo, "Dell Joins Japan Computer Push," *Advertising Age,* September 2, 1996, p. 15.

52. "Ruth Owades—A Budding Entrepreneur," *Sales and Marketing Management,* June 1992, pp. 32–33.

53. "Japan Is Dialing 1-800 Buy America: U.S. Catalogers Offer Bargains Shoppers Can't Find at Home," *Business Week,* June 12, 1995, p. 55; and Mari Yamaguchi, "Japanese Consumers Shun Local Catalogs to Buy American," *Marketing News,* December 2, 1996, p. 12.

54. Seanna Browder, "The Disappearing CD-ROM Players," *Business Week,* December 16, 1996, pp. 123, 124.

55. Based on consulting experience with a small direct marketing company in the computer industry, October 1995.

56. Paul Judge, "Why Firefly Has Mad Ave. Buzzing," *Business Week,* October 7, 1996, pp. 100, 104.

57. *Sales and Marketing Management,* April 1997, p. 14, from Cahners Business Confidence Index as reported in Robert S. Lazich, *Market Share Reporter* (New York: Gale, 1998) p. 1752.

58. Beth Wade, "That's No Invoice; That's a Marketing Tool," *Marketing News,* September 9, 1996, pp. 10, 11.

59. "Rare Philosophy," *Marketing Management,* Summer 1995, pp. 4–6.

60. "News," *Modern Distribution Management,* March 10, 1996, p. 2.

61. Peter Bieler, *The Business Has Legs* (New York: John Wiley & Sons, 1996).

62. Information in QVC Web site at www.qvc.com, on January 28, 1997.

63. Julie Schmit, "Microsoft Enters Net Shopping," *USA Today,* October 30, 1996, p. 4B.

64. Bart Ziegler, "Slow Crawl on the Internet," *Wall Street Journal,* August 23, 1996, p. B1.

65. Kathy Rebello, "Making Money on the Net," *Business Week,* September 23, 1996, pp. 104–118.

66. Joan Rigdon, "Microsoft to Sell Most Popular Software Through Resellers Using the Internet," *Wall Street Journal,* October, 16, 1995, p. B10.

67. Karen Kaplan, "Listening Boom: Music-Oriented Sites Lead the World Wide Web Hit Parade," *Los Angeles Times,* July 12, 1995, pp. D1, D7; Rebello, "Making Money on the Net."

68. Donna Rosato, "Fare Sales Land on Web," *USA Today,* July 25, 1996, p. B1.

69. www.travelbids.com/se-infoseek5a.htm, site visited June 11, 1998.

70. Ibid.

71. Robert Stone, *Successful Direct Marketing Methods* (Lincolnwood, IL: NTC Business Books, 1994).

72. Das Narayandas and V. Kasturi Rangan, "Dell Computer Corporation," Case #9-596-058 (Cambridge, MA: Harvard Business School Publishing, 1996).

73. Richard Miller, *Multinational Direct Marketing* (New York: McGraw-Hill, 1995), p. 14.

74. "Rare Philosophy."

75. Narayandas and Rangan, "Dell Computer Corporation."

76. "Gateway to Sell New PC Through Stores," *Los Angeles Times,* August 21, 1996, p. D2.

77. Ibid.

78. "Rare Philosophy."

79. Stone, *Successful Direct Marketing Methods.*

80. Judson, *NetMarketing.*

81. Jeffery Zbar, "Marketing to Hispanics: Hispanic Direct Mail Greeted by Open Door," *Advertising Age,* January 23, 1995, p. 34; and White, "Ethnic Side of Sears."

82. Paul Miller, "Expressed Out," *Catalog Age,* October 15, 1996, pp. 1, 24.

83. Amy Harmon, "Public Outrage Hits Firm Selling Personal Data," *Los Angeles Times,* September 19, 1996, pp. A1, A21.

84. David Nicholson, "Spamming Spreads Over Computer Networks," *Los Angeles Times,* September 9, 1996, p. D14.

85. Jane Hodges, "AOL Takes on Bulk E-Mailers," *Advertising Age,* September 9, 1996, p. 8.

86. Cuneo, "Dell Joins Japan Computer Push."

CASE 13

GATEWAY

WOULD YOU PURCHASE YOUR FIRST computer, sight unseen, over the phone or Internet? Millions have. In 1987 Ted Waitt, founder of Gateway, Inc. (formerly Gateway 2000), recognized a neglected market which would purchase PCs through direct marketing. Aiming to "offer buyers a logical alternative to the high markups, limited choices, and inadequate support common in the PC market," Waitt and his business partner, Mike Hammond, started selling computer peripherals and software to owners of Texas Instrument PCs. Soon Gateway began assembling its own PC-compatible systems. Using the direct channel, Gateway became a Fortune 500 company in less than 10 years.

Competing in one of the fastest-paced industries, Gateway knows how to forge relationships with customers without a strong retail presence. With growth rates of 30 percent or more annually, sales reached $6.29 billion in 1997.

Jim Taylor, senior vice president of global marketing, says "We ask customers to call up, spend more money on your credit card than you've ever spent before, for something you can't see and that, at the same time you order it, doesn't exist." Since Gateway only assembles computers once they have been ordered, Taylor notes, "we spend a lot of money trying to earn their trust." The investment has paid off. In its February 1998 cover story,

"Best PC Buys," *PC Computing* ranked Gateway number one in technical service among over 100 direct marketing PC companies. In the United States, more than 500 salespeople staff phone banks 16 hours a day. The company answers every call within two minutes, and is striving to do even better. Gateway also has 24-hour, toll-free support seven days a week for service and questions. According to Taylor, "In the electronic world, every contact with the customer is crucial and has got to reflect your emotional and moral claims."

To maintain a high consumer response, Gateway relies heavily on such direct response media as the Web, newspapers, television, magazines, catalogs, and others. Its Web site alone generates approximately $4 million a day in sales. The recently updated site enables customers to self-select according to their requirements, essentially assigning themselves to the appropriate market niche.

With an annual ad budget of more than $100 million, Gateway incorporates its South Dakota "heartland mystique" as a central part of its communications. For example, a recent television spot shows a Gateway production line virtually shut down until an employee remembers to say "thank you" to a coworker who helped him. Television is increasing in importance as a direct response medium for the company. Traditionally relying on such print vehicles as the *Wall Street Journal* to disperse information quickly, Gateway is now experimenting with creating a larger number of ads at a faster pace. A recent customer loyalty spot cost only $30,000 and was aired immediately after the company obtained favorable customer satisfaction data. Thus far, Gateway has been fairly conservative, relying mostly on cable. The problem, Taylor says, is "I can't buy media that gets so many people calling that it blows up our phone system." Print ads are another significant part of Gateway's communications, appearing mostly in trade PC magazines and newspapers. A greater number of print ads have started to appear in consumer books and home titles as well, since 80 percent of home PCs are bought by women, or with their permission.

Although the Gateway approach relies on dealing with consumers without the use of a retail intermediary, it is undergoing some significant changes. Recently, Gateway established a network of Country Stores to offer customers an opportunity to try different models, ask questions, and order a computer on the spot. The stores target areas with large university populations, upper-class residents, and other characteristics of Gateway's traditional buyers. The stores, which have a "down home" appearance, are inexpensive and flexible so that displays can be changed quickly. By the end of 1997, Gateway had 37 retail locations in the United States.

Gateway's success is not limited to domestic sales. In 1993, it opened a direct marketing and manufacturing operation in Ireland and since then has added showrooms in France, Germany, Japan, the United Kingdom, Sweden, and Australia. It has opened a manufacturing operation in Malaysia to serve the Asia-Pacific markets. Most recently, Gateway added a call center in Cyprus to serve Greece and the United Arab Emirates (UAE).

Waitt and Hammond have often been credited with pioneering the direct-market growth in the PC industry. According to Waitt, Gateway's future is promising. "Our strategic focus will be on expanding our customer relationships with enhanced products and services sold via the Web, on the phone, and in our stores to home consumers and business consumers around the world." Gateway's success can be marked by the 2.6 billion unit shipments it made in 1997 to customers around the world who—sight unseen—bought PCs at a good price.

1. *How does Gateway develop meaningful relationships with customers without a strong retail presence? What effect, if any, do you think its Country Stores will have on its direct marketing business? Explain.*
2. *On which types of direct response media does Gateway rely? How might its media needs differ from those of a major retailer?*
3. *This chapter discusses a number of decisions direct marketers must make when developing a marketing strategy. Discuss Gateway's decisions regarding target markets, pricing, and merchandise assortment.*

SOURCES: Gateway 2000 Web site, www.gw2.com, visited February 2, 1998; Gerry Khermouch, "Jim Taylor," *Brandweek,* October 20, 1997, pp. 102–105; Konstantinos Karagiannis, "Buying a Computer Direct," *Popular Electronics,* January 1998, pp. 14–15; Melinda Ligos, "From the Ground Up," *Sales and Marketing Management,* January 1998, p. 13; "Gateway 2000, Inc.," *Wall Street Journal Interactive Edition,* Company Briefing Book, visited March 27, 1997; and "Phone, Web Technical Support Ranked Number One," *PC Computing,* February 1998, p. 200.

Chapter 14

Integrated Marketing Communications

Objectives

1. Understand the objectives of integrated marketing communications.

2. Learn how the communication process provides the intended information for the market.

3. Learn about the communication mix, including personal selling, advertising, sales promotion, sponsorships, and public relations.

4. Know the factors that influence the communication mix.

5. Describe the steps in developing an integrated marketing communication plan.

6. Address diversity, ethics, and technology in communications.

THE "DOMINATRIX OF DOMESTICITY," THE New York Times *once called her. Some abhor her, some adore her. Like it or not, Martha Stewart's brilliant sense of publicity has you thinking about her—regularly. As with all great marketers, she saw a need, filled it with her formidable presence, and created an empire. It ranges from home improvement, interior design, and gardening to cooking, entertainment, and more.*

"Stewart is one of the best self-marketers in the industry," says Steve Cohn, editor of Media Industry Newsletter. *"She's amazing—she appeals to ordinary women as well as upscale types." According to Mike McGrath, a fellow magazine editor: "In the great anonymous era, she connects with people." The president and CEO of Time, Inc., Don Logan, credits both the magazine Stewart created and her "tireless marketing, promotion, and publicity efforts. The results speak for themselves."*

Stewart's empire now includes 18 books, a daily Emmy Award–winning television show, a syndicated newspaper column, a daily radio spot, a mail-order business called Martha By Mail, a line of $110-a-gallon paints, and the phenomenally successful magazine Martha Stewart Living. *Plans are under way for an Internet site with an "Ask Martha" format (like her newspaper column). All this is more than a cash cow. Within an integrated plan that is the envy of the industry, each division is used to cross-promote the others.*

"As a way to popularize the idea of information and learning, TV is second to none," says Martha. "And as people recognize the value of the TV show, they recognize the value of the magazine and the books. It's all very interrelated now." The show's promotion of the magazine is both innovative and effective. Acquiring new subscribers can be expensive—as much as $18 per name. So to reach circulation of one million could cost about $20 million. But cross-promotion drastically lowers the cost. On television, Martha points out, "we mention that all the recipes and source information are in the program guide of our monthly magazine. At the end of the show, there's an 800 number." In some months up to 50,000 new orders have poured in, and Martha Stewart Living *will soon exceed the two million subscription mark.*

For her books, all of which are still in print and selling, Stewart goes beyond the traditional multicity autographing tour. For her, bookselling is a year-round event, the main focal point being her innovative monthly charity lecture. She talks to groups ranging in size from 800 to 3,000, and she gets a local bookstore involved with the promotion. Her format usually includes a lecture and lunch (proceeds going to charity), followed by a book signing. According to Stewart, around 900 books are sold at each event, but the buyers that day later purchase more

THE CONCEPT OF INTEGRATED MARKETING COMMUNICATIONS

Which do you think would sell better—a poor product supported by great marketing communication or a great product supported by poor marketing communication? Actually, the product probably would not do well in either case. A good product that is poorly communicated is unlikely to be perceived appropriately by consumers. And a poor product, no matter how well it is promoted, will quickly become known for its lack of value. This is because social connections among people get the word around.

Marketers need to ensure that all elements of the marketing mix—product, price, promotion (communication), and place—are working together. This chapter deals with communication, which is broader than promotion but includes it within its scope. Recall from chapter 6 that a product's position is its image relative to competition in the mind of consumers. It would not make sense for Payless shoe stores to carry expensive brands. Nor would it make sense for Campbell's to charge less for its premium soup than its regular soup. Both would seem inconsistent in the mind of consumers. Nearly everything about a product communicates something to consumers. The gold label on Campbell's premium soups communicates quality. The very name Payless translates into lower-price shoes. Even where you buy a product says something. A study of doctors' offices revealed that many patients will skip the medical procedure or change physician if they feel uneasy in the office.[2]

Communication is the exchange of meaning between or among parties. It involves sharing points of view and is at the heart of forming relationships. You simply cannot connect with customers unless you communicate with them. **Promotion** is the process whereby marketers inform, educate, persuade, remind, and reinforce consumers through communication. It is designed to influence buyers and other publics. Although most marketing communications are aimed at consumers, a significant number also address shareholders, employees, channel members, suppliers, and society. In addition, we will see that effective communication is a two-way street: Receiving messages is often as important as sending them.

Integrated marketing communication (IMC) is the coordination of advertising, sales promotion, personal selling, public relations, and sponsorships to reach consumers with a powerful unified effect. These five elements should not be considered separate entities. In fact, each element of the communication plan often has a multiplier effect on the others. As we have just seen, Martha Stewart uses IMC to promote her products and brand name. Her strategic use of television, newspaper, radio, direct mail, and the Internet have resulted in an extremely successful business. Her recent efforts include a holiday promotion with Minute Maid, a deal with Kmart, and syndication of her TV show, which will now be aired six times a week.[3]

The IMC concept has three parts, as depicted in Figure 14-1, which this chapter will cover in order. First, it is important to consider the objectives of IMC, which need to be related to the overall marketing strategy. Second, marketers must be familiar with the communication process in order to be effective. Third, they must understand how each type of communication in the mix accomplishes a unique task. The key is to put them all together to achieve goals; this requires planning, budgeting, implementation, and feedback. Finally, we end the chapter with a look at diversity, ethics, and technology issues as they pertain to IMC.

According to Don Schultz, coauthor of *Integrated Marketing Communications: Putting It All Together and Making it Work,* two key goals of IMC are to establish a one-to-one relationship with consumers and to encourage two-way communication between a firm and its customers. One way companies are trying to achieve these goals is to orchestrate various el-

Communication
The process of sending and receiving messages.

Promotion
The process whereby marketers inform, educate, persuade, remind, and reinforce consumers through communication.

Integrated marketing communication (IMC)
The coordination of advertising, sales promotion, personal selling, public relations, and sponsorship to reach consumers with a powerful effect in the market.

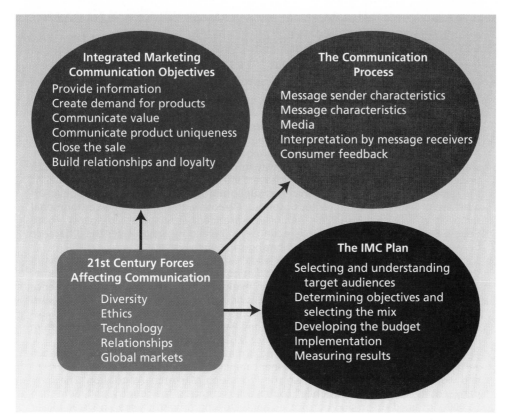

Integrated Marketing Communication Objectives
Provide information
Create demand for products
Communicate value
Communicate product uniqueness
Close the sale
Build relationships and loyalty

The Communication Process
Message sender characteristics
Message characteristics
Media
Interpretation by message receivers
Consumer feedback

21st Century Forces Affecting Communication
Diversity
Ethics
Technology
Relationships
Global markets

The IMC Plan
Selecting and understanding target audiences
Determining objectives and selecting the mix
Developing the budget
Implementation
Measuring results

Figure 14-1 *The Concept of Integrated Marketing Communications (IMC)*

ements of the promotion mix and create a brand experience directly with consumers. See the relationships feature, "From Integrated Marketing Communications to 'Intimate' Marketing Communications."

OBJECTIVES OF INTEGRATED MARKETING COMMUNICATIONS

Integrated marketing communications has numerous objectives. The most notable are to provide information, create demand, communicate value and product uniqueness, close the sale, and build loyal customer relationships.

PROVIDE INFORMATION

Ultimately, all communication is designed to provide some form of information. It gives consumers what they need to make informed choices within a reasonable time frame.[4] Objectives differ depending on the target audience's familiarity with a particular product. If it is relatively unknown, then marketers need to inform and educate the target audience. Often this communication introduces consumers to the product's benefits and uses. When it is working most effectively, information helps consumers make the buying decision. It provides data on a broad range of topics, including product characteristics, uses, availability, prices, and methods of acquisition. Yet, the tremendous number and variety of sources challenge consumers to select and process the most useful information. At the same time, marketers are challenged to create communications that contribute to the consumer's search for value in the marketplace or marketspace. Consequently, communications should be designed with consumer information needs in mind.

   In many cases, information is purely descriptive. Deloitte & Touche, for example, used an eight-page ad, entitled "Women at Work," to detail its initiatives to enhance the presence of women in the company. It also presented an ad as an article filled with information to inform consumers about the company's accounting, tax, and consulting services.[5] Another use of communication is to correct common misperceptions. For example, many consumers believe that frozen vegetables do not retain nutrients as well as fresh vegetables, but the opposite is true. Frozen food marketers have developed educational campaigns to inform consumers about their product benefits.[6]

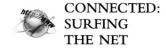

CONNECTED: SURFING THE NET

www.dttus.com

Learn more about one of the nation's leading professional service firms by visiting the Deloitte & Touche Web site. Find out about its specialized areas, services, solutions, and much more.

CONNECTING THROUGH RELATIONSHIPS

FROM INTEGRATED MARKETING COMMUNICATIONS TO "INTIMATE" MARKETING COMMUNICATIONS

What's more likely to turn you into a Snapple drinker? A 30-second television ad or a cold bottle right in your hand? In summer 1996 the Quaker Oats Company sent Snapple squads across the United States to give a sample to "every man, woman and child." As they made their way to parks, beaches, office buildings, and Little League games, a TV and radio blitz advertised an 800 number for a free sample. At the same time, the sampling promo was supported by outdoor advertising, point-of-purchase promotions, and Internet postings. "Obviously, this is more than a traditional sampling effort," said Russ Klein, senior vice president at Snapple's ad agency, Foote Cone & Belding in Chicago. "We're creating a happening for Snapple. It's the difference between getting a greeting card and having someone visit you."

Snapple's in-your-face—or "in-your-hands"—promotional strategy is what folks in the promo biz are calling *experiential marketing.* Aware that target audiences are becoming numb to ads and standard promos, marketers are creating a brand experience with consumers on a personal level. "There is an accelerating trend worldwide, toward the use of nontraditional marketing communications that link clients with their customers and allow real interaction," says Tony Pace, managing director of Momentum IMC, the event marketing unit of ad agency McCann-Erickson.

One hallmark of experiential marketing is that public relations tend to drive the advertising. Kraft Food's Oscar Mayer Wiener campaign hiked market share by 10 percent and won a 1996 Reggie Award from the Promotion Marketers Association. The company sent its campy "wienermobile" to supermarkets across the country, and more than 50,000 kids lined up to audition for a chance to sing "I wish I were an Oscar Mayer Wiener" on national television. The winner starred in the country's hottest TV ad slot: the Super Bowl. The miles of videotape shot during the auditions provided Oscar Mayer with a gold mine of images for future ads.

The best experiential marketing takes place on the street, where company representatives meet and mingle with consumers. Sega, the top brand in video games, goes even farther and gets its best customers to stage promotions. To get more intimate with its hard-to-nail-down and mostly male market, the company created a grassroots marketing army among product users. At 50 college campuses nationwide, students are paid to organize events and contests while giving away substantial amounts of merchandise for sampling and testing. By forging relationships with customers in this unconventional way, Sega claims it doesn't need a traditional promotion agency. Instead, it gets some of its best ideas for promos from kids off the street.

Sources: Judann Pollack, "New Marketing Spin: The PR 'Experience,'" *Advertising Age,* August 5, 1996, p. 33; Kate Fitzgerald, "Sega 'Screams' Its Way to the Top," *Advertising Age,* March 20, 1995, pp. 52–53; Betsy Spethmann, "Out of the Closet and into the Boardroom," *Brandweek,* March 4, 1996, pp. 22–26; and Betsy Spethmann, "Oscar's Top Dogs," *Brandweek,* March 11, 1996, pp. 22–23.

CREATE DEMAND FOR PRODUCTS

Communication helps create demand for products in global and domestic markets. It stimulates people to desire what they do not have and inspires them to earn the money to acquire items that improve their standard of living. Communication helps assure that products will be purchased in sufficient quantities to justify their development, production, and distribution. Today, the speed of communication allows companies to obtain worldwide demand in a short period. Many products marketed globally have coordinated IMC campaigns supported by high-tech information systems. Internet working—connecting personal computers to the network—makes it possible for companies to see what demand is being created by communication in various geographic areas and adjust product availability accordingly. Cisco Systems enjoys a 50 percent market share in the Internet-working industry and supplies 80 percent of all routers that direct Internet traffic. This type of technology allows companies to communicate throughout the world and rapidly build significant amounts of demand.[7]

Consider the movie *Jurassic Park,* which grossed $882 million worldwide in box office sales on a promotion budget of $150 to $200 million. Associated merchandise, marketed through 500 licensees, had sales of $1 billion on a $60 million promotion budget. What made this campaign so successful was the coordination of IMC by marketers across international borders to create demand. Participating companies included Kellogg in Canada; Weetabix in France, Portugal, and the United Kingdom; PepsiCo in Scandinavia; Coke, which leveraged its presence in Latin America; and MCA's sister company, Nissin Foods in Japan. It appears no corner of the world was left out. The tremendous sales reflect the successful use of IMC to increase demand on a global scale.[8]

COMMUNICATE VALUE

The search for value is complicated because consumers need to assess the benefits of a product relative to thousands of others. Marketers compete to provide value in keeping with consumers' willingness to pay. Consequently, much communication uses creative messages that help convey benefits. For example, Cutler-Hammer technical sales representatives learn about a broad range of sophisticated electronic products. They are taught how to communicate the benefits, functions, and features of each to the consumer. But to communicate value they must first identify how the customer will use a product. In the case of equipment sold to contractors, they find out how it will be installed. They can then point out cost-saving product attributes due to easy installation and reliable design.

Advertisers are often careful to depict scenes of consumers clearly benefiting from products. For its ShareVision video conferencing system, Motorola shows an executive using the technology and reinforces the advantages with text: "This revolutionary and affordable communication tool allows you to meet face to face with users around the world." The ad conveys the benefits available at a reasonable cost.[9]

COMMUNICATE PRODUCT UNIQUENESS

Marketers attempt to communicate uniqueness in order to differentiate their product from others. Burger King is broiled; McDonald's® is fried; Southwest Airlines is less expensive because it has no frills; Titleist is used by more professional golfers than any other ball, and so on. In each case marketers are attempting to distinguish this particular product from those of competitors. Marketers also use persuasive communication to convince consumers to switch from one brand to another. Messages compare a product's benefits, functions, and features to the competition. The goal is to illustrate your brand's unique value and build brand preference.

Dr. Martens, a shoe manufacturer, attempts to persuade consumers by using marketing communications that tell the company's history. The campaign describes how Dr. Klaus Martens, the founder, injured his foot while skiing. He then invented a rubber-soled shoe that provides comfort to people on their feet all day. The message is that Dr. Martens, having suffered foot pain himself, knows how to build a shoe superior to that of competitors.

CLOSE THE SALE

Communication also helps close the sale. Marketers want their product to be purchased. If the experience is good, chances are it will be repurchased. Thus, IMC seeks to move buyers to action the first time and then reinforce their positive experience so they will buy again and

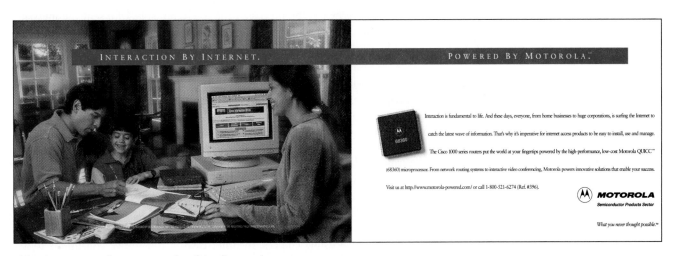

Advertisers want to show customers benefiting from products.

again. Today, customers are selecting when they want to receive communications, and often that is just prior to purchase. Many people use the Web to look up ads. Increasingly, newspaper, magazine, and television also are including Web site information so consumers can learn more or refresh their memory about what they have seen. These Web sites also are interactive, so the communication is more personal and involves the consumer. Purchasing is made easy when customers are told just where and how to buy.

BUILD RELATIONSHIPS AND LOYALTY

Once consumers have tried a particular brand, marketers remind them why they chose it in the first place and reinforce that behavior. In other words, communication helps maintain brand loyalty. Reminder communications reinforce the popularity of existing goods by reassuring loyal customers that they have made the correct choice. Because consumers tend to pay more attention to ads for products that they currently use, advertising is often meant to reinforce. For example, American Express card messages on television and in magazines remind consumers that "membership has its privileges."

THE COMMUNICATION PROCESS

The basic communication process is outlined in Figure 14-2. As you can see, messages move from the sender (marketer) to the receiver (consumer). Traditionally, communication has been seen as a one-way process. With the advent of one-to-one marketing through technologies such as the Internet, it is more useful to envision a two-way or continuous flow. Marketers need to start with a clear understanding of the target market, the objectives of the communication, and how to meet those objectives. They should also be aware that proactive customers have their own objectives and use the same process in reverse.

Let's look at the process. Effective communication can be difficult because consumers are bombarded daily by thousands of conflicting messages. Once marketers decide what to communicate, they must encode the message for the target market. It can be spoken, written, illustrated through pictures or diagrams, or conveyed by a combination of these. The encoded message then must be sent to consumers via one or more media: television, radio, newspapers, magazines, telephone, fax, personal contact, the Internet, and others.

Customers must decode, or interpret, the message that marketers send. Each customer's reaction will depend on personal background and experiences. One of the most important aspects of the communication process is feedback from the target audience. Sometimes it comes in the form of an action by the consumer. For example, if a campaign is designed to encourage product awareness, then positive feedback is an increase in the number of consumers who know about the product, and negative feedback is a flat or declining awareness. Such information is vital because it helps marketers judge whether the message accomplished its goal or needs to be adjusted.

One final element marketers must deal with when communicating to consumers is noise, that is, anything that interferes with a message being received. For example, after talking to a salesperson about a new sports car, you may want to buy it. But then a friend says: "It's a piece of junk." Your friend obviously interferes with the marketer's message. Noise can also occur if you are distracted from receiving the message or if you're not sure who sent the message. We will now look at each element of the communication process shown in Figure 14-2.

THE MESSAGE SENDER

Once marketers have determined that communication is in order, they initiate the process by formulating a message. As the sender, it is the marketer's responsibility to make sure the message is received by the targeted audience, is understood as intended, helps the audience be knowledgeable, and elicits an appropriate response.

Communications take valuable time from the receiver, so it is up to the sender to provide relevant information. Generally, a series of contacts is required. Once a relationship is created between the two parties, communication is much easier for two reasons: The sender learns the most useful information to supply, and the receiver is more inclined to listen. Effective communications obtain consumer responses that contribute to a company's goals. In some cases the message simply identifies the product so potential customers are more likely to include it in their set of possible choices. In other cases it may move consumers to act immediately.

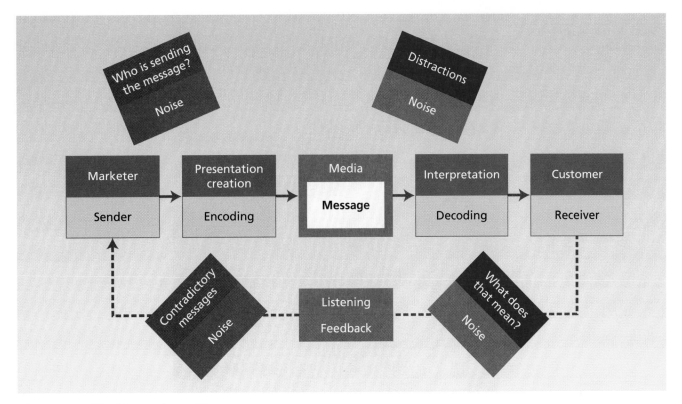

Figure 14-2 The Communication Process

The reputation of the sender—whether a person, a company, or some other organization—influences how consumers receive a message. In fact, when several sources communicate precisely the same message, it is received differently depending on the source. That's why marketers must select exactly the right person to carry their message. Sprint chose Candice Bergen as spokesperson after focus groups and other research showed that her credibility was strong with the target market.[10] PepsiCo recently signed a two-year contract with Green Bay Packers quarterback Brett Favre to endorse Mountain Dew. He will be featured in print and broadcast media across the Midwest, where he will have the most influence on consumers.[11] One person usually does not have high credibility with all segments of the population. Different consumers respect, admire, trust, and identify with different types of people. Even within one segment, it's difficult to identify a single spokesperson to whom everyone relates. That is why the famous milk mustache appears on so many faces.

What makes a source credible with a target audience? Generally spokespersons are judged according to their expertise, trustworthiness, and attractiveness.

Expertise Consumers attribute expertise to a spokesperson for many reasons. They may believe s/he has specialized training, a great deal of experience, or a thorough knowledge. Some companies hire engineers for industrial sales positions, believing that their academic degree lends special credibility. Doctors are highly credible spokespersons in messages for pain relievers. Children's Tylenol, for example, is promoted as "the first choice of pediatricians." Robitussin notes that it is recommended by physicians, pharmacists, and "Dr. Mom." Both campaigns are based on the credibility of its sources.

Consumers also tend to rely on someone with a lifestyle similar to their own, which accounts for the surge in advertising featuring "average" people. For example, "real" mothers tell why they like Luvs diapers, and "real" gardeners swear by Miracle-Gro. E-Plus, a German mobile phone company, has featured people with "normal" careers in their ads. Similarly, Volvo ran ads about "survivors," depicting people who had lived through a car accident in their Volvo.[12]

Trustworthiness Organizations such as the Underwriter's Laboratory, the American Medical Association, the American Dental Association, the Good Housekeeping Institute, and Consumer's Union have gained a great deal of credibility because of their trustworthiness. Not only do they have considerable technical knowledge, but also most consumers perceive them

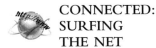

CONNECTED: SURFING THE NET

www.pepsi.com

Visit Pepsi World on-line and check out its latest promotional activities, from sports to music to movies and entertainment. You'll also be able to play intermix sound bytes and watch quicktime movie clips.

Marketers carefully select spokespeople to influence how consumers receive a message.

as unbiased. People tend to trust messages from "objective" sources. They also tend to discount messages from sources that stand to benefit in some way. Imagine that you are purchasing a VCR and the salesperson constantly emphasizes the importance of an extended warranty. If you know the salesperson gets a commission on warranty sales, then you are less likely to believe what s/he is telling you. If no commission is involved, then you are more inclined to trust the person.

Attractiveness (Personal Demeanor and Appeal)   It's not surprising that attractive, pleasant, likable spokespersons have influence. That's why they are selected to deliver messages. BellSouth uses celebrities who are actual customers, such as Muggsy Bogues, Courtney Cox, Naomi Judd, and Daisy Fuentes.[13] Telephone companies in particular are increasingly using famous people to endorse their products, due to the heightened competition resulting from industry deregulation. Michael Jordan signed a 10-year contract with LDDS WorldCom, while his teammate Scottie Pippen signed to endorse Ameritech Cellular. Other telecommunication endorsers have included pro golfer Corey Pavin, Atlanta Hawks coach Lenny Wilkens, and CBS Sports announcer Billy Packer.[14]

Often celebrities gain credibility in areas outside their expertise. For example, some movie stars have influenced political campaigns despite their limited political savvy. When famous endorsers are also informed, their power can be substantial. For example, actor Ted Danson is a knowledgeable and active supporter of ocean-protection legislation, as is Barbra Streisand for an agency combating global warming.[15] Athletes are obvious choices for promoting sports equipment and apparel, but the fame they have acquired on the court or playing field translates to other areas.

It's important to note that attractiveness involves all aspects of the source, whether sales personnel or any others who represent an organization. A company's general reputation also applies. Consider the damage to Exxon after 11 million gallons of oil were spilled in Alaskan waters. Since cleanup techniques are still low-tech, the environmental damage probably tarnished the company's image for many consumers.[16]

Encoding is the process of translating a message into terms easily understood by the target audience. We know from chapter 7 that information processing is a complex but very important aspect of the purchase decision. Marketers must encode messages so they are interpreted appropriately by the people for whom they are intended. For example, marketers of fine jewelry have traditionally encoded their messages to reach men—once the main purchasers of engagement rings and other gems as gifts. Today, however, women have higher disposable incomes and increasingly buy expensive presents for themselves. As much as 70 percent of all women's gold jewelry sales are now self-purchases. The Diamond Club International asks: "Who needs a husband when you can buy yourself two studs for the price of one?"[17] The company has encoded the communication to reach women with the message that they are independent and are entitled to splurge.

As we discussed in chapter 7, many messages are screened out by consumers. While some people seek information on their own, it is up to the sender to stimulate the consumer's interest in receiving a message. This involves grabbing attention and keeping it while the information is processed. Messages that are boring, uninteresting, or irrelevant are tuned out. In order to facilitate consumer understanding, communications should limit the amount of information conveyed at one time. We know that consumers take in only a little and that comprehension is based on their life circumstances and experiences. Consequently, effective messages present carefully selected topics in a context relevant to the target audience.

MESSAGE CHARACTERISTICS

There are countless ways to communicate a given message. One viewpoint or several can be presented. Recommendations or conclusions may or may not be included. Key points can be made at the beginning, middle, or end. Humor or fear can be used. And messages may or may not compare a product to those of competitors.

One-Sided and Two-Sided Messages A **one-sided message** presents only arguments favorable to the source. A **two-sided message** recognizes the arguments against a position and provides the recipient with why reasons are invalid. For example, a message for a fast-food chain might mention only the positive aspects of the ingredients and cooking methods. Or it might present both sides in response to a competitor's charge. When the source and receiver have relatively similar views, a one-sided message is most appropriate. When there is disagreement, a two-sided message often is most useful.

Recommendations or Conclusions A message can make recommendations or offer conclusions or leave that task to the receiver. Messages with conclusions are more easily understood, but when the audience draws its own, there is a stronger likelihood of acceptance. This is particularly true for highly educated consumers. If an advertising message is repeated, then the absence of any stated conclusion is likely to make the ad more effective. Repeated exposures give the target audience an opportunity to reach its own conclusions. If the marketer wants the message to have immediate effect, then the communication probably should draw direct conclusions. Rubbermaid launched a new campaign in response to smaller competitors, who were rapidly gaining market share. Since Rubbermaid wanted to influence consumers quickly, its ads were designed to focus on the numerous solutions its products provide to everyday problems. The campaign was reinforced with an 89-page book, *1001 Solutions for Better Living.*[18] This type of promotional effort draws direct conclusions for customers about product benefits.

Order of Presentation The placement of the key point of a communication affects how the message is interpreted and later recalled by buyers. More is remembered about the beginning and end of a message than its middle. Therefore, effective presentations usually open and close with strong statements. Weaker arguments are most often placed in the middle.

Humor Viewers like humorous ads because they are novel and enjoyable. But advertisers must be careful not to let humor obscure the message. There are several things to keep in mind.

- Be sure to mention the brand name within the first ten seconds. Otherwise, the communication runs the risk of inhibiting recall of key selling points.

- Subtle humor is more effective than bizarre humor.
- Humor must be relevant to the brand or the key selling point. Without this linkage, recall and persuasion are diminished.
- It is best not to use humor that belittles or makes fun of the potential user. Jokes about the brand, the situation, or the subject matter are usually more effective.[19]

Evidence is still inconclusive as to whether a humorous approach is more effective than a serious one. While humor tends to increase attention, it also may distract from or decrease acceptance of the message. Think about Nissan's memorable "Enjoy the Ride" communication, which aired during the 1997 Super Bowl. The commercial portrayed a flock of animated-puppet pigeons on a mission to soil a freshly washed Nissan.[20] The approach increased attention to accomplish its objective, which was to get people talking about the ad and paying attention to the Nissan name. This was followed later by non-humorous ads designed to support the "enjoy the ride" message.

Fear Appeals   Marketers sometimes use fear to gain the attention and interest of their audience. Campaigns by the American Dental Association warn that poor dental hygiene can result in tooth decay, gum disease, and loss of teeth. In some instances, advertisers play on fear for the safety of loved ones. A Michelin spot shows a baby floating in a tire and reminds parents, "You have a lot riding on them." An advertisement for seat belt use by the Michigan Association for Traffic Safety pictures a wheelchair: "It's your choice."

In many instances fear appeals are very effective. They can create higher attention and interest in the message. Consider the recent development of at-home kits testing for HIV, now marketed by companies such as Johnson & Johnson and Home Access Health Corporation. The latter runs an ad showing crossed fingers: "If this is your idea of an HIV test . . . it's time you learned about ours."[21]

Comparative Messages   In the 1970s, the Federal Trade Commission began allowing advertisers to name competitors in ads. Since then, a host of companies have chosen to compare their products with those of rivals. There have been sneaker wars, hamburger wars, beer

*Sometimes life insurance marketing
builds public awareness by using
fear appeals to persuade customers
to act on the message.*

wars, and cola wars. In each case, claims and counterclaims have been used in comparative messages. Do these techniques work? They certainly draw attention. Even though comparative messages allow marketers to present clear, objective arguments in favor of their product, many companies hesitate to use the technique. References to the competition may inadvertently cause the consumer to recall that product at the time of purchase. In addition, competitors may legally challenge claims of superiority or respond with comparative ads of their own.

In general, comparative messages may be more useful for companies with a lower market share, since they have little to lose by confronting the leader. For them, the potential gain in consumer awareness outweighs the likelihood that a large competitor will launch a counterattack. Royal Crown Cola used this tactic by showing Coke and Pepsi involved in a bizarre fishing contest for consumers. The intent was to remind people that there are other colas.[22]

MEDIA

The **media** are the means for transmitting messages from the sender to the receiver. There are three categories—personal, mass, and mixed—each with its advantages and disadvantages, as summarized in Figure 14-3.

Personal media involve direct contact, such as face-to-face communication or telephone conversations. These two-way exchanges allow for creative solutions to the consumer's problem. There is ample opportunity for relationships to form. Each party can assess the characteristics of the other. Although the telephone does not provide physical contact, it has dramatic cost advantages over personal encounters. Hot lines are an effective way to support customers after a sale. They not only help when problems arise with a product but also offer all kinds of advice that ultimately can maintain customer loyalty. The Microsoft On-line Institute provides consumer assistance and product training through a combination of self-paced tutorials and live instructors.[23] The disadvantage of personal media is expense. Each representative can only have a limited number of conversations, and the costs associated with hiring, training, and motivating people can be very high.

The mass media include television, radio, magazines, billboards, and brochures. Services are readily available to help plan for and acquire space in most markets around the world. CIO Communications, Inc., for instance, offers a resource center on the Web to assist with media planning.[24] Consequently, messages can be developed prior to being communicated through a range of nonpersonal sources. Since there are many media choices, nearly all customers can be contacted at a reasonable cost. The downside of using the mass media is the lack of interactive or two-way communication. Because it is impossible to get quick feedback, a great deal is spent beforehand on research that listens to the customer. Furthermore, ad preparation can be expensive and/or take a long time.

The mixed media approach combines personal and mass communication and has many of the benefits of both. First, material can be developed well in advance and offered in both print (fax) and audio (via Internet) formats. Advanced technology such as the PageFast software communication tool can connect fax machines to the Web. The promotion for PageFast reads: "If your firm depends on rapid customer response, and your customer base has access

Media
The channels through which messages are communicated.

	Examples	Advantages	Disadvantages
Personal Media	Face to face	Two-way communication	Expensive
	Telephone	Allows for creative problem solving	Time consuming
		Flexible tailoring of messages	Parties must be brought together at one time
		Immediate response	
	Television	Messages can be developed prior to sending	
	Radio	Low cost	Messages tend to be one way
Mass Media	Magazines	Many media choices	Preparations are expensive
	Newspapers	Reaches most customers inexpensively	Harder to obtain feedback
	Billboards		
	Brochures		
Mixed (Personal & Mass Combined)	Fax	Delayed or interactive	Receiver needs technology
	Internet	Two-way communication	Lack of consumer experience
	Answering machine	Low cost	

Figure 14-3 Media Advantages and Disadvantages

to the Web, give them an alternate method of letting you know they need your attention." This use of mixed media provides effective two-way communication at a low cost.[25] Second, because mixed media can reach large numbers simultaneously, the technique is very cost effective. A possible disadvantage is that fax and voice mail numbers are the property of the receiver, so the sender must be careful to respect privacy. A definite disadvantage is that many consumers lack the necessary technology or the experience to use it.

INTERPRETATION BY RECEIVERS: DECODING

Strong communications begin with an understanding of target audiences. People are not passive receivers of communications. In fact, they resist persuasion by refuting arguments, attacking the source, distorting messages, rationalizing, and tuning out. Many consumers regard marketing messages as "tricks" to make them purchase a particular product.

Refuting arguments is one way consumers resist persuasion. Weak messages may backfire as consumers create stronger counterarguments in their own mind. Another defense mechanism is to attack the source. Consumers may discount claims of comfort, prestige, or gas mileage because they don't trust the automobile company. All messages are automatically rejected. Attacking the source rather than the ideas being communicated is common in politics. Whenever politicians don't have a very convincing case, they are likely to strike out at the people who reject their arguments.

Intelligence and self-esteem have a lot to do with susceptibility to persuasion. Highly intelligent people are more likely to be influenced by logical, precise, and complex information. Others have to be very carefully led through an argument. Depending on the audience, marketers should let some people draw their own conclusions. It is not surprising that people with low-self esteem tend to be easily persuaded. They often rely on others in developing attitudes and making choices. Messages designed for such people should avoid complex arguments.[26]

CONSUMER FEEDBACK

Listening is an important way to learn what consumers think. Feedback is essential to a customer-focused company, and it helps the marketer adjust communications. Today, many organizations consider listening to be the first step in the communication process, even before the message is created. Through the consumer they determine needs and wants as well as how to structure communication.

THE COMMUNICATION MIX

TYPES OF COMMUNICATION ACTIVITIES

The five main types of communication activity are personal selling, sales promotion, advertising, public relations, and sponsorship. Figure 14-4 describes some characteristics of each type.

Personal selling
Face-to-face or other individual communication between a buyer and a seller.

Personal Selling **Personal selling** requires person-to-person communication between buyer and seller. Generally, this occurs face to face, although it also may involve the telephone, video conferencing, or interactive computer linkages. Despite its relatively high cost, personal selling continues to be the most important part of business-to-business marketing and is also significant in sales of big-ticket consumer items, such as autos, computers, and housing. The objective of most personal selling is to build loyal relationships with customers that result in profitable sales volume.

Companies are increasingly using personal selling to reach consumers. For example, door-to-door sales in the United States have risen 38 percent in recent years, and in international markets they total $57 billion.[27] Since personal selling provides two-way communication, it is possible to engage in a dialogue that leads to problem solving. Because this is generally the most expensive form of contact, salespeople are trained to do the best possible job of helping a customer find solutions through use of their product.

Advertising
Paid communication through nonpersonal channels.

Advertising **Advertising** is paid nonpersonal communication from an identified sponsor using mass media to persuade or influence an audience. It includes newspapers, television, radio, magazines, direct mail, billboards, the Internet, and point-of-sale displays. It is considered mass communication because the same message is sent throughout the targeted audience and the rest of the market. A major objective of advertising is to support product

	Personal Selling	Sales Promotion	Advertising	Public Relations	Sponsorship
focus	Person-to-person interaction	Support of sales activity	Mass communication directioned at target segments	Unpaid publicity that enhances the company and its products	Cash or resources in support of an event
Objective	Develop business relationship resulting in loyal customers	Obtain immediate sale and remind after the sale	Position the product and/or increase sales	Gain a favorable impression	Be associated with influential groups
Example	Pharmaceutical salesperson	Point-of-sale displays	Billboards	Press releases	Team sponsorship
	Computer and tele-communications sales	T-shirts with company name	TV ads	Charitable projects	Sport tournaments
	Retail sales	Special sales	Magazine ads	Civic leadership	Arts events
	Consulting sales	2-for-1 offers	Direct mail	Company spokesperson gives association speech	Association events
Appeal	Personal	Move buyer to action	Mass	Mass	Market segment
Cost per Customer	Very high	Low	Low to high	Very low	High to low
Amount and Speed of Feedback	A lot and immediately	A little and fairly fast	A little and delayed	A little and fairly fast	A lot and fast

Figure 14-4   *The Characteristics of Communication Activities*

positioning. The same basic theme usually is sent through all advertising channels. For example, television ads for Charmin have been reinforced by point-of-sale displays featuring Mr. Whipple, the "don't squeeze the Charmin" grocery clerk. Depending on audience size, cost per consumer can be very low. For example, although an ad for the 1997 Super Bowl had a price tag of more than $2.6 million per minute, the exposure per person averaged about two cents.[28] Because advertising plays a supportive role, it is sometimes difficult to determine just how well it works, in relation to other parts of the marketing mix. For example, the effects of accompanying shifts in product distribution and pricing often are felt more quickly.

Sales Promotion   **Sales promotion** is communication designed to stimulate immediate purchases using tools such as coupons, contests, and free samples. Since the approach generally is designed to stimulate immediate purchases, its effectiveness can be easily measured. Sometimes sales promotion is meant to remind customers after the sale, which contributes to relationship building. For example, a box of cookies may contain a discount coupon for the next box. Sales promotions usually last a short time. For the 1996 Summer Olympics in Atlanta, Coke's effort included a temporary theme park, in-store promotions, and a Web site, among others. To counter its rival, Pepsi made its biggest push ever with Pepsi Stuff. Consumers could use proof-of-purchase redemptions to buy brand-label merchandise unrelated to the soft drink. Although both endeavors were temporary, volume increased for both companies during the promotion.[29]

Public Relations   **Public relations** is the use of publicity and other nonpaid forms of communication designed to present the firm and its products positively. Because they are not paying for space, companies do not have total control over what is disseminated. The most common public relations channel is the news media. Of course, publicity can be negative. For example, a Swedish reporter claimed that a new formula of Unilever's detergents ruined clothes. Key competitor Procter & Gamble sent that information, along with its own confirming lab reports, to journalists throughout Europe. The Dutch Consumer's Council recommended that people refrain from using the Unilever detergent until the old formula was rereleased.[30]

Sponsorships   A major form of communication is sponsorships, which are reaching 10 to 15 percent of promotion budgets as we enter the 21st century. A **sponsorship** is the exchange of money (or some other form of value) in return for a public association with an event. Gen-

Sales promotion
Communication designed to stimulate immediate purchases, using tools such as coupons, contests, and free samples.

Public relations
Unpaid promotion designed to present the firm and its products in a positive light in the buyer's mind.

Sponsorship
The exchange of money (or some other form of value) in return for a public association with an event.

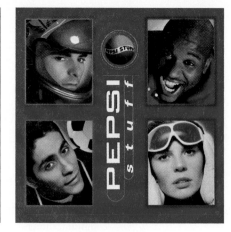

Pepsi has motivated purchases through its Pepsi Stuff promotions.

eral Motors' Cadillac and Buick divisions sponsor many Professional Golfers' Association tournaments. In fact, Cadillac has made the Seniors PGA Tour possible. Coca-Cola, PepsiCo, General Motors, Anheuser-Busch, United Parcel Service, and Nissan are among the largest sponsors of sports. Major League Baseball and Pepsi have a five-year, $50 million pact. The tagline, "Pepsi: the choice of Major League Baseball," will be prominently communicated.[31] Up to $5 billion is spent on sports sponsorships in the United States alone, approximately two-thirds of it earmarked for a specific event. Many college football bowls have obtained sponsors, such as FedEx for the Orange Bowl.

Sponsorships usually are integrated with all other aspects of the communications mix. General Motors takes its key dealers and business customers to the NASCAR racing events it sponsors, features the races in its magazine ads, and cites testimonials from NASCAR drivers. This benefits both parties to the sponsorship.

FACTORS AFFECTING THE COMMUNICATION MIX

Marketers must consider several factors in selecting the communication mix. The most important are whether the audience is the business-to-business or consumer market, whether a push or pull strategy is desirable, the product's stage in the life cycle, and whether opinion leaders will play a role.

Business versus Consumer Markets All forms of marketing communication are important in both business-to-business and consumer marketing. Yet, the emphasis is different in each area, as seen in Figure 14-5. Personal selling is most important in marketing to businesses, while advertising dominates in the consumer products arena. Sales promotion is equally important in both and outweighs advertising in business markets. Public relations is relatively less important in both. One reason for these differences is costs. Per exposure, television advertising costs less than a penny; a print ad about 1 cent; direct mail, $1; a telephone call, $10, and face-to-face personal selling, more than $200.[32] Although public relations involves no such expenditure, it cannot compare to the other forms in terms of effectiveness and the degree of message control.

Pull strategy

An attempt to influence consumers directly so they will "pull" the product through the distribution channel.

Pull versus Push Strategies Marketers attempt to influence the market through either a push or pull strategy, as illustrated in Figure 14-6. In many cases they use both. A **pull strategy** attempts to influence consumers directly. Communication is designed to build demand so consumers will "pull" the product through the channel of distribution. In other words, consumers ask retailers for the product, who in turn ask wholesalers, who in turn contact the manufacturer. One popular pull strategy for automakers is to offer consumers credit cards that provide rebates on new car purchases.[33]

While pull strategies tend to be used primarily for consumer products, they also have a place in business-to-business marketing. For example, marketers of electrical control and distribution equipment often target the purchasing agent with their messages. Sales representatives call on design firms, who then specify that particular electrical equipment in the engineering design.

414

Figure 14-5 Communication Mix for Business versus Consumer Markets

The **push strategy** involves communicating to distribution channel members, who in turn promote to the end user. This is particularly common in industrial or business-to-business marketing. Marketers often train distribution channel members on the sales techniques they believe are most suited to their products. The push technique is also used in retail marketing. When Intel decided to capitalize on its already strong brand name, it concentrated on the distribution channel, particularly on educating sales associates at the retail level. An entire program was developed, including point-of-purchase (POP) kits, literature, and a sales force that visited such major accounts as CompUSA and Computer City to teach personnel about Intel products. The "Intel at Retail" program was introduced at a trade show.[34]

Often, a push-pull strategy is appropriate. The combination approach sells to the channel and to the end user. This can speed product adoption and strengthen market share. As we learned in chapter 12, conflicts often occur between the marketing organization and its distributors. For example, in the food industry, retailers want to carry products that yield the greatest profitability. Since these may not be brands with the strongest pull, retailers may charge marketers for shelf space. Essentially, they are being paid to push the product to the end user. Using a pull strategy to create strong demand at the consumer level makes channel members more willing to handle the product.

Push strategy
An attempt to influence the distribution channel, which in turn will "push" the product through to the user.

Figure 14-6 Pull versus Push Strategies

Communications for the "Tickle Me Elmo" doll had to be altered to match the stages of its product life cycle.

Product's Stage in the Life Cycle By now it should be apparent that the communication mix is related to the product's stage in the life cycle. Consumers need to be informed and educated about new products, whereas they may need to be persuaded to purchase during growth and early maturity. Reminders and reinforcement are most appropriate in the mature and declining phases of the life cycle. Think about the holiday craze for the Sesame Street "Tickle Me Elmo" doll. To make consumers aware of the new product, Tyco sent 200 dolls to the producers of the Rosie O'Donnell Show. The Elmos were shown being tossed into the audience, and Tyco's promotion paid off. But when the dolls began selling out across the country, Tyco altered its communication approach by temporarily pulling television ads, hoping to avoid ill-will from consumers who could not find Elmo in stores.[35] In other words, communications were adjusted to match the stages of the product life cycle.

Opinion Leadership Marketing communications reach consumers directly and indirectly. Figure 14-7 illustrates both paths. In **one-step communication,** all members of the target audience are simultaneously exposed to the same message. **Multiple-step communication** uses influential members of the target audience, known as **opinion leaders,** to filter a message before it reaches other group members, modifying its effect positively or negatively for the rest of the group.[36]

One-step communication
Communication in which all audience members are simultaneously exposed to the same marketing message.

Multiple-step communication
Communications in which opinion leaders filter messages and modify positively or negatively their effect on the rest of the group.

Opinion leader
Influential member of a target audience who first screens messages sent by marketers.

Because of their important role, opinion leaders have often been called gatekeepers to indicate the control they have over ideas flowing into the group. Marketers interested in maximizing communication effectiveness nearly always attempt to identify opinion leaders. Opinion leaders are open to communications from all sources. They are more inclined to be aware of information regarding a broad range of subjects. They read a lot, talk with salespeople and other people who have information about products. Opinion leaders can have a sort of multiplier effect, intensifying the strength of the message if they respond positively and pass it on to others. Consequently, the resources used to gain support from opinion leaders are probably well spent.

Public figures are often opinion leaders. Consider the sales boost for several titles after Oprah Winfrey introduced her "book of the month club" feature. She has influenced so many consumers with her highly regarded opinion that her selections have become best sellers.[37] After Bill Clinton praised Walter Mosley's books in his 1992 campaign, sales rose tremendously. Mosley's first novel, *Devil in a Blue Dress,* even became a movie in 1995 as a result of the publicity.[38]

DEVELOPING THE IMC PLAN

Now that we have examined the factors influencing the process, let us see how an integrated marketing communication plan is built. The steps are outlined in Figure 14-8. The IMC plan should never be developed in isolation from the strategic marketing plan. It's the responsibility of strategic marketing personnel to define the role of communication in the overall marketing strategy. Usually, the IMC plan is designed to position the organization and its products in a manner consistent with that strategy.

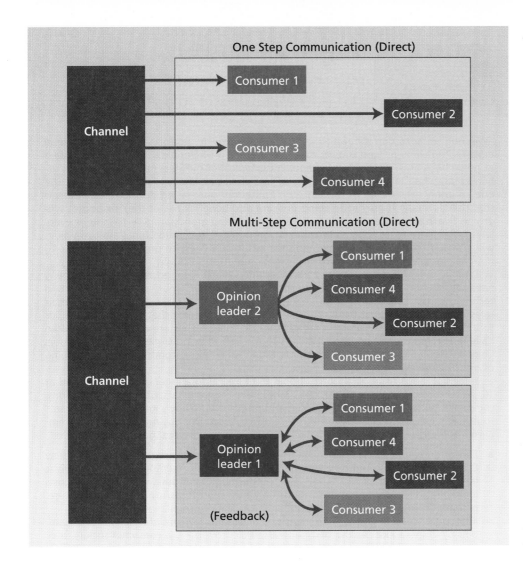

Figure 14-7 Opinion Leadership

SELECTING AND UNDERSTANDING TARGET AUDIENCES

Understanding the target audience is the most important part of communications planning. First, remember that the overall market needs to be segmented, and each segment should be treated uniquely. For every target audience, communications experts need to understand all aspects of consumer behavior: where, how, and why they buy as well as how they obtain and process information. In new and developing markets, companies sometimes must operate more by trial and error as they gradually come to know buying habits. For instance, as the People's Republic of China encourages more businesses to set up shop, multinationals are learning more about the children and youth segment of this burgeoning market. See the diversity feature, "Multinationals Target China's 'Little Emperors' with Ads and Promotions."

DETERMINING OBJECTIVES AND SELECTING THE IMC MIX

Consumers move from a lack of awareness about brands to purchase and loyalty. This process of increasing involvement can be described by hierarchy models. The most straightforward

---

Steps in the IMC Plan
1 Select and understand target audiences.
2 Determine the communication objectives and select the communication mix.
3 Develop the budget.
4 Implement.
5 Measure the results.

Figure 14-8 Developing the Communication Plan

CONNECTING WITH DIVERSITY

MULTINATIONALS TARGET CHINA'S "LITTLE EMPERORS" WITH ADS AND PROMOTIONS

"We used to go to dim sum on Sunday morning with the old folks," laments a Chinese mother, "but now my son is nine, he insists we go to McDonald's®. Otherwise he stays at home. What can we do?" This complaint is typical of mothers in China's cities. In urban areas, where a government policy of one child per family is strictly enforced, the one and only exerts a lot of influence on household purchasing decisions, especially if that child is a boy. These "little emperors" are also beneficiaries of the "six-pocket syndrome," with as many as six doting adults—parents and grandparents—to indulge every whim. There are more than 300 million children under age 14 in China, most of whom will grow up to be more wealthy than their parents. It's easy to understand why multinational companies are aiming their promotional efforts straight for the kiddies.

Danone S.A. of France, Nestlé of Switzerland, and U.S.-based H. J. Heinz Company have set up shop in China, marketing such foods as yogurt, milk, and cheese. Toy and technology companies like Bandai, Lego, VTech Holdings, and IBM are stepping up their sales efforts. For multinationals, Chinese children are the key that will open the door to a burgeoning market. Even companies with products that are not sold to children have redirected their promotional efforts to the younger set. General Electric sponsors China's version of Sesame Street in the hopes of instilling its corporate name in the mind of a future generation.

Television advertising is about to boom in China, with annual growth estimated at 10 percent or higher. And while the Chinese are less familiar with sales promotions, companies will need to provide coupons and point-of-purchase samples to spur parents to buy what they see on TV. Not much is known about the buying habits of little emperors and their parents, but advertisers have discovered several guidelines.

- **Education is a key value.** In China it's not uncommon for pregnant women to play English and Chinese tapes to their bellies to give their budding babies a linguistic head start. Mothers pay $70 for a VTech English alphabet desk, even though it costs more than they earn in a week. With only one child to assure the family's future, parents of little emperors are receptive to ads that emphasize learning.
- **Kids covet Western goods.** Nike shoes and Western blue jeans are seen as status symbols by Chinese kids. As the first generation to grow up in a consumer society, they are tuned in to messages of Western ads and don't want to "buy Chinese." Still, as consumer culture develops, advertisers will need to differentiate their products rather than just feature the "Western" label.
- **Chinese culture can't be ignored.** For thousands of years, Confucian tradition has emphasized respect for authority and family harmony. Ads in China uniformly portray happy families. Smart-aleck teens arguing with parents would not appeal to Chinese consumers. Advertisers must walk a thin line in marketing Western goods with a Chinese flavor. Coca-Cola China, Ltd., spent two years on market research before introducing a new fruit drink. Not only does Tian Yu Di (heaven and earth) feature a Chinese name, but also the attractive container has an image of China's Yellow Mountain and calligraphy by a Chinese master.

Sources: Helen Johnstone, "Little Emperors Call the Shots," *Asian Business,* September 1996, pp. 67–70; Sally D. Goll, "China's (Only) Children Get the Royal Treatment," *Wall Street Journal,* February 8, 1995, B1; and "Wooing Little Emperors," *Business China,* July 22, 1996, pp. 1–2.

---

of these is AIDA, which stands for attention, interest, desire, and action.[39] Figure 14-9 depicts AIDA and a more detailed version that includes awareness, knowledge, liking, preference, conviction, and purchase. For example, imagine that an in-line skater suddenly crosses your path and breaks your concentration (awareness). Next, you ask friends how they like their in-line skates, and you observe how others use the product (knowledge). Perhaps you rent a pair and have so much fun that you consider purchasing skates of your own (liking). By talking to friends and reading ads you develop a brand preference. Elaborate in-store displays and product guarantees convince you to buy a particular brand (conviction). Finally, you decide to purchase the skates with your credit card.[40]

As marketers plan their communication activities, they must keep the objective in mind. Is it to create awareness, build brand preference, or encourage purchase? The IMC mix will vary considerably, depending on the objective. To create awareness and product knowledge,

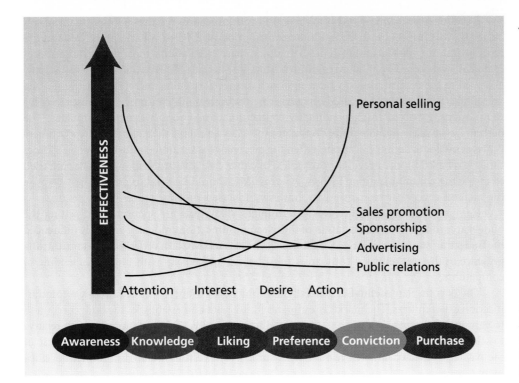

Figure 14-9 Effectiveness of Main Types of Communication at Different Stages in the Consumer Buying Process

advertising is very effective. It gains attention and even can lead to liking and brand preference. Once desire is created, however, sales promotion may be more useful. At this point the customer is more influenced by personal selling, sales promotions, and sponsorships. Attending a sponsored event could make the product so immediately salient that the consumer decides to buy. Sales promotions involving coupons, price incentives, or in-store samples may move buyers to action by reinforcing their conviction to try the brand. The effectiveness of personal selling increases dramatically in the later stages of the buying process. This is especially true for high-priced items in consumer markets, but in some business markets personal selling may be necessary just to gain attention. Although public relations appears to be least useful—because it tapers off after the attention stage and remains low compared to the others—keep in mind the lower cost. Other than the fairly minor expense of creating the public relations message, there is no cost for delivering it.

MasterCard targets 13 million college students by using all five types of communication. It provides scholarships to students in the American Marketing Association (sponsorship) and conducts free seminars on responsible finances (public relations). Through television spots and other media (advertising), cards with special features, such as low finance rates (sales promotion), are offered to the students. Often representatives visit campus to convince students to sign up for a card (personal selling), for which they receive a free gift (sales promotion).[41]

DEVELOPING THE COMMUNICATION BUDGET

The communication budget falls within expenditures for the entire marketing mix. Consequently, establishing the specific amount for IMC requires an understanding of the overall marketing strategy, the financial resources available, and the contribution communications is expected to make. In allocating IMC money it must be remembered that some activities can be started or stopped quickly, such as advertising and sales promotion. Personal selling often must be adjusted more slowly, since time is required to hire, train, and deploy the sales force.

The IMC budget is determined in two steps. First, the total allocation is decided. Second, the amount for each type of communication is assigned.

Determining the Overall Budget   The first issue is how much it will cost to accomplish the objective. Generally, communication objectives are established once a year. Two-thirds of advertising budgets for the following year are submitted to top marketing management during September or October, and nearly 80 percent are approved by November.[42] Most IMC budgets are based on one of the following: percentage of sales, competitive budgeting, payout plan, or cost of tasks that must be performed to accomplish objectives.

Deciding precisely how much to invest in communication requires a lot of financial calculations. It is important to establish the contribution of IMC to volume objectives and determine resulting profits and cash flows. In doing these calculations, most organizations forecast sales levels based on total expenditures. The latter include all costs that can be realistically allocated to the communication campaign such as special training and compensation for the sales force. The forecasts are based on marketing research about consumer responses to communications, expected IMC spending by competitors, and product demand estimates. The percentage of sales method simply estimates the sales level and then allocates a certain percentage of sales to communications. Often the percentage is set at the industry average. Sometimes it is based on the previous year's sales. In either case, the problem is that sales are used to create the communications budget, whereas IMC should be used to create sales. Because the method is very easy to administer, however, it is used widely.

Competitive budgeting involves determining what rivals are spending and setting the budget accordingly. The deregulation of the telecommunications industry probably influenced the budgeting strategies of large companies like AT&T and MCI. In order to maintain a strong presence in the market, such companies must be able to keep up with the IMC spending of competitors.

The payout plan method is generally used for new products that require high communication expenditures. The marketer estimates future sales and establishes the budget required to gain initial acceptance and trial of the product. Generally, IMC costs are very high relative to sales, in some cases even greater. The early expenditures are deemed reasonable because of the payback expected in later years. This is similar to investing money in product development.

The task method sets specific sales targets or other objectives and then determines what activities and amounts are required to accomplish them. This approach can be very complex and tends to be used by large organizations in highly competitive environments. Marketers must have very accurate information and considerable experience in order to develop the extensive models necessary. The task method is superior to the others because so much detailed attention is paid to how IMC contributes to accomplishing objectives.

Allocating the Budget   Communication works synergistically. In other words, as Martha Stewart suggested at the beginning of this chapter, investments in one type of communication may help other types accomplish their objectives. A salesperson benefits tremendously from awareness created by advertising and from purchase incentives due to sales promotion. The integrated aspect of marketing communication needs to be kept in mind when deciding the allocation for each activity. This process requires considerable and continuous dialogue among marketing team members. In many cases, data are fed into computer simulations that help determine the best allocations. In other cases, the team simply estimates what is required. In companies with major brands, an average of 18 executives are involved, including senior management media and advertising staff, marketing personnel, brand marketing management, and sales personnel.[43] The allocations may be determined by very specific objectives. When Nike wanted to increase traffic in retail outlets, it budgeted more for signage. When Westinghouse wanted to increase name recognition, it shifted resources from the sales force to advertising.

IMPLEMENTATION

Implementation of IMC plan tends to be done by functional specialists with considerable experience in their field. There are ample career opportunities in these areas—such as personal selling, advertising, and public relations—because each is multifaceted and challenging. Marketers strive to obtain uniquely talented employees and suppliers to carry out communication programs. No matter how good the plan, without creative and professional implementation, all is lost.

CAREER TIP   The Web is an abundant source for information regarding advertising, public relations, personal selling, and other areas. Use a search engine to obtain lists of organizations worldwide. You'll have an opportunity to explore your career of interest or research a specific company. You will also discover links to networks where you can post a resumé, receive daily news briefs, or access a job information service.

The first decision is how much to do in-house and how much to outsource. For example, personal selling can be done by company personnel, manufacturer representatives (private salespersons), or distributors. Likewise, companies must decide whether to do their own advertising and sales promotion or hire outsiders. Most large and medium-sized firms outsource much of their IMC implementation. Often representatives from these advertising and promotion agencies work on-site with the client's marketing executives and personnel. Chapters 15 and 16 will explain in more detail how to implement each type of communication activity.

Measuring IMC Results

It was John Wanamaker, a famous 19th-century retailer, who first said: "I know that half of the money I spend on advertising is wasted, but I can never figure out which half." He was referring to the fact that many messages may never reach much of the target audience. The real questions are, Who is reached by a communication, and what does it accomplish relative to the goals established in the plan?

Why is it difficult to estimate the results of communication? The major problem is isolating the effects of one part of the IMC plan to determine its relative influence on product performance. Most marketers start by identifying criteria or measures. Performance measures are variables or factors that tell us how well the organization or product is doing. Common measures are market share, sales level, and profitability. Other factors are often used, such as number of loyal customers, amount of brand recognition, brand image, and knowledge of the product.

Once performance measures are selected, the task of assessing IMC influence can begin. Very seldom is only one part of the IMC mix adjusted at a time, and competitors' activities are virtually never stable. So determining the precise effect of communication is rarely possible. When Nike introduces a new model, how much of its success can be attributed to pricing, product distribution, customer service, or promotion? Still, by monitoring IMC expenditures and performance measures for a large number of companies and then applying statistical analysis, researchers can get a good idea of the overall effect of IMC. This information is very useful in determining whether objectives are being met and whether changes are required.

ISSUES IN COMMUNICATION

Diversity

Effective communications are carefully targeted. The vast differences among consumers create opportunities for a wide variety of promotions to meet their needs. For example, 49 million Americans have some form of disability, and marketers are changing the way they communicate with these consumers. Long ignored, the one in five Americans who are disabled represent several substantial target segments.[44] Marketers now have a new vehicle for communicating with many of these consumers—the Internet.

Until recently the Web was not very user friendly for people with limited vision or dexterity. The Productivity Works of Trenton, however, created WebSpeak software, which reads computer screens out loud. It allows many people who have difficulty with traditional formats to browse and surf. This technology helps not only disabled consumers but also the large number of Americans who are illiterate.[45] It provides an interactive communication vehicle that has numerous opportunities, ranging from simple product descriptions to more persuasive messages.

Computer software is not the only way companies are connecting with disabled consumers. In chapter 11 it was pointed out that hotels are reaching out to this market segment. The travel industry is launching a public awareness campaign to communicate with both travelers and travel agents about promotions targeted at the disabled. The American Society of Travel Agents (ASTA) has produced a $25,000 video that illustrates industry efforts, and the number of travel agencies that specialize in arrangements for disabled consumers is also growing.[46]

Promotions in general are becoming more inclusive by depicting the disabled. MCI, for example, has a new advertising campaign featuring the themes of equality, freedom, and happiness. One television ad shows a deaf child, a grandmother, and a young man who are all connected to the Internet through MCI.[47] The print media are another forum for reaching the disabled. *We,* a magazine created for Americans with disabilities, has a circulation of 100,000. It provides marketers with a great medium for communicating about products and resources available to disabled consumers.[48]

ETHICS

Marketers must be careful about how they communicate. The American Marketing Association Code of Ethics states that acceptable standards include "avoidance of false and misleading advertising, rejection of high pressure manipulations, or misleading sales tactics, and avoidance of communications that use deception or manipulation." Despite these guidelines, the ethical boundaries for promotion are not always clear.

Communications targeting children have long faced public scrutiny. Under pressure from consumer groups and the federal government, R. J. Reynolds agreed to stop using the hip Joe Camel in its tobacco advertisements. The alcohol industry has also been accused of knowingly pushing products to minors. A survey by Competitive Media Reporting during one randomly selected week showed that the audience for beer commercials consisted primarily of youths under the drinking age. During an episode of *Beavis and Butt-Head,* in which Molson beer advertised, Nielsen media data showed that 69 percent of the viewers were under age 21. That same week Anheuser-Busch ran an ad during music video programming on BET, and 70 percent of the audience was younger than 21. The Beer Institute's guidelines note that "beer advertising . . . should not be placed in magazines, newspapers, television programs, radio programs, or other media where most of the audience is reasonably expected to be below the legal purchase age."[49] Are those standards ignored? In response to the controversy, Anheuser-Busch recently pulled its ads from MTV, and Coors has a policy of not purchasing MTV airtime at all.[50]

Communications perceived as inappropriate for children can create problems for a company even if health risks aren't involved. Consider PepsiCo's Mountain Dew "Extreme Network" campaign. The summer promotion offered beepers with six months of free airtime to consumers who mailed in 10 proofs of purchase and $29.99. Mountain Dew pledged to page thousands of the beeper owners weekly, giving them the chance to win various discounts and prizes. While some marketers viewed this as a trendy way to communicate, others saw it as a way to exploit a young, impressionable audience. Janine Bovsquette, vice president for marketing at Pepsi, says: "Beepers are the mainstream communications tool for the '90's. It seemed like the perfect fit." To reach its goal of 500,000 participants, Mountain Dew promoted to young people using ads in *Spin* magazine, promotional packaging, and commercials on MTV.[51]

TECHNOLOGY THAT BUILDS RELATIONSHIPS

In communications, marketers often use technology to reach consumers and establish relationships. New advances make it possible to connect with customers quickly. It is estimated that the number of on-line electronic mailboxes may double over the next two years, from 75 million to 150 million. E-mail is rapidly becoming as common a medium for communication as the telephone. In addition to the Web sites already developed for promotional purposes, new graphics formats enable marketers to send advertisements directly to consumers via e-mail. Netscape also offers a program called InBox Direct, which allows on-line editions of newspapers and magazines to be delivered directly to an e-mail address. Unlike traditional e-mail, the pages include the photos and advertisements just as they appear in the Web version.

Unlike the Web, e-mail communications can be targeted more directly to a select audience, providing them with information that will be useful for making a purchase. Another use for e-mail is electronic billing. The invoice appears on the screen, and the consumer need only enter a credit card number to pay. Customers may establish loyal relationships with companies who can provide this type of convenience.[52]

Clearly the Internet offers exciting new targeting opportunities that will increasingly affect the way marketers combine and orchestrate various communications activities to create the most effective IMC mix. In the next two chapters each of the five main activities that constitute the communications mix will be examined in more detail. Chapter 15 focuses on the mass communication activities of advertising, sales promotion, and public relations, including sponsored events. Chapter 16 is devoted to personal selling and sales force management.

CONNECTED: SURFING THE NET

Snapple

www.snapple.com

THIS CHAPTER'S RELATIONSHIPS FEATURE MENTIONS A number of companies that are taking integrated marketing communications to a new level and getting consumers involved. To learn more about this type of interactive marketing, visit the Web site of Snapple and answer the following questions.

1. Once you arrive at the site, make the "liquid connection." Knowing that communication is at the heart of building relationships, explain how the "liquid connection" makes this possible.
2. Opinion leaders are an important factor in the communications mix. How does the Snapple Web site identify and gain input from opinion leaders? Can you think of any other features the site could offer to maximize leaders' influence on others?
3. Integrated marketing communications has numerous objectives. List the objectives the Snapple Web site accomplishes. Explain.
4. Select a press release that shows how Snapple uses one or more of the five main types of communication. Describe the characteristics, objective, appeal, cost (low, medium, high), and amount and speed of feedback for that type or types.

IBM

www.ibm.com

THIS CHAPTER'S DIVERSITY FEATURE, "MULTINATIONALS TARGET China's 'Little Emperors' with Ads and Promotions," discusses the efforts of various companies to reach the millions of children in China. IBM is one of many multinationals stepping up sales efforts to plant its name in the mind of future consumers. In order to learn more, visit the IBM Web site and answer the following questions.

1. New technology often enables marketers to communicate with customers more effectively. List several products or services offered by IBM and explain how they help marketers connect with customers.
2. What does the IBM Web site offer for connecting globally? Why might message characteristics need to be adjusted for various countries?
3. The Internet is a combination of personal and mass media. What are its advantages and disadvantages? With this in mind, what features of the IBM Web site are more and less effective in communicating with customers? Explain.

CHAPTER SUMMARY

OBJECTIVE 1: Understand the objectives of integrated marketing communications.

Integrated marketing communication (IMC) is the coordination of all information to the market in order to provide consistent, unified messages. Since each aspect of IMC—personal selling, advertising, sales promotion, public relations, and sponsorships—tends to work synergistically, integration is very important. Marketing communication has six objectives. First, it should provide useful information that improves customer decision making and consumption. Second, it creates demand to ensure that products will be consumed in sufficient quantities to justify their development, production, and distribution. Third, it supplies knowledge about the value of products, such as their benefits, features, and functions. Fourth, it helps differentiate products by describing their

uniqueness. Fifth, it helps close the sale by moving customers to action. Finally, it is critical in building the all-important relationship with customers and in securing their loyalty.

OBJECTIVE 2: Learn how the communication process provides the intended information for the market.

Traditionally, communication was seen as a one-way process—from seller to buyer—without a feedback loop. Today, a two-way process is more realistic. The sender needs to specify objectives, as discussed above. The sender's characteristics are important determinants of how well messages will be received. Source credibility is determined by expertise, trustworthiness, and attractiveness (or appeal). Encoding requires translating the message into terms that will be easily understood. Since message interpretation depends on consumer life experiences, a thorough comprehension of consumer behavior is required to do an adequate job of encoding. Message characteristics also play a major role. Marketers need to decide whether a one-sided or two-sided message is better; whether to supply conclusions; the order in which information will be presented; whether to use humor or fear appeals; and whether to use comparative messages. The choice of media—mass, personal, or mixed—also influences communications. Today, mixed media like the Internet are becoming more important. Audiences are not passive receivers; they interpret information by processing it. Their intelligence and self-esteem are important factors here.

OBJECTIVE 3: **Learn about the communication mix, including personal selling, advertising, sales promotion, sponsorships, and public relations.**

The communication mix has five major components. Each has particular advantages. Personal selling involves face-to-face contact or two-way technology linkages, such as the telephone or Internet. This allows dialog and interactive problem solving. Advertising is paid, nonpersonal communication. It reaches all members of the audience with the same "mass" message. Sales promotion uses a one-way message to motivate purchase, usually in the form of short-term incentives to buy. Sponsorship is paid support of an event. It associates the sponsor with the event and its participants. Public relations is nonpaid communication (publicity) about a company and its products. These messages are sometimes broadcast by sources considered to be unbiased so they can have considerable credibility.

OBJECTIVE 4: **Know the factors that influence the communications mix.**

The communication mix is influenced by several factors. First, business-to-business and consumer markets use different mixes. The former are dominated by personal selling, while the latter are dominated by sales promotion and advertising. Second, marketers use a push or pull communication strategy. A push strategy communicates to channel members, who in turn communicate to end users. A pull strategy communicates with end users, who in turn demand products from channel members. Third, communications must be suited to the product's stage in the life cycle in order to have the greatest effectiveness. Finally, marketing communications do not always work directly on consumers. There is often a two-stage process whereby opinion leaders filter information before it reaches others in the market.

OBJECTIVE 5: **Describe the steps in developing an integrated marketing communication plan.**

The IMC plan is an outgrowth of the marketing plan. It has five steps. First, select and understand target markets. Second, determine communication objectives and select the IMC mix. Third, develop the IMC budget in line with the overall strategic marketing plan. Fourth, implement the plan. Fifth, measure communication results and adjust accordingly.

OBJECTIVE 6: **Address diversity, ethics, and technology in communications.**

Many media are not accessible to physically impaired individuals, and other avenues must be used. One is the Internet, especially through innovative software.

Marketers must be careful not to cross ethical boundaries in their communications. They should avoid false and misleading ads and sales tactics as well as high-pressure manipulation. Targeting children is a questionable practice because they may easily be misled or manipulated.

Communication technology is providing better ways to connect with consumers and create relationships. E-mail is one example. Software makes interactive communication easier and more rapid than ever before.

REVIEW YOUR UNDERSTANDING

1. What is integrated marketing communication?
2. What are the six objectives of integrated marketing communication?
3. What is the one-way communication process? How does it differ from the two-way process?
4. What are message sender characteristics and why are they important?
5. What is encoding?
6. What message characteristics should be considered? How does each influence effectiveness?
7. What are personal, mass, and mixed media? What are the characteristics of each?
8. What factors influence how messages are interpreted? Describe each.
9. What are the main categories in the communication mix?
10. What factors influence the communication mix? Describe each.
11. What are the steps in building an integrated communication plan?
12. How does diversity offer an opportunity and a challenge to communication?
13. What aspects of communication are covered by the American Marketing Association Code of Ethics?
14. Name one way communication technology is helping to build relationships with consumers.

DISCUSSION OF CONCEPTS

1. Describe the various goals of communication. What helps determine communication objectives?
2. Why is it so important for marketers to understand the communication process? How does that process affect the development and implementation of a campaign?
3. The way in which a message is communicated to consumers is critically important to its success. Name some of the issues involved in developing a message.
4. How do consumers distort messages? Have you ever distorted a message directed at you? How can marketers combat this problem?
5. Why is the source of a message so important? What are the

three characteristics of a good spokesperson? Do you think one spokesperson can communicate effectively with the entire market? Why or why not?

6. Briefly describe the five steps in developing a communication plan. How are the plan and the company's overall marketing strategy related?

7. List the pros and cons of each type of communication activity: personal selling, sales promotion, advertising, sponsorship, and public relations. What factors help determine which one to select?

KEY TERMS AND DEFINITIONS

Advertising: Paid communication through nonpersonal channels.

Communication: The process of sending and receiving messages.

Encoding: Translating a message into terms easily understood by the target audience.

Integrated marketing communication (IMC): The coordination of advertising, sales promotion, personal selling, public relations, and sponsorship to reach consumers with a powerful effect in the market.

Media: The channels through which messages are communicated.

Multiple-step communication: Communication in which opinion leaders filter messages and modify positively or negatively their effect on the rest of the group.

One-sided message: A message that presents only arguments favorable to the source.

One-step communication: Communication in which all audience members are simultaneously exposed to the same marketing message.

Opinion leader: Influential member of a target audience who first screens messages sent by marketers.

Personal selling: Face-to-face or other individual communication between a buyer and a seller.

Promotion: The process whereby marketers inform, educate, persuade, remind, and reinforce consumers through communication.

Public relations: Unpaid promotion designed to present the firm and its products in a positive light in the buyer's mind.

Pull strategy: An attempt to influence consumers directly so they will "pull" the product through the distribution channel.

Push strategy: An attempt to influence the distribution channel, which in turn will "push" the product through to the user.

Sponsorship: The exchange of money (or some other form of value) in return for a public association with an event.

Sales promotion: Communication designed to stimulate immediate purchases, using tools such as coupons, contests, and free samples.

Two-sided message: A message that presents arguments that are unfavorable as well as favorable to the source.

REFERENCES

1. "Martha's Way," *Success,* January-February 1997, pp. 31–32; Keith J. Kelly, "More Martha Stewart on TV Is OK'd," *Advertising Age,* August 26, 1996, p. 4; Mark Adams, "The Franchise," *Brandweek,* March 4, 1996, pp. MR10–13; Keith J. Kelly, "Magazine of the Year," *Advertising Age,* March 11, 1996, pp. S1, S11; and Martin Pedersen, "Martha Stewart Cross-Merchandising," *Publisher's Weekly,* December 12, 1994, pp. 19–20.

2. Lisa Bannon, "Cosmetic Surgeons Need to Pay More Attention to Appearances," *Wall Street Journal Interactive Edition,* February 4, 1997, www.wsj.com.

3. Judann Pollack and Alice Z. Cuneo, "Multitude of Deals Could Hurt Martha," *Advertising Age,* November 19, 1996, www.adage.com.

4. William Leiss, Stephen Kline, and Sut Jhally, *Social Communication in Advertising: Persons, Products, and Images of Well-Being* (Toronto: Methuen 1986); and George Stigler, "The Economics of Information," *Journal of Political Economy.*

5. Advertisement for Deloitte & Touche, *Fortune,* March 4, 1996, pp. 13–20.

6. "Will We Have Fewer, But Smarter, Consumers?" *Frozen Food Age,* November 1994, p. 20–22.

7. David Kirkpatrick et al., "Riding the Real Trends in Technology," *Fortune,* February 19, 1996.

8. Marcy Magiera, "Promotional Marketer of the Year: Spielberg & MCA Put Together Dream Team—and Herd of "Jurassic" Licensees Couldn't Be Happier," *Advertising Age,* March 21, 1994, pp. S1, S8.

9. Motorola advertisement, *Fortune,* March 4, 1996, pp. 24–25.

10. Kat Bertrand, "The Power of Personality," *Business Marketing,* August 1992, p. 24–28.

11. "Packers' Favre for Mountain Dew," *Advertising Age,* July 10, 1997, www.adage.com.

12. Volvo advertisement, *Advertising Age,* May 9, 1994, p. 34; E-Plus advertisement, *Advertising Age,* June 27, 1994.

13. Kim Cleland and Chuck Ross, "BellSouth Makes $185 Mil Call to Western Int. Media," *Advertising Age,* September 2, 1996, www.adage.com.

14. Kim Cleland, "Telephone Rivals Recruit Athletes to Score Attention," *Advertising Age,* February 2, 1996, www.adage.com.

15. Emily Yoffe, "Hollywood Help Us!" *Newsweek,* October 1, 1990, p. 71.

16. Henry I. Miller, "Red Tape Is Blocking Oil Spill Cleanups," *Wall Street Journal Interactive Edition,* July 10, 1997.

17. Tara Parker-Pope, "Jewelry Marketers Coax Women to Splurge on Fine Jewelry," *Wall Street Journal Interactive Edition,* January 7, 1997.

18. Raju Narisetti, "Rubbermaid Opens Door to TV, Hoping to Put Houses in Order," *Wall Street Journal Interactive Edition,* February 4, 1997.

19. Harold L. Ross, Jr., "How to Create Effective Humorous Commercials Yielding above Average Brand Preference Change," *Marketing News,* March 26, 1976, p. 4.

20. Bob Garfield, "Super Bust," *Advertising Age,* www.adage.com, site visited January 29, 1997.

21. Cyndee Miller, "HIV Kits Target Untested Market," *Marketing News,* January 20, 1997, pp. 1, 11.

22. Bob Garfield, "RC Hooks a Winner When It Goes Fishing for Some Individuality," *Advertising Age,* June 13, 1994, p. 3.

23. moli.microsoft.com/, site visited on February 10, 1997.

24. www.cio.com/marketing/commhome.html, site visited on February 10, 1997.

25. www.pagefast.com/, site visited on February 10, 1997.

26. M. Zelner, "Self-Esteem, Self-Perception, and Influenceability," *Journal of Personality and Social Psychology* 25 (1973): 87–93.

27. Tara Parker-Pope and Lisa Bannon, "Avon's New Calling: Selling Mattel's Barbie Doll in China," *Wall Street Journal Interactive Edition,* May 1, 1997.

28. Jeff Jensen, "Tagliabue Sees Big Score Ahead for NFL TV Rights," *Advertising Age,* January 20, 1997, www.adage.com.

29. "Heads of Top Soft Drink Brands Bring Budget Artillery, Smarts to Battlefield," *Advertising Age,* January 31, 1997, www.adage.com, site visited January 31, 1997.

30. Laura Wentz and Michael Vandos, "$300 Million Washout—Unilever Struggles to Save Power Detergents," *Advertising Age,* June 13, 1994, pp. 1, 4.

31. "Pepsi Unveils MLB Pact Details," *Advertising Age,* March 20, 1997, www.adage.com.

32. Barton A. Weitz, Stephen B. Castleberry, and John F. Tanner, *Selling,* (Homewood, IL: Richard D. Irwin, 1992), p. 7.

33. Gary Levin, "For Ford and GM Loyalty in the Cards," *Advertising Age,* March 28, 1994, pp. 5–18; Jonathan Berry et al., "Data Base Marketing: A Potent New Tool for Selling," *Business Week,* September 5, 1994, pp. 56–62.

34. Jainel Pinkerton, "Intel Turns Inside Out," *Dealerscope,* January 1994, p. 37.

35. Joseph Pereira, "Toy Story: How Shrewd Marketing Made Elmo a Hit," *Wall Street Journal,* December 16, 1996, pp. B1, B10.

36. Jagdish N. Sheth, "Word-of-Mouth in Low Risk Innovations," *Journal of Advertising Research* 11 (1971): 15–8.

37. Jacqueline Blais, "Oprah Nod Unnerves 'Rapture' Writer," *USA Today,* May 13, 1997, www.usatoday.com.

38. Michael K. Frisby, "First Fan's Club: President's Attention Makes Writer Soar," *Wall Street Journal,* January 2, 1997, pp. 1, 36.

39. E. K. Strong, *The Psychology of Selling* (New York: McGraw-Hill, 1925). p. 9.

40. Robert J. Lavidge and Gary A. Steiner, "A Model For Predictive Measurements of Advertising Effectiveness," *Journal of Marketing,* October 1991, p. 61.

41. Ray Waddell, "MasterCard Music Tour Targets College Market," *Amusement Business,* April 12, 1993, p. 5; and Howard Schlossberg, "College Master Values Program Targets 13 Million 'Independents,'" *Marketing News,* March 15, 1993, p. 5.

42. J. Thomas Russell and W. Ronald Lane, *Kleppner's Advertising Procedure* (Upper Saddle River, NJ: Prentice Hall, 1993), p. 138.

43. Fairfield Research, Inc., cited in "Beginning the End of the Seige," *Brandweek,* July 27, 1992, p. 34.

44. Associated Press, "Awareness Campaign Promotes Travel for the Disabled," *USA Today,* January 13, 1997.

45. Associated Press, "New Browser Allows Disabled to Experience Surfing the Web," *Wall Street Journal Interactive Edition,* February 2, 1997, www. wsj.com.

46. Associated Press, "Awareness Campaign Promotes Travel for the Disabled," *USA Today,* January 13, 1997.

47. Kim Cleland, "MCI Unreels a New Branding Effort," *Advertising Age,* January 6, 1997, www.adage.com.

48. "'We' to Bow in February," *Advertising Age,* December 27, 1996, www. adage.com.

49. Sally Goll Beatty, "Are Beer Ads on 'Beavis and Butt-Head' Aimed at Kids," *Wall Street Journal,* January 6, 1997, pp. B1, B6.

50. Ibid.

51. "Beeper Promotion Raises Concern over Ethical Marketing Practices," *Marketing Today,* August 1996, p. 8.

52. J. William Gurley, "E-Mail Gets Rich," *Fortune,* February 17, 1997, pp. 146–148.

CASE 14

NIKE

*I*N 1964, PHIL KNIGHT AND his former track coach, William Bowerman, began selling shoes made by a Japanese company, Onitsuka Tiger Co., out of the back seat of Knight's car. To gain more control of their marketing efforts, Knight and Bowerman developed the Nike brand, named after the Greek goddess of victory. A Portland State University design student created the famous "swoosh" for $35. It represents a wing, to "embody the spirit of the winged goddess who inspired the most courageous and chivalrous warriors." From the onset, Knight's philosophy has been that people root for a favorite team or athlete, not a product. So Knight sold "the athletic ideals of determination, individuality, self-sacrifice, and winning." Beginning in 1973 with track star Steve Prefontaine, Nike has actively sponsored athletes with these attributes. Today, it invests hundreds of millions annually to gain sponsorship of world-class teams and players.

According to CEO Knight, 1997, Nike's 25th year, was the best year yet. Profitability hit record highs, and revenues were up 42%—to $9.2 billion. Sales were so strong that Nike's increase equaled the total annual sales of the number three company in the industry. Knight attributes success to a number of factors.

- The company is based on one brand, which has a genuine and distinct personality, and tangible, emotional connections to customers the world over.
- It is rooted in sports, the fastest growing culture, growing so fast that it is becoming the one, true international language.
- Nike has been around 25 years and has grown each year because "our horizon is more than 12 months away."
- It is made up of 17,000 teammates who "stood this industry on its head."
- They include the brightest, most committed, most sought-after people in the industry.

- Nike returns have been 10 times the Standard & Poor's 500 index average over the last ten years. Just $100 invested in Nike in 1987 would be worth $3,094 today!

The company Web site claimed that 1997 "was about doing a lot of things right in a lot of different places: in the research lab and in the warehouse, on billboards in Atlanta and on 57th and Fifth in New York, on the soccer pitch in Germany and in the paint on the playgrounds of Chicago." Moreover, Nike's ability to coordinate integrated marketing communications that really connect with customers is outstanding. For example, the "swoosh" is so familiar that the name no longer needs to appear along with it.

Nike strategically coordinates its television and print ads, sponsorships, Web site, an 800 number, billboards, and other media to form an effective mix of communications. The athletes who deliver its message are a major factor. For example, Michael Jordan is generally considered to be the best basketball player in history. At a time when Nike profits were sinking, Knight selected Jordan to reestablish the company's image. Spike Lee filmed spots depicting Jordan as the basketball player whose talent (and Nike shoes) enabled him to fly. Approximately 35 ads later, Jordan was the most popular athlete in the country, according to New York–based Marketing Evaluations.

A number of other famous athletes have elicited a tremendous response from customers, including tennis players John McEnroe and André Agassi, baseball player Nolan Ryan, football's Deion Sanders, track stars Carl Lewis and Alberto Salazar, and basketball players like Charles Barkley and Scottie Pippen. And not to be forgotten is the young Tiger Woods, who has a $40 million contract with Nike. The charisma, talent, expertise, and personality of such athletes delivers Nike's message. According to its Web site, "Nike exists to be the best sports and fitness company in the world. We are here to inspire and motivate the athlete in all of us and advocate the love of sports. We live in the heart of sports and the athletes who play them."

And Nike is expanding its total market with integrated marketing communications. It is founder of P.L.A.Y. (Participate in the Lives of America's Youth), a multimillion-dollar program to promote healthy, active lifestyles among young people. There's also Niketown, a retailing effort to make a more personal connection with customers. Niketown stores feature basketball courts where customers can try out shoes, multiscreen televisions to display Nike promotions, and apparel autographed by Nike athletes.

Nike's June 1996 to May 1997 fiscal year was an amazing year for women's sports, beginning with Olympic gold for the U.S. women's soccer, basketball, and softball teams. Nike was at the forefront in sponsorships and involvement. When the company was launched 25 years ago, a mere one in 30 school-aged girls were involved in sports. Today that number has jumped to one in five. In 1996, Nike spent an estimated $15 million on communications directed at women, featuring tennis stars Mary Pierce and Monica Seles and volleyball player Gabrielle Reece. In 1997 its focus on women's sports reached new levels, including sponsorship of the WNBA and multimillion dollar contracts for such players as Lisa Leslie and Rebecca Lobo.

With a marketing budget of more than $250 million, Nike reaches consumers globally with events like Hoop Heroes, where Michael Jordan, Charles Barkley, and other Nike athletes help raise basketball consciousness in places like Shanghai, Melbourne, and Seoul. In the United Kingdom, Nike has begun expansion of a Customer Service Center, while in Brazil it has formed a partnership with Confedercao Brasileira de Futbol to sponsor the national soccer team. For World Cup 1998, Nike plans an array of media campaigns, product launches, and team endorsements. The telecasts are expected to draw an audience of 375 billion.

1. *Discuss how Nike uses IMC to position the company in a manner consistent with its strategy. Give examples.*
2. *How does Nike use athletes to influence the communication process? What characteristics of message senders do you think Nike considers the most important? Why?*
3. *This chapter discussed 21st-century forces affecting communication. Based on what you have read in the case and what you know about Nike, discuss how the company addresses these forces with its marketing communications.*

SOURCES: Nike Web site, www.nike.com; Sarah Lorge, "Marketing a Long Shot," *Sales and Marketing Management,* June 1997, p. 20; Linda Himelstein, "The Swoosh Heard 'Round the World," *Business Week,* May 12, 1997, pp. 76–80; Randall Lane, "You Are What You Wear," *Forbes,* October 14, 1996, pp. 42–46; and Steve Gelsi, "Everyone's Still Shooting at the Swoosh," *Brandweek,* February 5, 1996, pp. 30–32.

Mass Communications: Advertising, Sales Promotion, and Public Relations

Objectives:

1. Understand the concept of mass communication, including the relative use of advertising, sales promotion, and public relations.

2. Learn how technology, globalization, and ethics are playing major roles in mass communication.

3. Know the objectives, advantages, and disadvantages of advertising, as well as the sequence of steps in creating an advertising campaign.

4. Understand sales promotion objectives and what types of promotions are used to stimulate sales in business, trade, retailer, and consumer markets.

5. Understand the use of public relations in marketing.

How's this for a proposition: Millions of people from around the world stand in line and pay almost a billion dollars to see your ad. The press clamors at your door to discuss your marketing strategy, offering you endless public relations opportunities. In-store promotions bring instant recognition and appeal. Sound great? You're not the only one who thinks so. Mercedes-Benz, Timberland, JVC, Burger King, Eastman Kodak, General Mills, Hershey Foods, and Tropicana Dole Beverages agree. They spent a combined $250 million to be part of the greatest marketing adventure of the 20th century: Steven Spielberg's The Lost World: Jurassic Park, *which opened Memorial Day 1997. The opening weekend alone raked in more than $90 million, which broke all records.*

Mercedes took the opportunity to launch its new M-class all-activity vehicle, which was used in the movie. Commercials featured movie clips to enhance the tie-in. And Mercedes dealers had Lost World *displays to lure customers into the showroom. According to Marvin Sloves, chairman of Lowe & Partners/SMS, the advertising agency for Mercedes-Benz:*

We want to create marketing opportunities that give the client much more than product placement. . . . Increasingly, our clients are not only looking to involve themselves as advertisers, but as developers of unique programming that connects them emotionally to the lifestyles of their audience and customers. In the process, they build a stronger sense of customer loyalty and identification with their brands.

The biggest blitz came from Hershey Foods. Chris Kerwick, a brand manager at the company, said the promotion was Hershey's largest ever in scope. It included five new dinosaur-theme products, the candy industry's first holographic bags, and an on-pack consumer giveaway of Jurassic Park *"Survival Kits." Candy bars molded into dinosaur shapes and Reese's Pieces dinosaur eggs were just the start. And Hershey's did it all without much advertising support. "Dinosaurs have great appeal across all age groups, and we feel we can have a lasting impact with this promotion," says Kerwick. To promote the offer, the company used a freestanding newspaper insert two weeks before the opening and had 9-foot dinosaur displays in stores.*

Licensing is not just a major source of income to studios. It also helps in the overall marketing scheme. Clothing, toys, and a myriad of products from 70 licensees reinforced the brand image of Lost World. *It also was supported by an animated television series (from DreamWorks SKG, Spielberg's new studio), a comic book, and the possibility of another movie. Jim Klein, president of Universal Studios Consumer Products, believes that forging long-term partnerships is the highest priority, especially with the retailers who will sell the sponsors' products. "The key to winning at retail in this competitive arena is getting your products better presented," says Klein. Universal Studios customized point-of-purchase* Lost World *displays for retailers to strengthen the partnerships.*[1]

THE CONCEPT OF MASS COMMUNICATIONS: ADVERTISING, SALES PROMOTION, & PUBLIC RELATIONS

Today, mass communication helps companies connect with customers by providing information in exciting and creative formats. It adds tremendous value by informing people about the goods and services available in today's global markets. It's so pervasive that every few seconds, most of us are exposed to a message designed to influence our behavior. Consumers are bombarded by up to 3,000 marketing messages a day.[2]

In 1997 spending in the United States for mass communication was about $479 billion, and growth is about 7 percent annually. Much of the spending is for advertising (about $200 billion) but even more is for sales promotion (about $279 billion). Public relations is a distant third. The United States accounts for about one-third of the planet's spending on mass communication. And, mass communication in the rest of the world totals $921 billion, for a combined global figure of $1.4 trillion. About two-thirds is spent on consumer products, and one-third is spent by businesses marketing to other businesses.[3]

Much of the increase in mass communication is due to competitive factors, particularly the battle for brand strength. Familiar examples are Coke versus Pepsi, Kellogg versus General Mills, and MCI versus AT&T. Although the battle of the brands started in the United States, it has become global. Burger King and McDonald's® no longer just compete at home but in most cities around the world. And Pepsi and Coke are notorious for their vigorous rivalry in Brazil, Taiwan, and France. In fact, Coca-Cola has a worldwide ad budget of $750 million, almost double Pepsi's $400 million.[4]

Mass communication is composed of advertising, sales promotion, and public relations, as shown in Figure 15-1. Historically, techniques have changed according to advances in technology. Another recent influence is the need for standardization in global markets. Because mass communication is persuasive and powerful, there are many ethical issues for marketers to consider, but it is still a key way to connect with diverse customers. This chapter first looks at technology, global aspects, and ethics. Discussion then turns to advertising and its purposes. We describe the various categories of advertising, the agencies that create and place it, and the media that carry it to the consumer. Next, sales promotion is described as a means to get trial, stimulate immediate sales, and build customer relationships. Finally, a section on public relations and publicity addresses their role in corporate communications.

MASS COMMUNICATION IN THE 21ST CENTURY

In order to understand the future of mass communication, we start with a look at the role technology has played historically and will surely play in the 21st century. Second, we will see

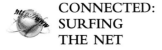

CONNECTED: SURFING THE NET

www.lost-world.com

Here's a chance to interact with exciting graphics, read the *Lost World* prologue, participate in Net-forum discussions, and read the inside story on the making of the movie. Visit the *Lost World* Web site and check it out.

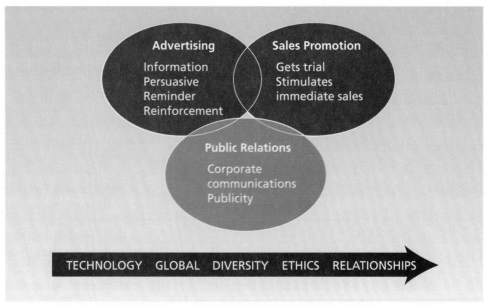

Figure 15-1   The Concept of Mass Communication in Marketing

how mass communication is occurring globally. Third, we will explore several serious ethical aspects of mass communication.

TECHNOLOGICAL PERSPECTIVE

The history of mass communication mirrors a number of technological advances.[5] Before the age of printing, street criers shouted merchants' messages, and shop signs often used pictures to identify their trade to a largely illiterate public. Movable type was invented around 1440, helping spread literacy, and 32 years later an advertisement for a prayer book was tacked to church doors. The word *advertisement* appeared in about 1665, when it was used as a header to describe announcements of commercial significance. By the mid-1700s, newspapers were popular and carried publicity and ads.

By the 1800s, mass communication through newspapers and handbills was abundant. When magazines were introduced in the mid-1800s, they provided an excellent way to communicate commercial messages. Professionals who did copywriting and advertising emerged because of this medium. By the mid-1930s, great ad agencies like J. Walter Thompson, Rubicam, and BBDO were successful. During that era, the growth of radio provided yet another medium for promotion and quickly surpassed magazines as the leading vehicle.

Although television came along in 1939 when NBC was established, not until the 1950s did television begin to surpass radio as a promotional medium. The combination of voice and video offered greater opportunities to reach consumers with a creative message. Ronald Reagan was one of the most popular spokespersons in the early days of television. Television now dominates, but magazines, newspapers, and radio still carry a significant proportion of promotional messages.

Whereas the traditional media revolutionized advertising and public relations, in recent years information systems based on computer technology have contributed dramatically to sales promotion growth. Computers have made it possible to track product movement at the retail level, thus enhancing the usefulness of all forms of sales promotion. Furthermore, computers will shape communication in even more exciting ways as we enter the 21st century. Until recently the process was strictly one way. The Internet now offers a two-way exchange, which is doing for mass communication what the telephone did for interpersonal communication.

GLOBAL MASS COMMUNICATIONS

Global advertising, sales promotion, or public relations occurs when a marketing team standardizes key elements of these activities across national boundaries. Since campaigns are usually used to support global brand strategies, companies such as Coca-Cola, PepsiCo, Procter & Gamble, BMW, Nike, Toyota, and Nestlé are leaders in this arena. Today, all the large advertising agencies have offices worldwide to support clients who seek global coordination. Due to cultural differences, marketers need to assess the benefits of standardized versus localized promotion.

Because standardization provides numerous economies, the cost of developing creative promotions can be shared across many markets. For example, when Gillette introduced the Sensor razor, a worldwide campaign used the same actors and dubbed in various languages.[6] Michael Jordan's fantastic slam dunks cost millions to produce, but they have the same appeal when used in Italy or Russia as in the United States.

Global standardization works best when customers, not countries, are the basis for identifying segments and when the product is compatible across cultures. It is also important for the firm to have similar competitors and an equivalent competitive position in most of the markets. Finally, promotion management should be centralized so that global marketing can occur.[7] A company like Kodak fits these criteria fairly well, although the imaging business does have regional differences. In Japan, Fuji is exceptionally strong, as is Agfa in Europe. Consequently, Kodak uses a standardized approach with adjustments for these local competitive conditions.

There are some serious drawbacks to global standardization. Cultural attitudes toward promotion differ. Singaporeans tend to regard it negatively, whereas Russian consumers are even more positive about it than Americans.[8] In addition, local audiences have certain cultural traditions. For example, when the National Football League created an international division to market outside the United States, it had to customize its programs to appeal to different cultures. To ensure marketing success, the NFL educated foreign consumers about U.S.-style football using a region-by-region strategy.[9]

CONNECTED: SURFING THE NET

www.fujifilm.com

Go behind the scenes at Fuji and find out what it takes to be a leader in imaging and information. Read Fuji's online magazine or investigate the company snapshot to learn more about its technology, products, global network, and profile.

Sales promotion and publicity often have a very local flavor. Each country has a unique promotion style, and most have legal as well as other restrictions. For example, Procter & Gamble found it was legal to mail free samples to consumers in Poland, a practice prohibited in many countries. What surprised them was that thieves stole the samples from mailboxes before they reached intended recipients. Ben & Jerry's Ice Cream ran a "Yo! I'm Your CEO" promotion in which people wrote essays about why they should be head of the company. The result was 20,000 entries from around the world. Although the new CEO was not chosen from among the entrants, considerable attention was drawn to the company's products.[10] And in England, Hoover Ltd. gave away free round-trip airplane tickets to New York or Orlando with the purchase of £250 in merchandise. The company underestimated demand and spent several million pounds more than it had budgeted.

ETHICAL ISSUES IN ADVERTISING, SALES PROMOTION, AND PUBLIC RELATIONS

The most serious ethical issue surrounding advertising, sales promotion, and public relations is deception. These communication methods are designed to be persuasive, but too much of the wrong type of persuasion can be misleading.

Deception occurs when a false belief is created or implied and interferes with the ability of consumers to make rational choices.[11] Purely descriptive information is seldom deceptive. But what about embellishment? Or what about the things left out? At what point does deception occur? Marketers must use a great amount of judgment to avoid being deceptive. An ad may show Michael Jordan soaring hundreds of feet to make a slam dunk in his Nikes, but no one is likely to believe that shoes make this possible. The exaggerated message is that Nike shoes will significantly improve the performance of the common athlete. But Nike lets you know that playing basketball well is also based on ability, training, and skill building. Nike emphasizes the point that personal dedication is important with ads such as their "Just Do It" campaign. And Michael Jordan is depicted as a hard-working and serious superstar. How exciting would it be to see Nike or Reebok simply describe the materials and design for their shoes? The outlandish puffery used by Nike would not be considered deceptive by most.

Marketers must walk a fine line between producing creative, stimulating messages and being deceptive. Even company slogans can come into question when they evoke strong emotions or make comparative comments. Pantene says: "Don't hate me because I'm beautiful." Hanes says: "Gentlemen prefer Hanes." Can shampoo really create jealousy, and do men really care about what brand of stockings women wear? Most consumers probably would not think these slogans seriously interfere with their ability to make informed choices. Are these catchy phrases fun and provocative or misleading?

When false information or exaggerated claims are used, deception is clear—and illegal. NordicTrack found that out. According to Jodie Bernstein, director of the Bureau of Consumer Protection, Federal Trade Commission: "Millions of consumers are searching for weight loss products and programs that are proven to work and NordicTrack appealed to that vulnerability with straightforward, quantifiable success claims. But the FTC challenges that NordicTrack based its claims on faulty surveys, and then mischaracterized the results in its advertising."[12]

Likewise, Eggland's Best Eggs used deceptive communication: "Imagine eating delicious, real whole eggs and not raising your serum cholesterol. People did. In clinical tests of Eggland's Best Eggs they ate a dozen a week while keeping within the limits of the Surgeon General's low-fat diet. And . . . their serum cholesterol didn't go up." But the company had no evidence to substantiate its cholesterol claims, and the FTC charged that its clinical studies were false.[13] To prevent this type of problem, some countries strictly prohibit puffery, and some even ban comparative claims.

France is one of many countries that frowns on deceptive advertising. A court in Paris banned the Philip Morris campaign claiming that secondhand tobacco smoke poses a smaller health risk than eating cookies or drinking milk or fluoridated water. This claim contradicts several U.S. surgeon generals, the American Medical Association, the World Health Organization, and the American Cancer Society, all of which have determined that secondhand smoke causes more than 50,000 nonsmoker deaths in the United States each year. No one has demonstrated anything like a similar risk for eating cookies or drinking milk or water. It can be concluded that Philip Morris acted unethically because they provided untrue information which some parents used to rationalize smoking around their own and other people's children.[14]

ADVERTISING

Advertising is paid, nonpersonal communication from an identified sponsor using mass media to persuade or influence an audience. The word is derived from the Latin *advertere*, "to turn toward."[15] Notice that advertising is paid for by an identified sponsor, so the audience knows the source of the message. In addition, it is a form of nonpersonal communication through mass media, such as newspapers, magazines, radio, and television. This allows advertising to be directed at relatively large audiences. But, there is no opportunity for the receiver to ask questions or for the advertiser to obtain immediate feedback. Consequently, planning is extremely important in order to create a successful ad the first time.

Advertising
Paid communication through nonpersonal channels.

THE MULTIPLE PURPOSES AND ROLES OF ADVERTISING

While advertising itself is powerful, it also plays an important support role for other forms of communication. In a famous McGraw-Hill Publishing Company ad, a grumpy purchasing agent stares directly at the viewer, saying: "I don't know who you are. I don't know your company. I don't know your company's product. I don't know what your company stands for. I don't know your company's customers. I don't know your company's record. I don't know your company's reputation. Now—what was it you wanted to sell me?" The ad goes on to explain that sales start before a salesperson calls—with business publication advertising. Whether alone or in support of other promotion methods, advertising informs, persuades, reminds, or reinforces.

Informative Advertising **Informative advertising** is designed to provide messages that consumers can store for later use. For example, an art museum may place an informative advertisement to make the community aware that a particular exhibit is on display. Often, the more information an ad provides, the better the response will be. A 6,450-word ad for Merrill Lynch brought 10,000 inquiries from interested investors. An 800-word ad for Mercedes-

Informative advertising
Messages designed to provide information that consumers can store for later use.

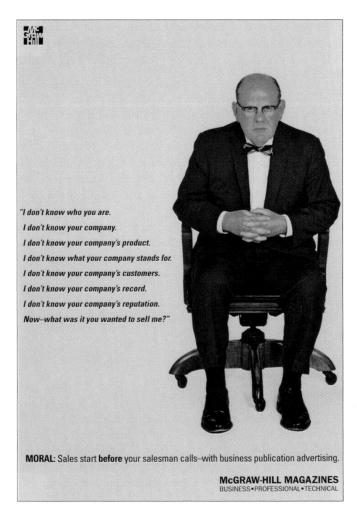

This famous McGraw-Hill Publishing Company ad explains that sales start with advertising.

Persuasive advertising

Messages designed to change consumers' attitudes and opinions about products, often listing product attributes, pricing, and other factors that may influence consumer decisions.

Reminder advertising

Messages that keep the product at the forefront of the consumer's mind.

Reinforcement advertising

Messages that call attention to specific characteristics of products experienced by the user.

CONNECTED: SURFING THE NET

www.mercedes.com

If you want to see some informative Mercedes-Benz communications, get connected. Visit the company's Web site, where you can find out about the latest news and events, technology and the environment, sports and leisure, the company history and future, and much more.

Benz was headlined: "You give up things when you buy the Mercedes Benz 230S. Things like rattles, rust and shabby workmanship." Sales for the car rose from 10,000 to 40,000. Many consumers want to be provided with as much information as possible about items that interest them.

Persuasive Advertising **Persuasive advertising** is designed to change consumers' attitudes and opinions about products as well as create attitudes where none exist. These ads often list the product's attributes, pricing, and other factors that influence the buying decision. They attempt to make the product choice important so consumers will think about the subject. In this way, the message recipient is asked to form an attitude first and then buy. For example, a Land Rover ad emphasizes the ability of its Range Rover to handle well on ice. The ad notes: ". . . no other vehicle performs more gracefully on ice than the Range Rover. The collaborative efforts of its remarkable all-terrain ABS, electronic traction control, and permanent four-wheel drive might very well make the difference between taking a drive and going for a spin."[16]

Reminder Advertising **Reminder advertising** keeps the product at the forefront of the consumer's mind. In some cases these ads simply draw a connection between the brand and some aspect of life. In other cases they reinforce past consumer behavior to encourage the next purchase. CompuServe's reminder campaign for its on-line service not only aired television spots in its top 20 markets, but also increased direct mail by more than 600 percent and ad inserts by 150 percent. All these told consumers that CompuServe is the solution when "life calls for deeper answers."[17] Reminder ads that stimulate the next purchase include the famous Burger King ad: "Aren't you hungry?" McDonald's® tried to move consumers into their restaurants with the slogan "You deserve a break today." The next campaign phase asked: "Have you had your break today?" The reminder was intended to spur more action from the consumer.[18]

Reinforcement Advertising To encourage repeat buying behavior, **reinforcement advertising** calls attention to specific characteristics of products experienced by the user. The key here is to communicate with the consumer about product features that created the greatest amount of satisfaction. These ads also reassure customers that they made the right choice. For example, ads for Dial ask, "Aren't you glad you used Dial . . . don't you wish everyone did?"

PROS AND CONS OF ADVERTISING

Advertising has many advantages. By controlling what is said, how it is said, and where it is said, marketers can develop standardized campaigns that run for extended periods. Over time, these help build a strong brand equity position. Moreover, advertising is a very cost-effective way to reach large audiences. For example, one 30-second network TV spot in prime time reaches on average 12 million households. At current rates, that's less than 1 cent per household of coverage. No other promotional method comes close to accomplishing that kind of exposure at such low rates.

The availability of such advertising media as television, radio, newspapers, magazines, and billboards makes it easy to reach most audiences. And because advertising is used so much, it's easy for marketers to find excellent agencies that can help research markets, develop campaigns, and manage the entire process. The advantages can be summarized as follows:

- Advertiser controls the content, presentation, and placement of messages.
- Builds brand position and equity over time.
- Cost effective for large audiences.
- Serves many communication needs—awareness, information, reminder.
- Available media make it easy to reach most audiences.
- Easy to find professionals to create effective advertising.

Advertising does have a downside. It's difficult to direct an ad at only the target audience—many others will be exposed to it. Because many consumers distrust ads and try to avoid them, advertising campaigns may need to run for a long time to repeat the message. It is not unusual for some companies or industries to spend hundreds of millions of dollars on advertising. For consumer cleaning products and children's games and toys, more than

16 percent of sales is spent on advertising. The motion picture industry spends more than 12 percent.[19] The disadvantages of advertising can be summarized as follows:

- Reaches many nonusers.
- High level of audience avoidance.
- Brief one-way messages.
- Can be costly in total.

CATEGORIES OF ADVERTISING

Advertising falls into various categories depending on its objectives, target audience, and type of message. Most marketers use one or more of the eight types described in Figure 15-2.

National or brand advertising, as the name implies, focuses on brand identity and positioning throughout the country. The aim is to develop a distinctive brand image in the mind of the consumer. Although this is often called national advertising, it is also the objective for global advertising.

Retail (local) advertising focuses attention on nearby outlets where products and services can be purchased. The emphasis is on attributes that will stimulate people to shop there, such as price, location, convenience, or customer service.

Directory advertising is a listing of businesses, their address, phone number, and sometimes a brief description in a publication such as the Yellow Pages. A short differentiating message can be critical since so many competitors also advertise there. Businesses usually consider directories extremely important because most consumers use them only when they are ready to buy a product.

Business-to-business advertising sends messages to a variety of organizations, ranging from health care providers to accountants, lawyers, and manufacturers. Often, technical content is communicated. In the health care field, for example, publications such as the *Journal of the American Medical Association* carry extensive advertising of pharmaceutical products of all types.

Institutional advertising is designed to communicate corporate identity and philosophy rather than messages about individual products. It describes the company's social and ecological responsibilities. For example, Toyota promotes its involvement in United States communities.

Direct response advertising targets individual consumers. Sales are stimulated through appeals by telephone or mail, and the product then is delivered to the customer's home or business. Companies like Federal Express and UPS have helped facilitate the dramatic increase in sales through mail-order catalogs.

Public service messages support such societal issues as the prevention of child abuse or smoking cessation. These announcements are usually created free by advertising agencies, and

Institutional advertising
Messages designed to communicate corporate identity and philosophy as opposed to product information.

Category	Description
National and Global (Brand) Advertising	Focuses on brand identity nationwide (globally). Aims to develop a distinctive brand image.
Retail (Local) Advertising	Focuses on local retail areas. Emphasizes positive attributes of retail outlets.
Directory Advertising	Company listings in a directory. Important to most businesses and retailers. Uses a short differentiating message.
Business-to-Business Advertising	Directed at professionals. Often communicates technical content. Common media include business publications and professional journals.
Institutional Advertising	Communicates corporate identity and philosophy. Describes social and ecological responsibilities of a company.
Direct Response Advertising	Appeals directly to individual consumers. Usual delivery methods are telephone or mail.
Public Service Advertising	Supports public issues. Usually created for free and media donate space and time.
Political Advertising	Aimed at obtaining votes for issues or political candidates.

Figure 15-2   *Categories of Advertising*

the space or air time is donated by the media. Sometimes they are partially supported by charitable organizations or the government.

Political advertising is aimed at influencing voters in favor of individuals or particular ballot issues. It has come under harsh criticism for mud slinging, negative and sometimes false accusations against political candidates, and the lack of focus on substantive issues.

ADVERTISING AGENCIES

Advertising agency
A business that develops, prepares, and places advertising for sellers seeking to find customers for their products.

Advertising agencies are independent businesses that develop, prepare, and place advertising in the appropriate media. Most companies outsource some or all of these services. In fact, more than 90 percent of all advertising is placed through outside agencies. Even very large corporations such as General Motors outsource. The cost effectiveness of outside agencies makes this a good choice for most companies. There are more than 10,000 ad agencies in the United States alone and probably an equal number around the world. As in any industry, there are several large agencies and many smaller ones. Big companies, such as Young & Rubicam or Saatchi and Saatchi, have offices in nearly every major country to provide the services required for global marketers.

In addition to full-service agencies, many specialize in certain advertising functions or in selected industries. For example, Creative Boutiques focuses primarily on developing ideas for advertising. In many cases, industries have certain unique needs. The health care industry is a good example. Durot, Donahoe, and Purohit of Rosemont, Illinois, is an expert in that kind of advertising, which requires knowledge of extensive regulation of health care ads by the Federal Drug Administration. Some agencies focus on certain target groups. Burmudez and Associates have expertise in the Hispanic market, and others specialize in various minorities.

THE ADVERTISING PLAN

The six major steps in developing a strong advertising plan are outlined in Figure 15-3. The process begins by setting objectives and next determining the budget. Then the theme and message are developed. The theme is the creative concept and the art and copy are used to convey the message. Next, media are selected, and a schedule is set. This is followed by creation of the ads. Finally, their effectiveness is assessed.

SETTING OBJECTIVES

Each objective should be developed in such a way that its accomplishment can be measured. Remember that advertising should support the communications plan, which in turn supports the strategic marketing plan. As Figure 15-4 suggests, the goals of informing, persuading, reminding, and/or reinforcing should be accompanied by specific objectives, such as increase sales, establish brand position, increase awareness, support the sales force or distributors, maintain awareness, or introduce a new brand.[20]

Figure 15-3 Steps in the Advertising Plan

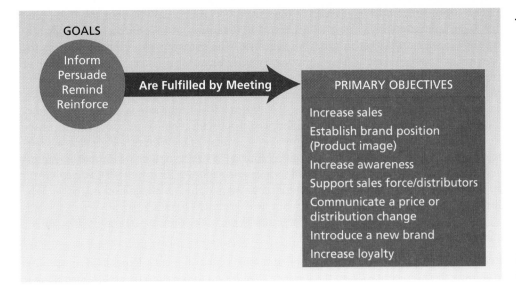

Figure 15-4 Advertising Objectives

DEVELOPING THE ADVERTISING BUDGET

As we mentioned before, advertising can be expensive in total although quite cost effective on a per person basis. In setting the budget, the first question to answer is how much will it cost to accomplish the objective? Most advertising budgets are determined using one of the following methods: percentage of sales method, competitive budgeting method, payout plan method, or task method.

The percentage of sales method for developing the advertising budget involves simply estimating the desired sales level and then allocating a certain percentage of sales to advertising. Often this percent is equal to the industry average. In some cases, the percentage of sales method is performed by taking a percentage of the previous year's sales and allocating it to advertising. The problem with this method is that sales are used to create the advertising budget when, in fact, advertising should be used to create sales. However, the method is used widely because it is very easy to administer.

Competitive budgeting involves determining what competitors are spending and setting the advertising budget accordingly. Large companies such as AT&T and MCI use this method. In order to maintain a strong presence in the eye of the consumer, many companies try to keep up with the advertising budgets of their competitors. AT&T has an ad budget of $673 million, which is a large amount for many smaller competitors to attempt to match.[21]

The payout plan method is generally used for new products that require high advertising expenditures. In this case, the marketer estimates future sales and establishes the advertising budget required to gain initial acceptance and trial of the product. Generally, these expenditures are very high relative to sales, and in some cases even exceed sales. The large expenditures are deemed reasonable because of the payback that occurs in later years. This is similar to investing money in product development.

The task method sets specific sales targets or other objectives and then determines what advertising activities and amounts are required to accomplish those objectives. This approach can be extremely complex. Advertisers who use the task method rely on very accurate information, experience, and develop extensive models developed for the purpose. It tends to be used by large organizations in highly competitive environments. It's superior to the other methods because so much attention to detail is paid in determining how advertising contributes towards accomplishment of objectives.

DEVELOPING THE THEME AND MESSAGE

Once objectives are in place and the budget has been established, it is time to develop the theme and message—the **creative strategy** that will govern and coordinate the development of individual ads and assure that their visual images and words convey precisely and consistently what the advertiser wishes to communicate. Be careful not to confuse this overall strategy with the creative work in putting a specific ad together. The message is a fairly straightforward outgrowth of the marketer's understanding of consumer behavior, infor-

Creative strategy
The strategy that governs and coordinates the development of individual ads and assures their visual images and words convey precisely and consistently what the advertiser wants to communicate.

mation processing, and the advertising objectives. For example, Whirlpool research found that Asian females are involved in 80 percent of household appliance purchases and that saving time is very important in their busy lifestyle. The company chose saving time as the theme. The creative strategy incorporated extremely busy Asian females and depicted their difficulty in finding time for family activities.[22] The implication is that buying a Whirlpool enables a busy woman to be with her family more often.

An **advertising campaign** is a series of different ads with the same creative strategy. Because one ad tends to have very little effect, campaigns are required to sustain the message and accomplish the objectives. There is usually an element of continuity, such as similar characters, music, or settings. The pink Energizer bunny keeps going and going through any number of ads. Other examples are Taco Bell's south of the border theme, the "What would you do for a Klondike bar?" promotion, Bounty's campaign as the "quicker picker upper," and the Taster's Choice ongoing soap opera between two apartment building neighbors.

To be effective, the theme and message must reach the consumer and must be creative, understandable, and memorable.

Advertising campaign

A series of advertisements with a main theme running through them.

Reaching the Consumer   An ad must first reach its target audience. **Exposure** is the process of putting the ad in contact with the market. Then it's up to the ad to communicate the message. A good advertisement addresses nearly every aspect of consumer behavior in a package that grabs interest and keeps it until the message is absorbed. Exposure does not ensure attention. As we learned in chapter 7, the perceptual process filters out a great deal. The ad must have what marketers call **stopping power**—the ability to gain and hold attention. Ads with stopping power are so attention getting that they interrupt whatever the person is doing. The best ads gain and hold attention because the consumer finds them interesting and relevant. They are often consistent with the buyer's lifestyle. Sometimes catchy music, humor, or an association with a celebrity works. Some phrases may gain immediate attention from certain people: weight loss, quick cash, retire early, pay off your debts, work at home, free, new, amazing, now, and easy.[23] These catch phrases have been so over-used by advertisers that many people immediately tune-out messages containing them.

Exposure

The process of putting the ad in contact with the customer.

Stopping power

The ability of an ad to gain and hold the consumer's attention.

Creativity   Originality and uniqueness are very important in advertisements. On the one hand, ads that are too unusual may not work because people have difficulty relating to them.

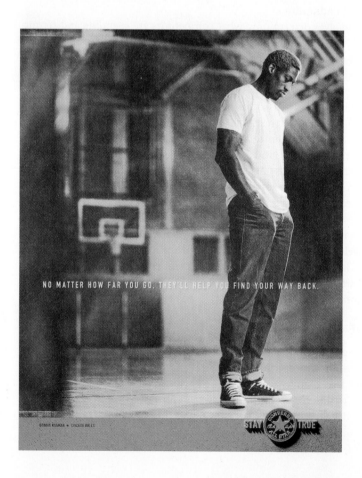

Sometimes ads use association with a celebrity to create stopping power.

On the other hand, creative, humorous, upbeat ads that provide some novelty tend to gain more attention than the same old thing. Recently, television ads for Energizer batteries spoofed the blockbuster movie *Twister*. A van of scientists driving around the country hoping to glimpse the famous bunny piques interest, and humor is injected when a supposed sighting turns out to be a woodchuck. Energizer's pink icon has made its alkaline battery the second best-selling, which shows that originality in advertising can make a difference. Coca-Cola also captured viewers with its computer-animated polar bears, considered a "heartwarmer, creative, and upbeat."[24]

Once attention is gained, consumers are likely to become aware of the message and internalize it. **Pulling power** holds the interest of the consumer to the end of the message. Most advertisers insist that the message must relate to some aspect of the individual's life. Celebrities, for example, have reference group appeal. A Pepsi ad in the 1980s featured pop star Michael Jackson and had enormous pulling power. It was rated one of the 50 best commercials of all time by *Advertising Age*.[25]

Pulling power
The ability to maintain the interest of the consumer to the end of the advertising message.

Understandability   While most ads don't attempt to say everything about a product, it's important that the information selected for communication be clearly understood. Otherwise, it will not be remembered. Procter & Gamble communicated the benefits of its detergent Cheer through a series of ads featuring a "silent deadpan presenter" who smudges garments with terrible stains. Viewers have a clear understanding of what the product can do when the items are pulled stain-free from a mixture of water, ice, and Cheer.[26]

Memorability   It's important that ads be memorable so that they are retained for some time. A high initial effect is useless if forgotten quickly. Consumers must remember ads until they actually purchase the product. One way to achieve this is through repetition. An ad usually must be seen at least three times before it moves into long-term memory. Jingles, slogans, and tag lines also help ensure recall. How many of the popular slogans listed in Figure 15-5 do you recognize?

SELECTING AND SCHEDULING MEDIA

Media Options   Media are the channels through which messages are transmitted from the sender to the receiver. Each medium has unique advantages and disadvantages, as described in Figure 15-6.

Newspapers   A highly credible and flexible medium, newspapers offer wide exposure to upscale adults. Many newspapers have prestige because of their positive impact on communities. They reach 90 percent of homes in a typical location, allowing for widespread coverage. Newspapers can also facilitate coordination between local and national advertising. Some effectiveness is being lost, however, as television becomes an increasingly important news source. Another competitor is information available on the World Wide Web. Few newspaper ads are fully read, and young adults rarely read newspapers. Circulation fell 3 percent nationwide between 1992 and 1995 during which time the number of dailies dropped from 1,570 to 1,532.[27] By March 1998 the decline had been reversed, however, with gain in circulation of almost 1.5 percent. The reversal occurred because "publishers realized that selling

Slogan	Product or Brand
Where's the Beef?	Wendy's Restaurants
Reach Out and Touch Someone	AT&T
Don't Leave Home Without It	American Express
Just Do It	Nike
Generation Next	Pepsi
Enjoy the Ride	Nissan
Breakfast of Champions	Wheaties
We Bring Good Things to Life	General Electric
Did Somebody Say McDonald's®?	McDonald's®
I Love What You Do For Me	Toyota
Good to the Last Drop	Maxwell House
Obey Your Thirst	Sprite
Sometimes You Feel Like a Nut	Almond Joy
Fly the Friendly Skies	United Airlines

Figure 15-5 Successful Advertising Slogans

	Advantages	Disadvantages
Newspapers	Wide exposure for upscale adults. Flexible; timely; buyers can save for later reference. High credibility.	Few ads are fully read. Young adults don't read them. Costs are rising. Alternate media are becoming more important news sources.
Television	Creative and flexible. Cost efficient. Credible.	Message is quickly forgotten. High production cost. Difficult to get attention.
Radio	Selective targeting possible. Mobile—goes with listeners. Low production costs.	No visual content. High frequency is required to reach many people. Audience research has traditionally been difficult.
Magazines	Target narrowly defined segments. Prestigious sources. Long life—can be passed along.	Audiences declining. Long lead times to develop ads. Need to use many different magazines to reach a lot of buyers.
Outdoor Ads	Low cost per exposure. Good to supplement other media. With color, lighting, and mechanization gets attention.	Can't communicate much. Difficult to measure results.
Internet	Considerable potential. Medium for relationship marketing. Customer driven and dialog oriented. Increasing number of users.	Little research to indicate proven effectiveness. Relies on consumers accessing the necessary technologies. Revenues still small. Difficult to target a specific audience. Difficult to measure results.

*Figure 15-6 Advantages and
Disadvantages of Various
Media*

Source: *J. Thomas Russell and W. Ronald Lane,* Kleppner's Advertising Procedure, *13th ed. © 1996. Adapted by
permission of Prentice Hall, Inc., Upper Saddle River, NJ.*

newspapers isn't much different from selling Coca-Cola or Crest. And relentless marketing has become standard practice."[28]

Television Television is also a credible source and is extremely cost efficient per person. It provides the creative flexibility to use both video and audio, allowing an unlimited range of spokespersons and themes. The disadvantages are high production costs and low recall of messages. Television is filled with advertising, which makes it difficult to gain the viewer's attention, and many consumers change the channel when commercials air. Consequently, television ads need to be rerun often to be effective. Due to increased Internet usage, television viewing may decline. A Nielsen survey reveals that television is watched less often in homes with a subscription to America Online. While no direct link has been established, studies will continue to look for correlations.[29]

Radio Very low production costs make radio an attractive medium. Furthermore, marketers can be extremely selective in targeting U.S. consumers because each market area averages 30 stations, each aimed at a specific audience. The problem has been limited research on local radio markets, but new computer systems are changing that. For example, a software program called Advance is assisting with postbuy analysis so that ad agencies can estimate the ratings for stations and specific air times.[30] Lacking visual content, radio spots require more repetition than television ads. As methods for audience rating improve, however, it should be possible to use fewer spots and evaluate more accurately their effect on selected segments.

Magazines Magazines also target well-defined consumer segments, and professional journals reach very specific groups. Although 92 percent of adults read at least one magazine per month, overall magazine readership is declining. Most adults (about 79%) consider magazine ads to be positive and helpful for making purchase decisions. In fact, there is evidence that consumers pay more attention to this advertising medium than to television.[31] In the past few years, many "small" magazines have been introduced to appeal to unique tastes, which makes more finely tuned targeting possible. The disadvantages of magazines are long lead times and high production costs for ads. In efforts to target more finely, new techniques for producing special ads are being designed that will bring costs down. Ultimately, the goal is

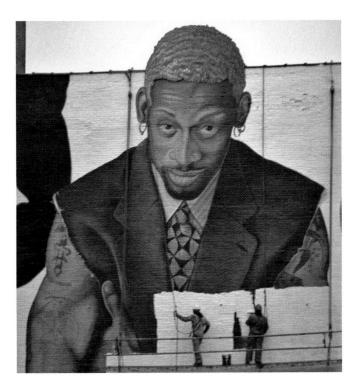

The 32 ft. outdoor painting of Dennis Rodman was so eye catching, it caused problems with traffic.

to get as close to unique customers as possible. To reach a large number of buyers, however, ads in many different magazines may be required.

Outdoor Advertising   Outdoor advertisements, primarily billboards, are very inexpensive per exposure, so they provide an attractive supplement to other media. With color, lighting, and mechanization, some billboards have fantastic stopping power. For example, 3M's billboard unit recently decided to spend $1 billion with Outdoor Systems of Phoenix because of this medium's effectiveness.[32] Outdoor advertisements can be so eye-catching that they distract motorists. Consider the 32-foot painting of Dennis Rodman displayed on a warehouse along the Kennedy Expressway in Chicago. It attracted so much attention in rush hour that it was removed in response to the concerns of traffic officials.[33] Despite their flashiness, outdoor ads can't communicate a great amount of information because people move past them so quickly. It's usually more difficult to measure the results of outdoor advertisements than other media.

The Internet   The Internet provides a relatively new medium that is both customer driven and dialogue oriented. This gives companies another way to develop customer relationships. The Internet has enormous potential. More than half of the 35 million Americans who are on-line have sought on-line information about a product or service.[34] A major advantage of Internet advertising is that all viewers are self-selected, so a high percentage have a strong buying inclination. Yet, there is still very little research on the effectiveness of the Internet, and revenues are relatively small.[35] Many Web sites are trying to overcome this problem by promising: "If your ad fails to produce a sale, it runs free of charge."[36]

This silo is considered to be the world's largest tomato can—a creative outdoor ad by Young & Laramore. An estimated five million cars have driven by the display in only five months.

CONNECTING THROUGH TECHNOLOGY

YAHOO! CORPORATION: FROM TECHIE TOOL TO HOT NEW AD MEDIUM

Every day 170,000 more pages are added to the World Wide Web, and every day more than two million visitors use the Yahoo! search engine to locate sites ranging from "anagram insanity" to "worm world." And if the $9 million company based in Mountain View, California, has its way, these visitors won't just type in a key-word and vamoose. Instead, they'll stay awhile to catch some music and news, play games, and glean information on topics of interest. Most important for the continued profitability of Yahoo!, these visitors will stay long enough to peruse ads from some of its 550 advertisers.

The transformation of Yahoo! from a techie tool to a digital destination says a lot about the continuing evolution of advertising on the Web's search engines. Organizations like Yahoo!, Lycos, and Excite sell advertising to turn a profit, and clients pay between $10 and $1,000 for every 1,000 "impressions"—Webspeak for the number of times a page is loaded by a consumer. At the end of 1996, Yahoo! had earned $19 million in ad revenue, but showing results to advertisers has been much more difficult than the company had imagined.

Search engines were designed to get site visitors in and out as quickly as possible. But for advertisers, this means that Web visitors don't linger over an ad, not the way viewers do when a commercial is smack in the middle of a *Seinfeld* episode. Yahoo! and the other major search engines are out to change this scenario. Karen Edwards, director of advertising at Yahoo!, marvels: "It's all happened so fast. Search engines are no longer search engines; we feel a lot more like media companies, providing information via various formats."

So far Yahoo! is the most aggressive of the search engines when it comes to attempting a makeover. It has launched regional versions such as Yahoo! San Francisco and Yahoo! New York, as well as several international editions, including Yahoo! Japan and Yahoo! Canada. There is Yahooligans for kids and Yahoo! for women, which offers gender-specific guides to entertainment, events, health resources, and information sources on the Web. There's even a customized version, with personalized content called My Yahoo! The biggest coup, of course, is the strategic partnership to create Yahoo! MTV, a cross between MTV Online and Yahoo!

By bringing together information in sites targeted at specific demographic or geographic groups, Yahoo! is not so different from a magazine publisher. For advertisers, the targeted sites will create a much more powerful medium than if Yahoo! had remained simply a vehicle for locating Web sites. The company's smart moves spurred stock analysts to upgrade their recommendations from a lukewarm "buy" to a "strong buy." Alan M. Braverman, an analyst with Credit Suisse First Boston, says that Yahoo! is the best positioned to take advantage of the huge growth in Web advertising expected in the next few years. On all counts it looks like advertisers and shareholders will have a lot to shout "Yahoo!" about. And by the way, the name isn't a hillbilly yell but the acronym for "Yet Another Hierarchic Officious Oracle."

Sources: Kim Cleland, "Searching for a Broader Role on the Web," *Advertising Age*, June 24, 1996, p. 34; Janice Maloney, "Yahoo! Still Searching for Profits on the Internet," *Fortune*, December 9, 1996, pp. 174–182; and Laurie Flynn, "Market Place: A Corner Turns for Yahoo and Other Internet Search Concerns," *New York Times*, February 11, 1997, p. D8.

The Internet is growing in popularity, but it relies on consumers owning or accessing the necessary equipment. As technology becomes less expensive and more user friendly, the effectiveness of this medium will improve greatly. It is difficult to target a specific audience today, but look for advances that will make it possible to attract specific segments and even specific (one-to-one) customers in the future. The technology feature discusses Yahoo! Corporation's attempts to advertise on the Internet.

CAREER TIP On June 10, 1998, Tony Lee, editor in chief and general manager of the *Wall Street Journal Interactive Journal*, announced a strategic alliance with Futurestep, the recruitment database developed by Korn/Ferry International, the world's largest executive search firm. Visit http://careers/wsj.com and click on the Futurestep icon to find the confidential Futurestep questionnaire. Fill it out and you will receive a personal profile by e-mail that explains your value in today's marketplace. Lee says you will also be considered for career opportunities with major employers worldwide.[37]

Media Popularity   Which media do the major advertisers select? Figure 15-7 illustrates advertising expenditures for the top 100 companies. The four types of television media account for about two-thirds, followed at a great distance by magazines, newspapers, radio, and outdoor advertising.

The Media Schedule   Media scheduling can be looked at as a plan within the advertising plan. This very exacting work involves a number of considerations: target audience analysis; reach, frequency, and continuity balance; media timing; and budgeting.

Target Audience   As you know, the marketing plan is always directed at specific market segments. Media planning begins by addressing those segments. Marketers have developed very detailed methods for defining target markets. For example, Clarita Corporation has developed PRIZM, which uses such variables as socioeconomic status, ethnicity, family life cycle, education, employment, type of housing, and location of housing to describe 40 audiences. In turn, these data are correlated with media usage patterns. The information helps determine which media are likely to influence the respective segments at various times and locations.

Media scheduling usually is done geographically and demographically. For example, Taco Bell, McDonald's®, and Burger King all compete for the fast-food dollar in the United States. But, Taco Bell targets males age 19–24, while the other two include families with children. Ad budgets reflect these additional segments, with Burger King and McDonald's® significantly outspending Taco Bell's advertising budget of $150 million.[38]

Once decisions are made about target audience and geographic considerations, media planners calculate the cost of communicating with the audience through various media. Media costs are generally expressed in units of cost per thousand, abbreviated as CPM (M is the Roman numeral for 1,000). The CPM for reaching the target audience is calculated as follows:

$$CPM = \frac{Advertising\ cost \times 1,000}{Circulation\ to\ target\ audience}$$

For example, suppose we are interested in reaching women with children under two years of age. We know that *McCalls* has 600,000 readers in this category, and an advertisement there will cost $60,000. The CPM of reaching our target audience is $100 ($60,000 × 1,000 ÷ 600,000 = $100). We can then determine the cost per person by dividing CPM by 1,000. In this case it is $0.10 ($100 ÷ 1,000 = $0.10).

Reach, Frequency, and Continuity Balance   Once media planners know the target audience and the cost of reaching it, they consider the reach, frequency, and continuity of the advertising campaign. **Reach** is the number of consumers in the target audience that can be contacted through a given medium. In the example above, the reach through *McCalls* is 600,000. **Frequency** is the number of times the audience is contacted during a given period,

Reach
The number of consumers in the target audience who can be contacted through a given medium.

Frequency
The number of times the audience is reached in a given period, usually per day or per week.

Media	Annual Expenditure	Percent of Total
Network TV	$9.7 billion	35.1
Spot TV	$4.9 billion	17.8
Cable TV	$1.9 billion	6.9
Syndicated TV	$1.6 billion	5.8
Magazines	$4.4 billion	15.9
Sunday magazines	$0.4 billion	1.4
Newspapers	$3.0 billion	10.9
National newspapers	$0.3 billion	1.1
Outdoor advertising	$0.4 Billion	1.4
Network radio	$0.5 billion	1.8
National spot radio	$0.4 billion	1.8
Yellow Pages	$0.1 billion	.4
Total	$27.6 billion	100.0

Source: Adapted with permission from the September 30, 1996 issue of Advertising Age. Copyright, Crain Communications, Inc. 1996.

Figure 15-7   Advertising Expenditures by Media for the Top 100 Spenders

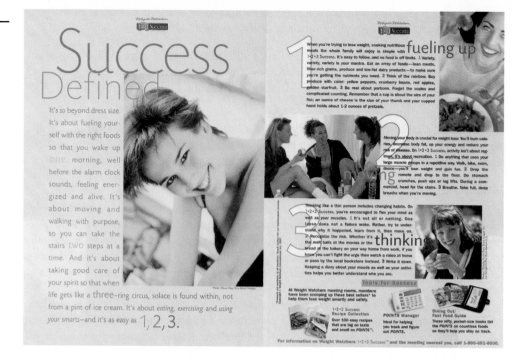

Consider the influence media timing may have had on Weight Watchers.

Continuity
The length of time the advertising campaign will run in a given medium.

Overexposure
Continuing to reach a prospect after a buying decision has been made or to the point that the campaign becomes tedious and actually turns off some potential buyers.

usually over four weeks. **Continuity** is the length of time the advertising campaign will run in a given medium. It is important to select a medium with enough reach, frequency, and continuity to gain the desired effect. At the same time, agencies do not want to waste funds. **Overexposure** refers to reaching a prospect either after a purchase decision has been made or so frequently that the campaign actually wastes money.

Media Timing   Products may be seasonal or purchased more frequently on certain days of the week. For example, suntan lotions are bought mainly during the summer and especially on weekends. Products such as soaps and cosmetics are purchased frequently all year round and may require constant advertising. Consider the importance of media timing for advertising weight loss products. About half of all dieters initiate programs between January and April. Weight Watchers and Jenny Craig, Inc., spent $30 million on television and print ads in January 1997 alone.[39]

To complicate matters, it's important to look at the activity of competitors. It may be necessary to counteract their campaigns or take advantage of times when they tend to promote less. Tactics include selecting media that competitors are not using or making adjustments to the scheduling, timing, and frequency of various advertisements.

Media Budget   Generally, the media budget is set according to the strategic marketing and communication plans. Marketers attempt to maximize the advertising effort within budget constraints, using one or a combination of media to achieve the most influence in the market. As part of the media plan, it's important to determine whether messages will be visual, verbal, or both. The amount of information to be communicated will influence the choice of media and consequently the budget. Recently, the costs of all forms have been escalating, so careful attention must be paid to the trade-offs among them. Fortunately, media competition helps the situation. Marketers from magazines, newspapers, television, and radio are constantly promoting their own vehicle. To accommodate clients, they are willing to provide help in media selection and scheduling.

CREATING THE ADS

This step in the ad plan involves both science and art. Creating ads can be as complicated as making a movie. The key is to know your objectives and the constraints imposed by the media, scheduling, and budget. What makes an ad outstanding and memorable? As with any creative process, it's difficult to determine precisely what people will like. To help answer that question, *Marketing*, a British journal, conducts a survey each month called "ad watch." British consumers are asked whether or not they remember a specific advertisement.

There are certainly many classics. The California raisins who "heard it though the grapevine" combined humor, visual novelty, and a great rock beat that caught the attention

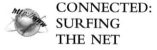

CONNECTED: SURFING THE NET

www.heinz.com

Has media timing brought about any changes in Weight Watchers communications recently? To find out, visit the Web site of Heinz, best known for its ketchup, but also owner of Weight Watchers Diet Program and a number of other successful brands.

of millions in the 1980s. Most people still remember Mikey, who willingly ate Life cereal. Other famous ads include the exciting outdoor scenes from Mountain Dew, and Air Jordan delivering the dunk for Nike. And nearly everyone (if old enough) can recall the little boy sharing his Pepsi with Mean Joe Green of the Pittsburgh Steelers after the game.

When diverse segments are part of the target audience, the advertisement must be created in such a way that it appeals to various tastes and preferences. Marketers also need to be aware of language differences, acceptable behaviors, ethnicity, and cultural norms. Many promotional efforts are now for a global audience, and that means communicating in as many as 3,000 different tongues and dialects.[40] To avoid costly mistakes, it is critical for marketers to research and understand the language(s) of a target market segment before they advertise to it. For example, "Pepsi Brings You Back to Life" was chosen by the company as the promotional theme in China, but the slogan translated into "Pepsi Brings Your Ancestors Back from the Grave." Coca-Cola selected Chinese characters (letters) that sound like its name but which mean "bite the wax tadpole." Imagine Chevrolet's surprise when it was reported that Nova in the Spanish market translates as "It won't go." In Italy, a campaign for Schweppes tonic water referred to the product as Schweppes toilet water, while Kentucky Fried Chicken's slogan in China became "eat your fingers off" rather than "finger lickin' good."[41]

Of course, not all diversity is ethnic or linguistic. Gays and lesbians, for example, may be unresponsive to ads that employ only heterosexual couples to represent the warm, loving relationships associated with use of the product. The diversity feature discusses Subaru's advertisements targeting gays and lesbians.

ASSESSING ADVERTISING EFFECTIVENESS

The effect of advertising can be assessed at two different points: before running the ad campaign and afterward. This kind of measurement is extremely important to determine what does and doesn't work so that the campaign can be adjusted.

Individual ads and campaigns may be tested beforehand to evaluate effectiveness before committing more funds. Various tests are used on the sample audience to determine whether the ad content has been stored in the consumer's memory. Both recall and recognition are considered important by advertising researchers. One test asks the audience what it remembers about an ad after a limited run in a particular medium. Two aspects usually are measured. **Unaided recall** asks the viewer to identify any advertisements s/he can recall, such as "What commercials do you remember seeing for automobiles?" **Aided recall** refers to content that can be remembered without seeing the particular ad. An example is: "Do you recall seeing a commercial for Cadillac?" By questioning several respondents, researchers determine both the unaided and aided recall scores. These tests may be conducted immediately following exposure to the ad or up to several days thereafter.

Unaided recall
The viewer is asked to identify any advertisements s/he can remember.

Aided recall
The viewer is given some specific piece of information about the ad before being asked if s/he recalls having seen it.

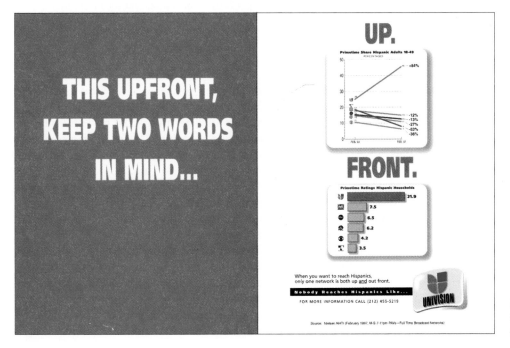

Univision is a popular network for marketers to reach a Hispanic audience.

CONNECTING WITH DIVERSITY
BREAKING TABOOS AT SUBARU

In spring 1996, Subaru of North America made a wild departure from the winding roads and dreamscapes that dominate most automobile ads. In a promotion for its all-wheel-drive Legacy station wagon, two women are pictured below a headline: "It loves camping, dogs and long-term commitment. Too bad it's only a car." Another version features two men, and it doesn't take too much imagination to realize that the couples in these ads are not "just friends."

Subaru risks offending a largely conservative general market by running ads that apparently endorse a controversial lifestyle. Why? Quite simply, like many marketers, Subaru sees the gay and lesbian market as an untapped gold mine. Highly educated and usually without dependents, gays and lesbians have a high level of disposable income. Geographic concentration in urban areas and a strong word-of-mouth network makes them easy to target. Most important, because these groups are sometimes frowned on by mainstream society, they actually welcome overtures from marketers. This well-heeled, easy-to-reach segment sees ads geared to them as "an act of courage."

Companies so far have taken two different tacks in advertising to gays and lesbians. The more timid approach is to "recycle" ads for the general market by placing them unchanged in gay media. For instance, American Express, Stolichnaya vodka, and Atlantic Records have run general ads in *Deneuve* and *Lesbian News*. The bolder approach is to create ads with specific gay themes and content, which is the path Subaru took. "You get a much better return for your advertising dollar" with gay-specific creative ads says David Mulryan, president of Mulryan/Nash NY, which developed the Subaru campaign and specializes in the gay and lesbian market. Hiram Walker thinks so, too. Its ads for Tuaca liquor show three young women looking coquettishly at one another with the headline: "Cool girl seeks sociable silent type to share la dolce vita."

There are still many risks associated with developing whole programs around this very new market. So far there is no body of research to provide measures of product or media usage in the homosexual community. A common mistake is to view the market as homogeneous. Gays and lesbians are two profoundly distinct segments, each with different attitudes, psychology, and purchasing patterns. And within each are subsegments based on age or lifestyle. For instance, older gays who came of age during more socially constrained times respond more to specific ads than do younger gays. Harry Taylor, publisher of *Out*, says that for his young readership "what's important is just putting [the product] in the medium."

Whether marketers choose to place general ads in gay media or craft gay-specific campaigns, the important message for these consumers is acceptance of their lifestyle. In a study by Yankelovich Panners, 6 percent of the 2,500 respondents who identified as homosexuals said they "want to feel accepted." For marketers the trick will be figuring out how to convey this acceptance without alienating more conservative consumers. Even Subaru, for all its boldness, has kept mum about its new ads.

Sources: Oscar Suris, "Advertising: Mum's the Word on Subaru Ads Aimed at Homosexual Consumers," *Wall Street Journal*, March 22, 1996, p. B2:3; Michael Wilke, "Ad Survey Shows Appeal of Gay Themes," *Advertising Age* , May 6, 1996, p. 19; Hazel Kahan and David Mulryan, "Out of the Closet," *American Demographics*, May 1995, pp. 40–47; and Cyndee Miller, "The Ultimate Taboo," *Marketing News*, August 14, 1995, pp. 1, 18.

Recognition means that you remember the ad when you see it again. This kind of remembrance is typically adequate for low-involvement products like chewing gum or soup. To test recognition, audience members are shown an ad and later are asked if they remember it. In other words, the ad is a stimulus during the testing procedure. One of the most popular types of recognition test is the Starch test, which is usually conducted after an ad has been run. Respondents leaf through a magazine containing the ad and are then asked if they remember seeing it. Next, a series of questions determines whether they associated the ad with the advertiser's name or logo and whether they read at least half of the copy. Because Starch tests have been run on so many ads, marketers can compare the scores of their ad to similar types. There are variations on the test for media other than magazines.

When persuasion is the objective of the advertisement, it is very important to go beyond simple memory tests and determine whether the ad influences attitudes or behavior. For this, marketers use persuasion tests, which essentially measure attitude change. For example, respondents may be asked to preview a particular television show with ads imbedded in it. They are then questioned about the program itself as well as brand preferences. Comparing the answers to measures taken beforehand, it's possible to determine the amount of attitude change.

SALES PROMOTION

Sales promotion is communication designed to stimulate immediate purchases using tools such as coupons, contests and free samples.[42] It is used frequently by most companies and it accounts for $177 billion in annual expenditures in the United States.[43] Notice that the definition focuses on immediate results and changes in the behavior of consumers or other channel members. In addition to its value as a short-term incentive, there is no doubt that sales promotion for many brands has a lot to do with long-term brand equity. This is particularly true of frequently purchased consumer items, such as Coke and Pepsi. Sales promotion plays an important role in reinforcing continuous usage and offsetting gains made by competitors. When brand switching occurs, sales promotion is a valuable way to regain consumer loyalty.

Sales promotion also stimulates trial. Many times, buyers are reluctant to try a new product because it may not perform as well as their existing one. Sales promotion reduces the risk by lowering the price or creating other incentives. Most consumers are now accustomed to having a trial opportunity at little or no cost. Car dealers offer test drives, and some companies provide free samples. MCI gives away free long distance minutes to college students, and IBM lets them use computers at college festivals.[44]

Whereas advertising and public relations increase awareness, sales promotion prompts people to action, resulting in immediate sales. By either increasing the perceived value of a product or reducing its price, sales promotion motivates customers to make an immediate purchase decision. Value is increased by providing a free gift, an unusual warranty, or some type of prize. Price may be lowered directly, with an introductory offer, or through coupons and rebates. In any case, the consumer recognizes an immediate opportunity and acts on it.

Although sales promotion generally has an immediate result, its long-term effects are less clear. It is most commonly used in conjunction with other forms of promotion, such as advertising, public relations campaigns, or personal selling. Consequently, it is usually seen as part of the total promotion package designed by the marketing communication strategists.

Sales promotion
Communications designed to stimulate immediate purchases using tools such as coupons, contests, and free samples.

TYPES OF SALES PROMOTION

Figure 15-8 depicts four different types of sales promotion: business-to-business, consumer, trade, and retailer promotions.

Figure 15-8   Types of Sales Promotion

Consumer promotion
Offer designed to pull the product through the retail establishment.

Trade promotion
An offer from a manufacturer to channel members, such as wholesalers and retailers.

Retailer promotion
An offer to the consumer that is sponsored by a retailer.

Figure 15-9 lists typical activities in each category. Business-to-business promotions usually involves trade shows, conventions, sales contests, and specialty deals, such as volume discounts and price sales. Sales promotion in the consumer market is directed at gaining a behavioral change by way of trial or actual purchase. Manufacturers use two basic approaches to influence the consumer, the sales pull and the sales push. **Consumer promotions** are manufacturer incentives offered directly to consumers, largely bypassing the retailer. They are designed to pull the product through the retail establishment with coupons, rebates, and other means that the manufacturer can control from headquarters.

Trade promotions are provided by manufacturers to distribution channel members. The objective is to give wholesalers and/or retailers an incentive to sell the manufacturer's brand. Essentially, these promotions make it worthwhile for the channel member to push the product to the consumer. Common incentives are advertising allowances and price reductions. For example, Ralston Purina may offer a 3 percent discount on Cat Chow to retailers. They may pass the savings on to the consumers in order to increase trade or may pocket the difference in order to increase profit.

Retailer promotions are directed at the consumer by the retail outlet. They are often confined to a local area, although large chains like Best Buy may run many of the same promotions at all locations. This provides a sales level sufficient to obtain quantity discounts from suppliers, which enables prices to be kept low.

Normally, the push and pull elements of the sales promotion strategy should work hand in hand. Trade promotions are usually coordinated with the firm's other sales activities. The sales force works to persuade customers (retailers or wholesalers) to purchase greater volume and push to consumers through retailer promotions. At the same time, consumer promotions are usually coordinated with ad messages about coupons and/or point-of-purchase displays tied into the advertising theme. This kind of one-two punch can produce dramatic results.

THE SUCCESS OF SALES PROMOTION

Sales promotion has become increasingly successful due to changing consumer lifestyles, better technology, and the changing structure of the retail industry.[45] Today's busy consumers are looking for ways to simplify purchase choices in order to save time. In addition, they want value, and they view sales promotion as a way of getting more for their money. Furthermore, one study shows that more than half of all households favor grocery brands that are supported with sales promotions.[46]

Technology helps marketers target sales promotions more precisely than ever before. Checkout scanners tell immediately which brands are purchased. Sorting machines identify which coupons and other redemption items are used, and tracking devices identify where purchases are made and by whom. It's now very easy for marketers to measure the effect of specific promotion activities on unit sales and profitability. For example, GTE developed a frequent shopper program for retailers that combine scanner data with information about consumers to reward the best customers, thereby improving relationship marketing. Companies supporting the program included RJR Nabisco, Scott Paper, and Philip Morris (for its Maxwell House, and Yuban brands).[47]

Another influence on the use of promotions is the changing structure of the retail industry. As large establishments such as Wal-Mart gain market power, they can compete more

Business-to-Business Promotions	Manufacturer Trade Promotions	Manufacturer Consumer Promotions	Retailer Consumer Promotions
Trade shows	Discounts	Coupons	Price cuts
Conventions	• off invoice	Rebates (refunds)	Displays
Sales contests	• off list	Samples	Free goods ("trials")
Specialty items	Allowances	Price packs ("cents off")	Retailer coupons
	• advertising	Value packs ("2 for 1")	Feature advertising
	• display	Premiums (gifts)	Patronage awards
	Financing incentives	Sweepstakes (prizes & contests)	
	Contests	Point-of-purchase displays	
	Spiffs	Cross-promotion	
		Continuity programs	

Figure 15-9 Major Types of Sales Promotion Activities

effectively with manufacturers' brands. To counteract this power, manufacturers use sales promotion to create a pull through the channel and thereby maintain their customer base. At the same time, they are engaged in tremendous competitive battles to maintain market share. A company that wants to hold share is almost compelled to use sales promotions commensurate with those of other major competitors, whether retailers or other manufacturers.

CREATING CUSTOMER RELATIONSHIPS AND LOYALTY THROUGH SALES PROMOTION

Sales promotion is an excellent tool for organizations that want to connect with customers through relationships. The purpose of relationship marketing is to create loyal, satisfied customers. Consumers can be very fickle, however, and marketers must keep that constantly in mind. Figure 15-10 describes the four main categories of buyers and strategies for marketing to each group.[48]

Current Loyals   As the name implies, current loyals are presently purchasing a company's brand. They range from intensely loyal users who buy because of their relationship with the company to people who are loyal because of simple convenience or price factors. It's difficult to persuade them to switch. One strategy used to maintain these customers is to reward their loyalty with personally targeted one-to-one promotions. This encourages them to continue using the brand and reminds them about the product they have been purchasing. For example, what is more personal than a birthday? Burger King began a kid's club in January 1990, and now more than four million children receive a bimonthly newsletter and coupons on their birthday. This builds a relationship and increases the loyalty of this important segment of consumers. Sales of Burger King children's meals have increased by 300 percent.[49]

Loyal consumers also may respond to sales promotions by buying a product in larger quantities or at a time when they normally do not purchase. For example, loyal users of Chi Chi's tortilla chips are likely to buy them in bulk, and a promotion is an opportunity to stockpile the product. Users of Starkist tuna may buy several cans when the brand is on sale. Once it is available at home, it is likely to be used more often. The competition is also preempted from selling their product until the consumer has finished the stockpile.

When a manufacturer owns two or more brands, current loyal customers are excellent candidates for **cross-selling**, promoting another of the brands or using one product to boost sales of another, often an unrelated product. Different companies also may work together to cross-sell. In 1997 Sony launched Station@Sony.com, which has been termed "one of the most ambitious destinations in cyberspace." It worked with a number of large companies as promotional partners, such as General Motors, American Airlines, Sears, and Visa International. The partners use banners, product placement, and promotional pods on the site to cross-sell their products.[50] This campaign appealed to loyal customers of all the partners, building relationships synergistically.

Switchers   Switchers purchase a number of different brands. Loyalty has decreased in recent years, and the percentage of consumers in the switcher category has become much larger. Consequently, many manufacturers and retailers focus on this group. In many cases, switch-

Cross-selling
Promotion in which the manufacturer of one brand attempts to sell another brand to the same customers, or the purchase of one product is used to stimulate the selection of another, often unrelated product.

Figure 15-10   Types of Buyers

CONNECTED: SURFING THE NET

www.7up.com

See firsthand how the uncola appeals to switchers. "Carbonate your brain" at the 7-Up Web site. Find out what 7-Up is doing for the community, keep tuned in to new music with "up beat," and enter a contest in "up for grabs."

ers cut their overall expenditures by finding the best deal at the time. They may switch regularly or only when they see an opportunity to increase value or decrease price.

Switchers are not likely to wait for an out-of-stock brand. Trade promotion aimed at maximizing inventory levels and store space works well with this group. Since they are interested in price and value, they respond to even fairly complex purchase offers. For example, several units of the same product can be bundled together, the amount of product can be increased for the same price, or the price can be reduced.

Some switchers are occasional users, purchasing infrequently or according to season. This is even true of churchgoers. In England, the Churches Advertising Network launched a series of ads targeted at this group around holiday time.[51]

Other switchers are simply seeking novelty or variety and change brands to alleviate boredom or monotony. Sales promotions work particularly well on them, since they are responsive to novel purchase opportunities. If the product is noticed at the precise time the variety seeker is interested in buying, then the manufacturer benefits. Seven-Up positions itself in a way that distinguishes it not only from colas but also from other uncolas. "When you want the taste of un, there's only one," is intended to reach the decision maker in households that purchase four or more soft drink brands.[52] A similar message is used for many 7-Eleven in-store promotions.

Price Buyers   The price buyer's only concern is cost. Most in this category want low prices, but a few choose only the most expensive brand. People in the latter category tend to ignore nearly all sales promotion, and they consider clipping coupons a total waste of time. In contrast, buyers after low prices are likely to purchase opportunistically, when they have funds and the product is on sale. They respond very well to price promotions: cents-off, two for one, buy a second one for a penny, limited time offers, and so forth.

Nonusers   Nonusers do not currently purchase a particular brand. Sales promotions are designed to create involvement, which may stimulate purchase. Again, cross-selling works to gain trial. For example, Starbucks used a popular coffee culture site to reach some of America Online's seven million subscribers.[53] In this case, sales promotion encourages nonusers to try the product. Prego urges fund-raising groups to use its book of suggestions, coupons, and helpful hints for event organization, nudging nonusers to try the company's products.[54] Some companies mail samples to nonuser's homes. Rather than throw the product out, consumers are usually willing to try it. In other cases, nonusers are supplied a trial under captive circumstances. An example is the complimentary snacks offered on airlines, such as branded peanuts, pretzels, and sodas. United Airlines serves Starbucks coffee on all flights.

BUSINESS-TO-BUSINESS PROMOTIONS

The four main types of business-to-business promotion are trade shows, conventions, sales contests, and specialty items. Often volume discounts and price sales occur in conjunction with these four activities.

Trade Shows   Trade shows are designed to bring marketers and customers together at a given location for a short period. They occur around the world and are an opportunity for companies to display existing and new product lines in ways that are convenient for customers. Nearly 75 percent of all firms use trade shows as a major promotion mechanism.[55] In the United States, nearly 6,000 trade shows take place every year, attended by approximately 80 million people.

Companies set up booths that are staffed by key personnel and salespeople, and it's not unusual for retailers and distributors to select the merchandise they will carry during the coming year. Consequently, business marketers may invest a large percentage of their promotional budget in trade shows. This is a very cost-effective way to meet a great number of potential purchasers. The cost of closing a trade show sale is estimated at around $350, compared to $1,100 for a regular business-to-business sale.[56]

Today, trade show information is heavily promoted and accessed on the Internet. The Trade Show Central Web site publicizes more than 10,000 events. A directory allows companies to find shows of interest and request information as well as register.[57] The site also provides exhibit costs, schedules, and listings of session topics and keynote speakers. Companies can quickly identify and select the event that will be the most beneficial in reaching potential customers.

Conventions Conventions provide another opportunity for marketers and buyers to meet. They are often sponsored by professional groups, such as the American Hospital Association, the American Medical Association, or the International Association of Certified Public Accountants. It is important to note that conventions are held around the world, giving marketers the chance to assess the level of global competition and gather ideas for new strategies. Although companies attend primarily to stimulate immediate sales, they also can take the opportunity to do long-range assessments of customer and industry trends. Marketing researchers often attend conventions and trade shows because so many qualified buyers are concentrated in one place. This provides a pool of readily available respondents, and schedules often permit in-depth interviews, focus groups, and surveys. These events are considered prime opportunities for data collection.

Sales Contests **Sales contests** for salespeople and dealers offer prizes for accomplishing specific goals. Most companies sponsor some type of sales contest from time to time and award trips, gifts, or cash, often at an annual sales convention. This type of sales promotion is designed to elicit immediate action by giving short-term rewards for short-term behavior. When incentives are tied to measurable and achievable sales objectives, they can be highly motivating.[58] Sales contests frequently are specific to product lines or market segments and are integrated into the overall selling and promotion strategy. Allied Signal designed an incentive plan targeted at its distributors, offering them a choice of gifts for increasing sales to retailers. This was an innovative way to encourage distributors to sell the product rather than just stock inventory.[59]

Sales contest
A competition for salespeople and dealers that awards prizes for accomplishing specific goals.

Specialty Items **Specialty items** are gifts for customers, usually sent through the mail or handed out by salespeople, with the organization's name imprinted on them. These include such items as pens, calendars, memo pads, T-shirts, sun visors, or hats. Generally there is no purchase requirement. AT&T runs a promotion on the Internet targeted at college students. The site asks them to register their name, address, and school information and in return they will be sent a free gift—a mousepad with the company logo. The site also offers links to free software, contests, and prizes as well as educational and promotional pages. The student's interaction with the site and the free gift are intended to help potential customers remember AT&T.[60]

Specialty items
Gifts with the organization's name that are provided to customers, usually given through the mail or by the sales force.

TRADE PROMOTIONS

Trade promotions are offered by the manufacturer to wholesalers or retailers. Five common types are discounts, allowances, financing incentives, sales contests, and spiffs.

Discounts One of the most popular trade promotions is discount or price-off arrangements, which reduce either the invoice or the list price. The invoice price is what the manufacturer charges to the distributor, while the list price is what the end customer is charged. If distributors choose to pass the price cut on to consumers, demand may increase. If not, distributor profit margins increase. Like all trade promotions, discounts encourage distributors to handle more of the company's product and to stimulate sales to consumers.

Allowances Allowances are funds given to retailers and wholesalers based on the amount of product they buy. Two typical allowances are for advertising and display purposes. For example, a retailer who purchases $5,000 worth of product may receive a $500 allowance to help

Approximately 80 million people attend trade shows in the United States every year.

Financing incentive
An offer to finance the retailer's inventory prior to its sale.

pay for advertising. Display allowances work the same way, except that the funds must be used for point-of-purchase displays in the retail outlet.

Financing Incentives **Financing incentives** help reduce the retailer's inventory carrying cost. This is commonly referred to as financing the "floor plan," which is the retailer's stock of inventory. For example, in the automobile business, dealers do not have to pay immediately for all the cars shipped to them. Instead, they pay a fee for having them in their showroom. Financing incentives come in a broad variety, but all are designed to get the manufacturer's product into the retail establishment.

Sales Contests and Spiffs Two other types of trade promotion are sales contests and "spiffs." In this context, sales contests reward the retailer for selling a certain level of product and often extend to the salespeople within the retail establishment. Spiffs are like a commission paid to salespeople in retail outlets who sell the manufacturer's product rather than a competitor's brand. These cash incentives are not uncommon for such items as cameras, televisions, mobile homes, and cellular telephones. Many people consider spiffs unethical because they encourage the promotion of one brand over others irrespective of its value to the customer. Because consumers are not aware of the spiff, they may believe the salesperson's motives are more "pure" than is actually the case.

Trade promotions are becoming prevalent worldwide. The Asia-Pacific Economic Cooperation (APEC) group, for example, identifies this as an area with significant potential to enhance regional economic cooperation. APEC established a working group to contribute to the development of economies through the use of trade promotion. A number of programs were created, including seminars, exchange of trade and industrial information, an international trade fair, and trade promotion training classes.[61]

RETAILER PROMOTIONS

Retailer promotions are directed specifically at the end customer and originate within the retailing organization. They seek to encourage consumers to purchase a product from a given location. Consequently, retailer promotions are often in-store or specific with regard to where the promotion can be exercised. Manufacturers may help with retailer promotions. Sony's "Modern Rock Live" campaign was one of the biggest promotions ever undertaken by the company. The vice president of personal audio/video marketing called it "a real value for consumers and a great traffic and sales builder for retailers." Sony provided kits to help outlets develop local tie-ins to the national promotion campaign, which used television, radio, and print advertising as well as a consumer Web site.[62]

The most common type of retailer promotion is price cuts. Retailers are likely to use these regularly to stimulate sales of certain product lines or to reduce inventory of older products. Also common are display promotions to direct attention to particular goods. Large national retailers are likely to send teams to work with local outlets in developing similar displays across the country. These teams are likely to be dispatched on a seasonal basis. The Gap, Inc., takes this approach for displays. Free trials are another type of retailer promotion. Local copy shops, for example, often offer a free color copy to induce customers to try their services. Retailer coupons are used relatively frequently and are often placed in local newspapers. Also popular is feature advertising on radio or television of discounted items, such as automobiles and mobile homes. It's not unusual for the retailer to be the spokesperson in these types of ads. Finally, patronage awards are very useful promotions. Generally, a card is punched or stamped each time the consumer shops at the retail outlet. When the card is filled, it's redeemed for free merchandise. The Cappuccino Cafe in Okemos, Michigan, redeems not only its own loyalty card but also those of competitors as a way to get new trials. Patronage awards, which stimulate loyalty to a given outlet, are particularly useful in local markets for creating a bond between regular customers and the retailer.

CONSUMER PROMOTIONS

Manufacturers use consumer sales promotions to influence their market share across all retailing outlets. There are several popular forms: coupons, rebates, samples, sweepstakes, price and value packs, point-of-purchase displays, and continuity programs.

Coupon
Certificate that entitles a consumer to an incentive to buy the product, usually a price reduction or a free sample.

Coupons **Coupons** are certificates that entitle a consumer to an incentive, usually a price reduction or free sample. Trade coupons are redeemable only at a particular store or chain, whereas manufacturer coupons are redeemable at any outlet. They are particularly appealing to manufacturers, because they can make a direct connection with consumers. Since manufacturer coupons create work for retailers, they may be given compensation or incentives for handling them.

Coupons are one of the most popular forms of consumer sales promotion.[63] Some consumers purchase a large percentage of their nondurable products through coupons. Research has shown that they have higher levels of education and income, live in urban areas, and are less loyal to brands or stores.[64] Many of them decide which coupons to use before they shop.[65] A recent national survey by the Nielsen Co. revealed that five out of six households use grocery coupons as an important part of their shopping. Yet, although manufacturers distribute $400 billion every year, only $6.25 billion is redeemed. Often people don't like to take the time to search for and cut coupons. And most newspapers or magazines are thrown out before the coupons are clipped. Brand loyalty is another factor, since coupons may not be available for the consumer's products of choice.[66]

Coupons are generally distributed as freestanding inserts (FSIs) in newspapers or magazines. They also may be sent in special mailings or as bill stuffers. Another technique is an on-shelf dispenser at the retail outlet, placed near the manufacturer's brand. Only about 2 percent of regular coupons are redeemed, 8.5 percent of checkout coupons, 9.8 percent of electronic coupons, and 13 percent of on-shelf coupons. Marketers try to identify the level of price reduction that will stimulate coupon use. If a 25-cent incentive will do as much as a 50-cent reduction, then the 25-cent incentive should be used.

Despite the popularity of coupons, Procter & Gamble says it will reduce and eventually eliminate them. Company research shows that 98 percent of the regular coupons issued each year in the United States are never redeemed. Furthermore, consumers prefer low prices to coupons. In response, Procter & Gamble has cut spending on this kind of sales promotion by 50 percent over the last five years and has reduced prices on its products by 6 percent since 1991.[67]

Rebates   Rebates are refunds given to consumers for the purchase of particular items. Psychologically, rebates make a larger impression than price reductions. For example, let's say an automobile manufacturer offers a $1,500 rebate or a 10 percent reduction in price for a $15,000 car. While the discount may be precisely the same, consumers are likely to see the rebate as greater. The reason is that the price discount from $15,000 to $13,500 is a perceptually smaller decrease than the $1,500 rebate. Since consumers usually have to mail a form to the manufacturer to get the rebate, they often will not bother if the amount is small. They also may lose or forget about the rebate. In those cases the company gets the sale without paying the incentive. Another advantage of rebates is that they leave higher margins for intermediaries.

Rebates tend to be particularly effective in stimulating trial of brands that are priced higher than those of competitors. Hewlett-Packard recently ran a $100 rebate on its Office-Jet printer-fax-copier products to stimulate sales. The offer, in combination with already low

Coupons are generally distributed as free-standing inserts in newspapers or magazines.

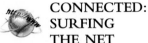

CONNECTED: SURFING THE NET

www.hp.com

"Customers around the world rely on Hewlett-Packard's broad array of products and services—in measurement, computation, and communication—to ready them for the 21st century." Find out if Hewlett-Packard has any rebate offers on-line by connecting to its Web site.

prices, was intended to target the estimated 31 million professionals who work at home. To get the rebate, customers had to submit a completed rebate coupon in addition to a proof-of-purchase sticker. They received their rebate six to eight weeks after the purchase.[68]

Samples Generally, samples are distributed via direct mail, door to door, or in stores. Sometimes coupons may be redeemed for free samples. This method is effective with new products or when targeted at people who lack experience with the brand. Occasionally, manufacturers attempt to renew an older product by providing samples. Co-op Promotions, which specializes in samples, packaged Off! insect repellent in one million Sunbeam barbecue grills for S. C. Johnson. Teldyne installed its shower massage in shower heads used by 35,000 bicyclists during a 15-city tour.[69] American Sampling, Inc., sends gift packs to 3.8 million new mothers annually, and companies like Market Source provide samples to college freshmen. Chesebrough Pond offered 80,000 samples and coupons of its newly formulated lotion to consumers in five different malls.

This kind of sales promotion requires very careful attention to detail because the cost of samples is high. One study found that 51 million coupons for a free product distributed through free standing inserts, FSIs cost $7 per thousand, while five million samples distributed through direct mail cost $80 per thousand. But the FSIs only converted 367,200 people ($0.97 per convert), while the mail samples converted 800,000 ($0.50 per convert.)[70]

Sweepstakes A sweepstakes is a contest in which participants' names are pooled, and the winner is drawn randomly. Most of you have experienced a twinge of anticipation upon receiving an envelope stating that you may have won millions of dollars. The objective of the contest is to get buyers to purchase the products included in the sweepstakes offer. Laws prevent the sponsor from requiring a purchase in order to participate. Sweepstakes promoters must provide full disclosure of the requirements for entering as well as the probabilities of winning.

A recent "Family Fantasy Sweepstakes" at Disney.com offered more than $200,000 in prizes. Participants could sign up to win Disneyland vacations, a GMC Jimmy, and a $5,000 shopping spree, among other prizes. The site encouraged consumers to enter daily, which also gave more exposure to Disney's Web site promotions.[71]

Price and Value Packs Price and value packs are cents-off or two-for-one offers. The cents-off variety is easiest to administer and receives a great deal of attention. The value pack, while more difficult to administer, gets more product in the hands of the consumer in a shorter period. Both are very flexible and relatively easy sales promotions to consumers. Value packs are different from premiums or gifts, which may not be related directly to the product. For example, in real estate sales it's not uncommon for the purchaser of a home to receive a free airline ticket to a vacation spot.

Point-of-Purchase Displays Point-of-purchase (POP) displays exhibit products at retail locations. Since up to 70 percent of purchase decisions are made in the store, the displays can be very important. Companies spend more than $12 billion annually on POP. More than 52 percent of carbonated beverage sales, 26 percent of candy/mint sales, and 22 percent of beer/ale sales are attributed to such displays.[72] They work best when tied directly to other messages or advertising campaigns. Generally, POP displays need to have a lot of attention-getting power and must focus the consumer's interest on the sales promotion and product at hand.

POP displays have a lot of attention getting power and can increase consumers interest in a product.

Many stores are using POP to connect with customers in an interactive and exciting environment. For example, customers at Niketown can hear the sounds of bouncing tennis balls and squeaking tennis shoes. Richard Nathan, head of RTC, one of the largest POP design companies in the United States, says: "It's sensory, it's visual, but not just for amusement. The best POP is not just fun; it informs you and shows you how to find products in a store."[73] A point-of-purchase display for Sega of America won an award at a trade show for its innovative design and widespread retail acceptance. The display, with wing panels joined by a glass case, had visual appeal and encouraged customers to stop and look at the products.[74]

Continuity Programs Continuity programs reward people for continued and frequent use of a particular product. A good example is the frequent flyer miles offered in the airline industry. While these usually don't stimulate more air travel, they are an incentive for a purchaser to travel with a particular carrier. The programs also are a recognized tool for increasing customer satisfaction. Nearly every airline offers frequent flyer miles, and most hotel chains now have similar programs. Hyatt, for example, offers free room stays after a certain number of regular stays. Continuity programs tend to run longer than other types of sales promotion because their basic objective is to promote long-term usage. Some airlines have used these programs for more than a decade, and most hotel chains plan to continue theirs almost indefinitely.

PUBLIC RELATIONS AND PUBLICITY

PUBLIC RELATIONS

Public relations (PR) is the use of publicity and other nonpaid forms of communication designed to present the firm and its products positively. A disadvantage is that the communication is not always controlled by the company. It can determine when to issue press releases and hold events, but it cannot control the press that independently decides whether to run the communication. Nevertheless, public relations offers several advantages not found with other types of promotion vehicles. Because gatekeepers—editors and news reporters—screen company-issued communication to ensure its accuracy, the public can have some confidence that the information it receives through public relations is truthful. In addition, PR provides editorial-type messages that can break through advertising clutter. The media cost is little or nothing, although development of the PR campaign can be expensive. Public relations can be used to establish the social responsibility of a good corporate citizen. Because of the typical content and source of messages, it is possible to reach upscale opinion leaders, who in turn spread the message. Furthermore, there are few legal restrictions on PR activities, making it a way to address numerous issues in a more balanced light than may be possible with advertising.

Public relations (PR)
The use of publicity and other nonpaid forms of communication to present the firm and its products positively.

Public relations is likely to focus on many publics, including employees, shareholders, community members, news media, and government. Rather than directly promote a particular product or brand, most PR messages have the appearance of objectivity. Many PR promotional campaigns center on social issues. For example, Avon supports breast cancer awareness in the United States, the prevention of violence against women in Malaysia, child nourishment in China, and AIDS prevention in Thailand. Toys "R" Us and Reebok offer gift certificates in exchange for guns. This type of public relations is known as *cause marketing* and costs $1 billion annually. One study found that 66 percent of consumers would switch brands if they considered the cause worthwhile. But the same study revealed that 58 percent of consumers believe cause marketing is insincere.[75] Effective PR requires activities consistent with the goals and objectives of the organization.[76]

The Washington Apple Commission supported the North American Free Trade Agreement (NAFTA) because its defeat would have cost the industry $150 million a year. It developed a PR strategy with a target market of 11 members of Congress. First, it started a letter-writing campaign by sending packets to almost 4,000 apple growers and shippers. The packet contained a sample letter to editors and congressional delegates as well as a fact sheet on NAFTA. Then, 51 agricultural producers in Washington State signed a letter endorsing NAFTA. Next, one apple grower went to Washington state with 150 other pro-NAFTA groups to meet with the president. This resulted in some free publicity on the television networks and the national wire services, who liked the idea of an apple grower talking to the president. The commission continued its show of public support but also focused its efforts on press conferences. Once again, two national wire services wrote stories on the industry. The PR effort resulted in a 10–1 vote in favor of NAFTA by the targeted congressional delegates. It also won an award from the National Agri-Marketing Association.

Public relations supports the marketing function in several ways.

- *Corporate communication.* Messages promote a better understanding of the organization among employees, shareholders, and other relevant publics.
- *Press relations.* Newsworthy information, such as new activities and personnel promotions, are provided to the media on a timely basis.
- *Lobbying.* Communication with legislators and government officials to promote or defeat legislation is a major activity for heavily regulated industries.
- *Product publicity.* Newsworthy innovations or new attributes of products can be promoted at little cost through the media.

PUBLICITY

Publicity is what is communicated about an organization in the public news media. Publicity can be positive or negative. Negative publicity detracts from the organization's image and can have serious effects on its market position. Most PR groups attempt to generate positive publicity through news stories and public service announcements. The more common avenues are press releases, news conferences, and the event sponsorship. The Internet increasingly is being used by marketers, both to spread publicity and to respond to crisis situations.

Press release

A statement written by company personnel and distributed to various media for publication at their discretion.

Press Releases and News Conferences A **press release** is a statement written by company personnel and distributed to various media for publication at their discretion. It includes information about the organization or product that marketers believe will be of interest to the public. The advantage of a press release is that the marketer has control over what information is provided. Many large organizations issue press releases regularly. This type of communication is used almost invariably when negative publicity needs to be countered. Rather than leave it to the media to track down the facts, companies provide the same information to all members of the press simultaneously. Press releases must be accurate, to the point, and based on hard evidence. If not, then the media will become skeptical about any material the company issues.

News or press conferences occur when reporters are invited to a meeting at which company officials make a public statement and usually respond to questions. As with press releases, companies have some control over news conferences.

Sponsored Events or Activities A very popular type of publicity is sponsored events or activities, especially for local promotion. Many companies sponsor rock or symphony concerts, sports teams, or youth groups. This gets their name before the public while contributing to the community. Various nontraditional activities are becoming popular publicity opportunities. To attract baby boomers, such companies as Audi, United Airlines, and Banana Republic have sponsored food and wine festivals, drawing as many as 5,000 attendees. Ford Motor's Lincoln is associating with mountain biking, arts, and hot-air balloon events.[77]

The Internet The Internet can be an ideal medium for publicity. In fact, it has spawned a new group of PR companies. Edelman Public Relations Worldwide is a leading creator of Web sites. Its services can be especially helpful when companies need to minimize negative publicity. For example, several bottles of Odwalla apple juice were found to contain *E. coli* bacteria. In less than three hours, Edelman created a site to provide consumers with information. It did the same for American Home Products after the death of model Chrissy Taylor, reportedly caused by inhaling Primatene Mist. The site was running within 12 hours and is still on the Web today.[78]

Other companies use the Internet to host chat sessions, which serve as a form of positive publicity. ICMA Retirement Corporation gives consumers a chance to interact with its president and CEO, Girard Miller. Robert Barkin, the company's vice president of public relations, says: "This is an opportunity for everyone with access to the Internet, whether they work in the public sector or not, to chat with one of the nation's leading authorities on retirement issues."[79]

Marketers who skillfully blend public relations and publicity into their communications mix can underscore and intensify the positive feelings created by other mass communications activities. In chapter 16 we will turn our attention to the most personal and individualized form of marketing communication—personal selling. Although one-on-one relationship building is key to effective personal selling, mass communications provides important support. It lays the groundwork for personal sales by creating deeper receptivity toward the company and its products.

 CONNECTED: SURFING THE NET

Subaru

www.subaru.com

THIS CHAPTER'S DIVERSITY FEATURE, "BREAKING TABOOS at Subaru," discussed the company's efforts to target advertisements to gays and lesbians. To expand your thinking about communication, visit Subaru's Web site and answer the following questions.

1. The Internet offers two-way interaction, making mass communication more personal. How does Subaru's site make this personal connection?
2. Whether alone or in support of other promotion vehicles, advertising informs, persuades, reminds, or reinforces. Which of these does the Subaru Web site best accomplish? Explain.
3. Each medium has unique advantages. Compare the advantages of Subaru's Web site to the other types of media discussed in the chapter. Select three which you think would be the most effective if used in combination.
4. Select a press release under the new product information category. If you were an advertiser for Subaru, what steps would you take to create the ad? Give examples of what you might do at each step, keeping the new product information in mind.

Yahoo!

www.yahoo.com

THIS CHAPTER'S TECHNOLOGY FEATURE DISCUSSED YAHOO!, a search engine on the World Wide Web. To learn more about Yahoo!, visit it's Web site and answer the following questions.

1. Go to the Yahoo! Information Center and find out about the Web launch program. What is it? Do you think this is an effective way to advertise? Why or why not?
2. How could Yahoo! use its Web site for public relations communication? Give an example of how it could help with positive publicity and minimize negative publicity.
3. From the press releases, select the April 8, 1997, article, "Yahoo! to Provide New Internet Advertising and Site Measurement Process." What advantages will this have for advertisers using the Web for mass communications? How might this change the way companies are able to connect with customers on the Internet?

CHAPTER SUMMARY

OBJECTIVE 1: Understand the concept of mass communication including the relative use of advertising, sales promotion, and public relations.

Mass communication helps companies connect with customers around the world. It adds value by providing information about the goods and services available. Expenditure on mass communication—advertising, sales promotion, and public relations—is increasing at about 7 percent annually in the United States and at a slightly higher rate globally. Roughly the same amount is spent on

sales promotion and advertising, but sales promotion is slightly ahead and is growing faster. Public relations is a distant third.

OBJECTIVE 2: Learn how technology, globalization, and ethics are playing major roles in mass communication.

The history of mass communication coincides with the development of communications technology, particularly print, radio, and television. Today, the Internet is adding an interactive medium. Global mass communication occurs when key elements of messages are standardized across regions and nations. Standardization has cost advantages when the same customer segments are found in many countries, but it has several limitations. The primary ethical issue in mass communication is deception. Puffery may be used to make a point, but care must be taken not to be deceptive. Some countries have very strict legislation that does not allow exaggerations of any sort.

OBJECTIVE 3: Know the objectives, advantages, and disadvantages of advertising, as well as the sequence of steps in creating an advertising campaign.

Advertising is highly controllable and works over time to build brand equity. It is cost effective for reaching large audiences. Its primary objective may be to inform consumers, to persuade them to buy, to remind them of the product, or to reinforce buying behavior and positive feelings about the brand. Advertising media are readily available, and it's easy for marketers to find help in creating effective campaigns. But advertising reaches many people outside the target audience, encounters a high level of avoidance, and can be costly. It also can communicate only brief, one-way messages. There are several different types of advertising: national, retail (local), directory, business-to-business, institutional, direct response, public service, and political. Generally, there are five steps in developing the advertising plan: set objectives, establish the budget, create the theme and message, select and schedule media, create the ads, and assess effectiveness.

OBJECTIVE 4: Understand sales promotion objectives and what types of promotions are used to stimulate sales in business, trade, retailer, and consumer markets.

Sales promotion is used to prompt consumers to action, resulting in immediate sales results. It is generally used with other forms of promotion, such as advertising, public relations, or personal selling. There are four types of sales promotion: business-to-business, trade, retailer, and consumer. Business-to-business promotions include trade shows, conventions, sales contests, and specialty deals. Trade promotions, which are offered by manufacturers to wholesalers or retailers, include discounts, allowances, financing incentives, sales contests, and spiffs. Retailer promotions, offered to consumers, include price cuts, displays, free trials, coupons, and patronage awards. Consumer promotions are manufacturers' offers, including coupons, rebates, free samples, sweepstakes, price and value packs, POP displays, and continuity programs.

OBJECTIVE 5: Understand the use of public relations in marketing.

Public relations activities are used primarily to influence feelings, opinions, or beliefs about a company or its products. An attempt is made to develop messages that at least have the appearance of objectivity. PR supports the marketing function in the following ways: corporate communication, press relations, lobbying, and product publicity. Common publicity-generating activities are press releases, news conferences, and sponsorship of events or activities. Because public relations messages are placed through public channels, the messages tend to be more credible and believable. They also tend to break through the advertising clutter and are relatively low in cost. Public relations can publicize the social responsibility of a good corporate citizen.

REVIEW YOUR UNDERSTANDING

1. Why is global standardization of mass communication useful?
2. How do deception and puffery relate?
3. What is advertising? What is its overriding goal?
4. What are the objectives of advertising, which also describe types of ads?
5. What are some of the advantages and disadvantages of advertising?
6. List the eight types of advertising. What is the focus of each?
7. Name the six types of advertising media. What are the advantages and disadvantages of each?

8. What is sales promotion? How is it different from advertising?
9. Briefly describe the four different types of sales promotion. What are the most common promotional activities within each category?
10. How does sales promotion help build relationships?
11. What is public relations? How is it unique from other forms of mass communication?
12. What are the pros and cons of public relations?

DISCUSSION OF CONCEPTS

1. Describe the five steps in developing an advertising plan. Which ones would you most enjoy working on? Least enjoy? Why?
2. Why is it important to develop a creative strategy before creating specific ads?
3. Which techniques are most commonly used to determine the advertising budget? Which one do you believe should be used and why?
4. What are the critical issues in selecting and scheduling the appropriate advertising media?
5. As with any creative process, it's difficult to determine precisely what people will like. When it comes to developing an advertisement, what are some of the characteristics that will tend to make the ad successful? Why?

6. In business, it's important to measure how well the organization performs certain tasks in order to make adjustments as necessary. How do marketers measure the effectiveness of advertising campaigns?
7. Marketers sometimes divide consumers into four categories of buyers. Briefly describe each type and the promotional activities that are likely to be successful with each.
8. List the most popular types of trade promotions. When is each type appropriate?
9. How do the advantages and disadvantages of public relations compare to those of other forms of promotional activities?

Advertising: Paid communication through nonpersonal channels.

Advertising agency: A business that develops, prepares, and places advertising for sellers seeking to find customers for their products.

Advertising campaign: A series of advertisements with a main theme running through them.

Aided recall: The viewer is given some specific piece of information about the ad before being asked if s/he recalls having seen it.

Consumer promotion: Offer designed to pull the product through the retail establishment.

Continuity: The length of time the advertising campaign will run in a given medium.

Coupon: Certificate that entitles a consumer to an incentive to buy the product, usually a price reduction or a free sample.

Creative strategy: The strategy that governs and coordinates the development of individual ads and assures their visual images and words convey precisely and consistently what the advertiser wants to communicate.

Cross-selling: Promotion in which the manufacturer of one brand attempts to sell another brand to the same customers, or the purchase of one product is used to stimulate the selection of another, often unrelated product.

Exposure: The process of putting the ad in contact with the consumer.

Financing incentive: An offer to finance the retailer's inventory prior to its sale.

Frequency: The number of times the audience is reached in a given period, usually per day or per week.

Informative advertising: Messages designed to provide information that consumers can store for later use.

Institutional advertising: Messages designed to communicate corporate identity and philosophy as opposed to product information.

Overexposure: Continuing to reach a prospect after a buying de-

cision has been made or to the point that the campaign becomes tedious and actually turns off some potential buyers.

Persuasive advertising: Messages designed to change consumers' attitudes and opinions about products, often listing product attributes, pricing, and other factors that may influence consumer decisions.

Press release: A statement written by company personnel and distributed to various media for publication at their discretion.

Public relations (PR): The use of publicity and other nonpaid forms of communication to present the firm and its products positively.

Pulling power: The ability to maintain the interest of the consumer to the end of the advertising message.

Reach: The number of consumers in the target audience who can be contacted through a given medium.

Reinforcement advertising: Messages that call attention to specific characteristics of products experienced by the user.

Reminder advertising: Messages that keep the product at the forefront of the consumer's mind.

Retailer promotion: An offer to the consumer that is sponsored by a retailer.

Sales contest: A competition for salespeople and dealers that awards prizes for accomplishing specific goals.

Sales promotion: Communications designed to stimulate immediate purchases using tools such as coupons, contests, and free samples.

Specialty items: Gifts with the organization's name that are provided to customers, usually given through the mail or by the sales force.

Stopping power: The ability of an ad to gain and hold the consumer's attention.

Trade promotion: An offer from a manufacturer to channel members, such as wholesalers and retailers.

Unaided recall: The viewer is asked to identify any advertisements s/he can remember.

REFERENCES

1. Jeff Jensen, "'Jurassic' Sequel Set to Be Promo Monster," *Advertising Age*, February 10, 1997, pp. 1, 46; Judann Pollack, "Hershey Creates World of 'Dino' Candy," *Advertising Age*, February 10, 1997, p. 46; Jeff Jensen, "Studios Take Supporting Role for Movie Licensees," *Advertising Age*, June 24, 1996, p. 45; Mark Gleason, "Mercedes is Going 'Jurassic,'" *Advertising Age*, June 17, 1996; and CNN Headline News report on New York Toy Fair, broadcast February 15, 1997.
2. Regis McKenna, "Marketing is Everything," *Harvard Business Review*, January-February 1991, pp. 65–79.
3. Ian P. Murphy, "Yearly 7% Growth Seen for Communications Spending," *Marketing News*, October 7, 1996, p. 8; "Marketing Communications and Promotion Strategy," www.pcola.gulf.net/tonypitt/mk15.htm, site visited on February 20, 1997; Kip D. Cassino, "A World of Advertising," *American Demographics*, November 1997, pp. 57-60; and, Robert J. Coen, "Ad Revenue Growth Hits 7% in 1997 to Surpass Forecasts," *Advertising Age*, May 18, 1998, p. 50.
4. "Heads of Top Soft Drink Brands Bring Budget Artillery, Smarts to Battlefield," www.adage.com, site visted on January 31, 1997.
5. The following history is taken from William Wells, John Burnett, and Sandra Moriarty, *Advertising* (Upper Saddle River, NJ: Prentice Hall, 1992), pp. 20–29.
6. Warren J. Keegan and Mark C. Green, *Principles of Global Marketing* (Upper Saddle River, NJ: Prentice Hall, 1997), p. 355.
7. Subhash C. Jain, "Standardization of International Marketing Strategy: Some Research Hypotheses," *Journal of Marketing* 53 (January 1989): 70–79.
8. William K. Darley and Denise M. Johnson, "An Exploratory Investigation of the Dimensions of Beliefs toward Advertising in General: A Comparative Analysis of Four Developing Countries," *Journal of International Consumer Marketing* 7, no. 1 (1994): 5–21; and J. Craig Andrews, Srinivas Durvasula, and Richard G. Netemeyer, "Testing the Cross-National Applicability of U.S. and Russia Advertising Belief and Attitude Meaures," *Journal of Advertising* 23 (March 1994): 21.
9. Jeff Jensen, "New NFL Unit Goes after International Fans," *Advertising Age*, November 18, 1996, p.10.
10. Associated Press, "Ben & Jerry's Names Odak to CEO Position," *Wall Steet Journal Interactive Edition*, January 2, 1997.
11. John R. Boatright, *Ethics and the Conduct of Business* (Upper Saddle River, NJ: Prentice Hall, 1997), p. 277.
12. Federal Trade Commission File No. 9423202, "NordicTrack Agrees to Settle FTC Charges over Deceptive Use of Study Results for Weight Loss Claims," released February 15, 1996.
13. Federal Trade Commission, "Eggland's Best Cholesterol Claims Called Deceptive," released March 13, 1996, www.ftc.gov, site visited February 18, 1997.
14. Federal Trade Commission, ASH (Action on Smoking and Health) Press

Release, "Philip Morris Deceptive Ad Campaign Banned in France," June 1996, www.ftc.gov, site visited February 18, 1997.

15. Wells, Burnett, and Moriarty, *Advertising*, p. 10.

16. Land Rover advertisement, *Fortune*, March 4, 1996, p. 50.

17. "CompuServe to Break New Branding Campaign," www.adage.com, October 13, 1995.

18. Associated Press, "McDonald's New Theme Sounds Like Old Theme," *Marketing News*, March 27, 1995, p. 5

19. "Advertising-to-Sales Ratios, 1993," *Marketing News* August 8, 1994, p. 38.

20. J. Thomas Russell and W. Ronald Lane, *Kleppner's Advertising Procedure* (Upper Saddle River, NJ: Prentice Hall, 1993), p. 24.

21. "Phone Battle Involves More than Just Budgets: Planning Critical for AT&T and BellSouth," *Advertising Age*, www.adage.com, site visited on February 20, 1997.

22. Richard Babyak, "Demystifying the Asian Consumer," *Appliance Manufacturer*, February 1995, pp. w25–w27.

23. *Marketing Update Newsletter*, exton.com, last updated January 15, 1997.

24. "Advertising Age's 50 Best Commercials," www.adage.com, site visited on February 14, 1997.

25. Ibid.

26. Ibid.

27. Elizabeth Gleick, "Read All about It," *Time*, October 21, 1996, p. 66.

28. Katrina Brooker, "Papers Lose Tweedy 'Tude, Find Black Ink," *Fortune*, June 8, 1998, p. 38.

29. Chuck Ross, "Online Homes Show Lower Usage of TV," www.adage.com, January 13, 1997.

30. Chad Rubel, "Radio Tunes in to Post-Buy Analysis of Advertising," *Marketing News*, June 3, 1996, p. 7.

31. Mediamark Research, Inc., *Doublebase 1988 Study: 19*, cited in "Study of Media Involvement," *Audits & Surveys*, March 1988.

32. Rhonda L. Rundle and James P. Miller, "Outdoor Systems' New Deal Aids Transition from Tobacco," *Wall Street Journal Interactive Edition*, May 2, 1997.

33. Steve Kloehn and Terry Armour, "Rodman to be Yanked from Mural," *Chicago Tribune*, April 4, 1996, www.chicago.tribune.com/sports/bulls/bslnr/bsrchive/rodman9.htm.

34. "Surfing Popular But Not Way of Life," *USA Today*, December 12, 1996, www.usatoday.com.

35. Harris Gordon, "B-to-B Marketing in the Interactive Age," *Business Marketing*, July-August 1996, p. A2.

36. Thomas E. Weber, "World Wide Wow: Sites Offer Advertisers a Money Back Deal," *Wall Street Journal Interactive Edition*, June 27, 1997.

37. "New Alliance at Careers.wsj.com" *WSJ New Features*, http://Listserv.dowjones.com, received via e-mail on June 10, 1998.

38. Karen Benezra and T. L. Stanley, "Slack-O Bell: Taco King Promo Tack hits where Genx Lives," *Brandweek*, November 7, 1994, pp. 1, 6.

39. Judann Pollack, "Weight Loss Rivals Boost Ad Budgets for New Year Rush," http://www.adage.com, January 6, 1997.

40. Brian Toyne and Peter G. P. Walters, *Global Market Management* (Boston: Allyn & Bacon, 1993), p. 250.

41. "International Marketing Nightmares," *Marketing Update Newsletter*, http://exton.com, updated on August 15, 1996.

42. Adapted from Peter D. Bennett, *Dictionary of Marketing Terms* (Chicago: American Marketing Association, 1988), p. 179.

43. "Marketing Communications and Promotion Strategy."

44. Terry Lefton, "Try It: You'll Like It," *Brandweek*, May 24, 1993, pp. 27–32.

45. Robert D. Buzzell, John A. Quelch, and Walter J. Salmon, "The Costly Bargain of Trade Promotions," *Harvard Business Review*, March-April 1990, pp. 141–149.

46. "Consumers Remain High on Promotions," *Marketing Times*, March-April 1993, p. 11.

47. Terry Lefton, "GTE Bails Out of Scanner Based Program," *Brandweek*, March 1, 1993, pp. 1, 6.

48. Shultz, p. 11.

49. Cyndee Miller, "Marketer Hoping Kids Will Join Club, Become Lifelong Customers," *Marketing News*, January 31, 1994, pp. 1–2.

50. Chuck Ross and Bradley Johnson, "Sky's the Limit for Sony's Ambitious Station Plans," February 3, 1997, www.adage.com.

51. "Church Reclaims Sunday with Ads," *Marketing*, December 16, 1993, p. 5.

52. Tim Davis, "Uncola Ads Target Larger Audience, Diet 7-Up Still in the 'Spot-Light,'" *Beverage World*, October 31, 1992, p. 19.

53. Bill McDowell, "Starbucks Is Ground Zero in Today's Coffee Culture," December 1996, www.adage.com.

54. Joan Flanagan, "Spaghetti Dinners Raising Friends and Money," *Fund Raising Management*, July 1994, pp. 29–32.

55. Business/Professional Advertising Association, 1992.

56. Pat Friedlander, "When Is It Time to Get a New Booth?" *Business Marketing*, February 1993, p. 48.

57. www.tscentral.com, site last updated March 29, 1996, site visited on February 14, 1997.

58. ttisms.com/oss/contests.html, site visited on February 14, 1997.

59. "The Incentive Edge: Case Study: Establishing Goals Simple & Specific," *Sales and Marketing Management*, May 1994, p. 8.

60. www.att.com/college/demogr.html, site visited on February 14, 1997.

61. "Asia-Pacific Economic Cooperation," www.apecsec.org/tpwgf.html, site visited February 14, 1997.

62. "Sony Electronics Announces National Modern Rock Live Retail Promotion," www.2.sel.sony.com/SEL/consuemr/ss5/press_releases/mrock.htm visited November 16, 1997.

63. Schultz, p. 31.

64. Capil Bawa and Robert W. Shoemaker, "The Coupon-Prone Consumer," *Journal of Marketing*, October 1987, pp. 99–110.

65. "Coupon Users Need Incentive," *Promotional Sense*, June 1992, p. 1.

66. "Coupons on Demand," www.wyattweb.com/freepage/s/sjm@bright.net/home.shtml, site visited on February 14, 1997.

67. Associated Press, "P&G: We're Committed to Cutting Coupons," *Marketing News*, January 6, 1997, p. 10.

68. "HP Announces $100 Rebate on its Office Jet Printer Fax Copier Products," October 23, 1995, http://hpcc998.external.hp.com/pressrel/oct95/23oct95k.html.

69. Lefton, "Try It: You'll Like It"; Laurie Freeman, "Direct Contact Key to Building Brands," *Advertising Age*, October 25, 1993, p. S2; and "Consumer Promotional Activity Rises," *Food Institute Report*, May 31, 1993, p. 3.

70. Lefton, "Try It: You'll Like It."

71. www.disney.com/survey/doc_sweeps2/ffmain.html, site visited on February 14, 1997.

72. Rebeca Piirto Heath, "Pop Art," *Marketing Tools*, April 1997, www.marketingtools.com.

73. Ibid.

74. "Eastar Copolyster by Eastman used in P-O-P Display for Sega of America Products," www.eastman.com/ppbo/displays/pr/sega.shtml, site visted on February 14, 1997.

75. Riccardo A. Davis, "Gun Exchange Strikes Nerve," *Advertising Age*, January 3, 1994, pp. 3, 38; Geoffrey Smith and Ron Stodghill II, "Are Good Causes Good Marketing?" *Business Week*, March 21, 1994, pp. 64–65; "Sponsors Sing a Profitable Tune in Concert with Event Promos," *Brandweek*, January 24, 1994, p. 20; and Nancy Arnott, "Marketing with a Passion," *Sales and Marketing Management*, January 1994, pp. 64–71.

76. "Best of Show—Public Relations Sowing the Seeds of Persuasion," *AgriMarketing*, April 1994, p. 64.

77. Elizabeth Jensen, "Marketers Lure Baby Boomers at Trendy Food-Wine Festivals," *Wall Street Journal Interactive Edition*, July 3, 1997.

78. Mark Gleason, "Edelman Sees Niche in Web Public Relations," *Advertising Age*, January 20, 1997, www.adage.com.

79. Kate Fitzsimmons, "Retirement Expert Girard Miller to Host Web Chat Session," *Wall Street Journal Interactive Edition*, July 10, 1997.

SUPER BOWL ADVERTISING

ONE OF THE MOST EXCITING Super Bowl games ever was the 1998 Denver Broncos 31–24 win over the Green Bay Packers. An estimated 133.4 million viewers saw the thriller, making it the third most watched program in television history. The game had a Nielsen media research rating of 44.5, indicating that two-thirds of U.S. viewing households were tuned to the game. But all the drama was not about football alone. Much of it had to do with the game behind the game—competition among the TV commercials that cost $1.3 million per 30-second spot. Bob Scarpelli, senior vice president and chief creative officer of DDB Needham, Chicago, says: "Super Bowl day is the Super Bowl of advertising. The Super Bowl has evolved to the point where people watch the ads more than the game." NBC sold 58 half-minute opportunities for advertisers to show off their talent. The goal is to keep viewers glued to their seats during the time outs that punctuate the on-field action. The risks and rewards of advertising during the Super Bowl are truly amazing.

Since many Super Bowl spots are seen just once, the punch must be exceptional. One technique is to involve viewers enough to pursue further contact. For example, Intel selected Steve Martin to narrate a "theft" from its labs. Suspects in the caper are introduced in the ad, and viewers are asked to visit Intel's Web site to vote on a culprit. Joanne Hasegawa, spokesperson for Intel, said the company was "really pleased with the results"—nearly 400,000 people voted. Mail Boxes Etc. extended the effect of its ad by inviting small businesses to join a contest, explaining in 100 words or less why they wanted to appear in an ad for the Super Bowl. About 3,500 small businesses responded. Likewise, Volvo used its Super Bowl spot to gain interest from the small group of heavy truck buyers—only three million people. Mike Delaney, top marketing executive for Volvo trucks, wanted to boost awareness but also needed to get involvement commensurate with the cost of the Super Bowl ad. Throughout the fall, Volvo hyped the game at its 200 dealerships and its 180 truck stops. About 12,000 entries were collected for a contest that would award a $120,000 truck. Volvo's Super Bowl commercial imbedded a message to let 25 entrants know that they were still in the running for the top prize. Similarly, an M&M Mars ad was designed to extend interest into a contest throughout the spring.

Most Super Bowl ads were stand-alone spots, but a cost of $1.3 million requires more than just a typical commercial. The advertising industry sees the event as a chance to showcase talent, and risks are often taken with content and even the timing of ads. Apparently the hands-down winner in 1998, as in some past years, was Anheuser-Busch. It's risky to show violence to animals, but in Budweiser's masterpiece, a lizard plots to assassinate the Budweiser frogs. In four hilarious spots that cost more than $5 million, the lizard's misguided scheme unfolds, and there were rave reviews. A survey taken the day after the Super Bowl, conducted by Saatchi and Saatchi, showed that Anheuser-Busch finished a strong first, with 56 percent of the respondents recalling

the ads. That compares favorably to the 36 percent Budweiser scored the previous year.

Even small companies willing to take a chance can win big with a single spot. The McIlhenny Company, maker of Tabasco hot sauce, took the chance and was hot, hot, hot with its entry. Network Associates, maker of antivirus software, used a spot to get name recognition. It spent $400,000 to produce an ad with two Warsaw Pact types debating whether a computer order to fire nuclear missiles was real or a hacker's attack. The tagline "Network Associates—who's watching your network?" heightened attention to the name as well as the real dangers of computer espionage.

Even the nature of the football game itself can influence the value of the ad. American Express had the risky final spot and teamed Superman with Jerry Seinfeld in a tremendously entertaining commercial. Given the closeness of the game, viewers stayed right to the end. What would have happened if the Packers had been leading big at halftime? As it was, American Express got the benefit of the exciting last stages of the game and the ad was powerful enough to grab attention, even in the midst of all the excitement.

Yet, many experts believe that Super Bowl advertising may not be a smart buy. Ted Bell, vice chairman, world wide creative director of Young & Rubicam, New York, says: "It's become advertising's in-joke, all these agency guys trying to outdo each other. It's about who can have the coolest commercial. It's self-indulgence on the part of the ad industry." According to Bob Scarpelli at DDB Needham, "Many clients want to be on the Super Bowl, just to be on the Super Bowl. The CEO wants his name on the Super Bowl. It's almost like bragging rights." Jay Schulberg, CEO of Bozell Worldwide, Inc., says: "I tell my clients there are more effective ways to spend $1.3 million."

1. *What should a marketer consider in deciding whether to advertise at the Super Bowl? Would this differ for a smaller organization versus a larger company?*
2. *What qualities must an ad possess in order to gain attention at the Super Bowl?*
3. *Recall one of your favorite Super Bowl ads and describe what elements made it successful from your perspective.*

SOURCES: Ellen Newborne and Roger Crockett, "More Bang for the Super Bowl Bucks," *Business Week*, February 2, 1998, p. 70; Skip Wollenberg, "Volvo Trucks, Mail Boxes Etc. Make Big Bets on Lone Commercials during Super Bowl," *Marketing News*, January 5, 1998, p. 25; Stuart Elliott, "Advertising: Post-Game Analysis of Super Bowl Statistics that Really Count—Commercial Winners and Losers," *New York Times*, January 28, 1998, p. D6; Eleftheria Parpis, "Playing for the Ring," *AdWeek*, January 19, 1998, p. 29; Steve Hamm, "This Year's Super Bowl Hero?" *Business Week*, January 19, 1998, p. 6; Scott Andron, "Volvo Trucks Buys Super Bowl Ad," *Greensboro* (North Carolina) *News & Record*, November 16, 1997, p. E1; and Kyle Pope, "NBC Scores Big with the Super Bowl; Game Is Among Most Watched Ever," *Wall Street Journal Interactive Edition*, January 27, 1998.

Personal Selling and Sales Force Management

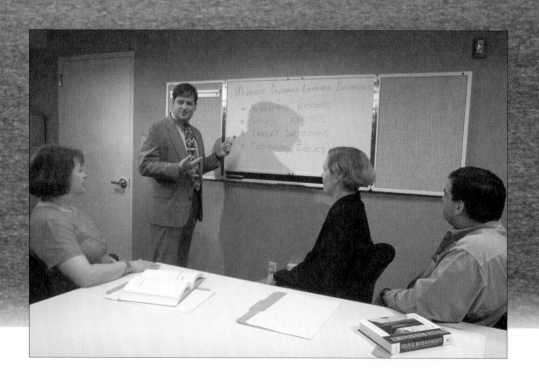

Objectives

1. Understand how selling evolved to a focus on relationships and what elements are involved in building them.

2. Know the responsibilities of salespeople and sales managers.

3. Identify and understand the steps in personal selling.

4. Learn the characteristics of strong salespeople.

5. Understand how to develop a diverse sales organization.

6. Explore how to implement sales actions, from setting quotas and compensating salespeople to evaluating and adjusting plans.

THE BUSINESS WORLD IS IN *constant change. To be successful, you have to adapt your skills and style to the dynamic nature of the market. Those that learn to adapt will survive and succeed. This is especially true in the competitive world of sales. Jonathan Ahlbrand has built his career around adapting to the needs of a changing industry. Currently, Jonathan is the Midwest Regional Manager of Distributed Learning for Simon & Schuster. How he got there, and the role that selling played in that rise is our opening story.*

Jonathan graduated with a degree in Geography. He spent the following two years as a photogrammetric analyst for a civil engineering firm. While he found the field interesting, he wanted a career that offered challenges plus high rewards for success. He also sought more interaction with people. Realizing that it was time for a change, Jonathan explored career opportunities in selling. After some investigation he selected the college publishing industry and procured a sales position with Merrill Publishing in Michigan.

This career move changed Jonathan's life forever. He knew he had found a market segment that fit his style and interests. He was Rookie of the Year his first sales year. The next summer, he was selected to participate in the Merrill Editorial Internship Program. In the following year, Merrill was purchased by Macmillan Publishing. That summer, Ahlbrand was one of three Merrill reps chosen for the Macmillan Career Development Program.

Success followed Jonathan to Macmillan. The next two years he saw continued growth in all aspects of his career. With a high interest in technology and a great sales record under his belt, Jonathan made a jump out of the text publishing industry to become manager of sales and marketing for a small Michigan-based software company. Jonathan's drive for success was a catalyst in propelling this company forward in the constantly changing market of sales automation software. Jonathan notes, there is a big difference between working in a corporate environment and small business environment. "I learned very quickly that I preferred the corporate environment. I cannot, however, discount the small business experience and the value it has added to my career."

Within a year, Jonathan was lured back to Macmillan as a senior sales rep. Shortly after his return, Macmillan was purchased by Prentice Hall. Jonathan was happy to learn that he would be slotted into a business and economics specialist position and would continue to call on most of the same schools in his former Macmillan territory. In the following years, he continued to perform well. His territory continued to grow and he was consistently within the top 10 of the business and economics specialists.

In the spring of 1996, he was designated as the regional media specialist and given added responsibilities of assisting his colleagues with media and technology related to sales and presentations. He was also selected to participate in the Prentice Hall Career Development Program. In the spring of 1997, Jonathan was promoted to Regional Sales Director for Simon & Schuster's College NewsLink Services. In December 1997, Jonathan was promoted to his current position as the Midwest Regional Manager of Distributed Learning for Simon & Schuster. His wide range of responsibilities include utilizing the educational assets of Simon & Schuster's Higher Education products and technology to address the needs of distance learning programs. He also fosters strategic partnerships between the company and educational institutions throughout the Midwest.

Through all the mergers, industry change, and career advances, Jonathan has focused on what he believes are the key factors in successful selling—long-term relationship building, creative problem solving, and adapting to change. Most importantly Jonathan develops relationships with customers that endure. "It is long term customers that provide stability in your sales. I always strived to be the first person customers call if they had a problem, were looking for a new solution, or had an opportunity to serve their own customers better. Everything I did as a sales representative is still a part of what I do now. Sales success is a solid foundation on which to build any business career."[1]

THE CONCEPTS OF PERSONAL SELLING AND SALES MANAGEMENT

Successful people nearly always "sell" their ideas. Broadly speaking, any time one party attempts to motivate the behavior of another party through personal contact, some form of selling takes place. When was the last time you tried to influence someone by expressing your point of view? Did you try to convince a friend to go to a movie you wanted to see or to a restaurant you wanted to visit? Whether intentional or not, you were engaged in the kind of communication that is at the heart of personal selling. It is through interpersonal contact that leaders influence the behavior of others. Although an attempt to influence people is not always labeled personal selling, it has the same characteristics. What makes personal selling a profession and not just interpersonal influence? It focuses on creating the economic exchange that is at the center of marketing. Salespeople sell customers on products.

Personal selling is one of the most prevalent and highest paid occupations in the United States. For every person employed in advertising, there are more than 30 jobs in sales.[2] More than 15.8 million Americans, nearly 10 percent of the workforce, are employed in professional selling. By 2000, at least 18 million sales positions will exist.[3] Furthermore, personal selling pays well, and compensation is rising dramatically. In 1996, top sales executives in some categories earned an average of $123,000, an increase of about 42 percent in two years; entry-level salespeople averaged about $40,000, up 25 percent in two years.[4] In November 1996, Hewlett-Packard boosted sales force compensation by as much as 25 percent to keep up with competitors like Oracle, IBM, and NEC.[5] It is not unusual for salespeople to make hundreds of thousands or more than a million dollars annually.

Whether you are planning a professional sales career or simply want to sell your ideas more effectively, you'll find this chapter very helpful. We begin by describing the different types of sales personnel and selling situations. Next, a comparison of various selling approaches emphasizes the importance of relationship selling. This is followed by a section on the responsibilities of the salesperson, both to the customer and to the company. We then walk through each of the steps involved in personnel selling—from planning and prospecting to closing the sale and providing follow-up service. The last personal selling section, which describes the four characteristics of strong salespeople, may help you determine if sales would be a good career choice.

While a salesperson in a small start-up company may work fairly independently (recall the lone Coach salesman in chapter 12), as a company grows its management must begin to think in terms of a sales force, sales teams, and sales managers. Good sales force management is needed to coordinate and inspire the efforts of these personnel and to integrate their efforts with the overall marketing plan. In the second half of the chapter we examine the five key functions of sales management: organizing the sales force, developing diverse sales teams, preparing forecasts and budgets, implementing sales actions, and overseeing sales force activities. We conclude with information about sales force automation.

PERSONAL SELLING

Figure 16-1 diagrams the topics in personal selling. We will examine each of these in turn.

TYPES OF SALES PERSONNEL AND SELLING SITUATIONS

The many titles for sales positions tend to describe the type of activity performed: sales executive, sales engineer, sales consultant, sales counselor, representative, account executive, account representative, territory representative, management representative, technical representative, marketing representative, agent, and sales associate. Many times the title of vice president is conferred on top-level salespeople who have important sales responsibilities but may have few if any people reporting to them.

Some common categories of salespeople are described in Figure 16-2. **Direct sales** occur when a salesperson interacts with a consumer or company in order to make a sale. **Missionary sales** are made by people who do not take orders but influence purchase by recommending or specifying a product to others. For example, textbook salespeople influence professors, who then require students to purchase a particular book for a class. Likewise, physicians prescribe drugs, golf professionals recommend a brand of clubs, and travel agents help select vacation packages.

The circumstances in which selling occurs can be categorized as executive and team selling, field selling, over-the-counter selling, inside sales, and global sales. Because each category involves a different setting, the activities of salespeople differ accordingly.

Executive and Team Selling   Although many people are employed in personal selling, the statistics don't count the numerous individuals with nonsales titles who spend much of their time on sales activities. Many executives, irrespective of their area, view personal selling as one of their primary functions. They not only communicate with the board of directors and employees in order to "sell" corporate policies but also frequently interact with major customers and suppliers.

Direct sales
Sales that result from the salesperson's direct interaction with a consumer or company.

Missionary sales
Sales made indirectly through people who do not obtain orders but influence the buying decision of others.

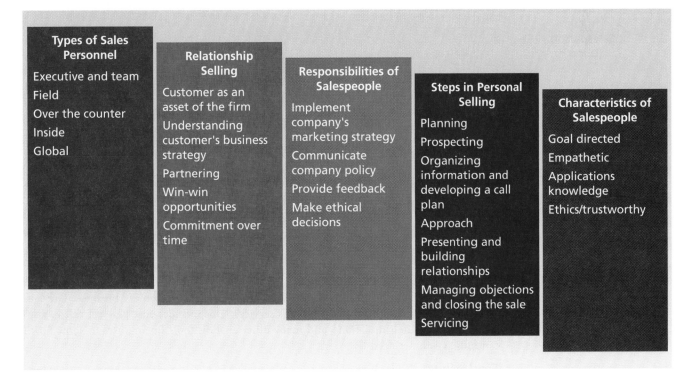

Figure 16-1   The Concept of Personal Selling

	ACTIONS	EXAMPLE
Telemarketing Representative (Direct) →	Uses telephone to contact customers to receive orders.	People who respond to callers of 800 numbers (Gateway 2000).
Inside Sales Support (Missionary) →	Works inside the seller's company to support the sales representatives who make face to face call on customer. Uses telephone and other non-face to face communication to help customers.	Westinghouse salesperson who sells without traveling to a customer's site.
Field Salesperson (Direct) →	Meet face to face with customers.	Nike salesperson calling on retail sporting goods chain.
Technical Salesperson (Direct) →	Meets face to face with customers to sell very technical products that need to be customized or explained in technical ways.	Square D salesperson (engineering background) calling on an electric utility.
Detail Person (Missionary) →	Meets with people who influence the sale of a company's products but may not purchase directly.	Eli Lilly salesperson who calls on doctors to increase prescription rate for Lilly products.
Service Salesperson (Direct) →	Sells intangible products, such as insurance and real estate, to a broad range of customers.	Prudential salesperson who sells a life insurance policy.
Retail Salesperson (Direct) →	Associates or clerks selling items in a retail outlet.	Saturn salesperson working in showroom.

Figure 16-2   Types of Sales Personnel

Team selling

Selling that involves people from most parts of the organization, including top executives, working together to create a relationship with the buying organization.

Team selling involves people from most parts of the organization, including top executives, who work together to create relationships with the buying organization. In one six-week period, Boeing sold more than $6 billion in 737s, 747s, and 757s to four major airlines. Corporate executives were deeply committed to the effort, although most of the responsibility still remained with the sales force. In a high-technology business like aircraft manufacturing, nearly every function gets involved in the sales process. At Boeing it is the salesperson's job to coordinate contact between the company and the technical, financial, and planning personnel from the airline. Even if the CEO is brought in, it is not unusual for the salesperson to remain in charge of the sale using the CEO where appropriate. The salespeople perform the leadership function because they know all aspects of their customers' business. They also must be thoroughly familiar with Boeing's services. This includes cost-per-seat calculations, computerized route simulations, and many other analysis tools Boeing uses to show how it can fulfill customer needs.[6]

Field Selling   Field selling occurs at a consumer's residence or at a customer's place of business. Field representatives spend most of their time, as the name implies, away from their company and near customers. Their job is to discover prospects, make contact, and create relationships. By working with customers in their own environment, field reps have ample opportunity to understand the customer's circumstances in depth. The best performers in field selling are often skilled at learning about the customer's situation and problems. Field sales in consumer markets include products like real estate, home building and remodeling, landscape maintenance, and even computers. For example, Hand Technologies sells personal computers in-home, where sales consultants can provide individual attention and have plenty of uninterrupted time.[7]

Field selling to businesses and distributors is also common. It is used for nearly every imaginable industrial product, for pharmaceutical sales to physicians and hospitals, and for selling consulting, accounting, and business management services to manufacturers and retailers. Merck, a leader in health care products, sends sales reps to hospitals, clinics, government agencies, drug wholesalers, and retailers, among others. Merck salespeople sold $16.7 billion in goods and services to other businesses and organizations in 1995.[8]

> **CAREER TIP** At Hewlett-Packard, field sales trainees are responsible for attending formal training classes and performance of appropriate projects. They develop sales through customer presentations, demos, trade shows, and territory management, as well as conduct customer and competitive research. Hewlett-Packard offers worldwide employment opportunities as well as leadership and development programs geared toward high-performing, high-potential sales professionals. If you think you might be interested in a sales career at Hewlett-Packard, connect to their Web site at: **www.jobs.hp.com/**. You will have an opportunity to learn about the company's recruiting process, events, and internships. In addition, Hewlett-Packard provides some valuable interviewing tips.

Over-the-Counter Selling   Over-the-counter selling occurs in a retail outlet. Examples include furniture, clothing, and jewelry stores as well as auto dealerships. Customers are drawn to the salesperson by the attraction of the store itself or by advertising and sales promotion. Salespeople need to be skilled at identifying the customer's requirements quickly, often in a single encounter, and at providing the appropriate service at the point of sale. Helping consumers the first time brings them back, which provides the opportunity to gain a loyal customer. It also creates good word of mouth, which brings in friends and relatives of satisfied customers. Successful over-the-counter salespeople tend to build loyal relationships by becoming knowledgeable about the unique tastes of customers. This occurs while working with them on numerous transactions over a long period.

Inside Sales   Inside sales involve one-to-one contact with the customer via the telephone. Mail-order companies are a good example. At L. L. Bean, sales representatives know the products, how they fit, how to ship them quickly, and how to repair and care for them. They provide customers with a helpful, pleasant experience so that they will be likely to use the service again.[9] Another example is the banks of telephone sales representatives who take orders in response to advertisements and infomercials. Sometimes they perform only a clerical function, since the consumer already is sold on the product, but many of these people do an ex-

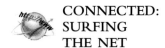

CONNECTED: SURFING THE NET

www.boeing.com

Learn more about the world's leading producer of commercial airplanes and its successful team selling effort. Go inside Boeing by connecting to its Web site. Read the latest top story, take a tour, read financial news, and much more.

Field sales occur in a customer's place of business or a consumer's home.

Inside sales involve connecting with customers via the telephone.

cellent job of answering questions and selling additional items. A variation is telephone marketers who solicit business by calling people at home or at work. Usually the intent is to sell products, but sometimes the purpose is to obtain a home visit for field salespeople.

Another form of inside sales is to work with established clients primarily by phone. Stock brokerage firms conduct much of their business this way. Many manufacturers and distributors have field reps and inside salespeople who work together with large customers. The reps solicit business at the customer's site, and inside sales personnel are ready at all times to provide technical support and take orders via the phone. This form of inside sales can be critical for industrial companies.[10] It is also a first job for many technical salespeople, since they can learn about company policies and products while receiving plenty of help with their first customer contacts. Once experience is gained inside, these people often take a field sales position.

Global Sales   It is difficult to overstate the importance of personal selling in global markets.[11] Many of these sales involve millions or even billions of dollars. For example, YTL Corporation selected Siemens AG of Germany and General Electric of the United States, among others, as bidders on a $750 million order for power generation turbines. One reason GE lost was its failure to send a top executive to help make the sale. YTL's managing director said: "I wanted to look them in the eye to see if we can do business."[12]

In the domestic arena, companies and their representatives often become accepted in a short period, but this may take years in a foreign environment. To overcome this resistance, many companies use domestic personnel from the host country to represent them. But this can cause problems if personal selling is not considered a prestigious occupation in that culture. Furthermore, finding and training qualified people can be challenging and expensive. Yet salespeople from the home office are less knowledgeable about the local business climate.[13] As a compromise solution, companies often rely on nationals to provide information and make initial customer contact but send salespeople from headquarters on regular visits to establish relationships and negotiate larger contracts. Pete Macking, vice president of sales for UPS, frequently travels abroad for that purpose. Although he has considerable overseas experience, he still works with foreign nationals affiliated with UPS.[14]

As the world gets smaller and companies send reps overseas, train local reps, or make cyber connections with different countries, cultural differences still loom large. For tips on global etiquette, see the diversity feature, "A Few Do's and Taboos for the Round-the-World-Rep."

RELATIONSHIP AND OTHER SELLING APPROACHES

All employees are important in building and maintaining customer relationships, but salespeople are critical because that is their primary responsibility. *One Size Fits One*, a popular book on the subject, says we are entering a world "where emphasis is less on building short-term satisfaction than on instilling long-term loyalty. And a world where relationships are the currency and the committed employees who maintain and nurture them are the primary source of competitive advantage."[15] If salespeople do not have the competencies and desire to build relationships one customer at a time, then no amount of support from all the other company employees will make up the deficit.

CONNECTING WITH DIVERSITY

A FEW DO'S AND TABOOS
FOR THE ROUND-THE-WORLD REP

Many selling skills that work in the United States also work overseas, but knowing how to act in certain cultures can make the difference in closing a sale. For instance, the simple thumbs-up sign that Americans use every day may offend a customer in the Middle East. And while health nuts often sip seltzer at a U.S. business lunch, in Japan it is bad manners to refuse a stronger drink. Here are a few global p's and q's gathered from a number of international business experts:

China

- Negotiating is an art, and there's no such thing as a quick sale. According to Chin Ning Chu, author of *The Asian Mind Game*, the Chinese "map out negotiating strategies, and follow the game plan until they get a contract the way they want it."
- The more sales reps know about the culture the better. "Chinese business people will accept Americans more if they make an effort to learn about their society," says Chu.
- Printed materials presented to buyers should be in black and white, since colors can have great significance for the Chinese.

Japan

- Gift giving at a first meeting is the norm. Consultants suggest a high-quality item with a designer logo or brand name.
- The neck is considered an erogenous zone; women sales reps are advised to wear high-necked blouses or a scarf.
- The ever-accommodating Japanese will rarely say no. Instead, they will say "maybe" or "that would be very difficult"—both of which essentially mean no.

Western Europe

- Two- or three-hour meals are not uncommon. Don't be in a rush to end a meal and talk business. Follow the lead of the host.
- In France, don't schedule a breakfast meeting. The French tend not to meet before 10:00 A.M.
- While many Europeans will discuss family matters, the Germans, the Swiss, and Scandinavians consider it rude.

Mexico

- Respect for seniors is always important. And it's customary to shake hands with everyone upon arrival and departure.
- A yes does not always mean yes. Mexican social etiquette makes it difficult to say no.
- In Mexico, as in China and Japan, business cards are used extensively. Sales reps should come armed with a large supply. Cards should be as descriptive as possible, noting any professional degrees or special titles.

Latin America

- Scheduling more than two appointments per day is unwise. Attitudes about time are casual.
- Emotions and trust are important elements in the buying process. No one purchases unless they're absolutely comfortable with the salesperson. According to David Charner of the English Resource Center in Caracas, Venezuela, which runs sales training programs: "Here we have to focus our training on searching for feelings, finding the hidden motivator that determines a buying decision."

The Middle East

- Always use the right hand to hold, offer, or receive materials. The left is used to touch toilet paper. People who write left-handed should apologize for doing so.

• In Egypt, paperwork and bureaucratic procedures make business processes slow. It may take a year or more to obtain a contract you could get in America in a week. And be careful not to tap two fingers together. It is a message that a couple is sleeping together.

Sources: Andy Cohen, "Getting to Yes, Chinese-Style," *Sales and Marketing Management*, July 1996, pp. 44–45; Andy Cohen, "Small World, Big Challenge," *Sales and Marketing Management*, June 1996, pp. 69–73; Andy Cohen, "Global Do's and Don'ts," *Sales & Marketing Management*, June 1996, p. 72; Marjorie Whigham-Desir, "Business Etiquette Overseas," *Black Enterprise*, October 1995, pp. 142–143; and "Mexico: Yes Does Not Always Mean Yes," *Business America*, p. 18; and. Roger E. Axtell, *Do's and Taboos Around The World,* New York: (John Wiley & Sons, 1994) is an excellent source about cultural etiquette.

Today, business strategies focus on creating relationships rather than simply selling products. Companies are entering into joint activities in record numbers, and selling organizations must work closely with customers to help them accomplish their goals. Sellers must understand the consumer's lifestyle or how the customer's business works. Consequently, sales organizations are shifting from traditional ways of doing business to a new emphasis on building relationships. The three basic sales approaches are shown in Figure 16-3: traditional sales, consultative sales, and relationship selling.

Traditional sales approach
Emphasizing persuasive techniques to get consumers to buy a company's products.

The Traditional Sales Approach   The **traditional sales approach** focuses on persuading consumers to buy a company's products, thereby raising sales volume. Remember that the Industrial Revolution produced goods in record quantities. Output grew more rapidly than demand. During the first half of this century, the purpose of personal selling was to stimulate sales. Firms no longer needed to find ways to produce more in order to keep up with demand. Instead, they had to sell more in order to keep up with increased production. The salesperson's focus was on pushing the company's products, especially features and functions, to increase the sales volume. Prospects were persuaded to buy. Techniques for persuasive selling,

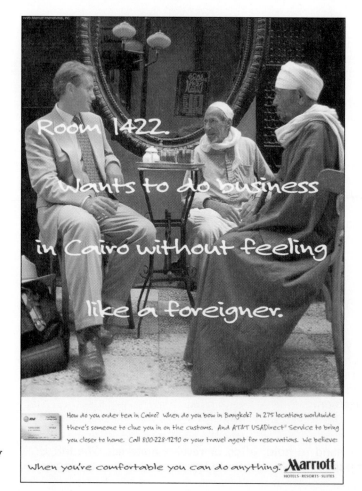

Salespeople must understand consumers' lifestyles and how their businesses work in order to build relationships.

	Traditional Sales	Consultative Sales	Relationship Selling
Focus	Understand your product	Understand customer's problems	Understand customer's business or lifestyle
Role of the customer	Prospect	Target	Asset of the business
Salesperson Focus	Persuasion	Problem solving	Partnering
Salesperson Role	Obtain sales volume	Advise customers	Building win-win circumstances
Objective	Profit through sales volume	Profit through problem solving	Profit through strategic relationships and customer satisfaction

Figure 16-3 *Major Sales Approaches*

which taught salespeople how to negotiate, were often the dominant subject of sales training courses. Essentially, sellers and buyers tried to see who could get the best deal.

The Consultative Sales Approach   For many organizations, the traditional sales era continued well into the 1970s. As the marketing function became more important, however, the sales function also took on new responsibilities. Marketing began to focus on serving customers, and selling had to change with it. **Consultative selling** means working closely with customers to help solve their problems. Salespeople are expected to understand how their company's products can do that. Essentially, the salesperson becomes an advisor to customers, rather than a negotiator seeking the best deal. In order for this type of selling to be successful, salespeople must work closely with the customer over an extended period. Consequently, this has been dubbed *long-cycle* selling.[16] Consultative selling stops just short of relationship selling.

Relationship Selling   **Relationship selling** attempts to forge bonds between buyers and sellers in an effort to gain loyalty and mutual satisfaction.[17] Because it promotes loyalty, it is in tune with the strategic nature of marketing. It recognizes that sellers and buyers benefit from one another's success. In today's consumer markets, people want to buy based on relationships with companies that can be counted on to enhance their lifestyle. Businesses are looking for partners who will help them compete. Relationship selling recognizes that the salesperson's role is to create value for the customer as well as the company. Typically, a great deal of work on both sides goes into building and maintaining relationships. The main aspects of relationship selling are discussed in more detail below.

Understanding the Customer's Business Strategy   The focus of relationship selling is to uncover strategic needs, develop creative solutions, and arrive at mutually beneficial agreements.[18] Salespeople must recognize that companies buy products to help them run their business better. By understanding the customer's business, salespeople are more likely to communicate in meaningful ways with the potential buyer. A. C. Rochester, a division of General Motors that supplies engines and fuel systems to the global automotive industry, "lends" sales engineers to clients to assist with product and program development. They help create product strategies and are very familiar with confidential aspects of the client's business. In effect, they become an integral part of the customer's marketing team.

The Customer as an Asset   Loyal customers should be viewed as an asset by the firm. Long-term contracts and repeat sales produce predictable sources of revenue. In fact, the worth of many businesses can be calculated by the size of the customer base, such as the number of subscribers of a cellular phone company. Customers are not viewed as prospects for a single sale or as targets for problem solving. Rather, they are partners in a relationship that produces long-term cash flows for the seller. At MCI, employees are rewarded not for the number of customers who sign up for services but for the number who stay signed up. Employees spend time with customers, learn what services they want, and develop ways to keep their business after the initial sale. MCI views loyal customers as an asset and works to create relationships that will maintain their loyalty.[19]

Consultative selling
An approach to selling in which sales personnel work closely with customers to help solve problems.

Relationship selling
Forging bonds between buyer and seller to gain loyalty and mutual satisfaction.

Partnering   Under the traditional approach, salespeople use persuasion to obtain orders, while consultative selling emphasizes the ability to solve customers' problems. In contrast, relationship selling focuses on partnering. Some partnerships are contractual, established through long-term written agreements. Some are noncontractual; that is, the buyer and seller enter into an implied agreement to do business together over time. In either case, a sharing of power occurs. In traditional sales, the balance of power is typically with the salesperson; in consultative selling it is with the customer. Relationship selling involves a symmetrical relationship—both parties have equal authority and responsibility. Both share information to help the other party succeed.[20]

Relationship selling replaces short-term thinking with a perspective that ensures value long after the sale is made. Consequently, just as much work is needed after the sale as before. A strong follow-through makes certain that partnerships are honored.

Negotiation

Discussion by two or more parties to arrange a transaction.

Building Win-Win Circumstances   Historically, buying and selling have involved negotiation. **Negotiation** can be defined as discussions by two or more parties to arrange a transaction. It requires give and take. To some it means that each party tries to maximize its own benefit relative to the other through a power position obtained during the interaction. To others, negotiation is a way to build relationships. In Japan and other cultures it is viewed as a long process that should involve every decision maker. Instead of being seen as conflict or struggle, negotiations can be regarded as information sessions that lead to win-win opportunities.[21]

Figure 16-4 describes the negotiating possibilities. When any party loses, the foundation for building a relationship diminishes greatly. And when one party gains a great deal more than the other, a relationship will not grow or will dissolve over time. A sound relationship requires that each party perceive it has gained value. In other words, lasting relationships involve win-win situations. Even in early meetings with customers, both parties need to win.

Managing Strategic Relationships   Account management refers to the activities of a salesperson or sales team to build and support the relationship with a customer. Many companies have an account manager for each large customer. At Compaq, for instance, these are managers for the top 1,000 accounts.[22] Consulting firms, advertising agencies, and manufacturers often have account managers. The GM Delphi division assigns them to work with the Chrysler, Ford, Toyota, Volkswagen, and BMW accounts as well as with their own GM assembly divisions. These managers concentrate their energies on maintaining the bonds between Delphi and the client. Account managers are particularly effective when the product supplied is important to the overall strategy of the buying company. For example, Delphi's components are critical to their customers' product designs. For some auto brands, Delphi produces most of the electrical systems, brake systems, and other components. Account managers spend considerable time with customers and carefully monitor satisfaction with products and delivery.

UPS World Wide Logistics sells third-party logistical support. Some clients want only basic services, such as low-cost shipping or warehousing. Others want more. According to the company's senior vice president of business development, John Sutthoff:

> Account managers are trained to understand the business strategies of our customers and to provide solutions that contribute to the success of these strategies. Often our account managers help customers build totally new strategies that result in stronger bonds with their customers. Consequently . . . account managers need to comprehend all aspects of business strategy as well as the competitive world our client's experience.[23]

The technology feature discusses how UPS uses technology to help the sales force.

Sales territory

All the actual and potential customers, often within a specified geographic area, for which the salesperson has responsibility.

THE RESPONSIBILITIES OF A SALESPERSON

Salespeople do not simply increase sales volume. Today, most view themselves as the marketing manager of a territory. This can be a geographical area, such as a city or region, or a single large account. Essentially, a **sales territory** is all the actual and potential customers for

Figure 16-4   Buyer-Seller Negotiations

	Buyer Gains	Buyer Loses
Seller Gains	Win-Win	Buyer negotiates poorly
Seller Loses	Seller negotiates poorly	Lose-Lose

CONNECTING THROUGH TECHNOLOGY

UNITED PARCEL SERVICE: SALES REPS AND LAPTOPS CREATE THE MISSING LINK

UPS has been delivering packages for close to a century, but until 10 years ago it didn't have a single sales rep. The world's largest shipping company had always focused on current customers, not on attracting new ones. Well, a lot has changed during the past decade. Heated competition from Federal Express, the U.S. Postal Service, and a number of small carriers has forced UPS to develop a new service menu for value-hungry businesses. Along with it has come a much more aggressive sales effort.

The company now employs about 3,000 reps and support staffers. To make sure they can keep up in the information-driven marketplace, UPS has invested $5.5 million in laptops and a communication system called LINK. By the end of 1995, everyone working on national accounts had a portable PC and training for a variety of software applications (including contact and customer management, to-do lists, contract implementation, calendars, e-mail, a report writer, faxing software, the Microsoft Office suite, and—whew—Netscape).

The shift from a paper-based system to an electronic one had dramatic results, especially in the area of contract implementation. The process used to take up to 90 days and now averages 15. Customers enjoy the benefits of the new contract that much sooner, and the transition has been smooth. LINK also allows information to flow more freely within the company, and between UPS and customers. "With the e-mail . . . we get messages throughout the day from the national account executives in the field . . . and that gives us good ideas on how to build strategies for customers in the future," says David Schuler, a national account manager for UPS. "We know what the competitive situation is around the United States and around the world. So we know early what's coming next—it's like having eyes and ears all around the country."

Clearly, UPS is benefiting from automation, and few at the shipping giant question the investment. Indeed, UPS plans to plug in a batch of cyber initiates every six months, until the entire sales force and all its support personnel are LINKed up. Says Schuler: "Once you get a little information, you want more. Because in sales, information is your weapon; the more you have at your fingertips, the easier it is to sell the customer. And in our industry right now, that's what the customers are asking for: information."

Source: Adapted from Melanie Berger, "The Missing Link," *Sales and Marketing Management,* Tools Supplement, December 1996, pp. 18–24.

whom the salesperson has responsibility. As marketing manager of a territory, the salesperson has several functions. The first is to implement the company's marketing strategy in that territory. The second is to communicate company policy to clients and potential customers. The third is to provide the company with feedback about the marketing environment, including the competition and customer needs and wants. Finally, salespeople must operate ethically.

Implement the Marketing Strategy In order to translate the company's marketing strategy into action, the sales force needs to have a basic understanding of all marketing functions. In many companies, salespeople have considerable leeway in applying the entire marketing mix to their territory, including which products to emphasize, which prices and discounts to offer, and which promotional materials to distribute. In other words, while their primary responsibility is to carry out the company's strategic marketing plan, they can use considerable judgment about how that will be done. At UPS World Wide Logistics, salespeople participate regularly in the marketing planning process. In this way they are fully knowledgeable about strategies and how to implement them.

Communicate Company Policy As agents of their organization, salespeople are responsible for communicating company policies to customers. A policy is a guide or set of rules the company uses in conducting business. Foot Locker's policy of total customer satisfaction means that products can be returned for a refund. Salespeople must honor this policy no matter what the circumstance. While company policies are relatively straightforward in most consumer sales situations, they can be extremely complex in business-to-business selling. For example, pharmaceutical sales representatives usually educate doctors about the proper use of certain drugs or medical equipment, but sometimes they are present when surgeons operate in order to answer questions about products should the need arise.

Companies are likely to specify exactly what salespeople can communicate. Also common are policies on appropriate product use, warranty issues, delivery, and pricing. By communicating such policies and enforcing them, salespeople help shape customer expectations, create good will, and maintain positive customer relationships.

Provide Feedback   Another important role of the sales force is to provide their company with information about customers, competitors, and market conditions. Salespeople are in constant contact with the market, and many companies have formal systems for collecting their information rapidly. Examples are portable personal computers with elaborate user-friendly programs or arrangements with customers to contact their computer systems directly.

Most salespeople have an array of sophisticated communication capabilities, including voice mail, e-mail, facsimile and satellite linkages, cellular phones, and pagers. This keeps them in touch 24 hours a day, seven days a week. Customer inventory levels (stock on hand), purchase orders, price quotations, shipping data, and promotional offers can be transmitted in both directions on-line. In addition, salespeople usually help forecast opportunities by describing the plans of current and potential customers that may affect future sales. Many times these estimates require careful analysis of a client's strategic plan. Hewlett-Packard, for example, uses an internal company network to forecast opportunities. It includes information ranging from customer testimonials and presentation materials to competitive data and can be downloaded to a PC in minutes.[24]

Salespeople also provide valuable information about competitors. By collecting and assembling this input from around the globe, Kodak can identify nearly every initiative competitors make. Let us say a salesperson in Austria identifies a rival's product introduction, new promotional campaign, or altered pricing strategy in that territory. The information can be evaluated at Kodak headquarters to determine the likelihood that markets elsewhere will be affected. In one case, Fuji strategies in one area of the world soon appeared in other areas. Because salespeople had provided an early warning, Kodak marketing executives were able to create a counterstrategy rapidly.

Make Ethical Decisions   Salespeople must exhibit excellent ethical judgment. With little supervision, they often have considerable freedom in what they do and say. Because performance evaluation frequently is tied to sales levels, there are strong pressures to put their own interests ahead of those of customers. Salespeople are likely to face ethical dilemmas regarding the company they represent and the customers they serve. It helps immensely if their company's philosophy is value creation for the customer as well as the organization. Let's look at these ethical dilemmas in greater depth.

Why does independence from supervision pose ethical issues? The company usually goes to great expense to hire, train, and support a salesperson. If s/he does not work hard, then the company may be denied sales. The amount of time spent selling is an issue of personal ethics. Most employers recognize that the job may require spending time on evenings or weekends with customers or doing paperwork. To compensate, there tends to be some flexibility regarding working hours, but an unethical salesperson may take advantage of the situation. For example, it may be relatively easy to shorten the workweek without being missed or to play golf repeatedly with clients, more with an eye to a low handicap than to building a relationship. A salesperson may add another job rather than devote full energy to the primary employer. And what about taking an MBA class during work hours without telling the company?

Other ethical issues arise with regard to performance objectives.[25] Most salespeople are evaluated at least partially on sales volume or profitability. This creates several temptations, including overstocking, overselling, or pushing brands that yield higher commissions. Overstocking occurs when customers purchase more than is required for a given period, which results in unnecessary inventory carrying charges. Imagine that you are a few thousand dollars short of your monthly sales objective. Suppose there is a distributor who relies on your estimates to restock inventory. If you put in an order for more than is needed, then you may gain a better performance evaluation, but you have behaved unethically.

Overselling occurs when customers request a lower-priced product that suits their needs and budget, but the salesperson supplies a much more expensive and more profitable product. Similarly, as noted in chapter 15, some companies offer spiffs for selling their product rather than a competitor's. Another unethical practice is to promise delivery when the salesperson knows the product will be late. The customer is prevented from ordering a competitor's brand, and when the delay becomes apparent, it is too late to obtain a substitute.

What salespeople communicate can also be an ethical issue. Puffery, or sales rhetoric so obviously excessive that customers recognize it as such, may not be in good taste but rarely is considered dishonest. Misrepresentation is far more serious. Salespeople are unethical when they give incorrect information, such as claiming their product is the same as another when it is not. Selling often involves verbal communication, and there may be little documentation other than an invoice after the sale. Whether spoken or written, intentional misrepresentation is illegal and can result in criminal or civil suits. Unintentional misrepresentation is at best a sign of incompetence in the salesperson and is grounds for canceling a contract. Ethical salespeople say, "I don't know, but I'll find out," rather than guess at the facts.

THE STEPS IN PERSONAL SELLING

Personal selling can be divided into seven stages, as outlined in Figure 16-5. Each step is explained in more detail below.

Planning   Sales planning translates the company's marketing strategy into territory plans and account plans. Territory management is extremely important. Salespeople must determine how the company's target marketing and positioning can best be applied in their territory. Because each area is different, it is important to make adjustments based on local conditions. Exceptional sales skills are of little use if calls are not made on the appropriate accounts with the right frequency and intensity. **Territory planning** determines the pool of customers, their sales potential, and the frequency with which they will be contacted about various products. The fundamental objective is to allocate sales time and use company resources to obtain the best results. Territory management is so important that many companies calculate to the minute what their salespeople do with their time. On average, salespeople spend 529 minutes per day (almost 9 hours) on the activities identified in Figure 16-6.[26]

Account planning establishes sales goals and objectives for each major customer, such as the sales volume and profitability to be obtained. Increasingly, account objectives include customer satisfaction, often measured by loyalty (repeat business). Account plans are based on an understanding of the customer's business and how the seller's products contribute to it. Elaborate account plans for major customers are common. For example, the AT&T sales team responsible for Ford Motor Company has a detailed description of its entire communication

Territory planning

Identifying potential customers, their sales potential, and the frequency with which they will be contacted about various products.

Account planning

Establishing sales goals and objectives for each major customer.

Figure 16-5   Steps in Personal Selling

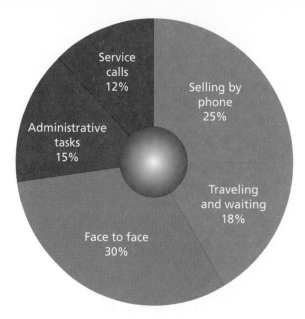

*Figure 16-6   Daily Activities of
Salespeople*

Prospecting

Seeking potential customers within the company's target markets.

Leads

All those who may have need of a company's product.

Prospect

A potential customer interested in the seller's product.

Qualifying

Examining prospects to identify those with the authority and ability to buy the product.

Qualified prospect

A potential buyer interested in the seller's product and with the attributes of a good customer.

Cold calling

Contacting a lead for the first time.

Center of influence

An opinion leader who can be quickly qualified as a potential customer because of his/her standing in the community.

picture. This required a massive effort to develop, but the millions of dollars in revenues make it worthwhile. The plan provides all the information necessary to build and maintain the AT&T relationship with Ford.

Prospecting   As the name implies, **prospecting** is seeking out new customers within the company's target markets. As illustrated in Figure 16-7, it involves three steps: obtain leads, identify prospects, and qualify them. **Leads** are the names of all those who might have a need for the product, a large pool that must be narrowed down to the most likely buyers. **Prospects** are potential customers who have an interest in the product. They may currently buy from a competitor, are former customers, or have shown interest in some way. **Qualifying** is the process of determining which prospects have the authority and ability to buy the product. It also determines whether they are desirable customers. A **qualified prospect** is a potential buyer interested in the product and likely to be a reliable customer.

A number of methods are used in prospecting: cold calls (canvassing), referrals, exhibiting at trade shows, networking, telemarketing, secondary data, and coupons and ads. These are shown in Figure 16-8.

Cold calling (canvassing) is contacting the lead for the first time, either by telephone, fax, or in person. The salesperson has no idea whether the person will be interested. A few prospects are likely to be found, some of whom may be qualified. Cold calling is warranted when there is little information about the market or when the product is likely to have universal appeal. Many consumer products are sold door-to-door, and cold calling is also used in business-to-business selling. It is not very popular with customers, but it can be a useful method if not abused.[27]

A variation of cold calling is the **center of influence** method, which identifies leads by contacting opinion leaders. Recall from chapter 14 that opinion leaders are open to communications with salespeople and are considered reference group models. It is common knowl-

Figure 16-7   Potential Customers

Cold Calls (Canvassing)	Going door-to-door.
Center of Influence	Identify opinion leaders and contact them for leads.
Referrals	Get customers or prospects to provide names of others.
Exhibitions & Demonstrations	Exhibit at trade shows or give speeches.
Networking	Contact friends, relatives, and associates to obtain leads.
Telemarketing	Phone people on lists.
Secondary Data	Obtain lists from companies like Dun & Bradstreet.
Coupons & Ads	The prospect responds to an ad or redeems a coupon.

Figure 16-8   Prospecting Methods

edge that the pharmaceutical industry has profiled every physician in the country according to opinion leadership. The leaders are more open to new products and also are more likely to influence colleagues.

Referrals are names of leads provided by a qualified prospect. This method can be very effective, since qualified prospects tend to associate with those who have similar attributes. Furthermore, compared to cold calling, the referral is likely to be receptive when the salesperson mentions the name of someone they both know.

Referral
A lead provided by a qualified prospect.

Exhibitions are an important way to obtain leads. About 85 percent of attendees significantly influence buying within their firm. This also is an inexpensive method. It costs 70 percent less to close a sale with these leads than with others.[28] In 1997, approximately 726,000 people visited the Detroit Auto Show.[29] An estimated one million attended the Chicago Auto Show that year, one of the largest and most prestigious in the world. Participants included both domestic and foreign automakers as well as specialty manufacturers and retailers.[30] Nearly every industry sponsors a trade show. Large halls such as Madison Square Garden in New York City, the Omni in Atlanta, and McCormick Place in Chicago provide facilities for thousands of organizations to display their products and obtain leads.

Networking involves contacting friends, relatives, and associates to obtain leads. Successful salespeople in most fields find this an important part of their business. Amway Corporation has had great success obtaining sales through networking. The company uses a system of independent agents who sell home care products directly to consumers. The agents obtain from customers the names of additional leads to contact.[31] Amway has had incredible success globally. In Japan, for example, it distributes about 130 consumer products through 980,000 distributors. Worldwide sales for fiscal 1996 were estimated at $6.8 billion.[32]

Networking
Contacting friends, relatives, and associates to obtain leads.

Telemarketing uses phone calls to contact lists of leads provided by marketing services and various directories. Organizations such as Dun & Bradstreet and Information Resources, Inc., provide listings of nearly every private and public organization as well as the name and title of executives, managers, and buying influencers. Many marketing services contact these leads to determine the types of products they purchase and other information. These interviews are then turned into lists of prospects and sold to various marketing organizations. AT&T has its own staff of telemarketers to find small business prospects for its products. Ford

Telemarketing
Making telephone calls to leads provided by marketing services or from other lists.

Exhibitions are a popular way to obtain leads.

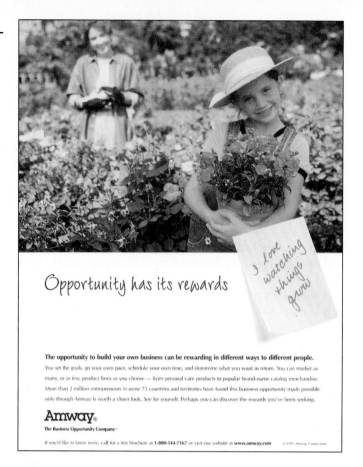

Amway obtains most of its sales through networking.

CONNECTED: SURFING THE NET

www.amway.com

By visiting the Amway site you can learn more about its extensive networking. And for fun, play a multiple choice game in which you match flags and countries.

Preapproach

Preparation by the salesperson for the initial meeting with a prospect.

hired the Phoenix Group of Farmington Hills, Michigan, to telemarket options to its leasing customers. In an effort to maintain loyalty, calls are especially targeted to those whose lease is about to expire.[33]

Secondary data sources can provide thousands of lists. Chapter 5 noted categories of secondary data, ranging from local libraries to company databases. Today, the information highway provides access to the names of nearly all U.S. companies and most international organizations. CD-ROM directories are another fast and effective source. Marketplace Business and PhoneDisc PowerFinder provide millions of names and phone numbers. The former is updated quarterly and lists 10 million U.S. businesses. The latter has search capabilities for every phone directory in the country. Both are tremendous sources for leads.[34] By using database technologies, companies also can qualify prospects. In some cases, the selling organization manages the database, but this is a highly specialized field. Because of the very costly technology and expertise required, most secondary data searches are outsourced.

Coupons and ads are another method for obtaining leads. Generally, coupons are placed in newspapers or magazines or sent through the mail. People who take the time to respond tend to be very interested and may have the attributes of a qualified prospect. A trend in magazine advertising is response cards that consumers mail in for free information after circling a number that corresponds to a specific ad. These cards give the seller a list of leads to pursue.

Organizing Information and Developing a Call Plan   **Preapproach** refers to preparing for the initial meeting by learning about the prospect. For consumers, just their address can yield socioeconomic information, such as the likelihood of sufficient income to purchase the product and even some general idea of tastes and preferences. Columbia TriStar Home Video has developed its own software for its sales force to use in learning about the large retail chain outlets they visit. In the case of businesses, the salesperson can obtain copies of the organization's literature and annual reports. These contain data on the firm's financial strength, organizational structure, objectives, plant locations, and sometimes even its purchasing philosophy. The salesperson's goal is to obtain enough information to develop an initial strategy for each call.

Once the preapproach phase is completed a call plan is developed to save time and minimize travel expenses. The **routing schedule** identifies which prospects will be called on and when. There are computerized programs to help with routing, or it can be done informally.

Approach The **approach** is the first formal contact with the customer. The objective is to secure an initial meeting and gain customer interest. It's usually a good idea to schedule an appointment; that will save time and puts the prospect in the frame of mind for a sales call. Many times, a letter of introduction before calling to schedule will help in obtaining the first appointment.

Many techniques have been developed for the initial approach. The most successful ones focus on the potential customer's business, such as a brief explanation of how or why the seller's product can help. It also is important to determine not just when the meeting will take place but how long it will last and its objective. Organizations with a strong reputation generally have an advantage in the approach stage. For example, Xerox or Kodak salespeople will have more success gaining an initial interview than will representatives of an unknown company.

Making the Case and Building Relationships The sales **presentation** is a two-way process: The salesperson listens in order to identify customer needs and then describes how the product will fulfill them. The most important part of any good presentation is listening. In fact, it is often said that successful selling is 90 percent listening and 10 percent talking. Unfortunately, many salespeople believe their role is to tell prospects about products. Instead, by asking questions, they should put the customer first and demonstrate that they have the customer's best interest in mind. The first contact is the first opportunity to connect with a customer.

Organizations generally have to train their sales force to be good listeners. This is a trait few people possess naturally. The training identifies ways to learn about the prospect's situation. It also teaches how to communicate that the salesperson is listening and is concerned about the customer's needs and wants. **Empathy** occurs when salespeople know precisely how prospects feel. Only when prospects know that the seller understands their needs and wants are they receptive to solutions the salesperson offers.

A popular technique for interfacing with customers is SPIN® selling. It stands for situation, problem, implication, and need payoff.[35] The approach resulted from research into what makes people successful at large sales. More than 35,000 sales calls were investigated. Companies like Xerox, IBM, and Kodak supported the study and have used the system successfully for years. Considerable training is required for people to become proficient with the technique. Essentially, it employs a sequence of probing questions that enlighten the salesperson and the client at the same time.

Situation questions help discover facts about the buyer's condition. Much of this can be learned before the interview so these questions should be limited.[36] Problem questions identify dissatisfaction with the current circumstances.[37] For example, the salesperson may ask: "What makes it difficult to use this type of product?" Implication questions follow, and these are crucial. They unearth the consequences of current problems and are likely to reveal important needs. For example, in response to questions about product safety, one customer began to realize that high insurance costs, low morale, and ethical issues were consequences or hidden costs.[38] Need payoff questions then explore why it is important to solve the problem.[39] In the SPIN® process, the buyer and seller establish the need for a product and the benefit of its ownership.

The first contact not only is an opportunity for the salesperson to make a case for a product but also may be the first step in building a relationship. While sales sometimes are made on the first visit, most occur later. Over time, the salesperson assumes different roles as the relationship develops.

Managing Objections and Closing the Sale One of the most important sales skills is the ability to overcome a buyer's objections. These may be raised subtly in many cultures. In the United States, for example, they often are disguised questions. A consumer may say, "I can't afford to purchase that automobile," but really is asking what financing is available, or how much it costs, or what are the trade-in terms. Assertive salespeople do not let the first objection stop the dialogue; they use it to advance the discussion. Most organizations have training programs to teach salespeople how to manage objections.

Routing schedule
A travel plan for calling on prospects that is developed to save time and minimize expenses.

Approach
The salesperson's first formal contact with the potential customer.

Presentation
A two-way process in which the salesperson listens to the customer to identify needs and then describes how the product will fulfill them.

Empathy
An interpersonal connection in which the salesperson knows precisely how the prospect feels and communicates that understanding.

Closing

The point at which the salesperson obtains the first order from the customer.

Follow-up

After-sales service to ensure customer satisfaction in order to obtain repeat business.

Closing means getting the first order. In many cases this is simple, such as asking directly if someone wants to buy the product or whether they will use cash or credit. In other cases, it involves elaborate contracts. Good salespeople know how important it is to help the buyer toward the final decision. You have probably tried on a suit or dress and heard the salesperson say: "Shall I have that measured for alterations?" or "Shall I wrap that for you now?" In business-to-business situations, the salesperson may ask if the purchaser is ready to make a decision or would like to discuss the issue more thoroughly. A caution is in order regarding closing.[40] If a buyer is not ready to make the commitment, then asking for an order prematurely can make the salesperson appear pushy and unconcerned with the buyer's needs. A great deal of sensitivity is required for an accurate reading of the buyer's state of mind.

Service There is a big difference between making a sale and gaining a customer. One sale equals one sale. The word *customer* implies something more than a single sale. In order to maintain relationships, salespeople spend significant time servicing accounts. They make sure products are delivered on schedule and operate to the buyer's liking. When there is a problem, the salesperson makes sure that it is resolved quickly and satisfactorily.

Follow-up occurs when a salesperson ensures after-sale satisfaction in order to obtain repeat business. Good follow-up reduces buyer's remorse. A bad feeling about spending a lot of money can be alleviated if a salesperson provides information that supports the decision. If that evidence is not forthcoming, then customers may quickly become dissatisfied. Follow-up also offers a way to identify additional sales opportunities. After the first step is taken, the second is easier. The salesperson who continues to work closely with the buying organization can uncover other needs to supply. Good service builds strong customer loyalty, which is the goal of partnership selling.

CHARACTERISTICS OF STRONG SALESPEOPLE

Hundreds, perhaps thousands, of studies have been done to determine what makes a good salesperson. Figure 16-9 describes the characteristics noted most often: goal direction, empathy, strong knowledge of applications, and ethics.[41]

First, strong sales performers tend to be goal directed. They spend adequate time on planning and then work according to the plans. They use their time effectively, which allows them to manage their territory efficiently. They are also highly competitive and obtain results in the face of stiff competition.

Second, because strong salespeople are empathetic, they are aware of the concerns and feelings of others. This means they can understand buyer behavior and have a customer focus. They see things from the customer's perspective. Most have very good listening and questioning skills that help them obtain this information.

Third, strong salespeople know how their products apply to the customer's situation. This requires technical competency as well as a good understanding of the customer's business.

Figure 16-9 Characteristics of Successful Salespeople

That combination allows the salesperson to solve problems for the customer creatively. Since each customer has a specific set of needs, each requires special attention. A salesperson must customize or assemble a mix of products that offers the best possible answer. In essence, the strong salesperson works with the customer to tailor a solution.

Fourth, salespeople must be ethical. The nature of the job often places them in difficult situations. Since good salespeople build relationships, they must be viewed as totally trustworthy, a requisite for creating partnerships. They seek out information when they don't know the answer to a question. They provide pertinent information. They try to help customers solve problems, whether or not a sale is involved. They have a record of keeping customers informed, of facing up to mistakes, and of not promising what they can't deliver.

Relationship selling requires that salespeople be more versatile, creative, and visionary than ever before. A strong salesperson works to harness all company resources for the customer's benefit.

SALES FORCE MANAGEMENT

The sales organization connects directly with customers. Personal relationships are what it's all about. Managers develop and guide the sales organization to make sure the connections are made in the right ways with the right customers. They lead others in order to carry out the overall personal selling portion of the communications mix. **Sales force management** is the marketing function involved with planning, implementing, and adjusting sales force activities. It is a tremendously important function for companies that stress customer relationships. Nearly every dimension of how salespeople behave with customers is influenced by how they are managed. Sales management teams keep this in mind when they recruit, train, and motivate salespeople. And, sales force management helps salespeople create lasting connections with customers by directing company resources to support relationship building.

Sales managers are responsible for the leadership and management of salespeople in order to accomplish the sales objectives established in the marketing plan. Sales managers make things happen through other people. They are not simply supersalespeople. They are vital in implementing the marketing strategy in companies like General Electric, Intel, Xerox, Kodak, Eaton Corporation, and thousands of others. Many marketing executives, especially in technology-driven firms, have made their way up through the sales manager route. To do an effective job, sales managers need a full understanding of marketing strategy and planning, each aspect of the marketing mix, and personnel management in addition to principles of selling and sales management.

Sales force managers perform many functions in support of the marketing strategy. Figure 16-10 describes the key functions: organize the sales force, develop diverse sales teams, prepare sales forecasts and budgets, implement sales actions, and oversee the sales force. These functions may be performed alone in a smaller organization or by a team of people in a larger company. The sales management team is comprised of representatives from personnel, who help with recruiting, training, and personnel records; from marketing (management) information systems, who provide necessary sales data; and, from customer service, who connect the sales force and their customers with manufacturing and logistics. Yet the overall responsibility for all the functions described in Figure 16-10 belongs to sales management.

ORGANIZING THE SALES FORCE

The characteristics of sales managers and the chain of command are important considerations in organizing the sales force. These and other concerns are of particular importance in global settings. The sales force may be structured by geography, by division or product line, or by market segment. Both the structure and the size of the sales group have a lot to do with sales coverage.

Sales Manager Types   The sales manager position can be executive, midlevel, or first-line, depending on responsibilities and scope of operations. At the top are national and international sales executives, often with the title of vice president. They usually report to the top marketing executive. In most companies, only one or a few people are in this position. Their management scope covers several products across a broad territory. In large companies, executive sales managers may have several other sales managers reporting to them, and they ultimately are responsible for several thousand salespeople. Midlevel managers, called regional managers when the sales force structure is geographic, supervise several other managers, called

Sales force management
The marketing function involved with planning, implementing, and adjusting sales force activities.

Sales manager
The person responsible for the leadership and management of salespeople in order to accomplish the sales objectives established in the marketing plan.

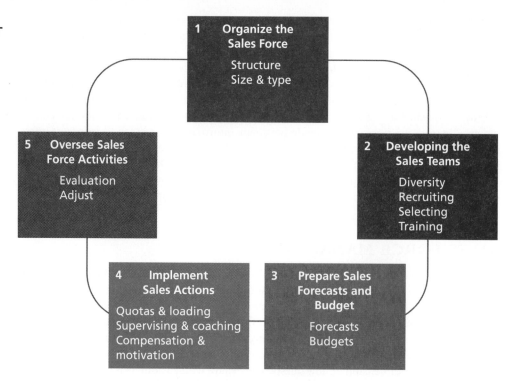

*Figure 16-10   Sales
Management Functions*

district managers or first-line managers, in a large area, such as New England or several countries. First-line managers oversee several salespeople who handle certain products or types of accounts in a limited geographic area. First-line managers who supervise field reps and retail salespeople usually have a sales force of eight to 12; those who supervise inside sales or telemarketing personnel are likely to have more. As a first assignment, some sales managers supervise only three or four people.

Sales structure

The organization of the reporting relationship between sales managers and salespeople.

Sales Force Structures   A **sales structure** is the organization of the reporting relationship between sales managers and salespeople. Sales organizations can be structured by geography, by product or division, by market segment, or by individual account. In some cases, all four are used. Figure 16-11 shows a typical geographical structure, topped by a general sales manager who reports to the vice president of marketing. Sales managers in the various geographical areas report to the general sales manager. Below them may be sales managers at the regional and district level, then territory representatives (salespersons).

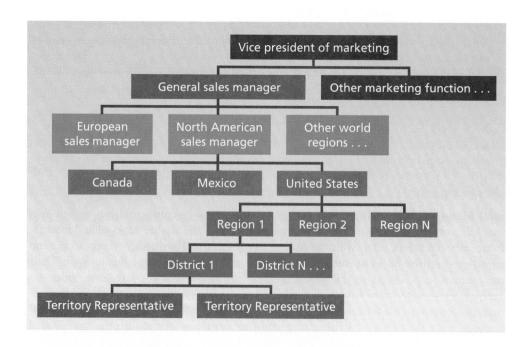

*Figure 16-11   A
Geographical Sales Force
Structure*

Figure 16-12   A Division or Product Line Sales Force Structure

Figure 16-12 illustrates the division or product line structure. Many companies are organized into divisions, and each may have a sales organization. Companies with very technical products are likely to use this sort of structure. For example, GM's Delphi division has a sales organization structured according to the components of an automobile: interior, exterior, electronics, and so forth. Each area requires a great deal of interaction among salespeople, designers, manufacturing personnel, and individual customers.

The third approach is to structure the sales force by market segment, as shown in Figure 16-13. Salespeople are focused on a given target segment, as outlined in the marketing plan. IBM has historically operated in this manner. It has one sales organization that sells to the financial community, another for universities, and yet another for manufacturing firms. The advantage is that salespeople focus on and truly understand the needs of a particular market segment. A company with a limited product line that has differing applications by segment would prefer this arrangement.

Many companies have a few customers who represent extremely large volume, called key accounts, house accounts, national accounts, or global accounts, depending on how they are managed. Major accounts may fit the 80-20 rule: About 80 percent of a company's sales volume comes from only 20 percent of its accounts. Although the percentages may differ considerably, the point is that major accounts are large, usually have unique sales needs, and are so important to volume and profitability that they require special emphasis. Major accounts are often managed by a separate sales group of a few very experienced people who report to the top sales executive. In other cases, they may be allocated to the midlevel area in which they are located. In some companies major accounts are assigned to sales managers who split their time between these customers and their management duties.

Developing the Sales Team

In order to develop the sales team, a good sales force must first be recruited, selected, and trained. Recruitment is the activity of attracting qualified prospects for the sales job. Selection involves choosing the strongest recruits for employment in the sales force. Training provides education and preparation to salespeople. In the United States it is a manager's responsibility to comply with the federal Equal Employment Opportunity Act. Hiring

Figure 16-13   A Market Segment Sales Force Structure

discrimination based on age, sex, race, national origin, religion, ethnic background, and physical handicap is strictly forbidden. Many countries have similar requirements that must be carefully followed.

Diversity in the Sales Force   Although the structure and size of the sales force are important, nothing is more critical for relationship marketing than the diversity of the sales organization. Managers must take care to develop a sales force that represents various groups. This enhances the ability of the organization to be sensitive to the needs of individual customers, thereby improving its relationship-building capacity. A diverse sales force provides a variety of insights, ideas, and perspectives, all of which make it easier to accommodate a dynamic and multicultural customer base.[42] Strong managers consider diversity in all stages of their sales force development, particularly including recruitment, selection, and training. For example, AT&T uses seven multicultural resource groups to ensure the hiring of diverse salespeople. In addition, 90 percent of AT&T's sales force has completed diversity training to increase sensitivity toward customers and fellow employees.[43]

While men traditionally have dominated the sales profession, many managers are finding that women have excellent relationship skills and often are more successful at selling. The mostly male readership of *Sales and Marketing Management* was asked: "Who is better at sales, women or men?" While 70 percent ranked the sexes as equal, 17 percent said women were better, compared to 13 percent who ranked men higher. Avon's CEO is committed to the promotion of women into sales management positions. The $4.5 billion cosmetic company has 86 percent female management—more than any other *Fortune* 500 company. To accomplish this, Avon rewards the improved representation of women and minorities in its annual bonus plan for managers. The importance of hiring women and minorities in the workforce also is a topic at conventions and is highly publicized within and outside the company.[44]

Many companies organize committees or task forces to promote diversity in the sales force. For example, IBM set up eight task forces to evaluate diversity and determine how to make such groups as women, African Americans, gays, and lesbians feel welcome within the company and its sales force. Levi Strauss established a committee to recruit diverse, qualified candidates for sales positions. In some cases, diversity goals are achieved by tying efforts to sales managers' compensation. This is true for Prudential Insurance.[45] The most common practices for insurance companies, however, include recruiting bilingual salespeople, using an affirmative action plan, and printing sales materials in languages other than English.[46]

Diversity training seeks to eliminate stereotypes and biases within the global sales force as well. It also addresses the unique tastes and preferences of the customer base as well as cultural practices that may be different. For example, Ford Motor Company uses this kind of awareness training around the globe because, according to its CEO, "it's very important for people to understand the different customer tastes around the world. People in China don't like exactly the same products as people in India."[47]

Recruiting   Effective recruitment attracts a qualified pool of candidates to fill the sales positions. The first step is to develop a job description specifying activities and qualifications. This written document spells out organizational relationships, responsibilities, and duties of the position.

The convenience of the recruiting site is important, which is why college campuses are often chosen. Many organizations use recruiting companies to find experienced candidates. Strong organizations spend a good deal of time identifying a pool of candidates. Northwestern Mutual Life Insurance has increased college hiring by 56 percent through aggressive recruiting. It offers mock interviews, career fairs, and resumé critiques on university campuses.[48] Companies like Hewlett-Packard and Motorola recruit through industry contacts, customers, and vendors. Both of these firms also are aggressively seeking out and developing recent college graduates for their sales force.[49] To find out more, contact your college placement office, or visit these companies on-line.

Selecting   Because good sales talent is in high demand, not only the company but also the candidate does the choosing. Sales managers must demonstrate sound judgment in selecting from a broad range of talents, and they also need to sell top candidates on opportunities with their organization. FedEx sales managers see recruitment and selection of sales candidates as one of their most important functions. FedEx is considered to have one of the best global sales forces. It selects candidates who can build relationships with a dynamic customer base spread over 200 countries.[50]

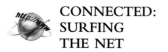

CONNECTED: SURFING THE NET

www.prudential.com

Find out more about Prudential's commitment to diversity by exploring the company's Web site. Also discover how Prudential is connecting through technology. Chairman and CEO Art Ryan says: "As we head into the next century, advances in on-line technology will offer us exciting, new opportunities to reach out to customers and to help them achieve financial security and peace of mind."

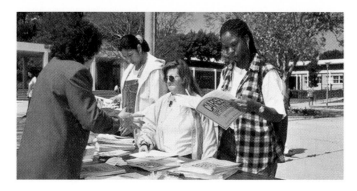

Many companies actively recruit salespeople on college campuses.

Although there is no definitive list of attributes that define those likely to become successful salespeople, the attitudes, skills, and knowledge of some individuals set them apart. Important personality traits include empathy, which allows a salesperson to understand problems from another's perspective; ego drive, which ties self-image and identity to job performance; and resilience, which allows a salesperson to bounce back from defeat. Also important is the ability to communicate, think analytically, and effectively organize and manage time. Knowledge of and experience with a product, industry, competitor, or company territory are also valuable qualities. Others include self-discipline, intelligence, creativity, flexibility, self-motivation, persistence, a personable nature, and dependability.[51]

Training Even the most qualified salespeople need continuous education. New hires need the most, but seasoned veterans also can benefit from advanced training and formal practice. Many sales executives believe training is critical for developing individual and team skills. Nabisco found that it increased morale, reduced turnover, improved relationship building skills, and developed a stronger sense of teamwork, all of which combined to increase sales dramatically.[52] Training programs are usually conducted regarding company policies and procedures, product and customer applications knowledge, sales skills, and territory and account planning.

Company policies and procedures can be very elaborate, specifying the exact relationship that salespeople are expected to have with customers. Policies range from mundane matters, such as sales account and entertainment budgets, to complicated issues, such as the types of special customer requests the company will honor. In today's sales environment, procedures often are highly complex. Among other things, they may involve understanding how to enter orders, how to service accounts, and how to create and maintain reporting systems between the selling and buying organization.

Training is necessary to understand the product's attributes and benefits. In technical sales jobs, products are often very sophisticated. In some cases training builds background information, such as a knowledge of electricity for electrical products or pharmacology for drug products. Salespeople learn not only about the technologies behind the product but also about how the product works. Teaching salespeople about new items is critical to the success of a pharmaceutical company like Merck. There is very little time between a product's FDA approval and its introduction to customers. With the help of physicians, Merck's 3,000 salespeople learn the product features in just one week. Merck also follows up to ensure that reps have a solid knowledge.[53]

Most organizations train new hires in basic relationship selling skills and experienced salespeople in more advanced techniques. The objective is to help the sales force do a better job of working with customers, listening, and finding ways to develop profitable relationships for each party. At Saturn, all sales reps go through a five-day program at company headquarters to learn about the company's customer-focused culture. Sales skills are developed in the context of the Saturn management philosophy.[54]

Many organizations use sales certification programs to enhance the skills and credibility of their sales force. These programs are usually provided by companies or associations which specialize in sales training. In this form of training, salespeople must attend classes, or in some cases take distanced learning courses offered over the Internet. Certificates are given according to the competency level attained. More than 50 percent of managers believe that a certification program would benefit their company, and 66 percent of consumers believe certified

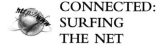

CONNECTED: SURFING THE NET

www.merck.com

Visit Merck's award-winning Web site to learn more about its sales training and leading pharmaceutical products.

salespeople are more credible. Certification is thought to demonstrate a defined level of competency and skill. Although such training is expensive, many organizations consider it a good investment.[55]

SALES FORECASTING AND BUDGETING

Forecasting and budgeting are important steps in allocating sales resources. The forecast estimates demand based on likely responses of buyers to future market conditions, sales force, and other promotional activities and marketing actions. Sales force budgets are generally set with the sales forecast in mind. Accuracy in the forecast and budgets is important, since production is scheduled to meet demand. When forecasts are lower than actual demand, customers go unserved. When they are higher than demand, high inventory carrying costs dramatically reduce profitability. Estimation methods vary from elaborate computer programs to fairly simple questioning of potential buyers. Even small companies, which are known for their ability to adjust quickly, depend on accurate forecasts.[56]

Environmental forecast

An estimate of the economic, political, and social factors likely to affect the level of spending for the types of products or services being forecast.

Sales Forecasting Most companies go through three basic steps in estimating demand—an environmental forecast, an industry forecast, and a company sales forecast. The **environmental forecast** examines the economic, political, and social factors likely to affect the level of spending for a product. Factors include unemployment, consumer spending, interest rates, business investments, and inventory levels. In general, information of this type helps determine whether economic conditions for the company's products are likely to be positive or negative. Environmental forecasting can estimate not only global, international, national, and regional trends but also very localized trends. Every year *Sales and Marketing Management* prints a "Survey of Buying Power," a tool that helps marketers predict sales of products based on environmental conditions, consumer age and wealth, and distribution channels.

Industry forecast

An estimate of the amount and type of competitive activity that is likely to occur in an industry.

Sales forecasts often use the industry outlook as a key element. An **industry forecast** estimates the amount of overall demand expected based on such factors as the industry business condition, amount of spending, number of new products, and communications budgets anticipated for competitors. In other words, this forecast projects the level of sales and marketing activity for the industry as a whole as well as for competitors likely to affect the company most directly.

Company sales forecast

A prediction of unit or dollar sales for a given period, in total or broken down by product, segments, or other categories, and based on the marketing strategy that will be put in place.

The **company sales forecast** is based on the overall marketing strategy. It forecasts unit sales and must be in line with marketing, financial, and operations plans. If not, then adjustments must be made to the sales forecast. The marketing plan is particularly critical. For example, a product positioned as a high-priced specialty item may have a low expected sales volume. For a product positioned as a low-priced commodity, the sales volume estimate probably will be higher. In addition, in order to do a good job of developing objectives, it is important to estimate demand with other departments in mind. Sales managers communicate about forecasts with many areas of the company to reconcile any differences. Since various departments may have specific objectives, such as cost containment, brand growth, and financial targets, this interaction is necessary. Estimates may be made for the entire company, a particular product, a geographic region, a market segment, or on some other basis.

CONNECTED: SURFING THE NET

www.whirlpool.com

Learn more about the world's leading manufacturer of major home appliances by visiting the Whirlpool homelife network. Use this 24-hour resource to check out "the clothesline," "appliance corner," "really cookin," and "family life." You can also search for company information. See what you can discover about its forecasting techniques.

It's important to remember that forecasts are only guesses. The more dynamic the situation, the less accurate the prediction is likely to be. Consequently, businesses in new fields may have more difficulty estimating demand than do businesses with mature product lines. In innovative, highly competitive industries it is hard to obtain reliable forecasts.

Some marketers mistakenly associate good forecasting with strong marketing. In fact, there are many examples of organizations that have forecast low sales volume and thus created less aggressive marketing strategies. Although they met their forecasts, they probably would have reached much higher sales levels if they had pursued an aggressive strategy. Most organizations recognize that perfect sales projections may mean the company is operating much too conservatively. Whirlpool Corporation believes a perfect forecast is possible only when a marketing group is performing below potential.

Forecasts are very important in deciding how to allocate company resources. Divisions that foresee high levels of sales are often given ample resources, such as additional salespeople, large advertising and promotion budgets, and lots of attention from product development and manufacturing. Consequently, the forecast can become a self-fulfilling prophecy. When forecasts are low, fewer resources are provided, and lower sales result.

Sales Force Budgets One of the most important tasks of the sales manager is to create and administer the sales budget. The three most common methods for setting the budget are a percentage of overall sales, in relation to competitors in the industry, or as projected costs for the sales tasks. The first method establishes the sales budget as a percentage of the historical sales level. Although simple to use, this method has a major flaw. The estimated increase over past sales results in a larger sales budget, but the situation should be the reverse. A larger sales budget should result in a higher sales volume. Despite this problem, many sales organizations base the budget on past performance. Essentially, a sales force that produces more is rewarded more resources in the future for its past success. A variation on this is to use the sales forecast to establish the budget. This is more acceptable because it looks at the future rather than the past.

The second way to determine the sales budget is through comparison with a competitor's budget. Industry data provide the number of salespeople and sales offices as well as sales expenditures for other companies. The sales budget is then set accordingly. One advantage of this method is that it emphasizes competitive activity in the marketplace. A disadvantage is that it is not based on an understanding of the actual costs of one's own sales activities.

Task-based budgeting looks at the tasks salespeople must perform in order to accomplish objectives. Careful thought is given to each aspect of the sales process and to estimating the associated costs. The items usually considered are salaries, recruiting, training, travel, sales promotion, staff and clerical expenses, dues, and supplies.

IMPLEMENTING SALES ACTIONS

Once the sales forecast and budget have been established, sales activity can take place. Sales managers set quotas, measure performance, determine compensation, and supervise, coach, and motivate the sales organization in such a way that objectives are accomplished.

Quotas **Quotas** are quantitative performance standards used to direct sales force activity. They also provide a way to evaluate performance. Whereas forecasts estimate results, quotas provide guidelines. They are one of the most important methods sales managers use to set and meet objectives. When quotas are exceeded, we would say that the sales force has produced beyond objectives; when quotas are not met, we would say that the sales force has fallen short of objectives. Overall, quotas are set in line with the strategic marketing plan. Most sales organizations use one of three types: sales volume, profit, or activity quotas.

Sales volume quotas establish unit or dollar objectives. Usually these are set for a market segment, product or service line, and average volume per customer. Typically, a quota for the entire sales organization is determined and then divided among the various sales regions and salespeople. During this process, salespeople and others are likely to provide feedback to sales executives regarding potential in their territory, the level of competition, and their belief about what is possible to accomplish. That information is combined with the sales forecast.

Sales profit quotas establish profitability objectives for customers, products, and market segments. Rather than volume, the focus is on the overall profit that can be made. This kind of quota is particularly important when sales actions like price negotiations or repeat versus new customers influence profit. It is also important when different products yield different profit.

Activity quotas encourage salespeople to engage in certain tasks, such as prospecting calls, service calls, sales calls, demonstrations, and new accounts visited. The focus is on customer contacts that will allow the company to implement its overall marketing strategy.

Quotas are generally used to determine some portion of a salesperson's compensation. The simplest procedure is to set the same quota (such as amount of sales) for all salespeople and provide bonuses to those who exceed it. This tends to be inequitable, however, because sales potential and competition are likely to differ from one sales territory to another. Consequently, sales quotas usually vary for different parts of the organization and different salespeople. Compensation is covered in more detail in a later section.

Performance measures Volume, profit, and activity quotas can be combined to measure performance, as shown in Figure 16-14. In this example the quota is based on sales volume, profit margin percentage, number of new accounts obtained, percentage of accounts retained, level of customer satisfaction, and number of new leads. Each factor is weighted in terms of importance. At the end of the sales period, the percentage of quota reached in each category is multiplied by the weight to determine the contribution of that category to achieving the total quota. In the example, sales are weighted at 40 percent, the quota is $500,000, and per-

Quotas
Quantitative objectives used to direct sales force activity and evaluate performance.

Sales volume quotas
Unit or dollar objectives, usually set by market segment, product or service line, and average volume per customer.

Sales profit quotas
Profitability objectives for customers, products, and market segments.

Activity quotas
Action objectives that encourage salespeople to engage in certain tasks, such as prospecting calls, service calls, sales calls,

	(1) Weight	(2) Quota	(3) Performance	(4) % of Quota	(5) Contribution to Total Quota: (4) × (1)
Sales in dollars	40%	$500,000	$525,000	105%	42%
Profit margin	20%	30%	33%	110%	22%
Number of new accounts	15%	25	20	80%	12%
Number of accounts retained	20%	100	120	120%	24%
Number of new leads	5%	25	50	200%	10%
				TOTAL:	110%

Figure 16-14 Quotas as a Measure of Performance

formance is $25,000 above that, leading to 105 percent of quota on that item. Multiplying by the weight, we get a 42 percent contribution to the total quota. Notice that when all these items are put together, this particular salesperson achieved 110 percent of quota (exceeded objectives by 10 percent). Performance exceeded the quota in all areas except the number of new accounts.

The performance measurement shown in Figure 16-14 can be used for several purposes. First, this person maintains loyal customers but seems to do little to increase the number of new accounts. The sales manager should discuss the situation to see whether training is needed or whether the territory has minimal potential for new customers. Second, since quotas can be used to motivate the sales force, the salesperson could be compensated for performing so well. Third, although the example provided here focuses on dollar volume, organizations often use this method to emphasize certain products or market segments consistent with their overall marketing strategy and positioning plan.

Compensation   A well-designed compensation plan should be geared toward the needs of both the company and the sales force. It should be developed with the overall sales strategy in mind. A compensation system not only helps motivate salespeople but also is important in keeping loyal employees. For obvious reasons, turnover is harmful in relationship marketing. Furthermore, satisfied salespeople work hard to develop loyal customers. It is almost impossible to build customer loyalty with a dissatisfied sales force.

The three basic elements of sales force compensation are salaries, commissions, and bonuses. A **salary** is a fixed amount paid regardless of specific performance. Salaries are usually based on education, experience, longevity, and overall professionalism. A **commission** is an amount paid in direct proportion to the accomplishment of specific short-term sales objectives. It usually is given for meeting or exceeding a broad range of criteria, including volume and profit by product, or according to customer type and loyalty. A **bonus** is a percentage of salary or fee paid in addition to other compensation for meeting long-term or unique goals. Bonuses are often given to the entire sales team for an outstanding effort, usually quarterly or annually.[57] Compensation plans can be based on salary only, commission only, or both, and sometimes bonuses as well.

Supervision and Coaching   Supervision and coaching are face-to-face interactions between the sales manager and a salesperson. Most managers spend considerable time working with their people in the field. Good managers communicate well and help salespeople determine appropriate sales actions. They provide guidance to keep the sales force operating according to the company's philosophies, policies, and marketing plans.

Essentially, sales coaching occurs when the manager aids in the development of skills. Similar to a voice coach or athletic coach, the sales manager gives advice and demonstrations that enable salespeople to do a better job. Feedback should be an objective, and positive incentives should be used as progress is made. Coaching usually involves visits with customers by the manager and salesperson. The sales manager observes and gives pointers afterward on sales techniques. Good coaches also address all aspects of selling—from time management to customer sales support or even interaction with other company employees. In some cases coaching is done through role-playing. The vice president of new business partnerships at American Express says: "The sales manager's role is to add value, whether it's with the customer or whether it's helping your salespeople prepare for their next round of sales calls. It's keeping an eye out for those common problems and opportunities that are coming up . . . you're always coaching, coaching, coaching."[58]

Salary

The fixed amount of compensation paid regardless of performance.

Commission

A form of sales force compensation in which the amount paid is in direct proportion to the accomplishment of specific objectives.

Bonus

A percentage of salary or a fee paid in addition to other compensation for meeting long-term or unique goals.

There are many appropriate coaching styles, but good coaches usually don't simply take over. They observe, ask questions, and listen. They communicate clearly and provide positive reinforcement for the activities that salespeople carry out well. Feedback from sales managers is invaluable because it helps salespeople understand their strengths and weaknesses.

Motivation   Most top salespeople are motivated by the very nature of the job. They find selling fascinating and want to excel in a competitive environment. Still, good sales managers can add to motivation by providing a positive organizational climate as well as financial and career incentives. Since many salespeople spend little time under direct supervision the systems for motivation must work well without the constant presence of the sales manager. A positive organizational climate exists when salespeople feel good about their opportunities and rewards. A positive climate also helps salespeople perform at the highest professional level.

Many companies use financial incentives. At ITT Sheraton, sales reps are rewarded with higher earnings for selling upgrades, such as rooms with an ocean view or access to the hotel business center. Only one month after the program was established, Sheraton's total revenue increased by 3 percent.[59] Although money is a strong motivator, other incentives often are just as important; examples are interesting work, appreciation from management, being well informed, job security, and liking fellow workers.

Ethical Issues in Motivation and Compensation   In striving to produce peak performers, sales managers may use several motivational approaches. If they push too hard in the wrong ways, then salespeople may be pressured to compromise ethical standards. When performance is poor, rewards may be withheld, or in extreme cases punishment may be used. Motivational techniques generally reward people for good performance. A key part of the management job, however, is to establish expectations not only in terms of sales volume but also regarding acceptable behavior. When managers focus exclusively on sales objectives, they are telling salespeople that the ends justify the means. This lack of attention to appropriate behavior in combination with pressure to perform can be considered unethical in itself. Let's look at three questionable practices.

- *Family pressure.* Salespeople are required to attend the annual sales meeting with their spouse (and perhaps other family members). Those performing well are rewarded publicly with free trips, gifts, or a large bonus. For the others, it is obvious to the family that they are low producers. Essentially, the company is interfering in family relationships with the intent of elevating sales.
- *Peer pressure.* The sales manager broadcasts performance results to all salespeople or in announcing sales contest winners points out a few low producers. Rather than private communications between the manager and the salesperson, overt peer pressure is being used to gain behavior changes. This would be like posting student names along with grades in the student newspaper. Is that an ethical way to motivate you to learn? Could this increase the pressure on students to cheat?
- *Termination.* All salespeople are rank ordered, and the lowest performers are asked to leave even though they may be performing very profitably for the company. This keeps all salespeople pushing for fear of losing their job. Since termination is devastating for most people, to avoid it they may put undue or unscrupulous pressure on buyers.

Even quotas, though less extreme than these scenarios, can be troublesome. They are generally considered useful tools, but some sales managers believe they lead to high-pressure tactics and thus are harmful to relationship building. That is why Saturn moved away from quotas in favor of salary incentives. Sears auto centers got into trouble when employees were charged with performing unnecessary work in order to meet sales quotas. An embarrassed Sears eliminated the system and switched to noncommissioned rewards based on customer satisfaction.[60]

OVERSEEING SALES FORCE ACTIVITIES

Once sales operations are in effect, management needs to evaluate them and in some cases make adjustments. Evaluation and control are the final steps in the management process. Sales activities nearly always can be improved. In fact, some of the strongest sales organizations are very flexible in meeting business challenges and competitive situations. This is particularly important in industries where changes occur rapidly. In general, most evaluation programs look at efforts and results, assess the company's influence in supporting performance, identify problems and opportunities, and take corrective action.

Salesperson performance can be evaluated behaviorally or by outcome. Behavioral performance is based on skills and the ability to meet the demands of the job. This includes such aspects as sales presentation, planning, teamwork, relationship selling, and technical knowledge. Outcome performance is measured by such customer-related factors as sales volume, market share, customer loyalty and satisfaction, and number of new accounts.[61]

In addition to evaluating individual salespeople, managers must regularly assess the entire sales force. This tells whether overall performance is strong. It may result in territory shifts, the addition of people, or other adjustments. The process gives both field reps and management an opportunity to learn whether the level of activity has produced the expected results. This often means doing productivity analysis to determine whether sales volumes have been reached, market shares have been accomplished, and the appropriate product mix has been sold to targeted segments. Usually, good evaluation requires looking behind the numbers to determine where the strongest and weakest results occurred and under what conditions.

Today, many companies use 360 degree evaluations; that is, salespeople are asked to evaluate their sales managers as well. This supports the team concept and helps break down the old barriers to joint progress. It is instrumental in helping sales managers improve. Since managerial success depends on working through others, this type of feedback is seen as absolutely critical in many companies. Pepsi uses the approach, and managers feel it provides important information about their leadership skills and how clearly they outline priorities for sales reps. The system helps managers improve their coaching of front-line salespeople.[62]

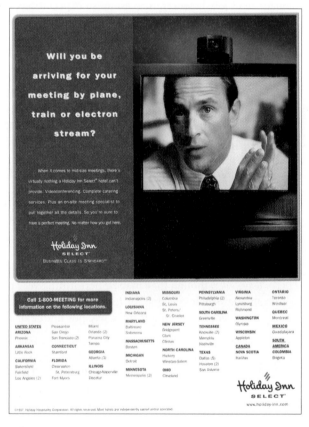

Holiday Inn and Sharp target salespeople by offering services for automated organization on-the-go.

SALES FORCE AUTOMATION

All sorts of high-tech tools are revolutionizing selling and sales management. **Sales force automation** is the use of technology to improve personal selling and sales management effectiveness. Texas Instruments credits sales force automation for much of the success of its 2,000 global field reps. Although orders for semiconductors increased 45 percent in one year, TI still met quality and delivery requirements for 95 percent of its customers. Gene McFarland, head of the company's worldwide marketing operations, says of the sales force: "We couldn't even come close to doing our job without the information technology that's in place here." TI sales reps communicate in real time with other parts of the corporation through a wide area network (WAN) that links 30 countries. Salespeople around the world can be coordinated by one manager who focuses on one account. This is important, since many key customers are global in scope. Also, using a TI software tool called Design-Win, reps are guided through the whole process of interacting with customers, from qualifying leads to getting the first order. The information is fed back to TI personnel ranging from R&D to procurement, so they can begin acting on it immediately.[63]

According to a *Sales and Marketing Management* study, the following technologies are the most commonly used by sales personnel:[64]

- Sales automation software   28%
- Notebook and desktop computers   24%
- Contact management/calendering systems   20%
- Cellular phones   16%
- The Internet   15%
- Paging   7%
- Wireless communication   6%
- Hand-held date recorders   3%

Gateway Systems Corporation of East Lansing, Michigan, has been a pioneer in sales force automation software. According to the director of marketing, Karen Griggs:

> Gateway's product, SYNERGIST Sales Portfolio (SSP), is designed to increase sales effectiveness on two levels. At the sales representative level, SSP facilitates the tracking of key account information, helps representatives monitor competitive inroads, and streamlines paperwork. At the sales management level, SSP allows managers to electronically collect critical pieces of information from the person closest to the customer—the sales representative. Furthermore, this information can be aggregated, analyzed, and provide indicators of the organization's performance within key target markets and accounts. And finally, SSP can serve as a communication vehicle from sales managers to their field sales representatives.[65]

Sales force automation facilitates communication and gives salespeople fast access to necessary information. The use of notebook computers, updated software, and other technologies has improved the overall effectiveness of personal selling and sales management. Managers and salespeople alike can coordinate, plan, and interact more efficiently than ever before. This helps develop stronger relationships within the sales force and with customers. The technology feature further discusses the use of technology as a sales force management tool.

Personal selling, like the mass communication activities we explored in the previous chapter, is a forceful means of implementing the promotion strategy element of the marketing mix. We have now examined three of the four basic elements in the mix: product, place, and promotion. The next two chapters are devoted to the fourth element—price. Chapter 17 surveys the many factors that affect pricing, both domestically and globally. Chapter 18 focuses on price strategy—its basis in value and the ways in which it is implemented.

Sales force automation
The use of technology to improve personal selling and sales management effectiveness.

CONNECTED: SURFING THE NET

UPS

www.ups.com

THIS CHAPTER'S TECHNOLOGY FEATURE, "UNITED PARCEL Service: Sales Reps and Laptops Create the Missing LINK," discussed the company's new aggressive sales effort. To expand your thinking about UPS and personal selling, visit its Web site and answer the following questions.

1. There are many types of sales personnel. Which do you think are the most prevalent at UPS? Find information on the Web site to support your answer.
2. What interactive functions does the site offer that connect with customers through technology?
3. Which of the three major sales philosophies do you think UPS emphasizes? Explain your choice.
4. Imagine you are a salesperson at UPS. What might your responsibilities be? Give examples.

Amway

www.amway.com

IN THIS CHAPTER YOU LEARNED ABOUT Amway Corporation, a group of independents who sell home care products through extensive networking. To expand your thinking about this form of personal selling, visit the Amway Web site and answer the following questions.

1. Selling occurs in several circumstances. Which does Amway use? What are the advantages of this form of selling?
2. In this chapter you learned four characteristics of strong salespeople. Imagine you are an Amway distributor. How would each of these characteristics be important to your success? Give examples.
3. Connect to Amway's global village and visit Hungary. Is Amway Hungary a good business opportunity? Why or why not? What problems would a global salesperson face? What is one way companies can overcome sales resistance?

CHAPTER SUMMARY

OBJECTIVE 1:   Understand how selling evolved to a focus on relationships and what elements are involved in building them.

Personal selling techniques have moved through three distinct modes: the traditional persuasive approach, consultative selling, and relationship selling. The latter is strategic in nature and involves developing long-term relationships that are mutually beneficial for buyer and seller. It requires that the selling organization understand the customer's business or lifestyle and treat loyal customers as assets of the firm. Typically this leads to partnering that creates value for the customer and the selling organization. The objective of relationship selling is to create steady profit through customer loyalty and satisfaction. Interactions with customers focus on win-win situations.

OBJECTIVE 2:   Know the responsibilities of salespeople and sales managers.

Most professional salespeople view themselves as the marketing manager of a territory. As such, they are responsible for implementing the company's marketing strategy within the territory.

They also communicate company policy to customers and potential customers. They are important sources of feedback and have a responsibility to convey this information to their organization. Salespeople must have excellent ethical judgment since they often operate without much direct supervision, are under pressure to boost volume, and have leeway in what they say to customers.

Sales force management is the marketing function involved with planning, implementing, and adjusting sales force activities. First, sales managers work with others in their company to organize the sales force, including its structure, size, and type. Second, they develop diverse sales teams through recruiting, selecting, and training. Third, they prepare forecasts and budgets. Fourth, they implement actions by establishing quotas, assessing performance, determining compensation, and supervising, coaching, and motivating the sales force. Finally, they evaluate sales activities and make any necessary changes.

OBJECTIVE 3:   Identify and understand the steps in personal selling.

The seven steps in personal selling are planning, prospecting, organizing information and developing a call plan, approaching a prospect, presenting a case and building relationships, managing objections and closing, and service. Sales planning translates the company's marketing strategy into territory and account plans. Prospecting involves seeking out new customers within the company's target markets. Next, sales personnel organize information and develop a call plan. To do this, they learn about prospects and prepare a routing schedule to identify which prospects will be called on and when. The approach is the first formal contact with the customer. The objective is to secure an initial meeting and gain customer interest. The next step is making the case and building relationships. This is done through the sales presentation. Sales personnel then manage objections and close the sale. One of the most important sales skills is the ability to overcome business objections. Closing means getting the first order. Service follow through is essential for developing customer loyalty.

OBJECTIVE 4: Learn the characteristics of strong salespeople.

First, strong salespeople are goal oriented. They use time well, manage their territory efficiently, and like to compete to obtain results. Second, they are empathetic; they understand buyer behavior, are customer focused, and possess excellent listening and questioning skills. Third, they have applications knowledge. They are technically competent, know their customers' business, and are good at creative problem solving. Fourth, excellent salespeople are ethical and trustworthy; they are honest, seek additional information when they don't know the answer, and make reliable partners.

OBJECTIVE 5: Understand how to develop a diverse sales organization.

Once the sales structure is determined, the sales organization is developed. Diversity is one of the most important aspects of a sales force because of its role in building relationships with multicultural customers. Strong attention must be paid to diversity when recruiting, selecting, and training salespeople. Recruitment seeks a pool of exceptional candidates and often takes place on college campuses. Selection is a choice process for the company and candidates alike, as both seek a good match. Training involves educating salespeople about company policies and procedures, product and customer application knowledge, relationship selling skills, territory and account planning, and diversity.

OBJECTIVE 6: Explore how to implement sales actions, from setting quotas and compensating salespeople to evaluating and adjusting plans.

Implementing sales actions involves several steps. Quotas establish the sales volume, profit, and activities expected from each sales person. They are used to direct action and evaluate performance. Supervision and coaching, which involve working with salespeople to improve performance, build self-esteem and skills. Motivation is also part of the sales manager's job. It depends on a positive organizational climate in which employees feel rewarded for the effort they make. Sales force compensation is developed with the overall marketing strategy in mind. It is designed to support the development of loyal salespeople, who in turn help create loyal customers. Salaries, commissions, and bonuses are used singly or in combination. Several significant ethical issues surround motivation and compensation. Managers must be careful not to use techniques that lead to unethical actions by salespeople. The final step in sales force management is evaluation and adjustment. Organizations must be flexible in order to maintain competitive advantage. This requires an assessment of individual salespeople and each part of the sales organization. Companies are beginning to use 360 degree feedback techniques to evaluate sales managers as well as the sales force.

REVIEW YOUR UNDERSTANDING

1. List several types of personal selling situations. Give an example of each.
2. What is relationship selling?
3. List the responsibilities of a salesperson.
4. What are the seven steps in personal selling?
5. What characterizes a strong salesperson?
6. What does closing mean?
7. Give three reasons why ethics are important to salespeople.
8. What are the five sales management functions?
9. List the types of sales forecasting. Briefly describe each.
10. What are three methods for setting a sales force budget?
11. What are quotas?
12. What is coaching?
13. What are three ethical issues surrounding sales force management?

DISCUSSION OF CONCEPTS

1. What are the key differences among the traditional, consultative, and relationship sales approaches? Which do you feel is most appropriate in a majority of circumstances? Why?
2. List the seven types of sales personnel. Under what circumstances would it make sense to have each type?
3. Why is it important for the salesperson to support the company's strategic marketing plan?
4. What is most important about each of the seven steps in personal selling? How do they form a process?
5. Describe some of the ways salespeople seek out new customers. Under what circumstances might each be appropriate?
6. Do you have the characteristics of a strong salesperson? Do you believe people are born with these, or can they be learned?
7. The job of the sales manager is to support the strategic marketing and communications plan of the organization. What are the key responsibilities of a sales manager?

8. Describe the methods a sales manager can use to set the sales budget. Which one do you feel is most effective? Why?
9. Training is now considered one of the most important factors in developing a strong sales team. What are the four major areas of training programs?
10. What is sales force automation, and how does it help sales managers and salespeople?
11. Is it acceptable to use family pressure to motivate salespeople? Why or why not?

KEY TERMS AND DEFINITIONS

Account planning: Establishing sales goals and objectives for each major customer.

Activity quotas: Action objectives that encourage salespeople to engage in certain tasks, such as prospecting calls, service calls, sales calls, demonstrations, and new accounts visited.

Approach: The salesperson's first formal contact with the potential customer.

Bonus: A percentage of salary or a fee paid in addition to other compensation for meeting long-term or unique goals.

Center of influence: An opinion leader who can be quickly qualified as a potential customer because of his/her standing in the community.

Closing: The point at which the salesperson obtains the first order from the customer.

Cold calling: Contacting a lead for the first time.

Commission: A form of sales force compensation in which the amount paid is in direct proportion to the accomplishment of specific objectives.

Company sales forecast: A prediction of unit or dollar sales for a given period, in total or broken down by product, segments, or other categories, and based on the marketing strategy that will be put in place.

Consultative selling: An approach to selling in which sales personnel work closely with customers to help solve problems.

Direct sales: Sales that result from the salesperson's direct interaction with a consumer or company.

Empathy: An interpersonal connection in which the salesperson knows precisely how the prospect feels and communicates that understanding.

Environmental forecast: An estimate of the economic, political, and social factors likely to affect the level of spending for the types of products or services being forecast.

Follow-up: After-sales service to ensure customer satisfaction in order to obtain repeat business.

Industry forecast: An estimate of the amount and type of competitive activity that is likely to occur in an industry.

Leads: All those who may have need of a company's product.

Missionary sales: Sales made indirectly through people who do not obtain orders but influence the buying decision of others.

Negotiation: Discussion by two or more parties to arrange a transaction.

Networking: Contacting friends, relatives, and associates to obtain leads.

Preapproach: Preparation by the salesperson for the initial meeting with a prospect.

Presentation: A two-way process in which the salesperson listens to the customer to identify needs and then describes how the product will fulfill them.

Prospect: A potential customer interested in the seller's product.

Prospecting: Seeking potential customers within the company's target markets.

Qualified prospect: A potential buyer interested in the seller's product and with the attributes of a good customer.

Qualifying: Examining prospects to identify those with the authority and ability to buy the product.

Quotas: Quantitative objectives used to direct sales force activity and evaluate performance.

Referral: A lead provided by a qualified prospect.

Relationship selling: Forging bonds between buyer and seller to gain loyalty and mutual satisfaction.

Routing schedule: A travel plan for calling on prospects that is developed to save time and minimize expenses.

Salary: The fixed amount of compensation paid regardless of performance.

Sales force automation: The use of technology to improve personal selling and sales management effectiveness.

Sales force management: The marketing function involved with planning, implementing, and adjusting sales force activities.

Sales manager: The person responsible for the leadership and management of salespeople in order to accomplish the sales objectives established in the marketing plan.

Sales profit quotas: Profitability objectives for customers, products, and market segments.

sales structure: The organization of the reporting relationship between sales managers and salespeople.

Sales territory: All the actual and potential customers, often within a specified geographic area, for which the salesperson has responsibility.

Sales volume quotas: Unit or dollar objectives, usually set by market segment, product or service line, and average volume per customer.

Team selling: Selling that involves people from most parts of the organization, including top executives, working together to create a relationship with the buying organization.

Telemarketing: Making telephone calls to leads provided by marketing services or from other lists.

Territory planning: Identifying potential customers, their sales potential, and the frequency with which they will be contacted about various products.

Traditional sales approach: Emphasizing persuasive techniques to get consumers to buy a company's products.

REFERENCES

1. Interview with Jonathan Ahlbrand on June 10, 1998.
2. Gene R. Luczniak and Patrick E. Murphy, *Ethical Marketing Decisions* (Boston: Allyn & Bacon, 1993), p. 185.
3. "Tomorrow's Jobs," *Occupational Outlook Handbook* (Washington, DC: Bureau of Labor Statistics, U.S. Department of Labor, 1995).
4. "Dartnell Corporation's 29th Sales Force Compensation Study," cited in Andy Cohen, "Leading Edge," *Sales and Marketing Management*, December 1996, p. 15.
5. Geoffrey Brewer and Christine Galea, "The Top 25," *Sales and Marketing Management*, November 1996, p. 39.
6. Bill Kelly, "How to Sell Airplanes, Boeing-Style," *Sales and Marketing Management*, December 9, 1985, pp. 32–34; Dori Jones Yang and Andrea Rothman, "Boeing Cuts Its Altitude as the Clouds Roll in," *Business Week*, February 8, 1993, p. 25; and Shawn Tully, "Boeing: Is 'The Lazy Bee' a Bad Rap Question," *Fortune*, January 25, 1993, p. 10.
7. Juan B. Elizondo, Jr., "Computer Firm Adopts Tupperware Sales Tactics," *Marketing News*, October 21, 1996, p. 19.
8. Merck & Co. 1995 Annual Report.
9. L. L. Bean home page, www.llbean.com, site visited on February 24, 1997.
10. Brett A. Boyle, "The Importance of the Industrial Inside Sales Force: A Case Study," *Industrial Marketing Management* 25 (September 1996): 339–348.
11. Warren J. Keegan and Mark C. Green, *Principles of Global Marketing* (Upper Saddle River, NJ: Prentice Hall, 1997), p. 366.
12. Marcus W. Brauchli, "Looking East: Asia, on the Assent, Is Learning to Say No to 'Arrogant' West," *Wall Street Journal*, April 13, 1994, pp. A1, A8.
13. Sak Onvisit and John J. Shaw, *International Marketing*, (Upper Saddle River, NJ: Prentice Hall, 1997), p. 539.
14. Interview by the author.
15. Gary Heil, Tom Parker, and Deborah C. Stevens, *One Size Fits One* (New York: Van Nostrand Reinhold, 1997), p. 2.
16. Gerald L. Manning and Barry L. Rease, *Selling Today* (Boston: Allen & Bacon, 1992), pp. 17–18.
17. See Joe Chapman and Stephanie Rauck, "Relationship Selling: A Synopsis of Recent Research," in *Developments in Marketing Science*, no. 18, ed. Roger Gomes (Coral Gables, FL: Academy of Marketing Science, 1995), p. 163.
18. Edward R. Del Gaizo, Kevin J. Corcoran, and David J. Erdman, *The Alligator Trap* (Chicago: Richard D. Irwin, 1996), p. 21.
19. "Marketing Briefs," *Marketing News*, February 2, 1997, p. 2.
20. For more information, see Lisa M. Ellram, "Partnering Pitfalls and Success Factors," *International Journal of Purchasing and Materials Management* 31 (April 1995): 36–44.
21. Dean Allen Foster, "Negotiating and 'Mind-Meeting,'" *Directors and Boards*, Fall 1992, pp. 52–54.
22. Geoffrey Brewer and Christine Galea, "The Best Sales Forces," *Sales and Marketing Management*, November 1996, pp. 38–70.
23. Personal interview with John Sutthoff in Atlanta, GA, 1997.
24. Brewer and Galea, "Best Sales Forces."
25. Robert J. Kapp, "Ethical Issues in Personal Selling and Sales Management," in *Ethics in Marketing*, ed. N. Craig Smith and John A. Quelch (Homewood, IL: Richard D. Irwin, 1993), pp. 539–555.
26. "Involvement of Salespeople in Different Daily Activities Varies by Industry," Report 7023.3, *Laboratory of Advertising Performance* (New York: McGraw-Hill Research, 1987).
27. Mark J. Astaria, "Cold Calling Rules and Procedures," 1995, http:www.seclaw.com/coldcall.htm, site visited February 21, 1997.
28. Roger S. Peterson, "Go Modular, Be Flexible to Control Exhibit Costs," *Marketing News*, December 2, 1996, p. 11.
29. Dave Phillips, "Auto Show Revs Up a Record in Attendance," *Detroit News*, January 21, 1997, www.detnews.com
30. Joseph Winski, "Auto Shows Lure People Who Buy," *Advertising Age*, March 22, 1993, pp. 524–525; and www.chicago_autoshow.com/, site visited on February 24, 1997.
31. "Richard Johnson of Amway Japan Challenging Japan's Sales Culture," *Institutional Investor*, May 1994, pp. 23–24; and "Edison Achievement Award Winners. Jay Van Andel and Richard M. De Vos," *Marketing News*, April 25, 1994, pp. E2, E8.

32. "Welcome to Amway Japan," www.amway.com/amway/globalv/japan/htm, site visited on February 24, 1997; and "Amway Posts Record Annual Worldwide Sales of $6.8 Billion at Estimated Retail," www.news wire.ca/releases/october1996/15/c2347.html, October 15, 1996.
33. Raymond Serafin, "Cars Look for New Lease on Loyalty," *Advertising Age*, July 11, 1994, p. 41.
34. "Prospecting for Business," *AT&T PowerSource Magazine*, www.att.com/hbr/check/prospect.html, site visited on February 21, 1997.
35. Neil Rackham, *SPIN Selling Fieldbook* (New York: McGraw-Hill, 1996).
36. Ibid, p. 11.
37. Ibid, p. 12.
38. Role-playing with executives witnessed by the author.
39. Rackham, *SPIN Selling Fieldbook*, p. 21.
40. Jon M. Hawes, James T. Strong, and Bernard S. Winich, "Do Closing Techniques Diminish Prospect Trust?" *Industrial Marketing Management* 25 (September 1996): 349–357.
41. For additional information, see Geoffrey Brewer, "Mind Reading: What Drives Top Salespeople to Greatness," *Sales and Marketing Management*, May 1994, pp. 82–88; Bruce K. Pilling and Sevo Eroglu, "An Empirical Examination of the Impact of Salesperson Empathy and Professionalism and Merchandise Salability on Retail Buyers' Evaluations," *Journal of Personal Selling and Sales Management* 14 (Winter 1994): 45–58; and Saul W. Gellerman, "The Tests of a Good Salesperson," *Harvard Business Review* 68 (May-June 1990): 64–71.
42. Kenneth Labich, "Making Diversity Pay," *Fortune*, September 9, 1996, pp. 177–180.
43. Allison Lucas, "Race Matters," *Sales and Marketing Management*, September 1996, pp. 50–62.
44. "How Avon's CEO Implements Diversity," *Sales and Marketing Management*, January 1997, p. 37.
45. Lucas, "Race Matters."
46. James O. Mitchel, "Winning with Diversity," *LIMRA's MarketFacts* 15 (January-February 1996): 22–26.
47. "Ford Motor Company: 346,990 Reasons for Success," Special Advertising Section, *Fortune*, April 15, 1996, pp. 149–192.
48. Brewer and Galea, "Best Sales Forces."
49. "Meeting of the Minds," *Sales and Marketing Management*, November 1996, pp. 72–74.
50. Brewer and Galea, "Best Sales Forces."
51. Robert D. Hiorich and Ralph Jackson, *Selling and Sales Management* (Chicago: Barons Education Series, 1993).
52. Robert Klein, "Nabisco Sales Soar after Sales Training," *Marketing News*, January 6, 1997, p. 23.
53. Brewer and Galea, "Best Sales Forces."
54. Ibid.
55. Earl D. Honeycutt, Jr., Ashraf M. Attia, and Angela R. O'Auria, "Sales Certification Programs," *Journal of Personal Selling and Sales Management* 16 (Summer 1996): 59–65.
56. Robin T. Peterson, "An Analysis of Contemporary Forecasting in Small Business," *Journal of Business Forecasting Methods and Systems* 15 (Summer 1996): 10–12.
57. Michele Marchetti, "Are Reps Motivated by Bonuses?" *Sales and Marketing Management*, February 1997, p. 33.
58. "Meeting of the Minds."
59. "Motivating Telesales Reps," *Sales and Marketing Management*, August 1996, p. 38.
60. "What Should Sears Do? Consultants Offer Some Unsolicited Advice to Chairman Brennan," *Chain Store Age Executive*, August 1992, pp. 36–38.
61. Ken Grand and David W. Cravens, "Examining Sales Force Performance in Organizations that Use Behavior-Based Sales Management Processes," *Industrial Marketing Management* 25 (September 1996): 361–370.
62. Michele Marchetti, "Pepsi's New Generation of Employee Feedback," *Sales and Marketing Management*, August 1996, pp. 38–39.
63. Tom Dellecave, "Chipping In," *Sales and Marketing Management*, Supplement, June 1996, pp. 35–37.
64. Tom Dellecave, "Technology Update," *Sales and Marketing Management*, June 1996, p. 108
65. Interview with Karen Griggs, March 4, 1997.

DURACELL

PEOPLE ALL OVER THE PLANET ARE demanding portable electronics from telephones, computers, toys, radios, and tape players to all types of hand held instruments and new forms of personal products. The variety of these devices is mind boggling, including such items as poison gas sensors, and even infusion pumps for drug treatment. While portability is booming, nothing is growing more rapidly than the need for batteries to supply power for all these gadgets. That is one reason Gillette recently purchased Duracell, the nation's leading supplier of batteries in the consumer market. The marriage appears to be an excellent match. Both organizations have strong sales operations targeted at retailers. And Duracell targets many other categories of accounts as well. With a 49 percent share of the $2 billion U.S. alkaline battery market, Duracell is in a good financial position to expand and is seeking share gains. One growth strategy is a new line of high-tech alkaline batteries, Duracell Ultra, designed specifically for cellular telephones, digital and flash cameras, mini disc players, and camcorders.

The consumer battery market, estimated at around $20 billion, is dominated by the established alkaline and zinc batteries, which sell at relatively low prices. These are the familiar AA, AAA, D, C, and rectangular nine-volt batteries. Duracell, Rayovac, Ralston Purina's Energizer, and Eveready brands are the big four battery companies worldwide. The U.S. manufacturers tend to be strongest in sales of the standard batteries. Panasonic and such companies as Sony, Sanyo, and Toshiba are large producers of specialized batteries for consumer products. Now Duracell has designed a new line to compete in the specialized battery category.

"Duracell's design strategy has been based on continually offering longer lasting Duracell alkaline batteries for a broad base of general purpose applications," states Ed DeGraan, president, Duracell North Atlantic Group. "But increasing power requirements from a growing and varied portable electronics device base call for innovations beyond a single general purpose battery in order to maximize battery life and device performance."

Duracell Ultra incorporates several patent-pending product features which reduce internal resistance for improved high current flow to meet the power demands of high-tech devices. In addition, Duracell Ultra features PowerCheck, the only on-battery fuel gauge tester, which has been recalibrated for use in high-tech devices.

According to the company, the Duracell Ultra performance advantage is readily apparent to consumers as they experience both longer run times and improved performance in high-tech devices. With cellular phones, for example, consumers can talk up to 100 more minutes or make 50 more two-minute calls using Duracell Ultra, rather than standard alkaline batteries. Consumers can take up to 150 more pictures and reduce flash recycling time by powering their flash camera with Duracell Ultra. Brighter flashlight beams and faster radio control cars are two more examples.

"Duracell Ultra will revolutionize the way consumers perceive and purchase batteries for their high-tech devices," said Peter Hoffman, president, Duracell Commercial Operations. "Since this product innovation provides consumers with exceptional performance and value, Duracell Ultra will become the flagship of our substantial Duracell brand."

Duracell management believes the quality of the sales organization is critical to the success of the traditional line and will be a great asset for the new product line as well. Account managers work with major retailers to develop strategies uniquely suited to their competitive situation. Duracell salespeople are trained in relationship selling and play an important consultant role for major customers. Monica Botwinski, a 1994 marketing graduate from a major university, is a member of the Duracell sales team. One of her accounts was Pamida, a mass merchandiser chain based in Omaha, Nebraska.

In order to help Pamida be successful during the Christmas season, she worked with people there to develop a strategy involving all aspects of the marketing mix. The product mix was determined by estimating potential consumer demand. The price was established on the basis of volume projections, competitor activities, and Pamida's profit objectives. The promotion strategy was developed not only around Duracell but also other products in order to increase storewide excitement and foot traffic. Finally, the location of Duracell products was carefully considered. Displays were customized to Pamida shoppers and placed in key locations to take advantage of cross-merchandising and impulse buying. The partnership approach increased Duracell dollar sales to Pamida by more than 44 percent, increased battery category sales by 20 percent, and increased battery category profitability by 38 percent. This sort of selling, which adjusts all parts of the marketing mix to the retailer's strategy and circumstance, is important to Duracell. Rather than simply sell to retail chains, who in turn have total responsibility for pushing the products, Duracell salespeople work together with the retailer's promotion personnel to develop marketing programs jointly.

Monica has recently been promoted to the position of Area Retail Operations Manager in Atlanta. As sales manager, she has 19 people reporting to her. In her new job she spends significant time recruiting on campuses as well as managing her district. She says, "this is an exiting and challenging time to step into this management position. And the introduction of the Ultra line provides vast new opportunities for our whole organization."

1. *A key part of the Duracell sales strategy involves working jointly with retailers to create marketing strategies. What responsibilities do Duracell account managers assume when working with key retailers? How are these responsibilities carried out when introducing a new line such as Ultra?*
2. *What are the similarities and differences in selling to retail chains versus other types of accounts? For example, Duracell*

sales reps also sell to universities, theaters, and companies that have a broad range of battery needs.

3. *What elements should sales managers consider in preparing the sales force for the new product launch?*

SOURCES: Duracell Web site, www.duracell.com; "They Only Live Once," *Fortune,* October 27, 1997, www.fortune.com; Jennifer Kulpa, "What's Ahead in Specialty Batteries," *Drug Store News,* October 20, 1997, pp. 74+; *RCR Radio Communications Report,* September 1, 1997, p. 44; interview with Monica Botwinski, Duracell North Atlantic Group, April 1998; "Survey—Battery Industry: Consumer Demand Sparks 'Revolution': Portable Power Supply has Come a Long Way in Recent Years," *Financial Times Surveys Edition,* April 4, 1997, p. 1. Duracell press release, New Duracell High-Tech Alkaline Batteries Maximize Performance in High-Tech Devices, February 18, 1998.

Chapter 17

Pricing Approaches

Objectives

1. Describe how pricing works with the other parts of the marketing mix.

2. Learn how economic factors such as demand and supply influence prices.

3. Understand the legal and ethical constraints on pricing decisions.

4. Use industry structure concepts to understand how competitors in different types of industries price.

5. Use competitive factors surrounding industry structure concepts to understand how pricing works in different types of industries.

6. Recognize the conditions that make international pricing complex.

YOU'VE DEVELOPED A REVOLUTIONARY NEW product in a $3.5 billion industry. The anticipated demand is so great that you delay your Japanese launch until June 1996 so that more units can be produced. In two hours, 500,000 units sell—one million in two days! The U.S. launch is delayed several times. Again, demand outstrips supply. By March 1997, Toys "R" Us, your biggest customer, still can't fulfill rainchecks from November 1996. The European launch is delayed again and again—and again. It seems that everyone wants your product. So you can charge anything you want, right?

That was the enviable position faced by Nintendo of America in September 1996, when it launched Nintendo 64 in the United States. Equipped with a 64-bit processor, the new machine boasted power equal to that of 10 Pentium chips bundled together. The quantum leap in graphic capability astounded players who used the in-store demo machines. Although clearly the best gaming system to date, it wasn't the only one available. Nintendo had led the pack with the early 16-bit systems but then languished by failing to provide a 32-bit machine. The new effort was meant to put them back on the map. Nintendo's strategy was to establish a huge user base as quickly as possible and then rake in the profits from the sale of game titles. But consumers first had to be lured away from competitors, such as Sega Saturn and Sony PlayStation.

Most new consumer technology products come out at a high price, which drops as the user base broadens or competitors enter the field. When Sega launched Saturn—the first 32-bit system—in Japan in May 1995, it charged the relatively high price of $399. Although Japanese consumers bought at that price, it was found to be too expensive for the critical U.S. market. Sega went down to about $330 for the U.S. launch. In September 1995, Sony PlayStation came out at $299. In an attempt to defend market share against Nintendo 64, both companies slashed their prices to $199 in March 1996.

The original price of Nintendo 64 was to be $249 for the system plus a game, but the latter was soon dropped from the planned package. The reason probably was manufacturing constraints, since Nintendo makes its own products and could not keep up with demand. Then came the shocking news in August 1996 that Nintendo's offering price would be $199. Sega responded in November by giving away three free games with the purchase of a Saturn CD-ROM system. Sales immediately jumped fivefold.

Obviously, system price isn't the only consideration. Sega launched with 10 games, Sony with 55. Nintendo planned to develop 10 games within four months, but limited manufacturing capacity caused massive delays. Also, the complexity of creating games for so revolutionary a system *continued to cause problems. Nintendo found out in Japan that a lack of games slowed sales of the system. With only four games available, after the whopping one million in two days, only another 200,000 units were bought for the rest of 1996. In addition, compared to a CD-ROM game for Sony PlayStation, R&D for Nintendo's game cartridges takes up to 12 times longer and costs about four times more. So a Sony PlayStation CD-ROM sells for about $50, while a Nintendo cartridge sells for $50 to $80.*

Some retailers took advantage of the shortages. Before Christmas 1996, a number of stores were advertising the system for $249, a steep 25 percent markup on the suggested retail. Desperate parents were willing to pay. In addition, while Toys "R" Us offered the standard prices on game cartridges (albeit via rainchecks), smaller retailers like Kay Bee Toys charged $5 to $10 more.[1]

The Nintendo case highlights many of the pricing issues marketers must address. Supply and demand, product differentiation, and bundling all play a role as competitors vie for loyal customers in domestic and international markets. This chapter explores the many facets of pricing that influence the exchange of value between customers and companies.

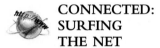

CONNECTED: SURFING THE NET

www.nintendo.com

Did you know that more than 40 percent of American homes own a Nintendo system? Find out more about the company and its pricing in the video game market by visiting its Web site. Visit headquarters, the product lab, or newsroom.

THE CONCEPT OF PRICING

You can purchase a totebag for as little as $2, but it probably won't have a special pocket for your cell phone or CD player. Chanel offers one with those features for around $2,500. Or perhaps you are in the market for a coat. You can spend less than $100 or much more. Nieman Marcus has a calfskin jacket for $3,975 and a cashmere trimmed with mink for $7,250.[2] A remarkably broad range of prices are charged for items that have similar functions. Ginseng roots grown for tea in Korea and other Pacific Rim nations sell for a few dollars, but a couple of ounces found in the wild can cost nearly $50,000. New cars range from $8,000 for a Geo Metro to more than $320,000 for a Rolls-Royce Bentley Azure. Even four years of college tuition can cost from several thousand dollars to well over $100,000 at a select private school or a prestigious foreign university.

Pricing plays a critical role in the allocation of resources in free market economies. Since prices fluctuate according to competitive forces, their rise and fall directly influence the amount of goods and services consumers are willing to purchase. Pricing is also critical for the firm. The amount consumers purchase times its price determines the total revenue a company receives. Long before a sale is made, marketers forecast consumer demand at varying prices. This influences the allocation of resources used to create, promote, and distribute products. Overall, prices have a dramatic effect in determining the overall profitability of the firm. Consequently, pricing is one of the most important and complex areas of marketing.

Seldom do we find one concept described by so many names. These "soften" the unpleasant feeling people may have when making payment. How many can you think of? Tuition is what you pay to go to school. Rent is what you pay for your apartment. An honorarium is paid for a speech. A retainer is paid to a lawyer. A fee is paid to a doctor. A premium is charged for insurance. Highways charge a toll. Dues are charged for membership. Assessments are used to calculate property taxes, the ongoing price for real estate ownership. A wage or salary is the price paid for work, and interest is the price paid for using money. Fares are charged for public transportation. Salespeople receive a commission for achieving a certain level of sales, and a bonus is the price paid for extraordinary performance. Whatever the name, price still signals that an amount is given up for the right to own or use something.

We have mentioned before that value comes from both the marketing organization and the buyer. In each case value is given up and received. **Price** is the exchange value of a good or service in the marketplace. We tend to think of price as a set amount of money that can be exchanged for a particular product. Yet, a good or service can also be exchanged for a different product through trading or bartering. Bartering simply bypasses the monetary system.

Price
The exchange value of a good or service in the marketplace.

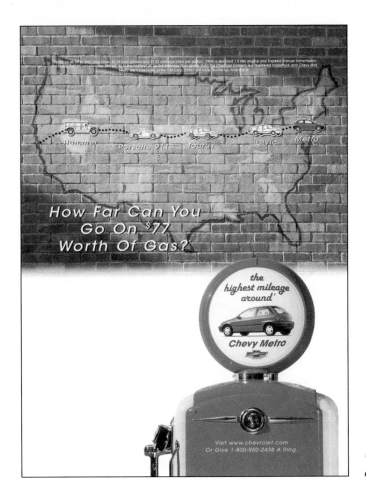

The Chevy Metro is designed and priced for people who want economical transportation.

PRICE AS PART OF THE MARKETING MIX

We have discussed many of the decisions concerning the elements of the marketing mix. Products, logistics, and promotion create value for buyers. Price captures value from buyers for the firm. It is how the firm recovers its costs for other parts of the marketing mix. All parts of the mix interact to establish the firm's positioning. In fact, good pricing decisions require analyzing what target customers expect to pay even before products are developed, distributed, and promoted. Marketers need to understand ahead of time what customers perceive to be good value. If too much is charged, then customers perceive that they are losing value, and they will spend their money on other products or purchase the minimum amount necessary. If too little is charged, then the firm can lose money, eventually become uncompetitive, and go out of business.

This chapter's diversity feature, "Family Bargain Uses Low Prices to Court the Invisible Consumer," describes a chain whose low-price strategy is carefully blended with other mix elements—product selection, store location, targeted promotion, and service features—to create superior value.

OBJECTIVES OF PRICE SETTING

Prices are set with profit, volume, competitive, and customer objectives in mind. First, businesses need to charge enough to make a profit, which satisfies owners (shareholders) and creates the financial resources needed to grow. Even nonprofits must have excess revenues over costs in order to keep pace with inflation and expand operations. Second, prices directly influence the quantity sold. Like profit, volume maintains or increases the size of the business. In addition to pleasing owners, financial health creates opportunities for employees to progress and prosper. Third, price can prevent competitors from taking your customers. Finally, proper pricing helps build customer relationships.

As with the chicken and the egg, it is difficult to determine what comes first, but profit, volume, competitive, and customer objectives are all linked. Figure 17-1 shows that the sat-

CONNECTING WITH DIVERSITY
FAMILY BARGAIN USES LOW PRICES TO COURT THE INVISIBLE CONSUMER

Executives at Family Bargain Center Stores want to fill a void. The population of its home state of California has changed dramatically over the last decade, and most retailers are neglecting the low end of the retail spectrum. Officials at the 131-unit chain based in San Diego are targeting the ethnic, low-income consumer with a strategy that stresses quality merchandise at low prices.

"We carry nationally recognized brands, essentially the same products found in major discount stores—but at prices substantially below theirs. We buy closeouts, overruns, and cancellations," says Family Bargain Center's president and CEO, William Mowbray. But that doesn't mean last season's goods. Fashion, he says, is just as important to the low-income consumer as it is to more affluent shoppers. People who shop at Family Bargain know you will find a shirt for $6 that would sell in the Gap for $34, or a pair of black Vans sneakers for $10 that would sell for up to $50 in a specialty shop. "This level of value is a powerful motivator for families struggling to buy necessities," says an analyst for Rodman & Renshaw, which published a report on Family Bargain in 1996.

Unlike most discount and specialty chains that purchase goods six months in advance of the selling season, Family Bargain buys when the season opens. "Within at least 10 days from the time we order," says Mowbray, "the goods are in the stores ready to be sold." And because the chain sells only apparel, not a mix of clothing and hard goods like most other discounters, Family Bargain's gross profit margin consistently averages around 35 percent, compared to the typical 28 percent.

Offering a combination of quality and current merchandise at good prices also pays off in customer loyalty. "I think one of the reasons for this is we tend to cater to our consumer more than other retailers do, building loyalty in the process," says Mowbray. The chain connects with its large Hispanic customer base by staffing stores with bilingual employees. The Rodman & Renshaw study says that "Family Bargain has developed a generic skill selling to ethnic groups. It does radio and flyers in numerous languages, including Russian, Punjabi, and Navajo." And Family Bargain doesn't expect customers to find them, it locates stores right where their target customers live. Its criteria for store siting are large Hispanic population, median household income of $25,000 (about half the national average), and a large percentage of children under age 14.

It's quite conceivable that the Family Bargain concept may turn into a national chain. "We think our concept can extend virtually everywhere in the U.S. because there are low-end consumers in all parts of the country," asserts Mowbray. And Wal-Mart, Kmart, or Target shouldn't be too surprised if a Family Bargain store appears next to them. In looking for a site, the company actually prizes locations near these discounters. "Wal-Mart in particular is a huge draw, which we typically benefit from," Mowbray says. The company's goal is to get the customer to think "I'll look for what I need in Family Bargain first, because if I find it there, I know I'll pay much less. Then, I'll go to Wal-Mart."

Source: Adapted from Jay L. Johnson, "The Invisible Consumer," *Discount Merchandiser,* June 1996, pp. 92–94.

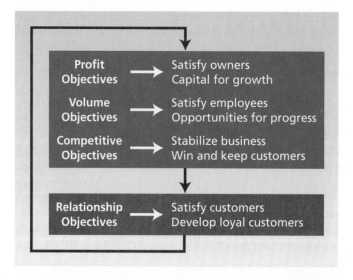

Figure 17-1   Prices Serve Several Objectives

isfaction of all parties to the business is in some way affected by price. Most important, when relationship objectives are met, we have satisfied, loyal customers who consistently produce revenues and profit. Yet it takes satisfied shareholders, contented employees, and a strong competitive position to make customers happy. Let's look at each set of objectives in turn.

PROFIT OBJECTIVES

Profit is critical for every business. Without it, investors will take their money elsewhere, and the business will cease to exist. In other words, you always need to price in order to make money. How do you do that? Simply stated, revenue minus cost equals profit. Price dramatically affects revenue. In fact, price times volume equals revenue. Later, we will see how price affects volume, which in turn affects cost. The point is that price plays a role in all the major factors that influence profit. To change profit, you simply increase or reduce price, volume, or cost. Since these three elements are so closely connected, the situation is very intriguing. Exactly how they interact is a big issue for marketers. For many businesses, a small change in price has a huge effect on profit. Let's say a business makes a 10 percent profit on sales. If nothing else changes, then a 3 percent price increase means that profits soar by 30 percent, up to 13 percent. A similar price decrease will have the opposite effect.

Price sometimes is designed to create maximum profits, but often satisfactory profits are the objective. Essentially, *satisfactory* means that the expectations of investors are met or exceeded. Satisfactory profits are based roughly on how much the company has historically made, plus how much similar companies make, plus the risks involved in the business. Profits are usually stated in terms of return on sales, a return on investment, or profit margin. A minimum return on investment is the amount you make when you put your money in a financial institution and earn interest. Since risks are involved in marketing a product, profits must be high enough to cover them. For example, Intel has a 25 percent return on sales. Intel prices products to make a profit margin of approximately 60 percent.[3] Satisfactory profit goals are designed to reflect what shareholders, management, employees, and customers believe are fair for all parties involved.

Profit maximization is often stated as the goal of pricing, but what price will achieve this? Since price interacts with volume and cost, it is hard to say. Furthermore, there are limits to what people will pay. Theoretically, to maximize profit you would increase unit price until just before unit volume declines, and that is the point at which profit is maximized. In other words, the greatest quantity is being sold at the highest price the market will bear. Economists call this *marginal analysis*. But marginal analysis needs to take into account the long-term picture. Customer demand fluctuates due to economic conditions and shifts in the marketing mix. Competitive pressures also make it difficult to know exactly which price maximizes profit in dynamic markets.

VOLUME (SALES) OBJECTIVES

The price charged often affects the number of units purchased. Firms must price in such a way that production is maintained at a stable or growing level. Too high a price may result in layoffs, and too low a price may cause difficulty in meeting demand, which means lost sales and damage to the company's reputation. In either situation, employees will be unhappy. In the first case they will lose income or a job; in the second case they can't serve customers adequately. As we will see in chapter 18, too low a price can even reduce the units demanded. Because it influences the overall amount to be consumed, price must be carefully set.

COMPETITIVE OBJECTIVES

Volume translates into market share, which creates market power. Many firms have specific market share objectives and price accordingly. Of course, many factors other than price contribute to high share. Although lowering price to increase share may reduce profits in the short run, it may cause competitors to restrict activities or withdraw from markets. Prices then can be raised later in the absence of competition. But certain predatory pricing is illegal, as discussed later in this chapter. Perhaps Nintendo had a market share strategy in mind when it entered the U.S. market with its 64-bit game system.

Aside from gaining share, pricing also can help the organization maintain its market position. Leaders try to establish the market price. Followers react to what the leaders charge. If either party wants to prevent pricing from being used to adjust demand, then it may choose

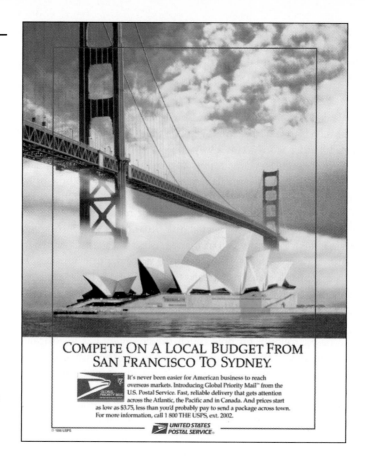

COMPETE ON A LOCAL BUDGET FROM
SAN FRANCISCO TO SYDNEY.

It's never been easier for American business to reach
overseas markets. Introducing Global Priority Mail™ from the
U.S. Postal Service. Fast, reliable delivery that gets attention
across the Atlantic, the Pacific and in Canada. And prices start
as low as $3.75, less than you'd probably pay to send a package across town.
For more information, call 1 800 THE USPS, ext. 2002.

UNITED STATES
POSTAL SERVICE®

The United States Postal Service uses nonprice competition and increases its advertising when appropriate.

one of two strategies. Status quo pricing maintains the same relative position: Every time a competitor makes a price change, rivals follow suit. Nonprice competition leaves price at a given level and adjusts other parts of the marketing mix, adding or subtracting value when appropriate. For example, advertising may be increased or decreased, extra product may be piggybacked on packages, or container size may be reduced. Of course, in the short term it is always easier to adjust price than alter other marketing mix variables.

RELATIONSHIP (CUSTOMER) OBJECTIVES

Prices can be established with customer loyalty in mind. This is at the heart of relationship marketing. The objective is to create sufficient value over time to develop repeat business. In this case, pricing signals the relationship the company desires with customers. This is called *value-based pricing* and is a major topic in the next chapter. Fundamentally, prices are set to provide value for the customer in both the short term and the long run. Your most loyal customers should benefit to some degree from the extra profit generated through the relationship. This can be accomplished by lowering the price to loyal buyers or by adding value to the product they receive. Most important, you must understand your customers thoroughly in order to learn what they value.

MAJOR FACTORS INFLUENCING PRICE

Pricing according to value concepts requires a grasp of several elements, as outlined in Figure 17-2. First, economic factors explain how the demand for and supply of products relate to price. Second, legal and ethical constraints affect pricing decisions. Since price plays a major role in determining how economic resources are distributed, the government and courts have taken a particular interest in pricing. Third, the competitive environment influences price. Marketers must understand how competitors differentiate their products and the effect that substitutes have on price. Fourth, understanding how the company's cost structure is influenced by price decisions is very important. Finally, numerous global factors affect pricing in domestic and international markets. Each of these areas is addressed in the following sections.

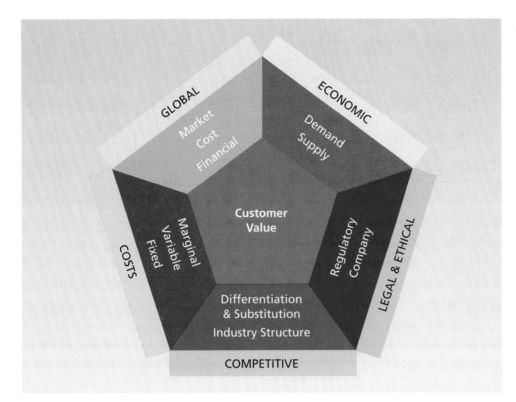

Figure 17-2   Factors Influencing Price

ECONOMIC FACTORS: DEMAND AND SUPPLY

Economists have developed elaborate theories about the effect of consumer demand and product supply. Both have a significant influence on pricing.

The Demand Curve   Demand is determined by the amount of product customers need, plus their willingness and ability to buy. Demand has a major influence on price. It is usually depicted by a demand curve, which is a graph showing quantity along the horizontal axis and different prices along the vertical axis. Marketers use the curve to estimate changes in total demand for a product based on differing prices. The **demand curve** describes the price elasticity of a given product. **Price elasticity** is the extent to which changes in what is charged affect the number of units sold. The formula for calculating it is

$$\text{Price elasticity of demand} = \frac{\text{Percentage change in quantity demanded}}{\text{Percentage change in price}}$$

Price elasticity is used to forecast responses to price changes and to define market segments. Knowing the price elasticity for company and competitor products is important in determining a pricing strategy.[4]

When price has a major effect on demand, the product is price elastic. When price has little effect on demand, the product is price inelastic. Figure 17-3 shows two demand curves, one for a price-elastic product (CD-ROMs) and the other for a price-inelastic product (heart surgery). CD-ROMs are useful but are not a necessity. If their average price is high, then consumers will demand very few; if the price goes down, then demand will increase dramatically. In contrast, most consumers who need heart surgery do not care about the price, especially if government or private insurance will cover the cost. Price changes in heart surgery are not likely to influence the total demand to any large degree.

When demand is elastic, prices tend to decrease over time. As Figure 17-3 shows, when the price of CD-ROMs drops from about $250 down to $50, sales increase from 1,000 units to more than 7,000 units, reflecting elastic demand. For heart surgery, as the price drops from $2,000 to $1,000, demand stays roughly the same. There are also effects on total revenue. In the elastic case it rises from $250,000 to $350,000 as increased volume more than compensates for the lower price. In the inelastic case, revenue declines from about $60 million to $35 million.

Demand curve

A depiction of the price elasticity demand for a given product.

Price elasticity

The extent to which changes in price affect the number of units demanded or supplied.

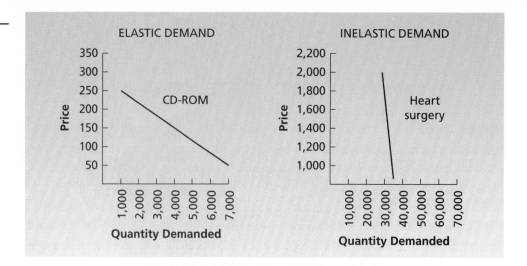

Figure 17-3   Demand Curves

Demand Sensitivity by Market Segment   In addition to the type of product, differences in market segments explain some of the variation in demand. Because the airline industry believes that the overall demand for business travel is less sensitive to price than the demand for leisure travel, pricing policies are designed specifically for each segment. Business travelers often purchase tickets at the last minute and are likely to pay full fare, whereas vacationers can plan well in advance and pay discounted rates. Fares are also lower for trips that include at least one weekend night, which seldom applies to business travelers. Their demand is inelastic because a certain amount of travel is required for the functioning of the firm. Leisure travelers not only have more elastic demand but also are more sensitive to price differences among airlines. Just before spring break, student newspapers are full of ads offering

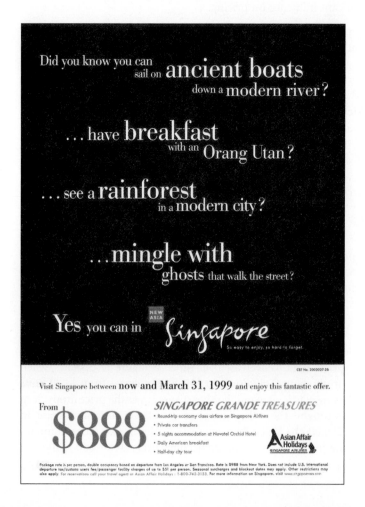

Leisure travelers have more elastic demand than business travelers.

trip packages at greatly reduced prices. Travel Express International, for example, has cruise or beach vacations for as low as $199 per person.[5]

Cross-Elasticity of Demand   We find **cross-price elasticity of demand** when the quantity demanded of one product changes in response to price changes in another product. For example, an increase in the cost of lumber in the building industry increases the demand for substitute products made of plastic and steel. At the brand level, an increase in the price of Coke increases the demand for Pepsi. Marketers use demand curves to describe price elasticity for a product class (all brands) or for a single brand. Price elasticity may differ for the total industry (that is, for all brands) versus an individual brand. Because gasoline is a necessity, variations in the average price charged by all producers may not affect demand dramatically. But Amoco may find that its demand is elastic if it charges a lot more than the industry average. In other words, cross-elasticity refers to the amount of demand for one company's product based on its difference from the average price. Therefore, the concept of elasticity applies to the total industry, whereas cross-elasticity applies to preferences for individual brands or substitutes. Several marketing factors are likely to have a significant effect on cross-elasticity. For example, a grocery product is likely to be influenced by shelf space allocation, product type, and brand market share.[6]

| **CAREER TIP** | At Amoco, pricing specialists use a combination of data to develop market-based pricing strategies and tactics for gasoline, as well as metrics to measure performance for strategies and execution. They are responsible for learning about market structure, product costs, competitive retail tactics, consumer behavior patterns, and price elasticities. They are also responsible for profit, volume, and margin results as well as for achieving other strategic and tactical goals. If you are interested in this kind of job or another career at Amoco, then view the current openings at **www.amoco.com/jobs/opport/opport.com**. |

Many marketing plans are designed to produce inelastic cross-elasticity for the brand. That means price is less important to buyers than brand attributes, so price competitors cannot lure them away. Consider Girbaud jeans, which typically retail for more than $70 per pair, whereas Levi's often sell for less than $30. Many consumers are willing to pay more for the Girbaud brand for prestige reasons or because they like its features.

To reduce the cross-price elasticity of their products, marketers may use any of the following approaches:[7]

- Position the product relative to costly substitutes. Maxwell House prices its Private Collection line close to premium whole-bean coffee brands.[8]
- Focus attention on unique features. Boston Whaler commands a premium for its line of recreation craft due to the company's reputation for safety. The boats can't sink, which is a major reason the U.S. Coast Guard selects the brand.
- Make it costly or difficult to switch. ABB Robotics trains users of its systems in programming and maintenance. Retraining on another system is expensive and time consuming.
- Make cross-brand comparisons difficult. Prudential says "get a piece of the rock," implying that its size is an asset in financial planning.
- Use price to signal status, image, or quality. The name Mercedes™ is synonymous with high price. One dealer says: "If customers have to ask the price, they can't afford it."
- Put price in the context of high value. Volvo emphasizes family protection. Assuring the safety of loved ones is a benefit that customers are likely to value more highly than the money they could save by purchasing a cheaper brand.

The Supply Curve   Price, which influences profit, also has an important influence on the willingness to produce. When price is higher, producers are willing to supply more. When profit margins are low, companies are likely to produce less. The supply curves shown in Figure 17-4 depict these relationships. In the elastic curve, an increase in unit price from $30 to $280 causes a dramatic increase in CD-ROM production, from 700 units to 6,500 units. In the inelastic curve, price hikes cause only a moderate increase in supply; there are relatively few trained surgeons, and they can squeeze only so many procedures into each day's schedule.

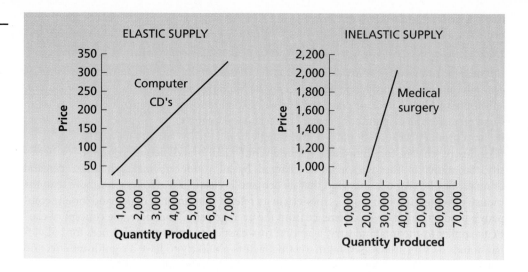

Figure 17-4   Supply Curves

Supply curve

A depiction of the price elasticity of supply for a product.

The **supply curve** reveals the amount that producers are willing to provide at each price. Theoretically, it operates very much like a demand curve, but different factors are at work. For example, companies with high fixed investment find it extremely difficult to exit the industry, so supply is inelastic. Another example is lawyers, who are generally reluctant to switch careers because they have invested heavily in education. When the price of legal services drops dramatically because of competition, lawyers are still willing to produce the same amount, reflecting the highly inelastic supply curve. When industry entry and exit are easy, supply tends to be more elastic. As prices rise, firms are willing to produce more; as prices decline, firms produce less or switch to other products.

Equilibrium Price   In theory, price plays a role in balancing supply and demand. In Figure 17-5, the equilibrium price for CD-ROMs—the point at which the supply and demand curves cross—is $150. At prices below that point, producers are increasingly reluctant to supply CD-ROMs; at prices above it, consumers are increasingly reluctant to buy. Market forces work to help balance supply and demand so that products do not go unused and customers do not pay more than is required. Economic theory suggests that, over time, most product prices are somewhat elastic. When prices are high, supply is likely to outstrip demand. Suppliers then lower prices until supply and demand come into equilibrium. When prices are too low, less is produced. Consumers are willing to pay more for scarce products, so supply increases until it is in balance with demand. In other words, supply and demand are related because changes in price affect how both suppliers and consumers respond. For example, the world ate 11 million tons of bananas in 1995, a 26 percent increase in demand over the previous year. Suppliers were able to respond because banana production was rising even faster.[9] There was a recent price increase, however, because poor weather conditions reduced the crop. Consumer demand probably will drop, suppliers will have to lower prices, and then another equilibrium point will be reached.

Figure 17-5   Supply and Demand Equilibrium

It is important to remember that supply and demand curves work perfectly only in economic theory, which assumes that most variables are held constant. In reality, the marketplace changes rapidly. Indeed, a main purpose of marketing strategy is to alter the supply and demand characteristics of an industry in the company's favor. For example, automakers are experiencing an imbalance in supply and demand due to greater popularity of light trucks. This has decreased purchases of passenger cars, causing large losses for the Big Three until they can reorient production in line with demand.[10] In many industries the tremendous diversity in market segments and individual firms introduces more variables than can reasonably be taken into account. Furthermore, it is very difficult to forecast demand and to predict what competitors will do. For all these reasons, attempts to influence elasticities through marketing strategies may not be very effective in practice.

LEGAL AND ETHICAL INFLUENCES ON PRICING

Both federal and state laws affect pricing decisions. In fact, pricing is one of the most legally constrained areas of marketing. Most regulations are designed to allow prices to fluctuate freely so that market forces can work. Some, however, protect consumers from unfair prices—those that are higher than the value created due to the manipulation of market forces. Pricing practices that are legislatively restrained or regulated include price fixing, price discrimination, minimum prices (unfair sales), price advertising, dumping, and unit pricing, each of which is described below. Figure 17-6 summarizes federal legislation on pricing.

While marketers certainly must take care to avoid outlawed pricing practices, many companies are equally concerned to avoid unethical pricing that could tarnish their reputation and erode consumer trust. Under "Pricing Ethics," the last topic in this section, we describe a number of questionable practices.

Price Fixing **Price fixing** occurs when one party attempts to control what another party will charge in the market. There are laws against vertical and horizontal price fixing. **Vertical price fixing** is an attempt by a manufacturer or distributor to control the final selling price at the retail level. The Consumer Goods Pricing Act of 1975 made all interstate use of unfair trade or resale price maintenance illegal. Retailers cannot be required to use the list price (suggested retail price) set by manufacturers or resellers. Freedom for retailers to adjust prices enhances competition, thereby reducing the overall average price to consumers. The passage of this law was controversial because manufacturers and wholesalers often want to control retail prices in order to maintain consistent positioning. Several practices for controlling retail prices are legal. The manufacturer or distributor may do any of the following:

- Own the retail outlet and establish its pricing policy
- Suggest and advertise a retail price
- Preprint prices on products
- Sell on consignment (own items until they are sold)
- Screen channel members, choosing only those with a history of price maintenance in their retail outlet

Price fixing
An attempt by one party to control what another party will charge in the market.

Vertical price fixing
An attempt by a manufacturer or distributor to control the final selling price at the retail level.

Act	Key Aspects
Sherman Antitrust Act 1890	Restricts predatory pricing (to drive competitors from the market) and makes it illegal to price fix.
Federal Trade Commission Act 1914	Set up the Federal Trade Commission, which is responsible for limiting unfair and anticompetitive practices in business.
Clayton Act 1914	Restricts price discrimination and purchase agreements between buyers and sellers.
Robinson-Patman Act 1936	Restricts discriminatory pricing that diminishes competition, particularly among resellers.
Wheeler-Lea Act 1938	Allows the Federal Trade Commission to investigate deceptive pricing practices and to regulate advertising of prices to help ensure that it does not deceive consumers.
Consumer Goods Pricing Act 1975	Eliminates price controls vertically and horizontally in the market so that channel members cannot set prices and so that retailers do not have to sell according to manufacturer or other channel member price schedules.

Figure 17-6 Major Federal Price Legislation

Horizontal price fixing
Agreement among manufacturers and/or channel members to set prices at the retail level.

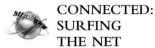

CONNECTED: SURFING THE NET

www.delta-air.com

You can compare airline prices on the Internet. The Delta Air Lines Web site has a number of features to help you determine your airfare. Not only can you make reservations and access destination maps, but also you can use interactive features such as the "fares and flight planner," "fares and quick flight," and "fare tips."

Price discrimination
A legally restricted practice in which a manufacturer or other channel member charges different prices to different retailers in the same marketplace.

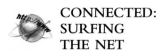

CONNECTED: SURFING THE NET

www.ames.com

Find out more about Ames's special discount program for seniors by connecting to its Web site. In addition, check out weekly sales prices, learn the company history, locate an Ames near you, and see a sampling of offerings.

Predatory pricing
Price cutting by large firms to eliminate small local competitors.

Horizontal price fixing is an agreement among manufacturers and other channel members to set prices at the retail level. The Sherman Act and the Federal Trade Commission Act outlaw these practices even if the prices are "reasonable." Violations of either statute can be severely punished with steep fines and/or prison sentences. In 1992, a number of major airline carriers (including TWA, Delta, American, USAir, United, Pan American, Midway, and Northwest) faced allegations of price fixing. Most denied wrongdoing, but many agreed to a settlement to avoid large legal expenses; a fine of $44 million was apportioned according to the case-related administrative costs of each carrier. The fiscal and managerial strain of the litigation helped push Pan American and Midway into bankruptcy. In addition, carriers were directed to issue more than $368.5 million in discount travel certificates to passengers.[11] More recently, Archer-Daniels-Midland admitted to participating in a global conspiracy to fix prices on two of its agricultural commodities. The penalty of $100 million was the largest criminal settlement in history.[12]

Signs of price fixing include cooperation among competitors on discounting, credit terms, or conditions of sale; any discussions about pricing at association meetings; plans to issue price lists on the same date or on given dates; plans to withhold or rotate bids on contracts; agreements to limit production in order to increase prices; and any exchange of information among competitors on pricing. The intent is to prohibit communication among competitors about pricing or any aspects of the business that may influence pricing levels.

On the international level, there are few antitrust sanctions to ensure fair competition. For example, in most countries impartial bidding processes are required, but in others the winners are secretly predetermined. In Japan this practice is called *dango* and is frequently used. In the United States and many other nations, it is known as bid rigging. U.S. trade officials estimate that substantial business is lost as a result of this practice. For example, U.S. builders have been prevented from competing for their share of the $500 billion Japanese construction market. Recently, the United States hired a Japanese law firm to file for $35 million in damages against 140 Japanese companies accused of rigging bids. This action resulted in a $32.6 million settlement.

Price Discrimination **Price discrimination** occurs when a manufacturer or other channel member charges different prices to retailers competing in the same marketplace. The Robinson-Patman Act of 1936 was designed to enhance competition by protecting small retailers against discounters or larger retailers who might obtain favorable treatment from suppliers. Today, this law is a major restriction on how manufacturers price. Essentially, the act permits manufacturer discounts only if the seller can demonstrate that they are available to all competing channel buyers on the same fair basis. Price fluctuations must be developed in such a way that both small and large buyers can qualify for discounts, or the discounts must be cost justified. The law specifies that it is illegal not only for sellers to engage in unfair practices but also for retailers to purchase products when they know that discrimination toward other retailers is occurring.

The Robinson-Patman Act involves a relatively complex issue. Differential pricing is allowed in many circumstances in which manufacturers are competing to gain or hold business. The law was designed to enhance competition by preventing restraint of trade. Essentially, violation occurs when manufacturers or other channel members charge differential prices that inhibit the ability of one retailer to compete with another. Acceptable price discrimination occurs when the differences are based on time, place, customer characteristics, or product distinctions. In other words, any time the marketing mix has been altered, price may reflect those changes.

Consider the annual fees associated with different credit cards. The issuer may charge affluent customers $100 a year for premium gold cards but suspend all fees for students. Discounts for senior citizens are another acceptable form of price discrimination. For instance, the Ames 55 Gold Card entitles customers age 55 and older to a 10 percent discount on merchandise bought on Tuesday.[13] These practices demonstrate how price deviates among consumer segments.

Minimum Prices Laws against so-called minimum prices, often called unfair sales acts, have been enacted in a number of states. These prevent retailers from selling merchandise for less than the cost of the product plus a reasonable profit. More than half the states have such laws in order to protect smaller retailers from larger competitors.[14] **Predatory pricing** occurs when large firms cut prices on products in order to eliminate small local competitors. Major

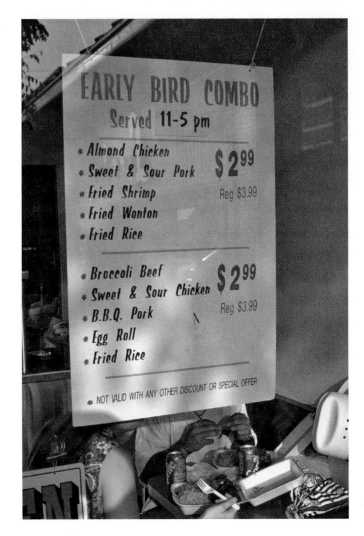

Senior citizens are often drawn to specials that take place prior to the traditional dining times.

airlines are sometimes accused of predatory pricing. ValuJet and other low-fare carriers have claimed that the big companies unfairly underprice them.[15] At the national level, the Sherman and Clayton acts prevent this. Other laws apply to intrastate commerce.

Loss leaders are items priced below cost to attract customers. In some states this practice is restricted. In others it is legal, particularly when it is not designed to injure specific local competitors. Most loss leaders are heavily advertised brands with strong appeal. For example, supermarkets may feature a special on name-brand laundry detergents that have wide appeal. Once in the store, customers are likely to purchase additional goods at normal or even elevated prices. McDonald's® and other fast-food chains can lower prices on burgers to increase traffic because their margins on soft drinks and fries make up the difference. Even investment companies like Charles Schwab use loss leaders. They waive fees on money funds to attract business, hoping that customers will later invest in other areas.[16]

Loss leaders
An item priced below cost to attract customers.

Marketers must be careful in using loss leaders. According to Donald Hughes, a former research manager at Sears: "You have to ask yourself how much money are you willing to spend to bring people into the store, because you have the problem of cherry picking, where people come in and buy only the loss leader, which foils your strategy."[17]

Price Advertising The Federal Trade Commission has set up permissible standards for price advertising. Essentially, these guidelines prohibit marketers from communicating price deceptively. Firms may not claim that a price is reduced unless the original price has been offered to the public regularly and recently. Price comparison with the competition cannot be made unless verification is provided. And premarked prices cannot be artificially increased as a point of comparison unless products are actually sold at that price in substantial quantities. In addition, a retailer cannot continuously advertise the same product as being on sale when that price has become standard at that outlet.

Many supermarkets use name-brand laundry detergents as loss leaders.

Bait and switch

An unethical practice in which sellers advertise items at extremely low prices and then inform the customer that the items are out of stock, offer different items, or attempt to sell the customer more expensive substitutes.

Dumping

Selling a product in a foreign country at a price lower than in the producing country and lower than its cost of production.

Predatory dumping

Pricing below cost to drive local firms out of business.

Bait-and-switch promotions are specifically outlawed by the Federal Trade Commission Act and various state statutes. **Bait and switch** occurs when the seller advertises items at extremely low prices and then informs the customer these are out of stock, offers different items, or attempts to sell the customer more expensive substitutes. In other words, when there is no intent to sell the advertised item, retailers are being dishonest.

Dumping   In the international market, one of the most common regulations relates to dumping, which is a form of price discrimination. **Dumping** occurs when a product is sold in a foreign country at a price lower than in the producing country and lower than its actual cost of production. Why do companies do this? It can be a very effective way to maximize profits, since global organizations cover many of their fixed costs through product pricing in the home market; they then price according to only their variable costs in other parts of the world. Dumping is illegal because it puts manufacturers in the local market at a disadvantage. In Latin America, for example, T-shirts have been imported from Asia and Panama for as little as 2 cents apiece.[18] Since 1990, China has been cited in more antidumping petitions in the United States than in any other country.[19]

Predatory dumping is pricing designed to drive local firms out of the market. Strong market share is gained, competitors are put out of business, and then higher average prices are charged. Some Japanese companies have engaged in this practice. In one case, Sony was selling television sets for less than $200 in the United States while charging more than $300 at home. Japanese companies also have been found guilty of dumping minivans in the U.S. market. Recently, Cray Research, a Minnesota manufacturer, accused NEC Corporation of Japan of trying to sell supercomputers to the U.S. government for less than one-fourth their value.[20]

Unit Pricing   Container sizes for the same item can vary considerably. In some cases the package may have similar wording, such as "giant" or "large economy" size. This makes it difficult for consumers to compare the price of products based on the size and type of packaging. The unit pricing legislation enacted two decades ago requires that certain types of retail outlets, especially food stores, display price per unit of measure as well as total price. For example, a 4-ounce can of tuna selling for $1.00 is also priced at 25 cents per ounce. In this way consumers can clearly see whether a larger size makes a price difference. The law is designed to help cost-conscious consumers make wise decisions at the retail level. In fact, according to a survey of customers, the most important attribute in stores is unit pricing signs on the shelves.[21]

Pricing Ethics   Ethical issues in pricing abound. For price-sensitive products they revolve around the creation of demand and delivery of value based on price. For price inelastic products, particularly because of the captive audience, gouging is an issue.

Although laws protect customers against unscrupulous pricing, we still find questionable ways of using price to increase demand. For example, an ad for dramatically reduced airfares states (in tiny print) that some restrictions may apply. When you call, you learn that so many restrictions apply that your choices are limited to a few seats and times. The Better Business Bureau of New York found that 14 of 29 airlines and car rental agencies left important restrictions out of their ads.[22]

Another way to increase demand is to make the product seem less expensive than it really is. Sometimes all costs are not clearly communicated. For example, you go to a car dealer and receive a price. After deciding to purchase, you notice a charge for administration ex-

Unit pricing legislation requires certain types of retail outlets to display price per unit of measure as well as item price.

penses on the invoice. The salesperson tells you that this is standard and was stated in small print on the sheets you were shown previously.

Perhaps you have noticed that your favorite brand of paper towel or pudding seems to disappear faster than it once did. Check the package. There is a good chance that the price remained the same but the size was reduced. Rather than pass on increased costs to customers, some manufacturers reduce the amount of product contained in a package. To obscure the issue, words like *new convenience package* are printed in small type. You're getting less value but may not be aware of it, because basic package design and price stay the same.

The captive customer creates a tempting target for some marketers. Because demand is already there, the question is how much to charge. Consider the cost of automobile parts. After an accident, you find that replacing one door will cost 20 percent of what you paid for the car. Are you likely to scrap it? It is true that handling and stocking inventory has to be included in prices, but it is a known fact that many companies make a much greater percentage on replacement items than on the original product.

Another way to reduce the amount delivered is to price on an all-you-want basis and then limit the supply. For example, a golf course or tennis club has a monthly fee for unlimited usage, but there are so many customers that you must wait an exorbitant amount of time for space. America Online did exactly that when it charged $19.95 a month for unlimited access. Members in California, Illinois, and New York filed a class action suit against AOL. A judge in Chicago approved a settlement agreement February 20, 1998. Part of the settlement provided refunds and credits to members who were on-line for selected times and experienced problems.[23]

COMPETITIVE FACTORS THAT INFLUENCE PRICE

When making pricing decisions, marketers must take the competitive environment into consideration. More specifically, it's important to look at industry structure and the potential for differentiating products through pricing strategies.

Industry Structure *Industry* may be defined broadly or narrowly for marketing purposes. It refers to a group of firms offering similar products. For example, Pizza Hut executives may view their industry as only establishments that sell pizza or as all restaurants in a particular price range. As with most other tools, marketers must make sure that the industry concept they use is relevant to the situation at hand.

To understand how competition affects price, we must look at industry structure as well as the behavior of individual firms. Industry analysis examines such aspects as the number of firms, whether products are differentiated, and the freedom of firms to enter and exit. Economists have identified four basic industry structures—perfect competition, monopoly, oligopoly, and monopolistic competition. Figure 17-7 shows how each type is likely to affect pricing and other forms of competition.

Type of Structure	Number of Firms	Product Differentiated or Homogeneous	Firms Have Price-Setting Power	Free Entry	Distinguishing Characteristics	Examples
Perfect Competition	Many	Homogeneous	No	Yes	Price competition only	Wheat farmer Textile firm
Monopoly	One	A single unique product	Yes	No	Constrained by market demand	Public utility Brewery in Taiwan
Oligopoly	Few	Either	Yes	Limited	Strategic behavior	Cereal maker Primary copper producer
Monopolistic Competition	Many	Differentiated	Yes, but limited	Yes	Price and quality competition	Restaurants Music industry

Figure 17-7 Industry Structure and Competition

Source: Karl Case and Ray C. Fair, Principles of Economics, 3rd ed. © 1994. Adapted by permission of Prentice Hall, Inc., Upper Saddle River, NJ.

Perfect competition

The industry structure in which no single firm has control over prices.

Monopoly

The industry structure in which one organization makes a product with no close substitutes.

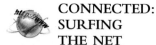

CONNECTED: SURFING THE NET

www.ticketmaster.com

See for yourself what kind of service charges apply to concerts and events. You can also check prices, order tickets, get venue and seating chart information, and much more at Ticketmaster online. See what's on sale in your area by exploring the company's weekly listing.

Oligopoly

The industry structure in which a small number of firms compete for the same customers.

Perfect Competition **Perfect competition** refers to an industry in which each firm has little if any control over prices. None is large enough relative to others to control factors of production or market demand. Usually, many small firms produce precisely the same product. Because they cannot dictate prices, their primary decisions revolve around how much to produce and how to produce it. Since firm size is small, it is generally easy to enter and exit the market. Profits tend to be generated not through price but economies of scale and cost reductions.

Monopoly At the opposite end of the spectrum from pure competition is **monopoly,** an industry structure in which one organization makes a product with no close substitutes. As the only firm in the market, the monopolist has a great deal of freedom in establishing price. Most monopolies exist because there are barriers to entry for competing firms. For example, governments in many countries establish sole providers for certain services, such as communications or public transportation. Generally, these are heavily regulated to prevent abuses, and prices are set by governing boards rather than company executives. Public utilities that are established as monopolies usually must have their rates approved by a commission whose job is to protect the public interest.

From time to time private enterprises can achieve monopoly status through control of a patent or scarce raw material. Sometimes entry barriers, such as the sheer size of initial investment, may keep competitors out. Intel has been called a monopoly because of its dominance as a technology supplier. Legal experts often refer to companies such as Microsoft and Intel as *essential facilities* because customers have to buy their products.[24]

Wanting lower concert prices for fans, Pearl Jam contended that Ticketmaster inflated the cost with an unwarranted charge, which added as much as 30 percent to the face value. The company argued that the service charge was used to secure venue arrangements, to guarantee performances, and sometimes for marketing purposes. It claimed that its activities may be misconstrued as anticompetitive because small-scale ticket services are unable to duplicate them.[25]

Oligopoly An **oligopoly** exists when an industry has a small number of companies competing for the same customers. Firms may behave in unusual ways to gain business, such as introducing a new technology, or they may combine a number of factors that can affect their use of price as a strategic tool. They tend to be large, and old rivals engage in strategies and counterstrategies over long periods. The global auto industry is a good example. Seven major companies around the world produce nearly all motor vehicles, and each firm is large enough to commit considerable resources to differentiate itself. Each gains competitive advantage over the others from time to time. A few small firms in a local market also can be considered an oligopolistic situation.

Because oligopolies are usually well established and have strong market position, it is difficult for new firms to enter. The incumbents also get to know one another well. Through intelligence gathering, they learn about their competitors' cost structure. Their detailed market knowledge gives them insight into the amount of profitability rivals are likely to generate based on various pricing decisions. Because members of oligopolies engage in moves and countermoves, planning is essential.

The problem with being perceived as a monopoly is never being seen as the leader you truly are.

◆

  It is often believed that change is welcomed only by new-comers to a situation. Indeed, those newcomers are often seen as the very catalysts of change. Pacific Gas and Electric Company has long recognized the changes that were coming to the California electricity market. We have done more than welcome change; we have helped initiate and encourage it.

PG&E, far from resisting the restructuring of the electric industry in our State, has been actively preparing for it. We are restructuring ourselves to make sure that our customers are well served. We will be a competitive leader in product price, customer service, safety and financial performance.

In fact, we look to a more competitive business environment to highlight the leadership qualities that have always been a part of PG&E.

PG&E

Pacific Gas and Electric utility is facing an increasing amount of competition.

Monopolistic Competition **Monopolistic competition** is an industry structure in which many firms compete for the same customers by differentiating their products. It falls somewhere between monopoly and pure competition but is much closer to the latter. Companies create brand loyalty to gain some of the benefits of monopoly. They control price by creating unique market offerings, such as nonfast-food restaurants in urban areas. Both price and quality are important in attracting customers and differentiating the product. Often there are numerous firms that are small or similar in size. Entry and exit are relatively easy, and the success of incumbents invites additional competitors. That's why several similar restaurants are likely to spring up when one starts doing well.

Strong marketing plans help organizations gain monopolistic advantages in highly competitive markets. They do this by creating subtle product differentiation. Rock groups are in this category. Stylistic differences enable you to differentiate among U2, Verve-Pipe, the Cranberries, and Spice Girls. And each commands a price differential for concerts. Monopolistic competition also is the structure of the athletic footwear industry. Nike, Reebok, New Balance, Adidas, and a few others compete more or less on subtle differences in products.

Differentiation and Price Competition Nonprice competition usually involves a differentiation strategy. **Differentiation** occurs when product attributes are stressed. Marketers try to demonstrate value and avoid any price reductions. In its purest form, a differentiation strategy relies on little or no mention of price. The relationships feature in this chapter, "Paying a Premium for Pet Care Nets Pampering, Too," focuses on ways in which quality pet products are differentiated beyond price considerations for many pet lovers.

Price competition adjusts prices to gain more customers or to establish a dominant position in the market. Recall that nonprice competition occurs when other marketing mix variables, such as product quality and promotion, are adjusted in response to competitors' pricing practices. Marketers need to understand the general approaches to price taken by their key competitors. This helps them anticipate overall market prices and what rivals are likely to do in response to price competition.

Marketing strategists study competitors in order to predict what they are likely to do under various conditions. Most companies respond in fairly consistent ways to price situations.

Monopolistic competition
The industry structure in which many firms compete for the same customers by differentiating their products and by creating unique offerings.

Differentiation
A strategy in which product attributes that provide value are stressed.

Price competition
A strategy that employs price adjustments to gain more customers or to establish a dominant position in the market.

CONNECTING THROUGH RELATIONSHIPS

PAYING A PREMIUM FOR PET CARE NETS PAMPERING, TOO

Carol Brandwein can easily drop $100 at her local pet supply store. She wants the best for her seven-year-old Bedlington terrier, Barnaby. Carol may spend $30 for a 40-pound bag of Nature's Choice premium dog food or $7.00 for Mr. Christal's luxury fur shampoo. While there, she may even enter Barnaby in a pet trick contest.

Americans like Brandwein lavish $20 billion a year on their beloved pets. A Barron's survey showed that seven out of 10 of us spend on our pets as if they were our children. Cashing in on this love-in are pet care businesses with prices at the high end of the spectrum. For instance, Colgate once sold its premium Hill's Science Diet exclusively through veterinarians. Now, it is one of dozens of brands available at the new breed of pet supply specialty stores popping up in malls all over the country. Huge national chains like Petco and PetsMart, as well as regionals like Pet Supply Depot in New England and Pet Food Warehouse in the Midwest, stock up to 12,000 items, and premium pet foods account for more than half their sales.

Grocery stores are losing out on this valuable product category not only because they can't carry the huge variety but also because pet supply stores give customers added value. Jeffrey Ross, president and CEO of Pet Supply Depot, a 17-store chain, says his affluent customers "want dollar value for their purchases. If they want to buy a premium dog food for their pet, they want to know why it's good, what it's going to do for them, and they want knowledgeable people. We have a continuing education program where we run four to six seminars a year for all our employees to make sure they're up on the virtues of premium food versus grocery food."

These specialty stores also host events for owners and their pets. In this business, building customer relationships means reaching out to poodles, gerbils, iguanas, and guppies. Pet Food Warehouse, a 25-store chain based in Minneapolis, holds costume shows, pet trick contests, and portrait sessions. Sometimes the owners take center stage. One store hosted singles night on Valentine's Day, and 200 people showed up with their pets.

"The point is that people are taking owning a pet as a real part of their lives," says Bill Lechner, general merchandise manager of Pet Food Warehouse. "The idea of just going down to the corner and picking up a can of cat food has changed, and now there's an emotional and social aspect of pet ownership. We realize it, and we promote it, foster it, and cater to it, because if you can get the pets in the store with the owners, they are going to stay in the store a lot longer than if they simply walk in, go to the food, get it, and go out."

Sources: Jerry Minkoff, "Perking up Pet Supplies," *Discount Merchandiser,* July 1995, pp. 30–32; Jerry Minkoff, "Pet Supply Depot: Netting a Share of the Animal-Lover Market," *Discount Merchandiser,* November 1995, pp. 46, 48; Jay Palmer, "Well, Aren't You the Cat's Meow?" *Barron's,* April 1, 1996, pp. 29–34; and Jerry Minkoff, "Pampering Pets = Persistent Profits," *Discount Merchandiser,* November 1995, p. 47.

Those that can produce at lower cost are more inclined to engage in price competition. Toyota, for example, was able to introduce a "dirt cheap" engine as a result of cost cuts. The new engine is one-third cheaper to make—a savings that can be passed on to consumers in the highly competitive auto market.[26] Even at lower prices Toyota can sustain a profit, while companies with higher costs are likely to lose money as prices drop. In countries where wage rates are low, such as Korea and Taiwan, production costs are low for many types of goods.

COST FACTORS THAT INFLUENCE PRICE

While prices should never be determined solely by cost, cost is critical information in making profitable pricing decisions. By understanding costs, marketers can judge profitability in advance. They can move resources to the highest-profit opportunities, avoid losing money, and gain better control of internal processes. By comparing costs with those of competitors, it is possible to assess production efficiency and estimate the relative profits each competitor can expect at various prices. This, in turn, helps anticipate the pricing choices available to competitors.

Types of Costs Costs are categorized in several ways. Most simply, accountants look at fixed and variable costs. Marketers also should consider marginal and incremental costs.

Mita uses price to establish a dominant position in the marketplace.

Fixed and Variable Costs   **Fixed costs** do not change in the short run. These are expenditures for items such as production facilities, equipment, and salaries. Often these are called *sunk costs* because, once committed, nothing can be done to lower them. They do not change very much no matter how many units of a product are sold. In service industries, salaries account for a large portion of fixed (sunk) costs. For example, hospitals pay nurses irrespective of the number of patients served. For airlines, payments for aircraft and hanger space, as well as salaries are fixed costs. The best you can do is use these costs more effectively. McDonald's® introduced the Egg McMuffin® so their facilities could produce revenues during more hours. That improved the effectiveness of their fixed costs.

Fixed cost

A cost that does not vary with changes in volume produced.

Variable costs change depending on how much is produced or sold. They are usually calculated for each unit of production. These costs include raw materials, warranty costs, and the aspects of payroll (such as commissions) that rise or fall depending on the units sold. In the airline industry, for example, variable costs include the commissions paid to travel agents and food served on planes.

Variable cost

A cost that changes depending on volume.

Total cost (*TC*) for a given period are calculated by multiplying the variable cost (*VC*) per unit times the quantity (*Q*) of units and adding the fixed costs (*FC*):

$$TC = VC \times Q + FC$$

Total revenues (*TR*) for a period are calculated by multiplying the price (*P*) per unit times the quantity (*Q*) of units sold:

$$TR = P \times Q$$

Profits (*PR*) are the difference between total revenues (*TR*) and total costs (*TC*):

$$PR = TR - TC$$

The average cost (*AC*) of each unit is the total cost (*TC*) divided by the quantity (*Q*) of units:

$$AC = TC/Q$$

Marginal costs

The expenditures incurred in producing one additional unit of output.

Marginal revenue

The income from selling one additional unit of output.

Incremental costs

Costs that go up or down based on volume; include both variable costs and certain fixed costs.

The average cost of each unit doesn't provide very much useful information for pricing decisions, however, because average costs are sensitive to volume. The more units sold, the lower is the average cost.

Marginal Costs   Unlike accountants, economists look at marginal costs and marginal revenues. **Marginal costs** (*MC*) are expenditures incurred in producing one additional unit of output. These costs often go down with each unit sold and stabilize at volume of production near full capacity. Marginal cost then increases because additional fixed costs must be added, such as more production machinery. Imagine an airline with a plane that normally flies half full. It would not cost much to add one passenger—the cost of another meal and the commission paid to the travel agent who sells the ticket. Yet any price the airline can get that is greater than that marginal cost adds to profit. The price of the new ticket sold would be the **marginal revenue** (*MR*), the income from one more unit of the product sold, usually the product price. But let's say the plane is full. Would you add another aircraft to take one more passenger? Obviously not, unless that passenger is willing to pay a huge price.

Economic theory shows that profits are maximized—total revenues (*TR*) minus total costs (*TC*) are greatest—when *MR* equals *MC*. In the airline example, we can continue to lower the price until all seats are gone, or *MC* (the price of food and commissions) equals the price of a ticket. Airlines do this to a degree by offering a few discount seats. But selling a ticket for the cost of food and the agent commission (about $35) is impractical. In reality, you won't often find many marketing executives sitting in their offices looking at graphs of marginal revenues and costs. Yet, like most good theories, this concept provides useful insights.

Incremental Costs   It was noted that fixed costs do not change with prices and sales volume. Many people assume that these are the costs of being in business. Also called overhead, these fixed costs may be higher or lower for different competitors. For example, higher overhead prevents Kodak from being as low in costs as many rivals, including Fuji Film of Japan. Kodak argues that its manufacturing cost is equally as low or lower, but equipment accounts for its inability to cut costs.[27] Fixed costs are extremely important in determining the profitability of a firm.

In practice, companies with high overhead may justify high prices if these reflect added value. Often they do not, yet decision makers push prices higher in an effort to obtain maximum revenue. The result may be even lower volume or reduced profit. If fixed costs do not add value for customers, they probably should not be a factor in pricing decisions. This is very difficult for many executives to accept because pricing to cover all costs (cost-based pricing) has been so prevalent.

Relevant costs for pricing decisions are **incremental costs,** costs that go up or down based on volume. Like variable costs, incremental costs are related to pricing because the price can affect the volume sold. Variable costs are always incremental. Only some fixed costs are incremental. For example, if a low price will increase demand to the extent that a new factory will have to be added to satisfy it, then the factory is an incremental cost and becomes a factor in the decision whether to lower the price. Once the factory is built, the cost becomes fixed or sunk. It has to be paid for no matter how much is produced. Pricing decisions that increase volume thus influence fixed costs, which in turn greatly influence the firm's cost structure.

Cost-Oriented Pricing   Both cost-plus and rate-of-return pricing are based on the company's costs. Cost-oriented pricing adds an amount to the product cost, called a markup, which is designed to yield a profit. A percentage markup can be added directly, or additional calculations can be made to determine what percentage rate of return the seller will receive. Either approach has serious problems, because each tends to ignore the customer and, to varying degrees, the competition as well.

Cost-Plus Pricing   Because of its simplicity, the cost-plus approach is popular. But, as the following example shows, it doesn't necessarily assure a profit. A local furniture store pays $750 to a wholesaler for a sofa and sells it to the consumer for $1,500, a markup of 100 percent. On the surface, it appears that the store has gained $750. But it has many costs to meet, such as salaries and overhead. When these are taken into account, and depending on overall sales volume, the retailer might actually lose money on this sofa and other items. Clearly, to determine whether the sale is profitable and/or precisely how much is made on the sofa a portion of the retailer's costs has to be allocated to each of the products sold.

Markups are popular because they are perceived to be fair or equitable for both the buyer and the seller. Standard markups have evolved in many industries to help indicate what amount is "fair." Manufacturers or wholesalers often suggest prices to retailers, or retailers form their own conventions. For example, an auto parts dealer may mark up brake assemblies by 40 percent and consumables such as oil by 25 percent. Since all similar retailers use the same basic markup structure, all have approximately the same retail price. Notice that the calculation is based on the wholesale price, which itself is a markup on the manufacturer's price.

Government contracts and some industrial contracts often specify that the seller must use cost-plus pricing. This is full-cost pricing because the markup is based on all costs, including allocations of overhead and other fixed costs. Sellers are expected to provide an accounting upon request. The difficulty lies in determining which costs to assign to which products. Again, even full-cost pricing largely ignores the value of the product to the customer.

Rate-of-Return Pricing A variation on cost-plus pricing, rate-of-return pricing is based on the breakeven point. Essentially, the method determines how many units must be sold at a particular price in order to cover fixed costs plus a profit on the investment made. The breakeven point is the amount sold at a given price on which the business neither makes nor loses money. Any volume beyond that point makes money. The breakeven point is calculated by dividing the total fixed cost (FC) by the difference between the selling price (P) of one unit and the variable cost (VC) of one unit:

$$\text{Breakeven point} = FC/(P - VC)$$

The difference between the price and the variable cost of a unit ($P - VC$) is called the contribution margin. It tells how much the sale of one unit contributes to covering fixed costs. Once these costs are covered, any remaining contribution is profit. Figure 17-8 shows the breakeven concept graphically.

As an example of rate-of-return pricing, assume that you decide to start a small business that will offer housepainting services to homeowners during summer vacation. You calculate that you will have to invest $10,000 in fixed (sunk) costs, including advertising and promotion, insurance, equipment, truck rental, and a salary for yourself. You feel that you should earn a 20 percent return ($10,000 \times 20\% = \$2000$) for having the idea, taking the initiative, and assuming the risk of losing your invested capital. Furthermore, you estimate that labor, paint, and other variable costs for each house will average $2,100, and with four workers your company can paint eight houses in four months. What is the average price you should charge for each house?

To answer this question, you first add your desired return to your fixed costs ($2,000 + \$10,000 = \$12,000$) to determine the total revenue contribution required. Then you divide that sum by the number of houses (units) to find the amount that each unit must contribute ($12,000 \div 8 = \$1,500$). Since the variable cost to paint a house is $2,100, you therefore determine that you must charge $2,100 + \$1,500 = \$3,600$ per house.

Notice in this example that profit is treated much like a fixed cost. This is because if you break even in a strict sense—that is, neither make nor lose money—then your project will not accomplish its profit objective.

Also notice that rate-of-return pricing ignores the customer and the competition. If homeowners consider $3,600 too expensive, then they may hire someone who charges less or

Figure 17-8 Breakeven Analysis

choose to do the work themselves. If they believe the price is very low, then they may be willing to pay even more. The pricing of competitors is important. Whether competitors are willing to paint a house for $3,000 or $9,000 will influence how consumers perceive your price.

Rate-of-return pricing also tends to ignore the scale of operations you could have. For example, if eight painters rather than four were employed, the fixed costs could be spread across sixteen houses rather than eight. That would lower the price, but you would have to supervise more workers while not making more profit. A major problem with the rate-of-return approach is that price will increase when demand goes down. For example, if only six houses are painted, the price for each rises by $500, to $4,100. Does this make sense? In the 1980s, U.S. auto companies lost share dramatically to foreign rivals. As demand for U.S. cars declined due to competitive pressure, Detroit increased prices to try to make up for lost unit sales, further reducing demand.

INTERNATIONAL PRICING

Pricing in global environments is affected by several factors not experienced in domestic markets. Also, because markets vary greatly among countries, international pricing is complex. Marketing executives must be knowledgeable about many issues and remain flexible in adjusting to unforeseeable circumstances. The major influencers on global pricing are market, cost, and financial factors, as outlined in Figure 17-9.

GLOBAL MARKET FACTORS

Market factors such as local demand, tastes and preferences, competitor activities, and gray marketing are important. All of these elements must be considered in international pricing.

Local demand can vary dramatically due to demographic, geographic, and political conditions. For example, China is the world's most populous country and is experiencing economic growth at a staggering rate. Yet few Chinese have enough income or even the space for most of the durable goods so common in the West. Consequently, many products for the Chinese market must be designed to be priced very low.

Subtle competitive differences can influence demand, even in fairly similar economic environments. In Europe, for example, some product categories—such as electronics and pharmaceuticals—have prices that vary more than 100 percent from country to country. One brand of portable television was priced at 434 deutschemarks (DM) in Germany and the equivalent of 408 DM in the Netherlands, 560 DM in Italy, and 596 DM in Spain. The European Union recognizes that differentials such as this cause difficulties.[28]

Globally, tastes and preferences also vary dramatically. A nationalistic bias for domestic products can make them less cross-price elastic in relation to imports. For example, in France, Germany, the United Kingdom, and especially Italy, consumers prefer vehicles made in their own country even if they cost more.[29] Generally, people in countries where domestic brands are preferred have high incomes and tend to be much less price sensitive across the board.[30] That means more latitude for premium pricing. Also, country-of-origin effects can work negatively or positively for imports. Germany's BMW and Mercedes both enjoy the reputation of excellent engineering in many markets, whereas all products from some countries are considered poorly made. Furthermore, consumer perceptions about an entire product class may vary. For example, unlike Americans, the British perceive little difference in photographic film and consequently are very price sensitive.[31]

Market Factors	Cost Factors	Financial Factors
Local demand	Distance and transportation	Exchange rates
Competitive conditions	Tariffs and homologation	Inflation
Availability of substitutes	Export duties, subsidies and controls	Government price controls
Gray marketing	Transfer pricing	

Figure 17-9   Influences on Global Pricing

The availability of substitute products also varies widely. The most obvious case is the substitution of automation for labor. Japan—with its high education level, high labor rates, and low unemployment—is highly automated, while Chinese producers use readily available low-cost human labor whenever possible. The market for high-priced robotics is mature in Japan, where many competitors are constantly seeking an edge, but demand is weak in China.

A notable feature of many foreign economies is the gray market, which has a significant effect on pricing. Many global companies manufacture in local markets so they can sell at lower prices there, but this also may lead to gray marketing.[32] **Gray marketing** occurs when pirated products made in a foreign country are imported back to the company's home market without approval. They are then sold at reduced prices, usually by unauthorized channel members. The importation of gray market goods is prohibited in the United States by a law that forbids bringing products into the country without permission of the trademark owner. Elsewhere in the world, restrictions vary, may not exist, or may not be well enforced. Many times the foreign-made product is of a different quality but bears the company label, so consumers are confused. In other cases, prices differ because of manufacturing costs, exchange rates, or other reasons. Caterpillar dealers in the United States recently faced price competition from company products illegally imported from Europe.[33] In another case, Duracell battery distributors in the United States bought the product at lower prices from Europe. Because of poor storage and age, many of these batteries were defective, which damaged Duracell's U.S. reputation, not to mention the confusion caused by considerable price inconsistencies.[34]

Gray markets can disrupt the best-laid plans of companies desiring selective or exclusive distribution. Any brand with some consumer following may find itself in this situation. For example, Yasuyuki Nambu buys new cars from U.S. sources (for example, from Cadillac dealers) and ships them to Japan for sale. He undercuts the selling price of authorized dealers by as much as 29 percent because he does not have their overhead.[35] The American dealers who supply Nambu are violating their franchise contract, which states they must not sell to unauthorized resellers.

Companies that want to ensure selective or exclusive distribution must take steps to eliminate gray market problems. If not, then the strength and motivation of the authorized channel will be seriously impaired. The company must clearly communicate to all members of the authorized channel the importance of following policy and upholding contracts. Their activities must be monitored, especially when significant gray market activity exists. Contracts with those who violate agreements must be terminated. Companies like Levi Strauss and Joico, a manufacturer of hair care products, vigorously follow such steps in operating their distribution channels.[36]

GLOBAL COST FACTORS

In calculating the costs of doing business internationally, it is not just distance that matters but the expense of moving goods from one country to another. Transportation and insurance costs escalate when borders are crossed, as do tariffs and red tape. Risks also increase, so prices must cover potential adverse circumstances.

Tariffs—taxes levied against incoming goods—contribute to costs and are sometimes added to price. They affect imports in nearly every country. Vehicle prices in Turkey are elevated nearly threefold by tariffs. In the United States, importers pay an average of 5 percent on all items, much more for some. For example, the U.S. tariff on orange juice is 35 cents per gallon, and on canned tuna it is 35 percent.[37]

Bureaucratic red tape often makes it difficult and expensive to enter a market. The Japanese use it as a barrier to foreign competitors. For example, they lock out international construction companies by claiming that Japan's dirt is unique, or they require considerable testing at border entry points for all sorts of products. Extensive red tape makes it difficult to import motor vehicles into Japan at competitive prices, and excessive regulations add more barriers.[38] Some European pharmaceutical companies claim that FDA regulations impede their access to the U.S. market.

The opposite of a tariff is an **export subsidy** paid by a government to encourage businesses to export. When you compete against these companies, essentially you're competing against their government as well. When they target a certain market, their prices can be more competitive because the subsidy covers much or all of their export costs. This may put nonsubsidized exports and domestic products at a pricing disadvantage. In other cases, govern-

Gray marketing
Importing products made in a foreign country back to the company's home market without approval.

Tariff
A tax levied against a good being imported into a country.

Export subsidy
Funding by a government to encourage businesses to export goods.

ments may restrict exports by adding costly duties, which raises prices in importing countries. During the first part of 1997, Russia restricted the export of platinum, forcing prices up around the world.[39]

Risk is also a factor in international business. When risk is high, prices must be raised. For example, selling in Russia is risky because of an unstable economy and the possibility of political takeovers. Anywhere in the world, a change in government can affect economic regulations and market access. Furthermore, a weak or indifferent government may permit greater corruption or lawlessness, which can mean that warehousing and distribution channels are insecure.

Transfer price

The amount a company charges its foreign affiliate for a product.

Transfer prices are the amounts that companies charge their foreign affiliates for products. This causes some interesting price variations across countries. By altering the transfer price, both local prices and profits can be dramatically affected. In this way, companies can manipulate their price in markets globally, affecting competition and their sources of rev-

---

 CONNECTED: SURFING THE NET

PetsMart

www.petsmart.com

THIS CHAPTER'S RELATIONSHIP FEATURE, "PAYING A Premium for Pet Care Nets Pampering, Too," discussed the segment of Americans willing to spend an amazing $20 billion a year on pets. In order to expand your thinking about pricing approaches, visit the PetsMart Web site and answer the following questions.

1. How does PetsMart use the marketing mix to persuade consumers to purchase Authority Premium Pet Nutrition? What role do you think price plays in the consumer's final decision? What should marketers do ahead of time to ensure that customers will perceive this product as a good value?
2. Prices serve several objectives. What are they? How do you think PetsMart meets/could meet relationship objectives? What aspects of the Web site help the company connect with customers?
3. Read "PetsMart concept" found in the corporate mission and position section. How does CEO Mark Hansen believe PetsMart beats the competition? How could industry structure, differentiation, and price competition affect the company's pricing decisions?
4. Imagine you are an investor in PetsMart. Examine the company's financial statement. Are you satisfied with profits? Why or why not? How can price affect all major factors that influence profit?

Amoco

www.amoco.com

IN THIS CHAPTER YOU LEARNED ABOUT a number of economic factors that influence price. Amoco was used to illustrate cross-price elasticity of demand. To learn more about factors influencing price as well as other pricing issues, visit the Amoco Web site and answer the following questions.

1. List the products Amoco sells. Do you think each product has an elastic or inelastic demand curve? Explain.
2. What determines demand elasticity? How does each relate to Amoco?
3. A number of factors influence international pricing. What opportunities is Amoco pursuing in China? How might demand vary there due to demographic, geographic, and political conditions?
4. Select an article from Amoco's *Onstream* magazine that illustrates how the company connects with customers through relationships, technology, globalization, ethics, or diversity. Explain why this connection is beneficial to the company.

enues. For example, Japanese auto supply companies can charge higher transfer prices for components going to assembly plants in the United States. This practice yields more profit in Japan and less profit in the United States. In turn taxes are paid in Japan, where the rate may be lower than in the United States. Ultimately, the tax savings mean that a lower price can be charged for the product in the United States.

GLOBAL FINANCIAL FACTORS

The primary financial factors influencing international prices are exchange rates, inflation, and government price controls. Exchange rates and inflation alter the value of currencies, while government price controls prohibit companies from moving prices upward at will. Controls are particularly troublesome when a rapid shift in exchange rates or inflation devalues the price put on a product.

Even money has a price, which is reflected in the exchange rate. The **exchange rate** is how much one currency is worth relative to another. On Thursday, February 27, 1997, it cost 120.69 Japanese yen to buy one U.S. dollar. That was down from 122.13 yen per dollar the day before.[40] When dollars cost less, anything valued in dollars costs less. The change noted above essentially meant that U.S. products sent to Japan became lower priced in yen, while Japanese products sent to the United States became more expensive in dollars. The difference was nearly 1.5 percent in a single day. Currency exchange rates can fluctuate considerably over time, affecting prices for imported and exported products.

Inflation is the tendency of a currency to be worth less over time. When inflation occurs, product prices along the supply chain increase. These are passed on in higher prices, so consumers have to spend more money to buy the same item. Most advanced nations now have low inflation rates, often around 3 percent or even less per year. In some countries inflation is extremely high and escalates monthly or even weekly. For example, in 1990 Procter & Gamble raised prices twice a month, by 20 or 30 percent, to keep up with inflation in some Latin American countries.[41]

Governments often use **price controls** in an attempt to keep inflation in check. Essentially, the maximum price increase allowable is set by law. Sometimes the controls are applied to all goods, sometimes they are selective, and sometimes they apply only to imports. In any case, they can make it difficult to earn a profit, so companies may not want to sell in that market. In Poland, for example, a shortage of cars and color television sets resulted from price controls, and many consumers who already owned these products resold them at a high price. This further discouraged production, since the black market price was 107 percent higher than the official price.[42]

Companies use many factors when making pricing decisions locally or globally. All of these factors are likely to influence price. However, as we will see in the next chapter, the actual pricing strategy must be well grounded in an understanding of how pricing captures value from the market. This requires knowing how customers define value.

Exchange rate
The worth of one currency relative to another.

Inflation
The tendency of a currency to be worth less over time.

Price controls
Government restrictions on the price that can be charged for a product.

CHAPTER SUMMARY

OBJECTIVE 1:   Describe how pricing works with the other parts of the marketing mix.

Pricing is an important element of the marketing mix. Price decisions are made along with product, promotion, and logistics decisions. Pricing is influenced by profit, volume, competitive, and customer relationship objectives. Consequently, pricing is important for nearly all aspects of the business.

OBJECTIVE 2:   Learn how economic factors such as demand and supply influence prices.

The demand curve helps us understand how price influences the amount of a product customers buy. The availability of substitutes, necessity, the portion of income spent on the product, and the timing of price changes affect the price sensitivity of demand. The supply curve tells how much product firms will provide at various prices. Usually, more is produced when prices are expected to

rise. By analyzing the supply and demand curves, it is possible to get some idea of future prices in an industry.

OBJECTIVE 3:   Understand the legal and ethical constraints on pricing decisions.

Both legal and ethical factors affect price. Laws prohibit both vertical and horizontal price fixing by U.S. firms. It is also illegal for manufacturers to sell to different parties at different prices, although some forms of price discrimination are acceptable. To control unfair price competition, many states regulate pricing minimums and the use of loss leaders. The Federal Trade Commission sets permissible standards for price advertising. For example, you cannot advertise a sale price unless it is really a sale and the items are available. International firms must sell at a high enough price to avoid violating anitdumping laws. Finally, unit pricing regulations help consumers make comparisons. To be ethical, prices should reflect a fair exchange of value, and marketers must be careful not to misrepresent the terms of an exchange. This requires clear communication of both price and value.

OBJECTIVE 4: Use industry structure concepts to understand how competitors in different types of industries price.

The four basic industry structures are perfect competition, monopoly, oligopoly, and monopolistic competition. In perfect competition, many firms vie to provide goods at the going price. A firm with a monopoly can set prices as high as the market will bear, although pricing by public utility monopolies is generally regulated in the public interest. In an oligopoly, a small number of competitors make pricing decisions based on their knowledge of one another's cost structures. Monopolistic competition tends to be based on product differentiation rather than price.

OBJECTIVE 5: Use competitive factors surrounding industry structure concepts to understand how pricing works in different types of industries.

Pricing decisions must consider variable and fixed costs, marginal costs, and incremental costs. Incremental costs, which are the most important, include variable costs and, often, some fixed costs, such as the cost of building a new factory to meet increased demand. Cost-oriented methods, such as cost-plus pricing and rate-of-return pricing, have serious drawbacks because they tend to ignore the consumer and competitors.

OBJECTIVE 6: Recognize the conditions that make international pricing complex.

Market, cost, and financial factors unique to global business must be considered in pricing. Market factors include local demand, competitive conditions, tastes and preferences, the availability of substitutes, and gray marketing. Important cost factors are transportation distance, tariffs, red tape, and export subsidies. Major financial considerations are inflation, exchange rates, and price controls. Risk is another influence on international pricing.

REVIEW YOUR UNDERSTANDING

1. List ten names for price.
2. Which constituents of a firm can be pleased with profit objectives, volume objectives, competitive objectives, and relationship objectives?
3. What are the major factors that influence price?
4. What is elastic demand? Inelastic demand?
5. What factors influence price elasticity?
6. What is supply and demand equilibrium?
7. What are the laws that affect pricing practices? Describe the restrictions.
8. Describe dumping.
9. What are two ethical issues regarding pricing? Explain.
10. What is industry structure? What are four structures that have price implications?
11. What are fixed and variable costs?
12. What are incremental costs?
13. What is cost-plus pricing?
14. What factors influence pricing in global settings?

DISCUSSION OF CONCEPTS

1. Prices are set with several objectives in mind. What are they, and how are they important to a company?
2. A company's pricing strategy is influenced by many factors: legal and ethical issues, economic conditions, the company's costs, the global environment, and competitors. What major effect does each category have on pricing decisions?
3. Product demand is influenced by price elasticity. What does this mean, and what effect does it have on a marketer's pricing policy?
4. Federal and state laws in the United States prohibit unfair pricing. What is meant by "unfair"? Give specific examples of

laws and briefly describe their objectives. Is this true of all countries?
5. How does the type of competition within an industry affect a company's ability to set prices? Briefly describe the major competitor-based pricing approaches.
6. What types of costs are relevant for pricing decisions? Which are irrelevant? Why? What are some of the main problems with cost-oriented pricing?
7. Despite its drawbacks, cost-oriented pricing is still used by many companies. Briefly describe the two types.

KEY TERMS AND DEFINITIONS

Bait and switch: An unethical practice in which sellers advertise items at extremely low prices and then inform the customer that the items are out of stock, offer different items, or attempt to sell the customer more expensive substitutes.

Cross-price elasticity of demand: The extent to which the quantity demanded of one product changes in response to changes in the price of another product.

Differentiation: A strategy stressing product attributes that provide value.

Demand curve: A depiction of the price elasticity demand for a product.

Dumping: Selling a product in a foreign country at a price lower than in the producing country and lower than its cost of production.

Exchange rate: The worth of one currency relative to another.

Export subsidy: Money paid by a government to encourage businesses to export goods.

Fixed cost: A cost that does not vary with changes in volume produced.

Gray marketing: Importing products made in a foreign country back to the company's home market without its approval.

Horizontal price fixing: Agreement among manufacturers and/or channel members to set prices at the retail level.

Incremental costs: Costs that go up or down based on volume; include both variable costs and certain fixed costs.

Inflation: The tendency of a currency to be worth less over time.

Loss leaders: An item priced below cost to attract customers.

Marginal costs: The expenditures incurred in producing one additional unit of output.

Marginal revenue: The income from selling one additional unit of output.

Monopolistic competition: The industry structure in which many firms compete for the same customers by differentiating their products and by creating unique offerings.

Monopoly: The industry structure in which one organization makes a product with no close substitutes.

Oligopoly: The industry structure in which a small number of firms compete for the same customers.

Perfect competition: The industry structure in which no single firm has control over prices.

Predatory dumping: Pricing below cost to drive local firms out of business.

Predatory pricing: Price cutting by large firms to eliminate small local competitors.

Price: The exchange value of a good or service in the marketplace.

Price competition: A strategy that employs price adjustments to gain more customers or to establish a dominant position in the market.

Price controls: Government restrictions on the price that can be charged for a product.

Price discrimination: A legally restricted practice in which a manufacturer or other channel member charges different prices to different retailers in the same marketplace.

Price elasticity: The extent to which changes in price affect the number of units demanded or supplied.

Price fixing: An attempt by one party to control what another party will charge in the market.

Supply curve: A depiction of the price elasticity of supply for a product.

Tariff: A tax levied on a good being imported into a country.

Transfer price: The amount a company charges its foreign affiliate for a product.

Variable cost: A cost that changes depending on volume.

Vertical price fixing: An attempt by a manufacturer or distributor to control the retail selling price.

REFERENCES

1. Joan Indiana Rigdon, "Nintendo Catches Up to Sony in Market for Most-Advanced Video-Game Players," *Wall Street Journal,* February 3, 1997, p. B3; Joan Indiana Rigdon, "Nintendo 64 Revitalizes Slumping Video-Game Market," *Wall Street Journal,* December 17, 1996, pp. B1, B4; Cyndee Miller, "Video Game Makers Brace for Yule Showdown," *Marketing News,* October 7, 1996, p. 12; Robert La Franco, "Take That, Nintendo," *Forbes,* June 3, 1996, pp. 96–97; Savuri Daimon, "Game Machine Makers in Dire Fight," *Japan Times Weekly International Edition,* April 1–7, 1996, p. 13; Sebastian Moffett, "Super Mario's Brothers," *Far Eastern Economic Review,* March 14, 1996, pp. 53–54; and "Nintendo Unveils Ultra 64 in Japan," *Discount Store News,* January 1, 1996, p. 42.

2. Laura Bird, "Retailers Turn Charity Events into Strategic Marketing Ploys," *Wall Street Journal Interactive Edition,* November 21, 1996.

3. David Kirkpatrick, "Intel's Amazing Profit Machine," *Fortune,* February 17, 1997, www.fortune.com.

4. James Stotter, "Applying Economics to Competitive Intelligence," *Competitive Intelligence Review,* Winter 1996, pp. 26–36.

5. Fax received from Travel Express International, March 10, 1997.

6. Walter Rockney and William Bommer, "Measuring the Impact of Product and Promotion Related Factors on Product Category Price Elasticities," *Journal of Business Research* 36 (July 1996): 203–216.

7. See Thomas T. Nagle and Reed E. Holder, *The Strategy and Tactics of Pricing* (Upper Saddle River, NJ: Prentice Hall, 1995), pp. 78–95.

8. Zina Moukheiber, "Oversleeping," *Forbes,* June 5, 1995, p. 78.

9. Christie Brown, "Banana Split," *Forbes,* August 12, 1996, pp. 94–95.

10. Alex Taylor III, "Why Detroit Can't Make Money on Cars," *Fortune,* September 9, 1996, pp. 36–37.

11. Brett Pulley and Bridget O'Brian, "More Airlines to Settle Suit on Price Fixing," *Wall Street Journal,* June 23, 1992, p. A3.

12. Ronald Henkoff, "Price Fixing: ADM Still Doesn't Get it," *Fortune,* November 11, 1996, pp. 30–34.

13. "Value Added Services Breed Loyal Shoppers," *Discount Store News,* May 6, 1996, pp. 56–59.

14. Richard J. Semenik and Gary J. Bamossy, *Principles of Marketing* (Cincinnati, Ohio: Southwestern College Publishing, 1995), p. 641.

15. Martha Brannigan and Asia Q. Nomani, "Airline Regulators Feel Pressure to Curb Major Carriers' Pricing," *Wall Street Journal Interactive Edition,* February 6, 1997.

16. Christine Dugas, "Look Beyond Yield for the Right Money Fund," *USA Today,* July 22, 1997.

17. Gene Koprowski, "The Price is Right," *Marketing Tools,* September 1995, http://www.marketingtools.com.

18. Larry Luxner, "Regional Integration Effects Produce Winners, Losers," *Bobbin,* November 1996, pp. 49, 51.

19. Nigel Holloway, "Sweet Smell of Excess," *Far Eastern Economic Review,* September 1996, p. 61.

20. Associated Press, "Japanese Company Defends Sale of Supercomputers," *USA Today,* May 12, 1997.

21. "Consumers Are Skeptical Again," *Progressive Grocer,* April 1996, pp. 40–46.

22. Jeff Wise, "On a Wing and a Prayer," *Adweek's Marketing Week,* October 23, 1989, p. 45.

23. Associated Press, "AOL Problems are Bad News for Businesses," *USA Today,* January 28, 1997, and www.usatoday.com; Richard Tedesco, "AOL Faces Three Class Action Law Suits," *Broadcasting and Cable,* January 20, 1997, p. 56; http://cmcnyls.edu/public/bulletins/aolcasap.HTM.

24. Dean Takahashi and Jon G. Auerbach, "Digital Raises Antitrust Issues as Dispute with Intel Escalates," *Wall Street Journal Interactive Edition,* July 24, 1997.

25. Charles Bilodeau, "Pearl Jam's War on Reality," *Consumers' Research,* June 1995, p. 24.

26. Valerie Rietman and Oscar Suris, "Toyota Motor Plans to Unveil Low Cost Engine Next Month," *Wall Street Journal Interactive Edition,* November 11, 1996.

27. Peter Nulty, "Digital Imaging Had Better Boom before Kodak Film Busts," *Fortune,* May 1, 1995, p. 80.

28. Stuart Sinclair, "A Guide to Global Pricing," *Journal of Business Strategy,* May-June 1993, p. 16.

29. Frank Verboven, "International Price Discrimination in the European Car Market," *Journal of Economics* 27 (Summer 1996): 240–268.

30. Chung Koo Kim, "The Interaction between Price and Long-Run Variables in a Multinational Brand Market," *Journal of Business Research* 37 (September 1996): 1–14.

31. Susan P. Douglas and C. Samuel Craig, *Global Marketing Strategy* (New York: McGraw-Hill, 1995), p. 228.

32. Paul Lansing and Joseph Gabriella, "Clarifying Gray Market Gray Areas," *American Business Law Journal,* September 1993, pp. 313–337.

33. Warren J. Keegan and Mark C. Green, *Principles of Global Marketing* (Upper Saddle River, NJ: Prentice Hall, 1997), p. 310.

34. Douglas and Craig, *Global Marketing Strategy,* p. 233.

35. David Holley, "Independent Auto Dealers Tap Discount Niche in Japan," *Los Angeles Times*, July 31, 1995, pp. D1, D5.

36. Based on the author's consulting experience in these industries.

37. Karl Case and Ray C. Fair, *Principles of Microeconomics* (Upper Saddle River, NJ: Prentice Hall, 1996), p. 558.

38. Clay Chandler, "U.S. Plans to Take Japan to WTO as Trade Controversy Continues," *Washington Post* 115 (1995): 3.

39. Associated Press, "Platinum and Palladium Rise on Doubts about Suppliers," *New York Times*, February 28, 1997, p. C5.

40. Bloomburg News, "Dollar Drops to Lowest Point in Four Weeks against the Yen," *New York Times*, February 28, 1997, p. C5.

41. Alecia Swasy, "Foreign Formula: Procter & Gamble Fixes Aim on Tough Market: The Latin Americans," *Wall Street Journal*, June 15, 1990, p. A7.

42. David G. Tarr, "The Welfare Costs of Price Controls for Cars and Color Televisions in Poland: Contrasting Estimates of Rent-Seeking from Recent Experience," *World Bank Economic Review* 8 (September 1994): 415–443.

CASE 17

TY, INC.

How would you like to get $1,500 for a product that cost you only $4.99? That's exactly what happened to a Nashville couple when they sold Peanuts the Elephant, a recently retired Beanie Baby. Chicago entrepreneur Ty Warner has been able to match supply, pricing, and demand to achieve extraordinary growth for his lovable little creations. The palm-sized beanbag animals were developed by Warner in 1993. To date, more than 80 Beanie Babies have been issued, with total sales topping $250 million annually and a 1,000 percent increase in orders between 1995 and 1996. Chocolate the Moose, Crunch the Shark, Bernie the St. Bernard, and all the others have caught on not only with kids but also with college students, parents, and grandparents. Priced under $5, they are affordable, collectible, and tradable. Beanie Babies can be seen hanging from bookshelves, peeking out of backpacks, and sitting on school desks. How did Ty Warner cause such a sensation? He focuses on three critical elements: a very affordable price for a quality product, the deliberate creation of scarcity, and extensive distribution that avoids large retailers.

According to *Forbes*, the empty-shelf strategy drives demand up. Warner believes careful manipulation of stock levels is important. "People are saying this Christmas will be the last, but every time we make a shipment, they want twice as many as we can possibly get to them. . . . As long as kids keep fighting over the products, and retailers are angry at us because they cannot get enough, I think those are good signs." In some parts of the courtry, Beanie Babies are so hard to find that a black market has developed. On several Web sites, critters like Chilly, a white polar bear, trade for $875, and Humphry the Camel goes for $900. In Canada, Maple Bear—a white bear with a Canadian flag on its chest—is popular. Sold only north of the border, this creature is sought in the United States because of its rarity.

The distribution strategy for Beanie Babies includes no licensing deals, no big ad budgets, and no selling to large national discount chains, such as Toys "R" Us and Wal-Mart. Such megastores can sometimes get away with raising the $4.99 price as high as $35. That is why Warner has always sold and shipped directly to thousands of independent gift stores. According to him, "It's better selling 40,000 accounts than it is five accounts. It's more difficult to do, but for the longevity of the company and the profit margins, it's the better of the two." After graduating from Kalamazoo College in 1962, Warner learned to sell through a selective distribution network when he worked for Dakin Incorporated, where he sold stuffed animals to specialty shops.

In addition to carefully selecting outlets, Warner limits the number of Beanie Babies a retailer can order to no more than 36 of each character per month. This maintains a good balance across the product line and a higher perception of value once the product is acquired. Although Beanie Babies are affordable, the restricted distribution presents a challenge in acquiring a full set, or even a particular favorite. By not selling to mass merchandisers, Warner can control demand at the retail level. Even knockoff efforts by discounters such as Wal-Mart (which sells $3.99 "Pebble Pets" made by Imperial Toy Corporation) have not had a significant effect on sales of Beanie Babies. According to Anne Nickels at Ty, Inc., the company is "very aggressive about protecting our copyright, and kids know the difference anyway, they're a lot smarter than marketers give them credit for."

It remains to be seen whether Beanie Babies will have staying power. Russ Berrie, the creator of trolls, sold only to independent gift stores and stayed away from discounters. Then the fad died. According to Berrie, "On April 12, 1993, at 1:42 p.m., every person in the U.S. stopped buying trolls. Ty is doing a terrific job, but he's got a blip up, and at some point that blip is going to have to come down."

Yet Warner's product line strategy keeps extending the life of this unique little toy. About every six months new Beanie Babies are added, while older ones are retired. The old Beanies increase in value as they become scarce, and the new Beanies have investment potential. Like baseball and football cards, Warner's affordable product almost immediately has value beyond the price paid. Terry Dahlberg, a salesperson at Ellie's Hallmark store in Davie, Florida, says customers anticipate the arrival of Beanie Baby orders. "They last two hours here. All hell breaks loose when they come in." Dalberg notes that at one point there was a waiting list of 170 eager purchasers.

Keeping track of all the orders by product configuration and amount is not easy. Recently, the company selected the Design Data Systems (DDS) order entry system. Software designed by Oracle Corporation and a work group at Ty, Inc., enables up to 100,000 orders per day to be processed with outstanding customer service. The system not only allows careful tracking of demand for various Beanies but also helps with supply from the manufacturers overseas. This has provided both effectiveness and efficiency in the marketing system.

People seeking new Beanie Babies can call an 800 number to locate shops that may have the product. No on-line ordering is planned for consumers at this time, but Ty, Inc., is investigating a Web site for retail orders.

A big challenge for Warner is to keep his product fresh and in demand. Certainly, the low price contributes to the toy's popularity. And there was a big boost when McDonald's® gave away a scaled-down version, called Teeny Beanie Babies, in Happy Meals®. For this biggest Happy Meal® giveaway ever, McDonald's® ordered nearly 100 million units from Ty, Inc. Despite the tremendous number, there was a sellout in many regions in the first few days of the promotion, a consumer frenzy not unlike that caused by the original Beanies. The craze may not last, but for now both customers and retailers are in hot pursuit of such animals as Zip the Cat, Lizzy the Lizard, and Web the Spider.

1. *How has Ty Warner used demand and supply to influence the sale of Beanie Babies?*
2. *If Warner had decided to sell Beanie Babies to such large retailers as Toys "R" Us and Wal-Mart, what effect might this have had on price and demand for the toy? Is Warner's distribution strategy effective? Why or why not?*
3. *In this chapter you learned that prices serve several objectives. How has Ty, Inc., fulfilled relationship (customer) objectives?*
4. *Why do you suppose the sale of knockoffs has not adversely affected the success of Ty, Inc.?*

SOURCES: Gary Samuels, "Mystique Marketing," *Forbes*, October 21, 1996, pp. 276–277; Johnny Diaz, "Beanie Babies Popular in Retail and Resale," *Knight-Ridder/Tribune Business News*, April 13, 1997, p. 413B; "Boffo Business in Beanie Babies," *Maclean's*, October 6, 1997, p. 10; Randy Weston, "Beanie Babies Blitz IS," *Computerworld*, April 28, 1997, pp. 1, 2; "Beanie Mania," *People Weekly*, July 1, 1996, p. 84; Linda Kulman, "Move Over, Tickle Me Elmo," *U.S. News and World Report*, April 28, 1997, p. 14; and Cyndee Miller, "Bliss in a Niche: Toymakers Find Success by Breaking with Tradition," *Marketing News*, March 31, 1997, pp. 1, 21.

Pricing Strategy

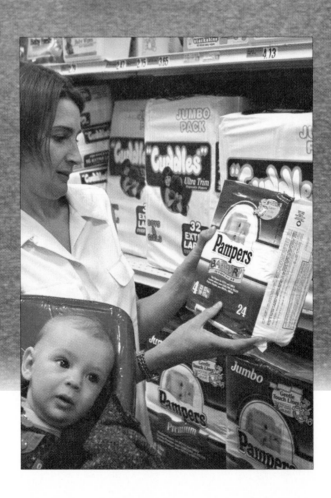

Objectives

1. Understand why an appropriate customer value proposition is a useful guide to pricing strategy.

2. Know what factors to consider when using customer- and competitor-oriented pricing methods.

3. Learn how pricing strategy is implemented by setting prices and communicating them to the market.

PRICING STRATEGIES NEED CONSTANT EVALUATION. PRICE is the easiest part of the marketing mix to change, and nothing has a more immediate effect on profit. Yet a lasting pricing strategy is critical for strong marketing performance. For consumer products, the 1970s and 1980s saw a dramatic increase in the use of promotional pricing, including special sales and coupons. But that strategy created headaches for marketers. Retailers would wait for special prices and then buy huge quantities, creating demand spikes that threw off production schedules. Consumers were confused by prices that sometimes fluctuated weekly.

In 1991, Procter & Gamble, the leading consumer products marketer, boldly went against the grain and changed its pricing system. Moving away from heavy product promotions, P&G instead instituted an everyday low-pricing strategy. Value pricing has allowed the company to eliminate more than 25 different short-term trade promotions. And it has provided more consistency for retailers and consumers. The new strategy also included cost cutting. By reducing the number of brands and sizes, and through better relationships with retailers, P&G has lowered expenses by $3 billion and plans to lop off another $2 billion. The goal is marketing costs at 20 percent or less of sales by 2000, down from 24 percent in 1996.

P&G realized that the redemption rate on coupons had dropped to less than 2 percent (of 300 billion coupons issued), down from 3.5 percent in 1983. Since 1991, P&G has cut its coupon budget in half while reducing prices by about 6 percent. "That equates to $2 billion in list-price reductions," says a spokesperson for the company. In the Boston area, for example, the retail price of Pampers was $10.49 in 1990, but each package had a $1.00 coupon toward the next purchase (in the region, only coupons up to $.99 could be doubled or tripled). Price reductions were first achieved by a subtle drop in content from 26 to 24 diapers. By 1997, the price was $7.99 with no coupons.

P&G continues to scan the environment for better ideas on how to use coupons. In December 1995, it cut couponing in three upstate New York cities—Rochester, Buffalo, and Syracuse—to test the results. At the same time, however, P&G broadened its use of checkout and direct-mail couponing, leading some consultants to think that the New York test is primarily aimed at freestanding inserts in newspapers. In fact, P&G mailed packets valued at about $20 to nearly 70 million homes— further evidence that it isn't out to kill off coupons. The company also expanded couponing in Phoenix and Tucson, Arizona, in August 1996.

Given the success of the everyday low-pricing strategy in the United States, P&G introduced it in Europe in 1996. The company's U.K. sales director urged retailers to support the program, pointing out that "shoppers have a pretty jaundiced view of promotions. Most think they're funded by higher pricing elsewhere. . . . Our research shows that 78 percent of shoppers would rather prices were cut at the expense of special offers."

Initial response by German and British consumers was rather hard to assess due to the immediate reaction from competitors. Supermarket giants Sainsbury's and Tesco slashed prices on in-store brands in an effort to maintain their edge. The P&G price change had brought the gap to less than 4 percent on dishwashing liquid, for example. So the store brands cut back enough to restore the usual 10 percent price difference.[1]

CONNECTED: SURFING THE NET

www.pg.com

If you haven't yet visited the Procter & Gamble Web site, check it out. Learn more about the company's value pricing and new couponing incentives from press releases and other company information.

THE CONCEPT OF PRICE STRATEGY

This chapter could just as well be titled "Delivering Customer Value." Pricing and value are so intertwined that you cannot talk about one without the other. Customers should receive an excellent value for the price they pay, and marketers should earn a satisfactory return. The objective of marketing is not simply to sell a product but to create value for the customer and the seller. Consequently, marketers should price products fairly, to reflect the value produced as well as received. Innovative marketers create value by offering, for example, a better product, faster delivery, better service, easier ordering, and more convenient locations. The greater the value perceived by customers, the more often they demand a company's products, and the higher the price they are willing to pay.

The firm is likely to incur higher costs when producing increased value. For example, it often costs more to make better products, create better distribution systems, or develop service facilities. Gillette can command higher prices because it invests in regular innovations in razor blades. In some cases, companies produce value by reducing their costs relative to those of competitors so that they can pass savings on to the customer in lower prices. That's what P&G did. Wal-Mart became a leading retailer by developing very focused marketing strategies that allowed dramatic cost reductions compared with rivals like Kmart. By passing most of the savings on to customers, Wal-Mart gained considerable competitive advantage.

Whether a company improves its position through innovative products, distribution, communication, or cost cutting, the trick is to find a balance between what customers are willing to pay and the costs associated with the strategy. Essentially, the price charged is what marketers think their product is worth. The price paid is what the customer thinks the product is worth. If both parties have a similar price in mind, there is a strong likelihood that each party will believe it is worthwhile to trade.

It is not easy to establish precisely what price both buyers and sellers agree is fair. We need to look at how customer value is derived, recognizing that people place different values on the products they buy as well as the relationships they have with companies. Several pricing strategies may work. It all depends on how price is perceived, how competitors act, and how a strategy is designed and implemented. This chapter will deal with these issues. First, we will explore using value as the basis for pricing. We will learn how critical it is for relationship marketing. Next, we will discuss the methods used for customer, competitor, and global pricing. Finally, we will see how marketers implement the pricing strategy.

VALUE AS THE BASIS FOR PRICING

Value-based pricing
A strategy that reflects value, not just cost.

To arrive at the proper balance between the needs of the market and the needs of the firm, it is important to understand value-based pricing. **Value-based pricing** recognizes that price reflects value, not simply costs. This is contrasted with cost-based pricing in Figure 18-1. Traditionally, firms assessed the costs of doing business, added a profit, and arrived at the price. Once it was set, the marketer's job was to convince customers that the product was worth it. If the marketer was not successful, then the price was lowered. If demand turned out to be higher than anticipated, then the price was raised. An important point is that the customer was the last person to be considered in this chain of events.

Value-based pricing begins by understanding customers and the competitive marketplace. The first step is to look at the value customers perceive in owning the product and to exam-

Figure 18-1   Value-Based versus Cost-Based Pricing

ine their options for acquiring similar products and brands. In other words, how much is the satisfaction gained from owning the product worth to them compared with what similar items or substitutes cost? Next, the marketer estimates the costs of production and necessary profit. To the extent possible, a similar analysis is usually done for each major competitor. Finally, product, distribution, and promotion decisions can be made. Notice that price is defined before developing the rest of the marketing mix. That way the marketer has a better chance of producing products at a volume competitive with rivals and of earning profits that satisfy the firm's financial objectives.

Many companies now use value-based pricing. General Motors builds most of its cars with a package of extra features that customers usually order, such as antilock brakes and automatic transmission. This makes the base prices slightly higher, but customers perceive there is more value in the purchase.[2] Although cost-based pricing is easier, it ignores the customer and the competition. Marketers know that it is impossible to predict demand or competitors' actions simply by looking at their own costs. Consequently, cost-based pricing is becoming less popular.

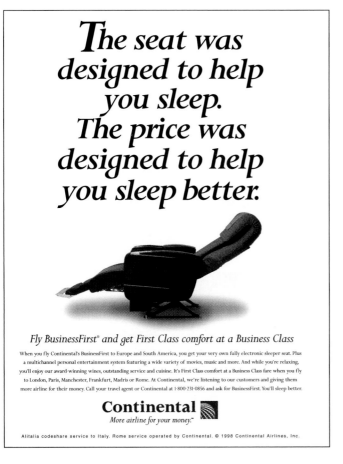

Continental uses value based pricing by offering "more airline for your money."

Even with a good knowledge of customers, competitors, and cost, the future is always uncertain. Therefore, value-based pricing should be seen as an approach or guide for making the judgments involved in pricing decisions. It requires a lot of experience and insight, and there is always an element of chance. With this in mind, we are now ready to examine the many factors that affect value-based pricing.

SOURCES OF VALUE

Value in use

The consumer's subjective estimate of the benefits of a particular product.

Value in exchange

The objective worth of a product in the competitive marketplace.

What is value? Generally there are two sources: value in use and value in exchange. **Value in use** is the customer's subjective estimate of the benefits of a particular product. **Value in exchange** is the product's objective worth in the competitive marketplace. Figure 18-2 describes these two concepts. Value in use is what economists call *utility*. The use value of a product is based on the buyer's needs and his or her understanding of the marketplace at a given time. For example, under normal circumstances a Snickers™ candy bar may sell for 50 cents. But after working several hours in a location where food is unavailable, a person may be willing to pay two or three dollars for it. In this case, the use value is high because of the buyer's circumstances. The exchange value is still 50 cents, the price established by competitive forces in the market.

Although prices are usually based primarily on value in exchange, companies also need to understand and manage buyer perceptions of the value of their products in use. Volvo has captured buyers at relatively high prices for years because of a reputation for durability and safety. The Volvo Saved My Life Club is not an advertising gimmick. On their own initiative, Volvo owners who had survived a wreck wrote to the company about their real-life stories. Volvo then developed a campaign of testimonial print and television ads to promote the safety and reliability of the car and enhance value-in-use perceptions of consumers.[3]

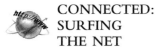

CONNECTED: SURFING THE NET

www.volvo.com

See members of the Volvo Saved My Life Club by visiting the company's Web site. There is also information about vehicle safety, design, and the company itself.

CUSTOMER VALUE IN PRICING

Because prices send powerful messages, it is extremely important that they reflect the customer value the company delivers. Customer value is derived from the product itself, the services surrounding it, the company-customer interaction, and the image the customer associates with the product. First, we will examine the connection between price and customer value. Second, we will find out how market leaders create customer value.

Price and Customer Value Strategies The relationship between price and customer value is illustrated in Figure 18-3. Federal Express, with its reputation for delivery 100 percent of the time by 10:00 A.M the next day, is perceived by many consumers as having a high price and high customer value. The U.S. Postal Service scores low on both dimensions. When FedEx introduced overnight delivery, it charged 25 times more than the USPS. Rather than undercut price, it redefined expectations of high customer value.

Buying market share

A strategy in which prices are set low for the short run to pull buyers away from competing brands.

Two hypothetical price strategies are indicated in Figure 18-3. Would it be practical for any company to use strategy A—high price and low perceived value? Clearly, few buyers would want to purchase from this company; they would give up more in price than they would gain in value. How about strategy B—low price and high value? Buyers would leap at the opportunity, but the company would be pricing at less than buyers are willing to pay. A strategy of this sort is called **buying market share,** that is, setting prices low for the short-run in order

Figure 18-2   Sources of Value

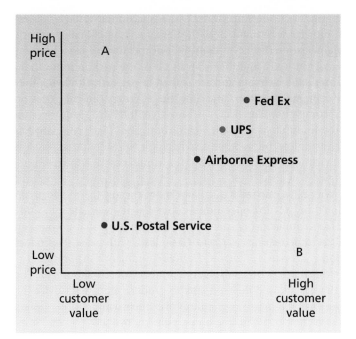

Figure 18-3   Price and Customer Value Strategies

to pull buyers away from competing brands. Japanese automobile producers used this strategy to enter the U.S. market. In the 1980s, the average Japanese import sold for nearly $2,000 below domestic makes and quickly took the lead among price-conscious consumers. By 1990, the Japanese were pricing vehicles up to $2,000 more than the Big Three but continued to sell because they had established an image of better quality.[4]

The strategy selected depends on the company's target market and the number of buyers who desire to purchase at each value/price position. Any price strategy has the potential to produce profit or loss depending on the volumes it obtains and the marketing costs associated with it. FedEx commands the lead in volume and revenues because so many buyers are willing to pay more for its services. UPS and Airborne Express are also successful but use different pricing strategies. In other businesses a high-value/high-price position may not appeal to many buyers. For stereo equipment, sales volumes are highest for low-price/low-value units. Nevertheless, Sony sells high-value/high-price units at a substantial profit.

Customer Value Propositions   *The Discipline of Market Leaders*,[5] a best-seller, shows how product leadership, operational excellence, and customer intimacy are the three ways to deliver customer value. Because different customers buy different kinds of value, it is not necessary to be the best in all these areas. After studying 80 companies, however, the authors conclude that an organization has to be excellent in one area and good enough in the other two to deliver what buyers want. Essentially, the customer value proposition for each of the three areas is (1) customers want the best products (product leadership); (2) customers want the best price (operational excellence); and (3) customers want the best solution (customer intimacy). Figure 18-4 describes how companies gain leadership in customer value by matching their strategy with what buyers want.

CONNECTED: SURFING THE NET

www.usps.gov

How do you rate the U.S. Post Office on customer value? The U.S. Post Office says, "Our goal is to evolve into a premier provider of 21st century postal communications by providing postal products and services of such quality that they will be recognized as the best value in America." Visit its Web site to learn about stamps, change of address, zip codes, postage rates, and services.

Figure 18-4   Leadership in Customer Value

Product Leadership The product leadership strategy builds customer value by differentiating the product. Nike and Intel come to mind. Both the design and functionality of their products are seen as offering high customer value, as does their overall level of customer service. Both companies invest heavily in R&D, and they stay ahead of the pack in innovation. Customers have grown to rely on their leadership and are willing to pay extra, knowing they will benefit from the product's supremacy. At the same time, these leaders can cut prices on old models, keeping even price competitors in check. For example, Intel dropped prices on its revolutionary Pentium Pro by almost 60 percent after its introduction.[6] Each company has very good operations to keep costs in line, but neither is striving for the absolute lowest cost in its field. Both also have good customer relationships, but few would describe them as pursuing customer intimacy strategies.

Operational Excellence Why can Casio sell a calculator more cheaply than Kellogg can sell a box of cornflakes?[7] For one thing, Casio's operational competencies translate into some of the lowest costs imaginable for manufacturing small objects. This means that no one can offer a lower price and sustain the same margins as Casio. Casio leads with price, its product design is adequate, and its customer service is equitable. Digital Equipment Corporation, using a similar strategy, recently slashed prices on its Alpha microprocessors by about half. The operational competence of Alpha has allowed the company to produce chips with twice the speed of Intel's Pentium Pro, yet charge almost no premium over their competition. Alpha's competence has been compared to "pricing a Porsche on par with a Toyota."[8]

Customer Intimacy How does Airborne Express take business away from giants like UPS and Federal Express?[9] Certainly not through product innovation and operations. Yet, Airborne is growing faster than either rival, with revenue increases of 20 percent annually since 1985. It acquired Xerox Corporation as a client with a customer intimacy strategy. By carefully targeting a few accounts and working closely with them to identify and serve their specific needs, Airborne has eliminated services the customers do not really want, thereby saving cost. The company shares the rewards of intimacy by passing some of the savings on to customers. Both parties win.

A variation on this theme can be seen in this chapter's relationships feature, "Banks Coddle Some Customers and Make Others Pay Their Way."

CUSTOMER, COMPETITOR, AND GLOBAL PRICING

Depending on the market context, customer-oriented, competitor-oriented, or global pricing may be used. Each of these approaches involves a different set of considerations, which are discussed in more detail below.

CUSTOMER-ORIENTED PRICING

Marketers who make pricing decisions should keep in mind the effect they will have on consumer behavior. Customers can't purchase everything they want, so they have to determine what will give them the "best value"—or, at least satisfactory value—for the money. But value is relative, not absolute. That is why exact prices are not nearly as important as price differences. Assessing value is difficult because time and energy limit the amount of information we can absorb, because expectations after purchase may not be met, and because price comparisons are hard to calculate. Consumers process information about prices in the ways described in chapter 7. As you know, psychological factors affect their decisions on a variety of issues, and pricing is no different. Among the most important influences on customers are reference prices, price awareness, the association between price and quality, the perception of odd-even prices, and limited offers. Also discussed at the end of this section is target pricing.

Reference price

The amount consumers expect to pay for a product.

Acceptable price range

All prices around the reference price that consumers believe reflect good value.

Reference Prices Consumers try to obtain satisfactory value, not necessarily the best value. They try to determine how much satisfaction will be gained by comparing the benefits and price of one product relative to another. In most situations it is simply not worth the time to make all the calculations necessary to identify the absolute best value. Instead, buyers use reference prices and a price range. The **reference price** is what consumers expect to pay, and the **acceptable price range** is all prices around the reference point that consumers believe reflect good value.

In many airports the price of food so far exceeds consumers' reference points and acceptable range that they are dissatisfied with purchases. The Greater Pittsburgh Airport Au-

CONNECTING THROUGH RELATIONSHIPS

BANKS CODDLE SOME CUSTOMERS AND MAKE OTHERS PAY THEIR WAY

In the world of retail banking, some customers are much more profitable than others, and banks are structuring their fees and services accordingly. First Manhattan Consulting Group in New York calculates that 20 percent of the customer base typically accounts for 200 percent or more of the profits in what the industry calls its retail business. Another 20 percent are marginally profitable, and 60 percent actually cost banks money. Driven by these percentages, bankers are developing strategies they hope will nurture the most profitable relationships and cut back on losers.

Banks usually make money on customers with high balances in either loan or deposit accounts and who are modest users of branch offices. Conversely, individuals with low balances who make frequent transactions at the teller window can be quite costly. Comstock Bank of Reno assigns letter grades to customers based on their profitability. An "A," "B," or "C" on the computer screen lets a teller or customer service rep know instantly how much attention to give a customer. Taking care of the A's at Comstock means personal phone calls from staff when certificates of deposit are close to maturing and going easy on the fees. "If I have a customer with $50,000 on deposit, I don't care what they do on their checking account," says branch administrator Jacqueline Entrekin.

The A's are worth special attention, bankers say, not only because they are very profitable, but also because they are likely to be recognized as such by others and to be tempted away. Dawn Foster, senior vice president of ActionSystems, a Dallas retail consulting firm, says research shows it takes about seven contacts a year—beyond routine teller transactions—to maintain a secure relationship with the best customers. So, astute bankers are sending them financial-advice articles, calling them from time to time, inviting them to seminars, and otherwise keeping in touch.

But what truly separates the A's from the C's are fees. Most banks now charge for transactions when small depositors make more than a certain number of monthly withdrawals from checking or savings accounts. They also charge a customer for making more than a specified number of telephone queries each month. In 1995, First Chicago Bank established self-service checking accounts and levies a $3 fee for most teller-assisted transactions. But it coddles its more profitable customers. Those who keep $2,500 in a checking account or $15,000 in combined deposits get a half percent off installment loan rates, automatic debit, free travelers checks, a free safe-deposit box, free computer banking, and half off on check orders.

Banks like First Chicago and Comstock are not trying to kick unprofitable customers out the door, but most wouldn't lament their loss. Consultants, however, encourage banks to take a middle road. Rather than impose fees on all unprofitable customers, they say, present them with a choice: Pay more or use certain services less. For instance, to encourage technophobes to give up tellers and use ATMs, banks can even give away cash premiums—$20 for every 100th ATM transaction. Instead of waiting in line to see a teller, customers may prefer to look at Andrew Jackson.

Source: Adapted from Bill Stoneman, "Banking on Customers," *American Demographics,* February 1997, pp. 37–41. Reprinted with permission. ©1997 American Demographics, Ithaca, New York.

thority requires concessionaires to use prices consistent with those in "typical" retail settings. The result is a unit volume of sales and a percentage of satisfied customers much higher there than in many other airports. An important point is that consumers respond more to price differences than to absolute prices. A reference price is often used to establish that difference. It represents the basis for judging value. For example, if a brand price is greater than a reference price, then the consumer perceives a loss in purchasing that product. If the brand price is less than the reference price, then the consumer perceives a gain.[10]

Researchers have found that consumers are likely to accept a price range for products and adjust their reference price accordingly. The brands lying outside the range will be rejected, and their prices won't be used in creating the reference price.[11] For example, you are looking for a mountain bike and expect to pay about $500 to $600. You find several bikes similar to what you want with price tags from $375 to $450. Your range shifts to about $400–$500, and your reference price drops to around $425. You also see bikes at $200 and $800 (a midpoint of $500), but those extremes do not figure in your calculations.

The reference price gives consumers an idea about the value they can expect. They can formulate the reference price in several ways:

- The last price paid
- The going price (amount paid most frequently)
- The believed fair price
- The average price
- The price limit (what most buyers will pay)
- The expected future price (price based on trends)[12]

Marketers also look at the differentiation value of their product's attributes to determine whether their brand is seen favorably or unfavorably. The buyer looks at the relative price and relative quality. If consumers tend to evaluate a product as better than others, then it has a positive differentiation value. This means that it may have higher demand or command a price on the upper end of the range. The opposite is true if a brand has a negative differentiation value.

Marketers often help consumers establish reference prices. How many times have you seen ads with the original price (manufacturer's suggested retail or list price) and a sale price? In this way, marketers attempt to create favorable differential price impressions. Other methods are "cents off," "everyday low prices," "new low prices," or promotions such as "1998 models at 1997 prices." Marketers must be careful, however, about price changes. If the frequency, length, and level of price promotions is not carefully managed, consumers' reference prices can be affected. As a result, consumers may lower their reference price.[13]

Price Awareness Business-to-business customers must be very price conscious. Each item they buy contributes to their costs and thus to their profits and competitiveness. Many of them keep extensive records using formalized purchasing systems designed to obtain the best value for the price. Consumers tend to be less aware of actual prices. Studies of grocery shoppers have found that people are inaccurate about the exact price they paid for an item 90 percent of the time, and they err by approximately 20 percent.[14]

Price/Quality Association and Product Categorizations When buyers have little information about a product, they often assume a relationship between its price and its quality. In other words, price is a surrogate for quality. A traveler who doesn't know the local hotels may select a medium-priced unit, expecting an average room, or the highest-priced hotel, expecting luxury accommodations. Ordinarily, the product delivered should be consistent in quality with its price relative to the competition.

Sometimes putting a very low price on a high-quality item may reduce demand by signaling low quality. Nike found that higher prices on many of its signature lines increased sales because consumers perceived that the price tag matched the company's image. Would it make sense to price Michael Jordan signature shoes the lowest? Prices that are inconsistent with perceived value can confuse buyers. Price indicates not only what we expect to give up or pay but also what we expect to gain. If these two are highly inconsistent, we distrust the seller, our own judgment, or both. The Hakeem Olajuwon brand of sneaker is priced at only $35. Hakeem's conscience will not let him endorse a more expensive product: "How can a poor working mother with three boys buy Nikes or Reeboks that cost $120? She can't. So kids steal these shoes from stores and from other kids."[15] The superstar is making a commendable effort, and buyers seem to be perceiving the value. Spalding, marketer of the shoe, reports strong sales.[16]

Marketers refer to the high end of a price range as the *ceiling*. Many companies establish ceiling prices from which reductions can be bargained.[17] In a product line with several levels of quality, there may be several ceiling prices. When consumers make few or no comparisons among brands, companies can charge prices at or near the ceiling. Companies with strong brands also can charge at the upper end. That is why Kodak is likely to price cameras at just under an $80 ceiling (or just under a $100 ceiling). It would be less profitable to charge $74.99 rather than $79.99. The $5 difference can add a lot to revenues but doesn't change the consumer's perception of value.

We know from experiments that price comparisons are made on a ratio rather than an absolute basis. If a Pontiac Firebird has a sticker price of $20,000 and is sold for $1,000 less, then that is seen as roughly a 5 percent discount. The same discount on a Firebird with a

How will the low price of Olajuwon's shoes affect kids' perceptions?

sticker price of $15,000 is seen as slightly larger, approaching 7 percent. Although consumers may not actually compute the percentages, their perception works as if rough calculations were made.[18] Pricing policy must take this into account.

Consider the error made by a discount copying service that didn't understand how prices are perceived. Major copy centers had established copy prices of approximately 4 cents per page. The discount firm offered the same service for 3 cents a page. This attracted a lot of customers and produced a substantial amount of sales. The difference of "approximately 25 percent" was enough to entice many students. When the major centers increased price to 5 cents and then 6 cents, however, the discounter followed with two 1-cent increases. At 6 cents per page, the 1-cent differential was perceived as much smaller—only about 17 percent. The discounter's sales volume declined with each price increase, although the 1-cent absolute differential in price was maintained.

Odd-Even Price Perceptions Prices that end in odd numbers tend to be perceived differently from even-numbered prices. Consumers have learned that discounters tend to use prices ending in a 9, 7, or 5. Before sophisticated computer systems and inventory control systems were available, retailers used these endings as a code: 9 identified a markdown; 7 a second markdown, and 5 a third markdown. Early discounters adopted the odd numbers for all their products to suggest sales prices. Today, odd numbers connote lower quality and price, while even numbers connote higher quality and price.[19] For example, Target and Wal-Mart appeal to the mass market with compact disks for $11.99 and $13.99, indicating a low price.[20]

Limited Offers Limited offers are often used by marketers to encourage consumers to buy types or quantities of products they had not planned to purchase. The special prices are meant to persuade consumers to stock up. Consider for example, the psychology behind a limit on sales. A special promotion for sugar may read "limit 4." Why? A study has found that people are more likely to buy an item that has a limit. This is similar to children who want candy because they are told they cannot have any. Furthermore, shoppers are more likely to buy an item with a limit of four rather than two.[21]

Target Pricing Customer-oriented pricing focuses on buyers' psychological information processing and their perceptions of value in use and value in exchange. **Target pricing,** which uses price to reach a particular market segment, is a very important strategy. It is a way of matching price with the value perceived by each segment. French-made Rosignol skis are carefully marketed to various types of downhill skier. Distinct lines are priced in relation to an individual's level of interest, ability, and income. Rosignol's all-mountain, high-performance Viper X attracts aggressive, experienced skiers who are willing to pay nearly $550. The 7SK, its top-of-the-line slalom race ski, also is priced at more than $500. For recreational skiers, there is the VC3, at a moderate $169, and the 5SM for skiers who like special terrain. Rosignol also created the DV7L series especially for women. As with most forms of customer-oriented pricing, target pricing requires a good understanding about what price communicates to potential buyers.

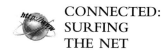

CONNECTED: SURFING THE NET

www.target.com

What other pricing approaches does Target use? Visit its Web site and find out. Check out "Super Target," the "quality discount super center for today's value-minded consumer," and "treatseats"—coupons discounting admission to popular shows, sports, and cultural attractions.

Target pricing
The use of price to reach a particular market segment.

Ditch the Joneses.

LINCOLN

Navigator from Lincoln. What a luxury [ ] should be.

The Loncoln Navigator uses target pricing to reach a market of upper income buyers.

COMPETITOR-ORIENTED PRICING

Competitor-oriented pricing focuses primarily on value in exchange, on the prices set by rivals. Leader-follower, going rate, discount or premium, and competitive bids are all price schemes of this type. Carried to its extreme, competitor-oriented pricing can lead to mutually destructive price wars.

Leader-Follower Pricing Duo-therm announced 10 percent higher prices for furnaces and air conditioners marketed to builders of manufactured housing. This was an invitation to others in this oligopolistic market to follow suit and increase profit for everyone. It was a large hike in an industry noted for being so price competitive that there is little or no profit. After a few days, rivals stuck to the original levels and began to win Duo-therm customers. Duo-therm then dropped prices more than 20 percent—8 percent below its original price—to show that it also could play price wars. This move won back customers and began to take some from competitors. Given the adverse effect on profitability of a prolonged price war, the major competitor then raised prices about 2 percent; Duo-therm then returned to its level before the increase. The competition followed. In the end, prices were 10 percent higher than originally. Duo-therm was the price leader, and other companies became the followers. All of them moved to a position of some profitability as average prices edged upward.

Competitor-oriented pricing often involves scenarios such as this. The leader-follower situation tends to occur in oligopolistic industries whose products have relatively inelastic derived demand. The leader usually has considerable strength—high market share, a loyal customer base, an efficient cost structure, moderate inventory, and a technological edge. Leaders generally can exercise power, as Duo-therm did, but often that is not necessary. The reason is that they create competitive environments which benefit followers by providing fair profits for all. Xircom, Inc., went from a $26 million to a $131 million company in less than four years. It changed its strategy to become the price leader in the market for mobile access services.[22] Good followers can also help create a positive industry pricing climate. In banking, most small and medium-sized institutions copy the products and pricing policies of larger competitors.[23]

Price leaders must show a willingness to defend their position when price becomes an issue. Yet, across-the-board cuts may hurt larger companies more, so it's important to be selective. When America West used price against Northwest's lucrative Minneapolis–Los Angeles route, Northwest did not retaliate in that market. It could hurt America West much more by hitting its Phoenix–New York route. Northwest introduced a limited-time fare, which signaled that it was willing to back off if America West increased its Minneapolis fare.[24]

Going Rate Pricing The **going rate** price evolves over time when no competitor has power over others so all price at a similar level. This is often the case in monopolistic competition

Going rate

The price that evolves over time when no competitor has power over others and all price at a similar level.

when product differentiation is very minor and firms attempt to gain loyalty while pricing at the going rate. For example, lawyers often charge the going rate per hour, which will vary considerably from one community to another. The going rate tends to avoid price wars. Because all providers charge approximately the same, and these prices are broadly communicated, buyers' price expectations are usually met. For example, Hewlett-Packard had to drop prices about 50 percent on Unix workstations to bring them in line with such competitors as Pentium Pro.[25]

Discount or Premium Pricing   Discount or premium pricing positions the company relative to competitors based solely on price. In most markets there are buyers who seek the cheapest products and those who seek the most expensive. Consider the sale of store brand hair coloring at very low prices and L'Oreal at very high prices. L'Oreal says its hair coloring is the most expensive "because I'm worth it." The Meijer food chain establishes the lowest price possible and asks: "Why pay more?"

Competitive Bids   We tend to think of bids as related to the purchasing function, but they also are a prevalent form of competitive pricing. Sealed bids are opened at a certain time, and the low price usually is the winner. An alternative is for buyers to look at bids as they are received and perhaps give feedback to sellers indicating they are too high. This is called open bidding, and it is intended to get suppliers to lower prices.

By understanding competitors, a company can greatly enhance its ability to win contracts at the highest possible price while still being the low bidder. Competitors often scale prices up or down to meet their own volume or cost objectives. By knowing competitors' capacity and cost structure, marketers can adjust their own bids.

Price Wars   **Price wars** occur when price cuts by one company spur similar reductions by competitors. These price-slashing battles can substantially lower profit margins. The consumer benefits, since products can be purchased below their value. The company most successful at cutting costs is usually the victor—if it can survive despite the meager profit margins. Large organizations with ample reserves have an obvious advantage.

As noted earlier, price wars have been especially common in the fast-food industry. Today, these restaurants frequently shave cents off individual items or offer larger portions at a

Price war

A cut by one company spurs similar reductions by competitors, resulting in price-slashing that can lower profit margins.

Autolite Platinum uses premium pricing, claiming it is "worth a little extra."

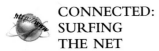

CONNECTED: SURFING THE NET

www.kelloggs.com

"Kellogg's Planet K is the place to find a world of cereal sensations. Start your globe trotting at Cereal City, the capital of crunch. Or pick another Kellogg's destination and get ready for your interactive itinerary." At the Kellogg's Web site you can also find out about the latest pricing strategies by accessing company news releases.

minimal price. In 1997, McDonald's® introduced its biggest discount ever, reducing the $1.90 Big Mac® to 55 cents with the purchase of fries and a drink. Called "Campaign 55®," for the year in which the first McDonald's franchise opened, it rotated the 55 cent price (in participating outlets) to Quarter Pounders®, McRibs®, the Arch Deluxe®, and even the Egg Mc-Muffin®. The aggressive strategy was a response to Burger King's 99-cent Whopper and low breakfast prices, which had been gaining market share.[26]

Some price wars are especially damaging. Recently, Kellogg, Post, and General Mills slashed cereal prices by as much as 20 percent. It is estimated that General Mills reduced earnings by $50 million and revenues by twice that.[27] Kellogg, which has dropped from 42 to 32 percent market share in the last decade, also had big losses. The war cut deeply into profits but had surprisingly little effect on sales volume.[28] It can be advantageous for a company not to participate in a price war. Heinz chose not to enter one recently and suffered no major losses as a result. In fact, share value increased by 2 percent.[29]

Another company that declined a head-to-head pricing battle is Netcom. Its alternative approach is described in this chapter's technology feature, "America Online, Inc.: A Tale of Two Pricing Strategies."

DIVERSITY: PRICING TO ATTRACT SENIOR CITIZENS

How would you like to find a population segment that is growing more rapidly than all others combined and with a median net worth twice the national average? That describes U.S. senior citizens, who average a net worth of more than $73,000. Since 85 percent of them do not work, they have the time to use their significant spending power.[30] A report by the U.S. Bureau of the Census predicts that the 65 and older crowd will double in the next 25 years in Nevada, Arizona, Colorado, Georgia, Alaska, Washington, Utah, and California. It is also estimated that 19 states will have more than one million seniors.[31] By 2030, according to World Bank forecasts, 16 percent of the world population will be 60 or older, and most will have 25 years of retirement.[32] Even Club Med has begun focusing on price-sensitive seniors, offering discounts at 14 resorts. Working with organizations such as the American Association of Retired Persons, Club Med has been very successful in reaching this group with reduced prices.[33]

Marketing experts on the elderly caution companies that all seniors are not the same when it comes to price sensitivity. A study by Roper Starch Worldwide found that one group, called "Free Birds" (median age 69, 13% of the population), are very cost conscious about everyday goods so they can spend lavishly on big-ticket items for themselves.[34] There is a shift in spending that affects pricing for the age categories above and below 68 years. The older seniors "save a lot and spend a little," while the younger group, which has benefited from a long period of economic growth, saves some and spends some.[35]

We have already noted that the graying baby boomers do not all fit the stereotype. They represent 23 percent of the U.S. population, and they control more than three-fourths of its wealth and half its discretionary income.[36] As the senior ranks continue to swell, we will see more use of segmentation and appropriate pricing strategies for this group. Web sites now specifically address highly active, high-income seniors who want to make good use of their disposable income. Some popular sites are SeniorNet, SeniorCom, and Seniors-Site.[37]

GLOBAL PRICING

Global pricing is complicated by many factors. One of the most important is government mandates that imported products cannot be paid for with cash; **countertrade** requires companies from the exporting nation to purchase products of equivalent value from the importing nation. Countertrade affects up to 30 percent of all world trade. When a nation's banking system is poor, countertrade may be the best form of pricing. It also provides government with a mechanism for stimulating exports. For example, it is estimated that 90 percent of Russian transactions for critical imports involve some form of countertrade.[38] In a bizarre deal, Polish coal was exchanged for concerts given by a Swedish band in Poland.[39] In other words, countertrade is a simple barter, the exchange of one good for another.

Although technically the term refers to government-regulated exchanges, countertrade also may be initiated by trading partners. There are many arrangements similar to barter that can benefit both parties. There may be tax advantages to not using cash. Agreements to purchase like values but without exchanging money can increase demand. A countertrade deal that covers an extended period can provide a lot of flexibility in scheduling, manufacturing,

Countertrade
Government mandates that imported products cannot be paid for with cash; instead, the exporting nation is required to purchase products of equivalent value from the importing nation.

CONNECTING THROUGH TECHNOLOGY

AMERICA ONLINE, INC.: A TALE OF TWO PRICING STRATEGIES

In 1996, with eight million people using its private network to chat, exchange e-mail, read news, or access the Internet or Web, America Online was considered a high-tech success. The company boasted more subscribers than any of its rivals, even though it charged higher rates: $9.95 for the first five hours and $2.50 per additional hour. With rates like these, cyber addicts racked up steep AOL bills and were easily lured by companies offering unlimited access for one flat rate. In December 1996, responding to heated competition from low-cost providers, AOL abruptly switched from pay-as-you-go rates to a monthly $19.95 for unlimited access. And its troubles began.

At first glance, the pricing change would seem a great success: AOL had a huge influx of customers, and demand soared. Average daily use per AOL member more than doubled, from 14 minutes a day in September 1996 to 32 minutes in December, when the new pricing kicked in. But more and more customers were listening to AOL's busy signal. The company hadn't anticipated the surge in demand by boosting its technical capacity. Customers felt the growth had come at their own expense and were enraged. Anti-AOL newsgroups proliferated on the Net, with titles like alt.america.online and alt.aol-sucks. The company even became the butt of Jay Leno's jokes. More damaging than bad press was the rash of class-action lawsuits from disgruntled customers. Instead of sending out free AOL software, the company was soon sending out rebates and refunds. It vowed to cut marketing to new customers and promised to spend $350 billion to increase technical capacity with new modems and service centers.

While AOL made a BIG mistake in not anticipating demand, its growing pains are perhaps unavoidable. Players in this very new industry lay out the ground rules as they grow. It's likely that consumers will see several more pricing schemes from AOL and its competitors. Just one month after AOL reluctantly announced its flat-rate pricing, some of its rivals abandoned theirs. One was Netcom On-Line Communication Service, based in San Jose, California. "We decided we could chase the industry and continue to spend more and more to provide lower and lower quality," said Netcom's chairman and chief executive David Garrison. But, he added, that "would be crazy." Instead, the company decided to phase out the "all you can eat" pricing and offer higher quality at higher prices to business users.

Internet watchers think Netcom's move makes sense. According to Andrew Winston, a professor of computer science, business, and economics at the University of Texas at Austin, it's an alternative to spending as much as $100 billion in the next few years to add network capacity. Says Winston: "One way to deal with congestion is to throw more bandwidth at it"—as AOL is currently doing. "But the other is to use a more intelligent pricing scheme that recognizes that there are users who have priority needs—people with businesses to run, financial traders, and others."

Sources: Amy Barrett, "For $19.95 a Month, Unlimited Headaches for AOL," *Business Week,* January 27, 1997, p. 35; Karen Kaplan, "The Cutting Edge: AOL's Growing Pains; How Its High-Tech Success Story Became a High-Profile Red Flag," *Los Angeles Times,* January 27, 1997, p. D1; Peter H. Lewis, "Netcom to Seek Profitable Niche: Internet Access Just for Business," *New York Times,* December 19, 1996, p. D8; and Joan Indiana Rigdon, "Netcom Scraps Flat-Rate Price for the Internet," *Wall Street Journal,* December 19, 1996, p. B11.

and shipping. Japanese and Dutch trading companies may have hundreds of these arrangements going at one time. The Japanese *keiretsu* system relies on cross-ownership, cross-ties in banking, and discrimination against outside buyers and sellers to form huge trading organizations.[40] By locking suppliers into the organization, enormous cost savings result. The major *keiretsu* are Mitsui, Mitsubishi, Sumitomo, Fuyo, Sanwa, and Daiichi.

International pricing also is complicated by the need to transfer funds. Payment is seldom direct, and generally a bank must be involved. This often requires a letter of credit that specifies the bank will pay a seller under various conditions. Because a good deal of time may pass between the settlement of an international deal and the transfer of products and funds, financing is critical. If it is poorly executed, then a lot of money can be lost.

Exchange fluctuations also influence global pricing. Companies that use value-based pricing tend to treat these fluctuations differently from those that use cost-plus pricing. As exchange rates go up and down, profit margins tend to vary. The cost-plus method simply increases or decreases price to keep the same margins, which changes what buyers pay. The value-based method tends to leave prices the same, varying instead the level of profit. Japanese companies exporting to the United States tend to maintain stable prices, reflecting their tendency to keep them in line with the market as well as profit objectives.[41] This works unless exchange rates fluctuate widely. The depreciation of the yen in relation to the dollar has meant that companies such as Nissan, Honda, and Toyota could lower U.S. prices. This has not had great effect on market share, however, because U.S. automakers have, in many cases, competitively reduced prices to maintain share. Many companies benefit in this way when the dollar is strong, but others are hurt. U.S. companies that use imported components from foreign companies have recently had to pay less, and profit has increased. Recently, some Asian currencies have been devalued. This has made U.S. products very expensive there. For example, students from Korea essentially pay much more for education in the United States now than they expected to pay only a year or so ago.

IMPLEMENTING THE PRICING STRATEGY

Once the overall pricing strategy has been chosen, it must be implemented. Since prices are easier to adjust than any other part of the marketing mix, they tend to fluctuate. Even companies with consistent pricing based on customer value make changes. Whether initiating a new strategy or adjusting an existing one, the first step in implementation is to set prices. The second step is to communicate them to the market. At both stages, ethical issues are involved.

SETTING PRICES

Fundamental Strategies for Price Setting
To set price, one of six approaches can be used: skimming, penetration, sliding down the demand curve, the price umbrella, everyday low prices, and promotional pricing. Companies can price high, low, or in between. Whatever the decision, it is sure to affect buyers and competitors. Figure 18-5 describes the fundamental strategies for price setting.

Price skimming

A strategy designed to obtain a very high price from relatively few consumers, who have the resources and desire to buy irrespective of price.

Skimming and Penetration Pricing These two approaches are discussed together because they are opposites. **Price skimming** is designed to obtain a very high price from relatively few consumers with the resources and desire to buy irrespective of price. The name is taken from the practice of dairy farmers, who once skimmed the valuable cream off the top of nonhomogenized milk and discarded the remainder or fed it to farm animals. Today, skimming is used by companies with innovations or fads. Marketers charge a very high price, thereby attracting only a small part of the total market. Because use value is high in a product's introductory period, a premium can be obtained. When more producers enter the market, prices tend to move downward as exchange value declines.

If companies perceive they can obtain a monopoly position for a short time, then they may skim to generate profits that provide investment capital for further innovations. To sustain skimming, companies must offer unusual products of the highest quality or artistic value. Many times this strategy does not produce loyal customers, since subsequent entrants eventually will offer a better value at lower price. In the past, IBM dominated personal computer sales, but as smaller companies entered the market it had to price more competitively.

Penetration pricing

A strategy that seeks the maximum number of buyers by charging low prices.

In contrast to skimming, **penetration pricing** seeks the maximum number of buyers by charging a low price. This approach is used for products that are very price elastic. If costs are sensitive to volume, then these will drop dramatically as share increases relative to competitors. This is a way to keep rivals from entering the market, since many companies avoid situations in which overall prices are extremely low.

The problem with penetration pricing is that losses are likely, especially in the short term. Because profit margins tend to be very small, demand must meet expectations in order to generate enough earnings. Furthermore, when customers buy only because of price, loyalty tends to be low. They are likely to switch to competitors offering an even lower price or innovations of higher value at a higher price.

Figure 18-6 summarizes the main features of skimming and penetration pricing, which are two ends of a spectrum. Because neither is likely to achieve strong buyer loyalty in competitive markets, most companies use pricing approaches that fall somewhere between these extremes.

Slide down the demand curve

Set a high price when a product is introduced and then lower it significantly as competitors enter the market.

Sliding Down the Demand Curve To **slide down the demand curve** means to descend from higher to lower prices. When launching its industrial control products, Texas Instruments has been known to use this strategy. First, management establishes a high price for an innovative product to skim the market. Second, when a major competitor follows with its version, Texas Instruments drops its price—sometimes only slightly, often a considerable

Strategy	Objective	When Typically Used
Skimming	High short-term profit without concern for the long run	No competitive products Innovation or fad Block competitor entry due to patent control, high R&D costs, high fixed costs, control of technology, government regulation, or high promotion costs Uncertain demand and/or cost Short life cycle Price-insensitive buyers
Sliding Down the Demand Curve	Gain short-term profits before competitors become entrenched without sacrificing long-term market share	Launch of high-technology innovations Slight barriers to competitive entry Medium life cycle
Price Umbrella Leadership	Encourage competitors to promote the product category to stimulate purchase of all brands and encourage competitors to follow the price leader	Several comparable competitors Growing market Stable competitors One or a few dominant competitors
Everyday Low Prices or Value Pricing	Appeal to buyers willing to shop for the "greatest" benefits for the money	Component parts in industrial markets Repurchased consumer products Mass merchandisers Established products
Promotional Pricing	Stimulate demand to introduce or reintroduce a product, neutralize a competitor, or move excessive inventory	Demand fluctuates seasonally or for a certain period Marketing "wars" or head-to-head competition Mass merchandisers Fashion items
Penetration Pricing	Stimulate market growth and capture market share; become entrenched to produce long-term profits	Large markets Products of broad appeal Long product life cycle Very price-elastic demand

Figure 18-5 *Fundamental Strategies for Price Setting*

amount. This aggressive strategy discourages or delays market entrants, and Texas Instruments obtains high short-term profit margins without sacrificing its long-term objective of penetrating the market.

The Price Umbrella DuPont is known for its leadership in innovations. It produces innumerable plastics, fibers, and chemicals used to create thousands of products. Because of its strength, the company is in a perfect position to use the **price umbrella;** that is, the leader prices high. Competitors can make fair profits at that level or even lower, especially if their costs are relatively low. Price leadership occurs when one or two companies price in such a

Price umbrella leadership
The leader maintains the price at a high enough level that competitors can earn a profit at that or lower levels.

Figure 18-6 *Skimming versus Penetration Pricing*

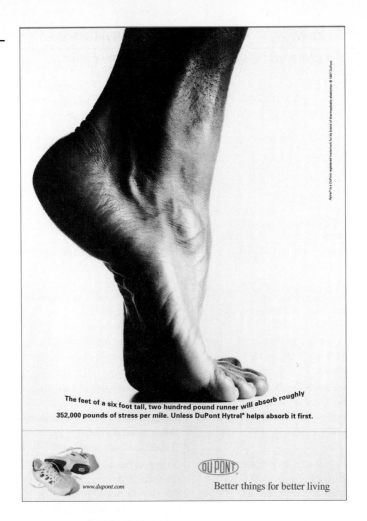

The feet of a six foot tall, two hundred pound runner will absorb roughly 352,000 pounds of stress per mile. Unless DuPont Hytrel® helps absorb it first.

www.dupont.com

DUPONT

Better things for better living

DuPont establishes prices commensurate with the high value it provides.

way that others follow them. In DuPont's case, marketers launch innovations after careful study of the product's likely contributions to customers and society. By assessing the use value relative to substitutes and other brands, DuPont establishes a price commensurate with the high value it typically offers. Along with the product, buyers receive DuPont's uncompromising customer support, which is based on an advanced distribution system, consultative and relationship selling, and service.

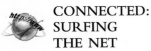

CONNECTED: SURFING THE NET

www.dupont.com

DuPont says: "We're a science and technology based global company of people who make products that make a difference in everyday life." Find out more about its leadership in product innovation by visiting its Web site.

CAREER TIP "DuPont is in a time of exciting changes. We are headed into the next millennium with future-based technologies, with innovative concepts, and with businesses that are very response driven." The company actively recruits for co-op/internships and regular full-time employment. Dan Burger, DuPont's European president, says the company concentrates on two global principles. The first is "to fully engage employees by connecting them more directly to business performance. The second seeks to empower employees by providing them with the tools and working environment they need to manage their development and their careers." Go on-line to find out about DuPont's major recruiting events and which campuses are regularly visited: **www.dupont.com/careers/index.html.**

Generally, DuPont's price is high enough to encourage other healthy companies to participate in the market. At the same time, because several competitors are promoting a similar product, demand is stimulated for the product category. DuPont even licenses its products to rivals in exchange for a percentage of sales revenue. Since these competitors do not have to engage in basic R&D, DuPont's leadership in product innovation is protected.

Everyday Low Prices Wal-Mart is famous for its **everyday low prices,** which on average are consistently lower than those of competitors. Sometimes this strategy is called *value pricing* (not to be confused with value-based pricing). In order for it to work, retailers need to develop extremely efficient (low-cost) operations. Wal-Mart has the most advanced computerized inventory control system imaginable. Rapid turnover (products don't sit on the shelves for long) and aggressive purchasing power provide the basis for keeping prices low. Target and Toys "R" Us also use this strategy—and pledge to meet or beat any competitor's price on any item. In this way, they maximize volume and keep customers from shopping around. Other examples are Dollar General and Family Dollar, which target low- or fixed-income families, a market often neglected. These stores' prices are developed to match the needs and shopping patterns of cash-strapped target customers, who often make frequent trips for a few items.[42] Baby Superstores, a 62-outlet chain, also relies on a consistently low pricing strategy to reach value-conscious parents.[43]

Everyday low pricing can be highly competitive on an international scale as well. For example, Zellers, Canada's low-price leader, used the slogan "lowest price is the law." Its profit margins shrank when Wal-Mart entered the Canadian market, and the two now compete intensely with their value-pricing strategies. The new Zellers slogan is "there's more than low prices," while Wal-Mart continues to implement cuts in order to offer the lowest regular prices to consumers.[44]

Promotional Pricing Companies such as Coca-Cola and PepsiCo, Burger King and McDonald's®, and Toyota and Nissan are nearly always engaged in some form of **promotional pricing**. These battles serve three purposes. First, the price discount is a way to make consumers notice the product. Second, immediate purchase is encouraged because promotional pricing gives consumers the impression that the price is likely to rise in the near future. Third, consumers are kept aware of the entire product category. The "wars" between Coke and Pepsi keep buyers loyal to cola at the expense of other soft drinks. Marketers in these two companies expect continuous challenges from one another as price interacts with other parts of the marketing mix to stimulate demand and produce minor market share shifts.

One kind of promotional pricing is loss leaders, used by retailers to lure consumers into their store. As you'll remember from the previous chapter, these products are priced at or below the retailer's cost. For example, the Meijer chain often prices milk very low compared with competitors. Because this item is purchased regularly by most consumers, its price tends to be remembered. For that reason, milk and similar repeat purchases provide shoppers with a ready source of comparison among rivals. At the same time, shoppers can benefit from the price reduction on most trips. Retailers make up for loss leaders by increased volume or higher prices on other items.

There are many other forms of price promotion. Although we usually assume that price reduction is most likely to stimulate demand, sometimes any message drawing attention to the product, including a price differential, will lead to purchase. Marketing research by a major pharmaceutical company revealed some surprising news. For many years, price promotions had been used to boost sales of selected prescription drugs. Each time the product was promoted at a reduced price by sales representatives, physicians prescribed it more. The assumption was that these products were price elastic for doctors, but the research found that most of them didn't know the price of these drugs and did not much care. Then why the increase in prescriptions? The study found that the price reduction gave salespeople a reason to discuss the product with physicians; drawing their attention to the product was what increased prescriptions. Subsequent research revealed that nearly any relevant sales message led to a rise in sales because, for established and commonly used drugs, many doctors prescribe the brand that first comes to mind—often the one discussed most recently with a sales rep. The point is that price decreases often stimulate sales, but the attention drawn to a product by price promotions also may be a factor.

Product Line Pricing Strategies

Consumers tend to use all products in a company's line as a way of making comparisons. Consequently, marketers use several strategies: product array, bundled, optional product, and captive product pricing.

Product Array Pricing Most companies sell several products. These may be offered within the same brand, such as different Chevy trucks, or in several lines, such as Chevy, Pontiac, and Oldsmobile. Prices need to be established across the entire product array. The difficulty arises because products are often substitutes for one another. Kodak film is sold at dif-

Everyday low prices
Prices that, on average, are consistently lower than those of competitors.

Promotional pricing
A strategy in which price discounts are used to get attention and encourage immediate purchase.

ferent prices depending on the shutter speed used to take pictures. Many speeds will work well enough for most amateur photographers, although a certain speed may be preferred for a certain shot. Many consumers select Kodak film at a premium price over rivals because of its reputation for lasting quality. They then must choose among film type and speed. Pricing often plays a major role in precisely which product is bought, since all the Kodak films are likely to be displayed close together. If price differences cause confusion, then consumers may become dissatisfied. Kodak is careful to price each product so that the differences help the photographer select differing value—what is best for action photos, landscapes, or flash shots. The various price points offer value for nearly every photographer. If one average price were used for all Kodak film, then competitors would quickly take share with dramatically lower prices.

Bundled Pricing   Products can be bundled or unbundled for pricing purposes. The bundled approach, which gives a single price for the entire offering, is used for standardized products, while unbundling is often used for customized products. For example, home builders use each method depending on the offering. Houses in a subdivision usually are priced to include carpeting, fixtures, and landscaping, whereas various items will be listed separately for custom homes. Even property and land preparation cost will be specified. The unbundling helps custom buyers assess the value to them of each item and make choices according to tastes and budgets. Packard Bell uses both approaches for its Platinum 2240, a Pentium machine with MMX technology. Among other features, it has a CD-ROM drive, a video accelerator, a sound card, stereo speakers, a fax-modem, and microphone. For some models these are bundled into one price offering; on other models they can be added depending on the customer's needs.[45]

Optional Product Pricing   Many products are sold as a base unit with optional add-ons. Cars are an obvious example. GM's new Corvette has a sticker price of about $38,000, but options may raise it as much as $5,000.[46] Add-ons for automobiles include CD players, sunroofs, and remote keys. Companies often price the base product low as a platform for selling other items. The telephone company does this. When you sign up for service, you also can buy caller ID and call waiting.

Captive Product Pricing   It is pretty obvious why Gillette prices its razors low. Once you own one, you will buy blades—perhaps for years. In a sense, you're a captive customer, but since razors and blades are not very expensive, the cost to escape is minor. But how about the cost of moving from Nintendo to Sony video games? You will need to purchase a new system (at approximately $200), and your current games no longer will be useful. New ones cost up to $70. Despite price cuts in the video game industry, you may not be able to afford switching from your Nintendo system.[47] The captive product strategy is used by many marketers. Internet access cellular phone companies price with a variation on the captive theme. They have an installment fee, then a fixed rate plus a variable usage charge. Often the fixed rate is set very low in order to obtain the more profitable usage fees.

COMMUNICATING PRICE

The second step in price implementation is to communicate with the market. This involves more than just advertising a figure. The price may have several components that are quoted in differing ways, and various kinds of price reductions can be offered.

Price Components   Let's say that Joan Martin purchased Rosignol skis, poles, and boots at the California Ski Company outlet. The package cost $800, and the total including tax was $848. Her roommate purchased the same package at a Winter Sports Equipment store for $800, but the total including tax was $893. She was charged $30 extra for binding installation and $15 for tuning the skis. Whether the buyer or seller pays for "extras" can make a substantial difference in price.

In consumer markets, there is wide variation in what is included in the price. Foot Locker will return your money if a shoe does not meet your expectations. If the support breaks down before you think it should, then you can take the shoes back for a refund or a new pair, no questions asked. While the Foot Locker price may be similar to that of other retailers, others may not provide the same level of customer service. Foot Locker's return policy is added value. The most common additions to price are these:

- Finance charges
- Installation fees

- Warranty charges
- 800-number assistance
- Replacement parts inventory
- Shipping and handling
- Training

It is important to communicate clearly the components that are included within a price quotation. If buyers are hit with unexpected charges for items they thought were included within the original price, dissatisfaction is likely. This is because many consumers believe this is unethical behavior on the part of the seller.

Price Quoting Price quoting is how prices are communicated to buyers. Some companies offer price quoting services. For example, many large insurance firms use InsWeb, an on-line comparative shopping service. In addition, some firms offer interactive quoting and comparison systems so consumers can feel confident they are getting a fair and reliable price.[48] Sometimes prices are stated clearly and directly, but often an indirect method is used. The **list price** (or suggested retail price) set by the manufacturer usually provides the reference point by which consumers judge the fairness of the market price. The **market price** is the actual amount buyers must pay for the product. Often the list price is much higher than the market price. For example, when Sony introduced the CD-R, a compact disk recorder, the list price was a shocking $28,000, but the market price today is much lower.[49] WebTV networks, another Sony product, were launched at a list price of approximately $330, which quickly dropped to a market price below $300.[50] The market price is likely to result from several types of reductions, including discounts and rebates.

Price Reductions Discounts are often given for cash payment, for purchasing large quantities, or for loyalty. Cash discounts are offered to consumers, business-to-business customers, and nearly all channel members. Many buyers look at the undiscounted price as a penalty for delayed payment. Discounts are incentives to speed cash flow from buyer to seller, and they are standard in many industries. It is common for cash discounts to be quoted in terms of a percentage reduction and a specific time for payment, most often 2/10, net 30. This says the buyer has a 2 percent discount if paid in 10 days, and full payment without a discount is due in 30 days. Many buyers pay within the first 10 days because a 2 percent discount figured over the remaining 20 days is equivalent to an interest rate of about 36 percent on an annual basis. Sellers use the discounts to speed payment and reduce losses due to bad debts. Many industries have increased their prices by nearly 2 percent to offset these cash discounts.

Quantity discounts, which are reductions for large purchases, are justified because the seller has lower costs when handling larger orders. That is, selling, order processing, billing, shipping, and inventory carrying costs are averaged over a greater volume. It is common for a supplier to use quantity discounts to entice buyers to purchase more and to achieve economies of scale for transportation and processing costs.[51] These can be offered at one time or on a cumulative basis. Corel Corporation, which offers Corel Office for NT at $1,995 per server, drops the unit price to $1,200 when 25 or more are purchased.[52] Another example is mutual funds, which often charge differing commissions, or "loads," depending on the amount purchased. One popular fund charges 4.25 percent for orders less than $50,000, 3.5 percent for $50,000 to $100,000, and 2.5 percent for more than $100,000. The buyer has up to one year to meet the commitment.

Patronage discounts are very similar to cumulative quantity discounts and they reward buyer loyalty. An example is a café that stamps a card for each cup of coffee bought and then gives a free cup when the card is full. Another variation is Sam's Club, a no-frills retail buying center developed by Wal-Mart, which offers discounts only to fee-paying members. Discounts should not be used, however, as the sole means for achieving customer loyalty. One study shows that in a three-year period, 60 percent of all discounted purchases were made by just 15 percent of consumers. Little market share is gained by discounts.[53]

Rebates reduce prices through direct payments, usually from the manufacturer to the consumer. Chrysler popularized this tactic in the 1980s, and now it has become difficult for the company to sell some cars without this incentive. In today's competitive car market, rebates are still a popular way to move cars off the lot.[54] As we noted in chapter 15, rebates may have a greater psychological effect on customers than discounts. The buyer perceives a rebate as a large amount of money. In contrast, the discount is seen as a small percentage of the total price. Remember, price differentials make the most impression on buyers. With rebates

List price
The price set by the manufacturer, and used by consumers as a reference point. Also called suggested retail price.

Market price
The actual price buyers must pay for a product.

manufacturers also are more assured that the rebates will not be partially absorbed by dealers. Sometimes, when discounts are given to dealers with the idea that they be passed along to consumers, part of the difference is kept by the dealer.

UNETHICAL PRICING PRACTICES

When marketers develop a pricing strategy, it should reflect the value perceived and received. This does not always happen. Abuses can occur through manipulation of the consumers reference price, quoting overcharged or misleading prices, or using discriminatory pricing practices. Unethical pricing can have legal repercussions, not to mention the risk of losing valuable customers.

As mentioned earlier, the reference price serves as a guideline to consumers. What happens when marketers manipulate that price in order to change the consumer's perception of what is "fair"? Three studies have addressed this issue.[55] When a reference price is set at an implausibly high level, it can influence perceptions about a fair price as well as the highest price. Therefore, it is important for marketers to establish reference prices with care.

Another unethical practice is to quote unclear or misleading prices, which can have serious legal consequences. For example, a $27.5 million lawsuit was brought against several TCI cable companies for quoting prices higher than published or approved rates. Some were charging double for certain services.[56] TCI also allegedly quoted installation prices for unwired homes to consumers with homes already wired, in addition to misrepresenting the costs for reconnection.[57] And consider the number of consumers who were unhappy when America Online automatically switched subscribers to the $19.95 flat rate option. The assistant at-

---

CONNECTED: SURFING THE NET

America Online

www.aol.com

THIS CHAPTER'S TECHNOLOGY FEATURE DISCUSSED AMERICA Online in "America Online, Inc.: A Tale of Two Pricing Strategies." In order to learn more about pricing changes and strategies, visit AOL's web site and answer the following questions.

1. What are the various pricing options AOL offers "to fit your lifestyle"? How does this pricing strategy recognize the varying needs of customers?
2. Under "Only on AOL" read the section on value. How does the company use value-based pricing to appeal to consumers?
3. How might consumer factors affect AOL's pricing strategy?
4. Imagine that AOL enters a price war with a major competitor. How may it affect the company, and who may ultimately benefit?

Bank of America

www.bankamerica.com

THIS CHAPTER'S RELATIONSHIPS FEATURE, "BANKS CODDLE Some Customers and Make Others Pay Their Way," discussed the structure of many bank fees and services. To expand your thinking about pricing strategy, visit the Web site of Bank of America and answer the following questions.

1. What features do you notice that help Bank of America connect with customers? Next, read "Corporate Banking." What is the company's relationship team, and what does it do?
2. How does the bank use limited offers to encourage customers to buy its products/services?
3. Which price-setting strategy or combination of strategies do you think would be most appropriate for Bank of America? Explain.
4. What is Bank of America's customer value proposition? Do you think its customers want the best price, best products, or best total solution? Explain.

torney general of Illinois wrote: "It is unfair and deceptive to substitute one level of service for another level of service at an increased price without obtaining the consent of the subscriber." In response, AOL refunded the money or gave credit to consumers who did not wish to be on the plan.[58]

Discriminatory pricing practices are often very controversial. Is it fair to charge a woman more than a man for dry-cleaning a shirt or for a haircut? This depends on a number of circumstances. Are the shirts similar, or is the service more difficult to perform for one gender versus another? Since most women have longer hair than men, perhaps it is more difficult or time consuming to cut. Nevertheless, studies have found that women do pay more than men for products ranging from haircuts to cars.[59] In 1995, with the Gender Tax Repeal Act, California became the first state to prohibit gender discrimination in pricing for similar services.[60] Even so, a number of California businesses continue to use different prices. A dry cleaner in South Bay charges a man $1.30 to launder a cotton shirt, while a woman pays $3.50 for a similar shirt.[61] Violators believe there is little likelihood they will be taken to court.

CHAPTER SUMMARY

OBJECTIVE 1: Understand why an appropriate customer value proposition is a useful guide to pricing strategy.

Pricing strategies are complex and must balance the needs of both the customer and the firm. Value-based pricing, which includes the concepts of value in use and value in exchange, is increasingly popular. Since customers seek differing types of value and competitors have a broad range of choices in how to price, other strategies are viable as well. In devising a pricing strategy, it is important to identify a customer value proposition that matches the capabilities of the organization. The three types of capabilities are product leadership, operational competence, and customer intimacy.

OBJECTIVE 2: Know what factors to consider when using customer- and competitor-oriented pricing methods.

Pricing strategies may focus on customers, competitors, or global factors. Customer-oriented pricing requires an understanding of reference prices, price awareness, price/quality association, odd-even perceptions, limited offers, and target pricing. Competi-

tor-oriented pricing considers leader-follower scenarios, going rates, discounting, and competitive bids. Some companies engage in price wars that can seriously affect industry and company profits. On a global scale, pricing may include countertrading or barter. Funds transfer and exchange rates also affect international pricing.

OBJECTIVE 3: Learn how pricing strategy is implemented by setting prices and communicating them to the market.

Implementing a price strategy requires setting and communicating prices. One of six fundamental approaches can be used to set prices: skimming, sliding down the demand curve, price umbrella, everyday low prices, promotional pricing, and penetration pricing. Product line pricing complicates matters. Options are product array, bundled, optional product, and captive product pricing. When prices are communicated, various components may be specified or only the overall price, and various reductions may be offered. Price communication must be done carefully to avoid unethical practices, such as false impressions about price or unfair discrimination.

REVIEW YOUR UNDERSTANDING

1. What is value-based pricing? How does it differ from cost-based pricing?
2. What is value in use? Value in exchange?
3. What three leader strategies match what buyers want?
4. What are reference prices? Give several categories.
5. What is a ceiling price, and how is it used in setting prices?
6. How are odd and even prices perceived?
7. When is going rate pricing used?
8. How is pricing used to attract senior citizens?
9. What are skimming and penetration pricing?
10. What is umbrella pricing?
11. List three aspects of product line pricing.
12. How are prices quoted?
13. What is discriminatory pricing?

DISCUSSION OF CONCEPTS

1. How are price and value related? What are the advantages of value-based pricing over the traditional cost-based approach?
2. What is the difference between value in use and value in exchange? How could a marketer use these concepts to improve profitability?
3. What is required if a company wants to use product leader-

ship, operational competence, or customer intimacy as the basis for establishing a customer value proposition? Give examples of each.
4. How does competition affect a company's prices? Briefly describe the major competitor-based pricing approaches.
5. We know that several factors influence consumer responses to

prices. What psychological factors should marketers keep in mind when using consumer-oriented pricing? Describe each.

6. How is a company's market position related to price leadership? What does this have to do with price wars?

7. Describe the six fundamental ways to set price. In what situations is each strategy typically used?

8. How does the communication of price present ethical dilemmas? Give examples of several questionable practices.

KEY TERMS AND DEFINITIONS

Acceptable price range: All prices around the reference price that consumers believe reflect good value.

Buying market share: A strategy in which prices are set low for the short run to pull buyers away from competing brands.

Countertrade: Government mandates that imported products cannot be paid for with cash; instead, companies from the exporting nation are required to purchase products of equivalent value from the importing nation.

Everyday low prices: Prices that, on average, are consistently lower than those of competitors.

Going rate: The price that evolves over time when no competitor has power over others and all price at a similar level.

List price: The price set by the manufacturer and used by consumers as a reference point. Also called suggested retail price.

Market price: The actual price buyers must pay for a product.

Penetration pricing: A strategy that seeks the maximum number of buyers by charging low prices.

Price skimming: A strategy to obtain a very high price from relatively few consumers, who have the resources and desire to buy irrespective of price.

Price umbrella: The leader maintains the price at a high enough level that competitors can earn a profit at that or lower levels.

Price war: A cut by one company spurs similar reductions by competitors, resulting in price slashing that can lower profit margins.

Promotional pricing: A strategy in which price discounts are used to get attention and encourage immediate purchase.

Reference price: The amount consumers expect to pay for a product.

Slide down the demand curve: Set a high price when a product is introduced and then lower it significantly as competitors enter the market.

Target pricing: The use of price to reach a particular market segment.

Value-based pricing: A strategy that reflects value, not just cost.

Value in exchange: The objective worth of a product in the competitive marketplace.

Value in use: The consumer's subjective estimate of the benefits of a particular product.

REFERENCES

1. Associated Press, "P&G: We're Committed to Cutting Coupons," *Marketing News,* January 6, 1997, p. 10; Jeff Neff and Pat Sloan, "P&G, No. 1 Again, Aims to Reinvent Marketing," *Advertising Age,* September 30, 1996, pp. 1, 20, 21, 24; Claire Murphy, "P&G Call for Low Prices Strategy," *Marketing,* September 26, 1996, p. 2; Judy Quinn, "Will P&G Test Mean Curtains for Coupons?" *Incentive,* April 1996, p. 7; Sean Brierley, "Supermarkets Defy P&G as Price War Breaks Out," *Marketing Week,* March 1, 1996, p. 9; and Ryan Matthews, "A Farewell to Coupons?" *Progressive Grocer,* March 1996, pp. 71–72.

2. Rebecca Blumenstein and Andrea Puchalsky, "GM's Midsize Cars Are Priced to Vie with Honda and Ford," *Wall Street Journal Interactive Edition,* November 11, 1996.

3. Lindsay Chappell, "Volvo, Saturn Cultivate Their Cult Following," *Auto News,* March 28, 1994, p. 12.

4. Alexander Hiam and Charles D. Schewe, *The Portable MBA* (New York: John Wiley & Sons, 1992), pp. 298–299.

5. Michael Treacy and Fred Wiersema, *The Discipline of Market Leaders* (Reading, MA: Addison-Wesley, 1995).

6. Ken Yamada, "Intel Road Map Loaded with Chip Price Reductions," *Computer Reseller News,* August 12, 1996, pp. 1, 242.

7. Ibid., p. 3.

8. Paul C. Judge, "Digital's Struggle to Save Its Alpha Chip," *Business Week,* December 30, 1996, p. 44.

9. Ibid., pp. 146–161.

10. Praveen Kopalle, Ambar G. Rao, and L. Joao Assoncao, "Asymmetric Reference Price Effects and Dynamic Pricing Policies," *Marketing Science,* 15, no 1 (1996): 60–85.

11. Joel E. Urbany, William O. Bearden, and Dan C. Weilbaker, "The Effects of Plausible and Exaggerated Reference Prices on Consumer Perceptions and Price Search," *Journal of Consumer Research* 15 (June 1988): 95–110.

12. See Michael H. Morris and Gene Morris, *Market Oriented Pricing* (Lincolnwood, IL: NTC Business Books, 1990), pp. 5–8.

13. "Consumers' Reference Prices: Implications for Managers," *Stores* 78 (April 1996): RR4.

14. Joel E. Urbany and Peter R. Dickson, *Consumer Knowledge of Normal Prices:*

An Exploratory Study & Framework (Cambridge, MA: Marketing Science Institute, 1990), pp. 7–8.

15. Brad Darrach, "A Different Kind of Superstar," *Life,* December 1995, pp. 92–93.

16. Mark Tedeschi, "Extreme Interest," *Sporting Goods Business,* February 10, 1997, p. 96.

17. Yongmin Chen and Robert W. Rosenthal, "On the Use of Ceiling Price Commitments by Monopolies," *Rand Journal of Economics* 27 (Summer 1996): 207–220.

18. Gilbert D. Harrell, *Consumer Behavior* (New York: Harcourt Brace Jovanovich, 1986), p. 68.

19. Checkmate Collection advertisement, *New Yorker,* April 4, 1988 and a J. C. Penney insert in September 1995 Newspaper Advertising Supplement, J. C. Penney Company Inc., NP08 W35 LDS Fall Wardrobe 266835.

20. Pete Hisey, "For Discounter in 1995, Growth Was 'Home' Grown," *Discount Store News,* August 5, 1996, pp. 45–46.

21. Vince Staten, "Can You Trust a Tomato in January?" *Library Journal,* July 1993, p. 179.

22. John T. Mulqueen, "Back on Track with Mobile Devices," *Communications Week,* September 23, 1996, pp. 73–74.

23. Robert Brooks and Darin White, "Don't Copy the Competition, Lead with New Markets," *Bank Marketing* 28 (May 1996): 13–17.

24. "Fair Game: Airlines May Be Using a Price-Data Network to Lessen Competition," *Wall Street Journal,* June 28, 1990, p. 1.

25. Kelley Damore, "HP Expands Midrange, Cuts Prices," *Computer Reseller News,* September 30, 1996, p. 10.

26. Richard Gibson, "Breakfast Takes Biggest Hit as Sales Slow across the Globe," *Wall Street Journal Interactive Edition,* February 26, 1997.

27. Judann Pollack, "Cereals to Pare Ad Plans," *Advertising Age,* June 24, 1996, http://www.adage.com.

28. Richard Gibson, "Kellogg Vows to Boost Market Share, but No Plan Is Unveiled," *Wall Street Journal Interactive Edition,* November 11, 1996.

29. "Heinz Meanz Business," *Marketing,* November 21, 1996, p. 25.

30. Robert F. Fletcher, "Marketing the Experience," *Executive Speeches,* April-May 1996, p. 1–4.

31. "Census Bureau Expects Elderly Population to Double in Eight States by 2020," *Health Care Strategic Management,* 1996, p. 9.

32. Marshall Carter, "The Coming Global Pension Crisis," *Foreign Affairs* 73 (November-December 1996): S1–16.

33. Cyndee Miller, "Boomers Come of Old Age," *Marketing News,* January 15, 1996, pp. 1, 6.

34. Ibid. p. 6.

35. Faye Rice, "Come of Age," *Fortune,* June 26, 1995, pp. 110–112 and 114.

36. Marjorie Coeyman, "Gray Matters," *Restaraunt Business,* November 20, 1996, pp. 42–50.

37. Peter Krasilovsky, "Lost in Space," *American Demographics* (Marketing Tools Supplement), October 1996, pp. 20–23.

38. Ann Ring, "Countertrade Business Opportunities in Russia," *Business America* 11 (January 1993): 15–16.

39. Sak Onkvisit and John J. Shaw, *International Marketing* (Upper Saddle River, NJ: Prentice Hall, 1997), p. 637.

40. Genay Hesna, "Japan's Corporate Groups," *Economic Perspectives* 15 (January-February 1991): 20–30.

41. Onkvisit and Shaw, *International Marketing,* p. 614.

42. Teresa Andreoli, "Value Retailers Take the Low Income Road to New Heights," *Discount Store News,* February 19, 1996, pp. 1, 19ff.

43. Duke Ratliff, "Baby Superstore Grows Up," *Discount Merchandiser* 36 (February 1996): 22–25.

44. Jim Fox, "Zellers Shifts Pricing Strategy," *Discount Store News,* October 21, 1996, pp. 3, 93.

45. Larry Blasko, "Packard Bell Brings High Performance without the High Price," *USA Today,* February 17, 1997, web.usatoday.com.

46. Kathleen Kerwin, "Not Your Father's Corvette," *Business Week,* December 23, 1996, p. 44.

47. Prices taken from Associated Press, "Sony Slashes Price of PlayStation System," *USA Today,* March 3, 1997, http://web.usatoday.com.

48. Mary Brandel, "Is the World Ready for Web Quotes?" *Computerworld,* April 29, 1996, p. 12.

49. Robert A. Starrett, "First and Second Generation Recorders: Less Choice, Less Confusion," *CD-ROM Professional* 9 (September 1996): 62, 64.

50. Stephen H. Wildstrom, "A Web Surfing Box for Peanuts," *Business Week,* September 16, 1996, p. 22.

51. W. C. Benton and Seungwook Park, "A Classification of Literature on Determining the Lot Size under Quantity Discounts," *European Journal of Operational Research,* July 19, 1996, pp. 219–238.

52. "Corel Office for NT Pricing Is Set," *Informationweek,* November 18, 1996, p. 32.

53. "Discounting Does Not Work," *Grocer,* July 27, 1996, p. 13.

54. Andrew Osterland, "Thanks, Lee," *Financial World,* December 16, 1996, pp. 34–35.

55. Tracy A. Suter and Scot Burton, "Believability and Consumer Perceptions of Implausible Reference Prices in Retail Advertisements," *Psychology and Marketing* 13 (January 1996): 37–54.

56. Price Coleman, "California Sues TCI," *Broadcasting and Cable,* May 27, 1996, p. 12.

57. Michael Katz, "TCI Accused of Customer Fraud," *Broadcasting and Cable,* May 13, 1996, pp. 50–51.

58. "America Online Plan to Change Pricing Draws Some Complaints," *Wall Street Journal Interactive Edition,* November 21, 1996.

59. Gerry Myers, "Why Women Pay More," *American Demographics* 18 (April 1996): 40–41.

60. "Civil Rights—Gender Discrimination," *Harvard Law Review* 109 (May 1996): 1839–1844.

61. Kim Boatman, "Cleaners Skirting California Unisex Pricing Law," *San Jose Mercury News,* January 14, 1996, www.sjmercury.com/news/local/sex/w1/4.htm.

CASE 18

HARLEY-DAVIDSON

*I*N 1903, THE FIRST HARLEY-DAVIDSON was sold—a single-cylinder, belt-driven two-wheeler. It was ridden for 100,000 miles by four owners without replacement of a single major component. The company still enjoys the reputation of producing outstanding, high-quality, high-value motorcycles. In the early days there were 151 motorcycle manufacturers, but only Harley-Davidson and Indian came through the Great Depression, and by 1953 Harley was the sole survivor. Today, it sells more than 130,000 machines annually and controls about 56 percent of the heavyweight bike market in the United States.

Much of the value of a Harley resides in its tradition—the look, sound, and heritage that have made it an All-American symbol. Customers include people like the CEO of Southwest Airlines, the head of AT&T, and *Tonight Show* host Jay Leno. The Harley V-twin engine designed in 1909 still turns heads across America with its throaty rumble, and the bikes are easily recognized by their teardrop gas tank and oversized instruments. According to Jeffrey Bleustein, a CEO and a Harley owner, the bikes "represent something very basic—a desire for freedom, adventure, and individualism."

Harley-Davidson CEO Richard Teerlink foresees continued growth. He believes that the Harley buyer is getting older, more affluent, and much better educated. The company is no longer dependent on the Hell's Angels crowd, and it has an audience that can really afford the higher-priced products. "There's a high degree of emotion that drives our success," says Teerlink. "We symbolize the feeling of freedom and independence that people really want in this stressful world."

Harley's are expensive compared to other brands, ranging from a Sportster at about $8,000 to the Electra Glide Ultra at $22,500. Furthermore, used bikes may cost far more than their original selling price. For example, a limited-edition model purchased new for $14,000 recently sold for more than $22,000. How is it possible to command such premium prices for a product that is slower and less fuel efficient than many of the performance bikes from Europe and Asia? Clearly, the competition has technological superiority.

Even if you were willing to pay $22,000 for a top-of-the-line Harley, until recently you would likely have to wait more than a year for delivery. Nevertheless, the bikes are so popular that the company plans to increase production to 200,000 by 2003, its 100th anniversary. Despite the fact that rivals like Yamaha have started creating look-alikes, Harley enjoys brand recognition and loyalty experienced by few other products.

With supply finally catching up to demand, Harley may have some interesting marketing challenges, particularly in the area of pricing. *Forbes* asks, "Is Hog Going Soft?" Although Harley's share of its class of bikes is well over 50 percent, five years ago it exceeded 70 percent. Industry consultant Donald Brown believes the company's lead is fading fast. Two years ago, dealers could obtain premium prices for bikes they did not yet have. Now that the machines are immediately available, prices are negotiable. Dealers now have plenty of new and used bikes in stock, including some of the models traditionally hard to find. The amount of stock may mean demand has been satisfied, and may present problems for future pricing. Scarcity makes buyers want Harleys more.

The price competition is also getting tougher. For example, Honda's American Classic lists for under $10,000, while Harley's similar Dyna Low Rider starts at about $13,500, a 40 percent premium. And Yamaha has made technical improvements, such as an easy-to-maintain shaft instead of a belt drive. Does that matter to bikers who wear T-shirts that say "I'd rather push a Harley than drive a Honda"? Sales of lower-priced models, such as Harley's Sportster, which enters the market at around $8,000 have declined more than 19 percent due to inroads by Suzuki's Intruder, Kawasaki's Falcon, and Honda's American Classic, which sell between $6,500 and $11,000. According to Gil Steward, sales manager of Harleys R Us, "Bikes are still selling, but the price is coming down." That means reduced profit margins.

One Harley distributor, Custom Cycle Works in Nashville, Tennessee, rents bikes to experienced riders who want the luxury of a Harley. The appeal, says Custom Cycle general manager Peggy Bowling, is that "people who ride Harleys have learned to enjoy life. I saw a T-shirt the other day that said 'If I have to explain it, you won't understand it.' That sums it up perfectly."

To compound matters for Harley retailers, most have complied with Harley-Davidson's request to upgrade their showrooms. This includes better location and decor as well as increased size to accommodate inventory in Harley accessories, clothing, and other items. So with margins shrinking at retail, dealers may be challenged to maintain their profitability. Pat Moroney, in Newburg, New York, says his store may have to increase volume: "By 2000, I may have to open an additional store to make the profit on 500 bikes that I now make on 300."

Today, Harley's overseas business is 30 percent of its annual total. Europeans like cruiser bikes but not Harley prices. In fact, some Hogs have recently been shipped back from Europe due to lack of demand. Harley may change its foreign product line in order to offer more affordable prices. But, says Teerlink, "any softening of demand doesn't appear to be a problem because Harley will simply cut back from producing so much."

1. *Describe the Harley-Davidson pricing strategy. What does the company's positioning have to do with its pricing strategy?*
2. *How does the fact that Harley has a relatively deep line of heavy bikes influence the pricing of each product within the line?*
3. *Create the customer value proposition that would allow Harley-Davidson to continue using a premium pricing strategy.*
4. *Should Harley alter its price, given strong price pressures from rivals? If not, what strategy should it pursue in light of industry developments?*

SOURCES: www.harley-davidson.com; Gary Strauss, "Harley Working to Stay Leader of the Pack," *USA Today,* November 5, 1997, www.usatoday.com; "Harley Davidson Plans Marketing Tactics after Indiana Headquarters Opening," *Knight-Ridder/Tribune Business News,* November 12, 1996, pp. 11–12B; Gina Fann, "Nashville, Tenn., Cycle Shop Finds a Niche Renting Harley-Davidson Bikes," *Knight-Ridder/Tribune Business News,* April 25, 1997, p. 42B; Dyan Machan, "Is Hog Going Soft?" *Forbes,* March 10, 1997, www.forbes.com; Gary Hamel, "Killer Strategies That Make Shareholders Rich," *Fortune,* June 23, 1997, www.fortune.com; and Ronald B. Lieber, "Selling the Sizzle," *Fortune,* June 23, 1997, www.fortune.com.

Photo/Ad Credits

Chapter 1 2 Jim Leynse/SABA Press Photos, Inc.; 7 © Norcom, Inc.; 9 Used with permission of L.L. Bean; 11 Used with permission of Frito Lay; 20 Used with permission of Land Rover North America; 21 Used with permission of American Express Incorporated; 22 Used with permission of Zenith Corporation; 23 © Daimler-Benz Research and Technology North America, Inc.; 25 © Pepsico, Inc.; 26 BARBIE and Associated trademarks are owned by Mattel, Inc. © 1998 Mattel, Inc. All Rights Reserved. Used with permission; 28 Used with permission of Philips Petroleum Company.

Chapter 2 36 Brian Seed/Tony Stone Images; 41 Used with permission of Lexus; 45 Used with permission of Jeep/Chrysler; 46 Used with permission of Snap-On Tools; 49 Used with permission of Xerox; 50 Used with permission of Bulova; 51 (**left**) © Churchill & Klehr Photography; 51 (**right**) © IBM Corporation; 55 Cynthia Johnson/Gamma-Liaison, Inc.; 57 Long Photography/Toyota Motor Sales, USA, Inc.

Chapter 3 62 © Kobal Collection; 67 Used with permission of Reebok Incorporated; 69 Bill Janscha/AP Wide World Photos; 71 Used with permission of Motorola; 77 Used with permission of Sketchers USA; 79 Douglas E. Curran/Agence France-Presse; 82 Robert Visser/AP Wide World Photos.

Chapter 4 92 James Leynse/SABA Press Photos, Inc.; 97 Used with permission of McNeil Consumer Products; 101 Courtesy of Lever Brothers Company; 102 Used with permission of G.E. Information Services; 103 Used with permission of Canon Computer Systems; 105 Used with permission of E.I. DuPont Corp.; 108 Used with permission of Swiss Army Brands; 110 Jim Havey/Havey Productions; 113 Travelpix/FPG International LLC; 114 Katsumi Kasahara/AP/WideWorld Photos; 119 Courtesy of Star Alliance and Young and Rubicam Ad Agency.

Chapter 5 126 Frank LaBua/Simon & Schuster/ PH College; 129 Michael Newman/Photo Edit; 131 Reprinted with permission of LEXIS-NEXIS, a division of Reed Elsevier, Inc. LEXIS-NEXIS are registered trademarks of Reed Elsevier Properties, Inc.; 134 Used with permission of Neilsen Media Research; 137 Used with permission of the Spalding Co.; 138 Jim Cummins/FP International LLC; 140 © Kimberly Clark; 142 Rhoda Sidney/PhotoEdit; 144 Leonardi/Gamma-Liaison, Inc.; 147 Alan Oddie/PhotoEdit.

Chapter 6 154 Used with permission of Gerber Products; 157 Randy Cole/COLE/Ecostock; 163 © General Motors Media Archive; 165 Used with permission of J.C. Penney and Cartel Creative; 170 Used with permission of Pepsico, Inc.; 172 Courtesy of Harley-Davidson Motor Company © 1998 Harley-Davidson. All rights reserved; 172 (**bottom**) Used with permission of Front Line Cap/Sports Specialities; 178 © Drew Friedman.

Chapter 7 186 Tom Wagner/SABA Press Photos, Inc.; 189 © Nikelodeon; 193 Used with permission of Timex; 194 Used with permission of United States Navy; 199 Used with permission of Nike; 202 R. Shock/Gamma-Liaison, Inc.; 203 Spencer Grant/PhotoEdit; 205 Used with permission of National Fluid Milk Processing Board and Bozell Worldwide; 206 Used with permission of Bijan Fragrances; 209 Used with permission of Aetna, Inc.

Chapter 8 216 Used with permission of ARAMARK Managed Services; 221 Used with permission of Timken, Inc.; 222 Used with permission of Enron; 223 © The Boeing Company; 227 Used with permission of Caterpillar, Inc.; 228 Used with permission of Zurich-American Insurance Group; 230 © The Haggin Group; 232 Used with permission of MCI; 233 © Churchill & Klehr Photography; 238 Used with permission of 3M; 240 Used with permission of 3M.

Chapter 9 246 Used with permission of Chevrolet; 250 Used with permission of Nicole Miller Eyewear; 252 Used with permission of Stickley, Inc.; 253 Used with permission of Gucci America, Inc. 259 Telegraph Colour Library/ FPG International LLC; 264 © Carolina Beverage, Corp; 266 Used with permission of BMW of North America. All other rights reserved to BMW of North America, Inc.

Chapter 10 276 © My Twinn; 281 Used with permission of General Electric; 282 Bob Carey/Los Angeles Times Syndicate; 283 Used with permission of Fallon McGalliot Ad Agency; 286 Used with permission of 3M; 288 Used with permission of Jerry Leff Associates and Howard Berman; 291 Used with permission of E.I. DuPont; 295 Used with permission of Chrysler, Inc.; 300 © Church and Dwight Co., Inc.

Chapter 11 308 Mark C. Ide/Simon & Schuster/PH College; 311 Hernandez/Gamma-Liaison, Inc.; 313 Mark Mellett/Stock Boston; 321 © Churchill & Klehr Photography; 325, 326 Used with permission of Kinko's Ventures; 328 Kelly Willens/AP/WideWorld Photos; 329 Remy Michelin/Allsport Photography (USA), Inc.; 330 Used with permission of the Malaysia Tourism Promotion Board.

Chapter 12 342 © Churchill & Klehr Photography; 347 Photographer Michael Furman; 349 Burger King® ad slick used with permission from Burger King Corporation; 358 Kerbs/Monkmeyer Press; 362 Churchill & Klehr Photography; 363 © Marshall Industries; 366 Used with permission of COSCO North America; 367 Used with permission of Port of Los Angeles.

Chapter 13 374 E.A. Wessman/Stock Boston; 377 Michael Newman/PhotoEdit; 379 Used with permission of Sears, Roebuck and Co.; 381 (**top**) Andre Jenny/Unicorn Stock Photos; 381 (**bottom**) Carolyn Schaefer/Gamma-Liaison, Inc.; 386 © American Multi-Cinema, Inc.; 389 (**top**) Used with permission of the United

States Postal Service; **389 (bottom)** Used with permission of Esprit; **392 (bottom)** Used with permission of Dell; **392 (column)** © Copyright CDNow, Inc. 1998 (All rights reserved).

Chapter 14 **400** Matthew Jordan Smith/Outline Press Syndicate Inc.; **405** Used with permission of Motorola; **408** Used with permission of National Fluid Milk Processing Board and Bozell Worldwide; **410** Used with permission of Life and Health Insurance Foundation; **414** © Pepsico, Inc.; **416** © Freeman Public Relations.

Chapter 15 **428** © Kobal Collection; **430** Used with permission of Universal Studios; **433** Used with permission of McGraw-Hill; **438** Used with permission of Converse; **441 (top)** Brent Jones/Stock Boston; **441 (bottom)** © Red Gold, Inc.; **444** Used with permission of Weight Watchers International; **445** Used with permission of Univision; **451** Charles Bennett/AP Wide World Photos; **453** Tony Freeman/PhotEdit; **454** Kerbs/Monkmeyer Press.

Chapter 16 **462** Frank LaBua/Simon & Schuster/PH College; **467 (left)** Michael Newman/PhotoEdit; **467 (right)** Ed Taylor Studio/FPG International LLC; **468** James Schnepf/Gamma-Liaison, Inc.; **470** Used with permission of Marriott International; **477** © Michael J. Schimpf; **478** Used with permission of Amway; **485** Amy C. Etra/PhotoEdit; **490 (left)** Used with permission of Sharp Electronic Corporation; **490 (right)** Used with permission of Holiday Hospitality Corp.

Chapter 17 **498** Cassy Cohen/PhotoEdit; **501** Used with permission of Chevrolet; **504** Used with permission of United States Postal Service; **506** Used with permission of Signapore Tourism Board; **511** Tony Freeman/PhotoEdit; **512** © Churchill & Klehr Photography; **513** Michael Newman/PhotoEdit; **515** © Pacific Electric and Gas. Reprinted from FORTUNE, June 24, 1996; **517** Reproduced with permission of Mita Copystart America, Inc. All rights reserved.

Chapter 18 **528** © Churchill & Klehr Photography; **530** Used with permission of Procter & Gamble; **531** Used with permission of Continental Airlines; **537** Barry Gossage/NBA Entertainment, Inc.; **538** Used with permission of Ford Motor Company; **539** Used with permission of Autolite; **544** Used with permission of E.I. DuPont, Inc.

Index

A

ABB Robotics, 254, 507
ABC Classification, 363
Abell, Derek, 107
A.C. Rochester, 250, 471
Academy of Motion Picture Arts and Sciences, 336
Accelerator principle, 226
Acceptance price range, 534
Access to Travel, 318
Account planning, 475–476
Ace Hardware, 261, 348
Action groups, 68
ActionSystems, 535
Active learning, 189
ActivMedia, 391
ADAC Laboratories, 55
Adam, Marc, 307
Adams, Russell, 27
Adams Mark Hotel, 318
Adidas, 515
Adoption process, 301
Advanced Configuration and Power Interface (ACPI), 302
Advanced Micro Devices, 373
Advanced Recovery, 347
Advent, 352
Advertising, 412–413, 418, 430, 432. *See also* Integrated Marketing Communications
   agencies, 436
   assessing effectiveness of, 445–446
   budget, 437
   categories of, 435–436
   creating the ads, 444–445
   direct marketing, 391
   ethics of, 432
   objectives, 436
   prices, 511–512
   pros and cons of, 434–435
   purposes of, 433–434
   selecting and scheduling media, 439–444
   strategy, 437–439
   Super Bowl, 410, 413, 461
Advertising Age, 439
Advocates, 237
AEI Music Network, Inc., 327
Aerosmith, 206
Aetna, 209
African-Americans, 203–204. *See also* Minority groups
Agassi, Andre, 180, 426

Age, 76–77
   market segmentation by, 162–164
   senior citizens' market, 209–210
Agfa, 431
Ahlbrand, Jonathan, 463
AIDA, 418
Aided recall, 445
AIDS, 331
Air bags, 82
Airborne, 533
Airborne Express, 8, 69, 386, 534
Air Express International, 369
Air Force, 8
Airline industry, 116, 255, 263, 392, 510
AirTouch Communications, 347
Air transport, 365
AirWeb Wireless Software, 288
Akers, Michelle, 153
Alcoholic beverages industry, 172, 176, 202, 257, 259, 266, 414, 422, 461
Alcoholics Anonymous, 333
Allen-Bradley Corporation, 285
Allianz, 227
Allied Signal, 451
Allocation, 356
Allowances, 451–452
All-Sport, 180
Allstate, 192
Alpo, 352
Alternatives evaluation, 190–191
Amana, 330
Amazon.com, 86, 127–128
AMC Entertainment, 386
American Airlines, 11, 258, 392, 449, 510
American Association of Retired Persons, 210
American Banknote Company, 334
American Cancer Society, 258–259, 432
American Civil Liberties Union (ACLU), 333
American Consumer Satisfaction Index (ACSI), 43
American Council of the Blind, 318
American Dental Association, 259, 407–408, 410
American Express, 20, 21, 67, 133, 251, 258, 392, 406, 439, 446, 461, 488
American Heart Association, 259
American Home Products, 456
American Hospital Association, 451
American Marketing Association (AMA), 5, 84–85, 145, 332, 335, 419

American Medical Association, 407–408, 432, 451
American Sampling, Inc., 454
American Society of Travel Agents (ASTA), 421
American Sports Data, 207
Americans with Disabilities Act (ADA), 318
American Youth Soccer Organization, 333
America Online (AOL), 146, 162, 388, 394, 440, 450, 513, 541, 548–549
America West, 538
Ameritech, 222–223, 235
Ameritech Cellular, 408
Ames department stores, 510
Ames Rubber Corporation, 55
Amoco, 522
Amway, 477, 478, 492
Andersen Consulting, 74, 106, 145, 239, 244–245, 255
Andersen Corporation, 176
Anderson, Dana, 133
Anheuser-Busch, 172, 257, 258, 259, 266, 414, 422, 461
Aniston, Jennifer, 206
Ann Taylor, 380
Antimerger Act, 81
AO Smith, 255
A&P, 261
APAC, 330
Applebaum, Irwyn, 64
Apple Computer, 121, 221–222, 290, 302
Application, positioning by, 180
ARAMARK Corporation, 95, 104, 106, 109, 216–218, 222, 228, 255, 315, 383
Arbitron Co., The, 145
Arby's, 160
Archer-Daniels-Midland (ADM), 255, 510
Arcidi, Ted, 310
Arco, 384
Arizona State University, 335
Armani, 253
Arm & Hammer, 180, 300
Armstrong, Neil, 95
Armstrong World Industries Building Products Operations, 55
Arrow Electronics, 351, 356, 373
Arthur Andersen, 264
Arthur D. Little, 53
Art Institute of Chicago, 11
Asahi Breweries, 257
Asia, 201
   trademark piracy in, 259

Asian-Americans
   social factors influencing consumer
      decisions, 203. *See also* Minority
      groups
Asian Mind Game, The, 469
Asia-Pacific Economic Cooperation
      (APEC), 452
Associated Grocers, 348
Assortment, 356
Assurance, 323–324
Astor Restaurant Group, 352–353
Asymmetrical digital subscriber line
      (ADSL), 372
A.T. Kearney, 53
Atari, 319
Atlantic Records, 446
AT&T, 11, 29, 30, 41, 46, 53, 55, 179, 203,
      218, 222, 226, 228, 237, 244, 267–268,
      284–285, 314, 344, 420, 430, 437, 439,
      451, 475–476, 477, 484
Attitudes, 198–199
Attractiveness, 408
Audi, 456
Audiophile, 352
Audubon Society, 82
Augmented products, 249–251
Aunt Jane, 261
Austad's, 393
Austin, Robert, 162
Australia, 325, 399
Autolite Platinum, 539
Automated vending operators, 383–384
Automatic Data Processing, 228
Automation, sales force, 491
Automobile industry, 231, 281, 356
Automobile Information Disclosure Act, 83
Automobile market, 187. *See also* names of
      individual car makers
Autonation, 380
Autozone, 378, 380
Avis, 180
Avon Products, Inc., 74–75, 86, 455

B

Baby Bells, 235
Baby boomers, 77, 162–163, 210, 540
Baby boomlet, 163, 164
Baby busters, 163
Baby Superstores, 545
Bachler, Steve, 47
Back order, 363
Back translation, 147–148
Bailey, Banks, and Biddle, 108
Bain & Company, 39, 41, 45–46
Bait and switch, 512
Bakery Music Company, 174
Banana Republic, 327, 456
Band-Aid, 266
Bandai Ltd., 115, 418
Banking, 535
Bank of America, 175, 203, 548

Bantam Books, 64
Banyan Systems, 147
Barbie dolls, 26, 298, 344
Bar codes, 363
Bargaining, 69–70, 241
Barkin, Robert, 456
Barkley, Charles, 426, 427
Barnard, Charles, 191
Barnes & Noble, 163, 320, 379, 380, 383
Bartering, 79
Barton, Neal, 105
Bath & Body Works, 327
Battoe, Joe, 133
Baxter International, 11
BayBank, 7
BBDO, 431
Beal, Dave, 306
Beanie Babies, 526–527
Beavis and Butt-head, 422
Bechtel, 255
Bedbury, Scott, 263
Beechon, 179
Beer Institute, 422
Behavior, segmentation by, 168
Belief, 198
Bell, Rich, 233, 234
Bell, Ted, 461
BellAtlantic, 244, 267–268
Bell Industries, 359
BellSouth, 235, 408
Benchmarking, 53, 139–140
Benefit
   positioning by, 179
   segmentation by, 169
Benetton Group, 261, 362
Ben & Jerry's Ice Cream, 28–29, 346, 432
Bergen, Candice, 407
Bergen Brunswig Corporation, 355
Berman, Gary, 202
Bernstein, Jodie, 432
Berrie, Russ, 526
Best, Roger, 152
Best Buy, 56, 320, 321, 346, 448
Best Products Company, 384
Betty Crocker, 262, 263
Bezos, Jeffrey, 127, 128
Bidding, competitive, 229, 510, 539
Bieler, Peter, 391
Big Sister/Big Brother programs, 333
Bill Blass, 184
Billboards, 440, 443
Bipolar adjective scale, 141
Black & Decker, 207, 260, 261, 348, 357
Black Entertainment Television, 204, 422
Bleustein, Jeffrey, 551
Blimpie, 353
Blockbuster, 376, 381, 383, 385
Bloomingdale's, 384
BMW, 41, 176, 178, 180, 250–251, 265,
      266, 284, 291, 431, 472
Boardman, Peter, 201
Body Shop, The, 29

Boeing, 10, 20, 22, 28, 74, 223, 288, 466,
      467
Bogues, Muggsy, 408
Bonus, 488
Booz, Allen & Hamilton, 132, 278–279,
      287, 293
Borden, Neil, 6
Borders, 379, 380
Bosch, 160
Bose, 352
Bosler Supply, 357
Boston Center for Strategy Research, 148
Boston Consulting Group (BCG), 100
Boston University Food Services, 217
Boston Whaler, 507
Botwinski, Monica, 496
Bovsquette, Janine, 422
Bowerman, William, 426
Bowling, Peggy, 552
Boy Scouts, 9, 333
Bozell Worldwide, Inc., 45, 461
Brands, 249, 257–268
   developing successful name, 266–267,
      273–275
   equity, 262–266
   maintaining value of, 266
   strategies for, 260–262
   top ten, 258
   trademarks, 258–259
Brandwein, Carol, 516
Brazil, 75, 148
Brigandi Coin Company, 393
Bristol-Meyers Squibb, 382
British Airways, 11
Brokaw, Tom, 144
Brokers, 344
Brookstone, 388
Brown, Donald, 551
Brunswick, 256
BSB Worldwide, 201
Budgets
   advertising, 437
   communications, 419–420
   media, 444
   sales, 486–487
Bugle Boy Clothing Co., 139, 149
Build-up segmentation method, 169
Bulova, 50, 352
Bundling strategy, 250, 546
Burger, Dan, 544
Burger King, 11, 30, 51, 119, 132, 141, 197,
      215, 258, 348, 349, 405, 430, 434,
      443, 449, 540, 545
Burkes, Ellis, 310
Burlington Air Express, 369
Burlington Coat Factory, 175
Burlington Industries, 139
Burlington Northern, 365
Burmudez and Associates, 436
Bush, George, 331, 391
Business analysis, 287
Business definition, 97–98

Business integration, 244
Business-to-business market, 7
   advertising, 435
   buying process, 227–241
   commercial, 219–221
   concept of, 218–219
   demand for, 226
   extractor industries, 220
   global, 226–227
   government market, 223
   institutions, 222
   Integrated Marketing Communications
     and, 414
   product classification, 254–255
   sale promotions, 450–451
   segmentation of, 223–225
   supply chain, 225–226
   trade industries, 221–222
   utilities, 222
Buyer's market, 17
Buying center, 236–238
Buying market share, 532–533
Buzzworm, 136
Byron's, 384

C

California Concepts, 382
California Lawyer, 231
California raisins, 444–445
California Ski Company, 546
Callaway, 352
Calvin Klein, 184, 212, 249
Calyx & Corolla, 387
Campbell's, 145, 258, 260, 402
Canada, 76, 314, 325, 405
Cannondale, 13, 133, 352
Canon, 103, 104, 266
Canteen Corporation, 383
Capital products, 254
Capitol Records, Inc., 263
Cappuccino Cafe, 222, 452
Carchoice, 380
Career Consulting Group, Inc., 130
Career Trak, 318
Carlson Co., The, 310–311
Carlzon, Jan, 105, 317
Carmax, 380
Carnegie-Mellon University, 288
Carnival Cruise Lines, 320
Carolina Beverage Corporation, 264
Carrefour, 385
Cartel, 80–81
Cartier, 379
Case analysis, 138–140
Cash cows, 100–101
Cashin, Bonnie, 343
Casio, 68–69, 534
Catalogs, 388, 389, 390
Catalog showrooms, 384
Caterpillar, 226, 227, 289, 302, 350, 360, 521
Catholic Church, 333

Causal research, 140–141
Cause marketing, 331
Caveat emptor, 17
Cave Automatic Virtual Environment
   (CAVE), 289
CBS, 222–223
CDnow, 376, 386, 392, 395
Ceiling, 536
Cellular phones, 298
Center of influence, 476–477
Centralized decision making, 174
Centrum Silver, 77
Century 21, 348
Cereal manufacturers, 208
Chad, 147
Chain stores, 383
Champ's Sports, 383
Chanel, 500
Chang, Eleanor, 203
Chapstick, 200
Charles Schwab, 69, 511
Charmin, 413
Charner, David, 469
Chase Manhattan Bank, 171
Chavez, Cesar, 68
Checkout scanners, 448
Cheerwine, 264
Chemical Bank, 160
Chesebrough Pond, 454
Cheskin + Masten/ImageNet, 139
Chevrolet, 197
Chicago Bulls, 89
Chicago Symphony, 333
Chi Chi tortilla chips, 449
Child, Julia, 391
Child Protection Act, 83
Children
   in China, 418
   consumer decisions and, 208
   marketing to, 215
Children's World Learning Centers, 94, 95,
   96, 97, 103, 110, 114, 132
Chilton Research, 139
China, 73, 75, 78, 177, 257, 367–368, 520,
   521
   children in, 418
   dumping by, 512
   sales tips for, 469
Chiquita, 258
Chlorofluorocarbons (CFCs), 74
Chou, Silas, 184
Christine Columbus, 133
ChrisCraft, 68
Chrysler, 20, 44, 46, 52, 82, 138, 140, 162,
   193, 225, 232, 254, 258, 269–270,
   294, 295, 296, 319, 391, 472, 547
Chu, Chin Ning, 469
Church & Dwight, 170
Churches Advertising Network, 450
CIA, 65
CIO Communications, Inc., 411
Circle K, 384

Circuit City, 377, 380
Citibank, 171
Citizen, 352
Citizens Bank, 57
Clairol, 352
Clarita Corporation, 443
Claussen, 298
Clayton Act, 81, 509, 511
Clinton, Bill, 70, 184, 416
Close, Glenn, 329
Closing the sale, 405–406, 479–480
Club, The, 180
Club Med, 210, 211, 540
Coach, 327, 342–344, 345
Cobain, Kurt, 206
Co-branding, 171
Coca-Cola, 4, 11, 24, 47, 89, 134, 157–158,
   160, 168, 169, 188, 196, 226, 249,
   257, 258, 261–262, 264, 266, 280,
   298, 329, 348, 364, 365, 405, 411,
   413, 414, 418, 430, 431, 439, 440,
   445, 447, 507, 545
Cognizant Corp., 145
Cohen, Nick, 180–181
Cohn, Steve, 401
Coil, William, 306
Cold calling, 476
Colgate-Palmolive, 170, 516
College football, 414
Colleges, 159, 235–236, 329, 330
Columbia TriStar Home Video, 478–479
Comcast, 314
Comedy Central, 139
Commercialization, 290
Commercial market, 219–221
Commission, 488
Committment, 45
Communication, 402. *See also* Integrated
   Marketing Communication
Compaq Computer, 15, 69, 253, 265, 346,
   347, 360, 362, 364, 472
Comparative messages, 410–411
Comparison, positioning by, 180
Compatibility factors, 172, 282–283
Competition, 11, 68–70
   brand names and, 265–266
   gaining information about, 65
   global, 47–48
   price, 503–504, 515–516, 538–540
   in professional services, 314
   in target marketing, 170
Competitive Media Reporting, 422
Component parts, 254, 255
CompUSA, 346, 376, 377, 380, 383, 393, 415
CompuServe, 131, 391, 434
Computer City, 346, 415
Computer industry, 6, 398–399. *See also*
   Internet; Technology
   cybercafes, 313
   games, 56, 299, 319, 499–500, 503
   in global market, 306
   information systems, 106

Computer industry (*cont.*)
  personal computer (PC), evolution of, 70–71
    software, 281–282
    ticketing, 340–341
Computer Sciences Corporation (CSC), 244
Comstock Bank of Reno, 535
ConAgra, 197
Concentrated marketing, 174
Concept testing, 287
Concern groups, 268
Conclusions, 409
Conditioning, classical and operant, 196–197
Conflict resolution, 240–241
  in distribution, 353–354
Connick, Harry, Jr., 184
Conoco, Inc., 281
Consolidated Edison, 222
Consolidated Metropolitan Statistical Area (CMSA), 76
Consultative sales approach, 471
Consulting organizations, 293
Consumer behavior
  in business-to-business market, 238–241
  decision making by, 190–191
  ethics issues related to, 212
  innovations and, 301–303
  involvement levels of, 188–191
  psychological influences on, 191–201
  service evaluation, 320–322
  social factors, 201–210
  tracking, 210–211
Consumer Bill of Rights, 81
Consumer Goods Pricing Act, 83, 509
Consumer Hotline, 333
Consumer markets, 6–7
Consumer Product Safety Act, 83, 268
Consumer Product Safety Commission (CPSC), 80, 269–270
Consumer protection laws, 81–82, 83
Consumer Reports, 43
Consumers
  feedback, 412
  Integrated Marketing Communications and, 414
  promotions aimed at, 448, 452–455
Consumer's Union, 407–408
Contempo Casual, 299
Continental, 531
Control process, 116
Control review meeting, 116
Convenience goods, 251–252, 349
Convenience samples, 144
Convenience stores, 384
Conventions, 451
Conza, Anthony, 352–353
Cool Hunt, 153
Coopers & Lybrand, 135
Co-op Promotions, 454

Coors Brewing Company, 172, 176, 266
Core business, 279–280
Core competencies, 103–106
Corel Corporation, 547
Core products, 248
Core service, 324–326
Core values, 96–97
Corlett, Candace, 210
Corning Telecommunications, 55
Corporate channel system, 349
COSCO, 366
Costs
  global, 521–523
  price and, 516–520
  reducing, 40
  structure, 40
  in target marketing, 171
Countertrade, 540
Country of origin, positioning by, 180
Coupons, 452–453, 529
Courtship phase, 231
Covergirl, 169
Cox, Courtney, 408
Cox Communications, 314
C-Phone, 302
Cranberries, 515
Crate & Barrel, 40
Cray Research, 512
Creative Boutiques, 436
Creative strategy, 437–439
Creativity, advertising, 438–439
Credit cards, 171, 510
Crime Tip Hotline, 333
Crocker, Betty, 27, 180
Crocker, William, 27
Cross-docking, 362
Cross-selling, 449
Crown Books, 379
Crystal, Billy, 329
CSX, 365
Culliton, James, 6
Cultural environment, 77–79
Culture, 201
Custom Cycle Works, 552
Customer-driven organizations, 18
Customer marketing era, 16, 17–18
Customers
  behavior of, 40–41, 41–43, 186–215
  channel management and, 354
  direct marketing, 387
  diversity of, 47
  efficient customer response (ECR) programs, 366–367
  future of connections with, 18–29
  global competition and satisfaction, 47–48
  importance of, in marketing concept, 4–5
  lifetime value of, 40
  microenvironment and, 66
  people systems, 105–106
  pricing and, 504, 534–537

relationship building, 44–47, 534
  satisfaction, loyalty, and quality concepts, 38–43
  satisfaction measurement program, 43
  understanding needs and wants of, 10–11
  value and, 11, 55–56
  value in pricing, 532–534
Custom Foot, 381
Custom Research Inc., 55
Cutler-Hammer, 233, 234, 241, 405
CVS, 252
Cybersource, 391–392
Czech Republic, 119, 254

D

Dahlberg, Terry, 526
Daiichi, 541
Dairy Mart, 384
Dakin Incorporated, 526
Dana Corporation, 55, 227
Dango, 510
Danone S.A., 418
Danson, Ted, 408
Danzas AG, 369
Databases, 131
  direct marketing, 387, 392–393
Data collection methods, 140–141
DaVinci, 244–245
Dayton Hudson Corporation, 383, 385–386
DDB Needham, 461
Decentralized decision making, 174
Decision makers, 237–238
Decision Technology Corporation, 147
Decline phase, 297
Decoding, 412
De-ethnicization, 164–165
Def Jam Records, 185
DeGraan, Ed, 496
Delaney, Mike, 461
Delco, 283
Delivery methods, 394
Dell Computer, 295, 373, 376, 377, 386, 392, 393
Deloitte & Touche, 145, 403
Delphi Automotive Systems, 109, 178–179, 225, 227, 472, 483
Delta, 510
Demand
  in business-to-business market, 226
  creating, 403
  prices and, 505–507
  sliding down the curve, 542–543
Deming, Dr. Edward, 53–54
Deming Prize, 53–54
Demographics
  in business-to-business market, 223–224
  environment, 74–77
  segmentation by, 160–164

Dennis, Keith, 247
Department stores, 384
Depression generation, 163
Depth, product line, 256
Design Data Systems (DDS), 526
Deskey Associates, 281
Details, 139
Detroit Auto Show, 477
DHL, 386
Dial, 434
Dialog, 131
Diamond Club International, 409
DiCamillo, Gary T., 124
Diet Coke, 46
Differentiated marketing, 173–174
Differentiation strategy, 108, 515
Diffusion process, 301–303
Digital Equipment Corporation, 265, 534
Dillard Department Stores, 354, 380, 384
DiPilli, Liz, 139
Direct channels, 344–346
Direct mail, 388
Direct marketing, 398–399
    advertising, 391
    catalogs, 388, 389, 390
    concept of, 376
    customer value, 387
    databases, 387, 392–393
    ethics in, 394–395
    growth in, 386–387
    on the Internet, 391–392
    by mail, 388
    merchandise assortment, 393
    message design, 393–394
    payment and delivery methods, 394
    pricing, 393
    target markets, 392
    telemarketing, 390–391
    television home shopping, 391
Direct Marketing Association (DMA), 394–395
Directory advertising, 435
Direct sales, 465, 466
Discipline of Market Leaders, The, 533
Discounts, 451, 539
Discount stores, 384
Discretionary income, 71
Discrimination, 197
Disney, Walt, 93
Disney Store, 93–94
Disposable income, 71
Distribution channels, 113
    centers, 362
    ethics, 85
    logistics, 359–369
    management of, 351–355
    organization and functions, 344–347
    wholesaling, 355–359
Distribution intensity, 349–351
Divergence, 326

Diversification, 281
Diversity, 48
    in advertising, 418, 445
    Barbie dolls, 299
    brand marketing, 267–268
    customer-centered markets, 47
    disabled travelers, 318
    future of, 25–26
    Integrated Marketing Communication, 421–422
    marketing issues, 201–204
    McDonald's approach, 350
    pricing plans and, 502, 540
    products designed for, 112
    researching youth, 139
    in retailing, 385
    in sales force, 484
    segmentation by, 161, 164–165
    senior citizens, 210
    social factors influencing consumer decisions, 201–210
Doctors, 402, 407
Dogs, 101
Dole, 68, 260, 261
Dole, Bob, 331
Dollar General, 545
Domino's Pizza, 177, 280, 360
Donna Karan, 185
Donors, categories of, 335
Door 2 Door, 313
Dorgan, Tim, 382
Dory, Leslie Dukker, 171
Dotterer, Dr. Lew, 8, 331–332
Dow Jones News/Retrieval Service, 131
Downs, Hugh, 391
Dr. J's, 153
Dr. Martens, 405
Dr. Seuss, 13
DreamWorks SKG, 429, 430
Dreyer's, 34
Drop shippers, 358
Drucker, Peter, 20–21
Dubrow, Burt, 30
Duke, Carol, 318
Dumping, 512
Dun & Bradstreet, 131, 477
Duncan Hines, 287
Dunlop, 352
Dun's, 387
Duo-therm, 538
DuPont, 68, 103, 105, 218, 244, 281, 291, 543–544
Duracell, 496–497, 521
Durot, Donahoe, and Purohit, 436
Dusenberry, Phil, 331

E
Early adopters, 302
Early majority buyers, 302
Eastman Chemical Company, 55
Eaton Corporation, 160, 255, 481

Ebel, 352
Echo bust, 163
Eckerd Corporation, 353
Economic order quantity (EOQ) model, 363–364
Economics
    income and spending behavior, 71–72
    prices and, 505–509
Eddie Bauer, 327, 388, 394
Edelman Public Relations Worldwide, 456
EDS, 255, 315
Edsel, 144
Education Alternatives, 315
Effectiveness, 11
Efficiency factors, 11
    in target marketing, 171
Efficient customer response (ECR) programs, 366–367
Eggland's Best Eggs, 432
Egypt, 470
Einstein, Albert, 134
Eisner, Michael, 93–94, 105–106
Elasticity, prices and, 505, 507
Electronic data interchange (EDI), 361
Electronic Data Systems Corp. (EDS), 145, 247
Eli Lilly, 94, 95, 98–99, 105
E-mail surveys, 147
Embassy Suites, 318
Emergency products, 251
Empathy, 44–45, 479
Employees
    ethics and, 57
    relationship with, 385–386
    in retailing, 377
    as stakeholders, 66–67
Encoding, 199–200, 409
Energizer, 179, 438
Englehart, Jim, 111
Enron, 222
Enterprise Rent-a-Car, 74
Entertainment industry, 259
Entertainment marketing, 328–329
Entrekin, Jacqueline, 535
EnviroGroup, 221
Environment
    recycling, 250–251
    U.S. laws protecting, 82
Environmental forecast, 486
Environmental Protection Agency (EPA), 80, 82
Environmental scanning, 65
E-Plus, 407
Equal Credit Opportunity Act, 83
Equal Employment Opportunity Act, 483–484
Equilibrium price, 508–509
Ericsson, 105
ESPN, 197
Esprit, 13
Essential facilities, 514

Ethics
    in advertising, sales promotion, and
        public relations, 432
    business relationships and, 235
    of channel management, 355
    consumer behavior influence, 212
    core values and, 96–97
    for direct marketing, 394–395
    in fulfilling commitments, 56–58
    future of, 26–29
    global environment for, 82–85
    in Integrated Marketing
        Communication, 422
    in marketing research, 148–150
    of nonprofit services, 336
    pricing and, 512–513, 548–549
    product imitation, 290–291
    product safety and liability, 269–270
    in retailing, 385–386
    in sales, 474–475, 481, 489
    target marketing and, 176
Ethiopia, 147
Ethnic background, 26
Ethnicity, 26
Europe, 520. *See also* countries by name
    automobile market in, 248
    business-to-business market in, 226
    cell phone competition from, 354
    import restrictions, 521
    ISO 9000, 52
    sales tips for, 469
European Community, 52
European Union (EU), 73–74
Evans, Mark, 48
Event marketing, 329
Eveready, 267
Everyday low pricing, 543, 545
Everything's A Dollar, 385
Evian, 139, 192
Exchange, value in, 8–9, 531
Exchange rates, 523, 541–542
Exclusive dealing, 354–355
Executive Accents, 390
Executive selling, 465
Expectations, 40–41
Expenditures, advertising, 443
Experience qualities, 320
Experiments, 140
Exporting, 118–119
Export subsidy, 521–522
Exposure, 438
Extractor industries, 220, 221
Exxon, 47, 221, 267, 408

F
Fair Credit Reporting Act, 83
Fair Debt Collection Practice Act, 83
Fair Packaging and Labeling Act, 83, 268
Family
    consumer decisions and, 207–210
    life cycles segmentation, 162

pressure on, 489
Family Bargain Center Stores, 502
Family Dollar, 545
Fanta, 157
Favre, Brett, 407
Fear appeals, 410
Federal Aviation Administration, 260
Federal Cigarette Labeling and Advertising
    Act, 83
Federal Communications Commission
    (FCC), 80, 107
Federal Deposit Insurance Corporation,
    313
Federal Drug Administration, 436
Federal Trade Commission Act, 81, 509,
    510
Federal Trade Commission (FTC), 80, 81,
    410–411, 511–512
Federated department stores, 354
FedEx, 8, 50, 52, 55, 69, 103, 106,
    173–174, 237, 365, 366, 386, 394,
    414, 435, 473, 484, 532, 533, 534
Ferron, J., 135
Field selling, 466–467
Filak, Doug, 67
Filene's department stores, 7–8
Film making, 63–64
Financing incentives, 452
Find/SVP, 164
Firefly Network, Inc., 387
Fireman, Paul, 152
First Interstate Center for Services
    Marketing, 335
First Manhattan Consulting Group, 535
Fisher, George, 104
Fisher-Price, 179, 261
Fitzpatrick, John, 201
Fitzpatrick, Sean, 162
Flagship Group, The, 277–278
Florida Orange Juice, 259
Florida Power & Light, 222
Florsheim, 383
Focus groups, 136–137
Folger's, 132
Follow-up, 480
Food and Drug Administration (FDA),
    80, 81
Food business, 98, 155–156, 384, 530
Food industry, 348
Foote Cone & Belding, 404
Foot Locker, 383, 546–547
Foot Traffic, 191
Forbes, Steve, 331
Ford, Henry, 17
Ford Motor Company, 46, 67, 82, 111,
    114–115, 135, 140, 144, 178, 190,
    198, 201, 219–220, 221, 223–224,
    234, 250–251, 254, 298, 456, 472,
    475–476, 477–478, 484
Forecasting, sales, 486
Forestry Systems, Inc., 117
Form utility, 8

Forward buying, 366
Foster, Dawn, 535
Foudy, Julie, 153
Fox, Mitchell, 139
Fox network, 29
France, 119, 177, 254, 385, 399, 405, 432,
    520
    nonprofit sector in, 332
    sales tips for, 469
    shopping patterns in, 115
    size and space in, 79
Franchises and franchising, 34, 383
    as distribution channel, 348
    in global market, 119
    growth of service sector and,
        315–316
Franklin, 162
Fred Pryor Seminars, Inc., 326
Freight forwarders, 369
Frequency, advertising, 443–444
Freston, Tom, 215
Freud, Sigmund, 192
Friskies, 352
Frito-Lay, 132–133, 176–177, 201,
    234–235, 257, 290, 291, 353
FTD florists, 192
Fuentes, Daisy, 408
Fugees, 185
Fuji, 80, 99, 104, 431, 518
Full-line forcing, 355
Futurestep, 442–443
Fuyo, 541

G
G. Heileman breweries, 176
Gag gifts, 251
Galvanometers, 138
Gap, The, 141, 376, 380, 386
Garrison, David, 541
Gatekeepers
    in business-to-business buying,
        236–237
    public relations and, 455
Gates, Bill, 20, 333, 382
Gates, Dr. Thomas N., 97
Gateway, 15, 393, 398–399, 491
Gatorade, 68, 179, 180
Gender
    automobile market and, 187
    segmentation by, 162, 185
Gender Tax Repeal Act, 549
General Agreement on Tariffs and Trade
    (GATT), 74
General Electric, 7, 66, 94, 99, 100, 102,
    103–104, 218, 237, 239, 256, 257,
    258, 261, 280–281, 296, 348, 418,
    439, 468, 481
General Foods, 266
Generalization, 197
General Mills, 6, 27, 31, 120–121, 267,
    429, 540

General Motors, 8, 29, 46, 82, 99, 109, 111, 119, 120, 140, 156, 171, 174, 178–179, 219, 223–224, 225, 227, 229, 235, 236–237, 246–248, 250, 254, 260, 261, 262, 267, 283, 296, 315, 329, 341, 344, 413, 414, 436, 449, 471, 472, 483, 531, 545, 546
Generation X, 163–164, 268
Geodemography, 160
Geography
    in business-to-business market, 225
    retail territory, 379
    sales force structure by, 482
    scope of, 117–118
    segmentation by, 160, 161
Georgetown University, 235
George Washington University, 336
Georgia Tech, 217
Gerasyova, Maria, 75
Gerber Products, 149, 156, 169, 261
Germany, 119, 310, 314, 399, 468, 520, 530
    business-to-business market in, 227
    freight shippers in, 369
    nonprofit sector in, 332
    sales tips for, 469
GI generation, 163
Gillette, 75, 118, 258, 345, 431, 496–497, 530, 546
Girbaud, 249, 507
Girl Scouts, 9, 335
Gitano Group, 350–351
Global marketing
    advertising, sales promotion and public relations, 431–432
    brand promotion, 266–267
    business-to-business, 226–227
    competition and satisfaction in, 47–48
    computers, 399
    entering, 116–120
    financial factors, 523
    future of, 24–25
    macroenvironment, 70–85
    physical distribution, 367–369
    pricing in, 520–523, 540–542
    product life cycle in, 300
    product lines in, 256–257
    research, 147–148
    retail, 386
    sales, 468, 469–470
    service sector growth, 312–316
    social class dimensions, 204–205
    style decisions, 201
    targeting, 176–177
    technology in, 70–71
    trademark piracy, 259–260
Globe Metallurgical, Inc., 55
Godiva, 253
Going rate pricing, 538–539
Goldberg, Whoopi, 329
Good Catalog Company, 388, 390
Good Housekeeping Institute, 407–408

Goods, 6–8
    for direct marketing, 393
    mix of, in retail, 380
Goodyear, 258, 346, 349
Gordon, Didi, 153
Gore, W.L., 291
Government
    business-to-business market in, 220, 223
    deregulation of services, 313–314
Granite Rock Company, 55
Gray, Bill, 104
Gray marketing, 521
Great Britain. See United Kingdom
Greater Pittsburgh Airport Authority, 534–535
Greco, Vinny, 29, 309–310, 348
Greece, 399
Green Giant, 177, 267
Greenpeace, 82, 333
Greenwald, Anthony, 196
Griggs, Karen, 491
Gross domestic product (GDP), 72
Grove, Andy, 265
Growth phase, 295–296
GTE, 55, 448
Gucci, 72–73, 253
Guess, 249
Guettler, Cindy, 27
Gustin, Carl, 45

H
Hagans, Phil, 350
Haley, Russell, 169
Hall, Edward, 79
Hall and Hall Global Trading, 119
Hallmark, 46–47, 48, 58, 93, 192, 204, 230
Hamilton-Hallmark, 351, 356
Hammacher Schlemmer, 388
Hammond, Mike, 398
Hanes, 432
Hanover pretzels, 261
Harding, Tanya, 207
Hard Rock Cafe, 380
Harley-Davidson, 44, 172, 259, 551–552
Harman/Kandon, 250
Hart, Shaffner & Marx, 349
Harvard Business Review, 97–98
Harvard Business School, 39
Hasegawa, Joanne, 461
Hasselblad, 352
Hayes, 344, 346
Hayworth, 297
HBO, 258
Healthrider, 388
Health Support Services (HSS), 217
Health Valley, 197
Heileman Brewing Company, 172
Helene Curtis, 352
Hello Direct, 393
Helms, Luke S., 175

Henry Ford Community College, 56
Herman Miller, 297
Hershey Foods, 66, 429–430
Hertz, 348
Heterogeneous group, 159
Hewlett-Packard, 6, 29, 57, 237, 258, 265, 288, 293, 453–454, 464, 467, 484, 539
Hickock, Allan, 263
Hilton, 119, 133–134, 337
Hines, Gregory, 164–165
Hiram Walker, 446
Hispanic Americans, 3–4. See also Minority groups
    National Hispanic Corporate Council, 202–203
    social factors influencing consumer decisions, 202–203
Hispanic Marketing Communication Research, 146
Hispanics, 78
H.J. Heinz Company, 15, 418
Hoffman, Peter, 496
Hoffmeister, David, 114–115
Hog Farm, 259
Holiday Inn, 68, 119, 348, 353, 490
Holland, 541
Home Access Health Corporation, 410
Home Depot, 267, 376, 377, 380, 383
Homer, Winslow, 144
Home Shopping Mall, 391
Home Shopping Network (HSN), 391
Homogeneous group, 159
Homosexuals, ads targeting, 445, 446
Honda, 107, 139–140, 172, 223–224, 265, 267, 269, 291, 295, 296, 542, 552
Honeywell, 288, 289, 345, 353
Hong Kong, 147–148
Hoover, 432
Horizon Instruments, 391
Horowitz, Joel, 184
Hotel industry, 119, 133–134, 318, 455
Household, 207
Howard, Juwaan, 98
Huffy, 13, 352
Hughes, 247, 384
Hughes, Donald, 511
Hull, Leighton, 350
Humor, 409–410
Hungary, 332
Hunt's Point Farm, 334
Hyatt, 455
Hypermarkets, 385
Hypermarket USA, 385
Hypothesis, 140

I
IAMS, 352
IBM, 7, 39, 55, 57, 66, 72–73, 221–222, 226, 255, 257, 258, 290, 344, 346, 376, 418, 423, 447, 464, 479, 483, 484

ICD Marketing Services, 205
ICMA Retirement Corporation, 456
Ideas, 6–8, 285–287
IGA stores, 261
IKEA, 383
Imada, Bill, 203
Imada Wong Communications Group, 203
Imitation, 290–291
Importing, 118–119
Impulse purchases, 251
Income, 71–72
Independent Grocers Alliance, 348
India, 75
    McDonald's in, 78
Indirect channels, 344–346
Industrial Light & Magic (ILM), 63–64
Industrial Marketing Manager, 143
Industry forecast, 486
Industry.net, 239, 241
Industry structure, 513–515
Inflation, 523
Information
    advertising and, 433–434
    data analysis, 132
    data types, 130–131
    decision making and, 132–134
    in Integrated Marketing
        Communication, 403
    marketing decision support system
        (MDSS), 129–130
    marketing information systems (MIS),
        128–130
    transaction-based information system
        (TBIS), 130
Information processing, 199–201
Information Resources, Inc., 145, 477
Information sources, 190
    in business-to-business market, 238–239
    professional seekers, 237
    systems, 106
Ingram Micro, Inc., 344, 346, 358
Innovations and innovators, 301–303
    success of, 282–284
    types of, 281–282
Institutions
    advertising by, 435
    business-to-business market in, 220, 222
InsWeb, 547
Integrated marketing communications
    concept of, 402–403
    consumer feedback, 412
    decoding, 412
    developing the plan, 416–421
    diversity and, 421–422
    encoding, 409
    ethics, 422
    media for, 411–412
    message characteristics, 409–411
    message sender, 406–408
    mix of, 412–416
    objectives of, 403–406
    technology, 422

Intel Corp., 264, 265, 268, 270, 280, 302, 341,
        345, 347, 351, 373, 461, 481, 514, 534
Intelligent Electronics, 346
Intent, 98–99
Intermediaries, 67–68
    in channel management, 355
    distribution, 344, 353
    in export/import business, 118–119
Intermodal transportation, 365–366
Internal markets, 8, 331–332
International, 224
International Association of Certified
        Public Accountants, 451
International Data Group (IDG), 226
International Labor Organization, 147
International Standards Organization
        (ISO), 52
International Trade Commission, 260
Internet, 15, 22–24, 420. *See also* Web sites
    advertising on, 81, 406, 439–440,
        441–442, 443
    business-to-business marketing on, 239
    catalogs, 388
    data on, 146–147
    development of, 281–282
    direct marketing on, 375, 376, 386,
        391–392, 393
    in Integrated Marketing
        Communications, 406, 411–412, 422
    NBA promotion on, 89
    physical distribution on, 113
    publicity on, 456–457
    research on, 65, 69, 137, 146–147
    services on, 235
    shopping on, 382
    sweepstakes on, 454
    tracking consumer behavior, 211
    trade show promotion on, 450
    Yahoo!, 442
Interplay Productions, 289
Interview techniques, 137
Introduction phase, 294
Inventory, 317, 363–364
Involvement levels, in purchasing
        decisions, 188–191
Iomega, 100
IPSCO, 330
IRI Research, 133
Isuzu, 120
Italy, 332, 520
Item, 255
ITT, 362
ITT Sheraton, 20, 72, 489
Ivory soap, 258

J

J. Paul Getty Trust, 336
J. Walter Thompson, 431
Jackson, Michael, 184, 439
Jagger, Mick, 184, 210
Jaguar, 250–251

Japan, 177, 254, 310, 325, 386, 387, 399,
        405, 523, 541
    attitudes toward competitors, 107
    bid rigging in, 510
    competition with U.S. firms, 47–49
    dumping by, 512
    freight shippers in, 369
    import restrictions, 521
    nonprofit sector in, 332
    quality award in, 53–54
    sales tips for, 469, 472
    shopping patterns in, 115
    U.S. restaurants in, 257
    vending machine use in, 383–384
    wealth distribution in, 72
J.C. Penney, 163, 380, 384, 385, 388, 391
J.D. Power & Associates, 41, 43, 134, 135,
        148, 149
Jenny Craig, Inc., 444
Jewel Osco, 382
Jiffy Lube, 267, 316
Jobs, Steve, 70
Joe Camel, 81
John Deere, 330
Johnson, Earvin "Magic," 331
Johnson, Steve, 239
Johnson Controls, 285, 315
Johnson & Johnson, 6, 27, 94, 96–97, 99,
        200, 224, 258, 261, 269, 410
Joico, Inc., 352, 357, 521
Joint decisions, 240–241
Joint marketing, 267
Joint ventures, 120, 263
Jones, Caroline, 176
Jones, Charles, 45–46
Jones, Lafayette, 26
Jordan, Michael, 14, 89, 98, 180, 206, 207,
        328, 329, 408, 426, 427, 431, 432,
        445, 536
*Journal of the American Medical
        Association,* 435
J.P Morgan and Company, 244
Judd, Naomi, 408
Judgment samples, 144
Jurassic Park, 404–405, 429–430
Just-in-time (JIT) system, 364
JVC, 429

K

K2, 352
Kaleidoscope Media Group, 231
Kanovsky, Gerald, 130
Kantas Group, The, 145
Kaplan Foundation, The, 334
Kawasaki, 172, 269, 552
Kay-Bee, 344
Kearns, David, 52
Keds, 210
Keiretsu, 541
Kellogg's, 174, 192, 248, 258, 405, 429, 534,
        540

Kelly, Ed, 217
Kelly, Pam, 299
Kennedy, John F., 18, 95
Kentucky Fried Chicken (KFC), 119, 257, 283, 386, 445
Kerwick, Chris, 429
Kestral, 352
Kikkoman, 164
Kimberly-Clark, 44, 140
King, Larry, 177
Kinko's, 285, 325–326
Kintetsu World Express, 369
Kiwanis Club, 333
Kleenex, 258, 266
Klein, 352
Klein, Jim, 429
Klein, Russ, 404
KLH, 352
Klondike, 438
Klugman, Rob, 176
Kmart, 15, 176, 218, 232, 256, 260, 351, 379, 380, 383, 384, 385, 391, 402, 502, 530
Knight, Phil, 11, 328, 426–427
Knowledge Discovery, 211
Kodak, 45, 80, 99, 104, 120, 133, 250, 256, 258, 261, 267, 268, 280, 353, 429, 431, 474, 479, 481, 518, 536, 545–546
Konika, 80
Korea, 310–311, 325, 542
Korn/Ferry International, 442–443
KosolClapp, Kamol Su, 174
KPMG Peat Marwick, 313, 315
Kraft Foods, 30, 47, 65, 111, 112, 120, 257, 261, 263, 267, 281, 382
Kroc, Ray, 350
Kroger, 222, 384
Kudrow, Lisa, 206
Kuhne and Nagel, 369
Kuwait, 315
Kuwait Mobile Telephones, 315

L
L.A. Vons, 136
Labeling, 268
Labeling of Hazardous Materials Act (LHAMA), 268
Lacroix, 352
Laggards, 302–303
Lake, Ricki, 177
Land, Edwin, 124
Land Rover, 20, 434
Language issues, 147–148, 267
Lanham Trademark Act, 83
Larson, Duane, 95, 103, 114
Larson-Mogal, Joshua, 289
Late majority, 302–303
Latin America, 405, 512
    personal space in, 79
    sales tips for, 469
Lauren, Ralph, 13

Laws, 79–82
    channel management, 354–355
    pricing, 509–513
    retailing, 385–386
La-Z-Boy, 267
LDDS WorldCom, 408
Leader-follower pricing, 538
Leads, 476
Learning, 196–197
Lechner, Bill, 516
Lee, 13
Lee, Tony, 442–443
Lefauvre, Skip, 44
L'eggs pantyhose, 358
Lego, 418
Leica, 352
Lenehan, James, 258
Leo Burnett Company, Inc., 133
Leona King Gallery, 332
Lep International, 369
Lesley, Lisa, 153
Leslie, Lisa, 427
Letterman, David, 391
Lever Brothers, 101
Levin, Martin, 44
Levi Strauss & Co., 3–4, 45
Levitt, Ted, 97–98
Lewis, Carl, 426
LEXIS-NEXIS, 131, 146–147, 160, 394
Lexus, 40–41, 169
L&F Products, 280
Licensing, 309–310, 429–430
    in global market, 119
LifeCycle, 197
Life cycle
    family, 208–210
    product, 293–300, 416
Lifestyle segmentation, 165–168
Lifetime value of a customer, 40
Likert scale, 141
Limited, The, 169, 344, 383, 387
Limited offers, 537
Lindemann, Kathie, 117
Line extension, 280
Linking pins, 237
Lipson, Paul, 334
Lipton, 197
Listening Ear, 333
Little Caesar's, 180
Little People of America, 318
Liz Claiborne, Inc., 281, 377
L.L. Bean, 8, 9, 22, 96, 387, 467–468
LM Ericsson, 354
Lobo, Rebecca, 153, 427
Lockheed Martin, 28, 223
Loehmann's, 384
Logan, Don, 401
Logistics
    integrated logistics management, 359–369
    order management, 361–367
    physical distribution, 360–361

López, José Ignacio, 235
L'Oreal, 539
Lorillard, Inc., 176
Los Angeles riots, 350
Loss leaders, 511
Lost World, 429–430
Lotus Development, 239
Louis Vuitton, 253
Low-cost strategy, 108
Lowe & Partners/SMS, 429
Loyalty, customer, 45–46, 406
    brand, 264
    frequent-purchaser cards, 191
    segmentation by, 168
    through sales promotion, 449–450
LSI, 70–71
Lucas, George, 63–64, 93
Lucasfilm, 63–64, 64
Lucky Stores, 379
Lufthansa, 119
Lutece, 50
Luvs diapers, 407

M
Macintosh, 196
Mack, 224
Macking, Pete, 468
Macmillan Publishing, 463
Macroenvironment, 70–85
Magazines, 267, 310, 340
    advertising on, 440–441, 443
    business-supporting, 197
Magnuson-Moss Warranty-Federal Trade Commission Improvement Act, 83, 269
Mail Boxes Etc., 461
Mail-order
    retail companies, 467–468
    wholesalers, 358
Mail surveys, 143
Malaysia, 330, 399
Malcolm Baldrige National Quality Award, 43, 54–55, 55, 61
Mall intercepts, 142–143
Mall of America, 381
Management
    consulting groups, 244–245
    functional, 236
    market, 292
    organizational structure, 291–293
    over product life cycle, 293–300
    of sales force, 481–491
Mansfield, Beth, 382
Manzi, Jim, 239
MapInfo Corporation, 160
Marginal analysis, 503
Marines, 8
Maritz Marketing Research, 145
Markdown, 382–383
Market development, 280
Market Facts, 145, 191

Marketing
    business-to-business, 216–245
    concept of, 4–5
    definition of, 5–9
    direct, 376, 386–395
    distribution channels, 344–351
    evolution of, 16–29
    information and research, 126–153
    integrated marketing communications,
        400–427
    mix decisions, 132–133
    myopia, 97–98
    nonprofit services, 332–336
    price as part of mix, 501
    purpose of, 9–10
    retailing, 376–386
    segmentation, 156–157
    services, 310–312, 340–341
    strategic marketing planning process,
        92–125
    strategy process, 12–16
Marketing concept, 9–10
Marketing environment
    culture, 77–79
    demographics, 74–77
    economic, 71–74
    ethics, 82–85
    laws and regulations, 79–82
    macroenvironment, 70–85
    microenvironment, 66–70
    technological, 70–71
Marketing intangibles, 316
Marketing Science Institute, 323
Marketing strategy process
    mix decisions, 14–16
    positioning, 13–14
    situation analysis, 12–13
    targeting, 13
Marketplace Business, 478
Market segment profile, 170
Market Segment Research, 164, 202
Market Source, 454
Marketspace, 24
Market testing, 288–290
Markup, 382
Marlboro, 258
Marlow Industries, 55
Marriott, 13, 40, 119, 255, 322, 326, 385, 470
Marriott Food Services, 200–201
Marshall, 373
Marshall Industries, 361
Marshall's, 384
Martens, Dr. Klaus, 405
Martin, Steve, 461
Marvin, Michael, 160
Maslow, Abraham, 192–193
Maslow's Hierarchy of Needs, 192–193
Mass communications, 428–461
Mass customization, 22, 175–176
Mass marketing
    development of, 16
    vs. segmentation, 157–158

MasterCard, 171, 181, 419
Materials handling, 363
Matrix, 352
Matsushita Electric, 73
Mattel, Inc., 26, 93, 298, 299, 302, 344,
    391
Maturity phase, 296–297
Maxwell, Brian, 169
Maxwell House, 507
May Company, 354, 384
Maytag, 330
Mazda, 174
McCalls, 443
McCann-Erickson, 162, 404
McDonald's, 4, 8, 11, 15, 29, 37–38, 47, 50,
    51, 74, 78, 89, 93, 103, 104, 114, 119,
    141, 163, 169, 179, 180, 197, 203,
    234, 258, 261, 288, 306, 316, 325,
    348, 350, 353, 368, 376, 386, 405,
    418, 429, 434, 439, 443, 511, 517,
    526–527, 540, 545
McDonnell Douglas, 289
McEnroe, John, 180, 426
McFarland, Gene, 491
McGinty, Andrea, 129
McGorrin, Mike, 110
McGrath, Judy, 215
McGrath, Mike, 401
McGraw-Hill Publishing Company, 433
MCI, 46, 174–175, 179, 181, 218, 232, 420,
    421–422, 430, 437, 447, 471
McIlhenny Company, 461
McKenzie & Company, 299
McKesson Drug Co., 348
McKinley, Robert, 171
McKinsey & Company, 117, 255, 293
McMein, Neysa, 27
McNeil Consumer Products Company,
    96–97
Meat Inspection Act, 81, 83
Media
    advertising, 439–444
    in Integrated Marketing
        Communications, 411–412
    schedule, 443–444
    segmentation by, 168
    timing, 444
Meers, Bob, 153
Megatrends 2000, 73
Meijer Thrifty Acres, 56, 261, 380, 539, 545
Melvoin, Jonathon, 206
Memorability, 439
Memory, 200–201
Men's Warehouse, 384
Mercedes-Benz, 23, 41, 177, 250–251, 258,
    291, 429, 433–434, 507, 520
Merck Pharmaceutical Company, 70, 97,
    467, 485
Merisel, 346
Merrill Lynch, 69, 105, 433
Merrill Publishing, 463
Mervyn's, 384

Message design, 393–394
Message sender, 406–408
Messener, Tom, 331
Metacrawler, 146
Metrics, 116
Metropolitan Museum of Art, 11, 333
Metropolitan Statistical Area (MSA), 76
Mexico, 72, 76, 119, 148, 469
Michigan Association for Traffic Safety,
    410
Michigan State University, 235–236, 333
Microenvironment, 66–70
Micromarketing, 174–175
Microsoft, 8, 18, 20, 68–69, 71, 98, 99, 101,
    204, 258, 263–264, 280, 282, 283,
    290, 295, 296, 302, 320, 333, 344,
    391–392, 411, 473, 514
MidAmerica Energy, 330
Midas, 193, 267
Middle East, 79
    sales tips for, 469–470
Midway, 510
Milk mustache ads, 205, 206, 407, 408
Miller, Girard, 456
Miller, Oral, 318
Miller, Thomas, 164
Miller Brewing, 172, 202, 266
Miller's Toys, 380
Miller-Tydings Act, 81
Milliken & Company, 52, 55
Milwaukee Electric Tool, 359
Minimum prices, 510–511
Minnesota-Based Educational Alternatives,
    Inc., 315
Minnesota Mining and Manufacturing. See
    3M
Minolta, 104, 352
Minority groups
    advertisements supporting, 446
    target marketing to, 155–156
Minute Maid, 402
Miracle-gro, 407
Misrepresentation, 475
Mission, 97–98
Missionary sales, 465
Misui, 541
Mita, 517
Mitsch, Ron, 306
Mitsubishi, 541
M&M Mars, 461
Mobil Oil, 221, 324
Molson, 422
Momentum IMC, 404
Monopolistic competition, 514, 515
Monopoly, 514
Monsanto, 330
Montgomery Ward & Company, 394
Moroney, Pat, 552
Morris, E. Scott, 153
Morton, 249
Mosley, Walter, 416
Motel 6, 13

Mothers Against Drunk Driving (MADD), 29
Motivation, 192–194, 489
Motorola, 52, 55, 71, 72–73, 104, 105, 121, 257, 288, 354, 361, 373, 405, 484
Motor Trend, 43
Mountain Dew, 197, 407
Movado, 253
Mowbray, William, 502
Mr. Christal's, 516
Mr. Goodwrench, 180
Mr. Hesel's Toy Shop, 380
MSAS, 369
MTV, 29, 201, 215, 259, 268, 422
Mulryan, David, 168, 446
Mulryan/Nash NY, 446
Murray, 352
Museum of Fine Arts (Boston), 7, 11, 144, 332, 374–376
Music industry, 29, 179, 201, 215, 259, 268, 422, 515
Mylanta, 162
My Twinn, 277–278

N
Nabisco, 114, 258
Nader, Ralph, 68
Nambu, Yasuyuki, 521
Name Lab, Inc., 266–267
NASA, 223, 230, 289
NASCAR, 414
Nathan, Richard, 455
National Agri-Marketing Association, 456
National Basketball Association, 89–90, 329
National Car Rental, 21
National Environmental Policy Act, 82
National Fish and Wildlife Foundation, 7, 332
National Football League, 431
National Geographic, 336
National Guard, 194
National Hispanic Corporate Council, 202–203
National Labor Relations Board, 385–386
National Organization of Women (NOW), 333
National Semiconductor, 121, 359, 362, 373
National Seminar Group, 318
National Trade Data Bank, 131
National Traffic and Safety Act, 83
Natural resources, 74
Nature's Choice, 516
Navy, 8, 194
N.E.A.R., 352
Neavill, Mike, 30
NEC, 69, 353, 464, 512
Needs, 192–193
Negotiations, 79
Neighborhood Report CompuServe, 131
Neighborhood Watch, 333
Neiman Marcus, 179, 343, 376, 384

Nescafé, 258
Nestlé, 257, 418, 431
Net Angels, 211
Netcom, 540, 541
Netherlands, The, 326
Netscape, 23, 99, 146, 239, 282, 320, 473
Network Associates, 461
Networking, 477
New Balance, 515
Newport Stripes, 176
News conferences, 456
Newspapers, 439–440, 443
    coupons in, 453
    public relations and, 455
New York Knicks, 20
New York Rangers, 20
New York Yankees, 230
NFO Research, Inc., 78, 145
Niche marketing, 174–175
Nickelodeon, 189, 215
Nickels, Anne, 526
NicoDerm, 258–259
Nicole Miller Eyewear, 250
Nielsen Co., 112, 134, 145, 422, 440, 453, 461
Nieman Marcus, 500
Nieto, Luis, Jr., 112
Nike, 4, 6, 11, 13–14, 56, 68, 89, 152, 180, 193, 199–200, 210, 249, 258, 280, 300, 328, 418, 420, 421, 426–427, 431, 432, 439, 445, 455, 515, 534, 536
Nikon, 104, 283
Nine West, 327
Nintendo, 56, 319, 499–500, 503, 546
Nippon Express, 369
Nissan, 139–140, 187, 188, 203, 204, 270, 291, 300, 410, 414, 439, 542, 545
Nissin Foods, 405
Nokia, 105, 354
Nonprobability samples, 144
Nonprofit markets, 7–8
Nonprofit organizations, 11
Nonprofit services
    ethics of, 336
    excess revenues, need for, 332–333
    fund-raising, 333–335
    types of, 332
Nonusers, 450
Norcom, 6, 7
Norcross fitness mall, 156–157
NordicTrack, 77, 194, 391, 432
Nordstrom's, 378, 379
North American Free Trade Agreement (NAFTA), 73, 455
North American Rockwell, 255
Northwest Airlines, 197, 222, 392, 510, 538
Northwestern Mutual Life Insurance, 484
Nova, 267
NovAtel Carcom, 294
NPD Group, 211
NutraSweet, 267
Nutri-Systems, 348

Nutritional Labeling and Education Act, 268
Nutro, 352

O
O'Brien, Louise, 45–46
Observation, 138
Ocean Spray, 68
Odd-even price perceptions, 537
O'Donnell, Rosie, 177, 416
Odwalla apple juice, 456
Off-price retailers, 384
Ohio State University, 329
Ohmae, Kenichi, 117
Oil of Olay, 77
Olajuwon, Hakeem, 536, 537
Oligopoly, 514
Olivetti, 121
Olympics, 217, 329, 413
Omaha Steaks, 388, 393
O'Neal, Shaquille, 89, 98, 208, 329
One-sided message, 409
One Size Fits One, 468
Onitsuka Tiger Co., 426
OpenMarket, 239
Operational excellence, 534
Opinion leadership, 416
Opryland Hotel, 385
Oracle, 464, 526
Orchids Only!, 390
Order management, 361–367
Oreck Corporation, 391, 394
Ore-Ida Foods, 382
Organizational objectives, 9
Organizational structure
    ethics of, 85
    and product management, 291–293
Original American Couch Potato, 259
Original equipment manufacturers (OEM), 356
Orlando Magic, 89
Oscar Mayer Weiner, 404
OTA, 352
Otis, 297
Outdoor advertising, 440, 441, 443
Outdoor Systems, 441
Outsourcing, 227–228
Overexposure, 444
Owners, 66–67
Ownership utility, 9

P
Pace, Tony, 404
Pacific Bell, 235
Pacific Gas and Electric, 515
Pacific Rim, 367–368
    business-to-business market in, 226
    trading bloc in, 73
Packaging, 268
Packard Bell, 546
Packard Electric, 49

Packer, Billy, 408
PAC Rim Consulting Group, 73
PageFast software, 411–412
Palmer, Cynthia, 29, 375–376
Pamida, 496
Pan Am, 510
Panama, 330
Panasonic, 496
Pantene, 432
Paramount, 386
Parker Hannifin, 285
Parlin, Charles C., 145
Partnerships, 232–235, 472
Passive learning, 189
Patek Philippe, 71–72
Patronage discounts, 547
Paul Mitchell, 352
Pavin, Corey, 408
Pavlov, Ivan, 196–197
Payless shoes, 402
Payment, 394
Pay packages, 488
PC Meter Service, 211
Peace Corps, 74, 193
Peapod, Inc., 395
Peapod Delivery Systems, 313, 382
Pearl Jam, 514
Peer pressure, 489
Pella Windows, 330
Penetration pricing, 542
Penn Central, 98
Pennsylvania Railroad, 80
Pentrax, 352
People for the Ethical Treatment of
      Animals (PETA), 333
Peppers, Don, 230
PepsiCo, 11, 24–25, 34, 47, 134, 168, 169,
      170, 177, 188, 201, 226, 257, 258,
      263, 266, 329, 348, 405, 407, 411,
      413, 414, 422, 430, 431, 439, 445,
      447, 490, 507, 545
Perception, 195–196
Perfect competition, 514
Performance, monitoring, 133–134
Performance measures, 487–488
Perishable, 317
Perot, Ross, 331
Personal interviews, 142
Personal selling, 412, 413
Person marketing, 328
Persuasion, 240–241, 434
Petco, 516
Pet Food Warehouse, 516
Petroleum Development Corporation
      (PDC), 221
PetsMart, 516, 522
Pet supplies, 516, 522
Pet Supply Depot, 516
PGA Tour, 336
Philip Morris, 176, 257, 281, 432, 448
Philips Petroleum Company, 28
Phillips, 283

Phoenix Group, 478
PhoneDisc PowerFinder, 478
Physical distribution, 113
Pic'N'Save, 385
Pierce, Mary, 427
Pillsbury, 263, 288
Pilot study, 134
Pinnacle Alliance, 244
Pioneer, 250
Pipelines, 365
Piper Jaffrey, 263
Pippen, Scottie, 408, 426
Pizza Hut, 11, 128, 257
Place decisions, 6, 14–15, 113, 115, 134, 330
Place du Grand Sablon, 380
Place utility, 8
Planet Hollywood, 380
Planning
      for direct marketing, 392–394
      in distribution, 353
      information and, 132
      Integrated Marketing
            Communications, 416–421
      in marketing, 5–6
      in personal sales, 475–476
      of products, 279–284
P.L.A.Y. (Participate in the Lives of
      America's Youth), 427
Playboy Enterprises, 101
Playskool, 30
Plaza Hotel, 253
Plunkett, Warren, 25
PMSI/Source Informaties, 145
Point Community Development
      Corporation, The, 334
Point-of-purchase displays, 454–455
Point-of-purchase kits, 415
Poland, 72, 540
Polaroid, 124–125, 352
Political advertising, 435, 436
Political marketing, 331
Politicking, 241
Pollak, Judann, 162
Population, 75–76, 143
Porsche, 116, 249
Portfolio planning tools, 100
Portugal, 405
Positioning, 13–14
      bases for, 179–180
      business products, 177–179
      concept of, 156–157
      map, 177
      repositioning, 180–181
      in retail market, 378–379
      in strategic marketing, 111
Post, 540
Postitech, 330
Power, John David, 135
Powerade, 180
Powerbar, 169
Power Bilt, 352
Powerhouse Gym, 309–310, 348

Power Information Network (PIN), 135
Prakken, Sue, 153
Prefontaine, Steve, 426
Prego, 450
Prentice Hall, 68, 463–464
Presentation, 479
Press releases, 456
Preston, James, 75
Price, 6
      customer concerns about, 40
      in marketing mix, 113, 116
      promotions based on, 454
Price buyers, 450
Price controls, 523
Price/Costco, 346, 353, 376, 384
Price discrimination, 510
Price fixing, 509
Price/quality, 179–180
Price strategy, 15–16
Price umbrella, 543–544
Price wars, 539–540
Price Waterhouse, 264
Pricing
      and channel management, 354
      communicating, 546–547
      competition and, 515–516
      competitor-oriented, 538–540
      concept of, 500
      cost factors, 516–520
      customer-oriented, 534–537
      demand and supply and, 505–509
      for direct marketing, 393
      diversity, 540
      ethics in, 84, 509–513, 548–549
      global, 520–523, 540–542
      industry structure and, 513–515
      laws about, 509–513
      new products, 499–500
      objectives of, 501, 503–504
      in retail, 379–380
      setting, 542–546
      value-based, 530–534
Prince, 20
Principal Financial Group, 330
Private labels, 261–262
Privatization, 314–315
PRIZM cluster system, 174
Probability sample, 143–144
Problem recognition, 190
Problem solving, 240
Process technology, 21–22
Procter & Gamble, 6, 25, 29, 30–31, 57, 75,
      101, 115, 149, 156, 162, 170, 177,
      179, 180, 255–256, 257, 258, 260,
      261, 265, 266, 292, 345, 351, 353,
      367, 413, 431, 432, 439, 453,
      529–530
Product, 6
      in business-to-business market, 225
      leadership, 534
      in marketing mix, 113, 114–115
      technologies, 104–105

Product array pricing, 545–546
Production
    agile systems, 22
    products for, 255
Production era, 16–17
Productivity Works of Trenton, 421
Product liability, 269–270
Product managers, 292
Product mix, 278
Products
    brands, 249, 257–268, 273–275
    business product classifications,
      254–255
    consumer acceptance of innovation,
      301–303
    consumer product classifications,
      251–254
    creating demand for, 403
    decisions, 132–133
    development of, 276–307
    differentiation of, 158–159
    dimensions of, 248–251
    ethics about, 85
    factors of, 239–240
    global, 256–257, 300
    life cycle of, 293–300, 416
    line, 255–257, 483
    management of, 278–279, 291–293
    packaging and labeling, 268
    safety and liability issues, 269–270
    service-goods continuum, 319–320
    stategy, 14
    technology of, 21
    vs. services, 316–319
Professional Golfers' Association, 414
Professionals, 314
Profit, 503
Pro hardware stores, 348
Projective techniques, 137–138
Promotion, 6, 402
    decisions, 134
    ethics about, 85
    in marketing mix, 113, 115
    pricing as, 545
    strategy, 15
Promotion Marketers Association, 404
Prospecting, 476
Prototypes, 287–288
Prudential Insurance, 192, 484, 507
Psychology, 165–168, 191–201
P-Trak, 394
Public relations, 413, 430, 455–456
    ethics of, 432
    publicity campaigns, 456–457
Public service messages, 435–436
Publishers, 143
Puffery, 475
Pulling power, 439
Pull strategy, 414
Purchase decision, 191
Purchase evaluation, 191
Purchasing agents, 235–236

Pure Food and Drug Act, 81, 83
Purina, 352
Push strategy, 415

Q

QS-9000, 231
Quaker Oats Company, 14, 118, 160, 199,
    404
Qualifying, 476
Quality, 11, 49–55
    assessments of, 51
    continuous improvement, 52
    control, 231
    definition of, 49–50
    dynamic, 51
    of life, 313
    perceived, 264
    quality function deployment (QFD),
      52–53
    of service, 318–319, 323–324
    static, 51
    total quality management (TQM),
      51–53
Quality function deployment (QFD), 52–53
Quality Value Channel (QVC), 391
Quantity discounts, 547
Quantum Chemical, 330
Quartermaine Coffee Roasters, 191, 211
Quick's Candy, 232
Quinlan, Michael R., 37, 38
Quintero, Paul, 334
Quotas, 487, 488
Quotes, price, 547
QVC, 376, 393

R

Rack jobbers, 358
Radant, Chris, 310
Radio, 329, 440, 443
Radio Shack, 377
Radley, Gordon, 63
Railroads, 365
Ralph Lauren, 111, 116, 174, 184
Ralston Purina, 448
Random digit dialing, 143
Range Rover, 250–251, 296
Raphael, Sally Jesse, 30
Rawlings, Martine, 233
Reach, advertising, 443
Reagan, Ronald, 331, 431
Rebates, 453–454, 547–548
Rebuys, straight and modified, 228–229
Recall, advertising, 445–446
Recalls, product, 269–270
Recognition, 446
Recommendations, 409
Recruitment, sales force, 484
Red and White, 348
Red Cross, 10
Red Devil, 281

Redhook Ale Brewery, 34
Red Hot Chili Peppers, The, 206
Red Lobster, 41, 58
Reduced cycle time, 52
Reebok, 68, 116, 152–153, 201, 208, 300,
    432, 455, 515
Reece, Elmer, 49
Reece, Gabrielle, 427
Reference groups, 205–207
Reference prices, 534–535
Referrals, 477
Reichheld, Fred, 39
Reid, C.L., 112
Reinforcement advertising, 434
Relationship marketing, 44–47
    business-to-business, 231–232
    importance of, 19–20
Reliability, 323
Reminder advertising, 434
Renault, 120, 178
Repair services, 377
Repositioning, 180–181
Request for quotation (RFQ), 229
Research, 129
    case analysis, 138–140
    data collection methods, 140–141
    depth interviews, 137
    design, 134
    ethics in, 85, 148–150
    exploratory, 135–140
    external, 145–146
    focus groups, 136–137
    global, 147–148
    in-company, 145
    observation, 138
    problem definition, 134
    projective techniques, 137–138
    quantitative, 140–144
    surveys, 142–145
    technology's effect on, 146–147
    on youth, 139
Research and development, 70–71
Resellers, 221
Responsiveness, 323
Restaurant business, 327
Retail
    advertising, 435
    return policies, 56
    salespeople, 466, 467
Retail cooperative, 348
Retailers and retailing, 327, 344
    concept of, 376
    diversity in, 385
    ethics, 385–386
    global, 386
    importance of, 377
    laws, 385–386
    promotions aimed at, 448
    sales promotions, 452
    strategy for, 378–383
    trade promotions, 451–452
    types of, 383–385

Return policies, 269, 319
Revenues, 40
Rhore-Poulenc Ericcson, 121
Riche, Marsha Farnsworth, 25
Risk
    in international business, 522
    product, 239–240
Ritz Carlton, 55, 61
R.J. Reynolds, 81, 176, 422
RJR/Nabisco, 448
Roadway, 366
Robbin, Jonathon, 174
Robb's Music, 319
Robert Wood Johnson Foundation, 333
Robinson-Patman Act, 81, 509, 510
Robitussin, 407
Rockefeller Foundation, 333
Rockwell, 330
Rodale Press Inc., 136–137
Rodin, Rob, 373
Rodman, Dennis, 89, 207, 441
Rodman & Renshaw, 502
Rogers, Martha, 230
Rolex, 13, 352
Rolleiflex, 352
Rollerblade, 258, 266
Roller Skates of America, 383
Rolls-Royce, 500
Romanelli, Dianne, 162
Room Service Deliveries, 313
Roper/Starch Worldwide, 166, 540
Rose, Dick, 343
Rose, Pete, 207
Rosen, Frederic D., 340
Ross, 352
Ross, Jeffrey, 516
Rossignol, 352, 537, 546
Rothman, Claire L., 341
Roundtree, Saudia, 153
Routing schedule, 479
Rowntree, 257
Royal Appliance, 351
Royal Crown Cola, 168, 411
R.R. Donnelley & Sons, 129
RUAN Transportation Management
    Systems, 330
Rubbermaid, 257, 267, 409
Rubicam, 431
Russia, 25, 75, 147, 256, 314, 522, 540
Ryan, Nolan, 426
Ryder System, 366

S
Saab, 225
Saatchi and Saatchi, 436, 461
Sabatini, Gabriela, 206
Safeway, 382, 384
Sainsbury's, 530
Saks Fifth Avenue, 253, 343, 384
Salary, 488
Salazar, Alberto, 426

Sales
    contests, 451, 452
    orientation, 17
    pricing and, 503
Sales and Marketing Management, 484,
    486, 491
Sales era, 16, 17
Salespeople
    characteristics of, 480–481
    responsibilities of, 472–475
Sales promotion, 413, 430
    business-to-business, 450–451
    consumer promotions, 452–455
    creating customer relationships and
        loyalty, 449–450
    ethics of, 432
    retailer promotions, 452
    success of, 448–449
    trade promotions, 451–452
    types of, 447–448
Sales territory, 472–473
Samples, 143–144, 454
Sam's Club, 384, 547
Samsung, 360
Sanders, Deion, 426
San Diego Zoo, 333, 336, 337
Sanwa, 541
Sanyo, 496
Sara Lee, 261, 273–275, 343–344
SAS, Inc., 67, 119
Sasser, Earl, 39
Satisfaction, 11
Saturday Evening Post, 145
Saturn, 44, 53, 162, 364, 366, 485, 489
Savvy Search, 146
S.C. Johnson, 454
Scandinavia, 405, 469
Scandinavian Airline Systems (SAS), 105,
    317
Scarpelli, Bob, 461
Scheimann, Sue, 139
Schenker, 369
Schneider National, 366
Schrader, Richard, 341
Schrandt, Robert, 57
Schulberg, Jay, 461
Schuler, David, 473
Schultz, Don, 402–403
Schultz, Howard, 34
Schweppes, 445
Science Diet, 352
Scientific method, 140
Scott Paper, 448
Scrambled merchandising, 380
Seagar, Bob, 197
Sea Land Service, 8
Sealy, 348
Sea Ray, 68
Search qualities, 320
Sears, 8, 30, 175, 249–250, 261, 270, 298,
        377, 379, 380, 384, 385, 449, 489,
        511

Sega, 404, 455, 499–500
Segmentation
    behavioristic, 161
    by benefit, 169
    of business-to-business market,
        223–225
    concept of, 156–157
    demographic, 160–164
    diversity-based, 161, 164–165
    geographic, 160, 161
    methods, 169
    psychographic, 161, 165–168
    VALS system, 166–168
    variables, 159–169
    vs. mass marketing, 157–158
    vs. product differentiation, 158–159
Segmented Marketing Services, Inc., 26
Segment leadership qualities, 171
Seimens, 121, 257
Seinfeld, Jerry, 329, 461
Selective attention, 195–196
Selective comprehension, 196
Selective exposure, 195
Selective retention, 196
Seles, Monica, 427
Self-image, 189
Self-reference criterion, 78
Seller, Jeffrey, 115
Seller's market, 17
Selling, personal, 463–464
    direct, 465
    executive and team, 465–466
    field, 466–467
    global, 468
    inside, 467–468
    missionary, 465
    over-the-counter, 467
    relationship approaches, 468, 470–472
    sales force management, 481–491
    salespersons' characteristics, 480–481
    salespersons' responsibilities, 472–475
    steps, 475–480
Sementelli, John, 309
Senior citizens, 540
Sentry, 348
Service, 480
    complexity, 326
    in marketing mix, 113
    quality, 49
    in retail, 379–380
Service Master, 316
Service Merchandise, 11, 384
Service Quality Indications (SQI), 52
Services, 6–8
    concept of, 310–312
    consumer evaluation of, 320–322
    expanded concept of, 327–332
    growth in, 312–316
    mix of, 324–327
    nonprofit, 332–336
    quality of, 323–324
    vs. goods, 316–319

SERVISTAR, 348
7-Eleven, 384
7-Up, 450
Seventh Generation, 286
SGS-Thomson, 121
Shaheen, George, 244
Sharp, 490
Sharper Finish, Inc., 347
Sharper Image, 388, 394
Sheaffer, 330
Sheraton, 322
Sherman Antitrust Act, 80, 81, 509, 510, 511
Sherwin-Williams, 344, 349, 377
Shimano, 196
Shopping goods, 252–253, 349
Shopping habits, segmentation by, 168
Shopping mall, 380–381
Shulstad, Craig, 27
Siemens AG, 468
Silicon Graphics, 289
Silverdome, 333
Simmons, Russell, 185
Simon & Schuster, 299, 463–464
Simple random sampling, 144
Simpson, O.J., 207
SIS International Research, 146
Situation analysis, 12–13, 109–111
Skeels, David, 175
Sketchers, 77
Skill Path, Inc., 318
SkillSearch, 322
Skimming, 542
Skinner, B.F., 197
Skipworth, Dick, 373
Skoda, 120
Skywalker Sound, 64
Slogans, 439
Sloves, Marvin, 429
Smart and Final, Inc., 356
Smashing Pumpkins, 206
Smith, Emmett, 153
Smith, Frederick W., 50
Smith Corona, 51
SmithKline Beecham, 179
Smithsonian Institution, 11
Snack industry, 164
Snap-On Tools, 46
Snapple, 14, 198, 199, 404, 423
SNET, 314
Snoop Doggy Dog, 184
Social class, 204–205
Social responsibility, 28–29
Social Security, 163–164
Society for Disability Studies, 318
Solectron Corporation, 55
Soloflex, 195, 267, 391
Solomon, 352
Somers, Suzanne, 391
Sommerville, Cindy, 313
Sony, 6, 19–20, 100, 250, 258, 260, 261, 283, 449, 496, 499–500, 546, 547
Southern Baptist Convention, 68

Southwest Airlines, 320, 405
Southwestern Supply, 359
Soviet Union, dissolution of, 120
Spago, 50
Spalding, 137, 168, 352, 536
Spamming, 394
Sparrow Health System, 8, 53, 331–332
Spartain Stores, 261
Specialized, 40
Specialty goods, 253–254, 349, 451
Specialty stores, 383
Speedo, 21
Spending behavior, 71–72
Spice Girls, 515
Spiegel, 203, 204
Spielberg, Steven, 259, 429
Spiffs, 353, 452
SPIN selling, 479
Sponsorships, 329, 413–414, 456
Sports marketing, 137, 171, 172, 300
Sportsmart, 383
Springer, Jerry, 30, 177
Sprint, 314, 407
Sputnik, Inc., 139, 142
SRI Consulting, 166–168
Stakeholders, 66–68
Standard Industry Classification (SIC) codes, 224
Standard Oil, 80, 267
Staples, 251–252, 376, 381, 383, 384
Star Alliance, 119
Starbucks, 34–35, 117, 263, 270, 450
Starch test, 446
Starkist, 68, 449
State Farm Insurance, 230
Statistical quality control, 53
Stay Fresh, 267
Steelcase, 297
Sterling Winthrop, 280
Stern, David, 89–90
Steward, Gil, 552
Stewart, Martha, 400–402, 420
Stickley, 252
Stockkeeping units (SKUs), 255, 363
Stolichnaya vodka, 446
Stopping power, 438
Storage, 317
Strategic alliances, 20
in global market, 120–121
Strategic business units (SBUs), 99–103, 224
Strategic direction, 98–99
Strategic Environment Initiative (SEI), 74
Strategic infrastructure, 99–106
Strategic marketing planning process
components, 109–111
concept of, 94–95
control process, 116
core vision and, 96–97
cross-functional planning team, 106
in global markets, 116–120
infrastructure, 99–106

intent, 98–99
mission, 97–98
mix plans, 111–116
organization vision, 95–106
strategy defined, 107–109
Strategic relationships, 472
Strategic window, 107
Strategy
definition of, 107–109
pricing, 528–552
Stratified random sampling, 144
Strauss, Levi, 3–4, 29
Streisand, Barbra, 408
Strohs, 266
Stroll, Lawrence, 184
Stuart, Donald, 133
Subaru, 174, 445, 446, 457
Subculture, 201–204
Subliminal perception, 196
Substitution, 69
Subway, 114, 316
Sumitomo, 541
Sunbeam, 454
Sun City retirement communities, 210
Sun Microsystems, 121, 218, 254, 285
Sun Trust Bank, 171
Super Bowl advertising, 410, 413
Supermarkets, 384, 530
Superstores, 383
Super Value, 348
Suppliers, 67–68
bargaining power of, 69–70
for direct marketing, 376
in retail, 382–383
Supplies, 255
Supply, prices and, 507–508
Supply chain, 225–226
Surveys
administering, 142–143
interpreting and reporting, 144–145
Surveys and Forecasts, 146
Sustainable competitive advantage, 108–109
Sutthoff, John, 472
Suzuki, 120, 174, 552
Swatch, 13
Sweden, 41, 72, 225, 399, 413, 540
Sweepstakes, 454
Switchers, 449–450
Switzerland, 418
freight shippers in, 369
sales tips for, 469
SWOT analysis, 110
Sykes, John, 215
SYSCO, 355, 357, 358
Szczsponik, John, 373

T
Tachistoscopes, 138
Taco Bell, 257, 438, 443
Tactics, 113

Take-down segmentation method, 169
Takeout Taxi, 313
Tandy, 349
Tangibles, 323
Target, 267, 379, 381, 384, 385, 502, 537, 545
Target audience, 417, 443
Target marketing, 13, 111, 169–177
    compatibility factors, 172
    competitive factors, 170
    concept of, 156–157
    cost and efficiency factors, 171
    in direct marketing, 392
    ethics of, 176
    finding new markets, 172
    global, 176–177
    in retail, 378–379
    segment leadership qualities, 171
    size and growth, 170
    strategies, 172–176
Target pricing, 537
Tariffs, 521
Taster's Choice, 438
Taylor, Chrissy, 456
Taylor, Harry, 446
Taylor, Jim, 398–399
Taylor, Morry, 331
Taylor Made, 352
TCG, 314
TCI, 314, 548
Teams, sales, 466, 483–486
Tech Data, 346, 357, 358
Technology
    base, 103–104
    brand names in, 265
    business-to-business market, 225, 239
    computer shopping, 382
    to connect with customers, 20–24
    in global macroenvironment, 70–71
    innovations and, 281, 282–284, 283
    in Integrated Marketing
        Communication, 422
    marketing research and, 146–147
    and mass communications, 432
    micromarketing and, 175
    pricing, 499–500, 541
    process, 104
    product, 105
    in research, 210–211
    in retail, 381–382
    sales through, 473, 491
    service sector growth, 312–313
    virtual reality in product design, 289
Teenage Research Unlimited (TRU),
    199–200
Teerlink, Richard, 551, 552
Teixeira, Josina Reis, 75
Telecommunications, 220, 222–223
Teledesic Corporation, 20
Telemarketing, 386, 388, 390–391, 466,
    477–478
Telephone surveys, 143
Teleshop, 391

TeleTech, 228
Television, 329
    advertising on, 440, 443
    home shopping networks, 391, 393
    and mass communications, 432
    programming, 30–31
    as promotional tool, 89
    talk shows, 177, 178
Termination, 489
Territories, 354, 475
Tesco, 530
Testing, product, 288–290
Test markets, 290
Tevis, 225
Texaco, 384
Texas Instruments, 55, 283, 345, 353, 361,
    372–373, 398, 491, 543
Textron Automotive, 7
T.G.I. Friday's, 310–311
THAI, 119
Thailand, 174, 176–177
Theater, promotion of, 115
Theme, advertising, 437–439
Thermo King, 267
Thiel, 352
Thighmaster, 391
Thom McAn, 180–181
Thompson Publishing, 239
3M, 238, 240, 280, 286, 306–307, 441
Three Musketeers, 177
Ticketmaster, 197, 340–341, 514
Tickle Me Elmo Doll, 416
Tier, 225
Tiger Electronics, 115
Timberland, 429
Time, culture and, 79
Time, Inc., 401
Time-It Lube, 191
Time utility, 8–9
Time-Warner, 222–223, 386
Timex, 193, 352
Timken, 221
Titleist, 168, 405
T.J. Maxx, 384
Tobacco industry, 81, 176
Tobias, Randall, 96
Todd, Barbara, 390
Toho and Shochiku Company, 386
Tommy Hilfiger, 184–185
Tooker, Gary, 71
Topco Associates, 348
Toshiba, 121, 373, 496
Total quality management (TQM), 51–53
Toth, Michael, 185
Toth Design and Advertising, 185
Tourneau, 352
Tower Records, 24, 174, 190
Toy Biz, 355
Toyota, 57, 67, 99, 120, 139–140, 291,
    360–361, 431, 435, 439, 472, 516,
    542, 545
Toy Safety Act, 83

Toys 'R' Us, 133, 344, 379, 386, 455, 499,
    526, 545
Trade industries, 220, 221–222
Trademarks, 258–259, 259–260
Trade promotions, 448, 451–452
Trade shows, 450
TradeWave, 239
Trading blocs, 72–74
Trading companies, 119
Training, sales force, 485–486
Transfer prices, 522–523
Transportation
    business-to-business market in, 220,
        222–223
    industry, 98
    in physical distribution, 364–366
TravelBids, 392
Travelers Group, 69
Travel Express International, 507
Trialability, 283
Triarc, 14
Trident Precision Manufacturing, 55
Tripp, Cindy, 77
Tropicana Dole Beverages, 429
Trout, Jack, 111
Truck jobbers, 358
Trucks, 364
Trust, 45
Truth-in-Lending Act, 81, 83
Truth in Packaging law, 81
TSI International, 239
TWA, 510
Twentieth Century Fox, 64
Twister, 439
Two-sided message, 409
Ty, Inc., 526–527
Tying arrangement, 355
Tylenol, 210, 407
Tylenol tampering scare, 96–97, 269
Tyler, Steven, 206
Tyr, 21
Tyson, Mike, 207

U
U2, 515
UCI, 386
Unaided recall, 445
Understandability, 439
Underwriter's Laboratory, 333, 407–408
Undifferentiated marketing, 173
Uniform Commercial Code (UCC), 269
Uniglobe, 348
Unilever, 354, 413
Union Pacific Railroad, 222, 365
United Airlines, 10, 34, 116, 119, 133, 171,
    222, 263, 388, 439, 450, 456, 510
United Arab Emirates, 399
United Kingdom, 325, 399, 405, 520, 530
    freight shippers in, 369
    marketing in, 177, 205, 314
    nonprofit sector in, 332

United Parcel Service (UPS), 8, 69, 100, 106, 173, 226, 230, 237, 255, 366, 414, 435, 468, 472, 473, 492, 533, 534
United States
 nonprofit sector in, 332
 shopping patterns in, 115
 size and space in, 79
 wealth distribution in, 72
United States Golf Association, 168
United States Postal Service, 504
United Technologies, 121
United Way, 333
Unit pricing, 512
Universal Studios, 386
Universal Studios, 429
University of Iowa, 330
University of Michigan, 329
University of Southern California, 333
University of Tennessee Center for Logistics Research, 132
Univision, 203, 445
Unsought products, 251
Upjohn Corporation, 134, 297
Upton, 384
Urbanization, 76
USAir, 392, 510
U.S. Air Force, 223
U.S. Army, 8, 192, 333
U.S. Bureau of the Census, 65, 76, 143
U.S. Department of Agriculture, 268
U.S. Department of Commerce, 117
U.S. Forest Service, 333
U.S. Immigration and Naturalization Service, 74
U.S. Patent Office, 65
U.S. Postal Service (USPS), 8, 69, 326, 388, 389, 473, 532, 533
U.S. Public Interest Research Group (PIRG), 268
U.S. Robotics, 68
U.S. West Airlines, 25
U.S. West telephone, 235
Use, value in, 532
Users, 237
Utilities, 220, 222

V

VALS segmentation system, 166–168
Value, 405
 delivering, 55–56
Value-based pricing, 530–534
Value chain, 55
Value Club of America, 391
Value packs, 454
ValuJet, 511
Valu-Rite, 348
Vanstar, 362
Variety stores, 385
Venture Stores, 267
Venture team, 293

Vermeer, 330
Vertical marketing system (VMS), 348
Verve-Pipe, 515
VF Corporation, 352
VH1, 215
Viacom, 189, 215
Vicary, Jim, 196
Vicks, 289
Victoria's Secret, 327, 393
Vidal Sasson, 350, 352
Video Express, 322
Virtual Emporium, 24
Virtual reality, 289
Virtual Vision, 288
Visa International, 171, 449
Vision, organizational, 95–106
V-8 juice, 180
Volkswagen, 120, 235, 249, 258, 300, 472
Volume, 503
Volvo, 162, 179, 250–251, 407, 461, 507, 532
VTech Holdings, 418

W

Wagoner, G. Richard, 247
Wainwright Industries, 55
Waiter on Wheels, 313
Waitt, Ted, 398–399
Walker, Bob, 146
Wallace Company, 52, 55
Wal-Mart, 56, 69–70, 75, 115, 133, 171, 175, 179, 261, 267, 269, 281, 317, 344, 345, 348, 351, 352, 358, 364, 376, 379, 380, 383, 384, 385, 391, 448, 502, 526, 530, 537, 545, 547
Waln, Shelley Lewis, 402
Walt Disney Co., 68, 89, 92–94, 99, 105–106, 111–112, 234, 258, 259, 326, 328–329, 330, 388
Walt Disney World, 53
Walton, Sam, 179
Wanamaker, John, 421
War babies, 163
Warehouse clubs, 384
Warehouses, 362
Warner, Ty, 526–527
Warranties, 269
Washburn Crosby Company, 27
Washington Apple Commission, 455
Water carriers, 365
Wealth, dispersion of, 72
WearGuard, 104
WebCrawler, 146
Web sites
 Amazon.com, 86, 127–128
 American Express, 20
 American Marketing Association (AMA), 84
 America Online, 548
 Ames, 510
 Amoco, 522
 Amway, 478, 492

ARAMARK, 218, 315
Arrow Electronics, 356
AT&T, 132
Avon, 86
Bank of America, 548
Barnes & Noble, 320
Blockbuster, 381
BMW, 176
Boeing, 467
Bugle Boy Clothing Company, 149
Carnival Cruise Lines, 320
Caterpillar, 302
CDnow, 392, 395
CIA, 65
Club Med, 211
Coach, 345
Coca-Cola, 157
CompUSA, 377
ConAgra, 197
Cutler-Hammer, 241
Deloitte & Touche, 403
Domino's Pizza, 177
Eli Lilly, 95
EnviroGroup, 221
FedEx, 50
Ford, 145
Frito-Lay, 291
Fuji, 438
General Electric, 281
General Mills, 31
General Motors, 248
Hallmark, 47, 58
Hershey Foods, 66
Hewlett-Packard, 454, 467
Hilton Worldwide, 337
Honda, 295
Honeywell, 353
IBM, 226, 423
Industry.net, 239, 241
Intel, 270
J.D. Power & Associates, 149
Johnson Controls, 285
Kellogg's, 540
Kimberly-Clark, 140
Kinko's, 326
Kmart, 232
Kodak, 80, 120
Kraft Foods, 120
Lost World, 430
Lucasfilm, 64
Malcolm Baldrige National Quality Award, 55
Mastercard, 181
Mattel, 302
McDonald's, 38, 368
MCI, 174–175, 181
Mercedes-Benz, 434
Merck, 485
Microsoft, 69
Mobil, 324
Motorola, 71, 257
MTV, 259

Web sites (*cont.*)
    Museum of Fine Arts (Boston), 376
    My Twinn, 278
    NASCAR, 414
    Nielsen Media Research, 134
    Nike, 200
    Nintendo, 500
    Nissan, 188
    Peapod, Inc., 395
    Pepsi, 407
    PetsMart, 522
    Powerhouse Gym, 310
    Procter & Gamble, 31, 530
    Quartermaine Coffee Roasters, 211
    Red Lobster, 58
    Rubbermaid, 409
    San Diego Zoo, 337
    Sears, 379
    Simon & Schuster, 464
    Snapple, 198, 423
    Spiegel, 203
    Staples, 384
    Starbucks, 270
    Subaru, 457
    Subway, 316
    SYSCO, 358
    Texas Instruments, 283
    3M, 240
    Ticketmaster, 514
    United Airlines, 133
    United Parcel Service (UPS), 237, 492
    U.S. Bureau of the Census, 65
    U.S. Patent Office, 65
    U.S. Postal Service, 533
    VALS 2, 166
    Volvo, 532
    Wal-Mart, 348
    Walt Disney Co., 94
    Weight Watchers, 444
    Westinghouse, 104
    Whirlpool, 486
    W.W. Grainger, 368
    Xerox, 48

Yahoo!, 457
Yamaha, 250
Webster, Frederick Jr., 106
WebTV, 283, 547
Weetabix, 405
Wehling, R.L., 30
Weight Watchers, 77, 267, 444
Wendy's restaurants, 51, 439
Westat Inc., 145
West Edmonton Mall, 381
Western Auto, 348
Westinghouse, 55, 103, 104, 110–111, 218,
    222, 297, 420
Wet Seal, 378, 382, 383
Wexler, Norman, 343
Wheeler-Lea Act, 81, 509
Wheelwright, George, 124
Whirlpool, 270, 438, 486
White, Al, 52
Whittier, Ron, 341
Wholesalers and wholesaling, 344
    defined, 355–356
    full-service, 357–358, 359
    importance of, 356–357
    limited-service, 358
    relationships, 358–359
    trade promotions, 451–452
    wholesaler-sponsored voluntary chains,
      348
Wholesaler-sponsored voluntary chains,
    348
Wightman, Baysie, 153
Wilkens, Lenny, 408
Williams, Pat, 89
Williams Sonoma, 40
Wilson, 168, 352
Winfrey, Oprah, 30, 177, 416
Winn-Dixie, 384
Winnebago, 330
Winns, 68
Winston, Andrew, 541
Wolf, 352
Woods, Danny, 310

Woods, Tiger, 207, 328, 426
WOOFS, 163
World Health Organization, 432
World Trade Organization, 74
World Wide Web. *See* Internet, Web sites
Wozniak, Steve, 70
WP-Studio, 147
W.W. Grainger, 358–359, 368, 388
Wyle Laboratories, 356

X
Xerox Corporation, 47–49, 48, 49, 52, 55,
    231, 258, 266, 479, 481, 534
Xircom, Inc., 538

Y
Yahoo!, 146, 442, 457
Yamaha, 107, 172, 250, 265, 551, 552
Yankelovich Partners, 185, 446
Yellow Pages, 435
Yellowstone Park, 299
Young, Steve, 206
Young & Laramore, 441
Young & Rubicam, 436, 461
Youth
    marketing to, 215, 249
    reference groups of, 206
YTL Corporation, 468

Z
Zellem, Mary, 390
Zeller's, 387, 545
Zenith, 22
Zientek, Annette, 133
Ziff-Davis Publishing, 387
Zip code segmentation, 160
Zollo, Peter, 199–200
Zytec Corporation, 55